Henry Clay

BOOKS BY ROBERT V. REMINI

Henry Clay

Statesman for the Union

Robert V. Remini

W · W · NORTON & COMPANY

NEW YORK · LONDON

FRONTISPIECE PHOTOGRAPH: Henry Clay, painted by George Peter Alexander Healy, 1845. *Courtesy of the National Portrait Gallery*

The illustration on page xxiii is of Henry Clay's home, Ashland. From a drawing by W. Lewis.

FIRST EDITION

The text of this book is composed in Galliard, with the display set in Caslon Shaded and Garamond Oldstyle. Composition and manufacturing by the Haddon Craftsmen. Genealogy chart by Ben Gamit. Book design by Marjorie J. Flock.

Library of Congress Cataloging–in–Publication Data

Remini, Robert Vincent, 1921–
    Henry Clay: statesman for the Union / Robert V. Remini.
      p.   cm.
    Includes bibliographical references and index.
    1. Clay, Henry, 1777–1852. 2. Legislators—United States—
    Biography. 3. United States. Congress—Biography. 4. United
    States—Politics and government—1815–1861. I. Title
    E340.C6R46   1991
    973.5′092—dc20
    [B]   91-9438

ISBN 0-393-03004-0

W. W. Norton & Company, Inc., 500 Fifth Avenue, New York, N.Y. 10110
W. W. Norton & Company, Ltd., 10 Coptic Street, London WC1A 1PU

1 2 3 4 5 6 7 8 9 0

In memory of my brothers
Vincent J. and William C. Remini

Contents

Photographs appear following page 354

There is an intuitive perception about [Henry Clay], that seems to see & understand at a glance, and a winning fascination in his manners that will suffer none to be his enemies who associate with him. When I look upon his manly & bold countenance, & meet his frank & eloquent eye, I feel an emotion little short of enthusiasm in his cause, and nothing short of absolute detestation & contempt for the cowardly baseness of those who *behind his back* accuse him of venality & corruption, yet in his presence, cower, like partridges before the hawk. Such a man as Henry Clay may well be betrayed into errors of passion & feeling, but it is impossible he should be guilty of those degrading vices of which *meanness* is a component part. He has too much sensibility. He suffers the slanders of interested enemies, and the slang whang of newspaper accusation to vex & harrass him exceedingly. . . . He is a great man—one of Nature's nobles.

— CONGRESSMAN EDWARD BATES
to his wife, Julia, February 25, 1828

Preface

"WHAT!" exclaimed the Nashville woman when I told her about my new research project following the completion of my biography of Andrew Jackson. "You're writing a biography of Henry Clay?" she gasped. "*Henry* Clay? Oh, General Jackson won't like that." Then, with a laugh, she added: "He might shoot you."

Well, he hasn't so far, and I doubt that he will, given his present location and the all-embracing expressions of forgiveness with which he departed this world. Besides, I don't consider myself disloyal to the Old Hero by writing a biography of Clay. I'm a historian, not a partisan or a propagandist.

Still, I've noticed many raised eyebrows among my colleagues in the academy when I explained my current interest. It does seem strange that having spent so many years of my life researching and writing the story of Jackson's remarkable course through American history, I should turn to his greatest political enemy and rival for my next scholarly undertaking. So perhaps some explanation is in order.

To begin with, I've always liked Henry Clay. Many times during my research into Jackson's life I found myself laughing out loud at some of Clay's caustic remarks in Congress. He had a wonderful, frequently self-deprecating sense of humor. Jackson lacked that characteristic. And many of Clay's speeches still carry an emotional wallop, at least for me, so I thought I'd like to get to know him better. Besides, as an old New Deal and Fair Deal liberal, I rather respected his efforts to use government to advance the material and social welfare of the nation. Furthermore, I was puzzled and fascinated by his hatred of slavery while, at the same time, he held dozens of slaves himself. And Abraham Lincoln called him "my beau ideal of a statesman, the man for whom I fought all my humble life." That, too, intrigued me. In addition, after many years of explaining Democratic principles and policies during the Jacksonian era in a number of books, I thought it was high time I became more intimately acquainted with the principles, policies, and leaders of the Whig party. I felt an expanded education into the political thought of the antebellum period would benefit my teaching as well as give me a better sense of the complicated historical forces at play during those years. Finally, I realized that Clay deserved a modern, scholarly biography. None had been written in fifty years.

After completing the Jackson *Life,* I had originally intended to go back and finish the biography of Martin Van Buren that I started as a doctoral student at Columbia University in 1947 under Dumas Malone. But since I completed my dissertation, two excellent biographies of Van Buren have been written recently, one by John Niven, the other by Donald Cole, along with a fine study of his administration by Major Wilson. The world, even the scholarly world, did not need yet a fourth work on the life and career of the Little Magician.

In preparing this biography of Clay, I was immensely aided by the availability of his papers. Unlike Jackson, Clay had most of his papers, dating from 1797 to 1843, already published in nine volumes when I started my research. What a difference that made. Instead of chasing around the country and half the globe looking for materials written by or to Clay, I found that most of them had already been gathered at the Clay Papers Project at the University of Kentucky in Lexington and published. Reading printed pages instead of manuscripts is a very exhilarating experience. I've often envied my twentieth-century colleagues, whose sources are mostly typescript, because of the ease with which they can manage their principal materials. Instead of struggling with impossible handwriting or pages in which the ink from one side had bled through to the reverse side, making reading next to impossible (and worse on microfilm), or contending with pages in which the correspondent first wrote down one side of a page, then turned the sheet ninety degrees and wrote across the face of the same page, instead of that, I could sit quietly in my study and read and understand every word of the text. What a blessing! I no longer had to scratch my head over a particular word or phrase or colloquial expression. Try figuring out the Shakespearean phrase "false as dicers' oaths," written in a ghastly hand, and one will get some idea of what I mean.

I am most grateful to my friend Richard Lowitt, who, upon hearing of my project, gave me his review copies of the first five volumes of *The Papers of Henry Clay.* Then the University of Kentucky Press graciously presented me with the remainder. Most especially—and here I cannot speak with greater emphasis of my gratitude—I am deeply in debt to Melba Porter Hay, current editor of the Clay Papers Project, who provided me with typescripts of Clay manuscript letters and documents written during the last eight years of his life. In addition, she furnished transcripts of any material the project received since publication of the *Papers* first began in 1959. Moreover, she has helped me track down information not generally available outside Kentucky. Not a single appeal for assistance or guidance did she refuse. Without her indispensable aid this biography would have taken many more years to complete. I owe her a very special salute.

In a different way, but most important in the assistance rendered in moving this book to completion, was the financial support provided by the University of Illinois at Chicago through its University Scholar's Program. And in conferring upon me the rank of Research Professor of Humanities, the university made possible the necessary time to do the writing and rewriting. It is impossible for me to thank adequately those administrators of the university who valued my past work sufficiently to provide the means to encourage this study to completion.

In the course of writing Clay's biography I became concerned about the degree of prejudice I might bring to it in view of my long association with Andrew Jackson and the Democrats. The Rockefeller Foundation provided a month's residence at its Study and Conference Center at Bellagio, Italy, where I was able to review and rethink what I had written in the first dozen chapters of the original manuscript. I am grateful to the foundation for granting this significant break during which I could assess my objectivity in narrating the events of the antebellum period.

At Ashland, Clay's home in Lexington, Bettie L. Kerr and Linda Brown supplied me with materials relating to the house along with several prints, postcards, and daguerreotypes of Clay and pictures of some of the furnishings of his house. Similarly Burton Milward helped me with information concerning the Clay monument at the Lexington cemetery by supplying a copy of the chapter on the cemetery from his recent book. Bruce and Virginia English of Ashland, Virginia, took me on a wonderful tour of Clay's birth site. Without them I would never have found the place.

James R. Bentley, the director; James J. Holmberg, the curator of manuscripts; Mary Jean Kinsman, the curator of photographs and prints; and Nettie Oliver, the staff researcher, at the Filson Club in Louisville placed the resources of the library at my service and gave a great deal of their time in answering questions and locating important documents and photographs. I am particularly grateful to Jim Holmberg for alerting me to every new Clay letter acquired by the Filson Club. Manuscripts were arriving even as this book went to press. Charles Bryan, the director, and Sara B. Bearss, the associate editor, at the Virginia Historical Society, identified many valuable documents in the society's library for me and showed me the coat John Randolph wore when Clay put a bullet through it. Unfortunately the coat now has so many moth holes that it is impossible to identify the one drilled through it by Clay's bullet. As always, John McDonough at the manuscript division of the Library of Congress went out of his way to assist my labors both at the library and other depositories in Washington.

James G. Barber of the National Portrait Gallery expedited my efforts to obtain copies of photographs in the Smithsonian and elsewhere around the country for reproduction in this book. Mary Ison of the prints and photographs division of the Library of Congress also aided my search for appropriate pictorial material. And Dr. Robert Tochia of the Union League of Philadelphia kindly contributed the transparency of John Neagle's great portrait of Clay which I have used for the dust jacket.

During the time my late brother Vincent, to whom this book is dedicated, lived in Louisville, he aided my research by copying Clay material at the Filson Club and the Clay Project at the University of Kentucky. He also provided food and shelter during my prolonged visits to Kentucky. I only regret that he did not live to see the results of our labors together.

My editor at W. W. Norton and Company, James L. Mairs, alerted me to the necessity of focusing a little more on Clay's character and personality and not getting completely lost in his political career. But I am especially grateful to him for agreeing to place all the footnotes in this book at the bottom of the pages to which they refer. And his editorial associate, Cecil G. Lyon, frequently used her good offices in many particulars to help smooth my way during the final months of editing the manuscript.

Now that I have intimately studied the lives and careers of both Andrew Jackson and Henry Clay, I suppose I shall be known hereafter as a Jackson man with feet of Clay. Jackson might not like that, but I suspect Henry Clay would find it highly amusing.

ROBERT V. REMINI

June 1990
Wilmette, Illinois

Chronology of Clay's Life
1777–1852

1777   *April 12* Born, Hanover County, Virginia
1781   Death of father, Reverend John Clay
1782   Mother, Elizabeth Hudson Clay, marries Henry Watkins
1785–1790   Attends Old Field School run by Peter Deacon and the school at St. Paul's
          Church in the district
1791–1792   Works in Richard Denny's drugstore in Richmond
1791   Clerks in chancery office of Peter Tinsley.
          Mother and stepfather depart for Kentucky
1792–1796   Reads law with Chancellor George Wythe
1796–1797   Studies law in office of Virginia Attorney General Robert Brooke
1797   *November 6* Licensed an attorney-at-law in Virginia
          November Migrates to Kentucky and settles in Lexington
1798   *March 20* Licensed to practice law in Kentucky
          April 25 Writes address to electors of Fayette County advocating emancipation
1799   Joins Lexington Masonic fraternity
          April 11 Marries Lucretia Hart
          Purchases residence on Mill Street
1800   *June 25* Daughter Henrietta born
1801   Daughter Henrietta dies
1802   Son Theodore Wythe born
1803   Elected to general assembly from Fayette County
          September 22 Son Thomas Hart born
1804   Defends Kentucky Insurance Company in Assembly, helps defeat John Adair's
          election to U.S. Senate, and assumes legislative leadership
1805   Daughter Susan Hart born
          October 10 Elected professor of law and politics, Transylvania University
1806   Purchases Ashland property
          Elected a director of Frankfort bank
1806   *November 7* Hired to defend Aaron Burr
          November 19 Elected to U.S. Senate

1807 *April 7* Daughter Anne Brown born
     Reelected to state legislature
     October 7 Elected trustee, Transylvania University
1808 *January 11* Chosen Speaker of the lower house
1809 *January 19* Fights first duel, with Humphrey Marshall
     Daughter Lucretia Hart born
1810 *January 4* Elected to U.S. Senate
     August Elected to U.S. House of Representatives
1811 Builds Ashland mansion
     February 15 Opposes recharter of First National Bank of the United States
     April 10 Son Henry, Jr., born
     November 4 Elected Speaker of U.S. House of Representatives (Twelfth and
          Thirteenth Congresses)
1812 Pressures Madison into asking for a declaration of war against Great Britain
1813 Adds wings to Ashland mansion
     July 5 Daughter Eliza born
1814 *January* Appointed one of five commissioners to negotiate peace treaty with
          Great Britain
     February 25 Sails for Europe
     April 13 Arrives in Gottenburg, Sweden
     June 2 Leaves Gottenburg for Ghent, Belgium
     August–December Participates in negotiating treaty
     September Informed of reelection to U.S. House of Representatives
     December 24 Signs Treaty of Ghent
     December Appointed to negotiate trade treaty with Great Britain
1815 *January 7* Leaves Ghent for Paris
     January–March Meets royalty and acquires nickname Prince Hal
     March 22 Arrives in London
     July 3 Signs trade convention with Great Britain
     July 22 Sails from Liverpool to New York
     September 1 Arrives in New York
     December 4 Reelected Speaker of U.S. House of Representatives (Fourteenth,
          Fifteenth, Sixteenth Congresses)
1816 *March 9* Supports enactment of Second National Bank of the United States
          (BUS)
     April 27 Supports first protective tariff
     August 30, September 14 Offered and rejects appointment as secretary of war
     September Daughter Laura born
     December 11(?) Daughter Laura dies
     December 16 Presides at formation of American Colonization Society
1817 *January* Offered and refuses office of secretary of war and mission to Great
          Britain
     November 9 Son James Brown born
     December Publicly supports Latin American independence
1817–1818 Assails policies of Monroe administration
1819 *January 20* Attacks General Jackson in House speech
     February Opposes Adams-Onís Treaty
     April 10 Borrows twenty thousand dollars from John Jacob Astor

February 15 Opposes Tallmadge amendment to Missouri bill

1820 *February 20* Supports Missouri Compromise and manipulates its final passage

October 28 Resigns as Speaker

1821 *January–February* Guides second Missouri Compromise through Congress and is dubbed the Great Compromiser

February 21 Son John Morrison born

Appointed chief counsel for BUS in Ohio and Kentucky.

Retires from Congress

Argues *Osborn* v. *Bank of the United States* before Supreme Court

1821–1824 Seeks to avoid involvement in Relief controversy

1822 Honorary degree of Doctor of Laws conferred by Transylvania University

April 22 Susan Clay marries Martin Duralde

August Elected to U.S. House of Representatives

November 18 Recommended for presidency by Kentucky legislators

1822–1823 Suffers lingering illnesses

1823 *June 18* Daughter Lucretia dies

October 21 Anne Clay marries James Erwin

December 1 Elected Speaker of U.S. House of Representatives (Eighteenth Congress)

1824 *January 14* Enunciates American System in House speech

February Opposes congressional nominating caucus

April Supports passage of Tariff of 1824

October 4 Repays Astor loan

November Defeated for President

December 4 Presents Lafayette to Congress

1825 *January 9* Meets with Adams and agrees to support him for President

January 28 Publicly accused of a "corrupt bargain"

February 12, 17 Offered and accepts office of secretary of state

March 28 Publishes address to congressional district explaining his support for Adams

April Supports U.S. participation at Panama Congress

August 11 Daughter Eliza dies

September 18 Daughter Susan dies

1826 *April 8* Duels with John Randolph

April Enunciates good neighborhood policy in U.S.-Latin American relations

1826–1827 Attempts to acquire Texas

1826–1828 Signs most-favored-nation agreements with Mexico, Denmark, Hanseatic cities, Prussia, Scandinavian countries, and Austria

1827–1828 Targeted for attack by Democrats

1827 *December 29* Publishes *Address* in response to charges by Jackson

1827–1828 Considers resigning as secretary of state because of continued illnesses

1828 *December* Rejects offer of appointment to Supreme Court

1829 Reluctantly resumes law practice

March Son Thomas arrested and jailed for nonpayment of debt

March 3 Resigns as secretary of state

May 16 Opens war on Jackson administration

November 25 Stepfather dies

December 4 Mother dies; older brother John dies

1830   *January–March* Visits New Orleans and environs
       June Attacks Maysville veto and Indian removal
       December 20—March 1831 Leaves Ashland for New Orleans
1831   *spring* Son Henry, Jr., graduates second in class at West Point
       October Son Theodore committed to "Lunatic Asylum of Kentucky"
       November 9 Elected to U.S. Senate
       December 13 Nominated for President by National Republican Convention
       December 15 Instructs Biddle to apply for recharter of BUS
1832   *May 7* Accepts nomination in person of Young Men's National Republican
           Convention
1832–1837   Leads congressional opposition to Jackson's appointments and policies
1832   *February* Supports tariff reform
       spring Guides passage of tariff and Bank recharter bills through Congress;
           Jackson vetoes Bank bill on July 10
       July 3 Wins passage of public land bill by Senate; postponed in House
       July Visits James Madison
       August Vacations at White Sulphur Springs
       October 10 Son Henry, Jr., marries Julia Prather
       November Defeated for President
       December Formulates tariff revision to meet secession threat by South Carolina
1833   *January* Forms alliance with Calhoun
       February Wins congressional approval of his Compromise Tariff and public
           land bill; Jackson pocket vetoes the land bill
       February Misses vote on force bill
       September–November Tours East Coast
       December 26 Introduces censure motions against Jackson and Taney
1834   *March 28* Wins passage of censure motions
       April 14 Refers to the Whig party as the new name of the opposition
       April 30 Attacks Jackson's protest message
       August Involved in stagecoach accident
       December Writes Senate committee report on French spoliation controversy
1835   *December 10* Daughter Anne dies
1836   *March* Opposes annexation of Texas
       March Supports deposit-distribution bill
       July Denounces Specie Circular
       December Elected president of American Colonization Society
       December 15 Reelected to Senate
       December 26 Opposes expunging of censure motion against Jackson
1837   *March 4* Attends Van Buren's inauguration
       April Accuses Jackson of precipitating panic
       October 5 Son Thomas marries Marie Mentelle
       September–October Attends special session of Congress and attacks
           administration economic proposals
       December Delivers presidential address to Colonization Society and suggests
           federal government subsidize return of blacks to Africa
1838   *January 9* Presents views on abolition of slavery
       February 19 Attacks Van Buren and Calhoun
       February–March Engages Calhoun in heated debates

June 7 Denied presidential nomination
1848–1849 *December–April* Winters in New Orleans
1849 *January* Injured in fall
      February 5 Elected to U.S. Senate
      April 11 Celebrates golden wedding anniversary
      July–August Vacations in Saratoga and Newport
      September Visits Van Buren at Lindenwald
1850 *January 21* Formulates compromise plan
      January 29 Presents compromise to Senate
      February 5 Gives first speech on compromise
      April 8 Accepts omnibus plan for compromise
      May 21 Attacks Taylor
      July Omnibus defeated
      August Vacations in Newport
      September 16 Assists final passage of compromise
1851 *March–April* Vacations in Cuba
      May 26, July 10 Acquires plot in cemetery, and writes last will
      December 1 Last speech in Senate
      December 17 Resigns from Senate
1852 *January* Meets Louis Kossuth
      June 29 Dies in Washington hotel
      July 1 Lies in state in Capitol Rotunda
      July 10 Buried in Lexington cemetery

Ashland

FILSON CLUB

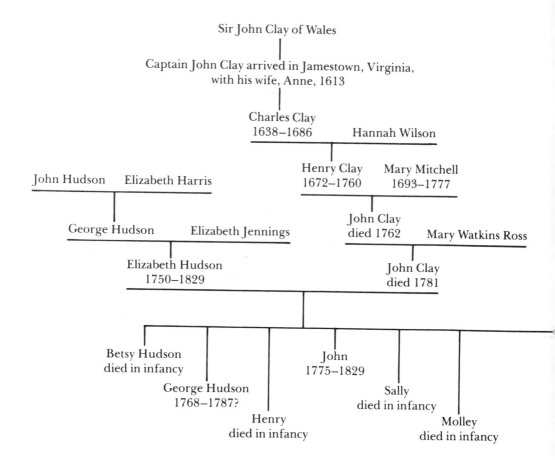

Sir John Clay of Wales

Captain John Clay arrived in Jamestown, Virginia,
with his wife, Anne, 1613

Charles Clay
1638–1686   Hannah Wilson

John Hudson   Elizabeth Harris   Henry Clay   Mary Mitchell
                                          1672–1760   1693–1777

George Hudson   Elizabeth Jennings   John Clay
                                                 died 1762   Mary Watkins Ross

Elizabeth Hudson   John Clay
1750–1829   died 1781

Betsy Hudson   John
died in infancy   1775–1829

          George Hudson   Sally
          1768–1787?   died in infancy

                    Henry   Molley
                    died in infancy   died in infancy

GENEALOGY OF THE CLAY FAMILY

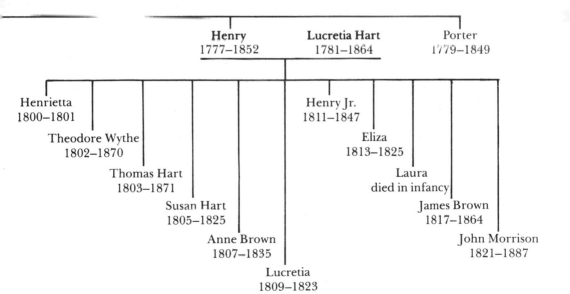

Henry
1777–1852

Lucretia Hart
1781–1864

Porter
1779–1849

Henrietta
1800–1801

Theodore Wythe
1802–1870

Thomas Hart
1803–1871

Susan Hart
1805–1825

Anne Brown
1807–1835

Lucretia
1809–1823

Henry Jr.
1811–1847

Eliza
1813–1825

Laura
died in infancy

James Brown
1817–1864

John Morrison
1821–1887

ABBREVIATIONS AND SHORT TITLES
USED IN THE NOTES

Adams, *Memoirs*   Charles Francis Adams, ed., *Memoirs of John Quincy Adams*
        (Philadelphia, 1874–1877), 12 volumes
ASPFR   American State Papers, Foreign Relations
Bemis, *Adams*, I, II   Samuel Flagg Bemis, *John Quincy Adams and the Foundations of
        American Foreign Policy* (New York, 1949) and *John Quincy Adams and the
        Union* (New York, 1956)
Benton, *Thirty Years' View*   Thomas Hart Benton, *Thirty Years' View* (New York,
        1865), 2 volumes
Calhoun, *Papers*   W. Edwin Hamphill et al., eds., *The Papers of John C. Calhoun*,
        (Columbia, S.C., 1959–), 19 volumes
Clay, *Correspondence*   Calvin Colton, *The Private Correspondence of Henry Clay*
        (Cincinnati, 1856)
Clay, *Papers*   James F. Hopkins et al., eds., *The Papers of Henry Clay* (Lexington, Ky.,
        1959–), 9 volumes
Clay, *Works*   Calvin Colton, ed., *The Works of Henry Clay* (New York, 1857), 6
        volumes
Colton, *Clay*   Calvin Colton, *The Life and Times of Henry Clay* (New York, 1846), 2
        volumes
CPP   Clay Papers Project, University of Kentucky, Lexington, Kentucky
Hone, *Diary*   Allan Nevins, ed., *The Diary of Philip Hone, 1828–1851* (New York,
        1927), 2 volumes
Jackson, *Correspondence*   John Spencer Bassett, ed., *The Correspondence of Andrew
        Jackson* (Washington, D.C., 1926–1933), 6 volumes
LC   Library of Congress
Mangum, *Papers*   Henry Thomas Shanks, ed., *The Papers of Willie Person Mangum*
        (Raleigh, N.C., 1950–1956), 5 volumes
Mayo, *Clay*   Bernard Mayo, *Henry Clay: Spokesman of the New West* (Boston, 1937)
NA   National Archives
Parton, *Jackson*   James Parton, *Life of Andrew Jackson* (Boston, 1866), 3 volumes
Poage, *Clay and Whig Party*   George R. Poage, *Henry Clay and the Whig Party*
        (Chapel Hill, N.C., 1936)

Polk, *Correspondence*   Herbert Weaver et al., eds., *Correspondence of James K. Polk*
        (Nashville, 1969–), 7 volumes
Poore, *Reminiscences*   Ben: Perley Poore, *Perley's Reminiscences of Sixty Years in the
        National Metropolis* (Philadelphia, 1886), 2 volumes
Remini, *Jackson,* I, II, III   Robert V. Remini, *Andrew Jackson and the Course of
        American Empire, 1767–1821* (New York, 1977); *Andrew Jackson and the
        Course of American Freedom, 1822–1832* (New York, 1981); and *Andrew
        Jackson and the Course of American Democracy, 1833–1845* (New York, 1984)
RG   Record Group
Richardson, *Messages and Papers*   J. D. Richardson, *Compilation of the Messages and
        Papers of the Presidents* (Washington, D.C., 1908), 20 volumes
Sargent, *Clay*   Epes Sargent, *The Life and Public Services of Henry Clay down to 1848*
        (New York, 1860)
Sargent, *Public Men and Events*   Nathan Sargent, *Public Men and Events*
        (Philadelphia, 1875), 2 volumes
Schurz, *Clay*   Carl Schurz, *Life of Henry Clay* (Boston, 1887), 2 volumes
Smith, *Forty Years*   Gaillard Hunt, ed., *The First Forty Years of Washington Society
        Portrayed by the Family Letters of Mrs. Samuel Harrison Smith* (New York,
        1906)
Tyler, *Letters*   Lyon G. Tyler, *The Letters and Times of the Tylers* (New York, 1896,
        1970), 3 volumes
Van Buren, *Autobiography*   John C. Fitzpatrick, ed., *Autobiography of Martin Van
        Buren* (Washington, D.C., 1920)
Van Deusen, *Clay*   Glyndon G. Van Deusen, *The Life of Henry Clay* (Boston, 1937)
Webster, *Papers, Correspondence,* and *Papers, Speeches*   Charles M. Wiltse et al., *The
        Papers of Daniel Webster, Correspondence* (Hanover, N.H., 1974–1986), 7
        volumes, and *Speeches and Formal Writings* (Hanover, N.H., 1986, 1988), 2
        volumes

Henry Clay

It has been my invariable rule to do all for the Union. If any man wants the key of my heart, let him take the key of the Union, and that is the key to my heart. . . .

— HENRY CLAY
speech in Norfolk, April 22, 1844

—— O N E ——

The Mill Boy of
the Slashes

P RESIDENT ANDREW JACKSON called him a "profligate
demagogue"—and that was among the more temperate of Old
Hickory's pronouncements about Henry Clay. "The *Judas* of
the West" came closer to expressing Jackson's real feelings about his rival. But
the President's most vicious verbal assault by far characterized Clay as "the
bases[t], meanest, scoundrel, that ever disgraced the image of his god—nothing too mean or low for him to condescend to, *secretely* to carry his cowardly
and base purpose of slander into effect; even the aged and virtuous female, is
not free from his secrete combination of base slander."[1]

Friendlier voices had better opinions of this singular statesman, like "Star
of the West," the "Great Compromiser," "Prince Hal," and "Harry of the
West." Most agreed with John Quincy Adams, however, that in politics as well
as in his private life Henry Clay was "essentially a gamester," a western riverboat gamester, who frequently took wild chances in hopes of a spectacular
"killing," just like most riverboat gamblers. Sometimes he "won big," and
sometimes he lost everything. As the Charleston *Mercury* wisely commented,
"Mr. Clay is a gamester in politics but not a cool one. His temper, unrestrained, exhibits frequent ebullitions from the excitement of the game . . . and
though he often wins a shrewd trick, and dips deeply into the bank, he loses in
the long run."[2]

Clay went after the biggest prize the country could offer, involving a

1. Andrew Jackson to Francis P. Blair, April 19, 1841, Jackson to Sam Houston, December 15,
1826, Jackson Papers, LC; Jackson to William B. Lewis, February 14, 1825, in Jackson, *Correspondence*, III, 276. When he was close to death, Jackson was asked if he had left anything undone.
"Yes," he allegedly responded, "I didn't shoot Henry Clay, and I didn't hang John C. Calhoun."
But Clay gave as good as he got. Jackson, he wrote, "is ignorant, passionate, hypocritical,
corrupt, and easily swayed by the basest men who surround him." Clay to Francis T. Brooke,
August 2, 1833, in Clay, *Papers*, VIII, 661–662.
2. Adams, *Memoirs*, V, 29; the Charleston *Mercury* is quoted in Merrill D. Peterson, *The Great
Triumvirate: Webster, Clay, and Calhoun* (New York, 1987), p. 381.

gamble he should never have attempted. As a result, the prize forever slipped
from his grasp. But he went after it again and again. By the time he suffered his
third humiliating failure he probably knew that it was beyond him. Not that he
stopped trying. Almost as long as he lived, he hungered and reached for the
office of President of the United States. And it could never be his. One of the
greatest statesmen of American history never had the opportunity to demonstrate how well he could lead the nation, advance the common good, and
improve the social and material well-being of the country.

Not only was Henry Clay of Kentucky a "typical western gambler" who
rarely resisted a "long shot," but whenever he gambled, he did it with a certain
amount of class. A wonderful sense of style always informed Clay's best efforts,
especially his most daring. That probably explains why many of his enemies
hated him with such fervor. He had a flare for the dramatic, a gift for the
outrageous. He did not annoy his political opponents so much as he infuriated
them. His thrusts could be deadly but were always exquisitely executed. And
he never failed to comment on the discomfort he had invoked, usually by
denying any intentional malice.

Some critics tagged him a charlatan, a liar, and a fake. There was indeed a
bit of the charlatan in him because of his extraordinary ability at self-dramatization. For example, he liked to describe his early life as one of almost total
deprivation. Oh, how he could tug at the emotions of his listeners when he
reminisced about his youth. Upon his arrival in Kentucky from Virginia,
where he was born, he said he had not yet reached his majority but was "an
orphan who had never recognized a father's smile, nor felt his caresses—poor,
penniless, without the favor of the great, with an imperfect and inadequate
education, limited to the ordinary business and common pursuits of life,"[3] all
of which was nonsense—or nearly so. Clay liked to proclaim himself "a self-
made man"—an extremely apt term, which he himself introduced into the
language—who rose from virtually nothing ("I inherited infancy, ignorance,
and indigence," he wailed[4]) and reached fantastic heights of everlasting fame
by dint of his own remarkable "genius." He probably believed what he said
about his youth. It certainly added to the legend that was popular at the time
about how greatness often arises from humble beginnings. The "rags to
riches" notion that Americans have enjoyed ever since the early nineteenth
century was studiously cultivated by Clay and his early biographers in the
belief that such a myth added to his stature and attractiveness. "He stands
among men in towering and barbaric grandeur," concluded one commentator,
"in all the hardihood and rudeness of perfect originality, independent of the
polish and beyond the reach of art."[5]

Actually Henry Clay's early life was considerably better than he pre-

3. *Congressional Globe,* 27th Congress, 2d session, pp. 376–377.
4. *Annals of Congress,* 18th Congress, 1st session, pp. 1311–1317.
5. Thomas F. Marshall made the statement in a public letter, quoted in Peterson, *Great Triumvi-rate,* p. 8.

tended, although it was not without hardship or misfortune. He was the seventh of nine children[6] born to the Reverend John Clay and his wife, Elizabeth Hudson, on April 12, 1777, three miles from Hanover Court House, Virginia, which was approximately sixteen miles north of Richmond. It was a low, swampy area and therefore commonly known as the slashes. The Reverend Clay was a Baptist preacher and a tobacco planter "of great dignity and eloquence"[7] whose ancestors arrived in America shortly after the founding of Jamestown.[8] His wife was fifteen years of age when he married her and came from a prosperous family. Elizabeth was later described as below medium height, "of well rounded form," with dark hair and eyes and ruddy complexion. Her son Henry inherited neither her dark hair nor her dark eyes. He had a fair complexion with extremely light hair, and his eyes were blue.[9] But he may have inherited her "great vigor of mind" and her "warm-hearted and imperious" nature.[10]

John and Elizabeth Clay, with their offspring, removed to the 464-acre homestead belonging to Elizabeth's father, George Hudson,[11] just a few months before Henry was born. This farm with its twenty-one slave hands supported the family in relative comfort. The house where the family resided rose to two stories, with dormer windows projecting from the steep roof and two large chimneys located at either end of the rectangular-shaped structure. It was hardly the home of an indigent family.[12]

6. He was named after an older brother who died four or five years earlier. See Zachary F. Smith and May Rogers Clay, *The Clay Family* (Louisville, 1899), pp. 6–7. Both Bernard Mayo and Glyndon G. Van Deusen in their biographies of Clay state that Elizabeth and John Clay had nine children. But Colton, *Clay*, I, 10, claims there were only eight. The discrepancy occurred because the ninth and last child died almost immediately on birth. In his will, dated November 14, 1780, John Clay named his living children and mentioned the unborn child that his wife was carrying. Apparently Henry Clay was not aware of the last sibling, a girl, who apparently died nameless at birth, and he probably assumed, therefore, that his parents only had eight children. No doubt he provided Colton with this information. In constructing the Clay family genealogy, I am grateful for the assistance of Nettie Oliver, staff researcher at the Filson Club Historical Society, Louisville, Kentucky.

7. Thomas Hart Clay, *Henry Clay* (Philadelphia, 1910), p. 15.

8. See genealogy chart.

9. Smith and Clay, *Clay Family,* p. 18; Clay's passport in the Filson Club, Louisville, Kentucky; George Bancroft, "A Few Words about Henry Clay," in *Century Magazine,* VIII (July 1885), p. 480. Henry Clay's wife, Lucretia, said that "he had when a young man the whitest head of hair I ever saw." J. O. Harrison, "Henry Clay, Reminiscences by His Executor," *Century Magazine,* XXXIII (December 1886), p. 179.

10. Thomas Hart Clay, *Henry Clay,* pp. 20–21.

11. A man of considerable importance at the time, George Hudson was an inspector of tobacco at Hanover Court House.

12. In 1834, when he was a senator from Kentucky, Clay mentioned that he was born in Hanover County, Virginia. Another senator asked which of two Hanovers might claim "the honor of giving birth to the Senator from Kentucky." Clay responded: "The place where that event happened, which enables me to stand before you, was between Black Tom's Slash and Hanover Court-House, or, to fix the spot more precisely, between the Merry Oaks and the Court-House, about half-way between them, and not very far from St. Paul's Church, at the vestry house of which I went to school several years." *Register of Debates,* 23d Congress, 1st session, pp. 1480–1485.

The Reverend John Clay—"Sir John"[13] to many of his more playful friends—made a strong impression upon his Baptist flock with his zealous preaching. In fact, at an earlier time he had gotten himself imprisoned for his rabble-rousing preaching which may account for his removal to Hanover County. Apparently "Sir John" preferred to minister to the masses and was something of a radical evangelical, none of which pleased the established church or the political authorities.

The colonials had already begun to stir in opposition to the crown, and the Baptists in Virginia took a lead in demanding religious toleration. The general discontent within the colony and elsewhere finally exploded into revolution and war when delegates from the several colonies met in Philadelphia and resolved that they had a right to be free and independent. Adopting a Declaration of Independence authored principally by Thomas Jefferson, the Virginia delegate, the Continental Congress pulled free from the British Empire and deliberately chose the path leading to war. Hanover County responded with patriotic fervor, and a company of volunteers, led by Patrick Henry, marched to Williamsburg to smite the royal brute.

Henry Clay, with his flair for the dramatic, always liked to boast that he was actually "rocked in the cradle of the Revolution."[14] And he was right to an extent. His early years in the slashes were filled with exciting and portentous events, only a few of which he remembered in later years. By the spring of 1781, when Henry was barely four years of age, Hanover was overrun with redcoats on horseback, commanded by Lieutenant Colonel Banastre Tarleton. They ravaged the countryside throughout the slashes, burning, pillaging, killing. Finally they invaded the Clay household, and a wide-eyed, horrified four-year-old child, clinging to his mother, watched in terror as the soldiers ransacked the house.[15] "I recollect in 1781 or '82," Henry Clay said some sixty years later, "a visit made by Tarleton's troops to the house of my mother, and of their running their swords into the newly made graves of my father and grandfather, thinking they contained hidden treasures. Though [I was] then no more than four years of age, the circumstance of that visit is vividly remem-

13. The first John Clay was indeed Sir John: Sir John Clay of Wales. His son, Captain John Clay, arrived in Jamestown, Virginia, in 1613. His wife, Ann, joined him in 1623. Captain John was Henry Clay's great-great-great-grandfather. "All I know, in the general," Clay wrote in 1845, "is that they [his paternal ancestors] came from England to the colony of Virginia, some time after its establishment, and settled, I believe, on the south side of James River. The descendants of the original stock are very numerous, and much dispersed, many of them residing in Virginia and Kentucky. A branch or branches of the family, remained in England, and among their descendants was [William Clay] recently quite a distinguished member of the British House of Commons." Clay added that his maternal ancestors also came from England and settled in Hanover County "about the beginning of the last century." Clay to Calvin Colton, March 5, 1845, and an undated note in Clay, *Works,* IV, 524.

14. *Niles' Weekly Register,* October 29, 1842, reporting a speech given by Clay in Indianapolis on October 5.

15. One tradition claims that after the ransacking, Tarleton left a handful of gold and silver coins on the table as compensation for the damage his troops had inflicted on the Clay household. As soon as Tarleton left, Mrs. Clay threw the coins into the fireplace. Schurz, *Clay,* I, 3.

bered, and it will be to the last moment of my life." Up and down the Virginia and Carolina frontiers Tarleton's cavalrymen butchered and pillaged. Both Henry Clay and another lad, Andrew Jackson, aged fourteen, living on the border between North and South Carolina, never forgot the horror inflicted by Tarleton's raiders.[16]

As the mature Henry Clay later recalled, his father, the Reverend John Clay, had died quite suddenly in the midst of this tumult and terror, and his freshly dug grave was desecrated by Tarleton's troops, looking for treasure. Young Henry had little or no remembrance of "Sir John." The only father he came to know was the man his mother subsequently married scarcely a year after John Clay's untimely death. At the age of thirty-three, Elizabeth Hudson Clay married Captain Henry Watkins, a twenty-six-year-old Virginia planter and militia captain who was her sister's brother-in-law. He was described as "an elegant, accomplished gentleman, of good blood, and of goodly wealth." Elizabeth had already borne nine children. She bore Watkins seven more.[17]

The four-year-old Henry inherited two slaves, James and "little Sam," from his father in a will dated November 4, 1780, and probated a year and a half later. His maternal grandfather, George Hudson, also left him "one negro boy, Ben" in his will.[18] So much for his later assertion that he was a "poor, penniless" orphan when his father died. Because the ideal of the "self-made man" added considerable luster to his reputation in the minds of his contemporaries, Clay nurtured the pretense of great poverty in his youth.

Another integral part of the Clay legend was the story about how he became known as the Mill Boy of the Slashes. To provide an example of his "filial and fraternal" devotion, local historians reported that, as a youth, whenever the meal barrel needed replenishing, he could be seen riding barefoot astride a mill bag thrown across the back of a pony on the road between his home and Mrs. Darricott's mill on the Pamunkey River. Those living along the route took to calling him the Mill Boy of the Slashes, and the story became an important part of the political biography of this "self-made" statesman.[19]

Most of the remainder of Sir John's estate went to his widow, who subsequently provided her second husband with a handsome dowry. The Hanover tax records of 1782 reveal that she owned 464 acres of land—taxed at twice the average rate of other farms in the county—thirty-two cattle, two vehicles, and sixteen slaves.[20] She also provided a sizable brood of children, but of the nine

16. Speech delivered by Clay in Indianapolis on October 5, 1842, *Niles' Weekly Register,* October 29, 1842; Mayo, *Clay,* p. 6; Remini, *Jackson,* I, 14–16.

17. Colton, *Clay,* I, 26; Thomas Hart Clay, *Henry Clay,* pp. 16–18. Elizabeth's eldest sister, Mary, married John Watkins, older brother of Henry Watkins.

18. Smith and Clay, *Clay Family,* pp. 54, 56. In the Reverend John Clay's will he also left a plantation in Henrico, called Euphraim, to his wife. Henry Clay later brought suit to recover it, arguing that it had been illegally sold to Richard Cocke. See Clay to Benjamin W. Leigh, December 7, 26, 1819, in Clay, *Papers,* II, 726–727, 735–736.

19. Smith and Clay, *Clay Family,* p. 13.

20. *Hanover Tax Lists, Tax Books, 1782–1792,* Virginia Archives, Richmond.

children she bore the Reverend John Clay, only three survived to maturity: John, Henry, and Porter.[21]

Henry Clay's formal schooling began at the Old Field School, presided over by Peter Deacon, an bibulous Englishman, who reputedly had come to this country "under a cloud." Young Henry learned to "read, write, and cipher" under the dubious instruction of this frontier itinerant. His education was meager in any event, and like so many other men of his generation who went on to national fame, Henry Clay later regretted the lost opportunity to secure adequate schooling, one grounded in the classics, history, and literature. In an age when knowledge of Greek and Latin were basic requirements for all educated men, Clay lamented this void in his background and said that it "remained one of his weak points through life." He advised a favorite son later on "to refresh your recollection of the dead languages. I never enjoyed the advantage of Knowing them, but I have remarked that those who do find a resource in them throughout life, and sometimes at a late period of it." He also felt that he had failed to apply himself adequately when he had the chance. "To attain the highest place," he counseled his son, ". . . you must make up your mind to labor incessantly. I never studied half enough. I always relied too much upon the resources of my genius."

Indeed, throughout his life, if Henry Clay had read more, labored harder at acquiring knowledge, studied some of the great works of literature, history, and philosophy, he would never have developed some of the limitations that later impeded his efforts as a statesman. "He was never such a student as a man intrusted with public business ought to be," wrote an early commentator. He had "a mind most gifted by nature," but as Clay himself admitted, he never cultivated it fully and relied too much on the resources of his genius.[22]

This "tall, awkward, slender stripling," dressed in "homespun butternut of his mother's making," attended a log schoolhouse with no flooring and a door that served as entranceway, window, and source of fresh air. At one point in Henry's early education the schoolmaster, in a fit of anger, struck him with a "magisterial blow" for some infraction or academic failure, the mark of which Henry Clay later said he carried for some time.[23] He also went to a school in the vestry house of St. Paul's Church for several years, and most probably his mother, and perhaps his stepfather, furthered his education in academic as well as practical skills.

But the greatest influence on his developing education was a number of public speakers who gave Hanover a reputation for oratory that was un-

21. Smith and Clay, *Clay Family,* p. 18ff. The first boy in the family, George Hudson Clay, was born in 1768 and died just before reaching his maturity. The second boy died in infancy.
22. Henry Clay to Henry Clay, Jr., October 21, 1828, April 19, 1829, in Clay, *Papers,* VII, 511; VIII, 30. James Parton, *Famous Americans of Recent Times* (Boston, 1867), pp. 51–52; Adams, *Memoirs,* III, 39. See also J. Drew Harrington, "Henry Clay and the Classics," *Filson Club History Quarterly,* LXI (April 1987), pp. 234–246.
23. "Anecdotes of Henry Clay," Clay Papers, Manuscript Department, Filson Club, Louisville, Kentucky; Colton, *Clay,* I, 19.

matched in any other part of Virginia. The most famous, of course, was Patrick Henry, and he could be heard in court and on the stump during the entire time that young Henry Clay was growing up. At a very early age the boy heard Patrick Henry,[24] acquired a keen interest in the "art of declamation," and began to train himself to become verbally fluent. He often acknowledged that he worked unceasingly to emulate the eloquence of the Hanover orators and that his later success in politics was the direct result of these efforts.[25]

Henry Clay was indeed one of the great public speakers of the early nineteenth century, but his art was different from that of Patrick Henry or any of the other distinguished Hanover orators. As he grew older, that difference became more noticeable. For example, Clay could not match Daniel Webster in declamation. His style was totally different. He was more a debater than an orator. There were not the majestic flourishes in the grand manner that oratorical eloquence normally dictated. Instead, there was something intimate in the way he spoke, something insinuating, friendly, warm—and highly emotional. Although he was frequently playful, witty, and loose, he could also slash, cut, and gouge when necessary. Invariably dramatic, if not flamboyant, he regularly mesmerized his audience with his histrionics. He was therefore always a popular speaker, and in Congress he instinctively knew how to appeal to the galleries and bring them to their feet, shouting and clapping. Most probably he attended many political meetings and courtroom sessions when he was a growing boy in Hanover, where he observed many models of every speaking style imaginable, both good and bad. Early in his education he recognized that the road to success lay in mastering the art of public speaking, and he did everything possible to acquire that mastery. He read aloud, recited from printed orations, and sat, watched, and observed how the art was practiced by some very distinguished revolutionary statesmen.[26]

As he grew, young Henry also learned to swim, become an expert horseman, and play a passable tune on the "fiddle." He was not as adept with the instrument as Thomas Jefferson or Patrick Henry, but he understood the personal joy and satisfaction of acquiring such a talent. And his "fiddle playing" assisted him enormously on the hustings when he ran for public office.

There was a sensitive and compassionate side to Henry Clay, even at an early age. A story was told that on one occasion he happened upon a runaway slave attempting to hide from his pursuers. He took pity on the runaway and surreptitiously brought him food. Later, when he learned that the unfortunate slave had been slain while resisting arrest, he burst into tears. Slavery always caused Henry Clay deep pain and anxiety. He owned slaves almost all his life, yet he anguished over the "peculiar institution" and called it "a great evil." He believed the words in the Declaration of Independence about all men being

24. Clay heard Patrick Henry at least twice. Thomas Hart Clay, *Henry Clay*, p. 19.
25. Clay to Lucretia Clay, March 6, 1840, in Clay, *Papers*, IX, 395; Mayo, *Clay*, p. 15.
26. Clement Eaton, *Henry Clay and the Art of American Politics* (Boston, 1957), pp. 13–14, 18; Mayo, *Clay*, p. 74.

equal, and he also believed that the words applied to blacks as well as whites "as abstract principle." Abraham Lincoln later adopted this position and repeatedly quoted Clay on it in his public speeches. Clay lamented that slavery had been bequeathed by "our ancestors" and claimed that if the nation could start all over again, he would oppose the institution and keep it from becoming a part of American society and culture.[27]

With the conclusion of the Revolutionary War and the establishment of peace, the new nation attempted the formation of a republican government under the Articles of Confederation. The problems that resulted in the years following independence—the so-called Critical Period—finally forced the convocation of a convention that wrote the Constitution and established a new federal structure of government. By the time the states ratified this document and put it into operation Henry Clay had entered his turbulent teenage years. George Washington was elected President of the new government, and although the Constitution succeeded in providing a stable and workable government, a number of disagreements between opposing political factions developed almost immediately. These differences ultimately produced the formation of two political parties: the Federalist party, led by Alexander Hamilton of New York, which provided unquestioning support to the Washington administration and advocated a strong central government, and the Republican party, led by James Madison and Thomas Jefferson, which frequently criticized the policies of the Washington administration and reemphasized the rights of the states.

In 1791 Captain Watkins decided to leave Virginia and follow his brother, John, to the new country that had been recently opened up beyond the Allegheny Mountains along the Ohio River, a region Daniel Boone had known as the "dark and bloody ground" of Kentucky. John Watkins had prospered and become a prominent citizen of Versailles, Woodford County, only thirteen miles from Lexington, and Henry Watkins hoped to improve his own situation by joining his brother in Kentucky. The entire region had once been claimed by Virginia, but it relinquished this claim to the central government in 1784 in order to advance the efforts toward creating a permanent union among the several states.

As they began their preparations for the grand removal, Watkins and his wife decided to leave young Henry behind in Richmond so that he might continue his education with a view toward becoming a lawyer, probably because he had shown considerable intellectual promise. They planned to get Henry installed in the chancery office through the good offices of Colonel Thomas Tinsley, the brother of Peter Tinsley, clerk of the High Court of Chancery in Virginia. In the meantime, Henry would be employed as a clerk in Richard Denny's drugstore in Richmond, where he would serve as errand boy.

27. See Clay's speech in Richmond, Indiana, in 1842, in Clay, *Works,* VI, 385–390. In his celebrated debates with Stephen A. Douglas, Lincoln referred to Clay no less than forty-one times. Edgar De Witt Jones, *The Influence of Henry Clay on Abraham Lincoln* (Lexington, Ky. 1952), p. 21.

So, at the age of fourteen, Henry moved to Richmond and worked at the Denny establishment for about a year, performing various tasks, such as running errands, delivering parcels, cleaning the store, and occasionally waiting on customers from behind the counter. If this early separation from his immediate family produced any psychological scars on young Henry, they went unreported. He never mentioned any hurt or bitterness about being left behind in Richmond. Quite possibly the separation encouraged in the boy an attitude of self-reliance and self-confidence, and strengthened his determination to succeed in the profession that had been chosen for him.

But Watkins was dissatisfied with the delay in getting Henry located in the chancery office and appealed to his good friend Colonel Tinsley and begged his intervention. The colonel finally yielded and spoke to his brother but was told that no position existed for the young man. "Never mind," the colonel reportedly stormed, "you *must* take him." And that apparently settled the matter. Young Henry Clay was appointed and thus began a career that eventually led him to his preeminent position as lawyer and statesman.[28]

When the fifteen-year-old lad first appeared in Peter Tinsley's office to begin his duties, the other clerks broke out in broad smiles, if not outright laughter, as he walked through the door. The young man was dressed in his best finery, a Virginia ("Figginy") suit of mixed silk and cotton cloth, pepper and salt in color, clean linen well starched, and the tails of his coat so stiff that they stood out from his legs at a forty-five-degree angle. He was quite a sight. But the other clerks soon learned that young Henry was no village bumpkin. He was an extraordinarily intelligent and diligent worker, friendly and fun to have around. He liked to have a good time and communicated a spirit of gaiety, frivolity, and comradeship. He picked up the office routine very quickly and was attentive to his duties. He soon came to the attention of the venerable chancellor himself, George Wythe, who regularly frequented Tinsley's office on official business. Wythe was the most learned jurist in Virginia, the law professor of Thomas Jefferson, John Marshall, James Monroe, and a host of other Virginia luminaries, a man of sterling character, and an excellent scholar of the classics to boot. He was a childless widower nearing seventy years of age, a signer of the Declaration, an effective advocate for the ratification of the Constitution in the Virginia ratifying convention, and a professor of law and the classics at the College of William and Mary.

Wythe inquired about Henry after observing him and his work habits over an extended period of time. Tinsley had nothing but praise for his newest clerk, whereupon Wythe, whose hand trembled so much that he could no longer write himself and needed a secretary,[29] asked to have Henry assigned to him as an amanuensis. Henry Clay's excellent handwriting was another factor

28. Colton, *Clay,* I, 19–20; "Anecdotes of Henry Clay," Manuscript Department, Filson Club, Louisville, Kentucky.

29. "When I first knew him," recollected Clay in 1851, "his right hand had become so affected with the rheumatism or gout that it was with difficulty he could write his own name." Clay to Benjamin B. Minor, May 3, 1851, copy CPP.

in his selection, and it remained wonderfully clear and readable to the moment of his death.

Tinsley naturally agreed to Wythe's request, and Henry began a four-year stint as private secretary to the most learned jurist in the state. "It proved to be mutually agreeable, and reciprocally beneficial," was the judgment of Clay's earliest biographer.[30] It was said that the chancellor's society and assistance became an extended seminar in the law, the classics, literature, history, and social refinement and grace. The boy tackled translations of Homer, Plutarch, and other classics. "I remember that it cost me a great deal of labor," wrote Clay in 1851, "not understanding a single Greek character, to write some citations from Greek authors, which he wished inserted in copies of his reports sent to Mr. Jefferson, Mr. Samuel Adams of Boston, and to one or two other persons. I copied them by imitating each character as I found them in the original works." Not understanding Greek, the young man nonetheless enjoyed "listening to his readings of Homer's Illiad and other Greek authors, so beautifully did he pronounce the language."

Young Clay also studied the law, especially Lord Coke, and read some history. Wythe's great forte lay in preparing the argument of a case, for which no one, attested Clay, excelled him in "thorough preparation, clearness and force."[31]

It is questionable how much time Wythe could spare his young assistant in the supervision of his reading and study, and as Clay himself later testified, there was no *systematic* instruction to the relationship;[32] but on balance, for the time, it was an incomparable education, one that could scarcely be matched anywhere in the country. Wythe took a bright, eager, talented, attentive, promising, and courteous sixteen-year-old student, and by the time Clay reached the age of twenty-one, the chancellor had molded him into an educated, cultivated, urbane, and articulate gentleman, with considerable knowledge of the law. Henry Clay never forgot the debt he owed George Wythe. "To no man was I more indebted by his instructions, his advice, and his example." In almost every particular George Wythe was the father Henry Clay had never had.[33]

There were two other important elements in the formation of Henry Clay that were apparent during this early period of his life. Because of his "passion for oratory," Henry organized and developed a "rhetorical society," for the purpose of "recitation and debate," among a number of young gentlemen of Richmond who later achieved reputations of distinction in serving their state and nation. Littleton W. Tazewell, Edmund W. Root, Philip N. Nicholas, Walter Jones, Thomas B. Robinson, John C. Herbert, Edwin Burrell, Bennett

30. Colton, *Clay,* I, 21.
31. Clay to Benjamin B. Minor, May 3, 1851, copy CPP.
32. Speech by Clay at Lexington, June 9, 1842, *Niles' Weekly Register,* July 9, 1842.
33. "Anecdotes of Henry Clay," Manuscript Department, Filson Club, Louisville, Kentucky; Clay to Benjamin Blake Minor, May 3, 1851, copy CPP. Clay named his first son Theodore Wythe Clay.

Taylor, and others participated in the formation of this debating society. They sharpened their legal and oratorical skills in this club and no doubt debated all the exciting political issues, foreign and domestic, confronting the new nation. They gained an excellent reputation in the community for the brilliance of their contests and arguments. Long before he entered a courtroom as a licensed attorney-at-law, young Henry had honed his considerable natural talent as a persuasive speaker to a high level of excellence.[34]

The second element in Henry's continuing development as an educated and accomplished gentleman was his introduction and acceptance into the best Richmond society. No doubt Chancellor Wythe provided the necessary initial entrée to this august community, but once he had gained admittance, Henry, by dint of intelligence and charm, despite his youth, won the right to become a part of that society. The society was indeed august, including such worthies as John Marshall, Bushrod Washington, Edmund Pendleton, Spencer Roane, and others of like accomplishments and stature in Richmond. Association, conversation, and probing verbal exchanges with such distinguished men helped refine and polish Henry's manners and deportment.[35] Whatever lingering awkwardness still clung to him on account of his youth and limited social background were soon wiped away. He became a confident, relaxed, and self-assured young man who mixed quite easily into any society he happened to encounter.[36]

The Richmond experience matured him in other ways. Socially Henry Clay could hold his own thereafter—anywhere and under any circumstance—but he also developed a devastating wit which occasionally got him into trouble. Lightning-quick with repartee, he could never resist the temptation to take advantage of an opening to display his deadly verbal rejoinders. For example, several years later Representative Alexander Smyth of Virginia, an excessively long-winded and tedious congressional speaker, turned to Clay and bragged: "You, sir, speak for the present generation; but I speak for posterity." Young Clay responded instantly: "Yes, and you seem resolved to speak until the arrival of *your* audience."[37]

At the very beginning of his career Henry Clay possessed a mighty weapon—a sharp, cutting tongue powered by a gifted mind—and he used it effectively. Unfortunately too many enemies were acquired over the years because he humiliated or embarrassed them with a quip or a thrust at a social or public function. But these assaults were mostly exceptions to his more gener-

---

34. Colton, *Clay,* I, 25.

35. There is a reference to Clay in a letter of John Marshall to Archibald Stuart, May 28, 1794, Marshall Papers, Virginia Historical Society, Richmond. "I have considered the record brought me by Mr. Clay," wrote Marshall, "and am really apprehensive that he is totally routed and has not a single rallying point left."

36. Colton, *Clay,* I, 26. Some of that refinement was lost in Kentucky but recovered when Clay began his career in Washington.

37. Sargent, *Clay,* p. 111.

ally relaxed and easygoing style. Everyone loved and admired the charming Henry Clay. He was the proverbial hail-fellow.

Reading law with Chancellor Wythe in preparation for examination for admission to the bar provided as rounded an education as anyone could expect in the late eighteenth century. But Clay himself should not be denied the credit that is his due. By virtue of his own exertions—"my own irregular exertions" was the way he put it[38]—he capitalized on everything and everyone provided him during the course of his five-year stay in Richmond. Because he was ambitious for fame and fortune even at an early age, he applied himself fairly assiduously to the task of self-improvement. For the remainder of his life Henry Clay reached for higher and higher honors and rewards. He had to struggle to achieve them, for certain character defects—his gambling instincts, his self-esteem that could easily lapse into arrogance, his acerbic tongue, to cite only a few—hobbled his efforts. They not only thwarted his own deepest hopes and dreams but ultimately denied to the nation at large the full benefit of his incomparable talents and abilities.

The capstone to Henry's early education came late in 1796, when Wythe arranged to place him in the office of the attorney general of Virginia, where the young man could further prepare himself for a career in law. Robert Brooke, former governor of the state and now attorney general, was the scion of a distinguished Virginia family, was educated at the University of Edinburgh, fought in the Revolution, and then achieved remarkable success as a lawyer and politician. He was the sort of person Henry desperately wanted to emulate, for he had shaped a career that appealed to the young man's own personal hopes for the future.[39]

Robert Brooke took the youth into his home, where Henry met Francis, a younger brother of the attorney general's, with whom he formed a lifelong friendship. Henry also met Thomas Ritchie, a brother-in-law, who later became a ruling power in Virginia politics and editor of the Richmond *Enquirer*. Ritchie always thought highly of Henry Clay's talents even though he opposed him politically because of his highly nationalistic views.[40]

Henry was now twenty years of age. Tall, reaching upward of six feet, and extremely thin, he carried himself in a loose, ambling, carefree manner. His legs and arms were long, his hands much smaller by comparison. He appeared confident and determined, as though he naturally belonged in the highest society and could hold his own against any competitor. At an early age young Henry seemed to know how talented he was, which knowledge probably explains his later arrogance. There was a sensitivity and mobility to his face that immediately registered his mood, his thoughts, and his feelings. His facial

38. Clay's speech in Lexington, June 9, 1842, *Niles' Weekly Register,* July 9, 1842.

39. Thomas Ritchie, *Reminiscences of Henry Clay* (Richmond, 1852), p. 2.

40. For Clay's influence on Ritchie, see Charles Ambler, *Thomas Ritchie: A Study in Virginia Politics* (Richmond, 1913), p. 23. The friendship between the two men ended over the "corrupt bargain." See Chapter XV.

expressions seemed to change constantly, particularly in conversation. Because of this characteristic, it was said that his portraits rarely achieved a true likeness. He appeared to have a small head, yet he wore a seven and five-eighths hat. He had a high forehead, a prominent and slightly arched and protruding nose, small blue eyes, and a wide mouth that looked like a long slash across his face. His thin, bloodless lips stretched so far that he could not whistle very well or spit tobacco juice with tolerable accuracy. Those lips frequently curled into a smirk in his public speaking and signaled his true meaning, even when his words did not. He frequently smiled, and his contemporaries always described that smile as "sunny" and "winning." Someone later said that Henry's face was a "compromise," put together by a committee, and although fun-loving, witty, and sometimes wild, he always looked like a Baptist preacher's son, just as Andrew Jackson's face had the dour expression of a Presbyterian elder. All told, Henry Clay was a man of "commanding grace" and charm, and those attributes compensated enormously for the fact that by and large, he was a singularly unattractive-looking man.[41]

During his residence in Richmond young Henry also began to formulate ideas about government and politics, the essentials of which he drew principally from the republicanism of the revolutionary generation and the states' rights philosophy of Jefferson and Madison. Although his political thinking absorbed a more nationalistic cast after he left Virginia, he never totally abandoned his commitment to states' rights. He identified himself with the Republican party early in his career, and James Madison later became something of an intellectual mentor.

Henry studied under Robert Brooke for about a year before presenting himself for examination for admission to the bar. On November 6, 1797, he appeared before Paul Carrington, William Fleming, and Spencer Roane, members of the Virginia Court of Appeals, who had been assigned the task of examining prospective attorneys, and presented his "legal Certificate" attesting to the fact that he had studied with Brooke in Henrico County. After examining him on his "Capacity, ability and fitness," the committee declared that "Henry Clay Gentleman . . . duly qualified" to practice as "an Attorney at Law" in the Commonwealth of Virginia.[42] He was now certified as a gentleman with a respectable profession, and he was still only twenty years old. Not a bad beginning for the "Mill Boy of the Slashes."

But the immediate problem for Henry was location, where to practice the law he had learned. Richmond was an inviting place for many obvious reasons, but it was also overrun with lawyers, many of them quite distinguished. To

41. This physical description mostly comes from Henry Clay's passport, no. 765, issued on March 8, 1851, Clay Papers, Manuscript Department, Filson Club, Louisville, Kentucky. The only physical characteristic the passport neglected to give, unfortunately, was his weight. Among many physical descriptions, see "Anecdotes of Henry Clay," Manuscript Department, Filson Club, Louisville, Kentucky, and Poore, *Reminiscences,* pp. 34, 79.
42. "License to Practice Law," Clay, *Papers,* I, 2–3.

struggle for recognition, place, and fortune in this agreeable but fiercely competitive city made little sense to him. There had to be a better place, where he could rise more rapidly. It did not take him long to think seriously about following his mother and her family out to Kentucky.[43] Already a number of his contemporaries had headed west. John Breckinridge, James Brown, and George Nicholas, all graduates of William and Mary and students of George Wythe, were just a few. Besides, there were wonderful reports about the flourishing business awaiting eager and capable lawyers. Land titles were in constant dispute because of earlier Virginia laws that allowed recorded entries in various locations, many without proper surveys, resulting in an overlay of claims to a single tract of land. As a consequence, lawsuits abounded, providing handsome fees for a veritable army of lawyers who had begun to descend on Kentucky. Like Andrew Jackson, who had left North Carolina a few years earlier to begin his law career in Tennessee, Henry Clay saw in the West the opportunity that the East could not promise or that might take years to achieve.

It would be a dangerous journey, one infested in places with hostile Indians, murderous renegade whites, and scheming Spanish intriguers. It meant hiking across the Allegheny Mountains, through the Cumberland Gap, and then along the Wilderness Road that Daniel Boone had marked out more than twenty years earlier. For a young man in his early twenties, just beginning his career, it was not a difficult decision to make. And it was hardly a gamble. It seemed like the most natural and logical thing to do.

So, in early November 1797, immediately after receiving his license, Henry Clay packed some essential belongings, including no doubt a few letters of introduction, and headed west.

---

43. What little immediate family still remained in Virginia had died off or moved away. His brother George died of smallpox at this time, and brothers John and Porter had gone to Kentucky.

Kentucky: The Dark and Bloody Ground

HAT WAS the Indian name for Kentucky: Dark and Bloody Ground. It seemed appropriate for this beautiful bluegrass country astride the Ohio River because over the years Kentucky's attraction had set tribes and nations at each other's throats. Bloody and dark. Now, at the close of the eighteenth century, it attracted adventurers and gamblers from every direction, especially Pennsylvania, Virginia, and North Carolina, and they sprawled north and south and west along the majestic banks of the Ohio River. This attractive, undulating land belonged to Virginia after the Revolution, and these new immigrants were squatters with shadowy claims at best to this rich land. They were later described as "blue beards, who are rugged, dirty, brawling, browbeating monsters, six feet high, whose vocation is robbing, drinking, fighting, and terrifying every peaceable man in the community."[1] They resented Virginia laws and claims and almost immediately began to agitate for home rule.

With the conclusion of the American Revolution the British were expected to abandon their forts on American territory in the Northwest and the Spanish to recognize the thirty-first parallel as the southern boundary of the United States. But neither country respected these provisions of the peace treaty ending the war. The British sat arrogantly in their forts, and the Spanish, once the English had ceded the Floridas back to them, claimed that the northern boundary of their territory ran from the mouth of the Yazoo to the Apalachicola, not the thirty-first parallel.

Thus, at the conclusion of the Revolution the United States seemed incapable of controlling what belonged to it by right of treaty agreements. And westerners quickly discerned the weaknesses of their government created by

1. Thomas D. Clark, *History of Kentucky* (New York, 1937), p. 6off. *Congressional Globe,* 26th Congress, 2d session, appendix, p. 65.

the Articles of Confederation. It could not protect them from Indian attacks, which were frequently initiated by the British and Spanish; it could not tax; it could not coerce; it could not impose its will on dissidents or rebels or anyone else.

Cut off from eastern seaport cities by the mountains, westerners found the Ohio and Mississippi rivers splendid means of transport to needed markets. However, the Spanish occupied the mouth of the Mississippi River and had no intention of obliging the economic needs of western Americans unless it served their purpose. What they did was encourage Americans to commit treason, to switch loyalties, to desert the United States and pledge their allegiance to the king of Spain. They fostered conspiracy—the so-called Spanish Conspiracy—and they enjoyed a fair amount of success at it because westerners craved free access down the Mississippi along with pledges that the Spanish would cease encouraging attacks by the Creek, Choctaw, and Chickasaw Indians.[2]

The intrigues with Spain by Americans and the threat of possible secession intensified when John Jay, the secretary of foreign affairs, attempted in 1786 to negotiate a treaty with Spain by which the United States would abandon the right to navigate the Mississippi River for twenty-five or thirty years in exchange for commercial concessions. The treaty never materialized, but the West was legitimately outraged that such an idea had even been contemplated by its government.

The constant squabbling between individual eastern states further discouraged westerners. Then the failure of Congress to do anything about creating new states after Virginia had ceded its western lands to the central government in 1784 seriously endangered the territorial integrity of the United States. George Washington commented on the danger in a letter to Benjamin Harrison on October 10, 1784. "The Western States, (I speak now from my own observation) stand as it were upon a pivot: the touch of a feather, would turn them any way."[3]

What made the difference, what completely reversed the situation, was both the passage in 1787 of the Northwest Ordinance, which formulated a policy for the territories leading to their admission into the Union as states "on an equal footing with the original States in all respects whatsoever," and the subsequent adoption of the Constitution, which created a tripartite government with enumerated powers. Now there was a new concept of Union. No longer was the United States a static collection of independent states quarreling among themselves over vested rights. This new conception of Union provided a dynamic expression of an expanding country, controlled by a central

2. Thomas D. Clark and John D. W. Guice, *Frontiers in Conflict: The Old Southwest, 1795–1830* (Albuquerque, 1989), pp. 11–14, 24–25, 27–28. The Archivo des Indias in Seville, Spain, contains many documents that reveal the extraordinary, not to say traitorous, relationship between westerners and the Spanish government.

3. John C. Fitzpatrick, ed., *The Writings of George Washington* (Washington, D.C., 1938), XXVII, 475.

government under the Constitution, in which new states would be added to the Union by its authority and action.[4] Shortly thereafter, on June 1, 1792, Kentucky was admitted as the fifteenth state in the Union.

Not that the ordinance or the Constitution ended conspiracy and intrigue among these robbing, drinking, brawling monsters. The peculiar conditions of western life invited reckless and desperate schemers, and their wild plans continued well into the nineteenth century. For a young man with gambling instincts and excellent legal and oratorical skills, like Henry Clay, the dark and bloody ground of Kentucky with its special economic needs and aspirations and its burgeoning political development proved a superb location to launch a spectacular career.

When Clay arrived in Kentucky in early December 1797, the state claimed a population of over 185,000 people. He decided to take up residence in Lexington but first stopped off at Versailles, approximately twelve miles from Lexington, to see his mother again and her family. He received a warm and encouraging welcome, full of reassurances about his future prospects. His stepfather had prospered. Currently the proud owner of nearly one thousand acres of land, eleven slaves, and five horses, Watkins had become a justice of the peace in Woodford County. No doubt Clay's decision to move to Lexington met parental approval, for his elder brother John had taken up residence in the town as a merchant and had succeeded so well that Porter, the youngest Clay brother, soon joined him. The twenty-year-old budding lawyer left Versailles with the comforting sense that he could visit his mother and family on a regular basis if he chose since the distance between them was slight.

When Clay arrived in 1797, Lexington, in Fayette County, was a delightful town in an attractive location. A later writer said that the countryside surrounding Lexington "beggars description. Poetry cannot paint groves more beautiful, or fields more luxuriant. The country is neither hilly nor level; but gently waving. All that is wanting to make it a paradise in scenery, is the prospect of lakes, rivers, and mountains." The community boasted upwards of two thousand inhabitants, black and white, who drank, gambled, swore, fought, cleared a wilderness, planted, established commercial enterprises and who lived in two hundred houses of one kind or another, many little more than rude wooden cabins hastily erected. But aspects of a wilderness had already begun to fade. Lexington was a thriving town with its eye to future expansion and growth. It claimed to be the center of trade in Kentucky, and its numerous factories, mills, and distilleries justified that claim. Hemp was the cash crop for the region, while farther north, near the Ohio River, tobacco was preferred.[5] When he arrived, Clay found a seminary, which became Transylvania Univer-

4. Peter Onuf, *The Origins of the Federal Republic: Jurisdictional Controversies in the United States, 1775–1787* (Philadelphia, 1983), p. 153.
5. Amos Kendall to F. G. Flugel, May 14, 1814, Kendall Papers, Manuscript Department, Filson Club, Louisville, Kentucky; Lewis Collins, *History of Kentucky* (Covington, Ky., 1878), I, 22–24; Clark, *History of Kentucky,* pp. 85–109. See also F. Garvin Davenport, *Ante-Bellum Kentucky: A Social History, 1800–1860* (Oxford, Ohio, 1943).

sity the following year, numerous churches, rude log cabins, two newspapers, a public library, a dancing school, as well as a number of dry goods shops, some of which offered the latest fashions available. Lexington is located in central Kentucky in the bluegrass country and was named after the famous revolutionary battle. It was a veritable "Athens of the West."[6]

Ordinarily a young man might have had great fears and doubts about settling in such a remote wilderness, but these new surroundings hardly troubled Clay. For one thing, he had a brother living in town, who may account for his decision to settle in Lexington; for another, a great many Virginians had settled in Kentucky and had established a cultural climate that was congenial and reminiscent of life back home; and for a third, several other Wythe protégés now practiced in Lexington, and Clay lost no time in contacting them and offering his services. Of course, with his penchant for and mastery of self-dramatization, Clay later carried on at length about how difficult it had been to relocate in Kentucky. He arrived in Lexington, he wailed, "without patrons, without the favor or countenance of the great or opulent, without the means of paying my weekly board, and in the midst of a bar uncommonly distinguished by eminent members. I remember how comfortable I thought I should be if I could make one hundred pounds, Virginia money, per year, and with what delight I received the first fifteen shillings fee. My hopes were more than realized. I immediately rushed into a successful and lucrative practice."[7]

He did indeed rush into success. Not that it happened overnight. He was young and had a great deal to learn about many things—Kentucky law, if nothing else—before his career could spiral upward. But he had so much going for him, so many talents, so much charm and charisma, all operating under the direction of a driving ambition, that the western people were bound to find him irresistible.

For the first few months Clay took time to acquaint himself with life and law in Kentucky. He assisted John Breckinridge, George Nicholas, James Brown (the local Wythe students), as well as other lawyers, and spent his time preparing briefs, reading cases, studying Kentucky law, collecting debts, getting to know people and the vicinity, and visiting his mother—anything and everything to make himself useful and serviceable.[8]

Not until March 20, 1798, did he go to the Court of Quarter Sessions in Fayette County, present his license, and request permission to practice law in Kentucky. After he took "the several Oaths by Law prescribed," he was duly authorized to begin his practice.[9] And it is truly remarkable how quickly he

6. The first library in the West was started in Lexington in 1795, and the first newspaper west of the Allegheny Mountains, the *Kentucky Gazette,* was established in Lexington in 1787.

7. Colton, *Clay,* I, 29–30.

8. See, for example, the memorandum of suits given to Clay by John Breckinridge, February 20, 1800, in Clay, *Papers,* I, 22.

9. "Record of Permit to Practice Law," [March 20, 1798], Clay, *Papers,* I, 3.

gained a statewide reputation as a knowledgeable, hardworking, and dependable lawyer.

Although he mastered the problems involving disputed land claims and thereby laid the foundation for a lucrative practice, he was especially known for his superb handling of criminal cases. He won enough acquittals and reduced sentences for his clients within the first few years of his practice to inflate his reputation to the highest level in the state. To a large measure this success resulted from his extraordinary histrionic powers. He delighted juries. He even mesmerized them at times. In court he frequently regaled the juries with funny stories and anecdotes, told with gestures and grimaces and emotional outbursts. He quickly learned the arts that appealed to westerners, and he unashamedly employed them to his advantage.

Clay also won acceptance among his new Kentucky neighbors because he could drink, carouse, swear, and gamble with the best of them. They thoroughly enjoyed his company. "He is rapid in conversation," reported one man many years later, "full of anecdote, and swears most insufferably. But this last quality is common to all Kentuckians." He even shucked off some of the refinement he had acquired in Richmond in an attempt to improve a "homey" character and appearance.[10]

Naturally Clay became a member of the local young men's debating or Rhetorical Society, as they called it, almost immediately upon his arrival in Lexington. The society discussed "questions of history, philosophy, and political economy , . . and profitably to the members." At first he just sat and listened to the other debaters without making any comment of his own. Then, one evening, after a lengthy discussion of some issue or other the members decided to take a vote. But Clay was overheard to remark that the question had not been exhausted. "Don't put the question yet," called several members to the chairman. "Mr. Clay will speak." Everyone in the room turned around to hear the society's newest member. All eyes converged on him. He was therefore obliged to rise from his chair.

"Gentlemen of the jury," he began. Everyone smiled or tittered. In an instant he realized his mistake and became momentarily confused. But the chairman and the other members urged him on, and he began again. His enormous self-confidence returned, and with the arrogance of the truly gifted he called out once again, "Gentlemen of the jury," and went on to deliver a rousing speech that brought his audience to its feet, applauding and cheering.[11] It was the best speech Henry Clay ever made, reported James Hughes, who was present and heard many of Clay's later efforts.[12] The years of dedication and practice in Richmond had come to full fruition. He did not patronize the members of the society or glibly recount anecdotes or funny stories, as he

10. John Nelson, ed., "Christopher Columbus Baldwin's Diary," *Americana,* XXVIII (July 1934), p. 337.
11. Clay to A. Wickham, January 17, 1838, in Clay, *Papers,* IX, 131; Colton, *Clay,* I, 78.
12. Colton, *Clay,* I, 78.

frequently did before juries. In this setting he provided a thoughtful, lucid examination of the question, but couched in sharply focused, exciting, and sometimes dramatic language. His versatility, his extraordinary verbal range, his powers of argumentation were the reasons for Clay's meteoric rise to prominence in Kentucky. He could stampede audiences when sufficiently inspired and lift them out of themselves. He could reduce them to screaming, yelling, cheering mobs. Frequently, during the course of a long congressional career, he so ignited the galleries that the presiding officer was forced to clear them to restore order. And he would stand at his place smiling with pleasure over his masterful display of verbal pyrotechnics.

But it must be remembered that this success was not simply a triumph of style, theatrical wizardry, manner, or tone, although his consummate artistry constantly informed his public efforts. There was more. There was always enormous substance in what he said. With all his stories and jokes and posturing, he made uncommon good sense when he spoke. He persuaded listeners; he did not bamboozle them.

His quick mastery of legal proceedings in Kentucky and his preparedness whenever he went to trial may be seen in an important case he handled in the Fayette circuit early in his career. In the course of the trial he was obliged to absent himself and leave the case in the hands of two associates. Unfortunately the associates were no match for their opponents. The case was about to be submitted to the jury when Clay reappeared in court. He knew nothing of the evidence submitted or the subsequent arguments among the counsels on the points of law. But he did know one thing: He knew the point on which the case turned. Consequently his statement to the court was so compelling "as to destroy the argument of the opposing counsel; and in less than half an hour after he entered the courthouse, the case was decided in favor of his client."[13]

It was this sort of thing that made his enormous reputation. And he had equal triumphs in criminal cases. Indeed, this was where he initially made his name as a lawyer, riding the circuit of the county courts and arguing before the Court of Appeals and the United States District Court at Frankfort, the state capital. One of his first and most important criminal cases involved the murder of a woman by her sister-in-law. There was never any question of guilt, so Clay pleaded for leniency on the ground of temporary insanity. The husband had forgiven the death of his own sister at the hands of his wife. Could not the jury imitate this mercy? It must have been a stellar performance, for the jury imposed a light sentence, and eventually the unhappy woman was restored to her husband and family.[14]

All this brings up another of Clay's many talents. A superb actor, he had a distinct flair for the theatrical, both in court and on the stump. He seems to

13. Colton, *Clay,* I, 80–81; see also the various memorandums of court action in Clay, *Papers,* I, 41ff.
14. Colton, *Clay,* I, 84–85.

have understood crowd psychology and the means necessary to excite his listeners. With juries he possessed a range of histrionic techniques by which to win them over and get them to agree to his pleas. And he acted with his whole body: arms; legs; torso; head; hands. He was six feet tall, long and thin, and he would bend and twist and gyrate to lend emphasis to what he said. But as observers constantly affirmed, Clay's movements and gyrations were always gracefully executed. Audiences sat entranced as they watched and heard him speak.

Furthermore, he radiated enthusiasm whenever he spoke. He always seemed caught up in the merit of his argument. Earnest, ardent, frequently passionate, he entranced his listeners by the enormous intensity of his presentation. One observer credited it all to his "sanguineous temperament." Clay himself put it more simply when he said that "his nature was warm, his temper ardent, his disposition enthusiastic."[15]

But perhaps Clay's "most unique and admirable" talent was his voice. "Whoever heard one more melodious?" asked one contemporary. "There was a depth of tone in it, a volume, a compass, a rich and tender harmony, which invested all he said with majesty. We heard it last when he was an old man, past seventy." All he said was a few words of acknowledgment to a group of women in the largest hall in Philadelphia. He spoke in an ordinary tone of conversation—nothing more. "But his voice filled the room as the organ fills a great cathedral, and the ladies stood spell-bound as the swelling cadences rolled about the vast apartment." Much has been said about Patrick Henry's "silvery tones," continued this commentator, but he did not possess "an organ superior to Clay's majestic bass." George Bancroft later remembered that "his voice was music itself, and yet penetrating and far-reaching, enchanting the listener; his words flowed rapidly, without sing-song or mannerism, in a clear and steady stream." Of course, he had a distinct southern accent touched with a slight western twang. For example, he said *"whar"* for "where" and *"thar"* for "there."[16]

Unfortunately, many, if not most, of Clay's early speeches have been lost because the reporters became so absorbed in his presentation that they failed to record what he said. Even his surviving speeches do not adequately carry the power and brilliance of his performances. Many contemporaries confirm the fact that it was never possible to convey the overwhelming impact, the utter magnificence of his presentations—especially those of his maturity—because they had to be seen and felt as well as heard to be appreciated. His eloquence, commented one man, "was absolutely intangible to delineation; . . . the most

15. George Bancroft, "A Few Words about Henry Clay," *Century Magazine,* VIII (July 1885), p. 480.
16. "Anecdotes of Henry Clay," Manuscript Department, Filson Club, Louisville, Kentucky; Bancroft, "A Few Words about Henry Clay," p. 480; Grace Greenwood, *Greenwood Leaves* (Boston, 1851), p. 326. Clay "inherited his incomparable voice" from his father, the Reverend John Clay, according to his grandson. Thomas Hart Clay, *Henry Clay,* p. 15.

labored and thrilling description could not embrace it." And it all came so naturally to him. "He was *an orator by nature*," said another. "His eagle eye burned with true patriotic ardor, or flashed indignation and defiance upon his foes; or was suffused with tears of commiseration or of pity; and it was because *he* felt, that he made *others* feel." What Henry Clay often accomplished went beyond mere eloquence. "It was something greater and higher than eloquence; it was *action*—noble, sublime, God-like."[17]

Small wonder his legal reputation in Kentucky grew so rapidly. Small wonder he soon acquired the reputation of a lawyer whose clients never suffered the death penalty for a capital crime. Not that the reputation was entirely deserved. As a matter of fact, the first criminal case he argued ended in defeat, and his client was hanged on circumstantial evidence for murdering his wife. Not much later a female slave confessed to the murder. Nevertheless, Clay's overall record as a lawyer was outstanding in both civil and criminal cases, and his practice expanded rapidly. In fact, within seven years of beginning his legal profession, Clay moved straight to the head of the Kentucky bar. Much of his business dealt with cases involving land, slaves, and the collection of debts. He represented many merchants and business entrepreneurs in these early years and felt he contributed valuable services to the industrial and economic growth of his state.[18] "It gives me real pleasure," wrote James Brown, his future brother-in-law, who had moved to New Orleans, "to hear from every quarter that you stand in Kentucky at the head o[f our] profession. May you soon grow rich. . . ."[19]

And he did make money (even if he failed to "grow rich"), not only from his expanding and lucrative law practice but from land speculation (which was the earliest and quickest route to wealth in the West) and later from investments in commercial ventures and manufacturing. His taxable holdings in Kentucky jumped from virtually nothing in 1798, when he first arrived, to more than six thousand acres of land (including town lots worth a thousand dollars), six slaves, and eight horses by the end of 1805.[20] He later bought property in Ohio, Missouri, Illinois, and Tennessee. He even owned a hotel in Lexington, and he acquired partial ownership of a hemp factory, a salt mine, and a resort in Bath County.

The money started to flow into his pocket rather steadily and handsomely with the beginning of the new century, but it flowed out almost as fast. For Henry Clay was an inveterate gambler, and he was not afraid of high stakes or taking wild chances. In his early years, like many westerners, Clay loved poker; later in life, like many Washingtonians, he became addicted to whist. In time

17. "Henry Clay: Personal Anecdotes," *Harper's New Monthly Magazine,* V (June–November 1852), p. 393.
18. See the various powers of attorney provided him by various companies in the Fayette District Court, Deed Book C.
19. James Brown to Henry Clay, March 12, 1805, Clay, *Papers,* I, 180.
20. "Tax Bill and County Levy," [ca. February 1, 1806], Clay, *Papers,* I, 217–218.

he became what Andrew Jackson called "the typical western gambler," who threw caution to the wind and might even sacrifice everything he possessed on a single throw of the dice. He told his friend Caesar Rodney in 1812 of his penchant for taking "chances," adding, "you know Rodney that I have always paid peculiar homage to the fickle goddess."[21]

Once, maddened by his losses in a game of brag, he even wagered his hotel. Senator William Plumer of New Hampshire later recorded the ease with which Clay won and lost hundreds of dollars, one night winning fifteen hundred, the next night losing six hundred.[22] As he grew older, the hundreds mounted to thousands.

Plumer also observed that Clay wasted little time reading and that he went out sporting almost every night: parties, balls, card games, and "frolics." He especially enjoyed female company. And women enjoyed him. One gentleman sent greetings and best regards from his daughter, "as in the case with most of her sex, your warm and staunch friend." It was later said (by a critic) that Clay set a very bad example in Washington for gambling, drinking, and carousing.[23]

Much of what Clay did, it should be remembered, was fashionable among westerners, especially the drinking and gambling. These were essential and normal parts of Kentucky living, and Clay accommodated himself to it quite rapidly. But as Nathan Sargent later insisted, Clay was no more a gambler than most southern and western gentlemen of that day. "Play was a passion with them . . . they loved its excitement."[24] Not only did Clay revel in the fun of winning money, but he also realized that the sport of gambling and the hard drinking and carousing had the approval and acceptance of his society. He was a rollicking "wildish fellow in those days," whose company everyone enjoyed in discussions over drinks, in arguments at the debating club, and in gossiping at the gaming table.

Clay was also an accomplished performer with the violin and was sometimes called "the fiddler of the Hanover slashes." He resembled many other Kentucky politicians in that they "owed not a little of their great personal popularity to the fact that they were skillful players on the fiddle." At the end of one festive evening, enlivened by many bottles and much fiddle playing, Clay brought the merrymaking to a smashing end when he set aside his fiddle and engaged in "a grand Terpsichorean performance . . . executing a *pas seul* from head to foot of the dining table, sixty feet in length . . . to the crashing accompaniment of shivered glass and china" while his companions laughed and applauded and cheered him on. The next morning he was presented with a

21. Clay to Rodney, December 29, 1812, in Clay, *Papers*, 1, 751.

22. Everett S. Brown, ed., *William Plumer's Memorandum of Proceedings in the United States Senate, 1803–1807* (New York, 1923), p. 608.

23. Lucius P. Little, *Ben Hardin: His Times and Contemporaries* (Louisville, 1887), p. 349, note; William N. Mercer to Clay, April 22, 1845, Clay Papers, LC; Gideon Welles, manuscript diary, June 28, 1846, Huntington Library.

24. Sargent, *Public Men and Events*, I, 47.

bill of $120 for the destruction, which he paid with a flourish and without batting an eye.[25]

Still, despite these sometimes wild antics, he never let them take control of his life; they never dominated his thoughts and passions. He indulged them, but he could just as easily walk away from them. He was too ambitious and intelligent to permit himself to lose sight of his major goals in the pursuit of his career. Although he liked to tipple, he usually knew when to stop. There were drunken sprees, of course, but they were not habitual or even typical. Overall, as even his enemies admitted, Henry Clay possessed a high degree of "social tact, suavity and grace of manner."[26]

A certain amount of coarseness acquired by Clay during his drinking and brawling years in Kentucky still clung to him when he went to Washington for the first time. But within a few years commentators noted with amusement, if not amazement, how he had polished away the rough spots and how the "chivalric standards of 'Old Virginia' " had reemerged.

In time Clay also came to realize that he must control his "passions" lest they damage his reputation as a thoughtful and serious legislator. And to a considerable extent, he succeeded. Some thirty years later Harriet Martineau recorded that he was an "impetuous" man by nature, "over which he has obtained a truly noble mastery. His moderation is now his most striking characteristic; obtained, no doubt, at the cost of prodigious self-denial on his own part."[27]

One other characteristic deserves mention in explaining Clay's great popularity with juries and among his future constituents: his delightful wit. He was so quick with an appropriate retort, so adroit, so spontaneous with a funny word or expression that few could match him. During the vote on the Tariff of 1824, for example, both Representatives Samuel A. Foot of Connecticut and Charles A. Foote of New York were expected to vote in its favor but surprised and disappointed Clay by voting against it. The bill passed anyway, and as Clay stepped down from the Speaker's chair, a colleague came up to him and remarked that they had done pretty well that day, all things considered. "Yes," Clay replied, "we made a good *stand,* considering we lost both our *Feet.*"

Once, when speaking in Congress, he had occasion to quote from *Hamlet,* the passage "Let the galled jade wince, our withers are unwrung." But instead of saying "unwrung," he said "unstrung." Two colleagues sitting near by hissed at him: "[T]he word is 'unwrung.' " Unfortunately the double prompting confused him. He drew himself up and with stronger emphasis made the word "unhung." The audience tittered over his embarrassment and

25. Little, *Ben Hardin,* pp. 38–39, 63, 251; R. T. Coleman, "Jo Daveiss of Kentucky," *Harper's Monthly Magazine,* XXI (August 1860), p. 352.

26. Little, *Ben Hardin,* p. 349.

27. Thomas Hart Clay, *Henry Clay,* p. 19; Harriet Martineau, *Retrospect of Western Travel* (New York, 1838), I, 174.

failed attempt at getting Shakespeare right. Then, with a gentle shake of his head and a long drawing out of the first word, he said: "Ahhhhh! Murder will out." The galleries not only laughed but applauded. The colleague who reported the incident could hardly believe the incident had not been faked. "I almost imagined he had slipped on purpose to show his adroitness in recovering."[28]

Actually Clay did not slip on purpose when quoting *Hamlet* because reciting poetry always presented a real problem for him. He invariably got it wrong. Once, in New Orleans, he was conversing with the actress Anna Cora Mowatt. "He took a deep interest in my professional exertions," she confessed, "and his encouragement was not sparingly bestowed." During their conversation Clay had occasion to quote from *Romeo and Juliet,* and as usual, he botched the passage, much to the lady's amusement. "I dare say I am *misquoting,*" he admitted apologetically. "I never could remember a line of poetry." He then told her how in one Fourth of July speech he mangled the poem "Breathes there the man, with soul so dead," and the audience had to come to his rescue, to the amusement of the crowd and his own intense embarrassment.[29]

Clay always had trouble with Shakespeare. "What is it," he asked a colleague one day, "that Shakespeare says about a rose smelling as sweet?" Because he wanted the quotation for a speech, he asked his colleague to copy the lines for him. Later, as he was delivering the speech, Clay disarranged his notes and could not find the quotation. Finally, in desperation, he turned to his audience and bawled: "A rose will smell the same, call it what you will."[30]

Clay was also an extremely sentimental man. "He was the most emotional man I ever knew," said one old friend. Tears came readily to his eyes, and he never tried to hide his emotions. On a steamboat one day the owners and operators of the ship refused to take any fare from him or anyone in his party even though they were rabid followers of Andrew Jackson. "I don't know when a trifling circumstance has moved me so much," he commented to a lady standing nearby. And "tears were standing in his eyes as he spoke." Indeed, anytime Clay got caught up in an emotional scene, tears would well up and his voice would quaver. He got carried away so often in speaking before Congress—describing the plight of Indians, for example—that when he concluded his face would be wet with tears and his handkerchief soaked.[31]

All the characteristics that constituted the unique personality of Henry

28. Sargent, *Clay,* p. 111; Colton, *Clay,* I, 108; "Anecdotes of Henry Clay," Manuscript Department, Filson Club, Louisville, Kentucky.

29. Anna Cora Mowatt, *Autobiography of an Actress: Or Eight Years on the Stage* (Boston, 1853), pp. 256–257.

30. Thomas Hart Clay, *Henry Clay,* pp. 400–401.

31. "I have seen his eyes fill instantly on shaking the hand of an old friend, however obscure, who had stood by him in his early struggles, and whom after a long interval he had suddenly met." Harrison, "Henry Clay, Reminiscences by His Executor," *Century,* p. 179; Mowatt, *Autobiography of an Actress,* p. 260.

Clay help explain his early legal successes in Kentucky. They also account for his bright and auspicious inauguration into the world of politics. The fighting, turmoil, and confusion among the "brawling, browbeating monsters" that had marked Kentucky's beginnings did not abate with its admission into the Union. The immediate problem was the degree of democracy sanctioned by the state constitution. By eastern standards that constitution was exceedingly liberal, indeed radical, virtually permitting universal manhood suffrage for whites. Still, that was not good enough for these egalitarian individualists of the West. They denounced the constitution as a perpetuator of tyranny, they attacked all three branches of the government, they excoriated the ruling "elite" as a self-perpetuating aristocracy that was devouring all the land and stealing all the money, and they demanded greater democracy in the form of direct election of the governor and senators. They even sought the gradual emancipation of the state's slave population! In brief, they wanted another convention to revise and further liberalize the constitution to bring it closer to the people.

The original constitution of 1792 provided for referendums in 1797 and 1798 on the advisability of holding a convention to revise the document. When Clay arrived in Kentucky, the agitation for the upcoming referendum in May 1798 had already mounted to near fever pitch. The debating clubs and newspapers were sharply divided over the feasibility of altering the constitution after such a short period, particularly in reconsidering the question of slavery. Some fervent Jeffersonian Republicans felt the would-be reformers verged on revolution, both economic and political. John Breckinridge had grave fears about the consequences of emancipation. And once the "browbeating monsters" freed the slaves, he reasoned, they would extinguish land titles and other property holdings.[32]

Clay totally disagreed. He attuned himself almost immediately to the more liberal and democratic elements in Kentucky society and jumped into the intense political discussion just about the time he petitioned to practice law. He wrote an address to the electors of Fayette County under the signature "Scaevola" (which had the happy effect of advertising his grounding in the classics), and it appeared in the Lexington Kentucky Gazette on April 25, 1798. It was a remarkable document in that Clay not only expressed his advocacy of gradual emancipation but called for a single-house legislature that could more easily and democratically express the will of the people. He dismissed the argument against change on account of the newness of the instrument. "Its infancy," he wrote, "is a powerful reason for amending it at the present time. . . . The longer a government operates, the greater is the difficulty of change." Look at Virginia, he cried. Its constitution "is as defective as one can be," yet "all amendatory attempts have proved abortive."

On the slavery question Clay was sincere and deeply moving:

32. Mayo, Clay, p. 66.

Can any humane man be happy and contented when he sees near thirty thousand of his fellow beings around him, deprived of all the rights which make life desirable, transferred like cattle from the possession of one to another; when he sees the trembling slave, under the hammer, surrounded by a number of eager purchasers, and feeling all the emotions which arise when one is uncertain into whose tyrannic hands he must next fall; when he beholds the anguish and hears the piercing cries of husbands separated from wives and children from parents; when, in a word, all the tender and endearing ties of nature are broken asunder and disregarded; and when he reflects that no gradual mode of emancipation is adopted either for these slaves of their posterity, doubling their number every twenty-five years. To suppose the people of Kentucky, enthusiasts as they are in the cause of liberty, could be contented and happy under circumstances like these, would be insulting their good sense.

"All America acknowledges the existence of slavery to be an evil," he continued, which injures both the slave and master. "The sooner we attempt its destruction the better." Authorizing the legislature to deal with the problem now or sometime in the future will cause no great danger. The legislators "can have no motive but public good to actuate them," and besides, there will always be a number of them who will hold slaves themselves.[33]

The argument is a trifle naive, but the sentiment is a great confirmation of Clay's generosity of heart and spirit. Like Jefferson and other enlightened Virginians, he understood the evil the institution also exerted on white masters. He knew it could not continue indefinitely.

As for the question of representation in the upper house, let reason prevail, he said. It is argued that the division of the legislature into two chambers reflects the principles of two classes of men—nobles and commoners—whose interests are distinct and different and must be protected. But such class distinctions have disappeared in this country, and therefore, the need of a senate has ceased. "What is the object of a representative legislature? It is to collect the will of the people, and to assemble the intelligence of the state, for the purpose of legislation. It is not necessary to this end that there should be two separate bodies of delegates." The will of the people is better expressed by the lower house, he declared, since its members are more numerous and come more immediately from the body of the people. Is it not "against the spirit of democracy" that fifteen men in the senate are equally qualified? And "why stop at fifteen, why not descend to two or one?" As for the senate's serving as a check on the lower house, "the will of the enlightened representatives of a free people should not be checked by any power upon earth, except it be the people themselves." Otherwise the aristocratic few manage the affairs of the many.[34]

This is a remarkable document from a young man who had just reached the age of twenty-one. Here was a Jeffersonian Republican with real flare, a fiery liberal somewhat in the tradition of Tom Paine. His spirited arguments were to attract the radical democracy throughout the state and give the con-

33. Clay, *Papers,* I, 4–5, 6.
34. Clay, *Papers,* I, 7.

servative mercantile and planter class a momentary concern. He had declared himself a bold and true democrat, totally in tune with the beliefs, aspirations, and sentiments of most Kentucky frontiersmen.

But he later retreated. In time he backed off from his more "radical" opinions. He found it more advantageous to curry favor with the establishment. He came to learn from firsthand experience the value of accommodating the interests and needs of the ruling elite in Kentucky. And although the referendum on the convention passed, the delegates chosen to review the constitution failed seriously to consider emancipation or provide the legislature with the right to interfere with slavery without the consent of slaveholders. If anything, slavery became more entrenched than ever in Kentucky. A more popularly elected senate was approved, however, along with a reform of the judiciary. John Breckinridge led his more conservative friends in accepting these alterations and thereby cemented over some of the extreme differences among Jeffersonian Republicans in the state.

It is instructive to note that although Republicans could differ vehemently over local politics, they stood together on national concerns. Naturally they applauded the opening of the Mississippi River to their trade in the Pinckney Treaty of 1795 with Spain, although they thought acquisition of New Orleans made more sense in the long run. But they exploded in violent opposition to the foolish attempt of a Federalist administration to muzzle political criticism and stifle Republican opposition. The X Y Z Affair, in which the French government stupidly demanded bribes through secret agents as the price of any diplomatic rapprochement, and the naval quasi-war against France that followed culminated in the passage of the detested Alien and Sedition Acts during the administration of President John Adams. These laws, passed in the spring of 1798, permitted the President to imprison or expel from the country any and all enemy aliens, they extended the length of time necessary for immigrants to become citizens, and they threatened both citizens and noncitizens alike with fine or imprisonment if they dared criticize Federalist policies or Federalist officials. This detestable demonstration of Federalist arrogance showed unbelievable contempt for the most basic understanding of liberty and justice. All the Jeffersonian fears about a powerful central government intent on imposing its will over everyone and everything became shockingly real. In Kentucky the reaction verged on the violent. "Sons of the Dark and Bloody Ground" denounced the government in powerful and sometimes frightening language as the enemy of human rights and happiness.[35]

In Lexington about one thousand people congregated on a field ground south of the town early in July to protest the hated laws. George Nicholas started things off with a heavy-handed speech about how the U.S. Constitution had been violated. But the crowd wanted and needed something more exciting and volatile. A few of the young bucks turned to Clay and shoved him

35. Dumas Malone, *Jefferson and the Ordeal of Liberty* (Boston, 1962), pp. 401–404.

forward with cries to let him speak. Suddenly the young man was lifted into a wagon. There, "in a torrent of invective," he thundered out all the pent-up rage boiling within this agitated mob. His "matchless voice" and his eloquence engulfed them as he condemned the tyranny that had inspired such villainy. The government had violated not only the rights of individuals by its attempts at censorship and blackmail but the sovereign rights of states as well by seeking to extend its powers beyond the limits imposed by the Constitution.

When he was done, there was silence. For many moments the crowd seemed transfixed. Then the noise began, first a rumble, followed by swelling applause, and finally an ovation. This tall, thin youth of twenty-one had hypnotized his audience and left it awed by his emotional flood of outrage. "Another Patrick Henry" was the opinion of many who heard the inspired Clay—and they knew whereof they spoke.[36]

The rally ended with Nicholas and Clay being carried on the shoulders of several stout fellows. They were deposited in an unhitched carriage and paraded "in triumphal procession" through the streets of Lexington as the assembled people saluted them with cheers and applause.[37] It was the first of many more such outpourings of popular approval and affection.

A few months later the Kentucky legislature passed a resolution drafted by Thomas Jefferson that declared the Alien and Sedition Acts null and void because they exceeded the government's constitutional power. It also declared that the rightful remedy for unconstitutional acts was "nullification by the state sovereignties." Virginia also protested in a resolution prepared by James Madison, and the Virginia and Kentucky Resolutions, or the doctrines of '98, as they were frequently called, reaffirmed the states' rights philosophy and the necessity of strictly limiting the central government's exercise of power.[38] These doctrines became an essential part of the intellectual baggage of most Republicans, including Henry Clay.

Clay's career at this juncture seemed to be burgeoning in every direction. Not only had he won the favor of the liberal democratic element in Kentucky society, but in 1799 he allied himself through marriage with the wealthier classes. And because of that alliance, he steadily evolved a more conservative cast to his economic and political thinking. On April 11—one day before his twenty-second birthday—he married Lucretia Hart, the youngest daughter of Colonel Thomas Hart,[39] who, like Clay, was a native of Hanover County in Virginia. Hart had moved first to Maryland, had helped organize the Transylvania Company, which financed the early settlers of Kentucky, and had arrived

36. George D. Prentice, *Biography of Henry Clay* (Hartford, Conn., 1831), pp. 23–25; Mayo, *Clay*, pp. 73–75.

37. Robert M. McElroy, *Kentucky in the Nation's History* (New York, 1909), pp. 224–225.

38. Malone, *Jefferson and the Ordeal of Liberty*, pp. 407–409.

39. Thomas Hart and his wife, Susanna Grary Hart, had seven children: three boys and four girls. Lucretia, the last, was very close to her sister Nancy, who married James Brown, a United States senator who later served as minister to France.

in Lexington in 1794 to better protect his thousands of acres of land. He now held extensive manufacturing and mercantile interests, boasted a substantial library and the first piano in Lexington. All this made the "fair" Lucretia a very attractive catch.

Lucretia was born in Hagerstown, Maryland, on March 18, 1781, and although she had attended a school for "Little Misses," she had no more intellectual interests than most girls her age at that time and place. Dark-eyed and dark-haired, lively and plain-looking—indeed, "a very plain and unadmired woman" by eastern standards—she nonetheless captured Clay's fancy. In describing her, all observers, even the most sophisticated and cynical in Washington, said she was "kind," "good," "domestic," and "above all discreet." During the many years she lived in the capital it was reported that she never made a single enemy.[40]

After a brief courtship Lucretia agreed to marry young Henry Clay. She was eighteen at the time of her marriage, and the wedding took place in her home on Mill Street in Lexington.

It proved to be a successful marriage, and Lucretia made a dutiful and loving wife. A spirited woman, she nonetheless tolerated her husband's swearing and his periodic gambling and drinking bouts. In fact, she was once asked if she minded her husband's habitual gambling. "Doesn't it distress you," sniffed a Boston matron, "to have Mr. Clay gamble?" Lucretia looked surprised at the question. "Oh! dear, no!" she replied very innocently, "he 'most always wins."[41]

Henry Clay himself may not have been an ideal mate, but years later the mature man offered a young female friend some advice about selecting one and the need to exercise caution and care. He was seventy years of age at the time:

Well; my dear Anna the time approaches when you are to sally out into the world, and perform your part in social circles. Will you allow me to make one or two suggestions of advice? Don't allow your affections to be too easily engaged. In youth, the heart is very susceptible, and we too often mistake its first emotions for a fixed & permanent attachment. You should be in no hurry to contract such an attachment. Why should you? The advantages you possess entitle you to the choice of all the young men in the U. States. Recollect that if you should make an unhappy choice there is no remedy. A life of misery and wretchedness is before you. Distrust, my dear Anna, all first impressions. Examine them thoroughly. Enquire if they are founded on the virtues, talents and good qualities of their object. If merely upon his good face, form, or personal appearance, do not allow your affections to be engaged. Consult always your good father, than whom there is no better judge of men. . . . I am almost tempted to ask you to promise me never to engage your hand, without hearing me on the merits of any person that may solicit it.[42]

40. Margaret Smith, wife of Senator Samuel Smith, was Lucretia Clay's close friend in Washington and commented on Lucretia's attributes in Smith, *Forty Years,* pp. 86–87, 332.
41. Poore, *Reminiscences,* I, 62.
42. Clay to Anna Mercer, April 5, 1848, copy CPP.

Clay surely did not choose Lucretia because of her "good face, form, or personal appearance" since she, like her husband, lacked physical beauty. Far more important were her amiable disposition and family connections, for the marriage placed Clay among the best and most influential economic and political circles in Kentucky. He now had impeccable connections that allied him to some of the most eminent families in the state. He married as well as his highest expectations could have demanded.[43]

As it turned out, Lucretia also proved to be a most competent manager and businesswoman, selling milk, butter, and cured hams to earn additional money when necessary. Because of her husband's frequent absences from home, she necessarily took over the management of their property. She made a practical study of agriculture when they later moved to a plantation. She supervised the overseer and became something of an "oracle" among farmers in the vicinity where they lived. It was reported that every time Clay left home he gave her a large check with which to manage their home. Upon his return she invariably returned the check to him with the remark that she had found no use for it. Lucretia loved her home and all the domestic chores associated with running it. She hated the social whirl in Washington that so attracted her husband later on. And she was an adoring mother (even if she rarely showed it) of the eleven children she bore her husband.[44]

Immediately after their marriage the couple moved into a residence on Mill Street purchased from Colonel Hart. The first child, Henrietta, arrived in June 1800 but died in infancy. The second child, Theodore Wythe, was born in 1802, followed by Thomas Hart in 1803, and Susan Hart in 1805. These responsibilities not only quickened Clay's determination to advance himself but sharpened his growing economic conservatism. Perhaps without realizing or thinking about it, he had become a supreme pragmatist, his eye restlessly prowling for every opportunity that he could seize to fatten the purse and exalt the name and reputation of Henry Clay.[45]

43. Smith, *Forty Years,* pp. 86–87, 332. Lucretia's grandson Thomas Hart Clay commented that "though never a beauty," she was a woman of great dignity and "always attracted attention and inspired respect." Clay, *Henry Clay,* p. 28.

44. Charles W. Coleman, Jr., "Ashland, the Home of Henry Clay," *Century Magazine,* XXXIII (December 1886), p. 167.

45. The Clays had eleven children in all. Thomas Hart Clay's bible, as printed in the *Kentucky Genealogist* (January–March 1959), I, 32–36, lists the birth and death dates for each of the Clay children as follows: Henrietta, born June 25, 1800, died May 5, 1801; Theodore, born July 3, 1802, died May 5, 1870; Thomas Hart, born September 22, 1803, died March 18, 1871; Susan Hart, born February 11, 1805, died September 18, 1825; Anne Brown, born April 15, 1807, died December 10, 1835; Lucretia Hart, born February 1809, died June 18, 1823; Henry Clay, Jr., born April 10, 1811, died February 23, 1847; Eliza, born July 5, 1813, died August 11, 1825; Laura, born October 16, 1816, died January 5, 1817; James Brown, born November 9, 1817, died January 26, 1864; John Morrison, born February 21, 1821, died August 1887.

THREE

The Burr Conspiracy

OVER THE NEXT several years Clay turned his full energies to the enlargement of his legal practice and reputation and to improving his connections with the best society of Kentucky. Not surprisingly he easily achieved his goals. He supervised his father-in-law's business affairs, attended faithfully the various courts at Lexington and Frankfort, and further developed his oratorical and theatrical skills before the various juries he addressed on behalf of his expanding clientele. He virtually inherited the legal practices of George Nicholas, James Brown, and John Breckinridge. Nicholas died in 1799, Clay's brother-in-law James Brown emigrated to Louisiana in 1804 after losing reelection to the United States Senate, and Breckinridge died suddenly at the age of forty-six after a brief political career as United States senator from Kentucky and then attorney general of the United States.[1] In keeping with his prospering career, Clay acquired additional landed property, some of which he rented as a source of extra income. He frequently received land in payment for his legal services and often acted on behalf of his clients through the power of attorney they gave him.[2]

Not long after his arrival in Lexington he joined the Masonic order in Lexington and started off as a junior warden. He discovered that virtually all the important men in town belonged to the order, so for the next several years he took an active and interested part in its activities. He was also elected a professor of law and politics at Transylvania University eight years after his appearance in Kentucky and became a trustee of the university from 1807 to 1813 and again from 1818 to 1830.[3] Slowly and steadily over the next several years he joined the necessary societies and acquired all the useful titles and

1. When Breckinridge first went to Washington after his election as senator, he turned over his law cases to Clay. Lowell H. Harrison, *John Breckinridge: Jeffersonian Republican* (Louisville, Ky., 1969), p. 139.

2. See the various mortgage deeds, powers of attorney, receipts, bonds, and other legal documents in the Clay, *Papers,* I, 8ff.

3. The trustees of the university elected Clay a professor of law and politics on October 10, 1805, and he served until the fall of 1807. During much of his life Clay actively supported and assisted the affairs of the university, including the recruitment of faculty.

honors that he deemed essential to the advancement of his career.

Clay suffered a few setbacks, however. For example, his first effort to gain political office ended in defeat when he decided to apply for the position of "Clerkship of the Senate."[4] He felt qualified since he had "lived in the Clerks office of the High Court of Chancery of Virginia, and acted some time as the Amanuensis of the Chancellor." And he had the political wit to invite the support of influential friends and business connections. Unfortunately none of it did him any good. He was passed over in favor of someone else.[5]

Not that it overly troubled him. As a matter of fact, he was rather pleased about the general course of political events both at home and at Washington City, the new capital of the nation. He supported the election of Thomas Jefferson for President along with other candidates running on the Republican ticket. The dismissal of Timothy Pickering as secretary of state and the resignation of James McHenry as secretary of war, even before the defeat of John Adams for the presidency by Jefferson in the election of 1800, seemed to please Clay most particularly.[6] The subsequent attempt by Aaron Burr, the presumed vice presidential candidate on the Republican ticket, to slip past Jefferson to snatch the presidency in the House election of 1801 did not elicit any known reaction from Clay. The "snatching" attempt—if it was one—failed in any event, and Burr was obliged to sit quietly for the next four years in the vice presidential chair.

The Jefferson administration elicited nothing but praise from westerners, especially after it had successfully negotiated the purchase of the vast Louisiana Territory in 1803. Now the sons of the "Dark and Bloody Ground" could float down the Ohio and Mississippi rivers to New Orleans and then into the Gulf of New Mexico without leaving the jurisdiction of the United States. It augured well for the stability and success of the Union. Any number of Kentuckians, including Clay's brother-in-law James Brown, migrated to the delta region in the hope of gaining a fortune in this newly acquired territory.

By the time of the Louisiana Purchase Clay had virtually reached the top of his profession at home. His business interests and contacts stretched across the state and into Illinois and Tennessee. He also maintained his relations, both financial and social, with eastern friends and associates. And he was not averse to requesting favors from his myriad contacts to advance his interests. For example, he asked his old friend Francis T. Brooke to "execute a small commission for me"—namely, the acquisition of statutes of the Virginia legislature relative to Kentucky that had been enacted prior to Kentucky's separation from Virginia. This material was "extremely difficult" to obtain in the

---

4. Clay to James Taylor, May 26, 1800 in Clay, *Papers,* I, 31.

5. Clay to Ninian Edwards, July 9, 1800 in Clay, *Papers,* I, 36–37.

6. "You have no doubt heard that Pickering is dismissed and McHenry resigned. The violent friends of [the Adams] administration seem to be quitting public service." Pickering and McHenry were two deeply committed Hamiltonian Federalists. Clay to Ninian Edwards, July 9, 1800 in Clay, *Papers,* I, 36.

western country, and Clay would enjoy a great advantage over other lawyers to have it in his personal library. Brooke obtained the material and forwarded it via a mutual friend, George Johnson.[7]

By this time any number of well-to-do Lexington merchants had decided to advance Clay's career in a more meaningful way and direction. They reckoned that his influence and talents should be felt beyond the courts and law offices and in the halls of the Kentucky legislature. They believed his skill before jurists could be replicated in the general assembly, where he would rise to even greater prominence and political power and thereby better serve the interests of his constituency. Apparently—or so the story goes—they did not even consult him in making the decision. He would be elected, they decreed, and that was the end of it.

Surely it was a decision that Clay wanted himself. That he had no direct hand in advancing his own nomination at this time may say something important about the extent to which his political shrewdness had developed. It was most assuredly better in this day and age to have supposedly "disinterested" citizens propose a candidate's nomination for office than have the candidate do it himself. If nothing else, it placed a greater burden on these "disinterested" citizens to do everything within their power to bring about the candidate's election. In any event, Clay was "brought forward" in the summer of 1803 while he was attending business at Olympian Springs, and without too much difficulty he was subsequently elected as one of Fayette County's four representatives in the general assembly. An early biographer claims that upon his return to Lexington Clay entered the canvass at last and took an active part in his own election. It was even reported that he was challenged to prove his fitness for office by demonstrating his marksmanship. The story goes as follows: Clay was haranguing a small crowd one day when a burly, bearded backwoodsman approached and peered intently at him.

"Young man," he snorted, "you want to go to the legislature, I see. Are you a good shot?"

Clay understood the importance of brag in the West, and even though he could barely shoot worth a "tinker's dam," he had no intention of admitting it.

"The best in the country," he lied.

"Then you shall go to the legislature," the bearded fellow replied. "But first you must give us a specimen of your skill. We must see you shoot."

Without missing a beat, Clay responded: "Well, put up your mark!"

The target was hung at eighty yards. Clay borrowed the backwoodsman's rife and supposedly hit the target smack in the middle. No one was more surprised over this feat than Clay himself, even though he admitted many years later: "I had never before fired a rife, and have not since."[8]

7. Clay to Brooke, December 30, 1801, Brooke to Clay, June 2, 1804, in Clay, *Papers,* I, 71, 137.
8. Sargent, *Clay,* p. 6; Prentice, *Biography of Henry Clay,* p. 25; Daniel Mallory, ed., *The Life and Speeches of the Hon. Henry Clay* (New York, 1844), I, 18–19.

It makes a pretty story, and whether it is true or not is not nearly as important as the fact that the people of Fayette County had long since decided that Henry Clay was one of them and that he belonged in the general assembly as their representative.

Clay took his seat in November 1803. From Lexington it was a relatively short distance to the neighboring Frankfort, the capital of Kentucky, and perhaps he had few illusions about what he could accomplish as a freshman legislator. For he had once commented to John Breckinridge that "our assembly . . . have indeed attempted much and done little; but I have heard it remarked, perhaps not improperly, that this is the best evidence of their superior wisdom."[9] The less government the better was the creed of many Republicans, as Clay knew only too well.

There were a goodly number of radical and backwoods democrats in the chamber, under the nominal leadership of the short, heavyset, beetle-browed Felix Grundy. These stalwarts fiercely contested the "Legal Aristocracy" that, in their opinion, ruled Kentucky for its own special interests and the interests of its wealthy clients. Clay now belonged to that "Legal Aristocracy" and could no longer expect the unquestioned support of the democracy, however much he may have once shared some of its political views.

Almost immediately upon his arrival in the general assembly, Clay signaled his intention of assuming an influential role in the conduct of legislative business as well as proving his ardent Republican partisanship to all his fellow assemblymen. He did so by introducing a bill to reduce the number of electoral districts from six to two for the upcoming presidential contest of 1804, in which Jefferson would run for reelection. This gerrymander was intended to negate totally what little Federalist support remained in this intensely Republican state.[10] It may have been overkill, but Clay was taking no chances in view of Kentucky's penchant for intraparty squabbling and the danger of a coalition between the Federalists and one of a number of splinter Republican factions. In any event, the bill passed, and not surprisingly Jefferson took all eight of Kentucky's electoral votes in 1804.[11]

Clay did not tangle directly with the democracy and its leader, Felix Grundy, until the following year, when Grundy began his campaign to annihilate the Kentucky Insurance Company. And it quickly developed into the same contest that occurred three decades later, when President Andrew Jackson decreed the destruction of the Second National Bank of the United States. This earlier contest with Grundy gave Clay experience in such warfare and provided his first major political victory in Kentucky.

The company in question had been chartered in 1802 and, among other things, granted exclusive rights to insure commodities transported on the Mis-

9. Clay to Breckinridge, December 18, 1800, in Clay, *Papers,* I, 45.

10. "Act for Choosing Presidential Electors" [December 24, 1803], in Clay, *Papers,* I, 123.

11. For his comments on the electoral bill, see Clay to Breckinridge, December 30, 1803, in Clay, *Papers,* I, 124–125. The Federalist candidate for President in this election was Charles C. Pinckney.

sissippi River and its tributaries. It was also authorized to issue negotiable notes, thereby allowing it to "transform" itself into a bank. Located in Lexington, it had become an extremely profitable company and greatly assisted the state's expanding economy. Investors in the company's stock received handsome dividends, and that included Henry Clay. Moreover, Clay's father-in-law sat on the board of directors.[12]

The democracy took exception to this reputedly "Federalist" device to advance the interests of the rich. To it the bank inspired every conceivable speculative and crooked trick to cheat honest folk. And Felix Grundy led the democracy into battle against the "monster." Unlike his first political encounter in which he supported the democracy, this time Henry Clay battled against it.

Grundy was approximately Clay's age but had come to Kentucky much earlier. He received his legal education from George Nicholas and was admitted to the bar at about the time Clay arrived in Lexington. Like Clay, Grundy had exceptional oratorical talents, and he soon became a leading Kentucky politician, representing particularly the Green River section of the state, the so-called south-side boys. Also like Clay, Grundy was passionately ambitious, and he therefore responded immediately to the swelling demands of the masses to humble the mighty Kentucky Insurance Company.

He did not disappoint them. In the general assembly he demanded the immediate repeal of the charter that had created the company. He railed against the "monied aristocracy" and the corrupting influence of its "ragmoney." He warned of the dangers to republicanism and their effect upon the virtue of the people. This bank must be obliterated, he declared, to prevent the economic enslavement of the democracy of Kentucky.[13]

Clay saw his opportunity. By meeting the challenge of Grundy's thrust, he could assume a role of immediate leadership in the lower house. Indeed, his wealthy Lexington constituents who benefited particularly by the activities of the bank expected him to do battle with Grundy. They expected him to champion the business and commercial interests of their community. And once girded, Clay did so with telling effect. Matching Grundy's oratorical flights in a powerful address to the lower house, he enumerated the importance and value of the bank to all citizens and classes in the state. Banking facilities were necessary for every category of commerce, he said, including farmers. Moreover, he warned, the charter provided by the state gave rights that could not be repealed without violating the property provisions of Kentucky's constitution.[14]

The oratorical heroics of the two men continued for a week before a

12. Elmer C. Griffin, "Early Banking in Kentucky," Mississippi Valley Historical Association, Proceedings, 1908–1909, II, 173–175.
13. For Grundy's part in this debate, see Joseph H. Parks, Felix Grundy, Champion of Democracy (Baton Rouge, 1940), pp. 20–29.
14. Kentucky House of Representatives, Journal, 1804, p. 95ff.

packed gallery and a throng of senators crowding the floor of the chamber. Finally the issue came up for a decision, and by the narrow margin of a single vote the bank survived. It was a close call, and Clay mistakenly thought "the institution has nothing to fear in future." He was appalled, he said, by "the most unheard of prejudices" expressed during the debate. "The ignorance of members on the subject was truly astonishing."[15]

Clay was roundly applauded by the entrepreneurial classes of the state, and Grundy just as roundly castigated.[16] Among the many charges leveled at "that unprincipled upstart," as many Bluegrass gentry called Grundy,[17] was the claim that during the debate he had accused the bank of issuing paper three times the amount of money in its coffers. Grundy appealed to Clay to confirm the fact that he had said no such thing. "We differed in opinion on the subject of the bank," he wrote. "That difference ought not to induce either of us however to wish, or even permit a false statement to be made to the prejudice of either." He professed he had merely stated that the bank could issue notes to any amount, so he asked Clay to transmit to him "a certificate" that he could publish, if necessary, corroborating his claim. If Clay did in fact respond to this request, his letter has not been found.[18]

But Grundy did not concede defeat. Not by a long shot. He had won enough concessions in the form of amendments to renew the contest at the next session of the legislature. Meanwhile, the fight was taken to the newspapers, in which pro- and antibank men either praised or vilified the two principal contenders in the legislative debate. Both sides geared up for the final showdown at the next session of the general assembly.

Grundy's support had grown considerably during the spring and summer. And he knew it, as did everyone else in the legislature. The "common folk" had turned out in large numbers at meetings and the polling places to support his cause. When the general assembly reconvened, he immediately won the first test of strength by managing the election of his friend General John Adair to the United States Senate to fill the seat relinquished by John Breckinridge, who had accepted appointment as Jefferson's attorney general. The year before, Clay had engineered Adair's defeat for a Senate seat. Clay had supported John Brown of Frankfort, but Grundy accused Brown of involvement in the Spanish Conspiracy. After six ballots in which Adair led all opponents, Clay suddenly threw the Brown votes to Judge Buckner Thruston of Lexington, who was more acceptable to a larger number of legislators, and he succeeded in defeating Adair. It was a masterful display of political legerdemain, and everyone gossiped and laughed about how poor John Adair "got workd out of his Election by the artful management of H Clay."[19]

15. Clay to Breckinridge, December 22, 1804, in Clay, *Papers,* I, 166–167.
16. See the many issues of the *Kentucky Gazette,* during the first half of 1805.
17. James Brown to Clay, February 27, 1806, in Clay, *Papers,* I, 221.
18. Grundy to Clay, February 4, 1805, in Clay, *Papers,* I, 171–172, and note 2.
19. Captain Jack Jouett to Breckinridge, December 24, 1804, John Breckinridge Papers, LC.

But that was last year. Now Grundy had turned the tables on Clay and won Breckinridge's Senate seat for Adair in 1805. It was a humiliating defeat for Clay. Grundy followed this successful move by renewing the fight over the bank. He claimed the charter was unconstitutional and had given the bank powers that jeopardized free government.

Clay responded in a series of speeches. But he failed. He went down to crushing defeat when both houses of the general assembly voted to strip the company of its banking powers. Grundy simply had the votes.[20]

One hope remained: a gubernatorial veto. And the governor, Christopher Greenup, obliged. He vetoed Grundy's bill on constitutional grounds.[21] It was a bold and fearless act, which few Kentucky governors had ever attempted before and for which he was publicly pilloried. With four votes to spare, the lower house overrode the veto and sent the repeal bill to the senate. It looked as though the bank were finished, especially after the repeal bill carried on its first reading in the upper house.

At this point Clay pulled a surprise move. Almost single-handedly he demolished the opposition and saved the bank. What he did was so clever and extraordinary that politicians talked about it for years. And it had all been so simple. Clay's ploy turned on the existence of a singular situation that affected only the Green River section, the section Grundy represented. It involved the fraudulent sale of thousands of acres of land south of Green River and the long deferment of payment due the state that had been engineered by the notorious logrolling "Green River Band" of legislators in the general assembly.[22] The "Green River debt" had become a scandal, long protected by the Green River boys. Now with the second reading of the repeal bill about to commence in the senate, Clay sprang his surprise. He introduced a bill to compel payment of the Green River debt, and he calculated that he had enough support from members of all the other sections of the state to win passage.[23] In effect he said to the Green River boys: If you override the veto, you repay the Green River debt.

It was like a lightning bolt. It paralyzed the Green River boys. In a scorching, scathing, lacerating speech Clay laid bare many details of the fraudulent land grants, and he went on to assert that if his bill passed and the debt was paid, taxes could be reduced throughout the state.[24]

Clay's blackmail was obvious to the Green River boys, and there was only one way for them to get it sidetracked: sustain the governor's veto in the

20. The arguments of the respective sides are given in detail in Mayo, *Clay*, pp. 172–176, and Parks, *Grundy*, pp. 20–29.

21. *Journal of the House, 1805*, pp. 83–87.

22. For Clay's discussion of this land scandal, see his speech in Congress, *Register of Debates*, 24th Congress, 1st session, pp. 1248–1249.

23. "Resolution Relative to Payment for Green River Lands," [November 22, 1805], in Clay, *Papers*, I, 211.

24. Mayo, *Clay*, p. 174.

senate. So they simply reversed themselves on the second reading of the repeal bill. The bill went down to defeat, and the bank was saved. Clay became forever more the darling of the Bluegrass gentry. And to no one's surprise, he was persuaded to forget about his bill for repayment of the debt.[25]

During these debates Clay proved he could speak with enormous passion and conviction, and he proved he could pull off political sleights of hand with speed and deadly skill. Ferociously intelligent, quick-witted, and politically astute beyond his years, he awed and maybe frightened many of his colleagues. "Henry is like a lion's whelp," marveled William Littell; "who shall rouse him up? The sound of his voice is terrible; yea, it is like the voice of many waters. He hath . . . humbled the mighty in the dust."[26] More and more Kentuckians were now predicting that Henry Clay would soon become a powerful force in the destiny of their nation.

The following session the state formally entered the "banking business" by chartering a bank in Frankfort with branches in the principal towns. In recognition of Clay's heroic efforts on behalf of sound finance in the state he was elected one of the bank's directors.[27] But the Lexington bank continued operating and turning a profit for its stockholders. Indeed, its charter was extended two years in 1818.[28]

Some Jeffersonian ideologues were disheartened, however, by what they regarded as Clay's fall from grace. His powerful efforts on behalf of the bank and his ideas and arguments sounded as though they had come straight from the canon of Alexander Hamilton. "I believe our Legislature in Kentucky are getting higher-toned every year," wrote a worried General William Russell, senator from Fayette, because of "the manner in which the banking System is relished in this State." And Clay was leading the way. "Since the rising of the Legislature Mr. Henry Clay has published a very lengthy circular and has circulated them amongst the people, though do not believe he has gained much credit therefrom, except from the banking party."[29] He seemed headed away from Jeffersonian Republicanism toward Hamiltonian Federalism.

In a sense Clay had indeed abandoned the arguments against banking that some found implicit in the language contained in Jefferson's advice to Presi-

25. Ibid., p. 174.

26. Quoted ibid., p. 175.

27. Opponents immediately accused Clay of using his position on the bank board to obtain funds for his political allies. "His ignorance is as great as his malevolence," Clay said about one critic, "for if he had known any thing about the operations of the Bank, he must have been convinced that I could never have promised to supply you with money from that quarter, no individual being able to control its measures." Clay was happy to hear that a printed defense had been issued by his friends. "The people only want information to do what is right," he said. Clay to John Ballenger, September 8, 1806, private collection, CPP.

28. An ironic note is the effort of Grundy to support a state bank bill immediately after Clay's coup against the Green River boys. Again Clay opposed this bill on the ground that the bank's notes would be issued solely on the basis of the state's credit, and the bill was defeated.

29. Russell to Breckinridge, March 1, 1806, Breckinridge Papers, LC. "Here I feel myself at a great loss for the want of Grundy or his talents," said Russell.

dent Washington in 1791 against chartering the First National Bank of the
United States. Clay had formed an alliance with the entrepreneurial forces of
the business and mercantile community against the individualistic democratic
forces of the countryside. That meant he favored the sound currency and credit
facilities that a well-operated banking system could provide; it also implied
that he would favor public works and subsidies to encourage and promote
industry.[30] But these ideas were not simply efforts to benefit the wealthy few,
according to Clay. In his mind such policies would advance the interests of all
groups, entrepreneurs and farmers, town folk and country folk. And his advocacy of them certainly did not mean that he had abandoned republicanism,
states' rights, or the Republican party. He still maintained his allegiance to
Jefferson and the national ticket. He still affirmed his commitment to states'
rights, even though older heads, like General Russell, feared for the future
course of the Republican party in Kentucky with someone like Clay in a position of power.

For the moment those fears slowly subsided. Banking played an important role in the state's continuing development, and farmers, who never could
understand how bankers made money, forgot their worries and conceded that
Clay might have a point. Not until the state was racked by economic depression in 1819 did the old hatred of banks resurface. Then political fireworks
exploded across Kentucky.

However, in 1805 Clay's triumph was complete. A few months later Felix
Grundy abandoned the political field by becoming a judge of the Circuit Court
of Appeals. But that hardly suited his interests or nature, and in 1807 he left
Kentucky for Tennessee. Now there was no one to challenge seriously Henry
Clay's leadership in the general assembly, and in 1808 he was elected Speaker
of the lower house. By this time he was the most promising politician of
Kentucky—without question.

Still, he did encounter periodic setbacks. His unrelenting efforts to move
the capital of the state from Frankfort to Lexington, for example, met repeated
failure. On one occasion, in speaking before the full house, he used the example of an inverted hat to make his point. Frankfort, he said, was walled in on all
sides by towering, rocky precipices and, in its general conformation, was not
unlike a great pit. "It presents," said Clay, "the model of an inverted hat.
Frankfort is the body of the hat, and the lands adjacent are the brim." Then,
altering his figure of speech, he claimed that Frankfort was *"nature's great
penitentiary,"* and if the legislators wanted to see the bodily condition of the
prisoners, all they had to do was observe the "poor creatures in the gallery." At
that moment he turned and pointed to the gallery, where a number of town
drifters were lounging about. When the members looked up to follow the

30. Clay's advocacy of the Ohio Canal Company in 1805 for the building of a canal around the falls
of the Ohio River at Louisville is an example of his developing advocacy of a policy of internal
improvements. He even sought federal aid, despite the fact that this ran counter to Jeffersonian
constitutional views.

direction of Clay's accusing finger, the frightened observers in the gallery went scampering off in all directions, as the chamber rocked with laughter. "This well-directed hit was successful; and the House gave their votes in favor of the measure." But it died in the upper chamber.[31]

A more serious setback was his near brush with disaster when on a lovely spring day in 1805 the gallant, delightful, suave, and sophisticated Aaron Burr came riding into Lexington. Here was the man who had tried to sneak past Jefferson to take the presidency in 1801. When that failed, he served out his term as Vice President—the position intended for him by the party in the first place—before returning to New York, where he quarreled with Alexander Hamilton and, in a notorious duel in Weehawken, New Jersey, "shooted dead great Hamilton."[32] If westerners chided him for his unseemly grab for office, they surely forgave him for his manly defense of his honor in killing Hamilton. The code duello was an essential and irrefutable component of Kentucky society, and no one questioned its importance in setting the standard for western honor, courage, and integrity.

His reputation and fortunes shattered in the East, Burr headed west to restore them. What he intended became confused in the minds of those who heard him because of the different stories he put out, but many westerners liked to believe that it involved something deliciously nasty toward the Spanish, something like the conquest of Mexico or the seizure of the Floridas. Whatever his intentions, they remain obscure to the present day. Still, he interested any number of important and influential westerners in his schemes. He bilked the romantic and wealthy Irishman Harman Blennerhassett, who lived on an island in the Ohio River near Marietta with his beautiful and accomplished wife. He encouraged the treachery of General James Wilkinson, who commanded U.S. troops in New Orleans, with talk of empires and great wealth. He huddled with Governor William Henry Harrison of the Indiana Territory, along with Senator John Smith of Ohio and former Senator John Brown of Kentucky. And he dazzled General Andrew Jackson in Nashville and got him to build boats for his adventure, using Kentucky bank notes to pay for them. Even Clay was inspired to write his friend the attorney general John Breckinridge and ask "if a War will take place. Such an event is peculiarly interesting to this Country. I believe it would not be unpopular. Perhaps this is a fortunate moment to repress European Aggression; and to evince to the world that Americans appreciate their rights in such a way as will induce them, when violated, to engage in War with alacrity and effect."[33]

31. "Henry Clay: Personal Anecdotes," pp. 394–395; Prentice, *Biography of Henry Clay*, p. 28.
32. The rhyme goes: Oh, Aaron Burr, what hast thou done?
                            Thou hast shooted dead great Hamilton.
                            You got behind a bunch of thistle
                            And shot him dead with a big hoss-pistol.
33. Clay to Breckinridge, January 5, 1806, in Clay, *Papers,* I, 216. On Burr and his conspiracy, see Milton Lomask, *Aaron Burr: The Conspiracy and Years of Exile, 1805–1836* (New York, 1982).

Burr's plans—whatever they were—started to unravel in the summer of
1806 with the founding of a Frankfort newspaper called the *Western World* to
advance the Federalist cause. Joseph Hamilton Daveiss, the U.S. district attorney, and his brother-in-law and the leader of the Federalists in Kentucky Humphrey Marshall led the movement to expose Burr. To Daveiss the intrigues
surrounding the former Vice President were nothing less than a continuation
of the old Spanish Conspiracy. He repeatedly warned President Jefferson of
the danger, but his appeals went unheeded.[34] The *Western World* then intensified the assault by claiming that the conspiracy consisted of dismembering the
Union, detaching the western territory, and adding Mexico and Florida to
form an American empire under the rule of Aaron Burr. What added zest to
this theory was the claim that many of the old Kentucky leaders, who had
dabbled in the Spanish Conspiracy and were now prominent Republicans,
aided and abetted Burr's plot. Conspiracy still stained the "Dark and Bloody
Ground," and according to these Federalists, the Republican party had a hand
in the treacherous deed.[35]

It was a cunning and devilishly clever act of revenge by Federalists to
disgrace Republicans and regain power. Humphrey Marshall supplied the
newspaper with one article after another to substantiate the charge, and the
public could not get enough of this spirited abuse of the ruling political elite.

Attorney General Joseph Hamilton Daveiss—his middle name was assumed and thus conveyed the magnitude of his Federalist commitment—went
before Judge Harry Innes, the federal magistrate in Frankfort on November 6,
1806, and requested authority for the apprehension of Aaron Burr on the
charge of preparing an attack against Mexico and bringing about the dismemberment of the Union.

Burr immediately sought legal counsel and wisely chose Henry Clay. "I
pray you to consider yourself my Counsel in the business moved by Mr D—a
more *technical* application will be made when I shall have the pleasure to see
you. . . ."[36] Clay, resentful of the obvious intrigue against the Republican cause
and no doubt convinced of Burr's innocence, readily accepted the offer of
senior counsel.

On November 9 Judge Innes denied Daveiss's motion. Instead, he advised the attorney general either to gather legal evidence to support his request
or to call for a grand jury investigation. At that precise moment Burr strode
into the courtroom to confront Daveiss, Clay and several other legislators and
friends trailing in his wake. The upshot of the encounter was the impaneling of

---

34. Daveiss wrote seven letters to Jefferson between January and July 1806 and two additional
letters to Secretary of State James Madison. He complained that he had tried "to awake this *snoring*
administration; but to no purpose." Quoted in Mayo, *Clay*, p. 239, who quotes Daveiss's own *A
View of the President's Conduct concerning the Conspiracy of 1806*, reprinted in *Quarterly Publication
of the Historical and Philosophical Society of Ohio*, XII (Cincinnati, 1917), p. 53ff.

35. Mayo, *Clay*, p. 233, citing *Western World* in the *Kentucky Gazette*, July 8, 1806, and following
issues.

36. Burr to Clay, [November 7, 1806], in Clay, *Papers*, I, 253.

a grand jury. But much to his subsequent embarrassment, Daveiss was not really prepared to provide all his evidence at this time and had to request dismissal of the jury when a key witness failed to appear. Burr, delighted by his victory, asked that the reason for the dismissal be recorded. He assured the court of his innocence and the likelihood of vindication if the case was ever reopened.

Clay believed him. So did the other counsel, John Allen of Frankfort. "Such was our conviction of the innocence of the accused," Clay later wrote, "that, when he sent us a considerable fee, we resolved to decline accepting it, and accordingly returned it. We said to each other, Colonel Burr has been an eminent member of the profession, has been an Attorney General of the State of New York, is prosecuted without cause in a distant State, and we ought not to regard him in the light of an ordinary culprit."[37]

At this juncture Clay was suddenly elected a United States senator. John Adair had resigned the office in pique after losing reelection to a six-year term by John Pope.[38] To serve out the remainder of Adair's term, the legislature, on November 19, 1806, elected its young hero, Henry Clay, by a vote of sixty-eight to ten, over George Bibb. Even Felix Grundy voted for Clay![39]

But before Clay could pack his bags and head for Washington to take up his duties for the short period that remained of Adair's term, Daveiss moved to impanel another jury to indict Burr. Presumably he now had the evidence necessary to make his case. Burr again turned to Clay and begged him to delay the start of his journey to Washington. "I must interest your professional aid in this business," he wrote, ". . . & various considerations will it is hoped induce you even at some personal inconvenience to acquiesce in my request."[40] But Clay was troubled on account of his new role as senator. He explained to Burr that there might be something in the nature of Burr's "enterprize" that might "militate" against his new duties, and therefore, it would be improper for him to continue as counsel.[41] Burr saw his point and tried to reassure him. He followed this up with a categorical denial in writing that he had ever promoted the dissolution of the Union in any shape or fashion. He had no desire to disturb the tranquillity of the country and had neither issued nor signed commissions to any person for any purpose. He owned no weapons, nor was anyone authorized to own firearms by his authority.[42] This crafty and decep-

37. This was written during the presidential campaign of 1828, when Andrew Jackson was charged with improprieties because of his association with Burr and his party responded by pointing to Clay's supposed involvement in the conspiracy. Clay's response took the form of a letter to Richard Pindell, October 15, 1828, in Clay, *Papers*, VII, 501–502.
38. Adair was completing John Breckinridge's term because Breckinridge had resigned to become attorney general.
39. *Journal of the House, 1806*, p. 60ff.
40. Burr to Clay, November 27, 1806, in Clay, *Papers*, I, 256.
41. This comes from a discussion Clay later had with William Plumer, Plumer Diary, LC, and reported in Clay, *Papers*, I, 257 note.
42. Burr to Clay, December 1, 1806, in Clay, *Papers*, I, 256–257.

tive disavowal of anything sinister or illegal set Clay's mind at ease—or nearly so—and he appeared in court on December 2 to answer the charges brought against his client.

But once again Daveiss opened the charade by asking for an adjournment because one of his witnesses had failed to appear.

Clay exploded. What a mockery of justice and respect for the law, he roared. To harass an individual with criminal accusations and haul him into a courtroom only to back away at the last minute because of insufficient evidence—and to do it not once but twice—was the height of whimsy and caprice. It was contemptible.[43] Nonetheless, the judge agreed to an adjournment because of the lateness of the hour but directed that they would reconvene the following day.[44]

There followed two days of testimony and bickering between Clay and Daveiss. Finally the jury concluded that the evidence was based on rumor and hearsay and unanimously acquitted Burr of "any thing improper or injurious to the government or the interests of the United States, or contrary to the laws thereof. . . ."[45]

The packed courtroom cheered. The shouts and applause testified to the crowd's belief in Burr's innocence and Clay's skill in defending his client. "A scene was presented in the Court-room which I had never before witnessed in Kentucky," wrote Clay at a later date. "There were shouts of applause from an audience, not one of whom, I am persuaded, would have hesitated to level a rifle against Colonel Burr, if he believed that he aimed to dismember the Union, or sought to violate its peace, or overturn its Constitution."[46]

Not only had Daveiss lost his case, but he, Humphrey Marshall, and the Federalist cause were thoroughly discredited. Immediately thereafter a gala ball and supper were given in Burr's honor, but Clay did not attend. He was anxious to start for Washington to take up his duties as senator. He later admitted that he had accepted the Senate seat because several of his clients had cases pending before the Supreme Court and had provided him with a purse of three thousand dollars to attend to their interests. Also, he thought that personal exposure in Washington, where he could meet the nation's distinguished political leaders, could hardly fail to help his career. Before leaving Kentucky, he received a visit from Burr, who thanked him for his sterling efforts and gave him letters of introduction to several friends in Washington.[47]

The day following his interview with Burr, Clay left for Washington, traveling by boat up the Ohio River and then by stagecoach over almost

43. "Defense of Aaron Burr," [December 2, 3, 1806], in Clay, *Papers*, I, 257–258.

44. The proceedings of the investigation can be found in the *National Intelligencer*, January 2, 5, 12, 1807, reprinting the accounts from the Frankfort newspapers.

45. Clay to Pindell, October 15, 1828, in Clay, *Papers*, VII, 501–502.

46. Clay to Pindell, October 15, 1828, in Clay, *Papers*, VII, 501–502.

47. Brown, ed. *Plumer's Memorandum*, p. 565; Clay to Pindell, October 15, 1828, in Clay, *Correspondence*, p. 208.

impassable roads. Actually "not a stage turned its wheels beyond Pittsburg," but within thirty years the country was "intersected with Stage Lines south from that point to New Orleans about 1500 miles (or by the rivers, 2000) and west about an equal distance, extending 200 to 300 miles up the Missouri river." At the very beginning of his national career he realized the transportation and communication difficulties between the western and the seaboard states, and quite possibly this recognition strengthened his convictions about the need to improve the means of getting from one section of the country to another. The country needed better roads, more internal improvements.

Naturally Clay was accompanied to the capital by his manservant, Aaron Dupuy. Later Aaron's son, Charles, continued his father's role as the master's personal servant. Clay did not take his wife since she was expecting their fifth child, Anne, born on April 7, 1807. But hardly had he begun his journey when he heard the most incredible news about Burr's activities in the West. It must have caused him quite a jolt. President Jefferson had issued a proclamation warning the nation of a military conspiracy and calling for the apprehension of those involved. On December 9 boats allegedly belonging to Burr were seized at Marietta on orders of the Ohio governor. Blennerhasset's island was captured by the Virginia militia, and the owner himself subsequently taken into custody. Clay could scarcely believe what he heard, but he had to admit that the government appeared "confident that Burr is engaged in treasonable projects. They speak of having received the most unquestionable evidence of his designs. The reduction of New Orleans first, the subjugation of Mexico afterwards, and ultimately the separation of the Western from the Eastern section of the Union are supposed to have been his objects."[48]

Clay continued his journey much depressed by what he had heard and undoubtedly fearful of its impact back home. Daveiss and Marshall had warned of the conspiracy and had tried to do something about it. And Clay had blocked them with all the skill and talents he had at his command. Now the Republican administration claimed to have proof that Clay had been wrong all along in his opinion and the Federalists correct. Clay shuddered. He still refused to believe what he had heard. He wanted to see the evidence himself.

Late in December Clay arrived in the nation's capital. Washington was an unimposing village, and its government buildings seemed strewn in all directions. Pennsylvania Avenue, the city's main thoroughfare, was frequently so muddy as to be impassable. The President's mansion, ringed by a rail fence, looked unprepossessing, and the Capitol building itself, which housed the Congress and the Supreme Court, was acquiring a new south wing. Grogshops, boardinghouses, and dry goods and grocery stores dotted the landscape. But the Federal City—or just the City, as many congressmen referred to it—had been laid out with a view to its future growth. Still, more than 150

48. Amos Kendall to F. G. Flugel, April 4, 1839, Kendall Papers, Manuscript Department, Filson Club, Louisville, Kentucky; Clay to Judge Harry Innes, January 16, 1807, in Clay, *Papers,* I, 270.

years transpired before it became a true metropolitan center.

Clay took his seat even though he was constitutionally under age. He was twenty-nine, and the Constitution stipulates that senators must be thirty. But no one seemed to notice or care, and Clay proceeded to business without being challenged. What he was asked to explain, however, came as no surprise. The Burr Conspiracy was on everyone's mind, and the congressmen queried him for details. Still, Clay defended the man. He swore that Burr was innocent, the victim of partisan persecution.[49]

Not until he called at the President's mansion to pay his respects did he finally acknowledge his mistake. The plot had been revealed to Jefferson by the infamous general James Wilkinson, who betrayed Burr when he feared his own involvement might be revealed. Wilkinson commanded U.S. troops in New Orleans but took bribes from the Spanish, as did Judge Benjamin Sebastian of Kentucky. The President showed Clay some of the documents implicating Burr in the conspiracy, and the young man at long last accepted the fact that Burr had lied to him and deceived him.[50] "It seems that we have been much mistaken about Burr," Clay woefully informed his father-in-law. "The energetic measures taken by the Administration have, I presume, entirely defeated him." At Burr's trial Clay said he would not appear for the government or for Burr. He had been "deceived" by Burr and would not give him "an opportunity of deceiving him a second time."[51]

Already Clay had received "strictures of some anonymous writer" for his part in the Burr Conspiracy. There would be more in the years to come. But he had no fear. "They give me no pain," he wrote, "as I am conscious of having participated in no illegal projects of Burr, and know that I will not be suspected of having done so by any who know me."[52]

49. Brown, ed. *Plumer's Memorandum,* pp. 548–549.

50. It is not absolutely certain that it was Jefferson himself who showed the documents to Clay. None of Clay's letters mentions Jefferson by name. He merely states that "The Government appear to be confident that Burr is engaged in treasonable projects." Clay to Innes, January 16, 1807, in Clay, *Papers,* I, 270. I have chosen to follow the statement of Mayo, *Clay,* pp. 265–266, who claims that it was Jefferson who spoke to Clay because Mayo was a scrupulous scholar and very careful of his facts. He even quotes Jefferson in the conversation but does not cite the source for his quotation. Another scrupulous scholar, Merrill Peterson, *Great Triumvirate,* p. 15, also follows Mayo.

51. Clay to Thomas Hart, February 1, 1807, in Clay, *Papers,* I, 273; George M. Bibb to C. A. Rodney, December 11, 1807, Miscellaneous Bibb Papers, Manuscript Department, Filson Club, Louisville, Kentucky.

52. Clay to Thomas Hart, February 1, 1807, Clay to William Prentiss, February 13, 1807, in Clay, *Papers,* I, 273, 280.

―――― F O U R ――――

The Duel

SEVENTEEN STATES constituted the Union on December 29, 1806, when the twenty-nine-year-old Henry Clay was sworn in as the junior senator from Kentucky. It was the beginning of the second session of the Ninth Congress, Vice President George Clinton presiding. Clay took his seat in the cushioned chair of scarlet leather provided in the semicircular chamber and adjusted rather easily to his august surroundings, despite his youth and the many distinguished men who sat close by. Unlike Andrew Jackson, whose first encounter with the upper house had been an unmitigated disaster, Clay had relatively little difficulty, although he readily admitted later on that he preferred the "turbulence" of the lower house "to the solemn stillness of the Senate Chamber."[1] The ever-dour, ever-critical Senator John Quincy Adams of Massachusetts took note of the young man, particularly after he heard him speak. Adams's colleague Timothy Pickering and Samuel Smith of Maryland, James A. Bayard of Delaware, Abraham Baldwin of Georgia, William Branch Giles of Virginia, and William Plumer of New Hampshire were some of the other distinguished men in attendance. Clay's Kentucky colleague was Buckner Thruston, whom Plumer described as a scholarly man, but "exquisitely delicate" when it came to the rough-and-tumble of Washington politics.[2]

With no possibility of his winning reelection to the Senate—apart from anything else his business interests dictated that he remain at home—Clay decided to enjoy what would be his short stay in Washington. He roomed at Frost and Quinn's boardinghouse near the Capitol with a number of Federalists, one of whom noted that he read little, gambled virtually every night, attended "all parties of pleasure," and quickly earned a reputation as a great favorite with the ladies. With his wife hundreds of miles away, Clay frankly admitted his intention of spending his time making this a spectacular "tour of pleasure."[3] He succeeded, too.

1. Clay to James Monroe, November 13, 1810, in Clay, *Papers,* I, 498.
2. Brown, ed., *Plumer's Memorandum,* p. 608.
3. Mayo, *Clay,* pp. 270–272; Brown, ed., *Plumer's Memorandum,* p. 608. "I still indulge the hope of dining on oysters at the ―――― city on Xmas day," Clay wrote before he had even reached

And neither his life as a hard-gambling, hard-drinking ladies' man nor his presence among the nation's distinguished leaders interfered or intimidated him one whit when it came to his duties as a senator. Unlike Jackson and others who remained virtually speechless throughout their first encounter with the upper chamber of Congress, Clay gave several impressive speeches of such eloquence as to draw the attention of some of the most critical and cynical of his fellow senators. John Quincy Adams, for example, recorded his impressions. "Mr. Clay, the new member from Kentucky," he wrote in his diary, ". . . is quite a young man—an orator—and a republican of the first fire."[4] These speeches involved favoring the erection of a local toll bridge across the Potomac, forbidding the further importation of slaves, and extending the federal circuit court system into Kentucky.[5] He was especially effective in arguing for internal improvements. Whereas Thomas Jefferson had grave doubts about the constitutionality of public works and had signed the national road bill only after admonishing the Congress to initiate the process to amend the Constitution accordingly, Clay had no fears, no qualms, no doubts whatsoever. He was a true believer in the principle of using the federal government to advance the prosperity of the nation through a program of internal improvements, for in Clay's mind such improvements benefited not one class or one section of the country but all of them. Such improvements would also tie the Union together more tightly. And even though Republican ideologues might throw up their hands in horror at such heresy, the "republican of the first fire" defended his creed as the emerging dogma of the new, young, pragmatic, entrepreneurially progressive generation that was about to inherit the legacy of the Founding Fathers. As a member of one committee he drafted a report on the building of the Ohio River Canal, which obviously meant a great deal to his constituents. The report noted "the great & national importance" of the project and how necessary it was for farmers seeking a market for their surplus products to get around the obstruction of the falls on the Ohio River. It called for the enactment of appropriate legislation, and Clay was described as supporting the proposal "with great ability & much eloquence."[6] Clay also supported legislation for the building of a canal to connect the Chesapeake Bay with the Delaware Bay. When John Quincy Adams charged logrolling in connection with this bill, Clay and several other senators blasted him with a fair degree of "acrimony."[7] By this time Clay had developed an impressive talent for sarcasm, and he began to display that talent ever more frequently in open debate. Natu-

---

Washington. Clay to Joseph M. Street, December 17, 1806, in the *Annals of Iowa,* V, no. 1 (April 1901), pp. 71–72, copy CPP.

4. Adams, *Memoirs,* I, 444.

5. *Annals of Congress,* Ninth Congress, 2d session, pp. 30, 92.

6. *Annals of Congress,* Ninth Congress, 2d session, pp. 92–93; Plumer, Diary, quoted in Clay, *Papers,* I, 286, note.

7. Adams, *Memoirs,* I, 460.

rally it sometimes earned him the lasting enmity of those who felt its sting.

Even at this early stage of his career he could not resist the overpowering temptation to show off the sharpness of his rapier tongue. Because of his youth, his brashness, his all-consuming desire to make a name for himself, and despite the fact that he sat in the Senate among the nation's first men, he could not refrain from indulging in theatrics for a quick kill. In the debate over building the Potomac bridge it was not enough to deliver a powerful speech in favor of the bill. He needed to draw blood. He stooped to ridicule and sarcasm to humble a Federalist opponent. He focused on Uriah Tracy of Connecticut and compared the man with Peter Pindar's magpie:

> Thus have I seen a magpie in the street,
> A chattering bird, we often meet;
> A bird for curiosity well known,
>   With head awry
>   And cunning eye
> Peep knowingly into a marrow-bone.[8]

It amused the Senate and presumably advertised the young man's erudition. Of course, Tracy had invited the stinging rejoinder by his rude observation concerning something Clay had said about the bill. Right at the start of his national career Henry Clay put everyone on notice that criticism of his remarks or behavior could bring an immediate and biting response. Derision and mockery proved such potent weapons to silence and intimidate opponents that Clay increasingly employed them to defend himself and his ideas.

While speaking, Clay frequently toyed with a snuffbox that always rested on his desk. It served as a stage prop at appropriate moments, just as did his spectacles later on. He acquired a taste for snuff early in his Washington career but had the good sense to recognize its possible ill effects on his vocal cords. So he never carried a box with him for fear of overindulging and harming "his splendid, silver-toned, melodious voice." Since the box on his desk was usually empty, or nearly so, Clay satisfied his craving by sampling the supply provided the members on a table close at hand. The elaborate ceremony he later executed as he applied the dust to each nostril was also part of his theatrics.

While in Washington he regularly stopped at a tobacco store to try "a pinch of fine maccaboy." When the clerk subsequently asked him if he wished to purchase the maccaboy, Clay would throw up his hands in horror and cite his fear of damaging his voice box. Once he and General Henry Dearborn entered the store and began sniffing away. Snuff injured some men's voices, declared Dearborn in his shredded, high-pitched, barely audible voice, "but it has never affected mine in the least." Clay loved to repeat this story, imitating (as only he knew how) Dearborn's piping tones to the delight of his audiences.[9]

8. Prentice, *Clay,* p. 37.
9. Sargent, *Public Men and Events,* I, 95.

Neither the Chesapeake nor the Ohio River bills, for which Clay had argued so impressively, survived through this session. Both were postponed. Even so, he deftly maneuvered in the "back rooms" and corridors of the Capitol to win support for a bill to create a commission to select a site for the Ohio Canal, and the ever-watchful Adams recorded that Clay had not only a talent for oratory but a taste for political management as well. The canal bill, he said, "had obviously been settled out of doors."[10]

Clay's constituents had long come to know that as a legislator he was a man who diligently served their interests. It explains one powerful reason why they kept returning him to office whenever he asked their support. And if he made mistakes from time to time, he usually erred on the side of reaching too far and too fast, to obtain advantages for the expanding commercial and political interests of his and their section of the country. But as he matured, Clay came to appreciate the similarity in many ways of western and eastern interests. The dynamic agrarian growth of the West had produced needs and goals comparable to those of the industrially developing East. Roads, bridges, canals, tariffs, subsidies, sound banking were some of the means by which their similar interests could be served—as well as the interests of the entire nation. In time he put it all together to form a coherent, intelligent, and farsighted program of national objectives to advance the material progress of the country.

Some Republicans—John Randolph of Virginia, for instance—were becoming increasingly rigid in their interpretation of republicanism, emphasizing the rights of the states and the need to hold the central government to a very limited exercise of power. Clay, on the other hand, moved in the other direction. He interpreted republicanism with an emphasis on the needs of the people to achieve maximum benefit from their association with the federal Union. The desire of westerners for improved roads to bring their surpluses to market was a good example of his thinking. The West was impeded in its growth because of limited transportation facilities, and this in turn slowed the process of establishing an indissoluble bond of people living great distances from one another. Small wonder the Spanish Conspiracy and similar plots periodically threatened to dismember the Union. The interests of all the people who were stretched over thousands of miles were not being adequately served by the federal government.

Clay had expected a good deal of debate in the Senate on foreign affairs, given the increasingly hostile actions of Great Britain against neutral powers, such as the United States, in waging its war against Napoleon.[11] Seizure of ships and cargo, impressment of seamen, and interference with trade were some of the tactics it employed to achieve its goal. Jefferson preferred to use economic sanctions, such as an embargo, to coerce Britain into a proper respect for American rights, but this stratagem ultimately proved futile. He sent

10. Adams, *Memoirs,* I, 463.
11. Clay to William Prentiss, February 13, 1807, in Clay, *Papers,* I, 280.

James Monroe to London to help secure a treaty that would at least end impressment and provide indemnity for illegally captured ships and cargo. But Monroe failed in his mission. He brought back a treaty so insulting and humiliating that Jefferson wisely refused to reveal its terms to the public or submit it to the Senate for ratification. It was as bad as the treaty negotiated by John Jay during George Washington's administration that had brought down on Washington's head the condemnation and anger of countless Americans.[12]

Clay therefore found the congressional session less interesting than anticipated because "no questions in relation to our foreign intercourse, involving such discussions have been agitated."[13] The likelihood of war did not seem to be in the offing, even though the struggle between Britain and France always posed the distinct danger of sucking the United States into the conflict.

Congress adjourned on March 3, and Clay, possibly sated for the moment with the sybaritic life he had led for the past two months, headed home. He had met all the great movers and shakers of the American world while in Washington, including the President, his secretary of state, James Madison, and Secretary of the Treasury Albert Gallatin, as well as some of the men, like John Quincy Adams, whose lives were to be intimately entwined with his own over the next several decades.

When Clay returned to Kentucky, he boldly and courageously agreed to serve as counsel for the ostracized Harman Blennerhassett, who had been imprisoned in Lexington by merchants who held him responsible for Burr's financial indebtedness. If there was any animosity against the young senator in Lexington because of his association with Burr and the conspiracy, Clay decided to confront it head-on rather than waste his time in endless rounds of defense and explanation. But before Blennerhassett could be tried for the civil action, he was hauled off to Richmond to face the greater charge of treason against the United States.[14]

This decision to defend Blennerhassett underscores another important aspect of Clay's character: his extraordinary personal courage. Pragmatic, ambitious, and realistic though he might be, he also stood up bravely for the things he deeply believed in or felt compelled to pursue out of a sense of duty. There were some things he could not and would not do, irrespective of political cost. For example, he hated slavery and said so—repeatedly. He lived in a slave state and held slaves himself, but he publicly denounced the institution as an abomination. While his courage in advertising his true feelings and beliefs brought the admiration of some—Abraham Lincoln, for example—it engendered anger and contempt in others.

Clay's personal test of his standing with the public over the Burr and

12. Dumas Malone, *Jefferson the President, Second Term, 1805–1809* (Boston, 1974), p. 482ff, 405–413.

13. Clay to Prentiss, February 13, 1807, in Clay, *Papers,* I, 280.

14. "Argument Relative to Harman Blennerhassett," [July 15, 1807], and Clay to Harman Blennerhassett, July 22, 1807, in Clay, *Papers,* I, 298–299, 300–301.

Blennerhassett matters came in the summer of 1807, when he stood for reelection to the general assembly. He took to the stump, where he was a master, and faced down his critics with all the oratorical and theatrical skills he so readily commanded. And he won—handily. He had made an honest mistake in his opinion of Burr, but so, too, had a lot of other Kentuckians. The people chose to excuse him for his mistake, as they did repeatedly over the years when he made other mistakes. They needed and wanted him in the legislature, where he could continue to attend to their interests. Naturally Humphrey Marshall and the other Federalists were deeply disappointed with the outcome, hoping to eliminate one of the strongest and most effective of their political opponents.[15]

The summer of 1807 also brought ominous news from the East. The British frigate *Leopard* had stopped and fired upon the USS *Chesapeake* in her maiden voyage when she refused to be boarded and searched for British deserters. The commanding officer of the American warship was forced to comply with the search order, and four of his sailors were dragged off the ship. In addition, twenty-one men were killed or wounded in the encounter. The humiliation felt by the nation on account of this incident seemed certain to lead immediately to war, and had Congress been in session at the time, a declaration of war might have ensued. Instead, Jefferson refused to call a special session of the Congress and made a determined effort to maintain peace by ordering all British ships out of American waters.[16]

In Kentucky the nationalistic fervor of westerners found a strong and vibrant voice in Henry Clay, who used many occasions on the stump and in the general assembly to express the outrage of the frontier against "our haughty and imperious foe."[17] It is not surprising, therefore, that on January 11, 1808, he was elected Speaker of the lower house. He was also elected a director of the Bank of Kentucky.[18]

In the late fall President Jefferson demonstrated his confidence and trust in Clay by asking him, through his attorney general, to serve as counsel should the government prosecute Burr in Ohio since it had failed to win its case of treason against him in the U.S. Circuit Court presided over by Chief Justice John Marshall. Clay reluctantly refused. "Having deceived me last winter, when I really believed him both innocent, and persecuted by Mr. Daveiss, he shall not deceive me again, now that I believe him guilty and meriting punishment." Had the trial been held in Kentucky, he might have consented to the

---

15. Mayo, *Clay,* pp. 304–306; Van Deusen, *Clay,* p. 44.

16. Malone, *Jefferson the President,* pp. 415–438.

17. Kentucky House of Representatives, *Journal, 1807–1808,* p. 63.

18. Ibid., pp. 37, 45–46. Clay was elected on the third ballot following the resignation of William Logan, who had been elected unanimously on December 28, 1807. Logan resigned to accept a judicial appointment. Clay was nominated for Speaker in the 1808–1809 session but lost to Logan. Ibid., *Journal, 1808–1809,* p. 4. Clay was elected a director of the bank on January 6, 1808.

request, but he could not go to Ohio because of his responsibilities in the legislature and the state supreme court.[19]

Nevertheless, the Federalists were not about to let the Burr affair slip away without wringing out of it every last ounce of political advantage. They harassed poor Judge Innes with demands that he be impeached, but Congress subsequently refused to do it. They attacked John Allen, Burr's other counsel, when he tried to win the nomination for governor. Under the circumstances, Clay felt compelled to reenter the controversy, and in a series of articles signed "Scaevola" and "Regulus" he lashed the "base malice" and electioneering "depravity" that had prompted the attacks.[20] Humphrey Marshall struck back at him with never-tiring zeal. He seemed obsessed with the need to drive Clay from politics.

Marshall was the brother-in-law as well as a cousin of John Marshall. Like the Chief Justice, he was tall, spare, intense, proud, and aristocratic. He stood six feet two inches in height, he had jet black hair and piercing black eyes, and he could speak with an emotional fire to match Clay's. He hated Republicans with a passion and lost no opportunity to plot their disgrace. Thus, when Clay offered a series of resolutions in the assembly expressing support and confidence in the national administration's efforts to respond to the war-provoking behavior of Great Britain, Marshall denounced the resolutions and the tyrannical behavior of the President in resorting to an embargo.[21] But the assembly sided almost unanimously with Clay. The single negative vote came from Marshall himself. Clay followed up this success by introducing his so-called homespun resolution. This resolution required all members of the legislature to wear only clothes of American manufacture. They would shun the "use of cloth or linens of European fabric until the belligerent nations respect the rights of neutrals by repealing their orders and decrees as relates to the United States." And that included Napoleon since he, too, had taken to seizing American ships and cargoes with his Berlin and Milan decrees.[22]

The debate on the resolution turned into a free-for-all. Marshall sneered at what he regarded as Clay's obvious demagoguery, and Clay replied in kind. The thrusts got deadlier and deadlier as they whipped back and forth across the chamber. Then Marshall called Clay a liar, and the young man lost control of himself. He lunged at his tormentor, arm raised high over his head. Other members intervened. One of them, who towered over the two antagonists, forcibly held them apart and in his marked German accent bellowed: "Come poys, no fighting here, I vips you both."

19. Clay to Caesar Rodney, December 5, 1807, in Clay, *Papers,* I, 311.

20. Clay, *Papers,* I, 328–334, 346–347, 349–353, 361–367.

21. See Clay's amendments of the resolution on foreign relations, [December 15, 1808], in Clay, *Papers,* I, 388–389.

22. "Resolution to Encourage Use of American Manufactures," [January 3, 1809], in Clay, *Papers,* I, 396–397.

Clay, still seething, lowered his arm. He glared at Marshall, his eyes flashing angrily. Then he slowly regained control of himself. He turned to the other
members and apologized for his behavior. "It is the apology of a poltroon!"
thundered the outraged Marshall.[23]

That did it. That was more than Clay could bear, more than the strict code
of southern honor would allow. That night he challenged Marshall to a duel.

Sir
                                                                      4 Jan. 9.
After the occurrences in the House of Representatives on this day, the receipt of
this note will excite with you no surprize. I hope on my part I shall not be disappointed
in the execution of the pledge you gave on that occasion, and in your disclaimer of the
character attributed to you. To enable you to fulfill these reasonable and just expectations my friend Maj. Campbell is authorized by me to adjust the ceremonies proper to
be observed.
    I am Sir   Yrs etc
                                         Henry Clay[24]

Marshall's response was swift and direct. "The object is understood," he
replied, "and without deigning to notice the insinuation it contains as to character, the necessary arrangements are, on my part, submitted to my friend,
Colo. Moore."[25]

That very same evening Clay informed his brother-in-law Thomas Hart,
Jr., of the dispute with Marshall in the general assembly and how it had "terminated by the use of language on his part to which I could not submit, & I
attempted to chastise him on the spot, but was prevented by the interference of
the House. . . . I shall want a brace of pistols and know of none that I can get
on which I would rely, except Mortons." He would also need powder and
wanted the best to be had.[26]

In the meantime, Clay's resolution was overwhelmingly passed after some
slight modifications with only Marshall and one other member opposed. The
resolution now stated that the people of Kentucky were urged to promote
domestic manufactures, and as a start, the members of the general assembly
would "discourage" use of European fabrics until American rights were respected on the high seas.[27]

23. Kentucky House of Representatives, *Journal 1809*, p. 93; Clay, *Papers*, I, 398, note 1; A. C.
Quisenberry, *The Life and Times of Hon. Humphrey Marshall* (Winchester, Ky., 1892), pp. 100–
103. A similar dispute occurred many years later on the U.S. Senate floor with Thomas Hart
Benton and ended with Clay's apologizing to the other members but refusing to apologize to
Benton. It did not end in a duel, however. Benton also apologized to the members but refused to
offer one to Clay.
24. Clay to Marshall, January 4, 1809, in Clay, *Papers,* I, 397.
25. Marshall to Clay, January 4, 1809, in Clay, *Papers,* I, 398.
26. Clay to Hart, January 4, 1809, in Clay, *Papers,* I, 398. The Morton referred to may have been
John H. Morton.
27. Kentucky House of Representatives, *Journal, 1808–1809*, p. 315.

Then, on Thursday, January 19, 1809, Henry Clay and Humphrey Marshall with their seconds and surgeons crossed the Ohio River at Shippingport near Louisville to a place immediately below the mouth of the Silver Creek in Ohio. It was commendable of the two men to take their quarrel to another state to settle and not further stain the "Dark and Bloody Ground" of Kentucky with any more gore from one of its sons. Such delicate feelings toward one's state were not uncommon. Andrew Jackson fought one of his duels in Kentucky to avoid violating the sacred soil of Tennessee. Of course, some states in the Union had laws against dueling, and one had to be mindful of whose soil one intended to pollute.

Ten paces were measured off, and the duelists took their positions. There would be three "preparations," or exchanges. According to the rules, "each gentleman . . . will stand as may suit his choice . . . and after the words attention! fire! being given, both may fire at their leisure."

"Fire!" came the call when all was ready. Marshall took aim, squeezed the trigger, and missed. Clay also fired and grazed Marshall just above the navel.

On the second preparation Marshall again missed. But Clay's "damned pistol snapped," and according to the rules, that constituted a fire.

On the third preparation Marshall's shot struck Clay in the right thigh, deflecting Clay's aim. Thereupon the young man "insisted on another fire very ardently, but his situation, resulting from the wound, placing him on unequal grounds, his importunate request was not complied with." The seconds then declared the proceedings over and pronounced the behavior of both gentlemen "cool, determined, and brave in the highest degree."[28]

Clay received a simple flesh wound, but it was not deemed serious since the bone escaped fracture. Still, said Clay, "prudence will require me to remain here [in Louisville] some days."[29] Several of his friends hastened to assure him that "Your firmness and courage is admitted now by all parties." They spoke of his "heroism," which, they said, "will serve to stop the mouths of all snivel faced Tories."[30]

But any number of assemblymen frowned on the practice of dueling in general, even though they acknowledged that it was "absolutely necessary sometimes for a mans dignity." They considered it especially improper for members of the legislature to engage in such behavior. Accordingly, on January 24 a resolution was passed in which both Clay and Marshall were said to deserve censure for engaging in a duel, despite the fact that they had shown

28. Clay to James Clark, January 19, 1809, in Clay, *Papers,* I, 400 and note 1. *Argus of Western America,* January 28, 1809, carries the rules of the duel.

29. Clay to James Clark, January 19, 1809, in Clay, *Papers,* I, 400 and note 1. Clay was taken to the tavern of John Gwathmey, in Louisville, where, he later wrote, "he remained during his short confinement from the very slight wound which he had received." Clay to the editors of the Washington *National Intelligencer,* January 24, 1825, printed in their edition of January 25, 1832.

30. James Johnson to Clay, January 28, 1809, in Clay, *Papers,* I, 401. See also William T. Barry to Clay, January 29, 1809, ibid., p. 402.

proper decorum in carrying it out "in another government, and consequently without the reach of this legislature."[31]

Although some of his friends tried to cheer him up by telling Clay that if his pistol had not "snapped," his "adversary must have fallen," the fact remained that he came near to getting himself killed. According to one witness, Marshall fired first on all three rounds. It took only one shot in a duel to snuff out the life of Alexander Hamilton, and Andrew Jackson—by no means the best shot in Tennessee—needed only one bullet to kill Charles Dickinson. Clay was a very lucky man to hobble away relatively unscathed. It would be a long time before he would risk that luck a second time.

31. James Johnson to Clay, January 28, 1809, in Clay, *Papers,* I, 401; and "Resolution of Censure for Arranging Duel, [January 24, 1809], ibid., I, 401.

—— F I V E ——

Emergence of a
Republican Ideologue

CLAY RECOVERED very rapidly from his dueling wound and returned to his legal and political careers with characteristic zest and energy. His law practice continued to expand, and he began to demand ever-larger fees for his services. By 1810 he was quite comfortable financially, and he dabbled—if that is not too modest a word—in various business enterprises that increased his personal wealth. He worked and attended a sizable homestead, raising various crops and cattle. He speculated in land, as did all economically aggressive westerners, and he invested in hemp, rope, sailcloth, and a number of other Kentucky products and industries. The state had begun to move very rapidly toward domestic manufactures in establishing small but flourishing mills and looms. It practically had a monopoly of the cotton bagging industry in the country, and it turned out more ropewalks than any other state, except Massachusetts. The manufacture of cottons and woolens, liquor, and salt had also become important industries in Kentucky. In addition, the state boasted of its gunpowder mills, both their number and quality. Clearly its economic development had shown spectacular growth since its admission into the Union, and Henry Clay, lawyer, politician, and entrepreneur, had developed right along with it.[1]

His family expanded as well. His first child had died in infancy, but by 1810 he had five children: two sons, Theodore (1802) and Thomas (1803), and three daughters, Susan (1805), Anne (1807), and Lucretia (1809). A sixth child and third son, Henry, Jr., was born on April 10, 1811. Likewise, Clay's political base had expanded and grown stronger. By 1810 he had become a potent force in Kentucky politics. He was reelected to the general assembly from Fayette County almost without campaigning. And in the legislature he com-

1. Davenport, *Ante-Bellum Kentucky,* passim; Clark, *History of Kentucky,* p. 109ff.; Lewis Collins, *History of Kentucky,* I, 45ff.

manded the attention, respect, and admiration of a large number of its members. He was a fluent, ardent, manly, hard-hitting, effective assemblyman, and none of his colleagues could match him in eloquence or verbal firepower. By 1810 his influence also extended to Washington, where he had friends and former colleagues who could serve his interests. He did not hesitate to call on them for assistance—usually to support the applications of friends and relatives for positions, some of which were extremely important.[2]

Easily reelected to the general assembly in 1809, Clay began what turned out to be his last term in the Kentucky legislature. On January 4, 1810, as the session came to an end, the legislature reaffirmed its collective admiration for him and elected Clay for a second time to the Senate of the United States, in this instance to complete the term of Buckner Thruston, who had resigned to accept appointment to the U.S. Circuit Court of the District of Columbia. In the lower house Clay received forty-four votes to twenty for Speaker William Logan, and in the joint house and senate vote he obtained sixty-one votes to thirty-one for Logan.[3] His letter of resignation from the house was necessarily written to Speaker Logan, and he took occasion to notice their rivalry for the senate seat. "It is in vain, sir, to attempt to express my gratitude to a partial country for this new mark of its esteem. . . . I cannot, however, refuse to myself this opportunity of bearing testimony to the frank, liberal, and honorable manner, in which, on your part, the competition between us has been conducted."[4]

It was an appropriate and gracious gesture. If nothing else, it confirmed how far Clay had come in perfecting his political skills. He did not bear political grudges as a general rule. And he never believed political differences should mar personal or social relationships. He could fly into a rage or indulge in personal attacks against opponents, using outrageous language, but then he would laugh it off as a momentary aberration. In an instant he would compose himself, quiet down, smile, apologize to his listeners for the outburst, and with a smirk slyly insinuate that he had been carried away by his enthusiasm and emotional commitment. He seemed to think that his victims understood that his barbs were not intended as personal slurs on their honor or character. It was the way the political game was played.

That was one thing Andrew Jackson never learned. He took politics very personally and got very angry if anyone abused him or dared criticize his behavior or opinions. And he harbored grudges for years against his detractors, sometimes a lifetime. Not Clay. When he died, claimed a partisan of the opposing party, "Clay left not an enemy behind him."[5] He truly understood

2. See, for example, his letter to Caesar A. Rodney, [April 10, 1809], and President Madison, April 10, 1809, in support of his friend Ninian Edwards for the position of territorial governor of Illinois, in Clay, *Papers,* I, 408–409.
3. Kentucky House of Representatives, *Journal, 1809–1810,* p. 121.
4. Clay to Speaker Logan, January 4, 1810, in Clay, *Papers,* I, 434.
5. Bancroft, "A Few Words about Henry Clay," p. 480.

what the rough-and-tumble of politics was all about. That was part of the enormous enjoyment he derived from the game. That explains his preference for the lower over the upper house. The senate was too quiet and solemn. The "turbulence" of the popular body was more to his liking.

Still, he had just been elected to the U.S. Senate, and he was happy to go. As a later commentator wrote, for those "who love dissipation . . . the game of politics . . . and those who make a study of strong minds under strong excitements," Washington is the place for them.[6] The first time Clay won election to the Senate he took it in part because of financial and legal reasons. Then, to his delight, he found that he thoroughly enjoyed—indeed, reveled in—the Washington social whirl and the larger political arena within which to operate. Furthermore, at the age of thirty-two he was beginning to aspire to higher office, and he needed to return to Washington to get a better sense of his future direction.

In traveling to Washington, Clay usually rode from Lexington to Maysville, then took a boat up the Ohio River, spending much of his time aboard either gambling or gossiping in the "ladies' saloon."[7] Then he boarded a stagecoach at Wheeling and went the rest of the distance overland. During the time he spent in the stagecoach he would charm all the other occupants, especially the ladies, with delightful and amusing anecdotes. People who met him on these trips invariably became lifelong admirers.

Clay took his seat in the Senate on February 5, 1810, and three weeks later, on February 22, he rose and delivered what became very typical of his later oratorical efforts in Congress. What was starting to evolve was the "essential Clay": his political philosophy, his intense nationalism, and his commitment to government encouragement and support for domestic manufactures and internal improvements. He successfully married political skill with intellectual conviction and a unique personal style. Unfortunately many of his efforts during his first, brief term as a senator went unrecorded or appeared only in an abbreviated form. Not until he participated in the second session of the Eleventh Congress were his remarks reported at length.

His first speech had fervor and bite. It breathed western passion to smite the foreign forces that unceasingly humiliated and shamed the American people. The restrictions against U.S. trade and the incitement of murderous Indians to plunge the frontier into a bloody battleground drove westerners mad with a need and desire for revenge. The Embargo and Non-Importation acts were monuments to ineffectiveness, and now the Senate seemed prepared to retreat even further with amendments to a measure sent up from the House, called the Macon Bill, which, when altered by the upper house, would do no more than restrict British and French warships from American waters.[8]

6. Martineau, *Retrospect of Western Travel*, I, 143.

7. Mowatt, *Autobiography of an Actress*, p. 258.

8. Irving Brant, *James Madison: The President 1809–1812* (Indianapolis and New York, 1956), pp. 126–129.

Clay stood at his desk, tall, angular, cadaverous and charged with a ferocious need to convey to his colleagues the indignation, exasperation, and fury of the western people. The bill sent up from the House, he began, was "a crazy vessel, shattered and leaky." But at least it offered some response to the "aggressive edicts of the belligerents." If it is emasculated by amendments, he trumpeted, "we are left defenceless, naked and exposed to all the rage and violence of the storm.

"I am for resistance by the *sword*," he cried. "No man in the nation desires peace more than I. But I prefer the troubled ocean of war . . . to the tranquil, putrescent pool of ignominious peace." If we cannot find peace and must select an enemy, he continued, "then am I for war with Britain; because I believe her prior in aggression, and her injuries and insults to us were atrocious in character." He went on:

> It is said, however, that no object is attainable by war with Britain. . . . The conquest of Canada is in your power. I trust I shall not be deemed presumptuous when I state, what I verily believe, that the militia of Kentucky are alone competent to place Montreal and Upper Canada at your feet. . . . Is it nothing to us to extinguish the torch that lights up savage warfare? Is it nothing to acquire the entire fur trade connected with that country, and to destroy the temptation and the opportunity of violating your revenue and other laws?

What can be done to breathe vigor and energy into the Macon bill? he concluded. "I entreat the Senate to recollect the high ground they occupy with the nation. I call upon the members of this house to maintain its character for vigor. I beseech them not to forfeit the esteem of the country."[9]

Here is the War Hawk to be. Here is the rabid nationalist, articulating the passionate confidence of the West to annihilate anything that threatened its pride, its prosperity, and its country.

Clay moved to recommit the bill to committee for improvement, but his motion was defeated by a vote of twenty to thirteen. The Kentucky senator had spoken heroically about resistance by the sword to old warriors of the Revolution. But what did he know about war and its misery in terms of national treasure and human life? "The conquest of Canada is in your power." What youthful nonsense! What would they fight with? A navy consisting of gunboats that could barely navigate rivers and bays? A near-empty treasury? The tired and weary men of an older generation shook their heads and counseled caution. The final upshot was the passage by both houses of Macon's Bill No. 2, which was a pathetic milksop indeed.[10]

President James Madison, who succeeded Jefferson in 1809, offered no leadership. The Republican party—such as it was—instilled no discipline. "Youngsters" like Clay, therefore, spoke up more and more in the "solemn

---

9. *Annals of Congress,* 11th Congress, 2d session, pp. 579–582.

10. The bill removed all restrictions but further stated that if either belligerent revoked its edicts, the United States would reimpose nonintercourse against the other belligerent.

stillness" of the Senate, and in the case of Henry Clay, they spoke with passion and conviction. Emboldened by the reactions of his colleagues, by his youth and temperament, by his genuine nationalism and concern for western development, he rose again on March 26 and delivered an important speech on domestic manufactures, important in that it marked his continuing development as an ideologue committed to a set of principles that he believed would foster the material growth of the nation and the betterment of all its people.

A bill concerning the purchase of war materials had come to the floor, and Clay's colleague John Pope had obtained an amendment instructing the secretary of the navy, when acquiring such supplies as cordage, sailcloth, hemp, and other naval stores, to give preference to those of American growth and manufacture. A Federalist, James Lloyd, Jr., of Boston, moved to strike out Pope's amendment, and that brought Clay to his feet.

In supporting the Pope amendment, Clay spoke not only from personal interest, the interest of the Hart family and many other Kentuckians with investments in hemp, but from his strong nationalistic sentiments and an ardent belief that manufactures were absolutely vital to this nation's future development and that the government should encourage and support such enterprises. He was beginning to form some of the ideas he later put together into an ideology of economic nationalism, which he called the American System. Also, he was beginning to forge the political alliance between the manufacturing interests of the East and the agrarian interests of the West, between the industrial North and the economically embryonic West, between an established older order of businessmen and a young, burgeoning class of western entrepreneurs.

The opponents of manufactures, Clay declared at the outset of his speech, worry about America's contracting the "indigence, vice and wretchedness" of Great Britain, but if "we *limit* our efforts by our own wants," we need not fear. "The invention and improvement of machinery, for which our age is so remarkable . . . will enable us to supply our wants without withdrawing our attention from agriculture; that first and greatest source of our wealth and happiness." At this point in his life Clay did not advocate the idea of America's becoming an industrial giant to compete with Britain. He wanted the country to remain fundamentally agrarian but to supply its own manufacturing needs. "It is important to diminish our imports," he added. "The nation that imports its cloathing from abroad is but little less dependent than if it imported its bread." National self-sufficiency is what he argued, and it was the first step toward an even stronger commitment later on to industrial growth.

Being Clay, being young, brash, a consummate actor, and an assured public speaker, he could not resist mocking the Federalist who had offered the amendment. Boston was a large commercial city, and Lloyd had simply reflected the interest of his constituents. "Dame commerce will oppose domestic manufactures," Clay taunted. "She is a flirting, flippant, noisy jade, and if we are governed by her fantasies we shall never put off the muslins of India and the cloths of Europe. But I trust that the yeomanry of the country, the true and genuine landlord of this tenement, called the U. States, disregarding her freaks, will persevere in reform until the whole national family is furnished by itself with the cloathing necessary for its own use." It was a deft thrust that drew guarded smiles from some of his colleagues.

"I entertain no doubt," he continued, that "in a short time" domestic manufactures in America, "fostered by government . . . are fully competent to supply us with at least every necessary article of cloathing. I therefore, sir, *for one* . . . am in favour of encouraging them . . . to such an extent as will redeem us entirely from all dependence on foreign countries. There is a pleasure—a pride . . . in being clad in the productions of our own families.—Others may prefer the cloths [of] Leeds and of London, but give me those of Humphreys-ville."[11]

And there was another consideration: national security. "Our maritime operations ought not . . . to depend upon the casualties of foreign supply," Clay said. With government help we could soon rid ourselves of any dependence upon Russia for hemp. Ten years ago there existed only two rope factories in Kentucky. Now there were twenty, as well as ten to fifteen of cotton bagging—and both industries were rapidly increasing. Pope's suggestion, therefore, possessed the double virtue of encouraging both the manufacture and the growth of hemp. Clay ended by stating that the three great subjects that demanded the attention of the national government were agriculture, commerce, and manufactures. Proposals to provide "a manly protection" for the rights of commerce had been rejected. Proposals to promote agriculture by building roads and canals had also been rejected—or rather postponed. "We are now called upon to give a trifling support to our domestic manufactories, and shall we close the circle of congressional inefficiency by adding this also to the catalogue?"[12] It was a splendid close to a short but well argued speech.

The Pope proposal survived. The Lloyd amendment was soundly defeated by the count of nine to twenty-two. Clay had articulated his position very precisely and in the process had clarified his own thinking and laid the foundation for his later advocacy of government support for public works and tariff protection for manufactures. Indeed, during this session his voting record showed his increasing commitment to the idea of government involvement in economic development, such as his support for increased duties on goods imported into the United States.[13] "A bill to augment the duties fifty per cent. has passed the House of Representatives," he told Adam Beatty, a close political and personal friend, "but I fear . . . it will not be concurred in by the Senate."[14] He was right. Although he supported the raise, he apparently did

11. Humphreysville, Connecticut, in 1810, had the largest woolen factory in the United States. Victor S. Clark, *History of Manufactures in the United States* (New York, 1929), I, 562.

12. Speech on domestic manufactures, March 26, 1810, *Annals of Congress,* 11th Congress, 2d session, pp. 626–630.

13. *Annals of Congress,* 11th Congress, 2d session, pp. 673–674.

14. Clay to Adam Beatty, April 23, 1810, in Clay, *Papers,* I, 470.

not speak in its favor. As he predicted, it was rejected as too extreme.

It was a sad end to a Congress that could not agree upon a course of action to counter the naval blows, property confiscations, and trade restrictions imposed by Great Britain and France. These acts were acts of "infamous treachery, if not open robbery," declared Clay. But would he go to war? Would he vote for war? Not against France, he said. "I scarcely know of an injury that France could do us, short of an actual invasion of our Territory, that would induce me to go to War with her, whilst the injuries we have received from Great Britain remain unredressed." We have hesitated, parleyed, and requested explanations instead of taking action. "A man receives a fillip on the nose, and instead of instantly avenging the insult, inquires of the person giving it what he means!"[15]

Although this session had been intellectually more important to Clay in the further crystallization of his ideas about America's future economic growth, it was a disappointment in other ways, not the least of which was Clay's inability to enjoy himself socially. Dolley Madison, the President's wife, had her parties every Wednesday evening, of course, but the young Kentuckian generally stayed away. For one thing, his health was bad during the entire winter of 1809–1810; for another, he was engrossed in his duties as a senator. He was more and more determined to make a strong impression back home in Kentucky, and as he well understood, the surest way of achieving it on a statewide basis was to deliver eloquent and passionate speeches of substance in Congress which (when reported in the newspapers) would stir the feelings and emotions of his constituents in Kentucky. To deliver such speeches took time and effort.

Not that he totally avoided the "gay and agreeable" life of the salon. He always enjoyed "spicy" gossip available at such functions for the ammunition it provided for quips about the sexual dalliances of the famous. For example, when Napoleon divorced the empress Josephine prior to his marriage to Marie Louise of Austria and forced his brother Jérôme to divorce his American wife, Elizabeth Patterson, the daughter of William Patterson of Baltimore, Clay indulged in a slightly ribald observation: "Bonaparte has repudiated the Empress. I suspect he is afraid of being denominated a fumbler, and wishes to operate on a subject more prolific than the Empress. His brother's wife Miss Patterson alias the Duchess has been figuring away here for some time, with her little son. I would recommend her to imitate her brother in law's example, and take to herself a good strong back Democrat. She looks as if she wanted very much the services of such a character."[16]

In speeches given later in his career Clay sometimes made reference to the behavior and characteristics of his colleagues or well-known personalities, some of which may have had sexual connotations. A number of the barbs he

15. Clay to Caesar A. Rodney, August 6, 1810, in Clay, *Papers,* I, 481. See also Clay to ?, February 8, 1810, copy CPP.
16. Clay to George Thompson, March 14, 1810, in Clay, *Papers,* I, 458.

aimed at James Buchanan, for example, fall into this category.

Before leaving Washington for home at the close of the congressional session, Clay spoke to his friend Caesar Rodney, the attorney general, and William A. Burwell, a congressman from Virginia and former secretary to President Jefferson, about his future political plans. He enjoyed the national scene in Washington very much, he told them, and believed he could play an important role in Congress, especially now that the country faced the increasing hostility and scorn of the European combatants. But he had to admit a preference for the excitement and turbulence of the lower house over the quiet dignity of the upper. He preferred action over discourse, movement over contemplation, ardor and impulsiveness over caution and circumspection. He lost patience with senatorial deliberativeness and irresolution. It was not his style. The tumult and agitation of the popular body, its rough, noisy, sometimes explosive mood were more to his fancy. There he could shine. There his ardor, his enthusiasm, his wit, his oratory, his dramatics, his easy and familiar style of speaking could be displayed to advantage. There he could have an impact. Besides, his experience in Kentucky had gotten him accustomed to the popular branch. When he came right down to it, he told James Monroe, "it was a mere matter of taste."[17]

Rodney and Burwell agreed, and they strongly advised him to return home, forget the Senate and seek election to the House of Representatives in the Twelfth Congress. Although he thought he could win a regular term to the Senate if he wished, encountering no opposition worth mentioning, Clay clearly appreciated his true political calling and instinctively made the right choice in deciding the future direction of his career.[18] He would finish out his senatorial term—that meant waiting until the fall of 1811 before he entered the House (presuming he was elected)—rather than leave a vacant seat in the upper house or force the appointment of another to replace him for the final session of the Eleventh Congress.[19]

So, upon his return home, he announced his candidacy. Immediately other prospective candidates withdrew. They would not waste their time on a hopeless cause. As Clay himself had predicted, there was no opposition to his decision to represent his district, and in August 1810 he was overwhelmingly elected to the lower house of Congress. Clearly he had a very strong political base in Kentucky, which he knew, and he seemed prepared now to utilize it for his own good and the good of the several interests he represented.

At the same time as his election to the House of Representatives, the foreign situation heated up considerably. Not only did a British warship attack the naval brig *Vixen* and shoot away her main boom, but the Spanish took exception to the decision of President Madison to occupy the region between

17. Clay to Monroe, November 13, 1810, in Clay, *Papers,* I, 498; Mayo, *Clay,* p. 360.
18. Clay to Caesar A. Rodney, May 27, 1810, in Clay, *Papers,* I, 472.
19. Clay to Adam Beatty, May 31, 1810, in Clay, *Papers,* I, 473.

the Mississippi River and the Perdido River in West Florida under the presumption that this region was part of the Louisiana Purchase. Madison tried to mitigate his theft, not with cash but with a proclamation that there would be subsequent "negotiation and adjustment"—whatever that meant.[20]

Naturally westerners were overjoyed by this "plunge to the Gulf." To them it was a necessary acquisition to provide national security from British and French attack from the sea. Moreover, it gave further protection to the commerce plying the Mississippi to the gulf, and it provided one small gesture by the national government in which the American people could take pride and comfort. Whether or not this region constituted a part of the Louisiana Purchase was unimportant. Expediency dictated its acquisition, and Henry Clay would argue that principle—if it can be called one—against anyone who challenged the seizure.

And to the deafening applause of westerners, he did exactly that upon his return to the Senate in the fall of 1810. He justified the seizure in a heroic oration. To a very large extent, his speech was aimed directly at his friends and neighbors out West. The President had officially informed the Congress of his action upon its return to Washington, insisting on the legality of his decision and calling upon the members to sustain him by providing the necessary legislation to complete the incorporation of West Florida into the United States. Dutifully the Republicans responded with a bill to extend the Territory of Orleans to the Perdido, but the Federalists ranted against it as likely to provoke war with Spain and possibly Great Britain.[21]

At that point Clay rose to respond. Again there was a certain amount of sneering in his opening statement, but this time it rang true and seemed justified. It was provoked because the Federalists had expressed sympathy for the plight of the unfortunate king of Spain. "I have no commiseration for princes," Clay retorted. "My sympathies are reserved for the great mass of mankind, and I own that the people of Spain have them most sincerely."

It was a deft rejoinder. He then went on to trace the history of the disputed territory and attempt—rather feebly—a logical case to justify the President's action. He also denied that the President had, by his proclamation, violated the Constitution and usurped the war-making power. Had Madison not acted as he did, Clay argued, he would have been guilty of failing to execute the laws faithfully.

The logic grew weaker as the tone and language intensified. Clay's powerful bass voice began to soar, and his body swayed from left to right. His arms waved, his index finger pointed; his head shot from left to right. "It cannot be doubted," he bellowed, "that if you neglect the present auspicious moment—if you reject the proffered boon, some other nation, profiting by your errors, will seize the occasion to get a fatal footing in your southern frontier. I have no

20. *ASPFR*, III, 397–398.
21. Mayo, *Clay*, pp. 364–367.

hesitation in saying, that if a parent country will not or cannot maintain its authority in a colony adjacent to us, and there exists in it a state of misrule and disorder, menacing our peace, and if moreover such colony, by passing into the hands of any other power, would become dangerous to the integrity of the Union . . . we have a right, upon eternal principles of self-preservation, to lay hold of it. This principle alone . . . would warrant our occupation of West Florida."

Here was another part of the essential Clay: the pragmatist. He was arguing expediency to make his case, and that made more sense to him and his western constituents than all the specious history and logic he had previously intoned. Self-preservation. Something many Americans could understand and accept. Such an argument would also be used to wipe out Indians and steal their lands.

But to exercise the U.S. right of seizure might bring on war with Spain, argued Federalists. And if Spain declared war, surely the British would join it. "Sir," Clay responded, "is the time never to arrive when we may manage our own affairs without the fear of insulting his Britannic majesty? Is the rod of British power to be forever suspended over our heads?" Whether we assert our rights by sea or by land, "this phantom incessantly pursues us. . . . Mr. President, I have before said on this floor, and now take occasion again to remark, that I most sincerely desire peace and amity with England. . . . But if she persist in a denial of justice to us, or if she avails herself of the occupation of West Florida to commence war upon us, I trust and hope that all hearts will unite in a bold and vigorous vindication of our rights."

Clay closed with a magnificent jingoistic, nationalistic, expansionist peroration, just the sort of thing to rouse his countrymen and even stir some of the senators clustered around him: "I am not, sir, in favor of cherishing the passion of conquest. But I must be permitted to conclude by declaring my hope to see, ere long, the *new* United States (if you will allow me the expression) embracing not only the old thirteen States, but the entire country East of the Mississippi, including East Florida and some of the territories to the north of us also."[22]

Clay's exuberant nationalism, his sense of a *"new* United States" were essential elements in his emerging political philosophy. An expanding nation, both territorially and industrially, directed by a dynamic and respected central government, lay at the very heart of his convictions about the future course of the American nation.

When the young Kentuckian returned to his seat, the Republicans in the chamber applauded vigorously. He had made quite an impression on them. The speech was the sort of thing the American people wanted to hear after all the humiliating blows to their pride that they had been forced to suffer over

22. "Speech on the Occupation of West Florida," *Annals of Congress,* 11th Congress, 3d session, pp. 55–64.

the past several years. They needed to believe that they could defend their
honor and freedom and that leaders existed who understood that fact. And
Clay's speech had enough Anglophobia in it to please the most demanding of
his western constituents.

But the Federalists were not at all impressed with Clay's arguments. Senator Timothy Pickering of Massachusetts presented his evidence against annexation by reading a letter written in 1804 by the French foreign minister Talleyrand to the American minister in Paris in which he expressly denied that the
United States had acquired West Florida in the purchase of Louisiana. But the
Republicans shot right back that the letter had been conveyed to the Senate in
secrecy and Pickering had violated the secrecy by reading the letter in public.

Straightway the presiding officer ordered the galleries cleared, and the
Senate went into executive session. One hour later the galleries were again
opened, and Henry Clay offered a resolution censuring Timothy Pickering for
the "public perusal . . . of certain papers with open galleries" without a special
order removing the injunction of secrecy placed upon them by the President,
which was "a palpable violation of the rules of this body."[23] The motion cun-
ningly deflected attention away from the evidence Pickering had brought forward; it also further charged the already tense atmosphere in the Senate chamber and triggered a good deal of verbal bickering. Finally, on a strict party vote
the censure passed.

The Senate also abandoned further action on extending the Territory of
Orleans to the Perdido, for the administration was now anxious to go further
and claim East Florida as well. On January 3, 1811, Madison asked authority to
take "temporary possession" of part of the eastern end of Florida "which may
be desired by the Spanish authorities."[24] In the Senate the President's message
was referred to a committee chaired by Clay. Four days later the committee
returned a report that included a bill to authorize the President to occupy "all
or any part of the Territory lying East of the River Perdido" and south of
Georgia and the Mississippi Territory and to use U.S. troops if necessary.[25]
The Congress enacted the bill on January 15, 1811. As Clay had said, expediency dictated that the safety and security of the United States required the
eventual acquisition of the entire peninsula of Florida.

These efforts by Clay certainly gained him a large, appreciative audience
among fire-breathing nationalists, Anglophobes, and expansionists in every
section of the country. His reputation steadily mounted as one of the leading
spokesmen for those who espoused a *new* United States" and who no longer
worried about "insulting his Britannic majesty." He was listened to and respected by ordinary citizens everywhere, especially the younger ones. And they

23. "Resolution Censuring Timothy Pickering," December 31, 1810, *Annals of Congress,* 11th
Congress, 3d session, pp. 73–74, 80. The word "palpable" was later crossed out.
24. *Annals of Congress,* 11th Congress, 3d session, p. 370.
25. The declaration or report and the bill along with amendments are included in Clay, *Papers,* I,
520–522.

not only heard and applauded his views on the safeguarding of American
rights from foreign attack but also listened to his ideas about how the nation
could attain economic power and prosperity. Representative John Randolph
of Roanoke subsequently dubbed Clay "the Cock of Kentucky."[26]

On February 11, 1811, the "Cock" made his last important speech in the
Senate during this session. It dealt with the Bank of the United States, an issue
that later formed another integral part of his Republican ideology. Only this
time the speech later became an embarrassment to him, for now he argued
against the Bank and against the power of the government to create it.

In 1791, over the strenuous objections of Thomas Jefferson and James
Madison, President George Washington had accepted the counterarguments
of Alexander Hamilton and signed the legislation creating the Bank of the
United States (BUS). The measure was meant to provide a strong banking
system throughout the country and secure stable currency and credit. Jefferson
and Madison regarded the Bank as unconstitutional, an unwarranted expansion of power by the federal government. Hamilton denied the argument,
claiming that authorization came from the implied powers clause of the Constitution. In any event, the bill, as enacted, granted a charter for the institution
to run for twenty years, and during that time some Republicans had come to
appreciate the value of a national banking system. For example, Albert Gallatin, the secretary of the treasury, clearly understood the splendid financial
services the Bank had provided the government and the country. He was
therefore extremely anxious to have the Bank's charter extended in 1811, when
it was scheduled to expire.

President Madison chose to stand aloof, despite his earlier constitutional
doubts. But more ideologically orthodox Republicans continued their opposition to the Bank. Because congressmen were almost evenly divided on the
subject, some of them regretted that Madison could not stir himself to provide
leadership and guidance. He was "little better than a man of straw," complained one Federalist, with not "half the independence of an old clucking
hen."[27] The House ended up postponing indefinitely the question of recharter—the vote was sixty-five to sixty-four—so Secretary Gallatin turned to
the Senate for help.

It came in the person of Senator William H. Crawford of Georgia, a big,
hulking, good-looking man with a bright, sunny disposition and a growing
army of admirers, both inside and outside the Congress. Like Clay, he had
been born in Virginia and then moved to another state to seek his fortune.
Also like Clay, he was a resourceful, intensely ambitious, and practical politician, who had already begun to think about the ways to propel himself into the
presidential chair. On February 5 he introduced a bill in the Senate to extend
the Bank's charter for another twenty years and, in the course of his remarks,

26. Mayo, *Clay,* p. 351.
27. Quoted ibid., pp. 374–375.

denied that the government lacked constitutional authority to create the BUS. He cited the power of Congress to levy taxes as the necessary constitutional authorization to establish such an institution. He also enumerated the many benefits provided by the Bank, and he urged his colleagues to transcend selfish interests of their states and their local constituencies for the sake of the nation as a whole.[28]

The appeal to patriotism and the call to reject selfish interests should have awakened a positive response in Clay's consciousness, but his own banking connections in Kentucky precluded any such response. He had been a director of the Bank of Kentucky as well as intimately associated with the Lexington Bank, which he had saved from the desperate attacks of Felix Grundy. Both these banks had now locked arms with other Kentucky banks in cries of protest against the BUS, whose conservative banking policies they frequently found stifling. Kentucky legislators, therefore, joined with legislators of a number of other states and instructed their congressmen to block recharter.

For personal as well as political reasons, Clay had his position already determined for him. And he decided not only to vote against recharter but to speak against it as well in order to answer the arguments put forward by Senator Crawford. What helped him was the long, tiresome, and foolish harangue delivered previously by Senator William Branch Giles of Virginia, who seemed to shift one way and then another but finally ended by opposing recharter. This awful diatribe gave Clay the opening he wanted. He rose to do battle on February 15 and later had to eat every word he spoke.

He began by making Giles the butt of a delightful, if apocryphal, joke. "He discussed both sides of the question, with great ability and eloquence," remarked Clay, in a deadpan tone of voice, ". . . both that it was constitutional and unconstitutional, highly proper and improper. . . ." It reminded him of Patrick Henry, who once got confused about which side he was pleading in addressing a jury and pleaded magnificently against his own client. "You have ruined me," cried the devastated client. "Never mind," responded Henry. Thereupon he turned back to the jury and continued his plea. "May it please your honors, and you, gentlemen of the jury, I have been stating to you what I presume my adversary may urge on his side. I will now shew you how fallacious his reasoning & groundless his pretensions are." And Henry proceeded to refute every argument he had just advanced, after which he won the case! "A success," laughed Clay, "with which I trust the exertion of my honorable friend [Senator Giles] will on this occasion be crowned."

The Senate roared. Giles made an easy target and a convenient victim for Clay's wicked tongue. Still, it started the speech off with a bang. Turning to Crawford, the young man needled him for having "gone over into the camp of the enemy." He then asked, "[I]s it kind in him to look back upon his former friends, and rebuke them for the fidelity with which they adhere to their old

28. Chase C. Mooney, *William H. Crawford 1772–1834* (Lexington, Ky., 1974), pp. 19–22, 24.

principles?" He twitted Crawford for wandering through the Constitution in a futile search for authority. At least Hamilton had stuck to general principles. But how wise had been the Founding Fathers, Clay continued, "to leave as little as possible to implication." Under the name of accomplishing one speci-fied object that is enumerated in the Constitution, the power implied ought not to be interpreted to embrace other objects that are not enumerated. Clay was especially concerned that a bank given one set of privileges will assume others, just like the South Sea, East India, and Mississippi companies, and everyone knew how ruinous those mistakes turned out to be.

What is this Bank as proposed? he asked. "It is a splendid association of favored individuals, taken from the mass of society, and invested with exemp-tions and surrounded by immunities and privileges." (Oh, how he regretted those words when the Jacksonians in 1832 threw them back into his face.) "All corporations enjoy exclusive privileges—that is the corporators have privileges which no other possess." He looked around the chamber. "Where," he asked, "is the limitation upon this power to set up corporations?"

He contended that only the states had the exclusive power to regulate contracts and the responsibilities between debtors and creditors. If Congress assumed an equal power, then it can confer upon slaves or children the ability to contract, even in contravention of states' rights.

As for the argument that the country was growing in commerce, wealth, and population, thus creating new energies, new needs, and new exigencies, fine, declared Clay, then amend the Constitution if necessary, but do not simply infer that the powers are already implicit in the document. "Once substitute *practice* for principle—the expositions of the constitution for the text of the constitution, and in vain shall we look for the instrument in the instrument itself! It will be as diffused and intangible as the pretended consti-tution of England," as subject to contradictory interpretation as the Bible.

"I conceive then, sir, that we are not empowered by the constitution . . . to renew the charter of this bank. . . ." Moreover, the power of the purse will be wielded by an institution "in derogation of the great principle of all our institu-tions, responsibility to the people," and will be "amendable only to a few stockholders, and they chiefly foreigners." Twenty years later these same senti-ments found forceful expression in Andrew Jackson's veto of the Bank bill, a bill concocted by Henry Clay himself.

Clay ended with another nationalistic outburst, another Anglophobic blast against an enemy intent on subjugating this nation, one way or another. "Wealth is power, and, under whatsoever form it exists, its proprietor" can wield it to our destruction.[29]

The speech provided moments of eloquence, particularly at the conclu-sion, when Clay allowed his emotions fuller play. And the opening jabs at

29. Speech on Bill to Recharter the Bank of the United States, February 15, 1811, *Annals of Congress,* 11th Congress, 3d session, pp. 209–219.

Crawford and Giles had a distinctly sporting flavor that was characteristic. His biographers, on the whole, have disparaged the speech, no doubt because it contradicted everything he later epitomized and because he himself eventually repudiated it as a youthful mistake. The basic arguments do not fit the other parts of his emerging ideology—what would become his American System— but they may be understood in terms of self-interest, political necessity, and his continuing commitment to states' rights. Apart from his personal concerns he was largely acting at the direction of his constituents in Kentucky. Clay was a very practical politician, just beginning his ascent to national fame and power. At this stage of his career he invariably did what was expedient—later, when politically unassailable at home, he could be more independent—and in 1811 it was highly expedient for him to oppose the Bank. He also genuinely believed the bill to be unconstitutional. Five years later he changed his mind—and with good reasons. But for the moment, with war hardly more than a year away, he needed to strike at what he thought were the forces detrimental to the safety and prosperity of this country. And the Bank seemed to be one of them. At war's end he was to have other thoughts.

Like the House, the Senate split over the measure, and it took the deciding vote of Vice President George Clinton to kill it. Clinton's speech, which he delivered in the Senate upon giving his casting vote, was written by none other than Henry Clay himself. And according to the Kentucky senator, that speech gained for Clinton "more credit than anything else that he ever did."[30] That casting vote later caused the administration considerable grief as it tried to find the money necessary to carry on a war with its traditional enemy.

30. Adams, *Memoirs*, VII, 64. Clay also said that it had been written under Clinton's dictation, "and he never should think of claiming it as his composition." Ibid.

SIX

Mr. Speaker

KENTUCKY APPLAUDED Clay for his vote and speech on the Bank, and several influential newspapers in the country, such as the Richmond *Enquirer,* noticed his oratorical efforts and praised his sterling address and its importance in defeating recharter. Some journals commented that his future already appeared extremely promising, both for himself personally and for the nation at large. An inference about possibly achieving the highest office in the land could hardly be missed.[1]

Washington society also congratulated him. He was not only a much admired orator, said Margaret Bayard Smith, wife of the senator from Maryland, but a delightful guest at all the important social functions in town. He exuded a reckless air, an ambience that added a measure of excitement to all the functions he attended, a feeling that he might even risk a social gaffe if the stakes were high enough. With such friends as William Armistead Burwell and Caesar A. Rodney, he attended many social "crushes and squeezes," regularly put in an appearance at Dolley Madison's Wednesday evening levees, drove out to Great Falls and to the Bladensburg spa for some relaxation, and witnessed whatever new theatrical performance might be available in the capital.[2]

Still, despite the reckless air, he generally conducted himself with the utmost decorum. He was always polite and accommodating, good-natured and friendly. His sometimes flamboyant social style—a style not everyone appreciated—abated somewhat this particular season with the late arrival in Washington of his wife, Lucretia, and the children. Moreover, under no circumstance would Clay ever embarrass or offend her in public. He had too much regard and sincere affection for her—and for himself—to make that mistake. Lucretia did not have the social pretensions of her husband, nor did she particularly enjoy the rounds of amusements a political life in Washington involved. Margaret Bayard Smith summed her up very skillfully when she wrote that Lucretia "is a thousand times better pleased, sitting in the room

---

1. Richmond *Enquirer,* March 12, 1811.
2. Mayo, *Clay,* p. 355.

with all her children round her, and a pile of work by her side, than in the most brilliant drawing room."[3] Lucretia attended the functions required of her, but her preferences were almost totally domestic, including remaining at their home in Kentucky if at all possible.[4]

Home in Kentucky meant Ashland, the name Clay gave the estate that had become his residence in 1806 and that was located about a mile and a half south of Lexington. The name derived from the native ash growing in the area, and to Clay it also conveyed a sense of serenity and peace. Ashland provided him with a refuge from the tumultuous world outside, a safe haven to which he might regularly escape from the burdens and hardships of public life. And almost from the day he acquired the property he planted spruce trees. "When I passed through the wilderness in 1797," he recollected, "I was much struck with the Spruce pine as a beautiful ever green. I am very anxious to propagate it on a little farm that I am improving near this place [Lexington]."[5]

The estate was modest in size when Clay began purchasing the property, but in five years he had added several hundred acres. When he returned to Ashland at the close of the congressional session in 1811, the estate probably comprised four hundred acres. It had been purchased for approximately ten thousand dollars.[6] And it was always a matter of pride to Clay that every stick and stone on the property had been purchased by him alone. Nothing of the Ashland estate came to him as a gift or an inheritance.

The original house on the property when the Clay family first moved into it in 1806 was a modest affair, like most other houses in the area at that time. It is uncertain when Clay built the elegant country house that became his permanent home, but it is presumed that work on the structure began around 1809 because Henry Clay, Jr., later claimed that he was born in the dining room of the house on April 10, 1811.[7] When completed, the mansion faced west toward Lexington and was made of brick. Reputedly designed by Benjamin Latrobe, it stood two and a half stories high, with one-story wings flung out right and left from the central house itself.[8] Most interesting is the fact that it resembled a Virginia country home in Prince George County owned by Na-

---

3. Margaret Smith to Mrs. Kirkpatrick, [summer 1811], in Smith, *Forty Years,* pp. 86.

4. Lucretia's health and spirits were quite good during her sojourn in Washington. Clay's health, on the other hand, was "somewhat precarious," he claimed. "I have never been without cold since my arrival here, and my gums are far from being well—indeed I fear that the disorder in them is progressing. I have some thought of consulting some eminent physician here [Washington] on the subject of them." Clay to Dr. Frederick Ridgley, January 17, 1811, copy CPP.

5. Clay to John Ballenger, September 8, 1806, private collection, CPP.

6. See the various property deeds for October 11, 1811, and November 16, 1811, in Clay, *Papers,* I, 592, 596–597.

7. Van Deusen, *Clay,* p. 72. Van Deusen cites Henry Clay, Jr.'s manuscript diary, now located at Ashland with a copy in the library of the University of Kentucky. However, the copy has a number of pages missing, including the one cited by Van Deusen, and those in charge at Ashland have no idea what became of the missing pages.

8. These wings were not part of the original house. They were added in 1813 or shortly thereafter, and they were designed by Benjamin Latrobe.

thaniel Harrison and thought to be designed by Thomas Jefferson.

After the wings were added, the house measured 126 feet long by 57 feet wide. The entrance bay had a colonnetted fan doorway with tall windows on either side. It led into a lofty octagonal hall, to the left of which was a small room that Clay used as an office. On the right an elliptical stairwell provided access to the rooms above. Directly opposite the front entrance were doors leading into the drawing room and dining room. A wide, arched doorway connected these two rooms. Running the entire length of the northern wing on each side of the house were narrow hallways between which Clay had built an octagonal-shaped library, paneled in ash and walnut, with a dome ceiling or skylight for greater illumination. Beyond the library there were bedrooms and a billiard room.[9]

A serpentine carriageway, approximately 225 yards in length, snaked its way to the mansion through a grove of cypress, locust, and cedar trees. The smokehouse, dairy house, carriage house, and slave quarters were located a short distance away. A lovely park running north and east, where Clay frequently took walks, added to the overall spaciousness and grandeur of the estate. Sloping lawns sheeted with bluegrass led to a forest of dogwoods, redbuds, pines, hollies, and other flowering and ornamental trees and shrubs. Tan-barked walks, shaded by hemlocks, ashes, and walnut trees, all planted by Clay himself, marked the paths through this park.[10] Lord Morpeth, one of a number of distinguished visitors,[11] claimed it looked more like an English park than anything he had seen in the United States. The house was insured by Clay on September 25, 1812, for eight thousand dollars but valued at ten thousand dollars.[12] Unfortunately this noble structure fell into disrepair and was pulled down shortly after Clay's death. A somewhat similar structure was erected in its place in 1857, and today the estate consists of no more than twenty acres.[13]

All during his return to Ashland after the adjournment of Congress, Clay was concerned about Lucretia's latest pregnancy and the possibility of her giving birth before they reached home. Fortunately things went smoothly. "Our journey out was better than I anticipated," he wrote. "We reached home several weeks ago, and since our return the event which occasioned us so much

9. "Ashland, the Home of Henry Clay," pp. 163–170.

10. Ibid., p. 164. "C. D. S." wrote an interesting description of the house and grounds in an article for the New York *Tribune* entitled "Visit to Mr. Clay at Ashland," May 25, 1845. It also included a loving tribute to the master of Ashland. It was reprinted in *Niles' Weekly Register,* June 21, 1845. See also ibid., July 1, 1843.

11. Other visitors included Harriet Martineau, Martin Van Buren, the violinist Ole Bull, Baron de Maréchal, and Count Bertrand.

12. Fire insurance policy, September 25, 1812, in Clay, *Papers,* I, 730.

13. The mansion was probably defective from the beginning, and because of poor materials used in the construction, moisture seeped into the walls and foundations. Clay tried several times to solve the problem but to no avail. F. Kimball, *Domestic Architecture of the American Colonies and of the Early Republic* (New York, 1922), p. 274; Clay Lancaster, *Ante Bellum Houses of the Bluegrass* (New York, 1975), pp. 56–57, 137–139; Richard L. Troutman, "Henry Clay and His 'Ashland' Estate," *Filson Club History Quarterly,* XXX (April 1956), pp. 160, 161.

solicitude, on the way, has occurred & has put me in possession of the stoutest son we ever had, with less inconvenience to Mrs. Clay than she ever before experienced."[14]

The birth of Henry Clay, Jr., on April 10 was indeed a happy occasion for the family, but it was one of the few such joyful events they experienced that spring as the likelihood of war with Great Britain intensified over the next several months. Napoleon, in a cynical move to outfox the Americans, announced his intention of withdrawing the Berlin and Milan decrees, thereby permitting President Madison, under the terms of the Macon's Bill No. 2, to reimpose sanctions against Britain. Of course, Napoleon had no intention of keeping his word. Poor Madison never realized that he had been duped. Rather than wait for positive proof of Napoleon's goodwill toward the United States, the President invoked the Macon bill and threatened to proclaim nonintercourse with Britain unless the orders-in-council were repealed within three months. Britain sensibly refused to repeal the orders until it had proof that Napoleon truly meant to carry out his declared intention. Neither America nor Britain budged from its position over the next several months, and time inevitably ran out.

Unfortunately, while these portentous events transpired, a war hysteria swept the country, particularly along the frontier. The problem of the Indian remained a constant threat to settlers in the West, and that problem was exacerbated by the presence of the British in Canada and the encouragement they gave to the Indians to harass and attack Americans. It reached a climax of sorts when the great Shawnee chieftain Tecumseh sought to build a confederation of Indian tribes and hurl it full force against the entire length of the frontier. The scattering of his forces on November 7, 1811, at the Prophet's Town on Tippecanoe Creek in Indiana by American troops commanded by General William Henry Harrison served only to whet the desire of settlers for the total destruction of the Indians, along with their British allies. A declaration of war by the United States might bring as one of its rewards the subjugation of Canada, and with it the termination of the Indian menace.

Clay himself had encouraged this militant spirit. In his speech on the Senate floor delivered a year before he had held out the promise of invasion and conquest.[15] Nor was he alone in delivering heroic speeches about what raw frontiersmen could accomplish on the battlefield. Southern expansionists predicted an easy victory against the Spanish in Florida if "the troubled ocean of war" was allowed to roll in. They presumed, of course, that war against Britain necessarily involved conflict with Spain. Both countries could yield a sizable empire. These War Hawks, as they were called, breathed a passion for Canada and Florida that reflected the aspirations and hopes of practically the entire frontier. By late summer 1811 Clay was predicting war as a certainty. "If

14. Clay to Caesar Rodney, April 29, 1811, in Clay, *Papers,* I, 557.

15. *Annals of Congress,* 11th Congress, 2d session, pp. 579–582.

. . . France is honest and sincere in her recent measures, I look upon War with G. Britain inevitable."[16]

Of course, the wily Napoleon continued to deceive President Madison, who had plunged ahead and reimposed sanctions against the British. When the Twelfth Congress assembled in Washington on November 4, 1811, the President was prepared to alert the representatives to the possible prospect of war.

Clay had decided to start for Washington and his new position as a member of the lower (but livelier) House of Representatives in ample time to arrive well before the start of the session. He left home about mid-October and moved rapidly across the mountains, as though he knew beforehand that something important would occur among Republicans prior to their taking their seats, and he needed to be present to participate in it. Moreover, he anticipated fireworks on the floor of both houses from the moment they were called to order.[17]

What surprised him upon his arrival was the number of new faces in the House, all relatively young (late twenties and early thirties), all born after the Declaration of Independence had been signed, and virtually all fire-breathing War Hawks. Many of them came from the South and West and had their glinty eyes fixed on either Florida or Canada. They included such worthies as John C. Calhoun, Langdon Cheves, and William Lowndes from South Carolina, Richard M. Johnson from Kentucky, Felix Grundy from Tennessee, Peter B. Porter from New York, and John Adams Harper from New Hampshire. And of course, there was Henry Clay from Kentucky.

Although few of these men had ever personally known the political oppression of British rule, they had nonetheless developed a powerful enmity toward Great Britain. In addition, they felt a deep need to express their enmity and translate it into action. They therefore looked for leadership from those, like themselves, who understood the necessity of strong measures to assert the rights of the nation, including a declaration of war if nothing else sufficed to bring redress. But they wanted men with legislative and debating experience in order to check the opposition of an older generation of statesmen who counseled caution and prudence and delay. They wanted men skillful in parliamentary maneuvering and the art of political manipulation. And it just so happened that a number of these young War Hawks joined the same congressional mess at the beginning of the session. Clay, George Bibb, who replaced him in the Senate, Grundy, Lowndes, Calhoun, and several others found lodgings in the same boardinghouse. They soon discovered in their conversations with one another that they entertained identical feelings of passionate resentment toward Great Britain. Their talk at times reached such a pitch of emotional intensity that they became known as the War Mess. And in their talk they declared their determination to find dynamic leadership, something President

16. Clay to Caesar Rodney, August 17, 1811, in Clay, *Papers,* I, 574.
17. Clay to Caesar Rodney, August 17, 1811, in Clay, *Papers,* I, 574.

Madison could not and would not provide. Indeed, among older and more experienced representatives, men who had been around for a number of years, there was no one who fulfilled their needs or wishes, no one who could lead the Congress so that the members might discharge their responsibility to preserve and protect the nation against its enemies.

No one, that is, except Henry Clay. The young, aggressive Kentuckian offered many of the qualities they demanded. He had experience in Congress, had more than a nodding acquaintance with many, if not most, of the leading figures in Washington, had youth and enthusiasm, had speaking talents of the highest order, had both talent and ambition to lead, and, most important of all, had already demonstrated to the country at large and his colleagues that he shared with them the same fiery determination to smite the British and force them to respect American rights. As a matter of fact, by the fall and winter of 1811–1812 Clay was telling many friends to expect a declaration of war against Great Britain unless the orders-in-council were revoked. "War, calamitous as it generally is," he wrote in late December 1811, "seems to me the only alternative worthy of our Country. I should blush to call myself an American were any other adopted, in the existing state of our affairs."[18]

There was another extremely important reason for Clay's selection as leader of these War Hawks: his charisma. Over the past several years he had developed the extraordinary skill of drawing people to him. This magnetic quality to his personality attracted followers and admirers, both male and female. His amiability, his love of conversation, his ready smile, his delightful manners, his devastating wit, his remarkable intellect, and his profound understanding of the momentous issues facing the nation—all combined to produce a dynamic and charismatic personality that most Washingtonians increasingly found irresistible. A few years later one young congressman from Missouri tried to explain it. He "grows upon me more & more, every time I see him," exclaimed Edward Bates. "There is an intuitive perception about him, that seems to see & understand at a glance, and a winning fascination in his manners that will suffer none to be his enemies who cooperate with him. When I look upon his manly & bold countenance, & meet his frank & eloquent eye, I feel an emotion little short of enthusiasm in his cause. . . . He is a great man—one of Nature's nobles."[19]

At another time, when General Thomas Glascock of Georgia took his seat in the House, a mutual friend came up to him and asked, "General, may I introduce you to Henry Clay?"

"No, sir!" came the stern response. "I am his adversary, and choose not to subject myself to his fascination."[20]

18. Clay told Caesar Rodney as early as August 17 that war was inevitable. See also his letters to John Parker, December 7, 1811, and William W. Worsley, January 4, 1812, in Clay, *Papers,* I, 574, 599, 611.
19. Edward Bates to Julia Bates, February 25, 1828, Edward Bates Papers, Virginia Historical Society, Richmond.
20. Horace Greeley, *Recollections of a Busy Life* (New York, 1868), p. 250.

Thus, when the Twelfth Congress convened, the War Hawks had not only their candidate for the Speaker's chair but an agreement on the strategy by which they hoped to elect him. On the evening before the session commenced, the Republicans caucused in order to arrange, among other things, the organization of the new Congress, starting with the Speaker. There was some sentiment for the distinguished former Speaker Nathaniel Macon of North Carolina, who had frequently served as the ideological mentor of other representatives in the past, including a former member, Andrew Jackson. He was a Republican of the old school, conservative, strong in his commitment to states' rights, and unswervingly loyal to his friends and allies. But therein lay the problem. Many congressmen expressed concern that if Macon became Speaker, he would reappoint his friend and ideological co-conservative John Randolph of Roanoke as chairman of the Ways and Means Committee. To put it bluntly, Randolph seemed to have descended from cloud-cuckoo-land. That he was eccentric everyone acknowledged. That he frequently ran out of control and became a royal nuisance was also acknowledged. But he could not be lightly dismissed or disregarded. He had to be handled with infinite care, for he was a wicked debater with a sharp and nasty tongue, and when he rose to speak in the House, his colleagues trembled with dread that he might single out one of them for a verbal pummeling. His high, shrill, feminine voice set one's teeth on edge, but colleagues suppressed their urge to laugh for fear of the humiliating consequences that might ensue. In the past he had pilloried Thomas Jefferson for his departure from pure Republican dogma as though he, Randolph, were the high priest of the party and keeper of the flame. Indeed, many understood that the Republican caucus had been called on Sunday night because of widespread concern that Macon would continue Randolph on this powerful committee and the members wanted to prevent such a calamity by finding another Speaker.[21]

All this provided the War Hawks with the opening they needed and had been counting on. Nothing of their plans had been revealed beforehand to other congressmen, even though they had been in Washington for the past several days, meeting and scheming and devising their strategy. Their preparedness, their eagerness, their insistence that strong congressional leadership was vital at this crucial moment, particularly with so many new, young, and nationalistic-minded representatives on hand, and, most especially, their proposal that Clay possessed the talent, energy, and decisiveness to make an outstanding Speaker, coupled with the generally accepted desire to block Randolph's reappointment to Ways and Means, all combined to win Republican acceptance of Clay as the new Speaker. Despite his youth, despite his obvious connections with the younger and more vociferous representatives in the

21. On Randolph, see Robert Dawidoff, *The Education of John Randolph* (New York, 1982); William Cabell Bruce, *John Randolph of Roanoke, 1773–1833* (New York, 1922), 2 volumes; Hugh A. Garland, *The Life of John Randolph of Roanoke* (New York, 1850), 2 volumes; and Russell Kirk, *Randolph of Roanoke: A Study in Conservative Thought* (Chicago, 1951).

House, and despite his limited experience exercising executive responsibilities, the caucus agreed to support his election.[22]

A rather simple explanation of what happened is in a story related by Nathan Sargent to the effect that the War Hawks first decided in caucus that they needed a Speaker who would enforce the rules and bridle Randolph, "for he disregards all rules." The group agreed. "Then," said another, "he must be a man who can meet John Randolph on the floor or on the field, for he may have to do both." Again there was agreement. "But where is the man who can do this?" asked one. "I'll tell you," called out Jonathan Roberts of Pennsylvania. "Young Harry Clay . . . is the very man to do it." All in the room vigorously nodded their heads in agreement because they knew him to be a "manly" sort of fellow, and so it was decided to make Clay their next Speaker.[23]

The following day, Monday, November 4, the House met to begin its business and immediately proceeded to choose its Speaker. On the first ballot Henry Clay was elected. He received seventy-five votes, while William W. Bibb of Georgia won thirty-eight, Macon three, Hugh Nelson of Virginia two, and Burwell Bassett of Virginia one.[24] It was an amazing feat: first, because Clay was a freshman and second, because it occurred on the first day and on the first ballot. And it was not a close victory. He had won by a margin of almost two to one over his nearest rival. It constituted a personal triumph for the Kentuckian and a triumph for the strong-willed, determined, and aggressive young War Hawks, who were intent on rescuing the nation from disgrace and humiliation. Some congressmen now referred to Clay as the "Western Star," destined for a bright and dazzling future.[25]

But little did these congressmen realize that they had given themselves a master, a man who would indeed provide strong but domineering leadership. He was to make the post the most powerful position in the nation after the President. Since the founding of the Republic under the Constitution no Speaker had realized the full potential of the office. No one had used it to move and shape national affairs in a direction that he, the Speaker, determined. All that now changed. Henry Clay refashioned the office and converted it into a mighty instrument for the exercise of extraordinary political powers. But Clay had to prove himself before he could freely exercise the immense latent authority in the office, and the sadistic bully from Virginia, John Randolph, sat waiting to test him.

As the thirty-four-year-old Clay mounted the podium following his election and took the heavily ornate Speaker's chair, positioned on a dais under a

22. John Adams Harper to William Plumer, February 6, 1812, in Plumber Papers, LC, cited in Mayo, *Clay*, p. 403, note 2.

23. Sargent, *Public Men and Events*, I, 130.

24. *Annals of Congress*, 12th Congress, 1st session, p. 330.

25. Mayo, *Clay*, p. 403. For an excellent discussion of the leadership provided in Congress by the War Hawks, see Harry W. Fritz, "The War Hawks of 1812: Party Leadership in the Twelfth Congress," *Capitol Studies*, V (Spring 1977), pp. 25–42.

splendid canopy, he stared out at his colleagues clustered in a semicircle in this elliptically shaped chamber with its fluted Corinthian pillars draped with velvet. He looked supremely confident and self-assured. Always the actor, he tried to project just the right touch of authority as he assumed his new office. He tried to exude a manner that appeared forceful and purposeful. The carefully predetermined movements of his body, head, arms, and hands when he spoke assisted in creating this appearance. But he began humbly, as was proper. "Gentlemen," he said, after taking his oath and turning to his colleagues. "In coming to the station which you have done me the honor to assign me—an honor for which you will be pleased to accept my thanks—I obey rather your commands than my own inclination. I am sensible of the imperfections which I bring along with me, and the consciousness of these would deter me from attempting a discharge of the duties of the chair, did I not rely confidently upon your generous support." He was sure they understood that he would always try to conduct the public business "in the most agreeable manner."[26]

He demonstrated immediately how he planned to "conduct the public business" and run the affairs of the House. Each day, as he assumed his seat, he always had a clear and distinct notion of what business would come before the House and what he wanted to accomplish, what he would say, and how he would behave toward particular matters to be discussed that day. When suddenly confronted with a problem or difficult situation, he reacted immediately, making lightning-quick decisions. Decide fast, he later counseled. Act. "And never give your reasons for the decision."[27]

In a bold and determined move he started off by assigning all the War Hawks to the important committees, and he saw to it that they held control of each one. Peter B. Porter, a House veteran of two years, was named to head the Committee on Foreign Relations. Clay also assigned Calhoun, Harper, Joseph Desha, and Grundy to that committee. For Ways and Means, he tagged as chairman Ezekiel Bacon from western Massachusetts, another War Hawk and a House veteran of four years who was skilled in finance. He assigned Langdon Cheves, a future president of the Bank of the United States, to this committee to lend his assistance. In addition, Cheves headed Naval Affairs, while David R. Williams from South Carolina became the chairman of the Committee on Military Affairs. By and large Clay tended to use Bacon, Cheves, and Williams, by virtue of their chairmanships, as his "floor leaders" in the House.[28]

This immediate, daring, and courageous assertion of his executive authority in placing young, intense, war-bent representatives into positions of power clearly announced Clay's intention to determine congressional action and direction. It was a power play at the very start of his term as Speaker, and he

---

26. *Annals of Congress,* 12th Congress, 1st session, pp. 330–331.

27. Robert Winthrop, *Memoir of Henry Clay* (Cambridge, Mass., 1880), p. 6.

28. *Annals of Congress,* 12th Congress, 1st session, p. 333, 343; Ronald Hatzenbuehler, "The War Hawks and the Question of Congressional Leadership in 1812," *Pacific Historical Review,* XLV (February 1976), pp. 11–13.

pulled it off brilliantly and without encountering any significant opposition from disappointed seniors. These older, more experienced representatives took the loss of the important assignments with grace because Clay went out of his way to assure them that their influence in the House would not be diminished, that he would consult with them regularly about pending legislation. And he kept his word. Indeed, throughout his career as Speaker he treated his colleagues with such fairness and evenhandedness—never using his power to build a personal faction to advance his own political ambitions—that it virtually guaranteed his reelection to the office every time he chose to run for it. Even when he drove his colleagues toward particular goals, even when he arrogantly dictated a course of action to them, he did so for what he believed were national purposes, not personal gain. And they knew it.

A great deal of decision making, as John Quincy Adams had noted earlier in watching Clay in action, occurred "out of doors." Clay proved to be very adept at using the Speaker's private chambers to determine policy and solicit support for particular measures before the Congress. He also worked closely with the committees he had appointed and had a direct hand in framing all legislation pertaining to the war. In the Kentucky general assembly, through observation and participation, he had learned how politics must be conducted to produce desired results, how to manage situations adroitly to compensate for unexpected reversals, how to bargain for votes to win passage of essential legislation. In Washington he wisely and skillfully applied what he had learned, thereby creating in time a powerful position from which to operate. He possessed a remarkable talent for leadership which he exercised freely, unhesitatingly, boldly, and sometimes impetuously. Henry Clay, wrote a reporter of the Boston *Courier*, "combines and directs the greatness of others, and thus, with whatever direction he takes, he moves with a resistless might." What helped him immensely, of course, was the indispensable ingredient of a coterie of loyal friends, the War Hawks, who provided him with a core of solid voting strength with which he could shape and manage the affairs of the House.[29]

In effect, for the first time Clay established the concept of the Speaker as the political leader of the House. He assumed this role with the full knowledge and cooperation of his war-crazed friends who wanted a Speaker who could drive the members into making decisions and into authorizing military action. The passionate desire for war by a determined faction of representatives combined with the presence of a bold, aggressive, and self-assured person like Henry Clay produced the revolutionary changes that redefined the functions and powers of the Speaker of the House of Representatives.

Unlike his predecessors, Clay was the first Speaker to insist on his full rights as a member to debate and vote upon any issue to come before the House. He rejected the institutional role intended by the Founding Fathers of

29. Adams, *Memoirs*, I, 463; Felix Grundy to Andrew Jackson, November 28, 1811, Jackson Papers, LC; Clay, *Works*, I, 182–190; Boston *Courier*, quoted in Peterson, *Great Triumvirate*, p. 381.

a presiding officer whose principal functions were to direct traffic and keep order, similar to those of the Speaker in the British Parliament. By retaining his rights to debate and vote like any other member of the House, Clay significantly distinguishing himself from the Vice President, who merely presided over the Senate and voted only to break a tie.

Over the next several years Clay also presumed the right to refer all bills introduced into the House to an appropriate standing committee. He thereby invested these committees with immense new powers by leaving them free to ignore those bills they disliked and to recommend passage of those bills they approved. In the past the House itself had formally instructed these committees on the legislation it wanted drafted and reported. What gave Clay vast new powers was the fact that he, not the House, chose the members of these standing committees. All this meant that he had freed the House from the influence and control of the President and made the chief executive virtually "subservient to the House."

One of the important ways in which Clay took control of House affairs was his enforcement of House rules, primitive though they were, especially in regulating debate. Repeatedly he called individual members to order when they tried to delay proceedings or prevent the taking of a final vote. To block filibusters, he employed the tactic of having one of his floor leaders move the previous question, which, when approved, automatically cut off debate. Then Clay would immediately call for a vote on the principal question then pending. He also arranged to direct the House into a Committee of the Whole whenever he wished to have an issue discussed without taking a binding vote and without dilatory motions.

But to a large extent his most outstanding talent in bringing the House under his dominance was his ability to find the ways of producing majorities for the bills he wanted passed. It was here that his charm, charisma, eloquence, geniality, intelligence, and political skill, factors few other men in the history of the House could match, made the difference.[30]

Also, in the exercise of his authority Clay showed consummate tact, shrewdness, and remarkable executive skills. For example, he treated John Randolph with a certain degree of deference but deftly hedged him in whenever possible to keep him from causing trouble. Although the beardless eccentric was given a seat on the Foreign Relations Committee, Porter, Calhoun, Grundy, Harper, and Desha could be expected to keep him in line—at least by outvoting him. Wisely Clay protected Randolph's right to speak and dissent, but when the Virginian presumed to take liberties with his position as a representative, Clay did not hesitate to rule against him, knowing full well that the members would uphold his ruling.

Almost immediately an occasion arose that brought the two men into open disagreement. Randolph liked to appear in the House dressed in riding

---

30. Neil MacNeil, *Forge of Democracy: The House of Representatives* (New York, 1963), pp. 67–69, 152, 25, 46, 345.

clothes and carrying a whip to command his dogs trailing behind him. On one occasion he even struck a colleague with a cane in defense of his dogs. The first time he brought one of his animals into the House, after Clay had been elected Speaker, the chair promptly ordered the doorkeeper to remove the beast. When Randolph objected, he was ruled out of order. The Virginian appealed to his colleagues to overrule the chair, but they refused. By this time, with war looming, the other Republicans could no longer abide Randolph's willfulness and disturbing eccentricities or his arguments and explanations of true Republican doctrine, especially as they related to the conduct of foreign affairs. It did not take long before even Randolph himself acknowledged Clay's influence and power. The "Speaker of the Ho of Representatives was the second man in the Nation," he conceded.[31]

Nevertheless, Clay and Randolph tangled repeatedly, neither one giving the other the edge. Year after year, session after session, they ranted or raged or sparred or debated with each other. But Clay never permitted the gadfly to assume control of House proceedings or put on a display of gross misbehavior. Probably they secretly admired each other or at least respected the other's talents and abilities.

Two stories—no doubt apocryphal—that throw some light on their personalities and constant feuding were told about them. On one occasion Randolph spotted Clay walking toward him. Both men seemed unwilling to let the other pass.

"I never sidestep skunks," snarled Randolph.

When he heard that remark, Clay quickly responded, "I always do," and jumped out of the way.

And some historians mistakenly believe that Randolph was referring to Clay when he said in one speech: "Fellow citizens, he is a man of splendid abilities but utterly corrupt. He shines and stinks like a rotten mackerel by moonlight."

The Speaker also tangled with other representatives, and on one occasion his passionate outbursts almost led to a serious confrontation. For reasons not exactly clear Clay got into a extremely heated debate with James Milnor of Pennsylvania and finally challenged him to a duel. Milnor, who later entered the Episcopal ministry, declined the honor of risking his life over something he regarded as trivial. Mutual friends stepped in and ultimately settled the dispute on terms agreeable to both parties. But this display of bravado by Clay proved to his friends that he was indeed ready at all times to act "on the floor or on the field."[32]

Obviously Clay had his critics right from the start, and they puzzled over

---

31. Langdon Cheves to Clay, July 30, 1812, in Clay, *Papers,* I, 700.

32. On Randolph, see Bruce, *John Randolph,* II, 197. Randolph was referring to Edward Livingston, not Clay, when he spoke about a rotten mackerel because Livingston had authored Jackson's Proclamation to the People of South Carolina on December 10, 1832, regarding nullification; see ibid., II, 766, note (a). See the New York *Daily Tribune,* November 22, 1848, for the dispute with Milnor.

his accomplishments for one so young and inexperienced. Some expressed their distinct distaste for his "Kentucky-style" political manner, what they regarded as his youthful inelegance and crudeness. One of Clay's severest critics, Josiah Quincy of Massachusetts, disapprovingly described the Speaker's oratory and manner of behavior. "Bold, aspiring, presumptuous, with a rough, overbearing eloquence, neither exact nor comprehensive, which he had cultivated and formed in the contests with the half-civilized wranglers in the county courts of Kentucky, and quickened into confidence and readiness by successful declamations at barbecues and electioneering struggles, he had not yet that polish of language and refinement of manners which he afterwards acquired by familiarity and attrition with highly cultivated men."[33]

Unfortunately Clay's ability to wield his authority effectively gave him delusions of power that were unrealistic. In time he presumed to act as though his will constituted the final decision in any dispute that arose in the House. His arrogance, his overbearing conceit, his presumptuousness eventually turned men against him. They recoiled from his brazen audacity, and they branded him with the nickname the Dictator. Indeed, it was later gossiped that on leaving a party at sunrise—not an unusual occurrence—Clay was asked how he could expect to preside over the House that day. "Come up," he laughed in response, "and you shall see how I will throw the reins over their necks."[34]

But here at the very beginning of his long and distinguished career he displayed the necessary restraint (with some exceptions) in dealing with his colleagues as their Speaker, and he steadily grew in their admiration and esteem. Thus, whenever he wished the position of Speaker, the members granted it to him, and he served as their leader for a total of ten years, longer than anyone else during the nineteenth century.

It should be added that at the start of his tenure as Speaker of the House, Henry Clay seemed to know instinctively the time-honored aphorism that the purpose of politics is power, that the purpose of power is to govern, and that the purpose of governing is to advance the welfare of the nation, even at the risk of sometimes supporting unpopular positions.

Although the President hardly seemed to know what direction to take in facing the problems of the nation in 1811 and 1812, his secretary of state, James Monroe, inclined toward favoring the position of the War Hawks. On various occasions he assured them that the President was in fact sympathetic to their demands for more vigorous action. But many other Republicans in Congress had no desire to assume a position of defiance toward Great Britain that could immediately jeopardize the peace and possibly plunge the country into war. Nor were they hell-bent on expansion like their colleagues from the West

---

33. Edmund Quincy, *Life of Josiah Quincy* (Boston, 1868), p. 255.
34. Samuel Arthur Bent, *Familiar Short Sayings of Great Men* (Boston and New York, 1882), p. 150.

and South. And there were other Republican factions, like the dissident Quids, whose leading spokesman was John Randolph and who, by their incessant preaching about strict constructionism, could make the orderly operation of government in achieving specific goals a difficult, if not impossible, process. Finally, there were the Federalists, who were forever muttering about the imminent breakup of the Union but whose number had steadily diminished in the recent past. They now constituted only 7 out of 34 senators and 37 out of 142 representatives. Moreover, they could not agree on a single foreign policy position. Most of them opposed a declaration of war against Great Britain, but a small minority welcomed an outbreak of hostilities in the hope that it would overthrow the administration.[35]

Obviously it would not be easy for Clay to manage this factious crowd and drive it toward purposeful and unified action, such as a declaration of war. For war was definitely his purpose by the close of 1811. Josiah Quincy of Massachusetts, one of the Federalist leaders, informed Harrison Gray Otis that "Clay our Speaker told me yesterday with some *naivete* 'the truth is I am in favour of war and so are some others—*but some of us fear that if we get into war you will get our places.'* "[36]

A verbal free-for-all commenced almost immediately once the House began its deliberations in December 1811. A Senate bill, sponsored by the antiadministration forces, sought to increase the army by twenty-five thousand for an enlistment of five years, despite the lack of money and the difficulty, if not the impossibility, of raising such a huge force. The President had been more modest and practical, asking for ten thousand enlisted for three years, but the Senate had scoffed at his meager request, concocted a bill that more than doubled the size of the projected army, and forwarded it to the House. It was met, according to Representative Peter B. Porter, with "a gust of zeal and passion."[37] But conservatives with some support from moderates denounced the increase as a violation of Republican dogma and a flagrant disregard of the President's request.

The brouhaha was well under way when Clay stepped down from his chair and actively entered the debate with a stupendous display of rhetorical fire. The House was sitting as a Committee of the Whole. He walked to the well, paused for a moment to make certain he had the full attention of every representative, and then started to speak in a quiet tone of voice. Within minutes the tone had hardened, the voice pitch rose, and the words quickly revealed his burgeoning lust for war. "The difference," he declared, "between

35. On the Quids, see Noble Cunningham, "Who Were the Quids?" *Mississippi Valley Historical Review,* L (September 1963), pp. 252–263; Norman K. Risjord, "1812: Conservatives, War Hawks, and the Nation's Honor," *William and Mary Quarterly,* XVIII (April 1961), pp. 196–210; and Norman K. Risjord, *The Old Republicans: Southern Conservatism in the Age of Jefferson* (New York, 1965), pp. 40–71.

36. Quincy to Otis, November 26, 1811, in Samuel Eliot Morison, *The Life and Letters of Harrison Gray Otis, Federalist, 1765–1848* (Boston and New York, 1913), II, 34.

37. *Annals of Congress,* 12th Congress, 1st session, p. 701.

those who were for 15,000, and those who were for 25,000 men, appeared to him [Clay] to resolve itself into the question merely of a short or protracted war—a war of vigor—or a war of languor and imbecility." For his part, Clay thought 15,000 men "too great for peace, and . . . too small for war." Yet the object of this force he understood to be distinctly war: "War with Great Britain."

And what would be gained? Rather, said Clay, answering himself, "what are we not to lose by peace? commerce, character, a nation's best treasure, honor!" He had no desire to dwell on the "catalogue of injuries from England." But he could not overlook the impressment of seamen, the illegal seizure of American property "which falls within her rapacious grasp," and the violation of personal rights, "rights which forever ought to be sacred" but "are trampled upon and violated."

It is claimed, Clay continued, that England was fighting "for the world" against tyranny. A noble cause, he allowed, but how can it best be achieved? Only by the "scrupulous observance of the rights of others," thundered the Speaker. "We are called upon to submit to debasement, dishonor and disgrace—to bow the neck to royal insolence. . . . Let those who contend for this humiliating doctrine, read its refutation in the history" of nations. "Let us come home to our own history; it is not by submission that our fathers achieved our independence." The "American character has been much abused by Europeans, whose tourists . . . have united in depreciating it." But he knew, as did anyone with a grain of common sense, that "the great mass of the [American] people possessed more intelligence than any other people on the globe."[38]

In the course of this belligerent bombast, Clay proposed a compromise in the form of an amendment to reduce the strain on the Treasury and thus mollify the most conservative Republicans. He suggested at first commissioning only the essential officers and the remaining officers when their regiments had been enlisted. But he stuck by the force of twenty-five thousand. That he insisted upon. He later told William Worsley that he considered such a force "the strongest war measure that could be adopted, short of an actual declaration of war, which I have no doubt will be made before we rise, unless England ceases her aggressions."[39] And his strategy of amendment worked. It succeeded in splitting the opposition and ultimately bringing about the passage of the bill.[40]

What Clay had done by his adroit compromise was move the country toward greater preparedness for war. He had also devised the strategy by which to win ultimate congressional acceptance of what the War Hawks were

38. *Annals of Congress,* 12th Congress, 1st session, pp. 596–602; also reprinted in Clay, *Papers,* I, 602–609.

39. Clay to Worsley, January 4, 1812, in Clay, *Papers,* I, 611.

40. The bill passed on January 6, 1812, by the vote of ninety-four to thirty-four. The Senate, however, rejected the amendments, and the House then accepted the original bill with its call for twenty-five thousand men.

attempting to achieve. And with the subsequent introduction of the revenue bills to pay for this military buildup—"taxes must be laid," Clay whispered to a friend[41]—the Speaker further guided the Republican party away from its traditional ideological moorings. The old Jeffersonian arguments about economy, minimal government, and reliance upon state militias rather than upon a standing army and navy for national protection were seriously undermined by the steady drift toward girding the nation for war against Great Britain and an invasion of Canada. The antiwar Republican doctrine of '98 was no longer a ruling principle. Conservative and more moderate Republicans naturally worried and fretted over this aberration from party doctrine. It was becoming increasingly clear that one wing of the Republican party, led by Clay, held more supernationalistic sentiments than strict orthodoxy would permit. Members of this wing seemed less certain about the necessity of states' rights.

Clay's speech and several subsequent speeches on the floor to support bills to raise volunteers and increase the naval establishment not only signaled his own continuing stray from strict Republican orthodoxy but demonstrated to his audience his extraordinary powers as an orator and actor.[42] His verbal pyrotechnics steadily improved with each succeeding speech. The chamber instantly hushed when he stepped down from his chair to engage in debate. Members not only respected his arguments because of their commanding substance but acknowledged their admiration for his remarkable rhetorical skills. A master of persuasion, he recalled for some the heroic sounds of the past, when a revolutionary generation cried out its need for independence. And because his themes were liberty, personal rights, and national sovereignty, he seemed transported. He frequently reached unusual heights of eloquence that placed him on a par with the greatest of the revolutionary giants.[43] Intense love of country, declared the Baltimore newspaper *Niles' Weekly Register,* exuded from "every line and word" of the Speaker's speech. It "breathes the language of an independent patriot."[44]

President Madison accepted the stronger army bill forced on him by the legislature. Although he had called for a smaller force, he was slowly accepting the fact that the controlling hands in Congress were intent upon war. Even conservative Republicans got dragged along. Nathaniel Macon, a most distinguished and respected representative from North Carolina, astonished his colleagues by delivering a speech any War Hawk would have been proud to acknowledge as his own.[45]

The appalling failure of leadership by the President and the hesitation and

41. Clay to ?, ca. January 10, 1812, in Clay, *Papers,* I, 613.

42. These speeches may be found in the *Annals of Congress,* 12th Congress, 1st session, pp 743–745, 910–919.

43. Mayo, *Clay,* p. 433.

44. January 4, 1812.

45. On Macon, see William E. Dodd, *The Life of Nathaniel Macon* (Chicago, 1903), and Noble Cunningham, "Nathaniel Macon and the Southern Protest against National Consolidation," *North Carolina Historical Review,* XXXII (1955), pp. 376–384.

concern of moderate Republicans only stiffened the desire of the War Hawks to go to war immediately to reassert American rights. Nothing less than the military defeat of the British—and a humiliating defeat, such as a successful invasion of Canada, was what they had in mind—could assuage their war lust. They needed to prove to the world once more that American freedom had been honestly obtained and that they had a right to be independent and respected by other sovereign nations. Many of them, like Clay, wished to have done with talk and diplomacy and argument. They yearned to rush into combat. And as they grew more impatient, their dissatisfaction with an impotent and irresolute administration became more vocal and raucous.[46] They could not back away from their aggressive stance without a concession from Great Britain. The humiliation would have been intolerable. On the other hand, plunging the nation into war risked a catastrophe that might annihilate American independence. Unfortunately the Congress as a whole was badly divided on the question of war and felt various political pressures pulling it in opposite directions.

And where did the public stand? What thoughts did it have about the necessity of war? To those ardent nationalists who winced at every insult against the national honor by Great Britain or raged over Indian attacks and believed their termination possible only with the capture of Canada, war spelled the solution of all their problems. Perhaps General Andrew Jackson of the Tennessee militia spoke for many of them when he addressed his militiamen and assured them that they were "going to fight for the reestablishment of our national charector . . . in fine, to seek some indemnity for past injuries, some security against future aggressions, by the conquest of all the British dominions upon the continent of north america." The "hour of national vengeance" had arrived, he shouted.[47]

But there were many other Americans, mainly Federalists throughout New England, who had a less exalted view about the ability of the nation to reek vengeance upon a powerful Britain. They also demonstrated concern for the effects of war on their commercial investments and what it meant in terms of their future political power.

Whereas the administration worried and stewed over leading the nation into war, Clay had absolutely no fears and no hesitations. Always ready to trust to chance, always prepared to stake his money on the game with the highest risks, he applied steady pressure on the Congress and the administration to let loose "the dogs of war." And in feeling his way forward, Clay knew he had one lever on Madison that could ultimately move him to action. The President

---

46. "Our President tho a man of amiable manners and great talents, has not I fear those commanding talents, which are necessary to controul those about him. He permits division in his cabinet. He reluctantly gives up the system of peace. It is to be hoped, that as war is now seriously determined on, the Executive department will move with much more vigour. Without it it is impossible for Congress to proceed." Calhoun to Dr. James MacBride, April 18, 1812, in Calhoun, *Papers,* I, 99–100. Brant, *James Madison: President,* seeks to portray Madison as a bold and vigorous executive, but that is not the way the War Hawks saw him.

47. Jackson to the volunteers, March 7, 1812, Jackson, *Correspondence,* I, 220–223.

desired another term in office so that like Washington and Jefferson, he would serve as chief executive for eight years—not four years, like the repudiated John Adams. To win reelection, he needed united support from all Republicans in Congress, and it had slowly been impressed upon him that the War Hawks would withhold their support unless he asked for a declaration of war. What strengthened their lightly veiled threat was the interest De Witt Clinton of New York had begun to show in challenging Madison's reelection.[48] This intelligent, arrogant, imaginative, handsome young politico had already begun to curry favor and support from the many factions that detested both Madison and the Virginia Dynasty. There was even talk of a possible Clinton-Clay ticket.[49]

Although the cabinet leaned markedly toward peace, James Monroe, the secretary of state, bent the other way. He could not by any means be called a War Hawk, but compared with his colleagues in the cabinet, especially Albert Gallatin, he was a flaming hotspur. In addition, he was reputed to be another possible rival to Madison's reelection, but he soon indicated that he had no stomach for a contest with his fellow Virginian. Most important, Monroe provided Clay and his friends with an ear and mouth into the inner workings of the Madison administration.

The War Hawks demonstrated the extent of their cooperation with Secretary Monroe when the administration was duped into buying from an Irish adventurer by the name of John Henry for fifty thousand dollars, the entire budget for the secret service, a sheaf of documents that purported to prove the involvement of Great Britain in a plot to bring about the dismemberment of the Union.[50] Clay immediately spotted its potency to propel the administration into action, and he assured his friends in Kentucky that it would "accelerate a declaration of war."[51] Madison laid the documents before Congress, greatly exaggerating their importance in a covering letter. As expected, they created a sensation. Even the more conservative Republicans stood up and demanded war.[52]

Clay acted on this opportunity by devising a means to force the administration's hand. First, after consulting with his friends and a few selected representatives, he held a meeting with Monroe in which he outlined a proposal that could be taken to the President for his approval and implementation. He then wrote out his propositions in a formal letter to Monroe. He called upon Madison to recommend in a confidential message to Congress a thirty-day embargo to be followed by a declaration of war. Madison should also advise the calling up of ten thousand volunteers.[53]

48. John C. Calhoun to Patrick Noble, March 22, 1812, in Calhoun, *Papers*, I, 95–96.

49. Mayo, *Clay*, p. 485.

50. Donald R. Hickey, *The War of 1812: A Forgotten Conflict* (Urbana and Chicago, 1989), pp. 37–38; Calhoun to Patrick Noble, March 22, 1812, in Calhoun, *Papers*, I, 96.

51. Clay to William W. Worsley, February 9, 1812, in Clay, *Papers*, I, 630.

52. *Annals of Congress*, 12th Congress, 1st session, p. 1162ff.

53. Clay to Monroe, March 15, 1812, in Clay, *Papers*, I, 637.

Despite his constitutional scruples about invoking an embargo, the President decided to recommend this measure, and Monroe so informed the House Committee on Foreign Relations. But instead of Clay's suggestion, Madison proposed a sixty-day embargo in the hope of avoiding the calamity of war, thus doubling the length of time available for resolution of American grievances before issuing an outright declaration of hostilities. The proposal came to Congress on April 1 and was accompanied by a very perfunctory message. In a secret House session Clay spoke up in favor of the proposal within minutes after it was delivered, despite the President's alteration of his original suggestion. He approved of it, he said, "because it is to be viewed as a direct precursor of war." He considered it a war message and nothing less. "It remains for us," he cried, "to say whether we will shrink or follow up the patriotic conduct of the president." As an American and a member of the House, Clay said he felt a pride that the executive had recommended this measure.

John Randolph interrupted him. He intoned the presence of the all-seeing "Being who watches and surrounds us" in questioning the need for action at this time. "The eyes of God are upon us," he pontificated. "He knows the spirit of our minds." Clay dismissed Randolph's concerns by citing the newest instance of England's perfidy in the revelations of John Henry. "Is this not a cause of war? We have complete proof that [Britain] will do every thing to destroy us—our resolution and spirit are our only dependence."

Randolph responded by charging the House with wasting its time in idle debate. For the past five months, he argued, there had been a steady push by the Speaker to commit the nation to war. Henry Clay, not Great Britain, was forcing the issue.

The Speaker gaveled him down, ruling him to order. Randolph challenged the ruling, and in a close vote the Speaker's decision prevailed.[54]

Despite attempts to lengthen the time limit of the embargo beyond sixty days, and despite Randolph's constant interruptions and tirades, the House passed a bill embodying Madison's proposal by a vote of seventy to forty-one. The Senate chose to alter the time to ninety days, which the House acceded to after considerable fuss, and Madison signed the bill on April 4.

Clay glowed. He enthusiastically informed his Kentucky constituents that the value of the embargo "consists in the notification it gives to preserve property at home, to bring in as much as is practicable from abroad, and to make preparations for that contest which cannot be much longer deferred."[55] Federalists, of course, had a different interpretation. They chose to regard the embargo as a means of avoiding war. And although Madison told Thomas Jefferson that the embargo was intended as a move toward war, his public

54. *Annals of Congress,* 12th Congress, 1st session, pp. 1588–1589, 1591, 1593–1594.
55. Clay to William W. Worsley, April 4, 1812, in Clay, *Papers,* I, 643. John C. Calhoun agreed with Clay. The embargo, he wrote, "is understood to be the prelude to war." Calhoun to Dr. James MacBride, April 18, 1812, in Calhoun, *Papers,* I, 100.

message was so ambiguous as to permit a variety of interpretations.[56]

Clay was given much deserved credit for winning passage of the embargo. He "was a flame of fire," commented one congressman. "He had now brought congress to the verge of what he conceived to be a war for liberty and honour, and his voice, inspired by the occasion, rang through the capital, like a trumpet-tone sounding for the onset."[57]

Shortly thereafter Congress authorized the raising of one hundred thousand militia for a six-month tour of duty. That seemed to seal the decision of the country to resolve its dispute with Britain by recourse to arms. The nation waited. But nothing happened. Weeks went by and although there was some good news from abroad, there was no letup by Clay and the other War Hawks in their ongoing demands for war. Britain modified its orders-in-council to some extent and indicated it would go further; it also made amends for the *Chesapeake* atrocity. Still, the War Hawks, with Clay at their head, discounted what they regarded as feeble efforts at redress. They had come too far to turn back. So they kept after Madison, urging him to cease his caution and timidity, to shake off the malevolent influence of Secretary Gallatin, and to act as the brave commander of the American nation as he should.

A Republican caucus committee, with Clay as its chairman, put the final and crushing argument to their case. A congressional nominating caucus was to meet in mid-May to choose the Republican candidate for President in the 1812 election, and Madison was given to understand how difficult it might be to secure solid congressional support for his nomination if he persisted in his moderation, hesitancy, and inaction.[58] When the President still balked, Clay did not hesitate to use stronger language. Madison "was plainly told that his being supported as the party candidate for the next Presidency depended upon his screwing his courage to a declaration of war." That about ended the matter. Thereafter it was boldly asserted that Madison had been bullied and black-mailed into finally acquiescing to a declaration of war. Josiah Quincy reportedly said that Henry Clay "was the man whose influence and power more than that of any other produced the War of 1812 between the United States and Great Britain."[59]

Unquestionably the Speaker had much to do with the decision to go to war, but Quincy exaggerates Clay's influence, at least at the very end. By the time the caucus committee met with Madison, the President had already resolved to go to war. His only problem—and it was the one thing over which he and Clay presently differed—was the timing. Madison wanted to hold off as long as possible, and the War Hawks stubbornly refused to go along with him.

All the while the War Hawks increased their pressure for war, John Ran-

56. Madison to Jefferson, April 3, 1812, in Gaillard Hunt, ed., *The Writings of James Madison* (New York, 1908), VIII, 185–187.

57. Prentice, *Biography of Henry Clay,* p. 82.

58. On the caucus, see Colton, *Clay,* I, 153, 161; Sargent, *Clay,* p. 14.

59. Quincy, *Life of Josiah Quincy,* pp. 259, 255.

dolph on the floor of the House single-handedly tried to thwart them. He raised innumerable objections to several proposals, and in one long speech he repeated rumors that a declaration of war had been determined for June 1.[60] He condemned the "plot" as a churlish submission to Napoleon, warned against pursuing a war without the military or monetary means of achieving victory, and predicted dire consequences for the mercantile community. Clay was repeatedly forced to call Randolph to order and finally took the extreme step of announcing a more rigid enforcement of House rules. He also determined—with Randolph screaming about the abridgment of free speech—that a proposition must be moved and seconded as well as receive approval by the House before it could be considered.[61] Almost daily there were verbal fireworks between the two men, and they pursued their exchanges in the pages of the *National Intelligencer.* However, there could be no doubt that the Speaker meant to exercise tight control of the House, particularly in dealing with mavericks who tried to thwart his will.[62] The House at last had a master.

Events picked up momentum when, on May 18, the congressional nominating caucus met to select the candidate of the Republican party. Eighty-three congressmen attended, and eighty-two voted for Madison with one abstention. John Langdon of New Hampshire was chosen for the vice presidency. At a second caucus, held on June 8 because Langdon declined the nomination, Elbridge Gerry of Massachusetts was substituted, after which Clay arranged for ten congressmen who did not attend the May 18 caucus to add their ballots to the final vote. All ten voted for Madison.[63] Three days later the President began to prepare a message asking Congress for a declaration of war.[64] It was a vigorous and appropriate statement of the reasons leading to the decision.

The message went down on June 1. Two days later the House reported a war bill and declared that this was the nation's "second war of independence." On the advice of the President, it agreed to debate the issue behind closed doors. Clay opposed secrecy, as did Calhoun and some of the other War Hawks, but they acceded to the wishes of the chief executive. The Federalists and Randolph opposed the war measure and demanded a public debate, but they eventually gave up the fight. An attempt to include France in the general declaration was given short shrift, even by Federalists.[65] Under Clay's absolute

60. *Annals of Congress,* 12th Congress, 1st session, pp. 1451–1461.

61. Clay defended the right of every public body to determine its own procedures, especially against "the whimsical or eccentric propositions of a disordered or irregular mind." In passing, he pointed out the defects of some of the rules and the need to adapt new ones. *Annals of Congress,* 12th Congress, 1st session, pp. 1462–1479.

62. *National Intelligencer,* June 18, July 8, 1812.

63. *Niles' Weekly Register,* May 23, June 27, 1812.

64. George M. Bibb to John J. Crittenden, May 21, 1812, Crittenden Papers, LC; Madison to Jefferson, April 3, 1812, in Hunt, ed., *Writings of James Madison,* VIII, 185.

65. Clay appreciated the grievances the United States had against France but tended to minimize them in comparison with American grievances against Great Britain. See Clay to Jesse Bledsoe, June 18, 1812, in Clay, *Papers,* I, 675.

control the debate moved swiftly and without any serious difficulty. When the Federalists attempted a filibuster to prevent a final vote, Clay arranged to have one of the War Hawks move the previous question, and shut off debate. He then put the principal measure to a vote, and on June 4 the House passed it, seventy-nine to forty-nine.[66] North of the Potomac the vote showed a slight majority in opposition to the war, while south of the Potomac the vote was overwhelmingly in support. The West unanimously favored war.

The bill went to the Senate, where it languished for several weeks. Without the determined leadership of the House Speaker the Senate took its almighty time in deciding on a course of action. There was considerable talk about amending the House bill from outright war to a simple policy of issuing letters of marque and reprisal, and this proposal almost passed. Not until June 17 did the Senate finally consent to the war bill by a vote of nineteen to thirteen. The following day, June 18, President Madison signed the measure, thereby recognizing that a state of war existed between Great Britain and the United States.[67]

Two days later the British government agreed to abandon its orders-in-council.

66. *Annals of Congress,* 12th Congress, 1st session, pp. 1617, 1625ff., 1637.
67. *Annals of Congress,* 12th Congress, 1st session, pp. 267–271, 297.

The Diplomat

IGHT FROM THE START the war was a disaster for the
United States—on every front. Not only did military defeats
abound, but the administration seemed singularly inept in
attempting to conduct the war effort. It knew not where to turn, so it did
nothing, or very little. It needed competent commanders and had no idea
where they might be found or how to go about tracking them down. As
strange as it sounds, Madison even considered appointing Henry Clay to command the American armies despite the fact that the Kentuckian had absolutely
no military experience whatsoever.[1] Capable commanders like General Andrew Jackson of Tennessee, who yearned and begged for appointments to
prosecute the war, were spurned for political reasons. Jackson's appalling conduct in defense of Aaron Burr at the latter's conspiracy trial was deemed sufficient cause to reject the irascible general without investigating his ability to
conduct a military campaign. Clay regularly urged the administration to appoint William Henry Harrison, the victor over the Shawnee Indians at the
Battle of Tippecanoe, who was not only a proven entity but extremely popular
in the western country.[2]

On the military front one disaster followed another. General William
Hull led an invasion of Canada, but with the fall of Michilimackinac on July
17, he abruptly terminated his invasion and rushed back to Detroit. He forti-
fied the city and then, apprehensive over the fate of its inhabitants, foolishly
surrendered it to a decidedly inferior force of British soldiers and their Indian
allies.[3] Other attempts at invading Canada were equally calamitous and sometimes ludicrous. Aggressive generals frequently marched their troops to the

1. The story was published in 1839 to assist Clay's presidential bid. Supposedly Madison finally
decided that the Kentuckian could not be spared from Congress. Irving Brant, *James Madison:
Commander in Chief 1812–1836* (Indianapolis and New York, 1961), p. 45.

2. Clay to Monroe, July 29, August 12, 1812, in Clay, *Papers,* I, 698–699, 713.

3. There are several excellent histories of the war. See Reginald Horsman, *The War of 1812* (New
York, 1969); J. C. A. Stagg, *Mr. Madison's War* (New York, 1983); Harry L. Coles, *The War of
1812* (New York, 1965); J. K. Mahon, *The War of 1812* (New York, 1975); and Donald R.
Hickey, *The War of 1812: A Forgotten Conflict* (Urbana, Ill., 1989).

border only to discover that their men stood on constitutional principles and refused to cross over, necessitating a rear-action homeward march. Even at sea, where early victories promised some respite from the dreadful defeats on land, a succession of disasters soon developed. The loss of control of Lake Champlain, the destruction of the frigate *Chesapeake,* and the successful establishment of a naval blockade of the entire eastern coast provided a series of jolts that shook American confidence in their ability to wage a triumphant war under this Republican administration. The blockade encouraged smuggling, especially in New England, and the loss of revenue to the government further weakened its ability to pursue the war. Britain recognized and acted upon the opportunity to foment civil discontent within the United States and possibly trigger a secession movement by excluding New England from the blockade. In apparent appreciation, Massachusetts and Connecticut refused to provide their militias to bolster the war effort.

When Napoleon retreated from Moscow shortly thereafter, with the Russians in hot pursuit, it appeared that Great Britain would soon find relief from its European conflict and could concentrate its considerable resources on subduing its former colonies. The likelihood of that happening further intensified the apprehensions of the American people.

Clay returned to Kentucky during the latter part of July following the adjournment of Congress. He tracked the war effort as carefully as the limited means of communication allowed. He wrote regularly to friends and associates in and around Washington, and he kept up a steady stream of letters to the secretary of state, James Monroe. With the invasion of Canada going so badly Clay (with the connivance of Governor Charles Scott) raised a relief expedition under the command of William Henry Harrison.[4] At one point he even addressed these Kentucky volunteers at their muster ground in Georgetown just prior to their departure. He told the soldiers that the reputation of the state depended upon them. "Kentucky was fam'd for her bravery," he cried, "—they had the double character of Americans and Kentuckians to support."[5]

When news concerning Hull's disastrous defeat first began to arrive in Kentucky, Clay urged the people to suspend judgment about culpability until they received further information. But he acknowledged to friends that confidence in the general "is utterly and irretrievable gone. . . . The most sober and deliberate are doubting his fidelity." Not much later Monroe informed him of Hull's "mortifying & humiliating" surrender, the result of the general's "want of energy" and "promptitude of decision." Monroe was happy to add that General Harrison would take command of a new force of volunteers from Kentucky, Ohio, Pennsylvania, and Virginia "and resume the conquest of upper Canada." Clay responded that the West had no doubt of Hull's treach-

4. Clay to William Henry Harrison, November 7, 1812, Harrison Papers, LC.

5. Clay's speech delivered on August 16, 1812, in Clay, *Papers,* I, 715. Clay told Monroe that if there was any problem with what he and Scott had done, the President could revoke their action. Clay to Monroe, August 25, 1812, ibid., I, 719–720.

ery in bringing about so calamitous a surrender. But whether it was treachery or cowardice or something else, it "was so shameful, so disgraceful a surrender that . . . he deserves to be shot."[6]

Still, the West had not succumbed to despair, Clay assured Monroe. Quite the contrary. It had awakened "new energies and aroused the whole people of this State." Groups of volunteers were constantly moving toward the theater of fighting. "Last night 70 lay on my farm" and quickly clustered themselves into "companies of 10—50—100 &c." His only fear, Clay said, was the danger of what the Indians might do. The "savages" may "fall upon our frontiers" once they elude the volunteers. Already "the most horrid murders" had taken place within twenty-four miles of Louisville, where twenty-two persons were "massacred." "Our policy, my dear Sir, must be changed towards these savages. . . . They must be made to feel the utmost vigor of Government." The President has been deceived about their intentions and "dispositions," declared Clay. The Indians were not peace-loving or friendly. "The natural propensity of savage man to War" account in part for his predisposition for bloody hostility, "without recurring to that most fruitful source of them, British instigation."[7]

The war news throughout the summer and fall of 1812 was uniformly dreadful, and Clay seemed so anxious to return to Washington that the family agreed to an early date of departure from Kentucky. Furthermore, traveling with a family necessitated moving at a slower pace, and this consumed precious time. As a matter of fact, Clay admitted that because he had had his family in Washington for the last congressional session and planned to take them along for the next session, "I had scarcely time to turn around me when I got home before it became necessary for me to set out again."[8] So he remained only briefly at Ashland, but it was helpful in renewing contact with his constituency and assessing the electorate's sense of the progress of the war effort.[9]

Upon his return to Washington in the late fall after a particularly slow and tiring journey—the group, beside himself, included his wife, three of his children, and servants—Clay got busy immediately with plans to augment the existing forces stationed along the northern frontier, never losing hope that Detroit might be retaken by a "coup de main."[10] But the failure of leadership on the part of the administration had become scandalous, and this fact deeply depressed the Speaker. Madison was totally unfit for the role forced upon him. He was suited to scholarly discourse on the principles of republican government, not to the vigorous command of men during wartime. It was all terribly

6. Clay to William Eustis, August 26, 1812, Monroe to Clay, August 28, September 17, 1812, Clay to Monroe, September 21, 1812, in Clay, *Papers,* I, 722, 726–727, 728.
7. Clay to Monroe, September 21, 1812, in Clay, *Papers,* I, 728.
8. Clay to William Taylor, November 20, 1812, in Clay, *Papers,* I, 737.
9. Clay to Noah Webster, December 19, 1812, in Clay, *Papers,* I, 747.
10. Clay to Monroe, December 23, 1812, in Clay, *Papers,* I, 748–749.

frustrating and disheartening, and Clay unburdened himself in a despairing letter to his friend Caesar A. Rodney.

It is in vain to conceal the fact—at least I will not attempt to disguise with you—Mr. Madison is wholly unfit for the storms of War. Nature has cast him in too benevolent a mould. Admirably adapted to the tranquil scenes of peace—blending all the mild & amiable virtues, he is not fit for the rough and rude blasts which the conflicts of Nations generate. Our hopes then for the future conduct of the War must be placed upon the vigor which he may bring into the administration by the organization of his new Cabinet. And here again he is so hesitating, so tardy, so far behind the National sentiment, in his proceedings towards his War Ministers, that he will lose whatever credit he might otherwise acquire by the introduction of suitable characters in their places.

Fortunately the Congress itself possessed real strength and purpose. There never was a legislature, declared Clay, more "disposed to adopt any and every measure calculated to give effect and vigor to the operations of the War" than the Twelfth Congress. So he did not completely despair, despite Madison's inadequacies and the string of recent military failures. The spirit and patriotism of the country were high, the "justness of our cause" was obvious to all, and the nation possessed the means to achieve victory. All these guaranteed eventual success, if one never forgot, "if you please," the luck of the draw. Clay certainly never forgot to pay peculiar and particular "homage" to the "fickle goddess."[11]

The change in the cabinet, mentioned in Clay's letter, proved to be as inept as the Federalian secretly feared. Even so, as a dutiful Republican, the Speaker felt obliged to defend the administration and its handling of the war against every attack and criticism leveled by the Federalists in Congress. And these attacks intensified as the disasters to American arms mounted with each succeeding month. Even though Madison had survived the challenge of De Witt Clinton, the so-called peace candidate, and won reelection as President in the fall election of 1812, the voices against the continuance of the war steadily mounted. The Federalists could hardly wait for the beginning of the congressional session in early December to flail away at the administration's miserable efforts to preserve the honor and integrity of the American nation. President Madison and his agents had brought nothing but disgrace to the nation. The war had been a mistake from the very beginning, they said, and it was time to extricate the country from it as quickly as possible.[12]

Congress began its verbal brawling between the pro- and antiwar parties immediately upon reconvening, and it reached a peak in the House when, early

11. Clay to Rodney, December 29, 1812, in Clay, *Papers,* I, 750–751.
12. Josiah Quincy of Massachusetts was particularly severe in his remarks and several times was called to order by a member of the war party of Republicans. See particularly his exchange with Bolling Hall of Georgia, in the *Annals of Congress,* 12th Congress, 2d session, p. 544ff.

in the session, David R. Williams of South Carolina introduced a bill to raise an additional twenty regiments of infantry for one year to invade Canada. The House went into the Committee of the Whole to debate the measure, and the wrangling over the bill offered the Federalists every conceivable opportunity to pillory the administration and present strong arguments against the further prosecution of the war. Josiah Quincy was particularly vitriolic. He not only labeled the administration despotic but lambasted Clay and his cohorts as "sycophants, fawning reptiles, who crowded at the feet of the president, and left their filthy slime upon the carpet of the palace." He even assaulted the beloved Jefferson, whom he had once tried to impeach. It was an overwhelming and devastating tirade.[13]

On January 8, 1813, Clay decided to intrude his own "sentiments" upon the subject in the deeply felt belief that he could not stand mute while Madison and his administration were systematically excoriated for the many misfortunes that had befallen the country since the declaration of war. The day was bitterly cold when he spoke, and although the chamber was icy and uncomfortable, no one paid much attention to it as Clay warmed to his subject. Apparently inspired, he spoke with great passion, and his speech electrified his audience. Later it moved and excited his countrymen everywhere. It was his best effort to date.

Clay began with an apology. He was unprepared to speak on account of ill health. Indeed, his health over the past two years had been generally unstable, possibly the result of diseased gums.[14] In any event, he quickly moved to a discussion of the bill at hand, assuring the opposition that he had no intention of wounding "the feelings of any *gentleman,*" even though that was precisely what he planned to do. He reviewed the measures taken during the past twelve years to maintain the peace. "No matter with what unfeigned sincerity the administration cultivates peace, the opposition will insist that it alone is culpable for any breach between the two countries. . . . If gentlemen would only reserve for their own government half the sensibility which is indulged for that of Great Britain, they would find much less to condemn." Thus, he exclaimed, while the administration pursued a policy of peace, what was the conduct of the opposition? "They are the champions of war—the proud—the spirited— the sole repository of the nation's honor—the exclusive men of vigor and energy. The administration, on the contrary, is weak, feeble, and pusillanimous—'incapable of being kicked into a war.' "

Clay continued in this vein for several minutes, smiting the opposition from one direction and then another and, of course, always insisting, like the splendid politician he had become, that he intended no incivility to any particular gentleman. "You find them [the opposition], sir, tacking with every gale,

13. *Annals of Congress,* 12th Congress, 2d session, p. 459ff. The attempt at impeachment failed by a vote of 117 to 1.
14. Clay to Dr. Frederick Ridgley, January 17, 1811, private collection, copy CPP.

displaying the colors of every party, and of all nations, steady only in one unalterable purpose, to steer, if possible, into the haven of power." During this time "the parasites of opposition" use "cunning sarcasm" and "sly inuendo" to suggest a conspiratorial connection between members of the cabinet and the French government, even though they know it to be false and can be substantiated only by outright lying. "The administration of this country subservient to France! Great God! how is it so influenced? . . . On what possible foundation does it rest?" Clay then went through a catalog of possible associations and connections, and he dismissed every one of them. Those in the opposition, he continued, forget that they stand on American soil. They are not in the British House of Commons but in the chamber of the House of Representatives of the United States. They would like to transform themselves, if they could, into little Burkes or Pitts or Chathams, forgetting the interests of America in favor of the interests of Europe.

Clay then turned to Quincy's observations about Jefferson. He regretted the necessity of defending the former President. "Neither his retirement from public office, his eminent services, nor his advanced age," said Clay, "can exempt this patriot from the coarse assaults of party malevolence. . . . How impotent is party rage directed against him!" Clay jeered. When Quincy is dead and long forgotten—or if he is remembered only as a member of a "treasonable" junto from New England, the Essex Junto—"the name of Jefferson will be hailed as the second founder of the liberties of this people, and the period of his administration will be looked back to as one of the happiest and brightest epochs in American history."

This defense of Jefferson and attack upon Quincy won the hearty approbation of every Republican in the chamber. Had the *Constitution,* the *Wasp,* or the *United States* opened up on "poor Quincy," chortled John A. Harper of New Hampshire, she could not have done a better a job than what the Speaker did to him. "Never was man more severely castigated or one who more richly deserved it."[15]

After thoroughly maligning Quincy, at the same time rejecting any malicious design to offend his victim, Clay then announced his intention of discussing the causes of the war, the reasons for continuing it, and the means by which peace might be secured. But physical exhaustion necessitated that he request a postponement of his remarks until the following day. Again it was a splendid theatrical device that heightened interest and attention to his speech and guaranteed an even larger audience when the House reconvened.

The next day Clay started right off with another assault, this time against the "conspirators" who plotted the dissolution of the Union by constantly alluding to the "Virginia influence"—namely, the preponderance of men, since the adoption of the Constitution, in the executive branch from the Old Do-

15. Harper to William Plumer, January 8, 1813, Plumer Papers, LC, quoted in Brant, *James Madison: Commander in Chief,* p. 134.

minion. The intent of these "conspirators" was clear, Clay thundered: to convince Americans that respectable northern yeoman were yoked with Negro slaves to draw the "car of southern nabobs." (This presumed dominance of southern slaveholding interests in party affairs later proved a highly useful argument by the opposition, even after the Virginia connection had long been forgotten.) Clay, of course, dismissed the claims of the "conspirators" as laughable since there was no way on earth that Virginia could monopolize the presidency over a protracted period of time.

Clay addressed the causes that had impelled the nation to war, observing that it "requires a great struggle for a nation, prone to peace as this is, to burst through its habits and encounter the difficulties of war. Such a nation ought but seldom to go to war. When it does, it should be for clear and essential rights alone, and it should firmly resolve to extort, at all hazards, their recognition." This was the reason above all others, protested Clay, why the war must continue, continue until American rights were acknowledged and respected.

If there be a description of rights which, more than any other, should unite all parties in all quarters of the Union, it is unquestionably the rights of the person. No matter what his vocation; whether he seeks subsistence amidst the dangers of the deep, or draws it from the bowels of the earth, or from the humblest occupations of mechanic life: whenever the sacred rights of an American freeman are assailed, all hearts ought to unite and every arm should be braced to vindicate his cause.

If the administration has erred, concluded Clay, it has erred on the side of "betraying too great a solicitude" for peace, "not in doing too little. . . . An honorable peace is attainable only by an efficient war." His plan, he said, would be to call out the ample resources of the nation, provide judicious direction, vigorously prosecute the war on land and sea, and negotiate a peace at Halifax or Quebec. "We once triumphed" over England, and if we plug our ears against the "councils of timidity and despair we shall again prevail." But if we fail, "let us fail like men, lash ourselves to our gallant tars, and expire together in one common struggle, fighting for *'seamen's rights and free trade.'* "[16]

It was a magnificent speech and firmly established Clay at the very pinnacle of party leadership. Not only had Congress and the administration taken the full measure of Clay's genius, but the entire nation soon divined his extra ordinary talents when its citizens read his speech in the newspapers. It received widespread notice and acclaim. Indeed, some Republicans worried that Clay had virtually eclipsed Madison, Monroe, and Gallatin as leader and spokesman of the administration.[17] The speech was regarded by many as the best statement to date in defense of this war against Great Britain. It put to shame those

16. *Annals of Congress,* 12th Congress, 2d session, pp. 659–676. Clay's espousal of seamen's rights was never forgotten. As late as the election of 1844 some seaboard cities still hailed his perpetual commitment to the issue. See chapter XXXV.

17. Brant, *James Madison: Commander in Chief,* pp. 134–135.

who demanded withdrawal without the necessary acknowledgment of American rights. "In conception he was forcible," said one. "In diction sublime. In eloquence impressive and in action great."[18]

The enlistment bill subsequently passed the House and the Senate, and it was signed by President Madison on January 29, 1813. Clay had every right to be pleased with the outcome and his role in bringing it about. Indeed, when the Twelfth Congress finally adjourned on March 3, the House voted him a resolution of thanks in recognition of his excellent discharge of "the arduous and important duties assigned him whilst in the Chair." Clay responded by acknowledging the constant support of every member of the House. If irritation occurred during the course of the debates, he said, consign it to oblivion and remember only "the many agreeable hours we have spent together."[19]

Just prior to his departure for home at the conclusion of the session, Speaker Clay and Senator William H. Crawford of Georgia, the president pro tem of the upper house,[20] the two linchpins holding the administration together in Congress, were given a farewell dinner by the French minister, Louis Barbe Sérurier. During the course of the evening Clay sidled up to Sérurier ("always in a tone of extreme circumspection") and sighed over his frustrated hopes for French aid in America's war with Great Britain. After all, it was almost a year since the declaration of war, he cooed, enough time surely for a friend to declare his intentions—that is, if he had any intentions. If not, it might become necessary "to shift to that which is offered us with our enemies," Clay said in an insinuating tone of voice. "For we must finally have points, wherever they may be in Europe, where we may carry our products and exchange them for our needs."[21] Naturally Sérurier reported this remarkable conversation to the foreign ministry in Paris.

A few days later Madison was inaugurated for a second term, after which Clay headed home to Ashland. Along the way he observed some troublesome indications of how badly the nation was accommodating itself for the possibility of a protracted struggle. He was particularly disturbed on reaching Ashland to find a general dissatisfaction among his constituency over the conduct of the war. No individual was singled out for criticism, but that made it only more difficult to counteract. He did what he could to reassure his constituents, even though defending "our Washington friends" was becoming well-nigh impossible, and he pointed to the future and asked the public to concentrate its hopes on the promise of a safer and happier life once the war had been brought to a successful conclusion.[22]

Clay returned to Washington for the start of the special session of the

18. John A. Harper, quoted ibid., p. 134.
19. *Annals of Congress,* 12the Congress, 2d session, pp. 1153, 1167–1168.
20. And soon to become U.S. minister to France.
21. Sérurier to Duc de Bassano, March 2, 6, 1813, quoted in Brant, *James Madison: Commander in Chief,* p. 147.
22. Clay to James Taylor, April 10, 1813, in Clay, *Papers,* I, 782–783.

Thirteenth Congress on May 24. And despite recent electoral gains by Federalists, Clay defeated Timothy Pitkin of Connecticut for the Speaker's chair by a vote of eighty-nine to fifty-four, with five votes scattered. In his message to the Congress the following day President Madison accused the British of in-humanity in the savagery unleashed against the western frontier. As the leading representative of the western communities Clay felt compelled to add his voice in outrage against the "plunder and conflagration of our little towns." He demanded a public report so that the "indignation of all Christendom" might be registered and the horror recorded in perpetuity "on the page of history." A resolution for a select committee to examine these charges and produce a report was adopted without opposition.[23]

Madison's message contained other dire information: The Treasury was depleted, the country was living off loans, and additional taxes were necessary to prosecute the war. Recruiting was at a standstill—or nearly so—and conscription was a political kiss of death. Although Oliver Hazard Perry and William Henry Harrison won victories in the West, the coastline was effectively blockaded, and all but two American frigates were bottled up in harbors for repairs or did not dare venture out to challenge a superior British fleet. The continuing collapse of Napoleon's power following his humiliating retreat from Moscow added to American misfortunes. More and more the need for an early end to the war was seen by the leaders of both the Republican and the Federalist parties as essential for the preservation of American liberty. Even Clay, the vehement and emotionally vocal nationalist, had his doubts about the wisdom of continuing the war if peace could be obtained without disgrace.

An opportunity to disengage came early in 1813, when the emperor of Russia offered to mediate between Great Britain and the United States. Madison could hardly contain himself. He rushed to accept the offer without first waiting to discern the reaction in Britain. He wanted so desperately to extricate the country from its agony that he risked another stinging insult from abroad similar to the one Napoleon had administered when he pretended to rescind his Berlin and Milan decrees. To conduct the negotiations, Madison appointed John Quincy Adams, currently the U.S. minister to Russia, and a former Federalist, James A. Bayard, a Federalist and recently resigned senator from Delaware, and Albert Gallatin, the secretary of the treasury. They were to meet with the British delegates in St. Petersburg, and they were instructed to press especially for a repudiation of Britain's policy of impressment. Gallatin and Bayard left the country on May 9—courtesy of a passport provided by the British fleet—to meet Adams in Russia.[24]

Then, in the summer of 1813, the country learned the awful news: The

---

23. *Annals of Congress,* 13th Congress, 1st session, p. 109.
24. Brant, *James Madison: Commander in Chief,* pp. 149–163; Ralph Ketcham, *James Madison: A Biography* (New York, 1971), pp. 550–551.

British government flatly refused to participate in the proposed negotiations. It was another embarrassing defeat for the Madison administration.[25]

Several months later Britain changed its mind as the dreary war in Europe and America dragged on with no sign of diminution. By early 1814 the conflict had become truly burdensome. However, this reversal did not mean acceptance of the Russian offer. Any future negotiations must be accomplished in a one-on-one situation. No intermediaries. Lord Castlereagh, the foreign minister, would have nothing to do with the Russian efforts at mediation, but he was willing to enter direct negotiations with the United States in either London or Gottenburg, Sweden. He said he wanted to keep "the business unmixed" with the affairs of the Continent. But the administration rightly surmised that Castlereagh feared the United States and Russia might find a common interest against Great Britain (such as the impressment issue) and conduct themselves in "concert" to the detriment of the British Empire.[26]

Acting with a little less haste, Madison informed Congress on January 6, 1814, that he had accepted the British offer but advised that preparations would go forward for continuing the war until such time as an actual treaty had been signed.[27] Madison appreciated the difficulty involved in the negotiations inasmuch as Castlereagh had declared that any solution to their mutual problems would have to be consistent "with the maritime rights of the British empire," all of which sounded as though the impressment of seamen would not be a negotiable issue.[28]

For this peace mission, and to maintain a politically balanced group of commissioners, Madison kept the nationalistic Adams and the Federalist Bayard. Because Bayard would probably support the British argument on impressment, Madison needed another strong nationalist to serve on the mission. At first he thought of William H. Crawford of Georgia, recently appointed U. S. minister to France, but that would mean pulling him out of France at a crucial time when Napoleon's empire was collapsing. The President immediately thought of Clay as a substitute. Not only was the Kentuckian a leading nationalist who could be expected to fight for American rights, but he was an outstanding and loyal supporter of the administration. Federalists were naturally alarmed over his nomination when it arrived in the Senate for confirmation, and several Republicans also expressed their concern. After all, Clay had no diplomatic experience at all, and if he conducted himself like a western

25. Brant, *James Madison: Commander in Chief*, p. 163.

26. See Monroe's instructions to the commissioners, January 8, 28, 1814, in *ASPFR*, III, 701–702.

27. The best secondary accounts of the treaty negotiations are Frank A. Updyke, *The Diplomacy of the War of 1812* (Baltimore, 1915); Bradford Perkins, *Castlereagh and Adams: England and the United States, 1812–1823* (Berkeley, 1964). A good popular account is Fred L. Engelman, *The Peace of Christmas Eve* (New York, 1962).

28. Castlereagh to Monroe, November 4, 1813, in *ASPFR*, III, 621. The offer was accepted on January 5, 1814. See Monroe to Castlereagh, January 5, 1814, ibid., 622–623.

hothead, he might do the negotiations more harm than good.[29] But the French minister, Louis Sérurier, was delighted with Clay's selection. It was the surest sign, he said, that the President "could offer to the nation of his inflexible resolution to maintain its rights and honor up to the last extremity."[30]

For his part, Clay said he did not find himself "at liberty to decline the duty which the Government has been pleased to assign me . . . although it is full of responsibility." It troubled him a little to resign his seat in the House—he preferred the seat to any other station under the government, he said—but Clay could not in good conscience decline the service that the President, "without solicitation on my part," had been pleased to offer him. He regarded acceptance as a patriotic duty. It may also have crossed his mind that it was a likely first step toward future appointment as secretary of state. And that position, in due course, he meant to have.[31]

Jonathan Russell was also included in the mission since the negotiations would be held in Gottenburg—the site selected by the President over London—and Madison intended to nominate Russell as U.S. minister to Sweden. Also, he had been chargé d'affaires in London at the start of peace negotiations. Later Albert Gallatin was added as the fifth peace commissioner.[32]

Despite some initial apprehension in the Senate, all the commissioners won easy confirmation, and on January 19, 1814, Clay resigned his post as Speaker of the House. By a vote of 149 to 9, a resolution thanking him for his conduct passed handily, and Langdon Cheves of South Carolina was chosen to replace him.[33]

Clay received his instructions from Secretary of State James Monroe on January 28. He was reminded of the President's inflexible position on impressment and that the "degrading practice" must cease. To assert American rights on this issue, the President was prepared to exclude all British seamen from U.S. vessels, exempting only naturalized citizens, and surrender any British sailor deserting to an American port. As for Canada and British instigation of Indian attacks, a cession of land would be in order (outright annexation of Canada was also suggested), but if this was refused, then previous treaty rights of British traders on American soil must be terminated. Also, there must be no

---

29. See, for example, Clay's most recent speech in the House on resolutions commending American naval heroes on January 4, 1814, in *Annals of Congress,* 13th Congress, 1st session, pp. 847–848, and his remarks in relation to Perry's victory in Clay, *Papers,* I, 847–848.

30. Sérurier to Bassano, January 24, 1814, quoted in Brant, *James Madison: Commander in Chief,* p. 240.

31. Clay to David Parish, January 23, 1814, Callery Collection, Historical Society of Delaware, copy CPP; Clay to a friend, January 17, 1814, in Clay, *Papers,* I, 856.

32. At first Gallatin could not be named a commissioner without his cabinet position's being declared vacant. But when he decided to remain in Europe following the refusal of the British to accept the Russian offer of mediation, the President was required by law to name a new secretary of the treasury. He appointed George W. Campbell of Tennessee. Gallatin was named a commissioner on February 8, 1814.

33. *Annals of Congress,* 13th Congress, 1st session, p. 1057.

limitation of American naval strength on the Great Lakes. For the rest Monroe referred him to the original instructions provided the commissioners sent to Russia. He also supplied Clay with a passport that named him "a Minister Plenipotentiary and Extraordinary."[34]

Clay proceeded to New York, where he was joined by Christopher Hughes, Jr., of Maryland, secretary to the mission. British Admiral Thomas Cochrane obligingly provided a passport for the twenty-eight-gun corvette *John Adams*—an ex-frigate that had been overhauled to provided greater seaworthiness and stability—in order to permit the ship's passage through the blockade without incident. Captain Samuel Angus commanded the corvette.

After what seemed like an interminable delay, Russell finally joined Clay in New York and together with William Shaler, another diplomatic functionary attached to the mission, sailed from New York on Friday, February 25, 1814. It was a miserable journey. The North Atlantic Ocean in winter can be a horror in any year, and 1814 was particularly bad. The crew proved less than competent, and the captain, according to Hughes, was mad as a hatter. "A Miracle we weren't drownd," he later wrote. For seven weeks they suffered, although Clay always had the saving talent to laugh under the most trying of circumstances. They arrived in Gottenburg on April 13, anchoring twelve miles from the city because of ice in the river. By mail they tried to get in touch with Gallatin and Bayard, who were supposed to be in Amsterdam, and John Quincy Adams, who was expected from Russia but did not leave St. Petersburg until April 28. Clay wrote privately to William H. Crawford in France and asked about visiting Paris after completing his duties as a commissioner. He hoped that he might be done with his work by July or August and wondered if there would be any danger to his traveling across France, in view of conditions in the country following Napoleon's demise and the occupation of Paris by the allies.[35] Later he revealed that Crawford had been "particularly kind" to him throughout his long stay on the Continent.[36]

About a week following their arrival in Sweden, Clay and Russell heard from Gallatin and Bayard in London. Recent events had taken a "bad" turn, said the commissioners, and were likely to have an "unfavorable influence" on relations between the United States and Great Britain. Not only had Paris fallen to the allies, but Napoleon had abdicated and was about to be sent into exile in Elba. The Bourbon monarchy had been returned to the French throne in the person of Louis XVIII, and a congress would soon convene in Vienna to arrange the peace terms and restore legitimate sovereigns to their rightful thrones. Universal peace had descended upon the European world, "from

34. Monroe to commissioners, January 28, 1814, in *ASPFR*, III, 701–702. Passport dated February 4, 1814, in Clay, *Papers*, I, 863. The passports supplied by Russia and Sweden name him an envoy extraordinary and minister plenipotentiary. Ibid., I, 864–865.

35. Clay to Crawford, April 14, 1814, in Clay, *Papers*, I, 877.

36. Clay to Charles Tait, August 19, 1814, Alabama Department of Archives and History, copy CPP.

which we are alone excluded." Under the circumstances both Bayard and Gallatin thought that Gottenburg was not a good site for their negotiations. "I do believe that it would be utterly impossible to succeed in that corner," declared Gallatin, "removed from every friendly interference in our favour on the part of the European powers, and compelled to act with men clothed with limited authorities and who might at all times plead a want of instructions." Gallatin suggested London as a substitute in order to remain as close as possible to Castlereagh. But Bayard thought a town in Holland preferable and felt they could rely on the "friendly dispositions" of William of Orange.[37]

Clay had no objections to a change of site but would not countenance a move to England. "I shall not consent to go to London," he flatly announced. The British were rejoicing over Napoleon's defeat and abdication and now demanded what they called "the chastisement of America." To attempt negotiations in such an atmosphere would be ridiculous. With all due deference to Gallatin, he wrote, it would be "further condescension" to gather at their "seat of Government . . . especially when we have yet to see the example in British history of that haughty people having been conciliated by the condescension of their enemy." Russell agreed, as he did to most things Clay proposed, and added that any change should be understood to have come at the instance of Great Britain in order to prevent any injury to the friendship between the United States and Sweden and Russia. So, while arrangements were undertaken in London for a new location for their deliberations, and Russell went to Stockholm to present his credentials as minister, Clay just sat and waited. He occupied his time with excursions in the vicinity, and at one point visited Trollhattan on the Göta River to see the Göta Canal, which was about forty-five miles north of Gottenburg.[38] He also socialized a great deal and dined at some of the great houses in the city. And of course, all the ladies found him charming and utterly delightful.

The British government finally suggested Ghent, in present-day Belgium, as a comfortable place to meet and conveniently located in neutral territory. Gallatin and Bayard readily agreed. It "may have the effect to facilitate & shorten the negotiations," they wrote.[39] And once Castlereagh had the names of the complete list of the American commissioners, he appointed their opposite numbers. They included: Admiral James Gambier, first Baron Gambier; Henry Goulburn, British undersecretary for war and the colonies; and Dr. William Adams, a reputed expert on maritime law.

Not an impressive crew, these British. The ablest among them—which is hardly saying much—was the young Goulburn, who later went on to become a member of the Privy Council and then chancellor of the exchequer. He knew

37. Bayard to Clay and Russell, April 20, 1814, and Gallatin to Clay, April 22, 1814, in Clay, *Papers,* I, 881–884.
38. Clay to Russell, May 1, 1814, Clay to Bayard and Gallatin, May 2, 1814, in Clay, *Papers,* I, 887–891.
39. Bayard and Gallatin to Adams, Clay, and Russell, May 17, 1814, in Clay, *Papers,* I, 919.

a great deal about Canada, its affairs and problems, and came to the negotiations prepared to thwart any and all efforts by the Americans to annex any part of that territory. He was especially anxious to obtain complete British control of the Great Lakes, something Clay would oppose with every ounce of energy he possessed. At one point Clay remarked that Goulburn was "a man of much *irritation,*" to which John Quincy Adams replied: *"Irritability . . . is the word,* Mr. Clay, irritability," and then, staring straight at the Kentuckian, added, ". . . like somebody else that I know." Clay laughed and retorted: "Aye, that we do; all know him, and none better than yourself."[40]

Dr. William Adams, the second British commissioner, possessed all the worst attributes of the British upper class. Educated at Oxford, "with pretensions to wit," like so many of his class, and a perfect "blunderbuss of the law," according to his American namesake, Dr. Adams disdained anything not properly British. Bayard said that he was "a man of no breeding. . . ." It all guaranteed some lively sessions once the commissioners gathered to begin their negotiations.

Admiral Gambier was another obnoxious sort, ever on the alert for any reason to explode but never getting any further than sustained testiness. He had served with valor and distinction in the navy and as a reward been elevated to the peerage.[41]

None of these men was the equal of his American counterpart—with the possible exception of Russell. But then they were never meant to conduct the negotiations. Unlike the American commissioners, who had wide latitude in conducting the talks, they were mere puppets, controlled and directed from London. By holding the meetings in Ghent, the British commissioners were close enough to London so that their discussions could always be referred to the home ministry for decision. Castlereagh and Lord Bathurst, secretary for war and the colonies, exercised tight control of the negotiations. The three British commissioners were little more than glorified messengers, carrying proposals and counterproposals back and forth across the Channel. "If we propose the alteration of a word," John Quincy Adams later wrote, "they must refer it to their government." It reminded him of the old joke: "My Lord, I hope your Lordship is well this morning," to which his Lordship replied: "Indeed, Sir, I do not know, but I will send a courier to my Court and inquire."[42] Such a hobbled arrangement necessitated long and drawn-out negotiations that wearied the Americans and drove them nearly mad. After a while they came to believe that the British government did not want to make peace; otherwise they would have sent more "powerful delegates."[43]

40. Adams to Mrs. Adams, December 16, 1814, in Worthington Chauncey Ford, ed., *Writings of John Quincy Adams* (New York, 1915), V, 237.
41. James Gallatin, *The Diary of James Gallatin,* ed. Count Gallatin (New York, 1926), p. 72; Adams to Louisa Catherine Adams, August 30, 1814, in Ford, ed., *Writings,* V, 108.
42. Adams to Mrs. Adams, December 13, 1814, in Ford, ed., *Writings,* V, 236.
43. Gallatin, *Diary,* p. 29.

Clay was immediately informed by Gallatin and Bayard of the proposal to meet in Ghent and given the names of the British commissioners. He in turn contacted Russell and Adams, who had recently arrived in Stockholm, and told them that he had ordered Captain Angus to ready his ship in order to transport them to Ghent, via Antwerp or Ostend. He himself had decided to travel overland by way of Copenhagen and Hamburg and expected to reach Ghent in three weeks.[44]

Clay left Gottenburg on June 2 and traveled slowly by coach so that he might enjoy the countryside along the way. He went via Denmark, Germany, and Holland; he reached Ghent on June 28. He seemed to like the Dutch and said "their Canals, their rich meadows extending as far as the eye can reach, without fences, and separated only by ditches filled with water, and covered with innumerable herds of the finest cows I had ever beheld, exceeded my expectations, much as they had been praised." Belgium, he thought, was inferior to Holland. But everywhere he went, he said, the climate was "execrable. No summer, no sun, eternal clouds, and damp weather."[45]

When Clay arrived in Ghent, the other commissioners were waiting—all save Gallatin, who did not arrive until July 7. But where were their British counterparts? The Americans waited for weeks for them to appear. It seemed the enemy was demonstrating once again its "haughty" disdain for its former colonial subjects. On display was "the well known arrogance of the British character."[46]

The American commissioners made the mistake of trying to live and work together in one location. They found quarters first at the Hotel des Pays Bas but then moved to the Hotel Lovendeghem on the Rue des Champs.[47] They remained together at this location probably in the hope of improving communication among themselves in order to present a stronger and more unified front to the British. Perhaps, too, they hoped to save on expenses. But their plan did not work out as expected. Here were five highly individualistic, highly opinionated, highly dissimilar, and singularly egotistical public servants all congregated within a confined area and each following his own perceived notion of what constituted the best treaty for the United States. The titular

44. Clay to Russell and Adams, May 31, Clay to Russell, May 31, and Clay to Bayard and Gallatin, June 1, 1814, in Clay, *Papers,* I, 928–930.

45. Clay to ?, August 19, 1814, copy CPP.

46. Clay to Monroe, August 18, 1814, in Clay, *Papers,* I, 963.

47. Jean Joseph Dons, lord of Lovendeghem and Ten Broecke, purchased the house in 1783 for fifty-six hundred pounds. The C&A Department Store now occupies the site at the corner of Veldstraat and Voldersstraat. On the side of the C & A building is a plaque in Dutch and English that reads: "Treaty of Ghent 1814–1964 Here resided from July to December, 1814 the U.S.A. delegation, headed by John Quincy Adams later VI President of the U.S.A. during the negotiations with the British plenipotentiaries leading to the signature of the Peace Treaty of Ghent on December 24th 1814." Beneath it is another smaller plaque which reads: "1814–1964 In appreciation of the Hospitality of the People of Ghent in 1814 to the five Americans negotiating the Peace Treaty: John Quincy Adams, J. A. Bayard, Henry Clay and Jonathan Russell. National Society United States Daughters of 1812."

leader was John Quincy Adams, a well-educated, experienced diplomat who tended from the outset to be antisocial. He constantly found fault with nearly every person who came within visual range. He was in "a very bad temper" long before they began their negotiations with the British, noted James Gallatin, who served as his father's secretary.[48] His Puritan background, his dedication to duty and untiring work habits, his keen sense of his responsibilities and rights as head of the delegation, his intellectual zeal and gloomy outlook—all these and a lot more set a model that sharply contrasted and soon conflicted with attitudes, deportment, and general ideas of some of the other commissioners, most notably Henry Clay. Adams was frequently demanding, testy, irritable, critical, and fussy. He overworked himself because unlike the others, he had brought no secretary—Clay had Henry Carroll as his private secretary—and spent hours and days copying documents.[49] He was also a man without humor who took offense at many of Clay's less fortunate efforts at wit. He was also shocked by Clay's lackadaisical approach to their responsibilities and particularly by his hedonistic style of living. "Mr. Clay annoys him," snickered James Gallatin.[50] At first Adams refused to sit at the same dining table with his colleagues because their behavior offended him. "They sit after dinner and drink bad wine and smoke cigars," he scolded in his diary, "which neither suits my habits nor my health, and absorbs time which I cannot spare. I find it impossible, even with the most rigorous economy of time, to do half the writing that I ought."[51] It is interesting that although all the other commissioners resented Adams's decision to dine apart from them, it was Clay who finally spoke to him about his seeming discourtesy and got him to change his mind and join the others in taking his meals.[52]

What sometimes annoyed Adams to distraction was Russell's readiness during their general discussions together to follow Clay's lead on every issue. The weeks Russell and Clay had spent together crossing the ocean and getting located in Sweden had resulted in a pronounced friendship. Consequently, Russell regularly acceded to Clay's suggestions or requests. In a sense Clay had become his mentor, and he probably saw in the Kentuckian a likely future supporter for his political ambitions.[53] He had served as chargé d'affaires in France and England and therefore had enough diplomatic experience to make him completely familiar with U.S. concern over neutral rights. Adams claimed that both he and Clay were "the two members of the mission most under the influence of that irritability which we impute to Mr. Goulburn. . . . There is the same dogmatical, overbearing manner, the same harshness of look and expres-

48. Gallatin, *Diary*, p. 27.
49. Clay to Henry Goulburn, September 5, 1814, in Clay, *Papers*, I, 973.
50. Gallatin, *Diary*, p. 27.
51. Adams, *Memoirs*, II, 656.
52. Ibid., II, 657–658.
53. See Russell's letters to Clay, April 26, May 8, 12, 16, 17, 22, 1814, in Clay, *Papers*, I, 886–887, 894–895, 901–902, 917–918, 920–921.

sion, and the same forgetfulness of the courtesies of society in both."[54]

James A. Bayard was totally different in every conceivable way. Educated at Princeton, he trained as a lawyer, went into politics, became an active Federalist, and participated in the decision to lift Jefferson into the presidential seat over Aaron Burr in the contested election of 1800–1801. He and Gallatin had preceded the others to Europe when the emperor Alexander offered his services in mediating a peace between the United States and Great Britain. Bayard went to Russia, where Adams was serving as U.S. minister, and apparently they got on each other's nerves. Bayard found the minister totally antisocial, harsh, and unbending. For his part, Adams had his usual negative thoughts about Bayard, whom he regarded as a little too loose-tongued for a diplomat. Happily, however, the two men eventually warmed (if that is the word) to each other during their weeks and months together in Ghent. Adams decided that Bayard was now *"another man"* entirely, always reasonable and in good spirits. He invariably referred to him in his letters to his wife as the *"Chevalier."*[55]

If Clay was the ablest and best-known politician in the group, Albert Gallatin was the most urbane, cultivated, and knowledgeable of European manners and society. Born and educated in Geneva, he migrated to America during the Revolution and tutored French at Harvard. He moved to Pennsylvania, helped cool tempers during the Whiskey Rebellion, and won election to Congress, where he attracted Republican attention because of his knowledge of economics. He was appointed secretary of the treasury by President Jefferson and achieved notable successes in running the nation's finances, particularly in reducing the debt despite the immense expenditure necessitated by the purchase of Louisiana in 1803. Like the "Chevalier," Gallatin had first gone to Russia when the emperor made his offer, and like Bayard, he grew in the estimation of the highly critical John Q. Adams. "Of the five members of the American mission the Chevalier has the most perfect control of his temper, the most deliberate coolness," wrote Adams, "and it is the more meritorious because it is real self-command. . . . I can scarcely express to you how much both he and Mr. Gallatin have risen in my esteem since we have been here, living together. Mr. Gallatin has not quite so constant a supremacy over his own emotions; yet he seldom yields to an ebullition of temper, and recovers from it immediately." Gallatin was good at blunting a nasty exchange with a "joke," something Adams greatly admired and envied. Gallatin could also be both flexible and stubborn, a rare faculty equaled by few other men. "His greatest fault I think," wrote Adams, "to be an ingenuity sometimes intrenching upon ingenuousness."[56] For his part, Gallatin had strong reservations about Adams because of his stubbornness and intellectual pretensions. In time

54. Adams to Mrs. Adams, December 16, 1814, in Ford, ed., *Writings,* V, 239.
55. Adams to Mrs. Adams, July 22, October 14, 1814, in Ford, ed., *Writings,* V, 66, 161.
56. Adams to Mrs. Adams, December 16, 1814, in Ford, ed., *Writings,* V, 238.

he came to believe that Adams could do the mission irreparable harm, so he spent a great deal of time placating the irascible New Englander.[57]

When the British commissioners finally appeared in Ghent, they initially located at the Hotel du Lion d'Or but then moved to the Hotel des Pays Bas, where the Americans had originally stayed. In arranging an introductory meeting of the two groups, the British offered to meet the Americans at their hotel, but the Americans preferred the British residence. So they finally convened on August 8, 1814 at the Hotel des Pays Bas. It was a former Carthusian monastery that had been converted into a factory and home by Lieven Bauwens, a Dutch entrepreneur. One entire wing of the former monastery had been rebuilt into luxurious apartments.[58]

By this time the allied victory in Europe was complete and the many disasters suffered by the Americans were generally known. This twin misfortune somewhat dampened American enthusiasm for holding firm on all their demands. Clay told William Crawford that they ought not to insist on the abolition of impressment, at least not if it stood in the way of completing a treaty. But he would hold firm on yielding American territory. That he would never countenance. Nor would he consent to any reduction of the American naval presence on the Great Lakes. Clay's sectional interest and concern were obvious throughout the negotiations, but he felt strongly that these items involved the honor and integrity of his country. Fortunately, the Madison administration decided to drop impressment as a *sine qua non,* and this new instruction reached the commissioners just as the envoys began their meetings.[59]

When the American and British commissioners completed the exchange of their respective instruments of authority on their first meeting together, Lord Gambier, the head of the British delegation, expressed a pious hope for the success of their efforts. Adams, the head of the American delegation, replied with a promise of civility and candor in their discussions. Then Goulburn offered an agenda: impressment; territorial boundaries for Indians to serve as a kind of buffer between Canada and the United States, which was termed a *sine qua non;* revision of the boundary between the United States and Canada; and reciprocal fishing rights. Adams responded by stating that the U.S. commission had instructions on impressment and boundaries but none on Indian territorial claims or fishing rights. Then he asked that neutral rights and a definition of a blockade be included on the agenda. He expressed sur-

57. Gallatin, *Diary,* p. 27.

58. Clay to Crawford, August 8, 1814, Crawford Papers, LC. The Hotel des Pays Bas is now a mental hospital.

59. Clay to Crawford, July 2, 1814, in Clay, *Papers,* I, 937–939. The original instructions to the American commissioners insisted that the abolition of impressment was a sine qua non to any peace treaty. But as the likelihood of gaining British acceptance of this demand steadily diminished, the administration decided to abandon it in the hope of winning a speedy and acceptable treaty. On August 8 the commissioners received this information from Secretary Monroe. Monroe to Plenipotentiaries, June 25, 27, 1814, in *ASPFR,* III, 704.

prise that Indian boundaries would be such an important point to the British, and Clay, Gallatin, and Bayard immediately chimed in and insisted on the American right to exercise complete sovereignty over the Indians and their lands within the limits of the United States. In return for the United States' yielding on the Indian question, the British commissioners offered to yield on navigation of the Great Lakes—that is, they would not dispute commercial navigation on the lakes by the United States, provided no American armed vessels patrolled them and no forts were erected along the shoreline. They also demanded free access to the Mississippi River and a reordering of the boundary around Maine and between Lake Superior and the Mississippi.[60]

The demands were preposterous.[61] Clay began wondering almost immediately whether the British were playing games with them. Their demands were so extreme as to cause him to suspect that they had no intention of writing a treaty.

In the ongoing discussions between the two missions individual differences of character and style emerged more distinctly and vividly. They revealed the wide gap between the objectives of the two countries and the interests and concerns of the participants, especially among the American commissioners. John Quincy Adams, as was his right as head of the U.S. delegation, prepared most of the notes, reports, and dispatches that emanated from his group, and of course, they tended to reflect his own views of what was needed or expected. From the start Clay expressed concern over this procedure and frequently prepared a statement of his own, much to Adams's annoyance.

The very first draft Adams composed elicited objections. One commissioner questioned the form, another the substance of virtually every paragraph of the text. "Mr. Gallatin is for striking out every expression that may be offensive to the feelings of the adverse party," noted Adams. "Mr. Clay is displeased with figurative language, which he thinks improper for a state paper."[62] James Gallatin observed: "Mr. Adams and Mr. Clay object to everything except what they suggest themselves."[63] Eventually Albert Gallatin took over the drafting of their official documents—which was what the others originally wanted—and because of his more European manner and style, which their English counterparts admired (they thought him least like an American),

60. Clay, Journal of Ghent Negotiations, in Clay, *Papers,* I, 952–955, 969; Adams, *Memoirs,* III, 8ff.; Updyke, *Diplomacy of the War of 1812,* p. 202. For Monroe's instructions to the plenipotentiaries, see his letters of February 10, 14, March 21, June 25, 27, August 4, 1814, in *ASPFR,* III, 702–705. For Castlereagh's instructions to the commissioners, see Robert Stewart Castlereagh, *Memoirs and Correspondence of Viscount Castlereagh . . .* (London, 1848–1853), X, 67–72, 90–91.
61. Even Lord Liverpool, the prime minister, thought the commissioners had misunderstood British policy and had gone too far. See Liverpool to Castlereagh, September 2, 1814, in Duke of Wellington, ed., *Despatches, Correspondence, and Memoranda of Field Marshall Arthur, Duke of Wellington* (London, 1858–1872), IX, 214.
62. Adams, *Memoirs,* III, 21.
63. Gallatin, *Diary,* p. 32.

he tended to become the spokesman for the group as the negotiations proceeded.

Gallatin also found himself mediating between Adams and Clay over personal matters, both small and large, that kept cropping up throughout the summer and fall. "Father pours oil on the troubled waters" as much as that could be done, said James Gallatin, but it was becoming tiring and irksome.[64] For one thing, Adams was accustomed to rise early—four-thirty in the morning was not uncommon—only to hear a card party breaking up in Clay's room. "I hear Mr. Clay's company retiring from his chamber," he gossiped in his diary. "I had left him with Mr. Russell, Mr. Bentzon, and Mr. Todd at cards. They parted as I was about to rise."[65]

These nightly gatherings that continued well into the next day nettled Adams. He clashed repeatedly with Clay. They were both "dogmatical," both overbearing, both harsh and frequently forgetful of common courtesies. Adams admitted as much. "An impartial person judging between them I think would say that one has the strongest, the other the most cultivated understanding; that one has the most ardency, the other the most experience of mankind; that one has a mind most gifted by nature, the other a mind less cankered by prejudice. Mr. Clay is by ten years the younger man of the two, and as such has perhaps more claim to indulgence for irritability."[66]

On one occasion tempers finally exploded in an exchange that produced some very strong and provocative language. (Clay had a particularly foul mouth when he lost control of himself.) And predictably it occurred over an extremely trivial matter. It concerned the selection of a messenger to take a communication, written by Adams, to the emperor of Russia in Vienna, where the great powers were convened in a congress to arrange the peace terms ending the Napoleonic conflict. Why the head of the mission would need to consult the other commissioners over such a trifle completely escaped the less formal Kentuckian. But always a stickler for correct procedures, Adams asked the others for suggestions as to names, he himself favoring the secretary of the legation to Russia who knew the emperor and Count Nesselrode, the foreign minister. Clay and Russell told him to do as he pleased but that they favored Mr. Shaler, who had been attached to the mission for that very purpose. Gallatin said that Shaler was not appropriate, whereupon Adams replied that he would send the communication by mail. Then, to make matters worse, Adams asked for suggestions about the proper mode of mailing the letter.

That did it. "Mr. Russell waxed loud and Mr. Clay very warm," chuckled young Gallatin. The air virtually turned blue. Adams reacted just as sharply in defense. "Mr. Clay said, with great heat and anger . . . that he should be

64. Ibid., p. 27.
65. Adams, *Memoirs,* III, 32.
66. Ibid., III, 32, 39; Adams to Mrs. Adams, December 16, 1914, Ford, ed., *Writings,* V, 239. Clay was thirty-seven years of age at the time.

ashamed not to take such a responsibility upon himself." Worse, he enveloped his remarks "with a scornful sneer"—which was one of Clay's less attractive habits when aroused and one he could never resist. Adams knew immediately that he should respond quietly and in a conciliatory manner, but, as he said, "I have not always a soft answer at my own command." So he lapsed into silence. But the set of his jaw and the look of his eye thundered his outrage and fury. The matter was dropped.[67]

Unfortunately there were many such clashes, and whenever they occurred, the other commissioners noted that invariably "Clay uses strong language to Adams, and Adams returns the compliment."[68] But Clay at least was careful not to let the administration in Washington get wind of the discord. He simply lied—outrageously. He told Secretary Monroe that "the most entire harmony prevails between my colleagues on the subjects of our mission. No former diversity of opinion here shews itself in the smallest degree. All are deeply sensible of the solemn nature of our duty. All are animated solely by the desire of advancing the interests of our common Country."[69]

Clay's irritability surfaced over yet another trifle, but one unrelated to Adams directly. The Society of Fine Arts and of Letters in Ghent named Gallatin, Bayard, and Adams honorary members, while the Society of Agriculture and Botany gave memberships to Clay, Russell, and Hughes. The two societies had drawn lots to decide the membership. When the Fine Arts Society held its next celebration, only Gallatin, Bayard, and Adams received invitations, but Gallatin had the impression that the invitations included the entire delegation. Russell refused to go, but Clay attended—after all, he hardly ever resisted a social gathering—"and was mortified on discovering the mistake." Practically all the Americans in the city were there by invitation, and what added to the embarrassment was a speech given by the secretary of the society explaining how Clay, Russell, and Hughes had been made members of the Agricultural Society and not the Fine Arts Society. Clay seethed. The next day he entered a formal complaint about being "misled" into attending the celebration and about the discourtesy of inviting three members and not the entire delegation.[70]

More serious matters also caused emotional outbursts. By the early fall the U.S. commissioners were getting frightening news of the progress of the war in America. Washington had been captured and burned by British troops, towns were also captured in Passamaquoddy Bay, and American troops failed to take Michilimackinac. What "wounds me to the very soul," wrote Clay to Crawford, "is that a set of pirates and incendiaries should have been permitted to pollute our soil, conflagrate our Capital, and return unpunished to their

67. Adams, *Memoirs,* III, 49–50; Gallatin, *Diary,* p. 28.
68. Gallatin, *Diary,* p. 28.
69. Clay to Monroe, August 18, 1814, in Clay, *Papers,* I, 966.
70. Adams, *Memoirs,* III, 58–59.

ships!"[71] These dreadful reports greatly disturbed the entire delegation, but Clay more "than any other of us," said Adams. "He rails at commerce and the people of Massachusetts, and tells what wonders the people of Kentucky would do if they should be attacked." Clay was indeed deeply offended by these disasters, especially the burning of the Capitol and the "President's house," and he said that he "could not help reflecting on the contrast" between Brussels—which "has been the continual seat of War, and been occupied at various times by all the great powers"—and Washington. In Brussels "the public edifices have escaped for ages the Barbarians torch." Not so Washington. Still, as a diplomat Clay should not have carried on the way he did—and in such a public manner. His behavior was inexcusable. He childishly indulged his anger.[72]

Clay had better news from home when his wife informed him in late September that he had been reelected to Congress.[73] But it was small comfort. As each succeeding note or message from the British commissioners became more dilatory and evasive, Clay grew increasingly "peevish and fractious." When American fishing rights within waters of British jurisdiction came up in the general discussions among the Americans, for example, he dismissed it as inconsequential, but when the question of British rights to navigate the Mississippi was mentioned, he grew indignant and raised strong objections. At one point he threatened to withhold his signature from a communication to the British delegation if it included the Mississippi question. As far as he was concerned—and this he repeated many times—"the Mississippi was destined to form a most important part of the interests of the American Union."[74]

The fisheries and Mississippi question recurred over and over in their discussions, and John Quincy Adams took a strong stand in favor of the fisheries while Clay, equally adamant, stoutly defended American rights to the Mississippi. The British claimed that the right of Americans to fish and dry their catch within British jurisdiction, acquired in the peace treaty ending the American Revolution in 1783, had been abrogated by the declaration of war in 1812.[75] If they granted the fisheries claim, the British thought they should be granted an equivalent right, such as the right to navigate the Mississippi,

71. Clay to Crawford, October 17, 1814, in Clay, *Papers*, I, 988–989.

72. "The loss of our Capitol filled me with grief, less for the loss of property than the loss of honor," Clay wrote. "This, I thank God, is in some measure recovered by the encouraging victories on Champlain, and the repulse before Baltimore." Clay to Captain Lloyd Jones, October 25, 1814, Columbia University Library, copy CPP.

73. A short time before, Crawford offered to recommend Clay as his replacement as minister to France, which Clay seemed anxious to accept. But when he was informed that his district had reelected him to Congress, he changed his mind. See Clay to Crawford, August 22, and October 17, 1814, in Clay, *Papers*, I, 972, 990.

74. Adams, *Memoirs*, III, 43, 60–61, 63; Clay to Russell, July 9, 1822, in Clay, *Papers*, III, 253.

75. "I think all of us (except Mr. Adams)," Clay recalled eight years later, "concurred in believing that the provisions respecting the Fishing Grants, *within the British exclusive* jurisdiction, and the navigation of the Mississippi, expired on the breaking out of the war." Clay to Russell, July 9, 1822, in Clay, *Papers*, III, 254.

which they held at the conclusion of the Revolutionary War, when the United States extended no farther west than the Mississippi River.[76] The right to fish in British waters was extremely important to New Englanders, and John Quincy Adams absolutely refused to surrender it. Besides, it was something his father had negotiated in the 1783 peace treaty and that made it sacrosanct. At the same time Adams did not think that the navigation of the Mississippi was terribly important and could be granted in return for a continuation of the fisheries right. Thus Adams, the easterner, was willing to yield an important western concern, while Clay, the westerner, was prepared to surrender an important eastern matter. Thereupon Gallatin, in his usual joking manner, suggested that the two questions be linked together: The British would be offered Mississippi rights in return for a continuation of the fishing rights.

Clay would have none of it. He argued that in making the offer, "we should lose both." But he was outvoted. Fortunately for him, the British rejected Gallatin's proposal since it necessitated traveling over hundreds of miles of American territory by Canadians to get to the Mississippi and the payment of a customs duty. They realized the right had little substantial value for them.[77]

These discussions among the Americans, often heated (especially between Clay and Adams) and sometimes stiffly formal, took place on a fairly regular basis. The American commissioners usually met together each day at 2:00 P.M. and talked for two hours, after which they had dinner. Most times they sat at the table until 6:00 or 7:00, conversing informally. Later they frequented the "coffee houses, the Reading Rooms, and the billiard tables"—all except Adams, of course, who used the time to take long walks.[78] Formal meetings with their British counterparts were less regular because every item and proposal raised by the Americans had to be referred back to London, and this necessitated weeks of waiting for a response. Because of these interruptions, Clay and the others had time to travel around the countryside, usually to Antwerp and Brussels. Their social life was quite active, of course, and all of them attended many dinner parties and card parties, which could run as late as 3:00 A.M. Clay was not particularly keen on these card parties because the stakes were too low. They bored him, and he "soon grew weary and impatient."[79] The fastidious Adams fretted over his many indulgences and the accompanying "relaxation of self-discipline. I have this month," he recorded, "frequented too much the theatre and other public amusements; indulged too

76. See draft of the original protocol and the protocol of the conference, August 8, 1814, in *ASPFR,* III, 706, 707–708.

77. Adams, *Memoirs,* III, 76; Clay to Russell, July 9, 1822, in Clay, *Papers,* III, 253–254. Liverpool, in effect, ordered a general retreat from the preposterous demands initially put forward. See his letter to the commissioners, September 3, 1814, in Wellington, *Despatches,* IX, 245. See also Castlereagh to Goulburn, August 28, 1814, in Castlereagh, *Memoirs and Correspondence,* X, 102.

78. Adams to Mrs. Adams, August 19, 1814, in Ford, ed., *Writings,* V, 89.

79. Adams, *Memoirs,* III, 60.

much conviviality, and taken too little exercise. The consequence is that I am growing uncomfortably corpulent, and that industry becomes irksome to me. May I be cautious not to fall into any habit of indolence or dissipation!"[80]

One breakthrough in the negotiations occurred when the British agreed not to demand the establishment of boundaries to designate the extent of Indian territory. It was obvious the Americans would never agree to such a demand, and the British decided instead to request the full restoration of Indian land held prior to the war.[81] At that point Adams prepared a note defending the American Indian policy, and he embellished it with all the moral justification he could muster. Clay said he agreed to everything in the note but thought that calling on heaven, God, and Providence was just so much "cant," to which Russell laughed out loud. Adams glared at both of them.[82]

Clay was encouraged not only by the British retreat from their original *sine qua non* regarding Indian territory but by the more recent news of General Andrew Jackson's victory over the Creek Indian's in the Battle of Horseshoe Bend and by the failure of the British attack upon Baltimore and their defeat on Lake Champlain at Plattsburg.[83] Now, if the British invasion from the Gulf of Mexico at New Orleans could be thrown back and if no new disaster occurred in the North, Clay told James Monroe, "I think we should make peace."[84]

It was generally believed by the Americans at Ghent that the British ministry would wait upon the results of the invasion of New Orleans before deciding on the final terms of a peace treaty.[85] In the meantime, the British suggested the principle of *uti possidetis*, on which to reach a final territorial settlement—that is, both sides retain what they possessed at the close of the war.[86] Here Clay was once again adamant. He would not yield a foot of American soil and insisted on a mutual restoration of territory taken during the war. He did believe that the British were still playing games with them, and he was inclined to show them that the Americans could play just as well. Clay was all for "playing *brag* with the British Plenipotentiaries," he said to John Quincy Adams. After all, "they had been playing *brag* with us . . . [and] it was time for us to begin to play *brag* with them." He asked Adams if he knew how to play the game. Adams shook his head. He had forgotten. "The art of it," explained Clay, "was to beat your adversary by holding your hand, with a solemn and confident phiz, and outbragging him." In an aside to Adams,

80. Ibid., 78–79.
81. Clay to Crawford, September 20, 1814, the British to the American commissioners, October 8, 1814, in Clay, *Papers*, I, 979, 982; Castlereagh, *Memoirs and Correspondence*, X, 102. The notes that passed between the American and British commissioners running from August 19 to October 31, 1814, can be found in *ASPFR*, III, 710–726.
82. Adams, *Memoirs*, III, 42, 43; *ASPFR*, III, 715.
83. Clay to Crawford, July 2, 1814, in Clay, *Papers*, I, 938.
84. Clay to Monroe, October 26, 1814, in Clay, *Papers*, I, 995–997.
85. Bemis, *Adams*, I, 210–211.
86. British to American commissioners, October 21, 1814, in Clay, *Papers*, I, 991.

Bayard added the observation that "Mr. Clay is for bragging a million against a cent."[87]

In the American response to the British suggestion, written by Gallatin, the commissioners said they would most assuredly not negotiate "on the basis of *uti possidetis* but only on the basis of *status quo ante bellum,* with regard to territory."[88] This rejection of uti possidetis brought a curt rejoinder from the British that since the Americans quibbled over or criticized every suggestion put forward to them, they should submit their own *"projet"* for a treaty.[89] The Americans readily accepted the challenge and over the next two weeks argued and debated what should be presented. Gallatin and Adams prepared drafts, with Clay, Bayard, and Russell suggesting amendments and alterations. What they finally proposed, even though they had doubts about getting it all, went as follows: the abolition of impressment, the definition of a blockade, indemnity for spoliations, a northwest boundary line at the forty-ninth parallel from the Lake of the Woods to the Rocky Mountains, and a mutual agreement not to engage the Indians in any future wars. One paragraph specifically mentioned "the state before the war as the general basis of the treaty"—that is, status quo ante bellum. But Clay chided the others on this proposal, saying the British would laugh at them. They would say, "Ay, ay! pretty fellows you, to think of getting out of the war as well as you got into it!"[90]

When the British finally responded to these proposals—after referring them back home—it was an almost total rejection of every article. Impressment, blockade, indemnities, the Indians—all were struck down. But at least it had become obvious from their response that the British themselves had abandoned the Indian boundary question, the principle of uti possidetis, and the exclusive military control of the Great Lakes.[91] They were more and more drawn to the idea of the status quo ante bellum, something that had developed in their thinking long before the Americans spoke of it.[92]

But Clay put forward another objection to a status quo treaty and said he would never sign one that continued the right of the British to trade with the Indians, "so help him God." Allowing the British this trade, he contented, provided too much opportunity for them to incite the tribes to warfare. "He said this in the harsh, angry, and overbearing tone which I, perhaps more than others," wrote Adams, "ought to excuse, as the involuntary effusion of a too positive temper. It always offends me in him; but I took no notice of it this day." As he spoke, Clay began ranting and swearing. He stalked back and forth

87. Adams, *Memoirs,* III, 101–102.

88. American to British commissioners, October 24, 1814, in Clay, *Papers,* I, 992; Gallatin, *Diary,* p. 32.

89. British to the American commissioners, October 31, 1814, in Clay, *Papers,* I, 998.

90. Adams, *Memoirs,* III, 68–69. See Clay's proposed note in Clay, *Papers,* I, 1003–1004.

91. Liverpool to Castlereagh, November 18, 1814, in Wellington, *Despatches,* IX, 438.

92. British to American commissioners, November 26, 1814, in Clay, *Papers,* I, 1001. See also the exchange of notes from November 10 to December 22, 1814, in *ASPFR,* III, 733–744.

across the room, repeating five or six times, "I will never sign a treaty upon the status ante bellum with the Indian article, so help me God!" The others chose not to bait him further and let the subject drop, but Adams shrewdly noted what had happened. "Mr. Clay," he wrote, "actually beat again a majority by outbragging us."[93]

The real reasons for British willingness to conclude the American war had to do with the situation in Europe. The Congress of Vienna was well under way, but a number of disputes that worried the British because they threatened the alliance had arisen among the allies. Talleyrand was clever enough to turn these dissensions to the advantage of France. The British were also anxious to avoid any discussion of neutral rights, and they constantly feared the moral intrusion of the Russians on the side of the Americans. Also, the state of British finances was another concern. Finally, the Duke of Wellington, commanding the occupation of Paris, expressed no real objection to leading the army against the Americans but warned that it would now involve control of the Great Lakes because Lake Champlain had been lost. He felt the wiser course was the immediate conclusion of a peace treaty.[94] Since it was clear that the British position at home, in Europe, and around the world would be immeasurably strengthened once the annoyance with the United States had been eliminated, the decision was reached to finish the business at Ghent on the basis of the status quo ante bellum.

Clay guessed as much.[95] Even when the British commissioners raised minor points (such as the slave trade and opening courts of law to nationals of both countries) that Adams thought were introduced as an excuse to break off negotiations and blame the failure on the Americans, Clay disagreed. He "was so confident that the British Government had resolved upon peace that he said he would give himself as a hostage and a victim to be sacrificed if they broke off on these points."[96]

The points were dropped. Indeed, the British dropped all mention of the fisheries, the navigation of the Mississippi, and the demarkation of a boundary from the Lake of the Woods westward.[97] When Clay read this latest note from the British, he happened to be in a particularly sour mood. His face registered his disdain at what he read. He much preferred an article in the treaty, he said, that formally admitted that the British right to navigate the Mississippi and the American right to the fisheries within British jurisdiction had been abrogated, even though Adams had warned that he would not sign any treaty forfeiting

93. Adams, *Memoirs*, III, 103; Clay to Russell, July 9, 1822, in Clay, *Papers*, III, 253.

94. Wellington to Liverpool, November 9, 1814, in Wellington, *Despatches*, IX, 425–426; George Dangerfield, *The Era of Good Feelings* (New York, 1952), pp. 80–81; Bemis, *Adams*, I, 216–217.

95. See Clay's letter to Monroe, October 26, 1814, in Clay, *Papers*, I, 996–997.

96. Adams, *Memoirs*, III, 112.

97. Bathurst to commissioners, December 6, 1814, instructions of December 19, 1814, in Castlereagh, *Memoirs and Correspondence*, X, 214, 221; British to American commissioners, December 22, 1814, in Clay, *Papers*, I, 1005.

the fisheries. The two men had tangled before on this issue, and Adams had cogently argued that such an agreement would have the appearance of sacrificing eastern interests to those of the West. The "disaffected in Massachusetts"—who were soon to meet at the Hartford Convention with the disaffected from other New England states to express their disaffection in a series of amendments to the Constitution—would say that the United States had "given up *our* territory and *our* fisheries merely to deprive the British of their right to navigate the Mississippi."

Clay showed contempt for the argument. He would have nothing to do, he said, with satisfying "disaffection and treason; he would not yield anything for the sake of them."

"But," replied Adams, "you would not give disaffection and treason the right to say to the people that their interests had been sacrificed?"

"No," snapped Clay. He would rather continue the war for another three years since he had no doubt that such a prolongation would "make us a warlike people, and that then we should come out of the war with honor."[98]

He was playing brag again. Only this time he was losing. The other commissioners, responding eagerly to the British concessions, agreed with Adams. Thereupon Clay proposed to break off the negotiations. More brag. He felt confident that Russell would support him, and he discounted Bayard and Gallatin as too eager for peace. So he went to Adams and asked him to join him in breaking off negotiations. Adams refused. There was nothing now to break off, said the New Englander.

"Well," replied Clay, "will you be of the same opinion tomorrow?"

"Perhaps not," Adams slyly responded, "but you can easily ascertain by asking the question again tomorrow."[99]

Gallatin and Bayard were astonished at Clay's truculent attitude. They could not imagine what was bothering him and termed it "mere unseasonable trifling." They proposed calling a meeting the next day with the British commissioners, but Clay wanted more time to consider the latest proposals. A vote was taken, and Clay lost.[100] It was a losing game of brag to the very end. So the British and American commissioners met the following day and for three hours hammered out the final terms of the treaty. It ended with an agreement to meet the next day, Christmas Eve, and sign six copies of the treaty ending the war on the basis of the status quo ante bellum.[101]

Clay offered no further objections. The terms of the treaty, he told Craw-

---

98. Adams, *Memoirs*, III, 101, 120. Later Adams got into a public quarrel with Russell about some of the disagreements among the American delegates, and Clay gave his recollection of their disagreements in a rather equivocal letter to Russell, July 9, 1822, in Clay, *Papers*, III, 252–257.

99. Adams, *Memoirs*, III, 121. Even the British suspected Clay of playing brag, using more elegant language in their report. See Goulburn to Bathurst, December 13, 1814, quoted in Dangerfield, *Era of Good Feelings*, p. 85.

100. The vote was three to one. Russell put the question and so did not vote himself.

101. For the treaty itself, see *ASPFR*, III, 745–748.

ford, "are different from what was expected [when] the War was made, but not perhaps dishono[rable] under existing circumstances."[102] Regrettably Clay chose to play the role of a carping critic during these negotiations at Ghent, particularly among his American colleagues. He contributed little toward arriving at solutions to problems when they arose. In fact, he himself frequently created the problems. Too often he sounded and behaved like a sectionalist, solely concerned with the interests of the West rather than the interests of the nation. He ended this unseemly performance by suggesting that they break off negotiations, and when he failed in his attempt, he simply allowed the signing to go forward without objection.

Still, he served a purpose, despite his constant provocations. A fiery nationalist, committed to safeguarding every inch of American soil, Clay made the British recognize that no treaty could be signed that diminished U.S. sovereignty or rights in any shape or form, despite all the military disasters recently sustained. And they eventually conceded his position. He also proved himself a strong counterweight to the inclination of Adams and Gallatin to accede to British demands if they did not affect eastern interests, particularly with respect to the Mississippi. Neither Bayard nor Russell was likely to put up much of a defense for western rights. Clay always pushed the British one step farther than his colleagues were willing to go, thereby increasing American maneuverability and better protecting what had already been conceded. It was a gamble that might have resulted in disaster, but he guessed that the odds were really in his favor. He kept up the pressure (his game of brag) to the end. If he had really intended to break off negotiations, as he threatened, he would not have remained silent at the end and signed the treaty.

The commissioners convened at 4:00 P.M. at the residence of the British envoys, and compared the six copies of the document, after which the eight men affixed their signatures. The document required the ratification of both nations before taking effect, but short of a catastrophe, such as the successful invasion of the United States via New Orleans and the Mississippi Valley, the commissioners expected the document to win speedy approval by both the United States and Great Britain.

The Treaty of Ghent settled none of the original issues that had precipitated the war. Nothing was said about impressment. Other issues such as claims and boundaries were relegated to future commissions. But it did call for the cessation of all hostilities and the return of territories taken by either belligerent. Indian lands would be restored to those held in 1811; that could cause a problem in view of General Jackson's treaty of August 9, 1814, with the Creeks wherein he obtained twenty-three million acres of land as the price of ending the war. As it turned out, the United States simply ignored this provision.

After the signing Lord Gambier expressed the hope that their efforts

102. Clay to Crawford, December 25, 1814, Crawford Papers, LC.

would provide a permanent peace. John Quincy Adams responded prophetically and handsomely. "I hope," he said, "it will be the last treaty of peace
between Great Britain and the United States."[103]

Although the greatest victory of American arms was yet to occur when
General Sir Edward Michael Pakenham led his troops to total disaster at New
Orleans on January 8, 1815, at the hands of General Andrew Jackson and his
Tennessee and Kentucky sharpshooters and saved the United States from possible military destruction, the Treaty of Ghent, as Clay told Monroe, "certainly
reflect no dishonor on us."[104] True, the terms of the instrument were not what
the nation expected when it declared war. Still, the pretensions of the British at
the start of the negotiations had been decisively resisted. More important, the
nation had been preserved whole, an Indian buffer state denied, and the way
prepared for the continued expansion of the United States across the plains
and mountains to the Pacific Ocean. The creation of a transcontinental nation
was not too many years away. And in turning back British efforts to thwart
that destiny, the Treaty of Ghent constituted a notable diplomatic achievement, one the nation would receive with delight and gratitude.

103. Adams, *Memoirs,* III, 126.
104. Clay to Monroe, December 25, 1814, in Clay, *Papers,* I, 1007.

— E I G H T —

"I Am Sick of Europe"

O N THE EVENING of the signing of the treaty a solemn service was held in the Ghent cathedral to give thanks for the restoration of peace between the United States and Great Britain. James Gallatin said it was a most impressive religious celebration. Four days later the Americans hosted a dinner for their British colleagues and a number of prominent townsfolk. About twenty-two individuals attended and were serenaded by the Society of St. Cecilia. First they played "God Save the King" and followed it with "Hail Columbia." Then Lord Gambier rose and proposed a toast to "the United States of America." John Quincy Adams responded by toasting "His Britannic Majesty."[1]

This would have been an excellent note on which to close the business at Ghent. Unfortunately the Americans took to wrangling among themselves and concluded their presence in Belgium with a squabble over the disposition of the documents involved in the negotiations. Clay, seconded by Russell and Bayard, wanted the books, maps, papers, and other effects to be sent to the Department of State, where they could be preserved and consulted in the future when necessary. "He said they might hereafter be interesting as historical records, and the Department of State was the proper place for them." Gallatin thought that all but the papers should be sent to London for possible use by himself, Adams, and Clay, who had been asked by the administration to proceed to the British capital to negotiate a general treaty of commerce with the British. But Adams, as head of the delegation, insisted on his right to retain the papers subject to further instructions from Washington.

At that point Russell asked for a vote on the question, but Adams refused to put the question. Thereupon Clay called a meeting of the others and drew up an "open letter" (signed by Russell, Bayard, and himself), which he presented to Adams, demanding the papers be forwarded to Washington in conformity with the wishes of the majority.

Adams refused the demand. "An act of the greater number without con-

1. Gallatin, *Diary,* p. 35; Adams, *Memoirs,* III, 131.

sulting the other members is not an act of the majority," he lectured.

At that Clay completely lost his temper. He started raging. "You *dare* not, you *cannot,* you SHALL not insinuate that there has been a cabal of three members against you; no person shall impute anything of the kind to me with impunity." Of course, there had been a cabal, and Clay's outburst could not hide it.

Adams held his ground. "What I *dare* say, I have dared to say in writing. Gentlemen may draw from it what inferences they please; I am not answerable for them. I am perfectly satisfied that your letter and my answer should be transmitted to our Government, and I assure you that if you do not transmit them, I shall."[2]

Clay backed off. He was not anxious to have such letters seen by the government. For Washington to learn that they had stooped "to a scramble after a few books and papers" would bring dishonor on them all. If Adams intended to return home with him aboard the *Neptune* in April, when they concluded their business in London, then he, Clay, would not pursue his objection. Adams admitted that the case ought not be referred to the government, and so the matter was dropped. The books, maps, and effects would go to London until Washington decided on their disposition, but in the meantime, Adams would keep the papers. Years later they turned up in the National Archives.

It was Clay's intention to return home immediately after negotiating the commerce treaty in London. He expected to get back to Washington in time to attend what he assumed would be an extra session of Congress meeting around May 20. In the interim, he told James Monroe, he planned to tour Paris and England "to see whatever is curious or instructive." It was inconvenient, he said, to leave Europe any earlier than April.[3]

Following the treaty signing, Clay remained in Ghent for two weeks, attending and enjoying a round of balls and parties to celebrate the conclusion of the peace treaty. He left Ghent on January 7 at six o'clock in the morning, but not before he had seen Adams and taken his leave. One of Clay's most striking characteristics was the often superb way he resolved personal feuds. He was a consummate politician. He never allowed a public dispute over policy to warp or injure his personal relationships if he could help it. He often went to considerable lengths to reassure the victims of his angry outbursts that he held them in the highest esteem and hoped that no words of his would impair their future conduct toward each other. There was an old Kentucky expression that he thought all politicians should subscribe to—namely, that one should watch a politician's feet and never mind what he says. In any event, he managed to placate Adams with soothing words, and they parted on good terms.

2. Adams, *Memoirs*., III, 142–143.
3. Clay to Monroe, December 25, 1814, in Clay, *Papers,* I, 1008.

Clay boarded the diligence, or public stagecoach, for Lille and then proceeded on to Paris. His friend William H. Crawford, the U.S. minister to France, welcomed him, gave him the grand tour of Paris, and introduced him to many of the leading families in residence. Clay was presented to the king at the Tuileries, where he met the court and any number of royal gentlemen and ladies. He attended a French lawcourt and witnessed a custody battle between the former king and queen of Holland over their eldest son, the future Napoleon III. He dined with Madame de Staël, as did most notable figures who came to Paris, and thought she was the "most extraordinary woman of this or any other age. . . . She seems to have been bestow[e]d on our race to vindicate the equal claim of the female mind to intellectual excellence."

On one occasion Madame de Staël playfully engaged the Kentuckian. "Ah, Mr. Clay," she said, "the English have been much incensed against you. I have been lately pleading your cause at London. Do you know they contemplated at one time sending the Duke of Wellington to command their armies against you?"

Clay thanked her for the "exertion of her eloquence in our behalf" but added that he "wished the British Government had sent the Duke."

"Why?" she responded with surprise.

"Because Madame, had we beaten the Duke, we should have gained immortal honor, whilst we should have lost none, had we been defeated by the Conqueror of Napoleon."

The next time that Clay visited Madame de Staël at her home she introduced him to the Iron Duke and related their previous conversation to Wellington. The duke graciously responded that "he should have placed a most notable feather in his cap had he beaten so gallant a people as the Americans."[4]

In short Clay had a grand old time in Paris hobnobbing with royalty. Because of it, he acquired the nickname Prince Hal, and many of his American constituents thought it a fitting title for him. The French rather liked him, too, although he spoke no French and communicated through interpreters. At parties he frequently sat on a sofa, surrounded by admiring women, the inevitable snuffbox in one hand, discoursing on the great subjects of American policy or European political conditions. Prince Hal could charm, even talking through an interpreter.

In view of the many military defeats suffered by his country Clay did not relish the idea of leaving this congenial city and journeying to London to conclude a treaty of commerce.[5] But around the middle of March 1815 Clay received word of General Andrew Jackson's tremendous victory over the British at New Orleans on January 8, 1815, in which approximately two thousand British soldiers were killed, wounded, or captured. The commanding general

4. Clay to Margaret Bayard Smith, March 1829, in Clay, *Papers,* VIII, 1.
5. Adams, *Memoirs,* III, 151–154.

of the British army, Sir Edward Pakenham, was also killed, along with many of his senior line officers. Prince Hal was jubilant. "Now," he reportedly said, "I can go to England without mortification." The only unpleasant aspect of this military victory was the cowardice supposedly demonstrated by the Kentucky militia on the west bank of the Mississippi River, where they were routed by a British force commanded by Lieutenant Colonel William Thornton. "I am mortified," wrote Clay, particularly since Jackson claimed that Thornton's troops would have been captured had the Kentuckians not fled the scene. Jackson was very severe with his criticism because the action of the Kentuckians slightly tarnished the magnificence of the victory. But he himself was partly responsible for the debacle on the west bank because he had not foreseen and guarded against the likelihood of a British thrust in that area. In any event, the Kentucky militia resented Jackson's censure of their conduct in his official report to Washington, and they did not forget it.[6]

At approximately the same time that news of the Battle of New Orleans reached Washington, the first copy of the Treaty of Ghent also arrived at the capital. Both joyous events triggered wild scenes of celebration throughout the nation. By these events the world had been served notice that the United States, a free country under a republican form of government, was here to stay. The nation could defend its freedom and sovereignty, even against a monarchy that had defeated the military genius of the age, Napoleon Bonaparte. The Senate speedily and unanimously approved the treaty on February 17, 1815, and the following day the President proclaimed it in force. Earlier the British had ratified the treaty, although Lord Liverpool had insisted that the war would not cease until ratification had been completed by both parties, thereby leaving open the option of keeping New Orleans in the event of a British victory over General Jackson.[7]

As Clay was preparing to leave Paris for London, Napoleon suddenly returned to France from Elba amid "astonishing scenes" of welcome from the people. It was more like a "triumphal entry" into Paris than a hostile invasion. "Wonderful age! wonderful man! wonderful nation!" exclaimed Clay. "The mind is not sufficiently tranquillized to speculate on the consequences of this great event. European peace is out of the question, but who will be the parties to the new War? Will they make war upon him, or he on them?"[8]

In any event, Clay went about his business as though nothing had changed and proceeded to London without any difficulty. He arrived on March 22, a journey of three days. He left behind his colleagues, who expected to join him shortly. He was annoyed at them for the delay since he was anxious to wrap up their diplomatic affairs and get home. "My own private wish," he told the secretary of state, "is . . . that the President" would turn the duty over

6. Schurz, *Clay*, I, 123–124; Clay to Crawford, March 23, 1815, in Clay, *Papers*, II, 11.
7. Liverpool to Castlereagh, December 23, 1814, cited in Bemis, *Adams*, I, 219.
8. Clay to Monroe, March 25, 1815; Clay to Crawford, March 23, 1815, in Clay, *Papers*, II, 11, 12.

to the U.S. minister to Great Britain since the question of a commercial treaty was "of little importance." He had been itching to get home for nearly a year. "I am more than ever attached to my native home," he said, "and to my friends there."[9]

Clay subsequently learned that John Quincy Adams had been appointed minister to the Court of St. James. Yet Adams took what seemed like an eternity to get to London since he had to wait in Paris for his credentials and an official communication of his appointment, as well as move his family from Russia to Great Britain.[10] In addition, Bayard was named to replace Adams at St. Petersburg, and Gallatin was scheduled to succeed Crawford as minister to France.[11]

On reaching London, Clay went immediately to see Castlereagh in the hope of getting the negotiations started, but the government was so absorbed in the catastrophe of Napoleon's return that it had no inclination to initiate talks over a commercial treaty with the United States. So he waited. "I am tired," he wrote to Bayard, "tired out with my absence." He wrote later: "My anxiety to return is extremely great."[12]

When Gallatin arrived in London, the two men were invited by Castlereagh to join him at his home on April 16 for an informal conversation on a wide range of topics. First off, Castlereagh wished to make reparation for the needless killing of American prisoners of war at Dartmoor Prison by British soldiers. He also seemed anxious to speed the release of approximately six thousand American prisoners held in Great Britain. His concerns were genuine, and the matter was quickly and amicably settled.[13] In addition, Castlereagh seemed inclined to venture upon some "general principles" as the basis for a commercial treaty, to which Clay agreed wholeheartedly since the likelihood of a renewed war in Europe meant that all the old questions that had arisen between the United States and Britain might come up again.[14] Castlereagh suggested that the entire matter of a commercial treaty be discussed by the Americans with their counterparts at Ghent, Henry Goulburn and Dr. William Adams, along with Frederick John Robinson, the vice-president (since the president was absent) of the Board of Trade. At first Clay and Gallatin objected to Castlereagh's suggestion since they had full powers to act, and the British "plenipotentiaries" none. But Castlereagh assured them that it was his

9. Clay to Charles Tait, August 19, 1814, Alabama Department of Archives and History, copy CPP.

10. Clay to Monroe, March 25, 1815, Clay to John Payne Todd, March 30, 1815, in Clay, *Papers,* II, 12, 16.

11. Because of ill health, Bayard refused his appointment and returned to the United States, where he died a week later, on August 6, 1815.

12. Clay to Bayard, April 3, 15, 1815, in Clay, *Papers,* II, 17, 19.

13. *ASPFR,* IV, 19; "Minutes of a Conversation between Castlereagh and Clay and Gallatin," [April 16, 1815], Clay to Jonathan Russell, May 10, 1815, Castlereagh to Clay and Gallatin, May 22, 1815, in Clay, *Papers,* II, 19–20, 23–26, 37–38.

14. Clay to Bayard, April 28, 1815, in Clay, *Papers,* II, 22.

understanding that both sides to the discussion would be on an equal foot-ing.[15]

After an initial and most agreeable meeting between the British and American plenipotentiaries, no further action resulted. Nothing happened. When three weeks passed without further word from the British government, Clay and Gallatin decided to depart for America, and they notified Castlereagh of their plans to return home aboard the *Neptune*. That announcement brought a swift reaction. Vice-President Robinson sought out Clay in the House of Commons, where the American was visiting, and, "after expressing his regret at the delay which he said was unavoidable owing to the pressure of business," requested an interview which Clay promptly agreed to.[16] At that interview Clay and Gallatin were invited to consider the possibility of a treaty to abolish all discriminating duties, open the East India trade, provide com-mercial terms on the basis of "most favored nation," and regulate trade be-tween the Canadian provinces and the United States. Furthermore, the British professed themselves ready to discuss such sensitive issues as impressment and blockades, although they did not hold out much prospect for a final agreement on these issues.[17]

It was an encouraging interview. As a result, Clay postponed his return to America. He now believed that something substantial might be accomplished with a little more patience. In the interim he led an active social life, dining with the earl of Westmorland, Lord Gambier, Sir James Mackintosh, Alexan-der Baring, Castlereagh, and the British plenipotentiaries. One "venerable earl" was asked how he liked his American guests and which one he preferred. "Ah," he exclaimed, "I enjoyed them all but I liked the Kentucky man best."[18]

And Clay liked them. Twenty years later, on meeting an English lady socially, he was "still full of the sayings of Castlereagh and Canning, of Lords Eldon and Stowell, of Mackintosh and Sydney Smith." Prince Hal genuinely liked British aristocrats and got along rather well with them. They, in turn, thought he was a right charming and witty fellow—for an American.[19]

At these parties—the London parties especially—the conversation invari-ably centered on Napoleon and the renewal of war. "The foolish cry of War every where resounds," Clay told James Monroe. "I hope the career of Block-ades, Orders, Decrees, Confiscations and Burnings will not again be run."[20]

Although Prince Hal enjoyed the London scene, he found it fearfully

15. Clay to Russell, May 10, 1815, in Clay, *Papers,* II, 25.

16. Clay to Russell, May 10, 1815, in Clay, *Papers,* II, 25.

17. Henry Clay's manuscript "Notes of Conversations with the British Plenipotentiaries," James G. Blaine Papers, LC; Clay to Bayard, May 17, 1815, in Clay, *Papers,* II, 29. For a full account of these talks, see "Notes of Conversations," and Clay and Gallatin to Monroe, May 18, 1815, ibid., 30–37.

18. Thomas Hart Clay, *Henry Clay,* pp. 402–403.

19. Martineau, *Retrospective of Western Travel,* I, 177; Thomas Hart Clay, *Henry Clay,* p. 403.

20. Clay to Monroe, March 25, 1815, in Clay, *Papers,* II, 13.

expensive, "greatly exceeding all my anticipations; and yet I kept not house, and was certainly not extravagant in my personal expences." He later told the secretary of state that an American minister abroad should adopt a "stile" of living that would avoid "the meanness which provokes ridicule, and the ostentation which challenges observation." Rather, "it should be one of neat simplicity, regulated by the habits of society in the Country where he resides, and admitting of the return of civilities and the dispensation of our respectable Countrymen of expected hostility." Under this rubric, he added, the present salary for a minister was "wholly inadequate to sustain the expences of such a stile of living at most, if not all, of the foreign Courts at which we have Ministers."[21]

On one of his excursions in the British Isles Clay visited the Smithfield Stock Show, where he observed Hereford cattle for the first time. He was so enthusiastic about the animals that he became a pioneer in importing the breed into the United States. Two years later he acquired two Hereford bulls and two heifers.

When John Quincy Adams finally arrived in London on May 25, he was quickly apprised of what had transpired in his absence. To speed matters along—both Gallatin and Clay were still anxious to return home aboard the *Neptune*—Gallatin prepared the draft of a treaty with two sets of articles, one relating to commercial matters only, the other to the "belligerent and neutral collisions" that had occurred in the past between the two nations. Clay wanted to move immediately on the commercial articles because he thought that they could be speedily concluded. Thus, when the British came back with a "counter-project" of a commercial treaty, Clay and Gallatin decided to stick with the negotiations even though it meant that the *Neptune* would sail without them.[22]

But the "counter-projet"[23] turned out to be so different from what Clay and Gallatin had expected—and what they had led Adams to expect—that the Americans wondered whether they should pursue the negotiations any further. Specifically the British requested the right to trade with Indians on American soil. And there were other differences involving discriminating duties and the East India trade. Clay said he had been "deceived" by the British and felt they were once again playing the game of brag. He was so annoyed that he strongly urged his colleagues to terminate the negotiations at once.[24] "I am sick of Europe," he lamented to James Russell, "and sicker of European poli-

---

21. Clay to Monroe, April 5, 1816, in Clay, *Papers,* II, 191.

22. Adams, *Memoirs,* III, 201, 204, 209, 220.

23. This counterproject may be found in *ASPFR,* IV, 13–15, and Clay, *Papers,* II, 44ff.

24. "We . . . asked and obtained an interview with Lord Castlereagh for the purpose of stating to him that we felt ourselves obliged to exercise the right which we had reserved to ourselves of withdrawing from the negotiation." They were urged to remain, however, and finally consented to do so. Entry, June 7, Clay's "Notes of Conversations," Blaine Papers, LC; Adams, *Memoirs,* III, 221.

tics. I will not trouble you with my distresses on this latter subject."[25] As usual Gallatin tried to be conciliatory and put a good face on the situation. For his part, Adams said little since he had not been involved in the discussions from the beginning and wanted to familiarize himself with the issues before taking a stand.

When the American commissioners again met with the British plenipotentiaries, the article relating to Canada was discussed first, and Gallatin and Clay protested that although the British wished to trade with the Indians within U.S. territory, they would not permit Americans to navigate the St. Lawrence River, even down to Montreal. The Americans wanted the right to carry their own articles to a British port for further export, allowing the British to export these articles exclusively in their own vessels. Clay, displaying his usual penchant for bluster, ranted at the British commissioners that it was not a ship they were talking about—not even a boat. "It was little more than the mere floating of rafts to be taken down in exchange for gewgaws from Europe."[26]

Dr. Adams bridled at the mention of "gewgaws." If Americans like gewgaws, he snapped back, they would quickly trade their lumber and flour to possess them. After all, that was the meaning of trade. Dr. Adams was quite insistent that this article be retained in the final treaty, and that was enough for Clay to repeat to his colleagues that they should break off negotiations. As far as Clay was concerned, there were only two courses of action for them: conclude an acceptable treaty or terminate discussions and go home.[27] Ultimately the article was thrown out altogether.

During these negotiations news arrived that Napoleon had suffered a total defeat at Waterloo. Fortunately the allied victory did not place any strain on the commissioners, and they finally brought their discussion to a conclusion on May 31 with a document they all felt comfortable in signing. All, that is, except John Quincy Adams. He thought the document accomplished very little—or maybe his discomfort was based on the fact that he had so little to do with it. In any event, he signed it reluctantly. "Only out of deference to you and Mr. Clay that I consent to sign it at all," he said to Gallatin, and only after it was agreed that the order in which the two nations were named in the heading, text, and signatory passages would be alternated. The British had presented copies of the treaty that named themselves and their sovereign first in every instance. Adams demanded that the names be alternated.

"Now, don't fly off in this manner," pleaded Gallatin.

"Indeed, sir," Adams replied, "I will not sign the treaty in any other form."

Gallatin finally relented. Although the British seemed indifferent to the

25. Clay to Russell, May 10, 1815, in Clay, *Papers,* II, 26.
26. Adams, *Memoirs,* III, 224.
27. Ibid., III, 227.

entire matter, Adams was determined that the United States receive full recognition as a sovereign and independent nation. This was an important consideration to the crusty New Englander. "Mr. Adams is really a thorn," James Gallatin scolded in his diary. "He is so absolutely 'Yankee' and of a common type. . . . Of course Mr. Adams is retarding matters with his pigheadedness."[28]

As far as Clay was concerned, the question of alternating names was a matter of supreme indifference. What was important about the treaty, he said, were the provisions abolishing all discriminating duties and providing a most-favored-nation treatment of each other's products, along with U.S. admission to the trade of British India (Calcutta, Madras, Bombay, and Prince of Wales Island).

The commissioners could not agree on the West Indian trade or trade with the Canadian provinces. Nothing was decided on impressment, blockades, or colonial trade restrictions. These were left to "future consideration and to other hands." With respect to impressment, "they make us strong assurances," reported Clay, "of guarding in future agt. causes of complaint on our part."[29]

And that concluded the negotiations. The convention—so called because of the limited extent of its provisions—was signed and dated July 3, 1815, and it was to remain in effect for four years.

By and large the convention merely affirmed existing practice. Only the prohibition of discriminatory duties was a new, bold, imaginative, and important policy, and it became one of the major principles of American foreign policy.[30] The convention itself became a model for similar agreements with other countries, particularly the most-favored-nation clause. Subsequent administrations attempted to obtain most-favored-nation guarantees when negotiating trade agreements with foreign powers. This Convention of 1815 was renewed within four years and continues in effect to this day.[31]

The signing ceremony took place on a Monday. Early the very next day, July 4, Clay bolted toward Liverpool, so anxious was he to escape Europe and return home. Indeed, he had flown into a rage when, just a few weeks before, the *Neptune* sailed off with William H. Crawford and the dying Bayard, but without him. He raced to Liverpool because of the many vessels scheduled to sail for America from that city. Although Clay expected Gallatin to accompany him home, the Kentuckian did not wait for him. "Mr. Gallatin was to start the same day," he told John Payne Todd, son of Dolley Madison, who had accompanied Gallatin and Bayard to Europe in 1813 as private secretary, "but is I presume in my rear." He arrived in Birmingham in two days, stayed overnight, and pressed on to Liverpool "so as to take advantage of the first good opportu-

28. Ibid., III, 243; Gallatin, *Diary*, pp. 73, 77.
29. Clay to Russell, July 1, 1815, in Clay, *Papers*, II, 26.
30. Bemis, *Adams*, I, 225.
31. The Senate ratified the treaty on December 19, 1815, after nearly two weeks of debate.

nity for New York or Philadelphia. Be you ready," he warned Todd, who was in Liverpool and was to accompany him home, "for like Patrick Coutts, when dying, I wait for no man."[32]

Clay, Gallatin and his son James, and John Payne Todd booked passage aboard the *Lorenzo* and sailed for New York on Saturday, July 22. It took nearly six weeks to cross the Atlantic because of fierce gale winds that slowed their progress, and they did not arrive in New York until Friday, September 1.

The two diplomats received a warm welcome in New York. They were provided a "superb entertainment" at Tammany Hall, six days after their arrival, in recognition of their invaluable contribution to ending the War of 1812. Both men were saluted with numerous toasts for advancing the nation's diplomatic reputation in Europe.[33] A week later, in Philadelphia, the "Democratic Citizens" honored Clay at a reception in the Washington Hotel, toasting him as "Our distinguished and worthy guest, *Henry Clay* of Kentucky, a genuine republican, and an enlightened statesman."[34]

Henceforth, in their discourse, public prints, and public events, Americans generally would repeat the obvious fact: that in Henry Clay they had a statesman of the first rank who seemed destined to guide and direct the future affairs of the nation.

32. Clay to Todd, July 6, 1815, in Clay, *Papers,* II, 59–60. Coutts was a merchant in Virginia who died in 1776 and may have made some remark as he expired about getting on with it. Gallatin had a slight indisposition that delayed his departure from London by a day. Adams, *Memoirs,* III, 249.
33. Washington *National Intelligencer,* September 11, 1815.
34. Ibid., September 15, 1815.

NINE

The Ambitious Politicians

CLAY'S HOMEWARD JOURNEY was filled with the raucous shouts of approval by his countrymen for his splendid
accomplishment in bringing the war to a "triumphant" con-
clusion. If he had had any doubts about the success of his mission abroad, they
were drowned out by the resolutions, toasts, and expressions of congratulations that inundated him during his first weeks and months at home. The
theme of these expressions was invariably the same: "Henry Clay: The Orator,
the Statesman and the Patriot."[1]

It was all very intoxicating. Clay's ego received an enormous boost. And
he was proud enough and ambitious enough not only to take enormous satisfaction from the adulation but to nurture the thought and hope that it would
lead to greater fame and honor. Very possibly this homeward journey began
the period in which Henry Clay would think very seriously about one day
occupying the presidential office. At the age of thirty-eight, he believed he had
achieved the rank of statesman, just as everyone said, and he may have begun
dreaming about how he might go about placing himself in direct line for the
presidency. It surely crossed his mind that the office of secretary of state was
not unattainable and would prove a perfect conduit to his goal. Indeed,
Monroe had already informed him that President Madison would like to appoint him to the mission in Russia to replace the deceased Bayard "& will be
much gratified to hear that it will be acceptable to you."[2] Clay had not the
remotest desire to return to Europe—"I am sick of Europe," he had said—but
it was clear from the invitation that the administration thought that in matters
of foreign affairs he was one of the best men available in the country. In any

---

1. Other toasts included:

"Our Guest, Henry Clay—We welcome his return to that country, whose rights and interests
he has so ably maintained at home and abroad."

"Our able negociators at Ghent—Their talents for diplomacy, have kept pace with the valor
of our arms in 'demonstrating' to the enemy that these states will be free."

To many of these toasts, Clay responded graciously: "The Memory of James A. Bayard."
Clay, *Papers,* II, 61ff.

2. Monroe to Clay, October 30, 1815, in Clay, *Papers,* II, 88–89.

event, his return to Kentucky marked the obvious emergence of an ambitious politician who had his eye fixed on higher office.

His pride in his performance abroad—considering all the additional time required of him before he could return to America—found greater expression in his belief that he should receive a more ample financial reward. He wrote to Gallatin and suggested that their salaries ought to extend, at the very least, to July 17, which would round out a term of eighteen months from the date of their commission. "This will allow two weeks after the signature of the Convention, which is not unreasonable for posthumous and incidental business."[3]

But Gallatin went him one better. He claimed their compensation had been allowed to July 22, the day they departed England. In addition, they should receive an allowance for traveling expenses involved in "the removal to the seats of negotiation," which for Clay meant expenses traveling from Gottenburg to Ghent and Ghent to London.[4] These items the Kentuckian subsequently claimed, along with a sum lost to him in rent to a landlord in Gottenburg, as well as stationary and newspapers in Gottenburg and London. And he swore he would pay not one cent of duties "for articles introduced for my own consumption." All told, Clay eventually received $27,517.95 in salary and expenses for the mission, of which $13,647.94 represented salary for the period from January 17, 1814, to July 22, 1815, based on a per annum salary of $9,000.[5] Some of his earnings while abroad—1,200 pounds or $4,444.44—were invested through the Baring Brothers company in 6 percent stock of the United States. Clay always had a sharp eye in matters of finance, and the Barings assured him that they had obtained the stock for him at the lowest price available.[6]

One would think that Prince Hal might want to spend a long vacation with his family after being away so many months. But no. As a lionized diplomat and statesman Clay looked forward with keen interest and real anticipation to his return to Congress in the late fall of 1815. He could hardly wait to return to Washington. And his easy reelection to the office of Speaker at the very outset of the congressional session in December only added to his growing sense of his stature and national reputation and what might result in the future.

Washington City lay in shambles after the British invasion. The President's House, the Capitol, and several of the executive buildings had been torched, and nothing remained of the books and papers housed in the Library of Congress. President Madison took up residence in the Octagon House on New York Avenue, while local inhabitants built a brick hall, located on the site

3. Clay to Gallatin, September 28, 1815, in Clay, *Papers,* II, 64.
4. Gallatin to Clay, November 23, 1815, in Clay, *Papers,* II, 100.
5. Account as minister plenipotentiary, Auditors Office, January 18, 1816, and Clay to Gallatin, December 5, 1815, in Clay, *Papers,* II, 130, 106.
6. Baring Brothers to Clay, June 30, 1815, and Clay to Lucretia Clay, July 14, 1815, in Clay, *Papers,* II, 53, 60.

of today's Supreme Court, so that Congress might conduct the nation's business until a new Capitol could be erected. The Senate met on the first floor of this "Old Brick Capitol," the House of Representatives on the second. Not until 1825 was the new Capitol finished, although it was ready for partial use by December 1819. The President's mansion, more frequently called the White House after it had been repainted and refurbished, received its new occupants in September 1817.[7]

Clay found most of the War Hawks present in the "Brick Capitol" after his return, including Calhoun, Lowndes, Richard M. Johnson, and Peter B. Porter, and as Speaker he promptly appointed Lowndes to chair the Ways and Means Committee and Calhoun to head a select Committee on the National Currency. Although it was no longer necessary to cope with financing the war, the national debt had ballooned, and revenues for its reduction were desperately needed. Moreover, a number of congressmen worried over the possibility of renewed aggression on the part of Great Britain and urged adoption of measures by which the nation might prepare itself against such an emergency. All in all, several of the young war leaders, including Clay, argued that Congress must address the larger question of national development if liberty and the happiness of the people were to be protected and advanced.

The larger question necessarily focused on the economy. Among its many effects on the nation, the War of 1812 compelled the United States to abandon its reliance on international trade and build its own independent domestic economy. Capital that had once gone into shipping and commerce was now being diverted into manufactures and industry. The factory system had been introduced from Great Britain when plans for a newly invented textile machine were secretly brought into the United States. And because of the great natural resources in the country and the increased supply of relatively cheap labor, the Industrial Revolution quickly established itself in America. The modernization of transportation and communication followed right along with the building of roads, canals, bridges, turnpikes, and highways in many states. These diverse economic changes in American life constituted a veritable "market revolution," which intensified the impact of capitalism on the lives of virtually every citizen in the country.[8]

"England is the most formidable power in the world," declared Representative Calhoun. "We, on the other hand, are the most growing nation on earth. . . . Will Great Britain permit us to go on in an uninterrupted march to the height of national greatness and prosperity? I fear not. . . . You will have to encounter British jealousy and hostility in every shape . . . to check your growth and prosperity. . . ."[9]

Clay reveled in the market revolution spreading across the country be-

7. Constance McLaughlin Green, *Washington: Village and Capital, 1800–1878* (Princeton, 1962), I, 61–68.

8. Harry L. Watson, *Liberty and Power: The Politics of Jacksonian America* (New York, 1990), pp. 28–29, 34–35.

9. *Annals of Congress,* 14th Congress, 1st session, p. 514.

cause he knew what it meant in terms of national security as well as the future prosperity of the American people. More than anything else during these months following his return from Europe, Clay revealed an ardent nationalism that had swelled to gigantic proportions as the result of his long sojourn abroad. Europe had taught him something that he had been barely conscious of—namely, the greatness of his country, the strength of its institutions, how much he loved it, and how committed he was to its future development and happiness. In several speeches he gave in the House at the outset of the first session of the Fourteenth Congress, Clay repeatedly lauded the military exploits of Andrew Jackson, Jacob Brown, Isaac Hull, Winfield Scott, James Lawrence, and Oliver Hazard Perry during the late war. "I love true glory," rhapsodized Clay. "It is this sentiment which ought to be cherished; and in spite of cavils and sneers and attempts to put it down, it will finally conduct this nation to that height to which God and nature have destined it."[10]

In the course of these patriotic effusions Clay also began to detail a program of legislation in response to his own concerns and those of the other War Hawks. The immediate purpose of this program was obvious: Strengthen the nation in order to safeguard its liberties. But his program, he said, would also stimulate industrial growth and raise the nation to higher levels of economic achievement. It would hurry the march to "national greatness and prosperity."

The general idea behind Clay's program had the strong backing of the administration. In his State of the Union message to Congress in December 1815, President Madison commented favorably on the concept of increased government responsibility for improving the welfare of the nation as a whole. Later Clay was rightly to insist that all his economic and political concepts were basically Madisonian.

Much of what Clay now thought about the direction the nation must take for the immediate future resulted from his experiences during the late war, or so he said. "Yes, sir," cried the Speaker in a major speech he delivered in the House on January 16, 1816, "I was in the neighborhood of the battle of Waterloo, and some lessons I did derive from it: but they were lessons which satisfied me that national independence was only to be maintained by national resistance against foreign encroachments; by cherishing the interest of the people, and giving to the whole physical power of the country an interest in the preservation of the nation."

The whole physical power of the country! His program, as it evolved over the next several years, was aimed at benefiting the entire nation. It was the only way, he said, by which the country could achieve its full potential to defend itself against those who would threaten its continued existence.

"We had been insulted, and outraged, and spoliated upon by almost all Europe—by Great Britain, by France, Spain, Denmark, Naples, and, to cap

10. Clay gave a number of speeches of this character. The one quoted here was given on January 29, 1816, and is reported in *Annals of Congress*, 14th Congress, 1st session, pp. 776–792.

the climax, by the contemptible power of Algiers. We had submitted too long and too much. We had become the scorn of foreign powers, and the contempt of our own citizens." That must never happen again, he stormed. And it will not, if the nation girds itself and builds "the whole physical power of the country."[11]

To do this, Clay proposed or supported or recommended a wide range of new measures, starting quite appropriately with the military. As he had in the past, he cooperated with former War Hawk allies, such as Calhoun, Lowndes, Porter, and John Forsyth of Georgia, along with several new members of the House, to provide for a substantial increase in the navy and the creation of a regular armed force of ten thousand men. The idea of a standing army alarmed many old Republicans, but Clay responded to their fears, even if he did not allay them, by citing how "Mr. Jefferson" had increased the existing "peace establishment . . . making a force precisely equal to the present peace establishment." It is the duty of Congress, Clay insisted, to provide for the augmentation of the navy to enhance national security, and, if the danger of war should escalate, then, he said, we must increase the army and arm the militia.

Moreover, Clay recommended a program of public works to enhance the nation's defenses. "Construct military roads and canals," he pleaded, ". . . that the facilities of transportation may exist of the men and means of the country to points where they may be wanted. . . . I would provide steambatteries for the Mississippi, [for the lakes around New Orleans] and for the Chesapeake, and for any part of the north or east where they might be beneficially employed. In short . . . I would act, seriously, effectively act on the principle that in peace we ought to prepare for war."

In addition to these purely military projects, he "would as earnestly" plead for the commencement of "the great work, too long delayed, of internal improvements." He wanted to see "a chain of turnpikes, roads and canals from Passamaquoddy to New Orleans" and similar roads crisscrossing the nation and "intersecting the mountains, to facilitate intercourse between all parts of the country, and to bind and connect us together." And such a national program must be federally funded.

Furthermore, he believed the time had arrived to "effectually protect our manufacturers." They need protection against foreign competition if they are to survive, he declared, and he felt the administration had given at least an "implied pledge to do so." For his part, Clay said he wanted protection, not so much for the sake of the manufactures themselves "as for the general interest." This was the only way to make certain that needed materials would be available when foreign sources of supply were cut off. There should also be a system of taxation, he insisted, to replace revenue from imports when war interrupted the flow of these imports. By these measures, he concluded, we will show that

11. *Annals of Congress,* 14th Congress, 1st session, pp. 776–778. These remarks dealt with a bill to repeal the direct tax levied during the war.

the "objects of domestic no less than those of foreign policy receive our attention."[12]

Granted these suggested measures were patriotically inspired to guard against the possibility of future aggression by a European power, but a large navy, a standing army, direct taxes, internal improvements, and the subsidization of industry also meant the further intervention of the national government into the economic operation of society, the further intrusion into the lives and affairs of the American people. That meant the further concentration of power in the central government at the expense of the states. And that was heresy—all of it. That was Federalist doctrine, not Republican. That was anathema to old-line Republican conservatives, and if Clay did not trouble himself about this departure from the true faith, John Randolph of Roanoke reminded him of it at every opportunity.[13] On several occasions other representatives came to Randolph's aid. "[John] Ross of Penna is skinning the Speaker with a handsaw," Randolph gleefully reported.[14]

But Clay was not alone. In translating this nationalistic program into law, he had the active assistance of several distinguished congressmen. Indeed, such representatives as John C. Calhoun and William Lowndes could take more credit than Clay for the final results achieved during this session.[15] And with southerners like Calhoun and Lowndes urging passage of this program there could be no question that it was inspired in large measure by patriotic reasons, not the advancement of northern industry.

Department heads of the administration also cooperated with the House leadership in this new attempt at national development. Their first important accomplishment together was the approval of a revenue bill that retained the principle of direct taxation introduced during the war along with other wartime duties, at least until a new tariff could be written. Later—in fact, during this very session of Congress, as it turned out—a tariff bill that Clay enthusiastically supported was introduced. He was particularly anxious to have such Kentucky items as "hempen and sail cloths" protected, but he was also concerned for the producers of woolen and cotton goods. In arguing for the bill, Clay said that the object of protecting manufactures was to have "articles of necessity" made as cheaply at home as they could be imported and thereby make the nation independent of foreign countries. He believed that within three years the United States could achieve this goal. Then other entrepreneurs

12. *Annals of Congress,* 14th Congress, 1st session, pp. 789–792.

13. No sooner did Clay return to the House than he again tangled with Randolph over a change in the rules. Clay took malicious pleasure in noting how "a certain gentleman" spoke "four and twenty hours without stopping" for no other purpose than to delay the proceedings of the legislature. But Randolph shot right back: "I labor under two great misfortunes—one is, that I can never understand the honorable Speaker; the other is, that he can never understand me." *Annals of Congress,* 14th Congress, 1st session, pp. 698–699, 723–730.

14. Randolph to Edward Cunningham, January 31, 1816, Randolph Papers, Virginia Historical Society.

15. Charles M. Wiltse, *John C. Calhoun, Nationalist* (Indianapolis and New York, 1949), p. 111.

"would not hesitate to enter into the business, because they would look to that liberal and enlarged policy which they might anticipate from the government at a future period."

The Tariff of 1816, the nation's first protective tariff, was passed on April 27, and it established duties of 25 percent on woolen and cotton goods and 30 percent on iron products. Clay, Calhoun, and some southern representatives supported the bill largely for nationalistic reasons. Northeasterners and westerners generally favored the bill because it advanced their economic interests, while many southerners opposed it for a variety of reasons, including ideological. Daniel Webster, congressman from New Hampshire, also opposed the tariff because he believed it would injure the shipping interests of New England.[16]

Clay's position on the tariff was frequently misunderstood and misstated both during his lifetime and afterward. He never approved protection across the board. He believed in selective protection, depending on the observed needs of the country and the necessity of promoting those industries and products that would advance the economic well-being and safety of the nation.

But the measure that was to provide Clay with his greatest political difficulties, now and some twenty years later, was the bill brought forward by Calhoun and his Committee on the National Currency to incorporate a Second National Bank of the United States (BUS). The First National Bank had been enacted into law with strong support by the Federalist party but over the equally strong objections of Jefferson and Madison and their Republican cohorts in Congress. It had expired in 1811, when a Republican-controlled Congress refused to renew its charter.

The War of 1812 taught many Republicans how foolish they had been to allow a financial institution that provided a safe and adequate currency to pass out of existence at the very moment it was most needed. State banks, many of which could only be described as "wildcat" in their operation, had rushed in to take advantage of this financial opportunity. During the war sounder banks drained into their vaults what little specie was available in the country, and most of these banks were located in New England, where the war was decidedly unpopular. Within two years of the start of the war every bank in the middle, western, and southern states was forced to suspend specie payment and rely totally on paper money. The value of the paper immediately declined; in fact, some of it was practically worthless. The government, in its efforts to obtain sufficient funds to finance the war, appealed to the New England banks for help, but these banks turned a deaf ear. Obviously a Second Bank of the United States was desperately needed, and President Madison in his message

16. *Annals of Congress,* 14th Congress, 1st session, p. 1272; Edward Stanwood, *American Tariff Controversies of the Nineteenth Century* (Boston and New York, 1903), p. 140ff.; Niven, *Calhoun,* p. 53; Wiltse, *Calhoun, Nationalist,* pp. 108–111; Maurice Baxter, *One and Inseparable: Daniel Webster and the Union* (Cambridge, Mass., 1984), p. 64.

to the opening of the Fourteenth Congress urged the necessity of creating a uniform national currency.[17]

The response of Calhoun's committee was almost an exact replica of the First Bank. The bill, introduced on January 8, 1816, provided for the chartering for twenty years of a national bank to be located in Philadelphia with branches in the other cities. The Bank would operate with a capital stock of $35 million, of which one-fifth would be purchased by the federal government (in coin, Treasury notes, or government stock) and the other four-fifths offered to the investing public. The BUS would be operated by a board of twenty-five directors, five of whom would be appointed by the President of the United States and the other twenty elected by the stockholders. The directors would choose a president to administer the day-to-day operations of the BUS along with the governing boards of the branch banks. The Bank would become the custodian of the public funds, and its notes would be acceptable for all payments due the United States. In return the Bank would transact, free of charge, the government's financial business, such as transferring funds from one location to another, and pay the Treasury a bonus of $1.5 million in three installments over a four-year period.[18]

The debate on the bill in the House occupied two full weeks. The war had convinced many skeptics about the need for a national bank, but opposition centered on whether this particular bank suited the nation's needs and, of course, whether Congress had the authority to create such an institution with its attendant "evils."[19]

On March 9, 1816, Clay stepped into the well of the House to support the legislation. His remarks drew widespread attention in view of his previous opposition to the Bank. Unfortunately his speech went unrecorded; but nearly three months later he addressed the people of his district at Lexington, and he probably repeated the arguments he had presented in the House. In any event, many of his constituents were upset by his reversal on the issue and demanded an explanation.

In his Lexington address Clay claimed that he had previously opposed the renewal of the Bank charter for three reasons: that he was instructed to oppose it by the legislature of Kentucky, that the BUS had abused its powers and had "sought to subserve the views of a political party," and that the power to create such an institution was not authorized by the Constitution. Now, as for the first reason for his earlier opposition, he claimed that the Kentucky legislature no longer objected and, in fact, that many of his constituents approved a new Bank and told him so. As for the second, he was sure the new BUS would learn

17. Robert V. Remini, *Andrew Jackson and the Bank War* (New York, 1967), p. 26; Richardson, *Messages and Papers,* I, 547ff.

18. Ralph C. H. Catterall, *The Second Bank of the United States* (Chicago, 1903), pp. 10–21; *American State Papers, Finance,* III, 57–61.

19. *Annals of Congress,* 14th Congress, 1st session, pp. 1437, 1440–1451; Wiltse, *Calhoun, Nationalist,* pp. 110–111.

from the mistakes of its predecessor and "shun politics." As for the third, although he believed the Constitution never changes, "the force of circumstances and the lights of experience may evolve" which "fallible persons" had not seen "at a former period." At the present time, he declared, "events of the utmost magnitude had intervened" to convince him of the Bank's constitutionality. Besides, the regulation of the currency was one of the highest attributes of sovereignty, and the state banks were no longer capable of assisting the Treasury in the operation of collecting and distributing the public revenue. It was the duty of Congress, he continued, to apply a remedy to prevent the possible "convulsion and subversion of the government" because of the wretched state of the currency. Clay recognized that his reversal would expose him to censure, but in light of what had happened since the beginning of the war he could no longer justify opposition to a national banking system. "That which appeared to him in 1811, under the state of things then existing, not to be necessary to the general government, seemed now to be necessary, under the present state of things." Since Congress, not the states, has the power to coin money, the "plain inference is, that the subject of the general currency was intended to be submitted exclusively to the general government." The need for a "general medium" was everywhere felt. Exchange varied from state to state, he said, and frequently in different parts of the same state. What was needed was a uniform currency, and the BUS would satisfy that need.[20]

Clay's conflicting speeches and votes on the Bank question was used against him by his opponents over the next several decades. His argument about obeying the instruction of the state legislature was remembered and cited against him in 1825, when he deliberately disobeyed an instruction from the legislature. And during the Bank War in the administration of President Andrew Jackson, his earlier speech in opposing the BUS was republished extensively by the newspapers of his political enemies. Later Clay admitted that his earlier opposition to the Bank was a mistake and that his change of heart was the only time in his life when he had reversed himself on a public issue.

In explaining this reversal (and several other future actions), Clay's critics, then and later, tended to dismiss his actions as those of a political opportunist, of a man with no fixed principles about government, a man who merely acted out of selfish ambition. But this criticism totally distorts the fundamental meaning of his life and thinking. Granted his pragmatism, granted his political legerdemain in maneuvering through various legislative thickets, still, Clay did espouse an ideology that made remarkably good sense to someone of his generation and circumstance.

To begin with, he firmly believed in a constitutional system that divided power between the states and the central government. He repeatedly affirmed

---

20. The speech was reported by Lexington's *Kentucky Gazette* on June 10, 1816, and is reproduced in Clay, *Papers,* II, 199–205.

his commitment to states' rights virtually to the day he died. And this was no pretense to curry favor with Republican conservatives. It was a genuine commitment. He had no problem with the idea of reserving certain governmental functions and powers to state and local governments. He understood that national power was limited and should remain such. He understood that in writing the Constitution, the Founding Fathers had delegated certain powers to the central government and reserved those not delegated to the people and the states. But where Jefferson and Madison agonized over specific powers, such as the constitutionality of allowing Congress the right to charter a national bank or appropriate funds for internal improvements, Clay could not understand the difficulty. Whenever the government needed to act to protect the national security and safeguard the welfare of the country at large, he readily found the "necessary" authority in the implied powers clause or other clauses of the Constitution because no government, he argued, could long survive if denied the means of protecting itself and providing for the needs of its people. The history of the government under the Articles of Confederation demonstrated that truth.

Perhaps better than anyone else of his generation, Clay also understood that differences of opinion among men would arise from time to time on a wide range of issues, not simply constitutional interpretation. Differences between the states and the national government, differences between sections of the country, between competing economic interests, and between classes could be expected as the natural consequence of a people engaged in disparate occupations scattered across a huge country. It was therefore up to statesmen to find the means to resolve these differences in order to advance the material well-being of the American people and, most especially, to prevent the "convulsion and subversion of the government." That was the reason he placed such reliance on compromise over the next several decades. Men were bound to disagree on principles and issues, he said; if they were unwilling to work out their differences through a process of give-and-take, the result could be catastrophic. The result could produce savage civil conflict.

It was so easy for critics to discount and discredit his many efforts at compromise and accommodation as the facile exercise of a shallow and unprincipled man. They failed to appreciate that he was really committed to something higher and more important than the right of Congress to establish tariffs, banks, and roads. He believed that the American constitutional system provided the means that enabled men who loved the Union above everything else and who sought the betterment of their constituents to "harmonize" their differences and reach amicable solutions. The word "harmony" resonates throughout his career. Over and over it appears in his speeches to the public and to his colleagues in Congress.

Harmony! Compromise! Union! These are the words that provide the clues that best explain Clay's thinking and political philosophy.

In any event this Bank bill passed the House on March 14, 1816, by the vote of eighty to seventy-one. The Senate, after making a few changes, also passed the measure, and it was signed by President Madison.[21]

The Second National Bank of the United States began its operations on January 1, 1817, with William Jones as its first president. Its short twenty-year history was to be turbulent and filled with controversy, and Henry Clay was to be a central figure in its final destruction.

As for the $1.5 million paid by the BUS for its charter, Calhoun introduced on December 26, 1816, a bonus bill by which the money would be used to establish a fund for the support of internal improvements. In a speech supporting the bill Clay said that he had long thought that there were no two subjects more worthy of attention by Congress than those of "Internal Improvements and Domestic Manufactures," and he expressed the wish that the Fourteenth Congress would gain the merit of "laying the foundations of this great work."[22] The bill passed on March 1, 1817, but President Madison vetoed it the day before he left office on constitutional grounds, despite Clay's personal plea to him to leave the decision on the bill to his successor.[23] In an unnecessary but gallant action Clay insisted on his right to vote to override the veto, but his effort went for nothing. By a count of sixty to fifty-six the override failed. For the Speaker that meant that a public works program would have to be approached along an entirely different route. And he had occasion to speak on the subject in connection with an appropriation to extend the Cumberland or National Road into Ohio.

The National Road, which led westward from Cumberland, Maryland, had been authorized by Congress in 1806, and appropriations for surveys and construction had been approved several times thereafter. Clay was "particularly zealous" in supporting the Ohio extension and said that he had seen many highways in Europe as well as America "but had never travelled on so fine a road" as the Cumberland turnpike.[24] By 1816 government support of public works had become an essential ingredient in Clay's overall program of national development, not only to advance military preparedness but to assist the nation's industrial growth.

Still another bill passed by Congress caused an uproar, this time among the electorate, including Clay's own constituents. Colonel Richard M. Johnson of Kentucky, the supposed slayer of the Indian chieftain Tecumseh in hand-to-hand combat, complained in the House that its business dragged along interminably because the representatives stretched out each session as long as possible since they were paid by the day. Clay assigned him to a special committee with Webster and others to look into the matter, and they reported out a bill that would change the compensation of House members from six

21. *Annals of Congress,* 14th Congress, 1st session, pp. 1127–1134. Earlier Madison had vetoed a similar Bank bill.
22. *Annals of Congress,* 14th Congress, 1st session, pp. 866–868.
23. Clay to Madison, March 3, 1817, in Clay, *Papers,* II, 322.
24. *Annals of Congress,* 14th Congress, 1st session, pp. 1306–1307.

dollars a day to fifteen hundred dollars per annum. Since Clay, as Speaker, would receive double compensation, he demonstrated remarkable courage (or insensitivity) in arguing for its passage. Most of the members of the House, even those who ultimately voted against it, supported the measure. Only Representative Benjamin Huger of South Carolina, who was "born to opulence," spoke at length against it.

Clay pounced on him. Not everyone had the same good fortune as Huger, he said. Would Huger, then, "reserve the seats here for the well born and the rich alone?" If nothing is done to compensate "the poor and middling classes," the net result would be a House filled with wealthy men. Clay thought that compensation should be such that financial ruin would not result from lengthy tenure. He himself had attended Congress, sometimes with his family and sometimes without, and although he received double that of other members, "he had never been able to make both ends meet at the termination of Congress." Furthermore, compensation should guarantee the independence of Congress against the influence of the executive branch. The laborer, Clay concluded, is worthy of his hire, and if he is denied the wages of honesty, "the wages of corruption may, in process of time, come to be sought."[25]

With little vocal opposition this compensation bill passed on March 19 by a vote of eighty-one to sixty-seven, and almost immediately the people cried out their indignation at this bald-faced raid upon the Treasury. Many voters swore that the congressmen responsible for this outrageous "salary grab" would be summarily dismissed from office in the fall elections. And there was poor Clay with a double portion in his hand!

The fall elections included not only the entire membership of the House and a third of the Senate but the next President of the United States. In deciding its candidate, the Republican party had traditionally held a congressional caucus to make its selection; but the caucus was running into popular disfavor, and many congressmen, including Clay, questioned the propriety of the nominating process. But what was the alternative? State legislatures? Such a method invited only disagreement and disunity. It would produce a whole raft of favorite son candidates, none of whom would receive a majority of electoral votes and would result in the election's going to the House of Representatives for the final selection of the President.

Among possible candidates for the Republican nomination, two names stood out from the rest: James Monroe and William H. Crawford. Monroe had surreptitiously tried to obtain the nomination eight years earlier and was generally believed to have given himself an edge in 1816 by bowing out in 1808 and entering Madison's cabinet. His position was strengthened when the administration eventually rallied behind his nomination. Crawford of Georgia was the former minister to France who became secretary of war in 1815.

25. *Annals of Congress,* 14th Congress, 1st session, p. 1174. On this bill, see C. Edward Skeen, *"Vox Populi, Vox Dei:* The Compensation Act of 1816," *Journal of the Early Republic,* VI (Fall 1986), pp. 253–274.

Crawford was an extremely popular man among congressmen, while Monroe was not. Monroe belonged to the old Virginia Dynasty and a great many Republicans had grown weary of the dynasty. They were looking for more active presidential leadership than they felt the Virginian could provide.

Crawford might well have gotten the nomination had he stood his ground and fought for it. But he was only forty-four, and he figured that if he withdrew in Monroe's favor, he would be the odds-on favorite eight years hence. Besides, he may have been reluctant to challenge the Virginia statesman openly. He unwisely presumed that if he gracefully bowed out at this time, Monroe would return the favor in 1824 and support his nomination.[26]

In any event, when the call went out for the Republican members of Congress to meet in caucus in the hall of the representatives on March 12, only 58 out of 141 members attended, no doubt because the call was sent out anonymously. A second call for a meeting on the evening of March 16 was duly signed by Jeremiah Morrow of Ohio and brought out 119 members.

Clay attended the meeting and immediately offered a resolution that it was "inexpedient" for the caucus to make any recommendation to the people for the offices of President and Vice President. The resolution was promptly rejected. Monroe and Crawford were placed in nomination, even though Crawford had instructed his managers to withdraw his name and throw their support to Monroe. As it turned out, neither of his two managers attended the caucus. In the subsequent balloting Monroe received sixty-five votes and Crawford fifty-four. Daniel D. Tompkins of New York was given the vice presidential slot.[27]

By the time the congressional session ended not only had the Republican ticket been named, but a rather remarkable program of national development that established the legislative agenda for the next several decades had been enacted. Banking and currency, the tariff, and internal improvement were to be the major subjects for congressional action and political debate until they were superseded in the 1840s by slavery and sectionalism that led the way to secession and civil war. The Fourteenth Congress had pointed the direction for the nation's immediate future, a future to be shaped by the government's increased participation in the nation's economic development.

When Clay returned home after the adjournment of Congress, he was stunned to find that he had become a pariah. His constituents were furious at his active participation in passage of and support of the Compensation Act. Clay was not the only one to feel the sting of public outrage. Fully two-thirds of the House and half the members of the Senate were dismissed from office during the fall elections. Even those who voted against the "salary grab" were

26. Mooney, *Crawford*, pp. 53–77, 173–175; Harry Ammon, *James Monroe: The Quest for National Identity* (New York, 1971), pp. 352–357
27. *National Intelligencer*, March 14, 18, 1816; Lynn W. Turner, "Elections of 1816 and 1820," *History of American Presidential Elections, 1789–1968*, ed. Arthur M. Schlesinger, Jr., and Fred L. Israel (New York, 1971), I, 305–306; Ammon, *Monroe*, pp. 356–357.

booted from office. The people in their wrath expelled both friend and foe of the despised legislation. Some of these luckless congressmen chose not to run when they first encountered the fiery blast of public disapproval; a few resigned rather than face the humiliation of dismissal.

By the time Clay reached Lexington he knew he was in for a fight for reelection. Not only did his constituents fault him for supporting the Compensation Act, but they also criticized him for assisting the creation of the Second National Bank. He soon learned that delegates from various militia companies in his district planned to nominate a candidate to unseat him. But Clay divined that it was really a scheme "not yet avowed openly, to bring out Mr. [John] Pope," former member of the Kentucky House of Representatives from Fayette County and United States senator from 1807 to 1813. A Federalist, Pope had the dubious distinction of being the only member of the Kentucky congressional delegation to vote against a declaration of war in 1812. "The scheme," Clay predicted, "will not take." He expected other militia companies to refuse participation in the "scheme," and he asked his supporters to work toward that end.[28]

Sure enough, Thomas T. Barr announced his candidacy for Clay's seat in early June, but when delegates met at John Highbee's tavern and nominated Pope, Barr withdrew on the ground that with a Federalist in the race he did not wish to split the Republican vote. But Clay knew the contest would be rough, even without a split vote. Mass desertion to Federalist ranks seemed probable, and he had his hands full trying to prevent it from happening.

Fortunately Clay was a superb public speaker, which Pope was not, and throughout the summer he stumped his district, reminding his constituents of his tremendous and useful talents, his past favors, his patriotism, and his importance in national councils. In almost every instance he was obliged to explain why he had opposed recharter of the BUS in 1811 and favored it in 1816. He frankly admitted his fault. "It is I who have changed and not the Constitution. The bank was just as constitutional in 1810 as at the present moment; but I did not think so" in 1811.

Then he turned to the Compensation Act. And here Clay frequently showed what a exciting and resourceful performer he could be on the stump. After citing his sacrifices in serving his constituents and calculating that the additional tax on his district came to no more than five hundred dollars, he cried: "Yet for this paltry sum you would quarrel with your representative, a man, who has thro' a long course of years been a *faithful* if not an able servant. Did I ever neglect your interests? Have I not done all in my power to serve you? When the wide ocean separated us, when far from my wife, children, friends, and country, did I forget you, or neglect your interest? No; through an arduous negociation I supported your rights, and signed a peace which astonished Europe."

He invariably ended these speeches by playing on the strong nationalistic

28. Clay to Willis Field, March 25, 1816, in Clay, *Papers,* II, 181–182.

feelings that the late war had generated among westerners. "But it is now sneeringly asked, what have we gained by the war? . . . If we have not humbled Great Britain, we have taught her to respect us; if we have not got redress for past wrongs, we have in the spirit we have displayed, a guarantee against future injuries." The nation had achieved glory at New Orleans, and Clay said he remembered the joy he experienced when he first heard the news of General Jackson's victory. "I would not exchange the feelings, the joy of that moment for all the sufferings and sacrifices, which the war has cost me. Go, then, censure me for this, for the war, for the peace, or some other great act of my life, but do not quarrel with me for the mean, pitiful consideration of my tavern-bills at Washington."[29]

As a stump speaker Clay had few equals. And he knew it. He could draw sympathy from a crowd even when it demanded his blood; he could take its outrage and turn it to his own advantage. In all his speeches delivered during the summer and early fall of 1816, he assuaged the wrath of his constituents and reclaimed their devotion and support. To some extent he did it by acknowledging and accepting their anger over the Compensation Act and promising to work toward its repeal when he returned to Congress.

There is a story, which may be apocryphal, concerning an old hunter who had always voted for Clay but had now decided to vote against him on account of the Compensation Act.

"My friend," said Clay, "have you a good rifle?"

"Yes," came the reply.

"Did it ever flash?"

"Yes, but only once."

"What did you do with the rifle when it flashed,—throw it away."

"No," said the hunter, "I picked the flint, tried again, and brought down the game."

"Have I ever flashed," asked Clay, "except upon the compensation bill?"

"No."

"Well, will you throw me away?"

"No, Mr. Clay; I will pick the flint and try you again."[30]

Collectively Clay's constituents also decided to try him again, but his majority hardly came to six or seven hundred votes. It was the only time in his long political career when the electorate of his district came close to throwing him away. What helped enormously was Pope's opposition to the war, and on that issue Clay cut him up rather badly in several speeches that amused and delighted his listeners.[31] Later Clay acknowledged that his offense for voting in favor of the BUS was worsened by his "still greater offence" in supporting the

29. Speech delivered at Sandersville, a short distance from Lexington, on July 25, 1816, reprinted in Clay, *Papers,* II, 216–221.

30. Schurz, *Clay,* I, 139–140.

31. George M. Blakey, "Rendezvous with Republicanism: John Pope vs. Henry Clay in 1816," in *Indiana Magazine of History,* LXII (1966), pp. 233–250. On Pope, see Orval W. Baylor, *John Pope, Kentuckian: His Life and Times, 1770–1845* (Cynthiana, Ky., 1943).

Compensation Act. But, he went on, "my Constituents had the grace to pardon me."[32]

During the canvass President Madison wrote and informed Clay that Alexander J. Dallas had made up his mind to resign as secretary of the treasury and would be replaced by William H. Crawford, the secretary of war. Madison asked Clay if "you will permit me to avail our country of your services" as war secretary. The offer provided a way out of his electoral difficulties if he needed it, but Clay refused to take it. "Several considerations appear to me to require that I should decline accepting the honor," he replied to Madison, although he did not specify what those considerations might be. No doubt he regarded his position as Speaker of the House as superior—and it was. Probably nothing short of the office of secretary of state—or the presidency—was likely to tempt him to change his station, now or in the immediate future.[33]

Good to his word, Clay spoke and voted for the repeal of the Compensation Act when Congress reconvened, although he was honest and courageous enough to state that he still favored a higher per diem rate of pay. In his speech, delivered in the House on January 14, 1817, he said he "agreed perfectly in the sentiment, that instructions given by the people are obligatory on the representatives," a principle "consecrated by the revolution, inseparable from all free governments," and one he hoped never to see abandoned in the United States. Nearly a decade later this statement came back to haunt him when he chose to disregard the instructions of the Kentucky legislature in the House election of 1825 and failed to support the "western" candidate for President. When he went home after the last session, Clay continued, he had not met a single individual who did not think that the Compensation Act was improper. But in every instance those constituents agreed that a modest increase in the compensation was just.[34]

In January 1817 Congress repealed the Compensation Act and raised the per diem allowance from six to eight dollars.

Besides the House and Senate seats, the fall elections of 1816 involved a presidential contest, and James Monroe had absolutely no trouble in winning it. He received 183 electoral votes to 34 for Rufus King of New York, the Federalist candidate. Only Massachusetts, Connecticut, and Delaware supported King. The vice presidency went to Daniel D. Tompkins, who had served as governor of New York during the War of 1812 and had come under considerable criticism for his disbursement of state funds.[35] Throughout his tenure as Vice President Tompkins was to cause the administration acute embarrassment because of his drinking problem, no doubt worsened by accusations of fiscal improprieties as governor.

32. Clay to Caesar Rodney, December 6, 1816, in Clay, *Papers,* II, 257–258.
33. Madison to Clay, August 30, 1816, and Clay to Madison, September 14, 1816, in Clay, *Papers,* II, 226, 233.
34. *Annals of Congress,* 14th Congress, 2d session, pp. 495–498.
35. Turner, "Elections of 1816 and 1820," I, 308–309; Shaw Livermore, *The Twilight of Federalism* (Princeton, 1962), p. 34.

Inasmuch as the Federalist party seemed on the verge of collapse because of the suspicions of treason relating to its involvement at the Hartford Convention, Monroe had few worries about winning his election. Indeed, Clay began calling him "the President elect" as early as December 1816.[36] There was considerable talk about whom Monroe would choose for his cabinet, and Clay indicated to anyone who asked him that "the gentleman now abroad"—namely, John Quincy Adams—was decidedly *not* the man to head the State Department. Clay obviously wanted the post himself and said so openly. He was clearly jealous of Adams and extremely sensitive to the possibility that the New Englander might be chosen over him. And the rumors were not what Clay wanted to hear when he returned to Washington. Increasingly they named John Quincy Adams as Monroe's likely choice.[37]

But Clay was distracted during the opening weeks of the second session of the Fourteenth Congress by the illness of his two youngest children. He had brought with him to Washington his entire family, except for his two sons Theodore and Thomas. The children had contracted whooping cough, and shortly after the arrival of the family in the capital, the youngest, Laura, died.[38] To add to his distress, his son Thomas was involved in an accident that required medical treatment. Because of Laura's recent death, Clay said that his wife was "unusually sensible to even the remotest danger."[39]

At the beginning of the session Clay was repeatedly asked to serve as a director of the new BUS. He resisted at first. Later, after several more requests, he informed the recently elected president, William Jones, that if he were not expected to give more than "casual attendance" in Philadelphia, he would gladly serve. Since he was not a stockholder, he asked Jones to repair the oversight and purchase five shares for him, adding, "I need hardly say to you that I do not wish this letter to be the subject of any conversation."[40] Although "conflict of interest" did not exist in the thinking of early-nineteenth-century politicians, Clay himself was unusually sensitive about the operations of the BUS, and he warned one friend about appointing a majority of Republicans to the boards of the branch banks. "To confine it altogether to one party," he warned, "is to make it what it ought never to be, a party institution. That was the objection to the old bank of the U.States. If we set the example, and the major part of the stock should get into Federal hands could we then complain if they were to exclude every Republican?"[41]

36. "The Federal party, as a party, is almost extinct," Clay told William D. Lewis, January 25, 1818, Clay Papers, Manuscript Department, Filson Club, Louisville, Kentucky. Clay to Caesar Rodney, December 6, 1816, in Clay, *Papers,* II, 258.

37. Clay to Caesar Rodney, December 6, 1816, January 19 and February 22, 1817, in Clay, *Papers,* II, 258, 288, 316.

38. Clay to Christopher Hughes, Jr., December 8, 1816, in Clay, *Papers,* II, 259–260.

39. Clay to Thomas Morris, December 14, 1816, in Clay, *Papers,* II, 261–261. Clay does not specify the nature of Thomas Hart's accident in this letter, and no other documentary information has turned up to indicate what it might have been.

40. Clay to Jones, December 17, 1816, in Clay, *Papers,* II, 262.

41. Clay to Thomas Bodley, January 4, 1817, in Clay, *Papers,* II, 277.

When he was passed over for a position on the board of directors—surely participation on the board called for more than "casual attendance"—Clay claimed he "was quite indifferent about the place." But the president of the BUS went out of his way to assure the Speaker that no slight was intended, for the Bank needed and wanted Clay's active support.[42]

By the middle of February 1817 the President-elect made it fairly obvious that he had chosen John Quincy Adams to serve him as secretary of state. Adams had a strong record as a diplomat, and Monroe was very anxious to placate New England's resentment over the continuing influence of Virginia in the operation of government. The decision to appoint Adams was bad enough, but to add insult to injury, Monroe asked Clay to accept the office of secretary of war. It almost seemed as though Monroe were intent on embarrassing the Speaker. That, of course, was not his intention at all. Most probably the new President recognized that both Crawford and Clay wanted the office of secretary of state since it historically led straight to the presidency, so he chose Adams in order to avoid taking sides in their apparent political rivalry. To his mind, the appointments of Adams to State, Crawford to Treasury, and Clay to War would produce the ideal cabinet, free of discord and strife. Perhaps. Since Crawford already held the Treasury post, he might have rejected the offer to keep his place except for the fact that he could not afford to give up the patronage connected with his post, nor could he afford to jeopardize what he erroneously thought would be Monroe's backing for the presidency in 1824.[43] So he remained at his present position. But Clay rejected the offer of the War Department "in the most decided manner," whereupon Monroe compounded his error by inviting him to take the mission to Great Britain. This, too, was immediately rejected.[44]

Inwardly Clay fumed. He was furious with Monroe. His future actions and behavior made that fact eminently clear. Nothing in his surviving papers indicates how he felt or responded to the two offers. He kept his own counsel and said nothing. But when the arrangements for the inauguration of the new President got under way, Clay gave the first open indication of his resentment. Since the House of Representatives could hold more people than the Senate, a committee of the Senate in charge of the inauguration requested that the House chamber be made available for the swearing in and that the senators be permitted to have their "fine red chairs" installed for the occasion. Clay, as Speaker, responded that "the Senate had not, as a body, any right to regulate the Hall of the House of Representatives, or to arrange the furniture thereof,

42. Clay to James Prentiss, January 11, 1817, and Clay to William Jones, January 12, 1817, in Clay, *Papers*, II, 283.

43. Clay to George C. Thompson, February 22, 1817, Clay Papers, Manuscript Department, Filson Club, Louisville, Kentucky; Crawford to Gallatin, March 12, 1817, Gallatin Papers, New-York Historical Society; Ammon, *Monroe*, p. 358.

44. Crawford to Gallatin, March 12, 1817, Gallatin Papers, New-York Historical Society; Adams, *Memoirs*, IV, 73.

or to introduce other furniture into it, without the concurrence of the House of Representatives. . . . The furniture of the Hall, such as it is, was very much at their service."[45]

It was petty. But that was another characteristic of the man. Sometimes he could be monumentally petty—and supremely audacious in his pettiness.

This stalemate resulted in the inauguration's taking place outdoors. A platform on which Monroe was to take the oath of office was erected some two hundred yards east of the Capitol. Fortunately the weather was unseasonably warm and sunny, and a large crowd of eight thousand turned out to welcome their new President.[46] The failure of the House and Senate to agree on the inaugural arrangements was blamed on Clay, and several observers cited the loss of the State Department as its cause. Whatever doubts there may have been about the Speaker's motives instantly vanished when he conspicuously absented himself from the inauguration itself. The snub, if it may be called that, was deliberate and calculated. It was another very petty action, totally uncalled for. But it showed the depth of Clay's disappointment. He was desperate to become secretary of state, and unfortunately that desperation ultimately killed all his presidential aspirations.

Clay's childish action also provided the opening signal of a war he had declared on the administration and all its works. If Monroe did not think him worthy of the State Department, Clay could and would demonstrate what that hurt could mean in terms of getting a legislative program through Congress. In effect, he challenged the President to a power struggle over who would control the machinery of government.

For the past several years Clay had strengthened the Speaker's authority and influence in Congress enormously. He appointed the members of all committees, including their chairmen; he effectively controlled all business to come before the House; he interpreted House rules to suit himself and usually had no difficulty in enforcing his decisions; he directed the House into the Committee of the Whole whenever he wished to allow general discussion on an issue without taking any action on it; and he set the temper and mood of the House by his manner and style, eloquence, and powers of argumentation. Moreover, his fairness, respect for the other members, obvious affection for the House, and ability to command, to direct, and authoritatively to administer the business of the chamber—all won the admiration of his colleagues. Small wonder that each time the House selected a Speaker, Henry Clay was elected on the first ballot. Having acquired all this power and influence, the Kentuckian now chose to use it to cripple, if not shatter, the administration of James Monroe. The hubris of the man was monumental. Unfortunately, it was to do him as much harm as it did the President.

It would appear that Henry Clay meant to control policy making for the

45. Clay to James Barbour, March 3, 1817, in Clay, *Papers,* II, 320.
46. Ammon, *Monroe,* p. 367.

new administration by locating that power in the House of Representatives. It was an important article of republicanism that the legislature was the legitimate centerpiece of government. Now Clay was to define that concept more precisely by asserting to the fullest the authority and prerogatives of the lower chamber.

The short session of the Fourteenth Congress ended with the inauguration, and Clay returned to Lexington shortly thereafter while President Monroe toured the middle states and New England. The presidential tour occasioned the remark of a Boston newspaperman that a new era had begun in the political history of the country, an "Era of Good Feelings." When Clay returned to Washington, his "feelings" were anything but "good," at least as far as the administration was concerned. Realistically it was probably impossible to expect an era of good feelings when so many men of different political ideologies were crowding into the Republican party now that the Federalist party no longer functioned on the national level. Those who wanted to expand the powers of the central government and those who feared such expansion both called themselves Republicans, and their ensuing disagreements and quarrels distinguished this period as something other than an era of good feelings.

Henry Clay immediately took command of the congressional forces that favored raising the tariff on selected commodities, encouraging public works, and generally providing a more active role for the government in advancing the prosperity of the entire nation. All this horrified traditional Jeffersonian Republicans. These Old Republicans, or Radicals, as they came to be called, eventually turned to the secretary of the treasury, William H. Crawford, for leadership, hoping to restore traditional Republican values and ideology through his election to the presidency in 1824.[47]

The power struggles likely to develop over the next several years promised to tear the party apart, and the men who were to figure prominently in those struggles, including Crawford, Clay, John Quincy Adams, and Calhoun, held important positions at the beginning of Monroe's administration. After encountering a great deal of trouble filling the post of secretary of war, the President finally offered it to Calhoun, who promptly accepted it. The completed cabinet included Benjamin Crowninshield of Massachusetts as secretary of the navy, who was another holdover from the Madison administration but who was shortly replaced by Smith Thompson of New York, and William Wirt of Virginia as attorney general.

Calhoun joined the cabinet in December and proceeded to infuriate Crawford by inaugurating his own presidential candidacy. And since the secretary of state was generally considered the next in line for the presidency, an advantage Adams fully intended to exploit, that produced at least four men

47. Robert V. Remini, *Martin Van Buren and the Making of the Democratic Party* (New York, 1959), pp. 28, 46.

involved in power plays to advance their particular ambitions.

But only Clay was scheming to sink the administration, and he began his nefarious work immediately upon the opening of the Fifteenth Congress in December 1817.[48]

48. Clay was again elected Speaker on the first ballot. He received 143 votes to 1 for Samuel Smith and one blank ballot. See his remarks on assuming the Speakership delivered on December 1, 1817. *Annals of Congress,* 15th Congress, 1st session, pp. 398–399.

TEN

The Party Disrupter

CLAY'S FIRST OPPORTUNITY to assault the administration came over the question of Latin American independence. Spain no longer enjoyed the loyalty of its colonies in the New World, and its decline in power encouraged revolutionaries to plot the overthrow of Spanish rule. Revolt spread across South America during the Napoleonic upheaval, and this struggle for independence naturally won the support of many Americans.

Clay was particularly enthusiastic over South American aspirations for self-rule and had expressed his feelings publicly on numerous occasions, beginning as early as 1813. Then, when President Madison in the final months of his administration, in response to Spanish protests, tried to strengthen the nation's neutrality laws to prevent the arming and outfitting of ships in American waters, Clay opposed the bill because it would be advantageous to Spain in its struggle to subjugate its American colonies. He declared that "it would undoubtedly be good policy to take part with the patriots of South America. . . . We have a right to take part with them, that it is our interest to take part with them, and that our interposition in their favor would be effectual." Clay said that he "considered the release of any part of America from the dominions of the old world, as adding to the general security of the new." He hoped "the people of South-America . . . might triumph and nobly triumph."[1]

Despite Clay's efforts, a bill to prevent Americans from arming and equipping vessels of war in U.S. ports passed on the final day of Madison's administration. Thus, when the Fifteenth Congress began its first session in December 1817, the Speaker prepared to get the new neutrality law repealed. It must be remembered that this Congress was the product of a popular outcry against

---

1. *Annals of Congress,* 12th Congress, 2d session, p. 663, and 14th Congress, 1st session, p. 789. On U.S. involvement in Latin America's struggle for independence, see Arthur P. Whitaker, *The United States and the Independence of Latin America* (Baltimore, 1941); Charles C. Griffin, *The United States and the Disruption of the Spanish Empire, 1810–1822* (New York, 1927); Halford L. Hoskins, "The Hispanic American Policy of Henry Clay, 1816–1828," *Hispanic-American History Review* XLII (1927), pp. 155–169.

the Compensation Act and was keenly alert to public opinion. Moreover, few veterans of the House had survived the electoral slaughter, and those who had, like Clay, had seniority and years of experience to enhance their power and authority. In his premeditated assault on the new administration the Speaker had every intention of invoking all his powers and skills to strike back at Monroe. Even before Congress convened, he said he would make Latin American independence—in particular the recognition of the new republics—a principal issue for action by the legislature. In effect, Clay set out to replace the executive as the controlling arm in the conduct of American foreign policy.[2]

In presenting his first message to Congress on December 2, 1817, President Monroe seemed totally unaware of Clay's "resentment" and intentions,[3] and he offered a "cautiously friendly" account of the struggle between Spain and its colonies and of his wish to continue a policy of "impartial neutrality."[4] On the very next day Clay took the floor in the House to respond to the President's message as it related to foreign affairs.

He stood for a moment in the well of the House, his eyes sweeping the chamber, alerting the members to the fact that he was about to make an important statement. His deep, resonant voice, which echoed around the hall once he began to speak, helped him signal his audience to attention. As usual he started quietly and slowly. He urged the members to instruct its Committee on Foreign Affairs to determine what new legislation was necessary to ensure to the American colonies of Spain "a just observance" of U.S. neutrality in the ongoing war between Spain and its colonies. It was his opinion, he declared, that though evidence existed to suggest that Congress should "interpose its authority." At least, when we were "skulking" about Europe in 1778 and 1779, imploring "legitimacy" or "one kind look" or aid "to terminate a war afflicting humanity," we had "one great and magnanimous ally to recognize us": France. But no nation had stepped forward to acknowledge any of the Latin American colonies in revolt, he scolded, his voice now revealing the intensity of his feelings. Such disparity demanded a just attention to their interests, he argued. And if he was correct in his allegations, then "they loudly demanded the interposition of Congress."[5]

2. "Our Government, I believe, sincerely wishes success to the cause," Clay wrote to William D. Lewis, "but it indulges apprehensions, with regard to the power of Europe, which I think groundless, and which I fear may restrain it from doing even the little which I think we ought to do, and which in my opinion would not compromise our peace or neutrality." January 25, 1818, Clay Papers, Manuscript Department, Filson Club, Louisville, Kentucky.

3. Monroe seemed anxious to placate Clay and gave orders that the Speaker was to be admitted to his presence even when the cabinet was sitting. On one occasion Clay refused a servant's invitation to enter the cabinet room, then in session, whereupon Monroe came out and "took him into the council." Smith, *Forty Years,* p. 141.

4. Ammon, *Monroe,* p. 387; Richardson, *Messages and Papers,* I, 583.

5. *Annals of Congress,* 15th Congress, 1st session, pp. 401–404. "The subject of the Independence of Spanish America, in which I take a very lively interest, may possibly lead to the formation of new political sects." Clay to William D. Lewis, January 25, 1818, Clay Papers, Filson Club, Louisville, Kentucky.

Clay's amendment was adopted without opposition in the House, although few members regarded the Latin American issue with the same fervor as did the Speaker. But before too many weeks passed, it had become increasingly clear what Clay was about. Secretary of State John Quincy Adams immediately recognized his designs on executive prerogatives. He had studied Clay's antics long enough in Europe to know how he operated and what lay behind his "mischievous" behavior. Determined to reassert the administration's right to conduct foreign affairs and possibly convince Spain to sell Florida, Adams reduced Clay's motives to simple political ambition—namely, a desire "to control or overthrow the Executive by swaying the House of Representatives." The Speaker, Adams noted in his diary, intended to secure the recognition of the government at Buenos Aires, seat of the United Provinces of Río de la Plata, and perhaps Chile. He "had already mounted his South American great horse," Adams continued, and had sent proposals to Monroe via Crawford "professing a wish to harmonize with the Executive as to the manner" by which his objectives could be achieved.[6]

Three weeks later, on Christmas Eve, Clay and his wife dined at the home of Secretary Crawford along with the Adamses, Calhouns, and several members of Congress. It was a pleasant dinner party until Clay "came out with great violence against the course pursued by the Executive upon South American affairs." It startled everyone in the room. Adams compared his behavior with that of another notorious representative. "Clay is as rancorously benevolent as John Randolph," he declared. "He has taken his stand of opposition from the first day of the session, and his object is evidently to make grounds for it." He held neither the public nor the administration "in suspense concerning his intentions," Adams added.[7]

A few days later Clay struck again. "Being gay, and warm with wine," he singled out Crawford at another dinner party and "told him he meant to follow up his attack." Then he burst out with "And I'll beat you, by ———!"

It was embarrassing, indeed shocking. It was a sorry performance and clear proof of Clay's hurt pride and determination to get even. Clay also envied Adams. *He,* not Adams, deserved to head the State Department because *he,* more than anyone else in Washington, had earned the right to succeed to the presidency in 1824. As a national politician with a long record of public service, as a popular congressman and an incomparable Speaker, he deserved the presidency after Monroe. So convinced had he become of the validity of this claim that he needed to show Monroe the penalty he could exact for the humiliation of rejection. Of course, he would never have blurted out his intentions if he had not had too much to drink. He realized his mistake the next day and quickly sought out Crawford and assured him that "he was very anxious to avoid collision if possible"—all of which Crawford relayed to Adams.[8]

6. Adams, *Memoirs,* IV, 28.
7. Ibid., IV, 30–31.
8. Ibid., IV, 40.

By this time most observers in Washington knew that the office of secretary of state constituted the high stakes in this political game because it had become the immediate stepping-stone to the presidency. No matter who held it, that person won instant recognition as heir apparent, even if he had shown no interest in the presidency or had not been considered a viable candidate by the party leaders. At the same time all the other likely candidates for the office became his rivals. Adams understood this. "My office of Secretary of State," he wrote in his diary, "makes it the interest of all the partisans of the candidates for the next Presidency (to say no more) to decry me as much as possible in the public opinion." He also understood why Clay had made his opposition to the administration and contempt of Adams so obvious. "Clay expected himself to have been Secretary of State, and he and all his creatures were disappointed by my appointment. He is therefore coming out as the head of a new opposition in Congress to Mr. Monroe's administration, and he makes no scruples of giving the tone to all his party in running me down." Adams noted that Clay went about the House of Representatives "sneering" at a passage of a letter written by Adams to Luis de Onís, Spanish minister to the United States, in which the secretary of state had "said that the United States, after waiting thirteen years for justice from Spain, could, without much effort, wait somewhat longer."[9] Clay really had fun with that unfortunate slip. Obviously he was intent on seizing every opportunity to embarrass the administration and ridicule the chief spokesman for its foreign policy. He would have given a great deal to drive Adams from the cabinet, but the likelihood of that happening was extremely remote.

However much Clay hoped to wreak revenge on an administration that had passed him over, he did in fact sincerely and wholeheartedly support Latin American independence. Long before Monroe took office and "rejected" him as first secretary—a full year earlier, as a matter of fact—Clay had advocated American recognition and support of the rebels of Central and South America. So when his motives in seeking to alter U.S. policy toward Latin America were attacked, he stoutly denied any personal rancor toward the President or jealousy of the secretary of state. "I had rather have my present station than any appointment in the gift of any executive under heaven," he protested. "I court no favors."[10]

The Speaker also locked horns with Monroe over internal improvements, an issue that was to excite political passions for the next two decades and pit rigid states' rights conservatives against those, like Clay, who broadly interpreted the Constitution to permit greater flexibility to the central government in deciding its legislative authority. Simply stated, the question involved the constitutional right of the government to engage in public works. Strict constructionists declared that the Constitution prohibited the exercise of such a power. Without the consent of the states, Congress was forbidden to under-

9. Ibid., IV, 62–63. The letter had recently been released to the public.
10. Lexington Kentucky Reporter, April 29, 1818.

take internal improvements. This had been the thinking of Jefferson and Madison. And Monroe agreed with them. To get around the difficulty, the President now suggested a constitutional amendment.

The issue came to a head when a select House committee, reporting on the President's suggestion, rejected it and proposed that the Bank bonus be earmarked for internal improvements, a proposal that President Madison had vetoed the year before. The advocates of states' rights, declaring themselves the true believers of the Jeffersonian-Madisonian-Republican faith, pounced on the proposal, and a floor fight immediately ensued. On March 7, 1818, Clay joined the fight, stepping down from his chair and delivering one of his most ardent exhortations in defense of federally sponsored public works. Clearly, this issue had become an essential part of his political philosophy. It was to constitute one of the cornerstones of his American System. It took a commanding position in his developing thoughts about where the nation should be headed as the market revolution advanced and the American people moved into an increasingly industrial age.

Clay's object in this speech was to prove, if possible, the constitutionality of public works. He started off by reaffirming his commitment to the rights of the states and declared that he had drawn his political principles from the same source as his conservative states' rights colleagues—namely, the "celebrated production of Mr. Madison" known as the doctrines of '98 or the Virginia and Kentucky Resolutions of 1798. Then he pronounced the reason that convinced him that the government did indeed have the necessary power under the Constitution to approve public works: that "it materially tended to effect that greatest of all . . . objects, the cementing of the Union." We must look at the whole Constitution, he argued, at the history of the times when it was written and adopted, and "above all, at the great aim and object of its framers." He would give to the Constitution "a liberal construction" to everything that relates essentially "to the preservation of this Union." Commerce, of course, was important, as well as the "circulation of intelligence" so necessary to the existence of our government. "But most particularly union and peace were the great objects of the framers of this constitution, and should be kept steadily in view in the interpretation of any clause of it."

But he would not argue expediency alone, he declared. The document itself provided the necessary authority. It clearly stated that Congress shall have the power to establish post offices and post roads. Clay then spent several minutes trying to convince his audience that the words "to establish" meant "to make." Thus Congress could make roads. He further contended that the power was authorized "by derivation," in that Congress's exclusive power to regulate interstate commerce could not be exercised among the "interior states," like Kentucky, Tennessee, Ohio, and Indiana, without this authority "to make" roads. Are we in Kentucky and other western states to be told that a "continued stream of riches was to flow into the Treasury of the United States, without a single drop falling to fertilize the soil through which it passes? Or, would it not be admitted that equal justice to all parts of the country required that the revenue should be more equally distributed for the benefit of the respective parts of it?"

And what of the right to build military roads to provide for the defense of the nation from foreign invasion? Are such roads constitutional? Of course, they are, said Clay, and I "would make a road for ordinary purposes under the power to make a military road."

Clay ended his lengthy speech by contrasting his own position with that of his opponents. Conservatives, he said, regard everything gained by the states from the central government "as something snatched from a foreign power. I consider it as a government co-ordinate with them, and the true construction, I think, is to give to it all that vigor and vitality which rightfully belong to it."[11]

Unfortunately, in this otherwise statesmanlike approach to the question of government responsibility in the face of an ever-changing society, Clay stooped to lecture the President about human nature and political realities. It was totally out of place and again demonstrated the extent of the Speaker's injured pride. Monroe had recently toured New England and commented on the absence of party spirit and the harmony he found throughout the country. The President presumed to suggest that because of this harmony, a constitutional amendment to allow internal improvements might be possible in the near future. "Sir," Clay said mockingly in his House speech, "I do not believe in this harmony, this extinction of party spirit, which is spoken of; I do not believe that men have ceased to be men, or that they have abandoned those principles on which they have always acted hitherto." He went on to liken Monroe's tour to that of kings as they entered the Théâtre Français or Covent Garden. Previously, he said, only "scoffs and abuses, groans and hisses" were heard from audiences that now "enthusiastically join in the general applause, and swell the triumph."

It was petty. And the more he protested that his motives had nothing to do with his craving for the State Department, the more his colleagues quoted Shakespeare's line "The lady doth protest too much. . . ." Protesting his innocence over something he had said or done became one of Clay's habitual vices. He never seemed to know when to keep his mouth shut and simply walk away from the controversy he had provoked. "I came here to serve my constituents and my country according to the constitution, my conscience and my best comprehension of the public welfare," he pontificated. "I am no grovelling sycophant, no mean parasite, no base suppliant at the foot of authority. I respect the co-ordinate branches of government, but will exercise my own

11. *Annals of Congress,* 15th Congress, 1st session, pp. 1164–1180. "There is no prospect at present of a continuation of the U. States road Westwardly from Wheeling. It will take place some time or altho' one may not be able exactly to say when. My best efforts, whilst I continue in Congress, shall be directed to the accomplishment of that favorite object." Clay to John Coburn, February 20, 1819, Clay Papers, Manuscript Department, Filson Club, Louisville, Kentucky.

rights with the freedom which belongs to an American citizen, without fear of the consequences."

A week later he went after the President again. Again the speech dealt with congressional power to construct roads and canals. He accused Monroe of providing "no reasoning, no argument in support of his opinion—nothing addressed to the understanding" of his constitutional objections to internal improvements. "He gives us, indeed, an historical account of the operations of his mind . . . [but] without a single reason." During Monroe's tour he ordered a road repaired near Plattsburg to the St. Lawrence River, Clay added, as well as several other roads. "If the President has the power to cause these public improvements to be executed," cannot Congress do the same? And if the President recommended the establishment of a National Bank, as he did, was this not a "stretch" of the implied powers clause of the Constitution that far exceeded anything the advocates of public works had proposed?

Clay then tried to stir the legislature to guard its rights. One branch of the government must not gain power at the expense of the other. "We are now making the last effort to establish our power; and I call on the friends of Congress, of this house, or the true friends of state rights . . . to rally around the constitution, and to support by their votes . . . the legitimate powers of the legislature."

But his appeal fell on deaf ears. The best he could get from the House was a paltry resolution that Congress could appropriate funds for the improvement of roads and canals. It would not claim the power to construct them.

Clay again challenged the administration by moving an appropriation of eighteen thousand dollars for a minister to be sent to the independent provinces of the river Plate whenever the President deemed it expedient to send a minister to the provinces. He went on to give a splendid speech about the blessings of liberty and the responsibilities involved because of U.S. commitment to its preservation. He protested that he did not seek to force American principles on other nations if they did not want them. However, "if an abused and oppressed people willed their freedom," then the United States should take cognizance of it and act in accordance with its stated ideals and interests. "In the establishment of the independence of South America," he declared, "the United States have the deepest interest." He went on to describe what an independent South America would mean to the United States in terms of economic and political advantages. Trade and commerce would expand rapidly, and a free Mexico could be expected to stand with this nation in case of foreign attack.[12]

John Quincy Adams sighed aloud. "There is no member of the House of Representatives friendly to the Administration who has spirit and ability and mastery of the subject adequate to withstand him," he complained. Neither by "weight of character, force of genius, nor keenness of spirit" were the members

12. *Annals of Congress*, 15th Congress, 1st session, pp. 1468–1469.

able to cope with their imperious Speaker. Clay's angry and sometimes acrimonious efforts, said Adams, "trammel the means of giving aid to the South American revolutionists."[13]

And these spoilsport tactics finally got to Monroe. "The subject which seems to absorb all the faculties of his mind," reported Adams, "is the violent systematic opposition that Clay is raising against his administration."[14]

Nevertheless, Monroe's friends in the House, under pressure from the administration, marshaled their forces against Clay's appropriation proposal and sent it down to resounding defeat, 45 to 115. The Speaker knew it never had a chance of passage, but he said his "main object was to awaken and interest public attention in the great struggle to the South. That object, notwithstanding the efforts to misinterpret and misrepresent my motives, have been fully accomplished." His motion went down to defeat, he declared, because the "whole weight of the Executive" was thrown against it. Even so, "we had in support of it a respectable vote of pure and unmixed Republicans."[15]

By this time Clay had completely revealed himself to the members of Congress as a querulous and sometimes spiteful critic of the administration, poised at any moment to launch a blistering verbal assault against Monroe and his first secretary over any available issue.[16] Most often Clay went after them over their lack of policy toward Latin America or the right of Congress to authorize appropriations for roads and canals. His sharp verbal thrusts frequently drew blood, yet no one seriously challenged him. He was a potent and nimble debater and parliamentarian, and those representatives who dared defend the administration suffered a severe and thorough thrashing.

Clay was looking for real trouble when he unwisely decided to make General Andrew Jackson the target and instrument for his next act of revenge against the administration. The general was extremely popular with the American people by virtue of his tremendous victory over the British at New Orleans during the War of 1812. He was also a very quick-tempered individual who could act rashly and ruthlessly if his behavior on or off the field of battle was criticized or held up to public ridicule.

The string of events leading up to Clay's decision to select the general as his next victim began with the conclusion of the Creek War, when Jackson defeated the Indians at the Battle of Horseshoe Bend in 1814 and imposed a draconian peace, the Treaty of Fort Jackson, in which he forced the Creeks to surrender twenty-three million acres of land, or roughly three-fifths of the present state of Alabama and one-fifth of Georgia. Many of the hostile Creeks fled into Spanish-owned Florida, where they encouraged the Seminoles to attack the American frontier. These incursions, and a continuing desire to

13. Adams, *Memoirs,* IV, 64–65, 66, 71.

14. Ibid., IV, 70.

15. Clay to Henry M. Brackenridge, August 4, 1818, in Clay, *Papers,* II, 590.

16. "Last winter Clay's principal attack was levelled against the President himself, but . . . this winter confined his hostilities to me." Adams, *Memoirs,* IV, 212.

force Spain into surrendering Florida to the United States, prompted President Monroe in 1818 to direct General Jackson to put an end to the Indian atrocities and to cross the Florida boundary line if necessary. The First Seminole War resulted, and it added another laurel to Jackson's already resplendent crown of military victories. He not only invaded Florida but seized it from the Spanish! He easily defeated the slight show of Spanish resistance at St. Marks and Pensacola, he also attacked the Indians and burned their villages wherever he could find them, and he executed two British subjects, Robert Ambrister and Alexander Arbuthnot, after they had been tried and found guilty in a military court of providing aid to the Seminoles.[17]

Jackson's exploits thrilled most Americans. But others, including Henry Clay, were shocked and outraged. Not only had the general engaged in open warfare against a foreign government without constitutional authorization, but he had executed two British subjects, both of which invited formal declarations of war from Spain and Britain. The Spanish minister to the United States, Luis de Onís, demanded an apology as well as Jackson's punishment. Members of Monroe's cabinet, especially Crawford and Calhoun, also recommended Jackson's censure. Only John Quincy Adams defended Old Hickory. He argued that the invasion was defensive and necessitated by circumstances. With the approval of the President, Adams later informed Onís that Jackson would not be censured or punished and that "Spain must immediately make her election, either to place a force in Florida adequate at once to the protection of her territory . . . or cede to the United States a province, of which she retains nothing but the nominal possession, but which is, in fact, a derelict . . . a post of annoyance to them."[18]

It was at this point that Congress reconvened in December 1818 for its short session. Clay not only had all the ammunition he needed to strike a damaging blow at Monroe and his administration but could also cut down General Jackson, who was beginning to emerge as a possible presidential contender. Not only was Jackson a genuine and beloved American hero, but as a Tennessean he could easily compete with Clay for western votes. He could also compete with Crawford and Calhoun for southern votes, as both those cabinet officers understood only too well.

Because of the mounting pressure among rival and ambitious politicians in Washington to force Jackson's censure, the general decided to face down his enemies. He vaulted over the mountains with incredible speed and arrived in the capital on January 23, 1819. Already the House Committee on Military Affairs had reported its condemnation of the executions of Ambrister and Arbuthnot, and Henry Clay had delivered his first major speech against the entire Florida invasion.

The Speaker stepped into the well of the House to undertake this new

17. For a detailed description of this war, see Remini, *Jackson,* I, 341–377.
18. Adams to Onís, July 23, 1818, in *ASPFR,* IV, 497–499.

attack on January 20. Feeling and looking supremely confident, as he usually did, he relished the thought of the row he knew his remarks would provoke. Long and lean of body, his eyes mischievously darting from side to side, and his wide mouth slightly curled into a deceptive smile, Clay proceeded to display the full range of his extraordinary speaking talents. He was eloquent and witty, dramatic and playful, knowledgeable and devastating. It was one of the best speeches of his entire life. It was the sensation of the session. Widely publicized in advance, the speech drew a record crowd, including all the social lions of Washington. The Senate adjourned to hear him. Foreign ministers assembled early in the House to make certain they could get seats to observe everything that transpired. The gallery was packed with ladies and gentlemen "to a degree that endangered it," reported one witness, "even the outer entries were thronged and yet such silence prevailed that tho' at a considerable distance I did not lose a word."[19]

Clay spoke for two hours.[20] And he was heroic in performance. Sardonic, frequently sarcastic, and generally amusing, he "more than once made the whole house laugh." Only the friends and admirers of Jackson sat stony-faced during the speech since the frequent explosions of laughter came "at their expense."[21]

Clay began by disclaiming any animosity toward Jackson or, for that matter, Monroe. Toward the general he had nothing but the "utmost kindness" and "most profound respect." He had no other interest in what he was about to say "other than that of seeing the concerns of my country well and happily administered." He then reviewed the events leading to the invasion. The Treaty of Fort Jackson, he said, positively shocked him. "A more dictatorial spirit he had never seen displayed in any instrument." Its demands humiliated the Creeks with their severity: first the surrender of an enormous landmass, then the right to build military roads and establish trading stations in Indian territory, and finally "the obligation of delivering into our hands their prophets."

At this point all the histrionic energies within him began to flow. He electrified his audience. "When even did conquering and desolating Rome fail to respect the altars and the gods of those whom she subjugated!" It does not belong to the "holy character" of our religion to use the bayonet to force "into the bosoms of other people" the precepts of Christianity. "But, sir, spare them their prophets! Spare their delusions! Spare their prejudices and superstitions! Spare them even their religion, such as it is! from open and cruel violence."

19. Margaret Smith to Anna Maria Smith, January 1819, in Smith, *Forty Years,* pp. 145–145. Mrs. Smith said: "As you will read the speech in the paper, I will not detail it, although I could repeat almost the whole of it. But in losing the voice and manner of Mr. Clay, much of the effect will be lost." This last statement was repeated by many contemporaries. There is simply no way to capture the full flavor of Clay's speeches because so much depended on his "voice and manner."

20. This was considered at the time as a very short speech and disappointed many in the audience. Clay had intended to talk longer, but his voice gave out.

21. Smith, *Forty Years,* pp. 144–145.

The tension in the House was now so palpable that everyone sat motionless, not daring to stir.

Look at the words of Jackson's treaty, Clay continued. What do they say? "The United States *demand*. The United States *demand,* is repeated five or six times." That treaty was the "main cause of the recent war," and it provides melancholy proof that "hard and unconscionable terms, extorted by the power of the sword and the right of conquest, served but to whet and stimulate revenge, and to give to old hostilities . . . greater exasperation and more ferocity."

Much as Clay hated to admit it, the fault of igniting this war "was on our side." And in pursuing the war, two Indian chiefs had been lured aboard an American naval vessel that flew a British flag. They mistakenly thought they had discovered allies and expected to find ammunition and powder. Instead, they found a hangman's noose. Because of an earlier massacre of a detachment of soldiers at Fowltown, the chiefs fell victim of American vengeance. "Hang an Indian!" Clay shouted. "We, sir, who are civilized, and can comprehend and feel the effect of moral causes and considerations, attach ignominy to that mode of death." Not the Indian. Once captured, he is considered by his tribe disgraced, and therefore, he cares not whether he is shot or hanged. But it was the first time Clay had ever heard of "in which retaliation, by executing Indian captives, had ever been deliberately practised."

Clay paused, for his voice had begun to give out. He looked down at the floor. The audience waited. The silence was deafening. After a few moments he continued.

As for the executions of Ambrister and Arbuthnot, what could he say? Jackson's defenders admitted that the executions were "only a wrong mode of doing a right thing." Where, cried Clay, in what code of law or system of ethics, will one find "any sanction for a principle so monstrous?" Quoting from Jackson's own letter to the secretary of war, Clay read the following: "These individuals were tried under my orders, *legally* convicted as exciters of this savage and negro war, *legally* condemned, and most justly punished for their iniquities." Clay looked up from the paper on which these words were written. He shot a momentary glance at his audience. Then, quietly, he added: "The Lord deliver us from such legal convictions and such legal condemnations!" These men, he continued, should never have been tried and executed without the proper authority of the law. Of course, Clay slyly added, he "most cheerfully" acquitted Jackson of any intention to violate the nation's laws "or the obligations of humanity."

Turning next to the assaults and capture of St. Marks and Pensacola, Clay continued to batter Old Hickory. "It was open, undisguised and unauthorized hostility," he bellowed, nothing more.

As these passionate bursts intensified, Clay did not exclude the President from his criticism. What should have been done by the administration seemed eminently clear to him. "We ought first to have demanded of her [Spain] to restrain the Indians, and, that failing, to have demanded a right of passage for our army. But, if the President had the power to march an army into Florida without consulting Spain, and without the authority of Congress, he had no power to authorize any act of hostility against her." He was not disposed, Clay said, to censure the President for failing to order a general court-martial of Jackson since Monroe undoubtedly intended to pardon him in recognition of his past accomplishments. But let us not "shrink from our duty. Let us assert our constitutional powers, and vindicate the instrument from military violation.

"Beware how you give a fatal sanction, in this infant period of our republic, scarcely yet two score years old, to military insubordination," Clay warned. "Remember that Greece had her Alexander, Rome her Caesar, England her Cromwell, France her Bonaparte, and, that if we would escape the rock on which they split, we must avoid their errors."

The Jacksonians listening in the House must have turned purple with rage when they heard those words. Comparing Old Hickory with such tyrants! But Clay reassured them. Naturally he would never compare the despots of the Old World with a hero of the New. He once again begged not to be misunderstood. He was far from "intimating that Gen. Jackson cherished any designs inimical to the liberties of the country." He believed "Jackson's intentions pure and patriotic." Clay thanked God that the general "would not, but he [Clay] thanked him still more that he [Jackson] could not, if he would, overturn the liberties of the Republic." The Speaker believed that "our happy form of government" was destined to be perpetual. And it will be, he declared, by our practicing virtue, justice, moderation, magnanimity, and greatness of soul; "by keeping a watchful and steady eye on the Executive; and, above all, by holding, to a strict accountability the military branch of the public force."

It was a blistering assault. Despite his careful attention to all the niceties of gentlemanly conduct dictated by his position and authority as Speaker, he nonetheless crucified poor Jackson. His remarks sank deep into the consciousness of both those who heard him in the House and those who later read the speech after it was printed in the newspapers. They caused quite a sensation.

Clay ended the speech with a bang:

He [Clay] hoped gentlemen would deliberately survey the awful position on which we stand. They may bear down all opposition; they may even vote the general the public thanks; they may carry him triumphantly through this house. But if they do, in my humble judgment, it will be a triumph of the principle of insubordination—a triumph of the military over the civil authority—a triumph over the powers of this house—a triumph over the constitution of the land. And he prayed most devoutly to heaven, that it might not prove, in its ultimate effects and consequences, a triumph over the liberties of the people.[22]

What an explosion rocked the House when he finished! The tension had been nearly unbearable. When Clay stopped speaking, the release from the tension resounded throughout the chamber in a fearful burst of noise. Cheers,

22. *Annals of Congress*, 15th Congress, 2d session, pp. 631–655.

groans, shouts, applause, bedlam. Representative Richard M. Johnson of Kentucky jumped to his feet and tried to rebut the speech, but no one was listening. Everyone was busy commenting on what he had just heard. At length Johnson gave up. "After speaking without being listen'd to . . . [he] begged leave to defer what he had to say to the next day." Everyone thought that was a splendid idea, and the House went into adjournment.[23]

Hours and days after the adjournment people were still discussing Clay's masterful hatcheting of General Jackson—and President Monroe as well.[24] They all agreed not only that it was one of Clay's greatest speeches but that "it was one of the ablest speeches ever delivered in the House."[25] In terms of its impact on his audience, the Speaker had never been more persuasive. He had never been more eloquent, more theatrical, more completely in command of his subject and his listeners. Never had he thrashed his adversaries more thoroughly.

But it was also one of the most foolish things Clay had ever done in his life. He was not nearly as outraged about Jackson's behavior in Florida as he pretended. It was just that the general made an easy victim for Clay to exploit in admonishing the administration about its failures in foreign policy. He chose to excoriate a man who was an extremely popular war hero, a man who had provided the nation with a much needed military victory at New Orleans to convince the world that the United States had the will and might to defend its freedom against all enemies, even the most powerful. To assault this man made no political sense whatsoever. Indeed, it was inviting public outrage. Moreover, Jackson was a very excitable and vengeful man who could not abide criticism. Not from anyone. To attack him, to mock him, to make him the butt of nasty innuendos in a well-publicized speech was certain to incite his wrath and that of his friends, to say nothing of the general public at large. Clay had so much to lose by this assault that his decision to go ahead with it defies understanding.

Except that he was a gambler. He took chances, enormous chances. The bigger the better. The stakes may have been high, but so, too, were the possible rewards. And Clay had enough pride and arrogance to presume, at this juncture of his life, that he could get away with it.

Another thing. At this particular moment Clay did not look upon Jackson as a potentially dangerous political rival, one who could do him political harm or about whom he needed to worry. After all, Jackson was a "military chieftain," not a politician. Even though some vague talk had begun to be whispered in the corridors of the Capitol about the possibility of a Jackson presi-

23. *Annals of Congress,* 15th Congress, 2d session, pp. 631–655.
24. That evening Margaret Smith gave an account of Clay's speech to Secretary of War John C. Calhoun. Later she described this conversation in a letter to Anna Maria Smith: "Considering I was very much animated by the scene of the morning, perhaps you will not be surprised at our conversing without any interruption until 9 o'clock." Smith, *Forty Years,* p. 147.
25. Adams, *Memoirs,* IV, 224.

dential candidacy, Clay paid it little heed. Also, he presumed that Jackson would know that his remarks were not personal, not really directed at him as much as at the administration. Politicians frequently exaggerated their concerns, and their hyperbolic remarks on a public platform were not to be taken literally. Unfortunately Jackson did not see it that way. All he understood was that Clay had impugned his patriotism and his loyalty.[26]

From the moment the general heard about and then read this speech he developed a ferocious and full-blown hatred for Henry Clay. This speech marked the beginning of a feud that lasted until the end of Old Hickory's life. It was a feud that ultimately resulted in Clay's exclusion from the one office he most desired.

Because the Speaker never thought that Jackson would take his remarks so personally and so much to heart, he went to the general's lodgings a few days later to assure him that he meant no harm, that he always divorced personal rancor from public discussion, and that therefore he (Jackson) should obliterate from his mind any thought or idea that Clay intended to malign or injure him. "To evince that I was not actuated by any personal enmity towards him, in the opinions and sentiments which I had expressed to the House of Representatives," Clay later recalled, "I waived the ceremony of the first call to which, as Speaker, of that house, I was entitled, and visited him in the first instance." Unfortunately Jackson was not at his lodgings when Clay called. The Speaker therefore left his card in the hope that the general would accept this gesture as a peace offering. But, sighed Clay, "my visit was not returned."[27]

In fact, Jackson was incensed by the gesture. "The hypocracy & baseness of Clay," he wrote to a friend and neighbor, "in pretending friendship to me, & endeavouring to crush the executive through me, make me despise the Villain. . . . I hope the western people will appreciate his conduct accordingly," he went on. "You will see him skinned here, & I hope you will roast him in the West."[28]

Jackson could hate with a biblical fury, and he now directed it totally against Speaker Clay. He also knew how to exact revenge, something the Kentuckian had to contend with for the next three decades. Because the general was proud and extremely sensitive about his military accomplishments, he never behaved in any manner that would bring discredit on those accomplishments. In this instance, therefore, he acted with great circumspection during his stay in Washington. He remained quartered with advisers, refusing all

26. Jackson to Major William B. Lewis, January 25, 30, 1819, Jackson-Lewis Papers, New York Public Library. And Jackson was no fool. He knew that Clay had used him to get at Monroe.
27. Clay to Josiah Stoddard Johnston, October 6, 1827, in Clay, *Papers*, VII, 1114–1115.
28. Jackson to Major William B. Lewis, January 25, 30, 1819, Jackson-Lewis Papers, New York Public Library. "But my Dr. Genl," Jackson wrote to General Francis Preston, on February 2, 1819, "read Mr. Clay speech, a man who has been in the habit of praising my conduct, writing me friendly invitations to visit him . . . [and] would you believe it, that after he had delivered his famous speech and before it was publish he waited upon me at my lodgings." Jackson, *Correspondence*, II, 409.

social engagements. When Secretary Adams invited him to dinner, he declined: "Major-General Jackson presents his compliments to Mr. and Mrs. Adams, and regrets that he and his family cannot accept of their polite invitation to dine; having determined to decline all personal attentions of this kind until the issue of the proceedings in his case now pending before Congress."[29] In every respect Jackson acted with all the propriety and dignity that he could easily summon when circumstances dictated. He could always impress people with his elegant and commanding presence. To many his manner seemed downright "presidential." Extremely slender and slightly round-shouldered, he stood six feet tall and had strong cheekbones, a lantern jaw, intensely blue eyes, a long, straight nose, and a mouth that "showed rocklike firmness."[30]

Jackson's strategy to counter congressional antagonisms over his Florida adventure succeeded remarkably well. Almost everyone had expected him to do something rash, and people were gratified to find that he could be the very soul of propriety. Thus, on February 8, 1819, by a vote of 63 to 107, the House voted down the majority report of its Military Committee disapproving Jackson's handling of the Florida affair.[31] No doubt the members appreciated the retribution the public would exact if its hero was censured or punished. A few days later Old Hickory left for a triumphal tour of the northern states.

Henry Clay not only had been beaten but had created for himself a potentially powerful enemy who could do him great injury. And it was so needless. He really had no quarrel with Jackson. Indeed, he rather liked and admired the general despite his reservations about the events in Florida. He had no need for a feud with a westerner who could trounce him nationwide in any popularity contest. As John Quincy Adams noted, "His opposition to Jackson is now involuntary, and mere counteractive."[32]

Clay's ambition had been so whetted by repeated successes as a legislator, an administrator, and a diplomat that the presidency seemed certain once Monroe stepped down from office. For that reason he had refused the War Department and the mission to England. "Last winter," said Adams, "he aimed at the unlimited control of the House of Representatives, and at the formation of a Western party" to succeed Monroe.[33] Now, in a single moment, he had created a political enemy who would dedicate himself to blocking his political advancement. Now he had committed against General Jackson the first of a series of mistakes that would forever keep him from the White House.

29. Adams, *Memoirs,* IV, 232–233, note.
30. Henry A. Wise, *Seven Decades of the Union* (Philadelphia, 1872), p. 80.
31. *Annals of Congress,* 15th Congress, 2d session, pp. 1136–1138.
32. Adams, *Memoirs,* IV, 243.
33. Ibid., IV, 242–243.

—— E L E V E N ——

The Great Compromiser

W ITH THE EXCEPTION of John Quincy Adams, the other members of Monroe's cabinet agreed that Jackson should be censured for his unauthorized and embarrassing Florida adventure. Even the President himself felt inclined to punish the general, but he wisely decided to take Adams's advice and defend Old Hickory in public and keep his private thoughts to himself. Meanwhile, Adams continued his negotiations with the Spanish minister in the hope that a treaty could be signed wherein Spain would relinquish all claims to Florida—both East and West.[1]

Secretary of the Treasury Crawford had his own private reason for wanting to censure Jackson. To begin with, when he decided to return land taken from the Creeks in the Treaty of Fort Jackson and turn it over to the Cherokees who claimed it, Old Hickory threw a fit. That was *his* treaty, and no bureaucrat in Washington had any right to alter its provisions. The general therefore presumed that Crawford had a hand in the congressional investigation of his conduct in Florida. These "hellish machinations," he growled, were the work of "Mr Wm. H. Crawford and Mr Speaker Clay," and "I shall await the 4th of march next when mr Clay has no congressional privileges to plead."[2] Crawford was also disturbed by Jackson's continuing emergence as a presidential candidate. He had been building a political faction over the last four years to strengthen his own candidacy and had been quite successful in his efforts because of his adroit use of the enormous patronage available to him as Treasury head. The general was a distinct threat to his developing plans to capture the White House.[3]

Secretary of War Calhoun pressed as well for Jackson's censure because the general had gone over his head and asked the President for authority to seize Florida, not simply to subdue the Indians, as Calhoun had instructed him

1. Ammon, *Monroe,* pp. 428–430.
2. Jackson to Andrew Jackson Donelson, January 31, 1819, in Jackson, *Correspondence,* II, 408.
3. Remini, *Jackson,* I, 324–325, 378.

to do. He, too, nurtured ambitions for the presidency and was soon to discover his northern support slipping away to Jackson.

All this meant that for the 1824 presidential election four or five or more men would be scrambling for electoral votes. Clay could face possible opposition from Adams, Crawford, Calhoun, and Jackson. Adams would do nothing to advance his own candidacy, of course, being above that sort of thing, but his position as secretary of state automatically propelled him to the front line of candidates.[4]

Naturally Clay concentrated on Adams as his leading rival. Jackson he dismissed as a military chieftain with no presidential credentials. Crawford could be a problem because of his control of a huge patronage, but Calhoun was too junior a national figure to cause Clay much concern at this time. In any event, it was Adams who needed to be cut down from his commanding position, and the Speaker exploited every opportunity over the next several years to question, criticize, disparage, and complain about the nation's foreign policy.

Latin America continued to be Clay's best line of attack. Not only did he honestly favor the independence of the provinces in revolt in Central and South America and believe the administration should recognize them as independent nations, but he also believed that Americans generally supported all efforts of subjugated people to free themselves from the tyranny of European monarchies. "I am highly gratified to find that my poor exertions in behalf of our Southern brethren meet with your approbation," he told one former congressman. "They were made from a sense of duty, and with the view of promoting the cause of liberty." He explained to another man that despite attempts to "misinterpret and misrepresent" his motives, he had seen enormous enthusiasm for "our Southern brethren" in their struggle for independence, particularly during the most recent Fourth of July celebrations.[5]

When Adams succeeded in concluding a treaty with the Spanish minister to the United States, Luis de Onís, involving the disposition of Florida, he mockingly revealed that Clay's atrocious behavior had helped produce the treaty. "Before the Florida Treaty was signed," he wrote, "Clay's tactics were to push the Executive, if possible, into a quarrel with Spain. As he did not play his game very skillfully, his impetuosity contributed to promote the conclusion of the treaty."[6] The treaty, signed on February 22, 1819, called for Spain to cede all Florida to the United States, in return for which the claims by American citizens against Spain would be assumed by the United States to the extent

4. Bemis, *Adams,* II, 11–18.

5. Clay to James B. Reynolds, June 26, and Clay to Brackenridge, August 4, 1818, in Clay *Papers,* II, 581, 590. Clay also thought that the subject of Latin American independence might lead to the formation of "new political sects." Clay to William D. Lewis, January 25, 1818, Clay Papers, Manuscript Department, Filson Club, Louisville, Kentucky.

6. Adams, *Memoirs,* V, 25. The Spanish hoped the treaty would block U.S. recognition or intervention in Latin America.

of five million dollars. One article, written by Adams, stated that all royal land grants in Florida made before January 24, 1818, would be confirmed by the United States; lands granted after that date would be declared invalid. Once the Spanish government conceded that it must cede Florida to the United States, it prevailed upon the king to make two enormous land grants just a month before the cutoff date and still another large grant a day after the deadline.[7]

In addition, the treaty provided a southern and western boundary line for the Louisiana Purchase. It was fixed at the Sabine, Red, and Arkansas rivers and thence westward along the forty-second parallel to the Pacific Ocean. In effect, this provision relinquished U.S. claims to Texas, a provision Clay immediately spotted as cause to denounce the entire treaty. Later many Americans, especially southerners, condemned Adams's "illegal" abandonment of legitimately purchased territory. Jackson was particularly vociferous in his denunciation; however, at the time the treaty was negotiated, he told Adams that he approved the boundary line, most probably because of his desire to put the entire Florida affair to rest as quickly as possible.[8]

On February 24 the Senate unanimously ratified the Adams-Onís Treaty. But that did not end the matter. Spain took nearly two years to give its consent to the treaty, mainly quibbling about land grants and possibly calculating that the delay would stall any American effort to recognize the rebel governments in Latin America. Simón Bolívar and José de San Martín were the principal revolutionaries leading the cause toward an independent Latin America, and their military efforts had virtually shredded Spanish military authority within the provinces.[9]

That two-year delay gave Clay ample time to renew his plea for recognition of the rebel governments and attack the treaty as a shameless giveaway of American territory.[10] Indeed, by the beginning of the first session of the Sixteenth Congress, he had become such a royal nuisance to the administration

7. Hunter Miller, ed., *Treaties and Other International Acts of the United States of America, 1776–1863* (Washington, 1931–1948), III, 20ff.

8. Adams, *Memoirs*, IV, 239; Jackson to Francis P. Blair, October 24, 1844, in Jackson, *Correspondence*, VI, 326; Jackson to Monroe, June 20, 1820, Monroe Papers, New York Public Library; Remini, *Jackson*, I, 389–390. The Senate had taken up its own investigation of the Florida seizure, and a select committee issued on February 24 a report that was extremely critical of Jackson's conduct with respect to the capture of Pensacola and St. Marks and the execution of Ambrister and Arbuthnot. The committee made no recommendation, and the Senate ordered the report printed and laid on the table—in effect killing it. The *National Intelligencer* carried the full report the following day, February 25, 1819.

9. For the Latin American independence movements, see Irene Nicholson, *The Liberators: A Study of Independence Movements in Spanish America* (New York, 1969); Daniel O'Leary, *Bolívar and the War of Independence* (Austin and London, 1970); and Don Bartolomé Mitre, *The Emancipation of South America* (London, 1893).

10. On December 8, 1819, the President told Adams that Clay had given notice that he intended to bring up the recognition question in Congress, but Adams assured him that "the South American question was too much worn out, and . . . there would be members enough in the House able and willing to maintain the argument against him. . . ." Adams, *Memoirs*, IV, 472.

172   HENRY CLAY

that considerable thought was given to replacing him as Speaker with someone less troublesome. But whom could Monroe find? Clay was so preeminently superior to any other man in the House that his ouster not only would be seen as an act of open warfare but would surely infuriate westerners and trigger a power struggle that could prove disastrous for the administration. Unseating him would further advertise Clay's criticisms and make them appear overly important. While it was burdensome to continue to allow the Speaker to take potshots at the President's Latin American policy, it would be infinitely worse to challenge him openly and thereby establish him as the administration's leading opponent, around whom other dissidents could rally.[11]

Besides, as everyone knew, Clay had acted responsibly as Speaker. He had not used his power in making committee assignments to build up a personal following with which to attack the administration. He played no favorites. His appointments reflected his commitment to national concerns, in that all sections and interests in the country were represented.

Perhaps his unwillingness to misuse the powers of his office explains his ultimate failure to defeat administration policies. Surely it weakened his position as a presidential candidate. In any event, Monroe wisely refused to allow Clay's ouster from office, and the Kentuckian was unanimously reelected as Speaker.[12]

The President's message to Congress on December 7, 1819, informing the members that Spain had failed to ratify the treaty, set Clay off on another round of verbal assaults over what he now believed was a misbegotten agreement to dismember the nation. "I mean to propose the recognition of the Patriots and the Seizure of Texas," he told his friend John J. Crittenden. "These two measures taken, and Florida is ours without an effort."[13]

But his efforts to ignite the House into action against the administration was severely hampered by the emergence of two new problems. In 1819 the nation suffered an intense economic depression—the Panic of 1819—undoubtedly triggered by the action of the Second National Bank of the United States to stabilize credit and currency by calling in its loans and imposing a tight-money policy on the country. The collapse was severe enough to force Clay to look to his own financial situation and conclude that he must retire from public service at the end of the session and give greater attention to his law practice.

Also in 1819, Missouri applied for admission into the Union as a slave state, thereby upsetting (if it was admitted) the balance between free and slave states. To make matters worse, James Tallmadge, Jr., of New York proposed an amendment to the enabling act that would prohibit the further introduc-

11. Ammon, *Monroe*, pp. 498–499.
12. James S. Young, *The Washington Community, 1800–1828* (New York, 1966), pp. 131–133.
13. Clay to Crittenden, January 29, 1820, in Clay, *Papers*, II, 769; Clay to Adam Beatty, January 22, 1820, Clay Papers, Manuscript Department, Filson Club, Louisville, Kentucky.

tion of slaves into the territory and free those born in Missouri upon reaching the age of twenty-five.

These two problems, but particularly the latter, absorbed the attention of Congress to the exclusion of practically everything else, and Clay found it next to impossible to arouse any concerted action to aid "our Latin American brethren" or force the abandonment of the treaty with Spain.[14]

Still, Clay did his best against these impossible conditions. For one thing, he discovered the sleight of hand engineered by the Spanish in getting three huge tracts of land "the day before" (as he wrongly stated to the President) the date stipulated in the treaty. Monroe was shocked by the revelation and told Secretary Adams that if it was true, "a most shameful fraud" had been "practiced upon us."[15] Basically Clay was correct in substance about what had happened but wrong on the exact dates of the grants. In any event, Adams had stumbled badly on the question, and he was forced to demand that the Spanish government repudiate the three land grants. This was eventually done, but it increased the delay in getting a final ratification of the treaty and gave Clay added ammunition with which to cannonade the administration.[16]

In speech after speech on the House floor he blasted what he called "the blunders of a most ill conducted negotiation." Onís surrendered less than his instructions permitted, Clay insisted, and Adams surrendered territory without the permission of Congress. At one point Clay offered two resolutions: first, a resolution declaring that the Constitution designated the Congress with the power to dispose of territory "and that no treaty, purporting to alienate any portion thereof is valid, without the concurrence of Congress," and second, a resolution that Texas was ceded without an adequate equivalent and ought to be repudiated.[17] At another time he touched on something important about the American psyche when he explained why we troubled ourselves over Florida. It was one of the earliest statements about Manifest Destiny. "We wanted Florida, or rather we *shall* want it, or, to speak yet more correctly, we want no body else to have it. We do not desire it for immediate use. It fills a space in our imagination, and we wish it to complete the arrondissement of our territory. It must certainly come to us." And in return for something we did not need immediately and would certainly possess in time, the administration gave away not merely Texas but five million dollars "and the excess beyond that sum of all our claims against Spain," which had been estimated at

14. "For the present we think here of nothing but Missouri," Clay wrote to Jonathan Russell, "and I doubt whether we shall find time, during the Session, to march upon either Texas or Florida." January 29, 1820, in Clay, *Papers,* II, 771.

15. Monroe to Adams, March 8, 1819, quoted in Bemis, *Adams,* I, 337; Adams, *Memoirs,* IV, 287.

16. Miller, ed., *Treaties,* III, 42–49; Philip C. Brooks, *Diplomacy and the Borderlands* (New York, 1970), p. 100ff.; Adams, *Memoirs,* IV, 289–291.

17. Clay to Russell, March 24, 1820, in Clay, *Papers,* II, 797; *Annals of Congress,* 16th Congress, 1st session, p. 1691.

from fifteen to twenty million dollars. The treaty was absurd. Even the secretary of state admitted that Onís was "authorized to grant us *much* more, and that Spain *dare* not deny his instructions." Clay declared: "Let us proclaim the acknowledged truth that the treaty is prejudicial to the interests of our country."[18]

The administration's policy, he thundered, was bankrupt. Instead of recognizing the rebel provinces as independent republics to play on Spain's fears, the government had adopted a policy of strict neutrality in the hope that it would win ratification of the Adams-Onís Treaty. What a pusillanimous course of action! he sneered.

The next day Clay followed up these sharp remarks with resolutions again calling for the appointment of ministers by the President to those South American countries that had established their independence. A month later, when the House got around to debating the resolutions, Clay tore into the administration once again. The President, he insisted, had virtually conceded that his policy in obtaining treaty ratification "had totally failed." Once again Clay pleaded for recognition, reminding his colleagues of "the help we received, in our day of peril, from the hands of France." Are we to wait upon Europe before deciding on a course of action? Shall we trail behind and wait until Lord Castlereagh, the British foreign minister, and Count Nesselrode, the Russian foreign minister, decide that recognition could be legitimately given? "What! after the President has told us that the recognition of the independence of nations is an incontestable right of sovereignty, shall we lag behind till the European powers think proper to advance?" He went on:

What would I give . . . could we appreciate the advantages which may be realized by pursuing the course which I propose! It is in our power to create a system of which we shall be the centre, and in which all South America will act with us. In respect to commerce, we should be most benefitted: this country would become the place of deposit of the commerce of the world. . . . We should become the centre of a system which would constitute the rallying point of human freedom against all the despotism of the Old World. . . . Why not proceed to act on our own responsibility, and recognize these governments as independent, instead of taking the lead of the Holy Alliance in a course which jeopardizes the happiness of unborn millions? . . . Our Institutions . . . now make us free; but, how long shall we continue so, if we mould our opinions on those of Europe? Let us break these commercial and political fetters; let us no longer watch the nod of any European politician; let us become real and true Americans, and place ourselves at the head of the American system.

As far as can be discovered, this was the first time Clay used the expression "American system," although the general idea had been intimated several years earlier. It was an expression that was to capture his fancy and that of his

---

18. *Annals of Congress,* 16th Congress, 1st session, pp. 1719–1731. Clay to Amos Kendall, April 16, 1820, in Clay, *Papers,* II, 823.

followers around the country and take on additional meaning over the next several years.

The friends of freedom in Europe, Clay scolded, believe "our policy has been cold, heartless, and indifferent" toward a cause that should "engage our affections and enlist our feelings." Whatever the House finally decided to do in the matter, he said, at least he had employed his best efforts, at a moment when he was preparing to retire from public life, to help a people whose lives and future happiness were at stake.

Freedom! What was the United States all about if not human liberty? How can the American people enjoy its blessings, he asked, and not feel the compelling obligation to extend a helping hand to those who suffer oppression and persecution? How can they honorably turn away from their duty to share with the rest of mankind this most precious gift.[19]

It was a stirring and powerful speech. And from that moment onward the name of Henry Clay became virtually synonymous with any effort to advance the cause of liberty. From across continents and across oceans revolutionary statesmen were to appeal to him for guidance and assistance in their efforts to liberate their people from the rule of tyrants and despots. His became the voice that rang out clearly and regularly for "the freedom of mankind."

And the speech proved convincing to a number of Clay's colleagues. "Much to his own surprise and to that of almost everybody else" the House passed this resolution by the narrow vote of eighty to seventy-five.[20] This was his single victory on the question—but an empty one since the Senate simply placed it on the table and adjourned shortly thereafter.

Still, a greater and more lasting victory awaited him. Clay had championed Latin American independence, something the Latin Americans did not forget. His speeches were translated into Spanish and "read at the head of the armies of the South American republics"; statues were later erected in his memory; and in 1927, on the 150th anniversary of his birth, representatives from twenty Latin American countries assembled in Washington to salute his contribution to Pan-Americanism and his devotion and support of their efforts at winning independence.[21] Clay believed the rebels had proved their capacity for self-government and their ability to throw off the Spanish yoke. They therefore deserved not only recognition but the full support of the American nation. To this day Henry Clay remains one of the very few highly respected American statesmen among Latin American nations.

The Spanish Council of State finally conceded that it had no choice but to approve the Adams-Onís Treaty. The constitutional Cortes agreed. The king added his consent, signed the document on October 24, 1820, and returned it

19. *Annals of Congress,* 16th Congress, 1st session, pp. 2223–2229.
20. Adams, *Memoirs,* V, 108.
21. "Latin American Homage to Henry Clay," *Bulletin of the Pan American Union,* 61 (1927), pp. 539–546; Martineau, *Retrospect of Western Travel,* p. 175.

to Washington. Because the six-month term stipulated for the exchange of ratifications had long since run out, the Senate was required to approve the treaty once again. Despite Clay's opposition, the Senate gave its consent on February 19, 1821, with only four dissenting votes. Two of those four votes, John Quincy Adams noted, were the "minions" of Henry Clay.[22]

Adams could not help gloating over his triumph. Crawford and his partisans had hoped the treaty would fail, bring disgrace to the secretary of state, and eliminate him as a presidential contender, "while Clay and his admirers here were snickering at the simplicity with which I had been bamboozled by the crafty Spaniard." Well, he had bested them all. "By the goodness of that inscrutable Providence which entraps dishonest artifice in its own snares," Onís, Crawford, and Clay had come a cropper, and he, Adams, had triumphed.[23]

Still, Clay did not give up trying to win recognition for Latin America. Not until March 8, 1822, did President Monroe finally agree that the time had arrived to accept the fact that independence had been legitimately won by many southern republics and that Congress should vote the necessary funds to acknowledge the existence of these new states. "Yes!" snickered John C. Calhoun, "the fruit has now become ripe and may be safely plucked!"[24]

Although the United States was the first nation to recognize Latin American independence, it came almost seven years after Clay had first proclaimed the duty of the United States to extend its support to those fighting for freedom. And many of his remarks about restraining European influence in Latin America clearly foreshadowed the major principles of the Monroe Doctrine.

Clay's friends naturally credited him with leading the way to Latin American recognition, but the friends of the administration stoutly denied it. Calhoun scoffed that Clay reminded him of the farmer who insisted that his neighbors sow their grain in January. But they objected on the ground that it was much too early. The farmer persisted. Month after month he nagged his neighbors until finally, at the proper time in the spring, they sowed their grain and it "turned out prosperous and abundant." Naturally the farmer took all the credit since he was the first one who insisted on its being sown.[25]

When Clay returned home to Lexington at the conclusion of the congressional session, he had let it be known on May 10, 1820, during his speech on Latin American independence, that he intended to retire from public life and would not seek reelection. His law practice had declined considerably because of his involvement in national affairs, and his finances were in dreadful shape because of the economic panic and his readiness to come to the assistance of close friends and relatives by cosigning promissory notes. Because of financial

22. Adams, *Memoirs*, V, 285–286.
23. Ibid., V, 290.
24. Van Buren, *Autobiography*, p. 306.
25. Henry R. Warfield to Clay, May 5, 1826, in Clay, *Papers*, V, 307.

need, he had borrowed twenty thousand dollars from John Jacob Astor, which had to be paid plus interest prior to August 1, 1822.[26] "The just claims of a large family," he wrote, "and the attention which is necessary to my private affairs" were additional considerations.[27]

Some Washington observers, however, suspected that he would only resign as Speaker and keep his House seat, at least until the end of the Sixteenth Congress in the spring of 1821. In that way he could go home, increase his law practice, and then return to Washington in the winter and attend the sessions of the Supreme Court (to conduct his legal business) and the sessions of the House of Representatives.[28]

As a matter of fact, Clay did keep his options open when he returned to Lexington in 1820. At a public dinner given in his honor he said he had decided "to retain for a time the privilege of resigning or not, as circumstances might require, the remainder of his present term." As it turned out, he did resign the Speakership but retained his seat until the end of the session in 1821.[29]

On June 7, 1820, within days of his arrival in Lexington, Clay placed a notice in the *Kentucky Reporter* which announced his intention to "recommence" his law practice and that he would attend the Fayette Circuit Court, the Court of Appeals, and the U.S. Circuit Courts at Frankfort and Columbus, Ohio. For the remainder of 1820 he devoted himself almost totally to his law practice and was rewarded by an immediate increase in his caseload. Not until late December, after Congress had reconvened, did he leave Lexington and head back to Washington.

As Clay journeyed back to the capital, he stared at the well-settled farms nestled along the roadside with a deepening sense of foreboding. The Missouri question had caused a furor during the previous session, and as Speaker he had several times descended to the floor to attempt a compromise. The core of the controversy centered on the Tallmadge amendment to restrict the further introduction of slavery into Missouri as well as to free those slaves born in the territory upon reaching the age of twenty-five. Southerners raged over what they regarded as northern skulduggery to block the expansion of slavery. First

26. See the bond for forty thousand dollars between Clay, Robert Wickliffe, and John W. Hunt to Astor, April 10, 1819, copy CPP. The interest on the twenty thousand dollars came to forty-two hundred dollars.

27. See the mortgage deed, April 10, 1819; Astor to Clay, May 20, 1820; receipt from John Jacob Astor and son, July 31, 1820; and Clay to Charles Wilkins and others, June 3, 1820, in Clay, *Papers,* II, 865–867, 863, 868, 885.

28. Adams, *Memoirs,* V, 121.

29. Toast and speech at Lexington public dinner, [June 7, 1820], in Clay, *Papers,* II, 869. At this same dinner Clay remarked upon the "three great topics" that had lately commanded his attention in Congress. These three included internal improvements, domestic manufactures, and the "great cause of Freedom in South America." He said he hoped that the doubts and scruples about internal improvements had been laid to rest once and for all. He therefore spent most of his speech on the value of manufactures to westerners, "expressing the conviction that their encouragement was absolutely essential to our prosperity."

it had been the Northwest Ordinance of 1787, which forbade slavery north of the Ohio River. Now it was the territory of the great Louisiana Purchase. Missouri was the first area totally west of the Mississippi River to seek admission into the Union, and if Congress presumed the right to restrict slavery in that territory, then there was no telling when or where the restrictions would end. Slave property was protected under the Constitution, argued the southerners, and Congress had no right to hamper its expansion into the territories. The fact that a New Yorker, Tallmadge, in the House and another New Yorker, Rufus King, in the Senate led the movement in favor of the restriction intensified southern anger because it looked to them like a purposely contrived northern conspiracy against the South. Not only did King have a reputation of opposing western expansion, but in the Constitutional Convention of 1787 he had strenuously opposed the clause permitting southerners the right to count three-fifths of their slaves in determining representation in the House of Representatives.[30]

The Missouri question reawakened all the old fears and apprehensions. At one point in the opening round of debates Representative Thomas W. Cobb of Georgia shook his fist at Tallmadge. "If you persist," he cried, "the Union will be dissolved. You have kindled a fire which all the waters of the ocean cannot put out, which seas of blood can only extinguish."

So be it! screamed Tallmadge in response. "Let it come!"[31]

It was not only slavery that powered the excitement and furor of the House debate but sectionalism as well, the fear by people from one section of the country that another would take an unfair advantage of them whenever the opportunity arose. For one thing both North and South were apprehensive over the other's gaining more votes in the Senate, so that the admission of any state with slavery necessarily required the admission of a nonslaveholding state. For another, the advent of the Industrial Revolution and the market revolution produced conflicting economic interests, with northerners concerned about possible competition between free and slave labor in the territories. Increasingly the North desired government protection from foreign competition in the form of tariffs and government-sponsored public works, such as the extension of the National Road. And just as increasingly the South opposed such measures as a violation of the Constitution because they involved government participation in economic actions to favor only one section which the other had to help subsidize.

When the Tallmadge amendment was first proposed on February 13, 1819, Clay spoke against it. Unfortunately this speech and several others he gave on the Missouri question went unrecorded. Frequently he spoke very

30. King was undoubtedly the leading spokesman to argue the northern position during the Missouri crisis. His speeches were reprinted in pamphlet form and in many leading newspapers, including *Niles' Weekly Register*. See Glover Moore, *The Missouri Controversy, 1819–1821* (Lexington, Ky., 1953), p. 56.

31. *Annals of Congress,* 15th Congress, 2d session, p. 1204.

rapidly, particularly when excited, and reporters found it next to impossible to keep up with him.

Despite the lack of a full text, many of Clay's ideas and arguments may be inferred from the responding speeches of other representatives, especially those who disagreed with him.[32]

To analyze Clay's initial speech on February 15, when he attacked the Tallmadge amendment, two things need to be remembered: First, it was well known that the Speaker—and at this time he still served as Speaker—regarded slavery as an evil, despite the fact that he was a slaveowner.[33] He realized only too well that slavery betrayed his own deepest ideals about liberty and free government. Second, it was equally well known that Clay was an important leader of what he called "The American Society for colonizing the free people of color of the U. States," or, more popularly, the American Colonization Society. The society had been founded on December 21, 1816, in a meeting at Davis's Hotel, in Washington, at which Clay presided and gave a speech. The purpose of the society, he said in this speech, was "to promote the colonizing of the free people of color in the U. States, with their own consent, in Africa."[34] Its subscribers included some, like Clay, who believed that slavery was evil and that the emancipation of blacks and their removal to Africa would ultimately solve the slavery problem, but it mostly included southerners who worried about the place of free blacks in their society and wanted to get rid of them. Over the next several years the society probably relocated approximately one thousand persons to what later became the independent Republic of Liberia. In 1836 Clay was chosen president of the society and remained president to the end of his life.[35]

But the solution of the slavery problem in the United States through gradual emancipation and removal to Africa was illusory. Still, Clay chose to believe it was the answer—the only answer—because it provided the means of escaping the horrible consequences of a political struggle between the rising number of abolitionists in the North and slaveowners of the South. A few years later he wrote:

> My opinions are unchanged. I would still in Kentucky support a gradual emancipation. So I would in Missouri. The question I think in any State is a good deal affected

32. Actually some of Clay's printed speeches were what he himself provided the reporters after they had been corrected and sometimes altered.

33. When he gave this speech, Clay owned a dozen slaves, and this number increased to approximately fifty over the next two decades. Just before he died, he claimed thirty-three. See Clay's list of taxable property, 1851, copy CPP. But during his lifetime he did free several of his slaves who had served him faithfully, and he seems to have been a relatively decent and caring master. Even so, he was forced on occasion to contend severely with runaways, and he sometimes imposed punishments on rebellious troublemakers.

34. Speech at organization of American Colonization Society, December 21, 1816, and Clay to Monroe, September 22, 1817, in Clay, *Papers*, II, 263–264, 384.

35. For the society, see P. J. Staudenraus, *The African Colonization Movement, 1816–1865* (New York, 1961). See also James M. Gifford, "Some New Light on Henry Clay and the American Colonization Society," *Filson Club Historical Quarterly* (October 1976), pp. 372–374.

by the proportion of the African to the European race. In this State [Kentucky] I do not think that so great [*sic*] as to endanger the purity and safety of society. But I nonetheless believe that this question of emancipation of slaves, as our Federal Constitution now stands, is one exclusively belonging to the States respectively and not to Congress. No man is more sensible of the evils of slavery than I am, nor regrets them more. Were I the Citizen of a State in which it was not tolerated, I would certainly oppose its introduction with all the force and energy in my power; and if I found myself unhappily overruled, I would then strive to incorporate in the law, by which their admission was authorized, the principle of gradual emancipation.[36]

No doubt some of Clay's ideas about emancipation and colonization came from his mentor, James Madison, and possibly Thomas Jefferson. Also, his background as a Virginian during his formative years may have had an influence. For colonization as a condition for emancipation was an old idea that appeared as early as a 1691 Virginia statute. Later, during the American Revolution, the Virginia house of delegates debated a plan for gradual emancipation that linked it to colonization.[37]

The question of why a man like Clay who abominated slavery would own slaves himself was frequently asked in his own day and later. Apart from the reason he frequently gave to such queries about the severe difficulties that would be imposed on his blacks by their sudden manumission, there are several other possible explanations. One lies in the fact that he, his wife, and their families were raised in a slaveowning society, and it had been part of their very existence from the beginning. Another involves his probable recognition that if he continued farming (which he loved), he might have to move from Kentucky (which he did not wish to do) to a free state.[38] He felt he could not operate a large plantation or successfully compete agriculturally in Kentucky without them. Also, his pragmatic personality probably had something to do with it—that is, he accepted existing conditions he could not immediately change. Instead, he hoped to convince Kentucky eventually to change its constitution[39] and lead the way to gradual emancipation, thereby helping the nation produce the solution to a seemingly impossible problem.[40]

Clay's initial efforts against the Tallmadge restrictions in 1819 argued that the Constitution clearly states that the citizens of each state shall be entitled to all the privileges and immunities of citizens of the several states, and since the Tallmadge amendment would deprive a Missouri citizen of his slave property,

---

36. Clay to J. Sloane, August 12, 1823, Houghton Library, Harvard University, copy CPP.

37. Drew R. McCoy, *The Last of the Fathers: James Madison and the Republican Legacy* (Cambridge, Mass., 1989), pp. 282–283. See also George M. Fredrickson, *The Black Image in the White Mind: The Debate on Afro-American Character and Destiny, 1817–1914* (New York, 1961).

38. This is what several slaveowners did, including the Virginian Edward Coles, who moved to Illinois and became the state's second governor.

39. He certainly tried to do this several times.

40. Clay's speech before the American Colonization Society makes clear his belief that when a state refused emancipation, then one should work toward incorporating gradual emancipation into the law.

it was patently unconstitutional.[41] He also argued the cause of humanity, as Representative John W. Taylor of New York called it, by insisting that the slaves would be happier, better fed, clothed, and sheltered if they were allowed to be "dispersed" over the entire country rather than remain "cooped up" in the South.[42]

Despite his efforts and those of Philip P. Barbour of Virginia, the principal speakers for the southern side of the argument, the Tallmadge amendment passed by a vote of seventy-nine to sixty-seven. However, the Senate scuttled it by the overwhelming vote of thirty-one to seven.[43] But that was not the end of it. The issue was carried over to the next Congress, and Clay began to fear that unless a compromise could be immediately reached, it would lead to the worst of all situations—namely, the creation of *sectional* political parties. More than that, the specter of disunion had already appeared. "The words, civil war, and disunion, are uttered almost without emotion," he told Adam Beatty, a close friend and Kentucky legislator, and one senator said he would rather have both than fail in the resolution.[44]

A glimmer of hope for a compromise was spotted at the beginning of the next session, when Maine, the northern district of Massachusetts, petitioned for admission as a separate state in the Union. Clay saw the possibility of compromise immediately and openly declared that unless Missouri was admitted unconditionally, there was little chance of winning Maine's admission. Of course, he knew he did not have the votes in the House to tie Missouri and Maine together, but he recognized the merit of doing so and predicted it would happen in the Senate. And so it did. On February 16, 1820, the upper house united the Missouri and Maine bills into one, with Missouri admitted as a slave state and Maine as a free state, and then passed an amendment to it, suggested by Senator Jesse B. Thomas of Illinois, prohibiting the extension of slavery in the territory of the Louisiana Purchase north of 36°30′, with the exception of Missouri.[45]

Clay's first speech in the new Congress on the Missouri matter, given on February 8, 1820, was a spectacular performance. He spoke for four hours, and it consumed the entire "sitting" of the House. Again, unfortunately, his speech went unreported, possibly because it was a spellbinder, as one observer noted. "His mode of speaking is very forcible," wrote Representative William Plumer of New Hampshire. "He fixes the attention by his earnest & emphatic tones and gestures." Those in the audience sat riveted to their seats because of the

---

41. "I think the Constitution perfectly clear against the proposed restriction," Clay wrote to Jonathan Russell, January 29, 1820, in Clay, *Papers*, II, 771.

42. *Annals of Congress*, 15th Congress, 2d session, pp. 1180, 1182; Moore, *Missouri Controversy*, p. 46.

43. *Annals of Congress*, 15th Congress, 2d session, pp. 1193, 321–322.

44. Clay to Leslie Combs, February 5, 1820, and Clay to Beatty, January 22, 1820, in Clay, *Papers*, II, 774, 766.

45. *Annals of Congress*, 16th Congress, 1st session, pp. 831–833, 424, 427–430.

passion and flood of raw emotion he unleashed. They saw in every movement he made "the uncontrolled expression of violent feelings," said Plumer. Clay frequently shrugged, grimaced, and twisted "his features, & indeed his whole body in the most dreadful scowls & contortions." But the Speaker was such a consummate actor that these scowls and shrugs and contortions looked perfectly natural. There was absolutely no appearance of "theatrical effect" or of playacting. And when he sneered, as he did quite often, not one person in the chamber missed his intent or where or upon whom it was aimed. "If there is any passion which he expresses with greater force than another," reported Plumer, "it is contempt." Indeed, during this Missouri speech, he was even accused of using a "repulsive gesture" (another of his unfortunate habits) to warn "us not to *obtrude* upon *him* with our New England *notions.*"[46]

One of his arguments in this speech—again inferred from the responses of other members—bears close attention, for Clay expressed his belief that the ultimate end of slavery would come if the laws of economics and population were permitted to operate. With time, he predicted, the country would be largely populated with white citizens, thus driving down the price of labor so that free labor would become cheaper than slave labor. Once that happened, the slave states would free their blacks and presumably ship them back to Africa. Clay also insisted that a restrictive bill would deprive Missouri of the right of self-government and the untrammeled use of its police powers.[47]

Clay worked desperately to bring about a compromise even though he understood the problem of getting an unrestricted Missouri bill through the House. It was "a shocking thing to think of," he told John Quincy Adams, but he feared "that within five years from this time the Union would be divided into three distinct confederacies."[48] To prevent this catastrophe, he summoned every parliamentary skill and talent he possessed. Still Speaker, he wheedled and cajoled and threatened and resorted to all manner of "out-door politics" to spare the country what looked like a headlong rush toward disunion. At one point he pleaded with the Pennsylvania delegation not to desert their southern brethren. In the hope of influencing the Quaker vote in that state through the medium of the aged representative Thomas Forrest, Clay "wielded the powers of pathos in a manner so sublime and touching, that the old man himself became restless, and half the House were in tears."[49] On another occasion he declared in a speech full of bluster and nonsense that he would return to Kentucky and raise troops to defend the people of Missouri and their rights.

46. William Plumer, Jr., to William Plumer, Sr., February 12, 1820, in Everett Somerville Brown, ed., *The Missouri Compromises and Presidential Politics, 1820–1825* (St. Louis, 1926), pp. 8–9; *Annals of Congress,* 16th Congress, 1st session, p. 1210.

47. Washington *National Intelligencer,* February 9, 1820; the speech of John Sergeant in *Annals of Congress,* 16th Congress, 1st session, pp. 1173, 1197, 1206. In a later letter to William S. Woods, July 16, 1835, Clay summarized both sides of the slavery argument quite concisely. Clay, *Papers,* VIII, 786.

48. Adams, *Memoirs,* IV, 526.

49. New York *Daily Advertiser,* April 18, 1820, quoted in Moore, *Missouri Controversy,* p. 95.

Everyone knew "this is all talk, intended to frighten us out of our purpose," but the situation was so volatile and dangerous that Clay would even resort to this sort of mindless threat if it would help the situation and lead to a compromise.[50]

But certain individuals on both sides would not remotely consider compromise. Northern restrictionists who would impose conditions on Missouri were as vocal and denunciatory as the quixotic John Randolph, who wanted total surrender on the question. "God has given us Missouri," he shrieked in his earsplitting voice, "and the devil shall not take it from us." He reportedly proposed that all the southern delegations would depart Congress in a body if Missouri were not admitted without restrictions.[51]

The House rejected the Senate bill that tied Missouri and Maine together with the Thomas amendment, whereupon the Senate informed the House that it would agree to no other. An impasse. So a joint committee of the two houses, to which Clay appointed a majority of conciliators who favored compromise, was formed to break the deadlock. The subsequent report of the committee on March 2, 1820, urged adoption of the Senate bill. But as a mollifying gesture toward the House, the three parts of the bill—a free Maine, a slave Missouri, and no slavery north of 36°30' in the Louisiana Territory—were subsequently separated into three individual bills of legislation. And strangely, what was unpalatable as a single dose was swallowed by the House in three separate gulps.[52] "The Southern & Western people talked so much, threatened so loudly, & predicted such dreadful consequences," explained William Plumer to his father, ". . . that they fairly frightened our weak-minded members into an abandonment" of their position against slavery in the territories.[53] Eighteen northern congressmen either voted to eliminate the restrictive slavery clause from the Missouri bill or absented themselves on the final vote. Three votes made the difference.

John Randolph called the "weak-minded" northerners "doughfaces." He claimed that he had known all along that *these would give way.—*They were scared at their own dough faces—yes, *they were scared at their own dough faces!*"[54]

The Richmond *Enquirer* on March 7, 1820, called the compromise solution "a sort of parliamentary *coup de main.*" If indeed it was a parliamentary

50. Plumer to his father, February 20, 1820, in Brown, ed., *Missouri Compromises*, pp. 11–12.

51. Quoted in Moore, *Missouri Controversy*, p. 93.

52. The same thing happened in the passage of the Compromise of 1850. The advantage of having three bills is that it gave each member the opportunity to shift votes—that is, approving one bill but disapproving another.

53. March 4, 1820, Brown, ed., *Missouri Compromises*, p. 14. Plumer admitted that there was "some danger" the Union might be dissolved, although he himself was not moved by such threats.

54. Quoted in Moore, *Missouri Controversy*, p. 104. It is not clear what Randolph meant by "doughface." Something half baked? Something children smeared on their faces and frightened themselves in the mirror? Or did he mean "doe face" in reference to the "timidity of the female deer"? Ibid.

coup, only Speaker Clay had the position, ability, authority, and determination to pull it off.

Still, the House was not yet out of the woods. Randolph was determined to scuttle the compromise. On March 3, the day after the crucial vote on the Missouri question, Randolph rose in the House and asked that the vote be reconsidered. Speaker Clay turned to him with a look of studied contempt. After a moment he announced that the hour was late, the members exhausted. The motion, he declared, would be postponed until the following day. At that time it would be in order.

The following day Randolph rose to have the vote reconsidered. Clay ruled him out of order until the routine business of the House had been concluded. Meanwhile, as Speaker he signed the Missouri bill and had the clerk deliver it to the Senate. When Randolph rose once more after the routine matters had been completed, Clay blithely announced that the bill had gone over to the Senate and could not be retrieved. The Missouri vote, already taken, was final.

Randolph started shrieking. What colossal arrogance on the part of the Speaker! he cried. What contempt for the members of the House! He appealed to his colleagues to overrule Clay, but before a vote could be taken, the clerk returned from his errand. The Missouri business was finished. Did the House really want to begin it all over again? By a vote of seventy-one to sixty-one the members refused to reconsider. The thought of reliving the agony of the past several months was too ghastly to contemplate, much less endure.[55]

It was one of the neatest and cleverest parliamentary tricks ever sprung in the House of Representatives—up to that time. It was Clay's concluding achievement as Speaker. On March 6, 1820, President Monroe signed the Missouri bill. Although the Union had been threatened, if not endangered, by the Missouri crisis, he had provided absolutely no leadership. That role was handsomely played by Henry Clay.

When the session ended and Clay returned to Kentucky, he resigned as Speaker[56] but decided to continue as a House member until his term ended with the short congressional session in 1821. The task of restoring his law practice consumed most of his time during the summer, fall, and early winter. Meanwhile, Missouri went ahead to write a constitution and form a state government, as required by the enabling act just passed by Congress. The enabling act also provided that Missouri's constitution must be "republican" and not in conflict with the Constitution of the United States.[57] Naturally it was assumed that Missouri would write a constitution permitting slavery and

---

55. *Annals of Congress,* 16th Congress, 1st session, pp. 1588–1590.

56. He resigned on October 28, 1820.

57. *Annals of Congress,* 16th Congress, 1st session, appendix, pp. 2555–2559. It is interesting that Maine was admitted to statehood on March 15, 1820, as part of the compromise agreement, but Missouri was not specifically admitted at that time. It was merely authorized to write a constitution and form a state government.

that Congress would automatically accept it. But Missouri acted out its own resentment against congressional dictation by inserting in its constitution a clause that outraged the North. The clause required the legislature to enact laws to forbid "free negroes and mulattoes" from entering Missouri. Because free blacks were citizens in a few states, the Missouri constitution violated the second section of Article IV of the U.S. Constitution, which declares that "Citizens of each State shall be entitled to all Privileges and Immunities of Citizens in the several States." The immediate reaction among many congressmen on learning of this "affront" by the Missouri convention was to scrap the compromise. "The [enabling] act," wrote Plumer, ". . . contained conditions to be performed by [Missouri] & by us,—she has failed to perform her part—she cannot therefore call upon us to perform ours—so that the act of the last session is in effect void—Missouri is still a territory."[58]

By the time Clay reached Washington in January 1821 after a long journey filled with depressing thoughts about possible disunion, he found Congress in an uproar. The struggle in the House began immediately over the election of the new Speaker. It took twenty-two ballots before the northerner John W. Taylor of New York was elected over the southerner William Lowndes of South Carolina.[59] Then the Missouri question was introduced; but southerners insisted that Missouri was already a state, and therefore, no further conditions could be attached to its admission into the Union. "They want the guidance of such a man as Mr Clay," mused Plumer, "who, with all his violence & impetuosity, knew better how to control & direct his party, than any man they now have here."[60]

Not until January 16, 1821, did Clay take his House seat. "When I got there," he later recalled, "I found the members from the Slave States, and some from others, in despair. All efforts had been tried & failed to reconcile the parties." The compromise was in clear danger of coming unglued. The Senate had gone ahead and adopted a resolution for the final admission of Missouri with a proviso introduced by Senator John H. Eaton of Tennessee that "nothing herein contained shall be so construed as to give the assent of congress to any provision in the constitution of Missouri . . . which contravenes" Section Two of the Fourth Article of the Constitution of the United States.[61] But when the House took up a resolution declaring Missouri admitted to the Union on equal footing with the other states, it went down to quick defeat.

Another impasse. As congressmen shouted back and forth at one another, nobody seemed certain whether Missouri was a state or a territory. Once again the nation seemed headed back on the road to conflict and disunion. "They

58. Plumer to his father, December 3, 1820, in Brown, ed., Missouri Compromises, p. 21.

59. Annals of Congress, 16th Congress, 2d session, p. 434.

60. Clay to William S. Woods, July 16, 1835, in Clay, Papers, VIII, 787; Plumer to his father, January 13, 1821, in Brown, ed., Missouri Compromises, p. 27.

61. Clay to William S. Woods, July 16, 1835, in Clay, Papers, VIII, 786–787; Annals of Congress, 16th Congress, 2d session, p. 102.

begin already to talk of dissolving the Union," reported Plumer, "of admitting the Missouri Senators in the other Branch, & of many other desperate schemes."[62]

The situation was so grave that "both parties appealed to me," Clay later remembered, "and after surveying their condition I went to work."[63] On January 21 the House entertained a resolution, offered by William Eustis of Massachusetts, which admitted Missouri on condition that the offensive clause referring to "free negroes and mulattoes" be expunged. It was almost immediately defeated. Then Clay rose on January 29 and moved acceptance of the Senate resolution. In his remarks[64] Clay did not believe the offending clause of the Missouri constitution created an impossible obstacle to admission because the legislators of Missouri would be bound by an oath to support the U.S. Constitution, which would take precedence over their oaths to support the state constitution. Besides, if the legislators enacted laws in conflict with the Constitution, they would be struck down by the courts. Then he warned the northern restrictionists to think hard about the consequences of denying Missouri's admission. It might open its land offices, sell land at cutthroat prices, and say to all Americans, *"Here is our soil, come receive it, and defend us."* Think what that might lead to, cried Clay. Missouri would extend its possessions to the Pacific, and if it "receded from the general government," Kentucky, Tennessee, and Ohio might join it.[65]

As the long and animated debates on the motion continued over the following days, both sides of the question slowly acknowledged that Clay, the slaveholder, was not politicking but intent solely on preserving the Union. He understood the present danger and the need to focus his attention exclusively on that single object. And in keeping with that goal, he changed his manner and tactics. He "assumed a new character," said Plumer. "He uses no threats, or abuse" as he had when he was Speaker. "All is mild, humble, & persuasive— he begs, entreats, adjures, suplicates, & beseaches us to have mercy upon the people of Missouri." And his manner and tone were soon adopted by other southerners who saw the worsening storm ahead and wanted desperately to avoid it. Randolph, of course, went his own way and denounced each concession that was proposed.[66]

On successive days in early February five different amendments to the motion were put forward and rejected, one after the other. Clay said he spoke almost every day for two or three weeks. Finally, after one fruitless five-hour session, Clay proposed that the Senate resolution be referred to a select committee of thirteen in the hope of finding a solution to the impasse. It was a clever and timely proposal.

62. Plumer to his father, December 14, 1820, in Brown, ed., *Missouri Compromises,* p. 24.
63. Clay to William S. Woods, July 16, 1835, in Clay, *Papers,* VIII, 787.
64. These must again be inferred from the remarks of others since his own speech went unrecorded.
65. Motions and speech on the admission of Missouri, in Clay *Papers,* III, 18–20.
66. Plumer to his father, February 2, 1821, Brown, ed., *Missouri Compromises,* pp. 30–31.

Wearied by the interminable debates, many congressmen wanted to be done with the problem. At a caucus of northerners they "all agreed that the people at large had become tired of the subject, & wish to see the controversy closed without further delay." Clay apparently sensed this. Moreover, he knew that Missouri would be rejected in any immediate House vote, so he yanked the resolution off the floor and into a committee room. "This was an artful measure on the part of Clay," declared the admiring Plumer, "& will I have little doubt be in the end successful."[67]

With Clay's help—or rather direction—in making his selections for this committee, Speaker Taylor chose thirteen men known to be conciliatory, eight from free states and five from slave, with Clay as chairman.[68] Not unexpectedly the eight were dubbed "doughfaces" by Randolph. The committee, called the Committee of Compromise, labored under Clay's close, indefatigable, and magnanimous supervision and control. Its members wrangled for a week, and at one point a majority agreed to do nothing. But Clay begged them not to ask to be discharged. The next day he "induced" a bare majority to accept a report. It was the best he could do, but under the circumstances that was all he could hope for or expect. The committee vote was seven in favor of the report and four against. Clay, Smith, Lowndes, William S. Archer, William B. Ford, and Aaron Hackley of New York constituted the majority.[69]

Clay presented the report to the House on February 10. It called for the admission of Missouri "upon the fundamental condition" that the legislature would never pass a law preventing "any description of person" from settling in Missouri who is or might become a citizen of any state in the Union. When the legislature gave its assent to this condition, the President would proclaim Missouri a state.

In presenting this report, Clay moved that it be referred to the Committee of the Whole,[70] and in the course of the debate he remarked that the amendment required only "the performance of a precise and simple act" which, when accomplished, would free "public deliberations from the agitation and disturbance" that had characterized the entire controversy. If we persist in our endless debates and acrimonious accusations, he declared, we cannot fail "to produce, and possibly to perpetuate, prejudices and animosities" which can destroy this Union. He concluded by "earnestly invoking the spirit of harmony and kindred feeling to preside over the deliberations of the House on the subject."[71]

Despite these efforts, the Committee of the Whole decided against the amendment, seventy-three to sixty-four. This resolution was taken up by the

67. Plumer to his father, February 2, 1821, Brown, ed., *Missouri Compromises,* pp. 29, 31.

68. *Annals of Congress,* 16th Congress, 2d session, p. 510.

69. Plumer to his father, February 2, 11, 1821, in Brown, ed., *Missouri Compromises,* pp. 32, 34. Plumer doesn't name the seventh, but he does mention that Sargent favored the restriction.

70. Clay himself moved the motion by which the House resolved itself in the Committee of the Whole.

71. *Annals of Congress,* 16th Congress, 2d session, pp. 1078–1080, 1093–1094,

entire House, which, after further debate, refused to concur,[72] and the amendment proposed by the Compromise Committee was adopted. Utter confusion! The House then went to a third reading of the Senate resolution, as
amended, and defeated it by the count of eighty to eighty-three.[73]

The following day Arthur Livermore of New Hampshire moved for a
reconsideration of the vote on the Senate resolution, whereupon Clay pleaded
with the representatives at least to keep the door open for a possible solution
to the problem. Randolph protested this violation of parliamentary procedure
as "tending to prostrate the great constitutional barriers which surround the
powers of this house." But the representatives yielded to Clay's plea (101 to
66), and even though he made another impassioned speech for conciliation, in
which he "alternately reasoned, remonstrated, and entreated with the House
to settle forever this agitating question," the members once more defeated the
third reading of the resolution by 82 to 88.[74]

The crisis was compounded the next day when the two houses of Congress met in joint session to count electoral votes for President and Vice President. James Monroe and Daniel D. Tompkins were the candidates of the
Republican party and had no opposition from the Federalist party, which was
virtually extinct on the national level. Indeed, Monroe had won all the electoral
votes save one from New Hampshire, which was cast for John Quincy Adams.
What caused a "stormy & tumultuous" session was the fact that Missouri had
cast its three votes in the election. Northern restrictionists protested that Missouri was not a state and therefore could not vote, while southerners and
westerners insisted that Missouri was indeed a state and had every right to cast
its vote. What made it all seem so ridiculous was the realization that Missouri's
vote would not affect the outcome one way or another. But nerves were so
frayed that even the most inconsequential matter could set off an explosion.
For example, the Senate insisted that its president should preside over the joint
meeting. The House believed that the Speaker should share the honor, and this
was the procedure they finally adopted, which John Quincy Adams called an
"unprincipled fraud" and an example of Clay's "overbearing influence." Clay
also moved that the representatives receive the senators standing and uncovered and provide seats on the right side of the chamber. He and Mark L. Hill of
Massachusetts were appointed a committee of two to receive the Senate.[75]

The president of the Senate, the gentle and courteous John Gaillard of
South Carolina, led the procession into the House chamber. The galleries were
jammed with spectators, and everyone knew (or feared) what was about to
happen. Everything went smoothly as the recording of votes got under way,

72. By a margin of eighty-three to eighty-six.
73. *Annals of Congress,* 16th Congress, 2d session, p. 1116. Clay placed the blame for the defeat on
Randolph and on Weldon N. Edwards and Hutchins Burton of North Carolina. Clay to William
S. Woods, July 16, 1835, in Clay, *Papers,* VIII, 787.
74. *Annals of Congress,* 16th Congress, 2d session, pp. 1120, 1145.
75. Adams, *Memoirs,* V, 278.

but when Gaillard handed the Missouri vote to the tellers, Arthur Livermore of New Hampshire rose immediately and objected to receiving it on the ground that Missouri was not a state. Gaillard looked stunned. Instead of ruling the objection out of order and plunging ahead with the count, he hesitated. Instantly general pandemonium broke out. Senator John Williams of Tennessee called for the withdrawal of the Senate, and before anyone realized what was happening, the Senate rose and withdrew from the chamber.

Speaker Taylor tried to restore order. But John Floyd of Virginia, "in a violent & frantic manner," moved that the Missouri vote should not be thrown out. Randolph seconded him "in a speech of extreme severity & violence." They both were "for bringing Missouri into the Union by storm," declared John Quincy Adams, "and for bullying the majority of the House into a minority." Randolph went on for several minutes "til at length Clay growing impatient . . . interrupted him, & after explaining with great force & dignity, & liberality the correct course of proceeding, moved to lay the resolution on the table & invite the Senate back again." While Clay was speaking, Randolph asked him to yield. Clay agreed, but when Randolph went on too long, Clay demanded the floor back. Randolph took his seat, "saying that he would give way to the honorable gentlemen in every thing but one."[76]

With respect to the Missouri vote Clay brought forward an ingenious resolution in which he proposed that the total electoral vote of the entire country would be counted with Missouri and without Missouri, thereby providing what he called a "go-by." In either event the result that Monroe had been elected President and Tompkins Vice President would be announced.[77] Randolph and Floyd noisily objected to the resolution, but the House decided to accept the "go-by." The Senate was then invited back to complete the official canvass of the electoral vote.

When both houses reassembled, another wild scene ensued. The vote was counted, and when Gaillard announced, to no one's surprise, that Monroe and Tompkins had been elected, Randolph and Floyd demanded to know whether the Missouri vote had been counted. At first Gaillard acted confused and shaken by the interruption, but then he replied that he had no other function than to declare the results and that he would not answer any questions.

Gaillard started to give the results once again, but Floyd jumped to his feet and "with menacing gestures, & in a tone of defiance & rage, exceeding any thing I ever saw," recorded Plumer, tried to prevent the vote from being declared. Randolph joined in the fray as the Speaker pounded his gavel.

"Order! Order!" shouted Taylor. Floyd tried to appeal the Speaker's rul-

76. *Annals of Congress,* 16th Congress, 2d session, pp. 1147–1153; Plumer to his father, February 15, 1821, in Brown, ed., *Missouri Compromises,* pp. 35–37; Adams, *Memoirs,* V, 277.

77. The resolution came from a joint committee with the Senate to determine the mode of counting the electoral votes, and Clay, John Sergeant of Pennsylvania, and Solomon Van Rensselaer of New York served on the committee. Clay reported the resolution to the House. In the resolution Clay substituted the letters *A* and *B* for Monroe and Tompkins.

ing, as did Randolph, but Taylor told them both to sit down. By this time cries of "Order" came from every corner of the chamber.

Gaillard then completed his announcement. Randolph, still on his feet, renewed his demand to know whether the Missouri vote had been counted. Again the chamber rocked to cries of "Order." Still, Randolph continued speaking even as Taylor instructed him to be silent and take his seat. Above the din a voice was heard calling a motion for the senators to retire. Gaillard quickly put the motion to a vote, and the senators bolted for the door. They were relieved to escape the lunatic scene.

Although the conduct of many individuals could be faulted during this ridiculous charade, said Palmer, that of Henry Clay was "honorable to himself & useful to his country. . . . [And] in all the subsequent scenes of disorder & confusion, [he] kept his party down, & thus brought the election to a close in peace, if not in tranquility."[78]

But the Missouri crisis remained. Was Missouri a state or not? The question still had to be resolved. And to that end Clay now summoned all his political talents. Only he had such control of the southern proslavery representatives and such respect from northern antislavery restrictionists as to bring about a successful compromise—if such was possible. And he knew it. Moreover, he worried about the fate of the Union if compromise failed, and he kept reminding his colleagues of that frightening possibility. He therefore worked feverishly for the next two weeks—again wheedling, pleading, entreating, beseeching[79]—to find a solution to their problem.

On February 22 he moved the appointment of a special committee of twenty-three men to meet jointly with any committee the Senate might select, and together the members would consider and report on the question of Missouri's admission. It was also the day that the Congress learned that the Florida Treaty had at last been ratified. That meant the loss of Texas, a prospective slave territory in the Southwest. This knowledge may have assuaged somewhat the determination of northern restrictionists to exclude Missouri. In any event, the House by a wide margin approved Clay's proposal along with his unprecedented suggestion that the members of the committee be chosen by ballot rather than be selected by the Speaker.[80] For the committee, he wanted the best men possible, those he believed would, like himself, put the Union before everything else. He was therefore permitted to draw up a list of names[81] for

---

78. Plumer to his father, February 15, 1821, in Brown, ed., *Missouri Compromises*, pp. 38.

79. Clay said: "I coaxed, soothed, scorned, defied them, by turns as I thought the best effect was to be produced. Towards those, of whom there were many from the free States, anxious for the settlement of the controversy, I employed all the persuasion and conciliation in my power." Clay to William S. Woods, July 16, 1835, in Clay, *Papers,* VIII, 787.

80. The vote was 101 to 55.

81. Clay to William S. Woods, July 16, 1835, in Clay, *Papers,* VIII, 787. It is an indication of Clay's political skill that he included John Randolph on his list. To exclude him promised a temperamental outburst on the House floor at every turn. The list also included a large number of northerners who he felt were influential among restrictionists but who seemed receptive to a settlement.

this committee—everyone knew this beforehand—and circulate it through the House. This in itself showed the growing temper of the representatives to resolve the problem.[82]

The House selected the twenty-three members on Friday, February 23, and Clay's name, naturally, headed the list. The following day the Senate approved the proposal and chose seven members to meet with the House committee. Clay immediately summoned the joint committee to continuous sessions throughout the weekend. He set before the members substantially the same proposal for conditional admission that he had previously recommended in the House. He reckoned it the only possible solution. None better had been suggested. But he told the joint committee members that compromise was hopeless unless they gave the recommendation a strong vote and followed through in their respective houses by giving it their wholehearted support. "Now, gentlemen," he later remembered saying to them, "we do not want a proposition carried here by a small majority, thereupon reported to the House, and rejected. I am for something practical, something conclusive, something decisive upon the question. How will you vote, Mr. A.? How will you vote, Mr. B.? How will you vote, Mr. C.?"[83] He was delighted to discover upon taking the vote that the Senate members unanimously approved the proposal and the House members nearly so.[84]

Clay had the resolution printed Sunday night, and the very next day, Monday, February 26, he laid it on the desks of the representatives. This he did without the specific order of the House, but he wanted to move as quickly as possible. He believed he now had the support necessary to bring about what was later called the Second Missouri Compromise.

In presenting the resolution to the House, Clay explained that Missouri would be admitted on the same footing as the other states, provided the Missouri legislature solemnly pledged that laws would never be enacted to deprive any citizen of any state the rights and privileges that were protected by the U.S. Constitution. The proposal was debated for an hour, and a few times there were some sharp exchanges, although nothing like what had occurred over the past several weeks. Clearly the House was "in a favourable mood." Among restrictionists "it was evident that we were losing ground," said Plumer.[85] The resolution now moved rapidly through its several readings, and when the final vote was called, some eighty-seven Representatives approved while eighty-one disapproved. Everyone must have let out a sigh of relief. Among southerners only Randolph voted no. Eighteen northerners voted for the compromise.

82. Benton, *Thirty Years' View,* I, 10.

83. *Congressional Globe,* 31st Congress, 1st session, p. 125.

84. Of the seven senators, six approved. Rufus King, the seventh member, did not attend, claiming health problems, which some interpreted as more mental than physical. Plumer to his father, February 26, 1821, in Brown, ed., *Missouri Compromises,* p. 42; Moore, *Missouri Controversy,* p. 156.

85. Plumer to his father, February 26, 1821, in Brown, ed., *Missouri Compromises,* p. 42.

Two days later the Senate approved the measure, twenty-eight to four-teen. Four months after this congressional action the Missouri legislature ac-cepted the condition for admission but added its claim that the Congress had no right to bind the state. On August 10, 1821, President Monroe declared Missouri the twenty-fourth state in the Union.[86]

Clay had done his work well. "I was exhausted," he later recounted, "and I am perfectly satisfied that I could not have borne three weeks more of such excitement and exertion." One congressman credited the final solution to Clay's "unexampled perseverance." While many others were raving, ranting, or wringing their hands, he devised a concrete proposal and caucused with indi-vidual representatives to win their "conversions." He worked into the early-morning hours, day after day, to bring the Congress to a final solution, win-ning votes for what he saw as the only way to perpetuate the Union. He cut corners on occasion and pulled off some sleight of hand maneuvers, but he felt justified in view of the enormous risks at stake.

The Second Missouri Compromise was almost totally Clay's doing. And everyone acknowledged that fact. People hailed him as the "saviour of his country," just as they had hailed General Jackson after the Battle of New Orleans. He was now called the Great Compromiser or the Great Pacificator. Thomas Hart Benton, soon to take his seat as Missouri's first senator, named him the "Pacificator of ten millions of Brothers." Langdon Cheves, president of the BUS, told Clay: "The Constitution of the Union was in danger & has been Saved."[87] And what he said was exactly true.

In time people forgot that there were two Missouri Compromises, the second far more dangerous and threatening than the first. They gave Clay credit for "the" Missouri Compromise of 1820, "despite his repeated declara-tion to the contrary." But not even he could deny that virtually alone he authored the final settlement that succeeded in bringing Missouri into the Union without bloodshed or the dismemberment of the American nation.[88]

---

86. *Annals of Congress,* 16th Congress, 2d session, pp. 262, 264, 390, 1238–1240; Moore, *Missouri Controversy,* pp. 156–158; Plumer to his father, February 26, 1821, in Brown, ed., *Missouri Compromises,* p. 43.

87. Moore, *Missouri Controversy,* pp. 157–159; Van Deusen, *Clay,* p. 148; Cheves to Clay, March 3, 1821, in Clay, *Papers,* III, 58.

88. Benton, *Thirty Years' View,* I, 10. "Never have I seen the Union in such danger," Clay wrote fifteen years later. Clay to William S. Woods, July 16, 1835, in Clay, *Papers,* VIII, 787.

─── T W E L V E ───

Retirement from Politics

UT A STORMY and potentially dangerous cloud remained.
The South took great exception to northern success at restrict-
ing slavery in the territories. Southerners had been forced to
accept this "violation of the constitution" because it was the only way to bring
Missouri into the Union. But they did it by sacrificing the right to take their
slave property wherever they wished without concerning themselves about
restrictions from Congress. Now, with the loss of Texas because of the Florida
Treaty, only a very few slave states could be carved from the territory south of
36°30′ while many more free states were likely from the area to the north.
Thereafter the acquisition of Texas became essential to the hopes and needs of
southern expansionists.

Although the Missouri Compromises had stabilized the nation and restored a degree of harmony after this devastating jolt over the question of
admission, the signs of future discord and disruption were clearly discernible.
Thomas Jefferson, living in retirement, warned that it was just "a speck on our
horizon" which might very well "burst on us as a tornado." It deeply alarmed
him. It was like hearing "a fire-bell in the night," he told Congressman John
Holmes.[1]

Other men heard the awful clang as well. Slavery had now entered political discourse at the very seat of government and had multiplied the already
existing divisions among the several states. Clay had gotten Congress past this
first scuffle because he was trusted by his southern colleagues and respected by
all. But now he was leaving the House, and there was fear over what might
happen without him. As a final act before his departure he introduced a resolution of thanks to the Speaker, John W. Taylor, on March 3. It seemed appropriate that the former Speaker should offer the resolution, but unfortunately
Clay did it gracelessly. He referred to Taylor's election as the first indication of
"our divisions" and ended by extending the thanks of the House for Taylor's

---

1. Jefferson to John Holmes, April 22, 1820, in P. L. Ford, ed., *Writings of Thomas Jefferson* (New York, 1892–1899), X, 157.

"assiduity, promptitude, and ability."[2] Adams said it was a "short, studied, but grossly indelicate speech.[3]

Clay was also indelicate enough to go to President Monroe and complain that he felt he had a "just claim to, at least, half an outfit" for his public services while participating in the negotiations in London following the conclusion of the treaty negotiations in Ghent. Since John Quincy Adams had received half an outfit, he thought he had a right to one, too.[4] Clay was feeling the severe financial burden brought on by the Panic of 1819, his many gambling debts, his promises to stand behind the loans of friends and relatives who sometimes defaulted because of the panic, and the lack of a steady income resulting from his inattention to his law practice. So he shrugged off the possible embarrassment in personally presenting his claim to Monroe. He submitted his request and thereby placed the President in an extremely uncomfortable situation. Normally the matter would go to the State Department for a recommendation, but in view of Clay's hostility toward Adams, Monroe asked his attorney general, William Wirt, for an opinion. He received a favorable report, which he laid before the entire cabinet. Clay knew about the report because Wirt told him, and he kept badgering Monroe to come to a decision about it. Nearly a year and a half later and several more attempts by the Kentuckian to force a ruling in his favor, the President finally decided to get rid of what had become an irksome situation and allow Clay—much to the regret of Secretary Adams—$4,280 for the half outfit.[5] For the moment, however, Monroe waited before informing Clay of his decision.

During these "negotiations," if they could be called that, Clay had the gall to go to Adams to attempt to enlist his support for his claim. But he had other reasons to approach the prickly secretary of state. For one thing, he wished to assure Adams that he harbored no ill will toward him and hoped that the feeling was mutual. Since he was about to return home and since he expected to become a presidential contender four years hence, he decided that he ought not to leave Washington without attempting some friendly gesture toward his irascible rival. It was good politics.

The decision had all the marks of Clay's political cunning. To prepare the way, Clay spoke to Henry Brush of Ohio and assured him that he entertained "no unfriendly or disrespectful sentiment" toward Adams. Brush was "gratified" by Clay's declaration and promptly reported it to Adams, who responded by saying that "there had never been between him and me any ill understanding of *my* seeking." What Adams objected to, however, were the "sneers and sarcasms" expressed by Clay in the House and in the anonymously written

2. *Annals of Congress,* 16th Congress, 2d session, pp. 1294–1295.
3. Adams, *Memoirs,* V, 314.
4. Clay to Monroe, March 1, 1821, in Clay, *Papers,* III, 54–55.
5. Adams, *Memoirs,* V, 329–330; Joseph Anderson to Clay, July 12, 1822, in Clay, *Papers,* III, 258.

abuse he received in the newspapers. There was no way he could respond to them, he said.

After his initial gesture toward Adams via Brush, Clay followed up his campaign by calling personally at the secretary of state's office. But Adams saw right through him. He knew Clay's game, and he now had a pretty good idea what prompted the Kentuckian's visit.

The two men stood in sharp contrast with each other. The long, thin, bony Clay sat smiling at the squat, heavyset, gloomy secretary of state. His manner was relaxed and affable while Adams's was stiff and formal. According to Adams, his visitor's "morals, public and private, are loose, but he has all the virtues indispensable to a popular man. As he is the first very distinguished man that the Western country has presented as a statesman to the Union, they are proportionately proud of him, and, being a native of Virginia, he has all the benefit of that clannish preference which Virginia has always given to her sons."

They talked politics for a great while and about Clay's impending retirement from public life. Then Adams made his move. He suggested that after two or three years Clay might like to accept a mission abroad. Getting Clay out of the country would clear away an important rival to Adams's presidential hopes.

Clay responded with all the consummate acting skill he possessed. He smiled and behaved as though a great honor had been tendered him. He said he was gratified and obliged to Adams for the offer, but the state of his private affairs, he declared, plus his duty to his family, forced him to refuse the gracious offer. He then said that he had just made a "liberal arrangement" with the Bank of the United States in which he had been engaged as its "standing counsel" in Kentucky and Ohio. He anticipated that this lucrative position would relieve him of all his financial difficulties over the next three or four years, after which, Clay slyly added, he would return to the House of Representatives, where he felt he could render the most useful service to the country.

No doubt Clay startled Adams by next admitting that he regretted how his views on South American affairs had differed with those of the administration and also that he had been forced to speak out in a most confrontational manner. "He hoped, however, that this difference would now be shortly over."

The cautious Adams eyed his visitor carefully. He defended the policy adopted and said that he, too, regretted the differences between them. He never doubted, he declared, that the South American countries would win their independence, but he also stated that "our true policy and duty" forbade any interference in the struggle.

Clay did not pursue the matter, and Adams acknowledged that time would decide who was right. The secretary of state also admitted to himself that the Kentuckian had "large and liberal views of public affairs," but if Clay were President, his administration would be a "perpetual succession of intrigue and management with the legislature." Still, Adams concluded, with respect to internal improvements, his results would be "honorable and useful."[6]

Although Adams was not fooled by Clay's visit and realized that the Kentuckian wanted his support for "half an outfit"—which the President had put on temporary hold—as well as to "magnify his own importance" and rightful claim to the presidency, still, it had been a cordial exchange. Both men regretted past unpleasantnesses. Each acknowledged respect for the other's talents and accomplishments. And a few days later Clay went out of his way to assure Adams that he had addressed his request for the "half an outfit" to the President because of special circumstances. In no way did he mean to show Adams a discourtesy by circumventing the State Department. "I should be extremely sorry," Clay declared to him, "if such an impression were made on the mind of one with whom, I shall always remember with satisfaction, that I have co-operated in some very important transactions of our common Country."[7]

The secretary of state needed to hear this, and when the two men ended their discussion, they shook hands. Thus, a possible breach between Adams and Clay, which could have widened in time and become irreconcilable, had been avoided. It would now be possible for each of them, in the future, to cooperate with the other.

Unfortunately Clay failed to perform a similar action with Andrew Jackson. He had made an initial effort to contact the general after the scorching speech he delivered in the House, but Jackson had left town. Foolishly Clay did not follow up his intention to seek an interview with Old Hickory. If he had, it might have saved him much pain and trauma in the future. Although Jackson could hate with fanatical fury, he was also capable of letting bygones be bygones if it suited his needs. He later resolved a long-standing dispute with Senator Thomas Hart Benton, and their dispute included a gunfight in which Benton's brother, Jesse, put a bullet in Jackson's shoulder. Probably Clay believed Adams could seriously challenge his bid for the presidency and therefore needed to be soothed and reassured. Jackson, on the other hand, was a "military chieftain," to use Clay's term for Old Hickory, with only the barest of credentials for the presidential office. His sole public service of note involved killing Indians, Britons, and Spanish—hardly the prerequisites for the office of chief executive. And although the general's close associates and some misguided riffraff around the country might support his candidacy, wiser and cooler heads, thought Clay, would immediately recognize that Jackson was not fit for an office previously held by such statesmen as Washington, Jefferson, and Madison.

6. Adams, *Memoirs,* V, 305, 323–326.
7. Clay to Adams, March 18, 1821, in Clay, *Papers,* III, 70.

It was a colossal blunder on Clay's part. A wound that the Kentuckian himself had deliberately inflicted, but one that might have been healed with determined effort, was allowed to fester and finally to produce a permanent rupture between the two men. It was a wound that did Clay more harm than it did Jackson, and it definitely kept him from his most cherished goal. As a result, the nation was deprived at the highest level of the outstanding talents of one of its greatest statesmen.

A few days after Clay's meeting with Adams a dinner was given for the departing Kentuckian by his friends at Brown's Hotel. He was toasted and feted and wined. And of course, he made a speech.[8] Adams said that an occasion like this was an English practice which Clay seemed desirous of introducing into this country. "It is a convenient practice," Adams grumbled, "for men who wish to keep themselves forever in the public eye. It is for such men a triple alliance of flattery, vanity, and egotism." The occasion gave Clay an opportunity to be clever and witty and set up "clap-traps."[9] But whereas in Britain the diners go around the table and everyone is toasted and gives a speech, thereby providing an evening of wit and conviviality, in America it was becoming a vehicle for politicians to advertise themselves and display their "disgusting egotism."[10]

Adams was being his usual dyspeptic self. What Clay was doing made a great deal of political sense. He was retiring from public service but at the same time alerting everyone that he intended to return in a few years after his financial condition had improved. Clay never intended his departure to be permanent, and he did not want his colleagues to get the wrong idea that they could write him off as a future participant in the affairs of the nation and as a presidential contender.

Having secured his position in Washington as best he could, Clay departed for Kentucky in mid-March. He was very anxious to return home and begin the arduous business of making himself financially independent. Naturally, upon his return his friends and supporters tendered him a public dinner at Higbee's Tavern on May 19 in recognition of his "enlightened efforts" on behalf of the people of the entire nation. They assured him of their regret over his departure from Congress and expressed the hope that "at no distant period it may be found compatible with your private duties for you to enter again on public life."[11] Clay expressed his intense pleasure in the support he had always received from his constituents. Whatever the future might hold, he said, "I shall ever retain a fond and proud recollection of the many signal testimonies of their kindness and confidence."[12]

---

8. Toast and response at Washington Banquet, March 14, 1821, in Clay, *Papers,* III, 68.

9. A claptrap was a trick or device to get applause, an expression designed to win applause.

10. Adams, *Memoirs,* V, 330.

11. William T. Barry and others to Clay, May 12, 1821, in Clay, *Papers,* III, 76–77.

12. Clay to Barry and others, May 14, 1821, in Clay, *Papers,* III, 78.

The Lexington to which Clay returned in the spring of 1821 was suffering severe distress on account of the Panic of 1819. What worsened the debacle were the reckless speculations in land, the proliferation of "wild-cat" banks, and the widespread borrowing within the state. And the people blamed their distress on the Bank of the United States for having initiated the economic collapse by calling in its loans and tightening its credit policy. "All the evils which the community in particular parts of the country has suffered from the sudden decrease of the currency, as well as from its depreciation," wrote William Crawford, "have been ascribed to the Bank of the United States."[13] The reaction produced considerable state legislation against this "intruder" from the East. Nobody had invited the Bank into the several states, but the "monster," as Jackson later called it, had a charter from the federal government permitting it to open branches and operate its business wherever it liked. Six states slapped taxes on the branches within their borders, and fourteen passed stay laws to prevent the Bank from collecting its debts. In Kentucky the legislature rushed to the relief of its citizens by enacting stay laws against foreclosures, abolishing imprisonment for debt, and chartering the Bank of the Commonwealth with permission to issue three million dollars' worth of paper.[14] This Commonwealth Bank had virtually no capital of its own, and whereas Alexander Hamilton had once described banking as a means of supplying a large circulating medium (paper) on a small base of specie—roughly a ratio between specie and paper of one to five—Kentucky was stretching that ratio, according to one historian, from nothing to infinity.[15]

All this proved a bit embarrassing to Clay because he had accepted a position as chief counsel to the BUS in Ohio and Kentucky to alleviate his own financial difficulties and was obliged to bring suit against many debtors in his own state.[16] "It is intended by some of the friends of good principles," wrote Francis P. Blair, treasurer of the Bank of the Commonwealth, "to make an effort to turn out the malignant directors in the Bank of Kentucky & put in others, if not of our politics, at least some who will not exert the whole power of the Bank according to . . . H. Clay."[17]

The political situation in Kentucky worsened over the next several years as a result of the radical measures passed by the legislature. Ultimately the state's Republican party split into two opposing factions: the Relief party, which naturally supported the radical measures, and the Anti-Relief party, which did

13. *American State Papers, Finance*, III, 508.
14. *Kentucky Gazette,* February 22, 1821, summarizes arguments favoring the Commonwealth Bank.
15. Bray Hammond, *Banks and Politics in America* (Princeton, 1957), p. 282.
16. Some of this resentment may be seen in the presidential election of 1824, when Jackson carried eleven Kentucky counties against Clay. "The Kentucky election returns of 1824 show that a core of opposition to Clay had already taken form in Kentucky," argues Frank Mathias, "The Turbulent Years of Kentucky Politics, 1820–1850," doctoral dissertation, University of Kentucky, 1966, p. 94.
17. Blair to Joseph Desha, December 22, 1822, quoted ibid.

not. The Relief party comprised small farmers and debtors for the most part. Its leaders included John Adair, William T. Barry, Anthony Butler, George Bibb, Amos Kendall, and Joseph Desha.[18] The Anti-Relief party consisted of merchants and wealthy farmers and was led by Robert Wickliffe, George Robertson, Ben Hardin, Thomas Flournoy, John Pope, and John J. Marshall. They brought suit against the new laws and won their case before the Court of Appeals, Kentucky's highest court. The Relief people retaliated by using their influence in the legislature to bring about the abolition of the Court of Appeals and the creation of the New Court with new justices who were expected to reverse the decision of its predecessor.[19] The old justices of the Court of Appeals denied the power of the legislature to pass such an act and refused to surrender their offices. Naturally this Old Court was sustained in its contentions by the Anti-Relief party.[20]

The struggles between the New Court and the Old Court, which carried forward the quarrel between the Relief and Anti-Relief parties, shaped Kentucky politics throughout the decade of the 1820s and beyond. Clay tried to duck away from the squabbles within Kentucky and hide his true feelings from public view, but he clearly sympathized with the Anti-Relief people and "exerted hidden influence in behalf of the Old Court."[21] But the struggle did Clay considerable political harm. The Relief men had a better insight into Kentucky's financial crisis and won an immediate following. They subsequently formed within the state a powerful anti-Clay faction that seriously undermined his political power base.[22]

In the wake of the Panic of 1819 economic conditions in Lexington deteriorated rather rapidly. Unlike Louisville, sprawled along the southern bank of the Ohio River, Lexington could not hope to develop a commercial river trade and moved instead into manufacturing, such as hemp, textiles, and iron. But competition from abroad hampered the city's growth, and Congress failed to provided higher protective rates in 1820 as anticipated. The city stagnated. Although it was no longer a frontier community and now boasted fine brick homes and public buildings in place of log cabins, its population hardly moved forward and seemed fixed at five thousand. Lexington still called itself the Athens of the West, and Transylvania University added genuine intellectual distinction to the city's name; but by the 1820s Cincinnati across the Ohio

18. Many of these men later moved into Andrew Jackson's Democratic party, and at least two of them, Barry and Kendall, held important positions in the Jackson administration.

19. The best account of the Relief War is Mathias, "The Turbulent Years of Kentucky Politics," pp. 19–65. See also Arndt M. Stickles, *The Critical Court Struggle in Kentucky* (Bloomington, Ind., 1929).

20. David Meriwether, manuscript memoir, Manuscript Department, Filson Club, Louisville, Kentucky.

21. Mathias, "The Turbulent Years of Kentucky Politics," p. 98.

22. Frank F. Mathias, "Henry Clay and His Kentucky Power Base," *Register of the Kentucky Historical Society*, LXXVIII (Spring 1980), p. 127; Mathias, "The Relief and Court Struggle: Half Way House to Populism," ibid., LXXI, 165.

River seemed to have a better claim to the cultural title.

Clay returned home to a struggling city. His own financial difficulties eased considerably once he devoted full attention to his duties as a practicing attorney. To get back on his feet took several years of hard work. But unlike many of his constituents, he eventually pulled himself back into total solvency. And more and more he identified himself and his interests with those of the Bluegrass gentry and the manufacturing classes of his state.

Once home, Clay devoted himself to his family, which had grown considerably over the years. He and his wife had a total of eleven children, two of whom had died prior to 1821. Henrietta, the first child, died shortly after birth. The second child, Theodore Wythe, born in 1802, attended Transylvania University and showed promise as a public speaker. Thomas Hart followed in 1803, then Susan Hart in 1805, Anne Brown in 1807, and Lucretia Hart in 1809. Henry Clay, Jr., came along in 1811, and Eliza in 1813. Laura, born in 1816, was struck down by whooping cough at the age of three months. Her death devastated Clay. James Brown Clay and John Morrison Clay, born in 1817 and 1821 respectively, completed the immediate Clay family. Of his eleven children, only four survived him. Several of his children died in their teens, twenties, and thirties. Tragedy regularly touched his family throughout Clay's lifetime.

Educating this tribe posed numerous problems, part of which was caused by the distance of the Clay home from the neighborhood school. But another and more serious problem involved the lack of parental direction and discipline at home. Both Clay and his wife were absent from Ashland for long periods of time, and the children frequently ran wild. During the absences Theodore and Thomas had attended "a very ill-regulated school in Jessamine County" and had been "left to their own management," according to a new tutor. Upon Mrs. Clay's return from Washington in 1814 she hired Amos Kendall, a young, shy, and awkward Dartmouth College graduate, to tutor all her children. According to local gossip, she had heard that a young man, "solitary and poor, lay ill of a fever" in a hotel in town. She brought him to her home and "nursed him with her own hands till he recovered." Kendall never forgot the debt he owed her.

When Lucretia discovered Kendall's background, she asked him to take on the education of her children and offered him three hundred dollars a year, board, and the use of her husband's library. Also, reported Kendall, she "assures me of his [Clay's] assistance when he returns, which, she thinks, will be in six months." Kendall accepted—in "the hope of profiting by Mr. Clay's friendship," which did not come about because of Clay's absence in Europe—on condition that he had the option of resigning after six months, provided he found a substitute. He lasted a little more than a year. "Thank God," Kendall told a friend, "I am now in a place, which I would not exchange for any other within my knowledge."

Kendall was appalled by the behavior of his charges. The two boys had gone to a school where there was "no regular government, either in school or at their lodgings." As a consequence, they suffered serious academic deficiencies and had developed uncontrollable tempers. The fact that the family indulged them compounded the problem. Worse, Clay was hardly home. The principal parent needed for their proper upbringing scarcely paid them much attention. Not to put too fine a point on it, Henry Clay was a wretched father. Not only had he been away for long periods—over eighteen months during his European tour of duty—but even when he returned home, he was constantly distracted by politics, his law practice, or the running of his farm. He simply had other things on his mind and left the training and education of his children to his wife, not unusual for the time.

The "three fine little girls" were also quite "passionate, and have never been governed at all," declared Kendall. "But they are by no means unmanageable." On one occasion the new tutor heard a noise in the kitchen and rushed in to find young Theodore in a great rage, brandishing a large knife and swearing and threatening to "stab one of the big negroes." Without waiting to learn the cause of the fracas Kendall grabbed Theodore by the collar, seized the knife from his hand, and hauled him out of the kitchen. "If he were my boy," wrote Kendall, "I would break him of such tricks if it cost blood."[23]

Here was one of the first signs of Theodore's developing mental instability—the possible result of an earlier blow to the head that fractured his skull. At the time of the accident the boy's head "was trepanned by Doctor Pindell," who informed the parents that the boy would surely go to an "insane asylum."[24]

With the father missing a good part of the year, the problem of discipline was worsened by the mother's inability or unwillingness to assert her authority. Lucretia Clay lacked a "steady hand" in administering discipline, said Kendall, although on occasion she was obliged to give the boys—usually Thomas—a "severe whipping. . . . I congratulated her with real pleasure," remembered Kendall.

On another occasion, during a large party given by his mother, Thomas threw a tantrum, and Mrs. Clay asked Kendall to remove him from her presence. "Not very tenderly," the tutor dragged the boy, kicking and screaming, into the office. Thomas fought like a tiger and cursed his tormentor.

"You damned Yankee rascal," he cried, "you have been trying to make

23. Kendall to F. G. Flugel, May 14, 1814, Kendall Papers, Manuscript Department, Filson Club, Louisville, Kentucky. William Stickney, ed., *Autobiography of Amos Kendall* (New York, 1949), pp. 115–124; Martineau, *Retrospect of Western Travel*, I, 156. For Clay's early attempts at educating his two oldest boys see his letter to ?, April 19, 1813, Clay Papers, Manuscript Department, Filson Club, Louisville, Kentucky.

24. Stickney, ed., *Autobiography of Amos Kendall*, pp. 115–124, 149; Smith and Clay, *Clay Family*, p. 127. The tradition in the family is that the blow on the head caused Theodore to be subsequently committed to a mental institution. However, John's mental collapse later on leads one to suspect that a possible cause may have been congenital. However, there is no real evidence one way or another.

yourself of great consequence among the ladies this evening."

Kendall cuffed him once or twice, but uncertain as to his authority about whipping the brat, he just "let him bawl." The next morning Thomas was quite contrite and wished to apologize to Kendall for calling him a "damned Yankee rascal." Fearing the laughter of his siblings if he did, Thomas went to his mother and asked her to intercede. Hand in hand they approached the tutor. The mother begged Kendall's pardon for her son, which the tutor readily and heartily granted. "Notwithstanding his foibles," commented Kendall, "he is an admirable boy."[25]

Although Kendall faced impossible odds in attempting to control this unruly gang when he first began his employment, he slowly brought them around. With a firm and steady hand, along with Mrs. Clay's willing and total support, he eventually won their respect and obedience. After that he was able to make genuine headway with their schoolwork. He found that all the children, with the exception of Theodore, had fine minds, Thomas particularly. None of them understood English grammar, nor had they been exposed to Latin. To attack both problems, Kendall put them to work on Caesar's *Commentaries,* requiring them to write out their translations in their notebooks. "This is with the design," he wrote, "not only of impressing it more strongly upon the memory, but of improving them in writing and in English grammar." Before he left the employ of the Clay family, Kendall had improved the children's manners, behavior, and minds to a very considerable extent.[26]

Kendall subsequently went to Frankfort, where he purchased and edited the *Argus of Western America.* On saying good-bye to Mrs. Clay, he felt so obligated to her that he awkwardly stumbled for words and could not make the proper acknowledgments as he had intended. "She has done everything for me in her power," he wrote, "and I reflect on it with gratitude."[27]

Kendall did not meet the head of the Clay household until a year later. By that time Clay had returned from Europe, and the former tutor was anxious to make his acquaintance, no doubt in the hope of "profiting" from it. "I found him a very agreeable man," said Kendall, "and was familiarly acquainted with him in half an hour."[28] Later, when the Relief struggle threatened to cause Clay public embarrassment, Kendall offered to help. "The *Relief party,*" he wrote, "are very jealous of you. It is important that this jealousy should not break out into public expression and criticism. . . . In this situation I can do much to suppress their jealousy of you. . . ." Clay thanked him "for your kind offer of your pen and your [news]paper, I am infinitely obliged; and no doubt

25. Stickney, ed., *Autobiography of Amos Kendall,* pp. 115–124, 149ff.
26. Ibid., p. 149. Because of Thomas's ability, he was placed under the direction of a Mr. S. Wilson. "I approve entirely of it," wrote Clay to Wilson, "and if you can reclaim him from his habits of indolence (I believe he has none worse) you will do me an essential favor." Clay to Wilson, March 3, 1821, copy CPP.
27. Stickney, ed., *Autobiography of Amos Kendall,* pp. 115–124, 149.
28. Ibid., p. 172.

I shall have occasion for the friendly employment of both."[29] Unfortunately Clay failed to nurture this friendship in as handsome a manner as the editor had anticipated, and Kendall subsequently joined the Relief party, deserted to the Jackson cause, and proved a troublesome adversary to Clay, in both Kentucky and Washington. Kendall said he was loath to abandon Clay, his former benefactor, because it might label him a "vile and ungrateful man,"[30] but his personal situation drove him into the Jackson camp when Clay could not or would not meet his financial demands. Moreover, he really preferred the Jacksonian position with respect to banks, in particular the Bank of the United States, and when friends of the general threatened to establish an opposition newspaper in Frankfort, Kendall unhesitatingly shifted sides.

In 1821, upon Clay's retirement from Congress, the seventeen-year-old Thomas Hart Clay received an appointment to West Point, thanks to his father's intervention with the secretary of war.[31] Thomas was "strikingly" superior to his brothers and sisters in intellect and entered the Military Academy on August 31, with every hope of success. Unfortunately he failed mathematics in his first semester, and he was discharged from the academy on February 28, 1822.[32] Then he seemed to disappear. "I entertain strong fears that he has not gone home," wrote his alarmed father, ". . . and I am apprehensive that he remains in the City of New York." Clay asked a friend to help him locate his son. "The truth is," he said, "and I say it with infinite pain, that I have lost all confidence in his stability. I would yet indulge the hope that he has some sense of honor and propriety left. And yet $100 was advanced to him at West Point upon the pledge, as I am informed, of his honor, to proceed directly home . . . In short, he fills me, my dear Sir, with inexpressible distress." Thomas surfaced in Philadelphia, where he heard his father was headed. Humiliated and depressed, the young man finally returned home.[33] This may have been the beginning of what later developed into an acute problem of alcoholism for Thomas.

That same year, 1822, the ten-year-old Henry Clay, Jr., was enrolled in the preparatory school of Transylvania University where he completed his studies with a Bachelor of Arts degree in July 1826.[34] Shortly thereafter, Susan Hart Clay left the household when she married Martin Duralde of New Orleans on April 22, 1822. Both Clay and Duralde put up a "Just sum of £50.

29. Kendall to Clay, June 20, 1822, Clay to Kendall, June 23, 1822, in Clay, *Papers,* III, 237, 240.

30. Quoted in Mathias, "The Turbulent Years of Kentucky Politics," p. 83.

31. Calhoun to Clay, May 19, 1821, in Clay, *Papers,* III, 82–83; Clay to Calhoun, June 23, 1821, in Calhoun, *Papers,* VI, 212. Calhoun said that Kentucky had received its full quota of appointments for the year, but since vacancies still existed at the academy, he conferred an appointment on young Clay.

32. Letter of archives technician at the academy to an editor of the Clay Papers, July 24, 1990, CPP.

33. Clay to Morris, February 25, March 8, 21, 1822, Clay Papers, New Hampshire Historical Society, copies CPP.

34. Receipt for entrance tuition, October 1, 1821, in Clay, *Papers,* III, 121.

current money" as a marriage bond.[35] A year and a half later another daughter, Anne, married the dashing James Erwin from Tennessee.

At this time Clay also began to attend the physical condition of his estate at Ashland. Like his children, it desperately needed his care and concern. An English visitor, William Faux, described what he saw at Ashland in October 1819, and his comments say a great deal about what Clay's long absences from home had produced. "The windows are broken, and the frames and doors are rotten for want of paint or tar; the gardens in a piggish state, full of weeds, the walks gullied by heavy rains; the grass borders and lawn, wild, dirty, and unmowed, and everything else inelegant; although the soil is rich to excess, and almost all kinds of vegetables spring spontaneously and grow all in the neatest order." In an enclosure near the house Faux saw the "finest after-grass and the coarsest hay in the world."[36]

The original two-and-a-half-story stone structure[37] now included two wings designed by Benjamin Latrobe in 1813. Although Ashland was basically a Federal house, the consciousness of spatial design achieved by the alterations and extensions Clay's architects introduced over the years foreshadowed the Greek Revival so characteristic of antebellum America architecture. Nearby a cluster of small buildings, including a kitchen, two conically shaped icehouses, a coach house, a stable, barns, a greenhouse, and a dovecote, serviced various family needs. The house itself was tastefully furnished and boasted several imported items from abroad. China and a pair of sofas had been brought by Clay from France, and the downstairs windows were framed in gold brocaded satin draperies brought from Lyons in 1815. A slave by the name of Charles Dupuy took charge of the mansion, under Lucretia Clay's direction, and served as his master's valet whenever Clay went to Washington.

Clay regularly increased the size of his estate by purchasing additional acreage and exchanging small plots of land with neighbors until his property reached a size of approximately six hundred acres. On this farm or plantation Clay raised a number of crops, but of these, hemp was financially the most important. Because of inferior processing, American hemp could not hold its own against foreign competition, and Clay was obliged to do what he could in Congress to keep out the foreign product. That naturally meant raising the tariff rates whenever possible. His belief in protectionism, therefore, was partly attributable to his own financial needs and those of his Kentucky neighbors. He had firsthand information about what foreign goods could do to the American farmer, and as a legislator he reacted appropriately and understandably. He experimented with different methods to improve his hemp, and he

35. Marriage bond, Clay, *Papers,* III, 198.

36. William Faux, *Memorable Days in America, Being a Journal of a Tour to the United States* (London, 1823), pp. 196–197.

37. In 1832 Clay said that estimates agreed that there were not 650 square yards of surface to the house, exclusive of windows and doors. Clay to Henry Clay, Jr., May 2, 1832, in Clay, *Papers,* VIII, 504.

took a lively interest in any modern machine that could aid in the production of a superior product.[38]

Clay also experimented with sugar beets and different grasses for pasture only to decide that the native bluegrass occupied a superior class by itself. In addition, the farm produced some tobacco, corn, wheat, and rye. The excellent Kentucky grass provided splendid feed for livestock. Hogs, goats, cows, mules, and horses were raised by the hundreds at Ashland. Clay took pride in his animals and plantation, and ten years later he boasted that "I have upwards of 500 acres and in another near it about 300 more. I . . . cultivate upwards of 200 acres of Indian Corn; 120 acres of other grains, and have upwards of a hundred head of horses & mules, upwards of 100 head of Cattle &c &c."[39] Over the next several years he began to breed Maltese jackasses, Arabian horses, Saxon and merino sheep, and English Hereford and Durham cattle. He imported cattle from abroad, and his racehorses were so superior and earned him so much prize money that Clay built a private racetrack at Ashland, one of the few such in Kentucky.[40]

To work this large and steadily expanding estate, Clay had a modest force of a dozen or so slaves. In a little over ten years that number more than doubled, mostly through purchases.[41] Overseers supervised and directed this work force, but they had to be constantly watched themselves lest they abuse the slaves. Clay truly enjoyed his life as a farmer as he watched his estate grow and prosper. "I am getting a passion for rural occupations," he wrote a little later, "and feel more and more as if I ought to abandon forever the strife of politics. I shall not be unhappy if a sense of public duty shall leave me free to pursue my present inclinations."[42]

Many years later a visitor to Ashland spoke to a local gentleman about Clay's standing among the farmers in the neighborhood. "Oh, none ranked higher," came the response, "except his wife."[43]

The steady improvement of his farm resulting from his attention to its needs matched the steady growth of his law practice, once he returned to Kentucky. Of particular importance to him, especially to his income, was his association with the Bank of the United States. As its chief counsel for the

38. Clay wrote an article entitled "Hemp" that was published in pamphlet form in *Western Agriculturalist and Practical Farmer* (Cincinnati, 1830). Copy in the Filson Club library, Louisville, Kentucky.

39. Clay to Richard B. Jones, July 5, 1831, in Clay, *Papers,* VIII, 371.

40. Clay to P. Irving, March 18, 1817, University of Kentucky Library, copy CPP. In 1808, with four other gentlemen, Clay purchased the celebrated "Turf Horse Buzzard" for the "extraordinary" price of fifty-five hundred dollars. Quoted in Mayo, *Clay,* p. 195.

41. In 1831 Clay claimed that fifteen slaves worked his farm; two years later he stated that "fifty or sixty, black and white" now constituted his family. Clay to P. Irving, March 18, 1817, University of Kentucky Library, copy CPP; Clay to Edmund H. Pendleton, July 22, 1833, in Clay, *Papers,* VIII, 659.

42. This was written during another enforced departure from national politics. Clay to James Brown, April 17, 1830, in Clay, *Papers,* VIII, 192.

43. Coleman, "Ashland, the Home of Henry Clay," p. 167.

Ohio and Kentucky area he was called on repeatedly to help collect outstanding debts as well as to defend the "monster" against an outraged citizenry that
hated its presence among them. So great was the economic distress and so
tireless were hapless debtors to escape paying what they owed that he was
forced to bring suit in hundreds of cases each month, amounting to hundreds
of thousands of dollars. It proved lucrative for Clay, if disastrous to many
farmers. And he was persistent in his efforts, preparing injunctions, deposi-
tions, deeds, certificates, and the like to protect his employer.

Clay kept the president of the BUS, Langdon Cheves, apprised of his
actions and of his many successes in suing defaulters. "I have therefore the
satisfaction to inform you, that we have obtained two hundred and eleven
judgments, in cases issuing from the Cincinnati office alone, and that there
were only about twenty cases continued . . . [and] these were continued owing
to some peculiar circumstances affecting them."[44] He also kept President
Cheves informed of the worsening monetary conditions in the West and how
they would be handled. "Our currency is continuing, in Kentucky, to get
worse," he said. "The depreciation of the paper of the Kentucky Bank has
reached twenty seven per Cent. If that bank should determine to take indis-
criminately the paper of the Bank of the Commonwealth, there is no doubt
that the notes of both banks will continue to experience a depretiation, and
that it will be progressive. . . . We shall persevere in our course of taking the
notes of neither of those Banks, as the general rule."[45]

The BUS had a prize in Henry Clay and showed its appreciation at every
turn. It rewarded him handsomely with an enormous annual retaining fee of
six thousand dollars.[46] And its president made clear that of all the presidential
candidates gearing up for the election of 1824, the Bank and its officers stood
foursquare behind Henry Clay.[47]

But this association with the BUS also had its negative aspects. The hundreds of debtors being hauled into court and having their property stripped
from them to satisfy the judgments obtained by Clay did not take the action
kindly. Clay may have won the admiration and support of the Bluegrass gentry
in Kentucky by his actions, but debtors, the poor, and the discontented turned
away from him in disgust. John Pope deserted to the New Court a few years
later and took several friends with him. Amos Kendall and Francis P. Blair,
president of the Bank of the Commonwealth, also deserted, and together they

44. Clay to Cheves, September 13, 1822, in Clay, *Papers,* III, 286.

45. Clay to Cheves, May 5, 1821, in Clay, *Papers,* III, 76. By 1827 the court struggle and Relief
system had cost Kentucky six hundred thousand dollars in unpaid notes due the Bank of the
Commonwealth. Mathias, "The Relief and Court Struggle," p. 174.

46. "The liberality of the [Bank's] allowance which has been made to me is such as to admit of my
time, almost exclusively, being applied to its service." Clay to Cheves, February 27, 1821, in Clay,
Papers, III, 51.

47. "Of the *trio* [Adams, Crawford, and Clay]," wrote Cheves, "I heartily wish you success." Like
many others, Cheves discounted the candidacy of Jackson. Cheves to Clay, November 9, 1822, in
Clay, *Papers,* III, 315–317.

were to form an anti-Clay faction that later became the basis of the Jackson party in Kentucky.[48]

The BUS retained Clay for the celebrated case of *Osborn* v. *Bank of the United States,* argued before the U.S. Supreme Court. The case developed when Ohio slapped a fifty-thousand-dollar tax on each of the resident branches of the BUS. When the Bank refused to pay, the state auditor, one Ralph Osborn, seized one hundred thousand dollars of its funds. Clay, on behalf of the BUS, won a federal circuit court order demanding the return of the money, but the Ohio officials refused to comply. He then instituted suit for damages, and the legislature responded by ordering the Bank out of Ohio.

The zealous Clay immediately pounced upon Samuel Sullivan, the state treasurer, when he defied the Court by refusing to surrender the money. He "left me but one alternative," Clay informed Cheves, "which I instantly pursued." A house was hired to serve as a jail, and Sullivan was seized and "committed for a contempt of the Court in disobeying the decree." But Clay showed compassion toward the other defendants. "I have thought it not necessary, for the present, to ask of the Court to imprison the other defendants, all of whom it is believed are sincerely desirous that the money should be given up." In incarcerating the treasurer the arresting marshal took the key of the treasury office and confiscated ninety-eight thousand dollars of the hundred thousand dollars. The marshal retained the remaining two thousand dollars for his commission. Sullivan was then released from custody. "There has been no tumult," Clay happily reported, "no violence."[49]

An appeal brought the matter to the Supreme Court. At issue before the Court was whether the Eleventh Amendment to the U.S. Constitution protected Ohio from this judicial interference in seizing the tax money and whether the agents of the state were responsible for their actions in carrying out state law. The Bank asked Clay to argue the case before John Marshall and awarded him another generous fee.[50]

In the decision *Osborn* v. *Bank of the United States,*[51] Marshall, speaking for the majority of the Court, struck down the Ohio law, just as he had invalidated a Maryland tax law in *McCulloch* v. *Maryland,* and he denied that the Eleventh Amendment applied. It was another judicial action limiting the states' protection from suits under the Eleventh Amendment, and like the *McCulloch* decision, it was an important victory of national over state authority.

The continuing vigor and sweep of Clay's efforts on behalf of the BUS included prominent Kentuckians as well as the less distinguished. A case in

48. Mathias, "Henry Clay and His Kentucky Power Base," p. 128.

49. Clay to Cheves, September 8, 1821, in Clay, *Papers,* III, 112–113.

50. "I will thank you," Clay wrote to Cheves, "to place with the Cashier of the Bank the $2000, the residue of my fee for conducting the suit in Ohio, and that which the Bank has had the goodness to allow me for the Supreme Court." Clay to Cheves, October 22, 1821, Clay, *Papers,* III, 129.

51. 9 Wheaton 738ff.

point was his suit against the powerful senator of Kentucky Colonel Richard M. Johnson, his brother, James, and others, in an action involving hundreds of thousand of dollars. Clay felt he had been placed in an embarrassing situation by bringing this action, and he was inclined to step aside and let someone else handle it. There was the danger, he said, that Johnson might expect a "favorable disposition" on account of their past association in Congress. At the same time, if he did back away, the Bank "might suppose that such a disposition had been exercised." But Clay knew his duty and proceeded with the case as though it were no different from any other. And he succeeded in winning a judgment in the Bank's favor.[52]

Clay also appeared before the Supreme Court to defend his state's confusing and controversial land laws which allowed squatters title to land after occupancy of seven years. There was a question whether, at the time of separation, the compact signed between Kentucky and Virginia regarding land grants placed certain restrictions on Kentucky's authority to enact the legislation in question. Clay and George M. Bibb were appointed by their state as commissioners to work out a solution with Virginia, whereupon the two commissioners requested a meeting with the Virginia house of delegates. The request was granted, and the two men journeyed to Richmond, where they were honored and toasted at a dinner given at the Eagle Hotel, where they were staying.[53] Clay met many of his oldest friends, going back nearly twenty-five years. Thomas Ritchie was one, and the two men "promenaded" the long hall of the hotel, reminisced about the past, and talked of their political differences, each protesting they had remained steadfast to "Virginia doctrines."[54]

On February 7, 1822, Clay spoke to the delegates, and his efforts demonstrated again his matchless skill as an orator. He naturally began his speech with a reference to Patrick Henry and other great Virginians whose voices had filled the chamber. He not unexpectedly referred to the fact that he had been born in Virginia and that Kentucky itself was the child of the Great Dominion. Then he argued his case for Kentucky's right not to be restrained in pursuing the land policies it did:

Virginia *would* not have restrained her from adopting the system in question. It would have been utterly inconsistent with her enlightened and parental views. You did not mean to erect a new state destitute of the powers to maintain a respectable existence. You did not intend to send forth, in the wide world, your first (and he hoped he might say) your favorite child, rickety and crippled, devoid of the faculties necessary to preserve itself. No, no, no. It was your munificent purpose to advance her liberally; to place along side you a stout and hearty member of the Union, supporting and perpetuating your principles of liberty; and giving additional strength to the nation. Yes, it was your noble intention to plant a new star in the bright firmament of the American Confederacy.[55]

52. Clay to Cheves, July 21, 1821, in Clay, *Papers,* III, 102.
53. Toast and speech at dinner, in Clay, *Papers, III, 171.*
54. Ambler, *Ritchie,* p. 88.
55. Speech, February 7, 1822, in Clay, *Papers,* III, 161–169.

It was a moving speech. Even so, the Virginia delegates refused to agree on an interpretation that the compact had not restrained Kentucky from passing the legislation in question. Virginia therefore went to the Supreme Court in the case of *Green* v. *Biddle,* with Clay arguing for Kentucky.[56] However, the Court subsequently ruled in Virginia's favor, stating that the Kentucky law violated not only the state's agreement with Virginia at the time of separation but the contract clause of the Constitution as well.

Although Clay lost this case, he impressed the learned associate justice Joseph Story with his ability to plead his cause. "Your friend Clay has argued before us with a good deal of ability," Story said to Justice Thomas Todd, "and if he were not a candidate for higher offices, I should think he might attain great eminence at this Bar. But he prefers the fame of popular talents to the steady fame of the Bar."[57]

Indeed, Henry Clay was one of the most gifted men of his age. He distinguished himself as a public speaker, a lawyer, a politician, and Speaker of the House of Representatives. He might have made a truly great President.

56. 8 Wheaton 1ff.
57. William W. Story, *Life and Letters of Joseph Story* (Boston, 1851), I, 423.

THIRTEEN

The American System

URING CLAY'S retirement from active politics he naturally kept a watchful eye on developments in Washington and around the country. The fact that he attended the Supreme Court to argue various cases meant he regularly saw all his old political cronies and learned all the political gossip and scheming going on, in and out of the halls of Congress. He also kept up a active correspondence. Not surprisingly it centered mainly on the next presidential contest. Almost all his correspondents told him that he should make a run for the office. His only serious opponent, they insisted, would be John Quincy Adams, despite the fact that the secretary of the treasury, William H. Crawford, had been campaigning for the office for some time and had an extensive political apparatus around the country that operated zealously on his behalf. Crawford "was the only candidate who had an *Organized Party*," wrote Langdon Cheves, the soon-to-retire president of the BUS. "The fact I believe is pretty well founded & it is of great weight."[1]

One of the most interesting and unusual letters Clay received at this time came from John Overton of Nashville, Tennessee. Judge Overton was a bank president, planter, lawyer and at one point reputed to be the wealthiest man in Tennessee. He was also General Jackson's close friend and adviser. Indeed, Jackson and Overton roomed together when the general first moved to Tennessee from North Carolina. In his letter to Clay, Overton said: "I can assure you, as far as I know the public mind, you will get all the Votes in Tennessee in preference to any man whose name has been mentioned," including Adams and Crawford. As for Jackson's candidacy, that was simply rumor. "In fact, I am almost certain that he will not [run], and my information is derived, from good authority." Clay's unfortunate attack on Jackson during the Seminole controversy "might in some measure Operate to your slight injury" in Tennessee, Overton allowed, "but the great mass of the people, would warmly Support you." Only Jackson, no one else, could beat Clay there. A surrogate

---

1. Cheves to Clay, November 9, 1822, Clay, *Papers,* III, 314.

would be defeated. Then, because of his close ties with Old Hickory, Overton asked Clay to "keep these matters to yourself."[2]

Clay believed what Overton told him. No doubt he wanted to believe it because Jackson, as a candidate, would seriously challenge him for western votes and Clay wanted the West to provide him with unanimous and solid support should he decide to declare himself a presidential candidate. Unquestionably the Kentuckian desired the presidency, desired it with a near-ferocious sense of yearning. He saw no other possible candidate as better qualified for the office. But could he win the necessary majority of electoral votes, particularly with several prominent men already mentioned as possible candidates and particularly in view of Crawford's *"Organized Party"* and the likelihood that the treasury secretary would be nominated by a congressional caucus?

To survey the country in an informal poll of his political friends, Clay decided in the spring of 1822 to write them and ask their opinions and predictions on the upcoming election. In his letters he said he doubted whether New York or Pennsylvania would offer a candidate, although Governor De Witt Clinton of New York, who had run unsuccessfully against James Madison in 1812, had been mentioned as a possibility. In view of the many past Presidents from Virginia, Clay also thought that both New York and Pennsylvania had strong claims, provided they brought forward suitable candidates. But none existed at the moment. "For myself," he told his friends, ". . . I was content to wait the termination of the period of Mr. Monroes successor, if a Northern Candidate arose who was likely to unite   the general confidence." There was no such candidate, he flatly stated. At the same time the South was "springing up" several possibilities, all junior in years and experience to Clay. So what did these friends think of the Kentuckian's chances? He himself thought he had solid support from Ohio to the Gulf of Mexico. Was it enough? "In respect to your State," what were the prospects? Up to the present, Clay continued, he had "repressed rather than stimulated" public sentiment of support, particularly in Kentucky and Ohio. But proper timing is essential to success. "One's name should not be held back too long."

One final question he posed before concluding his letter: "Ought [I] to go into the next congress?" What advice could they give? Should he again place himself directly upon the national scene or continue his present occupation at home as lawyer and "elder" statesman?[3]

In response to his queries, virtually all of Clay's friends urged him to run again for the House. Unquestionably, they said, he would be elected Speaker,

2. Overton to Clay, January 16, 1822, in Clay, *Papers,* III, 156–157.

3. Clay to Peter B. Porter, April 14, 1822, Adam Beatty to Clay, April 17, 1822, in Clay, *Papers,* III, 190–193. See also William Creighton, Jr., to Clay, May 2, 1822, Henry R. Warfield to Clay, May 30, 1822, Andrew Hynes to Clay, June 30, 1822, ibid., III, 204–206, 210–214, 243. Clay also wrote to Governor William Carroll of Tennessee and other leading politicians, but his letters and their replies have not been found. See Hynes to Clay, June 30, 1822, ibid., p. 243.

and again his great talents would demonstrate his superior qualifications for the presidency, not only to his colleagues but to the public at large. In addition, he would have a profound impact on legislation, and if a congressional caucus were called to name the Republican presidential candidate, it would be vital that he be present. "There is still another view, in which your being a member, would be very important," said Adam Beatty, a close friend and Kentucky legislator. "If no candidate get a maj[or]ity of the whole number votes, the ele[ction] is to be made by the H. of R. from [the] three highest. In this event your [being] a member will be very importan[t.]"[4]

Beatty made a powerful point. With so many candidates in the race the likelihood of the final decision ending up in the House of Representatives became all too obvious. According to the Twelfth Amendment to the Constitution, when no candidate receives a majority of electoral votes, the election goes to the House and the selection of President is decided by the members from among the three candidates with the highest number of electoral votes. As Speaker Clay would almost certainly become the next President. Who could match his popularity and leadership in the House?

The argument was incontrovertible. So Clay signaled to his constituents his willingness to run again for his old House seat, and in August 1822 he was duly elected to the Eighteenth Congress without opposition. Of course, he explained his decision as the wish of his friends around the country, a wish he felt obliged to honor. "I would have preferred remaining a year or two longer in private life," he told Langdon Cheves. "But my friends, every where concurred in thinking my presence there [Washington] might be material in relation to another object, and one must, though he should do it rarely, yield his own opinion to theirs."[5]

In making his presidential calculations beyond the decision to return to Congress, Clay figured he had the West virtually sewn up—"all the States from Ohio to the gulph [sic] of Mexico."[6] He had little to fear from John Quincy Adams in that area because of Adams's abandonment of Texas during the Florida negotiations with Spain and his known indifference to the British right of navigation on the Mississippi River during the Ghent negotiations. The West belonged to Henry Clay, he reckoned, and would give him a possible total of fifty-two electoral votes. Ohio strongly supported him because of his stand on internal improvements, such as the National Road, and the proposed Ohio Canal. Added to Ohio were his own state, Missouri, Indiana, and Illi-

4. Beatty to Clay, April 17, 1822, in Clay, *Papers,* III, 193. Other friends made the same point as Beatty. See, for example, John Norvell to Clay, November 14, 1822, ibid., III, 321. There were, of course, some negative responses to Clay's query about returning to Congress. William Creighton told him that remaining at home would advance his standing with the people. "The Country has already become disgusted with the intrigues of the Cabinet Candidates, and will turn from them to seek a private Citizen unconnected with the administration or Congress." Creighton to Clay, May 2, 1822, ibid., III, 205.
5. Clay to Cheves, October 5, 1822, in Clay, *Papers,* III, 292.
6. Clay to J. Sloane, October 28, 1822, Harvard University Library.

nois. The real question mark was Tennessee. And in August he received the disturbing word that the Tennessee legislature had placed Andrew Jackson's name in nomination for President. "It was a kind of resolution that hardly any member would vote against," he was told by a member of that legislature, "who was anxious for the *Political importance* of his own state."[7] This action caught Clay by surprise. He had trouble deciding whether it was meant to divide the West or intended as a "mere complement" to the general without any real expectation that it would be carried forward and seconded by any other state. "I think it may be asserted very confidently," Clay told his New York friend and active organizer Peter B. Porter, "that no other Western State will lend its support to him." Indeed, he was assured by Governor William Carroll of Tennessee and others that Jackson's name would be withdrawn when it failed to excite interest in other states and that he, Clay, would receive "the unanimous support of Tennessee."[8] It was wishful thinking.

In the East Clay knew he could discount New England. That section belonged totally to John Quincy Adams.[9] But the middle states gave him some hope of success, particularly in New York and Pennsylvania. Naturally he understood that he would encounter considerable opposition from the friends of Crawford. In New York the Crawford supporters (sometimes called Radicals because of their adherence to a strict states' rights philosophy which demanded a very limited interpretation of the federal Constitution) were led by Martin Van Buren, probably the most astute politician in the country, who had just been elected to the United States Senate.

For quite some time Van Buren, just like Clay, had been calculating probable electoral trends for the 1824 contest. He had dismissed John C. Calhoun because his views of the "Federal Constitution were latitudinarian in the extreme."[10] He dismissed Adams for the same reason, along with the secretary of state's indifference to partisan realities and the need for party discipline. Interestingly, Van Buren did not fault Clay on his principles—most probably because he recognized the Kentuckian's basic commitment to states' rights—but rather he doubted his ability to sustain himself as a presidential candidate during the long months ahead. He really wanted Clay to run as Vice President on the Crawford ticket—a seemingly unbeatable combination—and he worked through several mutual friends in the hope of breaking down Clay's resistance to the idea.[11]

At one point Van Buren approached Clay in Washington "and without the smallest invitation or encouragement on my part," said the Kentuckian,

7. Andrew Hynes to Clay, [July] 31, 1822, in Clay, *Papers,* III, 265.
8. Clay to Porter, August 10, October 22, 1822, Clay to Langdon Cheves, October 5, 1822, in Clay, *Papers,* III, 274, 292, 300.
9. "Give Mr. Adams, then, New England," Clay said in working out a score sheet on the election. Clay to Porter, June 15, 1823, in Clay, *Papers,* III, 433.
10. Van Buren, *Autobiography,* p. 513.
11. Remini, *Martin Van Buren and the Making of the Democratic Party,* pp. 37, 48–49.

broached the presidential question. First he talked about Calhoun, then dismissed him. Next he treated Adams's "pretensions" and dismissed him also. "Well," said Clay, that pretty much reduced the possibilities to "Mr Crawford and myself. I could not but feel (perhaps unjustly) that Mr. Van Buren's motive was to sound me." Knowing Van Buren's reputation as a consummate politician (the Little Magician was his nickname) and the creator of the Albany Regency, a political machine to run New York while he served the state as its senator in Washington, Clay kept up his guard. "I forebore to excite his interest or stimulate his ardor in my behalf," he said. That may have been one of Clay's major errors in judgment during this election.

A year later Clay saw Van Buren again. He walked up to the little man and jokingly began the conversation with: "You said last winter who would not be elected, but did not tell me who whould [sic] be; it is time for you to fill up the blank."

As was his custom, the cautious, courteous Van Buren smiled politely and then replied that it was much more difficult "in pronouncing an affirmative judgement than a negative one."[12] And there the matter rested for the moment.

As for Pennsylvania, Clay thought he had a good chance if only he had adequate newspaper support. Were the people of Pennsylvania told through a partisan press, he said, that by adding their state to those he had in the West, the election could be decided instantly in his favor, they might declare for him. Cheves told him that nothing had yet been decided in Pennsylvania and that the final decision might come down to a close contest among Adams, Crawford, and Clay.[13] But whatever Pennsylvania decided, it had become increasingly certain that the race would end up in the House of Representatives, making it all the more imperative that Clay once more win election as Speaker.

Clay's efforts to begin some kind of national backing for his candidacy were rudely interrupted during the fall of 1822, when during a business trip to Ohio he fell ill with a severe "bilious fever" "which gave my friends some alarm." He was treated with mercury and forbidden to travel. His condition was apparently so grave that a report circulated in Louisville that he was dead, a report carried in the Washington National Intelligencer.[14] As soon as he could regain his strength Clay immediately informed his friends that word of his demise was premature.[15] "The newspapers represented you, some weeks ago, as very dangerously ill," wrote his friend Benjamin W. Leigh of Virginia, "and one of them killed you outright—which your distant friends regard as a very

12. Clay to Porter, June 15, 1823, in Clay, Papers, III, 432.

13. Cheves to Clay, November 9, 1822, in Clay, Papers, III, 313–317.

14. Clay to William Creighton, Jr., August 23, 1823, University of Kentucky Library; Clay to J. Sloane, October 22, 1822, Harvard University Library; Clay to Porter, October 22, 1822, in Clay, Papers, III, 301; National Intelligencer, October 30, 1822.

15. Clay to Porter, October 22, 1988, Henry R. Warfield to Clay, December 10, 1822, in Clay, Papers, III, 301, 335–336.

unpardonable abuse of the freedom of the press."[16] Wrote another: "You was sick, I mourned over it—you died I wept for you—you regained your health, I rejoiced & thanked my God for your deliverance."[17]

But Clay was a lot sicker than he let on, and his illness persisted for months. A year later he was still under medical care. "My health, it is true, is extremely bad," he wrote in late August 1823, "and I am now confined at home by the endeavor to re-establish it." A month later he admitted that his health had not yet been "re-established, but is improving, and I begin to feel that I see land, or rather that I may not get under it."[18] By the time he returned to Washington to recommence his political career he had finally shaken off the lingering debility—or thought he had. "My health is greatly improved and nearly re-established," he reported on December 15, 1823. Of course, he understood that full recovery "is in my power; if I can take the necessary exercise, and particularly on horseback." Several months later he complained to Adams that he was suffering from a return of his "dyspepsia."[19]

Because John Quincy Adams was such a real threat to Clay's hopes for the presidency in 1824—his distinguished diplomatic record and his current position as secretary of state gave him an enormous advantage even though he did nothing himself to advance his candidacy—it is possible that the Kentuckian set in motion a plot to discredit his rival. John Floyd of Virginia initiated a campaign in Congress for the occupation of the Columbia River and the reorganization of the Indian Service; in the course of the proceedings he got a resolution passed calling upon the President to send to the House all the correspondence relating to the Treaty of Ghent. Presumably these documents would shed light on the Columbia River and Indian questions. But how did he know that? Floyd later admitted that in the winter of 1819–1820 he and a group of his friends in Congress had been discussing the Columbia River in relation to its importance to the fur trade when "one of the gentlemen" commented that the importance of the Mississippi River had been reviewed at length in Ghent and that something interesting might be revealed if the correspondence of the diplomats was made available to Congress. Who was this "gentleman"? Was he one of the diplomats present at Ghent? If so, it could not have been Bayard, who was dead, or Gallatin, who was in Europe. Was it Russell? But he did not come to Congress until December 1821. That left Adams and Clay. But Adams became the target of this "plot," as it developed, so naturally some men, particularly Adams, pointed an accusing finger directly

16. Leigh to Clay, November 9, 1822, in Clay, *Papers*, III, 318.

17. Henry Shaw to Clay, February 11, 1823, in Clay, *Papers*, III, 372.

18. Clay to Francis T. Brooke, August 28, 1823, Clay to John J. Crittenden, September 13, 1823, in Clay, *Papers*, III, 481, 488.

19. Clay to Nathaniel Rochester, December 13, 1823, in Clay, *Papers*, III, 538; Clay to James Erwin, January 7, 1824, copy CPP; Adams, *Memoirs*, VI, 364. It is not known what was really wrong with Clay. "Dyspepsia" was a catchall word for a variety of illnesses when doctors were baffled by a patient's symptoms.

at Clay and named him as the mysterious "gentleman." Senator David Barton of Missouri claimed "that the whole intrigue was understood in the Western States in it's true light—& that he had no doubt it was one of the artifices of Clay to render Adams unpopular & advance his own pretensions to the Presidency."[20]

Be that as it may, when the documents were produced by the President and turned over to the House, Jonathan Russell, now a member of Congress, saw to it that included was one of his own letters written to Monroe (after the negotiations had ended), a letter he marked "duplicate" instead of "copy." This letter incorporated changes from the original that put Clay and Russell in a favorable and Adams in an unfavorable light. As doctored, the letter seemed to support two accusations: that Adams at Ghent had been willing to trade away the navigation of the Mississippi River to safeguard the fishing rights of New England and that Adams had been willing to allow Great Britain the right to trade with the Indians below the Canadian border. Both these accusations would annihilate the secretary of state's political support in the West—and very likely other sections of the country. Not unexpectedly the letter also implied that Russell and Henry Clay had defended western interests.[21]

Adams erupted. He vented his anger in the secret pages of his diary, and he charged Clay with masterminding the entire plot. "Clay's conduct throughout this affair towards me has been that of an envious rival—a fellow-servant whispering tales into the ear of the common master. He has been seven years circulating this poison against me in the West, and I have now no doubt that Russell's letter was brought forth upon suggestions originating with him. Russell has all along performed for him the part of a jackal."[22]

In a brilliantly written statement, Adams defended himself by pointing out the discrepancies in the "duplicate" letter from the original. Then he published the whole in September 1822 under the title *The Duplicate Letters, the Fisheries and the Mississippi, Documents Relating to the Transactions at the Negotiations of Ghent.* He made a shambles of the arguments against him and in the process flattened Jonathan Russell. When it came to an interpretation and analysis of documentary evidence, John Quincy Adams had few contemporary equals. Those who challenged him usually came away severely mauled.

At this point Clay stepped in with a letter of his own dated November 15, 1822, and published in the Washington *National Intelligencer* on December 17, 1822. In effect it abandoned poor Russell. It expressed regret over the "unhappy controversy" yet claimed there were errors of fact and opinion in Adams's pamphlet—"no doubt unintentional"—which Clay did not wish to

20. Plumer, Jr., to Plumer, December 6, 1822, Brown, ed., *Missouri Compromises,* p. 77.
21. A detailed account of this "plot" can be found in Bemis, *Adams,* I, 485–509. It can also be traced in Adams, *Memoirs,* V, 240ff; VI, 3ff. Floyd's revelation about "one of the gentlemen" who suggested looking into the Ghent documents was published as a letter of August 14, 1822, in the Richmond *Enquirer,* August 27, 1822. See Bemis, *Adams,* I, 507.
22. Adams, *Memoirs,* VI, 49.

pursue at this time since the issue had been satisfactorily resolved nearly a decade before. Perhaps sometime in the future he might write a history of the negotiations when passions had cooled and it would not be necessary to "enter the field of disputation, with either of my colleagues." As for a conspiracy, "I had no knowledge of the intention of the honorable Mr. Floyd to call for [the correspondence], nor of the call itself, through the House of Representatives, until I saw it announced in the public prints." A modern historian has pointed out that Clay's ignorance of Floyd's "intentions" did not mean that he had not planted the idea of requesting the correspondence in Floyd's mind in the first place.[23]

There is no hard evidence to prove that Clay instigated this "unhappy controversy." Indeed, he swore he was not the culprit. He knew, he said, that in New England and "even at Richmond" that "it had been industriously circulated . . . that I had instigated the calls for the Ghent papers. Now, as in truth, that was a most unjust surmise against me." But the humiliated Russell denounced his former colleague and friend and later tried unsuccessfully to injure him politically. He failed to win reelection to the Congress, and he left the national scene "a broken man."[24]

Adams responded to Clay's public letter with one of his own, noting that the Kentuckian had not pointed out any specific error of fact or opinion in his pamphlet. But if Clay were to publish his account sometime in the future, he, Adams, would be "ready with equal cheerfulness to acknowledge indicated error and to vindicate contested truth." Privately Adams expressed the hope that Clay would publish his account, for "he had it in his power, & was determined to give him as severe a dressing as he had Russell—that in the former controversy he had purposely spared Clay, & confined his refutation to Russell; but that it was for no want of matter against the former, who was, in fact, as vulnerable as the latter."

Clay wisely decided against writing his account. He left the field entirely to his presumed adversary. Adams had triumphed. "He has come out of this controversy, not merely with success, but in triumph," declared Representative William Plumer of New Hampshire. If there ever was a plot to discredit the secretary of state, it boomeranged, and the controversy went a long way toward advancing Adams's presidential prospects. "It seems as if the enemies of Mr. Adams were determined to make him President, so injudicious & so unsuccessful have they been in their attacks upon him."[25]

For his part Clay told friends that Adams had deliberately tried to draw him into the controversy. He therefore had only two courses of action. (He later expanded them to four.) He could either remain silent or reserve the

23. Bemis, *Adams*, I, 507.

24. Clay to Porter, February 4, 1823, in Clay, *Papers*, III, 369.

25. Bemis, *Adams*, I, 508–509; *National Intelligencer*, December 19, 1822; Adams, *Memoirs*, VI, 116–118; Plumer, Jr., to William Plumer, December 6, 10, 21, 1822, in Brown, ed., *Missouri Compromises*, pp. 77, 78, 81.

"right of correcting errors on some future fit occasion." He chose the latter course and would take his time about responding. As far as the controversy itself was concerned, he believed that Adams was "clearly in the wrong."[26]

The drubbing Adams administered to Clay was offset to some extent by the action of several western states placing the Kentuckian in nomination for the presidency. The push got under way when the Missouri legislature on November 7, 1822, named him as its candidate. Kentucky (November 18) and Ohio (January 3, 1823) followed Missouri's lead.[27] Clay spent considerable time over the next several months to snag New York, Virginia, and Pennsylvania—he dubbed Pennsylvania the Keystone State—which he declared an unbeatable coalition. "I shall participate in no intrigues, enter into no arrangements, have no understandings with others formal or informal, make no pledges or promises," he told his friends in those states. "I am determined, if elected, to enter the office unmanacled, free to promote the interest of our Common country with the utmost of my exertions, and at liberty to command the best & most faithful public servants."[28]

He seemed to protest too much. For many, Clay's lust—no other word suffices—for the presidency had become so palpable, so obvious, so relentless that it troubled them. They acknowledged his talents. They admitted his experience. "But he would make a most dangerous President," they said. He was too ambitious. "On this account, he finds not many inclined to aid his ambitious views."[29] Unlike Adams, who tried to indicate his availability for the presidency without bludgeoning other politicians into declaring for him, Clay wore his ambition on his sleeve where everyone could see it. Many turned away in alarm.

Throughout his efforts to generate national support for his presidential bid Clay continually discounted the candidacy of Andrew Jackson. His correspondents from Tennessee, New York, Ohio, and elsewhere encouraged him in this misreading of public opinion.[30] His Tennessee boosters kept assuring him that Jackson's name would be withdrawn once it became obvious to everyone that he could not muster support in any other state. Clay himself continued to believe that the principal reason Jackson had been brought forward was at the behest of "persons to the Eastward, friendly to other Candidates" who wish to "produce divisions in the West."[31]

26. Clay to Francis T. Brooke, January 8, 1823. The four possibilities were: (1) remain silent; (2) wait until both he and Adams had retired; (3) undertake a correction of errors immediately; (4) reserve the right to speak later. Clay to Porter, February 4, 1823, in Clay, *Papers*, III, 367–368.

27. Clay gives some details of the Ohio caucus in his letter to R. C. Anderson, Jr., January 5, 1823, which he wrote from Columbus, copy CPP.

28. Clay to Porter, February 2, 3, 4, 1823, Clay to Francis T. Brooke, January 31, February 26, 1823, in Clay, *Papers*, III, 357–359, 364, 365, 368–369, 388.

29. Plumer, Jr., to Plumer, April 10, 1820, in Brown, ed., *Missouri Compromises*, p. 49.

30. See Clay's correspondence from the second half of 1822 to the close of 1823 in Clay, *Papers*, III, 290–501.

31. Clay to R. J. Meigs, August 21, 1822, Lilly Library, Indiana University.

By the end of 1823 it had begun to dawn on Clay and others that Old Hickory was a much more serious candidate than they originally suspected. When caucuses in Pennsylvania began dumping Calhoun in favor of Jackson, the other candidates suddenly took notice. Then Tennessee elected the general to the United States Senate so that the country might get a better look at his qualifications to hold political office. "You will have seen that Genl. Jackson is elected to the Senate," Clay wrote Benjamin Leigh in a bemused tone of voice. "I understand that the General has altered essentially his course of personal conduct; and has become extremely gentle, affable & conciliatory. It is said that he has extinguished some of his most antient [*sic*] and bitter enmities; and is on all occasions seeking to reconcile himself with his enemies. What would *you* think of receiving from him a sincere and cordial shake of the hand?"[32] But the real question was whether Jackson would extinguish his hatred of Clay and offer his hand when the two met at the commencement of the next Congress.

By the time the Eighteenth Congress convened on December 1, 1823, Clay was determined to make the session an engine for his advancement. "Seeing that the election is likely to come to the H. of R.," he wrote, "not a doubt is entertained that the probabilities there are strongly with me. On the first ballot it is likely that I should receive the vote of not less than eleven states."[33] For that reason "the great aim of my friends will be to secure my being one of the three highest" candidates with the largest number of electoral votes in the general election.[34]

Under the circumstances it was all the more necessary for Clay to win election as Speaker. He said he would avoid any doubtful contest for the chair, but at the same time he knew there might be a push to gain it for one of Crawford's allies.[35] He could not let that happen—and he did not.

On the first day of the session, by a vote of 139 to 42, Clay was elected Speaker over Philip P. Barbour, the Speaker of the Seventeenth Congress and the political ally of William H. Crawford. "It was most gratifying," Clay declared, "to my friends and myself. . . . It will have a beneficial influence on another election."[36] Just how he corralled the necessary votes can be imagined. He was one of the most skillful political operators in Washington (except when he gambled); only now he had acquired a certain suavity that hid the "out-of-doors" politicking he had practiced years before. After the election Clay was solemnly conducted to the chair, where in a few brief remarks he said he would "exert an anxious, faithful, and unremitting endeavor to fulfill the

32. Clay to Benjamin W. Leigh, October 20, 1823, in Clay, *Papers,* III, 501.

33. This quotation is taken from two letters, the first part from Clay to Porter, December 11, 1823, and the second from Clay to Josephus B. Stuart, December 19, 1823, in Clay, *Papers,* III, 535, 545.

34. Clay to Charles Hammond, January 3, 1823, in Clay, *Papers,* III, 561.

35. Clay to Porter, October 4, 1823, in Clay, *Papers,* III, 495. Actually Clay said that if there was a "disposition" to replace him, he would not oppose it. But he did not dare allow Crawford's friends to administer him a public humiliation.

36. Clay to Porter, December 11, 1823, in Clay, *Papers,* III, 534–535.

expectations by which I have been so much honored. And may we not indulge
the hope, that . . . all our proceedings may tend to sustain the dignity of the
House, to maintain the honor and character of the country, and to advance the
public welfare and happiness."[37]

Lucretia Clay did not accompany her husband on this trip to Washington
to witness his first victory on returning to national public life, so he took
lodgings at Davis's on Ninth Street near Pennsylvania Avenue. He was now
forty-six years of age with five sons, one unmarried and two married daughters, and a grandson, Martin Duralde III, born earlier in the year.[38] His prospects for the future never seemed brighter. From his high perch in the
Speaker's chair he watched and listened and responded to every opportunity to
advance his interests. In Congress perhaps only one other man was his equal in
political adroitness, and that man was Senator Martin Van Buren. Short in
stature, elegantly dressed, fair-complexioned, with "small brilliant eyes" under
a bulging forehead, the New Yorker possessed the "most fascinating manners"
imaginable. Like Clay, he was suave, polite to all and preferred compromise to
conflict. "Mr. Van and myself are very civil," Clay told his friend Peter B.
Porter, "but we have had no conversation in regard to the Presidential election."[39]

Early in the session Clay was surprised by a visit from the Tennessee
congressional delegation. They had come, they said, for the express purpose of
effecting a "reconciliation" between General Jackson and the Speaker. In discussing the past "misunderstandings," Clay related an incident that occurred
during a homeward journey in July 1819, when the Kentuckian happened to
stop at a tavern in the village of Lebanon near the Green River. He took a seat
at the door of the tavern and started reading. Suddenly it was announced that
General Jackson and his "suite" were approaching the tavern. Clay rose from
his seat as Jackson ascended the steps. He saluted the general, Clay swore, "in
the most respectful manner."

Jackson inclined his head slightly. "How do ye do Sir," he muttered as he
hurried into the tavern.

Several members of Jackson's "suite" paused to converse with Clay, and
after a short while the Kentuckian entered the front room to the tavern to get
his hat and have a final drink. Clay spotted the general reading a newspaper
"from which he did not appear to take his eye." After dawdling for a minute or
two in the hope that Jackson would look up and begin a conversation, Clay
finally gave up. He left without speaking or being spoken to by Old Hickory.

Oh, responded the Tennessee delegation, there has been a terrible misunderstanding. Jackson was "laboring under a complaint which rendered neces-

37. *Annals of Congress,* 18th Congress, 1st session, p. 795.

38. Eliza was ten years old. Susan married on April 22, 1822, and Anne on October 21, 1823. The
fourteen-year-old Lucretia Hart Clay died on June 18, 1823.

39. Robert V. Remini, *The Election of Andrew Jackson* (Philadelphia, 1963), p. 18; Clay to Porter,
December 11, 1823, in Clay, *Papers,* III, 535.

sary a quick retirement to the back yard." Clay nodded and then went on to assure his visitors that his Seminole speech had not been meant as an attack upon the general personally. They were opinions "sincerely entertained" and should not "render it necessary that there should be any personal hostility between us." As far as he was concerned, there was no obstacle, said Clay, "to prevent a respectful and courteous intercourse."

Those were Jackson's sentiments precisely, the delegates gushed. They therefore suggested that the two men meet and "without adverting to the past exchange friendly salutations, and be on terms of amicable intercourse for the future."[40]

Everyone agreed, and the group shook hands all around. A little later the delegation gave a dinner, and both Jackson and Clay attended. Reported the gleeful Clay: "Genl. Jackson has buried the hatchet and we are again on good terms. The Tennessee delegation has been remarkably attentive to me, and I understand are nearly unanimous for me, if Jackson be out of the way."[41]

What, then, of Jackson's supposed temper, the rage, the uncontrolled and undying need to exact revenge against all those who dared to fault him or his military record? Obviously it had limits. There was purpose and guile in his emotional tantrums. When it suited his purposes, he could run hot or cold. At this juncture he seemed as determined as Clay to win the presidency, and if that meant burying the hatchet with the Speaker, so be it. Indeed, during this first session of the Eighteenth Congress Jackson buried several hatchets, including the one involving Senator Thomas Hart Benton of Missouri.[42]

At this point it behooved Clay to encourage the general's friendship, and he seemed to understand that fact and act upon it. The two men attended several parties over the next few months, and Clay behaved with a degree of cordiality that not one of Jackson's friends could fault. Unfortunately their mutual bid for the presidency virtually guaranteed another misunderstanding somewhere down the road.

On the second day of this congressional session President Monroe sent down his message as required by the Constitution. In it he advanced the position that later became known as the Monroe Doctrine, a position Clay heartily endorsed, given his long struggle to win recognition of the Latin American republics. Clay favored any course that would protect the newly acquired freedom of the South American republics from the designs of the Holy Alliance, which was seeking to quell every revolutionary uprising against the "legitimate" authority of European monarchs. Clay told Secretary Adams that he thought the doctrine was the "best part of the message." He regretted that the United States had waited so long to acknowledge South American independence, "and he believed even a war for it against all Europe, including

40. Clay to Josiah Stoddard Johnson, October 6, 1827, in Clay, *Papers,* VII, 1114–1116.
41. Clay to Porter, December 11, 1823, in Clay, *Papers,* III, 535.
42. Remini, *Jackson,* II, 60–61.

even England, would be advantageous to us." As a matter of fact, Clay thought "of offering a resolution to declare this country an asylum for all fugitives from oppression, and to connect with it a proposal for modifying the naturalization law, to make it more easily attainable."[43]

As the session proceeded, Clay unfortunately began to show the more abrasive and querulous side to his nature—possibly on account of continuing ill health and the pressure he felt over the presidential election. The first instance involved a proposed pension of three hundred dollars for the *mother* of Oliver Hazard Perry which the Speaker stoutly opposed. Perry had been neither killed nor wounded in battle, and his wife and children had already been put on the pension list. To add his mother seemed ludicrous to Clay. Where would it end? Then Clay added: "It is not your heroes—God knows we have had enough of them within the last twenty years—every man now is a hero—it is not your heroes, but the body of the people, the men who fight your battles, to whom you are indebted for your safety and your eminence as a nation." Was this a disguised jab at General Jackson who was popularly known as the Hero of New Orleans? Clay would have registered surprise and annoyance had anyone suggested such a rude inference. In any event, the House rejected the proposed pension.[44]

The second instance was far more direct and personal. But it also provided Clay with another opportunity to make a ringing appeal in support of freedom throughout the world. The Greeks had revolted against Turkish rule, and Daniel Webster, newly elected to this Congress from Massachusetts, where he had moved, offered a resolution to defray the expense of a mission to Greece whenever the President should deem it proper to send one. Clay joined in support of the resolution. "It asks us to speak a cheering word to the Greeks," he said. "Gentlemen had only to say yes or no. . . . Let them say, distinctly, whether they would give so much encouragement as this to a nation of oppressed and struggling patriots in arms, or whether they would shut themselves up in a cold, shivering, contracted, but mistaken policy, which must in the end react upon ourselves." Just prior to making this speech, Clay had also offered a resolution informing the "Allied powers of Europe" that the American people would look with "serious inquietude" on any attempt by them to overthrow the "Independent Governments" on the American continent and restore those countries to Spanish rule.

There was tremendous sympathy in the United States for the Greek rebels, but John Randolph called the idea of interference with foreign nations regarding Greece and Latin America Quixotism. Ichabod Bartlett, a young member of the House from New Hampshire, spoke specifically against the Webster resolution by pointing out that American anger with the Holy Alliance was based on the claim by the alliance that it could interfere with the

43. Adams, *Memoirs,* VI, 224.
44. *Annals of Congress,* 18th Congress, 1st session, pp. 980–982.

governments of other powers. How, then, he asked, have we the right to interfere with the internal concerns of Turkey?

At that moment Clay interrupted to reprove the young man. Again he spoke movingly in support of the Greek rebels. He said he was shocked that some of his colleagues regarded the resolutions as Quixotism, as unjustifiable interference, as a war measure. "Those who thus argue the question," Clay scolded, "while they themselves give unbounded range to their imagination, in conceiving and setting in array the monstrous consequences, which are to grow out of so simple a proposal, impute to us who are its advocates, Quixotism, Quixotism." He paused, his facial expression registering his anger, "While they are taking the most extravagant and unlimited range," he continued, "and arguing any thing and every thing but the question before the House, they accuse us of enthusiasm, of giving the reins to feeling, of being carried away by our imagination. No, sir, the proposition on your table is no proposition for aid, nor for recognition, nor for interference, nor for war." His voice rose in volume as he went on:

Sir, the Turk with all his power, and in all the elevation of his despotic throne, is at last but man; he is made as we are, of flesh, of muscle, of bones, and sinews; he can feel; and, Sir, he has felt the uncalculating valor of American freemen in some of his dominions; and when he is made to understand, that not only the Executive of this government, but that this nation; that our entire political fabric, base, column and entablature, rulers and people, with heart, soul, mind, and strength, are all on the side of the nation he is crushing, he will be more likely to restrain, than to increase his atrocities upon suffering and bleeding Greece.

Suddenly he raised his fist high over his head. His eyes flashed, and the tone of his voice hardened. "Sir," he shouted, "has it come to this? Are we so humbled, so low, so despicable, that we dare not express our sympathy for suffering Greece, lest, peradventure, we might offend some one or more of their imperial and royal majesties?" If there be any reality to this "menacing danger," he cried, "I would rather adjure the nation to remember that it contains a million of freemen capable of bearing arms, and ready to exhaust their last drop of blood and their last cent, in defending their country, its institutions, and its liberty."

It was a noble utterance, a great speech. Once more he had eloquently declaimed on the subject of human freedom. Once more he had added to his reputation as the great spokesman for liberty. But then he stooped to chastise young Ichabod. Naturally, he first congratulated him on his *"debut,"* but he also said he would like to hear from him his proof "that it is our duty to lay prostrate every fortress of human hope, and to see with complacency the last outwork of liberty taken."

That was just the opening shot, and the sarcasm mounted as Clay continued. He even dared his opponents to vote against the measure. "Go home, if you dare; go home, if you can, to your constituents, and tell them that you voted it down—meet, if you *dare,* the appalling countenances of those who send you here . . . and tell them . . . that the spectres of cimetars and crowns, and crescents, gleamed before you, and alarmed you, and that you suppressed all the noble feelings prompted by religion, by liberty, by national independence, and by humanity.["][45]

Ichabod Bartlett jumped to his feet in protest. He felt it incumbent upon him "to rise and repel the charge of personality which had been cast by the honorable Speaker upon the opponents of the resolution." If the charge, "the loud voice, the menacing look, the sneering gesture" were aimed at him personally, he must hurl it back "as unjust, ungenerous, untrue." At least, Bartlett continued, Webster's defense of the resolution had been "an intellectual treat," but the Speaker's "insinuations" were unmerited, as unmerited as would be the insinuations of anyone who would say to Clay that "you, sir, have a great personal and political object in view" and since the entire country is "in a tempest" over it, you have chosen to "ride on the whirlwind and direct the storm." Also, Clay's advice to him was "gratuitous." Said Bartlett; "However inexperienced I may be . . . when I feel any need for lessons on the subject of political integrity, I feel myself of age to select my instructor."[46]

Young Ichabod gave as good as he got, but Clay was not about to let it go at that. The Speaker responded by declaring that if the gentleman had been aggrieved and requested an explanation, he would have been happy to provide one. "But," cried Clay, "he has chosen to go on, and to seek it in the manner we have just witnessed, and now let him get it where he can. On this floor he shall never get it from me." Bartlett, continued the Speaker, had also dared to allude "to a relation in which I stand to this country . . . and he has ventured to insinuate that the ground I have taken . . . has been influenced by motives derived from, or connected with, that relation." At this point the chair corrected Clay. Bartlett had specifically disclaimed the imputation of such motives.

"I know he disclaimed them," came the thundering response, "and yet he made them, sir—I know the import of words. If a man says a thing is black, and then tells me he meant by that to say that it was white, I know how to understand him; but if he did not mean to cast the insinuation upon me, I cast it back with scorn and contempt upon his own shoulders, and there it rests."[47]

It was an unseemly performance, quite beneath Clay's dignity. He should never have indulged in such a petty display of annoyance and pique. It was as though Clay felt that anyone who dared take exception to his cutting words and sneering demeanor challenged his position as leader of the House of Representatives. Here was the terrible paradox at the heart of Clay's genius. All too often he projected himself in a succession of roles. The statesman, the eloquent

45. *Annals of Congress,* 18th Congress, 1st session, pp. 1104, 1170–1178, 1113–1115.
46. *Annals of Congress,* 18th Congress, 1st session, pp. 1201–1202.
47. *Annals of Congress,* 18th Congress, 1st session, pp. 1201–1202.

orator, the defender of liberty, the charming, witty Prince Hal, the Great Compromiser could suddenly, in a flash, give way to the arrogant, petty, sardonic gut fighter, the gambler, the political opportunist. His impetuous nature too frequently drove him from one role to the other.

Richard M. Johnson declared "that Clay was the most imprudent man in the world, and had been altogether wrong in daring the members of the House opposed to his opinions on the Greek question to go home and meet their constituents."[48] The House did not act on Webster's resolution, and Clay chose not to bring it up again.

And Bartlett apologized. He knew he had drawn blood. Like the gentleman he was, he offered an apology. "My affair with Mr. Bartlett gave me great pain," wrote Clay shortly thereafter. "His attack was premidated [sic], stimulated and unjustified. What I said was to repel it in a manner to secure me tranquillity for the future. It has had that effect. I was clearly in the right and he clearly in the wrong. Such was almost the unanimous opinion here. It has been accommodated by an *apology* from *him*."[49]

Of infinitely greater consequence than these two minor but revealing incidents[50] was the beginning of the discussion in the House of several measures that Clay was to shape into a set of principles that he called the American System. As the various parts of the system were enunciated, explained, defended, and advocated by the Speaker, he took justifiable pride in presenting himself to the electorate as the Father of the American System, a title and program hailed by his partisans as his supreme contribution to the prosperity and future growth of the American nation.[51]

The idea of the system had been in his mind for years. In numerous speeches he had discussed several of its parts. Now he grasped the unity of his program as a unique expression of what needed to be done by the government to benefit Americans in all sections and among all classes and economic endeavors. It was a vision of progress, a bold reformulation of the relationship between government and society. But most important of all, in view of the near breakup of the Union occasioned by the dispute over the admission of Missouri, Clay's American System was intended to strengthen the bonds that tied the nation together into a single whole. It was intended to ensure the perpetuity of a *united* country.

The first element of the American System involved internal improvements. Both Presidents Madison and Monroe had taken a dim view of public

48. Adams, *Memoirs*, VI, 241.

49. Clay to [Charles Hammond], February 22, 1824, in Clay, *Papers*, III, 655.

50. Clay's speech on Greek independence was actually one of his greatest. He later regarded it as one of the half dozen most important speeches of his entire career.

51. The best statement of the American System is Marie-Luise Frings, *Henry Clays American System und die sektionale Kontroverse in den Vereinigten Staaten von Amerika, 1815–1829* (Frankfurt, 1979). Unfortunately, as of this writing, it has not been translated into English. I am very grateful to Frau Frings for a copy of her book. See also James Winkler, "The Political Economy of Henry Clay," doctoral dissertation, Fordham University, 1969.

works and rather regarded them as unwarranted by the Constitution. Indeed, Monroe vetoed a bill in 1822 to repair the Cumberland Road as unconstitutional. Nevertheless, Congress continued to consider legislation affecting internal improvements and tried to shape them so as to avoid presidential displeasure. Early in this session Clay himself made a flat-out statement that "he was one of those who do believe the power of making roads and canals to belong to the government."[52] The matter came to a head when a bill was introduced to appropriate thirty thousand dollars for surveys of those roads and canals that the President might deem militarily or commercially essential to the welfare of the nation. When the bill went to the full Committee of the Whole, Clay took the floor on January 14, 1824, to begin to expound on what became the first part of his American System.

In his speech he repeated his old arguments about the meaning of the word "establish" as used in the Constitution, which he claimed meant "to build," or "make," and he argued that the power to regulate commerce between states necessarily involved the right to construct canals. He also reviewed the meaning of the necessary and proper clause. As a supporter of states' rights he agreed with John Randolph that the nation operated under a limited form of government which had no powers except those that were expressly enumerated in the Constitution or those that were "necessary and proper" to effectuate the enumerated powers. The Constitution, he said, authorized the establishment of post offices and post roads. Mails imply roads; roads imply their preservation; their preservation implies the power to repair them.

The power to regulate commerce, he continued, "if it has any meaning, implies authority to foster it, to promote it, to bestow on it facilities similar to those which have been conceded to our foreign trade. . . . All the powers of this Government should be interpreted in reference to its first, its best, its greatest object, the Union of these States. And is not that Union best invigorated by an intimate, social, and commercial connexion between all the parts of the confederacy?" Roads and canals are also necessary to serve as part of the national defense to repel invasions, suppress insurrections, and enforce the laws.

"Let me ask, Mr. Chairman," he continued, "what has this government done on the great subject of Internal Improvements. . . ?" Precious little, he answered himself. Only the Cumberland Road, which by 1824 began in Maryland and terminated in Wheeling, traversing the states of Maryland, Pennsylvania, and Virginia.[53] Not a cent is spent for a western road, Clay continued, "and yet we have had to beg, entreat, supplicate you, session after session, to grant the necessary appropriations to complete the road." That road is neces-

52. *Annals of Congress,* 18th Congress, 1st session, pp. 999–1000.

53. "There is no prospect at present of a continuation of the U States road Westwardly from Wheeling," wrote Clay in 1819. "It will take place some time or other altho' one may not be able exactly to say when. My best efforts, whilst I continue in Congress, shall be directed to the accomplishment of that favorite object." Clay to John Coburn, February 20, 1819, private collection, copy CPP.

sary, he went on, so that "we should be able to continue and maintain an affectionate intercourse with our friends and brethren—that we might have a way to reach the Capitol of our country . . . to consult and mingle with yours in the advancement of the national prosperity." This is no western bill. It is emphatically a national bill, looks to great national objects without which "the Union, I do most solemnly believe . . . may, at some distant (I trust a far, far, distant) day, be endangered and shaken at its centre."[54]

The archconservative John Randolph of Roanoke challenged Clay's argument and alluded to the Speaker's apparent change of heart about strict construction of the Constitution. After all, Clay had opposed the recharter of the Bank of the United States in 1811 as an unwarranted expansion of federal power. Now a national banking system to control the currency and credit of the United States had become an integral part of his evolving American System. What had happened in the interim to cause him to change his republican principles?

Clay immediately responded. His opposition to the BUS in 1811 involved not only constitutionality but "the expediency of the measure." The war changed everything. Because of the war, the financial difficulties resulting from the absence of a national bank, and the obvious "urgent necessity of such an institution, I did, on further consideration, change my opinion." But so, too, did President James Madison, the Speaker pointed out. And so, too, did a lot of other sound Republicans. Obviously Randolph "has utterly failed" to recognize that there is not "the slightest contradiction between the principles I then held and those on which I advocate the present bill." Randolph argues, Clay continued, that if Congress does not possess the power to charter a bank, it necessarily follows that it has no power to construct internal improvements. He argues from extreme cases, such as his contention that the power of taxation is a power that may be carried so far as to take away a man's last dollar. "But, is this good argument against the existence of the power?"

On one point Randolph had agreed with Clay—namely, the Speaker's limitations as a grammarian, philologer, and critic when explaining the meaning of the word "establish." Clay shot right back: "I know my deficiencies. I was born to no proud patrimonial estate; from my father I inherited only infancy, ignorance, and indigence."[55]

Randolph saw his opening. "The gentleman might continue the alliteration, and add insolence."[56]

Touché! Randolph may have been a bit addled at times and eccentric beyond belief, but his razor-sharp tongue could still slice to the bone. Even so, Clay was more than a match for the feisty Virginian, and both men probably enjoyed their verbal bouts.[57]

54. *Annals of Congress*, 18th Congress, 1st session, pp. 1021–1041.
55. *Annals of Congress*, 18th Congress, 1st session, pp. 1311–1317.
56. Bruce, *John Randolph of Roanoke*, I, 451, note a.
57. "My conscience acquits me entirely of all blame towards that gentleman [Randolph], throughout all our acquaintance. He has ever been the assailant. I have ever been on the defensive. The H.

In any event the House passed the survey bill on February 11, 1824, by the vote of 115 to 86, with New England strongly opposed but the West solidly in favor.[58] The President signed the measure on April 30, 1824.

As the general survey bill worked its way through the House, another important part of Clay's evolving American System also began its tedious progress through Congress. Indeed, this issue constituted the very core of the entire system. It was a tariff specifically aimed at protection—selective protection. As part of the American System it had as its purpose not simply the protection of specific items to assist certain industries or particular raw materials. For Clay the tariff was a means of assisting all sections and classes through the dynamics of increased national wealth and power benefiting all Americans and uniting them in a common purpose and identity. He offered a planned national economy responsive to the new industrial age that had just begun to emerge within the United States.

Technically the first protective tariff was passed in 1816 and established duties on iron products and woolen and cotton goods. But the purpose of that tariff was revenue, not protection. The Tariff of 1816 had the support of the Northeast (with the exception of the shipping interests) and the West. The South voted strongly against it.

Agitation for increased protection followed the Panic of 1819, when Pennsylvania, the foremost manufacturing state in the nation, led the way in favor of tariff reform. Mathew Carey, head of the Pennsylvania Society for the Encouragement of Manufactures and author of *Essays on Political Economy,* and Hezekiah Niles, editor of *Niles' Weekly Register,* among others, organized efforts to move a real protectionist bill through Congress, and Speaker Clay used his considerable power in the House to bring about a new tariff law in 1820. The bill won passage in the House but died in the Senate.

Efforts to raise tariff rates were revived at the beginning of the Eighteenth Congress, and once again Clay stacked the Committee on Manufactures with protectionists, who reported out a bill to increase the ad valorem rates on numerous articles, both raw materials and manufactured products, and substantially raised the level of protection. The South immediately attacked it. To southerners involved in the raising and transporting of cotton, a protective tariff, as they saw it, worked to their immediate detriment and seemed to make the government a partner in enriching the North at their expense. They deemed it unfair for southern cotton growers to sell their cotton on an open market, where the laws of supply and demand determined the price of their commodity, and to buy on a closed market, where the price of manufactured

of R. has always taken part with me and against him in every collision that I ever had with him." Not unexpectedly Randolph and his friends chose Crawford as their presidential candidate, an action that "surprizes me," said Clay. Clay to Francis T. Brooke, March 16, 1824, in Clay, *Papers,* III, 674.

58. New York also opposed the measure since it was involved in building its own internal improvements, like the Erie Canal. The South was divided, with a majority opposed to the bill.

goods was determined by tariff laws that stifled foreign competition. Such South Carolinians as George McDuffie, James Hamilton, Jr., and Robert Y. Hayne argued vehemently against the bill, as did Philip P. Barbour of Virginia, against whose speech Clay rose on March 30, 1824, to plead on behalf of increased protection.

He started at eleven o'clock in the morning and kept speaking until three-thirty in the afternoon. He agreed to interrupt his speech to allow the Committee of the Whole to rise, and he completed his argument the next day.

As he rose to speak, Clay struck an attitude whose grace, one observer remarked, contrasted sharply with "the slovenly make of his dress." He held his snuffbox unopened in his hand, there was frequent putting on and taking off of his eyeglasses—two of his more usual stage props—and he began quietly and a little hesitatingly. But in a moment or two the magnificent voice began to swell as he warmed to his subject and he became "deliciously winning."[59]

He began by invoking "the MOST HIGH" to "shower on my country His richest blessings" and lend the speaker the moral and physical power to do justice to his cause.[60] (Clay regularly claimed moral superiority for all the positions he argued.) He then went on to describe the general distress throughout the country resulting from the Panic of 1819, and he declared that it had been brought on by the fact that the nation had fashioned its industry, navigation, and commerce on international trade based on a European war (the Napoleonic Wars) that had long since terminated. "We have depended too much upon foreign sources of supply," he said, and now that the war had ended, Europe no longer needed American commerce, navigation, and produce. The result had been an unfavorable balance of trade, unemployment, and the diminution of the quantity of money necessary for growth and expansion. "The policy of Europe refuses to receive from us any thing but those raw materials of smaller value, essential to their manufactures, to which they can give a higher value, with the exception of tobacco and rice, which they cannot produce." The United States must create new markets for itself if it is to make headway in the modern world, he said. "We must give new direction . . . [and] speedily adopt a genuine American policy. . . . Let us create also a home market, to give further scope to the consumption of the produce of American industry." Let us withdraw the support we now give to foreign industry. Let us protect our interests at home against the injurious effects of foreign laws and regulations. By creating new businesses, we increase employment and augment the national wealth. Protected raw materials could be sold to these new industries, and the resulting manufactured products would be bought by the producers of the raw materials. Each section of the nation would benefit, for "if we cannot sell, we cannot buy." The home market, Clay continued, "can

59. Martineau, *Retrospect of Western Travel*, pp. 165, 178. Martineau was describing Clay during another performance, but what she said applies equally to this speech.

60. The words Clay actually used were the power "to perform the solemn duties which now belong to his public station."

only be created and cherished by the PROTECTION of our own legislation against the inevitable prostration of our industry, which must ensue from the action of FOREIGN policy and legislation."

What can be done?

Is there no remedy within the reach of the government? Are we doomed to behold our industry languish and decay yet more and more? But there is a remedy, and that remedy consists in modifying our foreign policy, and in adopting a genuine AMERICAN SYSTEM. We must naturalize the arts in our country, and we must naturalize them by the only means which the wisdom of nations has yet discovered to be effectual—by adequate protection against the otherwise overwhelming influence of foreigners. This is only to be accomplished by the establishment of a tariff. . . .

A genuine American System! Clay believed that the adoption of his ideas and policies would benefit the entire country, north and south, east and west. It would encourage and support economic growth. It would increase employment, raise wages, improve prices for agricultural products, and immeasurably strengthen the power of the nation. Clay's nationalism never rang out more strongly, never more fervently. He pleaded with his colleagues to think of the future prosperity they had it in their hands to create.

Clay then took up the objections against the tariff, beginning first with the apprehensions expressed by southerners. He argued that by the improvement of American industry the South would have access to better and cheaper materials. He cited the cotton bagging industry in Kentucky and how it had lowered its price considerably; without protection it would again be prostrated by Scottish manufacturers. He went on to argue against the case made by Daniel Webster for laissez-faire, particularly against the fallacy of the "balance of trade."

The present stagnation of business injures the laboring class most of all, declared Clay. Lack of employment demoralizes workers and society. "The greatest danger to public liberty is from idleness and vice." And whereas in the past labor was the principal element in the production of manufactures, that is no longer true today. Modern inventions and vast improvements in machinery developed in the last few years "have produced a new era in the arts." Thus population and wages no longer constitute the determinants in calculating the "fitness" of a nation to develop manufactures. "Capital, ingenuity in the construction, and adroitness in the use of machinery, and the possession of the raw materials, are those which deserve the greatest consideration." To develop these "arts," the United States must devote its full attention and concern. For the difference between a nation with and without these arts may be best understood by considering the difference between a keelboat and a steamboat fighting the currents of the Mississippi River. With what ease the steamboat outdistances the keelboat, he cried. "Laden with the riches of all quarters of the world, with a crowd of gay, cheerful, and protected passengers," the steamboat slams into the currents or glides smoothly through the eddies near the shore. "Nature herself seems to survey, with astonishment, the passing wonder, and, in silent submission, reluctantly to own the magnificent triumphs, in her own vast dominion, of Fulton's immortal genius!"

Manufactures will never rise up in a country of their own accord, Clay said. History, both ancient and modern, proves that. There must be protection in order to overcome the uncertainty, fluctuation, and unsteadiness of the home market.

As for the argument that the Constitution did not authorize a protective tariff, Clay denied it. The Constitution clearly granted power to regulate commerce with foreign nations and between states, and the grant is plenary, without any limitation whatsoever. Clay was exasperated with the constant argument about constitutionality. If we attempt to build public works, he said, certain gentlemen argue that the Constitution forbids it. If we attempt to protect American industry from foreign rivalry and foreign regulations, the Constitution presents an insuperable obstacle. "This constitution must be a singular instrument!" Clay chortled. "It seems to be made for any other people than our own."[61]

Clay argued that his American System comprehended all the great diversity of economic interests within the nation: agricultural, commercial, navigational, and manufacturing. "The cause is the cause of the country and it must and will prevail." The North, East, and West demand protection. Will the South refuse it and watch the other sections form an independent state? What this bill proposes, Clay continued, is "mutual concession," fair compromise. It falls between absolute exclusion and unrestricted admission of foreign goods. Neither side wins; neither side loses. But all will ultimately benefit. "I invoke that saving spirit of mutual concession under which our blessed Constitution was formed, and under which alone it can be happily administered. I appeal to the South. . . . Nothing human is perfect. . . . Let us imitate the illustrious example of the framers of the Constitution, and, always remembering that whatever springs from man partakes of his imperfections, depend upon experience to suggest, in future, the necessary amendments."[62]

It was a stunning performance, a bold and mighty speech, a stupendous effort to win over his colleagues to his vision of what the United States could become: a great and powerful nation, materially prosperous, with a prosperity that would be shared by every citizen of every class and section. It involved sacrifices; it involved compromises. But the net result would lift the nation to world power and dominance. Henry Clay was one of the few early statesmen to have this vision of America's future greatness and provide the ideas to transform it into reality.

To win passage of this bill, Clay resorted to his old tactics. He pleaded,

61. In an earlier and briefer speech delivered on February 24, 1824, Clay said: "We have tried the raising of tobacco—we have tried horses—we have tried hogs—we have tried hemp: the industry of the country roams from object to object, trying every thing, and alike in vain. We want protection—we ask this government for protection—not against our brethren—not against other states, but against strangers." *Annals of Congress,* 18th Congress, 1st session, p. 1674.

62. *Annals of Congress,* 18th Congress, 1st session, pp. 1962–2001.

cajoled, manipulated, intrigued, and generally discharged the multiple duties of spokesman, organizer, chief strategist, and general factotum. Throughout the session he remained confident that he could ram the measure through the House. "We entertain high hopes of the passage of the Tariff," he told Peter B. Porter. "The South as usual is against it, but we trust that the confidence of opinion which happily exists between the West and the middle states will ensure the passage of that salutary measure."[63] And despite the masterly opposition of Daniel Webster, Robert Y. Hayne, and virtually the entire southern wing of the House membership, the bill passed on April 16 by the close vote of 107 to 102. The middle states and the Northwest voted solidly in favor, the South and Southwest solidly against, and New England split with a majority opposed. A month later the tariff, with amendments, survived a hard fight in the Senate, winning passage by a scant four votes, and President Monroe signed it into law on May 25, 1824. "We are all satisfied that without your great Exertions it would not have been carried," Clay was told by supporters of the bill.[64]

The Tariff of 1824 provided a general level of protection at about 35 percent ad valorem. It was not an especially high tariff, but it did hike duties on iron, woolens, cottons, hemp, and wool and cotton bagging. Clay was naturally pleased with his handiwork, although he expressed reservations. "The measure of protection which it extends to Domestic industry is short of what it should have been," he told George W. Featherstonhaugh, an Englishman who had settled in New York. "But we have succeeded in establishing the principle, and hereafter I apprehend less difficulty will be encountered in giving to it a more comprehensive & vigorous application."[65] James Madison wrote to Clay and indicated his own exceptions to the general principle of protection, but on the whole, replied the Speaker, "my opinions were not widely different from yours." Government ought not to interfere between capital and labor or between different classes of society, he agreed, but "it ought to interfere, in behalf of our own people, against the policy and the measures of Foreign Governments." Once again Clay admitted that the measure fell "short of what many of its friends wished," but considering the "sensibilities" awakened by it, perhaps the wiser course dictated "that we should advance slowly."[66]

63. Clay to Porter, January 31, 1824, in Clay, *Papers,* III, 629. "I think we have nothing to fear in the house," Clay wrote to Mathew Carey, "and if Genl. Jackson adhere to us, nothing in the Senate; for his vote there may be of material consequence." Clay to Carey, January 4, 1824, copy CPP.

64. G. W. Featherstonhaugh to Clay, April 24, 1824, Albany Institute of History and Art, copy CPP. Jackson supported the measure in the Senate.

65. Clay to Featherstonhaugh, May 26, 1824, University of Kentucky Library, Lexington, copy CPP.

66. Clay to Madison, May 25, 1824, Madison Papers, New York Public Library. "With views of the subject such as this," wrote Madison, "I am a friend to the *general* principle of 'free industry' as the basis of a sound system of political Economy. On the other hand I am not less a friend to the legal patronage of domestic manufactures, as far as they come with particular reasons for exceptions to the general rule, not derogating its generality." Madison to Clay, April 24, 1824, in Hunt, ed., *Writings of James Madison,* IX, 183–184.

The Tariff of 1824 was the first truly protective tariff in American history. Clay said that within a few years "it will have accomplished much." Indeed. But among the things he never expected were disagreements so violent that they almost led to bloodshed and civil war.

FOURTEEN

The Presidential
Election of 1824

ALL DURING the great debate over protectionism the presidential question was never far from the minds of congressmen in both houses, Clay's particularly. In taking such a strong and positive stand in favor of the tariff, he knew he was exposing himself to possible political damage. His principal rivals could hide their views to avoid offending any interest or section of the country. "The difference between them & me is, that I have ever been placed in situations in which I could not conceal my sentiments." And those sentiments had remained constant. "They have been formed & declared for these 12 years past."[1] Moreover, they were so essential to the future prosperity and happiness of the American people that he felt compelled to speak forcefully on them despite real concern over their political impact on the electorate. The tariff caused him the most problems, especially in the South.

Sometimes Clay became an utter bore on the subject. At the dinner given to honor the birthday of General Jackson on March 15, he "became warm, vehement, and absurd upon the tariff," reported John Quincy Adams, "and persisted in discussing it, against two or three attempts of [Senator John] Eaton to change the subject of the conversation. He is so ardent, dogmatical, and overbearing that it is extremely difficult to preserve the temper of friendly society with him."[2] Still, Clay believed that the American people would ultimately appreciate the value of his American System to the nation's future growth and would reward him with their confidence and support. He might at times seem too ardent and impetuous in advancing his system, too arrogant and opinionated, but he believed the electorate would discount such defects, recognize his statesmanship, and elect him its chief executive.

1. Clay to Francis T. Brooke, February 29, 1824, in Clay, *Papers,* III, 667.
2. Adams, *Memoirs,* VI, 258.

Indeed, virtually everyone who came into contact with Henry Clay had two opinions of him. All conceded his "talents in debate, & his adroitness in the management of individuals & deliberative bodies," reinforced by exquisite manners and a fascination that few could resist. But that constituted only part of his general portrait. "All admire him," admitted Willie P. Mangum of North Carolina, but "the column that presents so beautiful a Corinthian capital does not rest upon the broad basis of Moral confidence." In short, many believed that Henry Clay would "bargain with the devil" to advance himself, and this hesitation over his integrity lasted throughout his lifetime.[3]

There were speculations, rumors, reports, and hearsay gossip about the election all during the congressional session. At first the speculations centered on whether a caucus of House and Senate Republicans would be held to name their presidential candidate, a traditional practice that had the active support of the Radical followers of William H. Crawford. Clay himself did not believe a caucus would be held because of the number of candidates in the field and their unwillingness to risk defeat in the caucus against the strong organization of the Radicals, led by Senator Van Buren. Besides, the caucus procedure was regarded by many as old-fashioned and undemocratic. Since there was only one national party—the Republican party—its candidate, having no opposition, would automatically win election, and if that candidate was chosen by a clique in Congress, then the people no longer determined the election of their President. Selection of the chief executive would belong to Congress. "The Cause of a Caucus is on the decline," declared Clay, "and I do not think there will be one, unless in a state of despair the friends of Mr. Crawford determine to hold one of a minority of the republicans. I believe I should have nothing to fear from a Caucus composed of all Congress or of all the republican members, to the exclusion of Federalists. A different result might happen if the Caucus should be attended by *all* Mr. Crawford's friends, with but a partial attendance of the friends of other Candidates."[4] All things considered, Clay was certain the idea of a caucus would be abandoned. *"There cannot be any Caucus here,"* he emphatically told Peter B. Porter.[5]

It is extraordinary how wrong Clay could be in predicting future political developments, especially when they involved his own personal interests. In fact, throughout his entire career he was blindly optimistic about his chances for election to the presidential office and always chose to believe that the necessary electoral votes would materialize once he had announced his candidacy.

Martin Van Buren had no intention of allowing the caucus to go by

3. Mangum to Duncan Cameron, December 10, 1823, R. M. Saunders to Mangum, January 23, 1832, in Mangum, *Papers*, I, 83, 463.

4. Clay to Charles Hammond, January 3, 1824, in Clay, *Papers*, III, 560–561.

5. Clay to Porter, January 31, 1824, in Clay, *Papers*, III, 630. Clay let it be known that he was "decidedly hostile to a caucus." Calhoun to Samuel D. Ingham, June 1, 1823, in Calhoun, *Papers*, VIII, 80.

default. He knew his candidate would win nomination if he could get other congressmen to agree to attend. He worked diligently to convince his colleagues that they had a responsibility to the American people to follow tradition—a Jeffersonian tradition, he liked to remind them—and hold a caucus. On February 7 a notice appeared in the Washington *National Intelligencer,* signed by 11 Crawford supporters, summoning congressmen to a meeting to select a presidential candidate to be held on February 14. In the same issue a group of 24 congressmen, representing the Clay, Adams, Calhoun, and Jackson interests, stated that 181 of the 261 members of Congress "deem it inexpedient, under existing circumstances, to meet in Caucus."

The meeting went forward anyway. "Persuasions, threats, coaxing, entreaties were unsparingly used," Clay reported.[6] Some sixty-six members attended, and despite cries that "King Caucus is dead," the balloting began. Then, to the accompaniment of "heavy groans in the Gallery," Crawford was declared the Republican nominee, having received sixty-two votes, while two went to Adams and one apiece to Jackson and Nathaniel Macon of North Carolina. By proxy, two additional votes were also awarded to Crawford. The treasury secretary now joined the company of Jefferson, Madison, and Monroe. All had been nominated by a congressional caucus.[7]

Prior to the meeting Van Buren continued to hope that Clay could be talked into joining the Crawford ticket as candidate for the vice presidency. With "unwearied efforts" he worked to bring about such an arrangement and asked Senator Thomas Hart Benton[8] to serve as go-between. The Magician held "several conferences on the subject" with the Missouri senator, but when the gist of these talks reached Clay, the proposition was rejected out of hand. Clay insisted that his duty required him to seek the presidency and that under no consideration would he agree to second place on the Radical ticket.[9] With Clay unwilling to join the Crawford team, Van Buren then persuaded Albert Gallatin to run in his place, and he was duly nominated at the caucus on February 14.

The other candidates, including Clay, jeered the results. A rump caucus had defied the wishes of the majority of congressmen as well as the thousands of supporters of the other candidates. "Never was any political measure quite so unpopular in the United States," declared *Niles' Weekly Register* on March 13. If Crawford ever had a chance for election, "the *mere fact* of such a nomina-

6. Clay to Porter, February 15, 1824, in Clay, *Papers,* III, 640.
7. Stephen Van Rensselaer to Solomon Van Rensselaer, February 15, 1824, in Mrs. Catharina V. R. Bonney, *A Legacy of Historical Gleanings,* p. 410; Remini, *Van Buren,* p. 48; *National Intelligencer,* February 16, 1824.
8. Clay and Benton were related by marriage. Thomas Hart Benton and Lucretia Hart Clay were cousins, his mother being a Hart. Benton visited Lucretia many times at Ashland. Despite the repeated clashes in Congress between her husband and Benton, Lucretia was always happy to receive her cousin at Ashland, "for she was somewhat proud of her Hart blood." Harrison, "Henry Clay, Reminiscences by His Executor," p. 181.
9. Van Buren, *Autobiography,* pp. 665–666.

tion . . . must inevitably destroy all his prospects." What made it all the more monstrous was the fact that Crawford was desperately ill, too ill to serve as President if elected. He had suffered a paralytic stroke late in the summer of 1823, but news of his condition had been kept secret, with only a few men privy to the extent of his breakdown. When he finally recovered enough to be seen by congressmen, he could not recognize them because he was entirely blind in one eye and could barely see out of the other. "He walks slowly, & like a blind man," reported William Plumer. "His feet were wrapped up with two or three thickness over his shoes—& he told me that they were cold & numb."[10]

Despite these difficulties, the Radicals continued to support his candidacy. In their mind Crawford was the only one committed to limited government and strict construction of the Constitution. Better a President who was paralyzed and blind than one healthy and vigorous and likely to initiate improper legislative programs.

A disaster of sorts also struck down John C. Calhoun. His northern support had been steadily eroding over the months, and when his friends in Pennsylvania swung over to Jackson at a convention held in Harrisburg on March 4, 1824, he decided to give up the race. Jackson was nominated by the Pennsylvanians with only one dissenting vote. But then the convention went on to nominate Calhoun for Vice President. He received eighty-seven votes, with ten each for Clay and Gallatin, eight each for William Findlay and John Tod, and one for Daniel Montgomery, Jr. Under the circumstances Calhoun agreed to stand as a vice presidential candidate and postpone his ambitions for the higher office.

The race had now been reduced to Adams, Crawford, Jackson, and Clay, with Jackson looking stronger each month. If none of them received a majority of electoral votes, as was virtually certain, then the election would be determined in the House of Representatives from among the three men with the highest electoral vote. There was not the slightest doubt in anyone's mind, especially Clay's, that if the election did go to the House and Clay was one of the three, then he would be the next President. This time he was probably right. His popularity, his demonstrated ability, his long service in the House as Speaker, and his many favors to individual representatives all combined to assure his election. At first it was thought that Jackson would fail to win a place among the top three because of his limited experience and lack of "statesmanlike qualities." But his triumph in Pennsylvania coupled with Crawford's sudden illness and caucus nomination now raised the likelihood that he, Adams, and Clay would make it into the House. If so, Clay repeatedly stated, the final result was certain. "If I get into the House I consider my election secure; if Jackson should even get it [sic] into it, leaving me out, he cannot be elected."

10. Clay to Porter, February 15, 1824, in Clay, *Papers,* III, 640–641; Plumer, Jr., to Plumer, April 1, 1824, in Brown, ed., *Missouri Compromises,* p. 108.

"If he [Crawford] Adams and Jackson go into the House, Adams will be elected."[11] This belief that Adams would take the presidency if he, Clay, failed to get into the House was repeated in several letters more than a year before it actually happened. In other words, as far as Clay was concerned, only he and Adams had any real hope of winning election in a House contest. If he himself failed, then he would most certainly support Adams.[12]

Why Adams? Because he was the least objectionable of the three. Jackson was a military chieftain, nothing more. He was hardly the man to serve as successor to Washington, Jefferson, and Madison in the White House. That was the public reason Clay gave for his opposition to Old Hickory, and it was true enough as far as it went. But there was another reason, a more personal one. Jackson was Clay's only rival for western votes. He was the one person who could deny the Speaker a solid base of support from which he could build an electoral majority to propel him into the presidency. And this was a very important consideration. In a confidential letter to Richard Bache, brother-in-law of George M. Dallas, written in February 1824, Clay said that if the election went to the House and he, Clay, was eliminated, "Adams or Crawford will be elected." Jackson was virtually dismissed without another thought.[13] Six months later Clay wrote: "And you may rely upon it that he [Crawford] cannot be elected in that House [the House of Representatives] against any of the Candidates, except perhaps Genl. Jackson."[14]

As for Crawford, Clay excluded him because he was a broken man who could barely speak or see, much less govern. "You see nothing now in the papers respecting the health of Mr. Crawford," the Speaker told Peter B. Porter. "The truth is it is extremely precarious; he is greatly reduced, almost blind in one eye, and the other also affected. Those who know best his condition think it extremely doubtful if he will live through the Summer."[15]

John Quincy Adams was another matter altogether. He did not have the liabilities of Jackson or Crawford, although Clay had to admit that his relations

11. Clay to Porter, January 31, 1824, Clay to Francis T. Brooke, February 26, 1824, in Clay, *Papers,* III, 630, 662.

12. In a letter to Richard Bache on February 17, 1824, Clay did say that "If Jackson, Adams and Crawford should be the three highest, Adams or Crawford will be elected." Clay *Papers,* III, 645. But two weeks later he told Francis P. Blair, "If I do not go into the House, I think Adams will be elected." February 29, 1824, copy CPP.

13. Clay to Bache, February 17, 1824, in Clay, *Papers,* III, 645.

14. Clay to Peter B. Porter, September 2, 1824, in Clay, *Papers,* III, 825.

15. Clay to Porter, April 26, 1824, in Clay, *Papers,* III, 744. Clay summarized his concerns about Crawford in another confidential letter, this one to the Ohio publicist and an ardent supporter Charles Hammond:

"1. The Caucus nomination of him by *a minority.*

"2. The state of his health.

"3. The principles of administration which there is reason to fear will be adopted by him from his position and his Southern support." Clay to Hammond, October 25, 1824, in Clay, *Papers,* III, 871. Hammond edited the Cincinnati *Gazette* from 1825 to 1840, and during the presidential election of 1828 he edited *Truth's Advocate,* which contained some of the worst mudslinging in the entire election.

with Adams had been severely strained over the past few years. And of all the candidates, Adams's principles and ideas on political economy came closest to his own. To a certain extent the Speaker was amused by Adams's candidacy. The secretary of state would win New England, despite his apostasy from Federalism, because of sectional jealousy. And that was about it. Nothing else. He might take a few votes in New York, but his support in the South and West was virtually nonexistent. Still, Adams was a man of stature and accomplishment whose diplomatic and literary skills, among others, were widely acknowledged and admired. Of the four candidates he most approached the ideal set by the Founding Fathers for the chief executive. But as a politician Adams was a walking disaster. "Mr. Adams can not write himself into that office," Clay was told by his supporter Senator Josiah S. Johnston of Louisiana, "& every time he acts personally on the Election it will hurt."[16]

Clay's campaign to win the presidency in 1824 was based on a simple strategy: winning a place among the top three candidates to get into the House. To achieve the necessary electoral votes to accomplish that feat, he counted on the electoral votes of six western states: Kentucky, Indiana, Ohio, Illinois, Missouri, and Louisiana. This would give him 46 electoral votes out of a total of 261, and in early 1824 Clay was telling his friends: "There is not a doubt here about one of them." Then, if he could pick up scattered votes in the East, say, in New York, New Jersey, Pennsylvania, Delaware, and Maryland, it would virtually ensure inclusion in the House.[17] He also figured that if Crawford's health caused a faltering among his friends, Virginia might give Clay, its native son, all or a portion of its electoral votes. Indeed, throughout the summer and fall Clay's supporters in Virginia, particularly Francis T. Brooke, assured him that Crawford's withdrawal would throw the entire Virginia vote to the Speaker.[18]

Other Virginians thought differently. "It is generally believed that Mr. Clay would be the second choice of our State," wrote John Floyd, "but his course has been so strange and uncertain, to say the least of it, that it has given us great dissatisfaction to me particularly who was the medium of his friendly overtures; therefore *I know the whole.*" Obviously Clay's American System was a little too "latitudinarian" to suit many Virginians.[19] Also his "pliancy and laxity" in matters of "morals," according to Thomas Ritchie, a leader of the Richmond Junto and one of Clay's oldest friends. Apparently his "sporting" activities among the ladies in Washington turned Virginians away.[20]

Once Clay got into the House—presumably with Adams and Jackson— he figured it would be a simple matter to topple the general. "For all I can

16. Clay to Josiah S. Johnston, August 4, 1824, in Clay, *Papers,* III, 809.

17. Clay to Richard Bache, February 17, 1824, in Clay, *Papers,* III, 645.

18. Brooke to Clay, July 12, 1824, Clay to Josiah Johnston, August 31, 1824, Clay to Porter, September 2, 1824, in Clay, *Papers,* III, 773–794, 822, 825.

19. Floyd to C. W. Gooch, June 9, 1824, Gooch Family Papers, Virginia Historical Society.

20. Ambler, *Thomas Ritchie,* p. 89.

gather," wrote one, "Clay would as soon see the Devil President as J or A—and thinks that by management . . . he [Jackson] may be defeated so as to leave the real controversy between A & C."[21]

By the time Clay returned to Lexington in early June he was quite confident of his chances of becoming the next President. He could not actively campaign, of course, since self-promotion was frowned upon in those days, even in Kentucky. He tried not to worry, even though he must have known that Jackson might possibly drain away some of his western support. Listening to the political comment of ordinary citizens who did not know him, and reading local newspapers, should have alerted him to the danger, that of competing with a war hero out on the frontier. Still, he chose to believe that westerners could distinguish between statesmen and military chieftains and would vote intelligently. He remained blindly optimistic about his chances.

In July Clay went to Columbus, Ohio, to attend the federal district court on Bank business, but he enjoyed only limited success. "We lost two cases," he told Nicholas Biddle, the new president of the BUS, and two others were continued by the court.[22] Upon his return to Lexington Clay took a short vacation with his family "at one of our watering places"—probably Olympian Springs or Greenville Springs—and returned to Ashland at the end of August to wait out the results of the election. His optimism never faltered.[23]

In the election of 1824[24] six out of the twenty-four states in the Union chose their presidential electors in the state legislatures. Consequently, considerable lobbying among political brokers took place in those states before the votes were cast. Elsewhere local leaders played a vital role in determining how their states finally balloted, so they were regularly courted by the friends of the several candidates. As the election drew nearer, the attacks these friends leveled against their opponents grew fiercer, particularly between the partisans of Adams and Crawford. Since the two candidates were both cabinet officers laden with patronage—and Crawford had been very active in the disbursement of his largess—the two men had strong newspaper support in the leading cities,[25] and these newspapers flailed away at each other with a vengeance.

21. C. W. Gooch to Thomas Ritchie, April 24, 1824, Gooch Family Papers, Virginia Historical Society.

22. Clay to Biddle, August 7, 1824, in Clay, *Papers,* III, 804–805.

23. Clay to Johnston, August 31, 1824, in Clay, *Papers,* III, 821.

24. For the election of 1824, see James F. Hopkins, "Election of 1824," *History of American Presidential Elections, 1789–1968,* ed. Schlesinger, and Israel, I, 349–381; Paul C. Nagel, "The Election of 1824: A Reconsideration Based on Newspaper Opinion," *Journal of Southern History,* XXVI (1960), pp. 315–329; Donald J. Ratcliffe, "The Role of Voters and Issues in Party Formation: Ohio, 1824," *Journal of American History,* LIX (1973), pp. 847–870; and Logan Esarey, "The Organization of the Jacksonian Party in Indiana," *Mississippi Valley Historical Association Proceedings,* VII (1914), pp. 220–243.

25. "Although I believe the number of my personal friends is not exceeded by that of either of the other Candidates," wrote Clay, "there is a large, indeed, the larger, mass of the Community who do not stand in the relations of friendship to any of the candidates. On that mass the Secretaries are able to throw out, from their respective departments, a more intense & vivifying heat than I am

"The Conflict between Adams & Crawford grows fiercer," wrote Clay's supporter Josiah Johnston, "—see the [Washington] National Journal. [Richmond] Enquirer—[Washington *National*] Intelligencer. [Albany] Argus &c." Fortunately Clay escaped the melee. "This is one advantage at least you enjoy by having no press—you certainly provoke no hostility."[26]

Johnston worked sedulously for Clay's election. No other man did as much. He positioned himself in Philadelphia and regularly dashed up to New York to drum up support. Back and forth he shuttled between the two cities. Just a few votes from these protariff states could make all the difference in the world. He reported his findings and success regularly to Clay, and frequently several times a day.

The lack of adequate newspaper backing may have kept Clay out of the range of the guns of the Adams and Crawford press, but it meant that Clay's candidacy was not getting the attention it needed to inspire support. And rumors constantly circulated that he had dropped out of the race. "Having no press," Johnston told the candidate, "—It is impossible to present your claims or your Chances before the people—or to Counteract the United efforts of all parties to withdraw you from the Contest."

Johnston did what he could to remedy the situation and on September 16 happily informed Clay that the Philadelphia *Aurora* had agreed to come out in his favor. Johnston rushed copies of the announcement to Clay,[27] and the Committee of Correspondence in Philadelphia sent one hundred copies to supporters throughout the country. "It will gave a good effect," Johnston said. "It will Keep alive your Cause which sunk every where under the want of direction & management.—I had myself no idea untill the adjournment of Congress of the total want of Interest or Zeal or arrangement among your friends With a little activity & money a sufficient number of presses would have been engaged."

When Johnston heard that the *Patriot* could "be had in New York for some money," he raced to the city "to accomplish this object—It is in vain to strive against the United influence of the press without one," he said. And he succeeded in his mission. "I have made a running visit to New York," he told Clay. "Secured the Patriot & returned this morning. It will at least have the effect to disseminate the truth."[28]

As the campaign moved into the final weeks, this lack of organization and management started to dishearten Clay a little. He feared that his friends in the

---

capable of ejecting. The Cities are focal points for the collection and subsequent distribution of this heat. The evil is great but I have seen no conscientious course but that of patiently bearing it." Clay to Johnston, September 10, 1824, in Clay, *Papers,* III, 832.

26. Johnston to Clay, August 30, 1824, in Clay, *Papers,* III, 820.

27. For his part Clay had copies of election materials—circulars, addresses, broadsides—prepared by the Kentucky Committee of Correspondence and sent to committees in Philadelphia and New York. Clay to Johnston, September 19, 1824, in Clay, *Papers,* III, 842.

28. Johnston to Clay, September 19, 22, 26, 1824, in Clay, *Papers,* III, 843, 844–845, 851.

West would become discouraged because of the absence of eastern enthusiasm and support. He feared they would bolt to Jackson. He was also distressed by the reports of newspapers, especially the Washington *National Intelligencer,* that "I have not a friend in the New York Legislature," where the electors would be chosen.[29] And the Radicals never ceased urging him to drop out of the race in favor of Crawford and take the vice presidency instead. "The friends of Crawford are still very anxious to make you Vice President. . . . It is much a subject of Correspondence among them—They Count Confidently upon most of your Votes in that event—They say [Albert] Gallatin would not be in the way."[30] In addition, Clay had several communications from Adams's friends in New York suggesting that they form a coalition to divide the state's electoral votes. Unfortunately he rejected these overtures.[31] The vice presidential offer gave him pause, however. Although it was much too late to make a switch, he told his "Eastern friends" that if they "think proper to bring me forward for the office of V.P. I wish it distinctly understood that it is their own movement, unprompted by me."[32]

But surely he knew the risks involved. His ardent supporters, especially in the West, would be devastated if he withdrew, and he himself admitted that if "Mr. Gallatin were dropt, and Mr. Calhoun and myself only were run, Mr. Calhoun would be elected."[33] No, he must press on, however feeble his campaign compared with what his rivals had mounted.

It really bothered Clay that his advocacy of an American System had not excited the electorate and strengthened his candidacy. He could understand the opposition he engendered in the South because of his stand on the tariff. But that stand should have won him northern backing. "It is a little remarkable," he complained to Johnston, "that my support of the Tariff has excited against me in the South, a degree of opposition, which is by no means counterbalanced by any espousal of my cause in Pennsa. and other quarters, where the Tariff was so much desired."[34] The tariff was also cited as the cause of his weakening position in Louisiana, with General Jackson the immediate beneficiary, even though Old Hickory was seen by some "as much a Tariff man" as Clay himself, only "his conduct was more covert." Alarms were sent to Clay in September urging him to "have your services to Louisa. enumerated"—such as

29. Clay to Johnston, August 31, 1824, in Clay, *Papers,* III, 821.

30. Johnston to Clay, September 4, 1824, in Clay, *Papers,* III, 829. The Richmond Junto hoped to force the vice presidency upon Clay, even without his knowledge or consent, by getting New York (rather than Virginia since he was a native son) to nominate him for the position. "Mr. Clay's friends in Virginia are anxious that he should be taken up in this manner," wrote C. W. Gooch to Van Buren on September 4, 1824. "It will unite us most effectively. As to consulting Mr. Clay it is injudicious. Let him not be consulted, and the force of circumstances must urge him into an acquiescence. And this will be done, too, without hazard. . . ." Van Buren Papers, LC.

31. Clay to Porter, September 2, 1824, in Clay, *Papers,* III, 825.

32. Clay to Johnston, September 3, 1824, in Clay, *Papers,* III, 826.

33. Clay to Johnston, September 10, 1824, in Clay, *Papers,* III, 833.

34. Clay to Johnston, September 3, 1824, in Clay, *Papers,* III, 827.

his efforts on behalf of molasses protection—or he could lose five precious electoral votes.[35]

Despite his growing despondency, Clay labored to cheer his friends about his prospects. He tried to be honest with them and state the disturbing facts as he saw them, but he also held out the hope that they would ultimately succeed. "I think my friends have no occasion to despair," he wrote, "although it must be admitted that the issue of the Election continues very doubtful. Many circumstances may arise; many combinations of interest in other States may take place. And it appears to me that the best course for us to pursue is to persevere with hope and confidence."[36]

To add to his malaise, Clay's family had been generally unwell. Theodore had recently returned from New Orleans and had come down with "a threatening fever," said Clay, "and I have myself had a slight attack."[37]

Another blow of sorts resulted from the visit to the United States of the Marquis de Lafayette. He was in the midst of a triumphant return, and his appearance produced an outpouring of popular affection and goodwill. He excited interest and attention everywhere he went. He represented a hallowed history, a revolutionary generation, and although a foreigner, he had played a vital role in winning American independence. As he paraded across the country, he seemed to link the present generation with its glorious past, and the people saluted him as hero and liberator.

Clay and Lafayette had met in Europe, and upon the Frenchman's arrival in the United States the Kentuckian wrote to him and invited him to Ashland for a visit. An invitation to visit the many was also extended in a resolution offered by Clay at a public meeting. Lafayette responded to the Speaker in a letter written from New York. "Your kind Congratulations and Affectionate letter Are New testimonies of those Sentiments which I am proud and Happy to Have obtained from You and which are Most Cordialy [*sic*] Reciprocated," said Lafayette. ". . . it is My fond determination to Visit the Southern and Western States, and I Anticipate the pleasure to find Myself under your friendly Roof at Ashland."[38]

What possibly worked to Clay's political disadvantage from the Frenchman's visit was the fact that Lafayette undoubtedly reawakened American veneration for their revolutionary heroes. And some of these heroes still lived—like Andrew Jackson, for example, who had fought in the Revolution, suffered capture, assault by a British officer, imprisonment, and the loss of his immedi-

35. William L. Brent to Clay, September 3, 1824, in Clay, *Papers,* III, 828. "The people [of Louisiana] know nothing of mr Clay," wrote Isaac L. Baker to Jackson on May 3, 1823, "and are not for him." Jackson, *Correspondence,* III, 196.

36. Clay to Robert P. Henry, September 14, 1824, in Clay, *Papers,* III, 839.

37 Clay to John J. Crittenden, September 17, 1824, in Clay, *Papers,* III, 842.

38. Lexington *Kentucky Reporter,* October 4, 1824; Lafayette to Clay, October 18, 1824, in Clay, *Papers,* III, 868. Unfortunately Lafayette did not reach Kentucky until May 1825, and Clay was still in Washington at the time. However, they did meet in Washington in late 1824.

ate family. Of the four candidates, only he could claim participation, like Lafayette, in securing American freedom from the British.[39]

Perhaps the one bright note for Clay in this period of his life came when
he finally paid off the enormous debt he had owed John Jacob Astor.[40] It was a
tremendous relief to be free of this burden and it gave him great satisfaction. "I
. . . no longer am afflicted by fears of the condition in which I should leave my
family, if I were cut off suddenly." A few more years of his present prosperity,
he said, and he would be completely "liberated from debt."[41]

By October Clay had reluctantly come to the conclusion that his only
hope for success in the election centered on winning a healthy share of electoral votes from the New York legislature. "My entry into the House," said
Clay, "depends upon N. York. If that State divides its vote with either Mr.
Adams or Mr. Crawford and myself I shall be returned." Or if Adams took the
entire New York vote, then Virginia might abandon Crawford for Clay. In
either case the Speaker believed he would go into the House.[42] So he cleverly
began negotiations to find a running mate from the state who could best help
him secure the needed votes. However, his strongest supporter in New York,
Peter B. Porter, advised him that he did not think it wise to select another Vice
President from his state. The Virginia-New York axis, with Virginia selecting
the President and New York the Vice President, had provoked considerable
jealousy from other states, Porter said. That axis had been functioning since
1800, and it was time for a change. Even so, Porter obliged the Kentuckian and
threw out the names of two New Yorkers as possible candidates, Smith
Thompson and Nathan Sanford; only he doubted whether Thompson would
agree to stand for the office.[43] Ultimately Sanford won the support of Clay's
friends, and the Speaker said he was sure that Ohio and Kentucky would vote
for him. "I feel considerable solicitude in regard to the Vice Presidency, on
account of the American policy," said Clay. ". . . If during the next Administration, we should have both the President and Vice President against us, what
should we be able to effect in advancing the internal prosperity of the
Union?"[44]

Several times the friends of Adams in New York approached Clay's sup-

39. The newspapers carried descriptions of the General Jackson's hardships and pain in serving his
country. See Remini, *Jackson,* II, pp. 74–75, for an extended discussion of the impact of Lafayette's
visit on the campaign.

40. William B. Astor to Clay, October 4, 1824; memorandum on bond to John J. Astor, November 1, 1824, Clay to James Erwin, December 13, 1824, in Clay, *Papers,* III, 857, 874, 895. For the
amount and reasons for Clay's indebtedness to Astor, see Chapter XI.

41. Clay to James Brown, January 23, 1824, in Clay, *Papers,* IV, 38.

42. Clay to Hammond, October 25, 1824, in Clay, *Papers,* III, 871.

43. Porter to Clay, April 5, 1824, in Clay, *Papers,* III, 733. Clay had hoped to get Porter himself,
"but your unfortunate deafness forms an objection to you." Clay to Porter, February 15, 1824,
ibid., III, 641.

44. Clay to George W. Featherstonhaugh, October 10, 1824, Miscellaneous Clay Papers, Manuscript Department, Filson Club, Louisville, Kentucky.

porters with a proposition in which the votes would be divided, sometimes equally and sometimes on a two-to-one basis in favor of Adams, depending on who made the offer, but all these proposals had been summarily rejected.[45] Clay agreed with this action by his supporters. He did not care to engage in open and undisguised management at this point. Or perhaps he thought he did not have to go quite that far to win the necessary votes. Besides, he could hardly repudiate actions already taken by his friends. So he took the high road. "Be perfectly assured," he liked to tell his supporters, "that if I am elected, I shall enter upon the office without one solitary promise or pledge to any man to redeem; and if I am not elected, I will at least preserve unsullied that public integrity and those principles which my friends have supposed me to possess."[46]

But New York needed management, and Clay's friends made the incredible mistake (which they later acknowledged) of not agreeing to some kind of coalition with the Adams faction. For as it soon turned out, it was Crawford that Clay's friends needed to knock out of the race. And Crawford's Radical friends in New York, led by Van Buren, were strong and well organized. They were also determined to capture enough votes to place their candidate among the three to go into the House.[47] But they needed additional support in the New York legislature to achieve their object, and they were therefore willing to share a ticket with one of the other candidates.

But which one? Van Buren wrote to Joseph Gales, editor of the Washington *National Intelligencer,* and asked what he thought of dividing "the votes of New York with Mr. Clay or Mr. Adams." Gales promptly responded that if Massachusetts voted for Adams and "it is necessary to split the apple, the half had better be given to Mr Clay than to Mr Adams—for I begin to believe he will lose Ohio, where the People appear to be getting Jackson-mad!" Nine days later Gales changed his mind. He liked Clay "less and less," he said, because of his "indefatigable efforts to work into the Ho of Reps to get himself . . . elected to the first place."[48]

All things considered, Van Buren probably favored giving a share of the apple to Clay. Then, when the Kentuckian's followers claimed they were "disposed to take up Mr. Crawford as their second choice" should their own candidate bow out, that settled it.[49] A caucus meeting of Radicals on November 5 devised a ticket giving seven of New York's thirty-six electoral votes to Clay.

45. Porter to Clay, October 6, 1824, in Clay, *Papers,* III, 860.

46. Clay to Hammond, October 25, 1824, in Clay, *Papers,* III, 870–871.

47. Outside of Virginia and Georgia the Radicals could not expect much help from any other state—with the possible exception of Delaware—so they had to obtain as many New York votes as possible.

48. Gales to Van Buren, October 17, 26, 1824, Van Buren Papers, LC. Van Buren's political nemesis De Witt Clinton favored Jackson; that automatically excluded the general from the Magician's plans.

49. Ralph Lockwood to Francis Brooke, November 17, 1824, Clay Papers, LC.

When the New York legislature met on November 10, the Radicals rammed their ticket through the upper house, where they held a majority. "We could not avoid taking them [the seven Clay men] on also," Van Buren later advised Crawford in explaining the necessity of a split ticket, "as they came from districts which were entirely agt us. . . . We could not do without their votes & therefore had no discretion on the subject. The assurance given us was that if the rest of our ticket prevailed they would *certainly* vote with us & *probably* if it did not."[50]

In the lower house the situation was altogether different because there was such division among the three (Crawford, Adams, and Clay) factions that no one ticket could command a majority. So Van Buren did something incredibly stupid and underhanded. He advised the Radicals in the lower house to vote for the Adams ticket to break the deadlock and force the legislature to a joint ballot. By reducing the contest to Adams and Crawford at the joint meeting of the two houses, Van Buren presumed that Clay's friends would vote for the Radical candidate to form the winning majority since they had promised to do so once the Kentuckian had been eliminated. How he could come to such a harebrained conclusion when it was the action of the Radicals that had eliminated the Clay ballot in the lower house and produced the joint session defies understanding. Probably Van Buren assumed the Clay men would support the Crawford ticket in order to protect their seven votes. And the entire maneuver was done out in the open. The Radicals in the lower house foolishly broadcast their intention of voting for the Adams ticket. The announcement was so sudden and unexpected that the Clay men were thrown "into convulsions, & . . . made some inflammatory remarks."[51] Nonetheless, the Adams ticket was approved.

A "fouler" and more "dishonorable piece of management," wrote one of the Clay men, "could not in my estimation be adopted."[52]

As Clay's friends left the chamber, seething with rage over their betrayal, several of Adams's supporters, including Thurlow Weed, Henry Wheaton, and James Tallmadge, pulled them to one side. They were persuaded to attend a secret meeting that evening, November 12, where they were told they could avenge their wrong and pick up a few votes for their candidate. What that meeting produced was a split ticket. Since the joint meeting of the legislature could select electors only from the two tickets approved by the upper and lower house, the friends of Clay were forced to vote for the Crawford ticket if they wanted to elect their seven men on the joint ballot. But Adams's friends proposed that a split ballot be printed with the names of men taken from the two tickets already passed in the two houses. The Clay men would be removed from the Crawford ticket and added to a group of men taken from the Adams

50. Van Buren to Crawford, November 17, 1824, Van Buren Papers, LC.

51. Benjamin F. Butler to Jesse Hoyt, November 13, 1824, Miscellaneous Papers, New York Public Library.

52. Ralph Lockwood to Francis Brooke, November 17, 1824, Clay Papers, LC.

ticket. Thus the Crawford slate would fail, and Adams and Clay would divide New York's electoral vote. In addition, Tallmadge and Wheaton agreed to exert an "influence" upon the electors "to induce them to give to Mr Clay a sufficient number of votes to ensure his return [as a presidential candidate] to the House of Representatives." There was a tacit understanding that at least eight votes would go to Clay.[53]

Without giving it a second thought the Clay men approved the proposal, and Thurlow Weed spent Sunday morning at the offices of the Albany *Daily Advertiser* printing the split ticket.[54] On Monday, November 15, the two houses of the New York legislature met together to select the state's electoral vote, 157 members present and voting. After the canvassing had been completed, the Radical presiding officer drew the first ballot from the ballot box to start the counting. He stared at it in disbelief.

"A printed split ticket!" he gasped.

"Treason by G——!" screamed a Radical, jumping to his feet.[55]

Confusion ensued, but above the din could be heard the voice of James Tallmadge demanding the count be continued. After many minutes of screaming and shouting and exiting by outraged Radicals the counting resumed. The result showed that seven Clay electors had received ninety-five votes, twenty-five Adams men had seventy-eight votes, and the Crawford electors had seventy-six with three blanks. It was then agreed that twenty-five Adams and seven Clay electors had been chosen with the four remaining electors to be selected on the following day.[56]

But the skulduggery had not yet run its course. After all, this was New York politics. On the following day, when the joint session of the legislature met again to fill the four remaining slots, the Clay men switched sides and voted with the Radicals. They were fearful that Adams would receive so many votes as to destroy the possibility of the election ending up in the House of Representatives. Thus, Adams took twenty-five of New York's thirty-six votes, Clay seven, and Crawford four.

The Clay men were delighted with their handiwork. "Van B. looks like a wilted cabbage," they laughed; "his invincibles are beaten at last."[57]

One more round of double-dealing had yet to be played out, however. When the New York electors met on December 1 to cast their votes for President and Vice President, enough pressure had been brought to bear on them to produce several changes. One Adams elector, for example, switched to Crawford, and one Clay elector went over to Adams. Then, for some unac-

53. A. Conkling to John W. Taylor, December 24, 1824, Taylor Papers, New-York Historical Society; Roger Skinner to Van Buren, December 1, 1824, Van Buren Papers, LC.

54. Remini, *Van Buren*, p. 78.

55. Thurlow Weed, *Autobiography of Thurlow Weed* (Boston, 1883), pp. 123–124.

56. Remini, *Van Buren*, p. 80.

57. Henry Wheaton to S. L. Gouverneur, November 21, 1824, T. S. Smith to Gouverneur, November 15, 1824, Gouverneur Papers, New York Public Library.

countable reason, two of the Clay electors did not appear to cast their ballots, and their places were taken by Adams's friends. A third elector had been subjected to so many threats that out of sheer stubbornness or perversity he voted for Andrew Jackson.

But what about the assurances the Clay men had received from Tallmadge and Wheaton that they would exert an "influence" upon the electors to guarantee that Clay would get enough votes to go into the House of Representatives? Thurlow Weed argued that the pledge of votes to Clay—even the original seven—was made conditional upon Clay's carrying Louisiana, and when he lost Louisiana, "that left our friends free to vote for Mr. Adams."[58]

A likely story. As a matter of fact, the New York electors did not know the results of the Louisiana election at the time they voted. The New York electors met on December 1 while the Louisiana result was not known in the East until December 15 at the earliest.[59]

When the New York ballots were finally tabulated and sent to Washington, the results showed twenty-six for Adams, five for Crawford, four for Clay, and one for Jackson.[60] "The grand mistake," Porter dejectedly told Clay several months later, "in the policy of your friends in this State was in not closing at once with the offer made by the Adams men to divide the ticket equally. Many of us were fully impressed with the propriety of this course, but we could not bring a sufficient number into the measure, while it was practicable."[61]

The New York results were devastating for Clay. As the returns in the fall elections from other states (where the popular vote decided the selection of the electors) started coming in, the Great Compromiser began to read the full dimension of his defeat.[62] Kentucky voted overwhelmingly for him, giving him 17,331 popular votes to 6,455 for Jackson. Neither Adams nor Crawford received a single vote in Kentucky.[63] But Ohio, where Clay had expected a tremendous victory, proved disappointing and showed how much he had misread political developments. He won the state but with a plurality of only 798 votes over Jackson. "Your prediction," Clay told Francis Brooke, "has been well nigh being verified as to Genl. Jackson's taking the Western vote from me.

58. Weed, *Autobiography,* pp. 128.

59. John W. Taylor to A. Conkling, December 8, 1824, Taylor Papers, New-York Historical Society; Clay to William D. Ford, December 13, 1824, Clay Papers, Manuscript Department, Filson Club, Louisville, Kentucky; Adams, *Memoirs,* VI, 446; *Niles' Weekly Register,* December 25, 1824.

60. For all the maneuvering that took place before the final electoral votes were cast, see Remini, *Van Buren,* pp. 72–84.

61. Porter to Clay, January 14, 1825, in Clay, *Papers,* IV, 17.

62. "Had our expectations to the West been realized, the actual state of the vote at Albany would have been less material. But there unfortunately we have been also disappointed. . . . We have not yet heard from Louisiana, but I am prepared . . . to receive unfavorable intelligence from it." Clay to George W. Featherstonhaugh, December 9, 1824, Miscellaneous Clay Papers, Manuscript Department, Filson Club, Louisville, Kentucky.

63. Or if they did win a few votes, they were so small in number that they were disregarded in the final tallies.

My friends have prevailed over him in Ohio but only about 7 or 8 hundred votes."[64] The Indiana result was worse. Jackson received 7,343 votes, Clay 5,315, and Adams 3,095. Illinois also deserted Clay for Jackson. In the final tally in that state the general won 1,901 popular votes, Adams came next with 1,542, then Clay with 1,047, and Crawford last with 219. The West had all but abandoned Clay. He won Missouri, Ohio, and Kentucky for a total of thirty-three electoral ballots. The four he got from New York brought his total to thirty-seven.[65]

Of the six states representing his strategy for victory—Kentucky, Indiana, Ohio, Illinois, Missouri, and Louisiana—three had given their electoral votes to other candidates. Louisiana was the final blow. This was another state in which the legislature chose the electors.[66] Supposedly Clay had the votes of thirty-one out of fifty-eight members of the legislature with two additional votes expected to arrive before the election. But then "much misfortune attended" the final balloting. Two of his supporters were injured from an overturned gig and were unable to attend the final voting; three others deserted, "in consequence of false rumors" that Clay had withdrawn from the race. As a result the Adams-Jackson joint ticket won by a count of thirty to twenty-eight, thereby dividing Louisiana's vote between Jackson, who received three, and Adams, who was awarded two. "Thus," editorialized the *Argus of Western America* on December 15, 1824, "while the strongest man in the state got no votes at all, the weakest got *two*. Such is the consequence of political barter."[67]

When the popular and electoral votes were tabulated from every state, Jackson had a plurality of 152,901 popular and 99 electoral votes; Adams had 114,023 popular and 84 electoral votes; Crawford had 46,979 and 41 electoral votes; and Clay came last with 47,217 and 37 electoral votes.[68] Jackson won most of the South, Tennessee, Pennsylvania, New Jersey, most of the Maryland vote, Indiana, and scattered votes elsewhere. New England and most of New York went to Adams, while Crawford took Virginia and Georgia. In the vice presidential race John C. Calhoun won handily, receiving 182 votes to 30 for Nathan Sanford, 24 for Nathaniel Macon, 13 for Jackson, 9 for Van Buren, and 2 for Clay.

Since none of the presidential candidates had the necessary majority of electoral votes, the final decision on the next President belonged to the House of Representatives, and Clay was automatically excluded from consideration. Had he received the votes promised to his New York supporters in their secret

64. Clay to Brooke, November 26, 1824, in Clay, *Papers,* III, 887.

65. Missouri gave Clay 1,401 popular votes, Jackson 987, and Adams 311. Hopkins, "Election of 1824," I, 409.

66. The six states included New York, Louisiana, South Carolina, Delaware, Georgia, and Vermont.

67. Clay to Brooke, December 22, 1824, and Clay to Porter, December 26, 1824, in Clay, *Papers,* III, 900, 904–905.

68. Hopkins, "Election of 1824," I, 409.

meeting on November 12, he would have replaced Crawford in the House election. In that case he would have been elected President—unquestionably. "Had the vote there been given to me, as you had every reason to anticipate," he wrote to Peter B. Porter, "my entry into the H. of R. would have been secured, without taking into account of the contingency of the vote of Louisiana."[69]

How had he managed to do so poorly against a military chieftain and an invalid? Where had he failed? Clay chalked it up to four factors: "the discouragement of my friends—the power of the Atlantic press—the influence of Governmental patronage—the fabrication of tales of my being withdrawn, propagated so late as to accomplish their object before they could be contradicted."[70] Perhaps some or all of these factors entered the final equation, but what really blew Clay out of the contest was something over which he had no control and did not foresee: Andrew Jackson's unanticipated rise of political popularity throughout the nation, particularly in the West. Everyone knew he was a popular war hero, but few thought that popularity could be translated into electoral votes. Jackson's rise to political prominence annihilated Clay's previously unrivaled preeminence in the West, and it lost him enough votes to exclude him from House consideration.

"I laugh off, and bear with unaffected fortitude, our defeat," he told Porter. "We have no reproaches to make ourselves, and it is a source of high satisfaction that my character has not suffered but been elevated by the whole Canvass." To others he added: "My friends need entertain no fears about my bearing with grace and fortitude our defeat."[71]

Still, it must have been a stinging blow to his pride. He, the author of the American System, the Great Compromiser, the man best qualified to preside over the future development of the nation, beaten by men less worthy: by a political flyweight, a military chieftain, and a physical wreck.

He sighed. "I only wish that I could have been spared such a painful duty as that will be of deciding between the persons who are presented to the choice of the H. of R."[72]

69. Clay to Porter, December 7, 1824, in Clay, *Papers,* III, 892.
70. Clay to Porter, December 7, 1824, Clay to Josephus B. Stuart, December 6, 1824, in Clay, *Papers,* III, 891, 892.
71. Clay to Porter, December 26, 1824, Clay to Hubbard Taylor, December 25, 1824, 1824, in Clay *Papers,* III, 904, 905.
72. Clay to Porter, December 7, 1824, in Clay, *Papers,* III, 892.

FIFTEEN

The "Corrupt Bargain"

I N LATE NOVEMBER Clay headed for Washington by way of Monticello. He planned to visit Thomas Jefferson, stay a day or two with him, and then call on James Madison at his home, Montpelier, in Orange County, Virginia. Both former Presidents made it clear to those who called on them that they disapproved of the election of General Jackson. Madison would not comment further, but Jefferson said he preferred Crawford, although he reckoned Adams a "very safe man."[1]

On reaching Washington in early December, Clay roomed with Representative Robert Letcher from Lancaster, Kentucky, among others, in a lodging house on Ninth Street. Against his wishes, Lucretia Clay chose not to accompany her husband. "Her long absence from society," said her husband, "and the too rigorous economy to which she thinks herself bound to subject herself opposed [sic] in her view, obstacles to her accompanying me which I could not overcome."[2]

Clay therefore socialized in Washington on his own. He accepted almost every invitation he received to a party or dinner. And he gadded about the capital quite extensively, usually with a handsome lady on each arm.

Many years later Gideon Welles, admittedly a staunch political adversary and stern moralist, commented on the many changes that had occurred in Washington over a twenty-year span. "I think the place has also improved in its moral aspect," he added. "There is less drinking less gambling—and less lewdness, notwithstanding the increase of population. The deportment of the members of Congress has greatly improved. A few men can do much to debauch the public mind. I think the influence of Henry Clay was pernicious and of a most demoralizing tendency. This I say without partizan prejudice, and without any design to do him wrong. But he was in former days the champion in the vices to which I allude, and commended by the fashionable vicious as the

1. Clay to Francis Brooke, November 26, 1824, in Clay, *Papers,* III, 888; Plumer, Jr., to Plumer, December 24, 1824, in Brown, ed., *Missouri Compromises,* p. 125.
2. Clay to James Brown, January 23, 1825, in Clay, *Papers,* IV, 38; *National Intelligencer,* December 4, 1824.

true specimen of a free hearted man, who would not be controlled by a rigid morality."[3]

There can be no doubt that Clay led a rather free and easy life during his many years in Washington, particularly those times when unaccompanied by his wife. He could never be accused of possessing a "rigid morality," and his drinking and gambling did become excessive at times. But did the "lewdness" accusation—whatever that meant to Welles personally—signify infidelity? Quite possibly. James Hammond of South Carolina, who hated Clay and had an enormous sexual appetite himself, noted in his diary that "the very greatest men that have lived have been addicted to loose indulgences with women. It is the besetting sin of the strong, and of the weak also, of our race. Among us now Webster and Clay are notorious for it. . . ." John Quincy Adams commented in his diary about Clay's loose morals, both public and private, and Andrew Jackson, of course, claimed that "all who know Mr. Clay knows that individually he is void of good morals, and that he is politically a reckless demagogue [sic], ambitious and regardless of truth when it comes in the way of his ambition."[4]

Whenever Clay traveled on the Ohio River, it was reported that he "passed a large portion of his time in the ladies' saloon." There could be no question that Clay always went out of his way to enjoy the company of women. And he never failed to kiss a lady if the opportunity presented itself, even on the floor of Congress. On one occasion someone jokingly tried to estimate the number of ladies he had "affectionately saluted." Clay laughed out loud. "Kissing was like the presidency," he exclaimed; "it was not to be sought, and not to be *declined.*" And he was very accomplished at kissing because his "mouth was huge,—prodigeous." The "ample dimensions of his kissing apparatus," reported one man, "enabled him completely to *rest* one side of it, while the other side was upon active duty." But more often than not all this public kissing meant little. His correspondence with women shows him to be a warmhearted, caring, and sentimental man, but nothing in his letters suggest anything improper. So no absolute judgment can be rendered about his reputed lewdness. Suffice it to say that a number of contemporaries regarded him as a man with "loose morals," and that sort of gossip, innuendo, and implication did him considerable harm in future presidential elections as American society become increasingly concerned with moral reform.[5]

Within a few days of his arrival in the capital in December 1824, Clay threw himself into the social whirl. He also received the results of the election

---

3. Welles manuscript diary, entry for June 28, 1846, Huntington Library, Pasadena, California.

4. Carol Bleser, ed., *Secret and Sacred: The Diaries of James Henry Hammond, a Southern Slaveholder* (New York, 1989), p. 172. The notation occurs on December 9, 1846. Adams, *Memoirs,* V, 325; Jackson to D. G. Goodlett, March 12, 1844, in Jackson, *Correspondence,* VI, 275.

5. Mowatt, *Autobiography of an Actress,* p. 258; Jones, *The Influence of Henry Clay upon Abraham Lincoln* , p. 13. Even William Henry Harrison commented on Clay's "great admiration of female beauty." Harrison to Clay, September 20, 1839, in Clay, *Papers,* IX, 342–343.

in New York and knew with some certainty that he had been eliminated from the House contest. He held on to a glimmer of hope that Louisiana might rescue him, but around December 15 even that glimmer died. Now came the awful task of deciding the next President. "It is in fact very much in Clay's power to make the President," wrote Representative William Plumer to his father. "If he says Jackson, the nine Western states are united at once for him—If he says Adams, two or three Western states fall off—& Jackson must fail."[6]

Indeed, Clay did hold that awesome power, and he had been thinking about it for some time. He had long since decided he would back Adams. But was that really in his interest? Crawford was immediately dismissed, not only because of his health but because he was the man Clay should have beaten and whose friends had frustrated the Speaker in New York and in Virginia. The Speaker had hoped Virginia would turn to its native son on learning of Crawford's physical breakdown, but it had hung on to him to the bitter end. The Radicals "are full of professions to me and express great regrets that a different direction had not been given to their exertions," he told James Erwin, his son-in-law. "This resembles the eulogiums which are pronounced upon a man after his death. I cannot tell you who will be elected, most probably it will be either Genl. Jackson or Mr. Adams. And what an alternative that is!"[7]

But surely the military chieftain was not a real possibility in his mind. "I cannot believe that killing 2500 Englishmen at N. Orleans qualifies for the various, difficult and complicated duties of the Chief Magistracy." Clay had already expressed many of his reservations about the general to friends and had heard others from those he respected. Peter B. Porter, for example, stated that Jackson "is by nature a *Tyrant*— I mean no *unworthy* imputation, for I believe him to be a man of the purest honor & integrity, but his habits as well as his native disposition have always been to consider the law, & his own notions of justice as synonimous."[8] Porter hit the bull's-eye with that last comment. Jackson always did have the curious, if not dangerous, notion that he and the law were somehow "synonimous."

It had to be Adams. Much as he personally disliked the man, Clay had little choice. Still, he had no intention of declaring for the secretary of state until he had spoken to him and learned more exactly what he might "expect of him, in the event of his success; & then to determine on the course he shall finally pursue."[9]

Apart from everything else it made sound political sense to join Adams. It would mean the union of eastern with western interests in support of Clay's

6. Plumer, Jr., to Plumer, December 16, 1824, in Brown, ed., *Missouri Compromises,* p. 123.

7. Clay to James Erwin, December 13, 1824, in Clay, *Papers,* III, 895. The same expressions about the Radicals may be found in Clay to William D. Ford, December 13, 1824, ibid., III, 895.

8. Clay to Francis P. Blair, January 29, 1825, in Clay, *Papers,* IV, 47; Porter to Clay, January 14, 1825, in Clay, *Papers,* IV, 18.

9. Plumer, Jr., to Plumer, January 4, 1825, in Brown, ed., *Missouri Compromises,* p. 127.

American System, thus providing the system with a *national* constituency. Moreover, it would make Clay the obvious successor to the presidency, a succession unlikely to produce any sectional outcry of injustice. On the other hand, if he joined Jackson, as he knew many westerners, particularly members of the Relief party in his own state, wished him to do, there could well be an outcry against a long succession of western Presidents (possibly sixteen years) just as there continued to be against the long succession of southern Presidents.

Any thought of succession for Clay necessarily meant appointment to the office of secretary of state, the position he had long coveted. Would Adams offer it? On that he needed to wait and see. In any event, he told his friends "that the duty which I have to perform shall be fulfilled with an anxious and solemn determination to promote the public good, if I can discern it, and without the slightest reference to personal considerations."[10]

Meanwhile, the Speaker went about the important duties of his office, the first of which was the reception given to honor the Marquis de Lafayette. The two men breakfasted together on December 5, after which Clay formally welcomed the revolutionary hero in the House chamber, with members of the Senate in attendance, in a stunning flow of oratory for which he was already justly famous. Lafayette read a response that newspapers accused Clay of writing for him. Clay denied the charge but admitted that he had suggested "the most effective sentences."[11] In an extremely handsome gesture of the nation's regard and gratitude, the Congress voted Lafayette a two-hundred-thousand-dollar gift and a township of land, a bounty that astounded even Clay.

But the session had no sooner begun than the Speaker was besieged by the friends of the three presidential candidates to look favorably on their choice. After a time he needed a stick to drive them all away.

"My dear Sir," purred one of General Jackson's friends, "all our dependence is on you; don't disappoint us; you know our partiality was for you next to the Hero; and how much we want a western President."

Then a friend of the Radical candidate accosted him. "The hopes of the Republican party are concentrated on you. For God's sake preserve it—If you had been returned instead of Mr. Crawford every man of us would have supported you to the last hour. We consider him & you as the only genuine Republican candidates."

Next came an Adams friend "with tears in his eyes," who said: "Sir Mr Adams has always had the greatest respect for you, & admiration for your talents—There is no station to which they are not equal—Most undoubtedly you were the second choice of New England. And I pray you to consider seriously whether the public good & your own future interests do not point

10. Clay to Benjamin W. Leigh, December 22, 1824, in Clay, *Papers*, III, 901.
11. *Register of Debates*, 18th Congress, 2d session, pp. 3–4; *National Intelligencer*, February 23, 1852; Poore, *Perley's Reminiscences*, p. 76.

most distinctly to the choice which you ought to make."

The absurdity of it all amused the kingmaker. How can anyone withstand all this "disinterested homage & kindness"? he laughed.[12]

At one point General Jackson called at Clay's lodgings and, not finding him home, left his calling card. Clay returned the visit, although he later had no recollection of any discussion with Old Hickory except at a birthday party given by the Russian minister on December 24. The party provided the only occasion when Clay alluded to the approaching election in Jackson's presence—or so he said. The two men were standing in a group discussing internal improvements when Clay, looking squarely at the general, said: "if you should be elected President, I hope the cause will flourish under your administration." Jackson replied that it was a question of how much revenue could be appropriated for public works.[13]

Clay himself was not above sending out messengers to do a little courting of his own. He directed his colleague and messmate Robert Letcher to pay a call on John Quincy Adams. This occurred on December 12, just prior to the publication of the Louisiana returns. On this first visit Letcher simply discussed Kentucky's internal politics, the opposition developing against Clay from the Relief party, and the rumor that the Kentucky legislature might instruct the congressional delegation from the state on how to vote in the forthcoming House election. Letcher returned on December 17, but in the meantime, Adams had been informed that Clay was disposed to support him "if he could at the same time be useful to himself." On his second visit Letcher expressed concern that the Kentucky legislature might name Jackson as the candidate it wished its delegation to support because he was a westerner. He went on to say that he was not prepared "to act definitively in opposition to the will of his constituents."

At this point Letcher asked Adams directly what his "sentiments towards Clay were." Adams assured him that he harbored no hostility against the Speaker, although he adverted to Jonathan Russell's attack and admitted that he believed that Clay had a hand in it. But, said Adams, the controversy had ended to his advantage, and therefore, he felt no animosity toward anyone connected with the incident.

Letcher confessed that Clay's friends thought the Speaker had been wrong in writing his letter as he did. It had been written in a moment of excitement, Letcher insisted, and he assured the New Englander that Clay, too, was free of any hostility. As the discussion meandered along, both men oozing goodwill and mutual feelings of respect, Adams suddenly caught the full drift of the conversation: "that Clay would willingly support me if he could thereby serve himself, and the substance of his [Letcher's] *meaning* was, that if Clay's friends could *know* that he would have a prominent share in the Admin-

12. Clay to Francis Preston Blair, January 8, 1825, in Clay, *Papers*, IV, 9.
13. Clay to Josiah S. Johnston, October 6, 1827, in Clay, *Papers*, VI, 1116.

istration, that might induce them to vote for me, even in the face of instructions."

A prominent share in the administration! Obviously the office of secretary
of state. But the office itself was never mentioned. In fact, Letcher denied
having any authority from Clay for what he said, and he made no overt propositions—none at all. He had no need. Adams understood what he was saying.
It was clear what he was expected to do if elected with Clay's support.

The irony surely did not escape Adams. On any number of occasions he
had come close to telling the Speaker what a despicable person he thought he
was. His diary was filled with rancor against the man who continually caused
him grief. He believed that Clay had singled him out for personal abuse and
political annihilation—all because of his overpowering lust for the presidency.
He believed that Clay had repeatedly spread stories (about the negotiations at
Ghent, for example) characterizing Adams as a enemy of the West. He believed that Clay had initiated the Russell attack. He even harbored the belief
that the Speaker had quietly attempted to maneuver the congressional caucus
in 1820 to get himself nominated as Vice President by snatching it away from
its incumbent, Daniel D. Tompkins—which may or may not have been true.[14]
And this was the man he would have to live with as his secretary of state—that
is, if he were lifted into the presidential chair. Well, if that was the price of the
presidency, so be it. He would pay it. John Quincy Adams was just as ambitious as Henry Clay.

Letcher ended the discussion by invoking confidentiality, and Adams understood that he was expected to phrase his answers to any question that might
be put to him "in mere general terms."

A week later Letcher returned. Again they had a long conversation on the
election. The Kentuckian advised Adams how important it was that the election be decided on the first ballot. It could be done, Letcher declared, with the
support of all six western states. Adams doubted that Kentucky could be included in the six, but Letcher went to great lengths to reassure him. "I consider
Letcher as moving for Mr. Clay," the secretary of state noted in his diary, "and
this anxiety of a friend of Clay's that I should obtain the election at the first
ballot in the House, is among the whimsical results of political combinations at
this time—'Incedo super ignes.' "[15]

Walking over fire. Indeed. That night he entertained Henry Clay at dinner, along with Letcher, Martin Van Buren, John C. Calhoun, Edward Livingston, Louis McLane, and a number of other high-powered congressmen. At
least one of them tried to speak confidentially to Adams about how the House
election would go. It almost seemed as though Adams were enjoying all the
attention—in a whimsical sort of way, of course.

On January 1, 1825, Letcher put in another appearance. It now seemed

14. Plumer, Jr., to Plumer, November 24, 1820, in Brown, ed., *Missouri Compromises,* p. 56.
15. Adams, *Memoirs,* VI, 444–453.

certain, he told Adams, that the Kentucky legislature would instruct its House delegation to vote for the western candidate—obviously Jackson. But he also stated that the instruction would have no effect. "The vote of Kentucky in the House was fixed and unalterable." Then he started speaking about the past differences between the secretary of state and the Speaker "as giving concern to some of the members of the delegation." He therefore "intimated" that it might be an excellent idea if Adams and Clay got together and had "some conversation . . . upon the subject." Adams agreed.[16]

That evening a dinner was given in Lafayette's honor by members of Congress at Williamson's Hotel, and everyone of importance, including President Monroe, put in an appearance. About 150 members of Congress and 30 officers of the government, civilian and military, attended. Clay arrived in high spirits, ready to seize any occasion to display his wit and sociability. A hail-fellow throughout the evening, Prince Hal seemed determined to enliven the proceedings. Staring around the room, he spotted both Adams and Jackson. "Old Hickory was under par," reported Representative Louis McLane of Delaware, and the dour Adams looked his usual dyspeptic self. But "Clay was in fine spirits and amused himself a little at the expense of the *rivals*. J & A sat next to each other on the fire &c &c, a vacant chair intervening."

Clay saw his chance for a little amusement. Seated at the other side of the room, he suddenly rose, walked over to the two men, and plopped himself into the vacant chair. Then, "in his inimitable impudent significant manner," he said: "Well, gentlemen since you are both so near the chair, but neither can occupy it, I will slip in between you, and take it myself!" Everyone laughed—except Adams and Jackson.[17]

Sixteen regular toasts followed, one for Monroe's administration, others for Lafayette, to which they both responded briefly. After these regular toasts Clay rose and offered a salute to "General Simon Bolivar, the Washington of South America, and the Republic of Colombia." In the course of his remarks he took several jabs at "the infatuated monarch" of "wretched Spain," who sought "the impracticable hope of maintaining a rule in the new world for which he is utterly incompetent in the old."[18]

At one point in the festivities Clay whispered to Adams that he "wished to see him in private, & have a free & confidential conversation with him." Throughout the evening the Speaker had been remarkably civil and attentive to the New Englander, no doubt pleasing the secretary of state. Adams replied that he would be happy to meet with him whenever Clay found it convenient to call. "In a few days," whispered the Speaker.[19]

Clay had made his selection, and Adams may have guessed as much,

16. Ibid., VI, 457.
17. Louis McLane to his wife, January 13, 1825, McLane Papers, LC.
18. *National Intelligencer*, January 3, 1825.
19. Plumer, Jr., to Plumer, January 4, 1825, in Brown, ed., *Missouri Compromises*, p. 127.

although he was too shrewd and cautious to take anything for granted. A week later the Speaker wrote to a friend back home and told him what he had decided. Even though he knew there were many Kentuckians who wanted a westerner in the White House and expected Jackson to be named, Clay said that "the election of the General would give to the Military Spirit a Stimulus and a confidence that might lead to the most pernicious results." At least in "the election of Adams we shall not by the example inflict any wound upon the character of our institutions."[20]

The day after writing this letter—that is, Sunday, January 9—Clay sent a note to Adams asking if it would be agreeable for him to stop by that evening. At six o'clock he arrived and spent the next three hours conversing with the man he intended to seat in the White House. It was a conversation "exploratory of the past and prospective of the future." Clay detailed to Adams all the efforts exerted by the several managers of the other candidates to gain his support—efforts "so gross that it had disgusted him"—and he admitted that some of Adams's friends, acting without authority, of course, had also urged him to look favorably on their candidate. He therefore had thought it best to hold off making his decision, not only to give a decent time "for his own funeral solemnities as a candidate" (Clay could never resist a "whimsical" poke at himself) but also to allow his friends the opportunity to decide themselves the course most conducive to the public interest.

The time had now arrived to come to a decision, Clay announced. Looking straight at Adams, he asked the secretary of state "to satisfy him with regard to some principles of great public importance, but without any personal considerations for himself."[21]

This conversation was recorded by Adams in his diary. At the point when Clay asked him for a commitment on some principles of great public importance Adams abruptly ended his narrative. What did he say in response to Clay's request? Did he specifically endorse the American System? Possibly. Did he offer to make Clay his secretary of state? Probably not. There was no need. Both men understood each other's purposes and needs. By the time the conversation ended each knew what he could expect from the other. A few days later Adams told Representative Plumer in confidence that the conversation "went over all their past differences, the scenes in which they had acted together, their present views of policy, & their expectations of the future."[22]

Expectations of the future. It would be fascinating to know what they each said about their plans and hopes for the future. In any event, by the time Clay took his leave he "had no hesitation in saying," recorded Adams, "that his preference would be for me."[23]

20. Clay to Francis P. Blair, January 8, 1825, in Clay, *Papers,* IV, 9–10. At this point Blair had not yet deserted to Jackson. That came soon afterward.
21. Adams, *Memoirs,* VI, 464–465.
22. Plumer, Jr., to Plumer, January 11, 1825, in Brown, ed., *Missouri Compromises,* p. 131.
23. Adams, *Memoirs,* VI, 465.

Two days later the Kentucky legislature passed resolutions instructing its delegation in Congress to cast the state's vote for the western candidate in the House election. The legislature declared that it was "the wish of the people of Kentucky" that the western candidate receive the state's vote. Once it had become clear that Clay "would be left out of the House of Representatives," wrote William T. Barry, "the sentiment in favour of Genl. Jackson grew strong. [T]he disposition to express a preference for him over Mr. Adams [is] too powerful to be resisted."[24]

The resolutions created quite a "stir at Washington—and made Clay sick a day or two." But he quickly recovered, for he and others simply disregarded the instruction even though the official tallies of the balloting in the presidential election in Kentucky showed that Adams had not received a single popular vote. "The delegation I believe," said Clay, "feels perfectly free to vote, as its own judgment shall dictate, notwithstanding the recent request of the K. Legislature."

The delegation was indeed free to vote according to its best judgment, but it was also leaving itself open for bitter denunciation and possible retaliation at the next election.[25]

As though to rally the entire West behind him by offering an attractive inducement, Clay brought forward in the House an appropriations bill to extend the National Road. On January 17 he spoke at length on its behalf. The measure when passed would appropriate $150,000 to construct the road from Canton to Zanesville, Ohio; it would also complete surveys intended to extend the National Road so that its route would pass by the seats of government of Ohio, Indiana, Illinois, and Missouri.[26]

On January 24 the Kentucky delegation in Congress announced its decision to cast its vote for Adams. But it was not a unanimous decision. The Relief party members had become more and more disenchanted with Clay because of his refusal to support their cause, so they turned to Jackson. But they were outvoted, eight to four.[27] The same day the Ohio delegation also declared for Adams.

The public announcement of Clay's decision rocked the Congress. "We are in commotion," declared Robert Y. Hayne of South Carolina, "about the

24. William T. Barry to Clay, January 10, 1825, in Clay, *Papers*, IV, 11.

25. Clay to Josephus B. Stuart, January 15, 1825, in Clay, *Papers*, IV, 19; Nathaniel Ware to Samuel Brown, January 27, 1825, Samuel Brown Papers, Manuscript Department, Filson Club, Louisville, Kentucky. All the Kentucky newspapers understood that the resolutions instructed the delegation to vote specifically for Jackson. See *Argus of Western America*, January 12, 1825.

26. The bill, with amendments, was enacted and signed by the President on March 3, 1825.

27. David Trimble, Francis Johnson, Thomas Metcalfe, Robert P. Letcher, Richard A Buckner, Philip Thompson, David White, and Clay voted for Adams; Robert P. Henry, John T. Johnson, Thomas P. Moore, and Charles A. Wickliffe voted for Jackson. Wickliffe later alleged that Clay "endeavored to prevail upon him to vote for Mr. Adams. Such an allegation is entirely untrue," Clay retorted. "I have never sought in my life to influence Mr. Wickliffes vote on that, or any other question." Clay to N. B. Beall, July 9, 1827, Clay Papers, Manuscript Department, Filson Club, Louisville, Kentucky.

monstrous union between Clay & Adams, for the purpose of depriving Jackson of the votes of the Western States where nine tenths of the people are
decidedly in his favor."[28] When Martin Van Buren heard the decision, he was
thunderstruck. He could scarcely believe that Clay could commit such a political blunder and turn a deaf ear to overwhelming western sentiment. He frankly
warned of the consequence. If you do this, he told his Kentucky colleague
Francis Johnson, "you sign Mr. Clay's political death warrant. He will never
become President be your motives as pure as you claim them to be."[29]

Van Buren was wrong. Henry Clay signed his own political death warrant. The rumor was already afloat that Clay and Adams had entered a "monstrous union" by making a deal, a bargain, in which the Speaker would support
the secretary of state for President and the New Englander would reciprocate
by appointing the Kentuckian his secretary of state, thereby placing him in
direct succession to the presidency eight years hence. Furthermore, the West
was Clay's political base. To disregard the known wishes of this constituency
invited political retribution. Senator Thomas Hart Benton of Missouri later
said that Clay had violated the principle of *"demos krateo."* Indeed, he had. Clay
also raised the question, according to Benton, of the right of the demos to
self-government.[30]

But who said the people have a right to determine their President *directly?*
The election of the chief executive, according to the Founding Fathers, was
never intended to be a democratic process. An elaborate electoral college had
been constructed to keep the demos from immediately controlling the outcome of the process. It was up to the electors to decide the issue; if they failed,
then the decision belonged to the House of Representatives.

However potent this argument about what the Founders intended may
have been in 1824, it did not take into account the tremendous changes that
had occurred throughout the country since the adoption of the Constitution.
The nation was fast evolving from a republic to a democracy. The Industrial
Revolution, market revolution, and transportation revolution had helped trigger this phenomenon. In addition, the expansion of the country westward, an
improved standard of living, rising expectations of ordinary citizens, and other
factors all played a part in this evolution. State constitutions were being rewrit-
ten to expand the franchise. More and more people were demanding and
getting a recognition of their right to participate directly in the operation of
their government. They would get their democracy, one way or another. If
Clay chose to disregard their wishes, then he was risking his future. It may
have been one more indication of his inability to read the political signs of the
times accurately. "The result," Thomas J. Green predicted, ". . . will bring

28. Hayne to J. V. Grimké, January 28, 1825, Miscellaneous Hayne Papers, New-York Historical
Society.
29. Van Buren, *Autobiography,* p. 150.
30. Benton, *Thirty Years' View,* I, 49.

home to Clay such a political curse he can't outlive."[31]

On January 28, 1825, what some congressmen anticipated actually happened. An unsigned letter appeared in the Philadelphia *Columbia Observer* accusing Clay of promising House votes to elect Adams in exchange for the office of secretary of state. Now the reputed bargain was public knowledge.

Clay reacted immediately. He asked Joseph Gales and William W. Seaton, editors of the Washington *National Intelligencer,* to publish "A. Card" the next day. On January 31 it appeared:

> I have seen, without any other emotion than that of ineffable contempt, the abuse which has been poured out upon me by a scurrilous paper issued in this City[32] and by other kindred prints and persons, in regard to the Presidential election. The editor of one of those prints, ushered forth in Philadelphia, called the Columbia Observer . . . has had the impudence to transmit to me his vile paper of the 28th instant. In that number is inserted a letter, purporting to have been written from this City, on the 25th instant, by a member of the H. of R. belonging to the Pennsylvania Delegation. I believe it to be a forgery; but, if it be genuine, I pronounce the member, whoever he may be, a base and infamous calumniator, a dastard and a liar; and if he dare unveil himself and avow his name, I will hold him responsible, as I here admit myself to be, to all the laws which govern and regulate the conduct of men of honor.
>
> H. Clay
> 31 January 1825.

This challenge to the author to reveal himself and meet Clay on the field of honor provoked a flood of laughter when George Kremer, a Pennsylvania representative better known for his eccentricities of dress than anything else, piped up with the announcement that he would prove the truth of the charges. He neglected to say, however, whether he had authored the unsigned letter. Clay demanded a House investigation, and a week later a select committee chosen to look into the charges, headed by Philip P. Barbour, submitted its report without reaching a conclusion or revealing a single fact. Kremer had refused to testify, and therefore, the committee asked to be discharged.

Clay looked about as ridiculous as Kremer, and he even admitted later that "I ought to have omitted the last sentence in the Card." Other congressmen shook their heads in disbelief. Louis McLane, who was to cast Delaware's single vote for Crawford, said that "irretrievable ruin is his inevitable fate." Everybody loved and admired Henry Clay, but nobody trusted him. His ambition had gotten totally out of hand. The "monstrous union," or coalition, as it came to be called more commonly, "is so unnatural & preposterous," said McLane, "that the reports of no committees, nay all the waters of the sweet Heavens cannot remove the iota of corruption." The same thing applied to

---

31. Green to William Polk, January 29, 1825, Brown-Polk Family Papers, Filson Club, Louisville, Kentucky.
32. It was reprinted in the Washington *Gazette.*

Adams, "for so deep and universal is the indignation excited by the coalition, and the affair with Kremer, that from the moment of his election he will encounter an overwhelming opposition in both Houses of Congress [and] throughout the nation. The Jackson men are most violent & implacable."[33]

But what where Clay's alternatives? "That I should vote for Mr. Crawford? I cannot. For Gen. Jackson? I will not. I shall pursue the course which my conscience dictates, regardless of all imputations and all consequences."[34]

Still, he had a way out of his dilemma: refuse the office of secretary of state when Adams offered it to him. In fact, he kept telling friends that he had not made up his mind about what he might do. "I can enter in *any* situation that I may please," he correctly stated. But he was ambivalent. "Feeling really great indifference about any office, resting upon the will of one man, I do not know that I should accept the first place in the Cabinet, if offered."[35] But he really hungered for the office—desperately. The only question was whether he should accept it in light of the vicious accusations being hurled at him. "Shall I, under all the circumstances of abuse which surround me, go into the Department of State, if it should be offered to me? Whether it will be or not I really do not know."[36]

While Clay was going through this agony, John Quincy Adams was busily arranging other "bargains." John Scott, who alone would cast Missouri's vote, came to Adams and presented a list of the printers he wished appointed for printing the laws in Missouri. He also spoke about the application to the President for the removal of his brother as a judge in the Arkansas Territory for having killed his colleague on the bench in a duel. According to the laws of the Territory of Arkansas, no participant in a duel could hold public office. Adams replied by reassuring him about the printing patronage. As for the brother, the secretary of state responded: "There has been such an application made as long since as last summer. But as the President has not acted on it hitherto, I think he will not." Scott subsequently "voted for Adams, the way Clay told him to do." As President Adams made no move to unseat the brother. And when the brother's four-year term as judge ran out, Adams renominated him to the Senate, but it was very promptly rejected by the upper house.[37]

Two days before the House election Adams received Representative Henry R. Warfield, a former Federalist whose vote might break a tie in the

33. Clay to Robert Walsh, Jr., February 18, 1825, in Clay, *Papers,* IV, 75; McLane to Mrs. McLane, February 6, 1825, McLane Papers, LC. Representative Plumer told his father that "Clay's card is generally condemned." Plumer, Jr., to Plumer, February 6, 1825, in Brown, ed., *Missouri Compromises,* p. 136.

34. Clay to ?, February 1825, in Clay, *Papers,* IV, 54–55.

35. Clay to James Brown, January 23, 1825, in Clay, *Papers,* IV, 39.

36. Clay to William Creighton, Jr., February 7, 1825, University of Kentucky Library, copy CPP.

37. Adams, *Memoirs,* VI, 473; Bemis, *Adams,* II, 42–43. "Scott was irresolute," said Walter Lowrie, "until Clay got hold of him, he had him with him until late last night. And altho his inclination led him to vote for us, Clay had power to persuade him to vote for Adams." Smith, *Forty Years,* p. 185.

Maryland delegation. Warfield was concerned that if elected, Adams would exclude Federalists from office. Daniel Webster had the same fear. Adams reassured them both. To the charge that his administration would be "conducted on the principle of proscribing the federal party," Adams denied it absolutely. He repeated to Warfield "that I never would be at the head of any Administration of proscription to any party—political or geographical."[38] Webster was pleased to hear this disavowal and told Adams that the "Patroon," Stephen Van Rensselaer of New York, would also appreciate hearing similar assurances and that he would advise the Patroon to visit the New Englander to obtain confirmation firsthand.

Election day fell on Wednesday, February 9, 1825. A heavy snowfall pleased some apprehensive Washingtonians. Considering what was about to happen in Congress, the storm would keep the "lower classes," said Margaret Bayard Smith, from committing some act of "foolish violence."[39]

Representative Van Rensselaer trudged his way through the snow to attend this momentous session. When he reached the Capitol, Henry Clay was waiting for him. The Speaker invited Van Rensselaer into his private office, where Daniel Webster was also waiting. Previously Van Rensselaer had given his pledge to Van Buren not to vote on the first ballot for Adams, whom he did not like. In fact, he disliked all the Adamses. The New York vote was split, and Van Buren hoped to keep it that way for several rounds of fruitless balloting and then (with luck) step in to settle the question in Crawford's favor. Now Van Rensselaer was closeted with Clay and Webster and being hammered with arguments about why he should switch his vote to Adams. They told him that the election turned on his vote, they feared the collapse of government if Adams failed, and they described in lurid detail the consequences resulting from such "disorganization." Most particularly they "referred in very impressive terms to the great stake he had in the preservation of order from his large estate" in New York. What would happen to the great patroonship he had inherited, they cried, if he held out against Adams and the election resulted in a stalemate?[40]

Poor Van Rensselaer "staggered" out of the Speaker's office when they were done with him, visibly shaken by the words he had heard. Louis McLane found him "in tears litterally," ranting how "the vote of N. York . . . depended upon him" and "if he gave it to A. he could be elected most probably on the first ballot."[41] Alarmed, McLane sent a hurried message to Van Buren in the Senate to come quickly and speak to Van Rensselaer. But Van Buren refused. He had a pledge from Van Rensselaer, and he knew the Patroon was a very religious man and would not violate his oath.

38. Adams, *Memoirs,* VI, 499–500; Bemis, *Adams,* II, 43–45.
39. Smith, *Forty Years,* p. 186.
40. Van Buren, *Autobiography,* p. 152.
41. McLane to Mrs. McLane, February 9, 1825, McLane Papers, LC.

At the precise hour of noon the members of the Senate paraded into the hall of the House of Representatives and took seats in front of the Speaker. Spectators crowded the galleries, which included foreign ambassadors and other distinguished persons. For the next two hours the monotonous business of opening electoral certificates and counting the ballots proceeded slowly and solemnly. Then, to no one's surprise, John C. Calhoun was declared the elected Vice President, but no candidate for the presidency had received a majority of electoral votes. After that announcement the senators filed out of the chamber to allow the representatives to proceed with their constitutional duty and choose the next President. Tension in the room swiftly mounted.

The Speaker took his place at the podium. He then directed a roll call. As he did so, the representatives of each delegation seated themselves in the order in which the states would be polled—that is, running north to south along the Atlantic coastline and then south to north along the Mississippi Valley. Each state had one vote determined by the entire delegation, with a majority of states (thirteen) necessary for election. In the case of Delaware, Illinois, Mississippi, and Missouri a single representative decided the vote of his state. All the delegations received from the sergeant at arms separate ballot boxes, into which the secret ballots were deposited. Each state appointed its own tellers, who counted the ballots and then prepared the results on two separate slips of paper. These were submitted to a committee of tellers, divided into two groups to serve as a check on each other. Daniel Webster headed one group; John Randolph, the other.

In most of the calculations put forward prior to the election it was generally conceded that Adams could expect to receive the six New England votes and those brought along by Clay—namely, Kentucky, Ohio, Missouri, and perhaps Louisiana.[42] Illinois, as it turned out, also went to Adams by the action of its single representative, Daniel Cook, who may or may not have been bribed.[43] That gave Adams eleven states. He needed two more. And if Warfield did in fact have the deciding vote in Maryland and was satisfied with Adams's assurances about Federalist appointees, then the total would reach twelve. That was it.

Crawford, on the other hand, could count with certainty on no more than four states: Delaware, Georgia, Virginia, and North Carolina. New York was split; that was the way Van Buren wanted to keep it in order to strengthen his bargaining hand after several rounds of futile balloting. Jackson would take the remaining seven: Tennessee, South Carolina, New Jersey, Pennsylvania, Indiana, Alabama, and Mississippi. If this calculation proved correct, no candidate would have a majority and the House would have to continue balloting

42. Louisiana did go to Adams. Representative Henry Gurley "was friendly to Adams," and his vote tipped the balance. Plumer, Jr., to Plumer, February 13, 1825, in Brown, ed., *Missouri Compromises,* p. 138.

43. When Cook sought reelection, the people of Illinois defeated his bid because of his "betrayal." Thereupon President Adams awarded him a confidential "diplomatic junket to Cuba" paid for out of the contingent secret service fund. Bemis, *Adams,* II, 41–42.

until Adams, Jackson, or Crawford received thirteen votes.

As the balloting began, poor Van Rensselaer shivered. Finally, as was his habit, he lowered his head to the edge of desk, covered his eyes, and implored "his Maker" for guidance. When the ballot box reached his desk, Van Rensselaer removed his hand from his eyes. As he did so, he spotted a ticket on the floor bearing the name John Quincy Adams.

It was the answer to his prayers! Joyfully and with "great excitement" he picked up the ballot and stuffed it into the box. The presumed New York tie was broken when eighteen Representatives voted for Adams, fourteen for Crawford, and two for Jackson. According to Van Buren, Van Rensselaer's single vote gave Adams the thirteen states he needed to be elected the sixth President of the United States.[44]

Thus the election ended on the first ballot. When Webster announced the result—thirteen for Adams, seven for Jackson, and four for Crawford—the chamber reacted in stunned silence, probably because the election had ended so quickly. Clay no doubt breathed a sigh of relief. The end had come as he had hoped and expected. He then turned to the House and declared, "That JOHN QUINCY ADAMS of Massachusetts, having received a majority of the votes of all the states of this Union, was duly elected President of the United States for four years, to commence on the fourth of March, 1825." Partisan friends of Adams burst into applause, whereupon Clay ordered the galleries cleared.[45]

The deputy sergeant at arms called out the order: "The Speaker orders the galleries to be cleared. All must retire. Clear the galleries!"[46] Clay overreacted in this tense atmosphere, but his behavior was understandable under the circumstances.

"It was impossible to win the game, gentlemen," snickered John Randolph; "the cards were stacked."[47]

"May the blessing of God rest upon the event of this day!" said Adams when he received the news from Alexander H. Everett.[48] "The long agony was terminated . . . on the first ballot," Clay wearily wrote to Francis Brooke. ". . . the manner in which the whole scenic [sic] was exhibited in the H. of R. was creditable to our institutions and to our Country."[49]

Andrew Jackson Donelson, nephew, ward, and private secretary of General Jackson, said he was "sickened" by the result, not because of his uncle's

---

44. Van Buren, *Autobiography*, p. 152. Van Buren is the only source for the incredible story about Van Rensselaer's vote. William B. Fink in his article "Stephen Van Rensselaer and the House Election of 1825," *New York History*, XXXII (1951), pp. 323–330, denies that Van Rensselaer ever promised to vote for Crawford.

45. *National Intelligencer*, February 10, 1825. It is interesting that one of Clay's friendly newspapers in Kentucky—Amos Kendall's *Argus of Western America*—stated on February 16, 1825, that Adams was elected because of the "influence of Mr. Clay and an arrangement by which he is to enter the cabinet." At the time Kendall and Clay were still friendly.

46. Poore, *Perley's Reminiscences*, p. 25.

47. Smith, *Forty Years*, p. 186.

48. Adams, *Memoirs*, VI, 501.

49. Clay to Brooke, February 10, 1825, in Clay, *Papers*, IV, 62.

defeat but because "every corrupt act was employed to draw the Representatives from their responsibility to their constituents." More such corruption could be expected, he predicted. "The closing scenes of this nefarious drama is not yet acted out, nor will it be until the 4th of March when Mr. Adams is to seal with his oath all his corrupt bargains."

Corrupt bargains! Already the words were current. Everyone in Congress knew, or thought he knew, that the "nefarious drama" had one more act to go. "It is rumored and believed by every body here," wrote Donelson, "that Mr Clay will be made Secretary of State. . . . What a farce! That Mr Adams should swear to support the constitution of the U States which he has purchased from Representatives who betrayed the constitution, and which he must distribute among them as rewards for the iniquity."[50]

Andrew Jackson took his defeat as gracefully as he could, considering all the states he had won in the general election that deserted him in the House election. Writing two weeks later, he said he felt that he had behaved with dignity and self-control. Indeed, he had. "No midnight taper burnt by me; no secret conclaves were held; or cabals entered into, to persuade any to a violation of pledges given, or of instructions received."[51]

On February 10 Monroe gave a levee to honor the President-elect, and all Washington turned out to attend it. Adams and Jackson chanced upon each other, and without betraying a sign of disappointment or anger, the general shot out his hand in a gesture of sincere and hearty congratulations. An audible sigh of relief echoed across the room. But Clay was seen "walking about with exultation and a smiling face"—and "with a fashionable *belle* hanging on each arm."

"The villain!" snarled one man.

Another pointed at Adams. "There is our '*Clay President*' and he will be moulded at that man's will and pleasure as easily as clay in a potter's hands."

Still a third man said: "When Prometheus made a man out of clay he stole fire from heaven to animate him. I wonder where our speaker will get the fire with which he means to animate his Clay President."

"Not from Heaven, I warrant," laughed another.

It was quite a levee. Even Jackson's gesture of courtesy was criticized as "a useless piece of hypocrisy."[52]

The day following the election Adams told the secretary of the navy, Samuel Southard, that he would offer the Department of State to Clay.[53] The

50. Donelson to John Coffee, February 19, 1825, Donelson Papers, LC. Even Amos Kendall, who at this time was still friendly with Clay, stated in his newspaper that Adams's election was "attributed to the influence of Mr. Clay and an arrangement by which he is to enter the cabinet." *Argus of Western America,* February 16, 1825.

51. Jackson to Coffee, February 19, 1825, Coffee Papers, Tennessee Historical Society.

52. Smith, *Forty Years,* p. 183.

53. Adams, *Memoirs,* VI, 505. On Southard, see Michael Birkner, *Samuel I. Southard, Jeffersonian Whig* (Rutherford, N.J., 1984).

decision was as swift as it was expected. No other choice was possible. Apparently no other choice was even considered. Adams notified President Monroe of this decision the next day, and when he received a note from Clay that he wished to speak with the President-elect, Adams invited him to come to his home at half past six.

They met and talked for an hour. "I then offered him the nomination to the Department of State," recorded Adams.[54] Clay hesitated for a moment and then said he would take it into consideration and respond as soon as he had time to consult with his friends.

Naturally the Speaker knew the offer was coming, but he could not presume to query his friends beforehand, and in view of the public talk about a corrupt bargain—although he made light of any threatened opposition—it was politically imperative for him to hear all sides before coming to a decision.

Adams understood. He told Clay to take his time. The Speaker did mention the Kremer affair and said that he would have proved the existence of a conspiracy against him if the committee had been able to take Kremer's testimony. In fact, Kremer had supposedly offered to sign a document admitting a conspiracy, but members of the Pennsylvania delegation, specifically Samuel D. Ingham and James Buchanan, as well as Representative George McDuffie of South Carolina—had talked him out of it.[55]

It took Clay a week to come to a decision. He spoke to friends in the Washington area, wrote to others at a distance, and even heard from those who offered their opinion before it had been asked. For example, his good friend back in Kentucky John J. Crittenden argued in favor of accepting. "I think I can see the policy which dictated the charges . . . against you . . . of having 'made your bargain' with him. . . ." (Clearly the word "bargain" had reached even Kentucky.) "It is intended to intimidate you" from accepting, said Crittenden, because they "tremble to see you" as secretary of state. "They wish to obstruct your passage to it by heaping up the way with all the falsehood & calumny they can create & invest." Crittenden went on to say that he thought Clay should accept the post if it were offered.[56]

Other friends repeated this argument and added that he could hardly elect a President and then refuse to serve under him. Such behavior would tend to discredit his motives in voting for Adams. It might indicate that he had a low opinion of the President-elect and therefore had done the country a distinct disservice. Besides, if he accepted the post, he not only would endorse the new administration but could help formulate its policies and move it farther toward his goal of achieving a genuine American System.

No doubt an additional consideration was the knowledge that the encouragement of Latin American independence could be advanced by his taking

54. Adams, *Memoirs,* VI, 508.
55. Ibid., VI, 508–509.
56. Crittenden to Clay, February 15, 1825, in Clay, *Papers,* IV, 68.

over the office of secretary of state. Another thing: The western states, with a population nearing three million, never had had a President, a secretary of state, or any other commanding position in the government. They were entitled to recognition, said some of his friends, and it was about time they received adequate appreciation for their growing importance in the Union.[57]

But there were Cassandras as well. They reminded him of the Kremer affair and warned that if he accepted the offer, the "corrupt bargain" cry would accelerate and would dog him throughout his years as secretary of state. Still other friends countered this argument. Whether or not he accepted the appointment, they said, Clay could "not escape severe animadversion," and if he refused the office, his opposition could claim that Kremer's "patriotic" revelation had prevented the consummation of the bargain. Clay "ought not to give the weight of a feather to Mr. Kremer's affair" was their conclusion. These friends also contended that Adams would have great difficulty in finding a suitable replacement and that either of the other candidates would have made Clay the same offer if he had been elected.[58]

At length many of the opponents of the appointment changed their minds, said Clay, "and I believe they were finally unanimous in thinking that I ought not to hesitate in taking upon myself its duties." Only the "violent" friends of Calhoun, Crawford, and Jackson remained obdurately opposed to his appointment.[59]

So on Thursday, February 17, Clay asked for an interview, and at approximately 9:00 P.M. he informed Adams that he would accept the office.[60] Adams "would not have been my President," Clay wrote a day later, "if I had been allowed to range at large among the great mass of our Citizens to select a President; but I was not so allowed, & circumscribed as I was, I thought that, under all circumstances, he was the best choice that I could practically make."[61]

The public announcement struck the Jackson camp like a thunderclap. Colonel Richard M. Johnson of Kentucky rushed to Old Hickory with the news. The general listened to it calmly but did not betray the astonishment he actually felt. As long as Johnson stayed with him, he remained quiet and subdued. But no sooner did the colonel leave the room than the general let out a deafening roar that echoed across the nation. "So you see," he raged, "the *Judas* of the West has closed the contract and will receive the thirty pieces of silver. his end will be the same. Was there ever witnessed such a bare faced corruption in any country before?"[62]

57. William Creighton, Jr., to Clay, February 19, 1825, Clay to Brooke, February 18, 1825, in Clay, *Papers,* IV, 76, 73, Clay to Crawford, February 18, 1828, in Clay, *Correspondence,* p. 193.

58. Clay to Brooke, February 18, 1825, in Clay, *Papers,* IV, 73.

59. Clay to Brooke, February 18, 1825, in Clay, *Papers,* IV, 73–74.

60. Clay to Adams, February 17, 1825, with endorsement, in Clay, *Papers,* IV, 72.

61. Clay to Brooke, February 18, 1825, in Clay, *Papers,* IV, 74.

62. Jackson to William B. Lewis, February 14, 1824, Miscellaneous Jackson Papers, New-York Historical Society. "Mr Clay (*like Judas of old* it is said), *sold himself and influence* to Mr. Adams . . .

Because of all the rumor and talk about a bargain, even before the announcement of Clay's appointment, the news of his selection, when it came,
tended to confirm the fact that an agreement had indeed been reached prior to
the election. The "cause" was judged by the "effect", the reality of the appointment proved the existence of a prior agreement. Jackson put it very simply:
"Clay voted for Adams and made him President and Adams made Clay secretary of state. Is this not proof as strong as holy writ of the understanding and
corrupt coalition between them."[63] And the more Clay denied the corrupt
bargain charge, as he had to do constantly from 1825 onward, the more the
people disbelieved him and condemned him for his "betrayal." Many people
felt they had been cheated of their right to select their own President. "Corrupt" politicians in Washington had confiscated that right.

Jackson was just as sharp a politician as anyone else in Washington and
immediately spotted the lethal potential of the corrupt bargain charge.
"Would it not be well," he suggested to his campaign manager in Tennessee,
"that the papers of Nashville and the whole State should speak out with moderate but firm disapprobation of this corruption, to give a proper tone to the
people, and to draw their attention to the subject? When I see you I have much
to say."[64]

As he returned home from Washington, Jackson spoke to the many
crowds that came out to see him, crowds that wanted to cry out their chagrin
and disappointment over his defeat. In responding to them, Old Hickory
denounced "the rascals at Washington" for their villainy and described the
"*cheating* and *corruption*, and *bribery*" that had occurred in the House elec
tion.[65] Soon the Jackson newspapers around the country took up the cry:
"Corrupt Bargain." So, too, the press of the other defeated candidates. The
outcry was one of moral outrage against a coalition brought to power in total
disregard of the popular will. "There is no other corrective of these abuses,"
stormed the Old Hero of New Orleans, "but the suffrages of the people." If the
electorate "calmly & judiciously [apply] this corrective, they may preserve and
perpetuate the liberty of our happy country. If they do not, in less than 25
years, we will become the slaves, not of a 'military chieftain,' but of such
ambitious demagoges as Henry Clay."[66]

Before leaving Washington, Jackson had written a letter to Samuel
Swartwout of New York in which he mentioned Clay's reference to him as a
"military chieftain" as the reason for Clay's not supporting him in the House
election. The reference had appeared in a letter to Francis T. Brooke by Clay

---

for which, (it was predicted) he was to receive the appointment of Sec of State." Jackson to
Colonel Squire Grant, February 18, 1825, in Jackson, *Correspondence,* III, 276.

63. Jackson to D. G. Goodlett, March 12, 1844, in Jackson, *Correspondence,* VI, 274.

64. Jackson to Lewis, February 20, 1825, Jackson-Lewis Papers, New York Public Library.

65. Letters reprinted in the *Niles' Weekly Register,* July 5, 1828.

66. Jackson to Lewis, February 20, 1825, Jackson-Lewis Papers, New York Public Library.

and had been published in the Washington newspapers on February 12. Jackson's response contained such strong language that Swartwout knew the letter would make excellent political propaganda, so he published it, but without the general's knowledge or consent. The letter struck telling blows at the *"Judas* of the West." Jackson not only acknowledged his military record but reveled in it. "It is very true," he wrote, "that early in life . . . I contributed my mite to shake off the yoke of tyranny, and to build up the fabrick of free government; . . . I made an appeal to the patriotism of the western citizens . . . to support her Eagles. If this can constitute me a 'Military Chieftain' I am one. . . . Mr. Clay never yet has risked himself for his country, sacrificed his repose, or made an effort to repel an invading foe. . . . He who fights . . . must . . . be held up as a 'Military Chieftain': even [George] Washington . . . might be so considered, because he dared to be a virtuous and successful soldier, an honest statesman. . . ."[67]

It was a devastating letter and received wide newspaper circulation. But Jackson's patriotic self-praise provided an easy mark for one of Clay's more stinging rejoinders. "Gen. Jackson fights better than he reasons," he responded. He admitted his own "misfortune never to have repelled an invading foe" or led his countrymen to military victory. "If I had," he snidely remarked, "I should have left to others to proclaim and appreciate the deed."[68]

Those who claimed to understand Clay best credited his decision to accept the office of secretary of state to his ambition—his overreaching ambition. Friendlier voices, like General William Henry Harrison, contended that Clay accepted the post to advance western interests or that he could not refuse the offer because it "would have been said immediately that he had been driven from his intentions by the exposure of the intrigue."[69] Still others said that he was a gambler who enjoyed taking chances and that he had taken the supreme chance of a lifetime in order to properly position himself as the legitimate successor to the presidency. Sophisticated Washingtonians were amazed and perhaps a little amused at the violent reaction of the Jacksonians. After all, the offer "was anticipated, by everybody, as a matter of course."[70] Obviously the general's friends had found an issue with which to bludgeon the incoming administration and replace it in four years with the "virtuous" hero of the Revolution and War of 1812.

Was there a corrupt bargain between Clay and Adams? Probably not, although absolute proof does not exist and most likely never will. Observers in 1825 chose to believe what they found most congenial to their personal instincts and feelings. Still, a corrupt bargain hardly seems likely, for there was

67. Jackson to Swartwout, February 22, 1825, in Jackson, *Correspondence,* III, 278–280.
68. "Address to the People of the Congressional District," March 26, 1825, in Clay, *Papers,* IV, 163.
69. Harrison to David K. Estes, March 3, 1825, Louise Este Bruce Papers, Virginia Historical Society.
70. Plumer, Jr., to Plumer, February 16, 1825, in Brown, ed., *Missouri Compromises,* p. 140.

never any need for Clay to ask for and get a commitment that he would be appointed secretary of state. Once he gave his support to Adams, the office was automatically his. No doubt it would have been his had Jackson or Crawford been elected with his help, although Crawford might have offered the post to Van Buren. What the Speaker wanted was "a prominent share in the Administration," something Adams could give him in view of their similarity of outlook on national issues, such as support for internal improvements and the tariff. Both Jackson and Crawford were strict constructionists, who ideologically opposed these issues. Clay could support only Adams, not Jackson and certainly not Crawford. In his long conversations with Adams about "principles of great public importance," the Speaker undoubtedly satisfied himself that the New Englander would adopt the American System as the framework on which he would structure his administration. The office of secretary of state was incidental to the whole thing. Of course, Adams would offer it to him—it was "anticipated by everybody"—and of course, Clay would accept it after a decent and appropriate interval of consultation with friends.

Was there corruption in the House election? On Adams's part? Probably. If nothing else, the "deal" with Scott to protect the representative's brother from dismissal to order to obtain Missouri's vote in the House contest was very likely a violation of law. On Clay's part? Well, it depends on one's interpretation. He delivered Kentucky's vote in the full knowledge that he violated the instructions of the legislature and probably the wishes of the entire electorate of his state. The legislature had instructed the delegates to vote for Jackson;[71] moreover, the previous fall presidential election had been a contest between Clay and Jackson—no one else. According to the official count, Adams did not receive a *single* popular vote in the state. It was perfectly clear to Clay and everyone else that the people of Kentucky wanted Jackson if they could not have Clay. To award Kentucky's vote to Adams in the House election—as Clay and the other delegates had a legitimate (constitutional) right to do—was condemned as contemptuous of the people's will. It was an arrogant disregard of the principle of self-rule, a gross denial of the people's right to have their vote cast for the candidate of their choice. In the 1820s men committed to the ideals of republicanism called such behavior corrupt. Others would argue that Clay was put in Congress to exercise his best judgment in deciding what was good for the American people as a whole. And that is precisely what they believed he did.[72]

The consequences of defying popular will, however, can be catastrophic.

71. The instructions did not actually name Jackson; they stipulated that the delegates should vote for the "western" candidate, and neither Adams nor Crawford fitted that description.

72. Kendall in the *Argus of Western America,* November 24, 1824, reported that Adams received only fifty-five popular votes in Kentucky. Clay later argued that the Kentucky legislature had a right to instruct U.S. senators, since the legislature elected them, but not members of the House, who were directly elected by the people. Only the people of his congressional district could instruct him, he said, and they preferred Adams—which is probably false.

That is the only way to describe what the charge of a corrupt bargain did to Henry Clay. Moreover, it continued for the rest of his life. That single charge, more than anything else, forever kept him from his greatest ambition and most ardent wish: the White House. He later admitted that accepting the office of secretary of state was the stupidest thing he had ever done in his life.[73]

73. Speech in Lexington, June 9, 1842, in Clay, *Papers,* IX, 708–716.

—— S I X T E E N ——

Secretary of State

A FIERCE and lasting hatred now existed between the two western statesmen: Jackson and Clay. That hatred never ceased until Jackson died in 1845. And as long as that animosity continued, it guaranteed that Old Hickory would do everything within his considerable power to destroy Clay's ambitions for the presidency.

Clay also lost an old friend: Thomas Ritchie, editor of the Richmond *Enquirer*. The "corrupt and vile bargain," as Ritchie called it, "treacherously betrayed the South" and he forthwith suspended all friendly intercourse with Clay.[1]

Following his inauguration on March 4, 1825, as the sixth President of the United States, Adams sent his list of cabinet nominations to the Senate for confirmation. Heading the list was the name of Henry Clay, followed by Richard Rush and James Barbour. It had been the President's plan to retain Monroe's cabinet virtually intact, replacing himself at State with Clay and replacing Calhoun, the new Vice President, at War with General Jackson. In this way a true coalition of all the Republican factions (Adams, Clay, Crawford, Jackson, and Calhoun) could be united within the new administration. But Jackson let it be known immediately that he had no intention of associating with this "monstrous union," and Crawford resigned his office the day before the inauguration. So Adams picked Richard Rush of Pennsylvania, who had served as minister to Great Britain, to head the Treasury Department, and James Barbour of Virginia, the War Department. William Wirt agreed to stay on as attorney general, as did Samuel Southard as secretary of the navy. John McLean, although not yet a cabinet officer, also continued as postmaster general.[2]

Clay predicted there would be little opposition to his nomination in the Senate and estimated the negative votes at three or four. It came as quite a shock when fourteen out of forty-one Senators voted to refuse confirmation. Only John Branch of North Carolina chose to speak out against the appoint-

---

1. *Enquirer,* February 8, 1825; Ambler, *Ritchie,* p. 99.
2. Mary Hargreaves, *The Presidency of John Quincy Adams* (Lawrence, Kan., 1985), pp. 48–50.

ment because of the "suspicion" of alleged wrongdoing, but there was nothing in his remarks that needed clarification or refutation, so the Senate proceeded immediately to the vote. Jackson naturally voted against confirmation, as did two of his closest partisans. Most of the opposition to Clay, interestingly enough, came from the Radical party, although Van Buren, its leader in Congress, voted to support the appointment.[3]

"This was the first act of the opposition from the stump which is to be carried on against the Administration under the banners of General Jackson," recorded President Adams in his diary. True enough. In less than a year the factions of Jackson, Crawford, and Calhoun, under the superb direction of the master political operator Martin Van Buren, began to coalesce their forces with the aim of defeating the coalition of Adams and Clay and replacing it with Old Hickory. And they had an unbeatable issue with which to forge their alliance and win the election of 1828: the "corrupt bargain."[4]

On March 6 Clay resigned from Congress, and the following day Adams signed his commission. Clay took the oath of office as secretary of state on March 8 and began his new duties. When he received the commission, Clay was a little more than a month shy of his forty-eighth birthday. As his first act in office he resigned as counsel for the Bank of the United States in the states of Ohio and Kentucky. "I think it right to apprize you of the termination of that relation from this day," Clay wrote on March 8 to the Bank's president, Nicholas Biddle. The banker replied that he personally regretted the termination and that the board of directors had instructed him to convey its satisfaction with the "able & faithful manner" with which he had discharged his duties. It would be difficult for Clay to give up the "remuneration" he had received from the BUS, which Biddle said was "liberal as it was designed to be," but the new secretary of state received the rather handsome amount of $12,698.60 from the U.S. Treasury for his congressional services and travel expenses during the second session of the Eighteenth Congress, which helped mitigate the financial loss.[5]

At the time of his nomination Clay felt quite indisposed. He complained of a "cold or influenza" and was forced to take to his bed and summon a doctor. As a matter of fact, Clay suffered ill health throughout his term as secretary of state. Adams obligingly came to Clay's lodgings on several occasions to discuss the details of inaugurating his administration, such as appointments to foreign posts, in particular the selection of ministers to Great Britain and Mexico. Clay was perfectly satisfied with Adams's recommendation of Rufus King of New York to the Court of St. James, but he questioned that of Joel Poinsett of South Carolina to Mexico. He thought the newly elected senator from Ohio General William Henry Harrison might make a better appointment. Not that he had anything against Poinsett, but Harrison had

3. Adams, *Memoirs,* VI, 524–525; Remini, *Jackson,* II, 103; Bemis, *Adams,* II, 58–59.
4. Adams, *Memoirs,* VI, 525; Remini, *Van Buren,* pp. 123–146.
5. Clay to Biddle, March 8, 1825, Biddle to Clay, March 11, 1825, Joseph Anderson to Clay, March 16, 1825, in Clay, *Papers,* IV, 93, 103, 114.

solicited many endorsements for the post and seemed "exceedingly anxious" to get it. The President turned up his nose at the suggestion, and the mission went to Poinsett.[6]

Clay conducted his business from the State Department building at Pennsylvania Avenue and Fifteenth Street, the site of the north wing of the present Treasury Department building. The structure, 160 feet long and 55 feet wide, rose two stories high. Erected in line with the south facade of the White House, it was made of brick and featured a small portico with a modest colonnade in the Greek Revival style. The new secretary of state set to work immediately drafting instructions and dispatches for the various foreign missions around the world.[7] There were seven missions in Europe and seven on the American continent to direct, along with numerous consulates. The Patent Office also came under his supervision, and the business of that agency had increased to such an extent that Clay was forced to hire two additional clerks to handle all its affairs.[8] He worked twelve and fourteen hours a day, and it quickly sapped his strength. "I find my office no bed of roses," he told Francis Brooke. "With spirits never more buoyant, 12 hours work per day are almost too much for my physical powers." A month later he still felt the strain. "I have prepared instructions to six new and old missions, some of them reaching to twenty pages, and all requiring much reading of previous correspondence and documents relating to each. . . . This very day I have had interviews with four different foreign ministers on matters of great public importance, and each of considerable duration." It began to cross his mind that maybe he had made a mistake in accepting the office. Perhaps the diplomatic corridors of power were not for him after all. "I know my *forte* is the H. of R.," he wistfully noted. "But I will endeavor to do my duty in this new office, and if God grant me life and health I will disappoint and triumph over my enemies."[9] He finally told Adams that "his health was so much affected" that he wished to postpone preparing some of the instructions until he had gone home to Kentucky, collected his family, and returned to Washington. He was confident such a journey would improve his health, as it had done repeatedly in the past when he suffered the same complaint. He expected to get back around the middle of July. Convinced Clay would return at the earliest possible moment, the President urged him to take as much time as necessary in returning home.[10]

6. Clay to Adams, March 5, 1825, in Clay, *Papers*, IV, 88; Adams, *Memoirs*, VI, 523–524.

7. On Clay's foreign policy, see Margaret Ruth Morley, "The Edge of Empire: Henry Clay's American System and the Formulation of Foreign Policy, 1810–1833," doctoral dissertation, University of Wisconsin, 1972.

8. Clay to Louis McLane, January 14, 1826, in Clay, *Papers*, V, 33–35. McLane was chairman of the House Ways and Means Committee, and Clay had asked for an appropriation to hire three additional clerks in the department and another for the Patent Office. The requested legislation was not passed until March 2, 1827.

9. Clay to Francis Brooke, April 6, 1825, Clay to James Brown, May 9, 1825, Clay to Charles Hammond, April 4, 1825, in Clay, *Papers*, IV, 221, 335–336, 211.

10. Adams, *Memoirs*, VI, 533, 545.

Before he left the capital, Clay informed Adams of several conversations he had had with Pablo Obregón, the Mexican, and José María Salazar, the Colombian, ministers. Their talks centered on a proposed congress of American ministers from the hemisphere to meet in October in Panama to discuss matters of mutual interest and concern. Clay was very anxious to advance his policy of encouraging Latin American independence and cooperating with these liberated nations. He informed the President that it was his most "earnest" desire that a minister from the United States be appointed to attend this congress. Secretary Barbour, however, opposed the idea. Adams agreed to take the matter under advisement.[11]

On April 23, 1825, the quasi-official Washington newspaper *National Journal* carried an article outlining the proposed agenda for the congress in Panama. The agenda included military operations, such as freeing the islands of Cuba and Puerto Rico; ways of advancing the Monroe Doctrine to frustrate further efforts of colonization on the American continent; establishing principles of maritime law for the participating nations; and discussing relations with the black Republic of Haiti. Earlier, on March 18, 1825, an article, signed by "Mutius Scaevola," appeared in the Philadelphia newspaper *Democratic Press,* praising the purposes of the Panama Congress and urging United States leadership lest some other power, like Great Britain, assume that role. "Scaevola" (a name used by Clay several times in the past) proposed a Pan-American confederation for mutual defense against a non-American nation. Samuel D. Ingham, a staunch Jacksonian, later identified the author of this article as Henry Clay, although the secretary of state never confirmed or denied it.[12]

Adams held a cabinet meeting at Clay's suggestion to discuss U.S. participation in the congress, the upshot of which resulted in a decision to agree to attend as a neutral but with an understanding that the proposed October date for the meeting be put back to give more time for necessary preparations. Because of these sudden developments regarding the Panama Congress, along with growing administration fears that Cuba and Puerto Rico might be attacked by the newly liberated countries of South America, Clay could not get away from his duties until the middle of May.

To some extent he was apprehensive about returning home. Among other things, opposition to his actions in preventing Jackson's election had been steadily growing in Kentucky. In congratulating him on his appointment as secretary of state, Francis P. Blair nevertheless detailed the rancor that had been building up against him. "The Jackson party among us are quite vocifer-

11. Adams, *Memoirs,* VI, 536–537. For Adams's position on the question, see Charles Wilson Hackett, "The Development of John Quincy Adams's Policy with Respect to an American Confederation and the Panama Congress, 1822–1825," *Hispanic American Historical Review,* IX (November 1928), p. 505ff.
12. There is some question whether Clay actually wrote this article. See Bemis, *Adams,* I, 545, note 19, and Hargreaves, *Presidency of John Quincy Adams,* pp. 148–149.

ous," he said, "—reiterate the Kremer abuse, & seem to consider that your acceptance of the Office of Secretary, a greater outrage, than even defeating the election of General Jackson."[13] And Amos Kendall added the gossip that the struggle in Kentucky between the Relief (New Court) and Anti-Relief (Old Court) parties had been brought to bear on the House election "and that you at Washington have acted in concert with the old Judges and their friends in Kentucky." True, Clay had little regard for the New Court party and its measures, but he had tried to steer clear of involvement. Now, it seemed, he had been thrust headlong into the dispute. His role in electing Adams was being interpreted to the electorate by the Jacksonians as collusion between the Great Compromiser and the friends of the Old Court. "Passion is taking the place of reason," Kendall went on, "and you have little conception of the ferocious feelings by which many men, especially the old Judge Party, are actuated. Violence on one side begets it on the other, and a degree of heat is rising which not only puts an end to all fair and honorable discussion, but actually endangers the public peace."

Kendall ended his letter with a not-so-subtle hint about money. He needed a loan. Since the death of his wife had removed all her real property from his grasp, which he required to run his newspaper, he said he must have not less than two thousand dollars in specie. He could get it in Philadelphia or New York if he had friends in those cities. But, alas, he did not. "And now, sir, if you can tell me where I can borrow [this money] . . . I believe you will do me the highest favor in your power."[14]

Clay foolishly allowed his relationship with Kendall to fall apart. The editor was becoming desperate for money, and his continued loyalty and support could be purchased quite easily. He had already hinted that he would be happy to have a "public employment." Nothing difficult, of course. "If I were offered a situation not too laborious, with a liberal compensation attached to it, and left entirely free to sport my pen as I pleased, I should accept." Furthermore, he allowed that in the future the *Argus* might say some unflattering things about the new administration—after all, "I consider a newspaper, in some degree as public property"—but whatever critical comments might be written he swore, they would never "receive form, aid or polish from my pen."[15] These "subtle" hints were unmistakable. It would seem that Kendall was putting Clay on notice that unless he received financial help he would desert to the Jacksonians.

The secretary of state did in fact offer Kendall a position in Washington with a salary of a thousand dollars. Kendall turned it down. He wanted fifteen hundred dollars at the very least. Clay's response to this demand was almost

13. Blair to Clay, March 7, 1825, in Clay, *Papers,* IV, 91. The Kremer letters were circulated in many states "to excite a hostility" toward Clay. J. Wingate, Jr. to Clay, March 18, 1825, ibid., IV, 122.
14. Kendall to Clay, March 23, 1825, in Clay, *Papers,* IV, 134–136.
15. Kendall to Clay, February 19, 1825, in Clay, *Papers,* IV, 77–78.

curt. "I do not know that I could offer you any other than that which you thought it your interest to decline," he snapped.[16] So the relationship between the two men worsened with each passing month, although Clay may have thought that Kendall would never desert him out of a sense of loyalty to Lucretia Clay. Several times in the past Kendall had referred to that loyalty. "It is true, I owe no obligations to you," he wrote Clay as late as February 19, 1825, ". . . but I cannot separate you from Mrs. Clay whose kindness I never shall return by an attempt to destroy the popularity and hopes of her husband."[17]

Kendall was a strange, very complicated man, nearsighted, stooped, chronically ill, with prematurely white hair and a sallow complexion—unquestionably far homelier than Clay. Years later Thomas B. Stevenson, a staunch supporter, reported that he had seen the repulsive-looking Kendall in Frankfort. "The expression of his countenance excites the idea of a famished wolf," said Stevenson. "It makes one hungry just to look at his lean, lank jaws, his restless, eager eyes, and his voracious hooked nose."[18]

Clay showed Francis P. Blair—another wispy, jejune little man, who hardly weighed a hundred pounds—a trifle more courtesy than he did Kendall. In fact, he made a real effort to assure him that "although I think you have recently erred [in supporting the Relief party] . . . I beg you to be assured of my continued esteem."[19] Indeed, he was concerned enough about what was happening to his standing in Kentucky to write out a long address to the people of his congressional district. The address was published in the Washington *National Journal* on March 28 and reprinted in virtually every newspaper in Kentucky and all the important sheets around the country.

Clay tried to be precise, thorough, and clear in his presentation. And he generally succeeded. In the document he again acknowledged his mistake in seeming to imply a determination to call Kremer to account on the field of honor. That was not his intention, he said, for no man "holds in deeper abhorrence than I do, that pernicious practice." He also insisted that the House of Representatives had a legitimate right to select whomever it wished as President. It had a "discretion" in the matter, "for choice implies examination, comparison, judgment." Of the 261 electors, he continued, Jackson had only 99, whereas 162 other electors wanted someone else. The majority should indeed govern, but the majority had not expressed its will. "I was called upon,"

16. Clay to Kendall, October 18, 1825, in Clay, *Papers,* IV, 747.
17. Kendall to Clay, February 19, 1825, Kendall to Clay, April 28, 1825, in Clay, *Papers,* IV, 77, 306. Kendall came out against Adams in his *Argus of Western America* on September 20, 1826, but he said nothing against Clay and did not mention the corrupt bargain. That came later.
18. Stevenson to Clay, August 29, 1848, Clay Papers, LC. On Kendall, see James Douglas Daniels, "Amos Kendall: Kentucky Journalist, 1819–1829," *Filson Club Historical Quarterly,* III (1978)," 46–65; Lynn LaDue Marshall, "The Early Career of Amos Kendall: The Making of a Jacksonian," doctoral dissertation, University of California, Berkeley, 1962; and Baxter Ford Melton, "Amos Kendall in Kentucky, 1814–1829," doctoral dissertation, Southern Illinois University, 1978.
19. Clay to Blair, December 16, 1825, in *Globe,* March 16, 1841; Elbert B. Smith, *Francis Preston Blair* (New York, 1980), pp. 19–25.

he said, "to perform a solemn public duty, in which my private feelings . . . were not to be indulged, but the good of my country only consulted." He therefore dismissed Crawford because of ill health. He dismissed Jackson because a President "must be a STATESMAN," and Andrew Jackson "has [not] exhibited . . . the qualities of a statesman." If the general had such qualities, "the evidence of the fact has escaped my observation." Clay admitted that the resolution of the legislature had informed him that it was the "wish of the people of Kentucky" that he vote for Jackson, but the resolution did not inform him by what means this wish had been learned. Any number of other Kentuckians from his district had said that they left the matter to his good judgment, and "I felt myself bound, in the exercise of my good judgment, to prefer Mr. Adams." As for the "corrupt bargain," he, like Jackson, could state: "I entered into no cabals; I held no secret conclaves; I enticed no man to violate pledges given or instructions received."

Clay ended the address on a graceful note: "That I have often misconceived your true interests is highly probable. That I have ever sacrificed them to the object of personal aggrandizement I utterly deny. And for the purity of my motives . . . I appeal to the justice of my God, with all the confidence which can flow from a consciousness of perfect rectitude."[20]

The address went over very well throughout the nation, particularly in eastern states. "Its effect has been wonderful," Clay enthused. "It has swept clean from Boston to Charleston. . . . I have used in it a strain of irony and sarcasm which my friends need have no apprehension of my employing in my public correspondence." Letters praising its strength and lucidity immediately poured into his office—"I had, yesterday, the honor of receiving two such letters from the Chief Justice of the U.S. and the C. Justice of Virginia"—and he only hoped that it would have as powerful an effect on his constituents back home.[21]

But in one sense Clay did himself a distinct disservice. Although his constituents desired an explanation of his actions in view of the accusations leveled against him, the address also served to keep the issue before the entire electorate. It necessarily invited responses from his critics. Senator John H. Eaton of Tennessee, for example, got into a public shouting match with him for daring to suggest that he (Eaton) had been involved in writing Kremer's note.[22]

Clay finally escaped Washington around the middle of May, and his journey homeward proved to be one long salute for assisting the election of John Quincy Adams. He was toasted, feted, dined, and wined at virtually every large community along his route, he said. "My reception West of the Mountains so

20. Address to the people of the congressional district . . . , March 26, 1825, in Clay, *Papers*, IV, 143–165.

21. Clay to Charles Hammond, April 4, 1825, Clay to John Sloane, April 7, 1825, in Clay, *Papers*, IV, 211, 227; Clay to James Tallmadge, April 7, 1825, copy CPP.

22. The correspondence on this matter was published in the Washington newspapers. "Was ever any thing so silly as for Eaton to publish his correspondence with me? I am greatly deceived if he has not come out worse than he stood before." Clay to Brooke, April 6, 1825, in Clay, *Papers*, IV, 221. The Eaton-Clay correspondence is published ibid., IV, 191ff.

far has exceeded my expectations. . . . In all the villages through which I passed crowds of decent orderly citizens visited me and with much kindness & cordiality welcomed me." Halting his journey virtually every day necessarily slowed his progress, and the receptions sapped his strength. By the time he reached home he was exhausted. "Public dinners, Barbacues [*sic*] and Balls have left me but little leisure to restore my health or transact my private business," he told Samuel L. Southard, the secretary of the navy. But he was not "intoxicated" by these demonstrations. He accepted them "with perfect coolness," he said, as a sign of the "just indignation against the conspiracy of last winter."[23]

The private business Clay mentioned in his letter was the need to prepare his family for their removal to Washington. This involved renting Ashland during their absence, and auctioning off most of their household furnishings (beds, sofas, chairs, carpets, mirrors, chandeliers, piano, tables, clocks, etc.) and their livestock (horses, mares, colts, mules, English cattle, and merino sheep). The removal of a "tolerable large family" some five hundred miles from a residence of more than twenty-five years took considerable effort. But in due course the house was rented and the family effects were sold off. From the auction, held at noon on June 24, Clay realized five thousand dollars.[24] His "hard featured lady," Lucretia, was not especially happy about moving to Washington, but her daughter Susan, now married and living in New Orleans with her husband, Martin Duralde, and her two small children, urged Lucretia to take advantage of the opportunity. "I have heard that you regret leaving Ashland very much," Susan wrote, "but for my part I am very glad of it for I think you worked too much, stay'd at home too much and you were too much plagued there, at Washington you will be forced to go more into the world and although you will perhaps not like it much at first, you will soon get accustomed to it."[25]

By July 7 Clay thought he could begin the return journey with his family and so notified the President. In this letter he again noted the wonderful receptions he had received, particularly in Kentucky and among his own immediate constituents. "La Fayette's transit through the Country has hardly occasioned more excitement than my return. . . . There is not a murmur existing against me." But this was another instance of Clay's inability or unwillingness to read the clear political signals—especially negative signals—that were flying throughout the West. He acknowledged that some of his constitu-

23. Clay to Charles Hammond, May 23, 1825, Clay to Southard, June 17, 1825, in Clay, *Papers*, IV, 387–388, 447. See the various toasts, volunteers, resolutions, etc. in his honor ibid., IV, 381–442 passim.

24. See the advertisement of auction, June 13, 1825, and statement of auction sale, June 24, 1825, rental agreement with Nelson Nicholas, September 14, 1825, Clay to Adams, June 28, 1825, in Clay, *Papers*, IV, 435, 457–461, 642, 489. It was estimated in the auction sale that Clay owned about 120 sheep.

25. Edward Bates to Julia Bates, December 4, 1829, Edward Bates Papers, Virginia Historical Society, Richmond; Susan Clay Duralde to her mother and father, August 8, 1825, in Clay, *Papers*, IV, 570.

ents had disapproved of his House vote when they first heard about it, but they had been "converted," he declared, and had united in the general demonstrations of support.[26]

What Clay seemed unable to appreciate was the terrible rending of the Republican party in Kentucky. And that division had produced an opposition dedicated to his overthrow. The struggle between the Relief and Anti-Relief parties had grown more bitter and violent. And the state election in August only made things worse. The lower house was won by the Old Court (Anti-Relief), but the upper house was divided between the two factions. The apparent victory of the Anti-Relief party delighted Clay. "I am highly gratified with this result," he wrote. He congratulated his good friend John J. Crittenden on his election to the state house of representatives and then urged him to restore the Old Court judges to office and dismiss the New Court judges. "The pruning knife should be applied with a considerate and steady hand. . . . Where you have the power of appointment, put in good & faithful men." But the net result of the state election, as Kendall informed him shortly thereafter, was "that our contest here will be renewed and continued with more bitterness than ever." Worse, "the impression is general among the friends of the New Court," said Kendall, "that you have interfered in this question and thrown your influence against us. [And] . . . it is impossible to vindicate you satisfactorily."

Clay snapped right back: "I think your party is wrong; that they should hasten to forget the past, and unite, for the future, in advancing the true interests of the State, without indulging in unavailing regrets. As to the calumnies of which you and they believe themselves to have been the object, you should despise and outlive them."[27]

By the fall of 1825 no one could doubt that the Republican party in Kentucky had permanently split, with the Anti-Relief group supporting Clay and the administration, and the Relief group rallying behind General Jackson and his friends. In time the administration party in Kentucky and elsewhere in the country was called the National Republican party. The antiadministration, or Jackson, party became known as the Democratic-Republican or simply Democratic party.

Although Clay's health had not improved to the degree he had hoped during his sojourn at Ashland, he relied on his return journey to provide "more tranquillity and abstraction from the bustle and the crowd," which would renew his energies. But catastrophe struck along the way. When the family reached Cincinnati on July 12, Clay's youngest daughter, the twelve-year-old Eliza, came down with a fever. Dismissing it as the result of excitement over the trip, the family continued eastward. At Lebanon, Ohio, the child's condition worsened, and Clay called a physician who advised the parents not to

26. Clay to Adams, June 28, 1825, in Clay, *Papers,* IV, 489.

27. Clay to Crittenden, August 22, 1825, Clay to James Brown, September 4, 1825, Kendall to Clay, October 4, 1825, Blair to Clay, August 30, 1825, Clay to Kendall, October 18, 1825, in Clay, *Papers,* IV, 585, 619, 719, 603, 747.

move her any further. A week passed, and despite the application of several remedies, Eliza did not respond. "I am greatly mortified and distressed by the occurrence," Clay apologetically explained to Adams, but there was little he could do.

Several more weeks passed, and finally the doctor assured the father that the child would surely recover and that it was safe for him to continue his journey alone. As soon as Eliza was well enough, she was to resume the trip to Washington with her mother and the other members of the family. Torn between his responsibilities to his child and to his position as secretary of state, but virtually guaranteed the child's recovery by the doctor, Clay, with "some forebodings," finally decided to continue alone to Washington. He arrived on August 21.

He was not twenty miles from the capital when he read in the *National Intelligencer* that his daughter had died on August 11. The news devastated him. He was filled with remorse and guilt at having left his family at the critical moment. He wrote to his wife to offer some consolation "for the severe afflic-tion which Providence has seen fit to send us. . . . I cannot describe to you my own distressed feelings, which have been greatly aggravated by a knowledge of what your's must have been, in the midst of strangers, and all your friends far away." What more could he say except that "We must bow, with religious resignation, to decrees which we have no power to revoke."[28]

Eliza was the only unmarried daughter in the Clay family, and her mother had "anticipated much gratification from her society and from completing her education" in Washington. But that was now over. The two sorrowing par-ents, after Lucretia's arrival at the capital, moved into Mrs. Eliza Clark's board-inghouse until such time as they could find more appropriate lodgings. "I have not yet had it in my power to obtain a house," he said, "or even to look or enquire much about one."[29] On October 11 the family rented Richard For-rest's three-story brick house on F Street between Fourteenth and Fifteenth streets for an annual rent of five hundred dollars paid quarterly. Clay then had boxes and trunks of the family possessions—books, china, furniture, etc.— shipped by wagon from Ashland. "The rooms are very good," Clay wrote to his brother-in-law James Brown, the U.S. minister to France, "and sufficient in number for my reduced family."[30]

This terrible tragedy was followed by yet another. One month after Eliza's death a second daughter died. Susan Clay Duralde contracted yellow fever in New Orleans and after an illness of nearly a week died at 9:00 P.M. on Septem-ber 18, 1825. She was twenty years old. "The news of the death of her sister

28. Clay to Adams, July 21, 25, 1825, Clay to James Erwin, August 28, 1825, Clay to Lucretia Clay, August 24, 1825, Clay to Brooke, September 2, 1825, in Clay, *Papers,* IV, 546, 550, 598, 589, 615. The *National Intelligencer* carried the story of Eliza's death on August 20, 1825.

29. Clay to Henry B. Bascom, August 30, 1825, Clay to James Erwin, August 30, 1825, in Clay, *Papers,* IV, 600, 601.

30. Rental agreement with Richard Forrest, October 11, 1825, memorandum to Robert Scott, July 6, 1825, Clay to Brown, November 14, 1825, in Clay, *Papers,* IV, 728, 512, 823.

weighed heavily on her," George Eustis told Clay; "it depressed her spirits and perceptibly affected her death. . . . The deceased died of a malignant fever, as it is called here. The organs of the stomach were vitally affected thirty six hours before dissolution." Before dying the young woman moaned, "I regret to die without Seeing my Father & mother." These were her last words as reported to Clay. She left a husband and two children, the younger not yet weaned.[31]

Overwhelmed with understandable self-pity, Clay cried out his despair: "Ah . . . is it not cruel out of six daughters to be deprived of all but one! Age, grief and misfortune make us feel a great want, and God alone can supply that."[32]

Clay buried himself in work. It was all he could do. His poor wife worked through her grief as best she could. Susan was her favorite child, according to Nancy Brown, and her passing was almost unbearable. "I have never before found all the resources of my fortitude so entirely unavailing," the father groaned. "Great as have been the sufferings of Lucretia, on the occasion, the character of her sex or her mind has enabled her to sustain the shock better than I have done." Like a great many other women of this age who regularly faced the death of their children, she found consolation in her religion.[33]

If Clay had worked twelve and fourteen hours a day before he left Washington, he worked even longer hours after his return. But he undermined his health in the process and delayed any hope of recovery from his chronic illnesses. His friends registered their concern. "You must allow me to admonish you to take care of your *health*," Daniel Webster wrote him. "Knowing the ardor, and the intensity, with which you may probably apply yourself to the duties of your place, I fear very much you may over-work yourself." You must do two things, he went on. Never do today what can be put off until tomorrow or anything yourself that could be done by another.[34]

Over the next several months Clay tried to put his daughters out of his mind and focus instead on his duties. But at times he came close to a breakdown, and he had to steel himself against yielding to the overwhelming "affliction" he suffered. Fortunately John Quincy Adams was President, and he did what he could to adjust the needs of his administration to Clay's present indisposition and difficulties. For one thing, he did not intrude or interfere in the business of the department. As former secretary of state he knew more about the activities of the department, current problems, and the like than his successor. With eight years' experience running State, and with a long personal history in diplomacy as minister to the Netherlands, Portugal, Prussia, Russia,

---

31. George Eustis to Clay, September 20, 1825, Étienne Mazureau to Clay, September 19, 1825, in Clay, *Papers,* IV, 665, 659.

32. Clay to Charlotte Mentelle, October 24, 1825, in Clay, *Papers,* IV, 756. In addition to Eliza and Susan, Henrietta, Lucretia, and Laura had died. Of six Clay daughters, only Anne Clay Erwin remained.

33. Nancy Brown to Susanna Price, December 12, 1825, November 23, 1826, Brown-Polk Family Papers, Manuscript Department, Filson Club, Louisville, Kentucky; Clay to James Brown, November 14, 1825, in Clay, *Papers,* IV, 822.

34. Webster to Clay, September 28, 1825, in Clay, *Papers,* IV, 698–699.

and Great Britain, he could very easily have taken over. But he did not. Nor did he offer to step in. Because he respected Clay and his ability to run the department, he felt no need to stare constantly over his shoulder. "Mr. Clay is in deep affliction," recorded Adams in his diary, "having lost two daughters in the course of a month. . . . His own health is so infirm that he told me he feared he should be obliged to resign his office; but said he would try to retain it through the winter, and declared himself entirely satisfied with my conduct toward him, and with the course of the Administration hitherto."[35]

It is extraordinary that the two men got along as well as they did, considering their total dissimilarity in background, temperament, manner, and style. The one a hail-fellow, impetuous, enthusiastic, romantic, and high-spirited, the other moody, remote, cautious, forbidding, and austere; the one charming, outgoing, fun-loving, and invariably optimistic and naturally buoyant, the other reserved, cold, standoffish, dour, and fatalistic. Clay was pragmatic and opportunistic; Adams, moralistic and self-righteous. Not too long before they had cordially disliked each other. But in a relatively short period of time they had been able to forget the past and work together toward making a success of their partnership. They were united in their desire to show the electorate that this administration would add luster to the nation's glorious history. In terms of policy and program they agreed almost totally. Within a month of his appointment as secretary of state, Clay told a friend that "an entire harmony as to public measures exists between Mr. Adams and me."[36]

If nothing else, Clay won over the President by dint of hard work. Despite his mysterious health problems—possibly chronic bronchitis and bad teeth—Clay devoted himself unstintingly to achieving total success for the administration. Of course, it was in his own personal interest to attain that goal, but he genuinely sought the President's vindication by providing him with unwavering support and assistance. He not only consulted with Adams over major issues, both domestic and foreign, but labored long hours each day over the mind-numbing details of diplomatic paper work, for which he had little patience or interest. He assisted the President in putting together a national program of breathtaking originality and imagination, and Adams presented it to Congress on December 6, 1825, at the start of the Nineteenth Congress.

The message was a bold, courageous, and statesmanlike assertion of the government's responsibility to assist the advancement of the nation's intellectual and economic well-being. Its major themes and concepts were rooted in the American System, and it proposed a program of public works of startling magnitude.

This first of Adams's messages to Congress began naturally enough with a discussion of foreign affairs, and it gave an optimistic view of developing commercial relations. Then came the first important pronouncement. A con-

---

35. Adams, *Memoirs,* VII, 52.
36. Clay to Brooke, April 6, 1825, in Clay, *Papers,* IV, 221.

gress to be held in Panama of independent Latin American countries had been proposed "to deliberate upon objects important to the welfare of all," and the United States had accepted an invitation to attend. Already the republics of Mexico, Colombia, and Central America (or the Central American Federation) had sent deputations to Panama, and the President would shortly name the ministers to attend on behalf of the United States.[37]

Since the previous spring Clay had had a series of conferences with the ministers of Mexico and Colombia, Pablo Obregón and José María Salazar, at their request. Knowing Clay's advocacy of the principle of cooperation among independent nations of the Western Hemisphere, they solicited his aid in winning administration approval of the Panama Congress. The ministers did not wish to issue an invitation to the United States without prior knowledge that it would be accepted, so they assured the secretary of state that they did not expect the United States to abandon its policy of neutrality or engage actively in the ongoing war with Spain for Latin American independence.

Clay succeeded in obtaining administration approval despite Adams's less than enthusiastic endorsement. He reported back to the Mexican and Colombian ministers that the President could see much merit in such a congress in terms of settling disputed questions and strengthening the "friendship and amicable intercourse between the American powers."[38] At first Adams had several troubling questions he wanted answered before committing himself, but the responses he subsequently received through Clay so satisfied him that he gave his approval for U.S. participation in the congress.[39]

The Panama Congress was an enlightened effort to initiate a policy of cooperation and amicable discourse among the American nations. It would be the first Pan-American Conference, an idea originally formulated by Simón Bolívar, the great South American liberator.[40] For the United States, it was a Latin American policy that if adopted and pursued at the very beginning would have prevented countless problems and misunderstandings in the future. It was a policy far ahead of its time.

Unfortunately many congressmen abhorred the idea of such cooperation. To them it meant a shocking abandonment of the principles of neutrality contained in Washington's Farewell Address. In addition, they feared a lessening of U.S. independence in determining its foreign policy. And of course, Jacksonians opposed it on political grounds. Anything recommended by the "monstrous union" deserved to be cast out, they argued.

Adams's message to the Nineteenth Congress, according to the opposition, then continued to pile one "horror" on top of another. "In assuming her

37. Richardson, *Messages and Papers,* II, 868.

38. Clay to Adams, December 20, 1825, in Clay, *Papers,* IV, 927; Adams, *Memoirs,* VI, 536–537, 542.

39. Clay to Obregón, November 30, 1825, Clay to Salazar, November 30, 1825, in *ASPFR,* V, 837–838.

40. Bemis, *Adams,* I, 543.

station among the civilized nations of the earth," said the President, "it would seem that our country had contracted the engagement to contribute her share of mind, of labor, and of expense to the improvement of those parts of knowledge which lie beyond the reach of individual acquisition, and particularly to geographical and astronomical science." Accordingly he proposed the exploration of the entire northwest coast of the continent; establishment of a uniform standard of weights and measures, a national university, and an astronomical observatory ("light-houses of the skies" was his term for them); and the initiation of a broad program of federally sponsored internal improvements. These public works would include roads, canals, bridges, turnpikes, harbor and waterway installations, and other means of facilitating "communications and intercourse between distant regions and multitudes of men." The rationale for such a spectacular program was manifestly obvious. "The great object of the institution of civil government is the improvement of the condition of those who are parties to the social compact." Besides, "the spirit of improvement is abroad upon the earth. . . . Liberty is power [and that] . . . nation blessed with the largest portion of liberty must in proportion to its numbers be the most powerful nation upon earth." For the Congress, within its constitutional limits, to fail in its responsibility to improve agriculture, commerce, and manufactures and to fail to encourage the mechanical and "elegant" arts, the advancement of literature, and the progress of science for the benefit of the people "would be treachery of the most sacred of trusts." Then he dropped one final bombshell: ". . . Were we to slumber in indolence or fold up our arms and proclaim to the world that we are palsied by the will of our constituents, would it not be to cast away the bounties of Providence and doom ourselves to perpetual inferiority?"[41]

The conservatives in Congress could scarcely believe that in the year 1825 any President could propose such an outrageously exaggerated view of the constitutional powers of the American government. Roads, canals, a national university, a Panama Congress, "light-houses in the skies," indeed. This was the American System with a vengeance. And it was preposterous, stormed the Radicals. The "monstrous union" had produced a "monstrous" program. Many congressmen shook their heads in anger or disbelief, although the friends of the administration both in Congress and around the nation[42] immediately applauded its enlightened view of the responsibilities and opportunities available to this nation.

But the phrase "palsied by the will of our constituents" caught everyone's attention. What a contemptuous view of the electorate! chorused the Jacksonians. What arrogance and presumption! What a mockery of constitutional and limited notions of governmental power! Leave it to Adams and Clay, the

41. Richardson, *Messages and Papers,* II, 878–879, 881–882.
42. "Of the character of 'The Message'—it appears to me the first among that class of papers which have been, and still are, identifying the literature of the Glory of this—*Great Nation."* Richard Douglas to Clay, December 19, 1825, in Clay, *Papers,* IV, 924.

corrupt perpetrators of a "corrupt bargain," to advise the Congress to defy "the will of our constituents." Was this not further proof that the presidency had been stolen, that the people had been betrayed? And notice that remark about "Liberty is power." Every individual who understood anything at all about republicanism knew that liberty was the exact reverse of power, that the protection of liberty required the restraint of governmental power. "Sir," said Representative Willie P. Mangum of North Carolina, "this administration I verily believe will be conducted upon as corrupt principles, indeed more corrupt, than any that has preceded it. Bargain & compromise will be the order of the day."[43]

Thomas Ritchie could not believe a President would write such a message. "Are we really reading a state paper," he asked in the *Enquirer,* "or a school boy's Thesis?"[44] And Andrew Jackson, who had just resigned his seat in the Senate and had been renominated for President in the next election by the Tennessee legislature, wrote: "When I view the splendor & magnificence of the government embraced in the recommendation of the late message . . . together with the declaration that it would be criminal for the agents of our government to be palsied by the will of their constituents, I shudder for the consequence—if not checked by the voice of the people, it must end in consolidation, & then in despotism."[45]

Those conservatives especially concerned about the limits of government, who preached a narrow interpretation of the Constitution as basic to the Jeffersonian and Republican creed, were stunned by the content of the message. This was particularly true among the Radical members of the party, especially in Virginia, where they had remained loyal to Crawford in the late election despite his crippling infirmities. Consequently, one immediate effect of the message produced the election of an archconservative to the U.S. Senate: John Randolph of Roanoke, Clay's old nemesis, was chosen to complete James Barbour's term. And the message helped convince Martin Van Buren that the future belonged to the friends of Andrew Jackson and that he needed to lead his Radical associates into the general's camp. Thomas Hart Benton, who had supported Clay in the election of 1824, later confessed that the message "went to the construction of parties on the old line of strict . . . construction of the constitution."[46]

In fashioning his message, Adams consulted regularly with his cabinet, and the meetings lasted several hours each day. Clay did not like including in the message the idea of establishing a national university because in his view, it

43. Mangum to Bartlett Yancey, January 15, 1826, in Mangum, *Papers,* I, 231. Mangum was not speaking specifically about the message, but he undoubtedly had it in mind when he wrote this letter.

44. Quoted in the Albany *Argus,* December 9, 1825.

45. Jackson to John Branch, March 3, 1826, Branch Family Papers, Southern Historical Collection, University of North Carolina, Chapel Hill.

46. Benton, *Thirty Years' View,* I, 54.

did not rest upon the same constitutional principles as internal improvements
or a national bank. Otherwise he approved of the general arguments about
public works, although he "scrupled" over some of the details. His keen political instincts warned him that certain elements of the message could provide the
opposition with an opening to begin a general attack upon the administration.
"Mr. Clay was for recommending nothing which, from its unpopularity,
would be unlikely to succeed," the President noted. Others in the cabinet, like
Barbour, argued against anything "so popular that it may be carried without
recommendation. Clay good-humoredly remarked this alternate stripping off
from my draft; and I told them I was like the man with his two wives—one
plucking out his black hairs, and the other the white, till none were left." But
the final decision as to what would be plucked belonged to the President. The
"perilous experiment must be made," he wrote. "Let me make it with full
deliberation, and be prepared for the consequences."[47]

It is worth noting that this great and highly nationalistic state paper
caused the normally impetuous Clay to warn the President away from a potentially damaging encounter with Congress, while the normally cautious Adams
turned aside his doubts and hesitations and plunged ahead with his "perilous
experiment."

When the decision was finally made and the message published, Clay
reverted to his old optimism and predicted a positive response from the electorate. "Matters look favorably here," he told his newspaper friend Charles
Hammond, "especially in the H. of R. . . . I believe the great mass of the
American public is satisfied with the past, and sanguine as to the future." He
thought the message went particularly well "everywhere North of this place."
Of course, there were rumblings to the south and west. He also acknowledged
that it might have contributed to Randolph's election. Still, on the whole, he
anticipated strong popular support. "Its doctrines on Internal improvements
&c have given the offence in the ancient dominion; but that very cause must
have an opposite and friendly effect almost every where else. My belief is that
upon the whole it will be very popular."[48]

As the cabinet discussions made clear, Adams needed considerable assistance in the matter of practical politics. He preferred pursuing a nonpartisan
policy, especially in regard to appointments. Ability and integrity were his
principal concerns.[49] He made it a rule not to dismiss individuals whose politics conflicted with his own, as he had pledged prior to the House election. But
Clay tried to warn him against too close an observance of that troubling rule.

47. Adams, *Memoirs,* VII, 60–63.
48. Clay to Hammond, December 10, 1825, Clay to James Brown, December 12, 1825, in Clay,
Papers, IV, 891, 895.
49. Clay wrote to one applicant: "In respect to appointments to public office, there is great
solicitude always to select those who are honest, faithful & capable. Previous pledges or commitments for them, always embarrassing, will be avoided; and when vacancies occur the pretensions
of the different applicants will be justly weighed, without favor or partiality." Clay to Finis Ewing,
June 16, 1825, Brigham Young University Library, copy CPP.

"Mr. Clay . . . observed that with regard to the conduct of persons holding offices at the pleasure of the President," commented Adams, "the course of the Administration should be to avoid, on the one hand, political persecution, and, on the other, an appearance of pusillanimity." It was one thing for an individual to "indulge his preference" for a candidate prior to the House election, "but after it was decided," said Clay, "no officer depending upon the will of the President for his place, should be permitted to hold a conduct in open and continual disparagement of the Administration and its head."[50]

Adams conceded the principle but challenged that it could be done without difficulty. "Great delicacy" was needed in its application, he said.[51] The President tended to retain all those with whose work he was familiar. And some of these, like his postmaster general, John McLean, would betray him and give aid and comfort to the enemy. Even those appointments in which personal favor might be charged by the opposition could usually be defended on the basis of experience.[52]

Clay was forced to go his own way on the question of appointments, but he did it without acting disloyally to the President. He took away the printing patronage to publish the laws from editors who failed to support the administration, including Amos Kendall's *Argus of Western America,* which had come out in opposition. The withdrawal of this patronage constituted the final act that sent the former tutor scurrying into the Jackson camp.[53]

There were approximately eighty newspapers around the country that enjoyed the patronage of printing U.S. statutes, and within the first year of his tenure as secretary of state Clay had snatched it away from at least ten publishers. This was a modest number of replacements compared with what the Democrats were to inaugurate when they captured the White House. Still, it was unprecedented for the time. Clay continued this patronage policy throughout his tenure, shifting the printing from the initial ten to seventy-six journals, and was regularly lambasted by the Jacksonians for blatantly attempting to corrupt the press. The Nashville *Republican* lost its subsidy to the Nashville *Whig,* a sheet owned by a family possibly related to Clay; John Binns's *Democratic Press* of Philadelphia replaced a newspaper partially owned by the Jacksonian Samuel Ingham; and in Charleston, the *Patriot,* supported by George McDuffie and Robert Y. Hayne, was supplanted by the *City Gazette.*[54]

As far as he could control it, Clay distributed the patronage where he felt

50. Adams, *Memoirs,* VI, 546.

51. Ibid.

52. Hargreaves, *Presidency of John Quincy Adams,* p. 54.

53. Coupled with the Jacksonian threat to found a rival newspaper in Frankfort.

54. Culver Smith, *The Press, Politics, and Patronage: The American Government's Use of Newspapers, 1789–1875* (Athens, Ga., 1977), pp. 73–78. For an extended listing of Clay's substitutions, see Hargreaves, *Presidency of John Quincy Adams,* pp. 265–269. See also *House Documents,* 19th Congress, 1st session, no. 41, pp. 9–16, for Clay's report on publishers of the laws. The Jacksonians also accused Clay of nepotism in sending his son Theodore as a messenger with dispatches to Mexico.

it could do the most good. "Nobody can say that *I* neglect *my* friends," he later boasted "with one of his significant leers."[55] Consequently, the Jacksonians incorporated the charge of extensive corruption in the executive branch of the government in the presidential campaign of 1828. In his private letters Jackson himself hammered away at this "corrupt" policy. "The patronage of the government for the last three years," he growled in 1828, "has been wielded to corrupt every thing that comes within its influence, and was capable of being corrupted, and it would seem, that virtue and truth, has fled from its embrace. The administrators of the Govt has stained our national character." The approaching presidential election, he went on, "is a contest between the virtue of the people and the influence of patronage."[56]

The "perilous experiment" of the President's message when it went to the Congress on December 6 threw down a gauntlet that the opposition immediately picked up. The Jacksonians, now including the Vice President, John C. Calhoun; Senator Thomas Hart Benton of Missouri, formerly a Clay supporter; Senator Robert Y. Hayne, of South Carolina, a close ally of the Vice President's; Senator John M. Berrien of Georgia, a Crawford man and former Federalist, among others, planned to attack the Panama Congress proposal. At the same time, in a coordinated effort, the Radicals chose to concentrate their fire on the internal improvements section of the message. Indeed, the Little Magician, Martin Van Buren, rose almost immediately in the Senate with resolutions denying congressional power to build roads and canals and suggesting a constitutional amendment if the Congress intended to act on the President's suggestions. Naturally he had no intention of advocating such an amendment. The resolutions were meant to consume time and block the passage of bills to construct improvements. "The debate on my Resolutions will be extensive," he told his Regency. "I believe . . . that we shall be able in the end to break up all interference on the part of the Genl Govert without a previous amendment of the Constitution."[57] Almost immediately upon receipt of the message Van Buren approached the Vice President, now allied with Old Hickory, and asked how the Jacksonians planned to respond to it. Calhoun told him that the Panama mission would constitute the first major struggle between the administration and the Jackson party. Delighted with this response, Van Buren acknowledged his own opposition and assured the Vice President that he could be counted on to lend his support in defeating it.[58]

In the meantime, the President forwarded to the Senate for confirmation the names of the individuals to attend the Panama Congress as representatives of the United States. Clay had hoped to include his former colleague at Ghent Albert Gallatin as joint head of the mission with Richard C. Anderson, the

55. Joseph Hopkinson quoted Clay's alleged boast in a letter to Webster, April 13, 1827, in Webster, *Papers, Correspondence,* II, 189. Hopkinson had heard it from Robert Walsh.
56. Jackson to John Coffee, May 12, 1828, Coffee Papers, Tennessee Historical Society.
57. Van Buren to Benjamin F. Butler, December 25, 1825, Van Buren Papers, LC.
58. Remini, *Van Buren,* p. 105.

present U.S. minister to Colombia, but the President refused the recommendation, despite several requests. Subsequently Adams nominated Anderson
and John Sergeant of Pennsylvania as envoys extraordinary and ministers
plenipotentiary, and William B. Rochester of New York as secretary—all
friends of Clay.[59]

When the House of Representatives opened a debate on the Panama
question by calling for papers relating to the mission, the President rightly
suspected an organized opposition had been formed to defeat his administration. "This is the first subject upon which a great effort has been made in both
Houses to combine the discordant elements of the Crawford and Jackson and
Calhoun men into a united opposition against the Administration."[60] These
suspicions were confirmed almost immediately when the Senate began debating the nominations. Van Buren submitted a resolution proposing the debate
on the mission be conducted with open doors unless the publication of documents might prove detrimental to existing negotiations. He went on to request
that the President give an opinion on the matter. It was a deliberate ploy to
annoy the irascible President, and Clay advised Adams to tell the Senate that it
should form its own "judgment and responsibility." It asks for an opinion, said
Clay, and that is totally without precedent. "If you were to give it, they would
be more likely to abuse you for it than to respect it."[61]

Adams agreed. And back went his testy reply. He deemed it "my indispensable duty to leave to the Senate itself the decision of a question, involving
a departure . . . from that usage, and upon the motives of which . . . I do not
feel myself competent to decide."[62]

"Will you do me the favour," Peter B. Porter wrote to Clay, "to inform
me what Van Buren is doing at Washington. Is he leagued with the Vice
President?" What is he up to?

Clay's response was a fairly accurate account of the situation at the capital.
"I imagine that the V. Pres, V. Buren and their associates have not yet agreed
upon the terms of this most strange ————." The Senate, he continued, was
infested with a dozen or more men who were hostile to the administration at
all times. In addition, eight or ten were "secretly inclined" to opposition.
When the two groups united, they formed a majority. Nevertheless, predicted
Clay, the nominations would receive Senate approval.[63]

The verbal assault on the mission in the upper house was well organized

59. Clay to Gallatin, November 8, 11, 1825, in Clay, *Papers,* IV, 801, 814. At first Adams refused
the request because he thought the Congress would not approve the expense of an additional
minister. Later he extended the offer to Gallatin, who declined it, whereupon the President substituted Sergeant. Bemis, *Adams,* I, 547, 551.

60. Adams, *Memoirs,* VII, 111.

61. Clay to Adams, February 15, 1825, in Clay, *Papers,* V, 106.

62. *Register of Debates,* 19th Congress, 1st session, pp. 142–143.

63. Porter to Clay, February 17, 1825, Clay Papers, LC, Clay to Porter, February 22, 1825, Porter
Papers, Buffalo Historical Society; Clay to Brooke, February 20, 1826, in Clay, *Papers,* V, 117–
118.

and controlled—probably the result of Van Buren's masterful hand. Senator Hayne started off by voicing southern fear that the Panama Congress would discuss the suppression of the slave trade and the independence of Haiti. He asked whether representatives from an island controlled by blacks should be permitted to sit as equals with Americans. Then he answered his own question in a thundering voice: not while there were southern votes in Congress to prevent it.[64]

Van Buren followed and pronounced the mission "a *political connexion,* at war with the established policy of our Government." It was contrary to the no entangling alliances doctrine contained in Washington's Farewell Address and the many state papers of Thomas Jefferson. It was claimed, said Van Buren, that the Monroe Doctrine requires this nation to participate in the Congress. The secretary of state demands that the Senate "fulfill the alleged *pledge* of Mr. Monroe." This nation is not so pledged, cried the Magician. Association with such a congress places the United States in the same category as the hated Holy Alliance in Europe. "But I am against all alliances, against all armed confederacies, or confederacies of any sort."[65]

Senators Berrien, Benton, and Holmes followed the Magician with speeches of gargantuan length, all deliberately conceived to consume as much time as possible. Clay watched their tactics with growing anxiety. He was especially concerned over the activities of Calhoun's friends, like Robert Y. Hayne. "The Vice President," he wrote, ". . . is up to the hub with the opposition. . . . One of the main inducements with him, and those whom he can influence, is, that they suppose, if they can defeat or, by delay, cripple the measure, it will affect me."[66]

Indeed, that was exactly what they supposed. This was a diplomatic mission, concerning an issue (the liberation of Latin America) that Clay had long advocated and been identified with. To sink it in an endless congressional debate would go far to mar Clay's record as secretary of state and possibly to blast his immediate future ambitions.

It remained for Clay's old adversary in the House John Randolph to cap the Senate debate with one of his most outrageous performances. In a rambling, sometimes incoherent, funny, insulting, and devastating speech, filled with literary and classical allusions, among other odds and ends, and delivered with delightful insouciance, he roamed among a number of topics, including the Panama Congress, other parts of the President's message, the Constitution, and the "corrupt bargain." The Panama mission, he chuckled, had been brought about by the manufacture of letters purportedly sent from Latin America. In reality, he said, it was a "Kentucky cuckoo's egg, laid in a Spanish-American nest." The other senators sat in utter amazement at his performance; but they listened intently, and the Jacksonians enjoyed every moment of it. The

64. *Register of Debates,* 19th Congress, 1st session, pp. 154–174.
65. *Register of Debates,* 19th Congress, 1st session, pp. 237–262,
66. Clay to Crittenden, March 10, 1826, in Clay, *Papers,* V, 158.

presiding officer of the Senate, Vice President Calhoun, perhaps bemused and pleased by it all, made no effort to stop this abuse.

Eventually Randolph narrowed his sights on the corrupt bargain. Then, referring to two scoundrels—Blifil and Black George—in the popular novel *Tom Jones,* by Henry Fielding, he claimed that he had been "defeated, horse, foot, and dragoons—cut up—and clean broke down, by the coalition of Blifil and Black-George—by the combination, unheard of until then, of the Puritan and the blackleg."[67]

It was a stinging and nasty assault, one of a long series of verbal blasts at Clay. Only this one was far worse than any of the others. It touched a very sensitive nerve, it included not only charges of bribery and management but forgery as well, and it went unanswered. Clay had no way of responding in kind—except by demanding "satisfaction" in a duel.

Like most intelligent men in this modern age, Clay opposed dueling in principle, but he had been raised in a society that recognized dueling as the only appropriate means of defending one's honor when grossly insulted. Many states, including Kentucky, outlawed dueling—not that the restriction was regularly enforced. But what seemed to force Clay's hand was the publication just a few days earlier in the *United States Telegraph,* the leading Calhoun-Jackson newspaper in Washington, of an article in which the charge was repeated that management, bargain, and intrigue had brought the present administration to power in total disregard of the popular will.[68]

In a moment of panic and outrage Clay scratched out a brief note:

Sir   Washington 31 March 1826
Your unprovoked attack of my character, in the Senate of the U. States, on yesterday, allows me no other alternative than that of demanding personal satisfaction. The necessity of any preliminary discussions or explanations being superseded by the notoriety and the indisputable existence of the injury to which I refer, my friend General [Thomas S.] Jessup [*sic*], who will present you this note, is fully authorized by me forthwith to agree to the arrangements suited to the interview proposed. I am, Your obedient Servant
                                                H. Clay
The Honorable John Randolph[69]

It was a dreadful mistake. To summon to a field of honor a man believed by many to be something of a "cuckoo" himself invited ridicule and derision.[70] But Clay felt compelled to defend himself against such an unfair and un-

---

67. *Register of Debates,* 19th Congress, 2d session, pp. 389–404. By this time the vote on confirmation of the ministers had already taken place, but the issue was still alive in the House of Representatives, where the appropriation bill for the ministers was under discussion.

68. March 27, 1826. This paper was edited by Duff Green, and it was later rumored that Clay had challenged Calhoun to a duel and killed him. See Crittenden to Clay, April 27, 1826, in Clay, *Papers,* V, 277.

69. Clay to Randolph, March 31, 1825, in Clay, *Papers,* V, 208.

70. In Kentucky Clay friends said that it would have been better for him "to have disregarded the phrensy of the madman." John J. Crittenden to Clay, April 27, 1826, in Clay, *Papers,* V, 277.

provoked attack; otherwise he risked more of the same, both in and out of
Congress. By demonstrating in the strongest possible way that he would not
stand idly by and allow others—no matter who they were—to savage his
reputation and character might put a stop to any more of it.

A short time later Clay explained the reasons for issuing his challenge.
Randolph's assaults, he said, "were so gross repeated and unprovoked that I
could not longer bear them." The only thing that gave him pause was "the
opinion which is entertained by some, as to the state of Mr. Randolphs mind.
But I thought I ought not to be governed by that opinion which was opposed
by the recent act of my native state electing him to the Senate."[71] Randolph
promptly accepted the challenge, although at the same time he denied the right
of any "minister" of the executive branch of government to hold him responsible for words uttered in debate in the Senate.[72]

The seconds, General Jesup and Colonel Tatnall, succeeded in delaying
the duel for a week on technical grounds in the hope of preventing it altogether, but their efforts failed. They agreed that the combatants would use
pistols with a smooth bore and shoot at the word "fire," after which the words
"one," "two," "three," "stop" would be called out quickly to halt the proceedings.

The night before the duel Senator Thomas Hart Benton of Missouri,
visited the Clay family. He was a blood relation of Mrs. Clay—they were first
cousins—and upon his arrival he found the family in the parlor, the youngest
boy asleep on a sofa and Lucretia looking bleak and desolate because of the
recent deaths of her daughters, but nonetheless calm and apparently unaware
of what would happen the next day. Although some "alienation" had existed
between the two men since the House election, Benton wanted Clay to know
that there was nothing personal in his decision to go over to Jackson. Clay
could understand that attitude—it was one he always assumed himself—and
"expressed his gratification at the visit . . . and said it was what he would have
expected of me."

At noon the next day, several hours before the duel was to take place,
Benton went to see Randolph and told him of his visit the night before: the
domestic scene; the child asleep; Mrs. Clay tranquil and calm. How different
that may be tomorrow, Benton cried out. Randolph turned to his visitor and
"with a quietude of look and expression which seemed to rebuke an unworthy
doubt" said: *"I shall do nothing to disturb the sleep of the child or the repose of the
mother."* He then turned away.[73]

71. Clay to Charles Hammond, April 19, 1826, Clay to Francis T. Brooke, April 19, 1826, in Clay,
Papers, V, 253–254.
72. Randolph to Clay, April 1, 1826, Thomas S. Jesup to Clay, April 1, 1826, in Clay, *Papers,* V,
211–212. Clay "incurred no blame in calling him to the field," Randolph told Van Buren. He had
furnished Clay grounds for such a step on many occasions, "but he had always given the offense in
a way that left it optional with Mr. Clay to give the matter that direction or to let it pass." Van
Buren, *Autobiography,* p. 204.
73. Benton, *Thirty Years' View,* I, 70–74. Later Randolph said the same thing to Van Buren. See
Van Buren, *Autobiography,* p. 204.

Clay and Randolph faced each other at 4:30 P.M. on Saturday, April 8, at Little Falls bridge on the Virginia side of the Potomac River. The location was most important to Randolph because if he died in the duel, only the "chosen ground" of Virginia was scared enough "to receive his blood."[74] And he fully expected to die because, as he had said, he had not the slightest intention of returning Clay's fire. He later expressed his magnanimity in ideological terms. "I will never make a widow & orphans. It is agt. my principles."[75]

The place chosen for the duel was a small depression in a "thick forest," just across the river from Georgetown. As the preliminary arrangements were being discussed, Randolph's pistol accidentally discharged because it had been set on a hair trigger. Clay obligingly dismissed the mishap, and the two men took their positions. A distance of ten paces or thirty feet separated them.[76]

"Fire!" came the call. Both men took aim and fired—"happily without effect." Clay's shot hit the dirt near Randolph, and Randolph's shot struck a stump behind Clay.

Senator Thomas Hart Benton, who was observing these proceedings, rushed forward to mediate and stop the duel. Clay would have none of it. "With that wave of the hand with which he was accustomed to put away a trifle," Clay remarked, *"This is child's play!"* He then demanded another fire.

Randolph agreed, and they acted out this charade one more time. Clay's shot struck the same spot as before. And this time Randolph raised his pistol—and discharged it into the air.

"I do not fire at you, Mr. Clay," he called, and immediately advanced with outstretched hand. "Sir," he said, "I give you my hand." Clay met him halfway and shook hands with his adversary.

"You owe me a coat, Mr. Clay," Randolph laughed. One of the bullets had passed through his coat, very near the hip.

"I am glad the debt is no greater," replied the secretary of state.

And so ended this ludicrous duel. Two days later Clay and Randolph exchanged cards, and social relations were formally and courteously restored.[77]

---

74. Benton, *Thirty Years' View,* I, 71, 73. It should be noted that Virginia also outlawed dueling.

75. Willie P. Mangum to Charity A. Mangum, April 16, 1826, in Mangum, *Papers,* I, 274–275.

76. Benton, *Thirty Years' View,* I, 75–76; Charles King to Clay, April 12, 1826, in Clay, *Papers,* V, 233.

77. *Argus of Western America,* April 26, 1826; Benton, *Thirty Years' View,* I, 73–77. Randolph told Van Buren that at no time did he intend to take Clay's life because of his unwillingness to make Mrs. Clay unhappy but that after "certain occurrences" he had decided to wound Clay in the leg. His failure "to accomplish which design he attributed to an anxiety to avoid the *kneepan,* to hit which he regarded *as murder!"* Van Buren, *Autobiography,* p. 204. Randolph's damaged coat—yellow in color—may be found today in the Virginia Historical Society. However, it is impossible to distinguish the bullet hole from the many moth holes in the coat. A set of Randolph's pistols is also held by the society; however, they were not used in this duel.

The Discouraging World of Diplomacy

I T HAD BEEN the administration's hope that the U.S. represent-atives to the Panama Congress might leave for their post by the middle of January 1826. But it was not until March 14 that the Senate finally got around to voting on confirmation. By a tally of twenty-seven to seventeen for Anderson and twenty-six to eighteen for Sergeant, the upper house gave its consent and cleared the way for the ministers to depart for Panama.

But the House had yet to give its approval for the necessary appropria-tion, and once more the battle was joined. The friends of Calhoun, such Sam-uel Ingham of Pennsylvania, George McDuffie, and James Hamilton, Jr., of South Carolina, combined with the friends of Crawford, like Louis McLane of Delaware, John Forsyth of Georgia, and John Floyd and William C. Rives of Virginia, and the friends of Jackson, including James K. Polk of Tennessee and Charles Wickliffe of Kentucky to direct the assault.[1] The House had re-quested documents for its deliberations, but on Clay's advice the President held off sending them until the Senate had acted favorably on the nomina-tions.[2] Not until March 15 did the President respond to the House request, and once more a long debate ensued that consumed valuable time.

One happy consequence of the debate was the emergence of Daniel Web-ster as a leader of the administration forces and one of its principal spokesmen. Clay treated him as an ally, and he was repaid in a handsome salute in which Webster described the secretary of state's efforts as an attempt to create a great "American family of nations." "Black Dan," as he was sometimes called on

---

1. Hargreaves, *Presidency of John Quincy Adams,* p. 152.

2. "My own inclination was to have sent the message which I had prepared to the House, stating that my answer to their call must depend upon the decision of the Senate upon the nominations; but I have, in accordance with the views of Mr. Clay, postponed the message." Adams, *Memoirs,* VII, 115–116.

account of his swarthy complexion, or the "god-like Daniel" invariably began his speeches slowly and quietly, his right hand resting on his desk, the left one hanging limply at his side. His bushy eyebrows, deep-set eyes, dark complexion, and magnificent voice produced a hypnotic effect on his audience. As he became more agitated, his left hand worked itself behind his back and reached under his coattail, while his right hand swung through the air in great looping gestures. It was a source of considerable comfort for Clay, Adams, and other National Republicans to know that a splendid orator sat in the House of Representatives ready at any moment to rise in defense of the policies of the administration.[3]

Not until April 22, by a count of 134 to 60, did the House pass the appropriation bill. The Senate gave its approval on May 3, by a vote of 23 to 19, and the President signed it on May 4.[3]

It was a victory—of sorts. In the first major contest between the emerging National Republican and Democratic parties, the administration had scored a success. The debates and the voting demonstrated that a slight but workable majority for the Adams-Clay coalition existed in the Senate; a more respectable majority, in the House. But what made it all so troubling was the fact that the Panama mission was generally popular—everyone said so—yet the administration required the entire congressional session to win its approval.[4] A number of years later it was reported "that a Senator—understood to be Mr. Van Buren—on being rallied on the triumph of the administration party on the Panama mission, replied, *Yes; they have beaten us by a few votes, after a hard battle;* But if they had taken the other side, and refused the mission, we should have had them!' "[5]

Long before the battle had been won, Clay began to draft the instructions for the Panama ministers. What resulted was a state paper of major significance in the history of American foreign policy.[6] "These instructions," he later explained, "are almost exclusively my sole work. Without consulting any body particularly, I engaged in their preparation" and afterward submitted them to Adams and the cabinet for their information and approval.[7] It ran about eighteen thousand words and enunciated the Good Neighbor Policy—or, as Clay called it, a policy of good neighborhood. The secretary of state's obvious purpose was to commit the new republics to the principles of American foreign policy—that is, avoidance of war in Europe, opposition to further coloni-

3. Clay to Webster, [February 2, 1826?], in Clay, *Papers,* V, 81; *Register of Debates,* 19th Congress, 1st session, pp. 2011–2022. For an extended discussion of Webster's speech, see Maurice G. Baxter, *One and Inseparable: Daniel Webster and the Union* (Cambridge, Mass., 1984), pp. 122–123.

3. *Register of Debates,* 19th Congress, 1st session, pp. 462, 291.

4. Clay to James Brown, March 22, April 26, 1826, in Clay, *Papers,* V, 187, 273.

5. Sargent, *Public Men and Events,* I, 117.

6. Bemis, *Adams,* I, 556.

7. Clay to Robert Walsh, Jr., April 25, 1836, in Clay, *Papers,* VIII, 845.

zation in the Western Hemisphere, liberalization of the rights of naturalization and emigration, affirmation of free trade and the freedom of the seas, abolition of privateering, and an appropriate definition of legitimate blockade.

Clay emphasized at the outset of his instructions that no nation can be bound by any treaty to which it has not given specific and "legitimate" approval. American neutrality was not to be jeopardized by an action of an external body. By maintaining a policy of strict neutrality, he stated, the United States had been able to check any European disposition to assist Spain in reconquering its colonies. "Keeping in mind, therefore, constantly in view the settled *pacific* policy of the United States, and the duties which flow from their neutrality," Clay advised the ministers to be prepared to take part in discussions involving the continuing war against Spain by the new republics. By 1826 those new republics included Mexico, the Central American Federation, Colombia, Peru, Chile, and the United Provinces of Río de la Plata. As the result of a favorable response from Russia to an overture by the administration, said Clay, the United States deemed it highly unlikely that the Holy Alliance would intercede on the side of Spain. That understood, "there can be no necessity, at this time, for an offensive and defensive alliance between the American Powers. . . . Peace is now the greatest want of America." Next to bringing a halt to the war between Spain and the new republics, devising means to preserve and perpetuate peace among the American nations and with the rest of the world should have the highest priority. There were no old prejudices to combat, no outmoded practices to change, no entangling alliances to break. The American powers were free "to consult the experience of mankind, and to establish, without bias, principles for themselves . . . likely to promote their peace, security and happiness."

Clay went on to urge the ministers to be alert to the "great advantages" that might be derived from the meeting. "Such an assembly," he said, "will afford great facilities for free and friendly conferences, for mutual and necessary explanations, and for discussing, and establishing, some general principles, applicable to peace and war, to commerce and navigation, with the sanction of all America." The ministers must be particularly aggressive in matters of commerce, navigation, maritime law, and neutral and belligerent rights. Again and again Clay drove home the point that property rights on the high seas must have the same protection to which they were entitled on land. He carefully instructed Anderson and Sergeant to reject all propositions founded on "the principle of a concession of perpetual commercial privileges to any foreign Power." American nations, he said, must not grant commercial favors to a foreign power on this or any other continent (he had in mind Great Britain but did not mention it by name) which shall not be extended to every other American nation. He emphasized free trade as the guiding principle and urged the ministers to win its approval at Panama.

With respect to Cuba and Puerto Rico, Clay opposed any attempt by the new republics to invade and seize control of those islands, even under the guise of winning their liberation from Spain. A military expedition directed against Cuba, however well intentioned, he said, will inevitably "become a war of *conquest.*" Such a war would have a disturbing influence on the balance of power in the West Indies. In that event the United States might find itself "reluctantly drawn by a current of events" to assist the island's defenders.[8]

Next, he threw out the possibility of building a transisthmian canal. Henry Clay was the first American to give official expression to the idea of a canal.[9] It probably entered his thinking in 1825, when the envoy of the Central American Federation suggested to him that their two countries agree to a treaty giving each control of a water route through the Nicaraguan area. Clay showed "deep interest" in the idea of constructing a canal but not in the idea of a treaty. He followed up his discussion with the envoy by instructing the U.S. chargé in the Central American Federation to collect all data relative to the cost and practicality of a Nicaraguan water route.

Then, in 1826, when preparing his Panama Congress instructions, Clay expressed the hope that a canal might be built. However, he did not favor its construction by one country, nor should the benefits, he said in the instructions, be "exclusively appropriated to any one nation, but should be extended to all parts of the Globe upon the payment of a just compensation or reasonable tolls." Here was another example of Clay's extraordinarily enlightened view of how the United States should conduct its foreign relations not only with Latin America but with the rest of the world. He instructed Anderson and Sergeant to inform the ministers from the other nations that the United States would take a "lively interest" in the building of such a canal.[10]

Turning to other topics, Clay declared that in all probability the subject of Haitian independence would be broached at the congress. Recognition of that island as a sovereign and independent state could not be contemplated by the United States at the present time. Clay himself had no problem with recognizing Haitian independence, but the President did. "Considering the nature, and the manner, of the establishment of the governing power in that Island, and the little respect which is there shown to other races than the African," the republic was deemed only nominally independent because of the trade privileges accorded France as the price of its so-called independence.

Clay further advised Anderson and Sergeant to avail themselves of every opportunity to press upon the other nations "a free toleration of Religion"

8. Clay to Anderson and Sergeant, May 8, 1826, in Clay, *Papers,* V, 313–341; Clay to Robert Walsh, Jr., April 25, 1836, ibid., VIII, 845.

9. The idea itself was centuries old, something the Spanish had thought about, and the British as well.

10. John Bassett Moore, *A Digest of International Law* (Washington, D.C., 1906), III, 2; Dwight Miner, *The Fight for the Panama Route* (New York, 1940), p. 11; Willis F. Johnson, *Four Centuries of the Panama Canal* (New York, 1906), p. 44; Gerstle Mack, *The Land Divided: A History of the Panama Canal* (New York, 1944), pp. 172–173.

within their respective limits, just as it was done in the United States. "With us, none are denied the right, which belongs to all, to worship God according to the dictates of their own consciences."

In concluding these instructions, Clay reiterated how important it was for all the participating countries to strengthen their republican faith and that they acknowledge the solemn duty of every nation to reject all foreign dictation in their domestic concerns.

In evaluating his role as secretary of state, Clay later asserted that "my great work was the preparation of the instructions" and the protection he tried to ensure for free trade and "against spurious blockades &c. for which we have so long and so earnestly contended." He also contended that this state paper constituted one of the most important works of his entire life.[11]

In sum, this document proposed a Good Neighbor Policy over a hundred years before the more famous statement of President Franklin Delano Roosevelt. It basically summoned all nations of the Western Hemisphere to declare their commitment to the principles of freedom and self-determination that had formed the basis of the American government. Clay signed the document on May 8, 1826.

But it all went for nothing. None of these noble utterances ever came before the other American republics because the U.S. ministers never participated in any of the discussions of the Panama Congress. Richard Anderson left his post in Colombia but died of a tropical fever at Cartagena on July 24, 1826, while en route. John Sergeant refused to travel to Panama during the "sickly season" and offered his resignation. Clay rejected the offer because it meant fighting another nomination through the Senate. He therefore permitted Sergeant to delay his departure by several months.[12]

The Panama Congress convened on June 22 after a series of postponements to oblige the United States government. It adopted a number of accords involving treaties of alliance and mutual defense and then adjourned on July 15, because of impossible weather conditions, to reconvene at Tacabaya, Mexico, after the treaties had been ratified by all the governments involved. Former President James Monroe was invited to serve in Anderson's place to complete the work he had begun in his famous doctrine, but he wisely declined the honor. The U.S. minister to Mexico, Joel Poinsett, was appointed in his place. But this appointment required Senate confirmation, which could not take place until Congress reconvened in December. Even then the Committee on Foreign Relations dawdled over the nomination for six weeks before allowing it to go forward for approval. Sergeant finally arrived in Mexico City in Janu-

11. Clay to Anderson and Sergeant, May 8, 1826, in Clay, *Papers,* V, 313–341; Clay to Robert Walsh, Jr., April 25, 1836, ibid., VIII, 845; *Pan American Union, Bulletin* (Washington, D.C., 1927) LXI, 539–546. See also John Bassett Moore, *Henry Clay and Pan-Americanism* (New York, 1915).
12. Clay to Sergeant, May 5, 1826, in Clay, *Papers,* V, 303; Sergeant to Clay, May 8, 11, 1826, Clay to Sergeant, May 11, 1826, NA, RG 43, 59, copies CPP.

ary 1827, stayed six months, and returned home, leaving Poinsett to accomplish whatever he could. But the congress in Tacabaya, Mexico, never really took place because several of the signatories of the Panama treaties did not return, and only Colombia ratified the treaties. The one result affecting the United States was the strengthening of Britain's position in Latin America because of its active participation in the Panama Congress. The heightening of Britain's prestige came at the expense of the United States.[13]

The failure of the Panama Congress was a bitter blow to both Clay and Adams. Knowing the value and importance of his work on the instructions to the ministers, Clay asked Adams to request their publication by the Congress. But the Jacksonians blocked the move. Not until 1889 was the document conspicuously published in the proceedings of the first International American Conference in Washington.[14] Clay's pioneering role in advancing Pan-Americanism was finally acknowledged and applauded.[15]

Clay had better success in fending off Mexican and Colombian efforts to seize Cuba and Puerto Rico in their continuing war against Spain. Here the British were actively involved, and George Canning, the foreign minister, tried unsuccessfully to prod Spain into ending the war with its former colonies in return for a British guarantee of Spanish sovereignty over Cuba and Puerto Rico. When the Spanish monarch rejected the British offer, the likelihood of attack upon the islands by Mexico and Colombia intensified. And therein lay the danger for the United States. Any thrust against the islands by Mexico or Colombia virtually guaranteed European intervention, something the United States had to prevent at all costs. Besides, the location of Cuba threatened the safety of the United States once a powerful European state assumed control of the island. If anything, Americans took the position that Cuba ought to be absorbed by the United States—not that Clay or Adams had any immediate designs on it. General Jackson had seen the strategic importance of Cuba at the time of his invasion of Florida and had promised to seize it if President Monroe would provide him the necessary frigates.

Clay laid the problem before President Adams after receiving a number of warnings that the political climate in Cuba was "considered as Extremely critical . . . [and] Americans, Europeans & creoles all say that the present state of things cannot last long, that their commercial & agricultural prosperity is not only destroyed, but their personal safety Endangered."[16] With the full support of the President, Clay then initiated a number of moves. First, he warned Mexico against the threatened "liberation." In a long note to Joel Poinsett, the

13. Arthur Preston Whitaker, *United States and the Independence of Latin America, 1800–1830* (New York, 1962), pp. 582–584; J. Fred Rippy, *Rivalry of the United States and Great Britain over Latin America, 1808–1830* (Baltimore, 1929), pp. 227–246; Bemis, *Adams,* I, 557–560.
14. The instructions were actually published obscurely in the 1830 appendix to the *Register of Debates.* See Bemis, *Adams,* I, 560, note 68.
15. Joseph Byrne Lockey, *Pan-Americanism: Its Beginnings* (New York, 1920), p. 286ff.
16. Thomas B. Robertson to Clay, April 20, 1825, in Clay, *Papers,* IV, 271–274.

minister to Mexico, Clay instructed him to bring the principles of the Monroe Doctrine to the notice of the Mexican government. As for a possible invasion of Cuba and Puerto Rico, the United States, he said, "cannot remain indifferent to such a movement." It "could not see, with indifference, any change that might be attempted" to their present status. Should these islands come under the "dominion" of any power other than Spain, "and especially under that of Great Britain, the United States would have just cause of serious alarm." He further declared that the "United States have no desire to aggrandize themselves by the acquisition of Cuba. And yet if that Island is to be made a dependence of any one of the American States, it is impossible not to allow that the law of its position proclaims that it should be attached to the United States." A copy of this warning was also dispatched to Colombia.[17]

Next, Clay instructed Alexander H. Everett, the U.S. minister in Madrid, to inform the Spanish government that the United States "would entertain constant apprehensions" should the islands pass into the hands "of some less friendly sovereignty." Moreover, the "United States are satisfied with the present condition of those Islands, in the hands of Spain, and with their Ports open to our commerce, as they are now open. This Government desires no political change of that condition." Therefore, the war must end; otherwise the United States might be obliged to assume duties, "the performance of which, however painful it should be, they might not be at liberty to decline."[18]

Following these notes, Clay approached Russia. He urged Emperor Alexander I to use his "best exertions" to influence King Ferdinand VII of Spain to end the war with his former colonies in order to preserve and protect his sovereignty over the islands. The contest had become nothing more than a struggle "between an exhausted dwarf, struggling for power, and empire, against a refreshed giant combating for freedom and existence." Spain will surely lose the islands if the war continues, said Clay, along with the "revenue and aid so necessary to the revival of its prosperity." The President "cherishes the hope, that the Emperor's devotion to peace, no less than his friendship for Spain, will induce him to lend the high authority of his name to the conclusion of a war, the further prosecution of which must have the certain effect of an useless waste of human life."[19]

Clay sent similar (but much abbreviated) pleas to Britain and France,[20] but Europe took only slight notice of them. The Russian emperor simply passed along the appeal to Spain without a corresponding prod to end the war. George Canning offered the typical British tactic of recommending a tripartite (Britain, France, and the United States) declaration to oppose any transfer of

17. Clay to Poinsett, March 26, 1825, in Clay, *Papers,* IV, 166–177; Clay to Anderson, December 30, 1825, NA, RG 59, copy CPP.

18. Clay to Everett, April 27, 1825, in Clay, *Papers,* IV, 292–299.

19. Clay to Henry Middleton, May 10, 1825, in Clay, *Papers,* IV, 355–362.

20. Clay to Rufus King, May 11, 1825, Clay to James Brown, May 13, 1825, in Clay, *Papers,* IV, 366–367, 372–373.

the islands. Clay evaded the proposal, just as Adams had done in 1823 with another joint proposal that ultimately resulted in the Monroe Doctrine. But the obvious determination of the United States to block seizure of the islands discouraged Mexico and Colombia from proceeding further with plans for an invasion.[21]

However, a greater threat to Cuba's integrity occurred in 1827, when Great Britain, in a dispute with Spain over Portugal, plotted to stir a revolution on the island and seize it if war broke out. Clay rewarded Daniel P. Cook of Illinois, recently ousted from the House of Representatives by his constituents for his vote for Adams in the House election of 1825, by sending him on "a confidential diplomatic junket to Cuba paid for out of the contingent secret-service fund."[22] Cook was instructed to discover the extent of Cuba's ability to defend itself and whether the United States would need to intervene to prevent a successful invasion. It was the declared wish of the United States, said Clay, "that the actual posture of things in regard to Cuba should not be disturbed."

Cook lasted in Cuba only long enough to contract dysentery. He returned home within a month and then died en route to Washington before submitting a report.[23]

Ultimately the British threat in the Caribbean evaporated. But the irony in all these negotiations was the fact that Clay, who had long championed the liberation of Latin America, was himself largely responsible for delaying the independence of Cuba.

The secretary of state suffered another reversal in his dealings with the new Latin American republics when Mexico successfully resisted his feeble efforts to acquire Texas. Not only did he fail in his quest, but he stirred a considerable amount of distrust and animosity among the Mexicans by his inept handling of the problem.

Like many westerners and southerners, Clay believed that Texas had been acquired from France as part of the Louisiana Purchase of 1803. Its loss to Spain in the Adams-Onís Treaty of 1819, by which the United States acquired Florida and a boundary line that stretched to the Pacific Ocean, provoked considerable criticism in some quarters, especially among southerners, as an unwarranted divestiture of American territory. They resented northern reaction to the slavery issue in the Missouri debates and expressed chagrin over limiting the spread of slavery above the 36°30′ parallel within the Louisiana Purchase. They wished the government to apply itself diligently to the "reacquisition" of Texas, and Adams gave Clay a free hand to initiate the negotia-

21. William R. Manning, *Early Diplomatic Relations between the United States and Mexico* (Baltimore, 1916), pp. 88–165. Colombia and Mexico decided to place the matter before the Panama Congress, but the liberating or conquering project subsequently collapsed with the failure of the congress. Mexico, however, continued to have an interest in Cuba as late as 1829. Bemis, *Adams,* I, 560.

22. Bemis, *Adams,* II, 42.

23. Clay to Daniel Cook, March 12, 1827, NA, RG 59, copy CPP; Clay to Francisco Vives, March 14, 1827, in Clay, *Papers,* VII, 302–303; Hargreaves, *Presidency of John Quincy Adams,* p. 143.

tions with Mexico now that Spain had been expelled from the area. In addition, several hundred American families immigrated to Texas under an agreement worked out with Moses Austin and his son, Stephen F. Austin, in which the settlers acknowledged Mexican authority within the territory in return for sizable tracts of land and a guarantee of home rule.

In instructing the first U.S. minister to Mexico on his duties, Clay informed Poinsett that the President was committed to the boundary line between the two nations as arranged under the Adams-Onís Treaty but hoped that it might be moved back from the Sabine River to some line farther west, such as the Rio Brasso, Rio Colorado, the Snow Mountains, and even as far west as the Rio Grande. The present boundary line was simply too close to "our great western mart," New Orleans. Perhaps Mexico might like a boundary that would locate its capital more closely to the center of its territories, Clay cooed. "But if you shall find that the Mexican Government is unwilling to alter the agreed line in the manner proposed . . . you are authorised to agree" to the established line and to its demarcation as stipulated in the original treaty. More important, Poinsett was instructed to endeavor to win a treaty of commerce and navigation between the two countries based on the principle of reciprocity or most favored nation.[24]

Unfortunately Poinsett had a penchant for meddling. And when he arrived in Mexico City, he found the British chargé already well advanced in his negotiations toward a commercial treaty. So he foolishly proceeded to interfere in Mexico's internal politics in the hope of strengthening his position. He helped a group of business friends obtain a charter to organize a branch of the fraternal order of Masons based on the York rite, as distinct from the Scottish rite, which was already in existence and consisted of wealthy landowners and clergymen.[25] The rival groups of Masons quickly assumed political identification, and Poinsett soon found himself labeled an unwanted intruder into the internal affairs of Mexico. In the ensuing quarrels and riots the legislature of Veracruz called for the ouster from the country of the U.S. minister. U.S.-Mexican relations went into a steep decline and never veered from that unfortunate direction for the next two decades.

Poinsett defended himself, but Clay demanded his dismissal on the ground, as he told the President, that he had "indiscreetly connected himself with party movements and political Masonry in Mexico." Adams refused to accept this recommendation, at least until the Mexican government itself

---

24. Clay to Poinsett, March 26, 1825, in Clay, *Papers,* IV, 166–177. The argument that the boundary was too close to New Orleans, and therefore a threat to it, was also the argument of Andrew Jackson.

25. William R. Manning, comp., *Diplomatic Correspondence of the United States concerning the Independence of the Latin American Nations* (New York, 1925), III, 1649ff.; Dorothy M. Parton, *The Diplomatic Career of Joel Roberts Poinsett* (Washington, D.C., 1934), pp. 130–138; Hargreaves, *Presidency of John Quincy Adams,* p. 80.

should officially ask for it.[26] Not until October 1829 did Mexico get around to demanding Poinsett's recall. By that time Adams was out of office. His successor replaced Poinsett with an even worse minister, who indulged in a wide assortment of outrages, including bribery.

But Clay kept up his efforts to acquire Texas by authorizing Poinsett to offer a million dollars for a line redrawn at the Rio Grande, which would leave Santa Fe to the Mexicans but bring Texas into the Union. If that proved unacceptable, Clay suggested half a million for a line at the Colorado River. After renewed evaluation of the worsening political situation in Mexico and his own shaky position, Poinsett decided against following through with Clay's proposal.[27]

Poinsett had better luck in negotiating a commercial treaty. On July 10, 1826, he signed an agreement with Mexico based on the principle of most favored nation. But its ratification took an interminable length of time, in part because the Mexicans wanted a prior agreement from the United States reaffirming the old boundary line with Spain and in part because of U.S. opposition to the wording of a particular clause. Final ratification came only after Adams and Clay had left office.[28]

The sad inauguration of distrust and bitterness in the relations between the United States and Mexico began with the Adams administration, and the major blame for the immediate deterioration may be laid directly at the door of the principal participants: Poinsett, Clay, and Adams. The enlightened Policy of Good Neighbor as enunciated in Clay's instructions to the ministers at the Panama Congress did not operate with Mexico because the United States was too concerned about its own immediate and special interests: territory and commercial privileges. The idea that the United States could induce Mexico to give up its land as an act of friendship for a paltry sum of money showed contempt for and indifference to Mexican rights, dignity, and sovereignty.

Another boundary dispute that got nowhere involved the northeast corner of the nation between Maine and New Brunswick. The treaty ending the American Revolution described the boundary in considerably less than exact language. Both Massachusetts and Maine asserted claims to the Aroostook area along the St. John River. Authorities on the Canadian side of the border arrested an American settler in the disputed area, and the administration immediately instructed its minister in London, Albert Gallatin, who had replaced Rufus King, to propose arbitration. What ultimately resulted was an arrangement worked out in 1827 to settle the boundary dispute by mediation, inviting the king of the Netherlands to act as arbitrator. However, the king was unac-

26. Poinsett to Clay, July 8, 1827, Clay to Adams, August 17, 23, 1827, in Clay, *Papers*, VI, 752–753, 914–915, 950–951; Adams, *Memoirs*, VII, 277.
27. Parton, *Diplomatic Career of Joel Roberts Poinsett*, pp. 121–122; J. Fred Rippy, *Joel R. Poinsett, Versatile American* (Durham, N.C., 1935), pp. 106–117.
28. Hargreaves, *Presidency of John Quincy Adams*, pp. 81–82.

ceptable to the governor of Maine because he was seen as a friend of the British, and the governor warned that his state would reject any settlement "unfavorable to her interests." Not until 1831 did the king offer a solution to the problem. He proposed that the two countries split the disputed area equally. But Maine rejected the proposal. So the dispute dragged on and later degenerated into a vicious and bloody war between American and Canadian settlers.[29]

Winning access to the navigation of the St. Lawrence River had been one of the objectives of the administration in suggesting arbitration of the northeast boundary, an objective that was utterly hopeless and never seriously proposed to the British. Indeed, the acquisition of additional commercial advantages for the nation was the declared policy of both Adams and Clay at the very outset of the administration. It complemented the American System. The President hoped to implement that policy by operating under the broad principle of reciprocity and, failing that, the most-favored-nation status.

In actively pursuing all possibilities for obtaining trade equality, Clay won a fair degree of success. Later he liked to boast that the extension of the system of reciprocity, which he, Adams, and Gallatin first negotiated in the convention with England in 1815, was one of his most important achievements as secretary of state. That system was best accomplished in a treaty with Central America[30] in which the two nations agreed to import products of each other "on terms of entire equality. . . . This has been a model treaty," Clay wrote in 1836, "which has been followed in several treaties afterwards negotiated."[31]

Clay also concluded a series of treaties with foreign nations that involved either reciprocity or most favored nation, notably Denmark in 1826, Mexico in 1826, the Hanseatic cities in 1827, Prussia in 1828, the Scandinavian countries in 1827, and Austria in 1828.[32]

During his tenure as secretary of state, Clay concluded nine commercial treaties, more than any previous administration. There were also a few other agreements over monetary claims against foreign nations, but these were relatively inconsequential. The succeeding Jackson administration achieved a greater degree of success in this area. The treaties, in the main, represented Clay's commitment to protect and broaden American trade, as well as to establish the principle of free trade around the world.

29. Clay to Levi Lincoln, December 15, 1825, Clay to Gallatin, June 19, 1826, Clay to Charles Vaughan, November 17, 1827, in Clay, *Papers,* IV, 910–911, V, 440–475, VII, 1273–1274; Enoch Lincoln to Clay, September 3, November 16, 1827, in *ASPFR,* VI, 930–931, 933. See also Hugh L. Keenleyside and Gerald S. Brown, *Canada and the United States* (New York, 1952).

30. Central America or the Central American Federation began to disintegrate almost immediately, and by the end of Clay's tenure as secretary of state it no longer existed as a sovereign entity.

31. Clay to Robert Walsh, Jr., April 25, 1836, in Clay, *Papers,* VIII, 845–846. Clay's instructions for this treaty can be found in Clay to William Tudor, March 29, 1828, ibid., VII, 200–203.

32. Hargreaves, *Presidency of John Quincy Adams,* pp. 82–89. "Several of these," wrote Clay in 1836, "(those for example with Austria and Mexico) were agreed upon, but not actually signed, and were subsequently concluded in the name of the succeeding Administration." Clay to Robert Walsh, Jr., April 25, 1836, in Clay, *Papers,* VIII, 845.

The most spectacular diplomatic disaster—at least in terms of its political repercussions—was the failure of the administration to settle the West Indian trade controversy. This trade had once been important to Americans, but after the Revolution the British closed it down. Although trade with the British West Indies had relatively little importance to the American economy by the 1820s, still, it rankled that Britain could impose a system of monopoly and restrictions against foreigners for its own benefit and those of its colonies. The Congress retaliated in 1818 by shutting American ports to British vessels arriving from ports closed to American ships. At the time of its passage Henry Clay spoke most "decidedly" in the House in favor of the law. "When she [Britain] is thus made to FEEL the injustice of her policy towards us, she will yield to more reasonable counsels."[33]

And yield Britain did. Protests from its West Indian colonists convinced the British government of the necessity of revising the trade laws. So, in 1822, Great Britain lifted the restrictions, and Congress responded by once more opening American ports. John Quincy Adams, then the secretary of state, had a hand in drafting the congressional legislation. But he went further than necessary. He insisted that the law require that American ships be admitted into colonial ports on an equal basis with those of Britain or its colonies. This was a direct challenge to the British policy of imperial preference, and the British rejected it virtually out of hand.[34]

There matters rested until Clay assumed the office of secretary of state. Determined to advance the principle of free trade yet conscious of the legitimacy of the British position, he tried to convince President Adams that there was "more than plausibility in the British claims, and that we ought to concede something on this point."[35] Besides, Clay rather liked George Canning, the British foreign minister, and believed that relations of "the most perfect frankness & friendship" could be established with "such an enlightened minister." He had been shown a letter from Canning to Christopher Hughes, U.S. minister to Sweden, that apparently pleased him very much. "I should fall in love with Mr. Canning, if I were to read many more of such letters from him. . . . Under his ministry . . . Mr. Canning is placing England in her natural attitude, that of being the head of European liberal principles, political and commercial."[36]

33. *Annals of Congress,* 15th Congress, 1st session, p. 1717.

34. F. Lee Benns, *The American Struggle for the British West India Carrying Trade, 1815–1830* (Bloomington, Ind., 1923), pp. 42–44, 69–60, 83ff.; Vernon G. Setser, *The Commercial Reciprocity Policy of the United States, 1774–1829* (New York, 1969), pp. 226–227.

35. Adams, *Memoirs,* VI, 540.

36. Clay to Samuel Smith, May 4, 1825, in Clay, *Papers,* IV, 323–324. Adams noted in his diary: "Clay, H. brought letters from C. Hughes and S. Smith of Baltimore. Hughes's enclosed copy of an answer received by him from G. Canning, which has put him out of his wits with exultation— his letter is a dissertation to prove that the whole science of diplomacy consists in giving dinners; and Smith thinks that our diplomatic appointments have not strengthened the Administration." Adams, *Memoirs,* VI, 539.

Clay consulted about the problem with several congressional leaders, including Daniel Webster, John Holmes, James Lloyd, Samuel Smith, and others. "I should like . . . to have your views on the Colonial question," he asked Smith. "Do we not contend for too much in insisting upon the introduction into the W. Indies of our produce on the same terms with that of Canada?" Britain insisted that relinquishing preference was tantamount to surrendering sovereignty.[37]

Most of the responses Clay received counseled him to withdraw the Adams demand, Webster adding his doubts about the long-term importance of the trade.[38] In the meantime, William Huskisson, president of the British Board of Trade, in a series of speeches before Parliament, proposed a program of trade reform designed to raise the British American colonies "as rivals to the United States . . . so as to render for the future their union with the mother country more cordial and more efficient."[39] A decision on what action the administration ought to take was then deferred pending further clarification of Huskisson's proposals.

Clarification came soon enough. When Albert Gallatin reached London as U.S. minister, he learned that on July 27, 1826, a British order-in-council had suspended trade between the United States and the British West Indies, the Bahamas, Bermuda, and other British possessions in South America.[40]

To meet this new development, Clay directed Gallatin on April 11, 1827, to assure the British "that the Government of the United States, ever animated by an anxious desire to preserve, extend, and strengthen amicable relations between the two countries," hoped that the two nations might survey their present positions and ascertain how their differences might be reconciled. Clay thought that "a misconception of each others' views" had led to the present impasse. He said that an arrangement by convention—that is, by diplomacy rather than legislative act—might prove the most effective way of settling the difficulty. He further stated that the President was willing to recommend to Congress, at its next session, the suspension of U.S. restrictions.[41] Unfortunately, when Gallatin held his interview with Huskisson and Lord Dudley, then foreign minister, he got a flat rejection. Huskisson said "that it was the intention of the British Government to consider the Intercourse with the British Colonies as being exclusively under its controul, and any relaxation from the Colonial system as an indulgence to be granted on such terms as might suit the policy of Great Britain at the time, when it might be granted."[42] Under the circumstances Adams had no recourse but to return to Congress and inform

37. Clay to Smith, May 7, 9, 1825, in Clay, *Papers,* IV, 332, 338.
38. Holmes to Clay, June 8, 1825, Smith to Clay, June 25, 1825, Lloyd to Clay, June 27, 1825, Webster to Clay, September 28, 1825, in Clay, *Papers,* IV, 421–425, 468–475, 477–486, 695–698.
39. Richard Rush to Clay, March 26, 1825, NA, RG59, copy CPP.
40. Gallatin to Clay, August 19, 1826, in *ASPFR,* VI, 346–347.
41. Clay to Gallatin, April 11, 1827, in Clay, *Papers,* VI, 418–430.
42. Gallatin to Clay, September 14, 1827, in *ASPFR,* VI, 978–979.

the members of British unwillingness to negotiate. There was no alternative, said Adams, "but resistance or submission." He continued: "My own sentiment was in favor of resistance." He believed that the Congress should totally interdict trade with all the British colonies, both in the West Indies and in North America. But the decision belonged to Congress. He laid it all out before the members when they reconvened in December, and he included the full record of diplomatic correspondence.[43]

To escape further embarrassment, the administration forces in the House and Senate brought forward proposals which would provide nonintercourse beginning September 30, 1827, unless the President should receive assurances that the West Indian ports would be opened to American vessels. But the Jacksonians had a substitute bill that effectively delayed any action at all, and they rammed it through the Senate. The House would not agree, so nothing was done. Consequently, Adams was obliged to reinvoke the restrictions of 1818, which declared American ports closed to trade with the British colonies. This action was dated March 17, 1827; the British action became effective on December 1, 1826.[44]

It was a stunning diplomatic defeat. And the Jacksonians howled their delight over this debacle. Worse, the fumbling administration efforts over the West Indian trade had brought the Calhoun and Crawford forces closer together to form what Van Buren called a union of "planters of the South and the plain Republicans of the North" in support of the election of Jackson in 1828. Thomas Ritchie, leader of the Radical junto of Virginia and editor of the Richmond *Enquirer*, accused the administration of sectional bias in promoting certain New England economic interests detrimental to the welfare of the South and West. Other newspapers derided and mocked Adams's exalted reputation as a diplomat. "Our diplomatic President," the Jackson press jeered, had ruined "colonial intercourse with Great Britain." Who could question the qualifications for office of the "military chieftain" now that Adams had demonstrated his own ineptness? Surely Old Hickory could do no worse than the so-called experienced diplomat from Massachusetts and his "black-leg" coconspirator from Kentucky.[45] And as it subsequently developed, the West Indian trade was reopened during Jackson's administration.

Clay did his best to counter these criticisms by writing editorial articles excusing the administration and faulting Congress for failing to enact necessary legislation. These usually appeared in the Washington *National Journal* and the *National Intelligencer,* the two newspapers that now served as spokesmen for the National Republican party.[46] But Clay could not erase from the

43. Adams, *Memoirs*, VII, 166, 213.

44. Hargreaves, *Presidency of John Quincy Adams*, p. 107.

45. Benns, *American Struggle*, pp. 158–163; New York *Advocate*, October 28, 1827; Albany *Argus*, September 5, 1827.

46. Clay to Peter Force, February 25, March 25, 1827, Clay to Gales and Seaton, May 9, 1827, in Clay, *Papers*, VI, 239–240, 353–354, 534–536.

public mind the fact that the administration had suffered a devastating diplomatic defeat that should have been avoided. *"You may rest assured,"* the delighted Van Buren wrote to a friend as the West Indian negotiations collapsed, *"that the re-election of Mr. Adams is out of the question."*[47]

47. Van Buren to Harmanus Bleecker, February 25, 1827, Miscellaneous Van Buren Papers, New York State Library.

— EIGHTEEN —

Abominations

A S SECRETARY OF STATE Henry Clay was a great disappointment, to both himself and his friends. He was a statesman of enormous talent who had bold, exciting ideas that
might have inaugurated a splendid new chapter in foreign relations, especially
with Latin America. He worked long, hard hours to serve diligently and faithfully the administration and the nation. To some extent his diplomatic failures
may be attributed to the political hostility he had generated in Congress because of his alleged bargain with Adams. He struggled as best he could to
defend himself, but with each new effort he seemed to make himself look
desperate, if not ridiculous. With each passing year his protests of innocence
proved less and less convincing.

Clay's inability to cope with his problems also stemmed in large measure
from his continued illness that went back several years. Fatigue and influenza
troubled him throughout the winter of 1825–1826, and frequently the President was forced to go to Clay's home to conduct their business. The secretary
of state missed numerous cabinet meetings because of ill health, and several
times he seriously considered resigning his office and returning home for a
long period of convalescence.[1]

In addition to physical illnesses, he suffered from severe emotional
strain brought on by the tragedies of his double loss when his daughters died
and by the continued disappointments involving the behavior of his two eldest sons, Theodore and Thomas. Of Theodore, Clay said he was "prone to
indolence and dissipation." He had taken him to Washington in 1824 in the
hope of reforming him. "I was disappointed," Clay later wrote. "Whilst here
he engaged . . . in gambling . . . and lost $500. That sum I did refuse to pay."
Clay wrote to his third son, the sixteen-year-old Henry Clay, Jr., presently
studying at West Point, that all his hopes now rested with him. "I am the more
anxious about you," the father wrote in 1827, "because I have not much hope
left about my two older sons. Poor Thomas! he brought tears from me to

---

1. Clay was particularly prone to relapses after bouts with influenza. Adams, *Memoirs,* VII, 113.

behold him. He begins to shew, at his early age [twenty-four], the effects of a dissipated life—swollen face &c &c. He *promises,* but there I fear the matter will end. If you too disappoint my anxious hopes a Constitution, never good, and now almost exhausted, would sink beneath the pressure. You bear my name. You are my son, and the hopes of all of us are turned with anxiety upon you."[2]

Poor Henry Clay, Jr. What a burden to be thrust upon him at so young an age. No doubt he took pride in his father's confidence, but it involved living up to expectations that could prove difficult to meet. He must bring pride to his parents and serve as an example to his older siblings.

Clay's mental condition improved somewhat when he rented a charming house from Susan Wheeler Decatur, widow of Stephen Decatur, located across Pennsylvania Avenue opposite the White House. It was quite spacious and included a handsome garden. The family made their move in the spring of 1827 and furnished the house with many fine objects sent over by Clay's wealthy brother-in-law James Brown, the U.S. minister to France. "Our comforts," Clay said, were considerably increased by the removal. "We are now residing in the best house, I think, in the City."

Health permitting, the Clays entertained fairly regularly during the congressional session, usually on Wednesday. Margaret Bayard Smith, the wife of Senator Samuel Smith, reported that it involved a great deal of work for Lucretia Clay and that she was sometimes overwhelmed with company. There was a "large dining company every week and a drawing room every other week," said Mrs. Smith. When Clay dined at home, he never dined alone "but always has a social company in a family dinner,[3] which is really the trouble of a large one." Indisposed or not, Lucretia was obliged to accept all outside invitations "for fear of giving offence." And she understood how much her husband enjoyed and needed these social engagements, especially the card playing that invariably concluded an evening's activities.[4]

Problems for Clay and the administration seemed to escalate with each passing month. One vexing matter that arose for discussion among the cabinet members during their first winter together related indirectly to the Department of State, but more directly to the War Department. This problem concerned the presence of Indian tribes within state and territorial boundaries and

2. Clay to John Jamison, April 8, 1828, Clay to Henry Clay, Jr., April 2, 1827, in Clay, *Papers,* VII, 217, VI, 385. "Henry Clay's son is one of the new cadets," James W. Armstrong wrote to Willie P. Mangum on June 23, 1827. "I find him a very clever young man, no pride at all." Mangum, *Papers,* I, 312.
3. "I have waited about an hour to see you and ask you to dine en famille with me, but I have waited in vain. . . . If you come home in time I should be very glad . . . if you would come out & take pot luck with us. In the hope of seeing you we will not dine before half after two." Clay to N. B. Beall, no date, Manuscript Department, Filson Club, Louisville, Kentucky.
4. Clay to Henry Clay, Jr., April 2, 1827, Clay to James Brown, May 30, 1827, Clay to James Erwin, April 21, 1827, in Clay, *Papers,* VI, 386, 612, Susan Decatur to Clay, March 30, 1826, ibid., V, 205–206; Smith, *Forty Years,* pp. 212–213.

the question of Indian landholdings. Historically the United States acted through the treaty-making clause of the Constitution in acquiring Indian land titles. In the Monroe administration John C. Calhoun, as secretary of war, had proposed a new policy in the nation's dealings with the tribes. He suggested that the United States cease treating them as independent nations, a policy that General Jackson had urged upon President Monroe. The thinking behind this policy contended that the tribes were not sovereign or independent and were therefore subject to congressional legislation. A concomitant of the policy involved physical removal, removal beyond "the pales of law and civilization" of those Indians who refused to submit to federal law and control.[5]

Adams's secretary of war, James Barbour, suggested setting up a territory west of existing states and removing the Indians as individuals, not tribal members, to this territory, thus establishing a barrier between white and red settlements. What brought the matter to a head was the nettlesome problem of the Creek Indians in Georgia.

Following their defeat at the hands of General Jackson at the Battle of Horseshoe Bend in 1814, the Creeks had been forced by treaty into yielding twenty-three million acres of land in Georgia and Alabama. What little remained of Creek territory in Georgia was later surrendered under the Treaty of Indian Springs, negotiated by the Monroe administration. By the terms of this treaty the Creeks had until September 1, 1826, to relinquish the land. But Governor George M. Troup of Georgia wanted to hurry the process and opened talks with Creek chiefs for an immediate survey. Disagreements ensued, violence flared, and President Adams directed General Edmund Pendleton to intervene and investigate the cause of the trouble. The result of the investigation proved that the cession of land had been obtained without proper approval by the tribal chiefs. Adams refused to allow the survey to go forward and directed a renegotiation of the treaty. But the Georgia legislature insisted that the Treaty of Indian Springs was indeed valid and demanded its territorial rights. Adams and Troup now seemed headed toward open confrontation.[6]

At a cabinet meeting in December 1825 Barbour thought the problem of acquiring Indian land could be settled by incorporating the tribes within the states and "ceasing to make treaties with them at all, considering them as altogether subject to our laws." But Adams questioned the constitutionality of such a move. At this point Clay intervened with a most startling opinion. He started off by declaring that it was impossible to civilize the Indians, that there never was a "full-blooded Indian who took to civilization. It was not in their nature." He further suggested that the Indians were destined to extinction, and

5. Calhoun, *Papers*, III, 350. The policy was far more detailed than presented here. For Jackson's position, see Robert V. Remini, *The Legacy of Andrew Jackson: Essays on Democracy, Indian Removal, and Slavery* (Baton Rouge, 1988), p. 45ff.

6. Michael D. Green, *The Politics of Indian Removal: Creek Government and Society in Crisis* (Lincoln, Neb., 1982), pp. 110–115.

although he would never "countenance" any inhumanity toward them, "he did not think them, as a race, worth preserving." They were clearly "inferior" to the Anglo-Saxon race, and their breed could not be "improved." They were rapidly disappearing and would no doubt be close to extinction within fifty years. "Their disappearance from the human family will be no great loss to the world," he declared.[7]

Barbour looked shocked at this blatant contempt for so-called "inferior" human beings, recorded the President, "for which I fear there is too much foundation." Like it or not, Adams seemed to be saying, Clay's conclusions were probably correct. And those conclusions undoubtedly reflected the thinking of most Americans at the time.

If what Clay said was true, muttered Barbour after recovering from his shock, why bother quarreling with our southern friends for the sake of a disappearing race? Why not yield to Georgia? Otherwise the state will be driven into supporting General Jackson in the next election.

Adams snorted. As far as driving Georgia into Jackson's arms, "I felt little concern or care for that."[8]

Adams wanted to get rid of the Creeks, just like Troup, but he wanted it done "legally." Finally Troup took his complaints to the Georgia legislature, which adopted a resolution declaring illegal and unconstitutional any attempted abrogation of the Treaty of Indian Springs. Nevertheless, the federal government reopened negotiations with the Indians, and eventually enough pressure was brought to force the Creeks into surrendering their land. By the Treaty of Washington in 1826 they supposedly relinquished title to all the lands claimed by Georgia.[9]

But the trouble persisted. Total removal of all southern tribes seemed the only feasible solution to the Indian presence, according to many observers. Still, nothing happened. Congress would not act, nor the President. All the Adams administration could do was provide a feeble holding action in defense of the rights of the federal government against the rights of the states in regard to Indian lands. Ultimately the Jackson administration succeeded in enacting removal legislation, something Adams wanted but could not achieve.

A general condemnation of the administration's erratic Indian policy and behavior swept across the southern tier of states. The southern tribes blocked the march of settlement and civilization, complained the critics. The Adams administration had failed miserably to assist the states in expelling these "inferior" people and clearing the path for the advance of American civilization. Unquestionably the Indian question went a long way toward providing Andrew Jackson with solid southern support in the next presidential election.

Clay may not have fundamentally changed his racist opinion of Indians in

7. Adams, *Memoirs,* VII, 89–90.
8. Ibid., VII, 90, 92.
9. Green, *Politics of Removal,* pp. 116, 122.

future years, but after Jackson had successfully brought about the enactment of removal, he became a defender of Indian rights. He never again held a position to do anything substantial about the problem, but he did speak repeatedly on behalf of the Indians, especially for the benighted Cherokees. Toward the end of his life one Indian wrote and thanked him "for your kind and benevolent defence of my wronged and oppressed nation—The Cherokee people."[10]

The Indian question constituted only one failed policy. By 1827 the signs of the approaching public repudiation of the Adams-Clay coalition were clearly visible. Defeat and disappointment seemed the hallmarks of this beleaguered administration. The Jackson-Calhoun-Van Buren alliance had grown stronger and better organized. Their emerging party, the Democratic party, now had a hard-hitting and well-financed opposition newspaper in Washington, the *United States Telegraph,* edited by Duff Green, to concentrate, refine, and intensify the attacks upon the administration. Green devoted himself particularly to proving the truth of the corrupt bargain charge. Toward the close of the 1828 campaign the newspaper boasted a circulation of more than fifty thousand readers of its regular and "extra" editions.[11]

Clay made an inviting target in the campaign, and Green delighted in pillorying him at every opportunity. Patronage distribution, the "kingly pomp and splendour" of the State Department's operation, the gambling, the Burr Conspiracy—all came in for several rounds of criticism. Clay was even accused of using English paraphernalia in preparing notes, instructions, and other written materials in conducting his diplomacy. "O fie, Mr. Clay—*English paper, English wax, English pen knives, is this your American System!*" Green chortled. "However, let us be just towards Mr. Clay in one respect—his playing Cards are of American Manufacture. They are all made in New England—the 'land of steady habits.' "[12]

Paradoxically both Clay and Adams suffered considerable criticism, by both the opposition and their own friends, over their handling of the patronage. Naturally the Democrats faulted the pair for their wanton abuse of the power, and the administration's friends, the National Republicans, according to Clay, complained that the President had been "very unwilling to exercise his dismissing power merely from the fact of the indulgence of individual opinion without some malfeasance. Moderation and forbearance I think was the true policy for him."

Forbearance! That was hardly the way to conduct politics, as Clay knew only too well. Adams had hoped to draw upon all parties in his appointments, but he succeeded only in disappointing every one of them, including old-time Federalists, the fast-diminishing Radicals, Democrats, and National Republicans. In the distribution of the patronage, Clay despairingly wrote, the Presi-

10. Clement N. Vann to Clay, December 7, 1848, Clay Papers, LC.

11. *Telegraph,* April 10, 1828.

12. Ibid., February 16, 1828, "Extra" *Telegraph,* March 21, 1828.

dent "intended to neglect or abandon his friends to woo his enemies."[13]

The National Republicans begged for a more partisan approach in the operation of government because too many officeholders were secretly—and sometimes not so secretly—committing themselves to the Democrats. "It is but fair," one man lectured Clay, "we shd. meet 'Partisans' of Jackson, by 'Partisans' of Adams." So *Let the Administration not be afraid*" of blatant partisanship, for that is the only way you build loyalty and support and organization and win elections. "Your friends," Mr. Clay, said Joseph Learned, a Baltimore lawyer, "and the friends of Mr. Adams see . . . that the Executive favors have not been bestowed upon the friends of the Administration, although possessing *equal* qualifications, and *superior* pretensions. They have felt this neglect with sensibility, from one end of the continent to the other."[14]

One end of the continent to the other! It was a wretched situation that got worse with each year. Clay's friends also warned him that defections to the Democratic cause were increasing, even in Kentucky and even among his past associates. Some urged him to consider running for the presidency in 1828 in place of Adams. At least they might then have a fighting chance. At present they felt abandoned and neglected and exposed to every criticism and calumny leveled by the Jacksonians. But Clay absolutely refused "to overthrow the present Administration." We stand together, he said. "We are both guilty or both innocent of the calumnies which have been propagated against both, 'though chiefly directed out of K. against me." Such attempts, he readily recognized, could not fail but produce mischief. "The conduct of the Jackson party has left me no wish but for Mr. Adams's re-election."[15]

Several times Clay went to Adams about the patronage problem. Perhaps the most serious accusation he brought involved the postmaster general, John McLean. Clay charged McLean with "using perfidiously the influence and patronage of his office, which is very great, against the Administration." Secretary Barbour "also made the same complaint." But neither Clay nor Barbour could provide a "specific fact" that could be charged against McLean, and even though Adams judged McLean's conduct toward the administration as "worse than equivocal," he still refused to take action. Clay tried again with respect to the customhouse officers in Philadelphia and Charleston. He put it bluntly. The National Republicans, he said, "have to contend not only against their enemies, but against the Administration itself."

Adams admitted that the port collectors were "no doubt hostile" and used their offices against him. He also admitted "some justice" to the complaints of

13. Clay to James Tallmadge, March 16, 1826, Clay to Richard Peters, Jr., October 16, 1826, in Clay, *Papers,* V, 174, 799.

14. Peter P. F. Degrand to Clay, February 8, 1827, Learned to Clay, September 27, 1827, in Clay, *Papers,* VI, 176, VII, 1079.

15. Porter to Clay, May 1, 1827, Clay to James Taylor, January 17, 1827, Clay to Porter, May 13, 1827, in Clay, *Papers,* VI, 503, 76, 549. See also Clay to J. D. Hammond, February 21, 1827, Clay Papers, Manuscript Department, Filson Club, Louisville, Kentucky.

his supporters, but hard and convincing evidence of improper conduct could not be advanced. He therefore decided that since he could see "no reason sufficient to justify a departure from the principle with which I entered upon the Administration, of removing no public officer for merely preferring another candidate for the Presidency," he would take no action.[16]

Here was a monumental failure of political leadership. Surely Clay recognized this fact, despite his habitual optimism in the face of impending disaster. If anything, he struggled even harder to answer the criticisms and charges brought by the Democrats. He prepared statements, gave public speeches, traveled to important cities, and corresponded widely with supporters—everything possible to save an administration that would not help itself. But, as he said many times, he and Adams were linked together. If one went down, the other must follow.

And the Democrats were hell-bent on bringing down both men. The general himself had long since consigned Clay to perdition for his Judas-like betrayal, and he frequently regaled his guests at the Hermitage with stories proving the Kentuckian's involvement in efforts to corrupt Jackson's friends in Congress. One of the guests, Carter Beverley, a Virginian, who listened to the Hero's diatribe, published a letter in the Fayetteville *Observer* in North Carolina on March 27, 1827, a copy of which also appeared in the *United States Telegraph*. The general, according to Beverley, stated "that Mr. Clay's friends made a proposition to his friends, that, if they would promise, *for him,* [Jackson] *not* to put Mr. Adams into the seat of Secretary of State, Clay and his friends would, in one hour, make him, Jackson, the President."

Rearing up with all the outraged fury he could muster on such opportune moments, Old Hickory assured his guests that "he most indignantly rejected the proposition. . . . He would see the whole earth sink under him, before he would *bargain* or intrigue" for the presidency.[17]

When this latest accusation was brought to him, Clay swore it was "*utterly destitute of foundation,*" indeed "a gross fabrication," and he refused to believe that Jackson had made such an atrocious statement.[18] But Beverley stood by his account and wrote to Jackson and asked him to confirm it.

Always ready to remind the people of his and their betrayal, Jackson responded in a letter, dated June 5, in which he declared that a "member of Congress of high respectability," who he supposed acted with Clay's knowledge and approval, had visited him and said that "he had been informed by the friends of Mr. Clay, that the friends of Mr. Adams had made overtures to them, saying if Mr. Clay and his friends would unite in aid of the election of Mr. Adams, Mr. Clay should be Secretary of State." Furthermore, these friends of

16. Adams, *Memoirs,* VII, 349, 364, 163–164.

17. "Report of Interview," no date, possibly April 15, 1827, in Clay, *Papers,* VI, 448–449, note. Also quoted in Colton, *Clay,* I, 320, although the letter in Colton is slightly different. Beverley's letter was dated Nashville, March 8, 1827.

18. "Report of Interview," no date, possibly April 15, 1827, in Clay, *Papers,* VI, 448.

Clay declared that if Jackson "would say, or permit any of my confidential friends to say, that in case I was elected President, Mr. Adams should not be continued Secretary of State . . . they would put an end to the Presidential contest in one hour." To this request the general responded "that in politicks, as in everything else, my guide was principle, and . . . that before I would reach the presidential chair by such means of bargain and corruption, I would see the earth open and swallow both Mr. Clay and his friends, and myself with them."[19]

Clay was passing through Wheeling on his way home when he was shown a copy of Jackson's response. Now, at last, he faced an accuser of responsibility and position, a genuine "public accuser." Even though it had taken two and a half years since the election to flush him out, the general had "thrown off the mask" at last, voluntarily come forward, and "we are now fairly at issue."

Clay rejoiced, so certain was he that he could finally bring the entire corrupt bargain affair to a speedy and successful conclusion. "I consider that letter as insuring his condemnation, and my triumph," Clay wrote to his friend N. B. Beall. To his editor ally Charles Hammond, the secretary of state added, "I could not have wished the affair to take a more favorable turn. If it does not end in degrading Genl. Jackson, I am greatly deceived as to the character of the American people."[20]

In an address to the public written in Lexington on June 29, 1827, Clay issued a "direct, unqualified and indignant denial" of the charges. "I neither made, nor authorized, nor knew of any proposition whatever to [the candidates or their friends] for the purpose of influencing the result of the election, or for any other purpose." All "allegations, intimations and innuendoes" to the contrary "are devoid of all truth, and destitute of any foundation whatever." Clay then called upon Jackson to substantiate his charges, in effect to reveal the name of the congressman "of high respectability" who had initiated this calumny.[21]

Clay repeated his denials in a long and somewhat labored speech at a public dinner given in his honor at Lexington on July 12. He spoke before a gathering of nearly a thousand people at Noble's Inn and reviewed the entire history of the late presidential election. He complained about a certain "portion of the press" devoted to Jackson whose writings teemed "with the vilest calumnies against me." He pointedly noted Jackson's failure to report the alleged proposition to him at the time it occurred. "At the end of more than

19. Jackson to Beverley, June 5, 1827, in Jackson, *Correspondence,* III, 356–357. Beverley apologized to Clay many years later for getting involved in what he ultimately came to believe was a conspiracy against Clay. "Do you know the character of Beverly," Jackson asked a friend. "He is I believe a Bankrupt, both in fortune and character." Jackson to D. G. Goodlett, March 12, 1844, ibid., VI, 274.

20. Clay to Beall, July 9, 1827, Clay Papers, Manuscript Department, Filson Club, Louisville, Kentucky; Clay to Charles Hammond, June 25, 1827, in Clay, *Papers,* VI, 719.

21. The address was published in the *Kentucky Reporter* of Lexington, July 4, 1827; Clay, *Papers,* VI, 728–730.

two years after a corrupt overture is made to Gen. Jackson he now, for the first time, openly proclaims it." Why the delay? Why did he not come out when Kremer made his accusations? Why did he remain "profoundly silent" until now? Clearly "he has been faithless, as a Senator of the United States, or [he] has lent himself to the circulation of an attrocious [*sic*] calumny."

Looking squarely at his constituents, Clay then touched on a very sore point. It had been asserted and repeated a thousand times, he cried, "that I violated instructions which I ought to have obeyed." He paused only briefly. "I deny the charge," he cried, "and I am happy to have this opportunity of denying it in the presence of my assembled Constituents." He denied that the general assembly had intended to give an "*imperative* instruction."[22] Moreover, he denied the right of the legislature to issue a mandatory instruction to the people's representatives. The legislature had a right to express its opinion, he conceded, "but it is not obligatory."

Clay ended the speech with his usual dramatic flair. "I demand the witness," he thundered, "and await the event with fearless confidence."[23]

The congressman "of high respectability" turned out to be James Buchanan of Pennsylvania, whom Jackson named in a second letter to Beverley.[24] Reluctantly Buchanan came forward in a public letter printed on August 8 in the Lancaster *Journal* and acknowledged his interview with Jackson. But he hedged about what he really knew, insisted he had acted solely on his own responsibility, and protested that he was really trying to promote Jackson's election while advancing the hope of office for Clay. He was, in short, a meddler seeking his own advancement. At every turn in this letter he tried to "cover" and protect Jackson. But however he dodged and equivocated, it was clear that emissaries from Clay had never come to him with any offer pertaining to the presidential election.

Clay rejoiced that his salvation had come at last. The letter disclosed not negotiations on the part of Clay but negotiations on the part of Jackson's friends to secure the Hero's election. "The tables are completely turned upon the General," Clay gleefully wrote his friend Francis T. Brooke. "Instead of any intrigues on my part & that of my friends, they were altogether on the side of Gen. Jackson & his friends."[25]

22. Clay made a distinction between a request and an instruction in which, he said, a request was always addressed to representatives and an instruction to senators.

23. *Kentucky Reporter,* July 18, 1827, reprinted in Clay, *Papers,* VI, 763–777.

24. As early as July 9, Clay had been alerted to the identity of the congressman. "It was Mr. Buchanan, by whom Genl. Jackson expects to prove the charge," Clay acknowledged. ". . . I have as little objection to Mr. B. as almost to any other man, having it in my power to prove in regard to him what amounts to something very variant in its nature from any proposal originating with me or my friends." Clay to N. B. Beall, July 9, 1827, Manuscript Department, Filson Club, Louisville, Kentucky.

25. Clay to Brooke, August 14, 1827, in Clay, *Papers,* VI, 899. Later Jackson said that Buchanan "shewd a want of moral courage in the affair of the intrigue of Adams and Clay, did not do me justice in the expose he then made." Jackson to William B. Lewis, February 28, 1845, in Jackson, *Correspondence,* VI, 375.

Jackson, on the other hand, was livid over the Buchanan letter. "The outrageous statement of Mr. Buchanan will require my attention," he rumbled to his friend and neighbor William B. Lewis. Meanwhile, the hapless meddler apologized for misleading the general. "I regret beyond expression," he wrote, "that you believed me to be an emissary from Mr. Clay."[26]

Jackson and his friends had done a fairly creditable job of discrediting themselves regarding their accusations about a corrupt bargain, but Clay would not leave it at that. The Buchanan affair had severely undercut the one issue the Democrats believed would clinch the next presidential election for them, and indeed, Jackson said no more about it publicly. Only Clay refused to let it go. He would not walk away from it. He kept protesting his innocence— over and over and over. He never seemed to learn when the time had arrived to keep his mouth shut. Despite the excellent advice from some of his friends to have done with the filthy business once and for all, Clay began gathering testimony from congressmen and others, including the Marquis de Lafayette, to prove he was guiltless of the accusations leveled against him. And this testimony he planned to publish!

His Kentucky friend John J. Crittenden urged him not to go public with this documentation. "I think the evidence which your enemies have extorted," Crittenden wrote, ". . . have given the mortal blow to all their accusations & calumnies." By *their* very evidence, they have established *your* innocence. "They grow weary of the subject, & find that the stone which they have so ignominiously laboured to roll up the hill, is likely to return upon their own heads—As far as proof can go—proof called out by your accusers—given by your opponents—you stand triumphant—All that is wanting is a little silence & a little time."[27]

Silence. More than anything else Clay needed to be silent. But he could not. He would not. His whole life contradicted such a course of action. No, he would publish his documents in the mistaken belief that he would finally lay the entire matter to rest—forever.[28]

An Address of Henry Clay to the Public, Containing Certain Testimony in Refutation of the Charges against Him, Made by Gen. Andrew Jackson, Touching the Last Presidential Election, dated December 29, 1827, and consisting of sixty-one handwritten pages, was published as a thirty page pamphlet and reprinted shortly afterward in newspapers throughout the country.[29] Six months later

26. Jackson to William B. Lewis, September 1, 1827, Jackson Papers, Pierpont Morgan Library, New York; Buchanan to Jackson, August 10, 1827, Jackson Papers, LC.
27. Crittenden to Clay, November 15, 1827, in Clay, *Papers,* VI, 1265.
28. Clay admitted that his friends were somewhat divided about the expediency of again addressing the public, "but the major part of them concur in recommending it." Clay to Crittenden, December 16, 1827, in Clay, *Papers,* VI, 1363.
29. *Address to the Public* . . . (Washington, 1827). See also *Niles' Weekly Register,* January 5, 12, 1828. After publication of this address a cartoon entitled "Symptoms of a Locked Jaw" appeared. Jackson, dressed in a military uniform, is seated on a chair. Clay is on top of him and with his left

Clay published a supplemental "Appendix" of letters from congressmen that was half again as long as the original. Thus, as the presidential election drew closer, the poor, desperate man foolishly kept thrusting the corrupt bargain charge before the eyes of the electorate. He would not stop reminding it of the accusation.

Prior to publication Clay showed his effort to Adams, who offered only a single suggestion about the concluding paragraph. But the President really thought it all was a waste of time. He believed that the Jacksonians would succeed in their campaign of slander and vilification. "When suspicion has been kindled into popular delusion," he said, "truth and reason and justice spoke as to the ears of an adder—the sacrifice must be consummated before they can be heard. General Jackson will therefore be elected." But when the electorate discover—as indeed it must in time that Old Hickory is incompetent by both his ignorance and ungovernable passions, then the public would recoil from him in favor of Clay and it would be "irresistible."

Clay pondered Adams's words for a moment. Yes, he conceded, this reaction of public opinion was most probable. But, he added, "it would be so long in coming that it might go beyond his [Clay's] term of active life."[30] Under the circumstances he felt obliged to proceed with publication.

In the *Address* Clay said nothing new. He simply repeated and repeated the falsity of the charges against him. When he finally concluded, he struck a defensive posture: "Finding me immovable by flattery or fear, the last resort has been to crush me by steady and unprecedented calumny. Whether this final aim shall be crowned with success or not, depends upon the intelligence of the American people. I make no appeal to their sympathy. I invoke only stern justice."[31]

Clay's friends in the Kentucky legislature tried to assist him in his invocation of justice but succeeded only in worsening the situation. These friends hoped to move through the upper house a resolution completely exonerating him from any wrongdoing, but what they provoked was another investigation—a "self-constituted Court of Inquisition"[32]—demanded by the Jacksonians. And as it turned out, that investigation proved very damaging.[33] For one thing Amos Kendall, now totally identified with the Jacksonians in Kentucky, testified that he had been paid by Clay to publish articles attacking Adams in 1823 and, worse, that Clay had tried to bribe him with an offer of a clerkship in

hand holds the general's head in position as he sews Jackson's mouth shut with a needle and thread using his right hand. "Plain Sewing Done Here" is inscribed at the top of the picture.

30. Adams, *Memoirs*, VII, 382–383.

31. *Address to the Public*, in Clay, *Papers*, VI, 1395.

32. Adams, *Memoirs*, VII, 440.

33. "Your friends," John Crittenden later explained to Clay, "allowed themselves to be goaded & precipitated into the measure without much reflection." Crittenden to Clay, March 4, 1828, Crittenden Papers, Duke University Library.

the State Department in order to woo him away from his New Court-Relief party allegiance.[34] Kendall had the gall to twist his ravenous appetite for patronage into a bribe from Clay. The man was totally unscrupulous.

And there were other damaging disclosures. No doubt the worst was the revelation of the existence of letters written by Clay to Francis P. Blair concerning the last presidential election. But Blair refused to testify before the "Court of Inquisition," and his refusal was immediately interpreted as proof that the letters documented Clay's guilt in arranging a "corrupt bargain."[35] Clay also opposed disclosure.[36] As he told Adams, one of the letters, that of January 8, 1825, had been written "with too much levity" (his wicked sense of humor again) and could be misunderstood (particularly since some of his "levity" was directed toward Adams). Actually the letters only revealed Clay's criticisms of all the leading candidates in the election, but they could prove extremely embarrassing if published, considering his present relationship to Adams.[37]

At length Clay decided that suppression of the letters only tended to prove the corrupt bargain argument, especially among those prone to believe that politicians were habitual liars and conspirators. So he agreed to allow the inspection of the January 8 letter by concerned individuals. Kendall naturally published excerpts from the letter that he cleverly managed to distort into sounding suspicious.[38]

This messy, vicious, and enduring questioning of Clay's behavior and integrity during the House contest of 1825 continued throughout the presidential election of 1828 and beyond. It was the single issue that most harmed Adams's chances for reelection. It also proved to be a millstone around Clay's

34. *Argus of Western America,* September 26, October 10, 1827, February 13, July 9, September 3, 1828. For Clay's response to these charges, see his letter to John Harvie, June 5, 1828, in Clay, *Papers,* VII, 327–332.

35. Blair told Clay that he expected nothing from General Jackson by his desertion to the Democratic party and that he had "never deserted your [Clay's] banner until the questions on which you and I so frequently differed in private discussion—(State rights, the Bank, the power of the Judiciary &c.)—became the criterions to distinguish the parties, and had actually renewed . . . the great divisions which marked the era of 1798." As for not testifying he explained that he would not be party to any effort that would sully Clay's reputation. "My opinion at first was that any attempt to pry into private intercourse & confidential correspondence ought to be met with nothing but resistance." Blair to Clay, October 3, November 14, December 31, 1827, in Clay, *Papers,* VI, 1106–1107, 1261, 1404. For Clay's response, see his letter to Blair, October 19, 1827, ibid., VI, 1163–1164.

36. Clay to Blair, October 11, 1827, in Clay, *Papers,* VI, 1136.

37. In the letter of January 8, 1825, Clay described the efforts of the various managers of the three candidates—Adams, Jackson, and Crawford—to win his support. Adams's friends, recorded the President, were described as coming to Clay "with tears in their eyes. This was meant by him only as a joke upon my [Adams's] infirmity of a watery eye; but malignity will give it a construction as if intended to insinuate that in these overtures of my friends I myself participated." Adams, *Memoirs,* VII, 462.

38. What Kendall did was print the letter in a parallel column with Clay's June 29 address given in Lexington. See *Argus of Western America,* August 20, 1828.

own neck, one that he could never cut loose, and it forever destroyed whatever hope he had for winning the presidency himself.[39]

The summer and fall elections of 1827 clearly indicated the future direction of American politics. Despite a few encouraging signs in New England and some parts of the Middle Atlantic states, such as Delaware, Maryland, and New Jersey, elsewhere they were uniformly bad for the National Republicans. In the Northwest the Democrats had started to build smooth-running political operations, which brought excellent electoral results in Ohio, Indiana, Illinois, and even Kentucky. The outcome in Kentucky, said Clay, had "excited new hopes" among the Jacksonians "and, for the moment, created some depression amongst our friends." His Washington colleagues sympathized with him. "I hope you are recovered from such a *shock,*" wrote Daniel Webster. "There is, doubtless, much cause for regret, but *none for despair.* We have a year yet, before us, & I trust time will aid our efforts."[40]

If the Kentucky results disappointed and depressed Clay—and they did—the New York election positively devastated him. "These are the darkest pages of our history," he moaned. "Every man should awaken to the impending danger. None should under rate it; for it is perilous and alarming."[41]

As the discouraging electoral news continued to depress him, Clay became obsessed with the need to defeat Jackson's election in 1828. "One predominant desire prevails in my mind," he ranted to his friend Francis Brooke, "and that is that the country shall be preserved from the calamity of the election of Genl. And. Jackson. To accomplish that object I am willing to renounce forever public life, and to resign this hour the station which I hold." Clay was thoroughly convinced that the nation would find itself in immediate peril if the "military chieftain" won the White House. It was a gruesome thought. The "success of the Opposition is pregnant with the fate of the Republic," he warned his followers. "I shall tremble, in that event, for its durability."[42]

In assessing the causes for the electoral disasters that seemed to be building rapidly, Clay's friends, lieutenants, and pensioners from around the country kept repeating the identical weakness. "We are in the same disjointed state here as formerly," wrote a Pennsylvanian. "A great many well wishers . . . but no organization." One westerner explained it in terms of Jacksonian strength. "The opposition," he said, "are an organized corps, active and well disci-

39. Analogies are always invidious or worse, but I am inclined to believe that the corrupt bargain charge against Clay in one respect at least was somewhat akin to the Chappaquiddick incident involving Senator Edward Kennedy of Massachusetts more than a century later. Both events, in different ways and for different reasons, permanently terminated the presidential candidacies of these two very worthy men.
40. Clay to John F. Henry, September 27, 1827, Webster to Clay, September 28, 1827, in Clay, *Papers,* VI, 1073, 1084.
41. Clay to Hammond, November 16, 1827, in Clay, *Papers,* VI, 1270.
42. Clay to Brooke, November 24, 1827, in Clay, *Papers,* VI, 1311.

plined." In the South another man predicted that the "organization of the other side . . . *will be* stronger than all." Even in New England an alarm was sounded by Daniel Webster. The Jacksonians, he wrote, "& a few other cunning & indefatigable Caucus [Crawford] men control the movements, & arrange the organization of the party."[43]

Organization! The Democrats had it, and the National Republicans lacked it. As simple as that. The use of propaganda by the opposition was a good case in point. The Democrats, it seemed, had established "a chain of newspaper posts from the New England States to Louisiana, and branching off through Lexington to the Western States." These journals inundated the country with propaganda against the Adams-Clay coalition and in favor of the Old Hero of New Orleans. "We have at considerable expense," boasted Senator Levi Woodbury, "established another newspaper in the northern part of the state of New Hampshire. We have organized our fences in every quarter and have begun & shall continue without ceasing to pour into every doubtful region all kinds of useful information."[44]

Because of the unrelenting attacks upon his character and integrity and because of his determination to block Jackson's road to the presidency, Clay assumed much of the work of building a national party to match what the Democrats had achieved. To a large extent he worked with Daniel Webster to obliterate the "old political landmarks" and bring about the "amalgamation" of all those groups that supported the American System and John Quincy Adams and that feared the consequences of an administration presided over by an ignoramus. "It appears to me to be important," Clay explained to Webster, "that we should, on all occasions, inculcate the incontestable truth that *now* there are but two parties in the Union . . . and that all reference to obsolete denominations is for the purpose of fraud and deception."[45]

The first thing Clay tried to do was raise money, the essential ingredient for party making. "It seems to me," he reminded Webster, "that our friends who have the ability should contribute a fund for the purpose of aiding the cause; and if that be deemed advisable, the appeal should be made in the large cities where alone the capital is to be found. You stated, I think, last winter, that such a fund would be raised, and that I was authorized to address you on the subject. . . . If you coincide in these views, would it not be well for you to give an impulse to the creation of a fund for the above objects by conversation or other communication with some of our friends?"[46]

43. Sidney Breese to Clay, July 21, 1827, Clay Papers, LC; Crittenden to Clay, March 4, 1828, Crittenden Papers, Duke University Library, Sergeant to Clay, August 23, 1827, John Pleasants to Clay, May 4, 1827, Webster to Clay, May 18, 1827, Clay Papers, LC.
44. *National Journal,* February 27, March 10, 22, 31, July 24, 1827; *National Intelligencer,* March 13, 20, 1827; *United States Telegraph,* November 30, 1827, April 19, 1828; Boston *Statesman,* March 17, 24, April 3, 9, July 21, October 17, 24, 1828; Woodbury to Gulian C. Verplanck, August 29, 1828, Verplanck Papers, New-York Historical Society.
45. Clay to Webster, April 14, 1827, Webster Papers, LC.
46. Clay to Webster, April 14, 1827, Webster Papers, LC.

Webster and Clay made a splendid team. Through "conversation" and "communication" Webster pursued those businessmen who he believed appreciated the value of the American System and all it might provide in the development of an industrial nation and who could be coaxed into offering contributions. And it should be noticed that in pursuing this much needed cash, Clay recognized that the cities were the best places to locate the individuals who could provide it in the huge amounts necessary to run a successful campaign. After the money had been obtained, Clay then suggested to Webster where it could be sent to do the most good. For example, he singled out the Cincinnati *Gazette,* edited by Charles Hammond, as worthy of support.

This newspaper was doing outstanding work in bringing to the attention of the electorate the strange circumstances of Jackson's marriage to Rachel Donelson Robards. "In the summer of 1790," Hammond stated, "Gen. Jackson prevailed upon the wife of Lewis Roberts [Robards] of Mercer county, Kentucky, to desert her husband, and live with himself, in the character of a wife." In a later editorial Hammond summed up his complaint: "Ought a convicted adulteress and her paramour husband to be placed in the highest offices of this free and christian land?"[47] Whatever Clay's feelings about the manner and tone of Hammond's writings, he thought the editor should be encouraged. "C. Hammonds papers in Cincinnati," he declared, ". . . is I think upon the whole, the most efficient . . . gazette that espouses our cause. . . . I think he is every way worthy of encouragement and patronage. . . . Perhaps he might receive a present of a new set of types." Webster agreed that Hammond's journal was "certainly ably & vigorously conducted" and surely worthy of a "present." Webster thought he could obtain a set of types "for abt. 5 or 6 hundred Dollars which he would ship to Cincinnati immediately.[48] However, Hammond did not receive the types because Clay thought of "another & perhaps a better mode of accomplishing the object in view," which he said he would discuss with Webster when next they met.[49]

Meanwhile, Hammond intensified his assaults upon Jackson and his family. One of his most vicious and unconscionable editorials declared:

> ☛ General Jackson's mother was a COMMON
> PROSTITUTE, brought to this country by the
> British soldiers! She afterwards married a MU-
> LATTO MAN, with whom she had several chil-
> dren, of which number General JACKSON IS
> ONE!!![50]

47. Cincinnati *Gazette,* March 23, 1827, copy in the Jackson Papers Project, University of Tennessee, Knoxville; *Truth's Advocate and Monthly Anti-Jackson Expositor,* quoted in Remini, *Election of Andrew Jackson,* p. 152.

48. Clay to Webster, August 19, October 25, November 8, 1827, Webster Papers, LC; Webster to Clay, September 8, October 29, 1827, Clay Papers, LC.

49. Clay to Webster, October 17, 1827, in Clay, *Papers,* VI, 1156–1157.

50. Quoted in Remini, *Election of Andrew Jackson,* p. 153.

Jackson exploded when he heard about Hammond's statements concerning his marriage, but he burst into tears on learning about the attack upon his mother.[51] And he immediately suspected Clay as the culprit behind this latest dastardly and criminal act. Earlier Jackson had received a letter from "some person in Kentucky"—could it have been Kendall?—informing him that Hammond had visited Clay in the summer of 1826 and obtained from the secretary of state papers that Clay had purportedly collected for the purpose of attacking Rachel Jackson. Old Hickory had directed his friend Senator John H. Eaton of Tennessee to confront Clay with this information and demand an explanation. Clay admitted to Eaton that he had indeed seen Hammond but vehemently denied giving the editor any papers relating to Mrs. Jackson. "I have now no recollection that the case of Mrs. Jackson formed any topic of conversation between us when you were in Lexington," Clay wrote to Hammond two days later.[52]

Despite the denial, Jackson continued to name Clay as the culprit. "I have no doubt but Clay is at the bottom of all this," he confided to his friend John Coffee.[53] And this conviction further fueled his already overheated hatred for the Kentuckian.

I am determined to . . . lay the perfidy, meanness, and wickedness, of Clay, naked before the american people. I have lately got an intimation of some of his secrete movements, which, if I can reach with possitive and responsible proof, I will wield to his political, and perhaps, his actual destruction. he is certainly the bases[t], meanest, scoundrel, that ever disgraced the image of his god—nothing too mean or low for him to condescend to, *secretely* to carry his cowardly and base purpose of slander into effect; even the aged and virtuous female, is not free from his secrete combination of base slander—but *anough, you know me,* I will curb my feelings until it becomes proper to act, when retributive *Justice will vissit him and his pander heads.* [54]

Sewer tactics, unfortunately, became an integral part of this campaign, and Henry Clay shares some of the blame because of the financial support and encouragement he gave Hammond in spreading such malicious slander. But Clay felt justified. The Democrats were also descending into the gutter to conduct their campaign. They declared the Adamses guilty of premarital sex, and Adams himself was accused of pimping for the czar when he served as minister to Russia. "The course adopted by the Opposition, in the dissemination of Newspapers and publications against the Administration and supporting presses," Clay declared, "leaves to its friends no other alternative than that of following their example, so far at least as to circulate information among the people."[55]

51. James Parton, *The Life of Andrew Jackson* (New York, 1861), III, 141.
52. Clay to Hammond, December 23, 1826, in Clay, *Papers,* V, 1023–1024.
53. "He keeps himself under the cloak of Hammond who, he knows is beneath, every other notice than a cowhide." Jackson to Coffee, April 8, 1827, Jackson to Richard K. Call, May 3, 1827, in Jackson, *Correspondence,* III, 354.
54. Jackson to Sam Houston, December 15, 1826, Jackson Papers, LC.
55. *Telegraph,* March 13, May 20, 1828; Isaac Hill, *Brief Sketch of the Life, Character and Services of*

During the last twelve months of the presidential contest Clay worked himself to near exhaustion to defeat the opposition. Indeed, his health disintegrated to such an extent by the spring of 1828 that he virtually submitted his resignation as secretary of state. "He thinks his health is gradually sinking," reported President Adams, "and his spirits are obviously giving way under the load of obloquy, slander, and persecution which has been heaped upon him." Clay's health had become so bad that he found it impossible to discharge his duties. "A relaxation from public duties was indispensable," said Adams, "and he must go home and die or get better." The President described Clay's condition as "a general decay of the vital powers, a paralytic torpidity and numbness, which began at the lower extremity of his left limb, and, from the foot, has gradually risen up the leg, and now approaches to the hip." Adams advised him to consult a Dr. Huntt and take a few months' vacation. As his condition worsened, Clay really thought "he had little hope of surviving." Finally he agreed to go to Philadelphia to consult the celebrated Dr. Philip S. Physick and another doctor by the name of Chapman. Huntt did not think Clay's condition was life-threatening, and Physick and Chapman advised him to relax and escape for a while from public cares and duties.[56]

Clay probably realized that he could not resign because of its devastating political impact. He had to stick it out. So he stayed on—and worked the harder. Every month he corresponded with a large corps of politicians around the country, including Peter B. Porter and John W. Taylor of New York, Francis T. Brooke and John Pleasants of Virginia, John Sergeant and Philip S. Markley of Pennsylvania, Josiah Johnston of Louisiana, and his many friends in Kentucky, especially John Crittenden. He pleaded with them to form local committees, organize state conventions, and establish newspapers to counter the efforts of the Jacksonians. "It is part of the system of the friends of General Jackson," Clay told Brooke, "to make demonstrations—speak loudly—claim every body and every State, and carry the election by storm. The circumstance most to be deprecated is that this system has too much success in dispiriting our friends." He begged Brooke to convene a convention in Virginia to nominate Adams electors. Such a convention, he said, "can not fail to have good effect." Clay also urged that his American System be treated as the party's platform. He explained to Webster that the question of internal improvements

Major General Andrew Jackson, cited in Remini, *Election of Andrew Jackson,* pp. 117–118; Clay to Webster, October 25, 1827, Webster Papers, LC. There is no evidence that Clay supplied Hammond with material relating to Jackson's marriage, but he did provide information about the general's army career and tenure as territorial governor of Florida in 1821, among other things. At one point Clay cautioned Hammond about revealing his identity in using the information sent to him. "I need not suggest to your discretion," Clay wrote, "the expediency of avoiding a reference to my name in any use you may think proper to make of the a/c." Clay to Hammond, June 1, 1827, in Clay, *Papers,* VI, 632.

56. Adams, *Memoirs,* VII, 439, 517–518, 521–522, 541–542. Some of Clay's friends thought that he was in financial difficulties and that that was the cause of his distress. They offered him a sum of money, which he refused. He explained that although he was not free of debt, he did not require this assistance.

must be supported in New England "and that the West and Penna. should be made *sensible* of that support. . . . We must keep the two interests of D. M. & I. I. [domestic manufactures and internal improvements] allied, and both lend to the support of that other great & not less important interest of Navigation."

Health permitting and whenever he could spare the time, Clay went campaigning. In 1827 he swung over to Baltimore to attend an affair in his honor, after which he journeyed to Virginia to speak at several dinners. From that place he headed west to Ohio, Indiana, and Kentucky. In Cincinnati he was welcomed by a crowd estimated at five thousand. The following summer he appeared for three straight days in the Lexington town courtyard to shake the hand of every man who came to vote in the Kentucky state election. He was unsparing in his efforts to defeat the Democrats, so intense were his feelings about the necessity of reelecting Adams. Had he been the presidential candidate himself, he could not have labored more.[57]

Unfortunately for the National Republicans there were too few Henry Clays. And the greatest disadvantage under which the Adams-Clay coalition suffered was the lack of organization, which Clay recognized all along. The Pennsylvania returns in the state elections of 1827 provided yet another example of what most troubled the National Republicans. Except in the city of Philadelphia, Pennsylvania went Democratic. Not only had the Jacksonians nominated men who were well known and respected, but they required from their candidates "a pledge that they will vote for the General, as the indispensable condition on which they will be supported." This "superior management and activity . . . gave them the machinery of the Democratic party," and with it they "returned a majority of members to the General Assembly."[58]

This and other disasters all were duly reported to Clay by his lieutenants. As was his wont, Clay tried to put a good face on them. He acknowledged the problem but assured his friends that it would be solved. "The same want of organization which exists in N. York is wanted in Ohio," he wrote, "but the evil is about to be remedied." Just how, he did not say.[59]

As a result of these repeated electoral disasters, the Jacksonians took control of the Twentieth Congress when it convened in December 1827.[60] And the

57. Porter to Clay, March 15, 26, 1828, Taylor to Clay, May 7, 1827, Johnson to Clay, April 29, 1827, Markley to Clay, April 28, 1827, Pleasants to Clay, May 4, 1827, Lincoln, to Clay, May 24, 1827, Sergeant to Clay, August 23, 1827, Clay Papers, LC; Clay to Brooke, September 24, 1827, in Clay, *Correspondence,* p. 179; Clay to Webster, June 7, 1827, Webster Papers, LC; Leonard P. Curry, "Election Year—Kentucky 1828," *Register of Kentucky State Historical Society,* LV (1957), pp. 200–205; Clay to Adams, June 23, 1827, in Clay, *Papers,* VI, 713. For the toasts and speeches delivered during this campaign, see Clay, *Papers,* VI, VII, passim.

58. Washington *National Journal,* October 30, 1827.

59. Sergeant to Clay, August 23, 1827, Sidney Breese to Clay, July 21, 1827, Pleasants to Clay, May 4, 1827, Clay Papers, LC; Clay to Webster, November 8, 1827, in Clay, *Papers,* VI, 1244.

60. The first thing the Democrats did with their majority was defeat John W. Taylor as Speaker of the House. "The contest will be close," Clay said before Taylor's defeat, "and if luck did not seem to be running somewhat against me, at this particular point, I should say Mr. Taylor will be chosen." Clay to Francis T. Brooke, November 29, 1827, in Clay, *Papers,* VI, 1331.

leadership of the Democratic party meant to use its congressional control to fashion still further electoral advantages for its candidate. In particular the Democrats intended to write a new tariff bill that would win votes for Jackson in the states where he needed them most. "I fear this tariff thing," warned the fiercely radical southerner Thomas Cooper, "by some strange mechanical contrivance or legerdemain, it will be changed into a machine for manufacturing Presidents, instead of broadcloths, and bed blankets."[61]

Precisely. What the leaders concocted—most notably Senator Martin Van Buren and his henchmen in the House of Representatives—was a bill that favored the domestic products of New York, Pennsylvania, Ohio, and Kentucky, where Jackson was weakest; it also discriminated against the products of New England, especially the manufacturers of woolens, where Adams's electoral strength was deemed too formidable to crack. The result was a ghastly, lopsided, unequal tariff bill that looked to some as though it had been introduced to be defeated.[62] Actually the Democrats planned no such thing. They wanted to win passage of this tariff because they desperately needed the votes of the North and Northwest.[63]

Van Buren regarded the tariff as critical. As late as the previous July 1827 more than one hundred delegates representing thirteen states had convened in Harrisburg, Pennsylvania, to pressure Congress into providing adequate protection. This Harrisburg Convention, organized by Hezekiah Niles, editor of his own *Weekly Register,* and Mathew Carey and Charles J. Ingersoll of Pennsylvania, produced a memorial and a petition to Congress on August 3, signed by ninety-seven men, who appealed to the government to redress the grievances of American manufacturers and farmers. In addition, a schedule for increased tariff duties was suggested. Throughout the North the Harrisburg proceedings elicited general satisfaction, but in the South the reaction was predictably hostile.

Democrats hoped that Jackson's attitude on the tariff question, given a few years earlier in a letter to Littleton H. Coleman, would gain him votes in both the North and the South because it seemed to take a middle-of-the-road position. The general had declared that he favored a "judicious" tariff, and that remark turned out to be a very useful piece of campaign propaganda. With Old Hickory's permission it was published extensively throughout the nation. When Clay read it, he could not resist mocking its hopeless ambiguity. With "a

61. Cooper to Gulian C. Verplanck, May 1, 1828, Verplanck Papers, New-York Historical Society; E. Sage to John W. Taylor, February 17, 1828, Taylor Papers, New-York Historical Society. Clay said that the "responsibility of measures now rests with the Opposition." Clay to Crittenden, December 16, 1827, in Clay, *Papers,* VI, 1363.

62. Said Clay: "The house is now engaged in the discussion of the Tariff bill, reported by the Committee of Manufactures, which nobody believes has the least prospect of passing in that shape." Clay to N. B. Beall, March 21, 1828, Clay Papers, Manuscript Department, Filson Club, Louisville, Kentucky.

63. Robert V. Remini, "Martin Van Buren and the Tariff of Abominations," *American Historical Review,* LXIII (July 1959), pp. 903–917. See also Remini, *Van Buren,* pp. 180–185.

characteristic shrug of his shoulders, a toss of his head," and a smirk, he said: "Well by ———, I am in favor of an *in* judicious tariff!"[64]

The need to bolster Jackson's candidacy in the North convinced Van Buren that he must "adjust" the protection rates. And as his grotesquely conceived tariff bill worked its way through Congress in the spring of 1828, it instantly confirmed Clay's worst suspicions. "They do not really desire the passage of their own measure," he marveled, "and it may happen in the sequel that what is desired by *neither party* commands the support of both."

He was right on the mark. But Clay kept hoping that several proposed amendments in the House—especially an amendment to increase the duty on manufactured wool to a 40 percent ad valorem rate with a 5 percent increase each year until it reached 50 percent—would win approval and thereby benefit woolen manufacturers sufficiently to gain enough votes from the Northeast to guarantee passage of the entire measure. "This is now my wish, and my advice," he wrote. There were sufficient increases on the duties on raw wool, iron, flax, hemp, and molasses to satisfy New York, Pennsylvania, Ohio, and Kentucky; but without the proposed amendment, woolens received only a modest raise, and this infuriated New England. "Can we *go* the *hemp,* iron, spirit and molasses," queried Webster, "for the sake of any woolen bill?" Ultimately Clay's advice was taken by his friends, and the bill passed both the House and Senate in mid-May and was signed by President Adams.[65]

Undoubtedly the new tariff won Jackson important support in the West and New York, but it enraged southerners who dubbed it a Tariff of Abominations. Nevertheless, they had no wish to endanger Jackson's election and did not abandon him. Besides, where could they go? They could never support Adams. Indeed, many of them looked to Old Hickory as the future President to redress the wrong inflicted against them and repeal the hated measure.

Meanwhile, John C. Calhoun returned to his home in South Carolina to write out a statement, published anonymously by the state legislature as *The South Carolina Exposition and Protest,* in which he enunciated the doctrine of nullification. This work asserted a state's constitutional right to void any federal law within its boundaries that violated its basic rights. The tariff was such a violation, he said, and if it was not repealed, South Carolina had the right, as did any other state, to declare it null and void.

An integral part of Clay's American System—protection for domestic manufactures—had suddenly become a potentially lethal issue, one that could tear the nation apart and incite a bloody civil war.

64. Jackson to Coleman, April 26, 1824, in Jackson, *Correspondence,* III, 249–250; Van Buren, *Autobiography,* p. 240.

65. Clay to Crittenden, February 14, 1828, in Mrs. Chapman Coleman, ed., *Life of John J. Crittenden* (Philadelphia, 1871), I, 67; Clay to Porter, April 12, 1828, in Clay, *Papers,* VII, 225; Webster to Joseph E. Sprague, April 13, 1828, in C. H. Van Tyne, *The Letters of Daniel Webster* (New York, 1902), pp. 135–136.

A Vision of
the Future

THE MUDSLINGING intensified during the closing months of the presidential campaign, and Henry Clay came in for a hefty share of it. The bitterness of the Jacksonians was directed mainly at him. Their resentment, reinforced by the general's towering hatred for the Kentuckian, found expression in newspaper articles, pamphlets, stump speeches, and broadsides that regularly spewed forth from the burgeoning Democratic press and Democratic leadership throughout 1827 and 1828. True, Adams was mocked as a pimp, accused of living and conducting himself in a lordly manner, charged with extravagances in purchasing a billiard table and chessmen for the White House, and, of course, condemned for engaging in a "corrupt bargain" to steal the presidency from General Jackson. But Clay—ironically the noncandidate in this election—took far more heat and abuse because he was seen as the evil manipulator and dastardly schemer of the Adams administration. He was imagined the author of every vicious accusation against Jackson and his family. And the Democrats were determined to pay him back in kind.[1]

In addition, he was tagged as initiating the decision of the Kentucky delegation in Congress to disobey the instruction from home to vote for Jackson in the House election of 1825, an instruction the Democrats interpreted as the voice of the people.[2] And because of his reputation in some quarters as a carouser and gambler and womanizer, Clay was frequently described in the press as spending his nights at the gaming table, in the "revels of a brothel," and in other unspeakable places engaged in actions that violated both "the laws of God and man."[3] At one point he was accused of embezzling a legacy of

1. For an account of the charges and countercharges, see Remini, *Election of Andrew Jackson,* passim.
2. Clay to N. B. Beall, July 9, 1827, Clay Papers, Manuscript Department, Filson Club, Louisville, Kentucky.
3. *Argus of Western America,* July 16, 1828.

twenty thousand dollars left to Transylvania University by the late Colonel James Morrison, a charge wholly without foundation.[4]

The Burr Conspiracy also played an important role in this campaign because both Jackson and Clay were implicated. The Kentuckian defended his own involvement, but he stooped to intrigue in an unsuccessful attempt to obtain incriminating evidence against Jackson from Mrs. Harman Blennerhassett.[5] And Clay virtually salivated over the "Coffin Hand Bill," conceived and distributed by John Binns, a Philadelphia newspaperman. This masterful propaganda sheet detailed Jackson's military "executions" during the Creek War, when six militiamen were executed for attempting to return home when their enlistments expired. The names of the victims were posted across the top of the handbill, and under each was drawn a huge black coffin. Democrats responded to this damaging campaign leaflet by asserting that the militiamen were mutineers, thieves, and deserters who had been properly tried by a military court before their execution.

Another of Clay's efforts to sabotage the Jacksonian ticket was his apparent involvement in a scheme to discredit John C. Calhoun. The South Carolinian had joined forces with Martin Van Buren to organize the Democratic party and had been nominated in several states as Jackson's vice presidential running mate. Accusations of impropriety arose over a fortifications contract awarded to Elijah Mix when Calhoun served as secretary of war in the Monroe administration, and Calhoun immediately demanded an investigation by the House of Representatives. According to Duff Green, editor of the *United States Telegraph,* Clay huddled with Speaker Taylor, Daniel Webster, and several others to determine the composition of the investigating committee in the hope of dictating its final report. Although the committee subsequently exonerated Calhoun, it raised enough suspicions about corruption to add another layer of tarnish to the Democratic ticket.[6]

In the midst of this vicious campaign, in which Clay sullied himself more than he probably realized at the time, a sudden and unanticipated outbreak of violence in the western counties of New York threatened to refashion political alliances in both the Democratic and National Republican parties and terminate the careers of those public figures known to be members of the order of Freemasonry. This was the Anti-Masonic movement, which developed with the disappearance and presumed murder of a man named William Morgan.

Morgan, a stonemason living in Batavia, New York, had written a book allegedly revealing the secrets of the Masonic order, and when he rejected the pleas of friends not to pursue this spiteful act, he was arrested on a trumped-up

4. Clay was the executor of the Morrison estate. See *Kentucky Reporter,* September 22, 1827.

5. Clay to Peter B. Porter, March 20, 1828, Porter to Clay, March 26, 1828, Clay to Porter, April 2, 1828, Porter to Clay, April 6, 1828, Clay to Porter, April 12, 1828, in Clay, *Papers,* VII, 175, 190, 212, 216, 225.

6. *Telegraph,* January 13, February 14, 1827; *Niles' Weekly Register,* January 13, 1827; *National Intelligencer,* February 15, 1827.

charge and taken to prison on September 11, 1826. Upon his release Morgan was seized, hustled into a waiting carriage, and reportedly taken to Fort Niagara, where he may have been drowned. No one knew what had happened to this hapless man except that he had mysteriously disappeared.

Almost immediately a public outcry against Masons swept across the western counties of New York. Masons were denounced as aristocrats who controlled business, government, and the law and were not above depriving ordinary citizens of their basic rights in order to protect their special interests. At first this outburst seemed to reflect a democratic surge in the country aimed at protecting the rights of the majority against the privileges of an elite minority. Others interpreted the explosion as the consequence of many economic and political changes occurring in the nation which involved possibly profound psychological forces.[7] Whatever the reasons, the Anti-Masonic furor soon developed into a full-fledged political movement, intent on the expulsion of all Masons from public office. It soon produced such skillful leaders as Thurlow Weed and William H. Seward, and it spread rapidly from New York into New England and then parts of the Midwest.[8]

At the height of the disturbance word got out that General Jackson was a high-ranking Mason, "a grand king" of the order, so to speak. The revelation nearly flattened the Democrats in western New York. To make matters worse for the Jacksonians, evidence revealed that Adams was free "from all imputed criminality of that sort."[9] But the Democrats quickly rebounded by announcing their discovery that Henry Clay was also a Mason of some prominence. Van Buren's political machine, the Albany Regency, could hardly contain its delight. "I have just been told," wrote one excited New York congressmen, "by a distinguished Western member that Mr. Clay is a Mason of rank. He has been in Lodges, Chapters &c., with him. Cannot this be so used with Clay's friends in our Western Districts, or with the people, as to divert that question from mingling with the Presidential one? Suggest these matters to those who will use them to advantage."[10]

Clay made no bones about his membership in the Masonic order and explained his feelings regarding the Morgan affair to his friend and ally in New York Peter B. Porter. "I trust that I need not contradict to you the story of my having got up, or contributed, to the Anti masonic spirit prevailing in your State. I have looked upon it as one of those delusions to which men are unfortunately sometimes exposed. If Morgan has been murdered or carried

---

7. Henry R. Stanton, *Random Recollections* (New York, 1886), p. 25.

8. On Anti-Masonry, see Michael F. Holt, "The Anti-Masonic and Know Nothing Parties," *History of U.S. Political Parties*, ed. Schlesinger and Israel, I, 629–636, and the articles of Kathleen Smith Kutolowski, "Anti-Masonry Reexamined," *Journal of American History*, LXXI (1984), pp. 269–293, and "Freemasonry and Community in the Early Republic," *American Quarterly*, XXXIV (1982), pp. 543–561. See also Paul Goodman, *Towards a Christian Republic* (New York, 1988).

9. Quoted in Remini, *Election of Andrew Jackson*, p. 138.

10. Gulian C. Verplanck to Jesse Hoyt, January 22, 1828, in William L. Mackenzie, *Life and Times of Martin Van Buren* (Boston, 1846), p. 203.

into captivity, I certainly could not approve of it; but if the one or the other has been done, I presume it has been the work of some misguided individuals, which however reprehensible it may be, ought not to affect the whole order. I am myself a Mason, and although not a bright one nor a regular attendant of the Lodge, I respect the craft, and its members generally."[11]

He could not—would not—repudiate his membership. As a consequence, the issue worked to his distinct disadvantage over the next several years as the Anti-Masonic party grew in numbers, determination, and political strength.

Despite the charges made against him and Adams and despite the organizing skill of the Democrats, Clay continued to entertain high hopes for the success of the National Republican ticket.[12] Of course, he naturally inclined to optimism, but he did sincerely believe that the tariff and internal improvements issues would make the Jackson men in Congress "stand in such bold relief," because of their opposition to these issues, "that I think the public will not fail ultimately to pass a right judgment upon them."[13] These issues were essential to New England, Pennsylvania, and the West, and the solid support of these areas would virtually guarantee Adams's reelection.

As for the Democratic claim that they engineered the passage of the Tariff of Abominations because of its commitment to protection, Clay chose to believe that Americans would see through that blatantly cynical and dishonest appeal for votes and punish them at the polls for their hypocrisy.

Still, unfolding events of late, such as the tariff enactment, troubled him more than he was willing to admit. He redoubled his campaigning efforts, striking out at Jackson with increasingly angry words. At a citizens' meeting in Baltimore shortly after the passage of the tariff bill, Clay excoriated the unhealthy trend toward Caesarism, the worship of the military hero, "the Philips—the Caesars—the Cromwells—the Mariuses and the Scyllas." If it were physically possible, he said, and compatible with his official duties, "I would visit every state, go to every town and hamlet, address every man in the Union, and entreat them by their love of country, by their love of liberty, for the sake of themselves and their posterity . . . to pause—solemnly and contemplate the precipice which yawns before us!" If we have incurred divine wrath and it is necessary for Him to chastise His people with the rod of vengeance, "I would humbly prostrate myself before Him, and implore his mercy, to visit our land with war, with pestilence, with famine, with any scourge other than military rule or a blind and heedless enthusiasm for mere military renown."[14]

Small wonder Andrew Jackson hated Henry Clay with a consuming pas-

11. Clay to Porter, March 24, 1828, in Clay, *Papers,* VII, 186.
12. Clay to N. B. Beall, March 21, 1828, Clay Papers, Manuscript Department, Filson Club, Louisville, Kentucky. For a discussion of the parades, barbecues, and other hoopla employed during this election, see Remini, *Election of Jackson,* pp. 109–119.
13. Clay to Porter, April 2, 1828, in Clay, *Papers,* VII, 212.
14. Delivered in Baltimore, May 13, 1828, in Clay, *Papers,* VII, 272–273.

sion. And it glowed more intensely with each passing year. This speech amply revealed Clay's obsession over the terrifying thought of the military chieftain becoming President of the United States.

In late June Clay, sick in mind and body from his intense campaigning and fearful that his efforts all may have been in vain, returned to Kentucky. His health improved only moderately, so he stopped off for several days at White Sulphur Springs, Virginia, to take the waters. The Kentucky gubernatorial election in early August troubled him particularly since it would provide the surest clue to what would happen in the state's presidential contest later in the fall. He was anxious to help win the election of Thomas Metcalfe over the Democrat, and former friend, William T. Barry, and he knew that the opposition would leave "no stone . . . unturned to defeat him."[15] Happily, Metcalfe won the election—narrowly, as it turned out—but the Jacksonians captured the legislature. This mixed result therefore provided no reliable clue to what might happen in the fall election.[16] As usual Clay put the best face he could on the outcome. "Metcalfe is elected, and only elected, but still he is governor, and I do believe that it will be followed by a train of consequences that will ensure success in the more important election in Nov. . . . We need not despair. Our *chance* (I am sorry to be obliged to use that word) is best."[17]

In late August Clay headed back for Washington, intending to stop off again at White Sulphur Springs for a ten-day rest. "The state of my health, though improved, is such as to still require some nursing," he wrote.[18] The waters at the springs proved mentally beneficial, but by the time he reached Washington in early October he had already begun to think about his future in rather negative terms. "My present inclination," he told James Brown, "is to retire from public life after the 4th of March." Had he been thirty-five years of age, he said, he would consider returning to the House of Representatives. But since he was fifty-two, he no longer enjoyed the "strength and buoyancy" to get back into that arena. "In any event, I shall have the satisfaction to know that all the great measures of Domestic policy which I have espoused will be firmly established."[19]

Still, as late as the third week of October he kept predicting victory. "I yet think that Mr. Adams will be reelected," he told Daniel Webster, "but it is mortifying and sickening to the hearts of the real lovers of free Government, that the contest should be so close; and that if Heaven grants us success it will be perhaps by less than a majority of six votes."[20]

But as the electoral returns started to roll into Washington in the late fall,

15. Clay to Samuel L. Southard, July 2, 1828, in Clay, *Papers,* VII, 374.

16. Metcalfe defeated Barry by the vote of 38,910 to 38,231. *Argus of Western America,* August 27, 1828.

17. Clay to John Sloane, August 25, 1828, in Clay, *Papers,* VII, 439–440.

18. Clay to James Erwin, September 4, 1828, in Clay, *Papers,* VII, 457.

19. Clay to Brown, October 11, 1828, in Clay, *Papers,* VII, 490.

20. Clay to Webster, October 24, 1828, in Clay, *Papers,* VII, 516.

it was clear that the National Republican ticket had been crushed in an avalanche of organized enthusiasm for Old Hickory. Some 1,555,340 males voted in the election, and 56 percent of them supported Jackson. The general received 647,276 popular votes to Adams's 508,064. In the electoral college Adams's defeat was even more spectacular. Jackson swept virtually everything south of the Potomac River and west of New Jersey for a total of 178 electoral votes; Adams carried New England, Delaware, New Jersey, and most of Maryland for a total of 83 electoral votes.[21]

For many the results of the election were seen as a triumph of democracy over aristocracy, a victory for the ordinary citizen, the beginning of popular government. "How triumphant," enthused Andrew J. Donelson, nephew, ward, and private secretary to General Jackson, "how flattering to the cause of the people."[22] A "great revolution has taken place," sighed one National Republican. "A majority of more than *two to one*" defeated the coalition of Adams and Clay, explained Edward Everett to his brother, "an event astounding to the friends of the Administration and unexpected by the General himself and his friends. . . . [They] are embarrassed with the vastness of their triumph and the numbers of their party."[23]

When Kentucky swung behind Jackson by a handsome majority, Clay must have been mortified, although he masked his true feelings. "The people of Kentucky," Amos Kendall explained to Jackson, "cannot be induced by management, by art, by falsehood nor even by her attachments, to be unjust to our country's defenders, or give her sanction to a corrupt administration of the general government." If nothing else, he jeered, "the line of Secretary succession is broken," obviously referring to Clay.[24]

"We are beaten," conceded the dejected Clay to Daniel Webster in late November. And it is pointless to dwell on the causes, he added. Suffice it to say that we are the party with a program. "We are of the majority, in regard to measures; we are of the minority in respect to the person designated as C. Magistrate." We must retain the majority we have. Above all, he continued, "*we* ought not to prematurely agitate the question of the Succession. The nation wants repose." The agitations of the last six years entitle the people to rest. If they are disturbed again, he wearily wrote, "let others not us assume the responsibility."[25]

21. Robert V. Remini, "The Election of 1828," *History of American Presidential Elections: 1789–1968,* ed. Schlesinger and Israel, I, 492. New York's electoral vote was divided, with the larger portion going to Jackson.

22. Donelson to John Coffee, November 16, 1828, Donelson Papers, LC.

23. Robert Wickliffe to Clay, October 7, 1828, Henry Show to Clay, January 9, 1829, Clay Papers, LC; *Niles' Weekly Register,* December 6, 1828; Edward Everett to A. H. Everett, December 2, 1828, Everett Papers, Massachusetts Historical Society.

24. Kendall to Jackson, November 19, 1828, Chicago Historical Society.

25. Clay to Webster, November 30, 1828, in Clay, *Papers,* VII, 552–553.

As for himself, Clay told a number of friends that he had "enjoyed more composure" during the days following the defeat "than I have for many weeks." He was preparing, he said, early in the spring to return home, where he hoped to remain in retirement. He anticipated strong pressure from his constituents to return to the House, but "the point will be whether I can resist it or not." Meanwhile, "we must still struggle for our Country, in private life, and hope that Providence may yet watch over and preserve our Liberties."[26]

But he was really not very sanguine about the future. "I agree with you," he wrote his friend, N. B. Beall, "that the President elect has a path before him strewed with thorns. If he can carry the nation through all its present difficulties and his own, prosperously and safely, preserving the Union, the Constitution and our liberties, I will acknowledge, at the close of his career, that I have done injustice to his temper and capacity. Meanwhile I shall be a 'looker on in Venice,' anxious and struggling in whatever station I may be to preserve those great principles of freedom and policy to which I have hitherto dedicated my public life. My confidence in their success, it is true, is shaken. But they have been so interwoven with my very soul, that I will not abandon the hope of their final success and triumph whilst reason and life endure."[27]

To everyone who wrote him offering his condolences, Clay advised him to submit to the popular will. "To this decision of the people of the United States, patriotism and religion both unite in enjoining submission and resignation. For one, I shall endeavor to perform that duty." But without doubt, he resented having to bend his neck. It galled him. "As a private citizen, and as a lover of liberty, I shall ever deeply deplore it." The election of the military chieftain was an absolute horror to him, and he feared dreadful consequences as a result. "The military principle has triumphed, and triumphed in the person of one devoid of all the graces, elegancies, and magnanimity of the accomplished men of the profession."[28]

The dread that enveloped Clay about what might happen to the country with a man on horseback at its head troubled other National Republicans as well. Some of them wondered aloud whether something might be done about it, and one "sorry Knave" suggested that the election be brought into the House of Representatives "by some political legerdemain" by which five states would be induced to vote for Clay, thereby creating a third candidate and allowing the House to "overturn the Jackson victory." Clay called this "a most wild and reprehensible suggestion." As "calamitous as I regard the election of

26. Clay to James Brown, November 12, 1828, Clay to John Sloane, November 12, 1828, in Clay, *Papers*, VII, 534–536. The pressure to return to the House may be seen in the letters of John Crittenden to Clay, December 3, 1828, and James Brown to Clay, December 12, 1828, ibid., VII, 554, 565.
27. Clay to Beall, November 18, 1828, Clay Papers, Manuscript Department, Filson Club, Louisville, Kentucky.
28. Clay to Adam Beatty, November 13, 1828, Clay to Hezekiah Niles, November 25, 1828, in Clay, *Papers*, VII, 536, 548.

General Jackson," he wrote, "I should consider the defeat of his election, at this time, by any such means, as a still greater calamity."[29]

The calamities of the past several months only wearied an already tired man whose body and spirit seemed broken. Margaret Smith visited the Clays shortly after the start of the new year and was shocked at the secretary of state's appearance. He was stretched out on the sofa and covered, face and all, by a dark cloak that looked like a black pall. Suddenly he awakened and pulled the cloak from his face. After a few moments he slowly rose to a sitting position. "He was much thinner," said Mrs. Smith, "very pale, his eyes sunk in his head and his countenance sad and melancholy—that countenance generally illumined with the fire of genius and animated by some ardent feeling. His voice was feeble and mournful." Mrs. Smith "was shocked at the alteration in his looks." He had not been out of the house for a week and could scarcely sit up straight, she said.

As soon as he had roused himself, Clay tried to pretend that all was well. "Mr. Clay still keeps on the mask of smiles," wrote the discerning Mrs. Smith. The lady thought that Clay was so ill that he did not have long to live. For two weeks he had been unable to sleep without "anodynes." But he assured her that he was fine and was attending to business as he always did, although he did admit that he never had guests to dinner anymore and never went out. "I never liked Mr. Clay so well as I do this winter," she wrote, "the coldness and hauteur of his manner has vanished and a softness and tenderness and sadness characterize his manner . . . that is extremely attaching and affecting." He remained in perfect good humor, she continued; no bitterness "mingles its gall in the cup of disappointment." He even spoke of Jackson in a good-natured manner.

Clay caught her staring despondently at him.

"Why what ails your heart?" he asked as he took Mrs. Smith by the hand.

"Can it be otherwise than sad," she responded, looking at Lucretia Clay, "when I think what a good friend I am about to lose?"

For a moment Clay did not speak. He simply pressed her hand, and "his eyes filled with tears." Then he said: "We must not think of this, or talk of such things *now*." He pulled out his handkerchief, turned away, and wiped his eyes. Then he turned back, smiled, and started talking "as if his heart was light and easy."[30]

Clay's manner and behavior during these final months and weeks of the Adams administration filled his friends with wonder. Mrs. Smith credited it all to the strength and vigor of his mind. She thought he had greater intellectual power than any man she had ever met, and that included Jefferson and Madison. The intellectual strengths of those two Presidents came from education

29. *National Intelligencer,* November 18, 1828, Clay to Francis T. Brooke, November 18, 1828, in Clay, *Papers,* VII, 541.

30. Smith, *Forty Years,* pp. 256–257, 259, 276–278. Clay commented on his poor health in a letter to his son Henry Clay, Jr., January 26, 1829, in Clay, *Papers,* VII, 607.

and favorable circumstances, she argued, a combination of which took them to great heights. "Not so Mr. Clay. Whatever he is, is all his own, inherent power, bestowed by nature and not derivative from cultivation or fortune. He has an elasticity and buoyancy of spirit, that no pressure of external circumstances, can confine or keep down." Depressions only seemed to give him new vigor. "He is a very great man."[31]

Without commenting on the comparison with Jefferson and Madison, it is undoubtedly true that Henry Clay had a greater natural force of mind than any of his contemporaries. Unfortunately he recklessly squandered much of his talent as he pursued pleasure and the illusory goals of a driving ambition.

To add to his miseries at this time, his twenty-six-year-old son, Thomas Hart Clay, was arrested and jailed for nonpayment of his hotel bill in Philadelphia and other small debts. Although Clay immediately sent $250 to pay the bill and provide his son with enough money to return to Kentucky, he was advised that it might take three months before the young man could be released. Fortunately the hotel's owner accepted Clay's note, Thomas was released, and he promised to leave immediately for Lexington.[32]

Clay's one consolation at this time was the success achieved by his youngest son, Henry Clay, Jr., a shy and modest student at West Point, unsure of his ability and no doubt intimidated by his father's many successes. The young man delighted his father by his performance at the academy.[33] But with Jackson in the White House it was obvious to young Clay that he would go nowhere in the army, so with his father's encouragement and permission, he decided to study law after he graduated. The approving father offered some advice:

> . . . To attain the highest place, or even a respectable rank, in the profession of Law, you must make up your mind to labor incessantly. I never studied half enough. I always relied too much upon the resources of my genius. If I had life to pass over again, and, with my present information, could control my movements, I would not appear at the Bar before 24 or 25, nor until after two or three years, at the least, of close study. You must not however let your eagerness to enter upon the study of law occasion you to remit your efforts in your present pursuits.[34]

In the closing months of his administration Adams tried to reward Clay for his service and loyalty with an appointment to the Supreme Court, just as his father had done in placing John Marshall on the Court nearly thirty years earlier. Associate Justice Robert Trimble had died, and the President offered the vacancy to his secretary of state. But Clay refused it with thanks and

---

31. Smith, *Forty Years,* pp. 285–286.

32. Thomas L. Wharton to Clay, March 6, 1829, in Clay, *Papers,* VIII, 2–3.

33. "You are one of my greatest comforts," Clay wrote his son. Clay to Clay, Jr., November 14, 1828, April 2, 1827, Clay, Jr., to Clay, February 1, 1829, in Clay, *Papers,* VII, 611–612, VI, 385. Young Henry subsequently was graduated second in his class.

34. Clay to Clay, Jr., April 19, 1829, in Clay, *Papers,* VIII, 30.

suggested his friend John J. Crittenden as a replacement.[35] It was a gracious gesture on Adams's part, but Clay felt he needed to return to Ashland and attend to his health and his family's future. Besides, a seat on the bench suited neither his temperament nor his ambition.

On February 11, 1829, the President-elect, General Andrew Jackson, arrived in Washington. He was dressed in deep mourning. His beloved wife, Rachel, had died suddenly on December 22 of a heart attack, only a few weeks after her husband had triumphantly won the presidency. "My heart is nearly broke," Jackson sobbed to a friend several weeks later. The "partner of my life," "my dearest heart" had been assassinated by vile slanderers, by his political enemies. At least that was how Jackson interpreted her sudden death. And Henry Clay was the vilest of them all. On a tablet placed over Rachel's grave her husband had written: "A being so gentle and so virtuous, slander might wound but could not dishonor." The slander may not have dishonored her, but in Jackson's mind it certainly killed her. Several years earlier the general had said that Henry Clay was the meanest scoundrel he could imagine, that even the aged and virtuous female could not escape "his secrete combination of base slander."[36] Now, as he entered Washington to begin preparations to take over the government, it alarmed some National Republicans about what he might do if he accidentally ran into Henry Clay. For one thing, the general refused to go to the White House to pay his respects to the outgoing President. Some said it was because he blamed Adams for the attacks on Rachel that had appeared in the Washington *National Journal*. Others claimed that Old Hickory did not wish to risk the possibility of finding Henry Clay in the White House when he visited,[37] that something terrible might result. Adams repaid the discourtesy by refusing to attend Jackson's inauguration, just as his father had done in 1801, when Thomas Jefferson was inaugurated.

The announcement of Jackson's intended cabinet in February brought a snort of disapproval from most National Republicans. One man called it "the Millenium of the Minnows."[38] Clay was no less critical, but he couched his disdain in sarcasm. "The President-elect," he wrote, "feeble in body and mind, and irresolute, is surrounded by a host of ravenous expectants of office, & a corps of newspaper editors, gathered from the four quarters of the world. His intended cabinet is almost officially announced." It consisted of Van Buren for the State Department, Samuel D. Ingham of Pennsylvania for the Treasury, John H. Eaton of Tennessee for War, and John Branch of North Carolina for the Navy. "Upon such a Cabinet," Clay scoffed, "comment is unnecessary."[39]

35. Adams, *Memoirs*, VIII, 78, 82–83.

36. Jackson to John Coffee, January 17, 1829, Jackson to Jean Plauche, December 27, 1828, Jackson Papers, Tennessee Historical Society; Jackson to Sam Houston, December 15, 1826, Jackson Papers, LC.

37. Adams, *Memoirs*, VIII, 102.

38. William Wirt to William Pope, March 22, 1829 in John P. Kennedy, *Life of William Wirt* (Philadelphia, 1849), II, 228.

39. Clay to James Caldwell, February 24, 1829, in Clay, *Papers*, VII, 627.

Over the next several weeks the outgoing secretary of state closed down his operation. There was absolutely nothing new or interesting happening since the Congress was in no mood to conduct business. "The present administration," he said, "is winding up their public affairs, originating no new measures, and endeavoring to turn their Stewardship over to the successors, in the best state possible."[40] Since Van Buren had been elected governor of New York, his arrival in Washington to take over the State Department would necessarily be delayed, assuming, of course, that he accepted the position. But that was not Clay's problem, and he went ahead with plans to leave town as quickly as decency allowed. On March 3 he submitted his letter of resignation to the President, who added his acceptance of it, whereupon Clay took it to be deposited at the Department of State. Lucretia put up their furniture for sale, which netted $2,886.37, plus $405 for the champagne and wine. The rest of their personal effects were packed and readied for shipment back to Kentucky.[41]

On March 4, 1829, a bright, sunny, and balmy day, General Andrew Jackson was inaugurated on the east portico of the Capitol before a crowd in excess of twenty thousand. In his inaugural address, which few could hear, the new President spoke of reform, especially in the area of executive patronage, the liquidation of the national debt, and the enactment of a "judicious" tariff. But he did not directly attack the American System. That would come later. When the ceremonies concluded, the mob rushed to the White House and nearly tore it apart in their enthusiasm and happiness over the inauguration of "the People's President."[42]

Naturally Clay did not attend these ceremonies. But he read Jackson's inaugural address and was slightly amused by that part that promised to extirpate the alleged abuses of patronage in the executive department. If only there had been more such abuses, with a firmer hand wielding the patronage ax, the Adams administration might have survived for another four years. "Among the official corps here," he wrote to Francis Brooke, "there is the greatest solicitude and apprehension. The members of it feel something like the inhabitants of Cairo when the plague breaks out; no one knows who is next to encounter the stroke of death; or which . . . to be dismissed from office. You have no conception of the moral tyranny which prevails here over those in employment."[43]

A few days after Jackson's inauguration Clay's friends gave him a dinner at the Mansion Hotel, and upwards of a hundred persons attended in his honor. Although suffering from a severe cold, he delivered a short speech of farewell to his friends. He began by thanking them for the honor of their presence and

40. Clay to Francis T. Brooke, January 10, 1829, in Clay, *Papers*, VII, 594; Clay to N. B. Beall, November 18, 1828, Clay Papers, Manuscript Department, Filson Club, Louisville, Kentucky.
41. Smith, *Forty Years*, p. 285; auction lists, Clay Papers, LC.
42. Remini, *Jackson*, II, 168–172; Richardson, *Messages and Papers* II, 999–1001; *Argus of Western America*, March 18, 1829.
43. Clay to Brooke, March 12, 1829, in Clay, *Papers*, VIII, 8.

again struck the theme about how the American people needed repose from the agitations of the late election. Still, he had to admit that he "deprecated" Jackson's election not only because the general lacked the temper, experience, and service to discharge his duties as President but also because he was elevated "exclusively" out of admiration and gratitude for his military service. He feared the establishment of military rule and prayed to God that it would not happen. Andrew Jackson "has done me much injustice," Clay complained, "—wanton, unprovoked and unatoned injustice." It was inflicted for personal ambition and private resentment. But my relation to him is now changed, Clay continued. He is the President, and as long as he holds that office, patriotism demands that he be treated with decorum and respect. Clay hoped that "our free institutions" would continue unimpaired. While devotion to his country prompted him to express this hope, "I make no pledges, no promises, no threats, and, I must add, I have no confidence." He ended his speech by proposing a toast: "Let us never despair of the American Republic."[44]

On March 12 Clay took leave of the former President, manifesting, said Adams, "some sensibility at parting," which probably meant that he broke down and cried. As Mrs. Smith frequently observed, Clay was a very sentimental man of deep "tenderness and sensibility." He told Adams that he would leave the capital on March 13 and expressed the wish that he would occasionally hear from the former President.[45]

As the day of his departure from Washington grew nearer, Clay gave increasing thought to his future. Naturally he told everyone who asked about his plans that he had not yet decided what he would do other than rest and attempt to regain his health. But more and more he kept thinking about 1832, when Jackson's term as President would end. Would the man who was irresolute, surrounded by spoilsmen, and "feeble in body and mind" seek a second term? Surely this incompetent military chieftain would bring calamity to the nation, and if he did seek a second term, the people would certainly send him packing. Any number of friends had told Clay that the results of the recent presidential election would have been far different if he, not Adams, had been the candidate of the National Republican party. His western supporters assured him that in their section of the country "every vote would have been obtained for me." Add New England—since representatives from that section had "assured me . . . that I would have got a greater aggregate popular vote than Mr. Adams received"—as well as New York, New Jersey, and Pennsylvania, where his American System enjoyed widespread support, and the military chieftain would have been defeated.[46] Such delusions!

---

44. *National Journal,* March 10, 1829 reprinted in Clay, *Papers,* VIII, 4–6. The dinner was held on March 7 at 5:30 P.M. Former President Adams did not attend this dinner because he intended "to bury myself in complete retirement, as much so as a nun taking the veil." Adams, *Memoirs,* VIII, 107.

45. Adams, *Memoirs,* VIII, 111; Smith, *Forty Years,* p. 301.

46. Clay to Brooke, January 10, 1829, in Clay, *Papers,* VII, 594–595.

Central to Clay's thinking was his belief that a political alliance between the manufacturing states of New England and the middle states with the West was unbeatable because it rested on the solid foundation of the American System. The economic interests of these states, requiring public works and higher tariff rates, necessitated that they work together politically to win the protection and support that would advance their own and the nation's development and prosperity.[47] Clay's reasoning seemed irrefutable to him. American society was moving inexorably toward industrialism, and this dynamic would force the government, sooner or later, to respond to it in the ways delineated by Clay in his American System. There was no escaping this certainty. Thus, if New England, the West, and the middle states would act together politically, they could theoretically provide 164 electoral votes to the candidate of their choice, far more than the number needed to elect a President.

In addition, Clay convinced himself that Jackson's charisma and Adams's lack of it, rather than any defect in the American System or its importance to the eastern and western sections of the country, had produced the electoral calamity the previous fall. Adams's unwillingness and inability to provide political leadership and his failure to wield the patronage power to purge his administration of disloyal members, such as the postmaster general, also contributed to his defeat. Clay would never be guilty of those faults when he became President. And he could combine charisma with statesmanship, he believed, to win back the support of the electorate that had deserted to the Democrats.

Clay shared his thinking with a few of his friends. He asked his New England cronies if he could count on the support of their section should he consider running for the presidency in 1832. A few of his straitlaced correspondents were shocked by his crude inquiry. One of them, Edward Everett, went to President Adams to share this latest development. "Everett told me that Mr. Clay had embarrassed him very much yesterday," Adams recorded in his journal, "by enquiring whether he might depend upon the support of the Eastern States at the next Presidential election, and said that, if he could, he should be sure of that of the Western States." Everett responded to Clay by remarking that it was impossible to see what direction future events might take. Both Adams and Everett did agree, however, that if Clay returned to the House of Representatives, he would be the leader of the opposition but that he would never be elected Speaker. Indeed, they decided that Clay's future success would depend a great deal on "a course of events which cannot now be foreseen."[48]

Clay understood this. He understood that much would depend on "contingencies," as he called them, such as the "movement of competitors, the course of the new administration, the determination of Jackson as to offering

47. For a full development of this theme, see Frings, *Henry Clay's American System,* passim.
48. Adams, *Memoirs,* VIII, 86.

for a second term &c." But these contingencies would develop rapidly, he thought, possibly as early as next summer or winter. "The next six months— the next six weeks—may develope important events, and shed brilliant light upon our path." Meanwhile, he asked his friends to take no formal action on his behalf. He did not want the public mind to be disturbed from "the enjoyment of that tranquility, of which, after the late violent agitation, it has so much need."[49]

Once more the craving for the presidential office had started to dominate his emotions and his thinking. Once more his lust began to seep into his correspondence and intimate conversations. He could not help himself. As he rode out of Washington on March 13, 1829, headed for Lexington, passing and waving farewell to John Quincy Adams on Pennsylvania Avenue from his carriage, he seemed obsessed with the vision of returning four years hence as the eighth President of the United States.

49. Clay to Brooke, January 10, 30, 1829, in Clay, *Papers,* VII, 595, 610.

TWENTY

Enforced Retirement

OR WEEKS prior to his departure from the capital Clay had received numerous invitations to attend dinners, meetings, and other ceremonies in his honor as he journeyed homeward. He was torn between the need to see and hear the salutes of his fellow citizens and his desire to get to Ashland, where he could rest. Moreover, he knew such events had the potential for disaster. The campaign had been too recent, he said, passions had not yet abated, and prejudices still ran high and strong. He toyed with the idea of revisiting White Sulphur Springs for health reasons but decided against it because of the length of the land travel and the bad state of the roads.[1]

What resulted was a compromise. He refused some invitations, particularly those requiring him to detour from his route of travel, and accepted others where he thought the crowds would be friendly. On the whole the receptions were enthusiastic and sometimes boisterous. "My journey has been marked by every token of warm attachment, and cordial demonstration," he wrote from Wheeling. "I never experienced more testimonies of respect and confidence, nor more enthusiasm. Dinners, Suppers, Balls &c. I have had literally a free passage. Taverns, Stages, Toll gates have been generally thrown open to me, from all charge. Monarchs might be proud of the reception with which I have been every where honored."

Naturally he spoke to the crowds, often reviewing his career to date. He took pride, he said, in the role he had played in the War of 1812, including the peace treaty that ended it. He also took credit for winning recognition of South American independence, settling the Missouri question, and enunciating the paramount need of government support of industry and public works that formed the core of his American System. When he spoke of the new administration, he was careful to say that he wished it well. "The love of the country ought to predominate over all selfish and party views and interests."

---

1. Clay to Brooke, January 30, 1829, Clay to James Caldwell, February 24, 1829, Clay, *Papers*, VII, 610, 628. The invitations may be found in the Clay Papers, LC.

Such remarks usually earned him cheers and applause. Obviously, he said, Jackson enjoyed greater affection and confidence from the people than he, Clay, had recognized. "Let us henceforward substitute to mere personal contest, the higher and nobler struggle for principle, for liberty, for sound measures of national policy."

Because he was such a splendid orator and politician, Clay never failed to end his speeches with a phrase or sentiment that would stir his audience and ignite an explosive response. It was never so much what he said as the way he said it: the voice, the dramatic delivery, the gestures. And all of it, unfortunately, is forever lost.[2]

Clay and his family arrived home on April 6, "in pretty good health," he wrote, a journey that took more than three weeks. Along the way he noticed the many physical changes taking place in the country. Frontier aspects of western life had given way to the signs of advancing civilization. The parlors of several inns where they stayed overnight were now covered with French wallpaper, usually depicting hunting parties or some other pastoral scene. These parlors now boasted three or four rocking chairs, in which ladies were "vibrating in different directions, and at various velocities." There were also signs of industrial growth and urban expansion in many communities, and several times Clay used their presence to expound upon his American System to the local citizenry.

Upon reaching Ashland, the family had very little furniture but expected two wagonloads within two weeks. Clay found the house and grounds out of repair but less so than he had anticipated, and he thought he could put it all back into shape in a relatively short period of time. For some inexplicable reason—perhaps a need for sympathy for all the time he had spent away from home serving the nation and his constituents—he chose to exaggerate conditions on his estate when he made his first public appearance before his constituents on May 16. "Upon my return home," he declared to them, "I found my house out of repair; my farm not in order, the fences down, the stock poor, the crop not set, and late in April the corn stalks of last year's growth yet standing in the field, a sure sign of slovenly cultivation."[3]

Clay set about immediately to the many tasks involved in farming, stock breeding, and hemp raising. He instructed his friend John H. Ewing to pur-

2. See his speeches in Clay, *Papers,* VIII, 14–15, 19–20. To a predominantly Catholic audience, he ended with: "The Irish Catholic—success to his struggles for liberty." An Irishman by the name of George Sweeny heard his speech and wrote Clay to tell him that although he had not been "originally amongst the number of your political friends," he had since reversed himself because of Clay's obvious "great worth." Sweeny to Clay, April 10, 1829, ibid., VIII, 25.

3. Martineau, *Retrospect of Western Travel,* I, 73; Clay to James Erwin, April 9, 1829, Clay to Clay, Jr., April 19, 1829, Clay to Thomas Wharton, April 19, 1829, Wharton to Clay, May 1, 1829, in Clay, *Papers,* VIII, 23, 29, 30–31, 36. Clay ordered an ottoman and two Grecian hair sofas from his agent in Philadelphia, which he figured would cost him about seventy dollars. The agent estimated that the sofas would cost thirty-five dollars each and the ottoman fifty dollars. Speech on May 16, 1829, in Clay, *Papers,* VIII, 53.

chase fifty head of merino sheep, some of which he offered to friends and neighbors. For the past ten years he had been raising an improved breed of cattle—"Hereford Reds"—but had recently become aware of the "Improved Durham short horns" after reading *Hints for American Husbandmen,* published in 1827 by the Pennsylvania Agricultural Society. He decided to add this new breed to his livestock by obtaining a pair of two-year-old heifers.

He also enlarged his Ashland estate by purchasing more than one hundred acres, repaired his house and several other structures on the property, and built an icehouse.[4] He also bought, sold, and leased slaves. For example, he purchased a twenty-six-year-old slave and her two children for $422; he sold four men and a boy for $1,780; he leased a slave for 50 cents a day and hired a slave for $5 a month.[5]

In a conversation about slavery with a friend, Clay recollected his opposition to the institution and his unsuccessful efforts to abolish it at a convention held years before to amend the Kentucky constitution. Although he failed to get rid of slavery in his state, Clay did take credit for inserting several clauses in the constitution that might not have otherwise been approved. Two of these clauses stated that slavery shall not be abolished without compensation to the owner, and slaves shall be "treated with humanity" and shall not be "subjects of merchandise."[6]

Upon his return home Clay had no desire to resume his law practice if he could financially afford to give it up. He needed as much relaxation and rest at Ashland as possible. But if circumstances did dictate a return, then "it would not be with an intention to engage in business generally. The kind of practice which I should prefer would be simply to argue causes previously prepared." He particularly wanted to avoid the Court of Appeals because of its enormous docket and the great amount of time required to plead cases before it.[7]

Even so, Clay was obliged to resume arguing in the courts because of a special appeal from an old friend and wealthy supporter, Robert Wickliffe, whose son Charles had gotten into trouble. Apparently the young man quarreled with Thomas R. Benning, editor of the Lexington *Kentucky Gazette,* a Jacksonian newspaper, when the editor refused to identify the author of an article attacking the senior Wickliffe. Charles shot Benning to death. "It would greatly promote my security if you will consent to appear for him," the father wrote to Clay, ". . . & . . . it will in a great measure relieve my fears as to the result." Clay was reluctant to take the case in view of his inclination to give up law, and he had been away from a courtroom for more than four years; but he

4. Clay to Ewing, May 4, 14, 1829, Clay to Adam Beatty, June 2, 1829, Clay to Francis Brooke, May 12, 1829, Clay to John Hare Powel, November 5, 1829, in Clay, *Papers,* VIII, 37, 39, 40, 63, 122; Van Deusen, *Clay,* p. 233.
5. Clay's financial transactions involving slaves from 1829 through 1836 are summarized in Clay, *Papers,* VIII, 85–86.
6. Henry Clay, Jr., manuscript diary, University of Kentucky.
7. Clay to John F. Henry, April 16, 1829, in Clay, *Papers,* VIII, 27–28.

could not deny the father's appeal after all the senior Wickliffe had done for him. "I would have avoided doing so," Clay wrote Josiah Johnston, "if I could have avoided it honorably."[8]

Clay, his friend John J. Crittenden, and Richard H. Chinn defended young Wickliffe at the trial, which began on June 30. As everyone expected, Clay represented his client brilliantly. He had lost none of his histrionic flash and oratorical flourish. Five days later the jury acquitted Wickliffe after deliberating only a few minutes. The case "had such a triumphant issue," Clay reported a few weeks later, "that I have been greatly benefited by it, in this State, instead of being injuriously affected."

Unfortunately that did not end the matter. When the *Gazette*'s new editor, George J. Trotter, referred to Charles as Benning's cold-blooded murderer, young Wickliffe called him out, and Trotter killed Charles in the subsequent duel. Perhaps justice was served after all.[9]

In accepting the Wickliffe case, Clay had kept his eye carefully focused on what it would mean to him politically just in case he decided later on to work toward obtaining the presidential nomination of his party in 1832. If he did opt to run again, it meant that all his actions and words hereafter must be scrupulously tailored to that goal, it meant that he must repair his broken fences in Kentucky and around the country, it meant he must become a frequent and highly vocal critic of the administration, and it meant that he must seek another public office in the very near future to gain a national platform to conduct his campaign.

As early as the week following his arrival in Lexington, Clay told friends not to be surprised if he suddenly turned up in their districts. After all, "travelling is conducive to my health," he slyly remarked. Obviously he was extremely anxious to see and talk with his fellow Kentuckians. "I have been too much separated from them. I wish them to know me, as I desire to know them personally."[10] He also wanted to test public reaction to the new administration.

The first opportunity to assault the Jackson administration came at a public dinner tendered him at Fowler's Garden in Lexington on May 16. The dinner marked the town's official welcome and greeting to its favorite and returning son. Some three thousand citizens jammed into the garden and the surrounding grounds. They were liquored and dined on pork and beef and whiskey and rum. And then they were treated to a rousing stump speech as only Henry Clay could deliver it.

8. Robert Wickliffe to Clay, March 15, May 23, 1829, Clay to Johnston, July 18, 1829, in Clay, *Papers*, VIII, 9–10, 57, 77. Wickliffe was a very undependable ally, who later deserted Clay in the hope of assuming leadership of the party and advancing his family's political interests.
9. Lexington *Kentucky Gazette*, June 26, July 31, 1829; Clay to Josiah Johnson, July 18, 1829, in Clay, *Papers*, VIII, 77; J. W. Coleman, *Famous Kentucky Duels* (Frankfort, 1953), p. 69ff. At one point Clay was called "this windy orator of the West."
10. Clay to John Henry, April 16, 1829, in Clay, *Papers*, VIII, 27.

He began, as usual, with an apology. This time it was his voice. Once so strong and powerful, he said, it had diminished considerably because of delicate health and advancing age. (And perhaps too much snuff.) But he would do his best. He thanked them all for coming, especially those who had differed with him in the last campaign. He had no reproaches to make to them, only regrets. He extended the hand of friendship to them, just as cordially as he did to his steadfast supporters. "It is highly gratifying to me to know that they, and thousands of others . . . were unaffected towards me by the prejudices attempted to be excited against me."

Then Clay circled his quarry. The late administration had been accused of misusing the removal power, and the Jackson administration, at its outset, promised a program of reform with respect to executive patronage. But what had occurred? "Now persons are dismissed, not only without trial of any sort, but without charge." Expelled without means of support and often disqualified by age from the pursuit of other employment, they become the victims of an "intolerable oppression," the oppression imposed by "the will of one man," Andrew Jackson. Clay mentioned the name of Napoleon in his attack upon the President—he never failed to invoke the name of the French tyrant in these speeches if at all possible—and briefly contrasted the actions of the two generals. If a French soldier voted against Napoleon, he was "instantly shot," declared Clay. Likewise, a vote by a public servant against Jackson invites immediate dismissal. Knowing the transiency of tenure, officeholders will make the most of their uncertain offices, and "we may expect innumerable cases of fraud, peculation, and corruption."

Notice, Clay declared, the number of editors recently appointed to political office. They were the most vigorous in their denunciations of the National Republicans, and the most vulgar. If their appointments were based on devotion to Jackson, and not on their ability and capacity to serve the public, then the press has been rendered "venal" and in time will destroy the "cherished Palladium of our Liberty."

Of course, Clay wanted it understood that he was not imputing to Jackson any scheme to subvert liberty. "But I must say that if an ambitious President sought the overthrow of our Government, and ultimately to establish a different form, he would . . . proclaim, by his official acts, that the greatest public virtue was ardent devotion to him. . . . Such an ambitious President would say, as monarchs have said, 'I am the state.' " He would dismiss competent officeholders and replace them with those who have spoken and written on his behalf. He would subsidize the press in order to get his grip on one of the most powerful influences upon public opinion. He would "convert the nation into one perpetual theatre for political gladiators. There would be one universal scramble for the public offices." After each presidential election "we should behold the victor distributing the prizes and applying his punishments, like a military commander, immediately after he had won a great victory." General corruption would ensue until at last "some Pretorian band would arise" and, with the concurrence of the people, put an end to constitutional government.

As he continued, despite denials, Clay virtually accused Jackson of pursuing this very course of action. "The object of President Jackson appears to be to destroy an existing equilibrium between the two parties to the late contest," he contended, "and to establish a monopoly." He apologized if he offended anyone in his audience by this remark, but he had to speak the truth.

As for himself, he wished to remain in private life. Still, he was ready at all times to return to "the service of the Republic" whenever the people felt he would be useful and called him back. For the moment, however, he wished to "re-establish a shattered constitution and enfeebled health. . . . Retirement, unqualified retirement, from all public employment, is what I unaffectedly desire."

Clay closed with another emotionally charged outburst:

And now, my friends and fellow-citizens, I cannot part from you, on possibly this last occasion of my ever publicly addressing you, without reiterating the expression of my thanks from a heart overflowing with gratitude. I came among you, now more than thirty years ago, an orphan boy, pennyless, a stranger to you all, without friends, without the favor of the great. You took me up, cherished me, caressed me, protected me, honored me. You have constantly poured upon me a bold and unabated stream of innumerable favors. Time, which wears out everything, has increased and strengthened your affection for me. When I seemed deserted by almost the whole world, and assailed by almost every tongue and pen and press, you have fearlessly and manfully stood by me, with unsurpassed zeal and undiminished friendship. When I felt as if I should sink beneath the storm of abuse and detraction, which was violently raging around me, I have found myself upheld and sustained by your encouraging voices and your approving smiles. I have doubtless committed many faults and indiscretions, over which you have thrown the broad mantle of your charity. But I can say . . . that I have honestly and faithfully served my country; that I have never wronged it; and that, however unprepared I lament that I am to appear in the Divine presence on other accounts, I invoke the stern justice of His judgment on my public conduct, without the smallest apprehension of His displeasure.

Clay then proposed a toast: *"The State of Kentucky.*— A cordial union of all parties in favor of an efficient system of Internal Improvements adapted to the wants of the State."[11]

The toast fell short of his best efforts, but the closing peroration had enough emotional impact to rouse his audience to prolonged cheers and applause.

What was politically significant about the speech was not only the fact that Henry Clay openly declared war on the Jackson administration but the uncanny instinct he demonstrated in striking with his first blow at that precise point where the opposition was most vulnerable: rotation of office, the so-called spoils system. It was an issue he hung around Old Hickory's neck in the

11. Speech in Clay, *Papers*, VIII, 41–54.

hope of dragging him down to defeat in the next election. And Jackson was indeed vulnerable. He had condemned the patronage system as practiced by his predecessor. He had promised reform once he had assumed office, he had assumed a high moral ground in his campaign about how he would appoint none but the virtuous and intelligent, yet here he was initiating what looked like a "reign of terror."[12] Dedicated, experienced, and capable administrators, said Clay, were yanked from office and replaced with venal politicians and incompetent journalists.[13] Right from the start Clay located and exposed to public view what he called the deceit and corruption that had already started to spew forth from the new administration. Right from the start he described the new administration as "the compound of imbecility, tyranny, and hypocrisy." He repeated this phrase over and over in speech after speech, perhaps in the hope that it would have the same dramatic effect as the corrupt bargain charge.[14]

Not that other National Republicans failed to notice the opportunity opening up to them, but Clay exploited it early and often. He even feared that he might have been a little too enthusiastic in his denunciation. "I said a great deal also on the subject of late removals from office," he told Charles Hammond by way of informing him of his speech, "and perhaps here also overstepped the bounds of prudence. But I was a great way on this side of the limit of my feelings of abhorrence, on account of the compound of embicility, tyranny and hypocrisy, which the Cabinet at Washington now exhibits, and that was enough for me."[15]

The administration's removal policy provided Clay with the first of a total issues that convinced him that General Jackson could be beaten four years hence. He had faith in "the virtue and intelligence of the people" to see through Jackson's mendacity, notwithstanding their actions during the late

---

12. On removals at the beginning of Jackson's "reign of terror," see Parton, *Life of Andrew Jackson,* III, 206–227. See also Carl Russell Fish, *The Civil Service and the Patronage* (New York, 1905); Eric M. Eriksson, "The Federal Civil Service under President Jackson," *Mississippi Valley Historical Review,* XIII (March 1927), pp. 517–540; Sidney H. Aronson, *Status and Kinship in the Higher Civil Service: Standards of Selection in the Administrations of John Adams, Thomas Jefferson and Andrew Jackson* (Cambridge, Mass., 1964); and William F. Mugleston, "Andrew Jackson and the Spoils System: An Historiographical Survey, *Mid-America,* LIX (1977), pp. 113–125.

13. Actually Jackson's record of removals was not as bad as Clay chose to believe. See Remini, *Jackson,* II, 185–192. In the Post Office, removals during Jackson's first year in office constituted only 6 percent of the possible total, most of which came from New England, the Middle Atlantic, and northwestern states. Richard R. John, "Managing the Mails: The Postal System, Public Policy, and American Political Culture, 1823–1836," doctoral dissertation, Harvard University, 1989, pp. 248, 290, note 100. Without indicting Jackson personally, John notes the "genuine novelty of the partisan removals" inaugurated in Old Hickory's administration compared with practices of the past. Partisan removals in the Post Office Department, John argues, began under Jackson. Ibid., pp. 271–272.

14. Clay to Hammond, May 27, 1829, Clay to John L. Lawrence, May 28, 1829, in Clay *Papers,* VIII, 59, 61; Clay to N. B. Beall, July 14, 1829, Clay Papers, Manuscript Department, Filson Club, Louisville, Kentucky.

15. Clay to Hammond, May 27, 1829, in Clay, *Papers,* VIII, 59.

election. Changes abounded in every state, he said. "Reform, real and substantial, very different from the mock reform at Washington, I believe to be now going on throughout the whole Country. Its progress may be slow . . . but its ultimate accomplishment I believe to be certain." Unlike you "infidels," he told one newspaper editor, who require too much from the people, he, Henry Clay, was more tolerant and realistic. "You require that the people should never err, but be always right. I require them only to be *generally* right. The late election I look upon as an exception. You make it a rule."[16]

Clay advised friends that he would love to open the eyes of the public to the "shocking enormity" of Jackson's hypocrisy and "put down" the tyranny in Washington. "But whether I shall live or not to witness the restoration of reason, order, law and good government, is far from certain." He pretended he might not be available for a presidential run in 1832. For one thing, he was fifty-two years of age, and he would have to think long and hard, he said, before declaring himself a candidate for that noble undertaking.[17]

Fortunately the results of the August elections in Kentucky encouraged Clay in his thinking about announcing his candidacy. "Henry Clay yet lives in the bosom of Kentuckians," cried one man, "yes, in the bosom of America." National Republicans now controlled the Kentucky legislature, albeit the Democrats had captured most of the congressional seats. Clay credited the congressional losses to "bad arrangements," by which he meant bad organization.[18] In view of the legislative victory with "majorities friendly to me," Clay began to expect some declaration in the form of a resolution from the general assembly about his political future. After all, "Kentucky, during all the late contest . . . was silent," he wrote. "It not only did or said nothing in my behalf, but a most extraordinary species of exparte trial, in my absence, was instituted in her Senate. I am now a private man. Does she not owe something to an injured fellow Citizen; something to her own justice?"[19]

Apparently Clay wanted a presidential nomination from the legislature. Not that he would ever ask for it directly. He therefore suggested to his editor friend in Ohio Charles Hammond that an editorial in his newspaper might get the process under way. "You might say," Clay prompted, ". . . that whilst the Western States generally might forbear to act on the question, Kentucky might feel herself called upon . . . to express her confidence in and attachment to Mr. C." Hammond might also state in the editorial, Clay suggested, that Kentucky could not be expected to look with indifference on the "malignant attacks" on

16. Clay to Hammond, May 27, 1829, in Clay, *Papers,* VIII, 59.

17. Clay to John L. Lawrence, May 28, 1829, in Clay, *Papers,* VIII, 61.

18. Simeon Kemper to Barnes Rogers, August 5, 1829, Rogers-Woodson Family Papers, Manuscript Department, Filson Club, Louisville, Kentucky; Clay to Elisha Whittlesey, August 6, 1829, Clay to Hammond, August 12, 1829, Clay to Josiah S. Johnston, August 26, 1829, Clay to Adam Beatty, July 9, 1829, in Clay, *Papers,* VIII, 83, 88, 90, 75.

19. Clay to Charles Hammond, August 12, 1829, Clay to Josiah Johnson, August 26, 1829, in Clay, *Papers,* VIII, 88, 90. The ex parte trial relates to a resolution introduced into the Kentucky general assembly to authorize a committee of the whole to investigate the corrupt bargain charge.

"his [Clay's] character." Having thoroughly investigated the bargain charge, Clay went on, Kentucky "owes it to herself and to him to express her discredit of that calumny," which the state has not done so far. "Now that the contest is over . . . and Mr. C. in private life, an expression of her opinion might be made with propriety &c &c."[20]

A shrewd politician, Clay began to initiate his presidential campaign for 1832 by encouraging his friends to take up his cause, all the while keeping himself discreetly in the background. Still, he knew he needed to learn first-hand what the electorate thought about a possible candidacy on his behalf, whether he still commanded widespread support and loyalty. Quite frankly, in some parts of the country he was regarded as hors de combat. "Mr. Clay is so unpopular that he is remembered only to be condemned," wrote C. W. Gouch to Van Buren. "I cannot imagine any thing that can ever restore him to the confidence of the Virginia public—or ever make him popular unless, indeed all other public men become as bad or worse than he is."[21]

To test the waters locally, Clay decided to take a three-week "excursion" around his state, particularly the southern counties, and hear what his constituents had to say about his involvement in the corrupt bargain and whether they agreed with him that Jackson's administration to date was a "compound of imbecility, tyranny, and hypocricy." So he spent much of September 1829 on the hustings. And the receptions, once more, delighted him. At Russellville and Hopkinsville he spoke for three hours to no less than three thousand at each place, including "hundreds" from Tennessee. "Vast crowds flocked around me in all the towns," he reported, "and frequently on the Highways." At each of his stops he used the opportunity to "vindicate his character from the foul aspersions which had been cast upon him" and to explain why he had voted for Adams in 1825. He recited the accomplishments of the Adams administration—diminished debt, naval improvements, commercial gains—and recited all the benefits to accrue from an implementation of his American System, especially in "securing political independence and domestic security." However, "Southern demagogues," he warned, threatened to resist and subvert the American System if possible, even by force. They must not be permitted to thwart the need of northerners and westerners for tariff protection and internal improvements.

Not once in all these speeches did he mention his own future plans. Instead, he confined himself solely to a defense of the Adams administration and himself and to an explanation of the American System and its certain benefits in the years to come. And he avoided an all-out, hard-hitting, "direct attack" on the present administration. That would come later.[22]

Clay returned from his "extensive excursion" tremendously heartened.

20. Clay to Hammond, September 9, 1829, in Clay, *Papers,* VIII, 98.
21. Gouch to Van Buren, October 27, 1829, Gouch Family Papers, Virginia Historical Society.
22. Clay to Josiah Johnston, October 5, 1829, Clay to Charles Hammond, October 7, 1829, in Clay, *Papers,* VIII, 110, 112; speech at Hopkinsville, *National Journal,* October 31, 1829.

"Every sort of enthusiastic demonstration of friendship and attachment, on the part of the people, was made towards me. Barbecues, Dinners, Balls &c &c. without number." There was real danger of his developing the gout, he jokingly remarked, because he devoured so "many of their good dishes at their numerous festivals."[23]

Clay intended to put all this to good use. One of the first things he did was report it to his newspaper supporters and make slightly veiled suggestions to them. "An overwhelming majority of the people are with us," he told Hezekiah Niles. We must act upon it. He suggested to the editor of *Niles' Weekly Register* the necessity of not simply opposing the Jackson administration but to do it with *"cause."* If we keep silent, it will be construed as acquiescence and that will discourage our friends. "To prevent that discouragement, and to preserve and augment our strength we must raise a banner." But, he cautioned, "what may be proper for my friends may not be proper for me." Clay was confident Niles would understand him precisely.[24]

By early October 1829 Clay had begun mentioning a presidential nomination openly to a few friends. "The Legislature will do something at the next Session to testify its regard to me," he told Senator Josiah S. Johnston of Louisiana. But it might not be an outright nomination, he allowed. "Still," he went on, "events at Washington may possibly occur early in the winter to render necessary and to justify that measure."[25]

To Charles Hammond, he sent instructions about what should be said in Hammond's newspaper to get his bandwagon rolling. The Kentucky legislature ought to begin its resolution of support in his nomination, he wrote, with some "friendly expressions of attachment confidence &c," after which it might approve a policy of internal improvements and tariff protection, disapprove of the President's spoils system, say "something" on Jackson's plan to remove the Indians west of the Mississippi River and "probably something" in regard to the public lands—namely, disapproving of their surrender. Recently a movement had begun to make the federal government surrender to the states those public lands within their boundaries. The idea seemed to be aimed in part at uniting the South and West in favor of this land cession and in opposition to the tariff.[26]

What seemed to be emerging from the specifics of this letter was a program or platform by which Clay could challenge Jackson in the coming presidential contest, a platform on which he believed he could crush any opponent. "Whenever the contest should be between any other man and myself, not excepting the Hero," he had written just a few months earlier, "I believe a large majority (less in case he were the candidate) would be for me."[27]

23. Clay to Josiah Johnston, October 5, 1829, in Clay, *Papers,* VIII, 110.
24. Clay to Niles, October 4, 1829, in Clay, *Papers,* VIII, 109. Clay himself underscored the word "cause."
25. Clay to Johnston, October 5, 1829, in Clay, *Papers,* VIII, 111.
26. Clay to Charles Hammond, October 7, 1829, in Clay, *Papers,* VIII, 111–112.
27. Clay to John H. Ewing, May 4, 1829, in Clay, *Papers,* VIII, 38.

Clay occasionally complained about his impoverished childhood, but this engraving of the house where he was born in Hanover County, Virginia, hardly suggests poverty or deprivation. FILSON CLUB

During the presidential election of 1832 this engraving of Henry Clay by Jarvis Kellogg was widely circulated. NATIONAL PORTRAIT GALLERY

Louisville, on the Ohio River, viewed from Jeffersonville, Indiana, circa 1850. When traveling south to New Orleans, Clay usually rode from his home in Lexington to Louisville, where he picked up a steamboat to take him to the Mississippi River and then down that river to the Crescent City. FILSON CLUB

The Ohio River near Maysville, Kentucky, where Clay regularly found passage aboard a steamboat to take him up the river to Wheeling, Virginia, before he continued on to Washington by stagecoach via the National Road. FILSON CLUB

The scene below the bust of Clay depicts the American and British negotiators in Ghent, Belgium, seated around a table at which they concluded the terms of the peace treaty that ended the War of 1812. The engraving by W. J. Edwards was executed from a daguerreotype by Mathew Brady. FILSON CLUB

PEACE NEGOTIATIONS AT GHENT.

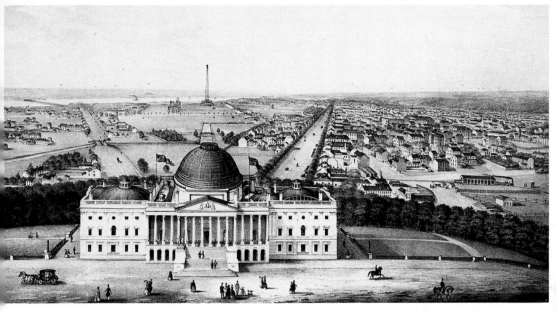

Washington from Capitol Hill around the time of the compromise debates in 1850. Visitors frequently commented that from the Hill they could see as far as Georgetown and across the Potomac River to Alexandria, Virginia. LIBRARY OF CONGRESS

Another but earlier view of the city of Washington with the Capitol on the right, during the presidency of Andrew Jackson. LIBRARY OF CONGRESS

The raccoon symbol was adopted by the Whig party in the election of 1840, and Henry Clay was subsequently known as the Old Coon or the Chief Coon. NATIONAL PORTRAIT GALLERY

The "hard featured" Lucretia Hart Clay, who rarely showed affection and, as she aged, became something of a recluse. She suffered many tragedies in her life, especially the deaths of all six daughters and two sons. FILSON CLUB

On the facing page, above: For many the golden age of debate in the U.S. Senate was when Henry Clay, Daniel Webster, John C. Calhoun, Thomas Hart Benton, and others wrestled with such momentous issues as the nature of the Union, slavery, and territorial expansion. Clay is standing in the rear. NATIONAL PORTRAIT GALLERY

On the facing page, below: This extremely popular engraving depicting the Great Pacificator delivering his famous speech in the Senate during the compromise debates of 1850 shows the Vice President, Millard Fillmore, in the chair, while John C. Calhoun stands to Fillmore's immediate left, Daniel Webster sits with his head resting on his left hand, William H. Seward is crouched at a desk at the extreme right, and Thomas Hart Benton is shown sprawled in his seat at the extreme left. NATIONAL PORTRAIT GALLERY

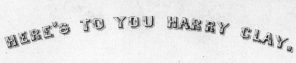

By 1844 party managers had reached the conclusion that songs and other hoopla attracted more votes than any other form of campaigning. This one was especially useful at taverns and other drinking places. NATIONAL PORTRAIT GALLERY

On the facing page: William Henry Harrison was virtually sung into the White House in the election of 1840, and this song was probably the best known during the campaign. "Tippecanoe and Tyler, Too," said the New York Whig Philip Hone, had "rhyme, but no reason in it."

TIP & TY.

A new Comic Whig Glee

Written for & dedicated to the

Democratic Whig Association

to the

BUNKER HILL CONVENTION.

New York Published by ATWILL *201 Broadway.*

O what has caused this great commotion, motion, motion, Our country

through, It is the ball that's rolling on, For Tippecanoe and Ty...ler too, For

Tippecanoe and Ty...ler too And with them we'll beat little Van, Van,

Van, Van, oh he's a used up man And with them we'll beat little Van.

"PLAIN SEWING DONE HERE"

"SYMPTOMS OF A LOCKED JAW"

This political cartoon depicting Clay sewing Jackson's mouth shut was for many years presumed to relate to the censure motion introduced in the Senate by Clay against Jackson in 1833. Actually the cartoon appeared in 1827, after Clay had published his Address in refutation of Jackson's charges about a "corrupt bargain." LIBRARY OF CONGRESS

For many Americans Henry Clay was both "a model of a man" and a "model of a statesman" who fought for liberty and the preservation of the Union against ambitious, jealous, and unprincipled politicians. Abraham Lincoln called Clay "my beau ideal of a statesman." LIBRARY OF CONGRESS

THE CLAY STATUE. A MODEL OF A MAN. DESIGNED BY THE GODDESS OF LIBERTY.

Political cartooning came of age during the Jacksonian era, and this is one of many that appeared during the presidential election of 1844 attacking the Whig ticket of Clay and Frelinghuysen. LIBRARY OF CONGRESS

Some 1844 banners proclaimed: "Henry Clay . . . Eleventh President of the United States" in bold letters and in minuscule type the words "nominated for" appeared after his name. NATIONAL PORTRAIT GALLERY

This waltz and quick step, written for the presidential election of 1844, prompted one wag to comment that William Henry Harrison had been sung into the White House and "if Mr. Clay should succeed it will be effected in some degree by dancing." NATIONAL POR-TRAIT GALLERY

Henry Clay conducted State Department business in this building at Pennsylvania Avenue and Fifteenth Street, NW. It was demolished in 1866 to complete the north wing of the present-day Treasury Department building. LIBRARY OF CONGRESS

The great triumvirate of the Senate: Prince Hal, Black Dan, and the Cast-Iron Man.
LIBRARY OF CONGRESS

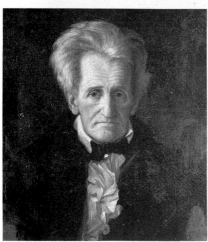

Above: Senator Thomas Hart Benton of Missouri supported Clay for the presidency when he began his career in Congress but later switched to Jackson. Big and blustery, with a booming voice, he and Clay screamed at each other during debates in Congress. "False, sir! False, sir! False, sir!" was one of Benton's frequent responses to remarks by Clay. NATIONAL PORTRAIT GALLERY

King Louis Philippe of France commissioned this oil portrait of Andrew Jackson by George P. A. Healy, and it was completed only days before Old Hickory died on June 8, 1845. Although a "perfect representation," according to one houseguest, it gave "rather the remains of the heroic personage than the full life." NATIONAL PORTRAIT GALLERY

At right: It was reported that whenever touring Americans in Italy viewed a bust of a Roman emperor or statesman, they instinctively exclaimed, "President Tyler!" NATIONAL PORTRAIT GALLERY

Daniel Webster, "Black Dan" himself, whose hypnotic stare, bushy eyebrows, bulging forehead, and especially monumental voice and matchless delivery commanded the attention and admiration of all who saw and heard him. NATIONAL PORTRAIT GALLERY

On the facing page, above: John C. Calhoun, looking handsome and youthful before disappointment, frustration, and resentment began to etch themselves into his face. Contemporaries invariably commented on his black, flashing, restless eyes. Clay jokingly called him John ("Crisis") Calhoun. NATIONAL PORTRAIT GALLERY

On the facing page, below: A nearly bald and elderly John Q. Adams in an oil painting by George Caleb Bingham, looking as crotchety, dyspeptic, and dour as his own diary frequently portrayed him. NATIONAL PORTRAIT GALLERY

None of the portraits and photographs of the Little Magician suggest his political adroitness, cunning, and managerial skills. But no doubt that is exactly how he wanted it. NATIONAL PORTRAIT GALLERY

On the facing page, above: A youthful and deceptively benign portrait of John Randolph of Roanoke by John Wesley Jarvis, circa 1811. One wag noticed, however, that a glove discreetly concealed his "pistol hand." NATIONAL PORTRAIT GALLERY

On the facing page, below: As part of his Portrait Gallery of Distinguished Americans, *published in 1845,* William Henry Brown, *"America's last great native-born silhouettist," executed this likeness of Clay in 1844. Brown frequently used paint and brush to sharpen details of his silhouettes, such as the scroll in Clay's right hand.* NATIONAL PORTRAIT GALLERY

This daguerreotype of Henry and Lucretia Clay, looking like an early version of American Gothic, *was probably taken on the couple's golden wedding anniversary, April 11, 1849.* FILSON CLUB

Theodore Wythe Clay, Henry Clay's eldest son, spent most of his adult life in this "Lunatic Asylum" in Lexington. Several of his emotional outbursts were triggered by his father's words or actions, but it is not known what they might have been. FILSON CLUB

By *1850*, *the date this lithograph was published, Louisville had become a thriving city and had developed a flourishing commercial river trade along the Ohio River.* FILSON CLUB

Clay's second son, Thomas Hart Clay, showed intellectual promise at an early age but then sank into alcoholism and indolence. Fortunately his marriage to Marie Mentelle helped him straighten out his life. FILSON CLUB

Clay's third and favorite son, Henry Clay, Jr., on whom many of the father's hopes rested. He was graduated second in his class at West Point and was killed in the Mexican War during the Battle of Buena Vista. FILSON CLUB

James Brown Clay, Clay's fourth son, who married money, served as U.S. consul in Lisbon during the Taylor administration, fought for the Confederacy, fled to Canada at war's end, and, like his father, died of tuberculosis. FILSON CLUB

The lovely city of Lexington, Kentucky, Clay's hometown, circa 1855–1856. All that is wanting "to make it a paradise," wrote one contemporary, "is the prospect of lakes, rivers, and mountains." FILSON CLUB

Ashland, Clay's stately home, built around 1809 and located one mile east of Lexington on six hundred cultivated acres, except for two hundred acres of park, where Clay raised hemp, rye, wheat, and other products and bred horses and Durham cattle "of the finest stock." The mansion was constructed of such inferior materials that within fifty years it had to be pulled down and rebuilt. FILSON CLUB

The drawing room at Ashland as it appears today. Visitors during Clay's lifetime frequently commented on several items in this room, including a bust of Theodore Frelinghuysen, a picture of Washington and His Family, *family portraits, and a "splendid large cut-glass vase standing upon a center table."* CLINE COMPANY

The dining room at Ashland as it appears today. CLINE COMPANY

Clay's library, the most beautiful room in Ashland. Octagonally shaped and paneled with ash and walnut, it has a dome ceiling to provide greater illumination. CLINE COMPANY

The master bedroom at Ashland as it appears today, with Clay's "Conversation Chair" in the foreground. CLINE COMPANY

Clay provided a testimonial to William Bell of Lexington, the maker of his bed. He admired the fact that it had been "put together without screws," and he pronounced it greatly superior to those in common use at the time. Moreover, it hardly ever required "any precaution to destroy bugs," he said, as it "affords no place of retreat to them." CLINE COMPANY

Conically shaped icehouses with walls extending sixteen feet underground, built by Clay shortly after he retired as secretary of state. CLINE COMPANY

This carriage was given to Clay by the citizens of Newark, New Jersey and is on display today in the carriage house adjacent to the Ashland mansion. CLINE COMPANY

Clay's passport to travel to Cuba with his servant James Marshall, issued on March 8, 1851, and signed by the secretary of state, Daniel Webster. It is interesting that a physical description of Clay is provided but nothing is said about Marshall except that he was "a free colored person." FILSON CLUB

Clay reportedly gave this fine daguerreotype by Frederick Debourg Richards, circa 1852, to the Norwegian violinist and composer Ole Bull. It has only recently become available to the public and may be seen in the National Portrait Gallery in Washington, D.C.
NATIONAL PORTRAIT GALLERY

A NATIONAL EPICEDIUM,

UPON THE

DEATH OF HENRY CLAY.

The Nation is called upon, by an inscrutable Providence, to mourn the loss of her great Statesman,—the Man of the Age,—whose superior efforts repeatedly effected a reconciliation of contending elements, and prevented the demolition of our Union.

He was the man who contributed so largely to American renown, throughout the world, and his name will be breathed with pride and affection while the principles of our Government endure, or their existence is remembered.

Born in Hanover County, Virginia, April 12, 1777—Died at Washington, June 29, 1852, aged 75 years.

To-day, his wing the eagle droops, and flies
 From sun-burnt crag, on vast mid-heaven peak,
With mournful sluggishness and sudden cries,
 And bitter sorrow in his startling shriek !
He falls, a smitten bird, to shades beneath,
 Where rays gleam not through the beclouded air,—
And I do hear, o'er the Golgothan heath,
 A cry, that tells grim Death has trodden there !

Heave, sorrowed breast ! and ye, mine eyelids, droop !
 A Nation mourns, and I must also weep !
And ye, his friends, uncovered, come and stoop,
 Where lies this John Patriot, in his deathly sleep !—
Toll, mournful bells ! and pierce the air, ye sounds—
 Ye doleful sounds, that speak such tones of woe !
And flash, ye lightnings ! to your utmost bounds,
 And bear the solemn tidings to and fro !

He sunk with quiet slowness, to his rest,
 And calmly knelt, at Death's approach, to bow ;
The Foeman hurled a barb into his breast,
 But peaceful still remained the victim's brow.
The great old man is dead ! and there he fell,
 Where he had stood triumphant many years ;
And now all men his glorious story tell,
 Ceasing, at times, to shed their grateful tears.

Sprung humbly from a non-historic stock,
 That boasts not blood, but true untrammeled soul,
He struck out fire from life's rugged rock,
 And kindled glory from the self-lit coal !
And, when a boy, he mused, upon his way,
 Athwart the *Slashes*, to the ancient *mill*,
Who knows what angel sent a friendly ray,
 To start the growth of his ambitious will !

He was ambitious for his Country's sake,
 Nor deemed it ill, himself to immolate
Upon her altar, though she would not take
 A sacrifice so Roman and so great !
Often has he with an heroic pride,
 Stood up to plead for Unity of Men,
Attracting patriot millions to his side,
 And binding them with charm of tongue and pen !

His arm the Nation's dignity upheld,
 His voice its glorious majesty proclaimed ;
He calmed the strife, when troublous ones rebelled,
 And for his Country's greatest glory aimed.
The learned called him *Cicero*, in speech,
 The People hailed him *Father*, like to him
Who plucked their Freedom from tyrannic reach,
 And sleeps 'n Fame that Time shall never dim !

His were the soul and mind, that planned,
 And brought forth peace, amid fraternal strife,
Checking dissensions in his native land,
 And breathing durance to Columbia's life !—
And die the man—how godlike in such days !—
 When gazed at by unnumbered eager eyes,
Who did that deed, unflattered by all praise,
 That saved our States upon a COMPROMISE !

And erst when moans of woe from bleeding GREECE,
 Whose butchered patriots bled in Scio's dust,
Came piteously beseeching for release
 From Turkish chains, rapacity and lust ;
He plead her cause, with eloquence sublime,
 And, linked in heart with granite WEBSTER, he
Was champion for Mankind of every clime,
 Whose heroes fought to make the People free !

Not sword in hand, did he ascend the height,
 Whose boughs of laurel bent to touch his head,
Nor won he honor by the flickering light
 Of burning towns, amid bemangled dead !
But by a greater path he rose on high,
 And grasped a quill the eagle's pinion from ;
Then wrote upon the star-bespangled sky,
 A glory to endure all age to come !

The grey-haired Sage of Ashland !—he is gone !
 No classic god more nobly passed away ;
And young Ambition, while the world rolls on,
 Shall strive to live and die *like* HENRY CLAY !
Heave, sorrowed breast ! and ye mine eyelids, droop
 Sad music peals his dirge—a Nation weeps !
O, ye his countrymen ! uncovered, come and stoop,
 Where lies this Patriot in his deathly sleep !

Hanzsche & Bro., Print., 21? Baltimore st.

BY J. F. WEISHAMPEL, JR.

Published and sold, wholesale and retail, at the Cheap Book Store, 264 Pratt Street, between Howard and Eutaw, Baltimore. Copy-righted.

The grief of the nation over the death of the "grey-haired Sage of Ashland" produced countless funeral odes, like this one.

A daguerreotype of Clay's funeral cortege taken outside Ashland on July 10, 1852.
HENRY CLAY MEMORIAL FOUNDATION

The general congressional elections in the fall of 1829 should have given Clay pause about the public mood. But as always he chose to look on the bright side. "Altho' the issue of the elections this fall is not as good as we could have wished, throughout the Union," he wrote to Peter B. Porter, "I see nothing in it to discourage." Why? Because the last presidential election was still too fresh in everyone's mind and the next too distant to cause the people to think seriously about it. With the new congressional session beginning in early December, and with the announcement of the administration's policy in the President's first message to Congress, there will be marked changes, he predicted, and they will "benefit our cause."[28]

And happily, there were other unexpected and recent events to "benefit our cause." The growing rivalry between Vice President Calhoun and Secretary of State Van Buren had become common gossip in Washington, which several friends regularly relayed to Clay. The question of the presidential succession lay at the heart of the rivalry, and the infighting in the cabinet already reflected the emerging competition between the South Carolinian and the New Yorker. Worse, a "petticoat war" had broken out among the wives of the cabinet members over the question of paying social court to the "notorious" Peggy O'Neal Timberlake Eaton, the wife of Secretary of War John H. Eaton. The morals of Mrs. Eaton occasioned any number of lewd comments[29] by Washington politicians, both National Republicans and Democrats, and many believed that Floride Calhoun, wife of the Vice President, led the fight to exclude Peggy from society. "You may think this Very strange," Clay was told, "that the admission of a certain Female into respectable Society at Washington should be made the basis of political orthodoxy . . . but strange as it may appear it is, no less Strange than true, Mr Van Buren has been the friend of this unfortunate Lady and has made every exertion to get her into Society . . . but the current of Female opposition could not be steme'd. . . . Such is the State of parties at Washington."[30]

Clay reveled in this delicious gossip. To his mind it only proved everything he had been saying about Jackson's incompetence and stupidity. That a constitutional crisis could develop within a matter of months over a question of female morality struck Clay as ludicrous. If only "the incompetency which he [Jackson] exhibits was as well known every where as it is at Washn," wrote Clay, the nation would turn from him in disgust.[31]

The President's first message to Congress in early December added to Clay's growing confidence about the certainty of defeating the general at the next election. In the message Jackson proposed that the tariff be modified to

28. Clay to Porter, November 22, 1829, in Clay, *Papers*, VIII, 128.

29. "Eaton has just married his mistress," wrote Louis McLane, "and the mistress of eleven doz. others." McLane to James A. Bayard, February 19, 1829, Bayard Papers, LC.

30. Robert P. Letcher to Clay, December 21, 26, 1829, Josiah S. Johnston to Clay, December, 1829, John Vance to Clay, December 28, 1829, in Clay, *Papers*, VIII, 158–160, 163–164, 164.

31. Clay to Jesse B. Harrison, January 3, 1830, Clay to James Brown, April 17, 1830, in Clay, *Papers*, VIII, 167, 192.

eliminate the "abominations" of the 1828 law; he explained his "rotation of office" policy, by which he expected to "reform and purify" the departments of government; he urged the removal of the Indians; and lastly, he wanted a modification of the present charter of the United States Bank, which was due to expire in 1836, because, he said, it had failed to establish a sound and uniform currency.[32]

After reading the message, Clay wrote immediately to Nicholas Biddle, president of the Bank, and congratulated him on the "public disapprobation" expressed by the President. "On two points you have reason to be thankful for the notice which was taken of you," he wrote. "It was premature; and . . . cannot fail to redound to your advantage." The President's "proscriptive system, under the delusive name of Reform," he told another, would surely open the eyes of the American public to the walking disaster that now presided over the affairs of the nation. As for the tariff, will it not provoke a "storm" in Congress? "Or shall we all be disappointed in that respect?"[33]

The Jackson administration seemed to be playing directly into Clay's hands by providing needed ammunition to help him reorganize and revitalize the National Republican party in support of his presidential bid four years hence. To further this advantage and stimulate party activity, Clay began thinking of touring the country with a trip to the South and another to New York and New England.

But these emerging plans were temporarily suspended by a series of tragedies that required his immediate attention. On November 25, 1829, Clay's stepfather, Henry Watkins, died after a short illness. Clay's mother was still alive but very feeble, and, said the son, "I fear will soon follow him." Clay offered to take her to Ashland to live with him, but she preferred to stay with her daughter, Patsy Watkins Blackburn, Clay's half sister. Ten days later she died at the age of eighty.[34] At about the same time Clay's eldest brother, John Clay, also died while descending the Mississippi River aboard a steamer. "It has thus pleased Providence to visit our family with severe afflictions," Clay lamented to his son.[35]

Despite these afflictions, Clay decided to go ahead at least with his plan for a trip to the South, a section of the country not particularly happy with his American System. Without touring the region extensively, he thought a short stay in Mississippi and Louisiana would give him a better feel for the political climate in the lower South and the extent of its opposition to the tariff and

32. Richardson, *Messages and Papers,* II, 1010ff.

33. Clay to Biddle, January 2, 1830, Clay to Jesse B. Harrison, January 3, 1830, Clay to Edward Everett, January 3, 1830, in Clay, *Papers,* VIII, 166, 167, 166.

34. Elizabeth Clay Watkins was buried in the country graveyard near her home, but in 1851 her son Henry moved her remains to the Lexington cemetery. Her tombstone reads: "Elizabeth Watkins Formerly Elizabeth Clay Born 1750 Died 1829. This monument, a tribute to her many domestic virtues Has been prompted by the filial affection and veneration of one of her grateful sons H. CLAY."

35. Clay to Henry Clay, Jr., December 2, 23, 1829, in Clay, *Papers,* VIII, 131, 160–161.

internal improvements. He had in mind a visit to his only surviving daughter, Anne Brown Clay Erwin, who was living in New Orleans, and his sons-in-law James Erwin and Martin Duralde. He decided to leave home around the middle of January and return about mid-March. His health was generally better— certainly better than it had been during his stay in Washington—but it still required care and attention, and this constituted another reason for limiting his travel.

As soon as he made up his mind to visit Louisiana, he wrote to Senator Josiah Johnston and explained his plans and intentions. "Tell me," he said, "how I can serve you whilst there, who is to be soothed, who to be won, to the support of your re-election. Whatever I can do on that subject, with propriety, shall be done."[36] And who could resist Clay's extraordinary ability to soothe and win? Who could resist his "fascination"?

Clay thoroughly enjoyed his short holiday. His journey down the Mississippi proved uneventful, and he remained almost entirely in New Orleans and its immediate neighborhood, venturing beyond on only two occasions. "I have been treated, throughout, with the greatest respect and attention," he wrote. Indeed, his visit was "attended with the highest gratification." When he appeared before the Louisiana legislature, the entire body, without distinction of party, including the Speaker, spontaneously rose to receive him. He was also invited to public dinners in Memphis, Vicksburg, Port Gibson, Natchez, and Baton Rouge and declined all of them except Natchez. And all these demonstrations, of course, misled him about his availability.[37]

He was relieved to find his daughter, grandchildren, and sons-in-law in excellent health. His grandson Henry Clay Erwin "talks quite plain," he reported, and his grandson James Erwin, Jr., "runs about every where and begins to say a few words." Duralde seemed relatively well-to-do, "and if he lives will become excessively opulent." Erwin, too, showed "great affluence, and has much capacity for business." Erwin and Clay considered purchasing a sugar plantation together but finally decided against it because of the likelihood of a slide in sugar prices. However, Clay did purchase a five-acre plot along the Mississippi River across from Baton Rouge.[38]

During his southern tour he went partying almost every night. He gambled at whist, danced with the ladies, gossiped about politics, drank more than he should, and generally had a smashing good time. Several of the ladies he met during this visit became lifelong friends.

The second week in March he traveled to Natchez, where he delivered a widely reported speech in the Mississippi Hotel. An enormous number of

36. Clay to Christopher Hughes, December 25, 1829, Clay to Josiah S. Johnston, December 25, 31, 1829, Clay to Daniel Webster, January 6, 1830, in Clay, *Papers*, VIII, 162, 165, 168.

37. Clay to Josiah Johnston, February 27, 1830, Clay to Philip R. Fendall, March 30, 1830, Clay to James Brown, April 17, 1830, in Clay, *Papers*, VIII, 177–178, 185, 192.

38. Anne Erwin to Clay, May 15, 1830, Clay to James Brown, April 17, 1830, Clay to James Erwin, March 14, 1830, in Clay, *Papers*, VIII, 206, 192, 181.

people crowded into the building, almost equaling the number that had honored General Lafayette a few years earlier. In the speech Clay made a handsome reference to Jackson's victory at New Orleans at the close of the War of 1812, and he also alluded to his own role as peace commissioner in Ghent. He obviously sought to portray himself as a statesman in retirement, above the clamor of partisan politics. He spoke of the American System, particularly the tariff, and insisted that it would do no harm to southerners despite arguments raised in Congress to the contrary. Has the consumption of cotton diminished since the passage of the tariffs of 1824 and 1828? he asked. "No, it has increased—greatly increased; and why? Because the protection extended by this policy has created a *new customer* in the American manufacturer."[39]

One Natchez merchant was so enchanted by Clay that he bolted the front gate to his estate, Mount Repose, and swore he would never open it until Clay was elected President. Unfortunately he was later required to build a new entrance.[40]

Throughout his tour Clay played the role of elder statesman to near perfection, so much so that even Jacksonians came to hear him and pay their respects. "Not an incident occurred at one of the largest public dinners that I ever assisted at, indoors, to mar the general satisfaction," he claimed. "I found myself there in the midst of equal numbers of both parties, with a Jackson man on my right and an Adams man on my left."[41]

"Nothing could surpass the warmth of my reception in Mississippi," Clay joyfully communicated to Senator Johnston. Then, the day following a dinner and ball given in his honor on March 13, in which both National Republicans and Democrats "vied with each other in their testimonies of respect," he started his homeward journey, ascending the river on the steamboat *G. Washington* and arriving home on March 26. He brought with him his seven-year-old grandson Henry C. Duralde, whom he pronounced "a fine sprightly boy." His wife, Lucretia, had not accompanied him on the trip, but he found her "cheerful and happy," especially since William Martin, the new overseer he had engaged before he left, proved to be an excellent choice. Martin, said Clay, "fulfilled all my hopes, and has put Ashland in better condition that I ever saw it at this early season of the year."[42]

The trip enormously encouraged Clay to pursue his ambitions for the presidency. By late March all doubts and hesitations about running had completely vanished. But he still could not say so openly. He knew he must be careful how he shared his decision with others. Thus, when asked by the public

39. *Niles' Weekly Register,* April 17, 1830.

40. This is a widely told tale in Natchez and was related to me by Kenneth P'Pool of the Mississippi Department of Archives and History.

41. Clay to Philip Fendall, March 30, 1830, in Clay, *Papers,* VIII, 185.

42. Clay to Johnson, March 25, 1830, Clay to Henry Clay, Jr., March 29, 1830, in Clay, *Papers,* VIII, 183, 184–185. Clay informed Johnston that the senator's reelection seemed certain, and indeed, his prediction was later confirmed.

about his intentions—and he was asked constantly—he responded with unbecoming coyness. He usually started off by saying that he was more and more attached to rural life and that it would take little for him to "renounce for ever the strife of public life." That out of the way, he then allowed that the decision about his running ought to rest with others. They could best judge when and how his name should be brought forward, if indeed it should be brought forward at all. And, he continued, "I am prepared to acquiesce in their will, whatever it may be." Some wanted him to wait before coming out with a declaration, but Clay thought that the conclusion of the present session of Congress provided a splendid moment to begin "such movements" as to draw all opponents of the administration together behind a National Republican presidential ticket.[43]

By this time Clay had convinced himself that he could carry Louisiana "against any one" and Mississippi "against anyone but Jackson." Then, if Virginia, Pennsylvania, and New York could unite behind him, he would carry the election.[44]

The following month Clay edged out a little farther. "If it be deemed expedient to present my name as a Candidate," he told Senator Johnston, the question of where and how it ought to be done will immediately arise. Clay thought that it should commence in the West, "*quickly* followed in New England." The thought had occurred to his friends, he said, that the process should start in Kentucky with a series of "popular nominations" in various counties immediately after Congress adjourned. This would "excite a spirit among the people" and result in an immediate victory in the August elections. "If we mean to act," he added, we must not delay because of the uncertainty in which it will leave our friends. "Already I am frequently spoken to and some times have been written to know if I am a Candidate. Of course, I give but one answer, which is that I shall never present myself as a Candidate."[45]

To Daniel Webster he declared that the National Republican party had three courses of action now open to it: abandon all opposition to Jackson's reelection, assuming he will run again; "hoist our banner and proclaim . . . our candidate"; or wait until the next session of Congress. The ultimate decision, as far he was concerned, rested with "my friends at Washington."[46]

Although he had kept open the possibility of taking other trips around the country, particularly to New York and New England, Clay changed his mind in early May because he felt they would look like open electioneering. Nothing could be gained from them, he added, and they would surely provoke resentment. Lately he had received numerous invitations that, in effect, would have initiated his campaign. "I have no intention of visiting the North or any other

43. Clay to Samuel Barnes, March 29, 1830, in Clay, *Papers*, VIII, 183–184.
44. Clay to Francis Brooke, April 19, 1830, in Clay, *Papers*, VIII, 194.
45. Clay to Johnston, April 30, 1830, in Clay, *Papers*, VIII, 199.
46. Clay to Webster, April 29, 1830, in Webster, *Papers, Correspondence*, III, 63–64.

place this summer, with any political object," he told Francis Brooke. "My own judgment is decided that I ought to . . . remain at home. Should I make any excursions this summer they will relate entirely to business or to my health." Daniel Webster agreed: "I advise you, as you will be much watched, *to stay at home.*"

Others disagreed. Peter B. Porter begged Clay to take his "long contemplated" visit to New York. It would provide a splendid opportunity, he said, to speak to the question of his membership in the Masonic order. In view of the developing Anti-Masonic fervor in the state, Clay needed to address the problem directly. "I have told them that you are a Mason," wrote Porter, "but that like most others of the old and most intelligent Members, you are not disposed to rate very highly the present usefullness or importance of the Institution. . . . That therefore you . . . for a number of years past ceased to take any active part in the transactions of the Society."[47]

Clay made his excuses to Porter about not honoring the plea and then stated his position on Masonry, reminding his friend that no opinion or explanation on the subject should be "communicated *as coming from me.*" He added:

> In regard to Masonry, I have heretofore freely expressed my feelings to you. I never was a bright mason. I never attached much importance to Masonry. In my youth I occasionally attended the Lodges prompted more by the social than the masonic principle. But I have long ceased to attend the Lodges, and have not been a regular member of one for many years. I never made a difference in my life, in any private transaction, or on any public occasion, between those who belonged to the fraternity and those who did not. I never entered a lodge in Europe. I do not recollect ever communicating myself as a Mason to any man in my life. I believe Masonry practically does neither much good nor harm. After saying this much, I must add that I would not renounce or denounce Masonry to be made President of the U.S. not from any force of any obligation which I stand under to it, but from the force of a much higher obligation that of honor.[48]

It had been Clay's original intention to visit Porter's home in Black Rock, as well as Saratoga, and then go on to New England. But all that had now changed. He used the excuse that his daughter, Anne Erwin, planned to visit him in a few weeks, along with several new Louisiana friends. The decision necessarily cost him a visit with his son Henry Clay, Jr., who was completing his studies at West Point. "I had hoped to be able to visit you this summer," he wrote his son, "but I now fear it will not be in my power."

The change in plans truly distressed him. Henry, Jr., was the boy in whom he had such great hope and who elicited his greatest love. Thomas Hart Clay constantly disappointed and upset him. The young man had gone to see his

47. Porter to Clay, May 23, 1830, in Clay, *Papers,* VIII, 212–213. See also Robert O. Rupp, "Parties and the Public Good: Political Antimasonry in New York Reconsidered," *Journal of the Early Republic,* VIII (Fall 1988), 253–279.
48. Clay to Porter, June 13, 1830, in Clay, *Papers,* VIII, 223.

father's 137-acre farm, called Clay's Prairie, on the Illinois side of the Wabash River near Terre Haute, with the idea of settling upon it if he liked it. But the father had "very bad accounts of his habits. I despair of him." And Theodore was worse. He now lived with his parents, and although he did not drink to excess as did his brother, wrote the father to Henry, Jr., "he has other habits almost as bad. He has the most unfortunate temper that ever afflicted any person, and seems soured with all the world." Then Clay burst out: "Oh! my dear Son no language can describe to you the pain that I have suffered on account of these two boys. My hopes rest with you and your two younger brothers," James and John.[49]

Although Clay wisely decided against a northern tour, he did begin to take a sharper look at what was happening in Washington and passed along to his congressional friends suggestions on appropriate responses to presidential misbehavior. For example, he thought it outrageous that the Senate had not "better fulfilled its high duties incident to the power of appointment." Senators ought to have rejected all of Jackson's appointments that replaced persons dismissed for political cause, all replacements of those approved at the last session, and "most of the printers, and most of the members of Congress."[50]

Jackson provided Clay with additional ammunition when he sent a ringing veto of an internal improvements bill back to Congress. It was a bill to extend the National Road from Maysville to Lexington, Kentucky, and Jackson claimed it was an imprudent expenditure of money. Moreover, he worried whether a system of internal improvements ought to be undertaken without a prior amendment to the Constitution that would explain and define the precise power of the federal government over it. This extension of the National Road ran totally within the state of Kentucky and strict constructionists argued that the federal government must not involve itself in small public works that were entirely local in their purpose and usefulness. This Maysville veto stopped just short of denying federal power over internal improvements. It did, however, affirm the right of Congress to appropriate money for defense and other national interests, but that was all.[51]

Jackson's Kentucky friends warned him that this veto would provide Clay with a weapon to harm them all. But the President stood his ground. "There is no money [in the Treasury] to be expended as my friends desire," he replied to one of them. "Now, I stand committed before the Country to pay off the National Debt . . . and I cannot do this if I consent to increase it without necessity. Are you willing—are my friends willing to lay taxes to pay for inter-

49. Clay to Edward Everett, May 6, 1830, Clay to Henry Clay, Jr., December 2, 1829, May 24, 1830, in Clay, Papers, VIII, 202, 131–132, 213. In June Clay gave Theodore the alternative of becoming a farmer and grazier or a cotton planter as the young man started off on an exploring expedition to Indiana, Illinois, and Missouri. Clay to Henry Clay, Jr., June 30, 1830, ibid., VIII, 231.
50. Clay to Webster, April 29, 1830, in Webster, Papers, Correspondence, III, 62.
51. Richardson, Messages and Papers, II, 1046–1055.

nal improvements?—for be assured I will not borrow a cent except in cases of absolute necessity."

Borrow money? "No," said the Kentucky Democrat, "that would be worse than a *veto* !"[52]

Clay was livid over the Maysville veto and deeply disappointed that the bill had been killed. He knew, of course, that the votes did not exist to override it in Congress. He therefore proposed to Daniel Webster and several others that the Constitution be amended to reduce the President's veto power. Interestingly, Clay chose to amend the Constitution respecting presidential power rather than state and define the right to authorize internal improvements. "We are all shocked and mortified by the rejection of the Maysville road," he told another friend. "Meetings of the people are contemplated. . . . At these meetings . . . public sentiment may be expressed, in terms of strong disapprobation of the act of the President. 2dy. in favor of Int. improvements . . . [and] proposing an amendmt. to the Constitution substituting a majority of all the members elected to Congress, instead of two thirds to pass a bill returned by the President." Such an amendment, he said, was quite within the spirit of our institutions. It was the right thing to do.

Clay also appreciated the political capital he would gain because of the veto, especially in the West, but that was only "a collateral consideration," he declared, in advancing "our cause." There was principle involved. "We shall be contending against a principle which wears a monarchical aspect, whilst our opponents will be placed in the unpopular attitude to defending it."[53]

At approximately the same time that Jackson vetoed the Maysville Road bill he also signed the Indian Removal Act, which began the process of removing the southern tribes of Indians west of the Mississippi River. Once again Clay spotted another issue with which to condemn and pillory the administration. "In regard to that most flagitious measure (the Indian bill)," he growled, it "threatens to bring a foul and lasting stain upon the good faith, humanity and character of the Nation." He therefore proposed the withholding of appropriations to carry the "abominable law" into effect and that the Senate reject all treaties brought before it that involved Indian removal. "If such a course should be deemed advisable, the violation of treaties existing, the upsetting of our Indian System, as it has been established from the commencement of our Independence, the inhumanity of the Indian law, its enormous expense, its interference with internal improvements, ought all to be set forth in vivid and striking colors." Public meetings should be assembled, he wrote, "resolutions passed, and our members of Congress instructed &c." If the Indians remain firm and refuse to enter treaty negotiations, "I believe they will ultimately be successful." Public opinion is with them, he said; "justice is on their

52. Van Buren, *Autobiography,* p. 324.
53. Clay to Webster, June 7, 1830, in Webster, *Papers, Correspondence,* III, 80–82; Clay to Adam Beatty, June 8, 1830, Clay to James F. Conover, June 13, 1830, in Clay, *Papers,* VIII, 220–221, 222.

side; honor, humanity, the national character, and our Holy religion all plead for them. With such advocates they ought to prevail, and they will prevail, if their friends are not too inactive."[54]

Obviously Henry Clay had come a long way since his remark in the Adams cabinet about how the disappearance of the Indian would be no great loss to the world. In just a few short years he had completely reversed himself on the subject. Now honor, religion, humanity, and religion all cried out for Indian protection. It would seem that Clay's change of heart resulted, to a considerable extent, from Jackson's espousal of removal and from the indignant protests against it from some religious groups around the country. Indian removal might prove a valuable campaign issue, and Clay joined in demands that the policy be nullified.

One final development in Washington also played into Clay's outstretched hand, and that was a dinner given to honor the memory of Thomas Jefferson at which President Jackson proposed a toast. "Our Union," he said. *"It must be preserved."* The toast was meant to convey Jackson's rejection and horror of the doctrine of nullification proposed by Vice President Calhoun and articulated several months later by Robert Y. Hayne in his famous debate with Daniel Webster on the Senate floor. This doctrine advanced the theory that a state retained the right to nullify any federal law within its boundaries that conflicted with the interests of the state. If three-fourths of all the states also nullified the offending legislation, then the law was repealed, just as if the Constitution itself had been amended. But if, after applying the doctrine of nullification, the state was coerced by the federal government, then the state had the right to secede from the Union. However, secession was meant as a last resort. The doctrine of nullification, said Calhoun, was intended to prevent secession.[55]

The "farce" of the Jefferson dinner in Washington, argued Clay, clearly indicated the future direction of the Democratic party. "It is to cry down all constructions of the Constitution; to cry up State rights; to make all Mr. Jeffersons opinions the articles of faith of the new Church; to hold out the notion of preserving the Union by conciliating the South, and to catch popularity by repealing Taxes &c." It marks the course of Democratic attack on the tariff and internal improvements. Well, he continued, it is fortunate that we know the plan of their campaign, and we ought to plan our own to defeat them. "We ought to recommend the repeal of all taxes that can be dispensed with on objects which do not come in competition with native products. To contend that the sacrifice of our American System is to propitiate G. Britain as well as the South. That to surrender it to the South is to sacrifice the great

54. Clay to Conover, June 13, 1830, Clay to Edward Everett, June 16, 1830, Clay to Jeremiah Evarts, August 23, 1830, in Clay, *Papers,* VIII, 222, 226, 255.
55. For full details of the Jefferson dinner, see Remini, *Jackson,* II, 233–236. On nullification, see Calhoun's "Exposition and Protest," in Calhoun, *Papers,* X, 445ff., and the biographies of Calhoun by Charles Wiltse and John Niven.

principle that a majority ought to govern; and to sacrifice the interests of three fourths of the Union to those of the remaining fourth &c &c."[56]

So Clay now had his complete platform, which he reviewed with a number of his political friends as he made his availability increasingly obvious. All the "planks" of his platform reemphasized Jackson's lack of statesmanship or inability to understand the crucial issues facing the nation. First, said Clay, there was the "failure" of Jackson's political appointments and the rejection by the Senate of some of them, such as Isaac Hill of New Hampshire and Henry Lee of Virginia. Then the President's "wild project of a bank; the Jefferson dinner; the Indian subject; [and] the attack on the Tariff." At other times Clay included support "of Int. improvements . . . [and] Against the nullifying doctrines of the South."

In all his political letters Clay railed most particularly against the Maysville veto. "He has lost the whole West, I verily believe," Clay declared. "The old buck is mortally wounded. He will run awhile, make a shew of vigor and fall." Thus by late spring Clay was telling his Kentucky associates that his friends in Washington had expressed "the most perfect confidence . . . in the success of our cause. They believe, if I live, that I will be elected against *any Competitor.*" Indeed, Senator Josiah Johnston of Louisiana assured Clay that when Congress adjourned, "our friends separated . . . with a full understanding, that you Would be the Candidate. & that that fact should be fully made known to the people."[57]

Throughout the summer of 1830 Clay received many expressions of support, and several correspondents asked for instructions on their future actions. He warned off his New England friends from taking the lead in providing a formal nomination. "Yet I believe the time for Legislative action," he continued, "will have arrived at the approaching winter Sessions." In the past we waited for our opponents to initiate the campaign, he said. "Henceforth, our flag should be unfurled, and we should march to the victory, which awaits us, with a prompt, fearless, and confident, step."[58]

And he really believed this. He had no conception of Jackson's phenomenal popularity with the American people. As always he was completely blind to the political reality that contradicted his belief that the American people would surely reward him for his outstanding services to the nation.

56. Clay to Conover, May 1, 1830, in Clay, *Papers,* VIII, 200.

57. Clay to John C. Wright, May 31, 1830, Clay to Adam Beatty, May 4, June 8, 1830, Clay to Francis Brooke, June 16, 1830, Clay to Thomas Speed, June 25, 1830, Clay to Johnston, June 20, 1830, in Clay, *Papers,* VIII, 217, 201, 220, 224, 230, 227.

58. Clay to Alexander H. Everett, August 14, 1830, in Clay, *Papers,* VIII, 249–250.

TWENTY-ONE

Presidential Nominee

O F PARTICULAR CONCERN to Clay as he moved steadily toward claiming the presidential nomination of the National Republican party was the growing "menace" of Anti-Masonry. The movement had intruded on the previous presidential election, but as his New York lieutenants repeatedly told him, it was only an "acorn" two years ago. Now it was a strong young tree. These lieutenants kept urging him to make a public statement about his membership in the organization—or repudiate it outright.

Clay would do neither. He absolutely refused to "renounce or denounce" Masonry to gain votes. That was a matter of honor to him.[1]

Supposedly Clay had left the Lexington Masonic Lodge on November 18, 1824. At least that was what the secretary of the lodge later published as a notice in *Niles' Weekly Register* on January 7, 1832. Whether he did or not,[2] Clay felt quite strongly that neither Masonry nor Anti-Masonry should be mixed up in national politics. What can a Masonic or Anti-Masonic President constitutionally do to promote the views of either group? he asked. Where in the Constitution is the power to put down or sustain Masonry? "The Sunday school, or Missionary or temperance or Colonization Societies might each as well attempt to elect a President upon the distinct ground of his attachment to one of those institutions." Clay also made it clear to his New York supporters that no explanation of his position be advanced in order to placate the Anti-Masons.[3]

---

1. See especially Richard Rush's letters to Clay, in Clay, *Papers,* VIII, 353ff. Said Clay: "I have been urged, entreated, importuned to make some declaration, short of renunciation of Masonry, which would satisfy the Anti's." Clay to Francis Brooke, June 23, 1831, ibid., VIII, 363. See also Clay to Colonel W. L. Stone, March 19, 1832, Miscellaneous Clay Papers, Manuscript Department, Filson Club, Louisville, Kentucky.

2. Clay was buried in 1852 with full Masonic honors under the Masonic ritual.

3. Clay to Porter, June 13, 1830, Clay to Joseph Gales, Jr., August 2, 1831, in Clay, *Papers,* VIII, 223, 381. Clay later said that he became a Mason in early life "from youthful curiosity and a social disposition." Clay to Emanuel C. Reigart, November 25, 1843, ibid., IX, 892. See also Clay to Jonathan Thompson, July 25, 1831, Clay Papers, Manuscript Department, Filson Club, Louisville, Kentucky.

In advising his New York friends on the question, Clay suggested that they allow the Anti-Masons the "right" to nominate a candidate for governor but not candidates for presidential electors; at the same time—as compensation, so to speak—he recommended that the National Republicans have the "right" to put forward a ticket for presidential electors but no candidate for governor. "Then the two parties would naturally unite," he brightly added. Naturally such an arrangement would benefit him personally, but he let that pass. "A conciliatory course on our part, toward the Anti-Masons, is wisest." Do not attack them. Leave that to the Democrats.[4]

Besides Anti-Masonry, what troubled Clay was the developing assault by the administration on his American System, starting with internal improvements and soon to include the Bank of the United States and the tariff. He wrote to Nicholas Biddle and repeated a rumor he had heard from his friends in Virginia that an attack on the Bank had been hatched in Richmond last autumn by Martin Van Buren during his visit to that city and would be the basis of the campaign for the next presidential election. Under the circumstances Clay advised the Bank's president against an early application for a renewal of the Bank's charter, due to expire in 1836. If you apply when Congress reconvenes, Clay told Biddle, "you will play into the hands" of those in the opposition. They will argue that the present charter still has a number of years to run and that therefore, there is no necessity to take action now. Moreover, they will contend that the public needs more time to consider the pros and cons of the question. Congress, always prone to procrastinate, will duck the issue. Meanwhile, the Democratic press will be marshaled to excite prejudices and appeal to every passion imaginable. Even were Congress to pass a recharter, the President would most certainly veto it, and the result would be an appeal to voters in the next presidential election. It would undoubtedly become "the controlling question in American politics."

But if recharter is delayed, continued Clay, when should it be brought forward? "I think," he said, answering his own question, "the Session immediately after the next Presidential election would be the most proper time. Then every thing will be fresh," the election over, "and there will be a disposition to afford the *new*[5] administration" the right to resolve the matter.

But suppose Jackson was reelected? If that happens, Clay continued, "he will have probably less disposition than he now has to avail himself of any prejudices against the Bank." He will also have less influence since he will be a lame duck. In sum, then, it was most unwise to go to Congress without something like a certainty of success, and it would be better to make application at the "first moment of calm" following the approaching presidential storm.[6]

4. Clay to Porter, November 21, 1830, Clay to John M. Bailhache, November 24, 1830, in Clay, *Papers,* VIII, 302, 304. His suggestion about the two electoral tickets fell on deaf ears.
5. Italics mine.
6. Clay to Biddle, June 14, September 11, November 3, 1830, in Clay, *Papers,* VIII, 223–224, 264, 287–288.

This is a very curious piece of advice that Clay offered Biddle, for after having locked up the presidential nomination of the National Republican party, he reversed himself totally. Obviously he predicated his advice solely on his presidential plans. For the moment delay seemed best. A year later he had just as many reasons to argue in favor of immediate action.

By the fall of 1830 Clay had begun talking seriously about the propriety of calling a national nominating convention to select the candidate of the National Republican party. There had been considerable speculation about convening such a convention, but it had never been tried before, at least not to nominate a presidential candidate. Anti-Masons had already announced their intention of holding a convention in September 1831 in Baltimore, in order to construct their ticket. Many National Republicans favored the idea, but not to select their presidential candidate since they believed they already had one in Clay. They simply wanted to use it to generate excitement for his candidacy as well as to pick his running mate. General enthusiasm for a convention prompted the Washington *National Intelligencer* on February 17, 1831, to recommend that one be held the following December in Baltimore, so that it could be near Washington. Almost instantly the suggestion found wide support from numerous states.[7]

Clay favored such a meeting because it was "essentially a proceeding of the people" and would bring together "respectable Citizens" from every section of the country and commit them to the outcome. At such a convention the delegates "form acquaintances, exchange opinions and sentiments, catch and infuse animation and enthusiasm, and return with a spirit of union and concert." Furthermore, he said, nomination by legislatures had one outstanding objection: Members were not elected for that purpose. In addition, a convention could also produce, and should produce, he continued, a "statement of those *broad principles* on which all nominations should be supported." He wanted his American System made the crux of the struggle between Democrats and National Republicans. He believed that Jackson could be defeated in 1832, provided the President's opponent stood firmly on a platform of internal improvements, protective tariffs, and sound credit and currency. The West had already deserted the President, he claimed. The present administration was so "wicked, passionate and corrupt" that it menaced the stability of the nation's institutions and jeopardized the welfare of the people. Under the circumstances the National Republicans could surely annihilate the Democrats at the polls. "We are for principles, for liberty, for the Constitution, for the Union. Let us then march directly to our object. . . . Let us hoist our banner and rally our friends and organize them for systematic action."[8]

As for his own candidacy, which everyone insisted was his without asking for it, Clay repeatedly insisted that he would not seek it and would cheerfully

7. Samuel R. Gammon, *Presidential Campaign of 1832* (Baltimore, 1922), pp. 60–61.
8. Clay to Hezekiah Niles, October 28, 1830, November 8, 1830, Clay to Francis T. Brooke, June 16, 1830, Clay to William B. Lawrence, November 21, 1830, in Clay, *Papers,* VIII, 281, 292–293, 225, 301.

support any other man the convention might see fit to nominate. Only National Republican principles mattered. Nothing else. Clay also claimed that he was enjoying his life of retirement. It had immeasurably improved his health. He spent more time with his family, and he could attend to the many duties incumbent upon a gentleman farmer.[9]

Recently he had purchased 111 acres of land adjoining Ashland from the John McNairs estate. He had in mind another piece of property that, if acquired, "would make Ashland all that I wish it in respect to quantity of land." He had also repaired the "horsemill" and moved it to the center of his estate. In addition, he built a new brick conical icehouse and said his farm now operated in "fine order." His daughter Anne and her husband had recently acquired a home, Woodlands, near Ashland where they resided during the New Orleans "sickly season." Having so many members of his family around him—increased in late October, when Anne presented him with his newest grandchild, Lucretia, named after the grandmother—quickened his pleasure of living in retirement. Clay's son James Brown Clay had entered Transylvania College, and John Morrison Clay was about to begin studies with the Reverend Benjamin O. Peers, an Episcopal clergyman, who ran a preparatory school in Lexington. Unfortunately both Theodore and Thomas were still committing "fresh indiscretions" at every turn. Theodore "seems to be doomed to misery and to render wretched all around him," while Thomas, during his stay at home, engaged "in two debauches, and the last threatened his life."[10]

As though to prove his disinclination to pursue a nomination, Clay told all his friends that he planned to spend the winter in New Orleans with his wife. "My purpose is to live there in great retirement whilst we stay." He truly loved the Crescent City and sometimes recommended it as one of the best places to live in the United States—except, of course, during the summer. But his real reason for going to New Orleans was business. Lucretia's sister Nancy Hart Brown, the wife of the former minister to France James Brown, had recently died, and Clay was obliged to attend to some business in connection with her estate. Louisiana law allowed a wife, upon her death, to dispose of one-half of the property held by her husband. Sister Brown had left her portion of a sugar plantation to her husband during his lifetime and to her sisters and brothers after his death. Furthermore, she designated Clay as one of her executors, and that was the reason for his trip. Also, he had other business interests to attend, and the weather in New Orleans compared with Lexington was far more congenial in the winter. So he decided to go and live for a season in "great retirement."[11]

Clay left Lexington on December 20, accompanied by his wife and his grandson Henry Clay Duralde. His daughter, Anne, and her family preceded

9. Clay to John L. Lawrence, March 7, 1831, in Clay, *Papers,* VIII, 328.
10. Clay to Henry Clay, Jr., October 31, 1830, in Clay, *Papers,* VIII, 284–285.
11. Clay to Henry Clay, Jr., December 9, 1830, in Clay, *Papers,* VIII, 309.

them to New Orleans by a few weeks. The family traveled by boat down the Ohio and Mississippi rivers, and when they arrived in Louisiana, they took up residence with Martin Duralde at his home about two miles from the city. They stayed in the area for a little more than two months, and Clay reported that his wife's health benefited enormously by passing the winter in the Deep South and that he, too, felt tolerably well.[12]

He may have thought he could live in "great retirement," but his renown brought almost daily visits from distinguished men in the area, including members of the Louisiana legislature and judges of the courts. On several occasions he took advantage of these visits to try to convince southern planters of the value of the protective system—and he liked to believe that they received his ideas favorably.

While Clay basked in the warmth of Louisiana hospitality, the nation was rudely shocked to learn of the breach between President Jackson and Vice President Calhoun. Nullification provided one issue of contention, the Eaton affair another, but then when Jackson learned of Calhoun's desire, as a member of James Monroe's cabinet, to censure him for his seizure of Florida, the rift widened. The Vice President compounded his troubles by defending himself in the newspapers, thus making a private quarrel public. He and his friends further alienated Jackson by blaming Secretary of State Van Buren for instigating the quarrel. The cabinet divided in its loyalties between Calhoun and Van Buren, and the National Republicans happily predicted that because of the split, the administration would henceforth be held in check in both houses of Congress.[13] All this was duly reported to Clay and added to his sense of contentment and well-being.

The family returned to Lexington in late March 1831, and a week later Jackson's cabinet resigned almost entirely. It was a constitutional crisis of enormous significance and added one more item to Clay's mounting agenda with which to pummel Jackson in the upcoming presidential election. "We cannot fail to profit by the controversy," wrote the delighted Clay. He sympathized with Calhoun and warned his friends away from attacking him. "Indeed *so far as relates to his personal controversy with Jackson,*" Clay wrote, "I think he has been wronged, and justice as well as policy prompts that he should, to that extent at least, be sustained." By this time the Kentuckian was strongly urging the convocation of a national convention, not for the purpose of a nomination, except for Vice President, he said, but to solidify the party, "excite passions," and strengthen the organization.[14]

Clay had already received numerous nominations from various committees and legislatures and even a few state conventions. National Republicans

12. Clay to Allen Trimble, December 18, 1830, Clay to Susan Price, January 28, 1831, Clay to Henry Clay, Jr., March 31. 1831, in Clay, *Papers,* VIII, 314, 322, 329.
13. Johnston to Clay, January 12, 1831, in Clay, *Papers,* VIII, 320.
14. Clay to Brooke, April 24, 1831, Clay to Thomas Speed, May 1, 1831, Clay to John Sloane, April 29, 1831, in Clay, *Papers,* VIII, 338, 344, 341.

meeting in convention on August 3, 1830, in Delaware, for example, placed his name in nomination, and Connecticut, New York, and Maryland followed shortly afterward. In September 1830 a political gathering in Winchester, Kentucky, resolved to hold a convention at Frankfort on December 9, to nominate, or so the members said, a presidential candidate who would endorse the American System. Some 290 delegates attended the Frankfort convention and, not surprisingly, named Henry Clay. Over the next several months additional nominations were announced in both eastern and western states.[15]

As a result, Clay came under increasing pressure to make himself nationally visible again, by openly declaring his presidential candidacy, by touring the North during the summer, or by winning election to the Senate seat occupied by John Rowan, who had supported Jackson's Maysville veto and who chose not to run again when his term expired in 1831. As a strong, articulate critic of administration policies Clay was urged by National Republicans to assert his party leadership in a more forthright and vigorous manner.[16]

Also, several prominent leaders, including former Radicals, such as Thomas Ritchie, who now supported the Democrats, badgered Clay to state explicitly his "Constitutional principles." But Clay hesitated about issuing any public statements that might be misinterpreted as an announcement of his candidacy. Besides, he said, if the electorate did not know where he stood by now, it never would. However, he did say privately that he regarded himself as a Madisonian, committed to the constitutional doctrines as stated by James Madison in his Virginia Resolution of 1798.[17] "I was with Mr. Madison then, I am with him now. I am against all nullification, all new lights in politics, if not religion. Applying the very principles of Mr. Madisons [sic] famous interpretation of the Constitution, in the Virginia address, I find in the Constitution the power to protect our industry, and to improve our Country by objects of a National character."[18]

Much as he disliked restating his views, Clay found himself doing precisely that as more and more friends asked for specific statements with which to marshal and arouse their state organizations. To Senator Johnston of Louisiana he provided four general principles:

1. Tariff protection in both theory and practice must be preserved.

2. Duties on foreign products can be reduced or repealed when not completing with domestic industries but must be maintained when they do complete.

3. Taxes ought not to be levied specifically for internal improvements, but surpluses of revenue should be applied to the promotion of public works.

15. *Niles' Weekly Register,* December 25, 1830.
16. Clay to John M. Bailhache, November 24, 1830, Clay to Brooke, April 24, 1831, in Clay, *Papers,* VIII, 304, 339.
17. This letter is one of Clay's strongest statements about his commitment to Madisonian republicanism.
18. Clay to Brooke, May 1, 1831, in Clay, *Papers,* VIII, 343.

4. Finally, the charter of the Bank of the United States should be renewed with any modifications suggested by experience.[19]

At one point Clay even addressed the Indian question that Jackson had shoved to the forefront of American consciousness with the Indian Removal Act. Clay wrote a letter to an Indian chief, John Gunter, expressing his regret over the treatment of the Indians, particularly the Cherokees, because of Georgia's determination to steal their lands. The treatment not only was unjust, he said, but inflicted a deep wound on the character of the Republic. The Cherokee Nation had the right to establish its own government, live under its own laws, be exempt from the laws of the United States or the laws of any individual state, claim the protection of the United States, and possess and enjoy its lands subject to no other limitation than that, when sold, they may be sold only to the United States. The policy of President Jackson, Clay continued, directly opposed those principles and thereby encouraged Georgia "to usurp powers of legislation over the Cherokee nation which she does not of right possess."

What can the Cherokees do? Well, said Clay, I have no answer to that question, but "I see clearly what they ought not to do." They ought not to make war. They must bear every oppression. Sooner or later the American people will redress these wrongs, he said. Sooner or later. Clay closed his letter with an offer of sincere wishes that the Cherokee Nation "may obtain justice . . . and may become a civilized, Christian and prosperous community."[20]

As for Georgia, Clay took a hard line. The Constitution, its treaties, and its laws must be faithfully and firmly executed, he told a friend. If Georgia submits, there is no problem; but if it rebels, then it must be "reduced to obedience, and that final effect of the struggle would add strength to the Union."[21]

Unfortunately Clay's change of heart respecting the Indians was never translated into the redress he spoke of when his party finally came into power in the 1840s. It was one thing to speak about injustice—especially as practiced by the other party—and quite something else to do anything about it when the power was finally available to put words into action.[22]

Despite the many potent issues with which to smite the opposition, especially Jackson's veto of the Maysville Road bill, the National Republicans continued to lose strength in Kentucky. The summer elections turned out "less favorably than we had hoped and believed." Clay sighed. He was at a loss to account for it, except to note the "means, some of them highly improper, of all sorts which the General Government brought to bear upon them." But that was a simplistic excuse that both sides employed to explain disagreeable elec-

19. Clay to Johnston, July 23, 1831, in Clay, *Papers,* VIII, 375.

20. Clay to Gunter, June 6, 1831, in Clay, *Papers,* VIII, 358–359.

21. Clay to Samuel Southard, February 14, 1831, in Clay, *Papers,* VIII, 323.

22. Rickey L. Hendricks, "Henry Clay and Jacksonian Indian Policy: A Political Anachronism," *Filson Club Historical Quarterly,* LX (April 1986), pp. 218–238.

tion results. The Maysville veto did indeed hurt the Democrats in some parts of Kentucky, as seen by the returns in the elections for the legislature. But the Jacksonians won a large majority of seats to the lower house of Congress, and that troubled Clay. There could be no question that Andrew Jackson was a fantastically popular individual, especially with the electorate on the frontier. The people loved and trusted him, despite his current problems with Calhoun and his cabinet and despite the unwelcome issues he sometimes raised, such as his attack on the Bank of the United States.[23]

If Clay could not win his own state in a presidential election, should he continue as a candidate for his party's nomination? The question haunted him, and he discussed it with Josiah Johnston. However, if he withdrew from the race, who would replace him? Friends tried to reassure him. The Kentucky election was not *as* favorable as expected, Johnston agreed, but it was favorable in some respects. Indeed, "I consider it a triumph," inasmuch as the National Republicans held a majority in the legislature and in a few months would choose a U.S. senator to replace Rowan. "We shall adhere to you," he told Clay. No one else is acceptable. "If you cannot be elected—no one can."[24]

But something was unquestionably needed to "reinvigorate" Clay's presidential candidacy, and more than one individual argued that he should stand for election to the U.S. Senate in the November election. Clay's own candidate for that post was his friend John J. Crittenden, who could have been elected the previous year had he been willing to vote for himself.[25] It was now anticipated that he would be easily elected in November. Well, said John Binns, editor of the Philadelphia *Democratic Press,* Crittenden must be persuaded, as a patriotic gesture, to step aside in Clay's favor. Then, after his election, Prince Hal could decline the honor, which would prove that he was still Kentucky's favorite son.

Resigning after the election was an idiotic suggestion, but many National Republicans did in fact favor Clay's coming into the Senate. It would materially benefit "the *cause,*" wrote Daniel Webster. "Every thing valuable in the Govt. is to be fought for, & we need your arm, in the fight." But what about poor Crittenden? He could be given another post, suggested one man. There would be absolutely no difficulty "in making you Gov," Crittenden was told, if you would defer to Clay.[26]

Although he came under increasingly heavy pressure to run for the Senate, Clay took no part in urging Crittenden to step aside.[27] He was skeptical

23. Clay to Edward Everett, August 20, 1831, in Clay, *Papers,* VIII, 387. Clay used stronger language about the summer election results in a letter to Senator Johnston: "I have been disappointed & mortified with the issue of our elections in the West." August 20, 1831, ibid., VIII, 389.

24. Clay to Johnston, August 20, 1831, Johnston to Clay, September 1, 1831, in Clay, *Papers,* VIII, 389, 395–396.

25. Albert D. Kirwan, *John J. Crittenden: The Struggle for the Union* (Lexington, Ky., 1962), p. 89.

26. John Binns to Clay, September 10, 1831, Webster to Clay, October 5, 1831, in Clay, *Papers,* VIII, 399, 416; A. R. Macy to Crittenden, October 14, 1831, Crittenden Papers, LC.

27. Kirwan, *Crittenden,* p. 90.

about risking election because he knew that the Jacksonians in the legislature were itching for the chance to defeat and thereby humiliate him.[28] Nor was he really desirous of the post. What undoubtedly convinced him to take the risk, other than the mounting pleas of his friends at home and around the country, was the fact that the administration did intend to strike down everything he believed "valuable" and important for the economic growth of the nation. Piece by piece his American System could be dismantled and cast aside. His arm was needed for the fight to prevent such a catastrophe, just as Webster had said, and so Clay consented to run.[29]

As a devoted friend of the Great Compromiser, Crittenden happily agreed to stand aside. He even took part in urging Clay to take his place. "There was no *collusion*, no rivalry, between us," Crittenden told his daughter. "All that was done was with my perfect accordance. I hope I shall always be found ready to do what *becomes me*. I have done so on this occasion and am satisfied."[30]

Not all the Crittendens were so obliging and gracious. One brother, Thomas, insisted that Clay himself had "some agency" in starting the movement to displace his brother, but John Crittenden put no stock in his brother's ridiculous claim.[31]

On November 9, 1831, the newly elected Kentucky legislature voted its choice for a seat in the U.S. Senate. In the upper house the vote was nineteen for Richard M. Johnson, eighteen for Clay; and one for Worden Pope. In the lower house Clay received fifty-five votes and Johnson forty-five. By only nine votes Henry Clay was elected U.S. senator.[32] Grumbled Clay: "I go to my post . . . with no anticipations of pleasure from occupying it."[33]

Not many weeks prior to Clay's election, the Anti-Masons held the first national nominating convention in American history. They convened in Baltimore on September 26, fully expecting to nominate John McLean, associate justice of the U.S. Supreme Court, as President. At the last minute McLean changed his mind and withdrew, and William Wirt of Virginia, former U.S. attorney general in the Monroe administration, was nominated instead, despite his past membership in the Masonic order. Because they were getting desperate to find a candidate and because Wirt had a national reputation and

28. Andrew Jackson faced the same risk when he agreed to run for the U.S. Senate in 1823, prior to his first presidential bid in 1824. See Remini, *Jackson*, II, 55–73.

29. Clay to Henry A. S. Dearborn, September 15, 1831, Clay to Samuel L. Southard, September 30, 1831, John Sloane, to Clay, October 15, 1831, William W. Worsely, October 22, 1831, Asher Robbins to Clay, October 25, 1831, Matthew L. Davis to Clay, November 2, 1831, Clay to James F. Conover, November 16, 1831, in Clay, *Papers*, VIII, 402, 410, 419, 421 423, 425.

30. Crittenden to Mrs. Chapman Coleman, November 18, 1831, in Coleman, ed., *Life of John J. Crittenden* I, 81–82. George Bibb, Kentucky's other senator, who supported the Maysville veto, chose not to seek reelection when his term expired in 1835. Crittenden was elected in his place.

31. Worsley to Clay, October 22, 1831, in Clay, *Papers*, VIII, 421.

32. *Niles' Weekly Register*, November 26, 1831. Governor Thomas Metcalfe certified Clay's election on November 10.

33. Clay to James F. Conover, November 16, 1831, in Clay, *Papers*, VIII, 425.

showed sympathy with their principles, the Anti-Masons decided that his past association with the Masons would not damage the party or his candidacy. They nominated him unanimously on the first ballot; then they selected Amos Ellmaker of Pennsylvania, a respected lawyer, for the vice presidency.[34]

Clay had advised his many friends that they ought not to get involved with the Anti-Masonic Convention in any way whatsoever. Let them meet and nominate, and let the person selected decide whether he will accept or not, said Clay. "And in Decr. next let our Convention decide with all the lights then before it. If a man can be found to accept the Anti Masonic nomination, as such, I am deceived if it do not prostrate him."[35]

Now the Anti-Masonic candidate had been named, and Clay was flabbergasted. Wirt was supposedly "zealously attached" to the National Republican party. Numerous letters to Clay from mutual friends described him as "firmly decided and cordially united with us." Now the truth was revealed. Sourly, Clay responded, "I suppose the ex-Attorney General found, in the magnitude of the fee presented to his acceptance, sufficient motives to silence all scruples as to the goodness of one cause . . . and for the desertion of another to which he stood pledged by the highest considerations of honor." More than ever, said Clay, we now see the wisdom of the National Republicans holding a similar convention in Baltimore. Every effort should be made to make it numerous, powerful, and respectable. In the meantime, the Anti-Masons, and Writ in particular, should not be attacked publicly, he directed. Although the convention delegates might conceivably think it politic to nominate Wirt themselves, most likely they will not, but it is prudent to "leave the door open to his party and him to unite with us."[36]

In late November Senator Clay started for Washington to take up his new duties. He brought along his wife and his grandson Henry Clay Duralde. His sons remained at home, except for Henry Clay, Jr., who had taken up residence in New Orleans to study law. The previous spring the younger Clay had been graduated second in his class from West Point, and at his father's suggestion had wisely given up soldiering—in view of the person who presided in the White House—and commenced the study of law. The young man thanked his father for "relieving me of the responsibility of a choice."[37]

The trip to Washington was most unpleasant on account of the cold. Winter arrived rather early and "continues up to this time with uncommon

34. On the first ballot Wirt received 108 votes, Richard Rush 1, and there were two blanks. On a motion from the floor Wirt's nomination was made unanimous. For details of the convention, see Gammon, *Presidential Campaign of 1832,* pp. 45–52.
35. Clay to Thomas Metcalfe, September 9, 1831, in Clay, *Papers,* VIII, 398.
36. Clay to James F. Conover, October 9, 1831, in Clay, *Papers,* VIII, 418. Clay thought that if the National Republicans nominated Wirt, not a single state would vote for him, with the possible exception of Vermont. Clay to William Greene, November 14, 1831, ibid., VIII, 424.
37. Clay to Southard, December 12, 1831, Clay, Jr. to Clay, June 21, 1831, May 7, 1831, in Clay, *Papers,* VIII, 431, 363, 347.

severity," Clay wrote on Christmas Day. "There have been already eight or ten falls of snow."[38]

But more than the weather troubled Clay, and troubled him profoundly. He was burdened by a terrible tragedy, but one not altogether unforeseen. Just a few weeks earlier Theodore had been committed to the "Lunatic Asylum of Kentucky" on the complaint of John Brand and his son, William Moses Brand. They believed "Theodore W. Clay Insane, & of unsound mind, & further that they consider the lives of themselves, & families, in danger from said Theodore W. Clay." A panel of twelve men, summoned by the sheriff, determined that Theodore was "a *Lunatic*" and should be confined. The asylum was located in Lexington, where Theodore spent most of the rest of his life.[39]

When the family arrived in Washington, they took lodgings in a very pleasant house near the general post office. The mess included Thomas A. Marshall of Kentucky and Daniel Jenifer of Maryland.[40] Naturally Clay's old friends and colleagues enthusiastically greeted him. By this time he and they knew the convention would nominate him, probably on the first ballot. He also received firsthand reports from his supporters, who had already begun to assemble in Baltimore for the convention. They reassured him of his certain nomination and the desire of the delegates "to fight the battle out." Clay wrote to Francis Brooke: "I wish I could add that the impression was more favorable than it is as to the success of such a nomination." But ever the optimist, he added: "Some thing however may turn up (and that must be our encouraging hope) to give a brighter aspect to our affairs."[41]

On Monday, December 12, 1831, the delegates of the National Republican party opened their convention in the saloon of the Athenaeum, a building at the southwest corner of St. Paul and Lexington streets, where the Anti-Masons had met several months earlier. Only 130 members arrived on opening day, but with each succeeding day the number increased until it finally reached 155. A total of eighteen states was represented: Maine, New Hampshire, Vermont, Massachusetts, Connecticut, Rhode Island, New York, New Jersey, Pennsylvania, Delaware, Maryland, Virginia, Ohio, Kentucky, North Carolina, Indiana, Louisiana, and Tennessee, as well as the District of Columbia. The following day the convention elected James Barbour of Virginia as its permanent president along with four vice presidents and two secretaries.

After Barbour had been duly installed and delivered a speech of apprecia-

38. Clay to Anne Erwin, December 25, 1831, in Clay, *Papers,* VIII, 437.

39. The complaint of the Brands was made on September 29, 1831, and the panel was summoned on October 3. See *Commonwealth of Kentucky* v. *Theodore W. Clay,* Fayette County Circuit Court, file no. 746, and Theodore W. Clay to Clay, January 8, 1832, in Clay, *Papers,* VIII, 442 and 442–443, note.

40. Clay to Anne Erwin, December 25, 1831, in Clay, *Papers,* VIII, 437.

41. Johnston to Clay, December 123, 1831, John Sergeant to Clay, December 12, 1831, Clay to Brooke, December 9, 1831, in Clay, *Papers,* VIII, 431, 430.

tion, Peter R. Livingston of New York, a former Democrat, rose and presumably made the first nominating speech in national convention history. At the end of his powerful harangue he placed the name of Henry Clay in nomination, and the delegates broke out "with loud and repeated plaudits." A roll call followed, and Clay was unanimously nominated to the "repeated cheers from a great crowd of spectators" in the hall. The next day John Sergeant of Pennsylvania was selected as the vice presidential candidate of the party.

Immediately following his speech and the roll call, Livingston hurriedly notified Clay of his nomination. The Kentuckian wrote out a short, simple letter of acceptance, which was read to the delegates and received with great applause:

> This manifestation of the confidence of a body, so distinguished, is received, gentlemen, with lively sensibility and profound gratitude. Although I should have been glad, if the Convention had designated some Citizen of the U. States, more competent than myself to be the instrument of accomplishing the patriotic objects which they have in view, I do not feel at liberty to decline their nomination. With my respectful and cordial acknowledgements, you will be pleased to communicate to the Convention my acceptance of their nomination, with the assurance that, whatever may be the event of it, our Common Country shall ever find me faithful to the Union and the Constitution, & to the principles of public liberty, and to those great measures of National policy which have made us a people, prosperous, respected and powerful.

On Thursday afternoon the delegates laid aside their business to visit Charles Carroll of Carrollton, the last surviving signer of the Declaration of Independence, to pay their respects. On Friday, December 16, the final day of the convention, the delegates listened to an "Address to the People" that excoriated Jackson for his failures as President, to wit: the spoils system; his conduct of foreign affairs; and his policies on the tariff, internal improvements, Indians, and the BUS. In his place the National Republicans offered Henry Clay, an "ardent, fearless, and consistent friend of liberty and republican institutions." As originator of the American System, the address continued, he deserved the support of all who favored domestic industry and internal improvements. As secretary of state he demonstrated his outstanding administrative qualities, and his "generous frankness and the captivating warmth of his manners" eminently fitted him for the presidency, where it is sometimes necessary to "conciliate the public favor." Compare these qualities with Jackson's read the address, "and may the goodness of Providence so enlighten your choice, [fellow citizens], that it may tend to promote the security and permanency of our excellent political institutions, and the true greatness of glory of our beloved country." On that prayerful note of hope, the convention adjourned.[42]

42. *Niles' Weekly Register,* December 24, 1831, reprinted in Schlesinger, and Israel, eds., *History of American Presidential Elections,* I, 540–566. Clay's letter of acceptance of his nomination may be found in Clay, *Papers,* VIII, 432.

After adjournment "the greater part" of the members rode down to Washington and visited Clay to convey their congratulations and thanks. It was a mass audience. Clay turned on the full force of his charm, and no one knew better how to delight or excite a crowd of well-wishers.[43]

A few months later, on May 7, 1832, a National Republican convention of young men, dubbed "Clay's Infant-School,"[44] met in Washington, D.C., to name their candidate. Some 316 delegates attended, chose Clay as their candidate, and drew up a party platform with planks taken directly from the American System. But what made this convention unique was the unexpected appearance of the nominee himself to accept the nomination and express the "deep and grateful sense which I entertain for the distinguished proofs which you have . . . given to me of your esteem and confidence." If he were elected President, Clay said, it would be his "earnest endeavor . . . to maintain, with firmness and dignity, [the people's] interest and honor abroad; to eradicate every abuse and corruption at home; and to uphold with vigor and equality, and justice, the supremacy of the constitution and the laws." Liberty must be preserved and transmitted to posterity, he continued, by "vigilance, virtue and intelligence." It was inseparably linked to the Union. Make no mistake about that. "The fate of liberty, throughout the world," he concluded, "mainly depends upon the maintenance of American liberty."

The delegates cheered wildly when he finished, and the shouting and applauding continued for many minutes. Then, slowly and deliberately, Henry Clay, the nominee of the National Republican party, went around the hall and shook the hand of each delegate and graciously thanked him for his support.[45]

43. Clay to Anne Erwin, December 25, 1831, in Clay, *Papers,* VIII, 437.
44. Sargent, *Public Men and Events,* II, 195.
45. Quoted in Remini, "The Election of 1832," I, 507.

TWENTY-TWO

"Scenes of Tergiversation, Hypocricy, Degeneracy, and Corruption"

NOT SURPRISINGLY, Clay's return to Washington, buttressed by his presidential nomination in Baltimore, immediately thrust him to the forefront of opposition leaders in Congress. "We have been called on by all the heads of departments, foreign ministers &c.," he informed his daughter, Anne, just a few weeks after his arrival. "I have every reason to be satisfied with the attentions which have been paid us."

In the minds of most congressmen, Henry Clay personified the National Republican party. He embodied all the principles and policies that the Jackson administration seemed determined to overthrow. He was virtually handed the reins of near-absolute party leadership when he returned to Congress, and he readily seized them, seized them with a growing sense of his ability to annihilate an administration he regularly described as "the reign of corruption & demoralization." Senator John Tyler of Virginia marveled at his sense of presence and demeanor. "Mr. Clay carries his head very loftily," Tyler told his daughter. "Age has bleached it very much, but his voice is as musical as ever, and his manners as attractive."[1]

The nation's capital had changed and grown considerably since the British left it in ruins. A building boom had widened the living space available to residents and transients and stretched streets and avenues into new areas within the District. Pennsylvania Avenue had been macadamized; Jackson

---

1. Clay to Anne Erwin, December 25, 1831, Clay to Ambrose Spencer, May 12, 1832, in Clay, *Papers,* VIII, 437, 512. Clay's preeminent position in the National Republican party may be noted in John Quincy Adams's *Memoirs,* VIII, 443ff., 449. Tyler to Mary Tyler, December 28, 1831, in Tyler, *Letters,* I, 428.

added the north portico to the White House; running water had been piped into the Capitol, executive buildings, and the White House; and by 1835 the Baltimore & Ohio Railroad, the newest form of transportation recently introduced, had opened a branch line to the capital. "Steam cars" of the B&O brought passengers to the city limits, where they were picked up and transported in an omnibus to the foot of Capitol Hill.

The new Capitol building stood on a twenty-two-acre plot and was enclosed by an iron railing. A beautiful and extensive view of the city, Georgetown, and even Alexandria across the Potomac River could be seen from the Hill on account of the "sudden declivity of the ground" immediately to the west. The Capitol ran a length of 352 feet and had a portico with a long flight of stairs that projected outward and consisted of a series of Corinthian columns rising 30 feet high and extending 160 feet in length. A lofty flat-topped dome rested in the center of the building, and each wing of the structure supported a similar but smaller dome.

Members of the House of Representatives assembled on the second floor of the south wing of the Capitol, while senators found their chamber in the opposite wing. Both halls were semicircular in shape and formed like an ancient Greek theater. The House chamber extended 96 feet at its widest and 60 feet at the highest part of the domical ceiling. The Senate chamber was smaller, 75 feet across and 45 feet high. A series of Ionic columns similar to those of the Temple of Minerva supported a gallery on the east side of the Senate room. And a goodly amount of Greek and Roman statuary and busts decorated both chambers, adding a peculiarly grand and elegant splendor to the young Republic's legislature. The Supreme Court found quarters in the basement of the building, making it relatively easy for some congressmen both to argue a case before the High Court and to attend to their legislative responsibilities.[2]

One of the first things Clay did after his arrival in Congress was notify Nicholas Biddle that he had changed his mind on the question of recharter of the BUS. He wanted the Bank president to apply for recharter at this session of Congress. "The friends of the Bank here, with whom I have conversed, seem to expect the application to be made." Although some doubt existed on what Jackson might do in the event of the passage of a recharter bill, "my own belief is that, if *now* called upon he would not negative the bill; but that if he should be re-elected the event might and probably would be different."

Why the reversal? Because he now had the official nomination of his party and he was certain he could defeat Jackson on the issue if the President dared veto a recharter bill. It was a blatant act of political self-interest. Biddle and his Bank would have to accommodate Henry Clay's presidential ambitions, like it or not. And Biddle had no choice. He could not afford to offend Clay, whose support was essential to the continued life of his Bank. Did Clay initiate the

2. Green, *Washington: Village and Capital*, I, 127–130; J. D. Steele, manuscript journal, 1820–1829, Huntington Library, Pasadena, California; Remini, *Jackson*, II, 55–56.

recharter question in the hope of provoking a veto? Quite probably.

Clay also decided that the Senate must punish Martin Van Buren for his malfeasance in office while serving as secretary of state and for his wicked involvement in the intrigue against Vice President Calhoun that brought about the disruption of Jackson's cabinet. Van Buren had resigned his cabinet post, and the President had appointed him minister to Great Britain. Although Congress was not in session when the appointment was conferred, the Little Magician had already departed for London. One of the Senate's first tasks on reconvening involved consideration of Van Buren's nomination.

"I think V. B. ought to be rejected," Clay had stated even before he was elected to the Senate. "Such a measure would cripple him and weaken the Administration." Moreover, the Magician deserved rejection because of his instruction to the previous minister to Great Britain, Louis McLane, requesting the same terms on reopening the West Indian trade that had been offered in 1825 to President Adams and for declaring his willingness to accept a settlement based on a legislative act rather than on a treaty, which the previous administration had insisted upon. In effect the Jackson administration had repudiated the policy of the previous administration and blamed Adams for failing to respond properly to British overtures to reopen the West Indian trade. All this naturally incited the wrath of the previous secretary of state, Henry Clay. "With the mark of the Senate's rejection on him," the Magician "will be powerless," Clay smirked.[3]

President Jackson's third annual message to Congress on December 6, 1831, caused no great outcry from the opposition, but the report of the secretary of the treasury, Louis McLane, produced a sensation. McLane's report on the Treasury proposed a scheme to modify the tariff, sell public lands to the states in which they lay and distribute the proceeds to all the states, pay off the national debt, sell the government's BUS stock, and recharter the Bank at the proper time with certain modifications.[4] Naturally Clay took great exception to these horrors. "The entire policy of the Government, in relation to every one of the great interests of the Country, is proposed to be changed. Was there ever a wilder scheme than that respecting the public lands?" As for the Bank question, Clay had difficulty divining the President's intentions. "The Executive is playing a deep game to avoid at this Session the responsibility of any decision of the Bank question," he concluded.

But some Democrats were also appalled by the report, especially by the administration's apparent retreat from its earlier and more combative stance on the Bank. "The Treasury Report," wrote Representative Churchill C. Cambreleng of New York, "is as bad as it possibly can be—a new version of Alexan-

3. Clay to Biddle, December 15, 1831, Biddle Papers, LC; Clay to Edward Everett, August 20, 1831, in Clay, *Papers,* VIII, 388–389.
4. *House Executive Documents,* no. 3, 22d Congress, 1st session, pp. 5–16. See also Remini, *Jackson,* II, 337ff., and John A. Munroe, *Louis McLane: Federalist and Jacksonian* (New Brunswick, N.J., 1973), pp. 310–313.

der Hamilton's two reports on a National Bank and manufactures, and totally unsuited to *this age of democracy and reform.*"[5]

Jackson had allowed the rather tame reference to the Bank question because McLane had linked it to the final payment of the national debt, something the President desired above everything else. But when Biddle responded favorably to Clay's request for immediate recharter and authorized a petition to Congress early in January 1832 to initiate the renewal, Jackson immediately reacted to this "treachery and malice" by reversing himself and decreeing the Bank's destruction. He would slay this monster, he raged, not cage it. He would veto any bill for recharter. His advisers assured him that Biddle's action was a political ploy for Clay's benefit in the coming election. The Bank president had dared intrude himself into the electoral process to get what he wanted. "Now as I understand the application at the present time," wrote the attorney general, Roger B. Taney, "it means in plain English this—the Bank says to the President, your next election is at hand—if you charter us, well—if not, beware of your power."[6]

Not only would a recharter bill need his guidance and powers of persuasion, the Kentucky senator reckoned, but the administration's declared intention to "modify" the tariff (whatever that meant) would also require his watchdog supervision. Moreover, he figured that Jackson planned to abandon protection by arguing that since the national debt would be extinguished within the next year or two, there was no need to continue building a surplus from the revenues generated by the tariff. The President intended "to break down the American system by accumulation of the revenue," reasoned Clay. Then he would entice the South to sacrifice the public lands by assuring southerners that it would further increase government revenues to the point where a sizable reduction of the tariff duties would become absolutely necessary. "A more stupendous, and a more flagitious project was never conceived," Clay cried.[7]

The South's opposition to a protective tariff had already spawned nullification, and the West's commitment to cheap land had produced a number of schemes to sell public land at reduced prices. One idea, which Clay supported, called for the money from the sale of land to be used for internal improvements. New England protectionists liked this scheme because it would not add to the surplus and, as a consequence, it undercut the argument favoring tariff reduction.

Thus, as the first session of the Twenty-second Congress began on

5. Clay to Francis T. Brooke, December 9, 25, 1831, in Clay, *Papers*, VIII, 429, 437; Cambreleng to Jesse Hoyt, December 29, 1831, in Mackenzie, *Life and Times of Martin Van Buren*, p. 230.

6. Remini, *Jackson*, II, 344; Taney to Thomas Ellicot, January 25, 1832, Taney Papers, LC.

7. Adams, *Memoirs*, VIII, 445; Clay to Brooke, March 28, 1832, in Clay, *Papers*, VIII, 481. On the question of public lands, see Daniel Feller, *The Public Lands in Jacksonian Politics* (Madison, Wis., 1984), and Malcolm J. Rohrbough, *The Land Office Business: The Settlement and Administration of American Public Lands, 1789–1837* (New York, 1969).

December 5, 1831, three major issues absorbed the attention and concern of the members and the President: the Bank, the tariff, and the distribution of public land sales. Each of these three, in Clay's mind, had enough firepower in it to blow the old man out of the White House.

As he resumed his seat in Congress, Clay never doubted that he would dominate the entire legislative process, just as he had in the past, and thereby claim his just reward from the American electorate when it trooped to the polls next fall to select the next President. After a theatrical entrance into the Senate, to the applause and shouts of approval from the gallery, he slumped into his overstuffed chair, a portrait of confidence and insouciance. He glanced around him at his distinguished colleagues, some of whom, like Thomas Hart Benton of Missouri, would joust with him repeatedly in heated verbal exchanges. Prince Hal smiled at John C. Calhoun, the presiding officer, who stared back at him, his demeanor stern and slightly forbidding. The arrogant, ardent, charming gamester had returned to enliven the debates of Congress.

Approaching fifty-five years of age, Clay was still tall, gaunt, bony, long-limbed, and homely. His face was narrow, accentuated by a straight, long, protruding nose and a balding, prominent forehead. A thin mouth, marked by bloodless lips, seemed constantly pursed and curved into a semismile. Furrowed cheeks and swept-back light gray hair added to his gaunt appearance.

A restless man and easily bored, Clay had no patience with the insipid and lengthy speeches that frequently droned on for hours in the upper chamber. While other senators harangued the galleries, he often sat in his chair licking a stick of striped peppermint candy. When the boredom became intolerable, he rose languorously from his seat and wandered over to the table of the Senate, where he executed elaborate motions as he prepared to sample a pinch of snuff from a silver box on the table.

But when Henry Clay rose to speak in that luxurious chamber, all the languor and apparent listlessness dropped away. The becoming smile, the bright, intelligent eyes, and the incredible voice animated his entire body. As he spoke, he gestured constantly, nodding his head, which "hung on a long neck." He stepped back and forth, or right to left, as he became more agitated and involved in what he was saying. "His arms, hands, fingers, feet, and even his spectacles, his snuff-box, and his pocket-handkerchief, aided him in debate." But it was the voice that constantly gripped his audience. "Rich, musical, captivating," it rose to the highest key he could command or sank to the lowest whisper without losing clarity, thrust, or precision. And coupled with his majestic voice was the intensity of his gaze as he spoke that mesmerized his audience. "He has decidedly the finest Voice that I ever heard, manly & commanding," commented one man, "with an eye that seems to pierce the inmost soul of those, whom he addresses."

Still, it was the content of his words, the intellectual power of his arguments, the eloquence of his declamation that commanded the respect and admiration of his colleagues. Whenever he gave a major speech, not only were the galleries and aisles on the floor jammed with foreign visitors and the public at large, but most of the representatives deserted their House to hear him.

Clay's style in debate was unique. His asides, spoken in an undertone, were often so clever, humorous, and sharp-edged that the audience listened very intently to him so as not to miss these delicious morsels. Once, when replying to an outraged Democrat, Clay paused as a sudden squall came up, thundering its presence and rattling the windows. "Storms seem to be coming in upon us from all sides," he remarked to the amusement of the other senators.

Frequently Clay tried to intimidate opponents. He could be exceedingly imperious in debate and show more than a touch of bad temper. During the Jackson and Van Buren administrations he often stooped to humiliation or cruel innuendo to humble defenseless victims. He seemed to think it was expected of him. On one occasion he bullied General Samuel Smith, a Revolutionary War hero. The eighty-year-old general, who had spent almost forty years in Congress, took a verbal pounding from the Kentuckian for reversing a previous position.

"The honorable gentleman was in favor of manufactures in 1822," taunted Clay, "but he has turned—I need not use the word—he has abandoned manufactures. Thus:

> "Old politicians chew on wisdom past
> And totter on, in blunders to the last."

The old man struggled to his feet. "The last allusion is unworthy of a gentleman," the general retorted. "Totter, sir, I totter! Though some twenty years older than the gentleman, I can yet stand firm, and am yet able to correct his errors. I could take a view of the gentleman's course, which would show how consistent he has been."

"Take it, sir, take it—I dare you!" jeered Clay in reply.

"No, sir, I will not take it. I will not so far disregard what is due to the dignity of the Senate."[8]

"I can never pardon Clay," Smith later wrote to his son. "I may forget but never can forgive. And yet my natural temper is forgiving. You know, that I cannot bear malice."[9]

A great number of outrageous scenes occurred during this first session of the Twenty-second Congress dealing with the three great issues, but possibly the most outrageous took place over the nomination of Martin Van Buren to serve as minister to Great Britain.

In mid-January 1832 the confirmation of Van Buren's nomination came

8. Poore, *Reminiscences,* I, 143–146; Hector Green to Ellen Green, October 6, 1840, Green Family Papers, Manuscript Department, Filson Club, Louisville, Kentucky; Adams, *Memoirs,* VIII, 466, 476–477.
9. Smith to J. Spear Smith, March 31, 1832, Smith Family Papers, Virginia Historical Society, Richmond.

to the Senate floor. A motion to table indicated immediately that it would be an ugly and brutal fight. The motion lost. On January 24 the debate began in earnest, and for two days a raging duel broke out between Clay, Webster, George Poindexter of Mississippi, Stephen D. Miller, and Robert Y. Hayne of South Carolina on one side, demanding rejection, and John Forsyth of Georgia, William L. Marcy of New York, Bedford Brown of North Carolina, and Samuel Smith of Maryland on the other, arguing in favor of confirmation.

Clay spoke on January 25. Looking bemused, urbane, and supremely confident, as always, he based his opposition mainly on Van Buren's instructions, as secretary of state, to Louis McLane in negotiating the West Indian trade. In repudiating the policy of previous administrations, said Clay, Van Buren had prostrated and degraded "the American eagle before the British lion." Moreover, he continued, Jackson had exceeded his authority in nominating Van Buren while the Senate was in recess. Then, seizing an opportunity to castigate the President over his rotation policy, Clay labeled it a "pernicious system of party politics," a system introduced from New York by its one time senator, Martin Van Buren. William L. Marcy, one of the Magician's ablest lieutenants, came to his friend's defense and made the colossal blunder of excusing Jackson's appointments policy by airily remarking: "To the victor belong the spoils of the enemy." It was a shocking admission and gave the National Republicans a telling quotation with which to bludgeon the administration during the election campaign. Spoils! However true the remark, it struck many senators as "semi-barbarous—and the utterance of that principle alone, lost Van Buren many, very many friends."[10]

George Poindexter chose to insinuate moral delinquency with reference to Van Buren's behavior toward Peggy Eaton, and Stephen Miller repeated some of the grossest innuendos. In response, Alexander Buckner of Missouri declared that "none but a liar—an infamous liar, would utter them."[11]

Vice President Calhoun gaveled Buckner to order. Thereupon Senator Forsyth sprang to his feet and denounced Calhoun for interrupting. "What right have you, Sir," he said, "to call a Senator on this floor to order. . . . You are grossly out of order for this interference." Shouts rang out, and the "low scurrillous slanders" that ricocheted around the chamber reached "a degree of malignity & vindictiveness never before exhibited in the Senate." Old wounds were ripped open. Calhoun's friends pilloried Van Buren for intriguing his way to power, and the New Yorker's friends responded by accusing the Vice President of lying and hypocrisy in the Seminole and Eaton controversies. All the while Clay and his associates added to the brouhaha with a catalog of nasty insinuations. "Clay gave a history of V. B. to shew how immoral he was,"

10. *Register of Debates,* 22d Congress, 1st session, p. 1320ff., 1325; Samuel A. Foot to William H. Seward, February 28, 1832, Frederick Whittlesey to Seward, January 25, 1832, Seward Papers, University of Rochester Library.
11. *Register of Debates,* 22d Congress, 1st session, p. 1341ff.

wrote a former congressman from New York. What hypocrisy! jeered the Democrats in response.[12]

With so many senators seeking revenge for one wrong or another, the idea of conferring on Calhoun the distinction of rejecting Van Buren's nomination occurred to several men. If there were a tie, Calhoun would cast the deciding vote. But to effect a tie required planning and organization, and no doubt Clay had a hand in it. It was "arranged" that George Bibb of Kentucky, who had promised to support Van Buren's nomination, missed the final vote. According to Francis P. Blair, writing many years later, Bibb was "ever the tool of superiors to whom he looked for support or elevation." At the start of his career he favored Clay, then deserted to Jackson, later "joined Calhoun and his nullifiers," and "fell out with him into Clays hands again and became the tool of the triumvirate [Clay, Webster, and Calhoun] in the conspiracy against [Van Buren]." He took instructions. He obeyed his superiors.[13]

And so it happened. Bibb failed to appear on the crucial day when the final vote was taken on January 25. Twenty-three senators voted no to the question, and another twenty-three said yes. All heads turned in the direction of the Vice President. Quietly and deliberately, Calhoun cast the deciding vote and defeated the nomination.[14]

"You have broken a minister," observed Senator Thomas Hart Benton of Missouri to a colleague seated beside him, "and elected a Vice-President." Minutes later Benton overheard Calhoun say: "It will kill him, sir, kill him dead. He will never kick, sir, never kick."[15]

Clay was delighted. "We have rejected V. Buren, and our friends are in high spirits." As for the talk that Jackson would select the Magician as his running mate when the Democrats held their nominating convention in May, Clay hoped it was true. "V. Buren, old Hickory, and the whole crew will, I think, in due time be gotten rid of. The attempt to excite public sympathy in behalf of the little Magician has totally failed; and I sincerely wish that he may be nominated as V. President. That is exactly the point to which I wish to see matters brought."[16]

Calhoun's open defiance of Jackson added to the growing rumor that a political alliance would soon be struck between the Vice President and Clay. Such an alliance could cause the President considerable difficulty in working

12. *Register of Debates,* 22d Congress, 1st session, p. 1341ff.; S. R. Hobbie to Azariah C. Flagg, January 29, 1832, Flagg Papers, New York Public Library, Marcy to Van Buren, January 26, 1832, Van Buren Papers, LC.

13. Blair to Van Buren, April 25, 1859, Van Buren Papers, LC. Samuel Prentiss of Vermont also absented himself.

14. *Register of Debates,* 22d Congress, 1st session, p. 1324.

15. Benton, *Thirty Years' View,* I, 215.

16. Clay to N. B. Beall, January 27, 1832, Francis Brooke, February 21, 1832, in Clay, *Papers,* VIII, 450, 465.

his will through the Congress. Sometimes Daniel Webster's name was added to this grand coalition, giving rise to the expression that the three men constituted a "Great Triumvirate."[17]

But Clay was cautious. Earlier he had warned his friends against any appearance of cooperation with the Calhoun faction. "Our principles are diametrically opposite," and we must not seem to lessen our attachment to them for political advantage. We should refrain from any attacks on the Vice President and his supporters, he added, provided it is consistent with our principles. "If they choose to attack the Administration let them march on their own line and conduct their own operations; and we on ours."[18] For the moment Clay wanted to wait and see what Calhoun would do next, whether he would make a run for the presidency himself or throw his support to Clay.[19]

And there was the question of what the Vice President and the nullifiers would do about the major issues that awaited the attention of Congress, in particular the tariff and the BUS. Clay had long since decided that Jackson's only policy lay in overthrowing each of the component parts of the American System, and he therefore worked out a strategy to block presidential action. With respect to the tariff, Clay needed to undercut the President's argument that a mounting surplus after the payment of the national debt justified sharp reductions of the tariff rates. He was determined to preserve protection even to the extent of increasing the rates on some articles; but in order to reduce the level of revenue, he was also willing to eliminate duties on goods not in competition with domestic products. At the same time he planned to divorce the public land issue from the tariff and support a bill to allocate the proceeds from land sales to internal improvements. This overall strategy would presumably appeal to northern manufacturers, western settlers, and southern planters.

Once he had this operating plan firmly fixed in his mind, he passed it along to his followers. "Mr. Clay laid down the law of his system," said one congressman, and he argued that the revenue must be reduced immediately by the total removal of duties on tea, coffee, spices, indigo, almost the entire duty on wines, and several other articles. There was no point in protecting products that were not grown or manufactured in the United States, he contended.[20]

Clay arranged to meet with twenty congressmen from both houses and work out the draft of a new tariff bill. One of those in attendance was John Quincy Adams, who had just begun his new career as a representative from his Massachusetts district and been selected to head the House Committee on Manufactures. In a joking way Clay asked the former President how he felt

17. See the editorials in the Washington *Globe,* for January and February 1832, especially January 28 and February 1.

18. Clay to Edward Everett, June 12, 1831, in Clay, *Papers,* VIII, 360–361.

19. Clay's speculations about Calhoun's future course of action are spelled out at length in a letter to Francis Brooke, April 1, 1832, in Clay, *Papers,* VIII, 484–485.

20. Adams, *Memoirs,* VIII, 445.

about "turning boy again to go into the House of Representatives."[21] Adams, as usual, failed to see the humor in it.

In presenting his strategy to this group, Clay was stupidly tactless. So determined was he to foil the President's program of "reform," and so confident was he of his leadership of the opposition, that he needlessly irritated a few of the assembled congressmen. "Mr. Clay's manner," recorded Adams, "with many courtesies of personal politeness was exceedingly peremptory and dogmatical." Few in the room questioned or criticized Clay's plan of attack, said Adams. They were as "obsequious as he was super-presidential." Adams was especially anxious to prevent any misunderstanding with his former secretary of state,[22] but he did wonder whether consideration had been given to the effect the elimination of so many duties, such as coffee, tea, indigo, etc., might have on the commercial community that had a large stock of these articles on hand. Also, he thought the proposed increase of duties on other items "would be a defiance not only to the South . . . but defiance also of the President, and of the whole Administration party."

An imperious, dogmatic Clay responded to these complaints. He dismissed the question about the reaction of the commercial community. As for defiance, he did not care whom his proposed new tariff defied. "To preserve, maintain, and strengthen the American system he would defy the South, the President, and the devil," he retorted.[23]

Still, Adams persisted in his belief that the South, already complaining of the inequity of the protective system, would be incensed over the proposed increases. But Clay continued to make light of the argument. The feeling of discontent, he argued, was almost, if not entirely, "imaginary or fictitious." After all, he had recently toured the Southwest and spoken to many of the leading men in Louisiana and Mississippi. He felt positive that the discontent, to a very large extent, had subsided. "Here is one great error of Mr. Clay," recorded Adams in his diary. Indeed.

The former President, like many others, easily divined Clay's motive in everything he said and did. A presidential election was approaching, and the Jacksonians meant to take credit for extinguishing the debt. So Clay argued in favor of repealing certain duties in order to deny the Treasury seven or more millions of dollars and thereby prevent the immediate elimination of the debt. On Clay's part, said Adams, "it was an electioneering movement, and this was the secret of these meetings, as well as of the desperate effort to take the whole business of the reduction of the tariff into his own hands."

Besides drafting the proposed new tariff, the secret committee considered meeting on a regular basis. Clay demurred. He said that such meetings would

21. Ibid., 443.
22. "I wished, however, most earnestly wished to give no just cause of offence to Mr. Clay." Ibid., VIII, 449.
23. Ibid., 445–446.

give the appearance of a permanent caucus to dictate measures to Congress. To get a formal decision on the question from the group someone proposed that it hold weekly meetings. The proposal was promptly voted down.[24]

Now, with a tariff schedule to his liking, separated from any mention of public lands, and a request for a recharter of the BUS forthcoming from its president, Clay prepared to take on Jackson and the Democrats. He made his first move on January 9, 1832. He submitted a resolution approved by the secret committee, (along with such individual senators like Daniel Webster), instructing the Committee on Finance to report a bill for abolishing duties on noncompetitive imports. Two days later he addressed the Senate in favor of his resolution. He claimed that the established policy of protection "stands self-vindicated," and therefore, there was no need to discuss it further. Rather, he insisted on the reduction of some duties and the elimination of others since the nation was approaching the termination of the national debt. In a virtual aside he expressed the hope that once the debt had been extinguished, the proceeds from the sale of public lands would be diverted for internal improvements. But he was preparing a bill on that subject, he said, which he would submit later in the session. The burdens of the people, he went on, needed to be relieved, and his proposal would do this without sacrificing the principle of protection and without undermining the American System.[25]

Southerners immediately objected. The suggested reductions, they declared, did not go far enough. They proposed deeper cuts. They wanted them sliced to the revenue level that would naturally destroy protection. And so the battle was joined.[26]

Just a few days before the submission of Clay's tariff resolution, a "memorial," signed by Nicholas Biddle for the recharter of his Bank, was brought to the Senate by George M. Dallas of Pennsylvania. Normally General Samuel Smith, chairman of the Senate Committee on Finance, would have presented the memorial to the upper house; but he was not considered aggressive enough to handle the issue in debate, so the responsibility was turned over to Senator Dallas.[27]

The House also began to address the tariff and banking issues within the Ways and Means and the Manufacturing committees. Thus by the beginning of the new year the two most important legislative items of the day were squarely before the Congress.

One other issue heightened political anxiety during the winter of 1832, when the Cherokee Indians sued in the Supreme Court for an injunction to allow them to remain in Georgia without being molested by state law. Georgia

24. Ibid., 443, 447–448.
25. Clay to Webster, January 8, 1832, in Webster, *Papers, Correspondence,* III, 141; Webster to Clay, January 8, 1832, in Clay, *Papers,* VIII, 443; *Register of Debates,* 22d Congress, 1st session, pp. 55, 66–75.
26. *Register of Debates,* 22d Congress, 1st session, p. 186ff.
27. Ralph C. H. Catterall, *The Second Bank of the United States* (Chicago, 1903), p. 223.

wanted them out of the state, and so did President Jackson. The Cherokees claimed they were independent, but Georgia insisted that they were subject to state law. In the celebrated case *Cherokee Nation* v. *Georgia* Chief Justice John Marshall denied that the Indians constituted a sovereign nation, but he also rejected Georgia's argument that they were subject to state law. The Cherokees, he said, were "domestic dependent nations," subject to the United States, as a ward to a guardian. They were not subject to individual states.[28]

But would President Jackson enforce this decision against the state? If he refused to enforce it, said Clay, "there is a virtual dissolution of the Union." For a state to disregard federal laws and treaties, even after their vindication by the High Court, and get away with it, terminates the government as we know it. There was a report, gossiped Clay, that Jackson told a Georgia representative that he hoped "Georgia would defend her rights!"

All this struck Clay as extremely troublesome. "Everything here is uncertain—the Bank—the Tariff—the Georgia question &c. Never have I seen any period of the Republic when all the future was wrapped in more doubt. I hope for the best and look for the worse."[29]

Clay's first major speech in the Senate on his tariff resolution occurred on February 2 and extended over a three-day period. Ostensibly in response to a protracted attack upon protection and public works by Senator Hayne of South Carolina, Clay delivered what was widely publicized as a "Speech in Defense of the American System," although it dealt more with the tariff than anything else.

For this first performance since his return in which the full range of Clay's enormous oratorical, intellectual, and histrionic powers on an important national issue would be demonstrated to the public, the Senate chamber bulged with spectators. They expected fireworks, and he did not disappoint them. They expected a dazzling display of his vaunted charm and ingratiating manner, and again he provided them with enough evidence of his seductive faculties to impress even the most critical Jacksonian. They expected passion and enthusiasm and vehemence, and over the three-day period he pulled all stops on these emotions.

He rose from his seat and was immediately recognized. Then he began slowly and quietly, as was his custom. Some of his words were hushed to a near whisper. He started off with a few courteous remarks about Senator Hayne (another custom) and then launched into a vivid contrast between the nation's present prosperity with conditions just prior to 1824. The tariff, the protective Tariff of 1824, he declared, had produced this transformation. The foes of the American System predicted a ruinous collapse with the advent of protection. "Every prediction which they made has failed, utterly failed." Instead of gloom

28. 5 *Peters* 1ff.
29. Clay to James Barbour, March 10, 1832, Clay to Porter, March 10, 1832, Clay to Edmund H. Taylor, March 28, 1832, in Clay, *Papers,* VIII, 472, 473, 483.

and distress, he said, we have "brightness and prosperity," and it resulted from American legislation fostering American industry rather than allowing it to be controlled by foreign legislation intent on assisting foreign industry.

At one point Clay tangled with Vice President Calhoun over the question of the tariff's constitutionality. The senator reminded the presiding officer that he, Calhoun, had not worried about that question in 1816, but the Vice President dismissed the objection by stating that constitutionality had not been debated at that time.

Clay then moved on to the demands of southerners for free trade. This reminded him, he declared, of the child who cries for the moon and stars. What these gentlemen really want, even if they fail to realize it, is the adoption of the British colonial system. They will bring about "the recolonization of these States under the commercial dominion of Great Britain." He then described what he believed conditions would be like as "colonists" dependent upon the "mother country" for their essential needs. "Their refuse goods, their old shop-keepers, their cast-off clothes good enough for us! Was there ever a scheme more artfully devised, by which the energies and faculties of one people should be kept down, and rendered subservient to the pride, the pomp, and the power of another?"

At this point Clay was shouting. "Sir, I can not go on with this disgusting detail," he angrily remarked. But he did. He piled one illustration, one statistic, one detail upon another, always interjecting short, dramatic, thrusting comments about the consequences to the nation's future prosperity.

As for the objection of the American System's deleterious effect upon the South, Clay simply denied it. The American System is beneficial to all parts of the Union, he contended, and absolutely essential to its larger constituency. Even if he could not demonstrate it to everyone's satisfaction, Clay felt compelled to assert as forcibly as he knew how that the American System benefited every section of the country. Moreover, the protective system had sustained the price of cotton over the past several years and averted a decline. Clay also denied that the South lacked the capacity to engage in the "manufacturing arts." But even if that assumption were true, he said, must those states that can manufacture be prevented from doing so? Surely South Carolina would not seek to thwart the economic growth of another section of the country. "Throughout her whole career she has been liberal, national, high-minded."

At one point General Smith interjected a reminder to the friends of the American System that they constituted a majority in the Senate and therefore should exercise their power in moderation. They must show mercy.

This was just the opening Clay wanted. General Smith, he cooed, also belongs to a majority—a political majority, for he is a Democrat. "Recall to your recollection the 4th of March, 1829, [Jackson's inauguration]," Clay roared, as he pounced for an easy kill, "when the lank, lean, famished forms, from fen and forest, and the four quarters of the Union, gathered together in the halls of patronage; or stealing by evening's twilight into the apartments of the president's mansion, cried out, with ghastly faces, and in sepulchral tones, 'give us bread! give us treasury pap! give us our reward!' . . . Go to the families who were driven from the employments on which they were dependent for subsistence . . . to the mothers . . . to the fathers who . . . [have been] stripped of all that was left them . . . and ask, what mercy was shown to them!"

Clay never could resist an opening to castigate the administration on its "spoils system," even when it had nothing to do with the issue at hand.

The fundamental principle on which free governments rest, Clay continued, as he returned to the basic question of his speech, is "that the majority must govern; from which there is no appeal but to the sword." That majority should govern wisely and justly, but if a minority can succeed in forcing the abandonment of measures that are essential to the interests of the majority by threatening the dissolution of the Union, as some South Carolinians had already done, then "the Union from that moment is practically gone." It might linger for a time in name and form, but its vital spirit will have disappeared. "I would intreat the patriotic people of South Carolina . . . to pause, solemnly pause! and contemplate the frightful precipice which lies directly before them. To retreat may be painful . . . but it is to retreat to the Union. . . . To advance, is to rush on certain and inevitable disgrace and destruction."[30]

At the tail end of his speech Clay mentioned reducing the revenue. The public would not tolerate the accumulation of an annual surplus once the national debt had been paid, he said, but the problem could be easily resolved by repealing duties on noncompetitive items. Then he concluded: "Let us then adopt the measure before us, which will benefit all classes—the farmer, the professional man, the merchant, the manufacturer, the mechanic; and the cotton planter more than all."[31]

Despite its frequent histrionic outbursts, its penchant for overkill, its wrongheadedness about southern interests and concerns, its statistical errors, its irrelevancies, and its overtly insincere courtesies it was a masterful speech, one of Clay's more triumphant efforts at influencing the minds and votes of his colleagues. It buttressed logical arguments with statistical data, all compellingly presented with humor, grace, passion, a touch of sarcasm here and there, and the force of personality and language. The speech was described by some as "the most powerful argument [in the science of public economy] that had ever been made." Henry Clay, said one contemporary, was "in the prime of his prime."[32]

Clay worked long and hard on the revised copy of the speech to prepare it for publication. He knew it would prove to be an important document in the presidential campaign and would influence many voters by its sincere and heartfelt appeal for the preservation of the Union.[33]

30. *Register of Debates,* 22d Congress, 1st session, pp. 55, 66–75.

31. *Niles' Weekly Register,* March 3, 1832.

32. Clay, *Works,* V, 435; Parton, *Jackson,* III, 451.

33. "That terrible long speech of mine in the Senate, which gave me less trouble in its delivery than it has since occasioned me," he wrote, "is now in the hands of the printer." Clay to Francis Brooke, February 21, 1832, in Clay, *Papers,* VIII, 465.

Clay not only won adoption of his resolution on the tariff but succeeded in maneuvering it from the Committee on Finance to his own Committee on Manufactures, where he could guard it and help shape its final form to win its passage through Congress. But the situation did not develop exactly as Clay had planned. A majority of all the antiprotectionists together with some of the Jackson tariff senators concocted a scheme to reduce the price of public lands and either transfer the lands to the states where they were located or distribute the proceeds from the sales among the states on an equal basis. Furthermore, they moved a resolution to commit the public land question to the Committee on Manufactures. "Can you conceive a more incongruous association of subjects?" howled Clay. Their object, he claimed, was to win antitariff support by sacrificing the public lands. By tying the two issues together, he contended, they expected to force him into abandoning western interests in public lands in order to safeguard the tariff.

But the Kentuckian knew how to scotch that plot, if not kill it outright. He planned to "disentangle the two subjects," make a separate report on the land question, and give another speech, which would expound his own ideas about what should be done. "I feel as if I were sitting upon a Volcano," he laughed.[34]

In addition to the "Volcano," Clay experienced intense personal melancholy during these debates. The condition of his son Theodore, who had been confined to the "Lunatic Asylum of Kentucky," caused him and his wife "inexpressible regret and anxiety." He had written several times to the unfortunate young man and sent him three parcels, but Clay's letters upset Theodore and caused him "the greatest excitement." So the doctors advised the father against making direct contact. Apparently Clay said some things that touched off a tantrum. Since Dr. J. C. Jordan, the physician attending Theodore, thought that horseback riding might be beneficial for his recovery, Clay directed that a horse and a pony be made available. The father also asked his younger son Henry Clay, Jr., who had accompanied his sister back from New Orleans to her second home in Kentucky, to visit Theodore. "It will be painful to you to visit Theodore, but is it not a duty?" the father wrote. The younger Clay reported that his brother, accompanied by Dr. Jordan, had visited him several times at Ashland. "I once thought his malady of a transient nature . . . but now I am fully aware of the extent of our afflication."[35]

Several times Theodore wrote to his father and his letters appear perfectly

34. *Register of Debates,* 22d Congress, 1st session, p. 638; Clay to Brooke, March 28, 1832, Clay to John H. Ewing, April 14, 1832, in Clay, *Papers,* VIII, 481–482, 492.
35. Clay to John Wesley Hunt, February 13, 1832, Clay, Jr., to Clay, April 7, 9, 22, 1832, in Clay, *Papers,* VIII, 462, 488–490, 496. Clay's letters to Theodore have not survived, so it is impossible to discover what he said in them that caused Theodore such distress. He may have sharply rebuked his son for quarreling with the John Brand family and getting into the predicament that caused his incarceration. Whatever it was, it did not keep Theodore from writing his father and asking for his help. "I observe what you say about my letters to him," Clay wrote to Henry Clay, Jr., on May 1, 1832, "and I must cease to write to him." Ibid., VIII, 502.

rational. They must have caused Clay infinite pain because they pleaded for release from confinement.

I have sometimes rode about and been seen by so many that it will rather be a wonder to many that I am not allowed to stay at Home, where I would be quiet and unmolested rather than in a Hospital. All who see me know that I am perfectly at my self. And I feel no reason why I should be subject to the will of others and not a free agent at least. My desires are lawful, and my conduct not in violation of any law, or the rights of any man. Why therefore I am thus restrained I cannot see, so long. No one has yet volunteered their friendly aid to me and I will not if I can chuse, be the slave of any man. . . . I have written a respectful request to the Commissioners and they have given me no answer. And I have no reason to believe they will. I expect therefore that Justice will be done to me, and hope that it will speedily. Either with Thomas [Hart Clay], or any where—I might find employment, if you do not wish I should return a while to Ashland will suit me. So I get my liberty, and the peaceable enjoyment of the bounties of providence I shall be satisfied.[36]

Throughout the congressional session Henry Clay, Jr., continued to give his father reports of Theodore's condition. His physical health was very good, said Henry, and he frequently spent a day or two with his sister, Anne, or his brother. The latest medical evaluation, from a Dr. Benjamin W. Dudley, stated that Theodore was "deranged upon two subjects, love and ambition. The first can only be cured by time, the second by humiliation. By humiliation he means that Theodore should be treated by all as an ordinary young man incapable of self direction." No particular deference should be paid to his opinion or judgment, said the doctor, and no indulgences should be rendered as a sign of respect. "In fine that we should appear entirely indifferent to his opinion or his mind." The doctor thought it was a mistake to allow him to go horseback riding and to send him political periodicals, as the father had been doing, because "it would seem to evince regard for his [Theodore's] opinions." Dr. Dudley concluded his report by stating that it would take a long time before Theodore would recover.[37]

To add to his anxiety and distress, Clay's own health worsened during the early spring. And the turmoil and excitement in Congress hardly helped his condition. "Naturally ardent, perhaps too ardent," he told Francis Brooke, "I can not avoid being too much excited and provoked by the scenes of tergiversation, hypocricy, degeneracy and corruption which are daily exhibited." He quit tobacco in "one of the two forms to which I had been accustomed, and will gradually discontinue the other." He said he also tried to stay calmer and not get too excited over the present direction of public affairs.[38]

The only good news he received was the announcement of the birth of

36. Theodore Clay to Clay, May 20, 1832, in Clay, *Papers,* VIII, 520.

37. Clay, Jr., to Clay, June 7, 1832, in Clay, *Papers,* VIII, 530. The problem involving love was not further defined in the letter. No sexual "derangement" is implied at all in the report, but this was a subject hardly ever discussed or mentioned in letters between family members at this time.

38. Clay to Brooke, April 26, 1832, in Clay, *Papers,* VIII, 499.

another grandchild. On April 23, 1832, his daughter, Anne, gave birth to a girl, whom she named Mary. Also his son Henry, Jr., announced that he was "intent upon a little 'affaire du coeur' " with Julia Prather of Louisville, whom he had met in November 1831. After studying her character, he "became more and more pleased with her" and finally offered her "my heart and hand." He told his father that she was, in all respects, "worthy of being your daughter and my wife."[39]

Otherwise Clay gloomily labored throughout the spring to force a new tariff and a recharter of the BUS through Congress. And to thwart the schemes of the antiprotectionists, he had to come up with a viable public land bill. Speaking as a member of the Committee on Manufactures on April 16, he reported out a bill in which his "distribution" plan was outlined in detail. He proposed to keep the price of land at the present level of $1.25 per acre and distribute the proceeds from sales—currently running around $3 million per annum—to the states for purposes of internal improvements, education, the colonization of free blacks, and the reduction of state debts. In distributing the money he would provide a bonus in the amount of 10 percent of the net proceeds to the seven new states of Ohio, Louisiana, Indiana, Mississippi, Alabama, Illinois, and Missouri in which the lands lay, the remainder of the money to be shared by all twenty-four states on the basis of their representation in Congress.[40]

This obvious political ploy to protect his western support, especially the fact that the bill had been drawn up by the Manufactures Committee instead of the Committee on Public Lands, brought immediate Democratic protests. So Clay's report and the bill were referred to the Public Lands Committee, which subsequently returned a different bill in which the price of land was lowered—to one dollar an acre at the outset and eventually to fifty cents—and graduated, and 15 percent of the sales were assigned to the seven new states and nothing to the other states. The rest of the money from the sales would be kept by the government.[41]

The electioneering intentions of both parties on the issue had now been completely revealed: To wit, in one of his messages to Congress, Jackson had suggested ceding the public lands to the states in which they lay, obviously courting western support. The Democrats, led by Senator Thomas Hart Benton of Missouri, knew that Clay opposed Jackson's suggestion, so they deliberately connived to embarrass and possibly injure the Kentuckian on the issue by forcing it into the Committee on Manufactures, where he was its only western

39. Henry Clay, Jr., manuscript diary, University of Kentucky library; Clay, Jr., to Clay, May 11, June 7, 1832, in Clay, *Papers,* VIII, 508, 529.
40. The report of the Committee on Manufactures was written by Clay himself and was a paper of major significance for both the National Republican and Whig parties. Clay later stated that it was one of the most important and valuable of his state papers. *Register of Debates,* 22d Congress, 1st session, p. 785ff. Mahlon Dickerson of New Jersey chaired the Committee on Manufactures.
41. *Debates in Congress,* 22d Congress, 1st session, appendix, p. 112ff.

member. Clay escaped the trap by bringing out a bill that would share the land sales with all the states (and he hoped win their appreciation) as well as lower the revenue and thereby protect the tariff. Infuriated by his escape (calling it a tariff, not a land bill), the Democrats invalidated the action of the Manufactures Committee and turned the measure over to the Public Lands Committee. They then secured a bill that would reward only westerners (and win their votes) and continue the building of a federal surplus so that they could argue for tariff reduction to gain southern votes.

By May Clay was exasperated. After six months "nothing" had been accomplished on the three major issues—tariff, public lands, and the Bank—so he urged that the sessions run to six hours and include Saturday meetings if necessary.[42] But the Democrats further delayed congressional action by taking time off to hold their nominating convention and, to no one's surprise, chose Martin Van Buren as Jackson's vice presidential running mate.[43]

On June 20 Clay gave another extended speech, this one in support of the land bill reported by his Manufactures Committee. He argued against giving the land away, to either transient settlers or the states. Such a policy would favor only speculators, for "it is a business, a very profitable business, at which fortunes are made." The federal government does not need the surplus once the national debt was paid, he argued, but the states could use it for education, public works, and the colonization of free blacks. He had no problem with the constitutionality of the colonization question since the states would handle it. "The evil of a free black population," he said, "is not restricted to particular States, but extends to, and is felt by all. It is not, therefore, the slave question, but totally distinct from and unconnected with it." He had often expressed his conviction that the federal government had "no constitutional power" over slavery. "That conviction remains unchanged." The states have the exclusive powers to regulate this subject, he declared.[44]

Finally, on July 3, 1832, after considerable lobbying, the Senate passed Clay's public lands bill rather than the measure proposed by the Public Lands Committee. The vote was twenty-six to eighteen. But southern and western opponents in the House won a postponement of the bill until the following session. It was defeated, said Clay, "only for want of time and from party spirit."[45]

Clay had somewhat better luck with the tariff. His committee proposed a bill on March 30 that incorporated all his expectations. In speaking on the measure, he claimed that "the fate of the protecting system" rested on it. Duties had been reduced between five and six million dollars, but the rates on

42. *Register of Debates,* 22d Congress, 1st session, p. 901.

43. *Niles' Weekly Register,* May 26, 1832.

44. *Register of Debates,* 22d Congress, 1st session, p. 1096ff.

45. *Register of Debates,* 22d Congress, 1st session, pp. 1174, 2853. The distribution percentage was slightly altered in the final version of the bill. Clay to Hezekiah Niles, July 8, 1832, in Clay, *Papers,* VIII, 551.

some articles had been jacked higher than the 1828 Tariff.[46]

The administration countered with a proposal that sought a compromise between the tariff demands of Clay and those of the nullifiers. Basically it recommended an overall cut from approximately 45 percent in 1828 to about 27 percent. This proposal went to John Quincy Adams's House Committee on Manufactures, which reacted favorably to it. Some adjustments we made to keep duties high on favored articles such as woolens, but the committee also deleted a few articles and generally lowered duties on noncompetitive goods. The bill was reported to the full House on May 16 and passed, despite southern opposition.

Over his strenuous objections, Clay's Senate tariff bill was subsequently tabled on the request of Mahlon Dickerson, chairman of the Committee on Manufactures, who asked his colleagues to await the bill from the House. Probably Dickerson acted on orders from the White House. But the Senate, under Clay's masterful guidance, made several important amendments to the House bill when it arrived, by raising rates on selected articles and then passed it early in July.

Unfortunately the joint committee of the two houses, prompted by the administration, rejected the Senate's amendments. "Clay was furious," wrote one senator, ". . . his defeat and mortification were signal and manifest."[47] But there was nothing he could do. It was July. Senators were suffering with the intense Washington heat; they wanted no more of this interminable debate, so they accepted the recommendations of the joint committee. Clay himself voted for the final bill even though he deeply resented what had been done to his handiwork. Still, he put a good face on his disappointment. Every principle, he said, "for which I contended at the commencement of the Session [has] been substantially adopted. 1st. The principle of adequate protection. . . . 2. The reduction of duties has been placed principally on the unprotected articles. 3. The duty on wines and silks has been greatly reduced."[48]

Southerners—especially South Carolinians—regarded passage of the tariff as a savage blow and a bitter defeat. "Bad as was the scheme of the [administration]," snorted Senator Robert Y. Hayne, "the bill from the House was much worse, and this is infinitely the worst of all."[49]

The President signed the Tariff of 1832 on July 14. The measure reduced revenues by approximately five million dollars and lowered most rates to 25 percent. But woolens, iron, and cottons retained their high protective schedules. Overall it remained a relatively high tariff.

While this debate over the tariff attracted considerable national attention because of southern threats of disunion, toward the end of June the public

46. *Register of Debates,* 22d Congress, 1st session, pp. 656–658.
47. George Dallas to Henry Gilpin, July 13, 1832, Dallas Papers, Historical Society of Pennsylvania.
48. Remini, *Jackson,* II, 360; Clay to Niles, July 8, 1832, in Clay, *Papers,* VIII, 551.
49. *Register of Debates,* 22d Congress, 1st session, p. 1217.

suddenly became aware of something far more frightening and immediate. The cholera that had swept Europe the year before had arrived in Canada and by June had appeared in New York City. Then, slowly, it continued to work its deadly way south. On June 27 Clay proposed a resolution asking the President to designate a "day of fasting, humiliation and prayer" that God in His mercy would spare the nation this scourge. "A single word," he remarked, ". . . as to myself. I am a member of no religious sect. . . . I regret that I am not. I wish that I was, and I trust I shall be. But I have, and always have had, a profound respect for christianity, the religion of my fathers, and for its rites, its usages, and its observances." The following day the Senate passed the resolution by the vote of thirty to thirteen.

Jackson, who regarded the resolution as a violation of the Constitution, contemplated a veto. It was the providence of the states and the pulpits, he declared, "to recommend the mode by which the people may best attest their reliance on the protecting arm of the almighty in times of great public distress." However, on a motion of John Quincy Adams the House tabled the resolution. Some Jacksonians mocked Clay's resolution as an overt appeal for popular applause. With his reputation as a man of "loose morals," Clay seemed hardly the person to call for public acts of piety. "Could he gain votes by it," sniffed one, "he would kiss the toe of the Pope and prostrate himself before the grand lama."[50]

The final item on Clay's agenda for the Congress involved a bill for chartering the Bank of the United States. But the President was determined to kill the "hydra-headed monster," as he called the BUS, and the members of his unofficial Kitchen Cabinet, who, on this issue, predominated over the official "parlor" cabinet, gladly encouraged and supported his malice against the Bank. Jackson believed the BUS was a threat to the liberty of the American people, and he wanted it terminated as quickly as possible.

But the pro-Bank forces in Congress charged ahead with their plans for recharter. In May Senator George M. Dallas of Pennsylvania reported a recharter bill, while in the House George McDuffie of South Carolina, chairman of the Ways and Means Committee, shepherded a similar bill to the floor.

Webster bore the brunt of the Senate fight for recharter, while Benton supported the President's position. Clay took little part in this debate. He spoke on June 2 and attempted to answer the Democratic charge that the Bank had interfered in political questions, particularly elections. He also vehemently denied that the request for recharter at this time was politically motivated.[51] But most of Clay's remarks were comments, not full-blown speeches. This question did not engage his best efforts, and he pretended that it played no

50. *Register of Debates*, 22d Congress, 1st session, pp. 1128–1129, 1130–1131, 1182; Jackson to Synod of Reformed Church of North America, June 12, 1832, in Jackson, *Correspondence*, IV, 447; Charles I. Rosenberg, *The Cholera Years: The United States in 1832, 1849, and 1866* (Chicago, 1962), p. 50.
51. *Register of Debates*, 22d Congress, 1st session, pp. 1018–1019.

significant role in the presidential campaign. He probably tried to hide his obvious concern for the measure, lest he unwittingly substantiate Democratic contentions about the Bank's involvement in political elections.

On June 11, despite the strenuous efforts of the Democrats, the bill passed the Senate by a vote of 28 to 20, and almost a month later, on July 3, it rode triumphantly through the House by the vote of 107 to 85. Clay was immensely pleased. "The Session has indeed been one of a succession of glorious triumphs for the Country and our cause."[52] Biddle expressed his delight as well. "I congratulate our friends most cordially upon this most satisfactory result. Now for the President. My belief is that the President will veto the bill."[53]

When told of Jackson's probable reaction, Clay laughed. "Should Jackson veto it, I will veto him."[54]

A week later the President did indeed veto the Bank bill. And what a message it was! It claimed the Bank was unconstitutional, despite John Marshall's decision in *McCulloch* v. *Maryland*. It said that control of the institution rested in the hands of the wealthy. "It is easy to conceive," wrote Jackson, "that great evils to our country and its institutions might flow from such a concentration of power in the hands of a few men irresponsible to the people." Not only did the President "vilify" the Bank and its practices, but he repeatedly asserted presidential authority and privilege. The Bank was the agent of the executive branch, and in Jackson's opinion, the charter conferred powers on this institution that were both unnecessary and dangerous to the nation.

Then the President ended his message with a powerful rhetorical flourish that the Democratic press was to use to splendid effect in the closing months of the presidential campaign. "It is to be regretted that the rich and powerful too often bend the acts of government to their selfish purposes," the President said. When laws are enacted that "make the rich richer and the potent more powerful, the humble members of society—the farmers, mechanics, and laborers . . . have a right to complain of the injustice of their Government." The true strength of the government "consists in leaving individuals and States as much as possible to themselves—in making itself felt, not in its power, but in its beneficence; not in its control, but in its protection; not in binding the States more closely to the center, but leaving each to move unobstructed in its proper orbit."[55]

It was a stunning and totally unexpected response. Friends of the Bank were appalled by its tone and substance. Nicholas Biddle likened it to "the fury of a chained panther biting the bars of his cage." It was, he told Clay, "a manifesto of anarchy."[56]

It was also superb propaganda for the election, something neither Biddle

52. Clay to Hezekiah Niles, July 8, 1832, in Clay, *Papers,* VIII, 551.
53. Biddle to Thomas Cadwalader, July 3, 1832, Biddle Papers, LC.
54. Robert C. Winthrop, *Memoirs of the Hon. Nathan Appleton* (New York, 1969), p. 35, quoted in Peterson, *Great Triumvirate,* p. 208.
55. Richardson, *Messages and Papers,* II, 1152–1154.
56. Biddle to Clay, August 1, 1832, Biddle Papers, LC.

nor Clay quite appreciated at the time. And Democratic newspapers seized on it. The BUS, they said, will "receive its death-blow from the patriotic Jackson, the man of the People. He has watched its corrupting power, its unwarranted abuses, and now . . . he will . . . put a period to its existence." It is virtually impossible, said the Washington *Globe,* the President's new mouthpiece, edited by Clay's former friend Francis P. Blair, "to describe, in adequate language, the sublimity of the moral spectacle now presented to the American people in the person of Andrew Jackson." The President had indeed taken a distinctly moral position on the question. He accused the rich of stealing from the poor and using the Bank as their instrument. On behalf and in the name of the people, then, he would destroy the monster.[57]

But the Bank bill did not end with the President's ringing message. Congress made one last desperate attempt to override the veto. The day following receipt of the message Daniel Webster rose and denounced both the President and his veto. He criticized its constitutional arguments, he disparaged its attitude toward the Supreme Court, and he censured its attempt to divest the Congress of its full legislative authority. "According to the doctrines put forth by the President," he scolded, "although Congress may have passed a law, and although the Supreme Court may have pronounced it constitutional, yet it is, nevertheless, no law at all, if he, in his good pleasure, sees fit to deny it effect; in order words, to repeal or annul it."[58]

The following day Henry Clay added his contempt for the President's arguments in another crowd-pleasing speech on the Senate floor. If possible, it was even more important than either Webster spoke because of Clay's reputation as a gut fighter who would pull no punches in giving Jackson his due. And he obliged his listeners. He called the President's action "a perversion of the veto power." The Founding Fathers never intended it for "ordinary cases," he insisted. "It was designed for instances of precipitate legislation, in unguarded moments." It was to be used rarely, yet Jackson had already vetoed four times in three years. "We now hear quite frequently, in the progress of measures through Congress," he cried, "the statement that the President will veto them, urged as an objection to their passage!" What sort of intimidating threat was that, he asked? The President, by virtue of his veto, expects to invade the legislative process and force his will upon Congress. That "is hardly reconcilable with the genius of representative Government." It was downright revolutionary.

Clay also warned of the economic and social consequences of the President's action. It would bring catastrophe. It resembled the doctrine of nullification, he declared. "For what is the doctrine of the President but that of South Carolina applied throughout the Union?"[59]

When he finished, Clay got a rousing reception from Bank partisans in the

57. *Globe,* July 12, 20, 23, 28, August 1, 6, 9, 17, 24, 30, 1832, and its reprints of editorials from other Democratic newspapers.
58. Daniel Webster, *Works of Daniel Webster* (Boston, 1864), III, 434, 446.
59. Clay, *Works,* V, 524–535.

galleries. He had played to them several times during the course of his speech, including a reference to Benjamin Franklin's celebrated fable about an eagle's carrying off a cat in the mistaken notion that it was a pig.

On July 13 Senator Thomas Hart Benton took the floor to respond to both Webster and Clay. This big, powerful-looking man was every bit the match for the "duplicate Senators," as he called Clay and Webster. He faulted them for criticizing Jackson's supposed misuse of power when the Bank of the United States exercised far greater power through its lending operations and was presently engaged in financing the defeat of the President in the next election. He said he was shocked by some of the things Clay had said about Jackson. They were "wanting in courtesy, indecorous and disrespectful to the President," Benton charged.

Clay jumped from his seat and denied the charge. He needed no instruction in etiquette and courtesy from a ruffian and street brawler like the senator from Missouri. Furthermore, he remembered back to 1813, when Jackson and Benton were enemies and had engaged in a gunfight with several other men, including Benton's brother, Jesse. Talk about disrespect. At least, taunted Clay, "I never had any personal recontre with the President; I never complained of the President beating a brother of mine after he was prostrated and lying apparently lifeless." And, I never said, as Benton said in the election of 1824, that Jackson was a murderer and a coward and that if he were elected President, congressmen would have to protect themselves by carrying guns and knives.

"That's an atrocious calumny," cried Benton.

"What," replied Clay, "can you look me in the face, sir, and say that you never used that language?"

"I look," boomed Benton, "and repeat that it is an atrocious calumny, and I will pin it on him who repeats it here?"

Clay's face flushed with rage. "Then I declare before the Senate that you said to me the very words."

"False! False! False!" screamed Benton.

Ladies in the galleries gasped in horror, while men roared their excitement at the likelihood of these two distinguished senators starting a fistfight. The chair gaveled for order. It took many minutes but finally the dignity of the Senate was restored.

"I apologize to the Senate," said Benton, "for the manner in which I have spoken—but not to the Senator from Kentucky."

Clay glared at his antagonist. Then the thin line of his mouth slowly stretched into a sly, contemptuous smirk. "To the Senate," he said, "I also offer an apology—to the Senator from Missouri, none!"

Half an hour later the two men shook hands, just as western politicians always did after they had abused and pilloried each other on the stump.[60]

60. Thurlow Weed Barnes, ed., *The Life of Thurlow Weed* (Boston, 1884), II, 42–43; Poore, *Reminiscences*, I, 144–145.

On this low note the debate over Jackson's misuse of power ended. Webster and Clay could not muster the necessary two-thirds vote. The twenty-two to nineteen tally in the Senate fell far short of the required number to override. On July 16, 1832, both houses adjourned.

Clay had high hopes that the Bank issue would defeat Jackson in the presidential election. Surely the American people now realized how essential the institution was for the financial stability of the country. Surely they realized that the President had assumed unconstitutional powers that would ultimately destroy the Union.

In the fall the American people had it in their power to unseat the tyrant and restore the country to legitimacy and sanity. Henry Clay returned to Kentucky on July 23 to await the verdict.

—— T W E N T Y - T H R E E ——

A Crushing Defeat

C LAY DEPARTED Washington[1] accompanied by his wife, his
grandson Henry Clay Duralde, four servants, two carriages,
six horses, a jackass, and a "Shepherds dog—a strange medley,
is it not?" he laughed.[2] He headed for White Sulphur Springs, where he
planned to rest for two weeks, but he stopped off along the way to visit his
friends Francis T. Brooke and James Barbour and their families in Virginia and
to pay his respects to James Madison. Clay always regarded his political thinking as fundamentally Madisonian in its republicanism, and he never failed to
send a copy of his major speeches to the great man.[3] He found his mentor
rather feeble in body but still perfectly sound in mind. Madison appeared to
him to take a lively interest in current events and "spoke with more freedom
than usual on public affairs."[4]

The Clay entourage spent a good part of August at the springs, where the
senator hoped the water would completely cure his present ailment. There was
a moment of near panic when he almost crossed the track of President Jackson
and family, who were headed back home to Tennessee. Fortunately the two
men missed each other. It would have been most embarrassing, although both
men were pretty adept at handling such unpleasant moments.

Clay was very heartened by the public displays of affection he received as
he passed among the electorate. "I believe the redemption of our Country

---

1. Before leaving Washington, Clay wrote a letter to Solomon Etting in response to a complaint
that the senator had used the expression "the Jew" in debate, which Etting said he and other Jews
found shocking. Clay did on occasion use this expression, in both his letters and his speeches, but
he assured Etting that he used it to describe a person, "not to denounce a Nation. . . . I judge of
men not exclusively by their Nation, religion &c, but by their individual conduct." He had many
Jewish friends, Clay insisted, such as Benjamin Gratz, with whom he had very close relationships.
"But I cannot doubt that there are bad jews as well as bad christians and bad mahometans." Clay
was never overtly anti-Semitic; he simply imitated what was all too common in his day. Walter H.
Liebmann, "The Correspondence between Solomon Etting and Henry Clay," *Publications of the
American Jewish Historical Society,* XVII (1909), pp. 81–82.
2. Clay to James Caldwell, July 30, 1832, in Clay, *Papers,* VIII, 556.
3. The "Madisonian platform" and Clay's commitment to it are succinctly stated in Daniel Walker
Howe, *The Political Culture of the American Whigs* (Chicago, 1979), pp. 49–50.
4. Clay to Robert S. Rose, September 10, 1832, in Clay, *Papers,* VIII, 574.

from an arbitrary and weak administration is at hand," he commented. But that was his opinion even before he left Washington (he predicted that Jackson would not get a hundred electoral votes), so the demonstrations only confirmed what he had already decided would be the final outcome of the presidential contest.[5]

Clay reached home on August 25 to find his eighty-six-year-old mother-in-law, Susannah Gray Hart, close to death, having sustained a fall a few weeks before. She lingered for a few days more, and her death deeply affected Lucretia. At the same time news arrived that the National Republican candidate for governor of Kentucky, Richard A. Buckner, had been defeated by his Jacksonian rival, John Breathitt, in the August election. "We have come home, therefore, to experience private distress and public mortification, growing out of the result of the late election," Clay groaned.[6]

It was a sign of worse to come, but Clay indulged his old propensity for self-delusion. He readily explained away such reverses and kept asserting that victory was ultimately assured. Buckner had lost the election, he decided, because he was a Presbyterian ("and against that sect most deep rooted, and inveterate prejudices exist") as well as because of the corrupt efforts of the administration to embarrass him and the influx of Tennessee voters in the counties bordering that state. It was inconceivable that "Jacksonism," as Clay sometimes called the President's reform program, could be popular with the western, especially the Kentucky, electorate. The causes for Buckner's defeat, he therefore concluded, were "wholly unconnected with the P. election."[7]

Clay's unrealistic interpretation of what was happening in Kentucky and around the country stemmed in large measure from the optimistic reports he received almost daily from his friends and supporters. Sometimes their evaluations were extravagant in the extreme. They did not want to believe that Jackson could be reelected—and perhaps reelected in a landslide. "You are destined to be the instrument of [the nation's] deliverance," Nicholas Biddle told Clay, "and at no period of your life has the country ever had a deeper stake in you." Reports from New York, Pennsylvania, Louisiana, Ohio, Indiana, Missouri, and New England were "most cheering," the senator wrote to his son, and there was every reason to hope that the Anti-Masons and National Republicans would coalesce in pivotal states prior to the election and commit themselves to Clay. He expected his American System, and Old Hickory's tyranny, spoils system, and vetoes of the Maysville Road and the BUS to "annihilate" the President.[8]

5. Clay to Philip Fendall, August 4, 1832, Clay to John Meany, August 4, 1832, Clay to Samuel Southard, July 21, 1832, in Clay, *Papers,* VIII, 558, 555; Clay to Jonathan Thompson, July 20, 1832, Clay Papers, Manuscript Department, Filson Club, Louisville, Kentucky.

6. Clay to Charles Hammond, August 27, 1832, in Clay, *Papers,* VIII, 563.

7. Clay to Hammond, August 27, 1832, Clay to Webster, August 27, 1832, Clay to Fendall, September 3, 1832, in Clay, *Papers,* VIII, 563–564, 565–566, 568–569; Clay to Jonathan Thompson, August 27, 1832, Clay Papers, Manuscript Department, Filson Club, Louisville, Kentucky.

8. Biddle to Clay, August 1, 1832, Biddle Papers, LC; Clay to Brooke, August 5, 1832, Clay to Henry Clay, Jr., August 5, 1832, Porter to Clay, August 30, 1832, Josiah Johnston to Clay,

Yet Clay was no fool. Normally a shrewd and astute politician, except when he gambled on long shots for immediate personal gain, he knew what was needed to win in this modern age. Several times he reminded his friends that party organization was the absolute key to success. "Let our friends organize throughout the State," he urged his leading supporter in Virginia; "let each County be divided into sections and let one or more members of your Comees, of Vigilance be designated in each to bring the voters to the polls, and I do incline to think that you would win the day." To another, he said: "If we could introduce every where an effective plan of organization, the State would go with us by at least 5000. I hope such a plan will be devised by the [state National Republican] Convention . . . and which ought to be composed of practical men." Clay expressed particular pleasure with the way Kentucky went about conducting the campaign. Through appeals to prominent individuals in the party, he told his Louisiana supporters, ample funds had been collected. Many farmers advanced "their fiftys and hundreds of dollars." The state felt that everything was at hazard, he continued, and even those who had retired from politics were among the most active of the party's friends.[9]

Clay also understood the value of good propaganda. He welcomed the publication of a campaign biography by George Denison Prentice.[10] He urged Biddle to have the speeches against Jackson's Bank veto reprinted and extensively circulated. It is a mistake, he said, to presume the public is well informed on any given subject. The people should be addressed "as if they knew nothing," and they should be educated in "plain, intelligible & forcible language." But Biddle went Clay one better. He reproduced and distributed thirty thousand copies of Jackson's own veto message in the mistaken belief that it documented the President's incompetence and wickedness. "The U.S. Bank is in the field," wrote a worried Senator William L. Marcy, "and I cannot but fear the effect of 50 or 100 thousand dollars expended in conducting the election in such a city as New York."[11]

Like Clay, the Democrats also appreciated the importance of organization in winning elections. Indeed, they were infinitely more adept at it than the National Republicans. For this election they had the virtual equivalent of a national party chairman. Amos Kendall, the onetime tutor of Clay's children and the fourth auditor of the Treasury in the Jackson administration, supervised the overall conduct of this campaign. He demanded organization, he urged the founding of partisan newspapers, he solicited funds, and he prodded

September 10, 1832, Clay to Southard, September 11, 1832, in Clay, *Papers*, VIII, 559, 560, 567–568, 573, 574–575.

9. Clay to Brooke, August 5, 1832, Clay to Adam Beatty, September 4, 1832, Clay to Johnston, October 6, 1832, in Clay, *Papers*, VIII, 559, 569, 580.

10. George D. Prentice, *Biography of Henry Clay* (Hartford, Conn., 1831).

11. Clay to Biddle, August 27, 1832, in Clay, *Papers*, VIII, 562; March to Jesse Hoyt, October 1, 1832, in William L. MacKenzie, *The Lives and Opinions of Benjamin Franklin Butler and Jesse Hoyt* (Boston, 1845), p. 113; Remini, *Andrew Jackson and the Bank War*, pp. 98–99.

politicians in the various states to trumpet the message of Jacksonian reform. "You must try by an efficient organization and rousing the patriotic enthusiasm of the people," he told one politico, "to counteract the power of money." To another he wrote: "Have you an organization in your state? Whether you have or not . . . send me a list of names of Jackson men good and true in every township of the state . . . to whom our friends may send political information. I beg you to do this *instantly.*"[12]

Another of Clay's former friends, Francis P. Blair, now edited Jackson's newspaper in Washington and regularly turned out hard-hitting and frequently vicious propaganda. The *Globe* proved to be as effective a party mouthpiece as the President could desire. It pilloried congressmen, editors, and any others who criticized Jackson's program. All this thoroughly delighted the President. "With my sincere respects to Kendall & Blair," he wrote from his home in Tennessee, "tell them the veto works well, & that the Globe revolves with all its usual splendor—That instead, as was predicted & expected by my enemies, & some of my friends, that the veto would destroy me, it has destroyed the Bank." Like Jackson, the *Globe* invariably referred to the BUS as the "monster," complete with twenty-seven heads and a hundred hands. The "Golden vaults of the Mammoth Bank" had been opened for bribery in this election, claimed Blair. "Let the cry be heard across the land. Down with bribery—down with corruption—down with the Bank. . . . Let committees be appointed in every township to prosecute every Bank agent who offers a bribe."[13]

After his desertion to the Jackson party, Blair felt very uncomfortable about what he had done, particularly as it affected Clay. On their first meeting after the break he seemed ashamed of himself.

"How do you do, Mr. Blair?" said Clay in his blandest manner on spotting the editor, at the same time extending his hand.

"Pretty well, I thank you, sir," came the sheepish reply. Then, for the want of something appropriate to say, Blair mumbled: "How did you find the roads from Lexington . . . ?"

Clay's "silvery tones" turned sharper. "The roads are very bad, Mr. Blair, very bad; and I wish, sir, that you would mend your ways."[14]

Blair chose to target the Bank or Nicholas Biddle, not Clay or Wirt, as the principal foe of this election. This enabled him, and other Democratic editors, to widen the contest into a broader examination of democracy and liberty. The struggle against the BUS, they contended, was a struggle to preserve American liberty and further the advance of democracy. "The Jackson cause," they in-

---

12. Kendall to ?, July 25, 1832, Kendall Papers, New-York Historical Society; Kendall to Gideon Welles, September 12, 1831, Welles Papers, LC.

13. Jackson to William B. Lewis, August 9, 1832, Jackson Papers, Pierpont Morgan Library, New York; *Globe,* September 5, 8, 16, 17, 1832. See also the *Extra Globe*s issued throughout the campaign.

14. Poore, *Reminiscences,* p. 104.

sisted, "is the cause of democracy and the people, against a corrupt and abandoned aristocracy."[15]

The National Republicans countered by accusing Jackson of tyranny and despotism. They argued that the President had annulled "two houses of Congress, the Supreme Court, and the Constitution of the United States." His Bank veto had raised the possibility of a financial calamity. Worse, the "Constitution is gone!" cried the Washington *National Intelligencer*. "It is a dead letter, and the will of a DICTATOR is the Supreme Law."[16]

The National Republicans also issued a number of political pamphlets raking over Jackson's so-called reform program. One of best of these, *A Retrospect of Andrew Jackson's Administration,* scornfully reviewed the record. In just four years, it read, Jackson had introduced a new requirement for office: "obedience to his will." Nearly a thousand officeholders had been dismissed, new offices created, and all filled with political hacks. In his use of the veto "Jackson has shown a strong propensity to intrude upon the legislative department, and by several successive acts of power has taken from Congress almost half of its powers, and from the Senate more than half." President Jackson "is an Usurper and a Tyrant," declared the *Retrospect,* "and our constitution and laws, under his Chief Magistracy, are but a dead letter."[17]

Perhaps more valuable than these pamphlets were the political cartoons published during the campaign. Cartoonists hostile to Jackson showed greater skill and ingenuity than those supporting the President, probably because the colorful Jackson made such an easy and inviting target. Many of these drawings related to the Jackson-Van Buren relationship and either spoofed Van Buren's dexterity in advancing his own presidential aspirations or ridiculed Old Hickory's reliance on the Little Magician. One such showed Jackson receiving a crown from Van Buren and a scepter from the devil; another depicted the President and others, attired as burglars, directing a large battering ram against the Bank's front doors; still a third, lampooning the spoils system, had a frolicsome red devil flying over the country with strings attached to his fingers, feet, and tail and jiggling the strings to make spoilsmen tied to the other end of the strings bounce and jump like puppets. One extremely popular cartoon showed Jackson and Clay dressed as jockeys and riding a race to the White House with Clay half a length ahead. But the one cartoon that achieved historical renown was entitled "King Andrew the First." In it Jackson is dressed in full regal attire, complete with ermine robe, crown, and scepter. In his left hand he holds a rolled document labeled "veto," and he stands on a tattered copy of the Constitution. At the top of the picture are the words "Born to Command."[18]

15. *Globe,* September 5, 1832, and reprints of editorials from other Democratic newspapers on September 15, 22, October 3, 6, 17, 20, 1832.

16. Cincinnati *Daily Advertiser,* reprinted in the *National Intelligencer,* September 6, 1832.

17. *A Retrospect of Andrew Jackson's Administration* (n.p., 1832), pp. 3–5, 6, 14, 15, 18.

18. Parton, *Jackson,* III, 424.

Both parties organized parades and barbecues and other popular forms of entertainment. Although the rules of the political game did not permit the candidates to campaign on their own behalf, whenever they moved across the country, they generated crowds, public dinners, and many outdoor celebrations. Naturally Jackson and Clay were obliged to acknowledge the acclaim with a few innocuous responses of a patriotic cast and tone.

The President returned to Washington in mid-September, no doubt to watch more carefully the actions of the nullifiers in South Carolina, who had denounced the tariffs of 1828 and 1832 throughout the summer and even threatened to secede from the Union. As he journeyed through Kentucky, Jackson was startled at the hysterical adulation he received. And this was Clay's own state! "Never have I seen such a gathering as met us in advance of Lexington three miles," the President told his nephew Andrew J. Donelson, "to say the least of the number, I may say 5000—and this too without any concert, or notification." The citizens of Lexington even honored him with a barbecue.[19]

As might be expected, Clay had a different interpretation of Jackson's tour through Kentucky. The journey had fired the indignation of a great many people, he claimed, and "has been turned with tremendous effect against him." It had roused the fighting spirits of the National Republicans. "I never witnessed on any former occasion so much activity zeal and firm resolution to triumph in Novr." Our friends have a "complete organization" and the "highest confidence of success."[20]

On the Bank question, Clay also differed with Jackson's opinion of the veto's effect. It "is now beginning to be seriously felt," he announced. Autumn was the season when westerners drove their horses, mules, cattle, and hogs to the eastern depots and other markets. In the past the Bank had always aided this operation "by supplying the means of driving them to market." Now its purchasing drafts, based on anticipated sales, had been suspended following the veto, causing a "considerable reduction of price" of the cattle and much annoyance and apprehension. "The veto is in every body's mouth," Clay reported, "and what is worse seriously felt in the purse."[21]

Any number of Americans were indeed concerned about the effects of the Bank veto, but when they came right down to it, they admired and trusted the President. They believed him patriotic and devoted to their interests. And they regarded the charges of corruption against the BUS as serious and in need of correction.

Because of the location of the central branch of the Bank in Philadelphia, Clay counted on winning Pennsylvania. He thought he might carry New York as well. "If we can get New York and Pennsa. without Ohio, or New York and Ohio, without Pennsylvania, we are safe; but if we lose both Pennsa. and

19. Jackson to Donelson, October 10, 1832, Donelson Papers, LC.

20. Clay to Matthew L. Davis, October 6, 1832, Clay to Johnston, October 6, 1832, in Clay, *Papers,* VIII, 579, 580.

21. Clay to Southard, September 11, 1832, in Clay, *Papers,* VIII, 574–575.

Ohio, even if we gain New York, we must be defeated. I hope our friends in Pennsa. will be fully aware of this state of things."

But Clay had no chance of winning Pennsylvania. Even the mayor of Philadelphia said he would "gain nothing on the Bank question in this State and will lose elsewhere. Attachment to a large monied corporation is not a popular attribute. The feeling of common minds is against Mr. Clay."[22]

By late October Clay's situation looked hopeless to some of his New England supporters. They reported that John Quincy Adams no longer favored his election and that the long-anticipated alliance with the Anti-Masons had completely stalled. In view of all this, and with the likelihood of Pennsylvania's anti-Democratic vote swinging to William Wirt, both Edward and Alexander Everett suggested to Clay that he withdraw, thereby allowing the National Republicans to throw their support to Wirt and thus unseat Jackson.[23] It was an absurd idea, but it showed the defeatist mentality among Clay's closest followers.

Only one really happy event occurred for Clay during these final months of the campaign, and that was the marriage of his beloved son Henry to Julia Prather, on October 10. The senator attended the wedding ceremony in Louisville and declared the "young lady of good fortune, and what is better, of amiable disposition, and cultivated mind." Unfortunately he took ill on his return home, and because the cholera raged along the Ohio River, especially in Louisville and Cincinnati, he predicted that the Democratic press would report his demise. "You may hear that I am dead with the Cholera," he wrote Francis Brooke. "I assure you upon my honor it is not true." The happiness occasioned by young Henry's marriage was dampened considerably by the death of Anne Erwin's daughter Mary, born just a few months before. The child had been sickly and feeble from birth. Still, it was extremely painful for the family to watch her slowly die.[24]

Deaths and disappointments. With but a single exception, they had seemed to dog Clay's path ever since his return home to Kentucky. Nevertheless, Clay kept up a confident front. In early November he was still telling friends that "I have great hopes and strong confidence in the defeat of Genl. Jackson." Surely the people had come to their senses and would make the right decision. "May the decision be such," he wrote, "as will heal the wounds of our bleeding Country, inflicted by the folly & madness of a lawless Military Chieftain!"[25]

22. Clay to Southard, October 23, 1832, in Clay, *Papers,* VIII, 588; B. W. Richards to John McLean, July 19, 1832, McLean Papers, LC. For Clay's New York support among workingmen, see Sean Wilentz, *Chants Democratic: New York City and the Rise of the American Working Class, 1788–1850* (Princeton, 1984), pp. 208–209, 212–213.
23. Everett to Clay, October 29, 1832, Abbott Lawrence to Clay, October 30, 1832, in Clay, *Papers,* VIII, 592–593, 594. See also Henry Dearborn to Clay, October 29, 1832, ibid., VIII, 592.
24. Henry Clay, Jr., manuscript diary, University of Kentucky Library; Clay to James Brown, October 23, 1832, Clay to Southard, October 23, 1832, Clay to Brooke, October 18, 1832, in Clay, *Papers,* VIII, 587, 584.
25. Clay to Charles Dorman, November 3, 1832, in Clay, *Papers,* VIII, 595.

If Clay did sense impending disaster and possible personal humiliation, he disguised it by assuring his supporters that the outcome hardly mattered to their cause. "Let the worst happen," he wrote Samuel Southard, "we shall carry a fresh infusion of vigor and power into Congress, and I hope be able there to check the mad career of the tyrant."[26]

And the "worst" did happen. By mid-November Clay knew that the American people had administered a crushing electoral defeat. He won Massachusetts, Rhode Island, Connecticut, Delaware, a majority of Maryland's vote, and his own state of Kentucky for a total of 49 electoral votes. Jackson took everything else, except Vermont, which went to Wirt, and South Carolina, which threw away its 11 votes on John Floyd of Virginia. The President received 219 votes; Wirt took 7. Of the popular vote, Jackson garnered 688,242, Clay 473,462, and Wirt an astounding 101,051. Van Buren was easily elected Vice President with 189 electoral votes, to 49 for Sergeant, and 7 for Amos Ellmaker, the Anti-Masonic candidate. South Carolina awarded 11 votes to Henry Lee of Massachusetts, and Pennsylvania gave 30 to its favorite son, William Wilkins.[27]

Besides Vermont, Wirt won a surprisingly large bloc of votes in Pennsylvania, New York, Massachusetts, and Connecticut and a smaller bloc from Ohio, Maryland, New Jersey, and Rhode Island, most of which would probably have gone to Clay had he been willing to cast off his Masonic membership prior to the Anti-Masonic National Convention. Clay performed reasonably well in New England (except for Rhode Island) and in some parts of the West, like Ohio, where internal improvements meant a great deal to the electorate. However, he was decisively defeated in Indiana and Illinois and barely won Delaware by a little more than 100 votes. He captured Kentucky by the count of 43,396 to 36,247,[28] but Tennessee gave Jackson 28,740 votes to Clay's 1,436.

The President took virtually everything south and west of the Potomac River. He also did remarkably well in the Middle Atlantic states, less well in New England, although he improved on his 1828 results by winning both Maine and New Hampshire. He had no opposition in Alabama, Georgia, and Mississippi. Maryland, voting by district rather than a general ticket, awarded him three of its ten electoral votes. However, two of Clay's electors did not cast their ballots when the votes were finally tabulated.[29]

Although the final totals of popular votes in this election are extremely inexact, there was no question that Jackson had won a smashing victory. One reason for the inexactitude of the vote was the fact that several states merely registered the vote count as "Jackson" and "anti-Jackson." In other words, the Clay and Wirt totals were merged. Furthermore, the Missouri vote for Clay is

26. Clay to Southard, October 23, 1832, in Clay, *Papers*, VIII, 588.
27. Sven Petersen, *A Statistical History of American Presidential Elections* (New York, 1963), pp. 20–21.
28. Clay apparently carried most of eastern and central Kentucky, while Jackson took the southern and western regions.
29. Remini, "The Election of 1832," I, 515.

never given; it is possible that the Jackson vote (5,192) merely represents the President's majority over the senator. Overall, Jackson received 54.6 percent of the vote, a rare achievement in presidential elections. Yet his popular majority declined by more than 1.5 percent over his 1828 showing, despite the fact that over 100,000 more voters went to the polls. No doubt some Americans disliked Jackson's policies or presidential style; also, the existence of the first third party in a political contest and the improved organizational structure of the two parties may account for Old Hickory's slight decline.[30]

Could Clay have won had he renounced Masonry and received the nomination of the Anti-Masonic party? Probably not. The numbers do not indicate the likelihood of that possibility, no matter which way they are juggled, particularly in the electoral college.

The final result mortified Clay. He was so discouraged that he considered resigning from the Senate. Why should he continue to serve the people when his only reward was their rejection? His spirits touched bottom. And his letters indicated the extent of his despair. "The dark cloud which had been so long suspended over our devoted Country," he wrote, "instead of being dispelled, as we had fondly hoped it would be, has become more dense, more menacing more alarming. Whether we shall ever see light, and law and liberty again, is very questionable."

"We are beaten, my dear Sir," wrote his New York friend Peter Porter, " 'horse foot &' but . . . we must bear it with what philosophy we can." Wrote Francis Granger: "Well, Weed . . . we have suffered a perfect Waterloo defeat."[31]

Apart from Jackson's extraordinary personal popularity, one reason for Clay's defeat may have been his inability to reach the general public. As one historian has astutely observed, Clay's ideas and his position on issues were often delivered in sophisticated economic and political speeches to his colleagues in the Senate and, when published, were principally read by "notables." Clay tended to address a politically informed public, and not the vast numbers of the American people. Unlike Jackson, he lacked the populistic instinct. He simply could not excite the majority's attention and interest in his vision of the nation's future.[32]

Furthermore, Clay had blundered in persuading Biddle to apply for a recharter of the BUS four years early, thereby provoking a presidential veto and providing the Democrats with a moral issue and unbeatable propaganda. Again, he gambled on a long shot for his own personal gain, and again he ensured his ultimate defeat.

30. Remini, *Jackson*, II, 391.

31. Clay to Hammond, November 17, 1832, Clay to Henry Clay, Jr., January 3, 1833, Porter to Clay, November 22, 1832, in Clay, *Papers*, VIII, 599, 607; Granger to Weed, November 13, 1832, Granger Papers, LC.

32. M. J. Heale, *The Presidential Quest: Candidates and Images in American Political Culture, 1787–1852* (London and New York, 1982), p. 112.

Finally, there were a great many people who distrusted him and worried about his all-consuming ambition, his ravenous appetite for the presidency. They also believed him morally wanting. The "corrupt bargain" still haunted him and continued to do so for the remainder of his life.

Clay had expected to delay his departure for Washington in preparation of moving into the White House. Now, as he told his son, "it seems that I must go to Washington this winter." Now he must face his friends and colleagues, face their embarrassment over expressing their feelings regarding his over-whelming defeat. It seemed to him at this time that he would be better off if he abandoned politics completely and devoted himself entirely to his farm and home.

But this mood of despair hardly lasted a month. And although his spirits would take time to become buoyant again, he soon began to regain his old enthusiasm and optimism. "We must go on to the last," he said, "with what spirit we can, to discharge our duty." After all, as he reminded his son, "I have . . . much reason to look back, with satisfaction, upon my public life, 'tho' it has not been free from a full share of thorns."[33]

Even his sense of humor over his defeat eventually peeked through. "I think I am entitled to your congratulations for our recent political defeat," he said with a straight face to one man. "Jackson had so completely put every thing into disorder, that we should have found it very difficult to mend fences and repair his injuries. Besides, perhaps he and his brother nullifiers of So. Carolina ought to settle matters themselves."[34]

Clay might make light of the looming crisis, but he knew eventually it had to be addressed and resolved. He had always regarded Jackson's behavior to-ward Georgia over that state's quarrel with the Cherokee Indians, despite the decision of the Supreme Court, as tantamount to an act of nullification.[35] In addition, the President's Bank veto had dismissed out of hand the High Court's opinion on the constitutionality of the BUS. And now that the South Carolina hotheads had started to take bold action against the tariff by calling a convention, there seemed to be taking shape a truly frightening constitutional emergency, one that might conceivably lead to bloodshed. Perhaps Clay needed to get back to Washington after all. Perhaps the country could still profit from his statesmanship.

But traces of his despair persisted. "It is under feelings of this kind that I expect, a week or two hence," he wrote on November 17, "to go to Washing-ton. There I fear I shall be unable, either to do good or to prevent mischief."[36]

Senator Clay was never more wrong.

33. Clay to Henry Clay, Jr., November 24, 1832, January 3, 1833, Clay to Hammond, November 17, 1832, in Clay, *Papers,* VIII, 600, 599, 607.

34. Clay to James Caldwell, December 9, 1832, in Clay, *Papers,* VIII, 602.

35. Clay to Henry Clay, Jr., November 24, 1832, in Clay, *Papers,* VIII, 600.

36. Clay to Hammond, November 17, 1832, in Clay, *Papers,* VIII, 599.

—— T W E N T Y - F O U R ——

Return to Triumph

AT FIRST Clay thought of waiting until Christmas before leaving for Washington, but the dread of a winter's journey, the good weather the nation enjoyed throughout the fall months of 1832, and the necessity of getting through, as fast as possible, the difficult moments when he first faced his colleagues convinced him to leave Ashland on November 28. His wife did not accompany him inasmuch as the second session of Congress was the short session "and not likely to be a very agreeable one." But his fifteen-year-old son, James Brown Clay, did join him since he was headed for Boston to enter the commercial house of Grant, Seaver & Co., a dry goods establishment located at 5 Liberty Square.[1]

As was his custom on beginning a long absence from home, Clay wrote a new will, which he entrusted to his wife. He named Henry Clay, Jr., one of its executors, as an expression of his confidence and pleasure in the young man. Theodore, who had been visiting the family lately and had conducted himself "quietly," returned to the asylum the day following the senator's departure, his mother "now fully convinced that he is deranged." Recently Lucretia had begun to look perpetually unhappy, mostly because her "two eldest sons are living sorrows to her. . . . One irreclaimably dissipated, the other insane and confined to a hospital." The regular and extended absences of her husband each year, leaving the overall supervision of the family and farm principally to her, added to her burden. A devout, churchgoing woman, she bore her "afflictions" with steadfast Christian fortitude.[2]

Because the weather cooperated, it took Clay only a week and a half to reach Washington, traveling via the Ohio River and the National Road from

1. Clay to Crittenden, November 28, 1832, Clay to James Brown, December 9, 1832, Clay to Henry Clay, Jr., December 30, 1832, in Clay, *Papers,* VIII, 601, 602, 606.
2. Clay to Henry Clay, Jr., November 24, 1832, Clay to James Caldwell, December 9, 1832, Anne Erwin to Clay, December 13, 1832, in Clay, *Papers,* VIII, 600, 602, 603; Edward Bates to Julia Bates, December 4, 1829 [but probably January 1830], Edward Bates Papers, Virginia Historical Society, Richmond; Smith, *Forty Years,* p. 324.

Wheeling, Virginia. The nation's economic growth and industrial development seemed more apparent than ever. Railroads had begun to finger their
way from city and city, and some men speculated that they would soon stretch
from the Atlantic to the Mississippi.

Clay arrived at the capital on December 9. After settling himself in his
Washington quarters, he found that the South Carolina situation had deteriorated so rapidly and so disastrously that he had no time to think about his
own unhappy predicament. He did not dwell on the late election, not even to
attempt an analysis of what had happened. It was useless to discuss it, he told
Francis Brooke. "From whatever causes it proceeded, it is now irrevocable."
The important question now centered on South Carolina and what was to be
done about its most recent action.[3]

The nullifiers had won an impressive victory in South Carolina's fall election, and Governor James Hamilton, Jr., immediately summoned the newly
elected legislature into special session. On October 22 the legislature, in turn,
called for a convention to meet at Columbia on November 19, 1832, to respond to the action taken by Congress in enacting a new tariff law. The convention, after it met, passed an Ordinance of Nullification on November 24, by
a vote of 136 to 26, which declared the tariffs of 1828 and 1832 "null, void, and
no law, nor binding" upon the state, its officers, or its citizens. After February
1, 1833, "it shall not be lawful," continued the ordinance, ". . . to enforce the
payment of duties . . . within the limits of this State." If the federal government
uses force against South Carolina, then the people of the state will consider
themselves absolved from all political connection with the people of other
states "and will forthwith proceed to organize a separate Government."[4]

In preparing his fourth annual message to Congress, delivered on December 4, the President had not yet learned the action of the Nullification Convention. The message, therefore, tried to be extremely conciliatory toward South
Carolina, at least until the state's intentions were better known. "As to nullification in the south," Jackson told his new Vice President, Martin Van Buren,
"I mean to pass it barely in review, as a mere buble, view the existing laws as
competent to check and put it down, and ask merely a general provision to be
enacted, to authorize the Collector . . . to demand of all vessels . . . where a state
. . . resist the collection of the revenue, the duty to be paid in cash."[5]

The message also attacked protectionism, and it called for the reduction of
the tariff to revenue level, the divestiture of the government's stock in the BUS,
the lessening of government-sponsored internal improvements, and the sale of
public lands to actual settlers at a price sufficient only to cover the government's costs in administering them, along with their eventual surrender to the

3. Clay to Francis T. Brooke, December 12, 1832, in Clay, *Papers,* VIII, 603.

4. *State Papers on Nullification* (Boston, 1834), pp. 29–31; William W. Freehling, *Prelude to Civil
War: The Nullification Movement in South Carolina, 1816–1836* (New York, 1966), passim.

5. Jackson to Van Buren, November 18, 1832, in Jackson, *Correspondence,* IV, 489.

states. The President also reaffirmed his support of Indian removal but said nothing about the Supreme Court's decision in the dispute between Georgia and the Cherokees.[6]

Jackson's conciliatory approach to the nullification danger struck some observers as most uncharacteristic. But when the news of the Nullification Ordinance of November 24 reached Washington, the fire-breathing, supernationalist President responded with his famed Proclamation of December 10, in which he warned South Carolinians that "disunion by armed force is *treason.*" Are you ready to incur its guilt? he asked. "If you are, on the heads of the instigators of the act be the dreadful consequences; on their heads be the dishonor, but on yours may fall the punishment."[7]

It was a superb state paper and a major statement in constitutional law. Abraham Lincoln later extracted from it the basic argument he needed to meet the secession crisis in 1861. The proclamation had a powerful nationalistic thrust and appealed to the patriotic sensibilities of Americans in all sections of the country.[8]

Jackson's about-face on nullification totally baffled Clay, as it did many other congressmen. "One short week," said the senator, "produced the message and the Proclamation—the former ultra, on the side of State rights—the latter ultra, on the side of Consolodation." But on the whole, Clay liked the proclamation, although he confessed it may have been a trifle strong, "which I cannot stomach." It ought to have been issued weeks ago, he declared, and might have had a better effect in allaying public fear and apprehension.[9]

Although the proclamation made it clear that Jackson would not tolerate South Carolina's violation of federal law, the crisis could be resolved if tariff rates were lowered across the board, and this the President meant to do as a gesture of conciliation. In brief, he hoped to scuttle protectionism, on which so much of Clay's American System rested. His secretary of the treasury, Louis McLane, began working with the chairman of the House Ways and Means Committee, Gulian C. Verplanck, to devise a suitable bill. Thus, as it soon developed, Clay was obliged to provide an alternate measure in order to protect the American System.

Around mid-December the senator turned his full attention to the problem. What he finally produced demonstrated anew the strength, originality, and flexibility of his mind in finding solutions to seemingly intractable political problems. In just a few days he devised the kernel of his solution, and he wrote

6. Richardson, *Messages and Papers*, II, 1157ff. A recent and excellent study of the nullification crisis is Richard E. Ellis, *The Union at Risk: Jacksonian Democracy, States' Rights and the Nullification Crisis* (New York, 1987).

7. Richardson, *Messages and Papers*, II, 1217–1218.

8. For a more detailed analysis of Jackson's proclamation, see Remini, *Jackson*, III, 17–23.

9. Clay to Brooke, December 12, 1832, in Clay, *Papers*, VIII, 603. According to John Tyler, Clay unhesitatingly pronounced the proclamation *"ultra-federal, black cockade."* Tyler to Clay, September 18, 1839, in Clay, *Papers*, IX, 341.

down a draft proposal for a new—a compromise—tariff. In it he acknowl-edged the sharp differences between pro- and antiprotectionists and how their disagreements had agitated the public mind and threatened serious conse-quences. He went on to propose, as a means of preventing a catastrophic civil war, that the existing tariff laws remain in force until March 3, 1840—virtually the end of the administration following Jackson's—at which time all the tariff laws would be repealed. From the present to 1840 no higher or other duties than those already existing would be laid. After that date all duties collected would be equal and laid for the purpose of providing only such revenue as the government needed to operate "without regard to the protection or encour-agement of any branch of domestic industry whatever."[10]

It was a breathtaking idea. To spare the country possible civil war and the breakup of the Union, Clay would sacrifice protection after a period of time during which industry could continue to enjoy the benefits of the present tariff schedule. In effect, it declared a truce for seven years. After that date protec-tionism would end. Both sides in the dispute could claim victory; both sides would achieve their immediate goals.

One of Clay's earliest biographers, a man named Epes Sargent, suggested that this compromise scheme was first conceived in Philadelphia.[11] Clay had gone to that city with his son James on December 13, to accompany the young man at least part of the way to his Boston destination. He alerted his brother-in-law James Brown, who had retired from his Louisiana plantation to Phila-delphia, of his coming but begged him not to advertise it because he wanted to avoid crowds and company as much as possible.[12]

Clay remained in Philadelphia almost three weeks. James went on to Boston shortly after their arrival, and Clay resided with his brother-in-law until January 2.[13] During that extended period, according to Epes Sargent, the senator consulted with a number of men about what should be done in the developing emergency. He spoke to Josiah Johnston, senator from Louisiana and his longtime adviser and valued friend, and a group of distinguished indus-trialists, including Messrs. E. I. du Pont, Bovie, Richards, and others. All of them expressed their concern over Jackson's intention to kill protectionism, and all of them wanted to know what Clay specifically planned to do about it.

During Clay's absence in Philadelphia, Congressman Verplanck, in the name of his Ways and Means Committee, brought forward a new tariff bill. But it was really Jackson's bill. The President later referred to the measure as

10. Draft proposal, inclosed in a letter by Webster to Hiram Ketchum, January 20, 1838, in Webster, *Papers, Correspondence*, IV, 263–264. Webster claimed he copied it from Clay's own draft.

11. Sargent, *Clay*, pp. 140–141. Van Deusen, *Clay*, p. 266, also cites Philadelphia as the place where the plan was drawn up. The fullest explanation of the scheme may be found in Merrill D. Peterson, *Olive Branch and Sword: The Compromise of 1833* (Baton Rouge, 1982), pp. 51–53.

12. Clay to Brooke, December 12, 1832, Clay to Brown, December 9, 1832, in Clay, *Papers*, VIII, 602, 603.

13. Clay to Henry Clay, Jr., December 30, 1832, January 3, [1833], in Clay, *Papers*, VIII, 606, 607.

"the Tariff bill prepared by McLain [*sic*] under my view."[14] Although this Verplanck bill, as it was called, did not propose to abandon the principle of protection, it did provide huge reductions, which would lower duties by 50 percent to the level of 1816, as amended in 1818. A few duties were raised. Even fewer, like coffee and tea, were removed from the free list. Most important of all, the reductions would go into effect over a two-year period—half in 1834 and the rest in 1835.[15]

Despite the fact that the Verplanck bill did not satisfy Jackson's declared desire to terminate the principle of protection, it did address South Carolina's principal grievance by erasing previous wrongs. The administration hoped the bill would be seen by the nullifiers as a gesture of friendship and a wish to reconcile past differences. But to protectionists the bill threatened economic disaster, even if it did preserve the principle of protection.

It may have been at this approximate time that Clay outlined his seven-year truce proposal to Brown, Johnston, and the group of industrialists in Philadelphia. With the Union in seemingly imminent danger, and with the administration proposing a "substantial repeal of the tariff," Clay had to come up with a plan that would satisfy the needs of the industrialists yet appease the clamor of the nullifiers—an apparent impossibility.[16] His scheme, as he proposed it to these industrialists, would gain them time with which they might seek additional popular support for their position and enjoy a period of security at the current high rate of protection. But the price was the announced abandonment of protection at the end of the seven-year period. Clay's plan would slow the process of abandoning the principle, but eventually protectionists would have to face the day when the rates would be lowered to revenue level.

Clay's willingness to abandon protection caused some men to question his motives and his commitment to principle. But the Kentuckian was never rigid in his ideological thinking. Like any intelligent politician, he understood that politics is not about ideological purity or moral self-righteousness. It is about governing, and if a politician cannot compromise, he cannot govern effectively. And Henry Clay knew that only a true compromise—one in which both sides sacrifice something to achieve a greater benefit—could win over the nullifiers and draw them back from a determined course of self-destruction.

In presenting his compromise, Clay no doubt recognized that if he spared the nation the agony of bloodshed, he would reclaim his shattered image as a party leader. He would be hailed as a great statesman, nimble-witted enough to find the solution to resolve the conflicting sectional interests that threatened

14. Jackson to Blair, August 12, 1841, Jackson Papers, LC. In a letter to Van Buren, Mahlon Dickerson said that it was generally understood that the bill was "drawn by your *Pet* McLane." January 11, 1833, Van Buren Papers, LC. All but one member of the Ways and Means Committee supported the bill as reported.

15. *House Report,* no. 14, 22d Congress, 2d session, p. 21.

16. Clay to Henry Clay, Jr., January 3, [1833], in Clay, *Papers,* VIII, 607–608.

the life of the nation. As an additional benefit, the abandonment of protection would surely swell his support in the South, where he desperately needed it. No doubt Clay's motives in deciding to lend his hand to the resolution of this crisis grew partly out of his pride and political ambition as well as his commitment to the Union and its republican ideals.

It is very likely that during these conversations in Philadelphia Clay outlined still another alternative plan, a backup, one that might be necessary to guarantee southern votes for a compromise. According to this second proposal, all the tariff laws would be repealed immediately, and a new law substituted with the following features: duties on all unprotected articles to be abolished forthwith, a reduction of 5 percent or 10 percent on protected articles, and the duties on the protected items "to be abated ⅓ or ½ three years and a half hence and seven years hence all duties for protection to cease entirely and a general ad valorem to be substituted upon all importations."[17]

As they listened to his schemes to save the Union, the industrialists no doubt realized that Clay, as the instrument of a reconciliation, would gain national recognition and acclaim that might eventually bring him into the White House. As head of the government, at some future date, perhaps he would find still another solution to restore the protective rates they wanted. Besides, Clay did not propose a permanent abandonment of protection. In any event, and for whatever reasons, they gave him their unqualified approval for the seven-year scheme. They also advised him, with respect to the second plan, to wait until he had an opportunity to speak with southerners upon his return to Washington.[18]

During his stay in Philadelphia Clay ran into Daniel Webster, who was returning to Washington from Boston. The two senators discussed the crisis facing the nation, and Clay showed his friend the seven-year proposal he had just explained to the committee of businessmen.[19] Webster was positively appalled by the plan since it surrendered the principle of protection. He had long since abandoned his original laissez-faire position on the tariff and now strongly advocated high rates of protection for northern manufactures. He later said he opposed Clay's plan at every stage of its development toward ultimate passage, and "so did three fourths of the Tariff interest in both Houses."[20]

When Clay returned to Washington, he closeted himself with a number of southern congressmen who did not support South Carolina's extreme reaction to the tariff question but who did insist on lower rates in any effort toward

17. John Tyler to John Floyd, January 10, 1833, in Floyd Papers, LC.

18. In a speech in the Senate, Clay later acknowledged this committee of businessmen as the real originator of his efforts at compromise, for they had come to him to save the manufacturing interests from ruin. *Register of Debates,* 22d Congress, 2d session, p. 968.

19. Sargent, *Clay,* p. 141.

20. *Congressional Globe,* 25th Congress, 3d session, pp. 172–173; Webster to Hiram Ketchum, January 20, 1838, in Webster, *Papers, Correspondence,* IV, 263–264.

compromise.[21] Moreover, "the *principle* involved," they said, constituted their "main concern." They had borne the protective system for ten or fifteen years, "in all its oppression." It was now time for a change. Senator John Tyler of Virginia, for example, had approached Clay immediately following the publication of the President's proclamation and told him flat-out of "the true glory which he had it in his power now to acquire" by coming up with a solution acceptable to both sides. Tyler "conversed freely" with a number of Clay's friends and "urged similar suggestions—and I begin to flatter myself that they have not been entirely disregarded."[22]

Clay rather liked Tyler, despite his Democratic commitment, and described him as opposed to both nullification and the actions taken by South Carolina. He very much hoped Tyler would be reelected to the Senate and urged his friends in Virginia to give him their support.[23]

In meeting with Tyler and other southern congressmen, Clay revealed his two plans and offered to surrender the *"principle"* in return for *"time."*

"Time," responded Tyler, "is of little importance to us." He wanted the surrender of the principle of protection, and he felt certain other southerners who rejected nullification would agree with him. After this initial meeting he offered to discuss Clay's proposals with some confidential Virginia friends and get their reaction.

Tyler turned first to the governor of Virginia and outlined what Clay had suggested. "I want your aid in this important matter," he told Governor John Floyd. "Consult *in the strictest confidence* with those around you and let me have your views. Bear in mind that the principle of protection is to be utterly abandoned—and the wound inflicted on the constitution thereby to be healed." As for the Verplanck bill, he continued, it most likely would pass the House, but its fate in the Senate was "doubtful in the extreme." For one thing, it laid a heavy hand on northern manufactures and might even annihilate some of them, such as the woolens industry. And if the Verplanck bill did become law, "what assurance have we that . . . [it] will be permitted to stand. Besides the protective principle is preserved." By accepting Clay's proposal, Tyler continued, we give northerners time to enjoy the present benefits of the tariff; they in return give us, after a period of time, the abandonment of protection. "When we talk of reconcilement and a restoration of peace," he declared, "would it not be better to have a peace de facto and embrace in true brotherly affection." Tyler was so taken with Clay's proposals that he was almost ready to "say to you that the battle is fought and won. My fears for the Union are rapidly dissipating."[24]

21. Sargent claims that Clay had no interviews with southern congressmen until he was about to submit his compromise bill to the Congress. Sargent, *Clay*, p. 141. But Tyler's letter to Floyd on January 10 disproves that statement.

22. Tyler to Floyd, January 10, 1833, Floyd Papers, LC.

23. Clay to Brooke, January 24, 1833, in Clay, *Papers*, VIII, 615.

24. Tyler to Floyd, January 10, 1833, Floyd Papers, LC.

Tyler's very positive reaction to the basic idea of a surrender of principle in return for time—one that drew increasing southern support over the following weeks—gave Clay an added incentive to try to manage a compromise through Congress, and it immediately revived his optimism about the role he could play and the "true glory" that might redound to his credit. In a single stroke he could reclaim all that he had lost in the recent electoral debacle. "It is among the possibilities that Henry Clay may yet be, south of the Potomac, what Andrew Jackson *has* been, the most popular man in the land."[25]

But what of the danger of another corrupt bargain charge—namely, that he had sold out his principles in return for southern support in order to position himself for another run for the presidency? Northern friends of protection were, like Webster, distinctly hostile to Clay's idea when they heard about it. They could easily charge him with self-serving betrayal.

Besides, there was the great temptation to do nothing and let the people suffer the consequences of their electoral folly. Let them now endure what the "madness of a lawless Military Chieftain" had brought. When it comes to conducting public affairs, Clay declared, there is a simple principle worth noting: "when we do not see a very plainly marked way, to do nothing." And considering how he had been treated by both the pro- and antitariff parties, he thought he ought to "leave them to fight it out as well as they can." We have no future, he despaired in a moment of weakness. "After 44 years of existance under the present Constitution what single principle is fixed? The Bank? No. Internal Improvements! No. The Tariff? No. Who is to interpret the Constitution? No. We are as much afloat at sea as the day when the Constitution went into operation. There is nothing certain but that the *will* of Andw. Jackson is to govern; and that will fluctuates with the change of every pen which gives expression to it."[26]

Thus, if Clay did nothing, a mad tyrant would set the nation's agenda and provoke havoc and bloody civil war. Jackson "has marked out two victims," Clay declared, "So. Carolina, and the Tariff and the only question with him is which shall be first immolated."[27]

Ultimately Clay shook off this despair and self-pity. He could not allow his disappointments and bitterness to determine his behavior and actions. As he said, the "lingering hopes of my country prevail over these feelings of a just resentment, and my judgment tells me that disregarding them I ought to the last to endeavor to do what I can to preserve its molestations and reestablish confidence and discord. I shall act in conformity with this judgment."[28]

Although the danger that his motives would be impugned was irrefutable,

25. William Hammet to Thomas White, February 11, 1833, Hammet Papers, Virginia Historical Society, Richmond.

26. Clay to Charles J. Faulkner, January 11, 1833, Clay to Brooke, January 17, 1833, in Clay, *Papers,* VIII, 611, 613.

27. Clay to Peter B. Porter, January 29, 1833, in Clay, *Papers,* VIII, 617.

28. Clay to Brooke, January 17, 1833, in Clay, *Papers,* VIII, 613–614.

then and later,[29] Clay elected to risk it. His instincts as a gambler told him that the odds were all in his favor. He could argue, as he subsequently did, that he was motivated solely by his love for the Union, not by presidential ambition, and that his plan was intended to prevent secession and civil war. If he succeeded, the people would hardly concern themselves with his reasons for sparing them the agony of bloodshed. They would hail him as the savior of his country.

This concern for the welfare of the nation was no deception. He did indeed act out of a deep commitment to the country and its people, even if he did understand the beneficial effect a victorious compromise would have upon his future presidential plans. In taking the course he ultimately pursued, Clay bent every effort to prevent the dismemberment of the nation. As he later said, "the key to my heart" was his love for the Union. He felt he must now take the initiative toward compromise in order to prevent the "military chieftain" from initiating a bloodbath in South Carolina.[30]

And with every new action taken by the President and South Carolina, a violent confrontation seemed absolutely certain. South Carolina showed no sign of backing away from nullification, and to strengthen its posture in Washington, an "arrangement" was devised whereby Robert Y. Hayne resigned as United States senator and succeeded James Hamilton, Jr., as governor, and John C. Calhoun resigned as Vice President of the United States and was elected by the state legislature to take Hayne's seat in the Senate. In this way a powerful mind and voice had been thrust to the center of the political arena in Washington to defend nullification and the rights of the states.

For his part, President Jackson responded to the growing emergency by submitting a force bill to Congress on January 16, 1833. He cited his obligation as the chief executive to enforce the laws and collect the federal revenue. Since an organized opposition to the collection of the revenue might commence in South Carolina on February 1, he asked that he be authorized to call out the state militia and use federal ships and troops should the application of force become necessary. He also requested permission to move the customs in order to force the nullifiers to go to considerable trouble to provoke a confrontation.

As the clerk read Jackson's force bill message to the upper house, the newly elected senator from South Carolina sat glaring intensely ahead of him. The words were droned out for more than an hour and a half. At their conclusion Calhoun demanded the floor and spoke for half an hour. This once-handsome man, whose face had now begun to show the scars of his disappointments and bitterness, spoke with "passion and excitement." He

29. In the past I, too, have questioned Clay's motives. But in studying his life close up, and not from Jackson's position, I have come to appreciate Clay's genuine commitment to and love for the Union as his first priority. See Remini, *Jackson*, III, 38.

30. The quotation about the key to his heart comes from a speech he gave in Norfolk, Virginia, April 22, 1844, copy CPP.

denounced the President for leading the nation into military despotism. Without provocation, in a time of peace, he stormed, "our Union stands on the eve of dissolution or the verge of a civil war." It was obvious, he cried, "that the country had now reached a crisis." But the senator's ranting and passion brought only a snicker from Jackson. "Mr. Calhoun let off a little of his ire against me today in the Senate," he chuckled, "but was so agitated and confused that he made quite a failure."[31]

Although Clay approved of providing the President with all necessary and constitutional power to execute the laws, he had no confidence that Jackson would refrain from abusing the power. He was sure Old Hickory itched to indulge "certain vengeful passions" against South Carolina. The tyrant would like nothing better than to drench the state in blood.[32]

To everyone's surprise the senator who stepped forward as the administration's spokesman in support of the force bill was Daniel Webster. A nationalist to the bone, who regarded nullification as a horror, the Massachusetts senator lavishly praised Jackson's proclamation, which he endorsed in every particular. To cynics he seemed to be offering to ally himself to the President with the expectation of switching parties and perhaps succeeding Jackson in 1836. It was rumored that he would even "wage the war with Mr Calhoun" in the Senate on the administration's behalf. Then, when he started accepting invitations for dinner at the White House, suspicion gave way to certitude that an alliance had been achieved. "I dined at the Palace, yes, Palace, a few days since," wrote Senator Tyler, "and found Mr. W. there in all his glory."[33]

Van Buren paled at the rumors. Besides his losing the possibility of succession, declared the disturbed Clay, the Magician's friends were also apprehensive that the passage of the Verplanck bill would raise Calhoun as a "successful vindicator of Southern rights" and keep Jackson in check from his intended assault on South Carolina.[34]

A bruising clash between Webster and Calhoun occurred in mid-February. The South Carolinian gave his first major and extended speech on February 15. He stood rigidly at his desk, tense, angry, resentful, even a little frightening. His eyes, hypnotic at times, roamed continuously around the packed chamber as though looking for some villain to identify and shame. He held his

---

31. *Register of Debates,* 22d Congress, 2d session, pp. 100–103; Silas Wright, Jr. to Azariah C. Flagg, January 19, 1833, Flagg Papers, New York Public Library; Jackson to Joel Poinsett, January 16, 1833, Poinsett Papers, Historical Society of Pennsylvania. Later on, whenever Clay wished to taunt Calhoun, he would mimic him with the expression that "the country had now reached a crisis."

32. Clay to James Brown, January 28, 1833, Clay to Brooke, January 24, 1833, Clay, *Papers,* VIII, 616, 615.

33. Tyler to Floyd, January 22, 1833, in "Original Letters," *William and Mary College Quarterly Historical Magazine,* XXI (1912), p. 11. "Few men understand, and can play upon the avarice and ambition of the human heart than Andrew Jackson," wrote William Hammet to Thomas White, February 4, 1833, Hammet Papers, Virginia Historical Society.

34. Clay to Brooke, January 24, 1833, in Clay, *Papers,* VIII, 615.

audience in a viselike grip as he poured scorn on the President's force bill, calling it a "Bloody Bill," a "War Bill," an unconstitutional declaration of war against his state.[35]

Webster responded with another eloquent statement on the nature of the Union, belaboring his point that the government was not a compact. "He hung his cause," criticized John Quincy Adams, "upon a broken hinge."[36] Webster made only one slip in an otherwise effective speech when he acknowledged that nullification might be justified if the Constitution was in fact a compact of states. Calhoun seized his opportunity to teach Webster a little history, and he almost got the better of him. John Randolph, sitting nearby, nodded his head in agreement as he listened. Although he regarded nullification as humbug and Calhoun a rude intrusion, he agreed with virtually everything the South Carolinian said. A hat lying on a seat in front of him partially obscured his view of Webster. "Take away that hat," he shrilled in his high, piercing voice. "I want to see Webster die, muscle by muscle."[37]

President Jackson delighted over Webster's spirited defense of his policy toward nullification. "Mr. Webster replied to Mr. Calhoun yesterday," Jackson told a Unionist in South Carolina, "and, it is said, demolished him. It is believed by more than one, that Mr. C. is in a state of dementation—his speech was a perfect failure."[38] Except for Thomas Hart Benton, the President did not have another really powerful voice to argue his case in the upper house. Therefore, Webster's support of everything the President said and did during the present crisis delighted Jacksonians but scandalized National Republicans. It was increasingly rumored that his desertion to the Democratic side was imminent.[39]

A final vote on the force bill came swiftly on February 20 despite Calhoun's repeated efforts to block its enactment. By a count of thirty-two to one, the Senate approved Jackson's request. All the nullifiers walked out of the chamber during the voting. Only John Tyler, who opposed the use of force against a sovereign state, as well as nullification, cast the single negative vote. Both Henry Clay and Thomas Hart Benton were among those not recorded.[40]

Clay really supported the force bill, although reluctantly because he had no confidence in Jackson's ability to execute it properly. He insisted he had left

35. Charles Wiltse, *John C. Calhoun, Nullifier* (Indianapolis and New York, 1949), p. 189; *Register of Debates,* 22d Congress, 2d session, pp. 519–553.
36. Adams, *Memoirs,* VIII, 526.
37. Wiltse, *Calhoun, Nullifier,* p. 194. For a different version of the Randolph anecdote, see Peterson, *Olive Branch and Sword,* p. 63.
38. Jackson to Joel Poinsett, February 17, 1833, Poinsett Papers, Historical Society of Pennsylvania.
39. An excellent account of the abortive efforts to bring about a Jackson-Webster alliance is Norman Brown, "Webster-Jackson Movement for a Constitution and Union Party in 1833," *Mid-America,* XLVI, (1964), pp. 147–171.
40. *Register of Debates,* 22d Congress, 2d session, p. 688.

the chamber a bit earlier because he was worn out with fatigue and did not expect a final vote to be called.[41] And he chose not to record his vote either on the "Engrossment, or the final passage of the Bill."[42] Because he was closeted constantly with southerners during these days of heated debate, in attempting to work out a compromise solution to the crisis, Clay probably felt it politically wiser to abstain from an open declaration of support for the force bill.[43] So he quietly disappeared and the next day said he could not "breathe the impure air of the Senate Chamber after dinner."[44]

Throughout the debate Clay was relatively quiet—but hardly inactive. He was involved in intense negotiations over a new tariff bill. And he was quite open about it. Even those in the opposition guessed what he was up to, and they gossiped and fretted about it constantly. Just prior to the passage of the force bill, Senator Silas Wright, Jr., of New York—Van Buren's leading henchman in the Senate—reported to the Albany Regency what he suspected was occurring in private between Calhoun and Clay. Calhoun, he said, will never permit the use of military force in his state and therefore will accept some "arrangement" with Clay to prevent Jackson from invoking the force bill. The Verplanck bill will somehow be jettisoned, Wright predicted, and Clay will step forward with a "peace offering" in the form of a substitute tariff, which Calhoun will immediately pronounce "an acceptable offering to S. Carolina." Then both the Clay and Calhoun forces will "join to put down the war bill as they call it." Thus Clay and Calhoun would get credit for preventing bloodshed and preserving the Union.[45]

41. Clay to Philip R. Fendall, August 8, 1836, in Clay, *Papers,* VIII, 862.

42. Webster to Joseph Hopkinson, February 21, 1833, in Webster, *Papers, Correspondence,* III, 219.

43. "You afterwards expressed to me," wrote John Tyler to Clay a few years later, "your dissatisfaction with the force Bill, and when afterwards you declared in the Senate, that had you been present you would have voted for it, am I mistaken in the fact that in a conversation afterwards with me you ascribed that declaration to the circumstance that the Northern members required you to make it as the condition of their support of the Compromise Bill." Tyler to Clay, September 18, 1839, in Clay, *Papers,* IX, 341.

44. Webster to Joseph Hopkinson, February 21, 1833, in Webster, *Papers, Correspondence* III, 219; *Register of Debates,* 22d Congress, 2d session, pp. 689–690. "I left the Senate the night the force bill passed about Eight OClock, whilst Mr. Webster was speaking, after the Chamber was lighted up. I left it, because I cannot endure the atmosphere of the room when lighted, I did not expect moreover that the vote would be taken that night." Clay to Philip R. Fendall, August 8, 1836, in Clay, *Papers,* VIII, 862.

45. Wright to Azariah C. Flagg, January 14, February 2, 1833, Flagg Papers, New York Public Library. See also Michael Hoffman to Flagg, January 15, 1833, ibid. Wright's suspicions come close to complete accuracy. His only miscalculations involved passage of the force bill and a belief that Webster was also involved in the "arrangement." Said Webster: "You have seen hints in the Newspapers, that Mr Clay & Mr Calhoun were in negotiation, to settle the Tariff question. Such is still the rumour, & I have no doubt *it is true.* What the precise plan is, or will be, I know not. It is understood Mr C[lay] will agree to almost any thing, in order to settle the question, save the Nullifiers & obtain the credit of *pacification."* Webster to Joseph Hopkinson, February 9, 1833, in Webster, *Papers, Correspondence,* III, 213.

Indeed, over the past several weeks Clay met privately not only with Calhoun[46] but with an increasing number of other congressmen as well, both northern and southern. Contacts with the southern representatives was arranged by his Kentucky colleague in the House Robert Letcher, who "was intimate with Mr. George McDuffie [of South Carolina] and other southern gentlemen."[47] Because Jackson made the force bill his first priority and all but forgot the Verplanck bill, Calhoun understood that unless he could come to an acceptable arrangement with Clay on the tariff, there was every likelihood that bloodshed would ensue and surely ruin his cause throughout the South. "Calhoun is, (politically), a dead cock in the pit," insisted Senator William R. King of Alabama. "The father of nullification under no circumstances can even receive the support of the Southern States."[48]

For Clay, the problem was not so much Calhoun and his southern sympathizers as it was the protariff senators, numbering eleven or twelve, who kept rejecting his scheme for compromise. Like Webster, they flatly refused to give up the principle of protection, even when Clay tried to assure them that he himself had not abandoned protectionism (at least not immediately and not permanently) and that for a specified period of time they had a guarantee of fixed rates at the highest possible level. This period of grace, he insisted, would provide industrialists with an enormous economic advantage. The manufacturers he met in Philadelphia acknowledged that fact, he argued. But most important of all, his plan would prevent the crisis from escalating into war. Surely they understood that compromise was the only means by which war could be avoided. And compromise meant sacrifice.

But some of these senators remained skeptical. In an attempt to invoke his ego and pride, they told Clay that his proposal would surely destroy him "in the public estimation" and that perhaps they ought to rally behind Webster and form a new party.[49]

Clay sought out each one of these senators and "interrogated" him individually. He held "two distinct meetings" of the entire group, "at the first of which he [Webster] attended, and to the last he was summoned."[50] Webster described Clay as obsessed with finding a compromise, calling it "his mania of pacification."

---

46. Senator Thomas Hart Benton of Missouri claims that the initial meeting between Clay and Calhoun, arranged by Representative Letcher, "was cold, distant and civil" because they were supposedly not on speaking terms. Later Calhoun warmed up when he allegedly heard that Jackson intended to have him arrested and tried for high treason. Benton, *Thirty Years' View*, I, 342–343. John Q. Adams met with John Davis, who admitted that he disapproved the "compromise between Clay and Calhoun and said Clay had stepped over the Potomac." *Memoirs*, VIII, 525.

47. Sargent, *Clay*, p. 141. Clay later regretted consulting so many congressmen, thus possibly jeopardizing eventual passage of the compromise. See Chapter XL.

48. King to Van Buren, January 9, 1833, Van Buren Papers, LC.

49. Clay to Biddle, April 10, 1833, in Clay, *Papers*, VIII, 636–637.

50. Clay to Biddle, April 10, 1833, in Clay, *Papers*, VIII, 637.

But the proposal put forward by Clay did not provide sufficient advantages to the protectionists to win them over. He had to offer greater inducements. Senator Tyler had said that *"time* is of little importance to us." But to the protectionists, it *was* important. Clay therefore revised his scheme to stretch out the time to a nine-and-a-half-year period. In addition, he would allow only minuscule reductions of the rates during this period. In other words, for nearly ten years there would be no tampering with the tariff; then the rates would drop off sharply on July 1, 1842, with duties standing at a uniform 20 percent ad valorem. Beyond 1842, duties would be levied to raise such money as the government might need to operate "until otherwise directed by law."[51]

This revised plan, which Clay personally wrote up for submission to Congress, evidently brought the protectionist senators around. Clay again spoke with them individually, "and I understood every one to agree substantially to the bill (for I had prepared a bill) except one, who finally voted for it."[52] No doubt Clay reiterated his most powerful argument—namely, that they must consent to the only action currently proposed to them or risk the breakup of the Union. Later the southern senators also agreed to the plan as revised since it was the principle, not time, that was most important to them. Calhoun was especially happy to give his consent, for it provided the necessary means of escape with honor for South Carolina. A compromise, a real compromise, had at last been struck.

On February 11 Clay, who had been all but silent for the past few weeks, rose in the Senate and announced that on the following day he would present a new tariff bill and make an extended statement in its favor. In so doing, he alerted the electorate that his genius had brought forth still another compromise, one he hoped would heal the nation's wounds and restore amity and harmony to its people.

"There is one man, and one man only, who can save the Union," cried John Randolph in a speech in Virginia, "[and] that man is HENRY CLAY. I know he has the power, and I believe he will be found to have the patriotism and firmness equal to the occasion."[53]

The nation knew it, too. A huge crowd massed inside the Senate chamber to hear the great man provide the details of his scheme. It was one of Clay's more triumphant moments in Congress as he stood before his colleagues on Tuesday, February 12, and spoke the words that would halt the danger of bloodshed.

51. Webster to Joseph Hopkinson, February 21, 1833, in Webster, *Papers, Correspondence,* III, 220; draft compromise tariff bill, in Clay, *Papers,* VIII, 619–620. To be more specific, the bill stipulated that after September 30, 1833, all duties over 20 percent would be reduced by one-tenth every two years until 1842; on January 1, 1842, one-half of the residue would be deducted; and on July 1, 1842, the remaining half would be deducted.
52. Clay to Biddle, April 10, 1833, in Clay, *Papers,* VIII, 637.
53. Garland, *Life of John Randolph,* II, 361–362.

He began by disclaiming any personal motive in offering his tariff bill.[54] His true object was the preservation of the Union and his American System. This could be done by protecting the tariff system, he contended, for the fall of that system by its sudden repeal would be "calamitous indeed." He also wished to stabilize tariff legislation by allowing time for a gradual reduction of duties to satisfy northern needs and reducing the duties to the revenue level to satisfy southern demands. After outlining the specifics of his bill, he publicly admitted that after eight and a half years "the principle of protection must be said to be, in some measure, relinquished." But that was the price of compromise. "I will admit that my friends do not get all they could wish for; and the gentlemen on the other side do not obtain all they might desire; but both will gain all that in my humble opinion is proper to be given in the present condition of the country." Here is a bill, he declared, that is founded on "that great principle of compromise and concession which lies at the bottom of our institutions." That principle produced the Constitution, and it has continued to "regulate us in our onward march, and conducted the nation to glory and renown."

Compromise: the true path, the only path, to national glory. Governing a nation, declared Clay, requires compromise and concession, not ideological absolutism. And in all compromises there must be mutual concessions. He regarded nullification as a dead issue, as indeed, it was. As for South Carolina, "I think that she has been rash, intemperate and greatly in error." But, he continued, "I do not want to disgrace her, nor any other member of this Union." He added:

> If there be any who want civil war, who want to see the blood of any portion of our countrymen spilt, I am not one of them. I wish to see war of no kind; but, above all, I do not desire to see civil war. . . . God alone knows where such a war would end. In what a state will our institutions be left? In what a state our liberties? I want no war; above all, no war at home. . . . [South Carolina] has been with us before, when her ancestors mingled in the throng of battle, and as I hope our posterity will mingle with hers, for ages and centuries to come, in the united defense of liberty, and for the honor and glory of the Union, I do not wish to see her degraded or defaced as a member of this confederacy.[55]

Here was Clay at his best. No sneers, no jabs at those who opposed him, no claim to moral superiority as justification for his action. Just a clear, straightforward, and statesmanlike assertion of what the Congress must do to resolve an issue that threatened to tear the nation apart.

The chamber rang with applause and cheers when he finished. But some northern protariff listeners in the audience sadly shook their heads in disbelief. Could this be the Henry Clay who had once argued so convincingly on the

54. In a letter to Francis Brooke, February 14, 1833, Clay said: "I was fully aware of all the personal consequences and personal risks to which I exposed myself [in presenting the bill], but 'what is a public man worth who will not sacrifice himself if necessary for the good of his Country.' " Clay, *Papers,* VIII, 623.
55. Clay, *Works,* V, 537–550.

necessity of protectionism for the future growth of the country? Obviously the Kentuckian was not the pure ideologue that they once thought. Obviously he had sold his principles for a mess of southern votes. Francis Granger of New York called the speech "mamby pamby." Never had Clay delivered "so washy an affair." And his tariff bill was a "perfect death blow to manufactures." One southerner exulted: "The 'American System' is as dead as Julius Caesar." Clay's old friends "are in a rage. They curse and damn him—and would consign him to perdition if possible."[56]

The bill a deathblow to manufactures? No such thing, as some manufacturers like du Pont, Bovie, Richards, and others already knew. It bought time. There would be no "fluctuations and agitations" for at least nine years, and manufacturers in every competitive branch of industry could use that valuable time to strengthen themselves against all foreign competition.

Clay no sooner sat down than Calhoun jumped up and announced that he approved the principles of the bill and would support it. The immediate reaction to this announcement was electric. A roar of delight and approval echoed around the hall. "Such was the clapping & thundering applause when Calhoun sat down that the Chair ordered the galleries to be cleared. The sensation was indescribable."[57] In an instant everyone knew that the crisis had passed, the Union been spared a possible civil war.

A select committee was formed to consider the bill, consisting of Clay as chairman; Calhoun; Webster; Felix Grundy, who proposed the committee; John M. Clayton of Delaware; William C. Rives of Virginia; and George M. Dallas of Pennsylvania. Clay liked the composition of the committee, although he knew that Webster would actively oppose the bill. On the other hand, Jackson was "mortified" by its composition. Surely a majority should be supporters of the administration, he snapped. "It is a direct insult to me."[58]

During the ensuing committee meetings such sharp disagreements over the bill broke out among the members that the likelihood of its passage seemed extremely problematic. In compensation for the eventual loss of the principle of protection, Clayton insisted on the inclusion of a home valuation clause. This clause would provide that after 1842 duties would be determined on the basis of valuation made at the port where goods were received rather than the port of origin, as had previously been the case. But southerners were known to oppose home valuation. It was unconstitutional, they argued, and it would defeat the purpose of the bill because an importer would include the amount of the duty in his evaluation and pass it along to customers, thus raising the tax a

56. Granger to Thurlow Weed, February 19, 1833, Granger Papers, LC; William Hammet to Thomas W. White, February 12, 1833, Hammet Papers, Virginia Historical Society, Richmond.
57. Hammet to White, February 12, 1833, Hammet Papers, Virginia Historical Society, Richmond.
58. Clay to Brooke, February 14, 1833, in Clay, *Papers,* VIII, 623; Jackson to Grundy, February 13, 1833, Whiteford R. Cole Collection, Tennessee State Library. Grundy, Dallas, and Rives were the Jacksonians on the committee. The President was particularly "mortified" over the appointment of Clayton to the committee because of his closeness to Clay.

good five to ten points beyond the 20 percent maximum. Clayton responded to these objections by insisting that without home valuation the bill was dead. With that announcement the committee members threw up their hands, rose from their places, and started to leave the room.

Clay halted them with an angry shout. "Gentlemen," he cried, "this bill has been referred to us, and it is our duty to report it, in some form or other, to the senate." He paused a moment. "And it *shall* be reported."[59]

The senators returned to their seats, defeated the home valuation amendment, and, by the close vote of four to three, agreed to report the bill back to the Senate.

Meanwhile, the private "arrangement" reached between Clay and Calhoun became public knowledge, even to the most naive. On February 15 the House of Representatives elected as its printers Gales and Seaton, the editors of the Washington *National Intelligencer,* over Frances P. Blair, editor of Jackson's mouthpiece, the Washington *Globe.* "A buzz of satisfaction went round the hall," recorded John Quincy Adams, when the result was announced.[60] The election of Duff Green as printer for the Senate followed almost immediately. Green was related to Calhoun by marriage and edited the Washington *United States Telegraph,* a highly vocal critic of the administration. These elections constituted a double blow for Jackson, for they involved subsidies to support these newspapers and they provided considerable political influence for the editors.[61] "Clay Webster & Calhoun," reported Representative Michael Hoffman to the Albany Regency, "aided by our disaffection elected Gales and Seaton printers to the House. I suppose the contract extended to the election of Green in the Senate."[62]

When the select committee reported the compromise bill back to the Senate, Clay spoke in its favor on February 21. Only now, in a sudden shift of position, he introduced the home valuation amendment, which his committee had just defeated, and urged its inclusion in the final bill even though he knew that Calhoun and other southerners hotly objected to it. But he was forced to gamble. He was forced to shift his ground—again. His friend John Clayton messed with Senators Samuel Bell of New Hampshire, John Holmes of Maine, Samuel A. Foot of Connecticut, Arnold Naudain of Delaware, Asher Robbins

59. Sargent, *Clay,* p. 144.

60. Adams claimed credit for the election in that he prevailed upon twelve Anti-Masons to vote for Gales and Seaton. *Memoirs,* VIII, 525.

61. "The influence of the B[ank]. united to the influence of Calhoun and Clay," said President Jackson, "elected those men printers to Congress to continue their abuse of the executive and weaken its influence and with a positive pledge that they will use all influence to recharter this hydra of corruption. Clays land bill enters into this bargain." Jackson to ?, March 24, 1833, in Jackson, *Correspondence,* V, 48.

62. Hoffman to Azariah C. Flagg, February 20, 1833, Flagg Papers, New York Public Library. The disaffections mentioned in the letter probably resulted from anger over Jackson's constant demands for the passage of the force bill as well as sympathy for southern fears over possible military intervention.

of Rhode Island, and Elisha Whittlesey of Ohio, every one of whom supported protectionism and insisted on home valuation as a sine qua non for his vote. And without their collective votes, as Clay recognized, the compromise bill could never pass. Fortunately Clayton wanted the passage of the compromise bill; he also wanted to prevent Jackson from raining fire and death on the South Carolinians. "Well, Clay," he said while looking at Calhoun and his friends, "these are fine fellows. It won't do to let old Jackson hang them. We must save them." To get the tariff through the Senate, let alone the House, the home valuation amendment had to pass.[63] That explains why Clay gambled on the southerners and introduced the amendment.

Clayton also wanted the passage of the public land bill, which Clay had reintroduced in the Senate and which had passed on January 25, 1833, by the vote of twenty-four to twenty. It was similar to Clay's land bill of the previous year, and protectionists favored it because it required the proceeds from the sales of public lands to go to the states for internal improvements, which would force the government to look to the tariff for its revenue. At the moment the land bill awaited action by the House.

The debate in the Senate over the Compromise Tariff raged for several days following Clay's introduction of the home valuation amendment. John Quincy Adams dropped by the upper house during the second reading of the compromise bill and reported that the debate was "brisk, animated, and somewhat acrimonious."[64] Calhoun insisted he would vote against the entire bill if the home valuation amendment passed, and Clayton responded that without the amendment he and his friends would vote against it. Simultaneously Clay pleaded for its passage. "The difference between the friends and foes of the compromise under consideration," he thundered in the Senate, "is, that they would in the enforcing act, send forth alone a flaming sword. We would send out that also, but along with it the olive branch, as a messenger of peace."

Then, in a dramatic move, he added a personal touch. "Pass this bill," he pleaded, "tranquilize the country, restore confidence and affection in the Union; and I am willing to go home to Ashland and renounce public service forever." In making this offer, he later insisted that he had two objectives: avert civil war and preserve the "policy of protection." He acknowledged that many would accuse him of acting solely out of personal political ambition. "Yes, I have ambition," he admitted, "but it is the ambition of being the humble instrument, in the hands of Providence, to reconcile a divided people, once more to revive concord and harmony in a distracted land."[65]

This disavowal of personal benefit went over well with the other senators. As Clay had been told by Clayton, it "will stop the cry of coalition—save

63. Clay to Clayton, August 22, 1844, Clayton Papers, LC. See also Sargent, *Clay*, p. 142; Benton, *Thirty Years' View*, I, 343.

64. Adams, *Memoirs*, VIII, 526.

65. Clay to Clayton, August 22, 1844, Clayton Papers, LC; *Register of Debates*, 22d Congress, 2d session, p. 742.

yourself & your friends from calumny, and your country from ruin."[66]

At one point Clay personally and privately entreated Clayton to free the southerners from having to accept the home valuation amendments. Let them off, he pleaded.

"No, sir, I will not," Clayton replied. "I know, in your magnanimity, you would let them off; but I will not. If they can't vote for a bill that is to save their necks from a halter, their necks may stretch. They *shall* vote for it, or *it shall not pass.*"

To make his point even stronger, Clayton threatened to move to table the entire bill, a motion that, if passed, would kill it for the session. He reportedly went to Senator Stephen D. Miller of South Carolina and said: "At the end of fifteen minutes I shall move to lay the bill on the table unless within that time you inform me authoritatively that Mr. Calhoun will vote for it."

The choice was clear: the tariff with the home valuation amendment or General Jackson figuratively marching at the head of forty thousand troops through South Carolina. With that threat hanging over their heads the Calhoun faction caucused near the colonnade behind the Vice President's chair and after a brief consultation decided to accept the amendment and with it the entire tariff.

Miller reported back to Clayton that Calhoun had given his consent to the amendment. "Very good," Clayton supposedly replied; "you have saved your necks from a halter." The home valuation amendment passed by a vote of twenty-six to sixteen.[67] Clay's gamble had paid off.[68]

While Clay worked his craft in the Senate, he did not forget the House, where all money bills must originate. The Verplanck bill still awaited final action, and the Democrats seemed to lack the leadership to drive the measure through. To a considerable extent, the fault belonged to the President, who had shown little interest in the bill. He focused entirely on the force bill. That was the measure he wanted. Thus Clay's supposition that Jackson intended to kill both protection and the nullifiers in South Carolina was incorrect. If the President had indeed meant to kill protection, he should have put all his weight behind winning passage of the Verplanck bill.[69]

The leadership vacuum in the House gave Clay his opportunity. He prevailed on his fellow Kentuckian Robert Letcher to move to strike out the Verplanck bill and substitute Clay's Senate bill. The move in the House came so suddenly that it caught the Jackson men off guard, and before anyone

66. Clayton to Clay, February 20, 1833, in Clay, *Papers,* VIII, 625.
67. Sargent, *Public Men and Events,* I, 239. All the nullifiers voted for the bill after Calhoun declared in the Senate that he understood that the amendment would not be so interpreted as to violate the Constitution or include the duties themselves in the valuation. Wiltse, *Calhoun,* II, 192.
68. Years later Clay wrote to Clayton, "You and I know positively that the act could not have passed without that [home valuation] principle. August 8, 1842, in Clay, *Papers,* IX, 753. And in a speech delivered on the tariff in 1844 Clayton specifically acknowledged the help of Bell, Naudain, Foot, and Holmes in devising the terms of the tariff. *National Intelligencer,* July 4, 1844.
69. Remini, *Jackson,* III, 41.

realized what was happening or could organize an opposition, the substitute bill passed to a third reading. "It swept like a hurricane," said the startled Adams.[70] On the next day, February 26, it passed the House by a vote of 119 to 85.[71] Scoffed Senator Benton: The administration bill "was arrested, knocked over, run under, and merged and lost in a new one which expunged the old one and took its place."[72]

No sooner had the Compromise Tariff passed the House than Clay announced the fact to the Senate. Although the home valuation amendment had squeezed through the Senate, the entire bill still awaited final action, and time was running out. Webster led the fight against the compromise because he sincerely believed it would sound the death knell of protectionism. Unfortunately he and Clay verbally fought out their differences on the Senate floor, and their exchanges added one last dramatic touch to the proceedings.

Their speaking styles were very different, yet both spoke so compellingly in their own way that they provided the packed Senate chamber with a lesson in discourse and argumentation. Henry Clay, Jr., came to Washington to visit his father and heard both men debate. He recorded his obviously prejudiced opinions, especially about Webster's style of oratory. He was disappointed, he said, in the Massachusetts senator's manner, and he had conceived a rather exaggerated opinion of his eloquence. "Yet I still consider him a great orator." Webster had a "deep masculine voice," young Clay recorded, and the lower tones were especially fine. Although he lacked grace in his movements like Prince Hal, he had a most "commanding countenance." He always looked grave, never smiled, and showed no evidence of wit,[73] but his arguments, invariably nationalistic in tone, were rock solid, and "his words which are pure English contain a golden meaning." He was not "so versatile and consummate a leader of debates as my father," wrote the younger Clay. But he possessed a power of "forming original and condensed opinions which is truly remarkable." He frequently drew references from the Bible, and these "are simple and affecting and often beautiful and sublime." He had also "accurately studied" the Constitution and the history of the United States, young Henry allowed.[74]

But Senator Clay, undoubtedly, was a far superior debater. His style was more relaxed and freewheeling, his movements always graceful, even when propelled by passion. When the Kentuckian spoke, listeners did not have the sense that they were hearing an oration, yet they found themselves utterly absorbed in his argument and fully persuaded by his logic and commanding language. His enthusiasm, his total involvement in his cause, and his frequent majestic flights of oratory mesmerized his audience. Clay's speeches also in-

70. Adams, *Memoirs*, VIII, 527.

71. *Register of Debates*, 22d Congress, 2d session, pp. 697–701, 715–716.

72. Benton, *Thirty Years' View*, I, 309, 310.

73. Actually Webster frequently demonstrated considerable wit in his speeches, and in conversation he had a fine sense of humor and cracked jokes. Martineau, *Retrospect of Western Travel*, I, 160.

74. Henry Clay, Jr., manuscript diary, University of Kentucky Library.

cluded witty asides, and his wit could delight or cut or reduce opponents to helplessness. To hear and watch these two great men cross verbal swords—as infrequently happened—must have been one of the great pleasures afforded Washington society during this Jacksonian era.

At this point in their association the two senators were, to say the very least, rather annoyed with each other. Webster kept insisting, "in a manner that I thought unfriendly," that the Kentuckian had abandoned the principle of protection. Clay also knew that a number of Webster's "Eastern friends" had it in mind to form a new party with the Massachusetts senator as its "sole head." Furthermore, Webster made "an unprovoked and unnecessary" allusion to Clay when he described Calhoun as struggling in a "Bog" and that anyone who came to his relief would share his "embarrassment." Clay complained: "Even the female part of the Audience understood to whom the allusion was directed."[75]

As the tariff debate renewed after the passage of the home valuation amendment, these various annoyances and disagreements between the two men finally bubbled to the surface. Spectators braced themselves as the Massachusetts senator rose to make his case against the compromise and the man who had proposed it. "The gentleman from Kentucky," rumbled Webster, "supports the bill from one motive, others from another motive." One wants to secure protection, the others to destroy it—and that is absurd.

The bill an absurdity! That is what Webster implied, and that remark really offended Clay. He heatedly responded that Webster "dislikes the measure, because it commands the concurrence" of both Calhoun and himself. But that is the essence of compromise, he lectured. The "gentleman from Massachusetts" condemns this "measure of pacification," Clay boomed with a slight edge to his voice that indicated he was moving toward nastiness, but he vehemently and consistently and loyally supports the administration's efforts to win final passage of the force bill. "Would the Senator from Massachusetts send *his* bill forth alone without this measure of conciliation?"[76]

That was a low blow. Webster hotly denied that it was *his* bill. He might have sarcastically added that Clay had conveniently missed casting his vote on the force bill, but he did not. That was hardly his style. So the moment of possible and serious friction passed. Later Clay told Francis Brooke that "Mr. Webster and I came in conflict, and I have the satisfaction to tell you that he gained nothing. My friends flatter me, with my having completely triumphed. There is no permanent breach between us."[77]

Although Clay may have known that Webster resented his position as unquestioned leader of the National Republican party, he did not want to quarrel with his colleague or back him into the Democratic party. Thus, when

75. Clay to Biddle, April 10, 1833, in Clay, *Papers,* VIII, 637.
76. *Register of Debates,* 22d Congress, 2d session, pp. 722–725, 729–742. Italics mine.
77. Clay to Brooke, February 28, 1833, in Clay, *Papers,* VIII, 628.

Webster tangled with Senator George Poindexter of Mississippi, a sinister-looking profligate, and might have provoked a challenge to a duel, Clay jumped in and acted as peacemaker. Webster had made an appropriate but contemptuous allusion to something Poindexter had said in debate, and Poindexter responded with *"I have the most perfect contempt for the Senator from Massachusetts."* When Clay heard that the exchange might "be made the basis of a serious proceeding," he wrote Webster and said he wanted to help prevent it in any way that would be honorable to both parties. A few days later Clay rose in the Senate, extravagantly praised Poindexter, sympathized with Webster, and expressed the "very great pain" that the entire Senate felt. He spoke on and on, virtually apologizing for both men and pleading that there be no cause for a permanent estrangement. He very nearly exhausted the Senate because of the length of time he took, but when he was through, both men apologized. Then they walked over to each other and shook hands. Virtually everyone in the chamber sighed with relief.[78]

To make certain that his own "conflict" with Webster did not get any worse, Clay wrote to Nicholas Biddle, who regularly provided Webster with financial handouts to ensure his continued support, and said: "I wish you would say all you can to soothe him. . . . You hold a large flask of oil and know well how to pour it out."[79]

While engaged in a general program of pacification, Clay buried the hatchet with another onetime adversary. John Randolph of Roanoke had peppered the Kentuckian with more verbal buckshot than anyone could remember. He was now feeble, desiccated, and near death. Most probably they each admired the other enormously for the singular, exasperating, excitable, and remarkably talented creatures they were.

The reconciliation took place quite by accident. "There was no explanation, no intervention," said Clay. Randolph had gone to the Senate one evening while the Kentuckian was speaking. "Help me up," Randolph commanded, *"I have come here to hear that voice."* Clay spotted him "looking as if he were not long for this world; and being myself engaged in a work of Peace," he walked over to Randolph when he had concluded his speech and extended his hand. Randolph seized it, and their salutations were "cordial on both sides." Ever the consummate politician, Clay later left his card at Randolph's lodgings, but the two men never met again. The Virginian died a few months later on May 24, after pronouncing Clay "a brave man. he is a consistent man . . . an independent man and an honest man." Still, when he died, he wanted to be buried facing west so he could keep an eye on Henry Clay. Just in case.[80]

When the Senate debate over the compromise tariff finally concluded

---

78. *Register of Debates,* 22d Congress, 2d session, pp. 655–666; Sargent, *Public Men and Events,* I, 241–243; Clay to Webster, March 2, 1833, in Clay, *Papers,* VIII, 629.

79. Clay to Biddle, March 4, 1833, in Clay, *Papers,* VIII, 630.

80. Clay to Brooke, March 11, 1833, J. W. P. to Clay, May 31, 1833, in Clay, *Papers,* VIII, 631, 645; Sargent, *Clay,* p. 120; Bruce, *John Randolph of Roanoke,* II, 36, 47.

after many days of acrimonious exchanges, the members voted on March 1. By the count of twenty-nine to sixteen the Compromise Tariff of 1833 was approved. On exactly the same day the House took up Clay's public land bill and passed it by a vote of ninety-six to forty.[81]

Clay was jubilant. It was a sweep. "Yesterday was perhaps the most important Congressional day that ever occurred," he wrote on March 2, "the Compromise bill, the Land bill and the Enforcing [Force] bill having all passed during it." He was particularly and justifiably pleased with the Compromise Tariff. "It will be popular every-where, even in the East," he confidently predicted.[82]

Then, as later, Clay was accused of abandoning not only protectionism but his entire American System. He steadfastly denied the accusation. He always insisted he proposed the compromise to "save the Tariff" and prevent "Civil War." He achieved both purposes. "It is not true that I ever abandoned the American System," he wrote to one man three years later. "It is not true that it is abandoned by the Compromise of 1833. It was, on the contrary, preserved by that compromise."[83]

What must be remembered was the fact that Clay never supported a high tariff per se. "I never was in favor of what I regarded as a high tariff," he later stated. He desired a tariff that would provide sufficient revenue for the operation of the government and "reasonable protection" to those industries that actually needed it, not protection across the board.[84]

But even his friends accused him of abandoning protectionism. They reckoned he had traded it off for southern support in his unending quest for the presidency. Jackson's threatened use of force had seriously undermined his southern strength, and Clay stood to profit from it by jettisoning protection from his American System.[85] Unquestionably Clay did consider all the political advantages to be garnered by his reversal of position, and they did affect his actions. But his chief purpose in proposing his Compromise Tariff and in his several shifts of position to win its passage was his desire to spare the Union the agony of conflict and secession.

With the passage of the Compromise Tariff, which the President promptly signed, South Carolina repealed its Ordinance of Nullification. But then it nullified the force bill in a feeble gesture of defiance. "They have committed a new folly in So. Carolina," said Clay, "by the impotent attempt to nullify the enforcing act. It should be laughed at and not treated seriously."[86]

---

81. *Register of Debates,* 22d Congress, 2d session, pp. 694–716, 1920–1921.
82. Clay to Brooke, February 28, 1833, in Clay, *Papers,* VIII, 628.
83. Clay to Philip R. Fendall, August 8, 1836, in Clay, *Papers,* VIII, 862–863.
84. Clay to James A. Meriwether, October 2, 1843, in Clay, *Papers,* IX, 863.
85. Robert Seager II argues this position in his article "Henry Clay and the Politics of Compromise and Non-Compromise," *Register of the Kentucky Historical Society,* LXXXV (Winter 1987), pp. 1–28.
86. Clay to Samuel L. Southard, April 22, 1833, in Clay, *Papers,* VIII, 639.

Indeed. The nation could well afford to disregard this latest "folly" and simply rejoice that nothing worse had occurred.

Thanks mainly to the heroic efforts of Henry Clay in working constantly for "pacification," the Union was saved and bloodshed avoided. In a moment of justifiable pride Clay told a reporter that it was "the most proud and triumphant day of my life."[87]

87. Quoted in Peterson, *Olive Branch and Sword*, p. 82.

The Great Triumvirate

PRESIDENT JACKSON signed both the force bill and the Compromise Tariff on March 2, 1833, but he waited until the Twenty-second Congress had adjourned and then pocket vetoed Clay's public land bill. It seemed like a spiteful act, and no doubt one of his principal reasons for killing the bill was its authorship by the man he so thoroughly despised. Clay insisted that if Jackson had applied his veto and returned it to Congress before adjournment, "we would have passed it, I believe, by two thirds."[1] Ironically the President might have gotten rid of Clay once and for all had he signed the bill. "Had the Land bill passed," the Kentuckian told several of his friends, "I should certainly not have returned to Washn. The state of that measure creates some doubt whether it is not my duty to go back once more." In repeating this sentiment to James Madison, his intellectual mentor, he also suggested that Jackson's use of the pocket veto was unconstitutional because he had failed to return the bill to Congress. In his response Madison gave Clay little support for his wishful opinion.[2]

Clay delayed his departure from Washington following adjournment in part because he was due to argue a case before the Supreme Court involving a writ of error from a Louisiana court and in part because "of the most violent cold I ever had." Since Daniel Webster was arguing the other side of the case before the High Court, John Quincy Adams went to hear them. Adams's verdict? "[D]ry as dust, and the eloquence of the champions could not make it otherwise." Clay was happy to find that in their appearance together before the Court there was "no breach between Webster and me. We had some friendly passes," he remarked to Francis Brooke, "and there the matter ended."[3]

---

1. Clay to James Brown, March 3, 1833, in Clay, *Papers,* VIII, 629–630. Jackson returned his veto message of the land bill to Congress on December 4, 1833. Clay continued his efforts (unsuccessfully) to win passage of his bill.

2. Clay to Samuel L. Southard, April 22, 1833, Clay to James Madison, May 28, 1833, Clay to Brooke, May 30, 1833, Madison to Clay, early June, 1833, in Clay, *Papers,* VIII, 639, 643, 644, 646.

3. Clay to Josiah S. Johnston, March 15, 1833, Clay to Brooke, March 11, 1833, in Clay, *Papers,* VIII, 633, 631; Adams, *Memoirs,* VIII, 536.

Clay's almost instant renown "in saving the Union" spread so rapidly around the country—indeed, the senator himself helped it along by sending more than a hundred copies of his tariff speech to leading political figures everywhere[4]—that he planned to take advantage of his reclaimed popularity and make a major trip around the Northeast. He hoped to go through Ohio to Buffalo, Niagara (he was especially anxious to see the falls), Montreal, Quebec, Saratoga, Boston, and several other parts of New England. Already there was talk of his running for the presidency in 1836, but Clay had no wish to think about that prospect until much later. "I really feel no disposition to enter again on an arduous & doubtful struggle for any office." Still, John Quincy Adams always believed that Clay could never resist the opportunity to try once more to scramble into the White House. His "vaulting ambition . . . overleaped itself . . . by the precipitation" with which he rushed to make another bid for the presidential prize, said Adams. The former President acknowledged Clay's eloquence and managerial powers but thought he had "less real talent, a weaker judgment, and far less consistency of principle" than a number of other National Republicans who might prove better choices in 1836. This critical assessment was shared by others. Benjamin Brown French, an astute observer of the Washington scene, believed Clay "to be heartless, and selfish; he is eloquent, but he lacks judgment very much."[5]

Clay left Washington on Sunday, March 17, and returned home via the National Road and a steamboat from Wheeling, Virginia. He arrived the first week of April, still suffering from his "violent cold." But the quiet and delights of farming at Ashland plus the nursing skills of his wife soon restored his health. "In the midst of Arabian horses, English cattle and Maltese Asses, I think I shall recover much sooner than I should have done in the corrupt atmosphere of the Capital."[6]

Clay genuinely enjoyed his farm and this time gave it more than his usual attention. He admitted that with the passage of time it provided "more & more interest for me." There is an enormous difference between farming "dead produce" for market, he declared, and the "rearing of all kinds of live stock," such as he engaged in. Watching the progress of jackasses, horses, sheep, cattle, goats, mules, and hogs from infancy to maturity "presents a constantly varying subject of interest, & I never go out of my house, without meeting with some of them to engage agreeably my attention."[7]

Having his family close about him was another delight. Theodore was

4. It cost Clay ten dollars to have 150 copies of his *Speech of Henry Clay, in the Senate of the United States, February 25, 1833, in Vindication of His Bill, Entitled "An Act to Modify the Act of 14th July, 1832, and All Other Acts Imposing Duties on Imports"* (Washington, 1833) published by the editors of the *National Intelligencer*. Clay to Nathaniel Williams, April 9, 1833, in Clay, *Papers*, VIII, 636.

5. Clay to Brooke, May 30, 1833, in Clay, *Papers*, VIII, 644–645; Adams, *Memoirs*, VIII, 521; Benjamin Brown French, *Witness to the Young Republic: A Yankee's Journal, 1828–1870*, ed. Donald B. Cole and John J. McDonough (Hanover, 1989), p. 35.

6. Clay to Biddle, April 10, 1833, Clay, *Papers*, VIII, 637–638.

7. Clay to Brooke, May 30, 1833, in Clay, *Papers*, VIII, 644.

temporarily home from the hospital; Anne was close by at the Woodlands and pregnant; and Henry, Jr., who had been admitted to the Louisiana bar but had decided to return to Louisville for reasons of health, gave up the law and with the help of his father and some money from his wife's family chose to devote his career to farming, "politics, history and the pleasures of science and litera-ture." Henry's wife was also pregnant and in July gave birth to a son. "In regard to its name," wrote the grandfather, "I shall certainly feel flattered if mine is given to it. . . . I should be most happy if the future fame of the new born should transcend any which his grandfather may have acquired." The child was duly christened Henry Clay III.[8]

With so much at Ashland to interest him and occupy his time, and after so many struggles to "maintain the public liberty," Clay felt that at the age of fifty-six he had earned the right to relax and enjoy himself and not worry about the future of the nation. But when he turned his thoughts from farm and family to the condition of the country, he conceded that he had grown less confident in the virtue and intelligence of the people and the stability of the nation's institutions. Are we not governed by the will of one man? he asked. Do not a majority of the people follow him no matter where he leads? He governs by enforcing the laws he favors and disregarding those he dislikes, even though the laws were passed by the representatives of the people and are manifestly for their own good. If Jackson were an enlightened philosopher and a true patriot, there might be some justification for such intense public adula-tion, "but when we consider that he is ignorant, passionate, hypocritical, cor-rupt, and easily swayed by the basest men who surround him, what can we think of the popular approbation which he receives?" Only one thing remains to complete the public degradation, said Clay, and that is Jackson's presumed right to name his successor. Martin Van Buren will unquestionably receive his blessing, and once the Magician is elected, the corrupt means of preserving and perpetuating power, now so successfully managed by the Albany Regency in New York, will be transferred to Washington.[9]

Clay shuddered at the thought of what might happen if Van Buren did in fact succeed to the presidency. When asked his thoughts about the present state of things and the prospects for the future, as frequently happened, "I answer, bad enough, bad enough, God knows. But what can I do? Have I heretofore ever ceased to warn the country against it? Worn out & exhausted in the service, why should I continue to sound the alarm, with no prospect of my being more heeded hereafter than heretofore? I want repose. I have reached a time of life when all men want it." Perhaps the country ought to try other men "who may be more successful, than I have been."

Clay seemed consumed with self-pity. But who could blame him? Even

8. Clay, Jr., to Clay, March 11, 1833, June 3, 1833, Clay to Clay, Jr., July 23, 1833, in Clay, *Papers,* VIII, 632, 648, 659.

9. Clay to Brooke, August 2, 1833, in Clay, *Papers,* VIII, 661–662.

distinguished men who agreed with his political philosophy "stood by with a cold indifference, without lending any helping hand. What can one man do alone against a host?" And it was a host, a host made up of the press, patronage, and a well-organized party—all directed toward training the masses to respond as the tyrant directed.[10]

Men of vision, men of character and learning, men who studied and understood the issues facing the nation, Clay believed, were turned out by the illiterate masses intent on following a charismatic but ignorant leader. With the advent of Jackson and "Jacksonism," the best men capable of serving the people were shunted aside in favor of the country's "refuse." If the Little Magician succeeded to the presidency, it would signal the triumph of a new political system that almost guaranteed the exclusion of statesmen from the highest electoral offices in the land. Soon some issue, one with tremendous potential for harm, would undoubtedly come along and command the attention of the nation, and without a Henry Clay, or someone of his stature, to find its solution, catastrophe might easily result. Slavery, for example. That frightening topic had already begun to emerge as an issue to rival Anti-Masonry in the passionate responses it generated. Abolition societies had been formed, slave rebellions of terrifying intensity, such as that of Nat Turner, had occurred, and some men interpreted South Carolina's nullification of the tariff as a mask to hide their larger concern about slavery. Even Clay admitted that this "peculiar institution," as Calhoun euphemistically called it, "lies at the bottom of many of the evils under which the Southern Atlantic States are suffering."[11]

Several concerned citizens, especially southerners, who expected a sympathetic response from Clay about their situation since he himself was a slaveowner, asked him for his views on the problem. "Several gentlemen from the Eastern States" also queried him about it. In response, Clay told them that slavery must be reckoned with on both the national and the state levels. On the national level he did not believe the government possessed the constitutional power to free the slaves without a constitutional amendment, although he thought it might grant aid for costs of transportation to ship the slaves back to Africa once they had been emancipated.[12] That left the issue up to the states. In Kentucky, he said, the institution exists in its most "mitigated form. Still it is slavery; and I for one . . . concur in the adoption of a system of gradual emancipation," just as he had thirty-four years before. But he did not think the question in Kentucky could be successfully agitated at the present time. For one thing, emancipation could be effected only by either an amendment to the state's constitution or compensation to present owners, and resources in Ken-

10. Clay to Brooke, May 30, 1833, in Clay, *Papers,* VIII, 645.

11. Clay to Richard Henry Wilde, April 27, 1833, in Clay, *Papers,* VIII, 641.

12. The idea of making the federal government the agent for the colonization of blacks was discussed by James Madison in his letter to Robert J. Evans, June 15, 1819, cited in McCoy, *Last of the Fathers,* p. 279. It is very likely that Clay borrowed this idea, as did so many others, from Madison.

tucky for compensation were inadequate. He also doubted whether the people were yet ready for an amendment to Kentucky's constitution. In the meantime, he thought that "a sensible progress, both in Europe and America, is making toward universal emancipation; and I think we had better leave to their full operation all the favorable concurring causes now existing than to make a premature and perhaps unsuccessful effort. Public opinion alone can bring about the abolition of slavery, and public opinion is on the march. We should wait in patience for its operation without attempting measures which might throw it back."

He noted Great Britain's progress toward emancipation and assumed that it would have a "powerful influence" in America and elsewhere. If it should be demonstrated in the British West Indies that crops could be cultivated just as well by freemen as by slaves, then "slavery will be stripped of one of its most plausible supports." And even though the federal government cannot interfere with the condition of the "unfortunate subjects" of slavery, nevertheless "it is perfectly manifest, I think, that you will have soon to alter materially the character of their labor. You will have either to find new products for it, or new markets for its present products."

For the moment, however, colonization was the only recourse for this country. "It is, I admit, a slow remedy, but it is to be remembered that slavery is a chronic disease, and I believe that in such maladies speedy recovery is not expected." All we can do is look forward to some distant time when slavery will cease to exist in the United States. "But I think it will not happen in our time."[13]

It is quite possible that Clay's own financial situation figured into his slow approach to a solution of the slavery question. After all, he stood to lose thousands of dollars if emancipation came suddenly and swiftly. But the evidence is really quite overwhelming that Clay did in fact believe that pressing for immediate abolition would definitely lead to disunion and civil war. That consideration outweighed any thought of monetary loss that would accompany the freeing of his slaves.

The Bank of the United States was another issue that might produce chaos in the country. At the outset of the War of 1812 the lack of a national bank nearly bankrupted the country, and one was immediately chartered when the conflict ended. It was the very Bank whose recharter President Jackson had vetoed last year. Clay still held out hope that the BUS could be rechartered. "Don't despair," he wrote Nicholas Biddle; "repose on recent victories for the present . . . and I do hope that at the next Session or the Session after, the Charter will be renewed."[14]

13. Henry Clay, Jr., manuscript diary, University of Kentucky Library; Clay to Richard Henry Wilde, April 27, 1833, Clay to Joseph Berry, June 15, 1833, Clay to James Brown, July 7, 1833, Clay to Thomas Speed, June 19, 1833, in Clay, *Papers,* VIII, 641, 650, 656, 653.
14. Clay to Biddle, March 4, 1833, in Clay, *Papers,* VIII, 630. See also his letter to Thomas Helm, April 20, 1833, ibid., VIII, 638. Clay thought that if Calhoun supported recharter in the next

In the midst of his happy repose at Ashland and gloomy thoughts about his future as a public figure, Clay became increasingly aware of the inexorable and calamitous movement of the cholera epidemic to the west. It appeared in Lexington on June 3 and within three days had killed more than fifty people. A week later it occasioned a virtual panic as shops closed, newspapers suspended operations, "and no one moving in the streets except those concerned with the dead or the sick." Daniel Webster, on an extended western tour, had planned to visit Clay at Ashland but was quietly advised to turn back when he reached Cincinnati. He wisely followed the advice. The "terrible scourge" raged with "uncommon violence" in Lexington, said Clay, where five hundred persons succumbed, a larger number than any other city in the country, with the single exception of New Orleans. Because of insufficient coffins to bury the dead, several corpses were enclosed in a single box, black and white interred in the same common grave. By mid-July the scourge had finally abated, and Clay told his friends that he had much "to be thankful for. . . . In a family of about sixty, white and black, we have had no deaths." His daughter, Anne, and her family at the Woodlands, his brother Porter in Frankfort, and Lucretia's family connections also miraculously escaped unharmed.[15]

"Living in the midst of death," Clay wrote his brother-in-law James Brown, "I feel the uncertainty of life." That uncertainty became a reality when he received word, shortly after the pestilence had broken out in Lexington, that his good friend, colleague, and staunch supporter Josiah S. Johnston had been killed aboard a Mississippi River steamboat headed for Natchitoches, Louisiana, when it blew up. Johnston's death meant the loss of a major political leader dedicated to Clay's elevation to the presidency. The Great Compromiser's most powerful and useful supporter in the Southwest was now gone, and the news of Johnston's demise left him shaken. "This event has filled me with grief," he wrote to Peter Porter. "He was among the truest and best of friends, and I shall never cease to deplore his untimely death." The following December he eulogized his friend in the Senate.[16]

Another tragedy occurred when his only living daughter, Anne, gave birth to a son who died within a few days. Infant mortality occurred quite frequently in the Clay family. As he had said, he seemed to be living in the midst of death.[17]

---

session of Congress, it might prove advantageous to the public and himself. "Not being in the habit of correspondence with him I cannot myself make the suggestion to him." Clay to Richard Henry Wilde, April 27, 1833, ibid., VIII, 641.

15. Clay to Henry Clay, Jr., June 7, 1833, Clay to Julia Clay, June 13, 1833, Clay to Peter B. Porter, June 16, 1833, Clay to Webster, June 17, 1833, Clay to James Brown, June 18, 1833, Porter Clay to Clay, July 21, 1833, Clay to Edward Everett, July 23, 1833, in Clay, *Papers,* VIII, 648, 649, 650, 651, 652, 658, 660.

16. Clay to Brown, June 18, 1833, John Sibley to Clay, May 22, 1833, Clay to Porter, June 16, 1833, in Clay, *Papers,* VIII, 652, 642, 651.

17. Clay to James Brown, October 8, 1833, in Clay, *Papers,* VIII, 664.

The grand tour of the North and East that Clay had planned for the summer had to be postponed, of course. At one point he even canceled it altogether, but in the fall, when the cholera outbreak abated somewhat, he changed his mind and decided to indulge himself and make an abbreviated trip. He could not resist sporting himself around the country and thereby satisfying his overwhelming need for a display of affection and gratitude by the very people who had rejected him twelve months earlier. He left Ashland on September 26, accompany by his wife, his son John, his grandson Henry C. Duralde, and two servants.

Before he left, he gave his overseer, William Martin, strict and detailed instructions about the management of his home and plantation. The instructions included which fields to plant and what and when to plant them, which animals and what produce to buy and sell, which fields to clear, what timber to cut, and which slaves to be hired out at the annual rate of approximately a hundred dollars plus room and board.[18] It was another sign that Clay truly enjoyed his life as farmer and stockman and might easily retire from public life.

The group reached Baltimore in early October, then circled from Philadelphia, New York, Providence, Boston, Charlestown, Worcester, Hartford, Springfield, Northampton, Pittsfield, Albany, New York, and finally back to Baltimore. From the very start of the tour it was one long triumph. "I am taken possession of, wherever I go," Clay joyfully informed his friends, "in spite of my remonstrances." Crowds turned out to cheer him; "lodgings and every luxury are provided for us at public expence." In New York City Philip Hone recorded in his diary that Clay was mobbed on his arrival and then escorted by one hundred gentlemen on horseback to the American Hotel. The Great Compromiser declined all public dinners but agreed to meet everyone who called on him. And he was showered with gifts, so many, in fact, that it became an embarrassment. In Providence he was elected to honorary membership in the Philormenian Society of Brown University "with all sorts of testimony of esteem." He also visited factories of various types, many of them "entirely new," and he expressed his astonishment at their "successful progress." The economic changes and improvements taking place in the country on account of the market revolution impressed him deeply and reaffirmed his belief in the merits of the American System and the wisdom of his party's principles and philosophy.[19]

Clay arrived in Boston aboard the steamboat *President* on October 21 "and was paraded round the streets in the midst of all the rain." The following day he went out to visit John Quincy Adams in Quincy. Adams noted the "great demonstrations of respect" shown the Kentuckian wherever he went,

18. Clay to James Brown, October 8, 1833, in Clay, *Papers,* VIII, 664; James F. Hopkins, ed., "Henry Clay, Farmer and Stockman," *Journal of Southern History,* XV (February 1949), pp. 91–95.
19. Clay to James Erwin, October 13, 1833, Clay to Silas Bailey, October 21, 1833, Clay to Henry Shall, November 3, 1833, Clay to John Pendleton Kennedy, November 10, 1833, in Clay, *Papers,* VIII, 664–666; Hone, *Diary,* I, 102.

but the dour former President thought this "fashion of peddling for popularity" was becoming all too common. Formerly confined to Presidents—Jackson had taken such a tour the previous spring—the practice had expanded with the growth of mass politics and allowed a candidate to travel around the country "gathering crowds together, hawking for public dinners, and spouting empty speeches. . . . Mr. Clay has mounted that hobby [horse] often, and rides him very hard."[20]

It was a long, tiring, exhilarating, and profitable tour. And it did Clay's psyche and emotional state of mind a world of good. He said he was "almost entirely prostrated by the unceasing excitement of the scenes through which, for a month past, I have been passing." But he delighted in every moment of it. Throughout the tour he purchased a considerable number of livestock, including five jackasses (one cost a thousand dollars alone), twenty-two sheep, and a Durham short-horned bull and heifer. In addition, he had four full-blooded English cattle given to him, and he purchased three others, "including a pair of full blooded Devons', the most beautiful of all the varieties of Stock."[21]

Clay and family finally reached Washington in late November and took the Samuel Ditty place on C Street near Pennsylvania Avenue, a small furnished house to the rear of Gadsby's Hotel. He paid $75 a month rent and spent $82.50 for painting, papering, plastering, and other minor repairs to make the lodging more comfortable.[22]

Shortly after his arrival in Washington Clay received a very distressing report from home. His son Henry Clay, Jr., now residing in Lexington, informed him that his Ashland estate looked neglected, with fences falling down, the winter provender untended, and the slaves not worked as they should. He blamed the situation on the overseer, William Martin, who frequently absented himself to attend his own affairs. Worse, Theodore had had to be recommitted to the "Lunatic Asylum." His mind was filled with "suspicions of plots and conspiracies," and Anne decided he must return to the hospital because of the "positive risk and danger of his going at large." Henry, Jr., as closest relation, gave his consent to the action and advanced fifty dollars and gave a five-hundred-dollar bond for Theodore's board. Finally, Thomas Hart Clay, who had been placed in charge of Ashland, had been drinking rather heavily since the father's departure. He appeared quite "addicted" to alcohol.[23]

It was one blow after another. Clay was powerless to do anything about his sons, except to provide whatever support possible, and he asked his son-in-law James Erwin, who lived closest to Ashland, to dismiss the overseer and hire

20. Adams, *Memoirs*, IX, 25.

21. Clay to Henry Clay, Jr., November 24, December 1, 1833, Clay to Thomas Hart Clay, November 25, 1833, Clay to Walter Dun, February 22, 1834, in Clay, *Papers*, VIII, 667, 668, 669, 700.

22. Clay to Brown, December 10, 1833, Clay to Philip R. Fendall, November 24, 1833, in Clay, *Papers*, VIII, 672, 667–668.

23. Henry Clay, Jr., to Clay, December 14, 1833, in Clay, *Papers*, VIII, 675–676.

an unmarried man if possible. Eventually John Headley replaced William Martin at an annual salary of $450.[24]

It was with such conflicting emotions—exhilaration over his recent tour and depression over conditions at home—that Clay turned back to his public duties and the continuing onslaughts of "King Andrew the First," the tyrant in the White House.

Over the summer and fall President Jackson had decided to remove the government's deposits from the BUS and thereby "kill the monster" once and for all. He dismissed his secretary of the treasury, William Duane, who refused to carry out the order of removal, and appointed Roger B. Taney as the new Treasury head. Taney initiated the removal of the deposits commencing October 1, 1833. Then Jackson dumped this fait accompli in Congress's lap, along with his veto message of Clay's land bill, when it reconvened in early December.

Removal of the deposits really frightened the country. Such a jolt to the financial system could spell disaster. Even Democrats were fearful, and many of them strongly opposed this high-handed action. Besides, money matters belonged to the province of Congress, not to the President. The secretary of the treasury acted on its behalf and was obliged to report his actions to the legislative branch of the government. Furthermore, Taney's appointment had not yet been confirmed by the Senate, so he was totally unauthorized, in Clay's opinion, to touch the revenue in any shape, manner, or form.

Actually Jackson did not propose to remove the deposits in a single action. He planned to draw out the funds as needed to operate the government; additional revenues, as they were received, would be placed in selected state banks, dubbed pet banks by the National Republicans. The President expressed enormous pleasure in this scheme and the likelihood of the early demise of Biddle's "monster." "We act solely on the defensive," he said with a straight face, "and I am ready with the screws to draw every tooth and then the stumpts." Unless he was very much mistaken, Jackson said he would have "Mr. Biddle and his Bank as quiet and harmless as a *lamb* in six weeks."[25]

But the lamb had teeth and a terrifying roar. Shortly after Taney issued the removal order, the board of directors of the BUS authorized Biddle to initiate a general curtailment of loans throughout the entire banking system. Biddle also restricted bills of exchange, refused to increase discounts, and ordered western banks of the BUS to purchase bills of exchange payable solely in eastern cities. All this was intended to apply such an enormous economic squeeze on the country that Jackson would be forced to rescind the removal order because of the public outcry. Said Biddle: "This worthy President thinks

---

24. Clay to James Erwin, December 21, 1833, Clay to Henry Clay, Jr., January, 17, 23, 1833, in Clay, *Papers,* VIII, 681, 690, 692. Martin was not immediately dismissed and stayed on as manager until 1835, at which time Headley replaced him.

25. Jackson to Van Buren, October 5, 1833, in Jackson, *Correspondence,* V, 216.

that because he has scalped Indians and imprisoned Judges, he is to have his way with the Bank. He is mistaken."[26]

The storm unleashed by Jackson's removal order and the subsequent action by Biddle struck the business community with immediate and devastating force. Merchants condemned the President's order as a "naked, bare-faced act of usurpation and mischief . . . a Proclamation of War." They branded Jackson a tyrant, for "tyranny is a disregard of the law and the substitution of individual will for legal restraint."[27]

It soon became obvious to the leaders of the National Republican party that removal could split the Democratic party right down the middle. Many Jacksonians had supported the President's veto. But removal! That threatened the financial underpinnings of American society. Mass desertions from the Democratic party might bring control of Congress into the hands of the opposition, where Clay was waiting to initiate another land bill and another recharter bill. "I consider that every movement which throws off a fragment from the Jackson party," wrote Duff Green, editor of the Washington *Telegraph*, "promises to swell our numbers. . . . You must see that every shock breaks loose some interest and that which our opponents lose we gain—We are in the field we must grow in strength."[28]

So sudden and disruptive was the Treasury order that even Daniel Webster, who had long lingered over the possibility of a political alliance with Jackson, drew back in horror and rejoined his old comrades in the National Republican camp.[29]

Throughout the fall months Biddle intensified his murderous squeeze. The Bank reduced its loans by $9.5 million just when business was expanding and in desperate need of credit and capital. The nation spiraled into recession and seemed headed into a major economic collapse.[30]

With the convening of the twenty-third Congress in December, a general cry of distress echoed across the country. Merchants in New York, said the son of Alexander Hamilton, "are really in very great distress nay even to the verge of General Bankruptcy." Senator John Tyler reported that "Bankruptcy to the North is almost general." The winter of 1833–1834 had produced such "appalling" distress, said another, that all the leading cities witnessed "great despondency pervading the trading part of the people." Even Clay admitted to

---

26. Biddle to Joseph Hopkinson, February 21, 1834, Biddle Papers, LC.

27. *National Intelligencer,* September 21, October 2, 4, 16, November 2, 1833.

28. Green to John Floyd, November 20, 1833, Floyd Papers, LC.

29. At the beginning of the session Clay felt that Webster had given himself "a fatal stab among his own friends" by his coziness with Jackson and that if he really deserted to the administration, "it will be with infamy." But Webster did not desert. Mangum to David L. Swain, December 22, 1833, in Mangum, *Papers,* II, 55–56.

30. Thomas Govan, *Nicholas Biddle: Nationalist and Public Banker, 1786–1844* (Chicago, 1959), p. 247; Catterall, *Second Bank of the United States,* p. 321.

his son that the "distress in the Eastern Cities is intense."[31]

The fault, lectured the senator, lay with Jackson for ordering the removal of the deposits. His unlawful, unconstitutional, high-handed action had brought the country to near financial ruin. And Clay expected to do something about it. He noted with growing pleasure the fact that a majority in the Senate had swung against the administration; unfortunately the House still held firm behind the President. Within a week Clay was boasting that he and his friends had so far "carried every measure" opposed by the administration. Things "have gone on swimmingly," he said. Unlike the President and his cohorts, however, we are rational and sensible men. "We mean to use with great moderation the power thus acquired."[32]

But before very long Clay began wielding that power with near-demonic determination to annihilate "Jacksonism." Never before had he seemed so driven, so obsessed, so consumed with the need to bring the administration to heel. He was absolutely convinced that the government had fallen into the hands of a lunatic and that he must exert every effort to challenge, outmaneuver, outwit, thwart, and circumvent Jackson's insatiable grasping after power. Encouraged by his triumphs of the previous session, totally convinced of his parliamentary powers to achieve his purpose, and exhilarated by the idea of again saving the country from chaos, Clay reveled in his presumed ability to command and control the United States Senate. Without realizing the extent or direction of his mania, he became as despotic, as dictatorial, as tyrannical as Jackson himself.

Clay spoke every day in the Senate, often several times in the day. He pleaded, cajoled, coaxed, and flattered his colleagues in long, powerful speeches that excoriated the chief executive and his misuse of presidential power. All of a sudden the quiet, sedate, drab, patrician, and uninteresting Senate of the United States became the arena for one of the greatest political cockfights in American history. Crowds appeared daily and filled every place to watch the bloody encounters between the President's maddened opponents and his equally agitated supporters. Just as he had transformed the House when he served as Speaker, so Clay now converted the Senate into an exciting, sometimes raucous forum for full-scale airings of every important national issue.

And Clay had help. Webster, now recovered from his momentary alliance with Jackson, sharpened his spurs and joined in the savage assault. Calhoun, too, periodically shrieked his fury at the President and bared his talons, although he liked to pretend that he was an independent fighter and not part of

31. James A. Hamilton to Van Buren, December 30, 1833, Jacob Barker to Van Buren, February 25, 1834, Jesse Hoyt to Van Buren, January 29, 1834, Van Buren Papers, LC; John Tyler to Mrs. Tyler, February 17, 1834, in Tyler, *Letters,* I, 485; Clay to Henry Clay, Jr., January 23, 1834, in Clay, *Papers,* VIII, 692.
32. Clay to James Brown, December 10, 1834, Clay to John M. Clayton, December 12, 1834, in Clay, *Papers,* VIII, 672–673, 674.

the assault team. This triumvirate,[33] this Great Triumvirate, as it was soon called, brought unaccustomed glory and notoriety to the Senate's proceedings that never before or since has been equaled. As has been said many times, it was the Senate's golden age.

This "Panic session" of the Twenty-third Congress was to witness not only a titanic verbal free-for-all among equally high-strung and temperamental politicians but the realignment of political forces brought on by the Bank War, nullification, the American System, and—most especially—President Jackson's conduct as chief executive of the United States.

Old Hickory's annual message, delivered on December 3, served as the opening signal for the brouhaha to follow, but the report of the new secretary of the treasury, Roger B. Taney, explaining the reasons for the removal of the deposits, really triggered the onslaught. Taney, as yet unconfirmed by the Senate in his new post, cited the following reasons for the removal: the Bank's involvement in elections, its corrupt practices, its interference with the payment of the national debt, Biddle's personal control of the Bank's funds, and the exclusion of the government's directors in formulating its operating policies, among a number of others.

Clay responded immediately, providing the administration notice not only that he would fight its efforts to destroy the nation's financial structure but that he would lead the Senate forces in the effort. "Mr. Clay is captain," reported Senator Silas Wright, Jr., of New York to the Albany Regency, "and he trains his troops daily and constantly. . . . How long this will be so we know not. Mr. Calhoun seems ambitious only to follow and ubci and Mr. Webster looks black as a thunk i i Hild and seems to go heavily."[34]

The secretary of the treasury, Clay began as he eased into his first skirmish with the administration, functions as the agent of the Congress in the handling of government funds. But the present incumbent has responded to a demand of the President that is unsanctioned by law and "dangerous to the liberties of the people." Increasingly Clay worried about American freedom, and he felt obliged to remind the Congress and the nation of the perils facing them as a consequence of Jackson's tyranny. Throughout this session, and indeed, for the remainder of his life, his speeches warned constantly against those actions that he feared threatened the "liberties of the people." As Lincoln later testified, Clay spoke often and brilliantly not only for the Union and against executive usurpation but for "the freedom of mankind."

The removal authority belongs by law to the Congress, not to the President, Clay continued in this initial attack against the administration, and Taney

33. In a letter to Webster, Nicholas Biddle wrote: "I only repeat what I have said again & again that the fate of this nation is in the hands of Mr Clay Mr Calhoun & yourself. It is in your power to save us from the misrule of these people in place, but you can only do it while you are united. It is for that reason that every honest man is anxious that you three should not be alienated from each other." December 15, 1833, in Webster, *Papers, Correspondence,* III, 285.

34. Wright to Azariah C. Flagg, December 11, 1833, Flagg Papers, New York Public Library.

therefore exceeded his authority. The full Senate, he declared, should itself investigate what happened, instead of referring the matter to a committee, and the Kentuckian wanted Taney to provide the names, locations, capitalizations, specie reserves, and general financial condition of the various state (pet) banks into which the government's funds were now being deposited. He also demanded that Jackson provide the Senate a copy of the paper, dated September 18, 1833,[35] read to the cabinet and widely disseminated, concerning the removal so that the Senate could decide whether it "be genuine or not."

That last demand had no other purpose than to annoy the President since the paper had already been published and circulated. Thus the Jacksonians, especially Thomas Hart Benton of Missouri and John Forsyth of Georgia, protested this "outrageous" demand upon the chief executive. Even so, under Clay's whip, the resolution carried by the vote of twenty-three to eighteen thereby providing the first real indication of the strength of the administration's opposition in the present Senate. And Clay expected to add to that strength in the coming months and maybe reverse the Democratic majority in the House. It can be done, he predicted, "If we have no *desertions.*"[36]

Jackson responded the next day to Clay's "impertinent" request by flatly rejecting it as an intrusion into his private communications with his cabinet. This rejection further alienated some National Republicans who did not always pander to Clay's leadership. "There is a tone of insolence and insult in his [Jackson's] intercourse with both Houses of Congress, especially since his re-election . . . ," noted Representative Adams. But the former President took pleasure in watching Clay get a taste of his own medicine. In the past, said Adams, the "domineering tone" had usually been the prerogative of the legislative, "and Clay has not been sparing in the use of it. He is now paid in his own coin."[37] Of course, Jackson also recognized that Clay would probably use the rejection for still more "impertinences" as well as for an excuse to launch his first major assault against the removal. Everyone seemed alert to the fact that the next time the Kentucky senator spoke on the floor it would be the start of a bare-knuckle, bloody fight with no holds barred.

The alarm went out several days later. "Clay opens his battery in the Senate on Thursday," December 26, wrote Representative Richard Wilde of Georgia, a pro-Bank member of the House Ways and Means Committee. "I have no doubt he will make a strong argument. He has prepared himself with care."[38]

35. The draft of this paper may be found in the Jackson Papers, LC, and a printed copy in Jackson, *Correspondence,* V, 192–203.

36. *Register of Debates,* 23d Congress, 1st session, pp. 23–37, 51–53; Lincoln to John M. Clay, August 9, 1862, in Roy P. Basler, ed., *The Collected Works of Abraham Lincoln* (New Brunswick, N. J., 1953), V, 363–364; Clay to Brooke, December 11, 1834, in Clay, *Papers,* VIII, 673.

37. Adams, *Memoirs,* IX, 51. "The call [by Clay] was a wrong step," remarked Senator Benton, "and gave the President an easy and graceful victory." Benton, *Thirty Years' View,* I, 400.

38. Wilde to Gulian C. Verplanck, December 24, 1833, Verplanck Papers, New-York Historical Society.

Indeed, he had. He planned to speak at length, giving facts and figures to document his arguments, and thereby send a thundering condemnation of the President reverberating around the nation. Everything Clay believed sacred and valuable and essential to legitimate government was "in imminent hazard" because of Jackson's despotic actions. "By means of the Veto, the power *as exercised* of removal from office, the possession of the public treasury and the public patronage, the very existence of Liberty and the Government is, in my judgment," he wrote, "in peril." He told his friends that he was embarked on a campaign similar to the one that ultimately produced the American Revolution. "I mean myself to open and push a vigorous campaign." He intended to haul the President before the bar of congressional justice in the Senate chamber and there present evidence that would bring about a censure of Jackson's conduct as chief executive of the United States.[39]

Clay himself noted that the Senate chamber was "crowded to overflowing" to hear "the first part" of his three-day extended examination into the monstrous actions of "this wicked administration." Even the corridors outside the chamber were jammed with people who could hear his voice but not see him. Clay savored the excitement and the notoriety to the fullest as he rose to address the assembled audience. Every facet of his enormous speaking talent came into play. And the intimate confines of the room allowed him to modulate his voice for greater dramatic effect, thereby taking full advantage of the excellent acoustics provided by the chamber's low-vaulted dome.

Clay stood at his place for a moment as he felt the palpable tension he had created. Then he began. He started by asking his fellow senators to censure the President of the United States and the designated secretary of the treasury. He did it by introducing two motions: the first against Jackson for his unlawful exercise of power over the United States Treasury; the second against Taney for the insufficient and unsatisfactory reasons given to the Congress for the removal of the Bank's funds.

Clay proposed something never done before or since. Because the Senate could not initiate impeachment proceedings, he asked instead for the President's censure. His action demonstrated the depth of his outrage over Jackson's behavior as chief executive, and it showed to what lengths he was willing to go to call a halt to that behavior.

The motions presented, Clay then launched into his formal address. To start, he charged the President with assuming "the exercise of a power over the treasury of the United States, not granted to him by the constitution and laws, and dangerous to the liberties of the people." The "rapaciousness" of this man in seeking to expand the powers of his office defied belief, thundered Clay in his first display of emotion. "We are in the midst of a revolution, hitherto bloodless, but rapidly tending towards a total change of the pure republican character of the Government, and to the concentration of all power in the

39. Clay to Brooke, December 16, 1833, in Clay, *Papers*, VIII, 679.

hands of one man." The President had paralyzed the powers of Congress through "an extraordinary exercise of the executive veto, not anticipated by the founders of the constitution, and not practiced by any of the predecessors of the present Chief Magistrate." The constitutional participation of the Senate in the appointing power "is virtually abolished" and reduced to "an idle ceremony." Because Secretary of the Treasury William Duane would not remove the deposits without first informing Congress, as he was required to do by law, the President had dismissed him and appointed Taney. Then Taney removed the deposits even though his appointment had not been confirmed by the Senate and he therefore did not have the authority to act. Such removal is nothing less than a deliberate and culpable usurpation of the power of Congress over the purse.

Jackson's revolution, his "rage for innovation," stormed Clay, moved beyond Congress and even extended to the judiciary. "Decisions of the tribunals, deliberately pronounced, have been contemptuously disregarded, and the sanctity of numerous treaties openly violated," as witness Jackson's ruthless treatment of the southern Indian tribes. In addition, the currency was undermined, internal improvements "crushed beneath the veto," the tariff indifferently considered and soon to be abandoned, so that by March 3, 1837, the government "will have been transformed into an elective monarchy."

In the paper that the President read to his cabinet but that he refused to send to the Senate, Clay continued, he stated in part that the responsibilities of the executive office included preserving *"the morals of the people, the freedom of the press, and the purity of the elective franchise."*

Clay paused. He looked around the chamber with a devilish grin on his face. "The morals of the people!" he guffawed. "What part of the Constitution has given to the President any power over 'the morals of the people'?"

Clay switched from sarcasm to outright anger when he reviewed Jackson's "utter contempt" of Congress in removing the deposits, and this contempt, he said, should not be permitted to stand unchallenged. The question before this house, cried Clay, centered on whether the protective barriers of civil liberties would "be prostrated and trodden under foot, and the sword and the purse be at once united in the hands of one man."

Clay's voice now rose in pitch and volume as he became more agitated. His arms flailed the air, his fingers sometimes spread wide, sometimes curled into a fist. The President, he charged, "neither by the act creating the treasury department, nor by the bank charter, has any power over the public treasury. Has he any by the constitution? None, none." At this point Clay was practically screaming, the word "none" being repeated at the highest possible pitch.

Finally Clay quieted. He let several moments pass before beginning again; only this time he totally altered his approach and reverted to subdued mockery and a sneering tone of indignation. The President, he said, had the temerity to claim that his right to initiate these outrageous deeds devolved upon him by virtue of the Constitution "and the suffrages of the American people." The suffrages of the American people! Since when and by what authority was there a "double source" of executive power under this government? "By what authority does the President derive power from the mere result of an election?" Gentlemen, Clay cooed, "I am surprised and alarmed at the new source of executive power which is found in the result of a presidential election. I had supposed that the constitution and the laws were the sole source of executive authority . . . that the issue of a presidential election was merely to place the Chief Magistrate in the post assigned to him." Obviously the military chieftain thinks otherwise. He proposes "that if, prior to an election, certain opinions, no matter how ambiguously put forth by a candidate, are known to the people, those loose opinions, in virtue of the election, incorporate themselves with the constitution, and afterwards are to be regarded and expounded as parts of the instrument!"

Clay closed with a magnificent peroration, delivered to the "loud and repeated applause" of a crowd whose emotions and feelings had been sent soaring by the thrusting and miraculous language of the speaker:

The land is filled with spies and informers, and detraction and denunciation are the orders of the day. People, especially official incumbents in this place, no longer dare speak in the fearless tones of manly freemen, but in the cautious whispers of trembling slaves. The premonitory symptoms of despotism are upon us; and if Congress do not apply an instantaneous and effective remedy, the fatal collapse will soon come on, and we shall die—ignobly die—base, mean, and abject slaves; the scorn and contempt of mankind; unpitied, unwept, unmourned![40]

The galleries and the lobbies exploded in prolonged shouts of approval as Clay finished and resumed his seat. Most agreed that it was his finest effort to date. Philip Hone, the New York merchant, heard the speech and pronounced it "one of the most eloquent appeals to the feelings of his audience that I have ever heard. It was solemn, energetic, and impressive." What undoubtedly gave the speech its great power was Clay's genuine belief that he was engaged in rescuing the nation from misrule and impending doom. Short of impeachment, at least a censure by the upper house might bring the tyrant to heel. "I said what I felt," wrote Clay to his friend Peter B. Porter, "and no one can feel more than I do. . . . And if I am to judge of the Speech by what has been said in its favor, I ought to be satisfied. That is much more than I expect will be the case at the White House."[41]

Indeed. The White House erupted in a towering rage. "Oh, if I live to get these robes of office off me," Jackson seethed, "I will bring the rascal to a dear account." He later likened the Kentucky senator to "a drunken man in a brothel," reckless, destructive, and "full of fury."[42]

40. *Register of Debates*, 23d Congress, 1st session, pp. 58–94; Sargent, *Public Men and Events*, I, 259. Clay's entire speech took three days to deliver, ending on Tuesday, December 31, 1833.

41. Hone, *Diary*, I, 117; Clay to Porter, December 26, 1833, in Clay, *Papers*, VIII, 683. Clay's remark that the nation was in the midst of a revolution, commented the New York *American* on February 4, 1834, was a "startling, and true as startling, declaration."

42. Parton, *Jackson*, III, 542; Jackson to Andrew Jackson, Jr., February 16, 1834, Jackson Papers, LC.

Clay's superb denunciation of executive despotism found powerful verbal support from Calhoun and Webster in speeches of enormous length and intensity, but neither equaled Clay's intellectual power and strength. "Mr. Calhoun took the floor," recorded Senator Benton, ". . . and did Mr. Clay the honor to adopt his leading ideas of a revolution, and of a robbery of the treasury."[43] But he could not add anything significant. The plundering of the Roman treasury by Julius Caesar, said Calhoun, was an act of virtue compared with Andrew Jackson's recent conduct. At least Caesar's seizure was done openly by an intrepid and bold warrior. "The actors in our case are of a different character— artful, cunning, and corrupt politicians, and not a fearless warrior. They have entered the treasury, not sword in hand, as public plunderers, but, with the false keys of sophistry, as pilferers, under the silence of midnight.

"With money and corrupt partisans," Calhoun growled, looking straight at the presiding officer, Martin Van Buren, "a great effort is now making to choke and stifle the voice of American liberty" by corrupting and managing the press, intimidating every department of government, and arranging a national convention to dictate the succession. When all this has been accomplished, the "revolution [will] be completed, and all the powers of our republic, in like manner, [will] be consolidated in the President, and perpetuated by his dictation."[44]

Daniel Webster, who chaired the Senate Finance Committee, spoke authoritatively but less vehemently than either Clay or Calhoun against the removal of the deposits, perhaps because of his recent flirtation with Jackson. Even so, he scored many telling constitutional points against the President's position. And each day thereafter one or more of the Great Triumvirate blasted the administration for its repeated crimes against the liberties of the American people.

At many points during the winter-long debate the presiding officer, Martin Van Buren, pretended not to hear the sledgehammer blows struck against executive despotism. So the Kentuckian decided to command his attention. In a voice soaring with sarcasm, he spoke directly to the Vice President and implored him to go to the White House and on bended knee "exert his well-known influence" over the old man and insist upon the restoration of the deposits. "And if I touch your heart," he melodramatically pleaded with Van Buren, "and persuade you to come to the rescue of your suffering country, I shall merit her gratitude and promote your glory."

When Clay's charming little game ended, Van Buren looked up from the book he was supposedly reading, gestured another senator into his seat as presiding officers and stepped down to the floor.

He walked straight toward Clay, looking directly at him. Suddenly it seemed that a frightful scene might ensue right on the floor of the United

43. Benton, *Thirty Years' View,* I, 411.
44. *Register of Debates,* 23d Congress, 1st session, p. 220.

States Senate between the Vice President of the United States and the nation's most distinguished senator. Would the elegant Magician brawl with the Great Compromiser in public? Seeing Van Buren approach, Clay slowly rose from his seat. Fascinated, he stared at Van Buren in growing disbelief. Spectators sucked in their breath, a few undoubtedly hoping for the worst.

At last Van Buren reached Clay's side. But instead of rebuking the senator in some provocative fashion, he bowed. Then, in a mocking voice to match anything Clay could produce, he purred: "Mr. Senator, allow me to be indebted to you for another pinch of your aromatic Maccoboy."

Dumbfounded, Clay simply waved his hand toward the gold snuffbox he kept on his desk. Van Buren sampled it and then leisurely returned to the chair of the presiding officer.[45]

The Great Triumvirate's relentless pounding of the President was dutifully answered each day by equally lengthy and eloquent speeches by the Democrats, notably Thomas Hart Benton ("Old Bullion," as he was now known), Silas Wright, Jr., and John Forsyth. Benton took four days to defend his chief, using most of the time to pummel Clay.

"The Senator from Kentucky," he rumbled in his big, reverberating voice, "calls upon the people to rise, and drive the Goths from the capitol." But who are these Goths? "They are General Jackson and the Democratic party—he just elected President over the senator himself." Perhaps the senator resents the drubbing he sustained in the election by the American people and is now attempting to exact revenge for his defeat and humiliation. As for the censure motion, Benton continued, that was totally improper because it charged the President with an impeachable offense and only the House of Representatives can initiate impeachment. How shall we respond to Clay's demand for censure? he asked. "I answer . . . to leave this impeachment to the House of Representatives [where it belongs] . . . and to those who have no private griefs to avenge."[46]

Forsyth and other Democrats chided Clay and his wrecking crew for approving the corrupting power of the BUS yet condemning Jackson's exercise of constitutional presidential power. They can abide Biddle's despotism but not Jackson's attack upon it. They pillory "King Andrew" but bend the knee to "Czar Nick."[47]

And back and forth it went week after week, both the triumvirate and its Jacksonian opponents mauling each other for all manner of corrupt acts and other assorted improprieties. John Quincy Adams stopped by the Senate one day, and as usual, he noted, "Mr. Clay was speaking. Between him and Silas Wright and [William] Wilkins [of Pennsylvania] and Webster and [Peleg] Sprague [of Maine] there was a sharp-shooting debate on the mere question

45. Stanton, *Random Recollections*, pp. 205–206; Hone, *Diary*, I, 117.

46. Benton, *Thirty Years' View*, I, 409.

47. *Register of Debates*, 23d Congress, 1st session, passim. See especially Senator Isaac Hill's speech, ibid., p. 791.

whether five thousand or six thousand copies should be printed" of a committee paper on Taney's deposit report. The debate was "very acrimonious."[48]

Almost anything said by a senator during these weeks touched off a donnybrook, and some of the arguments advanced by the Democrats on removal, declared Clay, "belong to the age of the British Stuarts" and were more alarming than the presidential acts themselves. "It is now contended that *all* Executive power is in the President," he snorted; "that he is to take care that *all* the laws are faithfully executed; that one will alone is to govern in that branch of the Government, to which all the Executive officers must conform; and that he has the power to remove, whenever he pleases." If these doctrines prevail, the executive will be "Supreme" and the other two branches of government subordinate to it.[49]

A number of Clay's suporters around the country thought he was too lenient on Jackson, considering the misery the old man had induced. The Kentuckian should not forget, they reminded him, that Congress possessed the ultimate weapon. "What are you going to do with that old reprobate in the white house will he be permitted to ruin the country with impunity. If you can get at him no other way *impeach* the old *scamp*."[50]

These encouraging responses from a certain portion of the electorate— and they increased throughout the winter—convinced Clay that he had the administration on the run. Washington, he noted, was "full of distress committees." That was a good sign. "The more the better," he added. Also, the continued desertions from the Democratic party, such as the recent one by Gulian C. Verplanck of New York, reassured him. Many of Jackson's "partizans are in much distress," wrote Senator Samuel Bell of New Hampshire, "under the impression that his lawless and reckless conduct and his obstinancy will prostrate the party."[51]

The President administered still another shock to his party when he decided to terminate the Bank's operation of paying pensions to Revolutionary War veterans. He instructed his secretary of war, Lewis Cass, to order Biddle to relinquish all the funds, books, and accounts relating to pensions to the War Department's commissioner of pensions. But Biddle refused to obey the order. It was, he said, just another detestable and flagrantly illegal action by the old reprobate to hold veterans as hostage in his unending war against the Bank. Clay agreed, and took to the Senate floor once again to defend Biddle against the usurper. The fact that the attorney general sustained the legality of the President's order did not impress Clay. He no longer respected the opinions of

48. Adams, *Memoirs,* IX, 87.

49. Clay to John R. D. Payne et al., February 1, 1834, Clay to Littleton W. Tazewell, February 1, 1834, in Clay, *Papers,* VIII, 692, 693.

50. Erskine Eichelberger to Clay, February 22, 1834, in Clay, *Papers,* VIII, 700.

51. Clay to Henry Clay, Jr., January 23, 1834, Clay to Brooke, February 10, 1834, in Clay, *Papers,* VIII, 692, 696; Bell to Joseph Blount, February 27, 1834, Autograph File, Harvard University Library.

any cabinet officer, he said, because they would be "instantaneously dismissed" if they disobeyed or contradicted the tyrant.[52]

At this point Webster wanted to reintroduce a bill to recharter the Bank, but Clay, as he explained to Biddle, totally disagreed. And his reasons showed how much more politically astute he was than the Massachusetts senator. The central question now "is the usurpation which has convulsed the Country," not the need for recharter. "The Bank ought to be kept in the rear; the usurpation in front." Later—perhaps next year—would be time enough to push for recharter. Nevertheless, Webster went ahead and presented a bill in the Senate which Clay refused to endorse. It distracted from the more urgent need to censure the President, and when Clay threatened to table, Webster reluctantly withdrew it. "Our friend wants *tone, decision,* and *courage,*" Webster sniffed.[53]

Clay never lost sight of the first goal of his party, and almost daily he brought in petitions and memorials, signed by thousands of voters, protesting the President's action. And with each presentation of a memorial he took another swing at the administration. "Gentlemen," he said on one occasion. "It is a question between the will of one man and that of twelve millions of people. It is a question between power—ruthless, relentless, inexorable power—on the one hand, and the strong, deep felt sufferings of a vast community, on the other." The people have the ability to bring about the restoration of the deposits. It all "depends on the People, and the demonstrations of their will. They can produce it."[54]

Clay particularly watched the upcoming elections in New York and Virginia. These would provide a sure sign, he said of current public opinion. Van Buren, in a private conversation with Clay, offered to bet him a suit of clothes on each of the New York elections. The senator responded with the remark that if the people sustained the administration, "I should begin to feel that our experiment of free government had failed; that he [Van Buren] would probably be elected the successor of Jackson; that he would introduce a system of intrigue and corruption, that would enable him to designate his successor."

This was a remarkable outburst on Clay's part in an otherwise innocuous exchange, and most uncharacteristic of him. It was one thing to abuse Van Buren on the Senate floor—that was part of the political game, and all the worthy politicians played it—but quite another to do it in private conversation. It demonstrated how deeply Clay was affected by the debate and what he sensed was happening in the country.

Van Buren looked flabbergasted on hearing the senator's words, hardly believing his ears. Still, Clay continued, no doubt carried away by the venom of his anger. "After a few years of lingering and fretful existence," he went on, "we should end in dissolution of the Union, or in despotism."

52. *Register of Debates,* 23d Congress, 1st session, pp. 462–463.
53. Webster to Biddle, March 25, 1834, Biddle Papers, LC.
54. *Register of Debates,* 23d Congress, 1st session, p. 718.

At that Van Buren burst out laughing. He chided Clay for entertaining "morbid feelings."

But Clay stood his ground. "I replied, with good nature, that what I had said I deliberately and sincerely believed."[55]

And he did indeed believe it. So much so that in early March he introduced four resolutions in the Senate to limit the President's power with respect to the removal of public officials from office. In effect the resolutions forbade the President from removing any official, with the exception of diplomatic appointees, without the concurrence of the Senate. Since appointment required confirmation, removal should also require confirmation. These resolutions were taken up briefly on April 7 and May 8 and then tabled.[56]

Clay's closing speech on the removal of the deposits took him two days. On March 27 and 28 he spoke in what he said was the longest debate (three months) in the history of either house of Congress. He urged the Senate to get on with a final vote on the censure resolutions. After nearly one hundred days it was time to act. Panic conditions throughout the country necessitated that the blame be fixed squarely on the President. "We are . . . not a complaining people. We think not so much of distress. Give us our laws—guaranty to us our constitution—and we will be content with almost any form of government."[57]

The censure resolutions finally came up for a vote on March 28. The censure of Taney passed by the count of twenty-eight to eighteen; the censure of Jackson was approved by the vote of twenty-six to twenty. Among the yea votes, those of Clay, Calhoun, Webster, Poindexter, Benjamin Leigh of Virginia, Peleg Sprague of Maine, and Theodore Frelinghuysen of New Jersey all were expected. Also, nullifiers and strong states' rights advocates, such as Willie P. Mangum of North Carolina, John Tyler of Virginia, William C. Preston of South Carolina, and George A. Waggaman of Louisiana, could have been anticipated. The remainder were no doubt deeply troubled by what Clay had called Jackson's revolution. Clay himself was not surprised by the outcome. "In the Senate our majority, on the resolutions which I offered, was as large as I ever expected."[58]

John Quincy Adams disapproved of the censure of the President and said so to several National Republican senators who consulted him about it. Adams spoke "very fully and with much earnestness" with these senators, but when the vote was finally taken, they agreed to a censure "under the domineering influence of Mr. Clay."[59]

55. Clay to Brooke, March 23, 1834, in Clay, *Works*, I, 383.

56. *Register of Debates*, 23d Congress, 1st session, p. 836, provides the four resolutions.

57. *Register of Debates*, 23d Congress, 1st session, pp. 1170–1177; New York *American*, April 1, 1834.

58. *Register of Debates*, 23d Congress, 1st session, p. 1187; Clay to James Brown, April 1, 1834, in Clay, *Papers*, VIII, 710.

59. Adams, *Memoirs*, IX, 116.

The domineering influence of Mr. Clay! Not much different from Jackson himself, criticized some National Republicans.

As though to add further insult, Clay next requested that the signers of the memorials to Congress be counted and included to the Senate's yeas and nays on censure. Clay estimated that well over one hundred thousand Americans had expressed their dismay over the removal of the deposits. It was an unnecessary display of his extreme pleasure in having brought down an unprecedented censure upon the head of the most popular man in the country, the President of the United States.[60]

The Washington *Globe,* edited by Francis P. Blair, immediately struck back. The perpetrators of this *"shameless libel,"* it said, were the "notorious stipendiaries" of the Bank. Their action amounted to *"the triumph of perfidy."* Without a trial, without a chance to answer the accusations, without regard to constitutional forms, the President had been found guilty of an impeachable offense. The twenty-six "stipendiaries" would have been "hissed out of the Senate if the voice of the people had been truly uttered by the members of that body." What was needed was the popular election of Senators so that it would cease being an "aristocratic" body under the dominance of an embittered demagogue.[61]

Clay delighted in the obvious pain he had inflicted on the President. Maybe now the people would realize the danger facing the nation and do something about it.

60. Benton, *Thirty Years' View,* I, 423.
61. *Globe,* April 1, 1834.

The Emergence of the Whig Party

THE BATTERING of the President continued throughout the month of April, and Clay got better and better at it. The restoration of the government's deposits to the BUS was now the senator's principal aim, and he hammered away at it repeatedly, virtually every day. But the more he pleaded and cajoled and demanded, the more Jackson refused to budge. When delegations visited the White House and begged the President to rescue them from the financial panic, he simply replied: "What do you come to me for, then? Go to Nicholas Biddle. We have no money here, gentlemen. Biddle has all the money. He has millions of specie in his vaults, at this very moment, lying idle."[1]

Nor would Biddle loosen his squeeze. He meant the financial suffering to go on until public pressure built up sufficiently to force Jackson to yield. Two strong-willed, arrogant, and determined men faced each other in deadly combat, and neither would give an inch, neither would compromise.

Clay did what he could in Congress, but moving Jackson proved impossible. On April 14 he gave another powerful speech, at which time he presented memorials from New York cities and towns demanding the recharter of the BUS and the restoration of the deposits. What made this speech historic was Clay's reference to "the patriotic whigs" in New York City who, he said, had just won an important electoral victory against the Democrats.

It was a great victory. It must be so regarded in every aspect. . . . And the whigs contended with such odds against them. . . . The struggle was tremendous; but what can withstand the irresistible power of the votaries of truth, liberty, and their country? It was an immortal triumph—a triumph of the constitution and the laws over usurpation here, and over clubs and bludgeons and violence there. Go on, noble city! Go on, patriotic whigs! follow up your glorious commencement; persevere, and pause not

1. Parton, *Jackson*, III, 549–550.

until you have regenerated and disenthralled your splendid city, and placed it at the head of American cities devoted to civil liberty, as it now stands preeminently the first as the commercial emporium of our common country. Merchants, mechanics, traders, laborers, never cease to recollect, that without freedom, you can have no sure commerce or business; and that without law you have no security for personal liberty, property, or even existence!

Clay pointed out in this speech that at the time of the American Revolution the Tories sided with the monarch against liberty and independence. But the Whigs contended against royal power and stood foursquare for freedom and independence. The contest today was no different, Clay argued. Partisans of the present administration sustain Jackson's illegal seizure of power "in the most boundless extent." They claim for him *"all"* executive authority. "They make his sole will the governing power." Every officer attached to the administration must obey his mandates—without question. If anyone utter a single murmur, he loses his employment. Even the public Treasury, hitherto sacrosanct and beyond his control, has been placed by his minions under his immediate direction.

"The whigs of the present day," declared Clay, drawing himself up to his full height of six feet and extending his arms outward, "are opposing executive encroachment, and a most alarming extension of executive power and prerogative. They are ferreting out the abuses and corruptions of an administration, under a chief magistrate who is endeavoring to concentrate in his own person the whole powers of government." They are contending for the rights of the people—all the people—for civil liberty, free institutions and the supremacy of law and the Constitution.

"Senators! . . . Let us perform our duty in a manner worthy of our ancestors." In this time of "trouble and revolution," amid the "general gloom and darkness" that now prevail, "let us continue to present one unextinguished light, steadily burning, in the cause of the people, of the constitution, and of civil liberty."[2]

This was one of Clay's relatively short speeches during this session but a "most happy and eloquent" one, for it recognized and pronounced the new name of the party that stood with him against the usurpation of power by an "imperial President." The name had been used locally in New York City during the spring election and may have been first invoked by Philip Hone, a wealthy merchant. Supposedly James Watson Webb, editor of the New York *Courier and Enquirer,* cited it in his newspaper at Hone's suggestion. According to another source, it may have been employed first by the Salem *Gazette* in Massachusetts. Whatever the origin, it was Clay's use and acceptance of the term in this speech, identifying the name Whig with everything he and his friends represented, that helped give it national prominence. Daniel Webster first employed the designation in a letter to Benjamin Welles on April 15. The

2. Mallory, ed., *Life and Speeches of Henry Clay,* II, 194–201.

Washington *National Intelligencer* used the label, "the Whig candidate," for the first time on April 14, 1834. By the summer of 1834 it was the common term applied to all those united with Clay in opposition to "Jacksonism" and the Democratic party.[3]

The New York Whigs made it somewhat official when they celebrated their electoral victory on April 15 with a meeting at Castle Garden. "Thousands" attended, including Peter B. Porter, Gideon Granger, Ambrose Spencer, and other "Whig officers of the Corporation." Said one anti-Jackson newspaper in advertising the meeting: "The Heavens smile upon our cause. The glories of a summer day cloudless and serene, will be reflected from the countenances of tens of thousands of freemen who will assemble this day [the fifteenth] to celebrate a triumph second to none achieved since the days of the Whigs of 1776."

At this meeting the crowd condemned the "mismanagement" in Washington that had produced "the evils of our condition": the ruinous public measures advanced by Jackson, the designation of Van Buren as successor to the presidency, the "irresponsible body of sycophants" surrounding the chief executive, and the overall abuse of power.

> To the last they shall fight for the laws of their choice
> And maintain them till Liberty slumber for ever.
> Then unite heart and hand,
> Like the famed Spartan band,
> And swear by the God of the ocean and land,
> That ne'er shall the Whigs of the Union be slaves
> While the earth bears a plant or the sea rolls its waves.

A week later New York had "a Whig General Committee" to direct party affairs.[4]

No sooner did Clay finish his speech on the Senate floor than Democrats recognized that he had just decreed a new name for their opponents. On April 22 the Washington *Globe* noticed the designation in an article entitled "Principles of the Alias Party" written by its editor, Francis P. Blair. "It is the custom with all offenders when they have disgraced one name by their crimes to assume another," wrote Blair. He claimed that the new party actually consisted of none but Tories, Federalists, National Republicans, and nullifiers who had banded together under the auspices of the monster Bank and "boldly resolved to take a name directly opposite to that which belongs to the founders of their

3. Hone, *Diary,* I, xii; II, 629; Dixon Ryan Fox, *Decline of Aristocracy in the Politics of New York* (New York, 1919), p. 367; E. Malcolm Carroll, *Origins of the Whig Party* (Durham, N.C., 1925), p. 123; Daniel Walker Howe, *The Political Culture of the American Whigs* (Chicago, 1979), pp. 88, 331, note 73; Webster to Welles, April 15, 1834, in Webster, *Papers, Correspondence,* III, 339–341. Nathan Sargent claims that he first suggested the Whig name. He wrote an article, he said, that proposed the change of name. It appeared in the first number of the Philadelphia *Star Spangled Banner* of February 11, 1834. Sargent, *Public Men and Events,* I, 262.
4. New York *American,* May 5, 1834.

party." By way of "metempsychosis," he laughed, the "ancient TORIES now call themselves WHIGS." But they fool no one. "By whatever false names the enemies of the Democracy may choose to be known they fortunately never fail to furnish us with a clue to their true sentiments."

By the summer the name of the Whig party had become so well known that Democrats disparagingly referred to it as the "Wig" party since everyone recognized that only lords and ladies wore wigs, while honest, God-fearing Americans had long since ceased wearing them or tying their hair into queues. This new democratic age of equality and individualism rejected everything connected with "ques and Wigs." Let everyone know the true identity of the opposition, jeered the *Globe*. "The Modern Wig—a cover for bald federalism."[5]

Several Whig newspapers immediately answered these gibes with a succinct statement of their intent and philosophy. Let the country know, they said, our intent and purpose: "The Rescue of the Constitution from hands that are violating it—the resistance and overthrow of *Tory* prerogatives, and an Executive grasping at, and exercising, all powers—these are the aim and the motives of the *Whig* party." As for the opposition, "Democracy now means approbation and unlimited support of Executive prerogatives. What is this then but *Toryism,* as originally understood under the Stuarts? It is therefore most appropriate that they who insist upon curtailing and controlling this prerogative of one man, should take the name of *Whigs."* And the new party will fight until "written law" shall be substituted "for an Autocrat, and his slaves of the collar,"[6] We take our direction from none other than Thomas Jefferson, who sanctioned this difference and division between contending political forces. "I consider the party divisions of WHIG and TORY," Jefferson was quoted as saying, "the most WHOLESOME which can exist in any Government, and well worthy of being nourished to keep out those of a more dangerous character."[7]

In a matter of a few weeks, claimed the New York *American,* the "great *Whig* victory in New York finds echoes from the lakes to the ocean," as National Republicans, Bank men, high-tariff advocates, friends of internal improvements, states' righters, some nullifiers, and especially the men who abominated Jackson, his policies, and his presidential style all crowded into the new party. By and large, they included men of wealth and learning—businessmen and professional men especially. But they also included some wage earners, who were caught up in the growth of manufacturing; and they embraced farmers, who needed internal improvements to carry their surplus products to market. According to the most recent student of the Whig political culture, they actually encompassed men in all occupations, classes, religions, and geo-

5. *Globe,* April 21, 22, November 8, 1834.
6. "Collar-men" was a term used at the time to describe sycophants.
7. New York *American,* April 18, 25, June 3, 20, 1834.

graphic locations. These men joined the Whig party not simply because of their fear of Jackson's exercise of unlawful powers but because they believed in programs and principles that contradicted the President's entire domestic policy. Many of them strongly supported the American System in all its particulars but, most of all, its fundamental assumptions about the importance of the role of the national government in advancing the country's happiness and welfare. They believed in policies that would improve, consolidate, and harmonize the nation, policies that would integrate private enterprise with public interest.[8]

On the other hand, Jackson and his followers tended to support laissez-faire economics and preferred state action to federal action in the legislative area. Jacksonians preached individualism[9] and egalitarianism, while the Whigs offered "the positive liberal state" in order to raise opportunity for all citizens so that they might achieve what has come to be called the American dream. Whigs thought of themselves as "sober, industrious, thriving people" who could improve society through careful planning and a program of enlightened economic and social legislation. For the most part, they wished to link themselves to the developing market revolution.[10]

Many Whigs tended to presume an identity of interests between capital and labor to promote the national economy, but Democrats accused them of seeking to manipulate the country's monetary resources in order to redistribute wealth for their own benefit and make it more unequal. Today many scholars regard Whigs as more modern and forward-looking than Democrats, that they recognized not only the economic realities of their existing circumstances but the obsolescence of the old order. They had faith in the future. They encouraged the new technology. They welcomed a modern, an industrial, a dynamic society. Democrats, on the other hand, especially the most conservative, were committed to an "old-fashioned" society and looked back with nostalgia on their virtuous and uncorrupted past.

In their political thinking, however, Whigs tended to be elitists and rather disdained the idea of a fully democratic electoral system. Unlike the Democrats, who repeatedly referred to the people as "good," "virtuous," "intelligent," and "capable of self-government," Whigs (including Clay[11]) had grave

---

8. New York *American*, April 25, 1834; Howe, *Political Culture of the American Whigs*, p. 13. Apart from my reading of the contemporary newspapers and the correspondence of some of the leading Whigs, I have relied on Howe's excellent study for most of my comments on the Whig party. See particularly pages 13–22. See also Charles Grier Sellers, Jr., "Who Were the Southern Whigs?" *American Historical Review*, LIX (1954), pp. 335–346.

9. On the question of individualism, Lawrence Frederick Kohl, in a most imaginative book, *The Politics of Individualism: Parties and the American Character in the Jacksonian Era* (New York, 1989), contrasts the Whigs with the Democrats.

10. The quotations come from Howe, *Political Culture of the American Whigs*, p. 20.

11. Clay's republicanism was basically the republicanism of James Madison, and the Kentuckian could point to his mentor's *Federalist* No. 10, wherein Madison wrote that "democracies have ever been spectacles of turbulence and contention; have ever been found incompatible with personal security or the rights of property; and have in general been as short in their lives as they have been violent in their deaths." *The Federalist* (New York, 1945), p. 59.

reservations about the ability of the masses to control and direct the future operation of the government. Whigs worried about a party-controlled democracy and emphasized the "representative" aspect of republicanism. In effect they favored rule by the wealthy, the better educated, and the more socially conscious, while many Democrats wanted to turn government over to the people—turn it over completely. The most extreme Democrats, Jackson particularly, would require the popular election of senators and judges (including Supreme Court judges), the abolition of the electoral college, limitation of presidential tenure, and the regular rotation of governmental officers.[12]

The Democratic press, led by the Washington *Globe,* constantly stressed the fact that the difference between the two parties was the difference between "the poor and the rich." And some Whig newspapers openly conceded that they had no problem with this simplistic explanation; only they insisted upon a more accurate definition of the word "rich." Asked the New York *American* on June 20, 1834: "Who are the rich men of our country? They are the enterprizing mechanic, who raises himself by his ingenious labors from the dust and turmoil of his workshop, to an abode of ease and elegance; the industrious tradesman, whose patient frugality enables him at last to accumulate enough to forego the duties of the counter and indulge a well-earned leisure." Merchants and traders and mechanics—these are the Whigs, proclaimed the New York *American,* and they maintain written law and legitimate authority against sycophancy and arbitrary rule by one man.

In their principles and policies both Whigs and Democrats had much to offer the nation in terms of its future power and greatness. And the two parties encompassed or touched upon almost every aspect of national life and institutions.

In view of Jackson's behavior—his many vetoes for reasons other than constitutional, his contempt of the Supreme Court and refusal to be guided by its judgments, his presumption in choosing Van Buren as his successor, his intrusion into and claim to coequality with the legislative process, his spoils system, his seizure of the Treasury through a secretary of the treasury whose authority to act had not yet been confirmed by the Senate[13]—the use of the term "Whig" by those who opposed these abuses seemed appropriate. Small wonder it won almost instant adoption.

In assuming the label "Whig," Clay no doubt hoped that he could saddle the Jacksonians with the everlastingly hated name of Tory, but he could not make it stick despite repeated efforts in countless speeches to identify his opponents with autocratic rule. Similarly, the Democrats frequently called Whigs Federalists in the hope of identifying them in the public mind with a thor-

12. For a more detailed discussion of Jackson's rather extreme democratic views, see Remini, *Legacy of Andrew Jackson,* pp. 28–44. And it should be remembered that when Jackson and the Democrats talk about the "people," they are referring to white males, not blacks, not Indians, and not women.

13. As a matter of fact, after eight months in office Taney's nomination still awaited submission by the President to the Senate.

oughly discredited and bankrupt party that had been tainted with treason following the Hartford Convention. This taunting of each other by Whigs and Democrats generated increasing heat as the congressional session moved into the steaming weeks of late April, May, and June.

"We have had one of the most extraordinary" congressional sessions in memory, wrote Representative Churchill C. Cambreleng of New York to Edward Livingston, just returned from his mission in France. The "most bitter and violent denunciations—with cries of ruin, panic and despair"—characterized the proceedings and "have succeeded in producing an excitement in the country which you have probably seldom seen even in times of embargo or of war."[14]

The excitement reached fever pitch the day following Clay's "Whig" speech, when President Jackson responded to the censure resolution in a special message protesting the insulting, intolerable, and unconstitutional action taken by the Senate. He was deeply hurt by the censure—Clay had scored a solid hit—and he had no intention of allowing the Kentuckian to get away with it.[15]

His protest message, dated April 15 and written to a large extent by his new attorney general, Benjamin F. Butler (also unconfirmed), with an assist from Taney and Kendall, wasted no time in registering the President's complaint. It excoriated the Senate for voting on charges that he had violated the Constitution, an impeachable offense, when such an action belonged exclusively to the House of Representatives. Jackson went on to claim that the appointing power resided solely with the President and that all executive officers functioned at his will.

Then he made a monumental slip. He boldly declared that "every species of property belonging to the United States"—whether land, buildings, provisions, or public money—came under the control of officers appointed by the President, responsible to him, and removable at his will.

He was dead wrong. Later Jackson was forced to issue a supplementary message because he feared he might be "misunderstood." Said he: "I think it proper to state that it was not my intention to deny in the said message the power and right of the legislative department to provide by law for the custody, safe-keeping, and disposition of the public money and property of the United States." He also repudiated the notion that he had claimed any power or authority not granted by the Constitution and the laws.

But the protest message made even worse claims. Jackson argued that he was "the direct representative of the American people" and responsible solely to them. Unlike congressmen, he scoffed, he was elected by *all* the people, and therefore, he served as their tribune.[16]

14. Cambreleng to Livingston, March 16, 1834, Livingston Papers, Princeton University Library.
15. Remini, *Jackson*, III, 151–152.
16. Richardson, *Messages and Papers*, II, 1289, 1291–1293, 1301, 1311, 1312–1313.

No previous President had ever made such an assertion. No President assumed such a remarkable relationship with the electorate. No President had ever stated point-blank that he was the head of the nation.

The message sent shock waves through the Senate. Clay and Webster were absent when it came down, but the words of the message were no sooner spoken by the clerk than Senator George Poindexter jumped to his feet and angrily moved that this "unofficial paper," as he called it, signed by one "Andrew Jackson," should not be received. Frelinghuysen and Southard of New Jersey and Sprague of Maine supported the motion while Benton and William R. King of Alabama vigorously opposed it.[17]

As soon as Webster and Clay resumed their seats, they immediately took charge of the response to the President's renewed encroachment on the authority and dignity of Congress. Clay offered a triple-headed motion declaring that Jackson's assertion of his presidential powers was "inconsistent with the constitution," that the Senate could not recognize the right of the President to protest a Senate vote as being illegal or unconstitutional, and finally that the protest message was "a breach of the privileges of the Senate and that it be not entered on the Journal" of the Senate.[18]

In the course of his remarks on April 23, Clay said he had heard that Jackson once told Napoleon's brother that he had made the emperor of France his model.[19] Not surprising, Clay jeered. But "the army and navy, thank God, are sound and patriotic to the core. They will not allow themselves to be servile instruments of treason, usurpation, and the overthrow of civil liberty, if any such designs now exist."[20]

However, it was Webster who delivered the great oration against the protest. Although Clay could add wit, intellectual bite, and deeply felt emotion, Webster provided the constitutional arguments to pulverize Jackson's claims. Regarded as the "Great Expounder and Defender of the Constitution," he fired away at the "outrageous contentions" contained in the message. He particularly savaged Jackson's claim to a special relationship with the electorate. "The Constitution no where calls him the representative of the American people," Webster stormed, "still less their direct representative." He denied emphatically that the President was chosen directly by the people. The college of electors, some of whom were chosen by the people and some appointed by state legislatures, elected him. "Where, then, is the authority for saying that the President is *the direct representative of the People?* . . . I hold this, Sir, to be a mere assumption, and dangerous assumption." Embarked on an illegal and unconstitutional course to restructure the government to the advantage of the chief executive, the President must be resisted and stopped dead in his tracks.

---

17. *National Intelligencer,* April 19, 1834.
18. *Register of Debates,* 23d Congress, 1st session, pp. 1450–1453.
19. Indeed, Jackson thought very highly of Napoleon Bonaparte.
20. *Register of Debates,* 23d Congress, 1st session, p. 1450.

Otherwise, cried Webster, there will be "ONE RESPONSIBILITY! ONE DISCRETION, ONE WILL."[21]

More than anything else, the protest message went a long way toward making the name Whig popular among those who abhorred Jackson's claim that he was the direct representative of the American people. "We can hardly yet believe . . . that any Chief Magistrate of this—republic?—could have dared to issue such a paper," the Whig press chorused. It was "presumptuous and insulting." Even Democrats worried over Jackson's claims. The Richmond *Enquirer* protested that the President was already strong enough, "and in some cases too strong." For a man so popular and respected as Andrew Jackson to set this precedent might prove catastrophic to the continued existence of a free nation. "Bold and bad men may come after him who may abuse his example." But the *Globe* had no such misgivings, although it acknowledged the significance of Webster's arguments. "The speech of Mr. Webster against the Protest," wrote Blair, "places him at the head of the self-named *Wig party*. He has thrown Mr. Clay and Mr. Calhoun entirely into the background. They must hereafter be considered 'the lesser lights' in the galaxy of disinterested worthies who maintain the cause of Bank power."[22]

Neither Clay nor Calhoun could hardly be described as sitting in the "background." Calhoun delivered a well-argued and angry speech in which he accused the President of placing himself close to the people in order to enlist them as allies "in the war which he contemplates against this branch of the Government." Jackson's doctrines meant the destruction of tripartite government, he said, the triumph of despotism, the end of republicanism.[23]

Clay's principal speech against the protest—he jabbed at it several times immediately after its delivery to the Senate—occurred on April 30. In this speech Clay unfortunately resorted to a personal attack on Jackson. He suggested that the President's head should be examined by phrenologists, such as Dr. Charles Caldwell of Transylvania University in Kentucky, who would undoubtedly "find the organ of destructiveness prominently developed. Except an enormous fabric of Executive power for himself, the President has built up nothing, constructed nothing, and will leave no enduring monument of his administration. He goes for destruction, universal destruction; and it seems to be his greatest ambition to efface and obliterate every trace of the wisdom of his predecessors."

Clay defended the Senate's right to censure the President and the reasons for it; he laughed at the arguments of the protest; and he insisted that Jackson was a dangerous tyrant and the protest nothing but a new form of veto, "an

21. Daniel Webster, *The Speeches and Writings of Daniel Webster* (Boston, 1903), VII, 139, 143, 144, 145, 147. For an extended discussion of Webster's speech, see Remini, *Jackson,* III, pp. 156–157.
22. New York *American,* April 22, 1834; *Enquirer,* April 21, 1834; *Globe,* May 12, 1834.
23. *Register of Debates,* 23d Congress, 1st session, p. 1646. Calhoun spoke on May 6, the day before Webster.

initiatory veto," wherein before legislative action is even prepared for the President's consideration, he notifies Congress of his displeasure and in that way initiates the kind of legislation he wants.

Clay also scored Jackson's contention that he was "the sole Executive" in which all other officers were his agents. That was "altogether a military idea," said the senator, "wholly incompatible with free government. I deny it absolutely. There exists no such responsibility to the President. All are responsible to the law, and to the law only, or not responsible at all."

Clay concluded by expressing the hope that the protest would turn out to be "the last stroke upon the last nail driven into the coffin—not of Jackson, may he live a thousand years!—but of Jacksonism."[24]

On several occasions Clay likened Jacksonism to the cholera. The difference? "Cholera performs its terrible office, and its victims are consigned to the grave, leaving their survivors uncontaminated. But Jacksonism has poisoned the whole Community, the living as well as the dead."[25]

With this personal assault on the President, Clay himself came under steady attack by Democrats, especially his inconsistency over the years on the Bank issue and the presumption that he was a "retained" stipendiary of the Bank. He admitted his reversal of position on the BUS in 1816 but argued that the experience of the War of 1812 had changed everybody. He also declared that for the past ten years he had had absolutely "no connexion" with the bank.

It was a clever deception. He meant no "official" connection. Actually he had received a five-thousand-dollar loan from a branch of the BUS in 1832.[26]

At length the debate on the protest message petered out and on May 7 the Senate took a final vote. By the count of twenty-seven to sixteen it rejected the protest and upheld its censure of the President's actions. Clay was so pleased that he bought himself a "Gold patent watch" for $107 to commemorate the day.[27]

But despite these victories in the Senate, the House of Representatives handed Jackson one triumph after another, all designed to bury the Bank of the United States forever. The most important of them came on April 4, when it passed a series of resolutions declaring that the BUS ought not to be rechartered, the deposits ought not to be restored, that the state (pet) banks should continue to receive the government monies, and that the BUS should be investigated to discover whether or not it had deliberately instigated the financial panic.[28]

24. *Register of Debates*, 23d Congress, 1st session, pp. 1559, 1564, 1575–1581. Clay used the expression "the last nail in the coffin of Jacksonism" in letters to friends. "Webster & Calhoun also mean to bestow on it [the protest] their devoirs." See Clay to John Pendleton Kennedy, April 28, 1834, in Clay, *Papers*, VIII, 721.

25. Clay to Alexander Coffin, June 11, 1834, in Clay, *Papers*, VIII, 725.

26. *Register of Debates*, 23d Congress, 1st session, pp. 1593, 1531; Biddle to Clay, August 1, 1832, in Clay, *Papers*, VIII, 557.

27. J. Joseph to Clay, May 7, 1834, in Clay, *Papers*, VIII, 724.

28. *Register of Debates*, 23d Congress, 1st session, pp. 3474–3477.

"I have obtained a glorious triumph," crowed Jackson. It totally scuttled any effort by the Senate to force recharter or the restoration of the deposits. "The Bank is dead," pronounced the attorney general.[29]

The Bank was indeed dead, but not Henry Clay. He waited, knowing the President had to come back to the Senate for approval of a number of important matters, not the least of which was the confirmation of his "collar-men." Before the session closed, the President would be required to submit his appointees, including Taney, to the upper house for its approval. Recess appointments without confirmation were permitted until the last day of the next session of Congress. At the moment a majority of the members of the cabinet lacked Senate approval. A lengthening list of ministers to foreign countries also needed confirmation. It was just another example, Clay wearily remarked, of Jackson's abuse of executive power and his disregard for the Constitution and the law.

Time eventually ran out for Jackson, and he was forced to submit his nominations, starting with Taney as secretary of the treasury. Clay was waiting. On Monday, June 23, the President submitted Taney's name, and on Tuesday the Senate rejected it by the vote of twenty-eight to eighteen.[30] The next day the *Globe* excoriated the Senate for its "indecent haste to immolate this excellent man on the altar of mammon." Led by Henry Clay, wrote Blair, the majority in the upper house cried out, *"Crucify him. Crucify him!"* But he will rise again, promised the editor. And his successor will be just as inflexible, for the President will entrust the department to *"none other."*

The Whigs then handed Jackson a second defeat. They rejected the nomination of Andrew Stevenson to be minister to Great Britain. They also rejected the President's nominations for appointment of the four government directors of the BUS—not once but twice. "Nicholas Biddle *now* rules the Senate," barked Jackson, "as a showman does his puppets." Again the Senate rejected Benjamin Tappan as U.S. district judge in Ohio and Martin Gordon as collector of the port of New Orleans. Then, at the end of the session, as another sign of its anger and spite, the Senate elected George Poindexter of Mississippi as its president pro tempore. This was a deliberate insult. The intensity of Jackson's hatred for Poindexter almost matched his contempt for Clay.[31]

Over in the House the Whigs provided yet another setback for the President. House Democrats were about to elect their new Speaker, and James Knox Polk, who had been a valiant and skillful soldier in the fight against the Bank, had Jackson's blessing for the post. But his colleague from Tennessee, John Bell, who had been silent on the Bank and rather fancied the job himself,

29. Benjamin F. Butler to Thomas W. Olcott, June 19, 1834, Olcott Papers, Columbia University Library.

30. Jackson immediately replaced Taney with Levi Woodbury of New Hampshire. Woodbury was confirmed unanimously on June 29.

31. *Globe,* June 24, 25, 30, 1834; Jackson to Edward Livingston, June 27, 1834, Livingston Papers, Princeton University Library.

hoped to attract support from the Whigs and the anti-Van Buren (mostly southern) Democrats. Polk expected the votes of the administration men as well as the nullifiers who believed that he, like them, opposed Van Buren's succession.

Polk would undoubtedly have gotten the position, except that the Whigs outfoxed him. They were expected to support a northerner. Instead, they chose as their candidate Richard H. Wilde of Georgia, a nullifier. Polk saw the danger and appealed to Senator Willie P. Mangum of North Carolina to rally the nullifiers behind his candidacy. But Mangum refused to be rushed. Rather, he watched the face of the enemy, Vice President Van Buren, who was presiding over the Senate. As the House balloted for the new Speaker, bulletins were hurried to the Senate with the results, and each time they arrived Mangum studied Van Buren's facial reaction. On the eighth ballot John Bell showed a large gain in votes. An expression of concern flickered momentarily over Van Buren's face, and in that instant Mangum knew that Polk was Van Buren's candidate. The alarm shot over to the House, the nullifiers bolted to Bell, the Whigs dropped Wilde, and on the tenth ballot John Bell of Tennessee won a majority and was elected the new Speaker.[32]

The result enraged Jackson. A big celebration had been planned for Polk in the White House, but it was abruptly canceled. When visitors came the next day to call on the President, the doorkeeper, Patrick, warned them that "if they would take his advice, they would as soon put their fingers into a candle, as to go [to the President's room], for he was in a miserable bad humor."[33]

It rankled Jackson that so many of his friends and neighbors had deserted him in the Bank War. John Bell, Davy Crockett, and Hugh Lawson White—all Tennesseans—sided with the enemy, and that drove him into a passion. White's defection hurt him deeply, for he was an old and respected friend. He "has permitted Mr Bell Crockett & Co, to make a bed for him," the President sadly wrote, "& he must sleep in it."[34]

Clay took one final swipe at the President before the "Panic session" ended. He attacked the operation of the Post Office Department, citing bribery, corruption, political favoritism, and financial malfeasance—all of which, or nearly all, were true. He noted that his onetime personal and political friend Postmaster General William Barry of Kentucky was incompetent, as was also true. Jackson knew Barry was unfit for the office, but he kept him on anyway because of his outstanding loyalty, especially during the Eaton scandal. Such behavior by the President, Clay angrily argued, only further documented the

32. *Register of Debates,* 23d Congress, 1st session, pp. 4368–4373; Mangum to Bell, June 15, 1835, Bell to Mangum, July 2, 1835, in *Tennessee Historical Magazine,* III (1917), pp. 198–200. On October 25, 1835, John Bell married Jane Erwin Yeatman, widow of Thomas Yeatman. She was a daughter of Andrew Erwin and a sister of James Erwin, the husband of Clay's favorite daughter, Anne.

33. Quoted in Charles G. Sellers, Jr., *James K. Polk, Jacksonian* (Princeton, 1957), p. 242.

34. Jackson to John Coffee, June 1, 1834, Coffee Papers, Tennessee Historical Society.

fact that Jackson abused the powers of his office.[35] Not surprisingly, nothing came of the charges against Barry.

The congressional session ended on June 30, and Jackson let out a sigh of relief. He had taken a verbal pummeling from the Great Triumvirate, but he had the satisfaction of knowing that he had killed the Bank forever. By late spring the financial panic in the country had begun to ease. The directors of the BUS forced Biddle to end his squeeze, and once that happened, normal business operations resumed.

On the final day of the session Thomas Hart Benton introduced in the Senate a proposal that the censure resolution be expunged from the record. Clay immediately sprang to his feet. It was most improper of Benton to make this proposal just as the Senate was about to adjourn, he declared. He instantly rallied his forces, and the proposal was voted down, twenty to eleven. But Benton announced his determination to "expunge" the record no matter how long it took. Each session of Congress thereafter he called for its passage, and it became one of the major points of violent argument between him and Clay.[36]

The Kentucky senator took particular pride in the leadership he had provided the Senate and the country against the tyrant. He now headed a reinvigorated party with a brand-new name. In listing the accomplishments of this session, he named the censure of Jackson and Taney, the several rejections of Jackson's nominees, particularly Taney, the passage of the resolution disapproving the removal of the deposits, the efforts to recharter the Bank and distribute proceeds from land sales to the states, and the attempts to curb presidential powers, especially the appointing power.[37]

If nothing else, "Jacksonism" had an implacable enemy in Henry Clay, and as long as there was breath in his body he swore he would stamp it out, however long it took.[38]

35. *Register of Debates,* 23d Congress, 1st session, pp. 2113–2116. Clay pointed out that only Senator Isaac Hill of New Hampshire defended Barry because Hill's brother had fifteen mail distribution contracts for the entire state.

36. *Register of Debates,* 23d Congress, 1st session, p. 2128.

37. Clay to Benjamin W. Dudley, July 31, 1834, in Clay, *Papers,* VIII, 737.

38. "Like you," Clay wrote Alexander Coffin, "I have sometimes almost despaired of our Country. The delusion has been so long, so dark, so pervasive, that I have occasionally feared that it would survive me; but, I thank God, it is passing off rapidly, and I trust that both you and I may yet live to see many brighter and better days." June 11, 1834, in Clay, *Papers,* VIII, 725.

The most recent study of the Whig party, and one I found particularly valuable, is Thomas Brown, *Politics and Statesmanship: Essays on the American Whig Party* (New York, 1985). Brown argues convincingly that the "core values" of the party consisted of "moderation, self-restraint, rational persuasion, and a positive passion for the public good." pp. 11–12.

TWENTY-SEVEN

Tragedy and Defeat

CLAY FACED a serious personal problem during the closing months of the session. His wife, Lucretia, became quite ill, and he feared for her life. The condition began in mid-February, and Clay described it as a "derangement of her stomach." It got so bad that she could eat nothing "without injury." She consulted several doctors, began a regimen of diet and exercise, but found no relief from her distress. She lost a considerable amount of weight, and her husband said she had been reduced to "a mere skeleton." As her condition worsened, Clay became more alarmed. "I fear she can not survive," he lamented to his son.[1]

The famed Dr. Philip S. Physick in Philadelphia was consulted, and he prescribed "tender mutton and beef" for breakfast ~~vince, she could hold it~~ ~~down, with his made without butter~~, and black tea. He also prescribed enemas, rhubarb at bedtime every night, "fresh hickory ashes and soot," and exercise such as walking or horseback riding. Clay also took her to Lee's Sulphur Springs near Warrenton for the cure, but the waters provided only limited benefit. It was finally decided to send her home in early May by way of White Sulphur Springs, accompanied by her son James Brown Clay, who found the mercantile business distasteful and, with his father's permission, had decided to complete his education and study law. Meanwhile, Clay remained in Washington until the close of the session.[2]

Once home Lucretia improved a little, but the summer months were especially difficult for her. She was finally diagnosed as suffering from dyspepsia "in an advanced stage." The "best physicians" in Philadelphia, Washington, and Lexington concurred on her condition and declared that "the cure is to be effected by diet, exercise and tranquility of mind." But she was a strong-willed woman and determined not to let her illness get the better of her. "She retains strength remarkably," said her husband, "keeps on her feet, and is even able to

1. Clay to Henry Clay, Jr., February 17, March 19, April 13, 1834, Clay to Julia Prather Clay, March 10, 1834, in Clay, *Papers,* VIII, 698, 704, 706, 714.
2. Physick to Clay, April 19, 1834, Clay to Henry Clay, Jr., March 19, April 24, Clay to James Brown, May 4, 1834, in Clay, *Papers,* VIII, 705–706, 715–716, 723.

take exercise on horseback." Not until the autumn did she really improve "when she changed the system of her medical treatment." From then on she began to recover, although it is not clear what changes in her treatment were undertaken.[3]

On his return home after the conclusion of the congressional session, Clay himself had a brush with near disaster that could have proved fatal. In descending a hill about one mile from Brucetown in Frederick County, Virginia, the stagecoach in which he was riding overturned. The horses pulled off the front wheels and dashed away with the driver in pursuit. A young man who was sitting next to the driver got entangled in the reins, slipped to the ground, and had the entire stagecoach fall on top on him. Clay, his servant, and a woman were inside the coach and scrambled out of it as quickly as possible. They managed to raise the stagecoach enough to pull the young man out of the wreckage. "But alas! it was of no avail. His neck was broke, his entrails seriously injured, he bled profusely at the nose, and never spoke." He died almost instantly. The young man was the son of the owner of the stage, and Clay wrote to the father to express his sympathy and explain what had happened. Clay himself sustained only a slight scratch on his leg, but he was lucky his injuries were no worse. The newspapers reported the accident, and he received expressions of concern and relief from as far away as London, England.[4]

Clay returned to Ashland to spend a relatively quiet summer, tending his wife and the operation of his farm. He set about improving his shorthorn cattle, Saxony sheep, Maltese asses, and Arabian horses. He also tried to entice Francis Lieber into coming to Lexington to assume the presidency of Transylvania University. He described Lexington to the prospective candidate as a community of six thousand surrounded "by a rich beautiful Country, unsurpassed in fertility." The city was "paved and watched and well built. All the professions and trades were practiced, and the city boasted three "Female academies" in addition to many other educational institutions. "Society is good, hospital and intelligent," Clay wrote. There were seven churches and three newspapers. Library holdings were scanty, so "our literary resources and Circles" could not be compared with those of Philadelphia. The university meant a great deal to Clay, and he worked on its behalf on numerous occasions. But despite his good efforts, Lieber decided against accepting the presidency because the salary was inadequate.[5]

On another educational front, Clay had trouble with his youngest son, John Morrison Clay. The boy had been enrolled in Edgehill Seminary in Princeton, New Jersey, run by Enoch Cobb Wines. Apparently young Clay

3. Clay to James Brown, August 2, 1834, Clay to John H. James, August 6, 1834, Clay to Francis Lieber, September 15, 1834, in Clay, *Papers,* VIII, 738, 739, 748.

4. Clay to Albert Humrickhous, July 6, 1834, Christopher Hughes, August 10, 1834, in Clay, *Papers,* VIII, 736. 742; *National Intelligencer,* July 12, 1834.

5. Clay to Lieber, September 15, 1834, Lieber to Clay, November 8, 1834, in Clay, *Papers,* VIII, 747, 750.

insulted one of the instructors and violated the discipline code. He was made to give a public apology before the entire school, a punishment which Clay thought excessive. The father protested to the headmaster. Considering his age and the nature of the offense, lectured Clay, a public humiliation would "exhibit him in a mortifying attitude, which would wound intensely the sensibility of any boy and might have a permanent injurious operation upon his future life."[6] Clay asked whether the headmaster intended to expel his son but was assured that John's apology ended the matter. The young man really wanted to leave the seminary and return home, but Clay would not allow it. Nor did John wish his mother to be informed of his misbehavior. Nevertheless, the father explained to his wife what had happened but reassured John that his mother was "highly pleased, as I was, with his manly settlement of it." The father realized his son was unhappy and wrote to "comfort him as much as I can."[7]

Clay's children caused him nothing but agony. Only Anne spared him pain. Harriet Martineau visited the Clay home in 1835 and described to a friend the family's "mournful domestic history." Theodore was insane, she reported, driven by the "violence of his passions"; Thomas was a "sot"; Henry, Jr., was "so jealous & irritable in his temper that there is no living with him"; and James, aged seventeen, and John, aged thirteen, gave "no great promise of steadiness. Mrs [Anne] Erwin is all that they can desire in a daughter; but she is the only survivor of six daughters. Is it not melancholy?" she commented.[8]

Indeed. Henry Clay was a man of deep personal sorrow that lasted much of his adult life.

The death of his brother-in-law James Brown on April 7, 1835, also sad denied the senator. Brown had been a devoted friend and supporter, financially and politically, and his passing only added to Clay's growing sense of futility and general malaise.

The Kentucky summer elections went well, however—"Our election has terminated triumphantly," he wrote one man—but the rest of the country seemed happy with Jackson, and the return to prosperity following the freakish panic was now blamed totally on Biddle. Clay began to suspect that the BUS was "hopelessly gone," and as a consequence, the Democratic party was gathering strength. The Whigs, on the other hand, seemed "cut up and divided against themselves," and the prospects for the future appeared "not a little discouraging."[9]

One reason for the party's condition was the lack of unanimity with respect to a presidential candidate for 1836 to face Martin Van Buren, recently

6. Clay to Wines, February 16, 1835, in Clay, *Papers,* VIII, 761–762.
7. Clay to Lucretia Clay, March 4, 1835, in Clay, *Papers,* VIII, 767.
8. Martineau to Reverend and Mrs. Samuel Gilman, June 12th [18]35, in John Spalding Gatton, "Mr. Clay & I Got Stung': Harriet Martineau in Lexington," *Kentucky Review,* I (Autumn 1979), p. 52.
9. Clay to William N. Mercer, August 13, 1834, Clay to Thomas Speed, November 1, 1834, in Clay, *Papers,* VIII, 743, 750.

nominated at the Democratic National Convention in Baltimore, along with
Richard M. Johnson of Kentucky as Vice President. Jackson had completed
two terms in office, and he chose the Magician as his successor, an action that
infuriated Whigs, particularly in the South. As always, Clay was willing to
stand again as his party's nominee, but he wanted overwhelming support from
Whigs in every section, and such signs were manifestly absent. In no conceivable way would he run and face the humiliation of another defeat unless he
could assure himself that he was the favorite and only standard-bearer of the
entire Whig party. But he had acquired something of the reputation of a loser,
so a number of Whig leaders started looking elsewhere, and this, too, added to
Clay's sense of despair. Like Jackson's term, his senatorial term would end with
the inauguration of the next President, and Clay began to ponder whether it
was worth running again. Present conditions could "hardly be worse," he
grumbled. "Blackguards, Bankrupts and Scoundrels, Profligacy and Corruption are the order of the day, and no one can see the time when it will be
changed." It reminded him of the English Civil War. "There is nothing wanting, to complete the paralel, but the Religious fanaticism, and that is supplied
by the fanaticism towards Genl. Jackson." He also indulged in self-pity again.
He often complained that the American people did not truly appreciate all he
had done for them. To put it simply, he felt "badly treated." He had had many
rewards, he acknowledged, but what he really wanted was repeatedly denied
him.[10]

Clay returned to Congress in the late fall of 1834 with conflicting feelings
about his future. He stopped off along the way to visit his youngest son at the
seminary and arrived in Washington in time to hear the President's annual
message. What concerned him the most about the message was the deteriorating relations with France over U.S. spoliation claims arising from the seizure
of ships and matériel during the Napoleonic Wars. The French had agreed to
compensation, but when the time came for payment of the first installment,
the Chamber of Deputies neglected to make the necessary appropriation. Jackson's impatience turned to anger when the Chamber, for a number of domestic
political reasons, repeatedly refused to honor its treaty obligations. What troubled Clay was the President's reaction, particularly the sharp, not to say provocative, language of his message regarding the claims. The President even
spoke of reprisals against French property in the United States.

Many others in Congress shared Clay's concern. Jackson's "rashness, in
advising a warlike measure, without waiting for the decision of the French
chambers at their approaching Session, seems to be generally condemned,"
claimed Clay. Very likely the French will take offense, he added. "In that event,
our difficulties will be greatly increased. Irritation begets irritation, and I
should not be surprised if, in the sequel, two gallant nations, hitherto enter-

10. Clay to Brooke, June 27, 1835, Clay to Christopher Hughes, August 25, 1835, in Clay, *Papers,*
VIII, 775, 798.

taining for each other the greatest respect, shall be found unexpectedly engaged in War."[11]

Chosen chairman of the Senate Committee on Foreign Affairs, Clay promptly demanded Jackson's instructions to the American diplomats in France relating to the dispute since July 1831. In the subsequent committee report to the Senate,[12] written by Clay, the justice of the claim was affirmed, but the report urged that peaceful means be pursued to achieve a settlement. It appended a resolution denying Jackson the authority for invoking reprisals against French property. Clay admitted on the floor of the Senate that he was concerned about French reaction to Jackson's threats, that they might range from prudent and cautious to aggressive and belligerent. His major address occurred on January 14, 1835, and he restated his agreement with the President over the justice of American claims but differed sharply with Jackson on the approach to the problem. Once again he attempted the role of pacificator to quiet possible French outrage yet reaffirm American rights to the spoliation indemnity.[13]

At one point in the debate Senator James Buchanan of Pennsylvania, formerly minister to Russia and the inept busybody in the corrupt bargain controversy during the presidential election of 1828, rose to challenge Clay and praise Jackson's handling of the problem. The Kentucky senator regarded Buchanan as an incompetent booby and flattened him with a single swipe. Given the arguments and facts presented in the committee report, said Clay, "he trusted it would not be out of his [Buchanan's] power" to understand and defend "the reasonings and conclusions of the committee."[14] Clay often had occasion to cut Buchanan down, and each time he did it the hapless Pennsylvanian simply slumped back into his seat with hardly a word in reply.

The Senate agreed to a reworded resolution stating that it was inexpedient to adopt any legislation at present with regard to the spoliation controversy, and this pleased the committee's chairman. "I hope," he said, "the whole proceeding in the Senate will turn the thoughts of the Nation on peace."[15]

Ultimately the controversy was resolved when Jackson publicly admitted

11. Clay to Henry Clay, Jr., early December 1834, in Clay, *Papers,* VIII, 751–752. On the French imbroglio, see Richard A. McLemore, *Franco-American Diplomatic Relations, 1816–1836* (University, La., 1941), passim; John M. Belohlavek, *"Let the Eagle Soar!": The Foreign Policy of Andrew Jackson* (Lincoln, Neb., 1985), pp. 90–126; and Remini, *Jackson,* III, 192–211, 222–237, 274–293.

12. Clay was very proud of this report and later included it among the state papers he compiled which he said possessed the most permanent value. The report "was so highly approved that it obtained the unanimous concurrence of the Senate—composed as it was of a large part of members bitterly opposed to me." Clay to Epes Sargent, July 16, 1842, in Clay, *Papers,* IX, 736–737.

13. Clay to John Forsyth, December 16, 1834, RG 59, NA, copy CPP; *Register of Debates,* 23d Congress, 2d session, p. 45; McLemore, *Franco-American Diplomatic Relations,* pp. 132ff; Belohlavek, *"Let the Eagle Soar!,"* pp. 116–119. King of Georgia, Sprague, Tallmadge, and Mangum also served on the committee.

14. *Register of Debates,* 23d Congress, 2d session, p. 200ff., 213.

15. *Register of Debates,* 23d Congress, 2d session, p. 215; Clay to Brooke, January 16, 1835, in Clay, *Papers,* VIII, 756.

that he had no intention of offending the French by his message and the French chose to accept it as an apology. The claims were paid in installments, and Jackson enjoyed another diplomatic triumph.

Whigs applauded Clay's report and resolution, claiming it healed the wounded pride of the French and convinced them that Jackson's menacing words would not be sanctioned by Congress. They contended that the report and resolution gave the French the incentive to pay the indemnity. "Thus has the patriotic majority in the Senate," commented Philip Hone, "once more interposed to save the country from a vexatious and unnecessary war, without the slightest sacrifice of national honor, although it is quite likely that Jackson will get the credit for it."[16]

At a dinner party given by Vice President Van Buren at the height of the tension over the controversy and attended by the secretary of state, several foreign ministers, judges of the Supreme Court, and others, Henry Clay suddenly strode into the room, looking smug and supremely self-satisfied. He thoroughly enjoyed the discomfort of the Democrats as they watched him circle the room and greet the various ministers, judges, and other guests. In the conversation that ensued, the topic soon centered on the favorable or unfavorable disposition of the French and British governments toward United States interests. Since several gentlemen present had been abroad recently, they ventured the opinion that American interests were best served with Tory ministries in both England and France.

In an instant Clay saw his opening.

"With your permission," he said in a reverential tone to the Vice President as he lifted his glass to propose a toast.

Van Buren nodded his approval.

"I proposed," Clay said with a smirk, "Tory ministries in England & France and a *Whig ministry* in the U. States!"

The company burst out laughing. Even the Democrats laughed, despite themselves. But poor Van Buren looked confused, for he "had no tact in warding off a sally or joke," commented Clay.[17]

Throughout the session Clay showed his mastery of verbal jabs to poke fun at the Democrats and publicly embarrass them. James Buchanan was a frequent target. A loyal Jacksonian, competent but unimaginative, colorless, conservative, and cautious, he made an easy target for the wicked Senator Clay. Six feet tall, heavyset, slow, he appeared slightly cross-eyed and was "as destitute of humor as an undertaker." On one occasion the Kentuckian stated that the "noble Whigs" declared their position on every issue that arose while the Democratic leaders just sat back and put their rank-and-file members forward to skirmish. "Come out," cried Clay, "come out like men and define your

16. Hone, *Diary,* I, 150–151.

17. Memorandum, 1834, Clay Papers, LC; Clay to Epes Sargent, September 26, 1843, in Clay, *Papers,* IX, 861–862.

positions. Let us hear from you; I call for the leaders of the party."

Buchanan rose and denied that he failed to give his position and opinion on every issue that arose, to which Clay, in his blandest manner, assured Buchanan that he had made no reference to him at all. "Far from it," he said. "I called for the leaders of the party."

Buchanan blanched. He appealed to the Senate, and Clay responded in his sweetest manner. He said he could well understand how Buchanan had fallen into error. "I often suppose that gentleman is looking at me when in fact he looks quite another way"—referring to the fact that Buchanan appeared cross-eyed. He then crossed his fingers on one hand to make his point more obvious. It was a brutal and needlessly vicious assault. "Your first blow was cruel, but magnificent," whispered a colleague sitting next to Clay, "the last savage warfare—tomahawking."

"Ah! d——n him," Clay replied, "he writes letters"—referring, of course, to Buchanan's infamous letter on the corrupt bargain charge.[18]

That was the less attractive side to Clay's wit when he stooped to a low level to make sport of another man's physical disability.

And he could never resist humiliating Buchanan. On another occasion while Buchanan was defending himself against the charge of disloyalty during the War of 1812 and had declared that he joined a company of volunteers when the British attacked Baltimore, Clay spotted his opportunity and pounced.

"You marched to Baltimore?" Clay asked.

"Yes."

"Armed and equipped?"

"Yes, armed and equipped."

"But the British had retreated when you arrived," said Clay with a straight face.

"Yes," responded Buchanan brightly.

"Will the Senator from Pennsylvania be good enough to inform us," Clay continued, "whether the British retreated in consequence of his valiantly marching to the relief of Baltimore, or whether he marched to the relief of Baltimore in consequence of the British having already retreated?"

The Senate exploded in laughter.[19]

It cannot be overemphasized that Clay's enormous verbal skills as well as his ferocious intellectual power and energy explain to a very large extent his extraordinary position of authority in Congress and the fascination he exerted on everyone, male and female. Few men wished to provoke one of the devastating onslaughts of the senator from Kentucky.

But not all his speeches were slashing assaults against his opponents. On

18. Thomas Ewing, "Anecdotes of Henry Clay," Filson Club, Louisville, Kentucky; Sargent, *Public Men and Events,* I, 287. Buchanan gave the appearance of being cross-eyed because of defective vision. Quite possibly he was nearsighted in one eye and farsighted in the other, conditions that caused him to tilt his head slightly forward and sideways.

19. Sargent, *Public Men and Events,* I, 288.

several occasions during this and the previous session Clay spoke seriously and soberly and compassionately, especially about the treatment the Indians had received from the administration. The Indians had suffered incredible hardships during their removal to the West, and the Cherokees elicited several appeals for their rights from Clay right up to the moment they were forced westward along what they called the Trail of Tears. "Alas! poor Indians, what rights can they assert against the State of Georgia, backed by the tremendous power of Genl. Jackson," he said.[20]

Harriet Martineau, the English traveler and writer, heard this speech and, like everyone else, was mesmerized by Clay's performance. Since it had been advertised beforehand, spectators jammed the chamber. Foreign ambassadors leaned against the pillars behind the chair, a group of Cherokee chiefs stood on the main floor listening "immoveably," and representatives appeared in the passages. One of the congressmen sat on the steps of the platform, his eyes glued on Clay "as if life hung upon his words." As Clay spoke, reported Martineau, "I saw tears, of which I am sure he was wholly unconscious, falling on his papers as he vividly described the woes and injuries of the aborigines." The audience shared his emotional distress. Even Webster drew his hand across his eyes. Only Vice President Van Buren, perched high in his chair as presiding officer, seemed bored. He yawned.[21]

Otherwise Clay appeared listless and detached during the final days of the Twenty-third Congress. "I am truly sick of Congress," he admitted to his son Henry, Jr. But he did express his happiness over the birth of another grandchild, Matilda, born to Henry and Julia, and he borrowed an additional twenty thousand dollars from John Jacob Astor in a four-year loan at 6 percent interest, of which seventy-five hundred dollars went as a loan to Henry, Jr.[22]

Fortunately this was the short session of Congress, and it adjourned at 3:00 A.M. on March 4. Clay stayed on in Washington several more days in order to argue three cases before the Supreme Court. Then he hurried home. But the trip was a misery. The ground was still frozen and covered with snow. It seemed more like January than March, he said. And along the way he became ill and had to interrupt his journey to recover and regain his strength.[23]

Politics continued to distress him, first because it was increasingly apparent that he lacked the confidence of the party to make a successful run for the presidency and second because there was no other candidate who could unite

20. See, for example, his speech on May 20, 1834, in *Register of Debates,* 23d Congress, 1st session, p. 1773, and his speech on February 4, 1835, ibid., 23d Congress, 2d session, pp. 289–300. Clay to John Howard Payne, December 23, 1835, in Clay, *Papers,* VIII, 811.

21. Martineau, *Retrospect of Western Travel,* I, 177–178. This was the finest speech she heard from Clay, she said.

22. Clay to Henry Clay, Jr., February 19, 1835, Astor to Clay, February 16, 1835, in Clay, *Papers,* VIII, 763. Matilda died in infancy.

23. Clay to Lucretia Clay, March 4, 1835, Clay to Southard, April 12, 1835, in Clay, *Papers,* VIII, 767, 769.

the Whigs in all sections of the country.[24] Daniel Webster had been nominated by the Massachusetts legislature and would undoubtedly carry New England. But the West actively disliked "Black Dan." He was not its sort. Instead, westerners preferred General William Henry Harrison of Tippecanoe fame, having won the Battle of Tippecanoe over the Shawnee Indians in 1811. Or they liked John McLean of Ohio, an associate justice of the Supreme Court, who had been angling for a nomination for years. Southern Whigs wanted Hugh Lawson White, the senator from Tennessee who, like John Bell, had deserted Jackson. They believed he stood an excellent chance of taking every southern state away from Van Buren. But three or four men running as the opposition to the Democratic candidate made no sense at all—unless, of course, there was a design to force the election into the House of Representatives.

Clay had no sympathy with Judge White's candidacy because he did not think the Tennessean truly represented the ideas and principles of the Whig party. And he thought Justice McLean was "entirely hors du combat." Of the others he definitely preferred "Black Dan," although to his dismay he recognized Webster's almost total lack of support in the West. Clay was willing to accept Harrison as a second choice, but he frankly regarded him as incompetent. "He is weak, vain, and far inferior to Webster," Clay wrote, "but I believe him to be honest and of good intentions." Furthermore, Harrison was "nervous . . . and excessively susceptible to flattery." Objectionable as he was—and not the least of it was the fact that "his pretensions are founded altogether on military service," just like Jackson—Clay still preferred him to either McLean or White.[25]

In time Clay reluctantly decided that there had to be two Whig candidates for the 1836 contest. To win northern and western votes, one of the candidates had to be Harrison, maybe Webster, or possibly McLean. Clay finally decided that whoever was chosen by the Pennsylvania Whigs should be the northern-western candidate.[26] It was the "keystone state," he said. The second candidate had to be a man who could embody "southern views, interests and feelings," and there was no other prospect than Senator White. Clay really resented having someone like White as a possibility. Still, he had little choice. There had to be a southern candidate because of "pre existing causes"—that is, because of southern opposition to the tariff, internal improvements, and the Bank. Yet all these causes had been eliminated, Clay insisted: The tariff had been compro-

24. Clay to William B. Rose, July 4, 1835, Clay to [John M. Bailhache] July 14, 1835, in Clay, *Papers,* VIII, 778–779, 882–784.

25. Clay to Southard, April 12, July 31, 1835, Clay to Christopher Hughes, August 25, 1835, in Clay, *Papers,* VIII 770, 795, 799. Richard P. McCormick answered his own question "Was There a 'Whig Strategy' in 1836?," *Journal of the Early Republic,* IV (Spring 1984), pp. 47–70, by arguing that there was no strategy because there was no national Whig party.

26. The Pennsylvania Whig Convention endorsed Harrison.

mised, internal improvements could easily be compromised in a public land bill such as he had proposed for several years, and "the Bank is dead." But southern voters continued to form their judgments on the basis of their opposition to these measures. What made it all the more damnable was the fact that many southerners would vote for Van Buren even though they despised him; at the same time they steadfastly refused to support any Whig who had espoused the measures of the American System.[27]

Ultimately Harrison, White, Webster, and McLean won endorsements from Whig legislative caucuses, local meetings, and state conventions. The Anti-Masons held no convention but managed to complicate matters by siding with Whigs in some states, like New York, and supporting Democrats in others, such as Rhode Island.[28]

Clay himself kept getting inquiries about whether he was available for a nomination, but as the summer stretched into the fall, he became more emphatic that he would not run. "The only condition upon which it would have been acceptable to me, that of my being desired by a majority, did not I thought exist; and I felt no inclination to engage in a scramble for it."[29] Besides, he enjoyed his life at Ashland, improving his breed of cattle, buying "Jacks & their jennys," and helping his sons get settled. He purchased land in Missouri for his son James, obtained letters of introduction for Henry, Jr., who was about to depart for Europe on a holiday with his family, and received an excellent report on John. The headmaster said that John's deportment "had been uniformly a model of propriety."[30]

Clay's real concern in the fall of 1835 was his beloved daughter, Anne. Apparently after another difficult pregnancy delivering Charles Edward Erwin on November 2, 1835, she encountered complications that genuinely worried the family. "I feel very uneasy about our dear daughter, Anne," Clay wrote his wife as he set out for Washington in mid-November. "I sincerely hope that she may get well, and that all my apprehensions may prove groundless." He visited his daughter before he left and later wrote that "she never looked upon me more sweetly or affectionately." He felt she had passed the critical period of her difficulties.

Clay was also concerned about leaving his wife at home. He greatly preferred her accompanying him. "But I hope and believe that this is the last separation, upon earth, that will take place, for any length of time, between us," he told her. Little did he know that his wife would never accompany him

27. Clay to William S. Woods, July 16, 1835, Clay to James Heaton, July 18, 1835, Clay to Brooke, July 20, 1835, Clay to Southard, July 31, 1835, in Clay, *Papers,* VIII, 787–788, 791–792, 793–795.

28. Joel Silbey, "Election of 1836," *History of American Presidential Elections,* ed. Schlesinger and Israel, I, 582–583, 584–585.

29. Clay to Christopher Hughes, August 25, 1835, in Clay, *Papers,* VIII, 798.

30. R. D. Shepherd to Clay, January 21, 1836, Richard Graham to Clay, September 13, 1835, Clay to Graham, June 1, 1837, Clay to Washington Irving, May 9, 1835, Enoch Cobb Wines to Clay, May 7, 1835, in Clay, *Papers,* VIII, 805, 801, 770, 771.

again to the capital. She disliked the society, the climate, and her husband's total preoccupation with the political world. She much preferred her home in Kentucky, visiting with her children and grandchildren and running a small yet profitable business selling milk and cured hams. And she never wrote her husband. Not a single letter.

In Washington Clay had a later report on Anne's condition from his colleague in the Senate John J. Crittenden. He was told that she now appeared to be out of danger. Still, Clay could not dispel a sense of apprehension. "My anxiety about her I cannot describe," he told Lucretia. "Our only daughter— and so good a daughter—there is no event that would so entirely overwhelm us as that of her loss." Indeed, Anne was the only survivor of six daughters, Henrietta, Susan, Lucretia, Eliza, and Laura, perhaps explaining in part Clay's overpowering fears for her life. He prayed for her every day, something he rarely did. He hoped soon to hear directly from Anne herself, and he wanted Anne's husband, James Erwin, to write him constantly. Erwin's letters had relieved him a good deal, but he still wanted regular assurances that she was recovering.[31]

On his way to Washington Clay again stopped off at Princeton to visit his son John, along with his grandsons Henry Clay Duralde and Martin Duralde III, who were now attending Edgehill Seminary as well. He was pleased with John's progress and reported that all three boys seemed "contented with their situations." Clay also went off on a short shopping excursion, buying two full-blooded Durham cows and assorted household items for Lucretia, including two dozen each of dessert forks, knives, and spoons, an oilcloth, and stair carpeting. By the time he got to Washington he was "a good deal fatigued" and suffering from a bad cold. But he figured a few days of rest would restore his health. He took lodgings in the M. A. Clements house on Pennsylvania Avenue along with Alexander Porter and John J. Crittenden.[32]

Then, on December 18, while laughing and talking and joking with some friends, the senator received a letter from Bishop Benjamin Bosworth Smith, rector of Christ Episcopal Church in Lexington, informing him that Anne had died on December 10 of complications following the birth of her son.

Clay fainted.[33] He dropped "as if shot." The shock was catastrophic. For the moment the blow nearly destroyed him. He had just opened a letter from home telling him that Anne was getting better. Now he had the news that totally shattered him.

"Every tie to life is broken," he wept when he regained consciousness. No one could comfort him, and for the remainder of the day he continued in a "state of distraction." He could not function. He could not stop crying. He found it difficult to breathe.

31. Clay to Lucretia Clay, November 19, December 9, 19, 1835, in Clay, *Papers,* VIII, 803, 805.

32. Clay to Lucretia Clay, December 3, 9, 1835, Clay to James Erwin, December 10, 1835, in Clay, *Papers,* VIII, 804, 805, 806.

33. Colton, *Clay,* I, 32.

"I have prayed for this dear child," he lamented; "night and morning have I fervently prayed for her; but oh! my prayers have not been heard."

Henry Clay was as completely devastated as anyone could be. Perhaps never in his life had he been so affected by death. The following day he summoned the strength to write to his wife.

Alas! my dear wife, the great Destroyer has come, and taken from us our dear, dear, only daughter. . . . If the thunderbolt of Heaven had fallen on me—unprepared as I fear I am—I would have submitted, cheerfully submitted, to a thousand deaths to have saved this dear child. She was so good, so beloving, and so beloved, so happy, and so deserving to be happy. Then, she was the last of six dear daughters, most of them at periods of the greatest interest and hope, taken from us. Ah! how inscrutable are the ways of providence! I feel that one of the strongest tyes that bound me to Earth is broken—forever broken. My heart will bleed as long as it palpitates. Never, never, can its wounds be healed.

He said he knew it was his duty to submit to the will of God. He regretted that he did not have the religious faith of his wife. He wept for poor Erwin. "To have lost such a wife as she was! In the midst of youth, with all her plans of happiness and improvements; and her five children! Poor orphans, what will become of you!"

Clay realized he ought to be comforting his wife. Instead, he was pouring out his own grief to her. "This dear child was so entwined around my heart; I looked forward to so many days of comfort and happiness in her company, during the remnant of my life, that I shall never, never be able to forget her. My tears, and thank God they have flowed almost in a continued stream, have been my only relief. Sleep, food, I have scarcely tasted either."[34]

To friends who offered words of sympathy he simply said that there were "some wounds which nothing can heal." Anne was altogether special and only twenty-eight years of age. "Never was father blessed with one more filial. . . . She was my nighest neighbour; all her tastes and pleasures and amusements . . . were similar to my own."[35]

Clay hardly functioned in the days and weeks following the news of Anne's death. When he finally spoke in the Senate on December 29, to introduce yet another public land bill, he broke down and admitted to his colleagues that he was "borne down by the severest affliction with which Providence has ever been pleased to visit me."[36]

He sat in his Senate seat because duty required it, but he hardly participated in its activities. He argued a case before the Supreme Court, again out

34. Clay to Lucretia Clay, December 19, 1835, in Clay, *Papers,* VIII, 808–809; Margaret Smith to Mrs. Boyd, Christmas Day, 1835, in Smith, *Forty Years,* p. 375.

35. Clay to Brooke, January 1, [1836], in Clay, *Papers,* VIII, 813.

36. *Register of Debates,* 24th Congress, 1st session, p. 48ff. "Clay is truly a noble fellow," wrote Thurlow Weed to Francis Granger, February 20, 1836, Miscellaneous Papers, New York State Library.

of a deep sense of duty. "I go out only to the Capitol and mix but little in society," he said. He felt very weary. And the weather added to his misery. Twenty-four snowstorms racked the East Coast during the winter of 1835–1836. "So that I trust there will never be any occasion of my again returning to this City after this Session. I am truly tired of it."[37]

Although Clay had another year to complete his senatorial term, he began to give serious thought to retiring. "I am tired of . . . public life," he said when it was proposed that he run for the office of governor of Kentucky. "I most unaffectedly desire repose."[38]

Perhaps what started to nudge him out of his self-absorption and sense of futility was the specter of slavery—in the newspapers, in debates, in discussions and private conversations—that mounted each month. Abolition societies continued to expand their operations and demands for emancipation. Several of their leaders, knowing his opposition to the institution, had begun to communicate with Clay and call for his help in advancing their cause.

"Your political career has placed you in the very front rank of bold defenders of equal rights," Lewis Tappan wrote to the senator. As secretary of state you responded instantly to the call of South Americans who "were suffering under political slavery, and panting for freedom." Is physical servitude less important? he asked. Can one advocate political equality for foreigners and not assist those in this country deprived of freedom? And compensation to the slaveholder is no solution, wrote Tappan. "Slaveholding is . . . a sin, and men ought not to be paid for ceasing to sin."[39]

It was only natural for men to look to Henry Clay, the "Great Pacificator," for solutions to grave problems as they arose, such as the emancipation of blacks. And Clay was not averse to speaking his mind openly on the subject. He was a member of the American Colonization Society and frequently spoke at its meetings. "That slavery is unjust & is a great evil," he wrote, "are undisputed axioms. The difficulty always has been how to get rid of it." Where there were few slaves in states the problem was negligible, and starting with Pennsylvania in 1780, a number of northern states had ended it. One answer, Clay suggested, might be to put off emancipation to some future time, say, 1850, and hold all slaves for life born prior to that year. All those born subsequent to 1850 would be freed at the age of twenty-eight. In this way "there would be very little if any diminution in the value of slave property," and free labor, as a consequence, would eventually be substituted for slave labor. "And you would thus gently & gradually free yourself from what has not been inaccurately characterized a great curse."[40]

37. Clay to Brooke, January 25, 1836, Clay to Lucretia Clay, January 23, 1836, in Clay, *Papers*, VIII, 821; New York *Herald*, March 21, 1836.
38. Clay to Thomas Speed, January 2, 1836, in Clay, *Papers*, VIII, 814–815.
39. Tappan to Clay, July 20, 1835, in Clay, *Papers*, VIII, 793.
40. Clay to William Henry Russell, July 18, 1835, in Clay, *Papers*, VIII, 789. The overall idea

But the time was not propitious for gradual emancipation, Clay declared. The issue had begun to generate feverish excitement all over the country. And where blacks predominated in a state, such as Mississippi, perhaps the only answer was colonization.[41]

As for immediate abolition, he opposed it, even though he had always believed that "every man, no matter what his color or condition, was entitled to freedom." But not now, not until it could be done without "injurious consequences." Like President Jackson, Clay sharply criticized the activities of northern abolitionists.[42] "I will not impute to them bad motives," he wrote to John Greenleaf Whittier in response to an appeal for assistance in the cause, ". . . but I must say that I think their proceedings are highly injurious to the slave himself, to the master, and to the harmony of the Union. I believe that, instead of accelerating, they will retard, abolition."[43]

The issue found sharper focus when General Antonio López de Santa Anna, president of the Mexican Republic, marched into Texas to reassert Mexican authority over the Americans who had migrated to Texas in the hope and belief that someday soon the United States would annex the territory. Most of these settlers were slaveowners from Tennessee, Alabama, and Mississippi who had moved to Texas because of the economic depression resulting from the Panic of 1819.

Santa Anna's action provoked the Texans into proclaiming their independence on March 2, 1836. Seven weeks later, on April 21, 1836, they defeated the Mexican Army at the Battle of San Jacinto and captured Santa Anna himself. Without wasting a moment, the Texas Republic sent a commissioner, Samuel Carson, to Washington in the hope of winning U.S. recognition of Texas independence and beginning the process of annexation.

When Carson told the President that Texas might have to initiate an aggressive war against Mexico to guarantee its independence, General Jackson laughed. "Where is your means, Sir, to carry on an offensive war against Mexico?"

---

about freeing slaves born after a particular date may have come from Thomas Jefferson. See Andrew A. Lipscomb, *The Writings of Thomas Jefferson* (Washington, D.C., 1903) XIV, 296–297; William W. Freehling, *Secessionists at Bay, 1776–1854* (New York, 1990), p. 126.

41. Clay to Thomas Speed, January 2, 1836, in Clay, *Papers,* VIII, 814.

42. In a speech delivered on March 9, Clay expressed "the strongest disapprobation of the course of the northern abolitionists, who are intermeddling with a subject that no way concerned them." He reiterated his support for gradual emancipation, although he had been taught from childhood that every man, irrespective of race, was entitled to freedom. If he were a southern slaveowner, Clay declared, he would resist emancipation in any form, gradual or otherwise, "because he would go for his own race, which was the superior race of the two; and because emancipation must necessarily give the inferior race, the course of time, a numerical preponderance."

This blatantly racist remark was typical of the thinking of most Americans in the mid-nineteenth century. And it extended to Indians as well as blacks. *Register of Debates,* 24th Congress, 1st session, pp. 778–780. Clay was speaking to a petition from Quakers in Philadelphia for the abolition of slavery and the slave trade in the District of Columbia.

43. Clay to Whittier, July 22, 1837, in Clay, *Papers,* IX, 64.

Carson brightly responded: "In the enthusiasms of the American people, their devotion to the cause of Liberty and the ways and means, to defray the expenses of War."[44]

The annexation of Texas would mean the acquisition of an enormous landmass that included among its population a large number of slaves. For Texas to enter the Union as a slave state not only would upset the equal balance between the number of free and slave states but would surely trigger a renewed controversy over emancipation. A war with Mexico might also ensue. Already companies of volunteers were forming in the western and southern states to help defend Texas's independence.[45]

The president of the Texas Republic, David G. Burnet, wrote to Clay shortly after the declaration of independence. "Our rights in the Soil of Texas," he said, "are founded in the holiest guarantees of national faith." We will never relinquish them, save with our lives. "To you Sir whose voice is always eloquent and never more powerful, than in Swaying the Sympathies of men and of governments, we look with confidence, for an advocate and a friend—To you, who took the feeble, distracted and vacillating governments of the South by the hand and introduced them to the great audience of nations—To you, the government of Texas appeals and asks a Similar favor."

Burnet wanted an early recognition of Texas's independence, which Clay, as chairman of the Senate Committee on Foreign Relations, could indeed assist. He assured the senator that he could not raise his voice in a more righteous cause and put the "diplomatic minions" of Mexico to silence.[46] Jackson, on the other hand, moved slowly on recognition. He feared the reaction of the rest of the world to a hasty move on his part, and of course, he feared for Van Buren's election in the fall. In no way did he wish to jeopardize the presidential contest. A Whig President to follow him was unthinkable.[47]

Clay entertained no such apprehension about the recognition of Texas's independence. In one speech he noted the "inhuman scenes" involved in the massacre of Texans at the Alamo but chose not to say more until his Committee on Foreign Relations concluded its deliberations on the Texas question. Not until June 18, 1836, did he bring forward the committee's report. In the report, which he himself wrote, he noted popular sentiment in favor of recognition, which, he admitted, the committee also shared. He then gave a brief history of U.S. policy with regard to recognition and explained that it was normally extended to governments "in practical operation" without asking

44. Carson to David G. Burnet, July 3, 1836, in *Diplomatic Correspondence of the United States, American Historical Association, Annual Report* (Washington, D.C., 1907), I, 101, 102.

45. Thomas N. Lindsey to Clay, May 22, 1836, in Clay, *Papers,* VIII, 851. "I am utterly opposed to risking the peace of the Country for outlaws & adventurers," declared the Whig senator Willie P. Mangum of North Carolina. His views were shared by many others. Mangum to Charity Mangum, May 22, 1836, in Mangum, *Papers,* II, 437.

46. Burnet to Clay, March 30, 1836, in Clay, *Papers,* VIII, 838.

47. Remini, *Jackson,* III, 360.

whether those governments had been rightfully brought into existence. There-fore, he concluded, the committee unanimously recommended that the inde-pendence of Texas be acknowledged by the United States whenever it received satisfactory information that Texas had "in successful operation a civil Govern-ment, capable of performing the duties and fulfilling the obligations of an independent Power."[48]

Clay wanted to leave the matter at that and proceed no further until the President provided additional information about the operation of the Texas Republic. Because so many Americans had assisted Texas in achieving its inde-pendence, Clay warned that this fact might strengthen European belief that the United States had "a desire of aggrandizing ourselves at the expense of our neighbors." The United States must also think about its future good relations with Mexico and give evidence of its ability to distinguish between eight mil-lion "unoffending" Mexicans and "Santa Anna—the blood-thirsty, vain, boast-ing, military tyrant."[49]

It was one thing to recognize Texas independence and quite another to annex it. Clay absolutely opposed annexation as long as Mexico and Texas remained technically at war. Nor would he concur in the annexation against the decided wishes of a large number of people in the United States, even if Mexico acknowledged the independence of Texas. But if any European power—especially Great Britain or France—were to attempt the conquest of Texas or aid Mexico in reconquering it, then, he said, "the U.S. could not regard any such attempt with indifference."[50]

Because of Jackson's hesitancy, Texas recognition took many more months. And annexation moved farther into the background. But the slave question remained and grew into horrendous proportions with each passing year, taxing the nation's statesmen to prevent it from exploding into a national crisis.[51]

Just before former President James Madison died in 1836, he was convers-ing with a friend about the agitation provoked by the abolitionists. Then he added: "Clay has been so successful in compromising other disputes, I wish he could fall upon some plan of compromising this—and then all parties . . . might unite & make him President."[52]

Madison's remark was relayed to Clay, and no doubt it gratified him

48. *Register of Debates,* 24th Congress, 1st session, pp. 1387–1388, 1759, 1846–1848.
49. Clay, *Works,* VI, 41–44.
50. Clay to Porter, January 26, 1838, Clay to Biddle, September 14, 1838, in Clay, *Papers,* IX, 135, 229.
51. "I think those Gentlemen at the South have been unwise who have expressed a wish for the incorporation of Texas *in order to strengthen the Slave interest;* and I should think it also unwise in Gentlemen at the North to avow the opposite ground, as a motive for action." Clay to John Greenleaf Whittier, July 22, 1837, in Clay, *Papers,* IX, 64.
52. George Tucker to Clay, June 30, 1836, in Clay, *Papers,* VIII, 859.

immensely. But at the moment the senator had no compromise to offer. Nevertheless, as the slavery question intensified in the following months and years, Clay slowly came to realize that his duty required him to continue his work in Washington, to stick it out and remain in the Senate if his state so decreed. It would be wonderful if all parties would unite to place him in the White House, but before that happened, he would first have to find the compromise to settle the growing discord over emancipation.

Meanwhile, he resumed his attacks on "Jacksonism" and tried once again to win passage of his bill to distribute to the states the proceeds from the sale of public lands. Because his scheme would allow states to use the money for internal improvements and would free tariff money for use in meeting the normal expenses of the federal government, it made a perfect package: It protected the tariff and advanced internal improvements. Unfortunately, with the repeated failures of his bill, the revenue kept ballooning because of the high tariff rates and the booming sales in public lands. One happy result of a burgeoning revenue was the liquidation of the entire national debt in January 1835, an event that provided another signal triumph for Jackson. But the surplus kept accumulating. Within a year the excess revenue in the Treasury had reached thirty-six million dollars. Something had to be done about it. Many, like Clay, complained that this handsome sum should be circulating in the marketplace, stimulating industry and creating jobs, not sitting idle in "pet" banks.

To encourage support for his public land measure, Clay proposed raising from 10 to 15 the percentage of revenue from land sales to go to the states in which the land was located. The remainder of the sales money would be divided equally among all the states.

Such an enormous largess brought greedy stares from southern and western states. Both Whigs and Democrats hungered after the money. But how could they get the bill past Jackson? Eventually both sides managed to sugarcoat the measure to win the President's approval. After Clay resubmitted his land bill on December 29, Calhoun took the floor to propose a bill to regulate the public deposits. Over the next few months what finally emerged was a distribution (from land sales) bill tied to a system of regulating and controlling the deposit (pet) banks, something Jackson desperately wanted to achieve. If he desired the regulation of the deposit banks, he must swallow his dislike of distribution. To make distribution more palatable to him, the bill specified that the revenue from all sources, not simply the money from land sales, would be distributed.[53]

Naturally such a vast outpouring of federal money into the coffers of the states would enhance Van Buren's chances for election to the presidency in the fall. So, with "a repugnance of feeling and a recoil of judgment," Jackson

53. For details of this bill, see Remini, *Jackson*, III, 318–325.

informed the Democratic leadership in Congress that he would accept this deposit-distribution bill.[54] The measure passed the Senate on June 17 by a vote of 40 to 6, and the House on June 22 by the vote of 155 to 38. Jackson affixed his signature on June 23, 1836.[55]

Clay rose in the Senate to express his gratification that the President had signed the bill. It was, he said, cause for "great rejoicing." However, he deplored the fact that his consent was first announced in the *Globe* rather than delivered to Congress. Such political behavior showed ignorance of "established usage" and disrespect toward the legislature.[56]

Actually Jackson entertained a far better opinion of Congress with the beginning of the new year. With each passing month the strength of the Democrats had increased in the Senate. Connecticut, Illinois, and Louisiana each sent a new representative to the upper house, and they all responded loyally to White House dictation. Then, when the Virginia legislature instructed its senators to vote in favor of Senator Benton's resolution to expunge the censure of Jackson from the Senate journal, John Tyler resigned rather than obey. He was replaced by William C. Rives, former minister to France and a loyal Jackson Democrat. Rives took his seat on March 14, 1836, and his arrival in the Senate marked a shift in the balance of power from Whig to Democrat.

With this majority in place, Jackson then began to feed additional nominations to the upper house. First came Roger B. Taney, nominated to serve as chief justice of the United States, replacing the deceased John Marshall. The nomination was confirmed on March 15 by a vote of twenty-nine to fifteen. The Great Triumvirate voted nay—naturally. After that, Amos Kendall was proposed as postmaster general, and he, too, was approved. To top off his series of victories, Jackson sent back to the Senate the nomination of Andrew Stevenson as minister to Great Britain. Quite appropriately it went to the Committee on Foreign Relations, and Clay brought in a recommendation that the nomination be rejected two weeks later. On March 16 the Senate confirmed Stevenson by a vote of twenty-six to nineteen. It was almost two years since Stevenson had been rejected in 1834. During that time the Senate had undergone thirteen individual changes in personnel, out of a total of forty-eight men, and of those thirteen, ten voted to confirm.[57]

By the time the Senate finally adjourned in early July, Jackson virtually had complete control of Congress. He even issued a Specie Circular on July 11, 1836, after the adjournment, in which he ordered that from August 15 onward nothing but specie (gold and silver) would be received for payment of public lands. Jackson took this action to stem the speculative boom in land sales that

54. Quoted ibid., III, 324. Jackson did ask for a few amendments, which were incorporated into the final bill.
55. *National Intelligencer,* June 23, 25, 1836.
56. *Register of Debates,* 24th Congress, 1st session, p. 1870.
57. *Senate Executive Journal,* IV, 520–522.

had recently occurred. By 1836 land sales had reached nearly twenty-five million dollars, with additional sales running up to five million dollars each month, and the President felt he must stop the spiral of inflation. But the circular was another marked disregard for the will of Congress, for Jackson issued it in the full knowledge that both houses disapproved and might have passed legislation to countermand it.

The Whigs erupted. The Washington *National Intelligencer* on July 14 denounced the circular "as a measure of the same arbitrary character as the removal of the public deposits in 1833, emanating from the imperious will of an irresponsible Magistrate." Clay called the circular "a most ill-advised, illegal and pernicious measure," so typical of a dictator. "One rash, lawless and crude experiment succeeds another," he wailed.[58]

Clay returned home accompanied by his fourteen-year-old son, John, who had contracted typhoid fever while visiting his father in early May. The boy had been "cupped, bled, blistered" and tended by his father with nerve racking concern that yet another child of his would die. "I wish his mother was present with us to assist in nursing him," wrote the worried Clay, "but he does not suffer for nurses." The father, along with his body servant, Charles Dupuy, slept in the same room with John every night of his illness, while a nurse watched over him during the day. Three doctors were engaged to attend him. "The fever was bilious, without intermission," reported Clay, and the headaches were severe and constant. Recovery was slow, but by the time the congressional session ended John was out of danger. The young man returned to Kentucky, continued his studies at Transylvania University, and on November 9, 1837, was admitted as a sophomore at Princeton University.[59]

Once back at Ashland, Clay faced the difficulty of helping care for seven grandchildren. The greatest burden fell on his wife, "and altho' the task is great," her improved health enabled her "to go through it." His own general health and spirits improved through the summer, and at some of the speaking engagements he accepted he seemed to have regained his old fighting form. For example, at one public dinner in Versailles, Kentucky, he appeared "in his accustomed manner, fervent, solemn, sometimes pathetic, sometimes playful, convulsing his audience with laughter." He gave Jackson a good thrashing, berating his Indian policy as one of "fraud, violence and injustice." The outrages against the Cherokees particularly distressed the senator, as well as the "miserable Black Hawk war"[60] against the Sauk and Fox Indians in Illinois and

58. *Globe,* August 31, 1836; speech at the Woodford Festival, Versailles, Kentucky, July 26, 1836, in Clay, *Papers,* VIII, 861.

59. Clay to Henry Clay, Jr., May 12, 1836, Clay to Margaret Bayard Smith, May 14, 1836, Clay to Thomas Hart Clay, May 19, 1836, Clay to Samuel L. Southard, May 23, 1836, Clay to Henry Clay, Jr., September 8, 1837, in Clay, *Papers,* VIII, 850–852; IX, 73.

60. The Black Hawk War broke out in 1832, when the Sauk and Fox Indians recrossed the Mississippi to return to their former lands in Illinois. White settlers panicked, and soon state and federal troops were summoned to expel the invaders. The war lasted only a few months, and Clay's son Thomas participated in it.

the "more disgraceful Seminole war," which had just broken out against the Indians in Florida and was to rage for the next six years. Of necessity he also attacked Jackson's handling of public monies and labeled him a "despot" whose "WILL . . . becomes the law." It was during this particular speech that he mentioned his thoughts about retiring from the Senate after the expiration of his present term. "Foul corruption" had penetrated so many departments of the administration that he felt incapable of preventing the evil from poisoning the entire government.[61]

Nevertheless, Clay believed that the American people would wake up to the corruption and defeat Martin Van Buren in the fall presidential election. "I think the political signs are highly auspicious," he told Samuel Southard. "I have now very great confidence in the defeat of Mr. V. Buren." But as so often had happened in the past, he disregarded all the political signs signaling impending defeat. The Whigs chose not to hold a national convention. In fact, some state meetings recommended against a convention. As a result, the party was split several ways, and the best that might be expected was an election that would end up in the House of Representatives, just as had occurred in 1824.[62]

Toward the close of the campaign—in late October—a great barbecue was organized close to Ashland, and Clay was invited to attend. He felt obliged to put in an appearance, and of course, he was asked to say a few words. He spoke briefly and expressed the hope that the people would defeat Van Buren. Finally, he said he would vote for Harrison because he thought he had the best prospects of whipping the Democrat. "Most certainly the General was not my first choice," he later wrote. "I should have preferred Mr. Webster to him, and so stated."[63]

Although Van Buren was denounced in the South as an abolitionist and the demon enemy of John C. Calhoun, vilified in the North as a southern sympathizer, and ridiculed in all sections of the country—by Henry Clay especially—as the handpicked puppet who would jump at Jackson's command, Van Buren amassed a popular vote of 764,198 in the fall election. This was slightly more (50.9 percent) than a bare majority. There was a considerable increase in southern voting, which helped Van Buren, as it turned out, and a slight falling off in some Middle Atlantic and New England states. In the all-important electoral college he won fifteen states for a total of 170 electoral votes.

The combined popular vote for all Whig candidates reached 736,147, representing 49.1 percent of the total. Harrison did surprising well by taking six states (Vermont, New Jersey, Maryland, Kentucky, Ohio, and Indiana) for a total of 73 electoral and 548,966 popular votes. That showing proved very

61. Clay to Dolley Madison, December 13, 1836; speech at the Woodford Festival, July 26, 1836, in Clay, *Papers,* VIII, 871, 860–861.
62. Clay to Southard, September 27, 1836, in Clay, *Papers,* VIII, 866.
63. Clay to Hugh Lawson White, August 27, 1838, in Clay, *Papers,* IX, 221.

instructive to Whig leaders. It said something about how the American people felt toward their war heroes.

Webster hardly made a showing at all. He won his own state, Massachusetts, for a total of 41,287 popular and 14 electoral votes. That was all. Clay had expected as much and, in the course of a long conversation with the Massachusetts senator several months before the election, "expressed to him the opinion of the expediency of his retirement from the contest, but he did not retire."

Hugh Lawson White took Tennessee and Georgia for 26 electoral votes, and South Carolina, where electors were still appointed by the legislature, awarded its 11 votes to Willie P. Mangum of North Carolina.[64]

"We are cursed with Van Buren for President," groaned Thurlow Weed, former leader of the Anti-Masonic party and now the Whig boss of New York. "This certainly only makes me hate [him] the more cordially." How could the people select such a sly and wily fox? he complained. "I have no confidence in a People who can elect Van Buren President. Depend upon it, his Election is to be the 'beginning of the end.' "[65]

Clay later admitted that the condition of the Whig party "was unfortunate. No mode was devised, and none seemed practicable, to present a single candidate in opposition to [Van Buren]." But his immediate reaction was one of concern about how the campaign was conducted. If a President can designate his successor, he said, "bring the whole machinery of the Government, including its 100,000 dependents, into the canvass," and thereby win the election, then a "fatal *precedent*" has been established that must be "rebuked and reversed, or there is an end of the freedom of election." Once then, it will be again attempted, and unless corrected by the people, it will become, in time, the established practice of the Country."[66]

The defeat marked the nation's continuing acceptance of "Jacksonism" and all its horrors, concluded Clay. It meant, in effect, Old Hickory would go on running the country for a third term.

But Clay resigned himself. "Not being able to find any satisfactory reason for not serving this the last Session of my term in the Senate," he wrote, "I think . . . I shall attend." Lucretia did not accompany him since she was needed at home to help care for the grandchildren.

Clay returned to the Clements house on Pennsylvania Avenue and shared a mess with his colleague John J. Crittenden, Senator Samuel L. Southard of New Jersey, and Representative John Calhoon—not to be confused with John C. Calhoun—of Kentucky. Shortly after his arrival in Washington Clay was informed that upon the death of James Madison the American Colonization

64. Petersen, *Statistical History of the American Presidential Elections,* pp. 22–24; Silbey, "Election of 1836," I, 595–599, 640; Clay to Hugh Lawson White, August 27, 1838, in Clay, *Papers,* IX, 221.
65. Weed to William H. Seward, October 25, November 25, 31, 1836, William H. Seward Papers, University of Rochester Library.
66. Clay to Brooke, December 19, 1836, in Clay, *Papers,* VIII, 872–873.

Society at its annual meeting had unanimously elected him its president. He acknowledged and accepted the election by declaring that the society had advanced the "only practical scheme ever presented" of ultimately separating the white and black races. Clay remained its president until his death in 1852.[67]

A short time later he was also notified that the general assembly of Kentucky, on December 15, had reelected him to the U.S. Senate. The vote was seventy-six for Clay and fifty-four for James Guthrie. He had strongly expressed his wish to retire, both publicly and privately, but "when I reflect upon the great and numerous obligations which I am under to the people of Kentucky," he wrote in finally accepting the election, ". . . I feel that there is no sacrifice which I ought not to make." He still believed he could make a difference in determining the nation's future direction.[68]

But this short session of the Twenty-fourth Congress proved disastrous as far as Clay was concerned. He gave strong support to a resolution introduced by Senator Thomas Ewing of Ohio to rescind the Specie Circular and, in the course of a long speech on January 11, 1837, predicted "a general panic throughout the country" if the administration's fiscal policies were not reversed. The circular would place such a premium on specie, he warned, that people would hoard it and gold and silver would soon disappear from circulation. He had no confidence in local banks to meet the needs of the community, and without the BUS, the nation faced the possibility of a devastating financial collapse because of rampant speculation in land, which had continued even after the circular went into effect. Clay assured his colleagues that rescinding the circular would not constitute an act of censure against the President. He had long fought the ascendancy of executive power, but, he went on, "its march has been steady, onward, and I lament to say, triumphant. It is now practically the supreme power in the State. . . . It is a monarchy in disguise."[69]

Senator William C. Rives of Virginia, a Democrat, offered a substitute resolution in which both specie and the notes of specie-paying banks would be acceptable for payment of public lands, and Clay was willing to support it as a compromise. Hard-money advocates, such as Jackson and "Old Bullion" Benton, rejected the notion of allowing paper to be used in land sales and faulted Rives for proposing it, claiming it was an act of spite because the party had failed to nominate him for the vice presidency. "Mr. Rives course is a strange one," fumed President Jackson. "I fear it springs out of jealousy."[70]

This split among Democrats—between so-called Conservatives, like

67. Clay to Philip R. Fendall, November 5, 1836, Clay to Southard, September 27, 1836, Clay to Dolley Madison, December 13, 1836, Clay to Ralph Randolph Gurley, December 22, 1836, in Clay, *Papers,* VIII, 868, 866, 871, 874. Calhoon subsequently left the mess because he was dissatisfied with his room. Clay to Southard, January 22, 1837, ibid., IX, 16.
68. *Niles' Weekly Register,* December 31, 1836; Clay to general assembly, January 16, 1837, in Clay, *Papers,* IX, 7–8.
69. *Register of Debates,* 24th Congress, 2nd session, pp. 360–376.
70. Jackson to Francis P. Blair, January, 1837, Jackson Papers, LC.

Rives and Senator Nathaniel P. Tallmadge of New York, who favored paper or soft money, and regular Democrats, who supported the administration's hard-money policy—augured well for the Whigs. That Clay would endorse Rives's substitute made the resolution only all the more unacceptable to Jackson. "The . . . schism in the party about Hard money, and Bank notes," Clay happily observed, ". . . may lead to some good results."[71]

To the President's shock and surprise the Ewing-Rives resolution passed the Senate on February 10 by the lopsided vote of forty-one to five. It had been referred to the Committee on Public Lands, which reported out a bill that in effect rescinded the Specie Circular, without naming it, by allowing bank notes in payment of all dues owed the government. Benton and Silas Wright fought hard against the bill, but most Democrats joined Clay and the other Whigs in its support.[72] Calhoun abstained. He felt an "explosion" imminent because of the "incredibly bad" state of the currency, so it mattered little, he said, what the Senate did.[73]

For the first and only time in its history the Senate also resolved the question of who would serve as Vice President. The Democratic candidate, Richard M. Johnson of Kentucky, had failed to receive a majority of electoral votes. Virginia gave its votes to William Smith out of resentment over the decision of the Democratic Convention to bypass Rives, and Maryland, Tennessee, South Carolina, and Georgia gave their votes to John Tyler. The Whigs had supported Francis Granger of New York. Consequently, Johnson received only 147 votes, as against 77 for Granger, 47 for Tyler, and 23 for Smith. Happily, the Senate was now safely Democratic, and on February 8, 1837, by a vote of 33 to 16, Richard M. Johnson was elected.[74]

But the action that remained forever fixed in the minds of both the administration's friends and enemies about this session was the renewed attempt of Thomas Hart Benton to have the censure of the President passed in 1834 expunged from the Senate's journal. "The people have called for it, in language not to be mistaken," said Chief Justice Taney, "& justice demands that it should be done."[75]

As long as Whigs controlled the Senate, it was impossible to expunge the record. But each year Democratic voting strength in the upper house mounted. "How changed is the Senate, even in one short year!" Clay sighed in February 1837. "I am truly sad when I reflect on our losses in that brief period, and look upon those who supply their places."[76] This was now the last session

71. Clay to Henry Clay, Jr., [January] 28, 1837, in Clay, *Papers,* IX, 20.

72. Jackson's own cabinet opposed the Specie Circular.

73. Benton, *Thirty Years' View,* I, 694–707; Wiltse, *Calhoun, Nullifier,* p. 301; *Register of Debates,* 24th Congress, 2d session, p. 21ff.

74. Silbey, "Election of 1836," p. 600; Leland W. Meyer, *The Life and Times of Colonel Richard M. Johnson of Kentucky* (New York, 1932), pp. 425–429.

75. Taney to Jackson, December 8, 1836, Jackson Papers, LC.

76. Clay to Benjamin W. Leigh, February 4, 1837, copy CPP.

of Jackson's administration, and there was a renewed sense that the expunging should be done before he left office.

On December 26, 1836, the third anniversary of the day on which Clay first introduced the censure resolution, Benton rose in the Senate and formally proposed that it be "expunged" and that the secretary of the upper house draw black lines around the censure "and write across the face thereof, in strong letters, the following words: "Expunged by order of the Senate, this ———— day of ————, in the year of our Lord 1837."

Benton and his friends organized their support with stunning efficiency, and on Monday, January 16, they began the debate on the resolution. It started slowly. Then, as darkness approached and the immense chandelier was lighted, a huge crowd filled every seat in the galleries, lobbies, and even the floor of the Senate itself. "The scene became grand and impressive." The "night was wearing away: the expungers were in full force—masters of the chamber—happy—and visibly determined to remain" and win the fight.[77]

Calhoun got to his feet. The battle was at last joined. He spoke in a soft voice, but he drove home his point. The Constitution says a journal shall be kept, he declared. If you expunge, how can it be kept? "It does the very thing which the constitution declares shall not be done." And why is it being done? he asked. "It is by dictation from the White House. . . . It is the combination of patronage and power to coerce this body into a gross and palpable violation of the constitution."[78]

There was a pause. Dead silence prevailed. All eyes then turned to Clay. Slowly his tall form rose. There was a "gentle bustle, as if all were striving to get a good view of him." He waited a moment, "and the Senate became still as death." He looked unusually grave, and when he finally spoke, his tone was subdued, "yet such was the peculiarly clear, silvery, sonorous quality of his voice that every word could be distinctly heard by every one in the chamber."

He began with a review of the background and origin of the dispute, which is what he frequently did in his Senate speeches. Then he argued the right of the Senate to "remonstrate against any executive usurpation" and do it "in language the most inoffensive and respectful," such as was done in 1834. "I believe the resolution of March, 1834," he said, "to have been true; and that it was competent to the Senate to proclaim the truth." How, then, and by "what article is contained your power to expunge what they [your predecessors] have done? And may not the precedent lead to a perpetual code of defacement and restoration of the transactions of the Senate?

"I put it to the calm and deliberate consideration of the majority if they are ready to pronounce for all time that, whoever may be President, the Senate shall not *dare* to remonstrate against any Executive usurpation whatever. For one, I will not."

77. Benton, *Thirty Years' View*, I, 719, 727, 728.
78. Ibid., I, 728.

It was a powerful argument. Even Democrats acknowledged it. The challenge, said one, was uttered in a "tone of proud, lofty, and indomitable defiance, and with an air of conscious, undeniable superiority."

Clay's face darkened; his voice rose in volume. Andrew Jackson, he declared, "has swept over the Government, during the last eight years, like a tropical tornado. Every department exhibits traces of the ravages of the storm." The Bank of the United States is only one example, and even though it was popular with the electorate, it now "lies prostrate" because it "incurred the displeasure of the President."

What object of his ambition remains unsatisfied? Clay cried. "When disabled from age any longer to hold the sceptre of power, he designates his successor and transmits it to his favorite! What more does he want? Must we blot, deface, and mutilate, the records of the country, to punish the presumptuousness of expressing an opinion contrary to his own?" By this time Clay was visibly angry. If the President is really the Old Hero that his friends proclaim, he should despise "all grovelling sycophancy." He should reject with scorn and contempt "your black scratches and your baby lines in the fair records of his country. Black lines! Black lines!" Clay bellowed, "Sir, I hope the Secretary of the Senate will preserve the pen with which he may inscribe them," present it to a senator (presumably Benton), and confer on him the title Knight of the Black Lines.

"The deed is to be done," Clay acknowledged, "—that foul deed which, like the blood-stained hands of the guilty Macbeth, all ocean's waters will never wash out." And when "you have perpetrated it, go home to the people, and tell them what glorious honors you have achieved for our common country. Tell them that you have extinguished one of the brightest and purest lights that ever burnt at the altar of civil liberty. . . . Tell them that, henceforth, no matter what daring or outrageous act any President may perform, you have for ever hermetically sealed the mouth of the Senate. . . . And if the people do not pour out their indignation and imprecation, I have yet to learn the character of American freemen."[79]

Here was yet another magnificent display of Clay's great eloquence and passionate delivery. The galleries broke into sustained applause. Even Senator James Buchanan, a victim of Clay's repeated assaults, said that Prince Hal had "enchained the attention of his audience." Thomas Hart Benton reluctantly admitted that it "was grand and affecting."[80]

Webster spoke last. He was not as passionate as Clay, perhaps because he had suffered "no personal griefs" from Old Hickory. His protest against the resolution, therefore, was brief and moderate. When he finished, there was a long silence. The question was called, and a vote ordered. Forty-three senators

79. Ibid., I, 729; *Register of Debates,* 24th Congress, 2d session, pp. 429–440.
80. *Register of Debates,* 24th Congress, 2d session, p. 440; Sargent, *Public Men and Events,* I, 337–339.

were present, five absent. In favor of Benton's resolution to expunge, twenty-four; opposed, nineteen. Among those against were Clay, Calhoun, and Webster.[81]

The secretary of the Senate took down the manuscript journal and opened it to March 28, 1834. As he did so, the Whigs walked out of the chamber to demonstrate their disapproval. It was 9:00 P.M. as the secretary drew a square of broad black lines around the censure and then wrote across its face: "Expunged by order of the Senate, this 16th day of January, in the year of our Lord 1837." The "darkness of the deed and of the house was well suited to each other," wrote Clay.

"The Senate is no longer a place for any decent man," he moaned. "It is rapidly filling with blackguards." It is "a place where ignorance and folly, corruption and ruffians have undisputed sway!"[82]

Whig newspapers published the names of those who voted to expunge in large, full-faced capital letters and heavy black lines drawn around them. Above the names was the title Clay had given them: "THE KNIGHTS OF THE BLACK LINES."[83]

Clay sustained one defeat after another at the hands of President Jackson. The Bank was dead. Tariff rates were slowly being reduced. Internal improvements had been blocked. And yet Old Hickory did not let up. He had one more blow to deliver. Two days before the end of the session the House of Representatives chose to side with the Senate against the President on the bill that would rescind the Specie Circular by allowing bank notes as payment for dues owed the government. The vote was 143 to 59, a rousing statement of opposition. Jackson promptly vetoed it. Virtually his last official act was a sharp slap at Congress, despite a Democratic majority in both houses.[84]

"Jackson played the tyrant to the last," marveled Clay. Could anyone doubt that "we are all expunged here," especially the Senate? "I shall escape from it as soon as I decently can, with the same pleasure that one would fly from a charnel-house."[85]

81. *Register of Debates*, 24th Congress, 2d session, p. 504.

82. Clay to Robert P. Letcher, January 17, 1837, in Clay, *Papers*, IX, 14; Clay to Benjamin W. Leigh, February 4, 1837, copy CPP.

83. Sargent, *Public Men and Events*, I, 342.

84. Jackson pocket vetoed the bill but wrote a brief message dated "March 3, 1837—11:45 P.M." It was never delivered to Congress but simply deposited in the State Department. Richardson, *Messages and Papers*, II, 1501–1507.

85. Clay to Noah Noble, March 4, 1837, Clay to Brooke, February 10, 1837, in Clay, *Papers*, IX, 37, 27; Clay to Benjamin W. Leigh, February 4, 1837, copy CPP.

TWENTY-EIGHT

The Panic of 1837

PERHAPS to show what class and style he possessed even in a "charnel-house," Prince Hal attended the inauguration of the new President on March 4, 1837. More likely he came because he rather liked Van Buren personally, despite his repeated attacks on the Magician's politics and associations. He witnessed what the Washington *Globe* called "the glorious scene of Mr. Van Buren, once rejected by the Senate, sworn into office, by the chief Justice Taney, also being rejected by the factious Senate"—and all in the presence of King Andrew himself. The newspaper noted with satisfaction Clay's presence at the ceremonies, along with Daniel Webster (Calhoun absented himself, however), and said they "seem to have caught the contagion of the fine day and glowing patriotism that surrounded them."[1]

But these happy thoughts and words about the contagion of the fine day and glowing patriotism that surround them hardly lasted two weeks. Suddenly a major financial calamity swept across the country. The New Orleans cotton market collapsed, and it bankrupted one of the largest New York dealers in domestic exchanges with connections to a variety of commercial and mercantile enterprises and banks. It touched off a chain reaction. In a matter of weeks dozens of companies slid into bankruptcy. The price of specie rose sharply and created a run on the banks, thereby forcing a suspension of specie payments by the banks. Such runs on New York City banks alone reached more than two million dollars. The safety of the deposit banks in the South and West were placed in immediate jeopardy. By the summer many of them had failed with losses totaling tens of millions of dollars. The "happy and prosperous" country that Jackson had turned over to Van Buren suddenly verged on total financial collapse. "The intelligence from the South, as to our Commercial embarrassments," declared Clay, "is dreadful."

1. *Globe,* March 8, 1837. In all probability Clay and Van Buren rather respected each other, even though they represented different outlooks on American life and politics. Being first-rate politicians, they were never completely estranged despite some sharp words Clay leveled against the Van Buren administration.

But who could doubt the cause? Beyond all doubt, said Clay, the measures of the government had produced "the present calamitous state of affairs." Perhaps now the people would open their eyes to reality. Perhaps now they would see that the iron will of one man had bankrupted the nation and endangered individual liberty.[2]

Actually a worldwide depression brought about the Panic of 1837. Jackson's killing of the BUS and issuance of the Specie Circular had virtually nothing to do with the onset of the financial collapse. Economic forces beyond the control of anyone in the United States brought the long period of industrial and agricultural growth to a screeching, if temporary, halt.[3] Jackson himself blamed the crisis on the "attempt by Biddle and the Barings, to take into their keeping the management of the currency, both in England and America." But no one could convince Clay or other Whigs that the Panic of 1837 resulted from anything but the disastrous fiscal policies of the Jackson administration. They specifically faulted the Specie Circular. "Every man who has become embarrassed by his own extravagant & improvident speculations," declared President Van Buren, "relieves himself from self reproaches by laying his misfortunes at the door of the Treasury order."[4]

For the summer Clay had planned to entertain and accompany Daniel Webster on his tour of the West and later to visit his son James, whom he had financially helped get located on a farm in Missouri.[5] But all that had to be canceled. President Van Buren hastily summoned the Congress into a special session in September to deal with the growing economic crisis. It meant that Clay would have to leave Ashland in mid-August at the latest. Only three times previously had the Congress been called into special session, and all three had involved wartime emergencies.[6]

Otherwise Clay spent a relatively calm and happy summer, enjoying an-

2. Clay to Alexander W. Stow, April 26, 1837, in Clay, *Papers,* IX, 43.

3. On the panic, see Reginald C. McGrane, *The Panic of 1837* (Chicago, 1924); Samuel Resneck, "The Social History of an American Depression, 1837–1843," *American Historical Review,* XL (1935), pp. 662–687; and Peter Temin, *The Jacksonian Economy* (New York, 1969).

4. Jackson to Blair, April 18, 1837, Jackson Papers, LC; Van Buren to Jackson, March 20, 1837, Van Buren Papers, LC.

5. Like many prominent Americans at the time, Clay speculated in land, especially military bounty lands. He first acquired a tract of military lands in Missouri in partnership with Colonel James Morrison which was later sold. At different times he also had property in Illinois, a farm at the confluence of the Missouri and Mississippi rivers across from Alton, Illinois, and a 40-acre plot at the juncture of the Grand and Missouri rivers. Clay purchased 680 acres of land at Richland near St. Louis, Missouri, to be operated by his son James. Clay really opposed James's removal to Missouri but acceded to it because "I desire most ardently, my dear Son, your happiness." In a short while the son complained of loneliness and unhappiness, and the father urged him to return to Kentucky. Clay to James B. Clay, January 22, 1838, in Clay, *Papers,* IX, 132. For Clay's land-holdings, see ibid., II, 578; III, 346, 627–628; VIII, 339, 649, 662–663.

6. Clay to James B. Clay, May 26, 1837, Clay to Richard Graham, June 1, 1837, Clay to Webster, March 28, 1837, in Clay, *Papers,* IX, 45, 46, 48, 40. "Mr. Webster and his lady and daughter have passed a week with us. They left Lexington yesterday. Their reception has been very cordial and I hope satisfactory to him." Clay to Alexander Hamilton, May 26, 1837, ibid., IX, 46–47.

other new grandchild, Anne Clay, born to Henry, Jr., and his wife, and helping care for the "seven Grand Children, left by my two daughters. Our house therefore has all the animation which it exhibited twenty years ago." In such a contented mood he counseled a friend about resisting depression and self-pity. He could have been talking about himself. "Few men have seen as much of the world as you have, or enjoyed more of it, or put more good things in and out of his mouth, or laughed more, or cracked more jokes. That . . . you should have surrendered yourself to ennui is too bad. For shame! No more ennui, no relapses. They are unworthy of you." Then, speaking of his own situation, Clay added: "I am here in the midst of tranquility and abundance. I have around me every thing to render me comfortable and independent. One deplorable event alone continues to prey upon me. If my beloved daughter had been spared me, I should have been more happy than most men at Sixty, which I have just reached."[7]

Adding to his happiness was the announcement that his thirty-four-year-old son, Thomas Hart Clay, the "sot," as Harriet Martineau called him, would marry Marie Mentelle, on October 5, 1837. "We shall see if that event will make him steady," wrote Clay. "I sincerely hope it may."[8] A year later the couple had their first child, Lucretia Hart Clay. Apparently the marriage did "steady" Thomas. No further complaints of his drinking appear in his father's letters.

Another cause for joy was the overwhelming electoral victories scored by the Whigs over their Democratic opponents in the summer election in Kentucky. It was a sure sign that the people placed the blame for the depression squarely at the door of the Democratic administration in Washington. The victories in Kentucky were soon repeated in other western states, and there was every reason to believe that the Democrats could be completely routed in the next presidential election.

It must have given Clay some satisfaction to know that his prediction last winter in the Senate about what would happen in the wake of Jackson's "experiments" with the currency and banking had come true. His prediction about financial disaster was fully realized. And he certainly relished the thought that "the Hero of the Hermitage has lived to hear himself cursed as bitterly and as loudly as any of his Class of whom History treats."[9] It was an act of justice long overdue.

Before long men around the country were writing Clay to declare their support should he agree to another run for the presidency in 1840. But it was far too premature to make any commitments. In fact, he was shocked to hear that a meeting of New York Whigs had publicly announced their intention to offer Webster as a candidate. How could they be so stupid? he asked. They

---

7. Clay to Christopher Hughes, June 18, 1837, in Clay, *Papers*, IX, 49–50.

8. Clay to Thomas Hart Clay, October 8, 1837, Clay to James B. Clay, October 19, 1837, in Clay, *Papers*, IX, 84, 87.

9. Clay to Christopher Hughes, June 18, 1837, in Clay, *Papers*, IX, 49.

leave themselves open to the charge that "their impatience will not allow them to wait until the fruit is ripe but prompts them to pluck it before it is mature." If we initiate a campaign for the presidency at this early date while the country is in the "paroxism" of suffering produced by the "disordered Currency and prostrated business," we expose "our patriotism to a charge of selfishness and insincerity." While it is true, he went on, that Webster was handsomely received during his recent tour of the West, do not be deceived. The people displayed "homage to his acknowledged ability," not any desire to support him for the presidency. "Ambition has a powerful blinding effect," he wrote—and he should surely know. "And I think Mr. Websters case is a shocking proof of it." Within six months of his devastating defeat last fall in the presidential election, said Clay, Senator Webster begins a long and arduous tour "with the evident purpose of becoming a Candidate again."

Clay made it clear that he wanted his friends to remain quiet, to do nothing to initiate campaign activities on his behalf. Their first object must be to seek union on a single candidate who would be acceptable to the great mass of Whigs. The last thing they needed to do was repeat the disaster of the previous campaign by fielding more than one candidate. He strongly favored a national convention once that candidate had been identified. And he thought the approaching special session might be helpful in finding that person. Would it be himself? Possibly. "Above all, I am most desirous not to seem, as in truth I am not, importunate for any public office whatever; nevertheless, if I were persuaded that a majority of my fellow-citizens wished to assign me to their highest executive office, that sense of duty by which I have ever been guided, would prompt obedience to their will; candor, however, obliges me to say, that I have not seen sufficient evidence of such a wish."[10]

Still, Clay kept getting letters from New York, South Carolina, Louisiana, Tennessee, Georgia, Ohio, Indiana, and elsewhere, he said, which declared that Whigs in these states preferred him above all others in the party. But what he could not and would not abide was "to be run down by other Candidates or would be Candidates on our own side." For them to bring up the "prejudices against me in the Jackson or V. Buren party," as though other candidates like Webster and Calhoun were free of such prejudices, was ludicrous. Without getting into invidious comparisons, he declared, if "my friends" wish to advance my candidacy, they might "point to my services, to my sacrifices, to the calumnies of which I have been the object if not the victim, to my early prediction of the fatal effects of electing Genl Jackson, to the uniformity of my opposition to him, and to my denunciation of those measures which have spread bankruptcy and ruin throughout the Land." But do not hold public meetings yet, he cautioned. It is far too premature.[11]

10. Clay to Matthew L. Davis, July 3, 1837, Clay to Waddy Thompson, Jr., July 8, 1837, Clay to George D. Prentice, August 14, 1837, Clay to the Committee of New York City Whigs, August 8, 1837, in Clay, *Papers,* IX, 54–55, 58, 69–71, 66–68.
11. Clay to Prentice, August 14, 1837, in Clay, *Papers,* IX, 69–71.

In mentioning prejudices, Clay obviously had the corrupt bargain charges in mind. They were invariably brought up each time he campaigned for the presidency. And he admitted that they "unfortunately accomplished their object," although he thanked "God that I have been permitted to live down those charges. . . . Our afflicted Country is now bleeding, in consequence of their success, and when its wounds will be healed God only knows."[12]

In any event, he hoped that the special session would "produce concentration" among Whigs so that they could find their candidate, defeat the Democrats, and rescue the country from further ruin.

Clay left for Washington in August, heading up the Ohio River to Wheeling and White Sulphur Springs, his favorite watering hole, and then on to the capital. His son John accompanied him on his way back to Princeton. In Washington Clay messed with Crittenden and Samuel Southard at Mrs. Handy's boardinghouse at the corner of Louisiana Avenue and Sixth Street. The special session began on September 4 and lasted until October 16.

President Van Buren sent down a message to the special or first session of the Twenty-fifth Congress on September 5, and after describing the financial crisis facing the nation and its causes—he cited the glut of paper money and credit for speculation—he went on to recommend the passage of legislation that would divorce the Treasury from the deposit banks. In effect he wanted an "independent treasury" system, one in which subtreasuries would be located in the leading cities to receive and disburse government revenues. The paper from state banks would not be accepted in payment of obligations to the government. Instead, he proposed issuing Treasury notes, which would be acceptable, a proposal that would obviously produce the happy result of expanding the supply of money in circulation. He also asked that the fourth installment of the Treasury surplus, due to be distributed on October 1, 1837, under the provisions of the Deposit-Distribution Act of 1836, be postponed.

Van Buren faced an extremely difficult situation in making these suggestions, for he walked a tight line between Democratic hard-money Radicals, like Benton—who were sometimes sneered at as locofocos[13]—and Democratic soft-money Conservatives, like Rives and Tallmadge. The two groups advanced conflicting ideas on the best approach to the fiscal crisis. By recommending Treasury notes and refusing paper money from state banks, Van Buren hoped to satisfy both sides of his party. "The Conservatives (for so they denominate themselves)," wrote Clay, "are said to be resolved to make battle with their quondam friends." Happily, the issue tended to give the Whigs

---

12. Clay to Seth Wheatley, August 18, 1837, in Clay, *Papers*, IX, 71–72.

13. This radical movement within the Democratic party originated in New York and received its unusual name when a group of radical Democrats used "locofoco" matches to light candles at a meeting held on October 29, 1835, in New York City after the more conservative Democrats turned off the lights. Locofocos argued for free trade, elimination of paper money, and the end of monopolies or the granting of favors or subsides to private business. Frequently the term "locofoco" was applied to all Jacksonians by the Whigs.

greater coherence than they had had in years and, at the same time, divide the Democrats and possibly initiate a new coalition of political forces. The "divorce bill," as some called the independent treasury plan, might become the "touchstone of parties," as several senators, including Buchanan, predicted.[14]

Clay saw all the political advantages now available to the Whigs on account of the financial crisis. He also realized that this special session provided him with an excellent opportunity to win identification as the man who could best lead his party to victory in 1840. Whigs would look for leadership. They would look for the man who could further coalesce the many groups that had come together to form their party. Long before he arrived in Washington, Clay knew he could be that man because he could provide unparalleled leadership, both in and out of Congress. Long before his arrival he had decided that he must demonstrate his indisputable right to the party's nomination. His actions and speeches throughout the session, therefore, all were aimed and calculated toward achieving that end.

But his task was a formidable one—especially in the Senate, where Democrats outnumbered Whigs thirty out of fifty-two. The contest between Whigs and Democrats would be much closer in the House, where the two parties split evenly in strength.[15]

Shortly after the President's message had been delivered, Clay called a meeting "of a small number of the members of the party" to plan strategy. Clay naturally dominated the group. He "was in so great a hurry that he took ground of opposition the very first moment after the reading of the President's message," even though not all the leading Whigs, including Daniel Webster, had arrived in the city. His haste only reminded everyone that he sometimes lacked control, that he was too "impetuous," too authoritarian.

At the meeting Clay particularly opposed Van Buren's recommendation to postpone payment of the fourth installment of the surplus revenue to the states on October 1. He believed that the Whigs should focus their attack on that part of the President's message, and he strongly "urged it upon the meeting."[16]

As the session got under way, Senator Silas Wright, the administration's leading spokesman, presented a series of bills to implement the President's proposals. Clay wasted no time in attacking them. He argued his views on the postponement of the distribution of the fourth installment of the surplus in his first speech in the Senate on September 15. In typical fashion he mocked the Democratic leaders, particularly Senator Wright. With one hand, he said, they take away funds from the states that could use them; with the other they turn

14. John Niven, *Martin Van Buren: The Romantic Age of American Politics* (New York, 1983), p. 423; Donald B. Cole, *Martin Van Buren and the American Political System* (Princeton, 1984), pp. 302–304; Clay to Henry Clay, Jr., September 8, 1837, in Clay, *Papers,* IX, 73; the Buchanan quote is taken from Major L. Wilson, *The Presidency of Martin Van Buren* (Lawrence, Kan. 1984), p. 62.
15. Cole, *Van Buren,* p. 306.
16. Adams, *Memoirs,* IX, 369.

over funds to those that will not use them. "That is to say, Government will not receive the paper of the country, and is about to create a paper of its own, which the country is expected to receive!" Thus "all the promises which have been made to us of the flowing of gold and silver all over the country—these promises of a better currency result in the issue of ten millions of paper money!"[17]

But the Senate dismissed Clay's arguments. By the vote of twenty-eight to seventeen it approved the President's suggestion to postpone the fourth installment of the distribution of revenue to the states. Clay voted against the bill. Later the Senate also passed a bill by a vote of twenty-five to six to issue ten million dollars in Treasury notes of denominations no less than one hundred dollars. Again Clay voted in the negative.[18]

He sustained yet another defeat on September 21, when Senator Wright brought in a resolution against the establishment of another national bank. Over the Kentuckian's strong objections, the resolution passed the Senate, thirty-one to fifteen.

The upper house then turned to the President's independent treasury plan. To everyone's surprise, John C. Calhoun came out in favor of it, but during the ensuing debate he added an amendment that would allow the government to accept both specie and the paper of specie-paying banks until 1840, after which nothing but specie would be accepted. John Quincy Adams dryly called it "Calhoun's bargain and sale of himself to Van Buren."

Calhoun a Van Buren man? That was the wonder of the decade. Even the President was startled by it. But the South Carolinian genuinely approved the idea of an independent treasury for the government. Besides, he had never been a Whig in the true sense. He cooperated with the Whig party and on many occasions joined his voice with that of Clay and of Webster to denounce the policies and practices of King Andrew. But that was the past. Now he felt a new era might begin, one in which he could play a commanding part.[19]

As debate over an independent treasury began, the Conservative William C. Rives offered his own bill, which would establish an association of state banks to serve as the fiscal agent of the government and mandate Treasury use of bank notes. And thus began the battle between the locofocos and their soft-money opponents.

Clay's major address to his colleagues and the American people came on September 25. It was a three-hour harangue. In it he attacked the independent treasury bill as ineffectual in correcting the disorders of the country and certain to bring about the "total subversion" of state banks. And why, he asked, is yet another new experiment being foisted on the American people? Why another untried expedient? "The people of this country are tired of experiments." If

17. *Register of Debates*, 25th Congress, 1st session, pp. 45–47.
18. *Register of Debates*, 25th Congress, 1st session, pp. 45, 1372.
19. Wiltse, *Calhoun, Nullifier*, pp. 342–356; *Register of Debates*, 25th Congress, 1st session, pp. 50–66; Adams, *Memoirs*, IX, 398.

this bill is passed, he predicted, the system will become "a vast and ramified connexion of Government banks, of which the principal will be at Washington, and every sub-treasurer will be a branch."

The destruction of the United States Bank, he charged, not only undermined the strong currency system that had existed but produced inflation, speculation, and finally the suspension of specie payments by the state banks. To make his point, he resorted to sarcasm. Van Buren's argument that the suspension of specie payments resulted from speculation was like arguing that a homicide produced by a gunshot was really caused by "the leaden ball, and not the man who levelled the piece."

The Panic of 1837 originated from five factors, said Clay: veto of the Bank bill; removal of the deposits from the BUS; the Gold Coinage Act of 1836, which reevaluated gold and silver on a ratio of sixteen to one; poor administration of the Deposit Act; and the Specie Circular. He might also have mentioned Jackson's veto of his land bill, for that bill, he claimed, would have distributed gradually and regularly the proceeds of land sales to the states and prevented the enormous surplus in the Treasury that culminated in the suspension of specie payments. All these factors, he went on, resulted from the despotic government created by Andrew Jackson and blindly supported by the Democratic party.

Clay then made a long fervent appeal for the economic advantages of sound, specie-backed paper money. And he resorted once again to his standard remedy: compromise. Some in the chamber grunted when they heard the word. But why not a compromise? he asked. Let us have both specie and paper, a "mixed medium" of two-thirds paper and one-third specie.

Clay expressed his surprise over Calhoun's acceptance of the basic idea of an independent treasury system, and he gave Rives's bill only tepid support. He thought the latter's suggestion impracticable but said he would vote for it over Van Buren's plan because "it is harmless . . . and looks to the preservation of the State banks."

Clay concluded by advising the Senate to postpone action on the independent treasury bill until December, when the next session of Congress was due to meet. He really believed that the only answer to the nation's problems was the establishment of another national bank, "that monster so frightful in the eyes of old maids, old bachelors, and old politicians." But he declared such action by Congress most unwise until the conviction of its necessity "is deeply impressed upon the people, and clearly manifested by them." Meanwhile, he said, "let us go home and mix with and consult our constituents."[20]

There was no reply to Clay's speech. Senator John King of Georgia moved to postpone the question until the following session. It was defeated, nineteen to twenty-seven, "the conservatives . . . voting agt. the postponement," reported Clay, "and some of our friends being absent."[21]

20. *Congressional Globe*, 25th Congress, 2d session, pp. 418–420; Clay, *Works*, VI, 61–86.
21. Clay to Southard, September 25, 1837, in Clay, *Papers*, IX, 80.

Again the Senate turned a deaf ear to Clay's advice when, on October 4, by a vote of 26 to 20, it passed the independent treasury bill with Calhoun's amendment attached. However, the House tabled it on October 14, by a vote of 120 to 107, with the Conservatives joining the Whigs to block its passage.[22]

Clay suffered another setback when he unsuccessfully argued against the issuance of Treasury notes. How can you be so inconsistent? he asked his Democratic colleagues in a speech on October 10. If the government can issue bank notes, how is it that the government does not have the power to create a national bank? "You resort to a Government paper currency, after having exclaimed against every currency except that of gold and silver!"[23]

As soon as he sat down, the Senate voted. The Treasury note bill passed, twenty-five to six, with Clay voting against it. And on that action the special session virtually came to an end. A few days later Congress adjourned.

The session was hardly one that Clay could point to with pride or a sense of accomplishment. True, the Democrats dominated the Senate, and in most instances the members voted strictly along party lines. Still, Clay had expected to achieve more in order to advance his presidential candidacy, and that he had failed to do. Quite possibly the failure arose from his attitude toward the present crisis. He took the position that the Whigs should adopt a "system of nonaction in Congress": propose nothing to address the depression and let the Democrats wallow in their own mudhole. Besides, he said, what can the Whigs do? Come up with another "Experiment"? The American people are sick to death of experiments. They had enough under Jackson. The only answer to the financial crisis, he pontificated, was another national bank, "and the public mind is not now . . . prepared for a National bank." But give it time. Perhaps in another year or so the people will finally see the wisdom of establishing such an institution and in due course elect a President who will oblige them.[24]

In any event, Clay returned home after the close of the session to wait and watch the results of the upcoming fall elections, especially the one in New York. He was getting weary of crossing and recrossing the mountains every few months, he said, but the only solution to that problem was permanent retirement. Lucretia had agreed to return with him to Washington for the opening of the second session in December but at the last minute chose to stay home. By this time she had totally given up the idea of ever setting up residence in Washington again. In the minds of some, she was becoming a recluse.[25]

The fall elections went spectacularly well for the Whigs, and New York was virtually "revolutionized." Clay likened the results to the capture of Lord Cornwallis at Yorktown and the defeat of Napoleon at Waterloo. "The People," he rejoiced, "with a spontaneous and enthusiastic rush to the Polls, re-

22. *Register of Debates,* 25th Congress, 1st session, p. 511. Earlier Rives's bill in favor of the state banks had been defeated, twenty-six to twenty-two.

23. *Register of Debates,* 25th Congress, 1st session, pp. 520–521.

24. Clay to Alexander Hamilton, December 6, 1837, in Clay, *Papers,* IX, 97.

25. Clay to Brooke, December 10, 1837, in Clay, *Papers,* IX, 101.

solved to rescue their Country from impending ruin. And they have rescued it, nobly rescued it. God bless them; God bless them forever!" Without organization, without leaders, without handbills, without "runners to stimulate exertion," the electorate forcefully rebuked the monstrous experiments of Andrew Jackson and his bankrupt Democratic party. The "brilliant" victories—and they occurred in Tennessee, Indiana, Maine, Rhode Island, Pennsylvania, and New Jersey as well as in Kentucky and New York—had resulted from the obvious economic plight of the nation, but also because of the support of the Conservatives. "We could not have succeeded without them," admitted Clay, "and without them we cannot maintain the ground which has been won by joint forces. They risked everything. . . . Both from principle and policy I shall give them the right hand of friendship." And he carried out his promise. Several times during the ensuing congressional session he invited the leaders of the Conservatives to caucus with the Whigs about their future actions.[26]

While Clay was striking this note of conciliation and cooperation with the Conservatives, John C. Calhoun in South Carolina virtually declared his separation from the Whigs. In a public letter to the Edgefield *Advertiser* published on November 16, he insisted that the Panic of 1837 had totally reordered political alignments throughout the country. Supporting the Whigs will undoubtedly help them to victory, he admitted, but it will do nothing for southerners. Whigs favor a consolidated government, protective tariffs, a national bank, and internal improvements which the advocates of states' rights abhor. If he and his friends assisted the Van Buren administration in its efforts to bring about the divorce of government and banking, he continued, political parties would again be formed "on the old and natural division of state rights and national" prerogatives, a division which most benefits the South and is "most congenial to our system."[27]

This Edgefield letter presumed to argue that Calhoun and the nullifiers had not changed their political philosophy in the slightest. It was the Democrats who had shifted their position and now conceded that banks and currency were beyond governmental control. "If once united," Calhoun wrote, "we will rally round the old State Rights party all in every section, who are opposed to consolidation or the overaction of the Central Government." The letter was an extraordinary display of verbal and political legerdemain but proved convincing to the voters of South Carolina. For nearly a decade nullifiers had been drilled into hating Van Buren with a passion. Now they were called to render him their support.[28]

Thus, as Congress reconvened in December to consider once more possible solutions to the Panic of 1837, the Whig party was gaining strength among

26. Porter to Clay, November 12, 1837, Clay to Robert Swartwout, November 21, 1837, Clay to Gulian C. Verplanck et al., December 8, 1837, Clay to Porter, December 5, 1837, Clay to Nathaniel P. Tallmadge, January 1838, in Clay, *Papers,* IX, 91, 93, 98–99, 96, 117.
27. Calhoun, *Papers,* XIII, 636–641; Wiltse, *Calhoun, Nullifier,* pp. 360–361.
28. Calhoun, *Papers,* XIII, 637; Niven, *Calhoun,* p. 232.

Conservative Democrats and losing it among supporters of states' rights. But this only reconfirmed Calhoun's contention that "the old and natural divisions" between parties were reasserting themselves.

When Clay returned to Washington, his first major engagement was his presidential address on December 12, 1837, before the twenty-first annual meeting of the American Colonization Society. Recently he had been getting more and more letters from leading emancipationists urging him to provide greater leadership of their cause, despite his antipathy toward abolitionism. "I have always cherished the hope," wrote James G. Birney, a former member of the Colonization Society and now secretary of the American Anti-Slavery Society in New York, "that you would be . . . the friend of Human Liberty. Most sincerely do I believe, that *you* could bring slavery to a speedy peaceful and happy termination throughout our country." So fixed in the public mind was the perception of Clay as the Great Compromiser that increasingly he was begged to utilize his wisdom and skill to find a solution to the slavery question and thereby spare the country the awful possibility of another national calamity.

Lewis Tappan, the New York philanthropist, again pleaded with him "to be *the man* who, at this junction, would nobly stand forth as the champion of human rights." But Clay only reaffirmed his abhorrence of abolitionists. "I most conscientiously believe that the Northern agitation of the question of Abolition is productive of no good," he responded to Tappan. "I believe it injurious to the unfortunate black race and hazardous to the harmony, peace and union of the whites." He then told Tappan abruptly and flatly that he had no time to discuss the matter further and doubted whether it would lead to any useful purpose.[29]

But Clay wanted everyone to know that he was no friend of slavery. "I think it an evil; but I believe it better that Slaves should remain Slaves than be set loose as free men among us." As for the recent argument of nullifiers that "slavery is a *blessing*," Clay regarded that notion as "indefensible, unintelligible, and brings reproach upon us."[30]

Clay set forth some of these ideas in his presidential address to the American Colonization Society. He congratulated its members on the extensive territory acquired by the society in Africa, where thousands of freemen had been transported and where eight flourishing settlements and towns "that abound in civilization" had been established. He reminded his audience that the society was founded to colonize free persons of color, not to perpetuate or abolish slavery or "let loose the untutored and unprepared slaves upon society." The members of the society, declared Clay, generally regarded slavery as a "deplorable evil," just as he did. The society had never promised to bring about the

29. Clay to Frederick Freeman, September 27, 1837, James Birney to Clay, December 22, 1837, Lewis Tappan to Clay, May 1, June 5, 1838, Clay to Tappan, July 6, 1838, in Clay, *Papers,* IX, 80–81, 111–113, 199–200, 212.
30. Clay to Cornelius C. Baldwin, August 28, 1838, in Clay, *Papers,* IX, 223.

separation of the two races by colonizing the Africans. "We promised only to
be the pioneer, and to show the practicability of the principle" of colonization.
A sudden and instantaneous separation, even if it were possible, would be
good for neither race, he concluded. It could be, in fact, a disaster.

Clay sincerely believed that colonization would work and solve the slavery
problem if enough money, say, one million dollars a year, could be raised.
Earlier he had hoped that the federal government would assign some of its
surplus to the states for this purpose. Barring colonization, no other solution
seemed feasible to Clay, and the alternative might be bloody conflict.[31]

The slavery question became a leading topic of debate in Congress during
its present session, although the President in his message spoke mostly about
the panic and the need for an independent treasury. Even Clay himself admitted to his friend Peter B. Porter that "we have been much excited here about
Abolition—that is some Southern Ultras, who are quite as mischievous as the
Abolitionists, have been."[32]

The ruckus began over the submission of petitions to abolish slavery in
the District of Columbia. The House had already passed a gag rule the previous May 18 by simply laying all antislavery petitions on the table. Clay innocently suggested that the petitions go to an appropriate committee, where they
could be studied "coolly and dispassionately." Later it could present a report
on its findings. Senator William C. Preston of South Carolina responded by
asserting that the petitions would stir up national excitement and therefore
should not be received at all. Clay replied by warning his colleagues of the
danger of inadvertently winning support for the abolitionists from those who
may oppose the emancipation of slaves but who support the "great republican
right of petition." Making martyrs of abolitionists would certainly not work to
the advantage of slaveholders.

Calhoun then joined the debate. He agreed with Preston about increasing
national excitement and cautioned against turning the Senate into a forum for
a discussion of abolitionism which could endanger the Union. Clay fired back
that he had no fear for the Union but hoped to "tranquilize every part" of it.
Furthermore, slavery in the District was different from slavery in the states.
Congress may not trifle with slavery in the states, he said, but it could, if it
wished, terminate it in the District. On that point, unfortunately, Clay saw no
possibility of its happening. "The actual abolition of slavery in the district is
about as likely to occur as the abolition of the Christian religion," he joked.
Besides, Congress has the right and duty to receive petitions on the subject. It
would be grossly improper to refuse them.[33]

The Senate chose to table the question, with most Democrats voting for

31. *Niles' Weekly Register,* December 23, 1837.

32. Clay to Porter, December 24, 1837, in Clay, *Papers,* IX, 114.

33. *Congressional Globe,* 25th Congress, 2d session, pp. 34, 37–38. See also William L. Van Deburg, "Henry Clay, the Right of Petition, and Slavery in the Nation's Capital," *Register of Kentucky
Historical Society,* LXVIII (April 1970), pp. 132–146.

tabling and most Whigs and Conservatives voting against. But Calhoun would not leave the matter alone. On December 27, 1837, he introduced six resolutions embracing the entire question of slavery and the nature of the Union. It advanced Calhoun's compact theory of the Constitution, emphasized the exclusive right of the states to control their own institutions, asserted that the federal government was the agent of the states and could not be the means by which one state might attempt to destroy the interests of another state, declared slavery safeguarded under the Constitution against any interference, claimed the abolition of slavery in the District would be a dangerous assault on the institutions of all slaveholding states, and (with obvious reference to Texas) insisted that any opposition to territorial expansion or the admission of new states based on abolitionism would threaten the Union.[34]

All along Calhoun had been headed toward a harder stand on the slavery question, particularly after he had failed to win passage of a bill in 1836 that would prohibit the circulation of antislavery literature through the mail. Clay opposed the bill at the time as unconstitutional and a clear-cut infringement of the freedom of speech and the press.[35]

With Calhoun's introduction of the six all-embracing resolutions, Clay was sure he had spotted the South Carolinian's game. "The professed object [of the resolutions] is Slavery—their real aim to advance the political interest of the mover and to affect mine." Calhoun had set two traps to "affect me at the South—one relating to Abolition, and the other to Texas."[36]

Because he regarded Calhoun's resolutions as "abstract . . . as a metaphysical mind can well devise," Clay countered on January 9, 1838, with six of his own. Before presenting them to the Senate, he prefaced them with the remark that the spread of the spirit of abolitionism in the North was a direct consequence of the perceived denial of the constitutional right of petition by Congress to abolitionists. Keep the question of abolition distinct from the right of petition, from the Texas question, and from all other subjects, Clay said. Let it stand by itself, "alone, unmixed with the rest of the community, without the general sympathy, and exposed to the overwhelming force of the union opinion of all who desire the peace, the harmony, and the union of this Confederacy." He then proposed his six resolutions:

1. Domestic slavery is subject to the exclusive control of the slaveholding states.

2. Petitions touching the abolition of slavery *in states* where it exists shall be rejected out of hand by the Senate.

3. Abolition of slavery in the District cannot be effected without breaking

34. *Congressional Globe,* 25th Congress, 2d session, p. 55. For Calhoun's compact theory of government, see Wiltse, *John C. Calhoun, Sectionist* (Indianapolis and New York, 1951), passim.

35. *Register of Debates,* 24th Congress, 1st Session, pp. 1728–1729; for a full discussion of the attempt to censure the mails see Remini, *Jackson,* III, 251–264.

36. Clay to Brooke, January 13, 1838, Clay to Porter, January 10, 1838, in Clay, *Papers,* IX, 129, 127.

faith with Virginia and Maryland, which ceded the land that created the District, even though it is within the full power of Congress to act in the matter. Such action, however, would seriously alarm the South beyond any conceivable benefit to the Union.

4. Abolition of slavery in the Territory of Florida, also within congressional power, would be inexpedient at present since Florida would decide that question for itself when it enters the Union as a state.

5. The Constitution provides no power to prohibit the slave trade or movement of slaves within and between slaveholding states.

6. The commitment of the American people to the Union is the surest bulwark of liberty.

In his remarks Clay brought up the question of petitions and declared again that the Constitution required the Senate to receive them. "If a man were to present me a petition," he said, "to grant him Ashland. . . ."

"Or Orozimbo," called out another senator, referring to Clay's prize Durham short-horned bull of which he was very proud.

"Or Orozimbo," Clay quickly conceded, "(whose death I am sorry to announce to the Senate, and he was a great loss, public and private,) I would, without the least apprehension for the loss of my property, put it in my pocket, or lay it upon the table." Will not the senator, he continued, recognize the difference between receiving a petition and granting it?

Clay pointed out to his colleagues the differences between himself and Calhoun. The South Carolinian "goes for strong language, menacing tones, and irritating measures; I for temperate, but firm language, conciliation, and for obeying the injunction of the Constitution in respect to the right of petition."

That last remark was pitched straight out to the American people so that they might note the contrast between the hothead and the statesman.

Clay concluded his speech with a domestic allusion. "In private life if a wife pouts, and frets, and scolds," should the husband threaten divorce or separation? Of course not. "He would approach the lady with kind and conciliatory language, and apply those natural and more agreeable remedies, which never fail to restore domestic harmony." At that the audience smiled its pleasure, and Clay took his seat.[37]

If Calhoun meant to puncture Clay's presidential candidacy, he ended up by puncturing his own. "I have borne myself in such manner," Clay wrote the following day, "as to lose nothing neither at the South nor at the North. Later he wrote: "I will turn the tables upon Mr. Calhoun."[38]

Clay himself had to admit that these resolutions and counterresolutions constituted a royal waste of time. "We have been engaged in the Senate . . . in

37. *Congressional Globe,* 25th Congress, 2d session, appendix, pp. 57–60.
38. Clay to Porter, January 10, 1838, Clay to Brooke, January 13, 1838, in Clay, *Papers,* IX, 127, 128.

the most unprofitable discussion that ever engrossed the attention of a deliberative body." But the Senate persisted in its attention, and after debating and
quarreling and amending Calhoun's resolutions, it adopted all but the last,
which it tabled. Again, in passing, the Kentuckian drew attention to Calhoun's
unwillingness to modify his resolutions while, at the same time, he, Clay,
accepted and voted for the first four of them. Clay's resolution regarding the
abolition of slavery in the District also passed after an amendment with a
comfortable majority.[39]

Several times during the debate Clay and Calhoun snapped at each other,
and on one occasion the Kentuckian asked the South Carolinian not to interrupt him with sudden outbursts or irrelevant questions. It proved to be the
first round of a prolonged battle between the two titans.

The second round came the following month, and it was a free-for-all.

39. *Congressional Globe,* 25th Congress, 2d session, appendix, pp. 60–62, 63, 65.

TWENTY-NINE

The War of
the Titans

THE BROUHAHA erupted in February. It had been brewing for months, ever since Calhoun deserted the Whigs and rejoined the Democrats. And Henry Clay initiated it.

The business of the Senate, under the direction of the administration's principal spokesman, Silas Wright, had turned back to the independent treasury plan. For a time the divorce bill looked as though it would sail through the upper house without ruffling the surface. Calhoun spoke in its favor, taking what he called "higher and broader grounds" in his arguments. Then William Rives and Nathaniel P. Tallmadge, the Conservative leaders, argued for a plan supporting state banks. Finally, on Monday, February 19, 1838, Clay rose to respond to the administration's proposal, and in the process he stooped to personal attacks against Andrew Jackson, Martin Van Buren, and his former comrade-in-arms John C. Calhoun.

Van Buren was an old hand at dealing with personal abuse, and he invariably reacted to it with aplomb. He smiled and appeared outwardly indifferent to criticism. His true feelings always remained hidden. But not Calhoun. He could not abide personal attacks—not from anyone—and least of all from those (practically everybody) who could not match the excellence of his "metaphysical thought processes."

Clay delivered a four-and-a-half-hour speech that left him exhausted but exhilarated. He began with yet another blast at Jackson, under whose direction, he said, "society has been uprooted, virtue punished, vice rewarded, and talents and intellectual endowments despised; brutality, vulgarism, and loco focoism upheld, cherished and countenanced. Ages will roll around before the moral and political ravages which have been committed will, I fear, cease to be discernible." Clay then referred—perhaps unwisely—to his vote for Adams in the House election of 1825. "Immediately after my vote, a rancorous war was commenced against me, and all the barking dogs let loose upon me. . . . But I thank my God that I stand here, firm and erect, unbent, unbroken, unsubdued, unawed, ready to denounce the mischievous measure of his Administration, and ready to denounce this, its legitimate offspring, the most pernicious of them all."

So much for Andrew Jackson. And now for Martin Van Buren. Has the Magician ever done anything to advance the honor and glory and welfare of the American people? asked Clay. "No, no; his country was not in his thoughts. Party, party, filled the place in his bosom which country should have occupied." He was nothing but the "tool" of the old reprobate, happy to carry out his frightful policies and principles.

As for Calhoun, what may be said about a man who once referred to his newfound friend Martin Van Buren "as an animal, crafty, skulking, and mean"? And why did he desert the Whigs? He wanted to prevent "the success of the common cause. He took up his musket, knapsack, and shot-pouch, and joined the other party. He went, horse, foot and dragoon, and he himself composed the whole corps." Oh, how often "have we witnessed the Senator from South Carolina, with woeful countenance and in doleful strains, pouring forth touching and mournful eloquence on the degeneracy of the time and the downward tendency of the republic?" What happened? In his Edgefield letter Calhoun claimed that the impeding victory, which "our common arms" were about to achieve, would "not enure to him and his party" but to the exclusive benefit of his allies and their cause. "I thought," thundered Clay, ". . . we had been contending together for our common country, for her violated rights, her threatened liberties, her prostrate Constitution. Never did I suppose that personal or party considerations entered into our views."

Clay now addressed the content of Calhoun's defense of the independent treasury plan. He called it "plausible, abstract, metaphysical, and generalizing." But, continued Clay, it had nothing to do with the real "business of human life." He then shredded Calhoun's argument point by point by assaulting its contentions and making light of its examples. It was one of Henry Clay's finest hatchet jobs.[1]

The speech, former Senator from North Carolina Willie P. Mangum wrote to Clay, was "one of the greatest, if not the very greatest, because of its practical & useful tone & pitch of character, that you have made in my time.—A little too spicy, perhaps, towards Mr. C—For you ought to remember, that truth often hurts more than the worst calumny." Senator Benton thought the speech "bore the impress of careful elaboration, and especially the last part."[2]

---

1. Clay, *Works*, VI, 94–133. "You saw Clays wanton and mad attack on the nullifiers," wrote Senator William C. Preston of South Carolina. "Was it not scandalous—In truth he was hurried away by his pruriency for a joke—but it was poison in jest." Preston to Mangum, [March 28, 1838], in Mangum, *Papers*, II, 517.
2. Mangum to Clay, March 26, 1838, in Clay, *Papers*, IX, 166; Benton, *Thirty Years' View*, II, 98. Calhoun winced with every thrust by Clay and his allies. "He *Mr. Clay* and the whole national

When Clay concluded his address, all eyes turned to Calhoun for his reply. Calhoun rose. He looked cold and forbidding. Harriet Martineau said he looked as if he had never been born and could never be extinguished. She called him the "cast-iron man." Calhoun stood motionless for a moment, as though pondering a great "metaphysical abstraction," and then solemnly announced that he would reply at his leisure. "Mr. Clay made a very long reply, but in the main very feeble and personal," he told his daughter. "I intend to give him, as good as he sent, and so informed him on the conclusion of his speech."[3]

It took him three weeks to respond. During that time "the cast-iron man" prepared himself to the utmost, even reading Demosthenes' oration "On the Crown." On Saturday, March 10, he finally gave the speech everyone keenly anticipated. The galleries, corridors, and lobbies were again packed with people as he stood at his place and began his address. Unlike Clay, whose hands, arms, head, and especially his eyes, emphasized his words, "whether gentle, persuasive, humorous, earnest, vehement, or denunciatory," Calhoun moved hardly at all. No action; he needed none; "it would have been out of place." His words went straight to the mark. They were simple, terse, clear, and direct. He peered steadily at the presiding officer, rarely at any of the other senators. Unlike Clay's voice, which was "soft as a lute or full as a trumpet," a voice of "wonderful modulation, sweetness, and power," Calhoun's voice was sharp, somewhat reedy, and he spoke quickly in near-staccato fashion "but with such a clear enunciation that every word was distinctly heard."[4]

Calhoun's oration, said Senator Benton, was masterly: "profoundly meditated and elaborately composed." Like Clay's, it was divided into two parts: one personal; the other substantive. He had attempted in all his speeches, he said, to avoid any remark that might be construed as personal or partisan. But the senator from Kentucky had replied with an ad hominem and premeditated attack on him. Why? Because he could not answer the argument advanced favoring the independent treasury plan nor even a particle of it, so he substituted personalities. As for Clay's contention that he had switched sides and positions, Calhoun denied it. He could never do such a thing. To prove his point, he then launched into an extended history of his career and positions on various subjects and issues during his long public service. He challenged Clay's interpretation of his Edgefield letter. The administration, he declared, had shifted its ground to the one he and the "whole State-rights party" occupied in 1834. It was not power or place that guided his actions but principle and

---

party are as bitter as gall," wrote the South Carolinian. "Their hired scriblers and press are daily misrepresenting in the grossest manner every thing I say or do." Calhoun to Armistead Burt, January 24, 1838, in Calhoun, *Papers,* XIV, 105.

3. Martineau, *Retrospect of Western Travel,* I, 149; Calhoun to Anna Maria Calhoun, February 24, 1838, in Calhoun, *Papers,* XIV, 157.

4. Sargent, *Public Men and Events,* II, 34; Benton, *Thirty Years' View,* II, 98; Cole, *Van Buren,* p. 333.

policy. "I, who have changed no opinion, abandoned no principle, and deserted no party— . . . to be told that it is left to time to disclose my motives! The imputation sinks to the earth. . . . I stamp it with scorn in the dust. I pick up the shaft, which fell harmless at my feet. I hurl it back. What the Senator charges on me unjustly *he has actually done*. He went over on a memorable occasion, and did not leave it to time to disclose his motives."

Now Calhoun began to react physically as he spoke—most uncharacteristically. When he said he stamped the charge with scorn in the dust, he actually raised his foot and brought it down on the floor with great force. And when he said he hurled back the dart, he looked squarely at Clay "with a look of intensified scorn, defiance, and triumph."[5]

The audience held its breath, for Calhoun had alluded to the corrupt bargain charge by his remark about "a memorable occasion."

Clay jumped to his feet. He felt ill, he said, and really should not have come to the Senate. "But as I *am* [here], I AM self-poised and prepared." Then with soaring sarcasm he added: "I ask not two or three weeks to prepare my speech in reply to the Senator from South Carolina."

Clay denied that he initiated the attack. "When I read in his [Edgefield] letter"—and here Clay held up a copy of the letter for all to see—"the unjust reproaches cast upon my friends and myself, I was most reluctantly compelled to change my opinion of the honorable Senator. . . . And after all he has said and published of those he lately acted with, can he really persuade himself that he occupies on this occasion a defensive attitude?"

Calhoun claims "he has left no party, and joined no party! No, none. He expects us to believe this, though we see him in frequent consultations and intimate association with the other party?"

At one point Clay focused his sights on the doctrine of nullification. He called it "a strange, impracticable, incomprehensible doctrine, that partakes of the character of the metaphysical school of German philosophy, or would be worthy of the puzzling theological controversies of the middle ages." Those words brought a snickering response from many visiters in the chamber.

Finally Clay turned to the corrupt bargain. The senator from South Carolina mentioned a "memorable occasion," he said. "If the senator means to allude to the stale and refuted calumny of George Kremer, I assure him I can hear it without the slightest emotion; and if he can find any fragment of that rent banner to cover his own aberrations, he is perfectly at liberty to enjoy all the shelter which it affords."

Representative John Quincy Adams had come into the Senate to hear the debate and sat close to Clay. Turning to Adams as he continued his speech, the Kentucky senator said: "Nor have I ever, for a single moment, regretted the vote I then gave for the eminent gentleman who sits beside me." His constitu-

5. Benton, *Thirty Years' View*, II, 98; *Congressional Globe*, 25th Congress, 2d session, appendix, pp. 176–181; Sargent, *Public Men and Events*, II, 37–39; Wiltse, *Calhoun, Nullifier*, pp. 380–382; Wilson, *Presidency of Van Buren*, pp. 104–105.

ents approved of his action, declared Clay, "and it is their glory as well as my own never to have concurred in the elevation of General Jackson."

He said he was proud and pleased that "I never in my life changed my deliberate opinion upon any great measure of national policy," except one. He opposed the Bank twenty-two years ago, he admitted, but like Madison, he changed his mind because of the financial disasters growing out of the War of 1812.

"We began our public career nearly together," he recalled, referring to Calhoun and himself; "we remained together throughout the war and down to the peace. . . . We concur now in nothing. We separate forever."

"Hoarse as he was," Calhoun responded that if Clay had not changed his principles, he had most certainly changed his company and now surrounded himself with the most distinguished members of the old Federalist party.

The two senators went back and forth with each other about whether or not they had shifted their positions in the last twenty years. There were brief, rapid rejoinders, but in this sort of debate Clay was clearly the master. Calhoun needed time to collect his thoughts, arrange his arguments, select his words. Clay did not. He was at his best in quick exchanges. "He was self-poised, ever ready; he could fire off-hand without rest."

According to one observer, Clay clearly had the advantage of Calhoun. He was adroit, animated, forceful, convincing. "Calhoun was not a ready debater." John Quincy Adams agreed, but of course, he sat there listening to Calhoun's allusion to a corrupt bargain. Clay drove the South Carolinian from his "defensive ground irrecoverably," the former President wrote. "There was rejoinder, surrejoinder, rebutter, and surrebutter. The truth and the victory were with Clay, who closed with a taunting hope that the settlement of accounts was as satisfactory to the Senator from South Carolina as it was to him."[6]

Clay himself was very gratified with his efforts. "I never was better satisfied with any Speech I ever made," he wrote his son. He told Nicholas Biddle that although he did not use the word "conspiracy" itself, he tried to prove in the speech that he felt there was in fact a "conspiracy" to destroy the entire banking system of the United States, starting with the BUS and ending now with an assault on state banks. "And I handled Mr. Calhoun without gloves," he gleefully added.[7]

But this battle did not end the war. Daniel Webster entered the contest two days later and gave what many considered the funniest, if not the finest, speech of his life. He joined forces with Clay to castigate Calhoun for his apostasy, and he did it with wit, sarcasm, and ridicule. It was truly a magnifi-

6. *Congressional Globe,* 25th Congress, 2d session, appendix, pp. 243–250, 632–641; *Niles' Weekly Register,* May 26, 1838; Sargent, *Public Men and Events,* II, 45; Wiltse, *Calhoun, Nullifier,* p. 382, gives a different reaction to the contest; Cole, *Van Buren,* p. 333; Adams, *Memoirs,* IX, 505–506.
7. Clay to Thomas H. Clay, February 23, 1838, Clay to Biddle, February 20, 1838, in Clay, *Papers,* IX, 150, 149.

cent demolition of Calhoun's pretense that he had pursued a consistent course throughout his political life.

"Where am I?" the Massachusetts senator mocked, rubbing his eyes. "In the Senate of the United States? Am I Daniel Webster? Is that John C. Calhoun of South Carolina," he said, pointing to the glowering nullifier, "the same gentleman that figured so largely in the House of Representatives in 1816, at the time the Bill creating a National Bank passed that body? What have I heard today? The Senator attempting to maintain his consistency . . . in my presence?"[8]

Never in the history of the Congress had there been such a debate, a debate of overwhelming dramatic and emotional power by three of the greatest statesmen and orators the nation had ever produced. The crowds that jammed the galleries, floor, and corridors enjoyed the unique experience of witnessing Clay's "glowing rhetoric," Calhoun's "nervous logic," and Webster's "overshadowing majesty."[9] Here in full view of the entire country was the Great Triumvirate tearing their coalition apart in oratory of unsurpassed eloquence. And they not only howled at each other's politics but over many months discussed and analyzed momentous national issues, such as slavery, abolition, expansion, depression, money and banking, public lands, and the nature of the Union. It was a stupendous moment in the parliamentary history of the United States. It set a level of debate never again equaled in this country.

Still another round in this war of the titans had to be fought before the contest ended. In the next Congress Clay tore into Calhoun again. He was goaded into it by the South Carolinian's decision to make personal peace with his longtime enemy President Martin Van Buren. A face-to-face encounter! It seemed unimaginable, inconceivable, totally impossible, in view of their past hostility and what it had done to the South Carolinian's hopes and plans for the presidential succession, but John C. Calhoun went to the White House, shook hands with the President, and completed his march back into the Democratic party that had begun during the special session of Congress in September 1837. At the Hermitage in Tennessee the aged but still active former President shrilled a warning. "Be careful of *Cateline*," Jackson cried, "he may be useful *but don't trust him.*"[10]

Calhoun's act of public "obeisance" was more than Clay could bear. At the first opportunity he crucified the South Carolinian on the floor of the Senate in language so provocative and outrageous that Calhoun could barely respond. Clay wanted to know the terms of the agreement between the President and the senator, what pledges made, what promises given. In view of the fact "that the distinguished Senator had made his bow in court, kissed the hand

8. *Congressional Globe,* 25th Congress, 2d session, appendix, p. 632ff.
9. Stanton, *Random Recollections,* p. 84.
10. Jackson to Blair, September 27, 1837, Jackson Papers, LC.

of the monarch, was taken into favor, and agreed henceforth to support his edicts," the American people had a right to know, said Clay, what commitments were consummated, what compromises completed.

Calhoun had indeed laid down the conditions on which he would return to the Democratic party, and according to his biographer, they amounted to "unconditional surrender." He not only saw his own future better served by association with the Democrats but also genuinely believed in the merit of the independent treasury. However, in his reply to Clay the South Carolinian angrily responded that he knew less about compromises and agreements than the senator from Kentucky. He recalled that "the Senator had a great deal to do with such things, in connection with a distinguished citizen [John Q. Adams], now of the other House."

Again a reference to the corrupt bargain.

Clay returned to the attack and continued with yet another defense of his actions in 1825, reminding everyone that Calhoun also supported Adams at the time and served as Vice President. As for compromise, Clay reveled in it. He praised the Compromise Tariff of 1833, noting that in spite of Calhoun's foot-dragging in working out its details, he, Clay, had saved the Union. Not only that, but he had saved the "gallant little State of South Carolina" from Jackson's wrath and fiery sword.

Calhoun laughed at Clay's egotistical claims about saving the Union. "The Senator was then compelled to compromise to save himself," he mocked. "Events had placed him flat on his back, and he had no way to recover himself but by compromise. . . . He was thus forced by the action of [South Carolina] . . . by my counsel to compromise in order to save himself. I had the mastery over him on that occasion."

"The senator says, I was flat on my back, and that he was my master," Clay roared in response. "Sir, I would not own him as a slave."

The audience howled. Clay felt the excitement of the chamber generated by his outburst, and he relished every moment of it as he continued his assault.

"He MY master! and I compelled by HIM!" Clay laughed angrily. "Sir . . . I saw the condition of the senator from South Carolina and his friends. They had reduced South Carolina . . . to a state of war; and I, therefore, wished to save the effusion of human blood, and especially the blood of our fellow-citizens."

The audience cheered. Rarely had the Senate experienced a greater sensation, a more perfect squelch. Calhoun was reduced to virtual silence.[11]

Calhoun's desertion to the Democrats and the reasons he assigned for doing so truly exasperated Clay. "I believe in private life he is irreproachable," the Kentuckian wrote, "but I believe he will die a traitor or a madman." His sole aim is to sow dissension between sections of the Union "and thus to

11. Clay, *Works,* VI, 165–168. The reference to Calhoun's biographer is Wiltse, *Calhoun, Nullifier,* p. 398.

prepare the way for its dissolution." Calhoun argues that from the beginning the government's action had been "ruinous to the South, and aggrandizing to the North!" This despite forty years of government in which "Southern men directed the course of public affairs!"[12]

Calhoun, of course, blamed Clay for all the nation's miseries. "Mr. Clay's American system, which poured countless millions into the treasury, taken from one section & given to another," he wrote, "was the source of all our oppression, disorder, and corruption. That had to be overthrown before reformation could possibly take place. Nullification & the deposite act effected that. They have between them dried up the source of corruption, patronage & power, and put an end *for the present* both to Congressional & Executive usurpation."[13]

Clay's heroic speeches, lasting four hours and more, took their physical toll. His health was not good in early 1838, and he admitted, "I am worked to death almost." There was no let up. "Company—Company—Correspondence—Correspondence, they are eternal & incessant." He might also have added: speeches and more speeches. He finally hired young Gales Seaton to serve as his amanuensis to assist him in his labors.[14]

And when all else quieted down, there were always his sons to burden his life. At this time his youngest, John, gave him "great pain." Princeton suspended the young man for taking a holiday in New York without permission. John's situation steadily worsened at the institution until it finally became so impossible that Princeton dismissed him the following year at his father's request. Clay admitted that his son had a tendency toward indolence. Like his oldest brother, the young man had a "high and irascible temper." Then another tragedy entered Clay's life when the newborn infant of Henry, Jr., died shortly after birth.[15]

On top of everything else a rather serious matter that momentarily turned Clay's attention away from his family's problems suddenly occurred in Washington. During the congressional session there took place a dreadful duel between two congressmen in which Clay was slightly involved. It developed when Representative Jonathan Cilley of Maine verbally attacked James Watson Webb, editor of the New York *Courier and Enquirer,* on the House floor. Representative William Graves of Kentucky, Clay's personal friend, attempted to deliver a reply from Webb to Cilley, who not only refused to receive it but also refused to provide a written explanation for his refusal. Graves regarded the refusal as an attack upon his honor, and the upshot was a formal challenge

12. Clay to Harrison G. Otis, June 26, 1838, in Clay, *Papers,* IX, 208.

13. Calhoun to Armistead Burt, December 24, 1838, in Calhoun, *Papers,* XIV, 498.

14. Clay to Thomas Hart Clay, February 23, 1838, Clay to Biddle, February 20, 1838, Clay to Henry Clay, Jr., March 2, 1838, Clay to James B. Clay, January 22, 1838, in Clay, *Papers,* IX, 150, 149, 152, 133.

15. Clay to James B. Clay, January 22, 1838, Clay to Porter, August 15, 1838, Clay to Richard Henry Lee, April 20, 1839, in Clay, *Papers,* IX, 133, 217, 308.

written out by Clay. The weary senator did so, he later admitted, in an attempt to soften its language in order to produce an amicable settlement of the dispute. His efforts failed. The two men met on February 24, 1838, across the Anacostia Bridge in Maryland, and on the third fire, using rifles no less, Graves killed Cilley. Clay was later accused of precipitating the duel, but he swore that he had no knowledge of the day, hour, or place of the meeting. "I only regretted my ignorance of it, because, if I had known it, I could have advised where the police might have been directed to arrest the parties & prevent the duel."[16]

Washington reacted in horror to this senseless slaughter. Official business came to a halt. An investigation resulted, and for weeks Congress debated a bill outlawing dueling in the District of Columbia. The Senate passed its version on April 9, with Clay voting in the affirmative, but the House let it die.

This barbarous duel, resulting in Cilley's death after two exchanges of fire, underscored the intense partisan feeling in Congress. It might never have happened otherwise. The duel had at least one meritorious effect in lowering the voices of the rancorous congressmen as they struggled through the final months of the second session.

The "retreat" of the nullifiers, led by Calhoun, into the camp of the Democrats unquestionably strengthened the position of the administration within Congress. Clay, Webster, and Rives led the fight against the independent treasury or subtreasury in the Senate, but the administration forces voted down their efforts to win passage of an amendment by Rives substituting a system of state banks for the subtreasury. Then, after killing Calhoun's amendment to gradually discontinue bank notes for debts owed the government, which might presumably attract Whig votes, the Senate passed the independent treasury bill on March 26 by the slim vote of twenty-seven to twenty-five.[17]

Included in the Senate bill was an amendment by Daniel Webster, supported by the administration, that, for all intents and purposes, rescinded the Specie Circular because it directed the secretary of the treasury not to discriminate as to the money (hard or soft) to be received in payment for debts owed to the government. But Clay saw immediately the political advantages the administration would derive by backing away (however slightly) from a strict hard-money policy. So he introduced a joint resolution on April 30 to repeal the Specie Circular outright. To his surprise, and probably the undermining of his intention to reap sole benefit from the resolution, it immediately drew strong Democratic support. It passed the Senate by a 34 to 10 vote, and the House by a 154 to 29 vote, with Democrats arguing that the circular had outlived its usefulness. Inasmuch as the House rejected the independent treasury bill on

16. Henry Wise to Clay, February, 25, 1842, Clay to Wise, February 28, 1842, in Clay, *Papers,* IX, 661, 662.
17. *Congressional Globe,* 25th Congress, 2d session, p. 264. Calhoun joined the Whigs and Conservatives to vote against the bill because his hard-money amendment had been struck out.

June 25 by 125 to 111, perhaps it was just as well that Clay introduced his resolution, despite the Webster amendment. Now the Treasury had full discretion to receive bank notes backed by specie.[18]

Unfortunately the friends of Clay and Webster took to squabbling over who should take credit for rescinding the circular. Since both men were potential Whig nominees for the presidency in 1840, the squabbling had purpose. "There is a morbid feeling among some of the friends of Mr. W.," wrote Clay, ". . . to claim for him the patronage of the late resolution. It was tweedle dum & tweedle dee, between his form and mine." Clay rightly claimed that his was the more appropriate for legislation and that the idea of doing away with discrimination against bank notes had been his when he proposed it more than a year before. "But," he added, "this competition about the resolution was unworthy of either of us."[19] True.

There were many actions by the Great Triumvirate during the sessions of the Twenty-fifth and Twenty-sixth Congresses that proved unworthy of them. But driving personal ambition and the further hardening of political lines between parties goaded them into excesses that only dimmed the luster of their well-deserved reputations.

In the ongoing struggle to win passage of the subtreasury system, the administration tried to obtain western support by proposing a new public land bill incorporating Senator Benton's graduation concept of reducing the minimum price of land. In addition, the administration proposed a preemption bill that would allow squatters on government land to purchase 160 acres at the minimum price before the land was offered for public sale. According to the Democratic leadership, the bill would give preference to "honest yeomen" over "greedy speculators."

Clay hated the whole idea of graduation and preemption. To start, it was a massive giveaway of government land. "We violate or disregard all the laws of supply and demand," he said. "We glut the market by throwing into it vast quantities of fresh land of unsurpassed fertility." Worse, under preemption, a "fraudulent, heartless, scandalous, abominable speculation" would be permitted.[20] "I consider the preemptioner a trespasser, and his occupation of the public lands, contrary to law, a trespass; and I contend that the property of the

---

18. *Congressional Globe,* 25th Congress, 2d session, pp. 324, 411–413, 478; Cole, *Van Buren,* p. 334; Wilson, *Presidency of Van Buren,* p. 109.

19. Clay to Porter, June 3, 9, 1838, in Clay, *Papers,* IX, 198, 203. In a letter to Nicholas Biddle, Webster claimed that he told Clay that he would introduce such a resolution upon his return trip from Boston. No sooner did he leave Washington than "Mr C. *brought forward a Resolution himself*— and some considerable bruit ensued, about his promptitude to aid the mercantile interest &c. &c. &c. So the world goes. Burn this—as it is libellous, in the extreme." Webster to Biddle, no date, c. late May 1838, in Webster, *Papers, Correspondence,* IV, 302. See also Webster to Roswell L. Colt, May 8, 1838, ibid., IV, 295.

20. Clay, *Works,* VI, 87–93; *Congressional Globe,* 25th Congress, 2d session, appendix, pp. 563–564.

People of the U.S. ought to be protected and guarded as strictly and securely as that of individuals."[21]

To Clay's shock and the surprise of practically everyone else in the chamber, Daniel Webster supported both graduation and preemption. He thought they would benefit actual settlers on a just and equitable basis. He was obviously soliciting western electoral support which only infuriated Clay. But between the Democrats and westerners they passed both graduation and preemption, Clay casting the only western vote against them. In the House the graduation bill failed, but preemption became law.

What made Clay's speeches on land policy particularly noteworthy was the care with which he composed them. As he did with so many of his efforts on other topics, Clay always constructed a historical framework with which to present his arguments. What contributed to his excellence as a speaker and a statesman was the profound regard he had for understanding the history of whatever subject was then under consideration by the legislature.

A year later he again failed to block Senate passage of a graduation bill. Fortunately for him, the House once more let the measure die. And in 1840 he engaged in another rancorous quarrel with Calhoun over a land bill that also failed.[22]

During many of the debates over the subtreasury, the panic, land policy, and abolition, there were periodic interruptions occasioned by dangerous events involving relations with foreign countries. Happily the Texas question had quieted. The United States recognized Texas independence at the close of Jackson's administration, but the drive for annexation had slowed when the Republic of Texas withdrew its request for annexation.[23] Also, Mexico had agreed to arbitrate the claims of American citizens.

But relations with Great Britain suddenly deteriorated in 1837, when an American vessel, *Caroline,* which was illegally transporting men and supplies between New York and Canada on the Niagara River to assist Canadian rebels, was seized and burned. One American was reported killed in the seizure, and angry accusations flashed back and forth across the border. Clay did not believe war with Great Britain would result, despite a great deal of loose talk along the frontier, but he did denounce the seizure as "a most unparalleled outrage." Following this incident, fighting broke out in 1839 among lumber-

21. Clay to John B. Dillon, July 28, 1838, in Clay, *Papers,* IX, 214.

22. Clay to John B. Dillon, July 28, 1838, in Clay, *Papers,* IX, 214; *Congressional Globe,* 26th Congress, 1st session, pp. 96–97, 202–203.

23. "I do not think that the question of annexation is one that ought to be considered or entertained at all, during the existence of War between Mexico and Texas," wrote Clay. "I would not for a moment consent to involve this Country in War to acquire that Country. Nor, if its independence were acknowledged by Mexico, and peace were established between them, would I concur in incorporating Texas in this Confederacy, against the decided wishes of a large portion of it. I think it better to harmonize what we have, than to introduce a new element of discord into our political partnership, against the consent of existing members of the concern." Clay to Porter, January 26, 1838, in Clay, *Papers,* IX, 135.

men in Maine and New Brunswick, Canada, along the Aroostook River. The cause of this so-called Aroostook War was a disagreement between the United States and Canada over the northeastern boundary as defined by the Treaty of Paris in 1783 which officially ended the American Revolution. Some twelve thousand square miles of territory were involved, and Americans claimed it all. In several speeches and comments in the Senate, Clay defended the claims of Maine and demanded that American rights be safeguarded. Pending arbitration of these disputes, however, he supported the President's efforts to quiet the frontier and preserve order.[24]

Clay exercised extreme caution in what he said publicly about these incidents since he was in obvious contention for the presidential nomination by the Whig party. Although he maintained the public posture that he was not a candidate and would do nothing to advance his cause, he still believed "there is *everywhere* an irresistable current setting in towards me." His only opposition was Webster or Harrison. Webster he dismissed as "unavailable" after his disastrous showing in 1836. And Harrison he regarded as an incompetent whom intelligent Whigs would sooner or later reject. What troubled him were the maneuvers of the friends of these two men to place them in nomination at local conventions. Their efforts invariably led to quarreling with Clay's friends. Indeed, Peter B. Porter warned the senator that in New York the friends of Harrison were "secretly urging every possible demonstration" for their candidate and maneuvering "to prevent any movement in the States favorable to you." These Harrison men, Porter went on, include "Anti Masons and Abolitionists" as well as Whigs. The leaders of the Anti-Masons—men like Albert H. Tracy, Francis Granger, John C. Spencer, and others—were "a herd of office seekers" and so numerous that there were not enough offices in New York to satisfy them. Porter urged Clay to tour the state at the conclusion of the congressional session to help his candidacy. But Clay demurred. It would be so obvious a campaigning ploy that even if he declared a thousand times, "I was *only* going to see your great Canal and other improvements &c. No body would believe me; and, what is worse, I should feel that I ought not to be credited."[25]

Clay chose to do his campaigning in a more subtle way. For one thing, he needed to get rid of Webster as a rival. It was a delicate matter, but he had to convince the Massachusetts senator that his candidacy was hopeless. Furthermore, his candidacy would set their friends to quarreling with each other and drive a wedge into the Whig party. "It is best for *him* and best for the common cause," Clay arrogantly announced. "It would be regarded as a measure of

24. Clay to Brooke, January 13, 1838, in Clay, *Papers,* IX, 129–130; *Congressional Globe,* 25th Congress, 2d session, pp. 496–497; 3d session, pp. 222–229; 26th Congress, 1st session, pp. 126–127. See Kenneth R. Stevens, *Border Diplomacy: The Caroline and McLeod Affairs in Anglo-American-Canadian Relations, 1837–1842* (Tuscaloosa, Ala., 1989).

25. Clay to Henry Clay, Jr., March 2, 1838, Porter to Clay, March 8, 1838, Clay to Porter, June 3, 1838, in Clay, *Papers,* IX, 152, 156–157, 198.

great magnanimity and his praises would be generally sounded."

So, in early June, to help Webster win a "resounding hymn" of Whig praise, Clay engaged him "in a long & friendly interview." He put the matter gently, "of course not in the form of advice, but of suggestion." Webster reacted just as gently and politely as Clay but said he "did not clearly see that he should abandon his position." Webster chose not to take offense at this obvious move to shoot him down, and he thereafter avoided any visible display of displeasure that might indicate a rupture of relations.[26]

Clay, too, behaved discreetly. Indeed, he exuded charm and sociability toward Webster—and toward practically everyone else—throughout the congressional session. He roomed at Mrs. Hill's boardinghouse near Gadsby's Hotel, but every month or so he entertained large groups of friends and colleagues at Joseph Boulanger's French restaurant. A great deal of drinking and card playing went on at these parties, so it was rather strange that the Temperance Society invited his support to win legislative action for its cause. "The Temperance cause has done great good," he allowed. "But if it resort to legislation—to coercion—it will be resisted & ought to be resisted. No man likes to have, or ought to have, cold water or brandy, separately or in combination, put in or kept out of his throat upon any other will than his own."[27]

One of Clay's dinner parties, numbering sixteen persons, cost him eighty dollars, not including the wine and four decks of playing cards. He loved to play cards, especially whist, although a year later he advised his son James against it. "Above all avoid dissipation," he wrote. "I hope you will never play at any game. After much observation and some experience I can say, with perfect truth, that he who is addicted to play loses money, time, sleep, health and character."[28]

And of course, Clay attended numerous dinner parties given by others, where his natural flair for brilliant conversation received full play. At one such party an observer remarked that she had never seen him "so interesting—nay fascinating." Clay sat at dinner next to a man who he knew opposed his politics. Yet they began a discussion of the administrations of Jefferson and Madison in which Clay said he preferred that of Madison and considered him after Washington the nation's greatest statesman and first political writer. His companion disagreed. Jefferson, he said, possessed a resilience and energy which carried the nation through many dangers, far beyond Madison's less energetic powers. "Prudence and caution—would have produced the same results," replied Clay. The two men continued the comparison, drawing on their large fund of historical memory. Within moments everyone at the table was listening in on the conversation, especially to Clay's comments. "So interesting was his conversation, so captivating his frank cordial manner that . . . I could have

26. Clay to Harrison G. Otis, July 7, 1838, in Clay, *Papers,* IX, 212–213; Irving Bartlett, *Daniel Webster* (New York, 1978), p. 156; Baxter, *Webster and the Union,* p. 268.

27. Clay to Edward C. Delavan, August 20, 1838, in Clay, *Papers,* IX, 218–219.

28. Clay to James Clay, May 22, 1839, in Clay, *Papers,* IX, 317–318.

listened all night," reported one of the guests, "and many nights with delight." History when read can be cold and stale, she continued, "compared with hearing it—the eloquence of language is enforced by eloquence of the soul-speaking eye and persuasive voice."[29]

Despite Clay's enormous personal charm, his statesmanship, his experience, and his preeminent position in the Whig party, many Whigs, particularly in New York, had serious reservations about placing him again in nomination for the presidency. No one doubted his talents or experience, but people also noted the many political enemies he had acquired over the years. That sharp tongue of his had cut down too many influential politicians. Also, he had run twice before and each time had performed badly. The fact that so many manufacturers, bankers, merchants, professional and businessmen preferred him only increased his liability in this advancing age of democracy. He was not a popular war hero, like Jackson—or General William Henry Harrison. Harrison, said one, "has not been so brilliant . . . [but he] possesses above all, that essential requisite . . . to wit, the favor and good will of the mass of the people—in other words *popularity.*"[30]

Another thing: Clay still bore the brand of the corrupt bargain charge. And it festered, reddened, and swelled once again to annoy and distract him. Indeed, the New York Harrison men probably resurrected it in order to eliminate him from the contest. One New Yorker wrote Clay and asked him for a copy of his defense of his actions in 1825. "There are many here in our city," he wrote, ". . . who are ever ready to apply the harsh epithets of—Bribery—Corruption &c. whenever the name of . . . Henry Clay is mentioned." Clay himself liked to believe that he had outlived the charge, and foolishly he sometimes made an oblique reference to it himself in Senate debates, such as promising to vote for a measure if the Kentucky legislature instructed him to do so.[31]

And Clay was even accused of being an abolitionist! Thus, while leading abolition newspapers in the North were beginning to attack him "as being ultra in my Slave notions," some southerners—nullifiers in particular, who liked to believe he headed a secret conspiracy to abolish slavery—actually indicted him "as being an Abolitionist!"[32]

It may have occurred to Clay that his apparent middle-of-the-road position invited attacks from both sides of the slavery question. In the hope of

29. Clay to Brooke, June 5, 1838, Clay to Harrison Gray Otis, January 24, 1838, in Clay, *Papers,* IX, 199, 275; four bills for food and drink, but mostly drink, from Joseph Boulanger, former chef in the Adams and Jackson White House, dated May 1, 1838, ibid., IX, 181; Smith, *Forty Years,* pp. 298–304. Mrs. Smith was discussing a dinner party given earlier, but it characterizes very well Clay's great talent for conversation.

30. Harrison Gray Otis to Clay, September 14, 1838, in Clay, *Papers,* IX, 229–230.

31. William Jones, Jr., to Clay, December 8, 1837, in Clay, *Papers,* IX, 98; *Congressional Globe,* 25th Congress, 2d session, pp. 166–167.

32. Clay to Rufus W. Griswold, July 28, 1838, Clay to Cornelius C. Brown, August 28, 1838, in Clay, *Papers,* IX, 215, 223.

clarifying his views, reinforcing his support among southern Whigs, and separating the most extreme abolitionists from the passive ones, like Quakers, he gave a powerful speech in the Senate on February 7, 1839, in which he condemned the "ultras" in uncompromising terms. He completely separated himself from the abolitionists on almost every point except his abhorrence of slavery itself. As always he gave a detailed history of the development of the "peculiar institution" since the adoption of the Constitution. He addressed the constitutional and legal questions involved in slavery and accused the abolitionists, by their agitation, of setting back emancipation half a century. "The slaves are here; no practical scheme for their removal or separation from us has been yet devised or proposed." So what can be done? Emancipation would only provoke a desperate struggle between the races for immediate ascendancy or produce such "instantaneous collisions" that would lead to bloody civil war. "Is it not better for both parties that the existing state of things should be preserved, instead of exposing them to the horrible strifes and contests which would inevitably attend an immediate abolition?"

What, then, is the answer? "Time," Clay devotedly hoped and believed. "Providence will cure all—abolition nothing. It may ruin all; it can save none.

"I beseech the abolitionists themselves," he concluded, "solemnly to pause in their mad and fatal course. Amid the infinite variety of objects of humanity and benevolence which invite the employment of their energies, let them select some one more harmless, that does not threaten to deluge our country in blood."[33]

Calhoun immediately rose from his seat to offer Clay high praise for at last understanding the true danger of the abolitionist movement. So spontaneous, so sincere, so fervent was Calhoun's reaction to Clay's speech that some wondered if another political alliance between northern money and southern cotton had been struck.[34] Abolitionists, of course, were appalled and disgusted by the tone and content of the Kentuckian's remarks. "His speech," wrote Calhoun, "is far from being sound on many points, but he has said enough to offend mortally the abolitionists, which will do much to divide the north & consolidate us."[35] Men like James G. Birney and John Greenleaf Whittier, who once idolized Clay, now cast him off as something loathsomely hypocritical. But Clay knew what he was doing—or thought he did. "My abolition Speech was made," he told one man, "after full deliberation. I expected it would

33. Clay, *Works,* VI, 140–159; Clay to Harrison Gray Otis, November 14, 1838, in Clay, *Papers,* IX, 248.

34. "Our friend Clay's speech," wrote Edward Everett to Webster, "excites great sensation here [Boston], which in the minds of some persons is increased by the remarks, with which Mr Calhoun is said to have followed it up. . . . Is it to be inferred from these expressions that there is a political understanding between Messrs Calhoun & Clay; and that the South is to be consolidated in favor of the latter as a Presidential Candidate." Everett to Webster, February 14, 1839, in Webster, *Papers, Correspondence,* IV, 343.

35. Calhoun to Armistead Burt, February 17, 1839, in Calhoun, *Papers,* XIV, 555.

enrage the Ultra's more than ever against me, and I have not been disappointed."[36]

Before delivering this speech, Clay had invited the opinion of several friends, including Senator William C. Preston of South Carolina. The conversation quickly turned to the probable impact of the speech on the electorate, and someone remarked that it would undoubtedly prove extremely offensive to the ultras on both sides of the question and could therefore endanger Clay's presidential prospects.

"I trust the sentiments and opinions are correct," snapped Clay in response. "I HAD RATHER BE RIGHT THAN BE PRESIDENT."[37] Here was the immortal utterance, the classic rejoinder, one that quickly entered the lexicon of American politics and was always to be associated with Clay's name.

Senator Preston spoke at a rally of Whigs in Philadelphia the following month and repeated Clay's deathless remark. Newspapers immediately picked it up and reprinted it around the country. It sounded noble and patriotic and appropriate to a statesman. Cynics and hard-nosed politicians smiled or laughed out loud when they heard it, but ordinary citizens thought it simply grand. Clay himself never denied that he said it.

Actually he would rather be both right *and* President. He had not abandoned his one enduring ambition, although at the age of sixty-two he thought that more than ever, he had to exercise care in the ways he went about achieving it. Webster was his immediate problem, and he could not shake a growing uneasiness that the Massachusetts senator meant to cut the ground from under him. That uneasiness turned to certainty when an article appeared in the Boston *Atlas,* a newspaper under Webster's control, blaming Clay for the Whig defeat in the recent Maine elections. Supposedly the Kentuckian's lack of popularity had caused the defeat. Therefore, said the *Atlas,* the Whig party should abandon those candidates who could not appeal to the masses and turn their support to General Harrison.[38]

Clay choked back his anger. "I am mortified—shocked—disgusted with the course of some men. I had hoped for better things of them." Did the editorial mean that Webster had withdrawn from the race and had become Harrison's promoter? "You have seen accounts of the intention of the Loco foco's to concentrate on Genl. Harrison," Clay wrote to a supporter. "I think the apple has been presented to him, but I have no reason to believe that he has accepted it." At first the senator refused to believe that Harrison was a viable

36. *Congressional Globe,* 25th Congress, 3d session, p. 177; Calhoun to Armistead Burt, February 17, 1839, in Calhoun, *Papers,* XIV, 555; *National Intelligencer,* February 11, 1839; Clay to Alexander Hamilton, February 24, 1839, in Clay, *Papers,* IX, 291.

37. *Congressional Globe,* 25th Congress, 3d session, p. 167; *National Intelligencer,* March 30, 1839; *Niles' Weekly Register,* March 23, 1839.

38. Harrison Gray Otis to Clay, September 14, 1838, Clay to Brooke, November 3, 1838, in Clay, *Papers,* IX, 229–230, 245.

candidate. What state south of the Potomac, he asked, had shown any disposition to vote for him? What western states, other than Ohio, would support him? True, the fall elections of 1838 had gone badly, but "why should I be held responsible for the issue of elections in States other than K.," Clay protested, "more than Messrs. W. & H?"[39]

Clay's suspicions about Webster and Harrison were further heightened when the Anti-Masonic National Convention met in Philadelphia on November 13, 1838, and nominated Harrison for President and Webster for Vice President. Webster knew about this beforehand, Clay charged, and approved the nomination. All signs indicate, he snarled, that collusion between the two men began in Washington during the last session of Congress with the distinct purpose of driving him, Clay, from the field. The attack started in Boston with the appearance of the article in the *Atlas* over the loss of Maine, and it continued in Cincinnati when another newspaper, the *Republican,* blamed the Whig loss of Ohio in the fall election on Clay. "*I* was assailed for losing Harrison's *own State,*" the Kentuckian shrieked in rage.

That settled it. Webster's plan of electing Harrison, Clay announced, absolved his friends "from all obligation to practice further silence & forbearance." Clay laid the blame for this connivance directly at the feet of Daniel Webster, for he did not believe that Harrison had the wit, cunning, or daring to attempt such a maneuver. The resulting struggle could mean a factional split in the Whig party, a danger that Clay fully comprehended. Indeed, he already observed signs that their inability to maintain unity could cost the Whigs the next election.[40]

Webster was unusually quiet during the third (short) session of the Twenty-fifth Congress. The winter of 1838–1839 found him regularly in the Supreme Court, arguing one case after another. When he did appear in the Senate, he said little, keeping his own counsel. "Mr. Webster has been here several weeks," Clay reported to his Whig friends in different states, "& wraps himself up, as far as I know, in perfect silence."[41]

But the emergence of General Harrison as the probable Whig presidential candidate in place of Clay caught the imagination of political leaders in all the northern states. Anti-Masons and abolitionists saw their opportunity to coa-

39. Clay to Harrison Gray Otis, September 24, 1838, Clay to Harry I. Thornton, September 16, 1838, Clay to Alexander R. Wyckoff, November 18, 1838, in Clay, *Papers,* IX, 233, 230–231, 250. Webster preferred Harrison over Clay, but he probably did not initiate the article in the *Atlas* and said so publicly. However, he did not repudiate what the editor had written.

40. Clay to Otis, December 13, 1838, Clay to Henry Clay, Jr., January 18, 1839, in Clay, *Papers,* IX, 251–252, 272–273; William P. Vaughn, *The Anti-Masonic Party in the United States, 1826–1843* (Lexington, Ky., 1983), pp. 180–181; Freeman Cleaves, *Old Tippecanoe: William Henry Harrison and His Time* (New York, 1939), p. 312. "The Whigs have now, with the blessing of God," Clay wrote to Jonathan Thompson, November 19, 1838, "the fate of the Country in their hands; and if they do not foolishly exhaust their power, in idle divisions among themselves, about this or that individual, they may bear it through gloriously." Clay Papers, Manuscript Department, Filson Club, Louisville, Kentucky.

41. Clay to Porter, February 5, 1839, Clay to Otis, January 24, 1839, in Clay, *Papers,* IX, 276, 274.

lesce their forces behind the general to thwart Clay's nomination. Of particular significance was the opposition of Thurlow Weed, who had swung from the Anti-Masonic to the Whig party a few years earlier and then managed the gubernatorial campaign that elected his protégé William H. Seward in the fall of 1838. Since Clay's friends in New York supported Seward, that in itself should have bolstered the Kentuckian's standing in the state. As a matter of fact, Clay was told by Peter B. Porter that "the Governor [Seward] & Thurlow Weed (who at this moment is decidedly the most important man, politically speaking, in the State) are not only friendly to your election, but warmly & zealously so." But Porter was deceived. A pragmatic, shrewd, and resourceful politician, Weed did not believe that Clay, a Mason and a slaveholder, could carry New York in a presidential election. In addition, unlike Harrison, the senator allegedly lacked mass appeal.[42]

Then another menace suddenly appeared to endanger Clay's candidacy. With the outbreak of the Aroostook War, General Winfield Scott—possibly the ablest commanding officer this nation has ever produced—had been sent to the Canadian border to restore peace. He subsequently persuaded the local governments of both New Brunswick and Maine to withdraw their troops, bringing the war to a speedy end. This masterful stroke, in addition to his earlier success in handling the difficult *Caroline* incident, enhanced Scott's popularity all along the northern frontier. Like General Jackson, the Hero of New Orleans, and like General Harrison, Old Tippecanoe, Scott suddenly acquired the nickname the Hero of Bridgewater. Politicians communicated this popular enthusiasm to Thurlow Weed. "Scott's name will bring out the hurra boys," wrote one. "The Whig party were broken down by the popularity . . . of old Jackson, and it is but fair to turn upon, and prostrate our opponents, with the . . . weapons with which they beat us." Thurlow Weed instantly identified Scott as a possible presidential contender. In fact, he now preferred him to Harrison.[43]

To make matters worse, the friends of Daniel Webster in New York, who also wished to get rid of Clay, rallied behind Scott and contrived a "triangular correspondence" game to defeat the Kentuckian. According to this scheme, three supposed supporters of Clay in different districts—Rochester, Utica, and New York City—would write to one another, and each would tell the others to do everything in their power to quicken support for the Kentuckian in their districts, "for I am sorry to say that he has no strength in this." Everyone would imagine wrongly that Clay's support in different parts of the state had

42. Glyndon G. Van Deusen, *William Henry Seward* (New York, 1967), pp. 61–62; Robert Gray Gunderson, *The Log Cabin Campaign* (Lexington, Ky., 1957), pp. 44–45; Porter to Clay, February 16, 1839, in Clay, *Papers,* IX, 287; Seward to Weed, May 23, 1838, Weed Papers, University of Rochester Library. On Weed, see Glyndon G. Van Deusen, *Thurlow Weed, Wizard of the Lobby* (Boston, 1947).

43. Henry S. Burrage, *Maine in the Northeastern Boundary Controversy* (Augusta, Me., 1919), p. 257ff.; Charles W. Elliott, *Winfield Scott; The Soldier and the Man* (New York, 1937), pp. 355–356, 367–382; M. Bradley to Weed, August 29, 1839, Weed Papers, University of Rochester Library.

vanished. Thus districts favorable to him, now supposing his nomination hopeless, would elect delegates opposed to him. By this contrivance General Scott was "to be made the cat's paw to defeat Mr. Clay."[44]

By the winter and early spring of 1839 it had become obvious to Clay that if he wanted the nomination, he would have to reach—and maybe fight—for it. So he began to stir himself. Besides publicly denigrating Webster's perform- ance in the Senate, Clay was assumed and widely believed for a time to have had a hand in attempting to win the reelection of William C. Rives to the Senate from Virginia. In that state the Conservatives naturally nominated Rives, while the Whigs chose John Tyler, and the Democrats John Y. Mason. This three-way split prevented an election, and it was indefinitely postponed. Rives informed Clay "in the most explicit terms" that he supported his presi- dential bid. At that point, it was later claimed, the Kentuckian and other congressional Whigs approached John Tyler's friends and offered the Whig nomination for Vice President if they would withdraw Tyler from the Senate race in Rives's favor. "To this arrangement Mr. Clay pledged all his influence and exertion," but he was warned that he might endanger his own nomination for the presidency by agreeing to the "arrangement." Still, according to the gossip about his interference, the Kentuckian was so certain of his nomination that he said he was willing to take the gamble. Tyler's friends were also gam- bling, but they figured that "the influences at work against Mr. Clay" would only improve their candidate's chances to win the vice presidential nomina- tion. As it subsequently developed, Tyler did in fact win second place on the Whig ticket, but not until January 1841 did Rives win election to the Senate.[45]

Clay also tried to win over Senator Hugh Lawson White of Tennessee, one of the Whig presidential candidates in 1836. He and John Bell sought out Henry A. Wise, who shared the same mess with White, and asked him to intercede. Since White was an extremely conscientious man of "stern virtue and the strongest sense of duty," Wise told Clay that there was only one way for him to approach the Tennessean. Wise would have to bend to his knees, look up with truth and innocence written all over his face, and say: "Judge White, Mr. Clay and Mr. Bell requested me to ask, Will you please stand out of Mr. Clay's way and give him your influence for the Presidency?"

Clay burst out laughing. Very well, he said, since honesty was always the best policy, proceed as necessary. Wise spoke to White, who confessed his preference for Clay. But he warned that the friends of Webster had gotten up the "triangular correspondence" game to defeat him and advised that Clay do

44. Porter to Clay, January 20, 1839, in Clay, *Papers,* IX, 273–274; Wise, *Seven Decades of the Union,* pp. 165–166.

45. Clay to Brooke, December 20, 1838, Clay to James Caldwell, March 18, 1839, in Clay, *Papers,* IX, 258, 296; Wise, *Seven Decades of the Union,* pp. 158, 161. Clay preferred Rives but repeatedly stated that he could not and did not play a part in the Virginia election, and I am inclined to believe him. See Chapter XXXI. Whatever he did, it is clear that he was motivated by a desire to win Virginia in the presidential election.

everything in his power to checkmate the scheme by having the primary nominations held early in the summer. White then set down certain conditions for
his support, all of which were later reported back to Clay. The Kentuckian
"distinctly made the pledges required of him by Judge White," but unfortunately he did not urge his New York friends to move up the date for convention elections. He thought this would constitute a grave and unwarranted
interference in the politics of the state.[46]

As Clay began to awaken to the many dangers confronting his efforts to
claim the Whig nomination, one great obstacle suddenly disappeared: Daniel
Webster departed for England in the spring of 1839. Before leaving, he prepared a letter that was released upon his arrival in London. The statement
announced his withdrawal from the presidential race. He thanked a Massachusetts convention for its nomination, but he said he chose to sit this one out.[47]

Webster had simply walked away from a fight he already knew he could
not win. In a stinging rebuke to Clay—considering his long association with
the Kentuckian and high regard for his talents—he did not indicate a preference among the remaining candidates.[48] He chose to let Harrison, Scott, and
Clay fight it out among themselves.

But by this time the "Mill Boy of the Slashes" meant to bend every effort
to have the prize for himself. A thumping Whig victory in 1840 seemed inevitable. Its presidential candidate could not fail. And no one but Henry Clay
deserved the honor of that victory. He had fought too long and too hard to be
denied. "Moderation, conciliation and decision, but above all firmness and
decision should be our course," he trumpeted. "May it be guided by wisdom
and lead to victory!"[49]

46. Wise, *Seven Decades of the Union*, pp. 162–169; Clay to Porter, April 15, 1838, in Clay, *Papers*,
IX, 173–174.
47. Webster to John Plummer Healy, with enclosure, June 12, 1839, in Webster, *Papers, Correspondence*, IV, 370.
48. However, Webster undoubtedly preferred Harrison because he believed the general had a
better chance of winning the election.
49. Clay to Jonathan Thompson, November 19, 1838, Clay Papers, Manuscript Department,
Filson Club, Louisville, Kentucky.

—— T H I R T Y ——

The Triumphal Tour

CLAY OWNED PROPERTY in Illinois, and occasionally he made a quick trip to the state to inspect it.[1] During one such visit he stayed overnight at a farm that had a fine herd of cattle. "A connoisseur and amateur of blooded animals," Clay enjoyed a tour of inspection with the owner, a farmer who "proved to be a Jackson man—red-hot." In the course of their conversation the farmer, who did not know the identity of his visitor, made some heated remarks about " 'that fellow Henry Clay' and of his bargain and corruption." The visitor suggested that the farmer might be mistaken and that there might not have been a bargain at all. But the farmer was positive. "Mr. Clay," he said, "was a very dangerous man."

Clay dropped the subject and retired for the night. A little later the farmer learned the identity of his guest. He was mortified by what he had said. In the morning he approached Clay, addressed him by name, and apologized for his rudeness.

Clay cut him off. There was no offense, he said, and therefore, no apology was needed. "You spoke your honest opinion," he continued, "which I hope you will find reason to change; but so long as it shall be your honest conviction I cannot object to your expressing it."

The farmer was nonplussed. But from that day forward he "was one of the most devoted friends Mr. Clay had in the State of Illinois."[2]

The story says a great deal about Henry Clay and about his relationship with the American people. Those who got to know him usually admired, respected, revered, sometimes idolized, and frequently supported him. Indeed, for those who knew him personally it was hard not to like Henry Clay. But the public at large did not really know him or completely trust him. It believed him guilty of a corrupt bargain in 1825 to thwart its will. It believed, like Jackson, that he was "void of good morals."[3] Some people even thought him a "very dangerous man."

1. Thomas Hart Clay attempted to work one of his father's farms in Illinois but gave it up shortly after the Black Hawk War.
2. Sargent, *Public Men and Events,* II, 15–16.
3. Jackson to D. G. Goodlett, March 12, 1844, in Jackson, *Correspondence,* VI, 275.

Perhaps in an effort to increase his "popularity" among the masses, and more certainly to bolster his sagging support in New York, Clay decided to tour the Great Lakes area, view Niagara Falls, as he had wanted to do for a long time, traverse the Empire State, and visit Montreal and Quebec. Despite the fact that a year before he had refused the pleas of his New York friends to make such a trip because it would appear like a vulgar act of campaigning, Clay now realized that the tour was necessary if he expected to capture the presidential nomination. "We never expect again," he wrote, "to have such great advantages in the contest." This was the supreme moment when Clay could finally win the presidency, and it all turned on winning the nomination.[4]

Early in the spring he notified his New York supporters of his intentions and that he planned an extensive trip through their state and a brief visit to Canada. He expected to leave Lexington around the beginning of July and take along his wife, if she would agree, and his two sons James and Henry, Jr. In view of his previous refusal to make the tour, Clay pretended both to himself and others that he was really indulging a long-held desire (which was real) to see the lakes and the falls and was fulfilling it by means of a short vacation. Thus he hoped to "tip-toe" along the northern frontier, swing into Canada, and then return to Washington by way of Albany, New York City, Philadelphia, and Baltimore—all this without giving the appearance of a political motive! And maybe he really believed what he said. "It is my anxious desire to proceed on the excursion as quietly, and with as little noise and parade as possible," he told Peter B. Porter. No speeches and no demonstrations. "This is due to the public pledges which I have made, to my own feelings, and, I think, to every consideration of policy."[5]

His New York friends were delighted. They had a strong organization in the state, but the growing popularity of General Scott, quietly encouraged by Thurlow Weed and Governor Seward, rightly worried them. A tour such as Clay proposed would go a long way to counteract that recent development. They agreed there would be no public dinners *with one single exception, however.*" You must speak in Buffalo, wrote Porter. The interior of the western end of New York was a hotbed of Anti-Masons and abolitionists. "It is particularly desirable that you should visit this section of the State."[6]

Clay demurred. "If I submit to my friends at Buffalo, how can I resist them at Rochester, and a hundred other towns in the West of your State?" How indeed. "I am firmly convinced that both policy and principle unite in recommending . . . [that I] avoid, in appearance and in fact, all electioneering."[7]

But it was really very foolish of Clay to think that on the eve of the Whig national nominating convention, scheduled for December 1839, he could un-

4. Clay to Benjamin W. Leigh, June 12, 1839, copy CPP.
5. Clay to Porter, May 14, 1839, in Clay, *Papers,* IX, 313.
6. Porter to Clay, May 26, 1839, in Clay, *Papers,* IX, 320.
7. Clay to Porter, June 6, 1839, in Clay, *Papers,* IX, 324.

dertake an extended tour without causing demonstrations, parades, speeches, and all manner of publicity and national comment. Perhaps it was time to forgo the pretense and drive as hard as possible to win the nomination. The Democrats were particularly worried about his possible candidacy and wanted to prevent it. "The old hero [Andrew Jackson] is electioneering with all his usual zeal," John Bell informed Clay. "He maddens at the idea that Ten. can be got to go for you, and if this state shall give her vote to you, my opinion is he will not survive such a result." He will burst a blood vessel! said Bell. His surrogate orators bemoan the "cruelty of putting his old and inveterate enemy into power to triumph upon him in his old age." He is not dead yet, they say, but your victory would surely kill him. "Spare him until the grave closes over him," shout these surrogates to the Tennessee voters. "Do not inflict this last insult upon the hero of N.O. and the Saviour of his country!" Oh, you should see how these partisans grind their teeth in rage and agony, said Bell, "when the shouts of the people rise in approbation of some sentiment expressed in your favor."[8]

So Clay decided to take the trip and appear in public, protesting all the while that it was a personal and private excursion. If nothing else, it would allow him to gauge popular reaction to his appearances. If the people turned out to be indifferent or hostile, there was still time to withdraw from the race. If they were warm and enthusiastic, perhaps they would show Whig leaders that he was indeed a popular candidate and could win the next election.

He set out in early July with the intention of passing hurriedly through Ohio—the home of General William Henry Harrison—to Cleveland to embark for Buffalo. He would visit a few friends along the way and inspect some land he owned. Lucretia would not accompany him, nor would Henry, Jr. Instead, James Brown Clay came up from Missouri to take the tour with his father. "He is very young, and I wish him to accompany me for his gratification & improvement."[9]

Although Clay shot through Ohio as fast as possible, he had the good sense to notify Harrison of his movements. A couple of months later Harrison responded. "No one who knows you would suspect you of poaching, but at any rate Ohio is a free Manor and you particularly ought to have as great privileges within her borders as any other person in the Union." Then, with an playful jab to the ribs, Harrison added: "Knowing your great admiration of female beauty, you must have been highly gratified, by your reception" as you toured. As for politics, the general expressed his embarrassment over his position as a rival for the presidency, "an office which I never dreamed of attaining and which I had ardently desired to see you occupy." But "fate" had decreed otherwise "and I await the result which time will determine."[10]

8. Bell to Clay, May 21, 1839, in Clay, *Papers,* IX, 317.
9. Clay to Porter, June 6, 1839, in Clay, *Papers,* IX, 324.
10. Harrison to Clay, September 20, 1839, in Clay, *Papers,* IX, 342–343.

Recently Harrison had indicated that if nominated and elected, he would serve only one term, something Andrew Jackson had advocated as a means of safeguarding the President from corruption. Senator Nathaniel P. Tallmadge of New York asked Clay whether he supported the idea of a single term. In response the senator said it would be an improvement of the Constitution because too often a President in his first term directs his thoughts solely to reelection "instead of being employed in devising measures for the advancement of the general weal." However, unlike Harrison, he did not believe a candidate should forswear a second term before election. It would be the equivalent of saying to the people: "Well you see I ask to be taken and tried only for a short time; you will soon get rid of me." At the same time he would be saying to rivals: "Give me your support for this brief term; I shall not be long in your way." If I am elected, declared Clay in conclusion, I must enter the office without previous pledges and left free to decide later what may be right and proper to do.[11]

On reaching the state of New York, Clay immediately discovered that Scott, not Harrison, was his principal rival, and with each passing day he became less and less scrupulous about giving speeches and appearing at public functions. He arrived on Saturday, July 13, at Niagara Falls, where he remained for nearly a week, viewing this natural wonder and visiting with political friends and supporters. These meetings further encouraged him to forget about appearing blatantly political and make a strong bid for popular support. He had too much to lose.

Clay moved on to Buffalo, where he was given a tremendous reception and dinner and where he delivered the first of a number of speeches in the state to win the electorate's affection and trust. Naturally he continued the charade about not wishing to be misunderstood about his trip. "Although my wish is to pass on quietly without display or parade," he said to the crowd, "I am penetrated with sentiments of gratitude for the manifestations of attachment and confidence with which I am honored in this beautiful city of the lakes. I thank you, most cordially thank you, for them all." He then continued speaking for about half an hour, mentioning the importance of protecting manufactures, the great improvements in canals, roads, bridges, and harbors, and the need to continue them. Finally he focused on the "radical maladministration of the government" in provoking a frightful depression. He ended by mentioning his own candidacy. He said he would retire from the contest if he could not promote union and harmony. "What is a public man worth," he concluded, "who is not ever ready to sacrifice himself for the good of his country?"[12]

What a lot of people remembered about the speech after he was gone—and indeed, it was mentioned in newspapers around the country—was the

<hr />

11. Clay to Tallmadge, June 18, 1839, in Clay, *Papers,* IX, 325–326
12. From the New York *Commercial Advertiser and Journal,* a Clay newspaper, reprinted in *Niles' Weekly Register,* July 27, 1839.

theme "Compromise, Concession & Union." This expression was the true tenor of all his speeches. It remained his major theme until his death.[13]

Since there had been little preparation for his arrival in Buffalo, the enthusiastic reception and demonstrations he received greatly pleased the senator. He also felt his speech went over well, and he agreed to meet larger crowds and attend other functions and dinners. Peter B. Porter told him that his visit had impressed many men who were "vacilating and undecided," and even Van Buren's "most respected and influential supporters" had been "drawn over" to him.[14]

Clay then traveled to Lockport, Rochester, Canandaigua, and Oswego. Whenever possible, he mended political fences, invited support for his nomination, sought to increase his "popularity," and withal tried to whip up excitement over his candidacy. He visited Congressman Francis Granger and a former congressman, Albert H. Tracy, in an effort to placate the Anti-Masons and abolitionists in the state. He also stopped off at Auburn to see Governor William H. Seward and stayed overnight at the governor's home, where he met local politicians. But Seward conveniently absented himself. A week or two later they accidentally met at Port Kent on Lake Champlain. The governor had tried to avoid Clay and weakly excused himself by stating that public duties and the travel associated with them had prevented an earlier meeting. Nevertheless, Seward made his position clear. All along he had said to associates that it was not a question of whom they preferred but whom they could elect. Speaking now as discreetly as possible, Seward mentioned the objections abolitionists expressed to Clay's candidacy.

The senator brusquely waved the objections aside. During his trip, he told Seward, "many Abolitionists had come to him confessing their Abolitionism but declaring their preference for and devotion to him." He also pointed to Granger and Tracy's support, as well as to the public demonstrations of affections he had everywhere encountered, as evidence of his strength in New York. Seward admitted that the demonstrations had indeed been "magnificent." But he stood his ground. The meeting was brief and a bit strained. Later Seward wrote to Clay and confessed that "among our friends in Essex, Clinton, St. Lawrence, Jefferson, Oswego and Cayuga, the spirit of the Whig party has been invigorated by your visit."[15]

Continuing his journey, Clay toured saltworks and the Erie Canal and went out of his way to meet, dine, and speak with local politicians as he cut across the western end of the state. And everywhere he appeared he encountered "enthusiastic demonstrations" from the masses of people who came out

13. Edward Everett to Webster, July 26, 1839, in Webster, *Papers, Correspondence,* IV, 382.

14. Porter to Clay, August 9, 1839, in Clay, *Papers,* IX, 334.

15. Seward to J. Randall, May 23, 1839, Seward Papers, University of Rochester Library; Seward to Weed, August 15, 1839, Weed Papers, University of Rochester Library; Van Deusen, *Seward,* p. 61; Seward to Clay, August 17, 1839, in Clay, *Papers,* IX, 335; Gunderson, *Log-Cabin Campaign,* p. 46.

to see him. "Quasi public dinners, suppers, vast concourses of people, Committees, & Speech" marked every mile of his journey from one end of New York to the other. He was passed along from local committee to local committee until he finally "escaped" into Canada, where he found that "respite" and freedom that had been denied him in his own country.[16]

In Canada Clay had scarcely gotten to within sight of Montreal before a committee from Burlington, Vermont, caught up with him and invited him to its city for a reception and public dinner, which he agreed to attend on his return from Quebec. Clay had great strength in New England, which he wished to preserve, even though that section did not claim a high priority during his current tour. New York and Pennsylvania were the two prizes he needed to wrap up the nomination and the election. And he could ill afford to risk their defection to either Scott or Harrison.

In Montreal he naturally met the governor-general of Canada, Sir John Colborne, and was cordially received. Pushing on to Quebec, he reached the charming city in early August, but by that time he was nearing exhaustion. So he hurriedly swung back into the United States and paid his respects to his supporters in Burlington.

Some Vermonters, Democrats especially, took exception to his call. "His temperature is not calculated for a northern latitude, for New England," one crusty state legislator scolded. "The bearing of the man is reckless, his moral influence is bad. His manners, & conversations are those of a man, who neither fears God, or regards man. Such is the impression Mr. Clay has left to the north. . . . There is some thing of the Puritan spirit still left with us. . . . We revere christianity, & hold in high respect the moral virtues, and no man can be long esteemed, who contemns religion, and disregards our moral relations. The pensioned Whigs may shout, but the yeomanry of New-England, maintain an indignant silence respecting Mr. Clay."[17]

This Vermont Democrat exaggerated his criticism. Still, Clay on occasion did offend many voters during his presidential campaigns because of his apparent indifference to or contempt for "moral virtues." Without realizing it, he unwittingly triggered the erroneous impression that he had little regard for Christian morality. In almost every instance that this happened during the tour it was provoked by a flash of humor, a foolish attempt to be playful (for example, instead of naming the state of Virginia he would playfully refer to it as the "dominion of the virgin queen"), or an ill-advised word. And the criticism hounded him from one election to the next.

After leaving New England, by boat and carriage, Clay lodged at Lake George and then moved on to Saratoga Springs, where he arrived on August 9.

It was "the meridian of the Saratoga season," recorded the New York City

16. Clay to Joshua R. Giddings, July 13, 1839, Clay to Francis Granger, July 19, 1839, Clay to Tallmadge, July 14, 1839, Clay to Porter, July 31, 1839 in Clay, *Papers,* IX, 330–333
17. Isaac Fletcher to James K. Polk, September 4, 1839, in Polk, *Correspondence,* V, 229.

merchant Philip Hone, and everyone of importance seemed in residence. "All the world is here," he wrote, "politicians and dandies; cabinet ministers and ministers of the gospel; officeholders and officeseekers, humbuggers and humbugged; fortune-hunters and hunters of woodcock; anxious mothers and lovely daughters." President Van Buren was also present, engaged in his own political fence mending.[18]

In their plans to honor Clay, the extremely wealthy Whigs who summered at the springs had tried to exclude public participation. "But it could not be; the movement is spontaneous, and the people seem determined to out-glorify the other [Democratic] party." What made it all the more remarkable was the presence of General Scott as well as Van Buren, and Scott was clearly "the rising sun" among many New Yorkers.[19]

Arrangements had been made for about eighty distinguished visitors to meet Clay on his approach to Saratoga and parade him into town. A fancy "collation" was provided, along with champagne, to maintain strength and high spirits for the march. Several committees from nearby towns also appeared and demanded the right to take part. Then they all lined up to made a grand entrance into Saratoga.

Clay sat in the lead barouche, preceded by Frank Johnson's musical band. After everyone got into position, Philip Hone said that "such a cavalcade was never seen before in the county of Saratoga." It stretched a mile and a half. The approach was announced by the firing of artillery from the distant hills, and they all marched straight to the United States Hotel. Here the streets leading to the hotel were choked with people, who shouted their welcome to "the man whom the people delight to honor." Since the large piazza in front of the hotel was filled with ladies, Clay's barouche had to be unhitched and dragged into position for the welcoming ceremonies.

Former Speaker of the House of Representatives John W. Taylor officiated and introduced Clay to the crowd. The senator was so overwhelmed by the attention he had received from so many wealthy and prominent Whigs that he spoke for more than an hour. Even Hone admitted that he went on too long for such an occasion, "but I suppose it was unavoidable," he added. After his seemingly endless speech Clay was conducted to his apartments amid the cheers of the men and the waving of handkerchiefs by the ladies.

That evening "the most splendid ball was given that was ever witnessed here." Bouquets of flowers and festoons of evergreens decorated the great dining hall, where eight hundred people came to pay their respects to Prince Hal. A larger collection of distinguished men and women had probably never been assembled in the country before, said Hone. Clay and his son were led into the room by several dignitaries while the band played "Hail Columbia."

18. Clay to Porter, July 31, 1839, Clay to Lucretia Clay, August 12, 1839, in Clay, *Papers,* IX, 333, 334–335; Louisville *Daily Journal,* August 9, 13, 14, 1839; Hone, *Diary,* I, 405–411; Cole, *Van Buren,* p. 347.
19. Hone, *Diary,* I, 411–412.

One old gentleman who said he admired Clay, although he himself was a locofoco, joined in the celebration. Finally he went up to Hone, who was seated at the head of the table, and exclaimed: "Almost thou persuadest me to be a Whig." Clay overheard the remark and in his brief speech that followed he said that this old gentleman had quoted Scripture and that he would quote a scriptual passage to him. "There is joy," intoned Clay, "on earth, as well as in Heaven, over one sinner that repenteth."[20]

Van Buren, Scott, and Clay not only stayed at the United States Hotel but occupied rooms on the same floor and relatively close to one another. As always the President showed Clay every politeness and courtesy, asking about Lucretia and expressing his regret that she had not accompanied the senator on his tour. On one occasion he chanced upon the senator in the hallway, and Van Buren, courteous as ever, said: "I hope I do not obstruct your way."

Without missing a beat, Clay replied: "Not here, certainly."[21]

A young lady by the name of Julia Gardiner, destined to be the first woman to marry a sitting President when she became Mrs. John Tyler, was introduced to Clay at Saratoga. Although still a schoolgirl, she appreciated "his attentions and the charm of his manner, which every one conceded," she later wrote, the women especially.[22]

At Saratoga Springs Thurlow Weed, the Whig boss of New York, came to see Clay. He wanted to make his own position absolutely clear. He said he was "warmly attached" to the senator and actually preferred him over all the others. But "I did not believe that he could be elected." In speaking this way to Clay, he said he was motivated by two considerations: concern that the great statesman should not be subjected to another mortifying defeat and that the Whig party should not miss its one great opportunity to win the presidency.

If Weed was honest about what he said, then it must have been a very difficult and perhaps a painful task for him to undertake. The two men met and talked for two days. Clay, as elder statesman, played his part exceedingly well. He could not have been "more courteous and kind," said Weed. But he did not hear what was being said to him. The New Yorker possibly dodged the corrupt bargain charge and the 1832 disaster, and since Seward had already mentioned the objections of abolitionists, he probably skipped that issue as well. Instead, Weed talked about the Bank controversy and related financial matters, none of which impressed Clay as detrimental to his candidacy. They went around and around, each trying to avoid offending the other. The senator finally suggested that when the national convention met in December, many of Weed's "apprehensions" would disappear. He felt there was a current setting in his favor "with accumulated strength"; he said that he could not and would not refuse the use of his name to the "troops of friends throughout the Union" who

20. Hone, *Diary*, I, 412–415; Weed to Seward, August 10, 1839, Seward Papers, University of Rochester Library.
21. Clay to Lucretia Clay, August 12, 1839, in Clay, *Papers*, IX, 334–335; Hone, *Diary*, I, 416.
22. "Reminiscences of Mrs. Julia G. Tyler," in Tyler, *Letters*, III, 197.

wished him to run. Therefore, he would wait to see what the convention decided and would "cheerfully and heartily acquiesce in the result of its deliberations."[23]

Weed left without accomplishing his mission. He could not deny that Clay, by his visit, had "awakened the zeal of his political friends." The masses, too, by their demonstrations and excitement seemed to acknowledge his noble genius. But behind the screams and shouts and cries of huzza, there were precious few votes to be had. Whigs adored him—no question—and acknowledged his statesmanship. But there were too many questions about his "moral values," the corrupt bargain, his record as a presidential loser, and whether he could lead them to victory in 1840.[24]

Clay moved on to Troy and Albany. He kept telling everyone that encouraging displays of popular enthusiasm on his behalf and promoting his "popularity" were the farthest things from his mind. "But the people—and they are sovereign in this matter—will not allow him to travel as he had intended," commented the *Commercial Advertiser and Journal.* Upon his arrival in a community, and without the slightest effort on the part of the Whigs to organize a demonstration, in either the cities or the countryside, "there was an immediate and spontaneous assemblage of citizens, in numbers far greater than that which received the president in the Saturday before." For Van Buren there had been weeks of preparation producing an "official and military pageant." For Clay there was "one day's notice," and the result was "an uprising of the people."[25]

"What an orator he was!" enthused an admirer many years later. "I heard him speak but once, yet that once I shall always remember. It was a good many years ago, now. It was in the immense car-house, or depot, at Syracuse. The crowd was immense; and every eye was turned toward the platform from which he was to speak, as if the whole crowd were but one expectant face." Clay rose—"tall, erect as a statue"—and looked around at the crowd as "if he were in an assembly of personal friends, as in truth he was." When he began to speak, the crowd hushed to "the most breathless silence," and "there was not a look of his eye, not a movement of his long, graceful right arm, not a swaying of his body, that was not full of grace and effect. Such a voice I never heard. It was wonderful!"[26]

Another reason people delighted in his speech was the funny stories he related. For example, he told them about his negotiations in Ghent, Belgium, to work out the details of the treaty to end the War of 1812. Many of the documents involved in the treaty were sent to the United States, and a few of them reached Kentucky, where they were read to Clay's constituents by "an

23. Weed, ed., *Autobiography of Thurlow Weed,* pp. 480–481; Hone, *Diary,* I, 416.
24. Weed, ed., *Autobiography of Thurlow Weed,* pp. 480–481.
25. *Niles' Weekly Register,* August 31, 1839.
26. "Henry Clay: Personal Anecdotes, Incidents etc.," p. 393.

odd old fellow" called Old Sandusky. While reading, Sandusky came across the
sentence "This must be deemed a *sine qua non.*"

"What's a *sine qua non?*" the Kentucky farmers called out.

Old Sandusky paused a moment, a little bothered at first by the interruption. But, said Clay, he "was fully equal to a mastery of the Latin."

"*Sine—qua—non?*" Old Sandusky repeated very slowly. "Why *Sine Qua
Non* is three islands in Passamaquoddy Bay, and Harry Clay is the last man to
give them up! 'No *Sine Qua Non,* no treaty,' he says; and he'll stick to it."[27]

The crowd roared its approval and ended with a long round of applause.

As Clay continued his tour, the demonstrations got larger and noisier. At
Troy he was escorted in a parade that stretched half a mile or more. And, of
course, he gave another speech. By this time he had reduced his performances
to a science. He spoke only thirty minutes—no more. He frequently told
anecdotes, and when he did, he would first pause, take out his snuffbox, carefully sample its contents, return the box to his pocket, and then launch into his
story, which was invariably amusing. And he played to the crowd. Did he need
to explain his position on national issues? he asked. "No," thundered back the
mob. Was there any man present who did not fully understand his opinions on
all measures and questions? Again, a rousing no from the audience. This back-
and-forth question-and-answer routine excited the crowd and provided a
rhythm and momentum that lifted all present to a state of near euphoria. He
then ended his address with his usual plea for Whig unity and perseverance and
an assertion that his party would defeat the Democrats and win the presidency.[28]

When Clay crossed the railroad bridge from Troy to Albany, the route
was one long march of cheering spectators. Ladies thronged the balconies of
their homes and public buildings, saluting their hero as he passed. As the
procession continued, "a shower of garlands, wreaths and bouquets, was
thrown into Mr. Clay's carriage, amid the waving of handkerchiefs and the
acclamations of the people."

At Albany Clay took the steamboat *Erie* and descended the Hudson
River. "It was more like a conqueror's voyage of triumph than like the passage
of a private citizen," commented one newspaper. Salutes were fired as he
passed river towns, and he was "cheered by loud huzzas of the people at the
landings." He stopped off at Kingston, went on to Poughkeepsie, Fishkill,
Newburgh, and then entered New York City in triumph.

The Whigs in the great city tendered him a brilliant reception. He landed
at the foot of Hammond Street and was escorted to Union Place and then
down Broadway to the Astor House. It was "the greatest cavalcade I ever
witnessed," said one. All Broadway was jammed with spectators; handker-

27. Ibid.
28. Ibid.; *Niles' Weekly Register,* August 31, 1839; *Commercial Advertiser and Journal,* August 20,
1839.

chiefs fluttered from windows; huzzas descended from rooftops. From an open barouche at the foot of City Hall he gave an extemporaneous speech. "His voice rang out so loud and clear that his words were distinctly reverberated from the wall of the Astor House." That evening Clay attended the Bowery Theater, and "a thousand voices shouted welcome till every rafter of the magnificent edifice shouted back again." What made it all the more remarkable was that these receptions had been accomplished with no expense and very little preparation or organization. Except for the reception for Lafayette in 1824, it was the grandest reception yet given to a visiting dignitary.

Clay crossed the river to Brooklyn, where he was greeted with a huge banner across Fulton Street:

H E N R Y   C L A Y
Welcome to Brooklyn

He was "paraded in triumph through the streets . . . strewed with flowers." The floor and seats of the barouche in which he was riding were also piled high with flowers. The next day he met the mayor of New York City and the Common Council and then received visitors in the governor's room in City Hall, where only one in twenty who went to see him could get anywhere near him. "The civilities of New Yorkers have nearly annihilated him," wrote Philip Hone, and he was frankly hoarse and quite fatigued. Even so, Clay that evening attended the theater, where he received another ovation.[29]

Since New York City was the center of his most important political strength in the state, he did everything possible to bolster Whig enthusiasm and encourage greater efforts on behalf of the party and himself. He put on display the full range of his charm, wit, affability, social graciousness, and personal charisma. His major speech on Wednesday, August 21, shamefully and excessively extolled the importance of the state in the nation's history. "From the moment that Burgoyne surrendered his arms and his army in New York," he declared, "a new light dawned upon the fortunes of our country; and whatever may have been our temporary reverses or partial defeats in other sections, they were all lost in the victory won on the plains of Saratoga."

During this New York visit Clay attended a reception of several hundred women at the American Institute. He rather enjoyed these special treats—his reputation with ladies was well known—and they greeted him on his arrival with "shouts of joy and congratulation." One "beautiful young girl" then presented him with a bouquet of flowers and a snuffbox made from the timbers of "Old Ironsides." He then gracefully presented one of the flowers to the "beautiful young girl."

When he left the city by train on Saturday morning for Philadelphia, he felt he had accomplished all he had set out to do in the Empire State. And

29. Stanton, *Random Recollections*, p. 153; Louisville *Daily Journal*, August 29, 31, 1839, copying the New York *Courier and Enquirer*; Hone, *Diary*, I, 417–418.

because he had been treated by the Whig politicians with such devotion and reverence, he also presumed that the outpouring of popular affection had convinced the leaders of the party that he was the man to head their ticket in 1840.

The Whig committee dutifully accompanied him to Philadelphia. Along the way the train made several stops in New Jersey to permit him to meet dignitaries and politicians, greet the crowds, and give short speeches. The Philadelphia committee joined his party at Bristol and arranged to have the rear car of the train detached from the other cars as it neared the city and then brought down the main track for a spectacular welcome.

The streets leading to the depot, reported one newspaper, "were crowded with carriages, omnibuses, coaches, gigs, wagons, horsemen and foot, awaiting the arrival of the expectant visitant." When he finally appeared, he looked haggard and drawn. The weeks of travel, receptions, speeches, meetings, and the excessive "civilities" of everyone he encountered had obviously exhausted him, and he was manfully trying to get through the next event without showing his weariness and distress.

After the welcoming ceremonies at the depot Clay was taken to a barouche, accompanied by Mathew Carey, and then driven to Independence Square, with a band playing and flags flying, to hear another address of welcome by Joseph R. Ingersoll. But Clay looked so tired and ill that they permitted him to forgo the ceremony and leave directly for his hotel. Several times he came out on the balcony of his residence to greet the crowds congregated below, each time saying a few words to satisfy their need to hear him speak. But "his hoarseness prevented any thing like a speech."[30]

Clay managed to get through all the Philadelphia activities without incident. He then headed to Baltimore, where he was again met by a large crowd, paraded through the streets, and welcomed at City Hall by the mayor. Feeling more rested, he delivered a thirty-minute speech "characterized by much of the varied ability—the playfulness,[31] the humor, the high patriotic feeling, and the fervid eloquence, which combine to produce in him, one of the most splendid and efficient orators of his age." During the speech he lamented the fact that ever since the destruction of the BUS the monetary affairs of the nation had fallen under the control of the Bank of England. The Jacksonians called our Bank a "monster," but "if it were a monster, it should always be recollected that we the people, had the control of its CAGE. It was bound in the iron meshes of a charter" and operated according to the needs and wishes of the

30. Louisville *Daily Journal,* August 31, September 2, 1839.
31. In this instance, according to newspaper accounts, Clay's "playfulness" consisted of the following: "His playful illusions to the state of friendly vassalage to the various committees of his friends, under which he had lived for some weeks past, and to his diversion for a short season into the dominions of the virgin queen, as a means of temporary relief from the pressure of well meant kindness, were exceedingly happy, and drew the most marked and approbatory responses from his hearers." *Niles' Weekly Register,* August 31, 1839.

American people. But the foreign monster has no such cage "and puts the screws upon the money market . . . regardless of the adverse effect upon this side of the Atlantic!" When he finished, "a round of applause arose that made the welkin ring."[32]

The campaign tour—supposedly a personal and private vacation—was a total success. Even his final swing home through Washington and Virginia stirred enthusiastic receptions along the way. At White Sulphur Springs Clay "found himself a prisoner in the hands of a zealous and united community. . . . One feeling, one spirit animated the breathing mass that surround him—it was a feeling of gratitude and veneration for the high service he had so often done his country."

Indeed, at this stage of his life Clay had reached a point of "veneration" by large numbers of the electorate. He was seen as the one man who could resolve seemingly irreconcilable differences. He was the first statesman of the land, they declared, "whose praise is now on the lips of every American of every party." The single toast he heard most often as he toured the country summarized precisely how the nation regarded him: "Our distinguished guest, HENRY CLAY—'The Great Pacificator.'"[33]

32. Ibid.
33. Ibid., September 7, 1839.

"Deceived Betrayed & Beaten"

CLAY HAD NO SOONER returned to Ashland in September than he began to contact ardent supporters around the country about the probable course their states would take in relation to the presidential election. In a word, he wanted their honest opinion about whether he should run or not. In view of some of the negative things he had heard in New York—most recently a false rumor that his withdrawal from the race was imminent—he needed to get a better sense of what the rest of the country thought. "I know of no one who will be more likely to communicate it than yourself," he told each of them. The information was frankly intended to "guide his own course" for the immediate future, and "I can hear accounts unfavorable to myself, with as much composure, if not with as much pleasure, as those of an opposite character."[1]

And they told him. Some assured him that he was the only possible candidate to head the Whig ticket, which was what he wanted to hear. But others advised his withdrawing in favor of Scott or Harrison. "Candor compels me to say," replied one, "that I greatly fear that your name would not be sufficiently potent to stem the current that has set, and is still running against us." In Indiana and Ohio "our opponents" strongly support Harrison. "They have not forgotten the old contest when their idol Gen. Jackson and yourself were in the field. They still retain a deep-rooted prejudice against you, repeating the oft-refuted charge of bargain, intrigue and management, between you and Mr. Adams, and they are beyond the reach of reason or arguments." Furthermore, although the Whigs in these states would not hesitate supporting a Clay candidacy if they thought his success was "probable," they "can not

---

1. Clay to Oliver H. Smith, September 14, 1839, Clay to Seward, September, 1839, in Clay, *Papers*, IX, 340, 347. Smith headed the Clay Whigs in Indiana. Similar letters went to Allen A. Hall and Thomas Washington in Tennessee, and Benjamin Leigh and Francis Brooke in Virginia, among others.

bear the idea of seeing you placed in a doubtful and desperate contest at this time."

It is truly remarkable how many Whigs desperately desired Clay as their President but withdrew their support from him because they did not want to subject him to the humiliation of a third defeat. They genuinely cared about him, so much so that they wished to spare him this personal humiliation. Better to deny him the nomination than witness his "disgrace" at the hands of Martin Van Buren. "How sad," commented one man.[2]

Clay learned at this time that Weed and Seward in New York had definitely come out in favor of General Winfield Scott. "A sort of panic has been got up," he was told. "A great many of your staunchest friends have yielded to its influence." Friends, indeed! Later he discovered how potent the drive for the "Hero of Bridgewater" really was. "To my very great surprize," Clay wrote, ". . . I found that the project . . . to run Genl. Scott had risen to an importance that I had never supposed it would reach." He also received direct evidence about the "triangular correspondence" scheme, a circular "from an assumed *friend of mine,* to influence the Whigs of N. York *against* me!" he snorted. This plus the rumor that he planned to withdraw truly infuriated him. In a letter to Governor Seward he was almost curt, and he told the governor that he had no intention of withdrawing at this time. "The truth is that I have formed no determination, one way or the other, about the matter; and on this occasion, availing myself of Mr. V. Buren's habit of non commitalism, I mean to remain uncommitted, until the proper moment arrives for a decision."[3]

By late fall there could be no doubt in Clay's mind that he had real problems in New York, Pennsylvania (where a second Whig convention, managed by the dour and forbidding Thaddeus Stevens, opted for General Harrison[4]), and some western states. Still, he could not make himself believe that after all the demonstrations he had recently witnessed that these two "military chieftains" could be preferred over himself. Besides, unlike Clay, neither Harrison nor Scott had support in all sections of the country. Except for the states along the border of Canada, what others favored Scott? And, in the election of 1836 Harrison had taken only three out of eight western states, one New England state, and three Middle Atlantic states. But he had received not a single electoral vote in the South.

Clay, on the other hand, felt he had support in all sections of the country.

2. Allen A. Hall to Clay, September 23, 1839, Oliver H. Smith to Clay, September 28, 1839, in Clay, *Papers,* IX, 344–345, 348–349. See also Willis Hall to Clay, November 20, 1839, ibid., IX, 355.

3. Willis Hall to Clay, November 20, 1839, Clay to Harrison Gray Otis, December 4, 1839, Clay to Seward, September 26, 1839, in Clay, *Papers,* IX, 355, 360, 347; Clay to Benjamin W. Leigh, November 17, 1839, CPP.

4. The first convention held at Chambersburg was dominated by Clay's friends from Philadelphia. Western delegates bolted and called for a "Union and Harmony Convention." A second convention was subsequently called, and Stevens, with the help of his henchman Charles B. Penrose won an endorsement for Harrison. Henry R. Mueller, *The Whig Party in Pennsylvania* (New York, 1922), pp. 58–60; Gunderson, *Log-Cabin Campaign,* p. 56.

Already he had received nominations or endorsements from Kentucky, Rhode Island, and Maryland. Moreover, south of the Ohio River he had no apparent competition. The Whig convention in Virginia endorsed him first, followed immediately by Mississippi, Louisiana, Alabama, and North Carolina. In addition, Clay had friends everywhere who had been working on his behalf for years. They had organizations that he, Clay, had urged and (in some instances) aided them to build. "Should you not forthwith proceed to organize the whole State and every County and City?" he told them. "Can you succeed without Conventions, Committees of Correspondence, Vigilance &c?" Besides these organizations, his statesmanship was acknowledged by everyone. Could Whigs dismiss all that in favor of a virtual unknown, like Scott, or elevate, as Nathaniel Beverley Tucker said, "such a poor creature" as Harrison?[5]

Clay decided to stick it out. It grieved him to see the Whigs so split just a few months before the convention. "Defeat and disaster do not, with them, seem to produce the usual effect of more concord and harmony," he wrote. Nevertheless, he felt obliged to stand his ground. In December he notified the Kentucky delegation now headed for the National Whig Convention in Harrisburg, Pennsylvania, that he would leave it to the convention to make the final choice, and if it turned out to be someone other than himself, then he would accept the verdict, and that nominee "will have my best wishes, and receive my cordial support."[6]

Clay had hardly arrived home from his tour, consulted friends, and attended some private affairs than it was time to pack and return to Washington for the beginning of the Twenty-sixth Congress. Although he felt reasonably rested after a few weeks at Ashland, he was bothered by rheumatism in his arm. He was also apprehensive about his children—nothing seemed to change— and worried about Julia, Henry, Jr.'s wife, who was pregnant once again and due to deliver in a few months. After Anne's untimely death his fears for the welfare of his family, especially its female members, intensified.

Upon his arrival in Washington in early December Clay appeared exceedingly restless and on edge. He moved his residence three times during his stay, perhaps giving some indication of his mood and the extent of his stress and anxiety.[7]

A rather painful episode occurred almost immediately upon his arrival at

5. Clay to Benjamin W. Leigh, June 12, 1839, CPP; Tucker to Clay, December 16, 1839, Clay Papers, LC; Gunderson, *Log-Cabin Campaign*, p. 43; Thomas E. Jeffrey, *State Parties and National Politics: North Carolina, 1815–1861* (Athens, Ga., 1989), pp. 95–96.

6. Clay to Oliver H. Smith, October 5, 1839, Clay to Nathan Sargent, October 25, 1839, Clay to Robert Swartwout, November 15, 1839, Clay to Thomas Metcalfe et al., November 20, 1839, in Clay, *Papers*, IX, 350, 352, 354, 357–359.

7. Clay to Thomas Washington, October 12, 1839, Clay to Lucretia Clay, January 24, 1840, in Clay, *Papers*, IX, 352, 383. Clay and his servant, Charles, first roomed at Mrs. Denny's boarding-house on Third Street, where his messmates included Rice Garland and Thomas W. Chinn. Then in February, he moved to Mrs. E. S. Arguelle's boardinghouse, opposite Gadsby's, where his messmates included Leverett Saltonstall and John Henderson. In the spring the three congressmen moved to Mrs. Cochran's boardinghouse on F Street. Clay to Lucretia Clay, February 12, 1840, Clay to Anne Saltonstall, May 31, 1840, ibid., IX, 385–386, 417.

the Capitol, painful in that it all but shattered his hopes for the nomination. Representative Charles F. Mitchell informed him that a poll had been taken among New York congressmen, and not a single member of the delegation believed that Clay could win their state's electoral vote. All but two thought that Scott could win handily. Clay received this devastating news with dignity and said he would communicate it to the Kentucky delegates headed for the Whig convention in Harrisburg. He would also tell them that he desired the nomination of the strongest candidate possible and would give him his full support. Millard Fillmore, who was present during this interview, said that the Kentuckian's reaction was "magnanimous and worthy of Henry Clay." When the New Yorkers had left, Clay penned a sad letter to his friend Peter B. Porter and predicted that Scott would be nominated. Everyone told him that he preferred the redoubtable "Harry of the West" and that nine-tenths of his constituents also preferred Clay, "yet they think that it is easier to carry nine to one than one to nine!"[8]

The "Democratic Whig National Convention"[9] began its meeting on December 4, 1839, at Harrisburg, capital of Pennsylvania, in the city's new Lutheran church, with twenty-two out of twenty-six states represented. Each state might cast its quota of electoral votes, and a majority of 128 votes was needed for nomination. As it turned out, the proceedings were dominated and managed by two men who were not delegates: Thurlow Weed and Thaddeus Stevens. Both men had been leaders of the Anti-Masonic party, both men were hardheaded pragmatists, and both men supported someone other than Henry Clay.

Weed, sometimes called the Jolly Drummer on account of his affability and persuasive charm, owned and operated the Albany *Evening Journal* and had built a political organization to rival Van Buren's Regency in New York. Tall, somewhat rugged in appearance, and a superb lobbyist, he had come to Harrisburg a week earlier to work his conviviality on the delegates for Scott. He had brought with him Horace Greeley, whom he had hired the year before to edit a political weekly. There was no question that Weed controlled the New York delegation, of whom twenty favored Scot, ten favored Clay, and two favored Harrison.[10]

Thaddeus Stevens was totally opposite in background, character, and personality. Lawyer, manufacturer, and real estate operator, he lacked Weed's personal charm and organizational genius. Rude, tactless, mentally scarred by a clubfoot and the premature loss of hair, he controlled the Anti-Masonic vote

8. Fillmore to Weed, December 2, 1839, Weed Papers, University of Rochester Library; Clay to Porter, December 4, 1839, in Clay, *Papers,* IX, 360–361.

9. This is what the convention called itself, and it is significant that it included the word "Democratic" because many Whigs, including Clay, rejected the right of their opponents to the exclusive use of the term.

10. Weed, ed., *Autobiography* of Thurlow Weed, p. 456ff.; Gunderson, *Log-Cabin Campaign,* pp. 29–32. See also Van Deusen, *Weed.*

in Pennsylvania by dint of hard work and uncompromising aggressiveness. Vindictive in thought and action, moody, and stentorian-voiced, he intimidated opponents to get what he wanted. He had put together in 1835 a coalition of Anti-Masons and Whigs that elected the obese and phlegmatic Joseph Ritner governor of Pennsylvania. Now Stevens had arrived in Harrisburg fully determined to win the nomination for Harrison. He wanted no part of Henry Clay because he was a Mason and a loser. Stevens achieved his first success when the convention seated two rival Pennsylvania delegations, one favorable to Clay and the other favorable to Harrison. This so-called amicable agreement actually gave control of the Pennsylvania vote to the Stevens group because it held a majority in the combined delegation.[11]

Stevens's hotel room became the center for plotting Whig strategy among those opposed to Henry Clay. Horace Greeley, as Weed's emissary, attended most of the meetings and helped strengthen the working tie between the New York and Pennsylvania managers, especially after they had resolved their differences over who should receive the nomination.[12]

When the convention began Clay had a clear plurality of the 254 delegates in attendance.[13] Once organizational matters had been cleared away and James Barbour of Virginia elected president of the convention, the managers of the Scott and Harrison forces proceeded immediately to extinguish that plurality. Peleg Sprague, a close friend of Daniel Webster's and a former senator from Maine, introduced a motion in which each state would appoint three delegates to a general committee. The members of the committee would canvass the preference of their states and then discuss and vote in secret on the possible candidates. If it appeared that a majority of the general committee favored a particular person, it would report that fact to the full convention. Presumably Sprague's motion sought to prevent floor fights. But one of Stevens's henchmen at the convention, Charles B. Penrose, amended the motion by requiring that the vote of a majority of each delegation would be reported as the vote of that state and that each state's delegation in the general committee would cast the full electoral vote of the state. In other words, the Penrose amendment called for the adoption of the unit rule. Worse, it negated the important minority strength that Clay held in Pennsylvania, Ohio, and New York. In effect, said one, it "effectually changed the body from a fair, open, honest convention into a closed-door conclave."

The Clay delegates instantly recognized the purpose of the amendment and fought it; but the combined efforts of the Weed and Stevens forces beat them back, and the amended motion passed. It was a "model contrivance of the few to govern the many," marveled Senator Benton. "A secure way to produce an intended result without showing the design, and without leaving a

---

11. On Stevens, see Richard N. Current, *Old Thaddeus Stevens: A Story of Ambition* (Madison, Wis., 1942), and Fawn M. Brodie, *Thaddeus Stevens* (New York, 1959).
12. Greeley to Stevens, December 10, 1839, Thaddeus Stevens Papers, LC.
13. Weed, ed., *Autobiography* of Thurlow Weed, p. 481.

trace behind to show what was done." Algebra and alchemy entered the formula, he chuckled. "Those who set the sum could work it; and the quotient was political death to Mr. Clay."[14]

Weed and Stevens then set about completing the formal execution of Mr. Clay. To those who pointed to all the delegates at the convention favoring "Harry of the West," Weed responded that they came from states the Kentuckian would surely lose in the general election, southern states in particular. Weed worked several delegations at this time, trying to get them to switch. When he found that they would not desert Clay, he asked them at least to designate Scott as second choice. Stevens was just as active for Harrison and had the additional advantage of Webster's withdrawal from the contest. He found that most of the New England delegations, after Webster, favored Old Tippecanoe.

An early informal canvass of the convention, with Michigan abstaining, confirmed what most suspected: Clay had the greatest delegate strength, polling a plurality of 103 votes from twelve states; Harrison came next with 91 from six states; and Scott last with 57 from three states.[15] New York was one of Scott's three states and gave him 42 votes. Not a single vote from that state went to Clay under the unit rule, even though ten men strongly favored him.

Before the general committee reached a decision on a candidate, Weed managed to convince the Connecticut committeemen to switch from Clay to Scott. When the Michigan delegation broke a deadlock in Scott's favor in another informal canvass, Clay's plurality dropped to 95 while Scott's vote rose to 68. Harrison remained at 91. At this point it looked as though Scott might become the compromise candidate, but Stevens managed to pull off a daring and cunning trick that turned everything around.[16]

He had in his possession a letter Scott had written to Francis Granger indicating a favorable disposition toward abolitionists. It was a crude effort on Scott's part to elicit their support. Stevens took the letter and visited the headquarters of the Virginia delegation. As he strolled around the room, he casually dropped the letter on the floor. When the Virginians, who had been considering naming Scott as their second choice, discovered it, they immediately caucused to decide what they should do. Alarmed that Clay might lose the nomination, and even more alarmed at the possibility of Scott's nomination, they decided to abandon Clay and switch to Harrison.[17]

The Scott bandwagon came to an abrupt halt. Weed saw immediately

14. *Proceedings of the Democratic Whig National Convention* . . . (Harrisburg, 1839), pp. 15–16. These proceedings are reprinted in Schlesinger, and Israel, eds., *History of American Presidential Elections, 1789–1968,* I, 700–713. Weed, ed., *Autobiography* of Thurlow Weed, p. 482; Sargent, *Public Men and Events,* II, 89; Benton, *Thirty Years' View,* II, 204.

15. For Clay: Rhode Island, 4; Connecticut, 8; Delaware, 3; Maryland, 10; Virginia, 23; North Carolina, 15; Kentucky, 15; Illinois, 5; Alabama, 7; Louisiana, 5; Mississippi, 4; Missouri, 4. Sargent, *Public Men and Events,* II, 91. Sargent mistakenly counts only 14 for Kentucky.

16. Gunderson, *Log-Cabin Campaign,* pp. 60–61.

17. Ibid., p. 61; Current, *Stevens,* p. 74, note 3; Alexander K. McClure, *Our Presidents and How We Make Them* (New York, 1900), pp. 67–68; Elliott, *Scott,* p. 380.

what was happening. He figured that on the next canvass the entire South would turn to Harrison and probably clinch the nomination. He could not and would not back a loser. That, he knew, was the first law of politics. So, with hardly a second thought, he bolted to Harrison.[18]

Clay's friends also saw what was happening. Again they tried to block the onward rush of the Harrison bandwagon. Unfortunately, despite their great strength in delegates, they did not have a manager of sufficient skill to counter the devious tactics of Weed and Stevens. The Clay supporters were ardent in their devotion and loyalty, but they lacked the political deftness to take control of the convention and bring about the nomination of their choice.

Since the general committee had still not made a recommendation, Cassius Marcellus Clay, a distant kinsman of the Kentucky senator, rose on Friday, December 6, and moved that the convention reverse itself and allow each delegate to designate "viva voce" his choice. In addition, he asked that the majority of their delegation cast the votes of absent members for them. It was the only way, he insisted, that the convention could obtain a "full, fair, and candid expression of opinion." But the motion was summarily assigned to the table.[19] Then Reverdy Johnson of Maryland moved that the general committee report its progress and then be dismissed from any further action. Again the motion was tabled. At this juncture it was generally understood that New York, Michigan, and Vermont had deserted Scott and that Illinois had abandoned Clay, for Harrison.

It was well after nine o'clock at night when the convention decided to take an hour's recess. Near midnight the reassembled delegates received the report of the general committee, which had voted Harrison, 148 votes; Clay, 90; Scott, 16. No vice presidential recommendation was submitted, and the convention adjourned without reaching a final decision.[20]

One of Clay's Kentucky managers at the convention—such as they were—wrote the senator immediately after the committee's vote was announced. "You have been deceived betrayed & beaten," lamented Leslie Combs, "by Northern abolition Anti-masonry and the Dutch & the Dane. . . . There has, in my opinion—been a deliberate conspiracy agt you by the friends of Mr Webster. Mr. [Alexander] Hamilton & Mr J. A. King of New York violated their instructions." Harrison did not get a single slave state vote, Combs continued, but neither did Clay win a free state, "except glorious *Rhode Island.*" Some delegates were so disgusted they considered leaving the convention and going home. "I shall not decide on my own course till tomorrow," Combs declared.[21]

Because there was a genuine possibility of the Clay supporters' bolting the

18. It has been suggested that Weed planned to switch all along and claim credit for winning the nomination for Harrison, but the evidence does not support this thesis. See Roy F. Nichols, *The Invention of American Political Parties* (New York, 1967).
19. *Proceedings of . . . Convention,* p. 18.
20. Ibid., pp. 18–20.
21. Combs to Clay, December 6, 1839, in Clay, *Papers,* IX, 362–363.

convention before the nominee had been selected, the other managers decided
to delay final voting on the general committee's report for twenty-four hours
in order to placate "the ardent friends of Mr. Clay, whose disappointment and
vexation found excited expression." Apparently these ardent friends could fret
and fume and shed tears but little more. As a sop to these hysterics, Weed and
Stevens agreed that "some prominent friend" of Clay's should be given the vice
presidential nomination. But to their surprise it became an exceedingly difficult task. No one wanted it—at least no "true" friend. In their desperate search
for a candidate the managers worked through the night and well into the
following day.

The general committee finally settled on Benjamin Watkins Leigh of
Virginia, who was indeed one of Clay's warmest friends. But Leigh immediately rose in the convention and declined the nomination. Weed then persuaded the general committee to advance the name of John M. Clayton of
Delaware. No sooner did the nomination reach the floor than Reverdy Johnson rose and read a letter from Clayton authorizing the withdrawal of his name
should it be presented to the convention. Weed's spokesmen insisted that the
instruction applied only to a presidential nomination, but Johnson persisted in
disallowing the use of Clayton's name. Tallmadge of New York and Southard
of New Jersey were next tendered the office, and both declined. "Finally, all
other efforts failing," said Weed, they turned to John Tyler of Virginia, who
had *"shed tears"* over Clay's defeat. A former Democrat, former governor,
former senator, and staunch states' rights advocate of the old school, he had
broken with Jackson over the Bank War and the Proclamation to South Carolina in 1832. In 1836 he consented to run on a Whig ticket with Hugh Lawson
White in Virginia, North Carolina, and Georgia and with William Henry
Harrison in Maryland. Clearly he did not object to the widespread use of his
name.[22]

The claim that Clay engineered Tyler's nomination in a deal to win the
Virginia Senate seat for William C. Rives is quite mistaken. Tyler actually
rejected the offer—supposing that it was indeed tendered—and continued the
senatorial deadlock until well after his nomination for Vice President.[23] Apparently those tears he had shed did the trick. They convinced delegates that he
was one of those passionate Whigs who idolized Henry Clay. Tyler attended
the convention, but no one thought to question his principles or his loyalty.
He himself later denied that tears had won him the nomination. He preferred
to believe—and there is an element of truth in his assertion—that as a states'
rights, anti-Bank Virginian he was chosen to balance the ticket and provide
southern votes. His acceptance, wrote one delegate, "was both a fraud and a
treachery."[24]

Actually the entire convention was a treachery. Clay thought it would be

22. Weed, ed., *Autobiography* of Thurlow Weed, p. 482; Sargent, *Public Men and Events,* II, 93.
23. Lyon G. Tyler, ed., *Letters and Times of the Tylers* (Richmond, Va., 1884), I, 591, 595;
Gunderson, *Log-Cabin Campaign,* pp. 62–63.
24. Sargent, *Public Men and Events,* II, 93–94.

an open convention, each delegate acting responsibly and in accordance with the will of his constituents. Not so. The Kentucky senator was delivered into the hands of a committee, and "the committee disposed of him in a back chamber." Rather neatly, too. "Double dealing and treachery accomplished the result the intriguers had been for months laying plans to effect."[25]

But Clay had the last word. And it was so noble and beautiful that the delegates went wild. On the final day of the convention the Kentucky delegation asked to read the letter Clay had sent about his position should the convention choose someone other than himself. In offering his "best wishes and . . . cordial support" to whatever ticket the delegates put together, he ruled out any possibility of the Clay men bolting the party. Weed and Stevens must have sighed with relief. Others broke down. Only a great man, they said, could act so magnanimously.

Diehard Clay men scorned the shouts and applause of the friends of the other candidates. "Having contumaciously cast the great leader of the party aside," said one, "they began lauding him with feigned sincerity and artful guile, *ad nauseam.*" Indeed, they did carry on about it—at great length. Probably they were really expressing their relief that the Whig party did not shatter over the treachery committed against a great statesman.

At the conclusion of the reading, Reverdy Johnson rose and moved the unanimous nomination of Harrison and Tyler. The delegates screamed their approval, and the convention adjourned.[26]

The united Whig party at last had a ticket: "Tippecanoe and Tyler, Too." Commented Philip Hone: "There was rhyme, but no reason in it." What the Whigs actually had besides a catchy slogan were two men who either knew little of the principles of the party or rejected them outright. The "poor creature" Harrison might disgrace the office, said one, but no matter. The presidency under Jackson had acquired too much power anyway, and Tippecanoe's election might be a beneficial antidote. "The throne is too high," he wrote Clay, "and it may be well to place a man upon it who will degrade it by his imbecility."[27]

Probably the man most responsible for Clay's defeat at the convention was Thaddeus Stevens. He not only turned Pennsylvania around but turned the entire convention around. And his reward? Nothing. He begged for office after the election and was stunned when he received not even a "crumb." And whom did he blame? Why, Henry Clay, of course. Who had greater reason for revenge? As a result, says his biographer, Stevens became more than ever a factionalist, not a true and regular Whig.[28]

25. Benton, *Thirty Years' View,* II, 204; Sargent, *Public Men and Events,* II, 92.

26. Sargent, *Public Men and Events,* II, 93; *Proceedings . . . of the Convention,* pp. 24–25. "Tis done & . . . Mr. Clay receives it in a manner to make one regret that it had to be so," wrote Francis Granger to Weed, December 9, 1839, Granger Papers, LC.

27. Hone, *Diary,* II, 553; Nathaniel Beverley Tucker to Clay, December 16, 1839, in Clay, *Papers,* IX, 367.

28. Current, *Stevens,* p. 75.

As Leslie Combs had declared to Clay, the National Whig Convention was controlled by Anti-Masons, abolitionists, and others who cared little about the program and principles of the party. As he looked back on it, wrote another delegate, the proceedings of the convention must be judged singularly unwise and unfortunate. "In fact, a gross BLUNDER."[29]

But Clay also had a hand in engineering his defeat. His Senate speech on February 7, 1839, against the abolitionists, more than any other single factor, undoubtedly prevented him from gaining a single northern state at the convention "except glorious *Rhode Island.*"

"I had rather be right than President," Clay had reportedly announced. So be it, responded the delegates.

At the very hour of his defeat Clay sat in a room at Brown's Hotel, drinking with several friends and waiting for news of his nomination. Although he had predicted Scott's success, he could not bring himself to believe that the Whigs would actually do it and reject him. The more he drank, the more he reassured himself. He began to carry on outrageously. "He made most singular exhibitions of himself," observed one man. "Open and exceedingly profane in his denunciations of the intriguers against his nomination," he started swearing "in words befitting only a bar-room in vulgar broil." Then, suddenly, he came awake to his gross behavior. There were strangers in the room, two of them dressed in black.

Clay turned to them. "But, gentlemen, for aught I know, from your cloth you may be *parsons,* and shocked at my words. Let us take a glass a wine." He walked to a "well-loaded" sideboard and poured several drinks. Then he left the room.

The strangers stared at each other in disbelief. Could this be the great Harry of the West, the Great Compromiser, Prince Hal? "That man can never be my political idol again," sadly commented one of the strangers to the other.

Clay crossed Pennsylvania Avenue to his boardinghouse to await the arrival of friends from Harrisburg. Several delegates returned to Washington by railroad and were met by a group of Whig partisans who had gone to the depot to greet the returning delegates. When they heard the news of Harrison's victory, they could not wait to relay it to Clay.

They found him seated in a chair. After they conveyed their stunning news, he jumped up. He started screaming and cursing and pacing back and forth across the room. "Such an exhibition we never witnessed before," reported one of the men who brought him the information, "and we pray never again to witness such an ebullition of passion, such a storm of desperation and curses." Clay kept stamping his feet as he paced. Finally he burst out: "My friends are not worth the powder and shot it would take to kill them!"

He named names. Daniel Webster, for one.[30] And his passion intensified

---

29. Sargent, *Public Men and Events,* II, 95.

30. "Webster is now openly avowed by Clay's friends," wrote John Catron to James K. Polk, "to

as Clay spoke, invoking the "most horrid imprecations" against his "friends." Shaking his fist and shouting as loudly as possible, he added: "If there were two Henry Clays, one of them would make the other President of the United States!"

The other men in the room tried to calm him. "If there were *two* Henry Clays," said one, "the continent would not be large enough to hold them, and they would not leave a morsel of each other; they would mutually destroy themselves."

Clay finally calmed down. As he did so, his anger and bitterness and hurt turned to self-pity. "It is a diabolical intrigue, I now know, which has betrayed me," he groaned. "I am the most unfortunate man in the history of parties; always run by my friends when sure to be defeated, and now betrayed for a nomination when I, or any one, would be sure of an election."[31]

Although Clay recovered from this shattering defeat and made a point of hiding his true feelings when making public appearances, he sometimes slipped into maudlin self-pity when drinking. Thereafter, said one man, "Mr. Clay was excessively intemperate in his habits, and more intemperate in exacerbation of temper and in his political conduct." Several needless quarrels erupted in restaurants or on the Senate floor on account of his wounded pride and disappointment. Sometimes his colleagues found him distant and "inapproachable," delighting his enemies, who "chuckled at his self-immolation."[32] The Democrats took particular pleasure in his humiliation. "Clay is broke down—& feels it," wrote one. He "looks as if he was placid & content—but it is plain enough that in debate his temper is very high."[33]

As soon as the convention adjourned, a number of delegates rushed to Washington to salute Clay and console him. More than ever they idolized him as a true patriot and statesman who would sacrifice his own ambition for the good of the party and the country. Some even told him that the friends of both Harrison and Scott admitted that if either one of these men were elected, "*Mr. Clay* will be the actual president of the U. States, direct their counsels and prescribe their future policy."[34]

Several days later a grand supper was arranged in his honor at Brown's Hotel on December 11. John Tyler attended and in a reply to a toast confessed that his nomination totally surprised him. But it was Henry Clay whom the

have been for Harrison, against Clay, previous to the Convention. I found it out at Phild. by accident, that the Webster delegates from Mass. were most anxious to exclude Clay, on their way to the Convention." January 3, 1840, in Polk, *Correspondence,* V, 367.

31. Wise, *Seven Decades of the Union,* pp. 170–172. It should be remembered that this entire scene was described by a man who was Clay's enemy and President John Tyler's henchman in Congress. The work was written in retrospect more than thirty years later. Most likely Wise added more than the facts warranted.

32. Ibid., p. 172.

33. John Catron to James K. Polk, January 3, 1840, in Polk, *Correspondence,* V, 367.

34. Porter to Clay, December 16, 1839, in Clay, *Papers,* IX, 367.

crowd wanted to hear, and he did not disappoint them. As he rose, every person in the room rose with him and cheered and applauded as they got to their feet. A wan smile flickered across Clay's face as he stared at his jubilant audience. Then all went silent as the participants resumed their seats to hear what Prince Hal had to say.

The Great Pacificator said all the right things. He congratulated them on their patriotic sacrifice in traveling hundreds of miles at the most inclement season of the year to meet, deliberate, and decide a momentous question. "You have made a unanimous nomination," he said, and surely no man can "object to what was done." If some were disappointed in the result, they were bound by patriotism, the hope of destroying a corrupt administration, and the need of establishing a purer and better government to accede to the nomination. "If," he continued in a most earnest and heartfelt tone of voice, "if I have friends . . . if I have any one that loves me—I assure them that they cannot do me a better service than to follow my example, and vote heartily as I shall, for the nomination which has been made."

The room exploded. Men wiped away tears as they cheered. It was a long while before the shouts died down and the speaker could continue.

"What is a public man worth to the country, in what does he show his patriotism," Clay declared, "if he is not always ready to sacrifice himself for his country." But there had been no sacrifice, he exclaimed. We have not been contending for Henry Clay or Daniel Webster or General Harrison or General Scott. "No! We have been contending for principles. Not men, but principles, are our rule of action. Look not then to Harrisburg but to the White House . . . not to the man who has been nominated, but to the Goths and Vandals at the Capitol. . . . Tell your constituents . . . to put forth all the energies they possess to relieve the land from the curse which rests upon it."[35]

The speech was intended to repair any rifts within the party that might have resulted because of his defeat. And Clay pronounced his speech so sincerely that it had the desired impact. "His speech had a soothing effect upon his disappointed friends," said one man, and they resolved to follow his advice and work hard to elect "Tippecanoe and Tyler, Too."

The speech proved again Clay's great patriotism and statesmanship. He was fiercely ambitious for the presidential office and terribly hurt when the Whigs asked him to stand aside for another, but he genuinely wished to see the party united behind its candidate so that the "Goths and Vandals" might be driven from power. Again and again he wrote to friends during the following months, urging them to support the ticket despite their "mortification" and "disgust." He told his family to behave as he did. "I have felt that it was the only course of honor good faith and duty," he wrote to his son Henry, Jr. "I have accordingly both publicly and privately expressed my determination to abide by and support the nomination. I shall be glad if you and my other connexions shall come to the same conclusion."

35. Speech, December 11, 1839, in Clay, *Papers,* IX, 363–364.

But to his dying day the loss of the nomination haunted him, and he always insisted that the Harrisburg convention violated a great principle: "that of conforming to the *known will* of their Constituents."[36]

Tippecanoe wrote him shortly thereafter. He had once admitted to the senator that he never expected to be his rival for the presidency, "an office which I never dreamed of attaining and which I had ardently desired to see you occupy." Now he had the nomination with every prospect of defeating Van Buren in the fall election. He thanked Clay for the "magnanimity" of his concession, effusively expressed his gratitude, and suggested they begin a regular correspondence. He invited Clay's advice during the campaign and asked his "opinion of the course I should persue" in answering attacks on his military career. As his friends had long since affirmed, he fully expected the Kentuckian to direct his counsels and prescribe his future policy.[37]

In the ensuing months Clay's intense disappointment gave way to resignation and ultimately to acquiescence in Harrison's place at the head of the Whig ticket. Not much later General Scott gave a banquet in Washington and invited all the Whig members of Congress. To the surprise of some, Henry Clay showed up and strode into the room "with his characteristic dignity." Scott, who had never met his former rival, immediately came forward to greet him and extended his hand. "I am happy to meet you, Mr. Clay," he said.

"I'll be d——d if you are, General Scott," came the reply.[38]

Clay returned to his senatorial duties, but he became "quite ill with a cold" and was forced to limit his activities and husband his strength and energy. The winter was particularly severe with more snow than he had ever seen, which made it very difficult to get around the city. He learned that his son James had, as expected, failed in his enterprise in Missouri and had returned home in the dead of winter. And he received a report (which ultimately proved unfounded) that his son-in-law James Erwin verged on bankruptcy that would implicate him to the extent of several thousand dollars.[39]

Despite his malaise, Clay accepted an invitation to visit Richmond in late February, on condition that nothing but "a quiet and unostentatious reception" would take place. That proved impossible. He soon discovered that there had begun "great preparations" for his arrival, which he feared would unduly tire him. He understood the need of Whigs to demonstrate their undying devotion and reverence for him, but he now wearied of these fatuous protestations. Something of his mood may be discerned from a letter he wrote to his

36. Sargent, *Public Men and Events,* II, 95; Clay to Otis, December 19, 1839, Clay to Henry Clay, Jr., December 14, 1839, Clay to William Jones, Jr., January 10, 1840, Clay to Ursin Bouligny, Jr., January 19, 1840, Clay to David Lambert, January 22, 1840, Porter to Clay, December 16, 1839, Clay to James Watson Webb, November 8, 1843, in Clay, *Papers,* IX, 368, 365, 373, 377, 382, 366, 885; Clay to John Strode Barbour, December 14, 1839, Miscellaneous Clay Papers, Virginia Historical Society, Richmond.

37. Harrison to Clay, January 15, 1840, in Clay, *Papers,* IX, 375.

38. Little, *Ben Hardin,* p. 342.

39. Clay to Lucretia, January 24, 1840, February 12, 1840, March 6, 1840, Clay to Henry Clay, Jr., February 22, 1840, in Clay, *Papers,* IX, 383–384, 386, 388–389, 395.

good friend Benjamin W. Leigh concerning the arrangements. "It was my most anxious wish, if I went to Richmond," he declared, "to be allowed to go there quietly, without any parade on my account. Why will you not allow me to do so? I have no doubt of the kindness towards me which prompts a desire for public manifestations; but *you*, I think, ought to conceive the state of *my* feelings which impels me to prefer the avoidance of all ostentatious display."[40]

Before taking this trip, Clay made one valiant stab at blocking passage of the subtreasury bill, which the administration had reintroduced in Congress. He trotted out all his old arguments about the worthiness of the BUS, the illegality of Jackson's seizure of executive power, and Van Buren's wickedness in perpetuating the spoils system. And he predicted, "thanks be to God! . . . a day of reckoning at hand." He compared the two Presidents Jackson and Van Buren to the Stuarts of Great Britain in their insatiable lust for power and prerogative. "The Scotch dynasty still continues," Clay thundered despite his "serious cold." "We have had Charles the First, and now have Charles the Second. But I again thank God that our deliverance is not distant, and that, on the 4th of March, 1841, a great and glorious revolution, without blood and without convulsion, will be achieved."[41]

His eloquent speech notwithstanding, his attempts to win postponement, and other efforts at amendment, all failed, and the subtreasury bill passed the Senate on January 23, 1840, by a vote of 24 to 18. More than five months later the House of Representatives also passed it, 124 to 107, through the combined efforts of the Van Buren and Calhoun forces. A severe downward turn of the economy that did not bottom out until 1843 and the failure of more banks seemed to demonstrate the need to sever the Treasury's ties with all financial institutions. As an appropriate symbol of his victory, the President signed the bill on July 4, 1840. But it had taken almost the entire length of his administration to achieve passage of this bill.[42]

Just as Clay was about to set out on his ten day-trip to Richmond, he received tragic news from home. Julia, the wife of his son Henry, Jr., had died on February 13, just two weeks after the birth of her son Thomas Julian Clay. She suffered a massive hemorrhage during the night. Henry, Jr., was inconsolable over his loss and sank into a deep depression. "Oh how desolate now appears the world to me," he scratched into his diary a week later. "She was the center of all my hopes. . . . Twice I have loved with a pure affection—twice I have built the temple of happiness. My dear Anne was its first inmate and then my Julia. . . . I cannot divest myself of the idea that my wife and sister are calling me to a place of more perfect rest."[43]

40. Clay to Lucretia, February 12, 1840, in Clay, *Papers,* IX, 386; Clay to Leigh, February 17, 1840, CPP.
41. Clay, *Works,* VI, 170–191.
42. *Congressional Globe,* 26th Congress, 1st session, pp. 139–141, 477, 495; Wilson, *Presidency of Van Buren,* pp. 133–139.
43. Henry Clay, Jr., manuscript diary, University of Kentucky Library.

The senior Clay wrote his son and tried to comfort him. The sudden, appalling, and unexpected tragedy, he wrote, "overwhelmed me with sorrow and grief." His earlier apprehension had proved justified. And the manner of Julia's death, so strikingly similar to that of his daughter, served only to deepen his pain and sorrow.

Yes, my dear Son, I do console and sympathize with you, from the bottom of my soul. But I hope that you will not forget that she has left you tender & responsible duties to perform towards the children of your mutual love and affection. These will require all your care, and I hope that you will command the fortitude requisite to the fulfillment of your duties to them. How one after the another are the objects which fasten me to the life passing away and leaving me with scarcely any wish but that I may soon follow them! Whatever might be my desire that must be my fate. During the short remnant of my life, I too shall need your kindness and affectionate attention. I beg therefore, on my account, as well as that of my dear Grand children you will take care of yourself.[44]

Over the next several days Clay tried to get some rest but could not. He wrote to his wife and commiserated with her. "Poor fellow; his life has not been long but he has had his full share of misfortunes." Clay realized that his wife's responsibilities would also increase in that she would have three additional grandchildren to look after. At least Julia's family could be expected to render some support. "We must submit to whatever Providence inflicts upon us," he sadly wrote.[45]

Despite this tragedy and his overwhelming sense of grief, Clay decided to go to Richmond after all in the hope that the journey and new scenes would help him "forget my sorrows." Besides, extensive arrangements had been made for his reception, and he felt he could not disappoint his friends. But it was a mistake. Although the reception surpassed in enthusiasm and cordiality anything he had witnessed before, he kept thinking of "the melancholy loss" the entire family suffered by the death of "poor Julia." These dreadful thoughts persisted for weeks, "and if our severe bereavement had not have forced its consideration upon me continually I should have enjoyed the trip very much."

During this trip he journeyed to Hanover, where he was born and which he had not seen for forty-eight years. Everything had changed, he reported, so much so that he scarcely recognized it. He found no markers for the graves of his father and maternal grandparents, and a crop of wheat was growing over their burial sites. He remembered the row of cherry trees; but few remained,

44. Clay to Henry Clay, Jr., February 20, 1840, in Clay, *Papers,* IX, 391. See also Clay to Mrs. Prather, March 24, 1840, Pope-Humphrey Family Papers, Manuscript Department, Filson Club, Louisville, Kentucky.
45. Clay to Lucretia, February 21, 1840, in Clay, *Papers,* IX, 392. A few months later Henry, Jr., turned up unexpectedly in Washington "in very bad spirits." Clay did what he could to help his son, and by the time the young man returned home the father felt Henry had improved "in his spirits." Clay to Lucretia, April 25, 1840, Clay to Thomas Hart Clay, May 12, 1840, ibid., IX, 409, 411.

and they looked as worn-out as he felt. His home was still standing but in a much altered state. He recognized, he said, the room where he was born. The church where he went to school for two years was still standing but in a very dilapidated condition. He met only one person in Hanover whom he recalled—an old lady of eighty by the name of Perrin, his mother's cousin, who was also quite decrepit and "not long for this world."[46]

Clay returned to Washington virtually decrepit himself. "I am sincerely and unaffectedly tired of remaining here, and wish to God that I was with you at home," he told Lucretia. "I am not well. . . . A few days more and I shall reach my grand climacteric."[47] For the next several months he had one severe cold after another, accompanied by extreme hoarseness. And this condition persisted well into the summer. He visited several doctors and medicated himself constantly with salts, camp pills, verbena cream, gum arabic, and assorted liniments, ointments, and lozenges. "I have begun again to rub the surface of my body every morning with Spirits and Salt. I must find some relief, or I cannot survive."[48]

Perhaps some of these ills were psychosomatic. There were so many disappointments, heartbreaks, and tragedies in his life. Triumphs, too, of course, but at this stage of his life Clay seemed overwhelmed by illness and grief and bitterness and disappointment. Like Lincoln, as one biographer wisely noted, Henry Clay was a man of deep, personal sorrows.[49]

46. Clay to Lucretia, March 6, 1840, in Clay, *Papers,* IX, 394–395. Today there is a marker on the site to designate the area of Clay's birth. A wooded area nearby is presumed to be the location of the graves of his father and grandparents, and an open field the location of the house where he was born.

47. Clay to Lucretia, April 2, 1840, in Clay, *Papers,* IX, 401. Clay would be sixty-three on April 12 and apparently thought he was going through "the change of life"—menopause.

48. Clay to Lucretia, July 7, 1840, in Clay, *Papers,* IX, 430–431 and note.

49. Van Deusen, *Clay,* p. 275.

THIRTY-TWO

"And Tyler, Too"

THROUGHOUT the spring and summer of 1840 Clay was inundated with invitations to appear at rallies and conventions to speak on behalf of the Whig ticket or attend barbecues in his honor. "Scarcely a day elapses that I do not receive four or five invitations," he declared. "If I could divide myself into a hundred parts, I should find full employment for each." Physically he could not begin to undertake such a program of appearances and speeches. Besides, he said, "I think self respect requires that I should not convert myself into an itinerant Lecturer or Stump orator to advance the cause of a successful competitor."[1]

Still, he could hardly appear indifferent to the success of Harrison and Tyler after promising his support. So he accepted a few invitations that would provide maximum national attention, even though he suffered continuous colds and hoarseness throughout the campaign and an overall sense of debility and fatigue. He agreed to speak at a national convention of young Whigs at Baltimore in early May, another near his birthplace in Hanover County, Virginia, in late June, and a third—most interestingly since it was close to Andrew Jackson's home—in Nashville in mid-August.

In all these speeches, and also in his brief unscheduled remarks at different places he traveled through, he emphasized the need for Whig unity. He constantly reiterated his acceptance of the decision of the Harrisburg convention to nominate Harrison as the man best suited to defeat the incumbent. "We are all Whigs, we are all Harrison men," he cried at a Baltimore rally. "We are united. We must triumph." Daniel Webster, recently returned from his trip to Europe, sat in the audience and may well have sensed a personal responsibility to respond to Clay's call for unity and amity. The two men rode in the Baltimore "Grand National Procession" in separate barouches, but if any lingering animosity existed between them, especially on the Clay's part, it did not show.[2]

1. Clay to Brooke, July 28, 1840, Clay to Jones Green, May 12, 1840, in Clay, *Papers*, IX, 436, 411.
2. Clay, *Works*, VI, 193; *Niles' Weekly Register*, May 9, 1840.

What really troubled the Kentuckian was the fact that the Whigs had not written a party platform at Harrisburg, while the Democrats, who convened in Baltimore on May 4 and nominated Van Buren for a second term, issued an extensive statement of their principles and policies. That annoyed and angered Clay. The Whig party, not the Democratic party, was the party of principles. "Our cause suffers from the imputation of the other side that the Whigs have no principles which they dare openly avow." So he set about rectifying the situation by writing such a platform—"a creed," he called it—"without committing any body," but setting forth "to the public some of the objects of a new administration."[3]

He passed his creed around to various Whig leaders and asked for their comments and suggestions. But the campaign was headed in a totally different direction, one of hard cider, rolling balls, parades, coonskin hats, log cabins, barbecues, and every high jink imaginable to get the country to "huzza" for "Tippecanoe and Tyler, Too," so Clay's high-minded creed was simply tossed aside. Who wanted to listen to lofty statements about the objects and purposes of government at a rally or barbecue? The electorate preferred nonsense and shout, laughed the Whig leaders, and they provided it to vulgar and unparalleled excess.

William Henry Harrison had a modest career to offer the American people in 1840, but the Whigs distorted it by their "improved" techniques of campaigning, first introduced by the Democrats in 1828. A native Virginian, like Clay, Harrison rose to a limited fame during the War of 1812 on account of his victory over the Shawnee Indians at Tippecanoe Creek in Indiana. During the war Clay used his influence with the Madison administration to advance the general's career. Harrison settled in Ohio and, after the war, won election at different times to both houses of Congress and received an appointment (thanks to Clay) as minister to Colombia. And that was about the sum total of his career, other than his unsuccessful run for the presidency in 1836.

When a Democratic newspaperman in Baltimore foolishly sneered at his candidacy, he unwittingly handed the Whigs a campaign slogan with which to trounce Van Buren. He wrote: "Give him [Harrison] a barrel of hard cider, settle a pension of two thousand dollars a year on him, and my word for it, he will sit for the remainder of his days in his log cabin by the side of a sea-coal fire, studying moral philosophy." The Whigs reacted immediately and pronounced Tippecanoe the "Log Cabin and Hard Cider" candidate, a virtuous man of modesty, simplicity, frugality, and common decency.

> Let Van from his coolers of silver drink wine,
> And lounge on his cushioned settee,
> Our man on his buckeye bench can recline,
> Content with hard cider is he.

3. Clay to John M. Clayton, May 29, 1840, in Clay, *Papers,* IX, 416.

So sang the Whigs. And it got worse as the campaign progressed. It almost seemed as though the Whigs intended to sing Harrison into the White House.

> Old Tip he wears a homespun suit,
> He has no ruffled shirt—wirt—wirt.
> But Mat he has the golden plate
> And he's a little squirt—wirt—wirt.

The campaign of 1840 went rollicking along with all manner of hoopla and political shenanigans. The Whigs capitalized on Harrison's military career, just as the Democrats had done previously with Jackson. They not only improved upon methods introduced in 1828 that would appeal to voters but invented other techniques like rolling balls—"Keep the Ball Rolling"—to whip up excitement for their candidate.

> What has caused the great commotion, motion, motion,
>   Our country through?
>   It is the ball a rolling on.
> For Tippecanoe and Tyler too—Tippecanoe and Tyler too.
> And with them we'll beat little Van, Van, Van,
> Van is a used up man,
> And with them we'll beat little Van.[4]

Sober-sided citizens were shocked at these antics, and some asked Clay about it. How could Whigs stoop to the level of Democrats and copy their coarse, not to say obscene, methods of campaigning? No doubt, they said, it was the consequence of nominating a "military chieftain," just like Andrew Jackson.

Clay replied that he, too, lamented the need to appeal to the passions of Americans, rather than their reason and judgment. Blame it on Jackson, he agreed. His party started it. But whatever is necessary to remove the present administration from office must be considered. "Corruption, Demagoguism, and Humbuggery will receive an accelerated movement" if Van Buren wins reelection, and the only alternative will be submission or "open & decided resistance by force." As for Harrison, he "may not fulfill all our hopes," but at least with him there is a chance of restoring the country to sanity and lawful, constitutional government.[5]

Andrew Jackson was also outraged by the antics of the Whigs and chalked it up to their contempt for democracy and popular rule. "The attempt of their

---

4. *Baltimore Republican,* December 11, 1839; Sargent, *Public Men and Events,* II, 110; Gunderson, *Log-Cabin Campaign,* pp. 107, 121.

5. Clay to William Browne, July 31, 1840, in Clay, *Papers,* IX, 437–438. Later Clay rather delighted in the nonsense. "I rejoice in all the popular movements, by which the current year is so much distinguished, demonstrating a fixed determination of the People to dismiss faithless and incompetent rulers." Clay to Philip W. Engs, September 26, 1840, ibid., IX, 444.

mummeries to degrade the people to a level with the brute creation has opened the peoples eyes,—it is saying to them in emphatic language, that they are unfit for self government and can be led by hard cider, Coons, Log cabins and big balls, by the demagogues, as can the lowering herd by his keeper and a baskett of salt."[6]

Jackson's reference to "Coons" has to do with a transparency introduced during the campaign which depicted a raccoon skin nailed to a wall near a woodpile and a barrel of cider. The "coon" then became one of the symbols of the Whig party and Clay himself was later known as the Chief Coon or the Old Coon.

One reason the Old Coon accepted the invitation to speak at the Harrison rally in Nashville may have been a wicked desire to torment Andrew Jackson.[7] Of course, Tennessee had a large number of Whigs, following behind John Bell and Hugh Lawson White, and the capture of the state from the Democrats would give Clay enormous pleasure.[8] Besides, he had received an invitation signed by 350 ladies of Nashville. "That of course, could not be withstood," he jokingly told a reporter. In any event, he returned home before Congress adjourned on July 21 (because of "fatigues incident to arduous service"), to rest up for the big event in Nashville. Harrison suggested that they meet on his return but warned that it "must appear to be accidental. Can you arrange such a one?" Unfortunately a conflicting schedule prevented the meeting.[9]

After a month-long rest at home, Clay and Senator John Crittenden took the relatively short two-hundred-mile trip from Lexington to Nashville in August, moving leisurely and stopping off regularly to address the crowds that immediately gathered when they learned of Clay's presence. He still suffered from hoarseness, which worsened each time he spoke outdoors. About twenty miles from Nashville a committee for the convention came out to greet him. And when they got to within two miles of the city, "a prodigious escort, military and Civil, on horseback, in carriages and on foot, with music bands &c" met them. It was one of the largest and longest processions he had ever witnessed, he told Lucretia. He rode through the streets in an open barouche

6. Jackson to Blair, September 26, 1840, Jackson Papers, LC.

7. When President Van Buren learned of Clay's intended visit to Nashville, he predicted that the Kentuckian would "affect great courtesy and respect towards you [Jackson], but that his malignity would seek some indirect avenue to reach your feelings; that he would endeavor to mask his attack so as to preclude you from repelling it." Francis P. Blair to Jackson, September 10, 1840, in Jackson, *Correspondence,* VI, 75.

8. Some politicians have insisted that there are really three states in Tennessee: east, middle, and west. Middle Tennessee, with its center at Nashville, was staunchly Jacksonian. But there was much resentment of Nashville's dominance in the state, so the other two areas tended to vote Whig.

9. *Niles' Weekly Register,* August 22, 1840; Clay to William C. Worthington, July 25, 1840, Harrison to Clay, August 6, 1840, in Clay, *Papers,* IX, 435, 438.

and was received "with the greatest enthusiasm, amidst the roar of Cannon, the ringing of Bells and Martial music."[10]

Clay spoke to the Nashville convention on August 17. The event was much anticipated in view of the fact that General Andrew Jackson sat grumbling in his home at the Hermitage only a few miles away. This seemed to rouse and excite the Old Coon. His hoarseness all but disappeared.

Clay was in rare form. His speech resonated with wit, sarcasm, spirit. And his audience loved it. He started off by asking where his old friend Felix Grundy might be. "Off in East Tennessee, stumping for Mr. Van Buren," someone shouted to him.

"Ah!" responded Clay, "at his old occupation, defending criminals." The audience roared.

Unfortunately, given his location, he launched almost immediately into a defense of his vote for John Quincy Adams in 1825. He just could not let the thing alone. Then he got nasty. He accused Jackson of appointing Edward Livingston, "a defaulter," as his secretary of state. Livingston had died four years earlier, and there was really no need to invoke his name this way. Also, Jackson had appointed Samuel Swartwout as collector of the port of New York, and Swartwout absconded with more than a million dollars, something Clay took pleasure in recounting at length. The senator concluded his speech by reminding everyone how the sons of Kentucky and Tennessee had fought side by side at New Orleans. Today, he said, they fight a different war against a "band of mercenaries . . . a band of officeholders, who call General Harrison a coward, an imbecile, an old woman!

"Yes," he cried. "General Harrison is a coward! but he fought more battles than any other general during the last war, and never sustained a defeat! He is no statesman! and yet he has filled more civil offices of trust and importance than almost any other man in the Union!"

Suddenly a voice called out from the audience: "Tell us of Van Buren's battles!"

"Ah," responded Clay, his eyes twinkling and his lips curled into a sardonic smile, "[let me] . . . tell you of Mr. Van Buren's three great battles." He fought general commerce and conquered him. He fought general currency and conquered him. He fought the Seminole Indians in Florida "and got conquered!"[11]

Jackson was livid when he heard about the speech, especially the comment about Livingston. He immediately scratched out a reply and sent it to the Nashville *Union* for publication. In it, Jackson recalled that when Clay was appointed secretary of state, he was charged "throughout the Union" with having bargained for it. "Under such circumstances how contemptible does

10. Clay to Lucretia, August 16, 1840, in Clay, *Papers*, IX, 439.
11. Clay, *Works*, VI, 215–219.

this demagogue appear," Jackson wrote, "when he descends from his high place in the Senate and roams over the country, retailing slanders against the living and the dead."

Clay could not let that low blow go unanswered and published an immediate response. He claimed he had been misunderstood by Jackson who did not hear his speech. Moreover, he had referred to the former President in his speech in respectful terms only to be assaulted with "insinuations and gross epithets . . . alike impotent, malevolent, and derogatory." No matter. They "have fallen harmless at my feet," he sniggered, "exciting no other sensations than that of scorn and contempt."[12]

The Whig press expressed its dismay over Jackson's coarse language. And this, they fussed, from a man who had held the highest office in the land. Compare the gracious response of Clay, they continued, with the "rude, ungenerous and uncalled for" language of General Jackson.[13] Philip Hone likened Jackson to a serpent coiled up in his unsanctified lair, collecting venom and squirting it through the columns of servile newspapers at the great men who opposed him.[14]

The Old Coon tried to do Old Hickory an injury by encouraging his Virginia friends to publish Jackson's letter alongside a letter of James Madison, written in 1828, declining to serve as an elector for John Q. Adams because he thought it was unbecoming for former Presidents to engage in partisan politics. Madison's letter, said Clay, "was characterized by all the delicacy and propriety which distinguished the conduct and writings of that eminent man." Jackson's, on the other hand, roundly criticized Harrison's abilities as a military leader and statesman and openly endorsed Van Buren's reelection. "It has occurred to me," wrote Clay, "that the publication of these two letters, in juxtaposition, would be attended with good effect."[15]

The Kentuckian returned home after his Nashville appearance much renewed in strength and spirit. Thereafter he campaigned very little; after all, during the last nine months he had been with his family only about four weeks. He spent the rest of the summer relaxing and trying to regain his health. He naturally rejoiced in the encouraging results of the summer and early-fall state elections and started predicting that Van Buren would win only six out of twenty-six states in the general election.

He was not far off the mark. A record number of voters trooped to the polls in 1840 and trounced poor "Van, Van, the used up man." Harrison

12. Both Clay's speech and Jackson's response were carried in the Nashville *Union,* August 19, and copies are located in the Jackson Papers Project, University of Tennessee, Knoxville. Jackson's notes on Clay's speech may be found in a memorandum dated August 17, 1840, Jackson Papers, LC. The Nashville *Whig,* August 21, 1840, carried Clay's letter.

13. *Niles' Weekly Register,* September 5, 1840; Nashville *Whig,* August 21, 1840.

14. Hone, *Diary,* I, 492.

15. Clay to Brooke, July 28, 1840, in Clay, *Papers,* IX, 436; Nashville *Union,* June 25, 1840, copy Jackson Papers Project.

received 52.9 percent of the popular vote, or 1,275,612, against 46.8 percent for Van Buren, or 1,130,033. A Liberty party, supported by abolitionists, attracted 0.3 percent, or 7,053 votes, for its nominee, James G. Birney. Harrison carried nineteen states, for 234 electoral votes, to Van Buren's seven states (Alabama, Arkansas, Illinois, Missouri, New Hampshire, South Carolina, and Virginia), with 60 electoral votes. Both houses of Congress were also captured by the Whigs. It was the high-water mark in the short history of the Whig party, a history spanning a twenty-year period, from 1834 to 1854. Nationally the Whigs were to win the presidency again in 1848, the Senate in 1842, and the House in 1846. And that was it.[16]

This was the one moment—starting March 4, 1841—when Whigs had the opportunity to legislate their dynamic program into law and demonstrate to the American people the value and importance of their policies and philosophy. Unfortunately the executive department included at the top a vain and egotistical incompetent pledged to one term in office and as his Vice President a rather rigid ideologue and former Democrat committed to states' rights and the interests of the South.

Harrison appreciated his limitations and understood the preeminent position of Clay within the Whig party. He also appreciated the Kentuckian's past help in securing for him a commission as brigadier general at the outbreak of the War of 1812 and his diplomatic appointment as minister to Colombia. But now, in 1840, *he,* not Clay, was the President-elect and could choose the men *he* wanted as advisers. Webster had been one of his earliest and strongest supporters and had performed heroically during the campaign, giving lively and enthusiastic speeches in various sections of the country. Whether Harrison would listen mostly to Webster or Clay had Whig leaders guessing and wondering.

In early November the President-elect notified Clay that he was coming to Frankfort, Kentucky, via Louisville, to see Charles A. Wickliffe to sell him some land he had acquired from his brother Benjamin. Wickliffe was a Whig but fiercely opposed to Clay personally and hostile to a national bank. Thus, the Harrison-Wickliffe meeting could be interpreted by some as a signal of the general's declaration of independence from Clay. In his letter to the senator Harrison suggested they see each other during his trip but then followed it up two weeks later with a second letter in which he expressed growing reservations about their get-together. A "personal meeting might give rise to speculations & even jealousies," he wrote, "which it might be well to avoid." So he

16. William Nesbit Chambers, "Election of 1840," *American Presidential Elections,* ed. Schlesinger and Israel, I, 680–682, 690. Andrew Jackson was shattered by the results. "Corruption, bribery and fraud has been extended over the whole Union," he wailed to Van Buren. The Democracy had been "shamefully beaten, *but I trust not conquered."* Jackson to Van Buren, November 24, 1840, Van Buren Papers, LC. See also Michael F. Holt, "The Election of 1840, Voter Mobilization, and the Emergence of the Second American Party System: A Reappraisal of Jacksonian Voting Behavior," *A Master's Due: Essays in Honor of David Herbert Donald,* ed. William J. Cooper et al. (Baton Rouge, 1985).

suggested that they communicate through a "Mutual friend or friends" since he did have some important matters to discuss with Clay and wanted his opinions.[17]

But the senator was not about to be maneuvered (intended or not) into looking foolish or cast out. After receiving the original letter, he immediately planned to meet Harrison in Frankfort and so alerted his friend, the newly elected governor Robert P. Letcher. The second letter in no way changed his plans. With characteristic audacity and decision he went to Frankfort, intercepted Harrison, and insisted that he visit Lexington. The President-elect readily capitulated. After all, Clay's position in the party, his magnanimous acceptance of defeat at the convention, his efforts during the campaign, and the near devotion shown him by most Whigs compelled the general to see the senator and accede to his invitation to visit him at Ashland, where they could talk further at their leisure and at length.

In their conversations, at both Frankfort and Ashland, Clay made it immediately clear that he did not want an appointment to the cabinet. Most probably Harrison intended to offer him the post of secretary of state—or so everyone assumed. Clay told him flat out that he was perfectly happy with his position in the Senate and would not change it. Considering Harrison's pledge to a single term, Clay's decision made considerable sense. He would certainly be the Whig candidate four years hence. He knew it, and several leaders around the country had already assured him of it.[18] Therefore, why should he get deeply involved in Harrison's administration and no doubt take all the blame for its failures and mistakes? In fact, Clay's good friend Peter B. Porter, of New York, advised him to take the mission to London so as to get far away from all the politicking that was likely to engulf the new administration.[19]

Harrison just listened. He did not appear surprised at Clay's decision, nor did he urge his host to change it. Since Webster would most likely get the State Department by default, Clay felt it necessary to explain to Harrison his feelings and relations with the Massachusetts senator. Again he was brutally frank. He admitted that his confidence in Webster had been badly shaken during the last eight years. Still, he felt that no Whig President could overlook him. So, if the general decided to appoint the Massachusetts senator to office, "it would not diminish the interest I felt in the success of his administration, nor my zeal in its support." But Clay added a condition. The administration would have to be conducted according to the principles "which I believed would govern it." Clay further mentioned that he had heard that some of Webster's friends

17. Harrison to Clay, November 2, 15, 1840, Clay to Robert P. Letcher, November 4, 1840, in Clay, *Papers,* IX, 450–452; Louisville *Advertiser,* November 19, 1840; Poage, *Clay and Whig Party,* pp. 16–17. Charles A. Wickliffe was the brother of Robert Wickliffe, a former Clay ally now out to replace the senator as leader of the Whig party in Kentucky.

18. Porter to Clay, December 14, 1840, in Clay, *Papers,* IX, 462.

19. Clay to Letcher, November 4, 1840, Porter to Clay, November 29, 1840, Clay to Porter, December 8, 1840, in Clay, *Papers,* IX, 451, 455, 458–459.

wanted him to go to the Treasury Department. That would be a mistake, Clay pronounced in a solemn voice. Webster "had not the requisite qualifications for that office," he declared. Indeed, in view of the fact that Webster owed Biddle's Philadelphia bank a total of $114,000, it seemed wise to reward him with an office involving different responsibilities.

When Clay mentioned principles, he certainly expected Harrison to understand what he was talking about. In particular, he had two things in mind: the chartering of a new national bank and adherence to the Compromise Tariff. And Harrison responded very favorably. In fact, Clay was impressed by the responses he received. "My main desire, in a long interview with him," wrote Clay shortly thereafter, "was to ascertain his views as to public measures; and I was happy to find him coinciding with those which I entertained."[20]

Since each passing day provided greater evidence that the Whigs would have real working majorities in both houses of Congress after March 4, 1841, Clay wanted to take substantial advantage of it. Abhorring Jackson's expansion of the executive powers and insisting on the supremacy of the legislature in any republican system, Clay thought that a special session of Congress should be called after Harrison took office in order to begin dismantling the Jacksonian economic program. And the President-elect, in their conversations, may have indicated his willingness to recall the Congress following his inauguration.[21]

It would seem that Harrison made a special point during his stay at Ashland to profess his "most ardent attachment to me," Clay later reported, which thoroughly pleased the senator. "He is animated by the best dispositions, and if he adheres to them, the Country will not be disappointed in his Admon."[22]

Although the two men talked about cabinet appointments—surely the clearest sign of Harrison's intentions and directions—the President-elect did not specify a single individual on whom he had decided to confer appointment. Clay wanted his old friend and ally in winning passage of the Compromise Tariff John Clayton of Delaware named to the Treasury Department and probably said so. But Harrison made it clear that talk of individual appointments was premature. Even so, Clay got the distinct impression that John J. Crittenden of Kentucky and Thomas Ewing of Ohio would win cabinet posts, with Crittenden becoming attorney general and Ewing the postmaster general. Both appointments, if made, would please Clay tremendously, especially Crittenden's, but he did not say so. In fact, he soon realized that his wisest course was to avoid any involvement whatsoever with the appointing process. Were

20. Clay to Brooke, December 8, 1840, Clay to Porter, December 8, 1840, in Clay, *Papers,* IX, 458, 459.
21. Clay to Thomas Speed, November 21, 1840, Clay to John C. Wright, January 22, 1841, Clay, *Papers,* IX, 453, 484. See also Clay's "Notes" for a newspaper article on the subject, February 4, 1841, ibid., IX, 495–496.
22. Clay to Clayton, December 17, 1840, in Clay, *Papers,* IX, 465–466.

he to interfere and make demands, he ran the risk of alienating Harrison and exciting his jealousy. Clay may have been the head of the Whig party, but he was not President. He needed to keep that fact firmly fixed in his mind, for quite soon thereafter Harrison indicated that he was apprehensive over Clay's future intentions with respect to the direction of his administration. "I must observe," the senator wrote in December, "that, notwithstanding professions of the most ardent attachment to me by Harrison, circumstances have transpired which confirm an opinion I have long since formed, that he is apprehensive that the new Administration may not be regarded as *his* but mine. Artful men for sinister purposes will endeavor to foster this jealousy. And to preserve my utility, I must avoid giving it any countenance."[23]

Clay left Harrison in Lexington on November 26 to hurry to Washington for the opening of the second, or short, session of the Twenty-sixth Congress. After March 4 there would be 133 Whigs as against 102 Democrats in the House and 28 Whigs to 22 Democrats in the Senate. Since Clay had a considerable economic program to present for enactment, he needed to start organizing his party as quickly as possible. But therein lay his problem. There were several strong factions within the Whig party—to wit, the friends of Clay, the friends of Webster, and a large number of southern Whigs committed, like Tyler, to states' rights. The Whigs, as a whole, formed "a coalition of persons, brought together from the four ends of our earth," said Harrison Gray Otis, ". . . & united . . . as yet in only one defined object—a change of men." Consequently, they could not agree upon a full, comprehensive program. What Clay needed to do, Otis told him, was to attempt the passage of only those measures "as all are agreed in." Only by such agreement would a broad foundation be laid for the formation of "a great 'Country party,' on primary principles and mutual concession, extending in every direction & embracing all the great interests of the Country." Anything else will tear the Whigs apart and condemn the party to ultimate extinction. Anything else and "the cossacks will be upon you in one or two years."[24] It was a prophecy that proved all too true.

Clay's mistake over the next few months and year was the belief that *his* principles and policies—namely, those embedded in the American System—constituted the core of Whig philosophy. And he expected to assume leadership in Congress to enact the system into law. Unfortunately not all men who called themselves Whigs—especially southerners—subscribed to Clay's philosophy, at least not in every particular. And the friends of Webster and Harrison were not about to acknowledge Clay's primacy of leadership. But the Kentuckian could not imagine any objection to his intentions. As one observer jokingly remarked, "If the two should go duck hunting together, Mr. Clay would ex-

23. Clay to Clayton, December 17, 1840, Clay to Brooke, December 8, 1840, Clay to Porter, December 8, 1840, Clay to James T. Austin, December 10, 1840, Clay to Jesse M. Christopher, December 9, 1840, in Clay, *Papers,* IX, 465–466, 457–460.
24. Otis to Clay, December 16, 1840, in Clay, *Papers,* IX, 465.

pect Mr. Webster to assume the office of spaniel, to bring out the birds, and the latter would not perceive that there was any degradation in his assumption of such an office."[25]

Only as President—and one in the mold of Andrew Jackson—could Clay expect to drive his great program through Congress. Instead, he foolishly presumed that he could reassert legislative authority under his direction, charter another national bank, pass his land bill, which would provide for internal improvements, and maintain protection on the basis of the Compromise Tariff. In addition, he believed that Congress should limit the chief executive's appointment, dismissal, and veto powers, as well as reduce the presidential tenure to a single term and bring the Treasury Department under the exclusive control of the legislature.

Talk about Jackson and the imperial presidency! Here was Clay at his most demanding and domineering. And in the final months of the Van Buren administration he did not hesitate to make his intentions absolutely clear to everyone. Arrogant and presumptuous, he stood in the Senate chamber, mocking the Jacksonians and predicting the early end of the subtreasury system. If the Democrats want "peace and harmony," he allowed, "we are prepared to meet them in a spirit of peace and harmony. . . . But if they are for war, as it seems they are, I say, 'Lay on, Macduff.'" After March 4, he gloated, there would be a general housecleaning and the restoration of constitutional government.[26]

By his presumption and arrogance Clay was headed for defeat and humiliation. And his comeuppance started to take shape in Ohio, where the President-elect wrote to Daniel Webster and offered him either the State or Treasury departments. Disregarding Clay's advice totally, Harrison tried to nudge Webster into assuming the Treasury duties since it would be more difficult to fill that post. But he left the final decision with the Massachusetts senator, and Webster subsequently chose the State Department, whereupon Harrison appointed Thomas Ewing to the important Treasury post.[27]

Clay sniffed his disappointment. He wanted Clayton for Treasury because he was a strong bank man and would work closely with the Old Coon, as he had in the past, in redirecting the nation's financial operations. He told Clayton that he had urged his appointment "in the strongest terms." Whatever could be done, he said, "I shall do to avail the public of your services in the Cabinet."[28]

As for Ewing, Clay learned that the movement on his behalf had a "northern origin," by which he undoubtedly meant Daniel Webster. So he went to Ewing and, as a friend, told him straight to his face that he did not approve his

25. Little, *Ben Hardin,* p. 180.

26. *Congressional Globe,* 26th Congress, 2d session, pp. 19–21; Clay, *Works,* VI, 232.

27. Baxter, *Webster,* pp. 273–274; Bartlett, *Daniel Webster,* pp. 174–175.

28. Clay to Clayton, December 17, 29, 1840, January 17, 1841, in Clay, *Papers,* IX, 466, 468–469, 480.

nomination. "I said to him, 'the people every where have pointed to you as P.M.G. [postmaster general] and you had better conform to that indication.' "

What effrontery! What impertinence! Such impolitic behavior can hardly be explained or understood except as another example of Clay's still-festering bitterness and disappointment. He apparently could not accept the fact that he was not the President of the United States. Fortunately Ewing chose not to take offense.

No sooner did Harrison arrive in Washington in early February than Clay went to see him to insist upon Clayton's appointment. Harrison handled the situation very well. He had no wish to quarrel with his visitor and so acknowledged Clayton's abilities and services and his great regard for the Kentuckian's advice, but he refused to budge.[29] As a result, Clay sustained a double defeat: Ewing got the Treasury post, and Clayton failed to get any spot in the cabinet at all.

The other appointments included Crittenden as attorney general, John Bell of Tennessee, secretary of war, George E. Badger of North Carolina, secretary of the navy, and Francis Granger of New York as postmaster general. The Granger appointment also rankled Clay. That former Anti-Mason was allied to Thurlow Weed, one of the important managers of Clay's defeat at Harrisburg. "I think Mr. C. must look about him or the rogues will cheat him," laughed William L. Marcy, the former New York senator. "To guard against such a contingency he ought to take care of his *out posts,* and the collectorship of N.Y. is the most important among them."[30]

Indeed. The office of collector of the port of New York was the most lucrative office at the disposal of the President. Not only was there a great deal of money involved in the position, but the collector possessed "more political power than any other man in Government with the exception of the President himself," said Peter B. Porter. For that office to get into the wrong hands could cause Clay's political operation in New York considerable grief. And Porter alerted him to the fact that Governor Seward and Thurlow Weed had decided on Edward Curtis for the post. Worse, Curtis had actively participated in Clay's defeat at the National Whig Convention, and he also had the support of Daniel Webster. Curtis was another former Anti-Mason and a shrewd political operator who could be expected to use the office to advance the interests of Clay's enemies. Moreover, said Marcy, he "is Mr. W.'s *factotum.*" Said another: "Mr. Clay must & does most deeply detest & despise him."[31]

Clay thanked Porter for his information and assured him that he would bend every effort to block the appointment. So, at the earliest opportunity, he

29. Clay to Clayton, February 12, 1841, in Clay, *Papers,* IX, 499.

30. Marcy to P. M. Wetmore, February 21, 1841, Marcy Papers, LC.

31. Porter to Clay, January 4, 1841, in Clay, *Papers,* IX, 471; Marcy to Wetmore, January 17, February 6, February 21, 22, 1841, Marcy Papers, LC; Aaron Clark to Willie P. Mangum, August 28, 1841, in Mangum, *Papers,* III, 223.

told Harrison that Curtis was "faithless and perfidious and in my judgment unworthy of the place."

Harrison appointed him anyway. And at one point during the conversation he turned to the senator and barked: "Mr. Clay, you forget that I am President."[32]

"Webster has prevailed," snickered William Marcy. It now appeared to many that an "implacable war" had broken out between the friends of Webster and Clay on no difference of opinion or principles but solely on partisan preferences. Webster, according to Clay's friends, was preparing to succeed Harrison, and it was obvious that he would have full control of Tippecanoe's administration. "The distresses of the victors," wrote Marcy, "begins to be laughably amusing to the vanquished."[33]

The building tensions within the Whig party went on public view in the Senate almost every day that Clay rose to speak. Sometimes he was playful, for example, in his speech on tariff duties when he read off the names of French wines and sighed and licked his lips and commented on the consumption of wine in America. "I venture to assert that there is more champagne wine consumed in the Astor House, in the city of New York, in one month, than any State south of the Potomac consumes in a year," he commented to the amusement of his audience. But more times than not he resorted to sarcasm, innuendo, and snide remarks bordering on malicious insult. Repeatedly he was called to order. His "indiscretions," said one man, showed that he lacked "self-command."[34]

And in an apparent display of perversity Clay went out of his way to defend the absent Daniel Webster, who had been attacked by Senator Alfred Cuthbert of Georgia over the slave trade. But when Cuthbert interrupted him, Clay lost control of himself. "I will not, I cannot, be interrupted. I will not permit an interruption. The practice is much too common . . . and I trust it will not be continued here." Cuthbert shot back something that was inaudible but that sounded "audacious" to the Senate reporter, whereupon Clay jumped to his feet and demanded "to know if the Senator applies to me? If he does, I will call him to order." Cuthbert sarcastically referred to Clay's habit of "using very provoking language to others." When the gentleman from Kentucky learned "proper courtesies towards his opponents," said Cuthbert, then he could expect "courtesy from him and not till then."[35]

32. Clay to Porter, January 8, 1841, Clay to Harrison, March 15, 1841, in Clay, *Papers,* IX, 473, 517; Tyler, *Letters,* II, 10, note 4. "I have the best authority for believing," said Senator Mangum, "that Mr. Clay was Constantly represented [to Harrison] as having a disposition to dictate the *Correct* policy of the Admn." Mangum to Charles P. Green, April 20, 1841, in Mangum, *Papers,* III, 145.
33. Wise, *Seven Decades of the Union,* p. 172; Marcy to Wetmore, March 18, 1841, Marcy to George W. Newell, February, 1841, Marcy Papers, LC.
34. Marcy to P. M. Wetmore, March 9, 1841, Marcy Papers, LC.
35. Clay, *Works,* VI, 227–270, 272–273.

"Clay's insolence is insufferable," wrote one Democrat, "and it will not be borne. Never have I seen power so tyrannically used as the new Senate are now using it, and every federal [Whig] senator bows servilely to the arrogant dictation of Clay."[36]

In a debate over dismissing Francis P. Blair as the Senate printer, Clay came close to disaster. He tangled with Senator William R. King of Alabama about Clay's statement that he "believed the Globe to be an infamous paper, and its chief editor an infamous man." The speech "was very violent and vituperative on the character of Blair," reported William L. Marcy. In reply King said he knew Blair and would "compare *gloriously*"[37] his character to Clay's. The Kentuckian bolted to his feet: "That is false, it is a slanderous base and cowardly declaration & the senator knows it to be so."

Spectators gasped. Slanderous, base, cowardly! Those were words that usually provoked a challenge to a duel, and everyone in the chamber knew it. In their horror the audience looked toward King, who slowly rose to his feet. After a long pause he said: "Mr. President, I have no reply to make—none whatsoever. But Mr. Clay deserves a response."

A duel! King's reply was a clear statement of intention. He then sat down and scribbled something on a sheet of paper. Clay realized what he had done and sat back in his chair, waiting for the inevitable. King left the chamber. A short time later Dr. Lewis Linn of Missouri carried a note to Clay, who read it and then handed it to Senator William S. Archer of Virginia. As seconds Linn and Archer were charged with arranging the details of the duel.

Fortunately the civil authorities intervened. The sergeant at arms arrested both men and bound the parties over to keep the peace. Clay appeared before two justices of the peace and posted a bond of five thousand dollars that he would maintain the peace, "and particularly towards WILLIAM R. KING." William Marcy, who witnessed the entire affair, said that there was "much solicitude to get it settled" but that Clay would have to give "an unequivocal apology." Clay agreed to do so on the floor of the Senate, and King then withdrew his challenge.

On March 14, in his most insouciant manner, Clay apologized for his language and behavior. He explained that he was carried away by his intense feelings toward Blair and no doubt should have remained silent. When he had done, King also apologized. A little later Clay sauntered over to the opposite side of the Senate and stopped in front of King's desk. In an ingratiating tone the Kentuckian cooed: "King, give us a pinch of your snuff?" The Alabama senator sprang to his feet and extended his hand. Clay seized it. The two men shook hands very vigorously as the spectators broke out in applause.[38]

36. A. O. P. Nicholson to James K. Polk, March 9, 1841, in Polk, *Correspondence*, V, 655.
37. Later Marcy said the word was not "*gloriously*" but "proudly." Marcy to Wetmore, March 12, 1841, Marcy Papers, LC.
38. *Congressional Globe*, 26th Congress, 2d session, pp. 245, 247–249, 256–257; *Kendall's Expositor*, April 15, 1844, in Clay, *Papers*, IX, 512; A. O. P. Nicholson to James K. Polk, March 9, 10, 1841, in

With the advent of the Harrison administration on March 4, everyone seemed to know that Webster had the inside track in determining policy and direction and that Clay was excluded.[39] Unfortunately the Kentucky senator had few options as to a course of action. "We must support this Administration," he dejectedly wrote John Clayton, "or rather, I should say, we must not fall out with it. . . . I have strong fears & strong hopes. And some times the one & sometimes the other predominate." Rather than make any additional demands on Harrison, he set about preparing the Whig program to offer the Congress once the President called the extra session. "I have a perfect Bank in my head," he told Clayton. "I should like to converse with you about it."[40]

But first he had to get Harrison to move on calling the special session. Weeks before, he had convened a caucus of Whig leaders and got their unanimous agreement that such a session was *"indispensible."*[41] This information was passed along to Harrison, but he did nothing. Possibly he resented the likelihood of Clay's assuming control of Congress after it reconvened in special session and probably legislating the Whig program without due deference to the White House.

Exasperated over the delay, Clay addressed a confidential letter to the new President on March 13—Congress was scheduled to adjourn in two days—and asked for an immediate decision on the matter. The letter was courteous but firm. "There is the imputation of vascillating counsels" in further delay, Clay wrote. To spare the President the bother, the senator presumed to enclose a rough draft of a proclamation "which I respectfully submit to your perusal."[42]

Harrison reacted angrily. In a letter to Clay he indulged his pent-up resentment "You use the privilege of a friend to lecture me & I take the same liberty with you—You are too impetuous. Much as I rely upon your judgement there are others whom I must consult & in many cases to determine adversely to your suggestions."

That letter struck Clay right between the eyes. And typically he read far more into it than the facts warranted. Pacing his room "in great perturbation" and crumpling the note in his hand as he paced, he snarled between clenched teeth: "And it has come to this! I am civilly but virtually requested not to visit

---

Polk, *Correspondence,* V, 654, 655; Marcy to Wetmore, March 9, 10, 12, 1841, Marcy Papers, LC. Marcy said that "Mr. Clay had to back out. He did it badly." Marcy to Wetmore, March 17, 1841, ibid. Poore, *Reminiscences,* pp. 259–260. Nicholson reported to Polk that he heard it was at the suggestion of Senator Wise that the sergeant at arms acted.

39. John F. Gillespy to James K. Polk, February 12, 1841, in Polk, *Correspondence,* V, 629; Cleaves, *Old Tippecanoe,* p. 339.

40. Clay to Clayton, February 12, March 3, 1841, in Clay, *Papers,* IX, 499, 510.

41. Clay to Letcher, January 25, 1841, Clay to John C. Wright, January 22, 1841, in Clay, *Papers,* IX, 484; Crittenden to Letcher, January 25, 1841, in Ann Mary Butler Coleman, ed., *The Life of John J. Crittenden with Selections from Correspondence and Speeches* (Philadelphia, 1871), I, 140. Marcy claimed that many Whigs in the House of Representatives opposed an extra session. Marcy to Wetmore, February 6, 1841, Marcy Papers, LC.

42. Clay to Harrison, March 13, 1841, in Clay, *Papers,* IX, 515.

the White House—not to see the President personally, but hereafter only communicate with him in writing!

"I was mortified," Clay shot back at Harrison, by the implication "that I had been . . . dictating to you or to the new administration—mortified, because it is unfounded in fact, and because there is danger of the fears, that I intimated to you at Frankfort, of my enemies poisoning your mind towards me." Clay denied dictation in the formation of the cabinet or in appointments. If expressing his opinions as a citizen and a senator constituted dictation, he said, then he was guilty. The alternative for him was retirement. But before he went into that happy state, he felt he could still render some service to his country in the Senate.[43]

And on that angry note, Clay slammed out of Washington and headed home, "breathing out rage and threatening all the way."[44]

The two men never saw each other again. But Clay had got no farther than Baltimore before his distress and anger and frustration crashed down on top of him and he suffered a physical collapse. He remained in Baltimore a week or more, regaining his energies, enough to drag himself to Ashland, where he knew he could get the rest and quiet he so desperately needed.

Harrison had every intention of calling an extra session, particularly after he had learned from Secretary Ewing that the country verged on insolvency and something needed to be done quickly about the government's revenues. But he wanted Clay to know that the decision belonged to him. It could not be dictated. His cabinet, especially Webster, agreed that the extra session should be summoned, so on March 17 he directed the Congress to reconvene on May 31. And that was almost his last important act. At the age of sixty-eight, William Henry Harrison died on April 4, from pneumonia. He was the first President to die in office.

Harrison had not been well, and when he contracted a severe cold during the inauguration ceremonies, it soon worsened into pneumonia. From the moment Clay saw Harrison in Frankfort the previous November he commented on his poor physical appearance. The general "is much broken" physically, noted Clay, his body "weather beaten."[45]

The senator was not surprised when he heard the tragic news, knowing, as he did, "his [Harrison's] habits and excitements." But another voice not far away let out a jubilant cry of thanksgiving. Andrew Jackson in the Hermitage praised "providence" for this deliverance. "A kind and overuling providence has interfered to prolong our glorious Union and happy republican system which Genl. Harrison and his cabinet was preparing to destroy under the dictation of the profligate demagogue, Henry Clay." Our happy land has been

43. Harrison to Clay, March 13, 1841, Clay to Harrison, March 15, 1841, in Clay, *Papers,* IX, 514, 516–517.
44. Marcy to Wetmore, March 25, 1841, Marcy Papers, LC.
45. Clay to Brooke, December 8, 1840, Clay to Porter, December 8, 1840, in Clay, *Papers,* IX 458, 459.

preserved, he exulted. *"The Lord ruleth, let our nation rejoice."*[46]

"Tippecanoe and Tyler, Too." The slogan had helped the Whigs to electoral victory. The "Tippecanoe part was gone," declared Representative Henry Wise of Virginia, "but the 'Tyler too' part of the Whig party was, by the act of God, left in power."[47]

From Ashland came a whispered prayer: "I . . . hope that he will interpose no obstacle to the success of the Whig measures, including a Bank of the U.S."[48]

46. Clay to James F. Conover, April 9, 1841, in Clay, *Papers,* IX, 518; Jackson to Blair, April 19, 1841, Jackson Papers, LC.
47. Wise, *Seven Decades of the Union,* pp. 180–181.
48. Clay to John L. Lawrence, April 13, 1841, in Clay, *Papers,* IX, 519.

THIRTY-THREE

The Dictator

URING the next several years, when the less attractive side of Clay's personality came increasingly into view, it should be kept in mind that no matter how badly he behaved he constantly dazzled people who came in contact with him, even when they differed strongly with him on policy and principles. "Haughty and imperious," wrote one, "Mr. Clay was nevertheless so fascinating in his manner when he chose to be that he held unlimited control over nearly every member of the party."[1]

"I don't like Clay," snapped John C. Calhoun. "He is a bad man, an imposter, a creator of wicked schemes. I wouldn't speak to him, but, by God! I love him."[2]

"Harry of the West" was, wrote Philip Hone, "the spoiled child of society." Everybody loved him, subscribed to his opinions, and found excuses for his foibles. And then, when it happened, as it regularly did, that the person or persons aggrieved by his momentary rashness expressed something like resentment, "he is so lovely, so soothing, so unconscious of unkind intention, that it all is forgotten in a moment." Clay's attitude would change in a flash. "My dear sir," he would gush, "how could you suppose I mean to offend you?—there was nothing farther from my thoughts, and I am astonished that you should think so." Suddenly the situation was reversed, and now the "assailant" received the apology and sympathy "which ought to have been bestowed upon the aggrieved party."[3]

In part, Clay's enormous charm, fascination, and ability to turn away resentment derived from his ability to tell amusing stories and anecdotes. Like Lincoln, the Kentucky senator was a *"raconteur"* of no mean ability. He always

1. Poore, *Reminiscences*, I, 273.
2. Quoted in Joseph M. Rogers, *The True Henry Clay* (Philadelphia, 1904), p. 250. The quotation may be apocryphal, although comments on Clay by Calhoun which resemble the quotation may be found scattered all through the Calhoun Papers, "except for the terminal paradox." Clyde N. Wilson, editor of the Calhoun Papers, to author, October 25, 1990.
3. Hone, *Diary*, II, 532.

seemed to have a homey tale in his intellectual baggage to deflect the outrage his savage blows sometimes inflicted. He always retained the talent, even when overly excited or agitated, to delight and amuse an audience or a caucus meeting or a roomful of dinner guests with his witty stories. And of course, he always told them with full "dramatic effect," sometimes resorting to dialect or mimicry.

Not all his stories served a larger purpose. Not all underscored a particular point at hand. Some sought to throw an opponent off guard or simply to enhance Clay's formidable reputation as a delightful guest and entertaining table companion. One story that always charmed his listeners—and it was told with appropriate inflections and gestures—concerned a stagecoach that stopped for supper at a small mountainside town. When the stage prepared to renew its journey, a colonel, in full regimental uniform and roaring drunk, insisted on riding with the driver. Presumably the fresh air would clear his head.

The coach had not gone far when the colonel fell off the coach and landed in the mud. Naturally the coach stopped to allow him to regain his seat.

"Well, driver (hic)," said the colonel as he struggled to his feet, "we've had quite a turn (hic) over, haint we?"

The driver assured him that the stage had not overturned.

"I say (hic) we *have*," shouted the colonel. "I'll leave it (hic) to the com(hic)pany. Haven't we (hic) had a turn (hic) over, gentlemen?"

No, there had been no turnover, they assured him.

The colonel looked crestfallen. "Well driver (hic)," he said as he struggled to regain his dignity, "if I'd known that (hic) I wouldn't a got out."[4]

Soon after Harrison's death some men began predicting that the collapse of the Whig party would be as sudden and as catastrophic as a stagecoach overturning—and that it would happen in the not-too-distant future.[5] Not all the wheels of the party were turning as they should: With northern and southern Whigs disputing over certain principles and policies the motion of the vehicle had become unsteady and had started to sway back and forth, and when Tyler made his position clear about certain Whig objectives, the conveyance seemed in imminent danger of overturning. If they had only known when they nominated Harrison and Tyler at Harrisburg what would happen in the months following the election, they surely would have concocted a different electoral ticket.[6]

4. Poore, *Reminiscences,* I, 164–166.

5. Marcy to N. Niles, April 18, 1842, Marcy Papers, LC.

6. Within four months Clay was to say on the Senate floor: "If at Harrisburg, or at the polls, it had been foreseen that General Harrison would die in one short month after the commencement of his administration; that Vice President Tyler would be elevated to the Presidential chair; that a bill, passed by decisive majorities of the first Whig Congress, chartering a National Bank, would be presented for his sanction; and that he would veto the bill, do I hazard any thing when I express the conviction that he would not have received a solitary vote in the nominating Convention, nor one solitary electoral vote in any State in the Union?" Clay, *Papers,* IX, 588.

On learning of Harrison's death, Clay chose to believe that the tragedy would make little difference to the enactment of the Whig program. Conveniently forgetting what he had said about Jackson's interpretation of the results of the 1832 election, Clay expected Tyler to accede to the obvious wishes of the electorate, as revealed in the last election, and initiate Whig measures to rescue the nation from depression and misrule. Indeed, for the first few weeks after hearing of Harrison's death, Clay kept referring to Tyler as the "Vice President" and insisted that "his administration will be in the nature of a regency." And regencies were historically and notoriously "weak." No doubt he also expected to direct the legislative process and immediately translate his American System into law. Even Democrats expected as much. "I fear that Tyler is such a poor weeping willow of a Creature," wrote Francis P. Blair to Jackson, "that he will resign all to the audacious depravity of the political black-leg."[7]

The "black-leg" hoped for a new start when Congress returned for the extra session. He even felt better. Physically his health had improved considerably since his breakdown in Baltimore, although he did not think his strength would be fully restored until the onset of warm weather. Mentally he felt exhilarated and ready to get back to work in Washington. In part his brightened spirits were based on the fact that he had known the fifty-one-year-old Tyler for more than twenty years and regarded him as a friend. He had admired the Virginian's courage and high sense of principle when Tyler resigned from the Senate rather than vote in favor of expunging the censure against President Jackson demanded of him by the Virginia general assembly. Clay said that Tyler had ability equal to that of Harrison. "He . . . is amiable, and I think honest and patriotic. His defect is want of moral firmness."[8]

Clay was also buoyed by his sense of Whig strength in Congress and the likelihood that the party could enact a speedy program of reform. And he knew what needed immediate legislative attention: first, repeal of the subtreasury and then a new national bank based on the experience with the old, "avoiding all mere experiments." Such a bank would have a capital stock of about fifty million dollars and the power to open branches in the several states. Clay also thought the Whigs should avoid touching the tariff during the extra session. The Compromise Tariff was due to expire on June 30, 1842, and any early tinkering with the rates would be needlessly provocative. "It will be time enough next winter" during the regular congressional session to tackle that matter, he said, when the question of home valuation would surely come up for discussion. He also expressed the hope that a new system of distribution of

7. Clay to Nathaniel B. Tucker, April 15, 1841, Clay to Henry R. Bascom, April 17, 1841, Clay to Waddy Thompson, Jr., April 23, 1841, Clay to Porter, April 24, 1841, in Clay, *Papers,* IX, 520, 522–523; Blair to Jackson, April 11, 1841, Jackson Papers, LC. Clay was not alone in thinking of Tyler as Vice President. Even the cabinet thought he would be styled "Vice President of the United States, acting President." Tyler quickly let it be known that he would assume all the powers, duties, honors, and titles accorded any President. Poore, *Reminiscences,* p. 269.
8. Clay to John L. Lawrence, April 13, 1841, in Clay, *Papers,* IX, 519.

the proceeds from the sale of public lands might be instituted. He shared some of these thoughts with Thomas Ewing, the secretary of the treasury, and Clay intimated that he expected full cooperation from the administration. "Let us have hearty & faithful co-operation between the President & his Cabinet, and their friends in Congress, and we cannot fail to redeem all our pledges and fulfill the just expectations of the Country."[9]

But within weeks Clay got his first intimation of possible trouble. He wrote to Tyler, saying all the appropriate things about his recent elevation to the presidency and promising full cooperation in achieving a successful administration. Tyler responded immediately. He confessed that he was not prepared to present Congress with a mature plan of public policy when it reconvened. He did expect the repeal of the subtreasury and any other necessary legislation to relieve the burdens of the Treasury. "As to a Bank," he said, "I design to be perfectly frank with you. I would not have it urged prematurely. The public mind is still in a state of great disquietude in regard to it." He pointed to the recent failure of Biddle's Philadelphia bank and the need to pursue the matter in a more thoughtful and deliberative manner—that is, the necessity of avoiding all constitutional objections to another national bank entertained by "a vast host of our own party to be found all over the Union."[10]

That letter should have given Clay pause—at least the need to be extremely careful before advancing legislation for a new bank. And he did understand the letter's meaning. Although he continued to maintain his confidence for the success of Whig measures in Congress, he now recognized that several of them faced real dangers. "I repair to my post in the Senate with strong hopes, not however unmixed with fears," he told several of his friends.[11]

Knowing the dangers, Clay pressed ahead with his schemes anyway. Thus the disasters that followed over the next several months were due in large measure to his own headstrong insistence on forcing the President and the Whig party into accepting what he, and he alone, had decided the American people had mandated in the election of 1840. He almost single-handedly shattered his own party by his obsessive desire to fashion a third national bank.[12]

9. Clay to Porter, April 24, 1841, Clay to Ewing, April 30, 1841, in Clay, *Papers,* IX, 522–523, 524–526.
10. Tyler to Clay, April 30, 1841, in Clay, *Papers,* IX, 527–529.
11. Clay to Brooke, May 14, 1841, Clay to Henry B. Bascom, May 10, 1841, in Clay, *Papers,* IX, 534,532.
12. Said Tyler: "My opinions on the subject of the power of Congress to create a national bank are permanently fixed, and that no power on earth could induce me to approve such a Bank bill as would alone satisfy the ultra-Federalists. This fact was as thoroughly known to Clay . . . not only by an acquaintance with my frequently avowed opinions, but from a conversation held with him upon the opening of the extra-session, he seized upon this as a favorable opportunity to press me to the *veto,* and by forcing me into a position of great awkwardness, to raise the cry of treason, to set all his presses upon me, and by exciting the passions of the Whigs to frenzy, to force them into an early committal for himself for the succession, and thereby to exclude all other competition." Tyler to Littleton W. Tazewell, October 11, 1841, in Tyler, *Letters,* II, 127–128. See also Tyler to Beverley Tucker, July 28, 1841, ibid., II, 54.

Clay got to the capital a full week ahead of the scheduled opening of Congress. He needed to get right to work organizing the Whigs in both houses if he expected to get his program through the legislature and adjourn by August. That meant regular caucus meetings, that meant providing an agenda at the very outset, and that meant asserting undisputed leadership of the party. It also meant inviting intense personal abuse for his audacity, arrogance, and dictatorship; but by this time he was used to such criticism, and it hardly troubled him at all. "Clay's game, to be plain," wrote Representative Henry A. Wise of Virginia, "was plainly seen. One thing which struck us at first was that he wished to play tyrant and dictator."[13] What made the Old Coon's task relatively easy was his acknowledged primacy in the party, the lack of any other Whig in Congress of comparable ability and daring, the enormous strength of his party in both the House and Senate, and a clear-cut program at hand, the details of which he had completely mastered. That program, as Clay finally enunciated it, went beyond the basic propositions of his American System. It now consisted of the repeal of the independent or subtreasury system; incorporation of a national bank; acquisition of an adequate revenue for the government by imposition of new tariff duties (including a temporary loan to cover the public debt); distribution of the proceeds of public lands; certain necessary appropriation bills; and some modification of the District of Columbia's banking system.[14]

One of Clay's first acts upon arriving in Washington was a visit to the new President to pay his respects. The courtly Tyler graciously received his guest and showed him every courtesy. Tall, standing a little over six feet, gaunt, with a high "retreating forehead," the Virginian had all the "features of the best Grecian model." In fact, his most prominent feature was his sharply defined aquiline nose. Two Americans in Naples happened to be present when a bust of Cicero was unearthed in an excavation. "President Tyler!" they exclaimed in unison.[15]

The President and the senator had a long and full conversation that touched on all the important issues, particularly the question of the Bank. Again Tyler expressed his reservations about a new one. He had just assumed

13. Wise to Beverley Tucker, June 27, 1841, in Tyler, *Letters,* II, 47. "Wise hates Clay," reported Representative David Hubbard of Alabama, "because he Clay repudiated his Quaker mistress (Philadelphia) and has transfered his affections to a New Paramour (New York). This is the foundation of the split in the Whig Ranks. Mr. Tyler desires to profit by it & intends running for the Presidency & expects to so shape his course as to compell our party [Democrats] as a choice of evils to take him up." Hubbard to James K. Polk, September 17, 1841, in Polk, *Correspondence,* V, 758.

14. *Congressional Globe,* 27th Congress, 1st session, pp. 22–23. Horace Greeley agreed with this program in almost every particular. The people expect Congress, he wrote, "to *work* rather than *talk* at this Session—the fruits of Statesmanship, not the flowers of declamation." The nation needs a sound currency, repeal of the subtreasury, and general retrenchment and reform. New York *Tribune,* May 24, 1841.

15. Anne Royall, *Letters from Alabama on Various Subjects* (Washington, D.C., 1830), I, 550, note; Oliver P. Chitwood, *John Tyler: Champion of the Old South* (New York, 1964), p. 253.

office, had little time to prepare for the special session, and frankly wanted the question postponed at least until December. But Clay would not yield an inch. He demanded a Bank *now*. After a while their discussion of the question became heated. The President's stubborn streak surfaced, and he finally lost his patience.

"Then, sir," he barked at Clay, "I wish you to understand this—that you and I were born in the same district; that we have fed upon the same food, and have breathed the same natal air. Go you now, then, Mr. Clay, to your end of the avenue, where stands the Capitol, and there perform your duty to the country as you shall think proper. So help me God, I shall do mine at this end of it as I shall think proper."[16]

Why was Clay so intransigent? Why gamble and risk a veto when he must have known that he could never override it in the Senate? No doubt several considerations, several of which were highly personal, shaped his attitude and behavior at this time. In part, as he frequently claimed, he wanted to reassert congressional supremacy in the American system of government that had been so thoroughly undermined by Andrew Jackson. Also, he regarded the Whig program as essential to the economic recovery and well-being of the American people and their future as a nation. The implementation of that program, therefore, had to be accomplished as soon as possible. Furthermore, he convinced himself that the election of 1840 constituted a mandate from the people to get on with the job of ending the depression, and everyone needed to conform to that fact whether they liked it or not. If, then, Tyler had constitutional problems with a new Bank, he should simply turn his head, hold his nose, and allow the legislation to become law without his signature.

But Clay also had personal demons to contend with in directing his behavior: ambition, pride, anger, arrogance, past disappointments and a need for vindication, and the enduring resentment that the people did not truly appreciate all his efforts on their behalf. ("Was ever man before treated as I have been & am now!" was his frequent nagging complaint.[17]) So, in the summer of 1841, he destructively decided to assert his absolute control over the Whig party and its course of action in Congress in order to show Tyler, Webster, and everyone else that *his* leadership and *his* agenda could best implement the victory of 1840. By so doing, he also believed he guaranteed his nomination for the next presidential campaign.

To some extent the interview between Clay and Tyler cleared the air. Not that it changed anything. In a brilliant display of executive leadership and administrative ability, not unlike those he developed during his early years as House Speaker, Clay went to work immediately to take command of Congress

16. Tyler, *Letters,* II, 33–34; see also Tyler to Tucker, July 28, 1841, ibid., II, 54. For a recent and scholarly treatment of the Clay-Tyler split, see Richard Gantz, "Henry Clay and the Harvest of Bitter Fruit: The Struggle with John Tyler, 1841–1842," doctoral dissertation, Indiana University, 1986.
17. Clay to Porter, January 16, 1842, in Clay, *Papers,* IX, 632.

and direct its legislative program. He frequently behaved arbitrarily and autocratically, listening only to those who agreed with him. He dictated the chairmen of all the important committees and sometimes even decided the membership of these committees in both houses. He was so spectacularly adept at administrative leadership that hardly a Whig, not even Webster's henchmen, dissented.

Here was the Andrew Jackson of the legislative branch! In time it cost him several friendships, including Ewing's temporarily, for he was particularly demanding on those closest to him. "He is much more imperious and arrogant with his friends than I have ever known him," Silas Wright told Van Buren, "and that you know, is saying a great deal."[18]

On one occasion Clay actually flew into a rage when a so-called Madisonian Whig, James Lyons, dared to attempt to argue the senator out of challenging Tyler over the Bank. After conversing with the President and discovering him "absolutely firm" on the question, Lyons tried to reason with the senator. He "talked with Mr. Clay and found him very violent." The Old Coon started screaming and actually said: "Tyler dares not resist. I will drive him before me."[19]

And so the inevitable quarrel began to unfold.[20] In Congress John White of Kentucky was elected Speaker, and Samuel Southard, an old and reliable colleague, installed as president pro tem of the Senate. Both men distributed congressional committee assignments as instructed by their leader. Clay himself headed the Senate Finance Committee, which would control all his major measures except the land bill. The chairmanship of the Public Lands Committee went to his friend Oliver H. Smith of Indiana, who could be expected to follow direction. Clay had the program and the votes, and he meant to succeed at long last in giving the country a real taste of Whig principles and policy.

"He predominates over the Whig Party with despotic sway," declared the New York *Herald* on July 30, 1841. "Old Hickory himself never lorded it over his followers with authority more undisputed, or more supreme. With the exception of some two or three in the Senate, and fifteen or twenty in the House, Mr. Clay's wish is a paramount law of the whole party." And how did the *Herald* account for this mastery? "His powerful intellect, courage, bold and determined spirit, and a perseverance that no difficulties can thwart or discourage."

It was awesome. Still, Democrats questioned how successful he would be with his agenda. They acknowledged his skill and boldness but thought that they themselves had the best talent in the Senate and with it could block the worst features of the Whig program. After all, their numbers included Silas

18. Poore, *Reminiscences,* I, 35; Wright to Van Buren, June 21, 1841, Van Buren Papers, LC.
19. Tyler, *Letters,* II, 41.
20. For a fuller discussion of the ensuing quarrel between Clay and Tyler, see David W. Krueger, "The Clay-Tyler Feud, 1841–1842," *Filson Club Historical Quarterly,* XLII (April 1968), pp. 162–177.

Wright, Jr., John C. Calhoun, Thomas Hart Benton, James Buchanan, and William Allen of Ohio. Against this very "strong phalanx," who among Whigs (besides Clay, of course) could champion their cause?[21]

But Clay was a "phalanx" in himself, as Democrats, Whigs, and the President soon discovered. And to put it simply, he had the votes. After assuming the chair of the Senate Finance Committee, he moved for the selection of a special committee of nine members to deal with the currency question and the selection of "a suitable fiscal agent," and he "seized" direction of this committee and arranged its membership so that six Whigs, one Conservative, and only two Democrats served on it.[22] "Mr. Clay is carrying every thing by storm," snarled one outraged Democrat; "his will is the law of Congress. His Speaker in the House has made the most outrageous arrangement of Committees. . . . It is the design of Mr. Clay to apply the gag very freely and to have but little discussion."[23]

True, Clay had something of a timetable in his head and repeatedly nagged his colleagues to stop wasting time with useless talk and get on with the business at hand. Even his friends sometimes "flinched." At one point he presumed to tell the other senators that they should emulate his daily schedule. He retired at night no later than ten, he said, rose at four or five, took exercise principally in the form of horseback riding for an hour or so, made his ablutions, took breakfast, read the newspapers, and was ready to go to work. If all the others in the Senate would pursue this course, they would "insure their health . . . pay their physician's bill" and begin work at eight or nine o'clock! Other senators could hardly believe him serious in making such an absurd suggestion. They defeated his suggestion by the vote of thirteen to thirty-one. "Clay's course is bold & reckless," commented William Marcy.

And the President was furious over his presumption. "Tyler wants him checkmated but does not want to do it himself by a veto."[24]

Clay mistakenly thought he could control the Senate without getting into too much difficulty. By turn, whenever he spoke, he could be cocky, haughty, reckless, and offensive—or reasonable, temperate, accommodating, witty, and charming. No one could predict how he might react to a criticism, an amendment, a suggestion. He told the Democrats that he would as soon attempt to convince them to vote the repeal of the subtreasury "as attempt to convince a convicted criminal with the rope around his neck that his conviction has been just and right." When Senator Levi Woodbury of New Hampshire chided him

21. Marcy to Wetmore, June 15, 1841, Marcy Papers, LC.

22. *Congressional Globe,* 27th Congress, 1st session, p. 12.

23. A. O. P. Nicholson to James K. Polk, June 14, 1841, in Polk, *Correspondence,* V, 698.

24. *Congressional Globe,* 27th Congress, 1st session, pp. 151–152; Marcy to George W. Newall [?], June 25, 1841, Marcy Papers, LC. According to Senator Mangum, the White House also flexed its muscles. "I was here in the darkest days of Jacksonism, as you know," he told Duncan Cameron, "& yet I have never witnessed such open & active efforts to bring executive influence to bear on Congress, as I have seen within the last fortnight.—And yet in the main, with little effect. June 26, 1841, in Mangum, *Papers,* III, 186.

because he had left the treasury secretary "to be whistled down the wind," Clay
responded by urging Woodbury to save "a little of his wind, which, from his
large size, he supposed was a commodity exceedingly useful to him."

Clay rarely missed an opportunity to mock Senator Buchanan. And many
times Buchanan asked for it. During one debate the Pennsylvanian regretted
that Clay "manifested so much excitability."

"Not at all; not at all," answered Clay. Then, in a soft, feminine voice, he
added: "I wish I had a more lady-like manner of expressing myself."

"I'm afraid the Senator will lose the proper intonation of his voice if he
pitches it on so high a key," Buchanan gaily responded.

"Not unlikely, as you put my voice so often in requisition," Clay answered, "I will modulate my voice to suit the delicate ear of the Senator from
Pennsylvania." Since Buchanan had a peculiarly sharp, high-pitched, nasal
voice, the galleries giggled over that remark.

When Calhoun pronounced the vote on one amendment as "the most
ominous vote yet given, Clay retorted: "Everything is ominous or a crisis, with
the Senator."

Calhoun brushed that aside. "I told the Senator in '37," he continued,
"that he would ride the Bank to death, as he had the American system, and
every other hobby which he had ever mounted."

"Well"—Clay laughed—"I will have a good horse and a pleasant ride."

Clay's arrogance became so intolerable during this extra session that other
senators labeled him the Dictator, to which he blithely replied: "Ask Charles
[his black servant] if I am not a kind master." Newspapers picked up Clay's
new "title," which Horace Greeley described as the "wretched slang of a profligate press about 'Clay dictation.' "[25]

The first item on Clay's congressional agenda was the repeal of the subtreasury system, and without wasting much time, he rammed it through the
Senate. His Finance Committee reported a measure to repeal, and five days
later it passed by a vote of 29 to 18. The House took more time but passed the
bill on August 9 by a vote of 134 to 87, and Tyler signed it. Jubilant Whigs
paraded from Capitol Hill to the White House. A catafalque with a coffin
labeled "The Sub Treasury" slowly moved along Pennsylvania Avenue, accompanied by a band, torchlights, transparencies, and fireworks. After saluting the
President, the mock mourners with the deceased in tow marched to Mrs.
Brown's boardinghouse at the corner of Seventh and D streets to receive Clay's
grateful acknowledgment of their ingenious demonstration.[26]

Next, Clay summoned Treasury Secretary Ewing to come forward with
the draft of a new Bank charter,[27] something they had been discussing for

25. *Congressional Globe*, 27th Congress, 1st session, pp. 13–14, 83, 222–223, 197–198, 328; Sargent, *Public Men and Events*, II, 128–129 and note; Poage, *Clay and Whig Party*, p. 56; *Tribune*,
July 17, 1841.
26. *Congressional Globe*, 27th Congress, 1st session, pp. 36, 312–313; Poore, *Reminiscences*, pp.
271–272.
27. According to Senator Willie P. Mangum of North Carolina, "it was at *his* [Ewing's] *special*

weeks. And on this question he knew the entire future relationship between Tyler and the Whigs would turn. "We are in a crisis, as a party," he told the governor of Kentucky. "There is reason to fear that Tyler will throw himself upon Calhoun . . . and detach himself from the great body of the Whig party. . . . If he should take that course, it will be on the Bank."[28]

Ewing had to respond, and on June 12 he submitted his plan of a Fiscal Bank of the United States, incorporated in the District of Columbia, to be capitalized at thrity million dollars, and authorized to establish branches in various cities, provided it obtained the consent of the states in which the branches would be located. Obviously the branching provision and the location of the Bank in Ewing's plan had been carefully crafted to allay Tyler's possible constitutional objections.[29]

Clay predicted as much. And it annoyed him. No branching powers without state consent! "What a Bank would that be!" he snorted. Although the Ewing plan presumably had the approval of the President, the endorsement of the cabinet, and the strong support of several highly placed Whigs, including Daniel Webster, it hardly achieved what the Whigs had long insisted was vital in a national bank. Clay faced a dilemma. He acknowledged Tyler's reservations about a Bank and the danger not only of a veto but that the President could be driven into the arms of Calhoun and his Democratic friends. Still, the Ewing Fiscal Bank failed to provide a true national bank. It was another experiment, and Clay was sick of experiments. He believed that the American people wanted "a real old-fashioned Bank; such an one as they and their fathers have tried, and experienced with benefits of." A "National Bank," he later shouted at his colleagues, not "a rickety, imbecile, incompetent local bank." So, taking an enormous gamble, he decided to risk presidential displeasure and write a bill worthy of himself and his party.[30]

Ewing's plan went first to Clay's select committee. Meanwhile, the senator caucused his Whig colleagues to consider the plan[31] and invited Ewing to his lodgings to rework the branching provision. Not surprisingly, on June 21, he reported to the Senate a different bill—his own—which essentially differed from the Ewing plan in its granting of unrestricted branching authority.

---

request Mr. Clay made a call upon the Treasury department for the Project, & never until at the moment, that the Project was in process of formation were difficulties either felt or apprehended." Mangum to Duncan Cameron, June 26, 1841, in Mangum, *Papers,* III, 182.

28. Clay to Letcher, June 11, 1841, in Clay, *Papers,* IX, 543.

29. *Congressional Globe,* 27th Congress, 1st session, pp. 48–49.

30. *Congressional Globe,* 27th Congress, 1st session, pp. 354–355.

31. These caucus sessions went on day after day, "four or five consecutive days," reported Senator Mangum, and each lasted for three hours or more. "The whole measure was canvassed in its principles & its details, with the minutest care . . . and all the consequences of disunion & discord, were fully considered & painfully canvassed, as they would affect the party & . . . the great interests of the Country, Commercial & political." Clay was very conciliatory during these sessions "not only on account of an imputed dictatorial spirit, made by our opponents, but beginning to be pretty openly insinuated by our friends." Mangum to Duncan Cameron, June 26, 1841, in Mangum, *Papers,* III, 184.

Gushed Horace Greeley's *Tribune:* "So brief, so clear, so forcible a document could only emanate from one of the master minds of the age."[32] While presenting his report, Clay said his committee regretted diverging from Ewing's position but thought that the secretary's plan was unsound and dangerous.[33] Requiring state consent for branching would prevent the government from operating equally in all the states and thereby would lose its uniform character as established under the Constitution.[34]

Clay's challenge—he gave "Tyler his choice to surrender or fight"[35] —brought a quick response from the White House.[36] Acting as spokesman for Tyler, Senator William Rives introduced an amendment to the bill requiring state assent to branching. As soon as Rives completed his remarks about the amendment, Clay attacked it. "No good—nothing, I fear, but unmixed mischief—can come of it," declared the Old Coon. But he spoke gently. He congratulated Rives for his spirit of compromise and conciliation. However, when Rufus Choate, senatorial successor to Webster, supported the amendment and stated that he *"knew"* the bill would not become law without it, Clay got testy and demanded that Choate reveal the source of his information. Obviously it came from Webster, and Clay wanted that fact openly acknowledged. He reacted strongly because he now realized "that not only the Palace but the Department of State was in the field against him. His native placidity was disturbed by this discovery."

Name your source, he cried. Choate refused. Clay went after him a second and third time for a response, but the Massachusetts senator held his ground. "I want a direct answer," Clay shouted at Choate during one exchange. The badgering and hammering continued for several minutes until the chair finally intervened and called both men to order. Representative Thomas Marshall labeled Clay "a sublime blackguard" because of his behavior, while the New York *Herald* denounced "the tyrannical insolence of Mr. Clay," whose "bullying disposition . . . causes him to forget himself sometimes." The next day Clay offered something approaching an apology.[37]

32. June 24, 1841.

33. The Whigs meeting in caucus gave special instructions to the committee on the plan, especially regarding the branching feature. Mangum to Cameron, June 26, 1841, in Mangum, *Papers,* III, 184–185.

34. Clay to Letcher, June 11, 1841, Clay to Ewing, June 14, 1841, [June 19, 1841], in Clay, *Papers,* IX, 543, 546, 548, *Congressional Globe,* 27th Congress, 1st session, pp. 79–81. Some congressmen thought Clay had an even more devious scheme in mind in proposing his own plan. He means "to drive Tyler *to a veto,*" declared Representative Wise, and then revert to "playing the 'Great Pacificator' again, instead of the dictator." Once he had thrown blame on the administration and its friends for the defeat of the bill, he would "then go back to Ewing's scheme in the spirit of *conciliation* and *compromise,*— two terms magical and fortune-making with him." Wise to Tucker, June 27, 1841, in Tyler, *Letters,* II, 47.

35. Wright to Van Buren, June 21, 1841, Van Buren Papers, LC. Wright also said that Clay gave "poor Daniel" the choice "to fight or run."

36. "Remember always that the power claimed by Mr. Clay and others," said the President, "is a power to create a corporation to operate *per se* over the Union. This from the first has been the contest." Tyler to Governor J. Rutherford, June 23, 1841, in Tyler, *Letters,* II, 50–51.

37. Marcy to Wetmore, July 3, 1841, Marcy Papers, LC; *Congressional Globe,* 27th Congress, 1st

The Democrats could barely hide their delight over these developments. "Our friends are in the highest spirits," wrote William Marcy, "—they think they see the certain & speedy dissolution of the Whig party." What gave them particular pleasure was the knowledge that Webster had joined Tyler "to embarrass the cause of Mr. Clay."[38]

The Great Compromiser then set about finding a way to enact a "real old-fashioned Bank" and skirt the objections of the President about branching. The Whigs, under his direction, caucused on July 12 and 13. They caucused practically every day, but these particular sessions were aimed at winning consensus on a compromise, since the bill, as presently framed, could not pass.

What Clay finally concocted was a variation of a scheme urged on him by his friend Peter B. Porter, who was visiting Washington at the time. He may also have heard of a similar idea, advanced by Representative John Minor Botts, a Virginia Whig, which supposedly had Tyler's approval. In making his argument for his suggested amendment, Porter pledged the support of other Whigs and named Senator William C. Preston of South Carolina in particular. Like everyone else, Porter knew the bill would never become law without some modification of the branching provision, and he assured Clay that his suggestion would carry and generate the votes in both houses to win final approval for the entire bill. His scheme called for a provision stating that each state retained the right to disallow a branch within its borders by enacting a law to that effect at the first session of its legislature following the passage of the Bank bill through Congress. What Clay added to this suggestion—possibly taken from Representative Botts—was a statement that whenever it became "necessary and proper" to establish a branch in any state, the Bank had the right to establish one, even if the state objected. He then introduced the scheme in the form of an amendment to his original bill.[39]

What a wretched "compromise." It hardly deserved the name and clearly shows the imprint of other hands since it lacks Clay's finesse in concocting such things. Not that the Kentuckian can escape blame for driving ahead with it. The section he added to the amendment revealed his intent to force branching on the country whether the President liked it or not. Consequently, he unwittingly convinced Tyler that he was engaged in a conspiracy to make him veto the Bank bill and "get all the credit" for at least attempting a possible compromise.[40]

Clay did not present the amendment to the Senate until July 27. He

session, pp. 140–145; Poore, *Reminiscences,* I, 275; Little, *Ben Hardin,* p. 342; New York *Herald,* quoted in Poage, *Clay and Whig Party,* p. 56, note.

38. Marcy to George Newell [?], June 25, 1841, Marcy to Wetmore, July 3, 1841, Marcy to John Knower, July 3, 1841, Marcy Papers, LC; Porter to Clay, July 23, 1841, in Clay, *Papers,* IX, 572.

39. Porter to Clay, mid-July, 1841, in Clay, *Papers,* IX, 565–566; Tyler, *Letters,* II, 55–57; Van Deusen, *Clay,* p. 349; Chitwood, *Tyler,* pp. 222–223.

40. Henry Wise to Beverley Tucker, July 11, 1841, in Tyler, *Letters,* II, 52; Marcy to Newell [?], June 25, 1841, Marcy to Wetmore, July 24, 1841, Marcy Papers, LC; Poage, *Clay and Whig Party,* p. 63.

allowed two weeks to expire because he needed additional time to win sufficient votes to get it and the entire bill approved. The Senate had been in
session for several hours when he rose to propose the compromise amendment. He said the purpose of the amendment was to allow the enactment of a
national bank in order to satisfy the "just expectations of a suffering people."
Rives pronounced the amendment a trick, but it squeezed through the Senate
by a vote of 25 to 24, with Preston voting in favor. The following day, by a
vote of 26 to 23, the upper house then approved this Fiscal Bank bill, as it was
called. The House, without suggesting amendments, passed it on August 6,
128 to 97, and sent it to the President.[41]

Ten days elapsed before Tyler responded. During that time many Democrats assumed that he would veto the bill and, as a result, that his cabinet,
except Webster, would resign in protest. Considerable betting occurred during these days on the possibilities of a veto and the mass exit of the cabinet.
Clay claimed that he did not know what Tyler would do, nor did the cabinet.
"There is a most agonizing state of uncertainty in the public mind," he wrote.
But with each passing day he became more and more convinced that Tyler
would veto, the consequence of which, he said, would be "the separation of the
President from the Whigs."[42]

The veto arrived in Congress on August 16. It was accompanied by hisses
and boos from the gallery while Benton shouted, "Bank ruffians," at the
"hooligans." "Clay sat in his seat, cool as a marble palace."[43] The veto had been
written against the advice of the cabinet, which virtually assured its resignation. Tyler objected to the branching provision, of course, as well as the Bank's
authority to discount notes. Moreover, he declared that any bank created "to
operate *per se* over the Union" was unconstitutional. The message was "broad
and sweeping" and sent the Democrats into a state of ecstasy. "It will do Old
Hickory's heart good when he hears of the Veto," rejoiced one. "We should
get the North Bend Glee Club to sing 'Tippecanoe & Tyler too,'" laughed
another. Said a third: "Egad, he [Tyler] has found one of old Jackson's pens
and it wouldn't write any way but plain and straitforward." The Democrats
were even more delighted when the Senate, three days later, failed to override.[44]

41. *Congressional Globe,* 27th Congress, 1st session, pp. 254, 256, 260, 314. On Clay's performance
Horace Greeley was downright rhapsodic. "The spirit of Henry Clay rises higher and higher as
difficulties grow thicker and mightier around him. His courage and constancy keep pace with the
demands upon him. *Crescit sub pondere virtus.* [Manly strength flourishes under heavy burdens.]
Always in his place, always ready, always courteous to those who treat him with ordinary courtesy.
. . . His whole bearing is dignified, courteous, and even conciliatory." New York *Tribune,* July 31,
1841.
42. New York *Tribune,* August 11, 16, 1841; Clay to Porter, August 8, 1841, Clay to Thomas Hart
Clay, August 15, 1841, in Clay, *Papers,* IX, 581, 584.
43. New York *Tribune,* August 19, 1841.
44. Richardson, *Messages and Papers,* III, 1918–1921; Robert J. Morgan, *A Whig Embattled: The
Presidency under John Tyler* (New York, 1974), pp. 41–42; Dabney S. Carr to Jackson, August 18,
1841, in Jackson, *Correspondence,* VI, 119; Marcy to Wetmore, August 18, 1841, Marcy Papers,
LC.

So delighted were the Democrats that a group of them went to the White House on the evening following the veto to congratulate the President, and their festivities almost became a riotous celebration. But the Whigs reacted angrily, and some of them, half drunk, congregated around the White House at 2:00 A.M. and beat drums, blew trumpets, and shouted: "Huzza for Clay!" and "A Bank! A Bank! Down with the Veto!" Although many of them had long expected a veto and had prepared themselves for the shock, still, they bitterly resented the action taken by the President. A few, like Webster, tried to make the best of it. He had a "carousal" at his house the following night and, after getting gloriously drunk, "swore he would stay in office."[45]

Those who claimed to know Tyler's thinking insisted that he was "in a state of high exasperation agt. Mr. Clay & his followers." He had been forced to veto the Fiscal Bank bill, making it appear that he opposed any national bank. He had already begun to speculate on his chances to succeed himself, and if he expected the Whig nomination in 1844—not beyond the realm of possibility since he controlled the patronage—he could hardly appear rigidly hostile to the idea of another U.S. Bank. Thus, when Whig friends visited him in an effort to reconcile their differences, Tyler responded eagerly and indicated the kind of Bank he might be willing to approve. Discussions immediately followed with members of the cabinet. Attorney General Crittenden alerted Clay, telling him that the President was willing to concede the power of branching with "all other usual banking business" except that of discounting promissory notes without state consent. Such a bill, the President later told his cabinet, could be passed in forty-eight hours. Alexander H. H. Stuart, a Virginia Whig, visited Tyler on a conciliatory mission and proposed a bill that converted agencies of the Bank into offices of discount and deposit in the states. Tyler again responded positively and told Stuart to go to Webster and have him work out the details. He "desired to have it back in three days, that he might sign it in twenty-four hours."

All of a sudden it seemed as though the entire political situation had been turned around. "As I rose to leave him," Stuart said, ". . . he held my right hand in his left, and raising his right hand upwards, exclaimed with much feeling: 'Stuart! if you can be instrumental in passing this bill through Congress, I will esteem you the best friend I have on earth.' "[46]

The Whigs immediately caucused and agreed to accede to the President's wishes. Senator John M. Berrien and Representative John Sergeant were charged with writing a bill in consultation with the cabinet and the President. The Whigs even agreed—in deference to Tyler—to dispense with the word

45. *Madisonian,* August 19, 1841, quoted in Chitwood, *Tyler,* p. 228; Marcy to Wetmore, August 18, 1841, Marcy Papers, LC.

46. Marcy to Wetmore, August 18, 1841, Marcy Papers, LC; Crittenden to Clay, August 16, 1841, in Clay, *Papers,* IX, 585–586; Chitwood, *Tyler,* p. 239; "Diary of Thomas Ewing, August and September, 1841," *American Historical Review,* XVIII (1912), pp. 99–100; Stuart's statement, in Benton, *Thirty Years' View,* II, 344, 350. The necessity for speed is conveyed in a remark of John Bell to Webster and Ewing. "Gentlemen you have no time to lose—if you do not attend to this today another bill less acceptable may be got up and reported. "Diary of Ewing," p. 102.

"bank" and call the agency the Fiscal Corporation of the United States.

"Heavens, what a name!" exclaimed Senator Benton. He preferred to call it this "Corporosity."[47]

Clay was scheduled to give his reply to the veto message on August 17, but fearing that his remarks might antagonized the already "exasperated" President, he was prevailed upon to postpone his speech until the nineteenth so as "not to disturb this concoction" that was presently being brewed.[48]

He spoke on Thursday for an hour and a half. Not surprisingly—considering what was going on between the Whigs and the President—he spoke calmly, moderately, temperately, and respectfully. Up to a point. He naturally expressed his sorrow over the rejection and said he had presumed that Tyler occupied the Madison position on the question of constitutionality. He charged the President with failing to reciprocate the friendly congressional spirit of concession and accommodation and scored the language of the veto as "harsh, if not reproachful." He needlessly pointed out that Tyler would never have been nominated at Harrisburg if his views on the Bank had been correctly known. Then he took up the President's objections one by one and wondered aloud why Tyler could not have suffered the bill to become law without his signature since he knew how Whigs and the people felt about it. He understood that Tyler might concur in the establishment of a Bank "and that some of our friends" were presently arranging it. "Whilst I regret that I can take no active part in such an experiment . . . I assure my friends that they shall find no obstacle or impediment in me." He closed with a passionate outburst: "Shall we adjourn, and go home in disgust? No! No! No! A higher, nobler, and more patriotic career lies before us. Let us here, at the east end of Pennsylvania avenue, do our duty, our whole duty, and nothing short of our duty, toward our common country."[49]

It was another one of "his most powerful and happy efforts," according to the admiring secretary of the treasury, Thomas Ewing, "exhorting expressions of rapturous applause from his most bitter enemies in that body, and thrilling his friends with delight."[50]

But Senator Rives did not applaud. Indeed, he took exception to Clay's speech and rose to defend the veto and Tyler's distinguished career before becoming President. He also took notice of Clay's past history, especially his anti-Bank arguments in 1811, and charged him with accusing the President of "perfidy." The speech was sharp and cutting and clearly nettled the Old Coon, who repeatedly interrupted. And since Rives had chosen to bring "*himself* within the lion's bound," the lion pounced on him when he concluded "with

47. "Diary of Ewing," p. 102; William N. Chambers, *Old Bullion Benton: Senator from the New West* (Boston, 1956), p. 253.

48. Benton, *Thirty Years' View,* II, 347.

49. Clay, *Works,* VI, 275–291.

50. "Diary of Ewing," p. 103. Reverdy Johnson reported the same reaction. Johnson to Mangum, August 24, 1841, in Mangum, *Papers,* III, 219.

unrestrained and unmitigated impetuosity and poured forth upon him the whole torrent of his feelings in the most high toned and powerful invective." Clay accused Rives of lacking party principles. "There he still stands, solitary and alone, shivering and pelted by the pitiless storm," the Dictator cried. Clay referred to those who would attempt the formation of a third party around Tyler but who could not collect enough recruits to "compose a decent *corporal's guard.*" Of course, Rives was not one of these, Clay hypocritically protested. And he hoped that the senator did not belong to "a new sort of kitchen Cabinet—whose object is the dissolution of the regular Cabinet—the dissolution of the Whig party—the dispersion of Congress, without accomplishing any of the great purposes of the extra session—and a total change, in fact, in the whole face of our political affairs."[51]

The words *"corporal's guard"* caught everyone's attention—including Tyler's—and it gained immediate and popular currency in referring to the President's congressional friends, such as Henry Wise, Thomas W. Gilmer, George H. Proffit, W. W. Irwin, Francis Mallory, and Caleb Cushing. It incensed Tyler, who complained that he was attacked and denounced by his own party. He regarded certain Whigs, the President said, "as his very worst enemies."[52]

The Fiscal Corporation bill sped through the House with minimum debate on August 23 in order to take advantage of Tyler's willingness to sign a Bank measure before he changed his mind. As a matter of fact, the President had already begun to develop second thoughts about what he had agreed to do. Why should he placate Whigs when they jeered and harassed and burned him in effigy? Why support a party that would most likely snub him in 1844 and nominate Henry Clay? Said an acute observer: Tyler "is convinced Clay is playing a game for himself and wishes to use him and when that is done will turn his back upon him." It occurred to Tyler that perhaps he should return to the Democratic fold. It was not beyond reason that the Democrats might select him as their nominee. In fact, Andrew Jackson was so pleased with his performance that within the year he had begun a correspondence with Tyler, and Old Hickory instructed the *Globe* to cease all criticism of the President.[53]

Clay's *"corporal's guard"* remark really nettled Tyler. The phrase was meant to invoke public ridicule, and it succeeded, especially after the publication of a letter written by Representative John M. Botts of Virginia accusing Tyler of treachery toward the Whigs and engaging in a conspiracy to form a third party with friendly Democrats and states' righters. But, said Botts, the

51. Clay, *Works,* VI, 291 296. "Mr. Tyler's conduct . . . betrays the grossest weakness, if not the basest treachery," wrote Reverdy Johnson to Mangum, August 27, 1841, in Mangum, *Papers,* III, 222.
52. "Diary of Ewing," p. 103. See also Tyler to Higgins, February 26, 1853, in Tyler, *Letters,* II, 164, note.
53. Marcy to Newell [?], June 25, 1841, Marcy Papers; Remini, *Jackson,* III, 481ff.

Whigs would *"Head*[54] *Captain Tyler, or die."* As the laughter in and out of Congress intensified, Tyler grew angrier. At length he decided that his chances for a second term were better with Democrats or his third-party friends than the Whigs. He also wanted "to get rid of his cabinet," and by reversing himself, he would surely drive them out. So he abandoned his own Bank measure. He informed his cabinet on August 25 that he would not sign the Fiscal Corporation bill after all and begged the members to use their influence to get it postponed. As Clay had said earlier, Tyler's one defect was "want of moral firmness."[55]

Like a shot, Webster contacted his friends to urge their cooperation in delaying a Senate vote on the bill. But it was too late for that. Clay would not cooperate, and some charged him with another attempt to embarrass the President. But even Senator Benton knew that accusation was false. "Mr. Clay had no such design. . . . The only design was to get him to sign his own bill—the fiscal corporation bill—which he had fixed up himself, title and all."[56]

Still, Clay was not without blame. He wanted to force the President's hand. And to do so, he was prepared to hold the revenue bill, then pending, as hostage and force the Bank bill to a final decision. "All the Locos" but one in the Senate agreed with him; but thirteen Whigs voted against the bank bill, and many of them "were much incensed at Mr. Clay's course." They charged him with "hurrying matters to a catastrophe," of forcing Tyler to veto once again and thereby compel the cabinet to resign and drive the President into the Democratic party. By this tactic, said some Whigs, the Old Coon could freely denounce the administration, assume dictatorial control of the entire Whig party, and announce his candidacy for President.[57]

Again the Whigs caucused, this time at Crittenden's lodgings. After several rounds of drinks a few of the participants decided to go to the White House and urge the President to attend their conference. They convinced him, and as Tyler entered Crittenden's house, Clay met him at the door.

"Well, Mr. President, what are you for?" cried the well-oiled Mr. Clay.

Tyler blanched.

"Wine, whisky, brandy, or champagne?" laughed the senator. "Come, show your hand."

Very quietly Tyler said he would have champagne.[58]

Clay had not publicly announced his support of the Fiscal Corporation bill, waiting for its submission to the Senate from committee. In the mean-

54. Meaning "to check."

55. Marcy to Wetmore, August 18, 1841, Marcy Papers, LC; Benton, *Thirty Years' View,* II, 349; "Diary of Ewing," pp. 103–104; Clay to John Lawrence, April 13, 1841, in Clay, *Papers,* IX, 519. On the cabinet crisis, see Morgan, *Whig Embattled,* p. 57ff. For Tyler's efforts to form a third party, see Robert Seager, *And Tyler Too* (New York, 1963), pp. 170–171.

56. Benton, *Thirty Years' View,* II, 350.

57. "Diary of Ewing," pp. 105–106.

58. Adams, *Memoirs,* X, 544–545; Van Deusen, *Clay,* p. 353.

time, he arranged, directed, steered, and conducted the remainder of his program through Congress, always hounding its members to move with greater
dispatch and not consume so much time with useless palaver. The Democrats
enjoyed Whig discomfort and needled the Kentuckian on his mad rush to
decision. Even the somber Calhoun suggested that if he, Clay, wanted to end
the session right away, all he had to do was withdraw the Fiscal Corporation
bill. "Never, never!" replied Clay. "No, not if we stay here till Christmas."[59]

So the bill came to the Senate floor on September 1. Although it fell
"short—far short," Clay announced, of the kind of bank the nation's needed,
he would vote for it because it would regulate exchange and control the supply
of a uniform currency. The following day he regaled his audience with one of
the funniest and most delightful performances of his entire career.

He described the "alleged disorders" at the White House on the evening
following the veto in which he claimed the "whole loco foco party in Congress" was present. "I think that I can now see the principal *dramatis personae*
who figured in the scene," he snickered. "There stood the grave and distinguished Senator from South Carolina. . . ."

Calhoun rose immediately from his seat to respond, but Clay would not
yield the floor.

"There, I say, I can imagine stood the Senator from South Carolina—tall,
care-worn, with furrowed brow, haggard, and intensely gazing, looking as if
he were dissecting the last and newest abstraction which sprung from meta-
physician's brain, and muttering to himself, in half-uttered sounds, 'This is
indeed a real crisis'!"

The chamber guffawed.

"Not far off stood the honorable Senators from Arkansas [Ambrose H.
Sevier] and from Missouri [Thomas Hart Benton], the latter looking at the
Senator from South Carolina, with an indignant curl on his lip and scorn in his
eye, and pointing his finger with contempt towards that Senator, whilst he
said, or rather seemed to say, 'He calls himself a statesman! why, he has never
even produced a decent humbug!' "

The spectators could not control themselves. They roared with laughter.

"The Senator from Missouri was not there," Benton shouted from his
seat.

"I stand corrected," responded Clay. "I was only imagining what you
would have said if you had been there."

Again the galleries erupted.

"Then there stood the Senator from Georgia [Alfred Cuthbert], conning
over in his mind on what point he should make his next attack upon the
Senator from Kentucky." More laughter.

"The honorable Senator from Pennsylvania [James Buchanan], I presume, stood forward as spokesman for his whole party; and although I cannot

59. *Congressional Globe,* 27th Congress, 1st session, p. 404.

pretend to imitate his well-known eloquence, I beg leave to make an humble essay towards what I presume to have been the kind of speech delivered by him on that august occasion."

Clay cleared his throat, raised the pitch of his voice to make it sound strangulated, and continued. " 'May it please your Excellency: A number of your present political opponents, in company with myself, have come to deposite at your Excellency's feet the evidences of our loyalty and devotion. . . . We have now come most hardily to thank your Excellency that you have accomplished for us that against your friends which we with our most strenuous exertions were unable to achieve."

The spectators could no longer contain themselves. They laughed and hooted and clapped their hands. It took many minutes before order could be restored.

Clay ended this uproarious speech on a much more somber note, taking direct aim at the President. He refused to believe, he said, that Tyler would desert to the Democrats. "The soil of Virginia is too pure to produce traitors. Small, indeed, is the number of those who have proved false to their principles and to their party." Clay then turned to the Democratic members. "No, gentlemen, the President never will disgrace himself, disgrace his blood, disgrace his State, disgrace his country, disgrace his children, by abandoning his party, and joining with you. Never, never!"[60]

Today it is nearly impossible, as contemporaries constantly commented, "to attempt to transfer to paper any just presentment of his lofty and impassioned eloquence," his wit, and his histrionic ability. His speeches had to be heard, not read, because there was simply no way to capture the passion, conviction, enthusiasm, and sheer splendor of his oratorical performances. To hear him at his best in Congress was a thrilling experience, a "noble intellectual treat" that virtually disappeared from public discourse after he passed from the scene.[61]

The Fiscal Corporation bill passed the Senate on September 3 by a vote of twenty-seven to twenty-two—almost a strict party vote.[62] Six days later the President returned his veto. Acting out of a sense of "constitutional duty," he faulted the national character of the bill and the exchange provision. And with that resounding negative all further attempts to establish a national bank terminated. Not until the next century would the country finally accede to Clay's arguments about the need for central banking in the United States.

Despite this paralyzing defeat—and the Whigs took the blow rather badly, cursing Tyler as a traitor, calling him "His Accidency," and burning him in effigy—the extra session produced a remarkably successful record. During

60. Benton, *Thirty Years' View*, II, 328; Clay, *Papers*, IX, 600–601.
61. "Diary of Ewing," p. 103.
62. *Congressional Globe*, 27th Congress, 1st session, pp. 418–419. The bill had already passed the House on August 23. For an excellent discussion of partisan behavior in Congress, see Joel Silbey, *The Shrine of Party* (Pittsburgh, 1967).

the many delays over passage of the two Bank bills, the other items on Clay's agenda were thrashed out in record time and enacted into law. A bankruptcy act, allowing debtors voluntarily to declare themselves insolvent, passed by mid-August, and Tyler signed it immediately. In early September a land bill making preemption permanent and allowing squatters to buy 160 acres at $1.25 an acre without competition won approval. The distribution provision of the bill stated that when the tariff rose above 20 percent, states in which the land was located would be assigned 10 percent of the sales, with the rest divided among all the states. Presumably these funds would be used for internal improvements. The passage of both the bankruptcy and distribution bills required a considerable amount of logrolling. To get southern and western votes for the bankruptcy bill, easterners had to accept distribution. And "the Distribution bill could not have been carried without the Bankrupt bill," the Kentucky senator told Governor Letcher.[63]

Clay's efforts in a conference committee of the two houses also resulted in some adjusted tariff rates (which in no way conflicted with the Compromise Tariff of 1833 because they were confined to the free articles) in order to help pay the national debt. And a loan bill was enacted to assist the government in meeting its expenses. It was during the debate on this measure that Calhoun contemptuously referred to Clay as "the Chancellor of the Exchequer.[64]

Despite this enviable record, Clay sourly commented that the Whigs presented the image of a body "with its head cut off." Congress had enacted "all our great measures, and one more [the Bankruptcy Act] than I thought was practicable at this Extra Session. If the President had been cordially with us what a glorious summer this of 1841 would be!"[65]

Disheartened and discouraged, four members of the cabinet—Ewing, Crittenden, Bell, and Badger—resigned within forty-eight hours after the submission of the second Bank veto.[66] Granger followed later. But Webster hung on. He could not accept the overlordship of Clay by abandoning Tyler, so he asked the President what he should do.

63. Clay to Letcher, January 6, 1841, in Clay, *Papers,* IX, 628. When Clay first submitted the land bill, Greeley pronounced it "one of the wisest and most beneficent measures of a long and useful public life. . . . We deeply regret that the country has not two Henry Clays; she cannot well spare one from the Senate, but she needs another in the House." New York *Tribune,* June 12, 1841.

64. *Congressional Globe,* 27th Congress, 1st session, pp. 243–246, 350, 372, 438; Norma Lois Peterson, *The Presidencies of William Henry Harrison & John Tyler* (Lawrence, Kan., 1989), pp. 98–99.

65. Clay to Ambrose Spencer, August 27, 1841, in Clay, *Papers,* IX, 594.

66. John Tyler, Jr., later recorded that the cabinet members "arranged with Clay that their resignations should be handed in the last day of the week, Saturday, September 11; but instead of all going in at once, it was concerted that the day should be consumed by the intervals between them, the last, that of Granger, Postmaster-General, being delayed until five o'clock P.M., thus rendering it impossible for action to be had by the President on the formation of a new cabinet that day. . . . As the President's private secretary I was present when the resignations were handed in to him, one after the other, and by his direction noted the time of the receipt of each by my watch. The first was received by the President at half-past twelve o'clock P.M., the last came to him at half-past five o'clock P.M." Tyler, Jr., to Lyon G. Tyler, January 29, 1883, in Tyler, *Letters,* II, 121–122, note.

"Where am I to go, Mr. President?" Webster asked.

"You must decide that for yourself, Mr. Webster," came the reply.

"If you leave it to me, Mr. President," said the secretary of state, *"I will stay where I am."*

Tyler rose immediately from his seat, extended his hand, and responded: *"Give me your hand on that, and now I will say to you that Henry Clay is a doomed man from this hour."*[67]

For some time the President had been planning to get rid of his cabinet; only he expected to do it after the extra session. He took it as another Clay discourtesy when he was forced to advance his timetable. He now fully expected to make a try for another term in office and had decided he needed a new team and other friends to help him in his quest.

As for Webster, his decision to remain in the cabinet "bodes no good to him," said William Marcy, even though the ostensible reason presented to the public—namely, the necessity of staying in office to complete the negotiations with Great Britain over the Maine boundary dispute—seemed perfectly legitimate. Clay thought that his continuance in the cabinet "must injure him to an extent that he will find it difficult ever to repair." Never one to hide his true feelings, he went to Webster and told him to his face what his fate would be if he pursued his present course. "I then said to him 'If you mean to continue in Mr. Tyler's Admon for the purpose of closing any incomplete business,[68] to which your attention and service are necessary, the public will approve your conduct. But if you identify yourself with it and remain indefinitely the public will condemn you.' " Webster just glared at him.[69]

As was their wont, the Whigs caucused again. This time they denounced the President, drafted an address to the public which boasted of the party's recent accomplishments, and listened to another funny, rousing, and emotional speech from their leader, Henry Clay.

"This is a dark night," he hissed. "There is no moon, and the little stars are slumbering in their beds, behind the dark canopy that is spread over the heavens." But do not despair, he counseled. "Let our hearts be cheerful. . . . We, Senators, will soon pass away, but our principles will live while our glorious Union shall exist." They had done their duty, he told them, but it had been temporarily arrested by a President "that we brought into power. [Benedict] Arnold escaped to England, after his treason was detected. . . . Tyler is on his way to the Democratic camp. They may give him lodgings in some outhouse,

67. John Tyler, Jr., to Lyon G. Tyler, January 29, 1883, in Tyler, *Letters,* II, 122, note. A discussion of Webster's role in the administration during these months may be found in Baxter, *Webster,* pp. 299–317.

68. Clay was alluding to the McLeod affair, not the boundary negotiations. Alexander McLeod, a Canadian, had been arrested by New York authorities for complicity in the destruction of the *Caroline.* See Albert B. Corey, *The Crisis of 1830–1842 in Canadian-American Relations* (New Haven, 1941), pp. 130–145.

69. Marcy to Wetmore, August 18, September 11, 1841, Marcy Papers, LC; Clay to John M. Clayton, November 1, 1841, Clay to John O. Sargent, July 29, 1843, in Clay, *Papers,* IX, 620, 841.

but they never will trust him. He will stand here, like Arnold in England, a monument of his own perfidy and disgrace."

He closed with lavish praise for the chairman of the caucus, Senator Nathan F. Dixon of Rhode Island, whose able and impartial discharge of his duties, he said, had always reduced "the most excited, the most boisterous . . . into lamb-like docility." Dixon responded by jokingly mentioning that although Clay looked absolutely earnest in what he had said about the chairman, "when you are all as well acquainted with the Senator as I am, you will give him full credit for sincerity, for any remarks he may make before ten o'clock at night, after that there may be some doubts."[70]

Thus ended the inglorious summer of 1841. Congress adjourned, and Clay paraded home to thunderous applause all along his route.[71] As the crowds waved at him and assured him of their approval of his behavior, there seemed little doubt that he would soon stand before them at the head of the 1844 Whig presidential ticket. Indeed, New York Whigs meeting in convention at Syracuse on September 7 had already passed resolutions supporting him. There also seemed little doubt that he could easily defeat Tyler—and Van Buren, too, should the Democratic party choose to nominated either of them.

"Behold him where he now stands," exulted the New York *Tribune* on September 21, "—a noble—an 'inspiring spectacle' . . . the PILLAR of the state. Around the pillar let us gather, for while it stands we shall be safe. . . . To Time alone will it yield—and then of its fragments we will make household gods to admonish us of our duty and remind us of what we owe to the true Republican—the Civil Hero of our country—HARRY OF THE WEST."

70. To the Whig Caucus, September 13, 1841, in Clay, *Papers,* IX, 608–609.
71. New York *Tribune,* September 29, 1841.

THIRTY-FOUR

"Like the Soul's Quitting the Body"

LONG BEFORE Clay left Washington, rumors abounded that he would resign his Senate seat. Most probably he himself discussed it with a few close friends. By the time he reached Ashland he had openly and freely confessed his decision to leave the Senate, probably before the close of the next session scheduled to begin in December. Apart from his anger toward Tyler for destroying their one chance of enacting a thoroughly Whig economic program and a burning need to get as far away as possible from the President and his *"corporal guard,"* Clay's declining health necessitated a long rest. He was plagued by continuous colds that hung on for weeks, accompanied by long periods of debility and weakness. At first he thought of retiring immediately upon his return to Ashland since "the *principle* of resigning" had been definitely decided, but he said he "could not bear to act so as to give even color to the reproach of desertion or infidelity towards friends," meaning he wanted to be absolutely certain that his successor would be a Whig personally devoted to him, such as the tall, homely, black-eyed, and heavy-browed John J. Crittenden. Finally, after much thought, he agreed to return to the Senate and resign sometime after the first of the year to take effect toward the end of March.[1]

Around the time Clay returned to Washington on December 5, 1841, he suffered another physical breakdown, starting with "a very bad cold," which confined him to his room for more than a week, followed by a mysterious swelling of his upper lip and nose that gave him intense pain. Some of his colleagues even commented that this seemingly vigorous man of sixty-four years, on the eve of another run for the presidency, suddenly looked old.[2]

1. Clay to Berrien, October 7, 1841, Clay to Porter, October 24, 1841, January 22, 1842, Clay to Brooke, October 28, 1841 Clay to John W. Allen, October 29, 1841, Clay to Nathaniel P. Tallmadge, October 30, 1841, Clay to John Sloane, November 6, 1841, in Clay, *Papers,* IX, 612, 616, 617, 618–619, 621, 636.
2. Clay to James B. Clay, December 10, 1841, Clay to Thomas Hart Clay, December 19, 1841,

The drain on his energies started to show immediately. In the pride of his political power, he seemed as "uneasy and restive as a caged lion," according to one observer. He absented himself frequently from the Senate, took an exceedingly diminished role in its proceedings, accepted no committee assignments, and several times postponed major speeches because of his indisposition. "I have been a looker on at Verona," he admitted to his friend Peter B. Porter in mid-January. Actually Clay was quite ill throughout the entire winter, even though it was an extremely mild winter with no snow to speak of and relatively comfortable temperatures.[3]

A crisis of sorts occurred on March 24, 1842. The day before, he had given a speech in the Senate lasting three hours. Suddenly he felt this "excruciating stricture in my left breast," which he thought had been produced by his colds or rheumatism. "I suffered great pain & was cupped[4] and purged," he told his wife. After three days the pain left him, "but I am much debilitated."[5] It is uncertain, but extremely likely, that he suffered a mild heart attack.

The continuing economic distress in the country, the distracted state of the Whig party, and the abominable conduct of Tyler no doubt added to Clay's distress. The nation faced "the spectacle of an administration without a party," he said, shunned by both Whigs and Democrats. Clay was now almost certain that the President with his *"corporal's guard"* would attempt the formation of a third party, assisted by Webster and his friends, particularly by Representative Henry A. Wise, "who has plyed him with flattery, and held out to him vain hopes of another Election." What Congress ought to do, Clay contended, was introduce more economy in the operation of government by limiting expenses wherever possible and abolishing unnecessary offices. And curtail executive power, he added, principally the veto power.[6]

In his message to the Twenty-seventh Congress at the opening of its second session, President Tyler addressed the continuing economic crisis and an empty treasury by calling for the creation of what he called the Exchequer, an agency to keep and disburse public monies, buy and sell domestic bills, and operate under the direction of a board located in the District of Columbia. It could receive deposits in limited amounts but could not make loans.[7]

Clay to Henry Clay, Jr., December 26, 1841, in Clay, *Papers,* IX, 623, 624, 625; Wright to Van Buren, January 12, April 2, 1842, Van Buren Papers, LC.

3. Poore, *Reminiscences,* I, 291; Clay to Porter, January 16, 1842, Clay to Lucretia, March 13, 1842, in Clay, *Papers,* IX, 632, 677.

4. Cupping was a medical procedure in general use at the time. It consisted of drawing blood to the surface of the skin at some appropriate place by creating a vacuum at that point, usually by applying heat to a cup

5. Clay to Lucretia, March 27, 1842, in Clay, *Papers,* IX, 688.

6. Clay to John M. Clayton, November 1, 1841, Clay to Tallmadge, October 30, 1841, in Clay, *Papers,* IX, 620, 619.

7. Chitwood, *Tyler,* pp. 291–293. "The Clay wing" of the Whig party, wrote Calhoun, "is deadly opposed to the [Exchequer] scheme." Calhoun to Wilson Lumpkin, December 26, 1841, in Calhoun, *Papers,* XVI, 20. See also Calhoun to James H. Hammond, December 31, 1841, ibid., XVI, 28.

Clay dismissed the suggestion with the remark that nothing could be made of it and nothing would be done about it. To think, he added, that Tyler believed the people were with him, and only politicians stood against him. "Poor deluded man!"[8] Well, he would soon learn differently.

As soon as he felt well enough, Clay introduced a series of resolutions in the Senate calling for three amendments to the Constitution. The first would restrict the chief executive's veto power by allowing Congress to override it by a simple majority rather than a two-thirds vote; it would also limit the pocket veto power by stating that bills not acted upon by the President during the final ten days of the session would become law if not acted upon by him during the first three days of the succeeding session. The second amendment would give Congress the power to appoint and remove the secretary of the treasury and the treasurer of the United States. Finally, the President would be forbidden to appoint members of Congress to any federal office during their elected terms of office.[9]

It was almost a month later before Clay felt physically capable of giving an extended address on these resolutions. His remarks began by tracing the history of the veto, starting in ancient Rome. The power was probably adopted by the Founding Fathers, he ventured, because of its general usage abroad and because they mistakenly believed that it might be needed for protection against the injurious effects of crude and hasty legislation. He pointed out the difficulty—no, the near impossibility of overriding a veto—since not a single presidential veto had been overturned by the Congress to date. He also explained how a chief executive like Jackson could intrude into the legislative process. The veto power necessarily drew after it, he said, "the power of initiating laws."

But Clay was realistic. He knew his resolutions would go nowhere. The difficulty of amending the Constitution was as great as overriding a veto. It was most unlikely, he continued, "whether any gentleman here present would ever live to see the Constitution amended; but still it was the duty of every friend of his country to use proper efforts to have it improved."[10]

Calhoun attacked Clay's arguments by insisting that the veto power constituted part of the checks and balances system that protected American liberty. He also pointed out that basic to Clay's argument was a belief in democracy, that the majority rules, which, he declared, must ultimately destroy minority rights. He made a very powerful argument in favor of the "republican" form of government erected by the framers of the Constitution, and he advanced his thesis that the solution to the problem lay in a "concurrent majority"—that is, the concurrence of all the separate, different, and even conflicting interests of the Union which would only then constitute a true majority. The

8. Clay to Henry Clay, Jr., December 26, 1841, in Clay, *Papers,* IX, 625.
9. *Congressional Globe,* 27th Congress, 2d session, p. 62.
10. Clay, *Works,* VI, 302–319.

two men engaged in several verbal tussles during this session, but their skirmishes generally lacked the fire and excitement of their previous engagements.[11]

And, as Clay predicted, the Senate made short work of his resolutions, giving them one day of debate and then forgetting them.

The members were much more concerned about repealing the six-month-old bankruptcy law. So many debtors had taken advantage of the new law that they created real concern for the protection of property. Consequently, a general cry went up around the nation for repeal. When the Kentucky legislature instructed its senators to vote for repeal, Clay refused (violating his own earlier rule on the matter[12]) and grew angry over the widespread report in the North that he had organized the movement for repeal. The House repealed the law by a vote of 126 to 94, but Clay's vote in the Senate saved it—at least for one more year.[13]

It was during the debate over this repeal that Clay and Senator Thomas Hart Benton took to screaming at each other—again. Clay had the floor, and during his remarks Benton—as was his wont—shouted something at him from his seated position. Clay bridled. "The Senator shall not address *me* in his seat," bellowed Clay, "and if he does, it shall be followed by language corresponding to such conduct." The senator from Missouri, he continued, did this all the time, calling, "False, false," at a statement by Senator Tallmadge during a recent debate. He is, said Clay, "an habitual disturber" of this body and clearly out of order.

"False, sir! False, sir! False, sir!" shouted Benton as the chair pounded his gavel and called both men to order.[14]

But the principal debates of the session centered on the tariff and distribution. The problem was the great need of the government for money, and obviously higher tariff rates could provide it. But while Clay favored a higher tariff to protect manufactures and secondarily to produce revenue, Tyler favored higher rates to meet the needs of the government and opposed them for purposes of protection.[15] The recently enacted Distribution Act stated that whenever tariff duties rose above 20 percent, the distribution of funds to the

11. *Congressional Globe,* 27th Congress, 2d session, pp. 160, 166, 187, 191, 203 and appendix, pp. 106–107, 164–168; Wiltse, *Calhoun, Sectionalist,* pp. 77–80. "The object of the whigs (the Clay part)," wrote Calhoun to A. O. P. Nicholson, "is to force us into the relation of opposers, or supporters of Tyler & his administration, so as to give them the control. It is our obvious policy, that they shall not succeed." December 18, 1841, in Calhoun, *Papers,* XVI, 7.

12. That senators should obey instructions from their legislatures because they are elected by them; representatives need not because they are elected by the people.

13. Clay to Porter, January 16, 1842, in Clay, *Papers,* IX, 632; Clay, *Works,* VI, 298–300.

14. *Congressional Globe,* 27th Congress, 2d session, pp. 216–217.

15. Clay regarded maintaining the provisions of the Compromise Tariff as a point of honor, at least until 1842. See his Senate speech of January 27, 1837, *Register of Debates,* 24th Congress, 2d session, pp. 564–576. The long economic depression following the Panic of 1837 required a revision of the tariff rates at the earliest possible moment.

states from land sales would cease. Clay favored distribution as a means of drawing off excess revenue. Increased revenue to the national government from land sales would justify lowering the tariff. Calhoun, of course, opposed the tariff; he also opposed distribution because like Clay, he saw it as a means of draining the Treasury and thereby forcing an increase in the tariff.[16]

The Compromise Tariff of 1833 was due to expire on June 30, 1842, at which time—according to one's interpretation of the law—the rates would either remain at a uniform 20 percent ad valorem or there would be no duties at all. Clay assumed the latter interpretation and expected the calamitous effects of the cutoff of revenue to force the President into requesting higher duties. Not until February did Clay finally move on the subject when he introduced resolutions calling for increased tariff rates along with repeal of the provision of the Distribution Law that required the suspension of distribution when the tariff rates rose beyond the 20 percent limit. And although Tyler would sanction higher duties to rescue the Treasury from its plight, he would not endorse distribution. Thus, once again, a situation developed to foster discord and further splinter the Whigs and prevent meaningful legislation.

Clay groaned. "All is confusion, chaos & disorder here," he exclaimed. "No system! No concert of action! No prospect of union and harmony!"[17]

Despite his discouragement, Clay never lost his sense of humor. Because Calhoun vigorously protested any increase in the tariff duties and contested the factual accuracy of many of Clay's claims regarding the history of the Compromise Tariff, the Kentuckian aimed several of his barbs at the South Carolinian—never forgetting, of course, the senator from Pennsylvania James Buchanan. In presenting a memorial from a group of ladies from New Jersey asking for higher duties on clothing—they must be "very beautiful indeed," the Old Coon clucked, "judging from their autographs"—Clay facetiously begged the "chivalry of South Carolina" in the person of its distinguished senator to "rush forward and protect their fair country women from foreign competition."

The bachelor Buchanan jumped in at this point to chide Clay for appropriating "all those fair ladies to protection" and leaving him with nothing but iron manufacturers to protect. Maintaining a straight face, Clay replied that his reason was simple: "The Senator had lived for thirty-five years and upwards, without having taken any fair lady under his protection."[18]

To Calhoun's charge that the Whigs had deliberately failed to reduce government expenditures in order to force the tariff above the 20 pecent limit, Clay countered with the argument that it was Calhoun's newfound friends in the opposition party who irresponsibly increased government expenditures.

16. Chitwood, *Tyler*, pp. 293–296; Wiltse, *Calhoun, Sectionalist*, p. 28. See also Peterson, *Presidencies of Harrison & Tyler*, and Morgan, *Whig Embattled*.

17. Clay to Porter, January 16, 1842, in Clay, *Papers*, IX, 632.

18. *Congressional Globe*, 27th Congress, 2d session, pp. 287–288. Actually Buchanan was just shy of his fifty-first birthday.

The transfer of Indian tribes from one side of the Mississippi River to the other had cost a fortune. The removal of Indians initiated by President Jackson produced a "vast and profligate" expenditure of millions. And the Seminole War still raged. The nation "has been sunk in the morasses of Florida" for more than seven years with no prospect for a speedy end. "Where, I ask again, are the monuments of all this expenditure? What has the nation got to show for its money?" Clay had been decrying this lunatic war for years. In 1838 he had written: "It seems to me, that it might be practicable, without affecting the National honor, to leave the Indians in the quiet possession of a portion of the Territory [of Florida], which will never be occupied, or at least not occupied within a century, by the whites, & thus terminate a war in which no laurels are to be reaped."[19]

In several of his three-hour speeches during this session Clay wandered from topic to topic in a somewhat disjointed fashion that underscored his weariness and dejection. He lacked his customary enthusiasm and verve. He needed to get away. He felt he must return home and take an extended rest.

Long after Clay resigned his seat, the tariff debate went on. Clay's resolutions eventually won approval and resulted in a bill—called the Little Tariff—which merely postponed for a month the reduction in tariff rates scheduled to begin on July 1. Tyler applied what Senator Preston called "his veto of the month," claiming it violated the principle of the Compromise Tariff of 1833. By this time Clay had retired to Ashland, but he kept up a steady barrage to his friends to hold fast to distribution. "I think you can not give up distribution," he told John Crittenden, "without a disgraceful sacrifice of Independence." But Tyler threatened a veto unless distribution was dropped. No matter, cried Clay. "The more Vetoes the better. . . . The inevitable tendency of events is to impeachment."

Congress tried again with a more permanent tariff but one that retained distribution. Tyler struck it down against the strong advice of Daniel Webster. "How deeply do I regret that I cannot have your full concurrence in this procedure," the President wrote his secretary of state. "But a Clay Congress can only be met in the way proposed—nor can the independence of the Executive or good of the country be otherwise advanced." Several infuriated Whigs, under the direction of John Minor Botts, tried unsuccessfully to initiate impeachment proceedings. Clay wholeheartedly endorsed the novel idea of an impeachment, but after Crittenden had warned him that Botts's behavior frightened off the more timid and prudent of their friends and therefore jeopardized Clay's presidential prospects, he reversed himself. Still, he agreed that impeachment deserved the consideration of "many minds," not simply Botts's.[20]

19. *Congressional Globe,* 27th Congress, 2d session, pp. 287–288, 347–348; Clay to Robert Swartwout, April 2, 1838, in Clay, *Papers,* IX, 168.
20. *Congressional Globe,* 27th Congress, 2d session, pp. 637, 688, 717–718, 762, 852, 923–926, 973, 1409ff. For the efforts at impeachment, see ibid., pp. 973–975, and 27th Congress, 3d session, pp.

Tyler took it all in stride. "Because I will not go with him [Clay], I am abused, in Congress and out, as man never was before—assailed as a traitor, and threatened with impeachment. But let it pass. Other attempts are to be made to head me, and we shall see how they will succeed."[21]

Finally, on August 30, 1842, by a very close vote, a tariff without distribution passed the Congress and won the President's approval. The Compromise of 1833 had provided a nine-year period during which industry could prepare itself for the loss of protection. But the Whigs decided in 1842 that manufacturers were not yet ready to face foreign competition, so they returned the general level of duties to those of 1832.[22] A separate distribution bill received a pocket veto.

Clay's retirement from the Senate began with the submission of a letter of resignation to the Kentucky general assembly on February 16, 1842. He said the time had arrived to quit the public service and return to his private affairs. If a Roman soldier could claim title to discharge after thirty years of service, surely "I, who have served a much longer period, may justly claim mine." He proposed that his resignation take effect on March 31, to give him time to complete various projects he had commenced. Actually this date was chosen to coincide roughly with the convention of North Carolina Whigs on April 4, scheduled to name him as their presidential choice. He wanted to vacate his Senate seat so that the nomination would occur immediately following his resignation. Apparently he felt the impact of the nomination on the country at large would be greater.[23]

Clay obviously needed to rest and attend to his personal affairs, but he also planned to get ready for the upcoming presidential election. Martin Van Buren had already begun an extended tour of the country in preparation for 1844, and Clay, ever gracious and charming, went out of his way to invite the former President to Ashland ("and make it your Head quarters") when he reached Kentucky. In addition to everything else, Clay felt a strong desire to escape Washington. "The President is moreover jealous, envious, embittered towards me," he said. And Clay reciprocated the feeling. The President had betrayed his friends and violated his word and his honor. "It is impossible for me to regard such a person, either in his individual or his official character with any other feelings than those of detestation." Both Tyler and Webster wielded

144–146. Preston to Clay, June 29, 1842, Clay to Mangum, July 11, 1842, Crittenden to Clay, July 15, 1842, Clay to Crittenden, July 16, 21, 1842, in Clay, *Papers,* IX, 720, 732, 734, 736, 739–740; Tyler to Webster, August 8, 1842, in Webster, *Papers, Correspondence,* V, 235; Chitwood, *Tyler,* pp. 297, 301–304. Clay called the veto of the Little Tariff "Mr. Tyler's last silly Veto." Clay to Mangum, July 11, 1842.

21. Tyler to Robert McCandlish, July 10, 1842, in Tyler, *Letters,* II, 173.

22. Howe, *Political Culture of American Whigs,* p. 120; Stanwood, *American Tariff Controversies,* II, 28–30.

23. Clay to General Assembly, February 16, 1842, Clay to Porter, February 7, 1842, in Clay, *Papers,* IX, 656, 647; Jeffrey, *State Parties and National Politics,* p. 136.

the patronage ax against him,[24] even to the extent of including one of the Wickliffes in the new cabinet. Clay's friends in Washington also suffered, as did those friendly newspapers around the country that printed the laws. Tyler's henchman Henry A. Wise began a campaign of slander by accusing Clay of encouraging and participating in the notorious Cilley-Graves duel. Wise was discredited but not before he had done considerable damage to Clay's reputation.[25]

For his part, Tyler thoroughly detested Clay for attempting to ruin his administration. His friends accused the Old Coon of scheming to become President, "even at the hazard of revolution. . . . I should not be surprised," wrote Abel P. Upshur, "to hear of popular outbreaks in all the large cities, and of desperate measures calculated to overthrow all law and all order." The Clay men constitute an extremely dangerous political party, said Upshur. "Look at their press. The secret whisper, the insidious scandal, and the open and profligate libel, are the weapons with which they carry on the war." But the effect will be counterproductive, Upshur prophesied. The "moral sense of the country" will rise up in disgust and again strike down Clay's feverish and persistent ambition to become President.[26]

For his own sake, for the sake of his friends and the future of the Whig party it made sense for Clay to distance himself from the capital as quickly as possible. Difficult though it would be, he had to bid farewell—possibly forever—to the Senate of the United States. John J. Crittenden, who had remained in Washington to argue several cases in court following his resignation from the cabinet, was chosen by the general assembly to take Clay's place, so nothing remained to complicate the Old Coon's immediate departure. One of Clay's last acts before leaving included a short speech against a resolution to refund to General Andrew Jackson a fine imposed on him in 1815 by a federal judge in New Orleans. The fine resulted from actions by Jackson during a period when martial law had been imposed on the city. But as he did in virtually every other struggle he had with Old Hickory, Clay lost this one, too. The fine, with interest, was refunded.[27]

The date set for Clay's farewell on March 31 fell on a Thursday. Virtually everyone in the city knew he would take formal leave of the chamber, and spectators crowded into every corner, lobby, and passageway to hear him speak—possibly for the last time. By half past one o'clock the formal business

24. "The Whigs are divided & distracted," wrote Calhoun. "I think the Clay portion is still much the strongest, but the force of patronage acts powerfully against them." Calhoun to Lumpkin, February 4, 1842, in Calhoun, *Papers,* XVI, 109.

25. Clay to Robert Swartwout, January 14, 1842, Clay to Van Buren, March 17, 1842, Clay to Pierce Butler, August 8, 1842, Clay to Graves, February 16, 1842, Wise to Clay, February 25, 1842, Clay to Wise, February 28, 1842, in Clay, *Papers,* IX, 631, 680, 752, 656–658, 661, 662–665. Wise did not repeat his accusation when writing his *Seven Decades of the Union.*

26. Abel P. Upshur to Beverley Tucker, March 6, 1842, in Tyler, *Letters,* II, 157.

27. *Congressional Globe,* 27th Congress, 2d session, p. 340. The fine was not paid until 1844, however. See Remini, *Jackson,* III, 478–479, 490.

of the day had been cleared away, and there being no other question before the Senate, Clay then rose to address it.

A hush came over the crowd. Everyone tensed. Finally he began. He spoke first of missing a vote on the tariff but quickly hurried to the main business at hand. "Allow me," he said in a near whisper, "to announce, formally and officially, my retirement from the Senate of the United States." He recollected that he first entered this body in December 1806—nearly forty years ago. From that time to the present "I have been engaged in the service of my country," he said. "History, if she deigns to notice me, and posterity . . . will be the best, truest, and most impartial judges; and to them I defer for a decision upon their value."

As for his public acts and public conduct, he wished to repeat what he had said many times in the past, that he sought no personal aggrandizement. "I have had an eye, a single eye, a heart, a single heart, ever devoted to what appeared to be the best interest of the country." Although the frequent object of "bitter and unmeasured detraction and calumny," he had also been sustained by warmhearted, enthusiastic, devoted, and loving friends.

Then, with deep and solemn emotion, he exclaimed: "What shall I say—what can I say—at all commensurate with my feelings of gratitude towards that State whose humble servitor I am?" He unfortunately fudged the truth in describing his underprivileged youth, how he arrived in Kentucky, poor, "without the favor of the great," an orphan. But scarcely had he stepped foot on the soil of Kentucky than "I was caressed with parental fondness," patronized with "bountiful munificence," and showered with the "choicest honors." Though he was calumniated frequently by many, Kentucky always threw its impenetrable shield around him and repelled the attacks of malignity.

His eyes filled with tears as he spoke. But he shook his head as though he had no time for such a display of emotion. His voice hardened, and he began again.

Recently he had been held up to the country as a dictator. "Dictator!" he cried. "If I have been a dictator, what have been the powers with which I have been clothed? Have I possessed an army, a navy, revenue?" At least his dictatorship had been distinguished "by no cruel executions, stained by no deeds of blood, soiled by no act of dishonor." True, he said, "my nature is warm, my temper ardent, my disposition in the public service enthusiastic," but those who supposed they saw proof of dictation in his conduct, have only mistaken that ardor "for what I at least supposed to be patriotic exertions." No doubt, he conceded, that ardor led him in the heat of combat "to use language offensive and susceptible of ungracious interpretation towards my brother Senators." If there be any present who entertained feelings of dissatisfaction with his past behavior, "I now make the amplest apology." And he said that he now took leave of the Senate without a single feeling of dissatisfaction toward the Senate itself or any of its members. He would leave with the hope that all personal animosities and jealousies that might have arisen in the past would be consigned to perpetual oblivion.

> And now, in retiring as I am about to do from the Senate, I beg leave to express my heartfelt wishes that all the great and patriotic objects for which it was instituted, may be accomplished—that the destiny designed for it by the framers of the Constitution may be fulfilled—that the deliberations now and hereafter, in which it may engage for the good of our common country, may eventuate in the restoration of its prosperity, and in the preservation and maintenance of her honor aboard, and her best interest at home. . . .
>
> May the most precious blessings of Heaven rest upon the heads of the whole Senate, and every member of it; and may every member of it advance still more in fame, and when they shall retire to the bosoms of their respective constituencies, may they all meet there that most joyous and grateful of all human rewards, the exclamation of their countrymen, "well done thou good and faithful servants."
>
> Mr. President, and Messieurs Senators, I bid you, one and all, a long, a last, a friendly farewell.[28]

Almost everyone in the chamber wept.[29] A few audible sobs could be heard. It "was something like the soul's quitting the body," wrote Crittenden to Governor Letcher.[30] It seemed to mark the end of an era because no one could conceive the Congress without the presence of Henry Clay. He had spoken for an hour and a half, and when he finally sat down, his face wet with tears, no one wanted to resume normal business even though it was only 3:00 P.M. As soon as Crittenden was sworn in as the new Kentucky senator, William Preston moved adjournment, commenting that "the deep sensation which had been sympathetically manifested" by Clay's farewell made it impossible to continue.

Senators hurried to Clay's side to shake his hand and say good-bye. He spoke to each one. After a long time he finally broke free and started to leave. Then he noticed Calhoun standing at a distance. He walked over to him, and the two men embraced in silence.[31]

Some Democrats sneered at the speech, and Senator Benton called it "a true theatrical performance." Indeed, it was. Senator Wright thought it an

---

28. Clay, *Works,* VI, 353–358; *Congressional Globe,* 27th Congress, 2d session, pp. 376–377.

29. "I don't know if the papers tell the truth as to the tears shed by Senators at Mr. C's valedictory," wrote Reverdy Johnson, "but if they did not, they must be more flint hearted than I am. Without the circumstances attending its delivery, I found my eyes to fill rapidly today in reading it, *Solus.*" Johnson to Mangum, April 2, 1842, in Mangum, *Papers,* III, 309.

30. Crittenden to Letcher, May 1, 1842, in Coleman, ed., *Life of Crittenden,* I, 177.

31. Sargent, *Public Men and Events,* II, 160. "It is to be hoped that the withdrawal of Mr. Clay from the Senate," Calhoun privately told his son, "will deprive the northern tariff wing of his party of their present preponderance. If it should, and the publick lands be restored, and proper retrenchments be made, publick credit may speedily be restored, and the finances placed on a safe foundation; but if that be not done, it is hard to say, what may not come." Calhoun to Andrew Calhoun, April 3, 1842, in Calhoun, *Papers,* XVI, 211.

egotistical display, and that, too, came close to the mark, for long stretches of the farewell were self-exculpating. There were too many might-have-beens, too many attempts at ducking blame. Still, it ended with an emotional wallop that few ever forgot.[32]

"The old coon is really and substantially dead, skinned & buried," gibed the delighted Andrew Jackson several months later. "Clay's political career is closed forever."[33]

Whigs totally disagreed. They fully expected Clay to head their ticket two and a half years hence, although a few began to wonder whether this obviously tired and worn-down warrior could lead the troops to victory. For the moment, however, they united in doing him honor. Organized by Willie P. Mangum and other friends and associates, the Whigs tendered him a dinner on April 9 to show "their respect for your virtues . . . and admiration of your talents." They saluted the force of his genius, the splendor of his eloquence, and the "fervor and purity of your patriotism." On the twelfth—his sixty-fifth birthday—they arranged a ball at the Assembly Rooms, which was "numerously and handsomely attended."

And there were other banquets and social engagements. But as the time approached to leave Washington, it became increasingly difficult for him to tear himself away. Debates continued in both houses of Congress, and Clay felt a twinge of regret that perhaps he had indeed said good-bye to all that forever. It was a depressing thought. At a dinner given by the Russian minister, Baron Bodisco, Prince Hal sat across the table from Senators Benton and Wright. To them, he looked "completely miserable." He hardly touched food or drink. "His face clouded, his tongue silent, and his air abstract and desolate," he seemed so unlike his usual self. Ah, conjectured Benton, he "lingers here, and seems loth to quit the stage."[34]

Benton may have been right. Clay waited almost a month before leaving Washington, and in some respects it really did seem like the soul quitting the body. As he departed the capital he so dearly loved, he no doubt devoutly hoped that his return would mark the inauguration of the administration of President Henry Clay.

32. Benton to Jackson, March 31, 1842, Jackson Papers, LC; Wright to Van Buren, April 2, 1842, Van Buren Papers, LC; Chambers, *Benton,* p. 257.

33. Jackson to Van Buren, November 22, 1842, Van Buren Papers, LC.

34. Mangum et al. to Clay, March 23, 1842, Clay to Mangum et al., March 24, 1842, private collection, copy CPP; Reverdy Johnson to Mangum, March 13, 1842, in Mangum, *Papers,* III, 304; Colton, *Clay,* II, 408; *National Intelligencer,* April 11, 14, 1842; Wright to Van Buren, April 2, 1842, Benton to Van Buren, April 14, 1842, Van Buren Papers. LC.

───── T H I R T Y · F I V E ─────

Texas

THE DESPONDENT former senator received a tumultuous reception upon his arrival in Kentucky—just the sort of thing to reawaken his naturally ebullient spirits. A committee met him in Maysville and accompanied him all the way to Lexington. Several other committees joined along the way. Parades formed without prior organization, church bells rang, and of course, Clay delighted his audience with several short but entertaining speeches. Almost immediately he began to feel better, and once he had settled down at Ashland and attended his farm and cattle, his previous indispositions seemed to disappear. The warming sun, he felt, cured his colds. Within a few weeks he looked like his old self again.[1]

Clay took a short vacation at the Blue Licks watering hole in Nicholas County, but for the most part he recuperated by spending long hours working the fields and building an "*enormous* Canal." The ditch ran a quarter of a mile long, three feet wide at the bottom and six feet at the top, and two and half feet deep. This would enable him to construct vats to water-rot his hemp. "I am executing here, in epitome, all my principles of Internal improvements, the American System &c." He said he planned to rig the entire navy with cordage made of "American Hemp—Kentucky hemp—Ashland Hemp."[2]

Clay's hemp was largely produced for a southern market that used it for cotton bagging. The hemp desperately needed protection against a superior variety from Europe. But Clay's southern customers abhorred the principle of protection, and that fact constantly placed the Great Compromiser in an awkward dilemma. The cotton market was severely depressed in 1842, and on his arrival home Clay noticed at once the continuing economic plight of his neighbors. "In what a sad condition has our unfortunate Country been brought by an unhappy series of events, during the last thirteen years! Embarrassment,

1. Lexington *Intelligencer,* April 19, 22, May 3, 4, 1842, quoted in Poage, *Clay and Whig Party,* p. 115.
2. Clay to Clayton, August 8, 1842, in Clay, *Papers,* IX, 754.

distress, ruin prevail among the people, throughout the whole land." But, he added, we must not despair.[3]

Clay had no sooner returned to Ashland than he received a number of distinguished guests. First came Lord Morpeth, Earl of Carlisle, who had been traveling around the United States since the first of the year. Of the many men he met in Washington, Morpeth thought Clay "much the most attractive." The Kentuckian invited him to Ashland, and the nobleman accepted. From New Orleans Morpeth ascended the river on the steamboat *Henry Clay,* which Harriet Martineau claimed had the highest reputation of any boat on the Mississippi River, "having made ninety-six trips without accident." Morpeth arrived in Lexington on May 4 and visited for several days. The two men got along famously, and the Englishman told his host that were it possible for him to participate in the next presidential election, "I should be quite ready already to tender you my vote." He noticed that Lucretia kept pretty much to herself during his visit but had many household responsibilities involving children and servants to keep her busy. She seemed quite efficient in managing the house, he added.[4]

Hardly had Morpeth left Ashland than former President Van Buren arrived. Traveling with James Paulding, the writer and former secretary of the navy, the Little Magician was on a fence-mending political swing around the country in preparation for the 1844 presidential contest. He had just visited with Jackson at the Hermitage. Upon his arrival at Ashland his host very "respectfully and kindly" inquired about the general's health; otherwise Jackson's name was never mentioned. Van Buren stayed four or five days in Lexington, and he and Clay had a grand time together.[5] In a peculiar way they rather admired each other, despite their many differences and the less than respectful things the Kentuckian had said about the little man from time to time on the Senate floor. But Van Buren understood the political game, and perhaps he liked the way Clay played it. Besides, there was no denying the Kentuckian's charm and personal warmth. They conversed for hours and reminisced and joked about many past events they shared. Though not as quick as Clay with a retort, Van Buren frequently held his own. "I found him interesting often," said Clay, "& some times amusing."[6]

---

3. Clay to Adams, July 24, 1842, in Clay, *Papers,* IX, 741.

4. Morpeth to Clay, April 16, 1842, in Clay, *Papers,* IX, 700; Martineau, *Retrospect of Western Travel,* II, 5; *National Intelligencer,* May 14, 1842; *Niles' Weekly Register,* June 21, 1842.

5. The portly former President enjoyed excellent health—he "tells me that he weights 172 lbs," reported Clay. Clay to Nathan Sargent, May 31, 1842, in Clay, *Papers,* IX, 704.

6. Van Buren to Jackson, May 27, 1842, Van Buren Papers, LC; Van Buren to Butler, May 24, 1842, Benjamin F. Butler Papers, Princeton University Library; Clay to Van Buren, May 12, 1842, Clay to Nathan Sargent, May 31, 1842, Clay to Crittenden, June 3, 1842, Clay to Mangum, June 7, 1842, in Clay, *Papers,* IX, 702, 704, 706, 708; Lexington *Kentucky Gazette,* May 28, 1842. Lexington gave the former President "a very good procession" and a magnificent reception. But Paulding admitted that he was growing tired of the interminable parades, dinners, receptions, crowds, and the like that he and Van Buren had had to endure.

Remarkably the two men talked little about party politics. In several letters Clay commented on how free their discussions had been of political affairs. Considering the likelihood that both men would be the presidential candidates of their respective parties, and considering Van Buren's proverbial caution, the absence of political talk might have been expected. Later they were accused of striking an agreement—"a bargain"—to oppose the annexation of Texas in order to keep it out of the 1844 campaign. But the accusation was totally false.[7]

Not that the election was far from their minds—particularly Clay's. Each day he received reports of meetings and conventions and public gatherings in which he was nominated. Throughout the summer and fall various state conventions chose him to head the Whig ticket. North Carolina, Maine, Vermont, Massachusetts, New York, New Jersey, Pennsylvania, Maryland, Delaware, Virginia, North Carolina, Georgia, Mississippi, and Kentucky—all declared him their presidential favorite, and although General Winfield Scott at first seemed like a possible rival, that likelihood never picked up speed and soon faded away. "The very mention of his [Clay's] name," wrote one of the organizers of the North Carolina Whig convention, "appears to brighten the countenance of every member and inspire him with fresh and increased zeal." Said another: "The name of Henry Clay is a Tower of Strength in these Mountains."[8]

Almost daily Clay received invitations to speak at political rallies around the country, and he even got calls to undertake a national tour. "As to the idea of my traversing the whole Union it would be physically impossible," he replied, "and if I attempted such a tour it would destroy me physically." Besides, he could not presume to act as the undisputed Whig candidate. He had to wait for the formal nomination, which would not take place until May 1844. Nevertheless, he needed to solidify his hold on his party and not permit another disastrous demarche—such as had happened in the election of 1840—to occur again. Since he no longer held public office, he needed a forum to advance his policies and ideas, and so he very carefully selected several places in which he planned to give major addresses.[9]

Most appropriately, the first one took place in his hometown at a grand barbecue on June 9. "They gave me a brilliant Barbecue," he told one friend. "There were, I think about 15,000 & some 3 or 4 hundred carriages."[10] Because

7. Clay to Sargent, May 31, 1842, Clay to Crittenden, June 3, 1842, in Clay, *Papers,* IX, 704, 706. In writing my biography of Andrew Jackson, I accepted the story about a Clay-Van Buren agreement without question. But after studying Clay's letters written at the time, I'm now convinced that it is totally without foundation. Remini, *Jackson,* III, 497. See also Cole, *Van Buren,* pp. 393–394.

8. C. L. Hinton to Mangum, April 5, 1842, Joseph Keener to Mangum & Graham, June 21, 1842, in Mangum, *Papers,* III, 315, 361.

9. Clay to Noah Noble, July 18, 1842, Clay to William H. Russell, July 27, 1842, in Clay, *Papers,* IX, 737, 747; H. W. Miller et al. to Mangum, March 8, 1842, Will A. Graham to Priestley H. Mangum, March 9, 1842 in Mangum, *Papers,* III, 300, 302.

10. Clay to J. T. Morehead, June 11, 1842, Clay Papers, Manuscript Department, Filson Club, Louisville, Kentucky.

there were many women in the audience, the Whig organizers decreed that no liquor would be served on the grounds. There was never any question that Clay would address this vast assembly, but some politicians feared he could destroy his candidacy with a verbal slip, a playful aside, or an impetuous flash of arrogance. One wrong word might reactivate all the old fears latent among the electorate and mobilize all his old enemies in the party who would love nothing better than to put him down. "He must hereafter remain a little quiet, and *hold his jaw*," counseled Governor Letcher. He must be extra-careful in what he says to the public.[11]

But these fears were groundless. The former senator performed to perfection at the barbecue. His two-hour speech was vintage Clay. Judge Robertson introduced him with a salute: "HENRY CLAY—Farmer of Ashland, Patriot and Philanthropist—the AMERICAN Statesman, and unrivaled Orator of the Age."

The tall, smiling, self-possessed statesman took his place on the platform, where he had enough room to move and swing his arms. Then he faced his audience. He opened with a series of jokes, beginning with a comment about the lack of alcohol after "the sumptuous feast" from which they had just risen. For his verbal efforts "you offered me nothing to drink but cold water," he complained in mock outrage. The audience giggled. He had nothing against temperance, he went on, as long as legal coercion was never used. Then he joked about why so many people had turned out: surely not to hear him, but to enjoy a "fat white virgin Durham Heifer." And he noticed the large number of "ladies" present and remarked on how their smiles, delicacy, and refinement guaranteed order, decorum, and respect in the proceedings. The crowd laughed and applauded.

Turning serious, he dredged up the election of 1824–1825 and his role in the election of John Quincy Adams. Then, for the first time in public, he admitted having made a mistake in accepting the post of secretary of state. "It would have been wiser and more politic in me to have declined accepting the office. . . . Not that my motives were not as pure and as patriotic as ever carried any man into public office." He lambasted Jackson for his charge of a corrupt bargain and launched into a blistering attack on Old Hickory's administration with its resulting ruin to the nation's economic structure and republican system of government.

Clay denied ever having reversed an opinion on any measure of national policy except the Bank of the United States. He denied ambition for high office and claimed he would remain a "passive spectator" in the current efforts to promote his candidacy for President. He also denied ever acting for personal gain and cited his many services to the nation, including his efforts to advance the interests of industry and end the nation's economic plight. "If these ser-

11. Letcher to Crittenden, May 19, June 21, 1842, Crittenden Papers, LC.; Poage, *Clay and Whig Party,* pp. 115–116.

vices, exertions and endeavors justify the accusation of ambition," he declared, "I must plead guilty to the charge."

As for the economic depression that still caused so much suffering, Clay blamed it on Jackson's veto of the Bank bill, the removal of the government's deposits from the BUS, and the "hard-money theorists" who had inflicted the Specie Circular on the country. As a cure he proposed strict frugality in public and private affairs and the creation of a sound currency through "some sort of national bank" that would be safe and free from government influence and interference, especially by the President. He also advocated a new tariff level that would provide an adequate revenue and reasonable protection for American manufacturers and producers, but one that would not increase sectional tensions. "Union is our greatest interest. No one can look beyond its dissolution without horror and dismay. Harmony is essential to the preservation of the Union."

Harmony! It was Clay's favorite word, and he used it repeatedly in speeches throughout the 1840s and through the last years of his life. It epitomized everything he believed and wanted to accomplish as a statesman. He strove desperately to "harmonize" all the different sections and interests in the country. It was the only way, he said, of preserving the Union.

Clay then dramatically cast Tyler out of the Whig party. The President's "dishonor and bad faith" had absolved Whigs from any responsibility or connection with the present administration. Unfortunately, he said, the American system of government did not imitate the British parliamentary system by which a vote of no confidence by Congress would require the chief executive to resign and go back to the people for their approval or dismissal.

Clay also took note of the Dorr Rebellion, which had occurred in Rhode Island. Thomas W. Dorr in 1841 had led a revolt against the state's franchise law of 1724, which restricted the suffrage to property holders. He and his followers framed a new constitution, abolished limited franchise, and set up a government with Dorr as governor. Martial law was decreed by state officials under the old colonial charter. Eventually the Dorr Rebellion was put down, and Dorr himself sentenced to life imprisonment. Clay condemned the uprising as the "work of Rebellion & Treason" intent upon social upheaval. It would "make Revolution—the extreme and last resort of an oppressed people—the constant occurrence of human life, and the standing order of the day." Democrats—who had no right to that name, he declared—encouraged and supported the Dorr Rebellion, along with its "dangerous spirit of disorganization and disregard of law."

He closed with a rousing call to political war:

Whigs, arouse from the ignoble supineness which encompasses you. Awake from the lethargy in which you lie bound,—cast from you that unworthy apathy which seems to make you indifferent to the fate of your country—Arouse, awake, shake off the dew drops that glitter on your garments, and once more march to Battle and to Victory. You have been disappointed, deceived and betrayed—shamefully deceived and betrayed. But will *you* therefore prove fickle and faithless to your Country, or obey the impulses of a just and patriotic indignation? As for Captain Tyler, he is a mere snap—a flash in the pan—pick your Whig flints and try your Rifles again.[12]

The speech—Clay called it his "Barbecue speech"—was reprinted in newspapers around the country and had a tremendous impact. It was perfectly timed and accurately pitched to the general mood of the nation. "No speech ever came, in better time and more admirably adapted to the state of the country and the condition of public opinion," commented Willie Mangum. It had an "electrical effect on the North & East," particularly coming at the same time as "the late absurd, insolent & extraordinary Veto." Clay's Kentucky friends were naturally delighted with the reception of the speech, but they still wanted him to lower his voice and remain out of sight. After his sometimes wild performances during the special session, he needed to quiet down, stay put at Ashland, and cloak himself with the mantle of sweet reason, moderation, and conciliation. He needs to be *"caged,"* snapped Letcher. "But he swears by all the gods he will keep cool and stay at home." Judge Alexander Porter added: "I hope the speech he made at Lexington will prove *his last speech.*"[13]

But Clay's blood was up. He knew how good he was at public speaking. If only the entire electorate could hear him, he could sweep the next election. And if only "ladies" had the franchise, he could win in a landslide. In fact, there was strong evidence that after Andrew Jackson, Henry Clay was "the most popular man in this broad nation," wrote Benjamin Brown French. Said another: "I think Henry Clay is daily gaining popularity."[14] Why not, then, take advantage of his oratorical ability and accept a few, limited out-of-state speaking engagements?

So he broke his promise and agreed to a series of public meetings at Dayton, Cincinnati, and Indianapolis. Naturally he denied any ulterior motive and simply claimed that he had given earlier promises to visit these cities. He encouraged Governor Letcher to accompany him, at least to the barbecue scheduled at Dayton since the Whigs of Ohio intended it as a salute to the Whigs of Kentucky.[15]

In late September Clay, accompanied by a large entourage, including Senator Crittenden, headed for Ohio. As he might have expected, his route

12. Clay, *Works,* VI, 360–384. On the Dorr Rebellion, see Marvin E. Gettleman, *The Dorr Rebellion* (New York, 1973), and George M. Dennison, *The Dorr War* (Lexington, Ky., 1976).

13. Mangum to Clay, July 4, 1842, in Clay, *Papers,* IX, 724; Letcher to Crittenden, June 21, 1842, Porter to Crittenden, July 21, 1842, Crittenden Papers, LC.

14. French, *Witness to the Young Republic,* p. 213; Nathaniel G. Smith to Mangum, August 22, 1842, in Mangum, *Papers,* III, 382. French was writing in 1850, but he said he had no doubt that Clay "has been and is now" the most popular man in America.

15. Clay to Joseph H. Crane et al., September 1, 1842, Robert C. Schenck to Clay, August 27, 1842, Clay to John W. G. Simrall et al., September 8, 1842, in Clay, *Papers,* IX, 761, 763.

attracted large crowds, and in several places, such as Maysville, he was obliged to stop and speak to the people. Unfortunately he could sometimes be carried away and end up speaking for several hours. Such out-of-doors efforts, day after day, took their toll, but he was clearly encouraged and exhilarated by the receptions he received.

The Dayton barbecue on September 29, splendidly organized by the Ohio Whig State Central Committee, drew from one hundred thousand to two hundred thousand people from several states, and during the proceedings a series of resolutions were passed nominating Clay for President and Governor John Davis of Massachusetts for Vice President. Both Crittenden and Clay spoke, but the latter was the main attraction. How many people in that tremendous audience could actually hear him is anyone's guess. Obviously a fraction. He naturally paid homage to General Harrison, the first Ohio President, and excoriated "Captain" Tyler. In this speech he orchestrated responses from the audience, getting them to respond "yes" or "no" or "the people" to appropriate questions. Otherwise he repeated many of the themes of his Lexington speech.[16]

On October 1, at Richmond, Indiana, however, he had a more interesting and significant encounter with his audience. No sooner had he completed his address than a Quaker by the name of Hiram Mendenhall presented a petition to him begging him as a patriot, philanthropist, and Christian to free his slaves and thereby set an example for other slaveholders in the nation. Clay's response to this surprise maneuver demonstrated once again his adroitness and quick-wittedness in handling awkward and potentially explosive situations.

He started off by reminding everyone that he was a private citizen, "a total stranger," traveling through Indiana. He was not an institution, like the Congress, to which petitions were usually addressed. Moreover, he was the equal of everyone in the audience, not someone superior, to whom one petitions for a favor. Then he asked Mendenhall how he would like it if he, Mendenhall, came to Kentucky and upon his arrival was petitioned to relinquish his farm and other property. "Would you deem it courteous and according to the rites of hospitality?" The law in Kentucky and many other states permits slavery, he said. The law may be wrong and ought to be repealed, but "you, Mr. Mendenhall and your associates are not the law-makers for us," and unless those laws are repealed, "we must continue to respect them . . . we must be excused for asserting the rights—aye, the property in slaves—which it sanctions, authorizes, and vindicates."

What prompts this petition? he rhetorically asked. The great Declaration of Independence, he answered himself, which declares that all men are equal. As an abstract principle, he continued, there can be no doubt of the truth of that statement. But in no society that ever existed can equality be enforced and

16. John Pfeifer, "Henry Clay and the Great Dayton Barbecue," *APIC Keynoter,* LXXXIV (Spring 1984), pp. 16–17; Clay, *Papers,* IX, 773–776.

carried out. Inequality exists everywhere. Large portions of the population—women, minors, insane, criminals, and "transient sojourners, that will always probably remain subject to the government of another portion of the community." Can anyone believe that the states, when they accepted the Declaration, tortured its meaning into a virtual emancipation of all slaves within their limits? "Did any one of the thirteen States entertain such a design or expectation?" In fact, had abolitionists seriously advanced their doctrines at the time of the Revolution, he contended, "our glorious independence would never have been achieved—never, never.

"I look upon it [slavery] as a great evil," he cried, something he had said repeatedly over the years. He deeply lamented its presence. But what can be done at the present time? "What would be the condition of the two races in those [slave] States, upon the supposition of an immediate emancipation? Does any man suppose that they would become blended into one homogeneous mass? Does any man recommend amalgamation—that revolting admixture, alike offensive to God and man." The races are different, he said, and can never be joined together in "the holiest rites. And let me tell you, sir . . . that in the slave States, . . . no human law could enforce a union between the two races."

If slaves were emancipated, what would happen? "A struggle for political ascendancy" would occur, he declared, with blacks seeking to acquire and whites seeking to maintain possession of the government. Another Dorr Rebellion would occur to subvert the existing political system, and then whites would be brought into complete subjection to blacks. "A contest would inevitably ensue between the two races—civil war, carnage, pillage, conflagration, devastation, and the ultimate extermination or expulsion of the blacks. Nothing is more certain."

Gradual emancipation is the answer, he thundered, and abolitionists have, by their antics, postponed by half a century what he called the "only method of liberation."

What Clay seemed to be saying in these remarks was that by virtue of the fact that blacks were indeed equal they had to be transported out of the country after emancipation to prevent them from initiating a bloody revolution by which they expected to displace whites as the ruling class. As for his own slaves, he continued, some half dozen of them cannot take care of themselves because of age, disease, and various other infirmities. And they cost him a great deal of money every year. Shall they be freed so they can end a wretched existence in starvation? Then there are infants. What about them? Still another class of blacks would not accept their freedom even if he should give it to them. "I have for many years owned a slave that I wished would leave me, but he will not. What shall I do with that class?"

Ask Charles, my personal servant, how I treat my slaves, Clay called to Mendenhall. Charles had traveled with his master over the greater part of the United States and some parts of Canada and had had a thousand opportunities to run away. "Excuse me, Mr. Mendenhall, for saying that my slaves are as well fed and clad, look as sleek and hearty, and are quite as civil and respectful in their demeanor, and as little disposed to wound the feelings of any one, as you are."

Finally, said Clay, he wanted to know what the petitioners were willing to do for his slaves. He had about fifty at that time, and he estimated their monetary worth at fifteen thousand dollars. To turn them loose upon society without any means of support would be an act of extreme cruelty. "Are you willing to raise and secure the payment of fifteen thousand dollars for their benefit?

"Go home, and mind your own business, Mr. Mendenhall," he scolded, "and leave other people to take care of theirs. Limit your benevolent exertions to your own neighborhood. Within that circle you will find ample scope for the exercise of all your charities. Dry up the tears of the afflicted widows around you, console and comfort the helpless orphan, clothe the naked, and feed and help the poor, black and white, who need succor; and you will be a better and wiser man than you have this day shown yourself."[17]

The implied and overt racist opinions by Clay in this speech and several others later on unfortunately reflected the beliefs of most Americans in the nineteenth century. Repugnant as they are today, they represented the considered view not only of slaveowners but of many northerners as well, including many abolitionists. American statesmen, like Clay and Jefferson and Madison, professed a belief in equality and eventual abolition but not at the expense of the white race and not if it endangered the Union.

The speech immediately won the approval of many Whigs and Democrats, who sincerely believed with Clay that abolitionists plotted to stir up trouble and could threaten the country's existence. But the speech only intensified the anger and strengthened the opposition of those committed to emancipation, those who believed that slavery was a national shame and needed immediate attention and resolution.

As a master Clay described himself in this speech fairly accurately. His treatment of his slaves reflected his unhappiness with the institution, and he always tried to provide adequately for the needs and comfort of his workers. One visitor at Ashland commented on the neatness and cleanliness of the slave quarters, which were surrounded by flowers and shrubs. "All the inmates are as happy as human beings can be." Some of them ran away on occasion, and sometimes Clay reported his loss in the newspapers and sometimes he simply let them go. Like most masters, he certainly could not abide an arrogant, a brazen, or a disrespectful slave. One of his slaves, by the name of Charlotte or "Black Lotty," sued for her freedom and that of her two children in 1829 in the Circuit Court of the District of Columbia. Clay had purchased her at the excessive price of $450 so that she could be united with her husband, Aaron, a

17. Clay, *Works*, VI, 385–390; Leonard S. Kenworthy, "Henry Clay at Richmond in 1842," *Indiana Magazine of History*, XXX (December 1934), pp. 353–358. See also Clay to Jacob Gibson, July 25, 1843, in Clay, *Papers*, IX, 745–746.

slave at Ashland. Taken to Washington to serve the Clay family, she visited her family in Maryland and decided to take her master to court. She lost her case, and when Clay ordered her back to Ashland and she refused, he had her thrown in jail. Her behavior caused consternation and insubordination among the slaves in Lexington and, wrote Clay to the person who had signed the order for her imprisonment, "I think it high time to put a stop to it." Until such time as he could arrange for her transfer home, "be pleased to let her remain in jail." Clay later freed her, as he did a number of other slaves, including Charles, his body servant.[18]

Four days after his Richmond appearance Clay performed again at the Indianapolis barbecue with approximately eighty thousand gathered to hear him. What made this speech unusual was the fact that he outlined something approaching a party platform for the Whigs, a program he had mentioned earlier to several friends. There were five planks: creation of a currency of uniform value, presumably by the chartering of another national bank; tariff protection; curtailment of executive power; a distribution law; and internal improvements. Another usual feature of this speech was his reference to Andrew Jackson. "God bless the old hero!" he cried. "I wish him no harm and, although he has injured me much, I would not, if in my power, spoil a hair of his venerable head." Apparently his remark about how Old Hickory had injured him did not sit well with the crowd, and it elicited some jeers and booing.[19]

Farther along in Columbus, Indiana, Clay discovered how much the electorate in Indiana loved the Old Hero. William Herod, a Whig congressman who had fought with Jackson at New Orleans and who introduced Clay, started off his remarks by shouting, "Hurra for Jackson."

Clay was incensed. In a state of "high excitement," he howled: "Hurra for Jackson, you say. Where is your country? I say hurra for my country, and the man that says hurra for Jackson, deserves not the name of a freeman, but he ought to be a subject of the autocrat of Russia, and have the yoke of tyranny placed upon his neck till he was bowed down, down to the very dust."[20]

And with that unseemly outburst the Old Coon ended this speaking tour. But despite the harassment he encountered in Indiana, the exposure and opportunity to express his ideas and principles strengthened his position as presidential front-runner of the Whig party. General Scott had virtually disappeared as a contender, and Daniel Webster only seemed to separate himself further from his old friends and allies. After successfully completing the

18. Clay to Philip R. Fendall, August 17, 1830, Clay Papers, Manuscript Department, Filson Club, Louisville, Kentucky; Clay to Philip R. Fendall, September 10, 1830, in Clay, *Papers,* VIII, 261–262; Van Deusen, *Clay,* pp. 311–312; Eaton, *Clay,* p. 120; Peterson, *Great Triumvirate,* p. 376. Clay freed "Black Lotty" in 1840.

19. Clay, *Papers,* IX, 782–784; Clay to Jacob Strattan, September 13, 1842, ibid., IX, 767; Poage, *Clay and Whig Party,* pp. 116–117.

20. Clay, *Papers,* IX, 785.

negotiations with Great Britain over the boundary between Maine and Canada, the secretary of state chose to remain at his post. Even after the Webster-Ashburton Treaty, which divided the disputed territory almost equally between the two countries, had won ratification in the Senate, he made no effort to resign. Instead, at a public dinner in Boston on September 30, he defended the administration, dismissed the idea of a new national bank as obsolete, endorsed Tyler's Exchequer idea, and again attacked the Compromise Tariff. He virtually declared himself an independent who was willing to cooperate with honorable men from both parties. Furthermore, he regarded any discussion of the Whig presidential candidate for 1844 as premature. As for Clay's possible candidacy, Webster privately informed his supporters in Massachusetts that *"he has no degree of reasonable prospect of being elected."* [21]

Clay was appalled by Black Dan's speech. "Was ever man so fallen as Mr. Webster?" Not a paragraph of his Boston speech should be taken seriously, he added. Clay considered making a formal written reply but soon thought better of it. Besides, his friends continually urged him to "keep cool" and act prudently. "I have some occasional fears that he [Clay] may write too many letters," wrote a worried Governor Letcher, "—still he is quite a *handy man* with a pen, and all his letters have some good reading in them." [22]

A more potent reason for overlooking direct or indirect criticism of his past activities was the necessity of turning his complete attention to personal affairs. Sometime during the late summer or early fall his son Thomas Hart Clay failed in a bagging and rope manufacturing venture he had established with his brother-in-law Waldemar Mentelle. Clay had financially assisted his son, and when bankruptcy threatened, he generously advanced "upwards of $30,000 under the hope that the markets would improve." He mortgaged Ashland, consisting of 515 acres of land, for twenty thousand dollars in negotiable notes. The notes were drawn for a period of five months beginning in November 1842 and were to fall due on April 15, 1843. To pay off these notes at the end of the five-month period, Clay decided to travel to New Orleans in an attempt not only to collect debts due him and secure contracts for the bagging and rope remaining in the company's inventory but to attend to some legal matters and possibly raise additional funds from political supporters and business associates in the area. [23]

He left Lexington in early December and stopped off at Natchez after a fatiguing journey down the Mississippi River. Aboard the steamboat he re-

21. Webster, *Papers, Speeches*, II, 332–353; Webster to John Plummer Healy, August 26, 1842, in Webster, *Papers, Correspondence*, V, 239. Samuel Appleton told Webster in November that "we do not hear of any more states nominating Clay, that jig is up, Coon Skins are as cheap now." Appleton to Webster, November 22, 1842, ibid., V, 252.

22. Clay to Clayton, November 2, 1842, in Clay, *Papers*, IX, 787; Letcher to Crittenden, June 21, 1842, Crittenden Papers, LC.

23. Clay to Nathaniel Silsbee, March 18, 1842, deed of trust for Ashland, November 15, 1842, partial statement of debts, November 23, 1842, in Clay, *Papers*, IX, 806–807, 789–790. Clay estimated his own debts at $19,391; his son owed him $20,000.

sorted "to books, to music, to the company of ladies, and sometimes to cards pour passer le tems."[24] Crowds assembled along the shore and wharves to shout and wave their welcome to him, "but an indescribable state of feeling prevented my having any agreeable excitement by these demonstrations," he told his wife. He had begun to understand how meaningless they could be in terms of electoral results.[25]

To his surprise he found the economic depression so widespread in the cotton markets and prices so much lower than he had anticipated that he could not find buyers for the hemp and rope. He lamented that he could see no alternative but the liquidation of Thomas's assets at a public auction. He contacted a number of prominent planters, but they had stored so much bagging and rope and had so little hope of improving conditions that they refused his appeals to agree to additional contracts. He moved on to New Orleans around the time of Christmas but found conditions just as bad. "Such is the extreme pressure of the times," he wrote, that collecting debts and obtaining contracts or loans were nearly impossible. "Everybody is very friendly & kind to me; but life appears cheerless and uncomfortable."[26]

Clay always enjoyed New Orleans, and he said his health vastly improved during his stay, except "I have had my usual share of bad colds, one of which now confines me to the House." On his arrival in the Crescent City he was greeted with a salute of one hundred guns from the Place d'Armes. Then a great procession escorted him to the home of Dr. William N. Mercer, where he was to reside during his visit. In the evening he was given a dinner at the St. Charles Exchange.

At one point he considered traveling to Cuba after leaving New Orleans, but the trip would take too long and he wanted to get back to Lexington in time for Thomas's auction. By late January he had collected all the debts he could—"I have succeeded better than I expected"—and that pleased him. He threatened suit over another debt, which brought about immediate arbitration. He sold some horses for $350 and his wife's hams, which were highly praised, and won a judgment in the Louisiana Supreme Court involving $9,000 paid by John B. Humphreys to the estate of James Brown, his deceased brother-in-law. He did not know Louisiana's unique civil code but said he admired its laws that protected women's property rights, something other states did not have the wisdom to adopt. "Women," he told the court in another one of his flights of oratorical excess, "are the pillars—aye, the Corinthian pillars—that adorn and support society; the institutions that protect women throw a shield also round children; and where women and children are provided for, man must be secure in his rights."[27]

24. Clay to William L. Hodge, October 24, 1845, private collection, copy CPP.
25. Clay to Lucretia, December 9, 1842, in Clay, *Papers,* IX, 790–791.
26. Clay to Lucretia, December 9, 1842, Clay to Thomas Hart Clay, December 12, 25, 1842, in Clay, *Papers,* IX, 790–791, 792–793.
27. Clay to Lucretia, January 18, 1843, Clay to Thomas Hart Clay, December 25, 1842, January

An incident that could have ended in tragedy occurred while Clay attended the disposition of the Humphreys estate. "A cracked man" entered the courtroom and fired a bullet into the ceiling. "I do not believe that the man had any design against any body," Clay assured his wife, but it was just "possible that my presence may have occasioned it." After the near assassination of President Jackson in 1835, public figures began realizing that they had become the targets of lunatics.[28]

Otherwise Clay's visit elicited nothing but goodwill. He saw all the power brokers in the region; attended numerous parties and receptions; visited Mobile, Baton Rouge, Vicksburg, Jackson, and Memphis; and made a special effort to exude charm and affability in every direction. His Whig hosts, in turn, provided a full measure of southern hospitality, and the people openly and fervently conveyed their excitement and pleasure at his presence among them. "The papers have not exaggerated the enthusiasm of my reception every where," he told Crittenden. At Baton Rouge he received "a very costly Saddle which was exhibited at the Fair." Even a locofoco presented him with a barrel of sugar.

The receptions truly delighted him and raised his spirits. "If pomp and parade, and displays of extravagant enthusiasm, by Democrats as well as Whigs, by women as well as men and boys, could afford me gratification, I had enough of it, God knows. I was gratified, although often much wearied." By the time he headed home on February 16, he had developed "strong hopes, and a pretty confident belief" that he could win Louisiana, Alabama, and Mississippi in the presidential election of 1844.[29]

Once home, Clay discovered that Thomas Marshall, the Ashland representative to Congress, had deserted to Tyler and with the help of the Wickliffes had attempted to "defame" the Great Pacificator. Clay immediately posted a notice on the courthouse door that he would address the electorate of Fayette County and defend himself. Marshall then announced that he would reply.

On the appointed day Clay gave another dramatic and mesmerizing speech. "I feel like the stag who has been long hunted," he groaned to the crowd with appropriate grunts and gestures, "and who returns at last to die on the spot whence he started in vigor and hope. The curs of party have been long barking at my heels, and the bloodhounds of personal malignity are springing at my throat but"—and then he rose to his full height, according to Leslie

22, 1843, Clay to Crittenden, January 14, 1843, memorandum of remittances from New Orleans, argument in Supreme Court, January 28, 1842, in Clay, *Papers,* IX, 793, 796, 797, 799, 800, 815; Poage, *Clay and Whig Party,* pp. 118–119.

28. Clay to Lucretia, January 3, 1843, in Clay, *Papers,* IX, 796. For the attempt on Jackson's life, see Remini, *Jackson,* III, 226–230.

29. Clay to Crittenden, January 14, 1843, Clay to Lucretia, January 18, 1843, Clay to Benjamin W. Leigh, March 17, 1843, in Clay, *Papers,* IX, 797, 798, 805. Not everyone was enthusiastic. "He [Clay] made no political capital by his visit," said a Democrat in Memphis, "—made a very weak speech, and as to his oratory, which we all were expecting to hear, we heard nothing of it." George W. Smith to James K. Polk, March 2, 1843, in Polk, *Correspondence,* VI, 234.

Combs, and looked eleven and a half feet high, and stared around with "flashing eyes on his defamers" in the crowd—"I SCORN AND DEFY THEM NOW, AS I EVER DID!"

As Clay concluded, the crowd searched around for Marshall to respond, but he was nowhere to be seen. The following day someone spotted Marshall and asked him if he thought "Old Hal" had given a great speech. "Not half as great," responded Marshall, "as you would have heard if I had replied to him; for if I did, the old lion would have been aroused, and such a speech he would have poured out as only he can make when thoroughly stirred up by opposition."

"But why didn't you reply to him?"

"Because I was a coward," confessed Marshall. "I did not dare attack the roused lion; and I thought prudence, in this case, the better part of valor; and I reckon it was."[30]

Clay also resumed active campaigning via his correspondence.[31] And he returned to the problems of his personal finances. The auction did not come up to expectations, and Thomas defaulted on his debt to his father. Clay therefore could not meet his mortgage payment and was forced to ask for a two-year ten-thousand-dollar loan. By August his situation was bad enough for him to go to John Jacob Astor, from whom he had received several earlier loans, and together with his son Henry Clay, Jr. and James Erwin, signed a bond in the amount of forty thousand dollars. Clay's share of this debt came to twenty thousand dollars and was due, principal and interest, on May 1, 1845.[32]

Clay also resumed his law practice. "What do you think of a young man like me resuming the practice of Law?" he kiddingly mentioned to John M. Clayton. He claimed he did it to help his son James, who was beginning a law practice in Lexington, but he also admitted that he was not unwilling to receive "liberal fees." Besides, an office in town would make him more accessible "to perfect strangers."[33] The office, located at 176 North Mill Street, was a small brick building, with plank flooring, plain furnishings, a log-stoked fireplace, and candles for illumination. Clay appeared in court on a few occasions, but he really had little time for his practice as the demands of the approaching election began to assert themselves on him, even though he appeared to have no viable Whig rival. Not even the New York "Intriguers of 1839," as he called Thurlow Weed, William H. Seward, and Francis Granger, could initiate a

30. Sargent, *Public Men and Events,* II, 161–163.

31. Clay even challenged James K. Polk to a public debate over the corrupt bargain issue when he heard from friends that Polk had made the subject "a frequent topic of discussion in your public addresses." Clay to Polk, May 20, 1843, in Polk, *Correspondence,* VI, 311–312.

32. Clay to Nathaniel Silsbee, March 18, 1843, Bond to Astor, August 17, 1843, in Clay, *Papers,* IX, 807; Clay to Lucretia, March 2, 1844, Thomas J. Clay Collection, LC. It is interesting that Andrew Jackson was also forced to borrow money because of the slump in the cotton market. See Remini, *Jackson,* III, 478, 488, 491, 514.

33. Clay to Clayton, April 14, 1843, in Clay, *Papers,* IX, 812.

movement against him. They seemed to have bowed to the inevitable.

So Clay's campaign started picking up speed. A collection of his speeches, which he had a hand in preparing, was published, and Epes Sargent brought out a campaign biography, as did Daniel Mallory and Calvin Colton. Of the Colton biography Prince Hal complained that there was "too much commendation and panegyric" in it. Exactly so. He also told Sargent that there were a number of state papers he had composed which he thought valuable and should be printed and distributed. These included his instructions to the U.S. ministers to the Panama Congress, the land report of 1832, and the Senate report on the French spoliation controversy. Not much later *The Henry Clay Almanac for 1844* was published in Philadelphia.

John S. Littel, president of the Clay Club in Germantown, Pennsylvania, published a collection of campaign songs in an attempt to emulate the 1840 campaign. Entitled *The Clay Minstrel, or National Songster,* it provided a wide variety of efforts, including "The Star of the West" sung to the tune of "Meeting of the Waters":

> There's not in the union, tho' we search it thro'
> A chief like old Hal of Kentucky, so true;
> And the one to restore our dear land so opprest,
> Is the bold Harry Clay, the bright *star of the West.*

Since "Yankee Doodle" was a popular and well-known tune it was pressed into service:

> Our noble Harry is the man
> The Nation most delights in;
> To place him first is now the plan;—
> For this we're all uniting!
> For farmer Clay then boys hurrah,
> And proudly here proclaim him
> The great, the good, the valiant Hal,
> And SHOUT WHENE'ER YE NAME HIM!

Because the country was seen as heading into stormy weather, Clay was depicted in another song, "Harry Clay and the Jackets of Blue," as the navigator of a ship symbolizing the country.

> The good ship of state is now driven ashore,
> The thunder howls round us, and dark tempest lower;
> The sea if fast rising—and break in the bay,
> And the hearts of the boldest are filled with dismay;
>
> Still will flounder, unless, with true patriot zeal,
> We get rid of the *lubber* who stands at the wheel!
> And take a *new* PILOT whose heart is *true blue*—
> And such we shall find in our Harry the true. . . .

Then give him the tiller—when he steps on deck,
His firmness and wisdom will save us from wreck.[34]

And a special march, "The Ashland March," was composed, presumably to accompany the electorate as it trooped to the polls.

As part of the campaign paraphernalia a great number of pictures and engravings of Clay were distributed. Previous attempts at a likeness proved very unsatisfactory, perhaps because he did not make a good subject in repose. So much the man of action, his mobile features defied precise definition when he sat motionless.[35] Commented Harriet Martineau: "All attempts to take his likeness have been in vain, though upward of thirty portraits of him, by different artists, were in existence when I was in America. No one has succeeded in catching the subtle expression of placid kindness, mingled with astuteness, which becomes visible to the eyes of those who are in daily intercourse with him."[36]

The Whigs of Philadelphia finally succeeded in obtaining a suitable likeness when they commissioned a portrait of the Great Pacificator by John Neagle in 1842. The artist executed a full-length portrait, depicting Clay as "Father of the American System." It is a large work, measuring more than nine feet three inches in length and six feet in width. Dressed in a black suit and tie, Clay stands on a plain platform of Kentucky marble and gestures toward a partially flag-draped globe that sits on a wooden tripod base with scroll feet. To symbolize the extension of American influence in the Western Hemisphere, the globe is turned to show the South American continent and the Isthmus of Panama. The background on the right side consists of an unfluted Doric column; the left side shows a plow, an anvil, a shuttle, and a ship under full sail. The plow represents agriculture, the shuttle the industries of cotton and wool textile, and the anvil the manufactures of iron products. "Their harmonious juxtaposition is meant to suggest a state of peaceful, productive economic cooperation."[37]

A superb engraving of this portrait by John Sartain in 1843 made it the best-known likeness of the Great Compromiser. Another engraving by Sartain from a full-length portrait by James H. Wise also circulated throughout the campaign. But Clay admired the Neagle likeness.[38] He told Neagle that it was "the judgment of my family and friends that you have sketched the most perfect likeness of me that has been hitherto made. My opinion coincides with

34. John S. Littel, *The Clay Minstrel* (Philadelphia, 1844), pp. 215, 168, 259.

35. On the various likenesses of Clay, see Charles Henry Hart, "Life Portraits of Henry Clay," *McClure's Magazine*, IX (September 1897), pp. 939–948.

36. Martineau, *Retrospect of Western Travel*, I, 173.

37. Robert W. Torchia, *John Neagle, Philadelphia Portrait Painter* (Philadelphia, 1989), p. 100. The symbolism of the entire work is excellently discussed in this study of Neagle.

38. The excellence of the likeness may be judged by comparing it with a daguerreotype done about 1845 and attributed to Mathew Brady. Neagle's portrait of Clay now hangs in the Union League in Philadelphia.

theirs. I think you have happily delineated the character, as well as the physical appearance of your subject." He also liked a painting by John W. Dodge depicting him as "The Farmer of Ashland." Engravings of both these portraits turned up everywhere over the next year.[39]

Clay was later asked if he had a coat of arms. No, he replied, and even if he had, he thought the use of it would be inappropriate. "In lieu of it, would it not be better to employ some object drawn from those interests which I have sought to promote in the National Councils? A loom, shuttle, anvil, plow, or any other article connected with manufactures, agriculture, or commerce."[40]

But one Democratic wag suggested that Clay's armorial bearings should never forget to include "a pistol, a pack of cards and a brandy bottle."[41]

There was one pleasant interruption in Prince Hal's autumn activities when his son James Brown Clay married Susan Maria Jacob, the daughter of John J. Jacob and Lucy Donald Robertson of Louisville on October 12, 1843. John Jacob was one of the wealthiest men in the South, and it greatly pleased Clay that his son had married so well.[42]

Throughout the late summer and early fall Clay took an increasingly active role in the election as the campaign gained momentum. He urged Calvin Colton to prepare a tract against the abolitionists with the aim of arousing the laboring classes against them. Tell them what the consequences of emancipation will be, he counseled: how blacks will disperse to the North and West; how they will compete with free laborers; how they will reduce wages and affect the "moral and social standing" of the Irish, Germans, and other nationalities; how abolitionists scheme to unite blacks and whites in marriage and thereby reduce the white man "to the despised and degraded condition of the black man." Show how the British cooperate with abolitionists, he continued, "for the purpose of dissolving the Union."

Clay felt strongly that the Whig party needed to stand tall and declare and defend its principles of self-government, order, law, and morality. It had been the "vice" of the party over the past ten years, he claimed, "to ally itself to the odds and ends of other parties, instead of resting upon the strength of their own numbers and their own patriotic principles. What sacrifices have they not made to gain Anti Masons, even abolitionists &c &c." Away with all that![43]

39. Clay to John O. Sargent, July 2, 1842, Clay to Epes Sargent, July 16, 1842, November 3, 1843, Clay to Nathan Sargent, August 6, 1843, Clay to Thomas Mittag, July 25, 1843, Clay to Neagle, May 29, 1843, in Clay, *Papers,* IX, 723–724, 736–737, 751, 840, 822, 880. At about this time Thomas D. Jones, a Cincinnati stonemason, executed a bust of Clay which the subject pronounced "a capital likeness." Copies appeared throughout the campaign of 1844. Clay to John P. Foote et al., October 17, 1844, in Lexington *Observer and Kentucky Reporter,* November 9, 1844.

40. Clay to Colton, September 16, 1845, Clay, *Works,* IV, 532.

41. Quoted in Van Deusen, *Clay,* p. 371.

42. Melba Porter Hay, editor of the Clay Papers, suspects that James was able to purchase Ashland after Clay's death because of his wife's inheritance. John J. Jacob died shortly before Clay.

43. Clay to Colton, September 2, 1843, Clay to John M. Berrien, April 23, 1843, Clay to Seargent S. Prentiss, April 27, 1843, in Clay, *Papers,* IX, 852, 812, 814.

Clay even began to entertain queries sent to him by mail, and some of his responses were published in the newspapers, with or without his approval.[44] One letter wanted to know his position on the Texas and Oregon questions. Great Britain had begun showing an interest in Texas with the intention of effecting an alliance with the Lone Star Republic, and both the United States and Great Britain jointly occupied the northwest corner of the continent, roughly from the Rocky Mountains to the ocean and from the forty-second parallel to 54°40′. Expansionists hungered for American occupation of both Texas and Oregon.

"Texas must be ours," trumpeted Andrew Jackson; "our safety requires it." Old Hickory also wanted Oregon since that, too, posed a possible threat to American security. "The important question, the Oregon and annexation of Texas," the Old Hero declared, "are now all important to the security and the future peace and prosperity of our union, and I hope there are a sufficient number of pure american democrats to carry into effect the annexation of Texas, and extending our laws over Oregon."[45]

So where did Henry Clay stand on these two vital questions? several correspondents wished to know. What did he think?

Clay responded immediately. He denied that anyone seriously contemplated the annexation of Texas. He had recently returned from the South, and he did not remember a single individual who expressed an opinion about it. Years ago he had announced his opposition to annexation in a letter to the Reverend William Channing. "My opinion, far from being changed, is strengthened and confirmed by subsequent reflection & subsequent events." Regarding Great Britain's design to "absorb" Texas, he did not believe it because it would "excite the hostility of all the great Powers of Europe," as well as the United States. As for Oregon, he was ready to defend American rights to the region, even to the point of war if it became necessary, but he did not favor an immediate occupation of the territory by the United States government. Such occupation would require a string of forts from the Rockies to the Pacific and a naval establishment along the coast to defend it—both at tremendous cost at a time of financial stringency. "I think our true policy is to settle and populate our immense territory on the East of those mountains and within the U. States, before we proceed to colonize the shores of the Pacific; or at all events postpone the occupation of Oregon some thirty or forty years." He also did not believe Great Britain threatened American claims to Oregon, and he seemed convinced that the long-standing proposal of the United States to settle the boundary at the forty-ninth parallel would eventually be adopted.

At the time these questions were posed Clay did not consider them important, and he really did not want to get involved with them. "I do not think

44. Clay to Lewis D. Campbell, November 29, 1843, in Clay, *Papers,* IX, 893.
45. Jackson to Blair, March 5, 1844, Jackson to Amos Kendall, April 12, 1844, Jackson Papers, LC; Jackson to Aaron V. Brown, February 9, 1843, in Jackson, *Correspondence,* VI, 201–202.

it right, unnecessarily, to present new questions to the public," he told John Crittenden. A recommendation for the annexation of Texas, in his opinion, would involve the United States in a war with Mexico, "and I suppose nobody would think it wise or proper to engage in war with Mexico, for the acquisition of Texas." The only reason the question was raised in the first place was to produce "discord and distraction." Still, the abolitionists might persist in their agitation over it, and rumors mounted that Tyler in his annual message to the Congress would call for annexation as a means of restoring his prestige and increasing his popularity so that he might retain his office for another term. Therefore, Clay told Crittenden, if the question arose in a serious manner and his opinion was demanded, then he would declare his opposition on several grounds: The country was large enough, acquisition would foment war and produce demands by nonslaveholding states for Canada in order to retain the balance between the slave- and nonslaveholding states, and it was wholly impracticable to accomplish. Unquestionably Texas would be settled "by our race . . . our laws, our language, and our institutions." But that could best be achieved if it remained free and independent.[46]

President Tyler, in his annual message to Congress in 1843, came very close to recommending acquisition, indicating his willingness to cooperate in any effort to bring Texas into the Union. Clay reacted with contempt. "Let Mr. Tyler recommend it, if he please, and what of that? The whole world will see the motive, and the impotency of the recommendation."[47]

As Clay worked himself ever deeper into the campaign, he huddled regularly with his close friends in Kentucky, especially Senator Crittenden and Governor Letcher. A superb politician, except for those times when he gambled on long shots, he understood the absolute importance of party organization for electoral success, and as he had done so often in the past, he urged his managers to attend to it. "What we most want is a system of general organization," he told Letcher. "There ought to be at N. York or Philada, a Central Comee. the whole Union; a State Comee. for each State, and local Comees, in every County & Township. And there should be an active correspondence carried on between all parts of the system. With such an organization we would, I think, be certain of victory." He also suggested plans of organization to several supporters—"wherever the plan has been put into operation its effects have been wonderful"—and identified particular individuals who he said were "capital workers." The Democrats always had superior organization compared with the Whigs, and that fact alone accounted for their many elec-

46. Clay to Robert S. Oakley, May 30, 1843, Clay to Thomas Worthington, June 24, 1843, Clay to Crittenden, December 5, 1843, in Clay, *Papers,* IX, 823, 828–829, 897–899. "I have no fears of the power of England on this Continent," Clay wrote to Thomas Worthington on June 24. "Twenty five years hence, our population will be near 35 million. . . . What can she do with us, when we have grown to that size?" But whenever known abolitionists asked Clay about annexation, he ignored their letters.
47. Clay to Leverett Saltonstall, December 4, 1843, in Clay, *Papers,* IX, 896.

toral successes—save for 1840. Then the Whigs had shown imagination and flare in their organizational efforts. That triumphant strategy, said Clay, needed to be repeated in 1844.[48]

Clay also began to think about a vice presidential running mate, although he had to keep it quiet so as not to give the impression that he was presuming nomination. He privately confessed to a few friends that John Clayton of Delaware was his first choice. But when Clayton publicly announced that he did not want the nomination, Clay considered Millard Fillmore, Winfield Scott, Francis Granger, John Davis, and John Sergeant as alternatives.[49] However, when the "Intriguers of 1839" started a movement, in the late fall of 1843, to win the second place for Daniel Webster,[50] Clay alerted his friends to the danger. Webster—increasingly uncomfortable over Tyler's steady move back to the Democratic party as a means of getting its nomination—had finally resigned from the cabinet in May. At first he seemed reluctant to renounce his apostasy from the Whig faith and wanted Clay to make the first gesture toward a reconciliation. But Clay refused. If there was to be a reconciliation, it was up to Webster to recant his abominations about the Bank. Finally, in a speech on November 9, Webster did reaffirm his loyalty to the Whig party and its principles concerning the tariff and banking. But he did it without apologizing for his previous statements and actions. Quite possibly he hoped the speech would help bring about a Clay-Webster ticket for 1844. Publicly Clay insisted that he had nothing to do with deciding the vice presidency, but privately he warned his friends that Webster could not be trusted. And to nominate him "would be shocking to the moral sense of our friends." Fortunately the movement for Webster found little support and soon died. It "had a still birth"—Clay laughed—"and that without any aid from me."[51]

Although several of his advisers urged him to keep his mouth shut and stay home and tend to his cattle and hemp, Clay decided to take another campaign swing during the winter months, avoiding, of course, any outward appearance that his visits to particular cities and states wore any "aspect of electioneering tours." The last swing had been through the Southwest, as Louisiana, Mississippi, and Alabama were then called. This one would take him through the Southeast—Georgia, North and South Carolina, and Vir-

48. Clay to Letcher, August 15, 1843, Clay to Nathan Sargent, September 2, 1843, Clay to James T. B. Stapp, November 16, 1843, in Clay, *Papers,* IX, 844–845, 853, 891.

49. Clay to Clayton, August 8, 1843, Clay to Buckner S. Morris, August 27, 1843, Clay to Henry A. S. Dearborn, July 13, 1843, Clay to Clayton, June 28, 1843, July 13, 1842, Clay to Berrien, April 23, 1843, in Clay, *Papers,* IX, 753, 759, 732, 831, 812.

50. "The rumor here [Washington] to day is also that Webster & Clay are again friends," wrote Barnwell Rhett to Calhoun, "and Webster is to be run as VP on Clays Ticket." October 7, 1843, in Calhoun, *Papers,* XVII, 491.

51. Porter to Clay, September 25, 1843, Clay to Porter, October 3, 1843, Clay to John L. Lawrence, October 5, 1843, Clay to Clayton, October 10, 1843, Clay to Berrien, October 27, 1843, in Clay, *Papers,* IX, 861, 864, 865, 868–869, 873. "My present purpose as far as you are concerned," wrote Nicholas Biddle to Webster, "is to avoid all scism between you & Mr Clay. I should for many reasons prefer in the first instance the union of the two names on the same ticket. . . ." Biddle to Webster, January 9, 1844, in Webster, *Papers, Correspondence,* VI, 8–9.

ginia. The trip would benefit his health by getting him into warmer climes and escaping the severity of a Kentucky winter, and he could always justify it by claiming prior acceptances of invitations to visit these states, which was true. "My plan is this," he wrote his Georgia friend the former Democrat and secretary of the navy John M. Berrien. "Business carries me to N. Orleans this winter, and I intend to proceed thence, via Mobile and the Southern route, through Georgia and So. Carolina to the North State. Thus I am brought to your State. Now what I desire is, to avoid visiting too many places" to meet "large concourses of my fellow Citizens." His health could be a problem, and therefore, he wanted to restrict his appearances to just a couple of rallies in each state. In particular he did not want to be "forced to make public Speeches. I never had any taste for them, intellectually, and they are physically very prostrating."[52]

Apart from considerations of health, the selection of the states to visit showed careful calculation. By this time Clay had decided that Van Buren would be his Democratic opponent. At first he thought the rivalry between the Van Buren and Calhoun factions within that party would eliminate the Little Magician. But if that happened, who could win the nomination? Certainly not Calhoun, the nullifier, and almost certainly not the untrustworthy "Captain" Tyler. No, it had to be the Magician, figured Clay, and Van Buren was most vulnerable in the Southeast, where he was cordially disliked for any number of reasons, especially his past enmity toward Calhoun and his role in the passage of the Tariff of Abominations. To lock up the South and add to it the West and New England, Pennsylvania and some of the other Middle Atlantic states, where Clay felt relatively secure, would produce a landslide in the electoral college. The prospect was so exciting that he began to tell his friends that "the victory of next year will dim the splendor of that of 1840. That is my *cool* judgment. You know I am never warm," he facetiously added.[53]

There was another reason for the selection of this route. He had never been to most of these southeastern states before, and he claimed that there were two places in the United States he earnestly wished to see: "one is the Eastern Shore of Virginia, and the other the Island of Nantucket; in both of which, the primitive manners customs and hospitality of the early emigrants to them from Europe, I understand, are admirably preserved."[54] So off he went on December 14, 1843, first heading for New Orleans to conduct some business, then followed by a six-month swing along the south Atlantic states ending in Washington—just in time for the Whig National Nominating Convention scheduled to begin in Baltimore.

On the journey south a rabid Democrat was invited to meet Clay, but he

52. B. F. Moore et al. to Clay, June, 1843, Clay to Moore et al., July 10, 1843, Clay to Berrien, July 17, 1843, September 4, 1843, Clay to James B. Everhart, December 12, 1843, in Clay, *Papers,* IX, 833, 834, 901. The "North State" mentioned in the letter is North Carolina.
53. Clay to Berrien, October 27, 1843, Clay to John Pendleton Kennedy, December 3, 1843, in Clay, *Papers,* IX, 873, 894.
54. Clay to E. P. Pitts et al., December 12, 1843, in Clay, *Papers,* IX, 901.

refused. He would not shake the Kentuckian's hand or be victimized by his celebrated "fascination." When told that Van Buren had shaken Clay's hand and visited him at Ashland, the Democrat refused to believe the story and offered to wager money that the tale was false. He was so positive that Van Buren would never shake Clay's hand that he consented to meet the despised Whig to learn the truth.

Clay turned on the charm. "I had a very pleasant visit from Mr. Van Buren," he assured the Democrat, "who spent two days with me at my house, and I should be very glad to return his visit if it were in my power, for, setting his bad politics aside, he is a very agreeable gentleman and right clever little fellow."

The Democrat just stared at Clay "confounded." He had "always entertained such hostile feelings" toward the Kentuckian. Now he admitted that Prince Hal "was a ———— clever gentleman, with neither horns nor hoofs, as he had been represented."

Clay repeated this story many times on his tour "with much humor and evident gratification."[55]

The prospective candidate arrived in New Orleans on December 23 and was immediately greeted by the populace as the undisputed choice of the Whig party to recapture the White House. Again he stayed with Dr. William Mercer on Carondelet Street, near the St. Charles Hotel, and spent two months there, taking care of his business, gossiping with politicians, and delighting the New Orleans belles. But mostly he met and talked with a fair number of traders who plied the Mississippi River in an effort to convince them of the importance of his economic ideas, particularly tariff protection.

This was his fifth trip to his favorite city. He had first visited New Orleans in the spring of 1819, followed by subsequent stays in the winters of 1829–1830, 1830–1831, and 1842–1843.[56] On this particular trip he shuttled up and down the river to Natchez and stayed with William St. John Elliot at his plantation, D'Evereux. And this time his political arguments, particularly his aversion to extreme measures on any of the major issues, gained a more receptive hearing. He was a "compromise man," he told all who spoke to him. In terms of protection he believed in a tariff that provided adequate revenue to the government and protection for those American industries that genuinely needed them. He even approved free trade with Canada but the principle of protection with Europe. To all intents and purposes he now favored a "judicious tariff." In view of the fact that he had sneered at Jackson for using that term twenty years ago and said he favored an "*in*judicious tariff" he was obviously making every effort to convince southerners and westerners that his present brand of protectionism would take a "middle ground" which could provide them with enormous financial benefits.

55. Sargent, *Public Men and Events,* II, 220–221.
56. Clay to William L. Hodge, October 24, 1845, private collection, copy CPP.

Since a great many southerners feared the rivalry of cotton growers in India when selling to the British, it made a great deal of sense to cooperate on protection with northern industrialists to whom they were selling more and more cotton. During Clay's previous visit to New Orleans he had found a depressed market. But the nation had begun to emerge from its long economic distress. Now industry had resumed full-scale production, unemployment had declined, and the farmer and plantation owner had once more found a ready market for their staples. In his public and private talks Clay assured his audiences that the Tariff of 1842 had brought the nation out of its depression.[57]

He also spoke of the need for distribution and a national Bank. But these were old and shopworn issues, and the people were growing tired of hearing about them.[58] The nation had gotten along without a Bank for nearly eight years, and few Whigs wanted to renew the struggle over creating a new one. Even the tariff seemed tedious. Economic issues—Bank, tariff, internal improvements—had lost their ability to excite and agitate the electorate. Increasingly the people were arguing over expansion, in particular the annexation of Texas. Newspapers carried stories about the question, and rumors constantly circulated that President Tyler was attempting to arrange a treaty of annexation.

A belief in "Manifest Destiny"—as John L. O'Sullivan, editor of the *Democratic Review,* later characterized expansionism—had begun to sweep the nation,[59] a sense that "Providence" had given the country a "right" to possess "the whole of the continent" in order to extend the blessings of liberty and self-government. Manifest Destiny became the newest slogan to excite the American public, and talk of economic matters only bored them.

All things considered, Clay, as a westerner, should have favored the acquisition of Texas. Kentuckians absolutely supported the idea since many of their kinsmen had relocated in Texas. Moreover, like many southerners, Clay had once denounced the Adams-Onis Treaty because it abandoned Texas to the Spanish. Most southerners believed that Texas was part of the Louisiana Pur-

57. Clay to Thomas B. Stevenson, July 21, 1849, Clay Papers, Manuscript Department, Filson Club, Louisville, Kentucky; Clay to Octavia Walton Le Vert, January 6, 1844, speech in late January in New Orleans, printed in the New York *Daily Tribune,* February 15, 1844, copy CPP; *Niles' Weekly Register,* March 20, April 13, 20, 1844. See also his speech to a committee of Tuscaloosa Whigs, late February or early March 1844, Raleigh *Register and North Carolina Gazette,* March 15, 1844.

58. Alphonso Taft told Webster that "I am credibly informed, that Mr Clay still makes a U.S. Bank a sine qua non, & gives it great prominence in his conversation wherever he goes. I omitted to say, that, among the causes which weigh heavily against the success of the Whigs under Mr Clay, the Compromise Act cannot be forgotten, in this State [Ohio]." Taft to Webster, April 7, 1842, in Webster, *Papers, Correspondence,* V, 292.

59. On Manifest Destiny, see Albert K. Winberg, *Manifest Destiny* (Baltimore, 1935); Frederick Merk, *Manifest Destiny and Mission in American History* (New York, 1963); Thomas R. Hietala, *Manifest Design: Anxious Aggrandizement in Late Jacksonian America* (Ithaca, N.Y., 1985); and Reginald Horsman, *Race and Manifest Destiny: The Origins of American Racial Anglo-Saxonism* (Cambridge, Mass., 1981). See also Thomas B. Jones, "Henry Clay and Continental Expansion, 1820–1844," *Register of the Kentucky Historical Society,* LXXIII (July 1975), pp. 241–262.

chase, and therefore, the Monroe administration had had no right to give it away.

Clay knew all this. Yet he turned his back on Texas because he thought it would divert the electorate from the "important" issues of his American System. At first he did not think the question seriously concerned the people. Then he believed it had been deliberately raised by abolitionists and southern extremists like Calhoun and his friends to distract the Whig party and divide the nation. Just as the Jacksonians always wished to mute the question of slavery in national debate, Clay wanted to squelch all talk about immediate expansion. "I shall regret very much . . . if the Whig Party should, in a *body*, vote" in favor of annexation, he told his friend John Crittenden. "Such a vote would be utterly destructive of it, without the possibility of securing Texas."[60]

So, as he began his extended tour through the Southeast, he spoke about nothing but his American System. Several times he had to apologize to his audiences for repeating ideas and arguments they had heard from him a thousand times before. Still, he persisted in haranguing them about something they did not especially want to hear. Only his great oratorical and histrionic powers kept them from yawning in his face.[61]

He should have known better. He should have sensed the shifting mood of the electorate. But his political instincts deserted him. His grasp of political reality failed him. Every day he was bombarded by letters about Texas, and in private conversation as well. But he was too arrogant and opinionated to accept the notion that the American people were sick to death of banks and tariffs and internal improvements. National issues must be the issues *he* decided upon. As undisputed head of the Whig party he could not tolerate any challenge to his supreme authority. Like Jackson, he presumed to know what was best for the nation and the American people. The electorate must listen and follow.

Just prior to his departure from New Orleans, Clay received information that "greatly surprized" him and should have roused him from his false perception of public thinking. It was so startling that he could not believe it to be true. He had heard that in a secret vote, "or in some other way," some forty-two senators had advised Tyler that they favored and would confirm a treaty of annexation. Worse, negotiations had already begun, and a treaty would be "speedily concluded &c." This information staggered Clay. "Is this true?" he asked Senator Crittenden. "Do address me instantly. . . . If it be true, I shall regret extremely that I have had no hint of it."[62]

Indeed, much of it was true. Tyler, with the help of his new secretary of state, Abel P. Upshur, had virtually completed all the details for a treaty, but its

60. Clay to Crittenden, December 5, 1843, in Clay, *Papers*, IX, 899.
61. On Clay's tour, see Dorman Picklesimer, Jr., "To Campaign or Not to Campaign: Henry Clay's Speaking Tour through the South," *Filson Club Historical Quarterly*, XLII (July 1968), pp. 235–242.
62. Clay to Crittenden, February 15, 1844, Crittenden Papers, LC.

submission to the Senate had been delayed when Upshur was accidentally killed in an explosion aboard the USS *Princeton*. Tyler chose Calhoun to succeed Upshur, and the South Carolinian accepted, having declined twice before, in order to assist in bringing about the annexation of Texas and with it the expansion of territory open to slavery. Once Calhoun took office, the treaty was signed and submitted to the Senate on April 22. Tyler had clearly outmaneuvered everyone, particularly Clay. Annexation was no longer academic but real and "most alarmingly political."[63]

Back in December Crittenden had warned Clay what Tyler was about, but the "Star of the West" chose to ignore it. However, about the time he left New Orleans for Mobile on February 24, and after learning about the secret senatorial vote, Clay began to consider whether he should write a public statement of his views on the subject.

No, chorused his friends. His well-known lack of restraint might result in a catastrophic blunder. The issue had become too explosive to be quieted by another one of Clay's published letters. Whigs could elect him handily, they protested, if only he would hold his tongue. "If St. Paul had been a candidate for the Presidency," wrote one, "I should have advised him to cut the Corinthians and not let the Hebrews even see his autograph."[64]

When Clay arrived in Mobile the day after his departure from New Orleans, he stayed at the home of Dr. Henry Le Vert and his charming wife, Octavia, who gave him a "splendid ball." Clay thoroughly enjoyed Octavia's company and frequently wrote her, virtually to the end of his life. In his letters he invariably referred to Octavia as "my ever dear friend." He remained for a week with the couple, recovering from a bad cold he had contracted in New Orleans, before moving on to Montgomery and Columbus. He reported to Lucretia that he was overwhelmed with kindness and generosity. "My greatest difficulty is to restrain the enthusiasm of my friends and to avoid the entertainments which they are pressing me to accept." His youngest son, John, had joined him just before he left New Orleans, and together with Clay's servant, Charles Dupuy, they were to complete the tour and probably get home sometime in May.[65]

The candidate gave more speeches in Columbus and Macon, staying overnight at the home of Mrs. Thomas F. Foster in Columbus. At Milledgeville, suffering from a fresh cold, he was introduced at a rally by Governor George Walker Crawford. During the course of his remarks Clay declared that William H. Crawford had been his first choice for President during the election of 1824–1825 until Crawford's stroke made his candidacy impossible. Again, he launched into a defense of his role in the House election since that old chestnut

63. Poage, *Clay and Whig Party,* p. 136.

64. Edward W. Johnston to Willie P. Mangum, September 14, 1843, Mangum, *Papers,* III, 468.

65. Clay to Octavia Le Vert, June 25, November 6, 1846, Clay Papers, Manuscript Department, Filson Club, Louisville, Kentucky; Clay to Lucretia, March 2, 1844, Thomas J. Clay Collection, LC.

had been revived once again by his enemies because of his likely nomination. In fact, he frequently told his listeners that in undertaking this nonelectioneering trip, he had had no intention of making speeches, but the circumstance of the wonderful and enthusiastic receptions he had received at every stop forced him to convey his gratitude and then add a few words about his position on various national issues. "In spite of myself I have been drawn out at Macon, Columbus, and this place [Milledgeville]," he wrote to William C. Preston, "to make speeches of more than an hour's duration at each, in the open air, and I find unless I stop that I shall get the Bronchitis. I am now as hoarse as a circuit rider."[66]

In giving these speeches, Clay deserved a lot of credit for frequently facing down his many critics, seen and unseen, who desired his political destruction. Georgia had long fought for the expulsion of the Cherokee Indians and almost provoked a confrontation with the federal government on account of it. The situation was resolved by the Treaty of New Echota during the Jackson administration, which provided for the removal of the Indians to the territory beyond the Mississippi River. Clay had voted against that treaty. Now he stood before Georgians and explained that the treaty had been "induced by *corruption*"—as indeed, it had—and therefore, he had not been able to vote for it.[67]

Clay and his son journeyed on to Savannah and arrived on Thursday, March 21. Nearly the entire city turned out to greet him. Some fifteen hundred congregated at the railroad depot to escort him into the city proper and then to the home of Senator John M. Berrien and his wife. The following day he gave another two-hour speech at the Pulaski House, speaking mainly about the Bank. He became very playful in this speech, complaining about the Democrats who constantly sought to poison the public mind against him. He had not brought to Georgia war, pestilence, or family, he protested. With a twinkle to his eye and a smirk on his face he said he would not bear away any of the "fair daughters of Georgia, whom he saw before him," even if he could. After all, he had "an estimable wife at home, with whom he was sufficiently blest already."[68]

At Savannah Clay wrote to Crittenden acknowledging receipt of two letters written in response to his queries about Texas. In this reply Clay revealed that he was seriously considering making a statement on the subject upon his arrival in Washington despite the objections of some of his friends in Kentucky. He had received numerous requests from various groups around the country for his stand on both the Texas and the Oregon questions. Since he would be a candidate, they said, he should explain his position to the entire nation.[69]

66. Clay to Preston, March 20, 1844, copy CPP.

67. *Niles' Weekly Register,* April 20, 1844.

68. Ibid., April 13, 1844; Frankfort *Commonwealth,* April 2, 1844.

69. See, for example, the letter from citizens of Charleston. "Are you for or against the annexation of Texas?" they asked. "Are you for or against giving the notice [about Oregon] required by the

"I think I can treat the question," Clay declared in his responding letter to Crittenden, "in a manner very differently from any treatment which I have yet seen of it, and so as to reconcile all our friends, and many others, to the views which I entertain." Again his arrogance and presumption came into full play, but Crittenden, being an old friend, quite understood. Clay really seemed to think that he could write a letter that would settle the matter by "harmonizing" all the divergent opinions on the subject and put it to rest, just as he had done so many times in the past. *His* views would bring harmony and peace. Clay went on to state that in the South he found no real agitation for annexation. His audiences loved his position on the principle of protection, so Crittenden ought to inform Whig senators from the South "that they may with perfect safety and confidence vote against the fraudulent tariff which is cooking up in the House."[70]

By the time he reached Augusta, Clay was beginning to feel the strain of all the receptions, dinners, barbecues, and balls he had attended, to say nothing of the many speeches he had given. From Augusta he had planned to visit Madison and Greensboro, but because of fatigue, he canceled these appearances. He begged his friends at his next stop in Columbia, South Carolina, to dispense with parades, meetings, and receptions. "And no public speeches," he added. "I find I must restrain the excitement to which I am constantly exposed. Quiet, quiet, quiet, is my greatest want."[71]

At Columbia Clay rested several days at the home of William C. Preston, now president of the College of South Carolina.[72] Then, accompanied by Preston and Wade Hampton, he moved on to Charleston, where he was welcomed and received the city's "highest demonstration of respect and homage."

The firing of guns signaled his arrival. A line of march formed, headed by a "schooner rigged boat," manned by sailors and drawn by a car proclaiming Clay's commitment and advocacy of "Sailor's Rights."

"Welcome, thrice Welcome, bright Star of the West" proclaimed the many banners lining the streets.

He was escorted to a theater to meet the "ladies" of the city and give a two-hour speech, which induced "enthralling attention." After that came a dinner and ball at the Charleston Hotel.[73]

Treaty with Great Britain . . . and take possession of that country?" Charleston *Mercury,* April 4, 1844, copy CPP.

70. Clay to Crittenden, March 24, 1844, Crittenden Papers, LC. Clay's intention to make this statement in Washington is repeated in a letter to Willie P. Mangum, April 14, 1844, in Mangum, *Papers,* IV, 76.

71. Frankfort *Commonwealth,* April 9, 1844; Clay to Preston, March 20, 28, 1844, copy CPP.

72. Clay apparently gave one short speech of no particular moment to the cabinet makers of Columbia in early April. He said that his only "surviving full brother," Porter Clay, was once an excellent cabinetmaker. Knoxville *Register,* May 1, 1844, copy CPP. He also intended to leave for Charleston on April 4, but a cold and his fear that travel during Easter week would offend "the religious community of Charleston" forced him to delay his departure. Charleston *Courier,* April 4, 1844, copy CPP.

73. *National Intelligencer,* April 15, 1844, copying the *Charleston Courier* of April 8, 1844; *Niles'*

Clay staggered on to Wilmington[74] and reached Raleigh, "City of the Oaks," on his birthday, April 12, at 6:00 P.M. to find it brilliantly illuminated in his honor. Some ten or fifteen thousand Whigs greeted the sixty-seven-year-old statesman with transparencies and blaring bands. "Never, while we live, do we expect to see again as proud a day . . . as Saturday last. Ten thousand Whigs—some say fifteen—forsaking their homes and business . . . were here in Raleigh . . . with banners and badges and other insignia of the Whig party, to welcome *their* great leader and the country's benefactor—HENRY CLAY." They then escorted him to the home of Governor John Morehead.[75]

On the morning following his arrival in Raleigh Clay gave a major speech on Whig principles[76] from a platform at the Capitol, after which he attended a barbecue where he was actually mobbed.[77] In desperation he made for a tree and braced his back against it. Then he turned to the mob, his wit at the ready.

"Ah! you have tree'd the old coon at last!" he cried, to which the happy and inebriated crowd responded with repeated cheers for the "Old Coon," the "Bright Star of the West."[78]

The day before Clay left Raleigh he sat down—tradition claims he seated himself under a great white oak tree on East North Street—and wrote the letter on Texas that ultimately destroyed his presidential bid. Why he chose this particular moment, rather than wait until he reached Washington, as he originally intended, is not clear. Perhaps he feared he would be too preoccupied to give the matter the full attention it deserved, or he may have been concerned about the degree of opposition it might receive from his friends in the capital, particularly Crittenden. Undoubtedly he had consulted with Preston, Hampton, Morehead, and others on its advisability, and probably all of

---

Weekly Register, April 13, 1844, copying the Charleston *Courier* of April 1; Frankfort *Commonwealth,* April 23, 1844.

74. Where he gave another speech, declaring: "I am a Whig! I am so because I believe the principles of the Whig party are best adapted to promote the prosperity of the country. . . . I place *country* far above all parties." He said he could never expect other men to conform altogether to his opinions, "any more than in selecting a wife (and here he turned playfully to the ladies,) a man can expect his lady love to be free from all possible defects." Raleigh *Register and North Carolina Gazette,* April 9, 1844, copy CPP.

75. Raleigh *Register,* April 16, 1844.

76. The speech treated trade, industry, banking, public lands, executive power, and abolition, but not Texas. "We want a National army, a National navy, a National post office establishment, National laws regulating our foreign commerce and our coasting trade, above all, perhaps, we want a National currency. The duty of supplying these national means of safety, convenience and prosperity must be executed by the general government, or it will remain neglected and unfulfilled." The speech was considered an important statement of Whig doctrines and was reprinted widely in newspapers and published in pamphlet form as *Mr. Clay's Speech, Delivered in the City of Raleigh, April 13, 1844* (n.p., 1844).

77. "Clay was in fine spirits, and in the best humour," reported Benjamin W. Leigh, "he made an excellent speech, but as he was not excited by the collision of debate, he did not rise to any of *his* high flights of eloquence." Clay made no personal comments throughout the speech and referred to Tyler only once. The Whigs reportedly consumed seven thousand pounds of meat at the barbecue. Leigh to Mangum, April 22, 1844, in Mangum, *Papers,* IV, 114.

78. Poage, *Clay and Whig Party,* p. 121; Van Deusen, *Clay,* pp. 363–364.

them agreed that the time had finally come for him to speak his mind on the subject. Even if they had not agreed, more than likely he had made up his mind, and nothing they could say would change it.

In going public, he felt obligated, he said, by a sense of "duty." Moreover, "I do not entertain the slightest apprehension of any injury to our cause from the publication of my opinions. On the contrary I believe it would be benefitted and strengthened."[79] Once again he totally failed to comprehend the political signs of the day.

This Raleigh letter, dated April 17, 1844, reviewed the history of U.S. relations with Texas, and Clay repeated his contention that this southwestern area constituted part of the Louisiana Purchase but had been relinquished in the Adams-Onís Treaty. Texas, he said, "was sacrificed to the acquisition of Florida." That being the case, it was idle and ridiculous, "if not dishonorable," to talk of resuming title to Texas, as though the United States had never parted with it. As far as he understood the situation, Mexico had not abandoned its claim, and for the United States to attempt to acquire Texas would constitute an act of war. "Of that consequence there cannot be a doubt. Annexation and war with Mexico are identical."

He did not look upon such a catastrophe with the lightheartedness of some, he said. "I regard all wars as great calamities, to be avoided, if possible, and honorable peace as the wisest and truest policy of this country." Some assume, he continued, that Mexico could be easily conquered, but they forget that Great Britain or France might come to its aid because each was "jealous of our increasing greatness, and disposed to check our growth and cripple us."

Even if Mexico consented to annexation, he did not think that Texas ought to be admitted into the Union because of the decided opposition by a "considerable and respectable portion of the Confederacy" that could cause discord and distraction throughout the nation and possibly endanger the Union. Statesmen must eradicate prejudices between sections and groups and cultivate harmony to foster contentment among all parts of the country. Clearly the acquisition of Texas would vastly benefit the slaveholding South and disturb the balance of political power. Nothing could be more fatal than strengthening one part of the confederacy against another part. There would be constant rivalry between them. Today it might be Texas, tomorrow Canada, in order to right the balance. And on and on.

Clay also mentioned the Texas debt the United States would be required to assume—thirteen million dollars, he conjectured[80]—which only added to the imprudence of acquisition. Finally there had not been a general expression of public opinion on the subject, and without that mandate extreme caution should be exercised by the President and Congress.[81]

Clay sent the letter to Crittenden with instructions to have it published

79. Clay to Mangum, April 14, 1844, in Mangum, *Papers,* IV, 103.

80. The treaty signed on April 12, 1844, called for the United States to assume the public debt of Texas up to a total of ten million dollars.

81. *National Intelligencer,* April 27, 1844.

by the Washington *National Intelligencer* on a day he and other friends—specifically Willie P. Mangum, John M. Berrien, and Alexander H. Stephens—might determine—that is, whether to publish it before or after Clay's arrival in Washington. He had the concurrence of George Badger, Governor Morehead, and Edward Stanly, who were with him in Raleigh and had read the letter. Clay added that he had no objection to modifications of its phraseology. But under no circumstances would he consent to the suppression of the letter or an unreasonable delay of its publication. Next week would be acceptable. He also stated that he felt perfectly confident about the ground he had taken and had no fear of the consequences because he knew that Van Buren, the likely Democratic candidate, also opposed annexation. "We shall therefore occupy common ground." If Van Buren did change his position and come out in favor of the acquisition of Texas "it will be so much worse for him." The public mind was fixed on the presidential election and hardly concerned with Texas.

How did Clay know what position Van Buren would take unless they had discussed it at Ashland? Neither man ever acknowledged collusion, and at the time of their interview Clay repeated to several friends that he and Van Buren talked very little politics.

Clay's disclaimer about collusion should be believed because an agreement between the two men defies common sense. It would surely appear to the public, and especially politicians, like another "corrupt bargain." Clay could ill afford another such scandal, and he was not so stupid as to fall into such a trap. And even had he risked a wild, idiotic gamble, the cautious Van Buren had too much political sense to agree to such risky business.

How, then, did Clay know? Possibly he inferred it from several offhanded comments the former President expressed during their many talks at Ashland or from previous remarks over the years. Possibly it had been leaked, just as Clay's opposition to annexation was leaked before the publication of the Raleigh letter. Whatever the source of his information, Clay seemed anxious to force Van Buren's hand. The Magician's "present attitude renders it necessary that I should break silence."[82]

Clay's letter shocked Crittenden when he received it.[83] Once more the Old Coon had rushed into battle, demonstrating again a complete lack of restraint, and there was nothing that Crittenden or anyone else could do about it. And the instructions accompanying the letter were quite specific. So it appeared in the *National Intelligencer,* on Saturday, April 27, the same day the Washington *Globe* published a letter from Van Buren to Congressman William H. Hammet of Mississippi expressing his own opposition to annexation. This coincidence—and it was coincidence—generated all kinds of rumors about how and when this convenient disposal of the Texas issue had been decided upon.

82. Clay to Crittenden, April 17, 19, 21, 1844, Crittenden Papers, LC.
83. Kirwan, *Crittenden,* p. 175.

The letters sent shock waves across the country.[84] The two ostensible candidates had told the American people something many of them did not wish to hear.

The letters proved to be unintended time bombs. Van Buren's had a very short fuse before blowing him up. Clay's took a little longer.

84. Buchanan to Jackson, April 29, 1844, Blair-Lee Papers, Princeton University Library.

THIRTY-SIX

"The Old Coon Is Dead"

C LAY COMPLETED his nonelectioneering tour of the Southeast with a swing through Petersburg, Norfolk, and Ports-
mouth, regaling their citizens with demonstrations of his oratorical prowess and proclaiming the "cherished honor" he felt at "having been
born in this Ancient and renowned Commonwealth." Some, like Thomas
Ritchie, editor of the Richmond *Enquirer,* challenged his claim. "I swear," the
Old Coon cried, ". . . that I was born in the Slashes of Old Hanover!" The
audience erupted with cheers and applause. "I am"—and here Clay let his voice
swell with emotion—"a native of Virginia, and I will continue to be a native
born citizen of this proud Commonwealth, the avowals of *Tom Ritchie* to the
contrary notwithstanding!"[1]

What a campaigner the Old Coon could be when emotionally engaged. If
the entire nation had only heard him speak on these occasions, he undoubtedly
would have been swept into the White House many times over.

Whig newspapers in Kentucky proclaimed his tour an unparalleled success. "His progress was one grand, unbroken triumphal civil procession, never
equalled in this country unless in the case of Gen. Lafayette," proclaimed the
Frankfort *Commonwealth* on May 7, 1844. "Mr. Clay, undoubtedly, is infinitely the most popular man in America and he certainly is the greatest of
American orators and Statesmen."

Clay reached Washington aboard the steamboat *Osceola* on April 26, just
prior to the publication of his Raleigh letter, and stayed at the home of his
friend William A. Bradley.[2] Like the Kentucky newspapers, he was ecstatic

1. Speech in Petersburg, April 19, 1844, Jonesboro, Tennessee, *Whig, and Independent Journal,*
May 1, 1844, copy CPP. Several years earlier John Tyler wrote: "Mr. Clay is undeservedly obnoxious to many in the Whig ranks. While Tom Ritchie held sway, he poisoned the public mind
against him. He taught the Demagogues to declaim against him and to slander him. . . . But the
prejudices then engendered against Mr. Clay still have their influence over the minds of many."
Tyler to Henry A. Wise, December 16, 1838, in Tyler, *Letters,* III, 74. Ritchie actually knew where
Clay had been born but could not bear the Old Coon's taking advantage of it in the election.
2. *National Intelligencer,* April 27, 1844.

over the receptions and demonstrations of support he had received at every city he visited. More than ever he was convinced of electoral victory in the fall elections. He claimed the Whigs would win Illinois, Missouri, Arkansas, Alabama, Louisiana, Mississippi, and Georgia. In actual fact, the *Democratic* candidate for President took every one of them. Here was another example of Clay's overconfidence in his ability to attract popular votes. Here was another example of his exaggerated, if not distorted, interpretation of his electoral invincibility. Of the six states he visited on this tour, only one, North Carolina, voted Whig.

Still, Clay had accomplished a number of worthwhile objectives. He repeatedly proclaimed the importance and value of the Whig principles of government to the American people.[3] In his last speech in Norfolk, after reiterating these basic principles, he asked what principles the leaders of the Democratic party espoused. "I am . . . a Whig . . . and have Whig principles. What the Democratic principles are I know not. They assail our principles without letting us know what they themselves maintain."[4]

Throughout his many speeches Clay trumpeted the notion of nationhood, the union of many people in various sections engaged in advancing the well-being of all. And perhaps for the first time he enunciated in Raleigh a doctrine that might have paralyzed some of the Founding Fathers yet was destined, decades later, to become the doctrine by which the nation secured the greatest prosperity and individual protection imaginable for its citizens. Said Clay: It is the duty of the central government, not the states or anyone else, to supply all the necessary "national means of safety, convenience and prosperity" for the American people.

Convenience and prosperity? Absolutely. The federal government must lead the way, he said. It must encompass whatever concerns the welfare of everyone. Otherwise the progress of this nation will be arrested. Although Clay might have denied the expansion of executive powers, for obvious political reasons, he nonetheless strongly advocated the continuing expansion of the powers of the national government to achieve the total well-being of all its citizens. Whatever dealt with the safety, prosperity, and happiness of the people came legitimately within the scope of the central government.

In fact, when Clay learned about the invention of the "electro magnetic telegraph," he immediately tagged it as a matter for governmental management. In the hands of private individuals, he said, it could be used "to monopolize intelligence and to perform the greatest operations in commerce and other departments of business. I think such an engine ought to be exclusively under the control of government," he went on, "but that object cannot be

3. He repeatedly cited a national bank and currency, national army and navy, a tariff for revenue with incidental protection to industry, distribution of the proceeds of the public lands, and a curb on the President's assumption of powers not conferred by the Constitution.
4. Speech of April 22, 1844, in *The Campaign of 1844* (Frankfort, Ky., 1844), pp. 77–78.

accomplished without an appropriation by Congress to purchase the right of the inventors."[5]

Here, then, was the beginning of what Abraham Lincoln and the Civil War would later accomplish—namely, a redefinition of the meaning of American liberty. No longer did it mean freedom *from* governmental power, as it had since the inauguration of the Republic; Clay now proposed that it meant freedom of opportunity, the ability of all Americans to achieve a life of "safety, convenience and prosperity," buttressed by the power of the central government.[6]

Just as Clay reached Washington and his Raleigh letter appeared, Whigs from around the country headed for Baltimore to name their national ticket. The city pulsated with excitement. "At every avenue, railroad-depot, and wharf, wherever coaches, cars, and steamboats, could disengage their passengers, there was a scene of animation exhibited that bespoke the anticipation of some great event." People crowded the sidewalks, clustered near hotels, and chatted, laughed, and cried huzza. As each new delegation arrived in town, banners appeared, music sounded, parades formed. All the hotels and boardinghouses were filled to capacity. Even private homes were thrown open to accommodate the swelling numbers of politicians and their followers.

The Whigs, with triumph radiating from their gleaming eyes, met in the Universalist Church on Calvert Street on Wednesday, May 1, at 11:00 A.M. Clay badges hung conspicuously from every buttonhole. Clay portraits, Clay ribbons, Clay hats, Clay cigars, Clay banners, Clay songs, Clay marches, Clay quicksteps, Clay caricatures enveloped the city. "Oh, the rushing, the driving, the noise, the excitement!" To see it and hear it and feel it was sheer ecstacy, said one man.[7]

The convention quickly organized itself under the presidency of Ambrose Spencer of New York. Then Clay's friend Benjamin Leigh of Virginia took the floor to state that the convention need not trouble itself with the usual form of nomination since everyone had but a single candidate in mind. He therefore proposed that Henry Clay of Kentucky be nominated unanimously. The hall exploded in applause and shouts and cries of "yea," and the resolution was adopted by acclamation. A committee consisting of John Berrien of Georgia, Jacob Barnett of Ohio, William S. Archer of Virginia, Abbott Lawrence of Massachusetts and Erastus Root of New York was directed to inform the candidate of his nomination.

5. *Mr. Clay's Speech, Delivered in the City of Raleigh, April 13, 1844* (n.p., 1844); Clay to Alfred Vail, September 10, 1844, Alfred Vail Papers, Smithsonian Institution Archives. Clay also recognized that getting the appropriation from Congress would involve questions of constitutionality and expediency. I am grateful to Professor Richard R. John of the College of William and Mary for making this letter available to me.
6. On Lincoln and the "new birth of freedom" concept, see James M. McPherson, *Abraham Lincoln and the Second American Revolution* (New York, 1991). I rather suspect that a good deal of Lincoln's thinking on the matter came directly from his "beau ideal," Henry Clay.
7. Sargent, *Clay*, p. 231.

When delegates suggested inviting Clay to attend the proceedings the following day, Reverdy Johnson rose and read a letter from the nominee declining such an offer out of a "sense of delicacy and propriety," which he hoped his friends would understand.

"That's right," cried a voice in the crowd.

"Just like him," shouted another.

And once more the convention flooded the hall with cheers and whistles.

The committee conveyed the decision of the convention to Clay, and he accepted the nomination "from a high sense of duty, and with feelings of profound gratitude." He requested the members to express to the delegates the "very great satisfaction" he felt over "the unanimity with which it has been made."

When the convention turned to select a vice presidential running mate, several possible candidates, including John Clayton, George Evans, and John McLean, immediately declined. Four nominations followed: Millard Fillmore of New York, John Davis of Massachusetts, Theodore Frelinghuysen of New Jersey, and John Sergeant of Pennsylvania, with 138 votes needed to win. On the first ballot Frelinghuysen took a commanding lead and never lost it. He was declared the nominee after the third ballot.[8]

Frelinghuysen's nomination came as a surprise to almost everyone, including Clay, but the former New Jersey senator had earned the respect and admiration of many Whigs because he represented a Christian and moral leadership that could add real strength to the party. Frelinghuysen was president of the American Tract Society, among other Protestant groups, and had been a strong critic of Jackson's Indian policy, arguing for numerous religious groups that opposed removal. He had given "his head, his hand, and his heart . . . without stint," read the Whig platform, "to the cause of morals, education, philanthropy, and religion."

"The nomination of Mr. Frelinghuysen was no doubt unexpected by you," Clay wrote to Thurlow Weed, "as it certainly was by me. I think nevertheless it is a most judicious selection."[9]

The convention presented a platform hardly worthy of the name. In one short paragraph it summarized everything Clay had espoused on his recent tour. And it included not a word about Texas. Of course, the Raleigh letter had been published only a few days before and might not have been known by some of the delegates. Most probably northern and southern Whigs simply contented themselves with Clay's earlier position—namely, the less said, the better.

The following day a Young Men's Ratifying Convention met in Balti-

8. *Niles' Weekly Register,* May 4, 18, 1844.

9. Whig platform, "Election of 1844," *History of American Presidential Elections,* ed. Schlesinger and Israel, I, 807; Clay to Weed, May 6, 1844, copy CPP. In response to a letter from Frelinghuysen, Clay declared: "Your nomination took me by surprize, but it was an agreeable surprize." Frelinghuysen to Clay, May 11, 1844, Clay to Frelinghuysen, May 22, 1844, copy CPP.

more and lustily cheered the Clay-Frelinghuysen ticket. There were processions, band playing, and flag-waving, and "the display of banners &c was superb," commented Hezekiah Niles. Webster spoke at the meeting and formally brought an end to his differences with Clay by his strong words of support. The two great Whig leaders were reunited at last. They had had no correspondence, "direct or indirect," since 1841.[10]

Democrats held their convention in Baltimore nearly four weeks after the Whigs concluded theirs. And where the Whigs displayed remarkable unity and a growing sense of victory, the Democrats, by contrast, seemed distracted, perplexed, and distraught, particularly over Van Buren's action on Texas, which they had plenty of time to read and digest before the convention. "I do not think I ever witnessed such a state of utter disorder, confusion and decomposition as that which the Democratic Party now presents," commented Clay. "Many believe that their Convention will not abandon Mr Vanburen and take up some one else."[11]

Andrew Jackson, still alive and still shouting into the ears of Democratic leaders, pronounced Clay "a dead political Duck" when he read the Raleigh letter. But Van Buren's letter completely surprised and "unmanned him." He admitted: "I have shed tears of regret. I would to god I had been at Mr. V.B. elbow when he closed his letter." But there was no turning back now; "the die was cast." So he wrote the Magician and frankly told him that "it was impossible to elect him," as impossible as it would be "to turn the current of the Mississippi." Under the circumstances, Van Buren could not be the Democratic candidate. Someone else—someone who favored annexation—must take his place. Jackson's personal choice was his protégé James Knox Polk of Tennessee.[12]

A great many Democrats, particularly the Calhoun wing of the party, agreed about getting rid of Van Buren. When they met in convention in Baltimore on May 27, they turned against the Magician and on the ninth ballot nominated Polk, the nation's first dark horse, along with George M. Dallas of Pennsylvania for Vice President. They adopted a party platform that said all the right things, according to the canon of Andrew Jackson, about banks, tariffs, and internal improvements, but it also called for the "reoccupation of Oregon and the reannexation of Texas at the earliest practicable period."[13]

Thus, with a single stroke, the Democrats had virtually annihilated Clay in the South[14] and in every other place where expansionism was the dominant

10. *Niles' Weekly Register,* May 4, 1844; Clay to Nathaniel Beverley Tucker, January 11, 1845, copy CPP.

11. Clay to Weed, May 6, 1844, copy CPP.

12. Jackson to Francis P. Blair, May 7, 11, 1844, March 10, 1845, Jackson Papers, LC. The letter to Van Buren himself is missing, but its existence is confirmed in Jackson's letter to Blair on May 11. Undoubtedly Van Buren destroyed the letter, as he did others by Jackson that he found too embarrassing and that he did not wish posterity to see.

13. Schlesinger and Israel, eds., History of American *Presidential Elections,* I, 799–801.

14. Not all southerners favored annexation. Some southern Whigs feared abandonment of their section by slaveowners, leaving behind debt and a ravaged land. Michael A. Morrison, "Westward

issue. It was later falsely reported that when Clay heard the name of the man to oppose him, he blurted out, "Beat again by hell," presumably because he realized that his strength in the South had suddenly dissipated.[15]

"Who is James K. Polk?" asked a startled nation. Although he had been Speaker of the House of Representatives and a former governor of Tennessee, "Young Hickory," as Democrats liked to refer to him, was hardly known. But did anyone think this relatively obscure politician could defeat the Great Pacificator? Could anyone seriously contrast his threadbare credentials for the presidency with those of the nation's most distinguished statesman? "This nomination may be considered as the dying gasp, the last breath of life, of the 'Democratic' party," declared the *National Intelligencer* on May 20.

"Are our Democratic friends serious in the nominations which they have made at Baltimore?" queried Clay. Well, so much the worse for them. The nominations "could not be better for our cause." His only regret, he said with a touch of unintended arrogance, "is that persons more worthy of a contest with us had not been selected." Having gotten that fatuous remark off his chest, he resumed a more intelligent attitude. In politics, as well as war, he warned, "it is a wise maxim . . . never to despise an enemy, and to prepare for battle as if he were the most formidable foe," as if "Napoleon or Wellington were in the field."[16] Not that he really believed what he said. Clay simply reminded himself that he ought to believe it.

Hordes of well-wishers crowded around the Kentuckian in Washington to congratulate him on his nomination and certain victory in the fall. Virtually the entire two Whig conventions from Baltimore marched through his rooms. By the time he departed for Ashland, nursing a chronic cold, he was weary but happy, "unwell but not seriously," confident and assured but aching to assume "the offensive instead of the defensive position and carrying the war into Africa."[17]

It was truly a great misfortune that the tradition in American politics at the time did not permit Clay to carry the war into Africa. Because of his unsurpassed oratorical powers, he would have made an excellent campaigner, provided he kept his head and resisted the efforts of hecklers to rattle or bait him and throw him off stride. But he understood the role he must play. He must return to Ashland and act like the senior statesman everyone knew him to be and keep absolutely quiet, allowing the managers of the Whig party to direct the campaign.

Apart from his natural inclination to involve himself in the excitement of

the Curse of Empire: Texas Annexation and the American Whig Party," *Journal of the Early Republic,* X (Summer 1990), p. 237.

15. Thomas C. Reyburn et al. to Clay, September 1844, John Pendleton Kennedy Papers, copy CPP.

16. Clay to Willie Mangum, June 7, 1844, Clay to John P. Kennedy, June 10, 1844, Clay to John M. Berrien, July 16, 1844, copies CPP.

17. Clay to S. W. Whiting, May 9, 1844, Clay to Octavia Le Vert, May 13, 1844, and another of no date but probably late spring 1844, Clay to John Sloane, May 21, 1844, copies CPP.

elections, Clay itched to take a more active part in the canvass because of the repeated low blows he sustained from Democrats, especially abolitionists, to prove him unfit for office. The campaign of 1828 had hit a low mark in vulgarity, which threatened now to be repeated.

The mudslinging began at once. One handbill, typical of many others, written by the Reverend Abel Brown, an abolitionist, labeled Clay "that notorious *Sabbath-breaker, Profane Swearer, Gambler, Common Drunkard, Perjurer, Duellist, Thief, Robber, Adulterer, Man-stealer, Slave-holder, and Murderer*!" It also accused the candidate of "Selling Jesus Christ!" because he traded in slaves.[18] Another revolting pamphlet, entitled *Henry Clay's Moral Fitness for the Presidency,* stated: "The history of Mr. Clay's debaucheries and midnight revelries in Washington is too shocking, too disgusting to appear in public print."

Not unexpectedly, the hoary-headed corrupt bargain charge came in for extended notice, and even Andrew Jackson participated in it by publicly reaffirming his belief that a deal had been struck. There was no possible way Clay could live down this charge, but it still rankled, and he seriously considered responding to it all over again. He wanted to prove—in fact, he claimed he had the evidence—that the bargain story had been concocted by the Jacksonians. Only the refusal by some of the witnesses to get involved thwarted his purpose. He privately called Old Hickory a slanderer. "We should have a pretty time of it with one of Jackson's lieutenants at Washington and another at Frankfort, and the old man in his dotage at the Hermitage dictating to both." The best Clay could do was to authorize the publication of his letters to Francis Blair. They proved nothing, though a "playful" reference to John Quincy Adams's "infirmity of a watery eye" necessitated a letter of apology to the former President.[19]

Clay's reversal on the Bank issue gave the Democrats ammunition to attack him as a man without principle who would shift his position on any question to turn a vote. They also charged him with advocating free trade—a charge that really infuriated Clay. They claimed he said one thing to southerners and the exact opposite to northerners. They even put it to rhyme:

ORATOR CLAY

Orator Clay had two tones in his voice:
　　The one squeaking thus and the other down so,
And mighty convenient he found them both—
　　The squeak at the top and the guttural below.

Orator Clay looked up to the North;
　　"I'm for a Tariff Protective," said he;

18. Frankfort *Commonwealth,* September 17, 1844. It was first reprinted in the New York *Morning Courier and Enquirer,* August 23, 1842.

19. Clay to John Sloane, May 21, June 14, 1844, Clay to Benjamin W. Leigh, July 20, 1844, Clay to Adams, October 26, 1844, copies CPP; Clay to Sloane, June 20, 1844, Letcher to Clay, July 6, 1844, Clay to Thomas B. Stevenson, July 18, 1844, in Clay, *Works,* IV, 488–490, 491, III, 458.

> But he turned to the South with his other tone,
>   "A Tariff for revenue only 'twill be!"
>
> Orator Clay to the North, with a squeak:
>   "I'm for a Bank, for a National Bank!"
> Orator Clay to his friends at the South:
>   "I confess my opinions are not very rank!"
>
> Orator Clay was a Mason of note—
>   Not a secret, a sign, or a word did he slip;
> But orator Clay all his secrets forgot,
>   And really couldn't remember the grip!"[20]

What made it all so infuriating was Polk's bald-faced claim that he supported protection. Although known to have opposed the tariff in the past, Polk wrote a letter to John K. Kane of Philadelphia in which he said he had sanctioned "reasonable" protection for home industry! And it delighted the Democrats. "Your letter to Kane will kill Clay," gloated Andrew Jackson Donelson.[21] Clay urged his friends to expose Polk's hypocrisy and provide evidence of his hostility to protectionism. "Nothing has surprised me so much as the attempt now making in Pennsylvania to represent Mr Polk as the friend and myself as the foe of Protection. If it should succeed I shall distrust the power of the press and of truth."[22]

The Whig press responded to the Kane letter, but its message lacked punch. "Mr. Polk is a loco, out and out, of the free trade school," it chorused. "He is for Free Trade and every other Loco abomination; and against every Whig principle and measure." A simple statement, but it hardly roused the electorate to condemn Polk's outright hypocrisy and theft of the Whig position on protection.[23]

Clay's past dueling record, particularly his supposed role in the Graves-Cilley affair, received extended coverage by the Democratic press. Inquiries demanded to know his position on dueling, and some asked him outright if he would fight during the election if challenged.[24]

He was also denounced as a man without any religious affiliation—which was true—who only talked of Christian morality but did not live it. Clay privately admitted that although "I am not a member of any Christian Church,

---

20. Quoted in Arthur K. Moore, "Anti-Clay Songs from the Campaign of 1844," *Filson Club Quarterly*, XXVI, no. 3 (July 1952), p. 230.

21. Polk to Kane, June 19, 1844, Donelson to Polk, July 16, 1844, in Polk, *Correspondence*, VII, 267. "The Tariff, it must be confessed is rather a favorite in Pa.," John Galbraith told Polk, "we have so many iron and other factories." June 17, 1844, ibid., VII, 258.

22. Clay to Clayton, August 29, 1844, Clayton Papers, LC; Clay to Joseph R. Ingersoll, August 29, 1844, copy CPP.

23. *The Campaign of 1844*, p. 158.

24. Alexander Plumer et al. to Clay, July 15, 1844, in *Kendall's Expositor*, September 3, 1844; Clay to Plumer, August 1, 1844, Lexington *Observer and Kentucky Reporter*, September 4, 1844; Clay to J. G. Goble, August 16, 1844, *The Campaign of 1844*, p. 198.

I have a profound sense of the inappreciable value of our Religion, which has increased and strengthened as I have advanced in years; and I sincerely hope that I may yet be inspired with that confidence in the enjoyment of the blessings, in another state of existence, which it promises, that disarms death of all its terrors." Prophet Joseph Smith demanded that he explain what would be his rule of conduct toward members of the Church of the Latter-day Saints if he were elected. Clay's response proved unsatisfactory, and Smith denounced him as a "frail man," adding: "What have you done that will exalt you? Can anything be drawn from your *life, character,* or *conduct,* that is worthy of being held up to the gaze of this nation as a model of *virtue, charity, and wisdom?*"[25]

Reports circulated that Clay regularly attended horse races on the Sabbath in the District of Columbia and that he had bet and won a thousand dollars on one such race. "It is an infamous falsehood, from beginning to end," protested Clay, "without the smallest color of foundation for it. . . . The charge is a vile and atrocious fabrication." Democrats also pointed out that in violation of the Constitution, he had taken his seat in the Senate some thirty years earlier before he had reached the age of thirty and therefore must have perjured himself. "I neither took, nor was required to take, any oath with respect to my age," explained Clay in response.[26]

Although he had witnessed and participated in many campaigns in the past, he could scarcely believe the distortions reported about his personal and public life. "The Loco's, beyond all question," he told one friend, "are every where making the most desperate efforts by the most devilish means. They have so metamorphised me that you will not be able to recognize me when I next see you."[27]

Perhaps some of the most potent assaults came from the pen of Amos Kendall and were printed in *Kendall's Expositor,* condemning Clay as *"the embodiment of Whig principles,"* those immoral principles of aristocrats who seek to increase their natural advantages by manipulating laws and reshaping society to make the government an "Aristocracy of Wealth." Clay's excessive habits of drinking, swearing, and card playing testify to his immorality, wrote Kendall. "A hundred years hence . . . Andrew Jackson will as far outshine Henry Clay . . . as the bright sun . . . outshines the pale moon."[28]

Clay's well-known "appreciation" of feminine charms also drew attention from the Democrats. However, "ladies" would have none of him, they insisted.

> The democrats will be triumphant;
> The ladies their charms will display.

25. Smith to Clay, November 4, 1843, Clay to Smith, November 15, 1843, in Clay, *Papers,* IX, 881, 890–891; Smith to Clay, May 13, 1844, Clay to Fernando C. Putnam, October 9, 1844, copies CPP.
26. Clay to F. M. Wright, October 21, 1844, in Lexington *Observer and Kentucky Reporter,* November 27, 1844; Clay to Thomas M. Bond, September 10, 1844, copy CPP.
27. Clay to Richard Henry Bayard, September 14, 1844, copy CPP.
28. August 14, 27, September 10, 1844.

> And so no man will they marry,
>> Who will vote for old Henry Clay.
>
> The Whigs all their humbugs are trying,
>> In hopes they'll carry the day,
> But so long as the ladies are with us,
>> No votes will they get for old Clay.[29]

One widely circulated Democratic pamphlet began with this arresting and eye-catching statement spelled out in bold, black type:

Christian Voters!
Read, Pause and Reflect!
Mr. Clay's
Moral Character.[30]

The burden of most Democratic stump speeches throughout the campaign centered on "Mr. Clay," reported Philip Hone, "with vituperative attacks upon his moral character. He was denounced as a gambler, libertine, and Sabbath-breaker, and the moral and patriotic yeomanry shouted [in response] . . . down with the profligate candidate of the Whigs.' "[31]

The Democrats truly enjoyed making the "Old Coon" the butt of their jokes and sly innuendos. In the past he had tormented a legion of Democrats. Now it was his turn to feel the sting of ridicule. They even produced a parody of Hamlet's famous soliloquy to mock him, and they called it "Clay's Soliloquy":

> To be, or not to be, that is the question:—
> Whether next "Fourth of March" shall see me seated
> With all due pomp and circumstance upon
> The presidential chair: or the base rout
> Of Loco Focos shall defeat my purposes?
> To hit—to miss—no more: Ay, if we hit,
> To end this curs'd uncertitude, these doubts
> We coons are heirs to—'tis a consummation
> Devoutly to be wished. To hit—to miss;
> To miss perchance the "spoils"—ay, there's the rub;
> For in the loss of them what else may come,
> When we have shuffled off this 'lection coil,
> Must give pause.[32]

And where the Democrats left off the abolitionists nicely stepped forward to continue the deadly barrage. They took particular offense over Clay's statement to Hiram Mendenhall. Since he hated slavery, they felt he should have been more responsive to their pleas, and they therefore struck back at him with

29. Moore, "Anti-Clay Songs," p. 230.
30. Quoted in Van Deusen, Clay, p. 371.
31. Hone, Diary, p. 712.
32. Moore, "Anti-Clay Songs," p. 228.

all the moral outrage they usually reserved for the most notorious defenders of the "peculiar institution." They denounced him as a slave dealer and slave catcher. They charged him with cruel behavior toward his servants, whipping them, chaining them, selling them when they disobeyed him, and deliberately breaking up families in the process. They even accused him of advocating the slavery of white folk. This atrocious fabrication came about during the Missouri debates when a Vermont congressman inserted into the record his interpretation of "the *effect* of certain words used" by Clay a year earlier—to wit, "If gentlemen will not allow us to have black slaves they must let us have *white ones,* for we cannot cut our firewood, and black our shoes, and have our wives and daughters work in the kitchen." At the time Clay never noticed what the Vermont congressman had inserted into the record. When it finally surfaced during this election, Clay vehemently denied saying any such thing. "I . . . assert, with the utmost confidence, that I never used the words. . . . I am confident of it because I never entertained such a sentiment in my life."[33]

As though to instruct Clay on what ought to be his conduct, the abolitionists rallied behind a former Alabama slaveholder who now fervently opposed slavery, James G. Birney of Michigan. Nominated by the Liberty party, along with Thomas Morris of Ohio for Vice President, Birney siphoned away from Clay many votes from key northern states. Indeed, that was the only reason for his nomination, according to Nathan Sargent. "I am convinced, [Birney] ran for no other purpose than to defeat Mr. Clay," touring in those places where he could do the Whigs the most harm. Clay's distant relative Cassius Marcellus Clay, who was the most outspoken abolitionist in Kentucky, tried to help his cousin by speaking on his behalf among abolitionists in the north. But southern Democrats reprinted some of Cassius's speeches and either claimed he was Clay's son or so garbled the report that some southerners believed the speeches were actually delivered by the candidate himself.[34]

Poor Clay was so misrepresented, so victimized by lying propaganda that he could barely keep up with it in providing responses or corrections or denials. "I believe I have been charged with every crime enumerated in the Decalogue," he told John Clayton.

The Old Coon tried to rise above it. "I laugh at the straights to which our opponents are driven. They are to be pitied. . . . They have no other refuge left but in personal abuse, detraction and defamation."[35]

33. *National Intelligencer,* July 1, 1820; Clay to John White, May 6, 1844, in *The Campaign of 1844,* p. 92; Frankfort *Commonwealth,* July 2, 1844; Clay to A. G. Seckel, August 8, 1844, copy, CPP.

34. Sargent, *Public Men and Events,* II, 242. With respect to the relationship between Clay and Cassius Clay, Kentucky newspapers claimed that it was "very remote. Their fathers were 2nd or 3rd cousins." See Frankfort *Commonwealth,* October 8, 1844. And the Clays from Alabama also claimed kinship. According to C. C. Clay, Jr., his father "& yr. great orator, Henry Clay, were distantly related, but could never trace the relationship." C. C. Clay, Jr., to S. M. Duncan, May 30, 1856, R. Baylor Hickman Collection, Manuscript Department, Filson Club, Louisville, Kentucky.

35. Clay to Clayton, August 22, 1844, Clayton Papers, LC.

Robert Wickliffe, General John M. McCalla, and James Guthrie formed a particularly vicious group of Kentucky scandalmongers. Clay was not only an habitual gambler, they contended, but a chronic liar and an inveterate drunk. McCalla, for example, circulated tales that Clay had gambled on board the steamboat from Wheeling to Maysville every time he returned from Washington—without exception. And when Clay went to Blue Licks in Nicholas County for a few days of rest in late August, McCalla spread the word that he had won several hundred dollars at the gaming tables instead of taking the waters as he claimed.[36]

In order to turn nativist prejudices to Clay's advantage, Whigs planted stories to the effect that Clay wanted to tighten the immigration and naturalization laws. The sharp rise in foreign immigration, especially among Germans and Irish, generated a growing antiforeign and anti-Catholic sentiment in several states. With the outbreak of Catholic-Protestant riots in Philadelphia, nativist resentment produced an organized American Republican party in New York and Pennsylvania demanding stiffer naturalization laws. Whigs in the two states sided with the "Natives." They rather looked down on all immigrants, but especially the Catholic Irish and Germans, and they decried the deleterious influence of immigrants in the political affairs of the big cities, all of which—combined with the dreadful spectacle of the Philadelphia riots—outraged Catholics.

Clay was deluged with requests from both Whigs and Democrats for an opinion on the naturalization laws.[37] "How am I to comply with the wishes of both parties? . . . What right have my opponents to attribute to me a wish to alter the naturalization laws?" Still, he felt he had to say something, but the best he could provide sought to make distinctions between those already naturalized, those awaiting naturalization, and those who might arrive in the future after the passage of a new naturalization law. Then, fearing to offend nativists, he conceded that perhaps some "additional restrictions," such as the extension of the probationary period, might be imposed on the process of naturalization. But he really resented these attempts to introduce new issues into the presidential canvass. "I learn," he told Thomas Ewing, "that representations are industriously made in certain quarters that I am opposed to all foreigners, and that I am in favor of depriving those who have been naturalized of all their rights and priviliges." These were outrageous lies, he said, and should be countered with the many contrary opinions he had expressed in the past. Ewing agreed that he could be easily exonerated, but Frelinghuysen unwittingly complicated the process. The active involvement of the vice presidential candidate with evangelical Protestants offended Catholics, "who are goaded almost to madness by what they consider a concerted attack upon their religious liberty & their

36. Lexington *Observer and Kentucky Reporter,* August 31, 1844.
37. He was even accused of belonging to the Native American party, a charge which he denied. Clay to Andrew G. Burt, October 9, 1844, copy CPP.

political rights." To agree with any statement about modifying the naturaliza-tion laws now, said Ewing, "will be seized upon by our adversaries . . . as an approval of, or a concession to the savage & intolerant spirit by which they were dictated." Say nothing, he counseled Clay. Our friends will understand; our *"enemies . . .* are entitled to no answer."[38]

But the possible defection of Catholics troubled Clay. He asked John Pendleton Kennedy if the Maryland Democrats were engaged in efforts "to unite the Catholics against us? And if so, with what success." Of particular moment was the situation in New York City. So he wrote to Governor Wil-liam H. Seward to get him to speak to Archbishop John Hughes in the city and assure him of Clay's goodwill. Seward had too many engagements to comply personally with the request, and Thurlow Weed was off to the West distribut-ing "funds & documents." Thus John Lee, a former congressman, called on Hughes and carried a letter from the governor and a copy of Clay's letter to Seward.

The archbishop received Lee cordially and asked him to assure the candi-date of his "highest respect," that he recognized the difference between Clay's sentiments "& the sentiments & conduct of the intolerant Whigs." He wished Clay success but gently ventured the opinion that "his brethren would be divided on the Presidential vote."

Hughes's underlying and none-too-subtle message, however, had fright-ening implications. And if too many Catholics sided with the Democrats, the result could be devastating in a very important state. What made it worse, said Seward, was the ever-increasing size of the abolitionist vote in New York. He estimated that it now reached sixteen thousand. If the abolitionists joined the Catholics against the Whigs, the state would be lost. And Birney had made it clear that although both Polk and Clay were slaveowners, abolitionists should "deprecate" Clay's election more than Polk's because the Old Coon was men-tally superior to Young Hickory and could therefore do more harm to their cause. So Seward told Clay that he was chiefly directing his efforts toward inducing the abolitionists "to abandon Birney & vote for you, as the only means of preventing the annexation of Texas."[39]

Like Birney, what many of Clay's critics held against him, it seemed, was his outstanding ability. They did not want a statesman in the White House. They preferred men of lesser talents. Clay "may be a more brilliant orator" than Polk, conceded the Richmond *Enquirer* on October 28, "but we do not want splendid eloquence to conduct the executive department." He may be a

38. Clay to William P. Thomasson, July 8, 1844, Clay to Ewing, June 19, 1844, Ewing to Clay, June 23, 1844, copies CPP. On nativism and the riots of Philadelphia, see Ray Billington, *The Protestant Crusade* (New York, 1938) and Michael Feldberg, *The Philadelphia Riots* (Westport, Conn., 1975).

39. Clay to Kennedy, September 16, 1844, Kennedy Papers, LC; Lee to Clay, November 2, 1844, copies CPP; Dwight L. Dumond, ed., *Letters of James Gillespie Birney, 1831–1857* (New York, 1938), II, 853; Charles Sellers, "The Election of 1844," *History of American Presidential Elections,* ed. Schlesinger and Israel, I, 790.

"more dashing politician" than his opponent, "but we do not want any high flying and daring politician, who soars even beyond the constitution" in pursuit of some "extravagant object. . . . We want no aspiring, 'moon-reaching' president."

Late in the campaign Clay decided to try his hand again at placating both sides of the nativism issue by making another public statement. And, of course, he thought he could do it without incurring the wrath of either the nativists or recent immigrants. He wrote a confidential letter to James Watson Webb, editor of the New York *Courier and Enquirer,* the sense of which he wanted conveyed to his eastern supporters.

> Every pulsation of my heart is American and nothing but American. I am utterly opposed to all foreign influence in every form and shape. I objected in the Senate to Aliens being allowed any privileges under our preemption laws. . . . I am in favor of American industry, American institutions, American order, American liberty. Whilst I entertain all these feelings and sentiments, I wish our Country, forever, to remain a sacred asylum for all unfortunate and oppressed men whether from religious or political causes.[40]

But this letter, so full of patriotic sentiment, could scarcely disguise the fact that a burgeoning alliance between Whigs and nativists was under way, nor could it hide Clay's obvious attempt to appease both sides of an explosive political issue. "The Catholics are with us," cheered Democrat John Catron, "& the other side will keep them so, no fear of that."[41]

Clay had returned to Ashland in late May 1844, and throughout the remainder of the campaign he put in many exhausting hours of mental labor, answering countless letters from local and national politicians, as well as the general public, and writing suggestions to Whig leaders and editors (especially Gales and Seaton of the Washington *National Intelligencer*) on ways to counteract Democratic and abolitionist propaganda. He made a few local public appearances but nothing that could be criticized as outright electioneering. He desperately tried to keep his political wits about him and avoid mistakes that could jeopardize the campaign.

But Polk also showed a keen mind for political strategy. The first thing he did was to declare publicly that he would not seek a second term in office if elected. This action had the happy effect of pulling the party together by encouraging the defeated rivals—Van Buren, Lewis Cass, Buchanan, Calhoun, and others—to support the ticket in the hope of inheriting the Democratic leadership in 1848. He neatly skirted the tariff issue with his Kane letter, and he endorsed the party platform for the reannexation of Texas and the reoccupation of Oregon. Young Hickory also made excellent use of Old Hickory.

---

40. Clay to Webb, October 25, 1844, copy CPP. The reason Clay did not want the letter published was his recent pledge "to the Public to write no more letters for publication, on public affairs, prior to the presidential election." Ibid.

41. Catron to Polk, June 8, 1844, in Polk, *Correspondence,* VII, 215.

Knowing how much the former President hated the Kentuckian, Polk encouraged Jackson to restate publicly his belief in the corrupt bargain. And he also prevailed upon him to talk Tyler out of running as an independent. At first Tyler hesitated, but after thinking it over and pondering Jackson's arguments in favor of retirement, the President agreed. "Your views as to the proper course for me to pursue in the present emergency of public affairs," Tyler wrote Jackson, "has decided me to withdraw from the canvass." He made it official in a public announcement on August 20.[42]

It was now a contest between the Old Coon and the Young Hickory with little thought given to the Liberty party candidate. In fact, many Whigs even found it extremely "difficult . . . to believe that J. K. Polk is serious opposition."[43] Victory seemed absolutely certain. Nevertheless, they tore into the Democrats with a heightened sense of the importance of the election—and a heightened sense of the importance of humbug in winning it. The united Whigs had learned many important lessons about campaigning from their experiences in 1840, and they tried to resurrect most of them. Songs, hats, buttons, canes, snuffboxes, cigar cases, shaving mugs, banners, campaign ribbons, Clay Clubs, parades, barbecues, and, of course, the "coon" played an important role in winning the attention of the electorate and attracting votes. And Clay balls became quite the fashion. Harrison had been sung into the presidency, noted Philip Hone, and "if Mr. Clay should succeed it will be effected in some degree by dancing."

But Clay was no Tippecanoe, and 1844 was a pale imitation of the log cabin campaign. For one thing, Clay's stature as a statesman and peacemaker militated against successfully utilizing his image for the shenanigans of a mindless campaign. Still, the Whigs did their best.[44]

> The skies are bright, our hearts are light
> In Baltimore the Whigs unite,
> We'll set our songs to good old tunes
> For there is music in these "Coons."
> Hurrah! Hurrah! the country's risin'
> For Henry Clay and Frelinghuysen.

At barbecues the faithful were encouraged to sing all the new campaign songs:

> Hurrah for Henry Clay,
> Nobody care for Tyler,

---

42. Charles Sellers, *James K. Polk: Continentalist, 1843–1846* (Princeton, 1966), 114; Jackson to Polk July 26, 1844, Polk Papers, LC; Tyler to Jackson, August 18, 1844, in Jackson, *Correspondence,* VI, 315.

43. John M. Morehead to Clay, October 29, 1844, Clay Papers, LC.

44. Hone, *Diary,* II, 652–653. An excellent summary of the paraphernalia used in this campaign may be found in Roger A. Fischer, *Tippecanoe and Trinkets Too: The Material Culture of American Presidential Campaigns, 1828–1984* (Urbana and Chicago, 1988), pp. 49–59.

> Van Buren's out of the way
> And Polk will soon burst his boiler.

> You'd better keep your Polk away
> Or we will cover him o'er with Clay;
> The Coons will never stop or balk
> But eat up *berries, Polk and stalk.*

Poor Clay. These were hardly comparable with the rousing and delightful "Tippecanoe and Tyler, Too," or "Van, Van Is a Used Up Man" songs. Perhaps the most popular of the lot was this one:

> The moon was shining silver bright,
> The stars with glory crowned the night,
> High on a limb that "same old coon,"
> Was singing to himself this tune:—

> Get out of the way, you're all unlucky,
> Clear the tracks for old Kentucky.

The jokes and cartoons were not much better. The coon symbol helped somewhat, and the chicken was made to represent the Democrats. Stories about tying a live rooster in a basket on top of a "loco pole" and a tied coon at the end of another pole brought the obvious conclusion. "Cooney's appetite made him uncomfortable and he gnawed his way to freedom, went up the loco pole, and made short work of the chicken."[45]

It soon became apparent that the Whig campaign lacked "excitement, zeal, or clamor for Clay, neither on the water nor on the land." No Clay flags decorated the "towns, cities and boat-landings," reported one man, at least none from Nashville to Philadelphia. The "gloss is worn off of Clay," William Marcy assured Polk. "The attempt to get up something like the log cabin *fooleries* has thus far failed."[46]

If nothing else, Clay had the women's vote. "The ladies were all 'Clay men,'" marveled Nathan Sargent with a straight face, even though their husbands, fathers, and brothers preferred Polk. The wife of Hendrick B. Wright— the man who presided over the National Democratic Convention!—organized a group of women who prepared Clay badges, flags, and banners. "Though my husband is a *Polk* man," asserted Mrs. Wright, "I am a *Clay* man; in fact, the ladies are all Clay men. The Whigs are to have a great gathering . . . and we ladies, several of us the wives of Polk men, are preparing banners and badges for the occasion." She offered one "of our most beautiful Clay rosettes" to an astonished Pennsylvania Democrat. "You ought to delight to follow so noble a chief as Henry Clay," she scolded him.

---

45. *Campaign of 1844,* passim; see also various issues during the summer of the Lexington *Observer and Kentucky Reporter* and the Frankfort *Commonwealth.*
46. Samuel H. Laughlin to Polk, June 28, 1844, Marcy to Polk, June 28, 1844, in Polk, *Correspondence,* VII, 293–294, 297.

What a pity for the Old Coon that it took another seventy and more years before passage of the Nineteenth Amendment gave women the right to vote.[47]

Despite Whig efforts to re-create another log cabin campaign, there were a number of serious and intelligent attempts to win support for the Whig ticket. John P. Kennedy brought out a splendid *Defense of the Whigs,* which described the evolution of Whig economic thought from James Madison's program of 1815. He also pointed out the migration of Federalists into the Jackson party. "I have read it with uncommon satisfaction," Clay wrote the author. "It is composed with great ability." A "cheap edition" should be published, he advised, and placed "in the hands of and studied by all the Clubs." Clay also provided an anecdote for a future edition about how Federalists became Jacksonians. It seems Federalists joined the general because they knew him to be "a rash intemperate and violent man, and if elected, would throw every thing into confusion, and the Federalists might again get into power!" Laughed Clay: "There was patriotism for you!"[48]

But the electorate had its mind on something besides Whig principles, songs, coons, roosters, and the like. Texas and slavery increasingly commanded national attention. When the treaty of annexation, signed by representatives of Texas and the United States, went to the Senate for ratification, it was accompanied by a letter written by the new secretary of state, John C. Calhoun, to the British minister to Washington, Richard Pakenham. In the letter Calhoun deliberately raised the dread issue of slavery. He contended that the treaty had been signed to protect American slavery from British efforts to emancipate slaves in Texas and advance the cause of universal abolition. The treaty represented U.S. efforts to block that "reprehensible" intention. In effect Calhoun had placed annexation *"exclusively* upon the ground of *protection* of *Slavery* in the *Southern States!"* And a great many men knew his reason—or thought they did. He planned to kill the treaty with his letter, they said, because he knew it would "drive off every Northern man from the reannexation" and give him "a pretext to unite the whole South upon himself as the Champion of its cause." That way he could create a Southern Confederacy and "make himself the great man of this fragment."[49]

Whatever Calhoun's reasons, the letter killed the treaty. On June 8, to hardly anyone's surprise, the Senate rejected it by the vote of thirty-five to sixteen. The Whigs and northern Van Buren men united against it, but blame for the defeat was laid directly at the feet of John C. Calhoun. He meant all along to keep Texas out of the Union, Jackson was told, in order "to make it a means of seperation between the slave holding and non Slave-holding States and part of a New Confederacy of the former."[50]

47. Sargent, *Public Men and Events,* II, 245–246. See also Hone, *Diary,* II, 653.

48. *Defense of the Whigs* (New York, 1844), which later appeared in an inexpensively bound pamphlet edition by Horace Greeley. Clay to Kennedy, June 10, 1844, copy CPP.

49. William B. Lewis to Jackson, April 26, 1844, Francis Blair to Jackson, May 2, 19, 1844, Jackson Papers, LC.

50. Blair to Jackson, July 7, 1844, Jackson Papers, LC.

Clay expressed delight in the treaty's defeat—he called it "Mr. Tyler's abominable treaty"[51]—and hoped at last the issue would disappear, at least until after the election. But instead of keeping quiet, as his supporters repeatedly advised, he once again wrote a letter and once again splattered himself with the ink of controversy.

Stephen F. Miller, editor of the Tuscaloosa *Monitor,* sent him an editorial he had printed in his paper on June 19. The article attempted to contradict the construction given by southern Democrats to a particular passage in Clay's Raleigh letter in which he used the term "Confederacy." But Miller went on to say in his letter to Clay that the Texas question "is pushed here with great assiduity by the Democrats" because they have no other grounds with which to attack their opponents.[52] Some very sound southern Whigs truly regretted Clay's Raleigh letter, he continued, in that "you did not leave a door open for annexation at a future time." Many months ago Clay could have won Alabama easily in a contest with Van Buren, but now Democrats "boast that Polk and Texas will sweep the state."[53]

Clay responded immediately in what came to be called his first Alabama letter. And no one who read it after publication doubted for a minute that in writing it, he was trying desperately to reclaim the South by softening his stand against annexation. "Personally, I could have no objection to the annexation of Texas," he declared, "but I certainly would be unwilling to see the existing Union dissolved or seriously jeoparded· for the sake of acquiring Texas."[54]

That single sentence shocked and outraged northerners at the same time it offended southerners. It straddles the issue, his critics contended, he has pulled back from his original position. He wants it both ways: appease southerners about annexation at some future date, and reassure northerners about his opposition to annexation at the present time. "Mr Clays letter has caused much depression, & some consternation, among his friends," Edward Curtis reported to Webster, "& great exulatation among his enemies." It was, said another, "Mr. Clay's political death-warrant."[55]

What Clay really tried to assert in this letter was his belief that annexation would come in due course but that it should be done at the proper time and in an intelligent, controlled, and carefully directed fashion. It should not come about because of some wild expansionist craze for additional territory that would promote disharmony within the nation, precipitate an international crisis, and possibly undermine the orderly development of the market revolu-

51. Clay to Stephen H. Miller, July 1, 1844, in Clay, *Works,* IV, 490–491.

52. Even the tariff "has lost its terrors with the people," said Miller, since it is now better understood.

53. Miller to Clay, June 20, 1844, in Stephen F. Miller, *The Bench and Bar of Georgia* (Philadelphia, 1858), II, 386–387.

54. Clay to Miller, July 1, 1844, in Clay, *Works,* IV, 490–491.

55. Curtis to Webster, September 1, 1844, in Webster, *Papers, Correspondence,* VI, 53; Sargent, *Public Men and Events,* II, 244.

tion that was so essential for everyone's future prosperity and happiness.[56]

Although Clay no doubt hoped to salvage his deteriorating electoral position by writing this letter, he was not motivated solely by a pragmatic bid for votes. His was a courageous and farsighted warning about how the nation could be polarized between two sections over the issue and thereby jeopardize, if not terminate, the continued existence of the Union. Unfortunately that was not what many interpreted as the meaning of his letter, and he succeeded only in driving away both pro- and antiannexationists.[57]

When it became clear that the letter did not have the effect he intended, Clay claimed he was misinterpreted. So he wrote a second letter on July 27 in a brave but foolish attempt to eliminate any misunderstanding about where he stood. This time it went to Thomas M. Peters and John M. Jackson and was published in the Tuscumbia *North Alabamian* on August 16, 1844. This time he inflicted on himself a mortal wound.

He began by providing a short history of how he had authorized an overture to Mexico to reacquire Texas when he was the secretary of state. Nothing came of this overture because Mexico repeatedly declared that it considered annexation an act of war. "I thought then, and still believe," wrote Clay, "that national dishonor, foreign war, and distraction and division at home were too great sacrifices to make for the acquisition of Texas."

But what would he do if elected President? To that question he said he had no hesitation in declaring that "far from having any personal objection to the annexation of Texas, I should be glad to see it, without dishonor—without war, with the common consent of the Union, and upon just and fair terms." As for slavery, he did not think it would affect the question, one way or another. "It is destined," he wrote, "to become extinct, at some distant day, in my opinion, by the operation of the inevitable laws of population"—that is, at some future period the country would be overwhelmingly populated with white citizens, thus driving down the price of labor so that free labor would become cheaper than slave labor. Therefore, he concluded, with respect to the annexation of Texas, he would be guided, if elected, by the state of public opinion existing at the time. He would be governed by his "paramount duty of preserving the Union entire, and in harmony."

The Whigs despaired. The Democrats rejoiced. "Things look blue," groaned Thurlow Weed. "Ugly letter, that to Alabama." Seward agreed. "Every body droops, despairs. . . . It jeopards, perhaps loses the State." The letters, said John C. Wright, had "given the rascals a new impulse. Liberty men, Locofocos and timid Whigs use the letter as bug-a-boo to the anti-annexation." The "public mind is excited," he added, ". . . is feverish, and unstable." Joshua Giddings told Clay the same thing and claimed the letters had produced a very unfavorable impression in Ohio. And Pennsylvania had

---

56. Morrison, "Westward the Curse of Empire," pp. 224, 230, 231.
57. Poage, *Clay and Whig Party,* pp. 143–144.

the same reaction. Clay "is as rotten as a stagnant fish pond, on the subject of Slavery & always has been," wrote one antislavery former congressman. "Confound him and all his compromises from first to last—he is just the man to make some diabolical compromise by which the lone star shall have a place in our galaxy."[58]

Again, it was a courageous, if misbegotten, statement of his moderate position. But it was unrealistic of him to try to divorce slavery from Texas. The two were inextricably bound together by this time. Even so, Clay recognized clearly that the slavery issue could destroy his party and the Union, and he tried desperately to separate it from the Texas issue, for which there now appeared to be a mounting and irresistible national desire.

Clay spent the next several weeks trying to assure everyone that his Alabama letters in no way conflicted with the Raleigh letter. "Could I say less? Can it be expected that I should put myself in opposition to the concurrent will of the whole nation?" Still, with all the unfavorable reaction pouring in on him, Clay continued to believe that the Texas question would do him no harm and "that we shall get a majority of ⅔ of the slave states."[59]

The Alabama letters irreparably undermined Clay's candidacy. He was accused of waffling, of saying anything to win votes.

> He wires in and wires out,
> And leaves the people still in doubt,
> Whether the snake that made the track
> Was going South, or coming back.

To make matters worse, Clay got into a controversy with his abrant cousin Cassius M. Clay, who had published a letter in the New York *Tribune* of August 13 in which he predicted that the candidate would lose three or four slave states because of his opposition to annexation. Moreover—and this really knifed poor Clay even though it was unintentional—C. M. Clay said the candidate was no emancipationist, "but I believe his feelings are with the cause. I know that those most immediately within his influence approximate to myself in sentiment upon the subject of slavery." Let no one mistake the real issue of this campaign, he wrote. It was *"Polk, slavery, and Texas"* versus *"Clay, Union, and liberty."*

Such a political gaffe, however unintended, required immediate repudiation. In an unequivocal statement to the Lexington *Observer and Kentucky*

58. Weed to Granger, September 3, 1844, Granger Papers, Buffalo Historical Society; Seward to Weed, September 2, 1844, Weed Papers, University of Rochester Library; Wright to Clay, September 5, 1844, in Clay, *Works,* IV, 492–493; Poage, *Clay and Whig Party,* pp. 145–146; Clay to Giddings, September 11, 1844, in George W. Julian, *The Life of Joshua R. Giddings* (Chicago, 1892), pp. 164–165.
59. Clay to Epes Sargent, August 7, 1844, copy CPP. Clay said he expected the Whigs to win New York, Pennsylvania, Virginia, and Ohio. He lost all but Ohio. Clay to William B. Campbell, October 26, 1844, copy CPP. See also Clay's letters to Edgar Atwater, September 18, 1844, and John Purdue and G. S. Orth, September 19, 1844, in *Kendall's Expositor,* October 22, 1844.

Reporter, published on September 4, Clay provided it: "MR. C. M. CLAY'S LET-
TER WAS WRITTEN WITHOUT MY KNOWLEDGE, WITHOUT ANY CONSULTATION
FROM ME, AND WITHOUT ANY AUTHORITY FROM ME. . . . SO FAR AS HE VENTURES
TO INTERPRET MY FEELINGS, HE HAS ENTIRELY MISCONCEIVED THEM. I BELIEVE
HIM TO BE EQUALLY MISTAKEN AS TO THOSE IN THE CIRCLE OF MY PERSONAL
FRIENDS AND NEIGHBORS, GENERALLY."

Clay went on to explain once again his real position on slavery and emancipation; but enormous harm had been done his cause, and nothing he could
do would repair it. Not much later the Democrats intercepted a private letter
Clay had written to his cousin in which he complained that in the South he was
described as an abolitionist and in the North as an "ultra supporter of the
institution of slavery." He was neither, he said. C. M. Clay apologized to him
and assured him of his friendly intentions, but with such friends the Old Coon
was surely headed for political extinction.[60]

Finally Clay was obliged—no doubt at the extreme urging of his supporters—to write to the editor of the Washington *National Intelligencer* and give
a pledge that he would speak out no more on national issues until after
the election. He reaffirmed his opposition to Texas—as though retracting the
Alabama letters—and regretted that he was so misunderstood around the
country. This final letter left the unfortunate impression that Clay had lost
control of his own campaign. He seemed irresolute, undecided, hesitant, no
longer the great statesman but a worn-out political hack.[61]

Two weeks prior to the election Clay still believed he would win—and
maybe improve on Harrison's showing in 1840. Overconfident, consumed
with desire for the presidency, unable to recognize the political reality of Texas
and abolition, insisting on the preeminence of such issues as the Bank, tariff,
and land sales, and incapable of believing the American people would choose a
lesser man over himself, Henry Clay went down to ignominious defeat. For
the third and last time the American people rejected him as their President.

It was shattering and overwhelming, the more so because it was totally
unexpected. "A mere *Tom Tit,*" had triumphed over the "old Eagle," groaned
John Quincy Adams.[62] "Henry Clay, the man of giant intellect . . . the orator
and the statesman . . . has fallen, never, in all probability, to rise," wrote the
Frankfort *Commonwealth* on December 3. "James K. Polk, the pigmy in intellect, the mistrusted of his own neighbors—without principles—the mere politician . . . is elevated to the highest office in the gift of the American people."

Andrew Jackson exulted. Clay "is really a *dead Coon,*" he had written two
years earlier. Now he knew it had finally come to pass. "I thank my god that the

60. Poage, *Clay and Whig Party,* p. 147; Clay to C. M. Clay, September 18, 1844, in Cassius M.
Clay, *The Life of Cassius Marcellus Clay* (Cincinnati, 1886), pp. 101–102. See also S. Starkweather
to Mangum, September 30, 1844, in Mangum, *Papers,* IV, 201. See also Stanley Carton, "Cassius
Marcellus Clay, "Antislavery Whig in the Presidential Campaign of 1844," *Register of the Kentucky
Historical Society,* LXVIII (January 1970), pp. 17–36.
61. The letter was published in the *Intelligencer* on October 1, 1844.
62. Adams, *Memoirs,* XII, 103.

Republic is safe & that he had permitted me to live to see it, & rejoice," the dying man declared. "I can say in language of Simeon of old, Let thy servant depart in peace, as I have seen the salvation of the liberty of my country and the perpetuity of our Glorious Union."[63]

But it was a close election—very close. Polk's percentage of the popular vote stood at a mere 1.4 percent over Clay's—that is, 1,337,243 for Polk, and 1,299,062 for Clay. Only 38,181 votes separated the two. Birney received 62,-300 votes. The vote in the electoral college, however, was much wider. Polk received 170 votes to Clay's 105.

Clay captured eleven states. At the start of the campaign he could count on Kentucky and the New England states, minus Maine and New Hampshire, where the Democrats had strong organizations, for a total of 40 votes. He had expected his southern tours to strengthen his position in that section of the country, but his Raleigh and Alabama letters surely caused him grave injury. "I [have] been among the common people & I live with them & talk with them," wrote one Alabama planter. "I know their views and . . . reasons for voting for Polk. ¼ of the vote in the Dist went for him on account of Texas. They say the poor man can get lands cheap & all this sort of talk if Texas is anext."[64] Of the southern states, only North Carolina supported Clay. He also won Tennessee—Polk's own state. In the past Tennesseans had twice rejected Polk's gubernatorial bid, and now they handed him an additional humiliation. Clay also took New Jersey, Delaware, Maryland, and Ohio. All the rest went to Polk.

Clay's critical losses were Pennsylvania and New York: Pennsylvania by 6,332 votes and New York by 5,106 votes. And New York, with its sizable thirty-six electoral votes, might have been salvaged. Polk won it by slightly more than 5,000 votes, with Birney taking a whopping 15,812 (including many Whigs) who might have gone to Clay. The addition of New York's vote would have given Clay the election.[65]

"The partial associations of Native Americans, Irish Catholics, abolition societies, liberty party, the Pope of Rome, the Democracy of the sword, and the dotage of a ruffian [Andrew Jackson]," declared John Q. Adams, defeated the Great Pacificator, and they "are sealing the fate of this nation, which nothing less than the interposition of Omnipotence can save."[66]

63. Jackson to Blair, October 29, 1842, Jackson to Kendall, November 23, 1844, Jackson Papers, LC; Jackson to Andrew J. Donelson, December 2, 1844, Donelson Papers, LC. In a letter to Van Buren, Jackson had written: "The old coon is really and substantially dead, skinned and buried. Clays political career is closed forever—he must now really retire upon ashland there to repent of all the evils he has brought, and attempt to bring, upon the country." November 22, 1842, Van Buren Papers, LC. To Blair, Jackson added: "Mr. Clay will now have leisure to take care of his fences, and short horn Durhams." November 29, 1844, Jackson Papers, LC.

64. H. C. Cummingham to Alexander H. Stephens, December 21, 1844, quoted in Morrison, "Westward the Curse of Empire," p. 246.

65. Michigan also provided a narrow victory for Polk. He received 27,759 votes to Clay's 24,337, a difference of 3,422 votes. Birney garnered 3,570 votes. Michigan had only five electoral votes so its capture alone by Clay would not have changed the outcome. These electoral returns can be found in Schlesinger and Israel, eds., *History of American Presidential Elections*, I, 861.

66. Adams, *Memoirs*, XII, 110.

The Whigs in New York attributed their defeat to the "abolitionists and foreign Catholics." Birney sold out to locofocoism, wrote Millard Fillmore, and "our opponents by pointing to the native Americans and to Mr. Freling-huysen, drove the foreign catholics from us, and defeated us in this state." As president of the American Tract Society, former president of the General Union for the Promotion of the Christian Sabbath, vice-president of the American Sunday School Union, and soon-to-be president of the American Bible Society, Frelinghuysen automatically offended Catholics. Martin John Spalding, the future archbishop of Baltimore and a Kentuckian by birth who admired Clay, declared he would vote for Prince Hal but not Frelinghuysen. Informed that he could not vote for one without the other, Spalding responded: "Then I shall not vote for Mr. Clay."[67]

One thing should be clear, Ambrose Spencer told Clay: "The naturalization laws must be altered . . . & the door forever shut on the admission of foreigners to citizenship, or that they undergo a long probation—I am for the former." Germans and Irish "can never understandingly exercise the franchise," he went on; because of "their ignorance [they] are naturally inclined to go with the loafers of our own population."[68]

William Seward also conceded that the "jealousy" of Whigs against foreigners and Catholics, the "unhappy tragedy" in Philadelphia, which awakened religious prejudices, and the readiness of Whigs to express their approval of changing the naturalization laws in preparation for disfranchising citizens already naturalized roused "the entire population" against Clay. In addition—although Seward did not say so explicitly—the candidate's unbelievably inept handling of the Texas issue drove any number of New York antislavery men out of the Whig and into the Liberty party.[69]

Clay replied to Seward that he felt "the severity of the blow most intensely . . . [and] still more for my country and my friends." He himself described "the general wreck of our Cause" to "a most extraordinary combination of adverse circumstances. If there had been no Native party . . . or if the recent foreigners had not been all united against us; or if the foreign Catholics had not been arrayed on the other side; or if the Abolitionists had been true to their avowed principles; or if there had been no frauds, we should have triumphed."[70] If.

As in almost every election in American history there had been frauds—on both sides. But in this election several instances undoubtedly altered the

67. Fillmore to Clay, November 11, 1844, Clay Papers, LC; Sargent, *Public Men and Events,* II, 249. Martin John Spalding was consecrated a bishop in 1848 and appointed archbishop of Baltimore in 1864. In 1844 he was engaged in pastoral work in Lexington and Louisville and had won a popular following as a lecturer in the United States and Canada.

68. Spencer to Clay, November 21, 1844, Clay Papers, LC.

69. Seward to Clay, November 7, 1844, Seward Papers, University of Rochester Library.

70. Clay to Seward, November 20, 1844, in Frederick W. Seward, ed., *Autobiography of William H. Seward* . . . (New York, 1877), pp. 733–734; Clay to Clayton, December 2, 1844, Clayton Papers, LC. Clay also believed that if Clayton had been nominated for the vice presidency in Baltimore the "Catholics would not have been so united against us, and I am not sure that a different issue of the election might not have taken place."

final outcome. In Louisiana, for example, the state was clearly lost to Clay because of fraudulent voting. John Slidell organized the Creoles in New Orleans and sent "a steamboat load of roughs" from the city to "colonize" Plaquemine Parish and thereby "secured the defeat of Henry Clay in Louisiana." Also, in New York City some fifty-five hundred immigrants (mostly Catholics) had been naturalized in the three months prior to the election, "and about twice that number in other parts of the State, ninety nine-hundredths of whom of course voted against us." According to Epes Sargent, "We have been robbed of our lawful President by the seven thousand fraudulent votes cast for Mr. Polk in this city [New York]." On the other hand, claimed Philip Hone, New York merchants, professional men, and those who worked by their skill and went "to church on Sundays, respect[ed] the laws and love[d] their Country" voted for Clay. Four years later Clay himself included Pennsylvania as a state also lost to him by fraud. James Buchanan went around the state stumping for Polk and insisting "that Mr. Polk *was* a *tariff* man, and a *better one* than Mr. Clay," even though he knew full well that Polk opposed "the whole doctrine of protection." He *"intentionally"* deceived the people of Pennsylvania. "What is to be apprehended," Clay declared, "is that he [Zachary Taylor, the Whig candidate in 1848] may be cheated out of Penna, as I was in 1844."[71]

Whigs around the country commiserated with the defeated statesman. Frelinghuysen told him to look to a brighter future and accept the loss with Christian fortitude and resignation. "As sinners, who have rebelled against our Maker we need a Saviour or we must perish. . . . Let us then repair to Him. He, will never fail us, in the hour of peril & trial."[72]

Philip Hone said something very prophetic. "The result of this election has satisfied me that no such man as Henry Clay can ever be President of the United States. The party leaders, the men who make a President, will never consent to elevate one greatly their superior." Besides, a statesman takes a position on all the leading issues and consequently makes enemies in different states. "What is meat in one section is poison in another." So it will probably happen again in the future that the best men will be shunted aside in favor of those less conspicuous and less talented.[73]

President John Tyler gloated. "My own opinion is that we had better now leave off abusing Mr. Clay altogether," the President wrote. "He is dead and let him rest."[74] Other men wept. Congressman Augustine H. Shepperd of North Carolina wrung his hands over the fact that Henry Clay "could get more men

71. Poore, *Reminiscences,* I, 528; Central Clay Committee of New York City to Clay, March 4, 1845, in Lexington *Observer and Kentucky Reporter,* March 22, 1844, copy CPP; *Niles' Weekly Register,* November 2, 1844; Sargent to Clay, November 26, 1844, Hone to Clay, November 28, 1844, Clay Papers, LC; Sargent, *Public Men and Events,* II, 240; Clay to P. R. Fendall, October 28, 1848, Miscellaneous Clay Papers, Filson Club, Louisville, Kentucky; Frankfort *Commonwealth,* November 19, 1844.
72. Frelinghuysen to Clay, November 9, 1844, Clay Papers, LC.
73. Hone to Clay, November 28, 1844, Clay Papers, LC.
74. Tyler to J. B. Jones, [1844], in Tyler, *Letters,* III, 114. Earlier Tyler called Clay "the most obnoxious man in the Union. Tyler to Mrs. Waller, September 13, 1844, ibid., III, 155.

to run after him to hear him speak, and fewer to vote for him, than any man in America." Others predicted the inevitable demise of the Whig party as well. After all, Clay and the party were virtually synonymous, and the latter could never survive without him. "When he disappears from the publick stage," Calhoun prophesied, "the Whig party will disperse and new political combinations must follow." For Calhoun, the Great Compromiser had always been a "great disturbing power" in the councils of government, distracting the South and blocking the West from "its true position." Calhoun's contention had great merit. Without Clay, or someone of his stature and strength, the Whig party could never survive its many distractions and afflictions.[75]

Most Whigs placed the horrendous defeat directly on Clay's shoulders. His entire political life, they said, repeated the same deadly faults and "has caused most of his own mortifications; as well, as kept the whigs out of power"—to wit, "a determination to *lead,* rather than to be advised . . . to *originate* and *stamp,* upon his friends, all the measures of his party, to be advocated." And, perhaps most deadly of all, "he was always too ambitious."[76]

Daniel Webster agreed. Although he conceded the many complex factors involved in the defeat, he thought that Clay bore a major portion of the responsibility for the disaster. "He would have triumphed over all these things," Webster wrote to Edward Everett, "but for two causes;—his Alabama letter,—& a general feeling throughout many parts of the Country . . . that his temper was bad—resentful, violent, & unforgiving."[77]

And Clay talked too much and wrote too many letters, all of which conjured up in the minds of the electorate a man who would say and do anything to win the White House. Many voters believed that in his efforts over the years to compromise opposing positions he had repeatedly and cynically shifted his positions to advance his political ambitions. He "wired in and wired out" on too many issues, like slavery, annexation, and the tariff. He could not be trusted.

The loss of the presidency caused Clay infinite pain. "I will not disguise, my dear friend," he wrote to Mary Bayard, "that I felt the severity of that blow, more perhaps because two weeks ago it was altogether unexpected by me here." To another he wrote: "My own heart has bled and still bleeds for my Country, for my friends, and for myself, although it is perhaps to me of no great importance." He had expected to be a "humble instrument" to bring the government back to its former purity and provide a degree of justice to "able,

75. Seager, "Henry Clay and the Politics of Compromise and Non-Compromise," p. 6; Calhoun to Francis Wharton, September 17, 1844, in J. Franklin Jameson, ed., *Correspondence of John C. Calhoun, Annual Report of the American Historical Association for the Year 1899* (Washington, 1900), II, 616–617.

76. John Wilson to Mangum, September 9, 1846, in Mangum, *Papers,* IV, 484.

77. Webster to Everett, December 15, 1844, in Webster, *Papers, Correspondence,* VI, 63. Interestingly, the Boston *Morning Chronicle* on November 27 attributed the defeat first to the congressional session of 1841, next to the nomination of the Old Coon, then "Henry Clay's moral character," and finally to the treatment of the Liberty party by the Whigs.

enlightened, and patriotic friends. That hope is now forever fled."[78]

In public he hid his sorrow. "I see him daily," said his friend and neighbor Leslie Combs, "& my heart bleeds when I look upon his noble countenance—serene & calm as a summer day. No mock-heroic disdain of popular approbation & yet a high consciousness of unrewarded public services & unappreciated merit. I never saw him bear so lofty a presence. He utters no complaint, although he considers himself forever off the public stage."

To a group of friends who visited him Clay claimed to be relieved from a "load of anxiety. . . . Now, I hope to spend the remainder of my days in peace and quiet."

"Great God," shouted one man, "to what degradation has our country brought herself?"[79]

Many others had the same thought. "The malign influence which wrought Mr. Van Buren's overthrow in the Convention, being now triumphant," editorialized the *National Intelligencer,* "menaces the peace of the country. . . . All social institutions and the harmony at least of the whole social structure is endangered."[80]

Looking at a Democratic victory banner waving over the slave market in Washington, a Whig from Vermont bitterly exclaimed: "That flag means *Texas,* and *Texas* means *civil war,* before we have done with it."[81]

78. Clay to Bayard, November 18, 1844, private collection, copy CPP; Clay to Joseph Hoxie, December 4, 1844, copy CPP.
79. Combs to W. W. Boardman, November 28, 1844, Miscellaneous Papers, Manuscript Department, Filson Club, Louisville, Kentucky; speech by Clay, ca. mid-November 1844, unknown to Clay, November 12, 1844, copies CPP.
80. November 11, 1844.
81. Quoted in Sellers, *Polk, Continentalist,* p 159.

THIRTY-SEVEN

"This Most Unnecessary and Horrible War with Mexico"

ONE OUGHT NEVER to speculate on what might have been. It is an idle exercise. But sometimes the possibilities are so enticing and so fateful to the course of history that they cannot be resisted.[1] The election of 1844 provides one such example. Had a third of Birney's New York votes (or approximately five thousand) gone to Clay, not only would the outcome have seated the Kentuckian in the White House, but the Texas question would have been handled in a more conciliatory manner and the Mexican War might never have occurred. Without that war and the enormous increase of territory it provided, the nation would not have quarreled over dividing the ceded territory between what would be open or closed to slavery. Clay himself later mused about what might have been. Had he defeated Polk, he wrote, "there would have been no annexation of Texas, no war with Mexico, no National debt . . . no imputation against us, by the united voice of all the nations of the earth, of a spirit of aggression and inordinate Territorial aggrandizement."[2] The only thing Clay did not mention, for the obvious reason that he was dead when it happened, was the real possibility, as some commentators later claimed, that there might never have been a Civil War.[3]

1. In writing *Public Men and Events,* Nathan Sargent also felt obliged to conjecture on what might have occurred to the history of the United States if Clay had won election, II, 253.
2. Clay to Epes Sargent, February 15, 1847, copy CPP. Clay also said he would have "preserved the protective system" and advanced internal improvements. Clay to Sylvester Schenck, April 8, 1847, New York *Tribune,* August 4, 1875, copy CPP; Clay to ?, April 8, 1847, *National Intelligencer,* April 27, 1847.
3. In 1867 Henry C. Carey, the distinguished economist and journalist, argued that there would have been no Civil War if Clay had beaten Polk in 1844. Howe, *Political Culture of American Whigs,* p. 120.

But Clay did lose the election. He never had the chance to be that "humble instrument, in the hands of Providence" by which the government could be restored to its former purity and the country "saved from the impending dangers."[4] He never had the chance to help steer the nation toward nonviolent emancipation. In three presidential elections the American people rejected him. The first two times he ran against an impossible hero, a man of towering popularity. But how could he lose a third time? And against a relative unknown and one widely believed to be third-rate?[5] In large measure the fault was his own. His character defects, as Webster mentioned in his letter to Edward Everett, were such as to turn the electorate away from him.[6] Many Americans loved him, of course, but many more distrusted him.[7] He always appeared cocky and overconfident, as though he were doing the people a favor by running for office. That was certainly true in 1844. Whereas Andrew Jackson virtually made himself synonymous with the masses and genuinely enjoyed meeting them, Henry Clay did not. Clay seemed disappointed in the American people because they failed to appreciate his great sacrifices on their behalf. They failed to comprehend the program he had devised for their benefit and the benefit of future generations. They failed to acknowledge his efforts to resolve differences and find compromises to avoid conflict and restore peace and harmony. They failed to adequately recognize his statesmanship. Clay always knew he possessed talents far exceeding those of anyone else of his generation. And it showed. He invariably behaved as though he knew what was best for the American people, whether they agreed or not. This condescension, this superior tone, this arrogance seemed to suggest a basic mistrust of the people's capacity for self-government. With time, ordinary citizens sensed his prejudices, his attitudes, and his lack of "sincerity" and consequently refused him the one office he desired above all others.

But Jackson also behaved as though he knew what was best for the people, such as his decision to destroy the United States Bank and remove the Indians west of the Mississippi River. Yet with all of Jackson's arrogance and domineering presumptions he constantly and loudly professed his belief in the people. He saturated his public and private papers with his commitment to democracy. "The people are sovereign," he repeated again and again. "Their will is absolute." He honestly believed this, and the people recognized it, believed him sincere, and therefore trusted him. No such democratic sentiment appears regularly in Clay's public or private pronouncements. When they do emerge, they have neither the fervor nor the intensity of Jackson's. Clay did frequently speak with patriotic enthusiasm and zest, and there can be no question that he loved his country and worked strenuously to preserve the Union. But democracy? He really preferred a more republican system in which

4. Clay to Crittenden, November 28, 1844, Crittenden Papers, LC.

5. Frankfort *Commonwealth,* November 19, 1844.

6. Webster to Everett, December 15, 1844, in Webster, *Papers, Correspondence,* VI, 63.

7. As Harriet Martineau once said, "Mr. Clay never satisfied me of his sincerity on the great question [slavery] of his time." Martineau, *Autobiography* (Boston, 1877), I, 379.

an oligarchy of talent and wealth would have the controlling voice.[8]

Still, if Clay could not match Jackson's exalted commitment to democratic rule, he was light-years ahead of him on the question of slavery. Clay truly abhorred the "peculiar institution" and hoped to have a hand in leading the nation back to accepting the inevitability of eventual emancipation. He was the president of the American Colonization Society, which sponsored the removal of free blacks to Liberia,[9] and although his health forced him to miss many of its annual meetings, he remained its president to the end of his life. But in attempting to neutralize the annexation question with his Alabama letters in order to prevent the issue of slavery from destroying the Union, he suffered a humiliating electoral defeat.

Clay also emancipated "some eight or ten" of his own slaves. In fact, a month following his defeat in 1844 he freed his manservant Charles Dupuy.[10] Jackson, on the other hand, accepted the "peculiar institution" as part of the "great compromise" that brought about the Constitution. He never freed a single slave, and sometimes he threatened his blacks with unspeakable cruelty.[11]

The weeks and months following his narrow defeat were very difficult for Clay. Not a day passed without friends, neighbors, politicians, and perfect strangers trooping to his home to express their heartfelt sorrow over the outcome of the election. "I am endeavoring to separate myself as much as I can from this world," he told Epes Sargent, "but, in spite of all my wishes for seclusion, great numbers call to see me at this place, and as I know that their purpose is friendly and respectful, I have not the heart to receive or treat them unkindly." And no sooner did the pain of defeat begin to abate than he would

8. Remini, *Legacy of Andrew Jackson*, pp. 7–44. During the debate in 1842 over Clay's resolution to limit the President's veto power, Calhoun chided him for suggesting that the majority spoke for the nation. Clay backed off somewhat by insisting "that he meant a majority according to the forms of the Constitution." *Congressional Globe*, 27th Congress, 2d session, appendix, p. 164, note.

9. It was suggested to him that one of the islands of the Pacific Ocean might be a better place to send free blacks since they seemed reluctant to return to Africa. Clay thought it a poor suggestion. "With respect to the repugnance of the Free blacks to going to Africa, it arises out of their disinclination to leaving the place of their nativity. They would, in the sequel, be equally opposed to going to the Pacific, or anywhere else beyond the United States. I adhere to all my opinions, often and sincerely expressed, that Africa, from whence their Ancestors were drawn, is the best quarter of the Globe in which they can be beneficially colonized. In expressing this opinion, I mean to offer no opposition to any other. . . . In, whatever mode the U.S. may get rid of the Free Blacks, I believe it will be better for them and for the whites." Clay to Thomas W. H. Moseley, November 4, 1845, Thomas J. Clay Papers, LC.

10. Clay to Joshua R. Giddings, October 6, 1847, in Julian, *Life of Giddings*, p. 209; deed of emancipation for Charles Dupuy, December 9, 1844, recorded in Fayette County Deed Book 22, p. 299, copy CPP. In 1846 the abolitionist press tried to prove Clay's cruelty to his slaves with a distorted account of conditions at Ashland by one of his runaways, Lewis Richardson, who escaped to Canada. But Richardson was really a violent, drunken, unmanageable, and disgruntled man, whom Clay was happy to lose.

11. Remini, *Jackson*, III, 51. In fairness it should be pointed out that by the 1840s Tennessee law made it almost impossible to emancipate slaves. Jackson's worst cruelties applied only to runaways.

receive "a bewailing and deploring letter from some distressed friend," and the pain would return. "Then indeed my heart bleeds, for the moment, for my Country and my friends." But some of the strangers who intruded on his privacy were "excessively (what shall I say?) oppressive. I am obliged to supply, when these strangers come, all the capital of conversation. . . . They come to look and to listen, and a monysyllable is all that I can sometimes get from them. I am occasionally tempted to wish that I could find some obscure and inaccessible hole, in which I could put myself, and enjoy quiet and solitude during the remnant of my days." Many of these individuals stupidly mentioned the calumnies to which Clay had been subjected, and he would reply that he wished to forget them and their "vile authors" as soon as possible. "I hope God will forgive them. I do not desire to soil myself by any contact with them."[12]

Clay spent a great deal of time during the winter of 1844–1845 "reading and studying interesting theological works," and he said he had benefited immensely from these readings "and by my reflections on them." In time he recovered his sense of humor and even gave short, amusing speeches about his electoral defeat. "Some of his opponents were like those of Tom Brown's Doctor Fell," he said:

> I do not love you, Dr. Fell,
> The reason why I cannot tell;
> But this alone I know full well,
> I do not love you, Dr. Fell.[13]

What he had come to believe, or so he said, was the awful fact that the American people did not love him. But that was not precisely true. They did love him, they did appreciate him— up to a point. His defects of character, his apparent waffling on some issues as though he would say anything to capture votes, and the superior air he frequently exuded combined to scare off sufficient numbers of the electorate (and party managers) each time he ran for President. He never truly grasped the fact that the people did not completely trust him and therefore would not risk placing full executive powers into his hands.

And he was unlucky. Andrew Jackson once claimed that luck played a significant part in his rise to fame.[14] Any number of times luck deserted Clay, the most obvious, of course, being his failure to get the nomination in the 1840 contest. He could have defeated Van Buren in that election. Any Whig could. And one did.

Fortunately Clay had farm and cattle to occupy his mind during this dreadful period of his life. When Philip Hone visited him a short time later, the New Yorker commented on the excellent condition of Clay's home and estate.

12. Clay to Sargent, January 11, 1845, Clay to Mary S. Bayard, February 4, 1845, May 7, 1846, copy CPP; Clay to John Carr, January 11, 1845, in Clay, *Works*, IV, 521; Clay to Octavia Le Vert, January 22, 1845, Clay Papers, Manuscript Division, Filson Club, Louisville, Kentucky.
13. Stanton, *Random Recollections*, pp. 153–154.
14. Remini, *Jackson*, I, 124.

"I never saw so fine a farm," Hone recorded in his diary; "his crops of wheat, Indian corn, and hemp are in the highest degree of perfection, his trees (nearly all of which were planted by himself) magnificent, and the stock do credit to the pastures on which they are reared."[15]

Calvin Colton visited Clay for two months to research his biography of the great man, which proved to be a healthy distraction since they were "in daily communication." The Great Compromiser gave generously of his time, suggested contacts, corrected factual errors to portions of the manuscript, and generally provided full support for the project. "I hope you will get successfully through it," he wrote Colton after his departure, "to accomplish which, I hardly need say, will require great patience, much research and study, and a large measure of candor and impartiality."[16] A little later he sat for another portrait by George P. A. Healy. He hated to do this because it was so time-consuming, tiresome, and boring. It was "a most unpleasant occupation, altho' he [Healy] seems to be an artiste of real talent." Clay suggested to John Crittenden that he have his portrait done. Healy charged only $150, but "you must make up your mind," Clay wrote, "to rather unusually long sittings."[17]

For a time Clay considered returning to New Orleans for the winter—again he was plagued with colds—and taking a brief trip to Cuba. An excursion to Cuba had been on his mind for several years, and there was a steamboat that regularly traveled between New Orleans and Havana. But he eventually decided against a southern tour for both financial and personal reasons.

During these months Clay was swamped with gifts and other tokens of the respect and gratitude of his many admirers: pairs of silver pitchers; a silver waiter; saddles; canes; jewelry for Lucretia, some of which was encrusted with diamonds; snuffboxes; books; prized animals; farm equipment, quilts; and clothing such as hats, boots, and cravats.[18] Babies were named after him, marble statues and portraits were commissioned, and stone columns proposed in his honor to be erected in the capitals of Virginia and Kentucky.[19]

15. Hone, *Diary,* II, 807.

16. Clay to Mary Bayard, February 4, 1845, copy CPP; Clay to Calvin Colton, April 28, 1845, in Clay, *Works,* IV, 528–529; Calvin Colton, *Last Seven Years of the Life of Henry Clay* (New York, 1956), p. 20; Clay to Colton, February 3, 1845, in Clay, *Works,* IV, 521–522.

17. Clay to Henry Clay, Jr., June 21, 1845, Henry Clay Memorial Foundation, Lexington, Kentucky, copy CPP; Clay to Crittenden, July 7, 1845, Crittenden Papers, LC. This portrait of Clay is presently hanging in the National Portrait Gallery, Washington, D.C.

18. When Clay first announced his candidacy, a group of his friends hired cabinetmakers in Philadelphia to execute a great Gothic bedroom suite which would be a gift to Clay for his personal use in the White House. With his defeat his friends sold the furniture to Daniel Turnbull, who purchased it for his plantation Rosedown, in St. Francisville, Louisiana, where it is presently located. The suite was so large that Turnbull was obliged to build a wing on the north side of his mansion to accommodate it. The suite consists of a bed, an armoire, a dresser, a cheval mirror, and a washstand.

19. The Clay Papers in the Library of Congress have many letters acknowledging or announcing these gifts. In one letter addressed to "My dear little Namesake" he offered this advice: "Your parents entertain fond hopes of you, and you ought to strive not to disappoint them. They wish you to be good, respected, eminent. You can realize all their most sanguine hopes, if you firmly resolve to do so, by judicious employment of your time and your faculties. Shun bad company,

Perhaps the most useful gift he received was the cancellation of the enormous debt he had incurred on account of his son's business failure.[20] Clay seriously considered selling Ashland to meet the debt and thought he might receive $70,000 for the entire estate. But a number of prominent merchants and manufacturers learned of his plight and decided to do something about it.[21] They did not wish their names divulged to Clay, nor did they wish to embarrass him by handing him a sum of money. So they quietly raised $25,750 and simply paid the debt and said nothing about it. The next time Clay went to the bank with a payment on a portion of the note due he was told by the cashier that there were no notes.

"There is nothing here against you whatever, Mr. Clay," said the cashier.

"What do you mean?" replied the astonished statesman.

"I mean, sir that your friends have paid every dollar you owed."

"My friends! who are they?"

"They desire their names kept secret. It was done through their appreciation of your services to the country and their respect for you."

Clay burst into tears. "Did any man ever have such friends," he sobbed.[22]

After he had learned of Clay's discovery, Abbott Lawrence assured the grateful man that an even "larger sum of money" could have been obtained if needed. Indeed, *"much more* if I were to make a general appeal to your friends."[23] A year later Clay was able to write: "It is true that I am not rich; but I am now nearly free from debt, and I possess a competence to enable me, to live in comfort during the remnant of my days, and to fulfill some of the duties of hospitality."[24]

Clay's euphoria in winning relief from his oppressive indebtedness was

and all dissipation. . . . Study diligently and perseveringly. You will be surprised at the ease with which you will master branches of knowledge, which on a first view, will frighten you. Make honor, probity, truth, and principle your invariable guide. Be obedient, and always affectionately respectful to your parents. Assiduously cultivate virtue and religion, the surest guarantee of happiness both here and hereafter. In your intercourse with your fellow beings, be firm, but at the same time, bland, courteous, and obliging. Recognize at all times the paramount right of your Country to your most devoted services, whether she treat you ill or well, and never let selfish views or interests predominate over the duties of patriotism." July 7, 1845, printed in Morton and Griswold, *Western Farmer's Almanac* (Louisville, Ky., 1859), p. 5, copy CPP.

20. On March 13, 1845, John Tilford informed Henry White in Philadelphia that Clay owed $7,000 to the Northern Bank of Kentucky which was secured by a mortgage on Ashland; $10,000 to various individuals in New Orleans; and another $8,500 to John Jacob Astor, the remainder of the $15,000 owed by his son Henry, Jr. John Tilford to Clay, February 17, 1845, Clay to Tilford, February 22, 1845, Clay Papers, LC; Lawrence to Clay, March 20, 1845, William B. Astor to Clay, April 28, 1845, Clay to Tilford, August 4, 1845, copies CPP. Clay to Octavia Le Vert, May 20, 1845, Clay Papers, Filson Club, Louisville, Kentucky.

21. Some of the men in the Boston area who contributed $500 or more included Abbott Lawrence, Jared Coffin, Thomas H. Perkins, Nathan Appleton, Peter C. Brooks, William Appleton, Edmund Dwight, Theodore Lyman, and William Lawrence. The names of the subscribers were listed in a book entitled *A Testimonial of Gratitude and Affection to Henry Clay.*

22. Jesse E. Peyton, *Reminiscences of the Past* (Philadelphia, 1895), pp. 20, 23.

23. Lawrence to Clay, March 13, 1845, Clay Papers, LC; Lawrence to Clay, March 20, 1845, copy CPP.

24. Clay to William B. Wedgwood, July 30, 1846, copy CPP.

rudely shattered by the sudden and catastrophic mental breakdown of his youngest son, John. In March the father noticed decided symptoms of the young man's "mental aberration." By April the father had reported that John was becoming "more and more deranged" and might have to be confined to the Lunatic Asylum of Kentucky in Lexington. Then, on April 3, John went roaming in the woods until 2:00 A.M. He was "wild and boisterous in his language" and often incoherent, although he did not attack anyone. He threatened to take his own life, and Clay was obliged to place him in the hospital. Apparently he had developed a "passion for Miss J——" and was rejected. The passion "revived," said the father, and John attempted to see the young lady, but she, "being advised of his situation, properly declined to receive him." He was led off quietly to the hospital and offered no resistance. In view of John's repeated mental breakdowns it can be presumed that there was more to this collapse than unrequited love.[25]

When the desperate man entered the "lunatic asylum," his derangement was reportedly worse than that of his brother Theodore when he was first committed. Fortunately, unlike his brother, John did not become violent. This terrible tragedy to the second of his sons left Clay a nearly broken man. "I find it extremely hard to bear this last sad affliction," he wrote. "It has put in requisition the utmost fortitude I can command." What made it all the more horrible was that John's "reason is sufficient to enable him to comprehend his situation, and to feel his confinement with the keenest pain." If only John were unconscious, said Clay, "we should be less afflicted. That is the condition of his brother [Theodore], and I fear will ultimately become his own." The father worried, too, about Lucretia and what this latest calamity would do to her. Fortunately her resignation to the will of God enabled her to bear this sorrow. She handled it "better even than I do," said Clay.

Happily, after a month of confinement in the asylum, John's condition improved dramatically and he seemed totally rational. "I pray to God," wrote Clay, "that he may so continue." The doctors thought it an excellent sign and consented to permit John to leave the hospital.[26]

Clay's other sons hardly gave him much solace. Henry, Jr., who lived in Louisville, was unsuccessfully attempting a political career. The father kept inviting him to move back to Ashland to be near his own two children and possibly "to mark out some business in which we might be both beneficially engaged." But Henry chose to stay where he was.

At this time Clay assisted Thomas and James in building new homes in the Lexington area. In 1837 he had purchased at auction a portion of property

25. Clay to Henry Clay, Jr., March 17, April 2, 5, 1845, Henry Clay Memorial Foundation, Lexington, Kentucky, copy CPP. As far as can be discovered John suffered at least three breakdowns. Toward the end of Clay's life John experienced an undisclosed incident that seriously worried his father. However, he recovered.

26. Clay to Henry Clay, Jr., April 5, 8, 27, May 6, 1845, Henry Clay Memorial Foundation, Lexington, Kentucky, copy CPP.

that adjoined Ashland. Then he had a house, called Mansfield, built on the site for Thomas. He also helped James finance the building of Clay Villa nearby. And beginning in October 1846, the brothers began a small business of making bricks on the Mansfield property. Thomas had three children: Lucretia, Henry, and Thomas. James, who practiced law in Lexington, had one daughter, Lucy. Everyone who knew Clay and knew what his family life was like, pitied him. "The great statesman's house is very desolate," commented Harriet Martineau. To be so honored, so admired around the country yet to live in such a dreadful home! Horrible.[27]

Once Clay had stopped feeling sorry for himself and the causes that had produced his humiliating electoral defeat, he began to speculate on the future and on the condition and direction of the Whig party. First off, he did not see any wisdom in dropping the "Whig" label, as some suggested, and assuming a new name by joining the Native American movement, thereby strengthening its organization. He admitted that "I have great sympathy with that party," but if the two parties united, the Democrats would then charge "that it was the same old party, with a new name or with a new article added to its creed." And the Democrats would still retain the immigrant vote. "I can only make suggestions," he wrote to John Clayton. "I think we should stand by our principles and by our arms and continue to endeavor to enlighten the public." We lost only by a hair out of 2.5 million who voted, he added. The Whigs may be the minority party, but it embraces "a large portion of the virtue, wealth, intelligence, and patriotism of the Country." It "is a great power, which judiciously wielded may yet save the Republic." We may be discouraged—that cannot be avoided—but we must "not yield to ignoble feelings of despair."

Clay knew from several correspondents that the Whig party in the South had been dispersed and that it would be impossible to evaluate the situation until "the heat & smoke of the conflict have passed away." Under the circumstances the Great Compromiser thought that the Whigs in Congress ought to hold an early meeting to consider their position and "adopt some system of future action." He thought they ought to let the Democrats pursue their particular purposes because the public must be allowed to experience the opposite systems of the two parties. Otherwise we will never "settle down in a stable and permanent policy." As for himself, although many had urged him to return to the Senate, he wished it understood by one and all that he had not the remotest thought of doing so, even if a vacancy occurred.[28]

By the beginning of 1845 Clay watched the Tyler administration in its

27. Martineau, *Retrospect of Western Travel,* II, 176. She said the same thing in a letter to her friends, the Reverend and Mrs. Samuel Gilman, June 12, 1835. "But you will, of course, keep this mournful domestic history to yourself," she added. Gatton, " 'Mr. Clay & I Got Stung,' " p. 52.

28. Clay to Clayton, December 2, 1844, Clayton Papers, LC; Clay to Crittenden, November 28, 1844, January 9, 1845, Crittenden Papers, LC; William C. Preston to Clay, November 23, 1844, in Clay, *Works,* IV, 503. Although Clay indicated disinterest in running for Congress again, he needed some franked envelopes to attend to all his correspondence, so, on occasion, he asked his congressional friends to send him a supply.

final days trying to "cook up" some scheme to annex Texas. What made it all the more pathetic was Tyler's hypocrisy. The President professed to support a strict construction of the Constitution, yet here he was arranging the annexation of Texas by a joint resolution of both houses of Congress in favor of such action, rather than by submitting a treaty of annexation for ratification by the Senate, as required by the Constitution. The motivation behind this ploy was obvious: A treaty took a two-thirds vote of one house, while a joint resolution needed only a simple majority in the two houses. Two majority resolutions were much easier to obtain than a single two-thirds treaty vote, so that was the route to annexation that Tyler took. The President and the Democrats "forfeit all consideration of respect to principle," declared Clay. He really thought the question should be left to the President-elect. His great fear, as he said many times, a fear shared by others, was the "disturbance" annexation would cause to "the Territorial balance of the Union." Such a disturbance could "lead to its dissolution."[29]

According to the House version of the joint resolution, Texas would be admitted as a state, its debt and public lands would remain its own, four additional states could be carved from its territory, but slavery would be prohibited in any of those states if they extended north of the Missouri Compromise line of 36°30'. The resolution passed on January 25 by a vote of 120 to 98. "God save the Commonwealth!" Clay snorted.[30]

In the Senate Thomas Hart Benton proposed as a resolution that the President be authorized to appoint five commissioners to negotiate all the terms of annexation, and when this had been completed, "a state formed out of the present republic of Texas" would be admitted into the Union.[31]

The differences between the two resolutions were ironed out shortly after Polk arrived in Washington to prepare for his inauguration.[32] Robert J. Walker of Mississippi introduced an amendment in the upper house giving the President the option of choosing between the House and Senate proposals. On February 27 this amendment squeezed through the Senate by the narrow vote of twenty-seven to twenty-five, the House accepted it the following day, and President Tyler signed the amended joint resolution on March 1, 1845, just three days before he was scheduled to leave office. Then, on Sunday, March 2, he sent a messenger to Texas offering annexation under the terms of the House resolution.[33]

29. Clay to Crittenden, January 9, 1845, Crittenden Papers, LC; Clay to Nathaniel Beverley Tucker, January 11, 1845, copy CPP.
30. *Congressional Globe,* 28th Congress, 2d session, p. 190 and appendix, pp. 309–314; Clay to John Pendleton Kennedy, January 31, 1845, copy CPP.
31. *Congressional Globe,* 28th Congress, 2d session, pp. 378–382.
32. "He [Polk] is for Texas, Texas, Texas," reported Senator Willie P. Mangum, "& talks of but little else." Mangum to T. R. Caldwell, February 20, 1845, in Mangum, *Papers,* IV, 468.
33. *Congressional Globe,* 28th Congress, 2d session, pp. 362–363; Seager, *And Tyler Too,* p. 283; Chitwood, *Tyler,* p. 360ff.; Peterson, *Presidencies of Harrison & Tyler,* pp. 255–257.

"Texas is ours," cried the Democrats. From the Hermitage the feeble voice of Andrew Jackson echoed the happy shout. "I not only rejoice," he gasped, "but congratulate my beloved country Texas is reannexed, and the safety, prosperity, and the greatest interest of the whole Union is secured by this . . . great and important national act."[34] From Ashland no such joyous reaction passed Clay's lips. He had long since accepted the inevitable, but he thought the way in which it was achieved violated constitutional forms. "The unconstitutional manner, more than the simple act, of Annexation ought to fill every enlightened patriot with alarm and apprehension. It will, I fear, totally change the peaceful character of the Republic." He said he would not be surprised to witness an insurrection in Canada, followed by U.S. recognition, "and finally a resolution of Annexation passed by a majority of the two houses of Congress! . . . And the annexation of Canada may be followed by that of California—Mexico—Cuba &c &c until the identity of the Nation is lost in dilution."[35]

Clay's fears were greatly intensified when President Polk, in his inaugural address, declared that the United States had a "clear and unquestionable" title to Oregon. The area had been jointly occupied by Great Britain and the United States since 1818, and it stretched from the forty-second parallel to 54°40′ and from the Rocky Mountains to the Pacific Ocean. If the United States declared its intention to terminate joint occupation, that action virtually constituted the first step toward a formal declaration of war.[36]

Clay shivered over this "headlong course" by Polk with respect to Oregon. He thought it much too premature to attempt the settlement of the Pacific coast with its problems of defense "when we have quite enough to defend the coast of the Atlantic Ocean and the Gulph of Mexico. . . . I am very apprehensive, my dear sir," he told his friend John Lawrence, "that we are shortly to have war with both England and Mexico." By itself, Mexico might not start anything, except possibly through nonintercourse to injure U.S. commerce and manufactures. "But Mexico, acting as an ally of Great Britain, is capable of inflicting upon us much mischief, especially on the Pacific." Clay even wrote to Lord Ashburton, expressing his hope that some means might be devised to avert "the calamity of a War between the U. States and G. Britain, respecting a territory so distant from them both, and at present so unimportant to either."[37]

Just a month following this letter to Lord Ashburton, the nation went into mourning over the death of Andrew Jackson on June 8. After twenty and more years of intense physical suffering and a long, protracted final illness, the Old Hero, who once regretted he had not shot Henry Clay or hanged John C.

34. Jackson to Francis P. Blair, March 10, 1845, Jackson Papers, LC.

35. Clay to John R. Thompson, April 23, 1845, copy CPP.

36. Richardson, *Messages and Papers,* IV, 373–382. On Polk's diplomacy, see David M. Pletcher, *The Diplomacy of Annexation: Texas, Oregon and the Mexican War* (New York, 1973).

37. Clay to Lawrence, April 30, 1845, Clay to Lord Ashburton, May 14, 1845, copies CPP.

Calhoun for the good of the country, died peacefully. But before his death he issued a general amnesty toward all his former enemies. Although Webster eulogized the former President before the New-York Historical Society and called him a man of "dauntless courage, vigor, and perseverance," who on several occasions had shown "wisdom and energy," Clay apparently made no public comment. But who could doubt his feelings about Jackson's accomplishments or wisdom? Old Hickory had led the nation from one disaster to another, according to Clay, and by his tyrannical actions had seriously undermined the nation's constitutional structure.[38]

Clay got into something of a controversy in the summer of 1845, involving his distant cousin Cassius M. Clay. It seems that Cassius had started an abolitionist newspaper in Lexington called the *True American*. Threats of violence from proslavery advocates resulted in the physical destruction of the press on August 18, 1845, by a Committee of Sixty, on which James Clay served as secretary. Fortunately Cassius escaped with his life. He wrote an angry letter to the senior Clay accusing him of "having given sanction and approval to the lawless action." He also accused Clay of leaving town for the Blue Sulphur spa in Virginia and refusing to help save his life "if things were pushed to extremity." Cassius demanded a response. "When I remember that I have devoted all the days of my manhood—my purse and my honor to the success of the whig cause," he angrily wrote, in order to promote "your personal elevation, I" insist upon an explanation. Apparently Clay did not respond, and Cassius went public with his complaint and denounced the statesman for his treachery.[39]

By the time Clay returned from his brief holiday at the spa the situation had quieted down considerably, but the incident became one more weapon for abolitionists to use against him should he decide to abandon his retirement. At the moment he had no such thoughts. He was looking forward to another trip to New Orleans, having skipped it the previous year. He wanted to take care of some legal business and sell his hemp, bagging, and some mules as well as a supply of Lucretia's celebrated hams. Indeed, Lucretia had built a respectable, though small, local business selling hams and milk.

Clay needed to escape "our more rigorous winters," he said, and "preserve" rather than "acquire health." He did not add (and it might have been more important than all the other reasons he gave) that he needed to get away from a dreadful home environment. Clay was approaching sixty-nine years of age, and he had decided that at this stage of his life he must preserve what little remained of his energy and strength. "I have appropriated my winters to the south," he said, planning to spend as many more of them in New Orleans and environs as possible.

An early and bitterly cold winter kept Clay from leaving Lexington for

38. *Niles' Weekly Register,* July 5, 1845.
39. Cassius M. Clay to Clay, September 25, 1845, Thomas J. Clay Papers, LC.

New Orleans until December 18. Then his trip downriver encountered numerous delays because the boat was stopped for days by floating ice in the Ohio River and by low water on the bars. "On one occasion only I believe were we in danger," he explained to his wife, "being enclosed in the Ice without being able to move the wheels or to steer the boat." Finally, when the boat did get under way, it was carried off helplessly by the mass of floating ice and was thrown against a ledge of rock. Fortunately no one was hurt.[40]

The Mississippi proved no better, and the boat got stuck on several bars. It took almost four weeks for Clay to reach Natchez, where he remained for several days to recuperate from his harrowing adventure and attend to some legal matters. A week later he arrived in New Orleans and again took up residence with his friend Dr. William N. Mercer in his new home.

To Clay's intense disappointment he found that the steamboat that ran from the city to Havana had been discontinued. He had counted on taking an excursion to Cuba, but now he opted against risking a sea voyage on a sailing ship. During this period he wrote regularly to his sons James and Thomas because of his concern for his livestock. He asked them to make certain that Ambrose Barnett, his overseer, paid particular attention to his stock. "The brood mares and the young Jacks I am very anxious about," he said. In response, Thomas gave him "a terrible account about losses of my stock" on account of the dreadful winter they had suffered. Clay himself did not escape the wintry blasts, even in New Orleans, and he came down with a severe case of influenza. "For ten days I have been quite ill with it, in so much that Dr. Luzenburg daily attended me four or five days. Nearly all last week I was confined to my room." His condition deteriorated so badly that he canceled plans to visit his charming friend Octavia Le Vert and her family in Mobile. Following his recovery he started back home on March 21 aboard the steamboat *Harry of the West* with the intention of stopping off in St. Louis to sell the land he owned jointly with James. He reached home in late April, after an absence of four months.[41]

Clay arrived in time to learn that Congress, following months of debate, had finally passed a resolution giving notice to Great Britain of terminating joint occupation of Oregon. Polk signed it on April 29. The action frightened Clay over what might happen next. "I have never been, during the last years, and am not now, without fears, for the peace of the Country." For one thing Britain might ally itself with Mexico, and together they could swiftly conquer Oregon and wreck American commerce. Clay still did not think that Mexico would act single-handedly, but what he did not know was that Mexican troops

40. Clay to Dudley Selden, June 4, 1846, Clay to Christopher Hughes, August 17, 1846, copies CPP; Clay to Lucretia, January 12, 19, 1846, Thomas J. Clay Papers, LC.

41. Clay to Thomas, January 24, 1846, Clay to Mercer, March 23, 1846, Clay to Nathan Sargent, April 28, 1846, copies CPP; Clay to Thomas, February 2, March 9, 1846, Clay Papers, LC; Clay to James, February 2, 1846, Clay to Lucretia, January 19, February 17, March 16, 1846, Thomas J. Clay Papers, LC; Clay to Octavia Le Vert, March 17, 1846, private collection, copy CPP.

had already crossed the Rio Grande in large numbers as a result of Polk's orders to General Zachary Taylor to advance his troops into the disputed area between the Nueces River and the Rio Grande. Polk took this action when Mexico refused his offer of thirty million dollars for California, New Mexico, and a boundary for Texas at the Rio Grande.[42] Not surprisingly the troops of the two countries skirmished, and in the action sixteen American soldiers were killed or wounded. When Polk received this information, he asked Congress for a declaration of war on May 11, 1846. Both houses quickly obliged him, and Polk signed the declaration on May 13.[43]

Fortunately Polk's bluster over Oregon resulted in Britain's offer to divide Oregon. There were several reasons why Britain preferred compromise to conflict, many of them economic. In any event, the United States accepted the offer, and Secretary of State James Buchanan and the British minister to the United States, Richard Pakenham, signed a treaty that divided the disputed territory at the forty-ninth parallel. Polk submitted it to the Senate, and it was ratified on June 15, 1846, by a vote of forty-one to fourteen.[44]

The United States had thereby isolated Mexico, the better to ravish it after first militarily defeating it and reducing it to total humiliation and submission.

"This unhappy War never would have occurred if there had been a different issue of the Presidential contest of 1844," Clay exclaimed to Horace Greeley, editor of the New York *Tribune*. "I foretold" it, he cried, yet "I lament its existence. A war between two neighboring Republics!" Clay also "foretold" in this letter the doom of the Tariff of 1842. "A law will be passed protecting favored interests (Iron, Coal, and Sugar, for example) and leaving all others to the mercy of Free trade." And he was right. The Tariff of 1846, sometimes called the Walker Tariff after its chief author, Secretary of the Treasury Robert Walker, became law on July 30, 1846. It considerably moderated protection on many items (reducing rates to about 25 percent), although it did not, as Clay predicted, apply free-trade principles to the others.[45] Following this revision of the tariff, Congress reenacted the independent treasury system.

With the trumpeting of war sounding across the nation after its declaration by Congress, thousands of young men, including "my son Henry, who

42. *Congressional Globe,* 29th Congress, 1st session, pp. 716, 720; Frederick Merk, *The Oregon Question: Essays in Anglo-American Diplomacy and Politics* (Cambridge, Mass., 1967), pp. 368–388; Clay to Nathan Sargent, April 28, 1846, copy CPP.

43. John S. D. Eisenhower, *So Far from God: The U.S. War with Mexico, 1846–1848* (New York, 1988), pp. 41–68. See also K. Jack Bauer, *The Mexican War, 1846–1848* (New York, 1974), pp. 48–49, 68–69; and Seymour V. Conner and Odie B. Faulk, *North America Divided: The Mexican War, 1846–1848* (New York, 1971). Although this war has been studied many times, Justin Smith's two-volume *War with Mexico* (New York, 1919) is still the most detailed and valuable. See also his *Annexation of Texas* (New York, 1911).

44. *Congressional Globe,* 29th Congress, 1st session, p. 1223.

45. Clay to Greeley, June 23, 1846, copy CPP. Clay's belief that this "unnecessary War with Mexico" would have been avoided "if there had been a different result of the last Presidential election" is also asserted in his letter to John B. Bibb, October 20, 1847, Clay Papers, Manuscript Department, Filson Club, Louisville, Kentucky.

goes as Lt. Col." in the Second Kentucky Volunteer Regiment, volunteered their services. "We cannot but admire and approve the patriotic and gallant spirit which animates our Country men," said Clay, "altho' we might wish that the cause in which they have stept forth was more reconcilable with the dictates of conscience." He was pleased that the Oregon controversy had been amicably settled and hoped there would be a quick termination of the war with Mexico.[46]

Father and son embraced in a tearful farewell, with the senior Clay presenting young Henry with a pair of pistols to carry with him into battle. But there was more anguish to be endured. The pain of watching the departure of his son to Mexico to face the hazards of armed conflict was intensified by another mental breakdown of his son John. Apparently it was not severe enough to require hospitalization, and he soon seemed "restored to the use of his mind." But it distressed Clay enough to send him hurrying to the Blue Licks spa to find "some relief" from his "severe domestic affliction."

Upon his return to Ashland Clay suffered another blow. A favorite grandson, Martin Duralde III, died in Philadelphia after undergoing "frightful convulsions from a congestion of the brain." For the past eighteen months the twenty-three-year-old man had endured the effects of a "hoemorrage of the lungs" and had traveled from New Orleans to Cuba to Old Point Comfort in Virginia seeking a cure. "He failed in accomplishing his object." And the grandfather was obliged to pay for the funeral expenses. Writing to the doctor who attended Duralde at the time of his death, Clay cried out his own pain and despair: "Ah! my friend, I hope you have had a less measure of affliction than has fallen to my lot. Death, ruthless death, has deprived me of Six affectionate daughters, all that I ever had, and has now commenced his work of destruction, with my descendents, in the second generation." He said he accepted the will of "an All-wise and merciful Providence" who had spared him so many years in order "to witness and to feel these great domestic misfortunes."[47]

Not much later Clay received frightening news when he learned that his son Henry, Jr., had sustained a "serious accident in Mexico" and might "never recover the perfect use" of his arm. Henry had joined General Zachary Taylor's army, which had won the battles of Palo Alto and Resaca de la Palma in early May before crossing the Rio Grande and capturing Monterrey in late September. Because Taylor had then allowed the Mexican troops to withdraw after the battle and had agreed not to advance for eight weeks, the President repudiated his truce agreement, snatched away three thousand of his veteran troops, and replaced Taylor in command with Major General Winfield Scott. "Taylor is very sore," reported the recovering Henry to his father, and considered the incident the "result of an intrigue" between Scott and Secretary of

46. Clay to Octavia Le Vert, June 25, 1846, copy CPP.
47. Clay to Francis Lieber, August 20, 1846, Clay to William N. Mercer, November 14, 1846, copies CPP; Dr. George McClellan to Clay, September 17, 1846, Thomas J. Clay Papers, LC; Clay to McClellan, September 24, 1846, copy CPP.

War William L. Marcy. But Polk had no love for Scott either since he was a very likely candidate for the Whig presidential nomination in 1848.[48]

Infuriated over his treatment, Taylor contacted friends back home and poured out his resentment. One of the most important of his friends was Senator John Crittenden, who had begun considering Taylor as a presidential contender in 1848. But Crittenden exercised extreme caution in initiating a Taylor campaign since he knew that Clay was still the first choice for President of many Whigs and that the Old Coon had not publicly announced his future intentions. The best anyone could get out of Clay in late 1846 was the statement "that I have never said to any one that I would or would not be a Candidate for the Presidency at the next election. I have remained perfectly passive." For the moment, however, he felt the party should move slowly and cautiously and not trouble itself over its possible candidate.[49]

But as the war continued, Clay became more and more critical of the administration, and he started to feel once more the excitement and the need to try another run. "You speak of the War with Mexico," he wrote his good friend Octavia Le Vert. "What a waste of precious human life. . . . And what a waste of treasure too!" Polk had no comprehensive military strategy, he added, and "how Genl Taylor is to keep up his long line of communication and receive indispensable supplies of provisions, munitions of War, and re-inforcement, God only knows, for I am sure neither the President nor Secretary of War does."[50]

It pleased him, of course, to hear from such notables as Horace Greeley that the "great mass" of Whigs, "who act from the heart rather than the head, protest that they won't hear of any other candidate than the old one, at least until he publicly and peremptorily refuses to run." But Clay would not oblige them. He kept his silence. At the same time he began to think more favorably of announcing his candidacy "at the proper time."[51]

There was also talk of his returning to the Senate, especially if some of the

48. K. Jack Bauer, *Zachary Taylor: Soldier, Planter, Statesman of the Old Southwest* (Baton Rouge, 1985), p. 167ff; Clay to Octavia Le Vert, November 6, 1846, Henry Clay, Jr., to Clay, February 12, 1847, copies CPP.

49. Kirwan, *Crittenden,* pp. 203–204; Clay to Daniel Mallory, October 12, 1846, Clay to Epes Sargent, October 17, 1846, copies CPP. See also Taylor's letters to Crittenden, January 3, February 13, March 25, 1848, in Crittenden Papers, LC.

50. Clay to Le Vert, November 6, 1846, copy CPP. Writing to William Mercer, Clay said: "The plan of the Campaign for conducting the Mexican War has been most unwise and unskilful. I think, in making the Rio Bravo [Rio Grande] and Camargo the base of military operations. It should have been (if any invasion of Mexico were decided on) to have taken La Vera Cruz, or to have blockaded it by land and water, and marched the Army from that point, or its neighbourhood, to the attack of the City of Mexico, if it were to be attacked." Clay to Mercer, November 14, 1846, copy CPP. The administration later adopted this strategy.

51. Greeley to Clay, November 15, 1846, Clay to John S. Littell, November 17, 1846, Clay Papers, LC. All Clay would say to Greeley was that "whilst I have deliberately foreborne to say yes or no to any one . . . I will say to you that it depends on conditions as to my life, health, vigor of mind and body, and general manifestations of a desire to place me at the helm." Clay to Greeley, November 21, 1846, copy CPP.

Whig leaders put up a fight against nominating him for the presidency. "This wretched principle of *availability*," acknowledged John Pendleton Kennedy, means that the presidency may fall "forever into the hands of the men whose mediocrity shall shield them equally from the praise or censure of the people."[52]

But what about a return to Congress? If Clay were excluded from another presidential run, would it not be wise to bring him back to the Senate, where his statesmanship could continue to serve the nation? No, not at this time, replied Clay. "I not only have no desire but I entertain a particular disinclination to return to it [the Senate]."[53]

Meanwhile, he spent the winter of 1846–1847 in New Orleans, again residing with Dr. Mercer and promising Octavia Le Vert this time to visit her in Mobile. He found the Crescent City "less gay" than in the past because of the war. And he dined one evening with General Scott, who was on his way to Mexico to take command of the army.[54]

Clay made one silly speech to the New England Society of Louisiana in New Orleans that included a very stupid remark. It was a pathetic attempt to sound patriotic. He started off by remarking how unaccustomed he was to public speaking these days—that earned him a big laugh—and how, upon seeing various military officers and generals in the room, "I felt half inclined to ask for some little nook or corner in the army, in which I might serve in avenging the wrongs to my country." That last remark brought the anticipated round of applause. "I have thought that I might yet be able to capture or to slay a Mexican." That was a crude and contemptible appeal to the highly volatile war fever of his listeners, and of course, it won him another round of applause. The remark about killing a Mexican was meant to be a joke, which some of his friends understood. "But did *others? No!*"[55] The speech was printed in the New Orleans *Picayune* on December 23 and later raised a number of eyebrows in many quarters of the country.

A better speech was given at a general meeting for the relief of famine-stricken Ireland. The Irish generally voted against Clay, but this speech undoubtedly softened their harsh opinion of him. He also visited Baton Rouge to attend an agricultural fair, and of course, he went to Mobile to see his good friend Octavia Le Vert, accompanied by the former governor of Tennessee, "Lean Jimmy" Jones.[56]

With the war going so well—General Stephen W. Kearny marched from

52. Kennedy to Clay, December 15, 1846, copy CPP.

53. Clay to Kennedy, December 27, 1846, Clay to Thomas R. Stevenson, December 19, 1846, copies CPP. On December 8, 1846, the Frankfort *Commonwealth* reported that many Kentucky newspapers had been advocating Clay's return to the Senate.

54. Clay to Le Vert, December 19, 1846, copy CPP.

55. Christopher Hughes to Clay, September 14, 1847, Clay Papers, LC.

56. Lexington *Observer and Kentucky Reporter,* January 23, 27, February 20, 24, March 6, 10, 27, 1847.

Fort Leavenworth to San Diego, California, in the summer and fall of 1846, capturing Santa Fe along the way—Clay began considering what might be the outcome. If Mexico was conquered, what could be done with it? Relinquish it? Annex it? Annex a country of eight million who spoke another language, obeyed other laws, and differed "from us in religion and race"? How could it be done without disturbing the peace and prosperity of the American nation? he asked. "These are very, very grave questions," he added.[57]

What intensified the gravity of these questions was the ever-escalating problem of slavery. In the summer of 1846 David Wilmot, a Democratic congressman from Pennsylvania, attached to an appropriation bill in the House of Representatives a proviso that declared that slavery must not exist in any territory to be acquired from Mexico. The idea that a southern conspiracy had produced the war in order to strengthen the slave power in the country was widely believed in New England, and the Wilmot Proviso was therefore seen by many as a means of blocking any effort to expand the slaveholding areas of the nation. The proviso passed the House on August 8, but the Senate killed it two days later. Nevertheless, for the next few years the proviso was reintroduced and repassed in the House over the strenuous objections of southerners. But each time it won approval in the lower house, it suffered defeat in the Senate. In terms of the next presidential election, the issue of the Mexican War had now been further complicated by congressional action, or lack of it, on the Wilmot Proviso.[58]

The horror of that brutal war came crashing down on Clay the day following his return to Ashland after a four-month absence. It was a beautiful day when he arrived, "a bright sun shine beaming all around." But the next day, while the family was sitting at dinner, Clay's son James entered the room "with grief depicted in his countenance, and related the sad and melancholy event which had befallen my beloved son on the bloody Battle field of Buena Vista." The battle took place on February 22 and 23, 1847, near Monterrey. General Santa Anna, with Polk's assistance, had returned to Mexico from exile in Cuba and led his troops north to engage Taylor's army. The Americans numbered five thousand, the Mexicans around fifteen to twenty thousand, and what should have been a rout of the American Army turned into a glorious victory. In the engagement young Clay was wounded, shot through the thigh. He ordered his men to withdraw, surrendering to one of them the pistols his father had given him. "Leave me, take care of yourselves," he said. "Take these Pistols to my father and tell him, that I have done all I can with them, and now return them to him." As the enemy approached, Clay tried to hold them off with his sword, but the Mexicans bayoneted him to death. General Taylor, the victor of the Battle of Buena Vista, wrote to the father to inform him of his

57. Clay to Kennedy, December 27, 1846, copy CPP.
58. Epes Sargent to Clay, February 27, 1847, Clay Papers, LC; Charles B. Going, *David Wilmot, Free Soiler* (New York, 1924), pp. 94–105, 159–201; Chaplain W. Morrison, *Democratic Politics and Sectionalism: The Wilmot Proviso Controversy* (Chapel Hill, N.C., 1967), p. 15ff.

son's gallantry and to express his "deepest and most heartfelt sympathies for your irreparable loss." Under his leadership, wrote Taylor, "the sons of Kentucky, in the thickest of the strife, upheld the honor of the State and of the country." A fellow officer sent the father a lock of Henry's hair, taken from his head after his body had been brought into the camp, which Clay wore in a "breast pin" and later bequeathed to his grandson Henry Clay III.[59]

The news shattered the father. His favorite son, his namesake, on whom he had pinned his greatest hopes and who even resembled him, had given his life for "this most unnecessary and horrible war with Mexico." Tears streamed down his face as the full realization of what had happened sunk in. Devastated, he bowed his head, covered his face with his hands, and gave full vent to his grief. "Alas," he later wrote, "there are some wounds so deep and so excrutiatingly painful, that He only can heal them, by whose inscrutable dispensations they have been inflicted. And the death of my beloved son is one of them." The persons and things "upon which I had most placed my heart, have one after another been taken in succession from me."

"Oh God!" he cried out, "how inscrutable are thy dispensations." His one solace, he said, was in the knowledge "that my dear Son preferred, if death were to come, that he should expire on the field of battle, in the service of his Country."[60]

Expressions of condolence poured in from people in every part of the country, including former President Martin Van Buren. President Polk sent nothing. The body of the slain hero was returned to the family and buried in Frankfort on July 20, 1847, with an appropriate monument added three years later.[61] The tragedy had such a profound effect upon Clay that it drove him to

---

59. Clay to Mary S. Bayard, April 16, 1847, copy CPP; "Death of Lieut. Col. Henry Clay Jr." lithograph by N. Currier, National Portrait Gallery, Washington, D.C.; Taylor to Clay, March 1, 1847, private collection, copy CPP; Cary H. Fry to Clay, March 22, 1847, copy CPP. For Whig opposition to the Mexican War, see John H. Schroeder, *Mr. Polk's War: American Opposition and Dissent, 1846–1848* (Madison, Wis., 1973). But Robert W. Johannsen in his *To the Halls of the Montezumas: The War with Mexico in the American Imagination* (New York, 1985) shows how popular the war was with a large number of Americans, particularly those outside New England.

60. Clay to William Mercer, April 1, 13, 1847, Clay to John A. Dix, April 13, 1847, Clay to Richard Henry Wilde, April 10, 1847, Clay to Josiah Randall, April 2, 1847, copies CPP; Clay to John Clayton, April 16, 1847, Clayton Papers, LC; Clay to Joshua R. Giddings, October 6, 1847, in Julian, *Life of Giddings,* pp. 208–210. "Circumstances of alleviation exist," Clay wrote, "but alas! my heart constantly tells me of the irreparable loss which I have suffered." Clay to Thomas Moseley and P. H. Olmstead, May 14, 1847, Clay Papers, Manuscript Department, Filson Club, Louisville, Kentucky.

61. See the Clay papers for the various letters of sympathy Clay received. One letter included a poem, the last stanza of which reads:

> Weep not for thy son;
> He has gone to his rest,
> And the turf lies soft, on a soldier's breast.
> What! weep for the brave one? Bright laurels he wore,
> He soared like the eagle, he died at the sword.

Julia Towler to Clay, June 2, 1847, copy CPP.

religion. From his letters it is clear that his decision to join the church had been on his mind for some time, but this latest calamity may have settled the matter. On June 22, 1847, in the drawing room at Ashland, Henry Clay was baptized, along with his daughter-in-law Marie Mentelle Clay and her four children, by the Reverend Edward F. Berkley of Christ Church according to the forms of the Episcopal Church. He took "the Sacrament of the Lord's Supper" on July 4, in the Chapel of Transylvania University in Lexington, and on July 15 he was confirmed in the same chapel by Bishop Benjamin B. Smith. Perhaps, said Clay, all the tragedies and suffering he had endured were intended to "detach us altogether from this world" and "prepare us for, another and a better world."[62]

On the face of it, particularly in view of his previous life-style, Clay's action of becoming an Episcopalian seemed totally out of character, and indeed, any number of Americans accused him of hypocrisy. Cynical politicians, of course, ascribed the worst motives to his conversion. "His joining an aristocratic church," declared one, "does him no good here, among the go-to-meeting portion, of christians. And among the great mass, of the 'meek and lowly,' it will do him harm. I consider it rather farcical."[63]

Most likely Henry's death in and of itself did not bring about Clay's conversion. Probably—and here it is impossible to speak with any degree of certainty—a number of factors bore down on him. The accumulation of family deaths, especially the deaths of his six daughters; the mental breakdowns of two of his sons; possibly a sense of guilt over the many tragedies that had befallen his children; the repeated electoral defeats; and his poor health and advancing age all combined to drive him into the church. He needed respite from his many woes, and he may have finally come to believe that his last hope of finding it lay in the arms of Mother Church.

Andrew Jackson had once predicted that Clay would either join the church or die a drunkard.[64] The Old Coon chose the church.

62. Thomas H. Clay to Samuel M. Duncan, December 28, 1858, Clay Papers, Manuscript Department, Filson Club, Louisville, Kentucky; Clay, *Works* III, 53; Clay to Mercer, April 1, 1847, copy CPP; Colton, *Last Seven Years in the Life of Henry Clay,* p. 52.

63. J. B. Mower to Mangum, October 18, 1847, in Mangum, *Papers,* V, 84.

64. Francis P. Blair to Van Buren, August 25, 1847, Van Buren Papers, LC.

THIRTY-EIGHT

The Sage of
Ashland

THE NOTABLE American victory over a vastly superior Mexican force at the Battle of Buena Vista propelled General Zachary Taylor, or Old Rough and Ready, as he was popularly called, to the front rank of possible Whig candidates for the presidency in 1848. It also nudged Clay away from his state of passivity regarding the nomination. Shortly after learning of his son's death on the battlefield, he informed John Clayton that he would consider placing his name before the country as a presidential candidate. For a fourth try? Former President John Tyler saw Clay at the Blue Sulphur spa in Virginia the previous summer and thought him "old as his gait indicates. Can it be that he looks to '48? Is the fire of ambition never to be extinguished?"[1] Apparently not. At least not yet.

All his life Clay was a savagely ambitious man. There can be no doubt about that. His ambition colored everything he did. It even took precedence over his family and all other personal relationships. Not until his final years, after he had become desperately ill, did his fierce drive for the nation's highest office finally come to rest. Only then did he find peace of mind, and he found it in the knowledge that at last he had reached a stage of his life when he was motivated solely by the welfare and future prosperity of his country, not by personal ambition.

Throughout much of his life Clay's actions to some extent had been self-serving because of his desperate need for the presidency. Even as late as 1847, at the advanced age of seventy, his hunger for this office had not abated. "Up to the battle of Buena Vista," he wrote at this time, "I had reason to believe that there existed a fixed determination with the mass of the Whig party, throughout the U.S., to bring me forward again. I believe that the greater

---

1. Tyler to C. A. Wickliffe, August 24, 1845, Preston Davie Papers, Virginia Historical Society, Richmond.

portion of that mass still cling to that wish, and that the movements we have seen, in behalf of Genl Taylor, are to a considerable extent superficial & limited."[2]

Apparently the beginning of a canvass for Taylor once again stirred Clay's ambition and pushed him from his noncommittal position. But he had conditions for running again: good physical and mental health and a conviction that his services "were demanded by an unquestionable majority of the Country." He discounted Webster as a possible rival, except in Massachusetts, along with Judge John McLean, whose name was inevitably raised (usually at his own urging) every four years but never went anywhere. That left the two "military candidates," Generals Taylor and Scott, neither of whom Clay felt possessed presidential qualifications. Of the two, he thought Taylor the more straightforward, sincere, and honest, with the bluntness of a soldier but "with nothing of the petitmaitre about him." But would the Whigs nominate someone like Taylor without knowing whether he held a single principle in common with them? Were the image of a hero and "availability" all that mattered? Had the experience with Tyler not taught them anything?

Moreover, Clay abhorred the idea of committing "the future destinies of the Republic . . . to Military Chieftains." It would give the nation an irresistible impulse toward war and conquest. It would encourage the idea of Manifest Destiny, the notion that the nation by some divine right should expand beyond anything it needed to provide for the people's happiness and prosperity. Clay said he did not regard the election of General Harrison as a commitment by Whigs to a preference for military men. After all, Harrison was as much distinguished in his civilian as in his military career, if not more so, Clay said repeatedly. To test the waters, "in a quiet way," and get a sense of public reaction to his possible candidacy, he told Clayton that he would visit the East Coast during the summer and hoped to meet him so that they could further discuss his future.[3]

Clay knew, of course, that he could still count on widespread support among the party faithful. "We have Clay men among us," wrote one Whig, "that swear everlasting confusion and destruction, to every body and every thing, that is not 'Clay,' that if, he's not elected, no Whig shall be." Even so, another segment of the Whig party, far more "prudent and sagacious" and yet "seriously and devoutly Mr. Clay's friends," fear bringing him forward again, "dreading that awful calamity—defeat." They believed the Old Coon had "outlived his popularity, that he never can again, be, A. No. 1."[4]

At about the same time that Clay opened up the possibility of another run for the White House, the Washington *National Intelligencer,* on April 24, began leaking rumors to the effect that Nicholas Trist, one of Clay's appointees

2. Clay to Daniel Ullmann, May 12, 1847, copy CPP.
3. Clay to Clayton, April 16, 1847, Clayton Papers, LC; Clay to Daniel Ullmann, August 4, 1847, in Clay, *Works,* IV, 543–545.
4. J. B. Mower to Mangum, March 12, September 21, 1847, in Mangum, *Papers,* V, 57, 81.

to the State Department who had survived the many changes of administrations, had been sent to Mexico on a secret mission to negotiate a treaty of peace. According to the leak, Trist was expected to demand the cession of all Mexican territory north of 26° and running from the Gulf of Mexico to the Pacific Ocean. But Trist's actual instructions from President Polk called for a guarantee of the Rio Grande as the boundary of Texas, the acquisition of New Mexico and California, and the right of passage across Tehuantepec. In return the United States would pay Mexico up to thirty million dollars.[5]

On the military front General Scott had landed with his troops at Veracruz, captured it, and headed for Mexico City, where Santa Anna was waiting for him. Another American military triumph would give the Whig party two victorious generals as presidential contenders, while the poor Democrats had no one of equal military stature to rival them.

By late spring Clay had become more outspoken in his condemnation of the war. As he prepared for his eastern tour, he began to make his feelings more publicly known. "Yes! Gentlemen," he told one group of antiwar activists, "I entirely concur with you in deprecating this Mexican War, the causes which brought it about, & the manner of its commencement. I sincerely wish that every bayonet and sword employed, in its prosecution, by both belligerents, were converted into sythes, ploughshares and axes, and they dedicated to their respective uses in the innocent and peaceful arts of life."[6] He also began to consider the issues he might raise in the campaign: protection, for one; the causes of the war and the manner of its conduct, for another; also, the burgeoning national debt as a direct result of the war; and, of course, internal improvements and the alarming increase in presidential powers. After all, these constituted the basic dogmas of the Whig party. But some of these issues were so old and threadbare that few Whigs cared to campaign on them again. Rather than a weary loser like Clay, they much preferred a candidate with the glamour of military victory to enhance the campaign, and never mind tariffs and public works and the veto power.[7]

On July 24 Clay began his "quiet" tour of the East Coast. He naturally headed first for White Sulphur Springs, where he stayed for a week before departing for Baltimore and Philadelphia. His immediate goal, he told several correspondents, was to go to Cape May in New Jersey and "enjoy a Sea bath, which I have never in my life before had an opportunity of doing."[8]

On his arrival at the depot in Philadelphia he received one ovation after

5. Clay to Adam Beatty, April 29, 1847, private collection, copy CPP; Bauer, *The Mexican War,* pp. 282–287.

6. Clay to William Passmore et al., June 1, 1847, copy CPP.

7. Clay to Daniel Ullmann, August 4, 1847, in Clay, *Works,* IV, 543–545.

8. Clay to Daniel Ullmann, August 4, 1847, in Clay, *Works,* IV, 543–545; Clay to Mary S. Bayard, August 7, 1847, copy CPP. During his journey he happened upon Senator Thomas Hart Benton, and they cordially greeted each other to the surprise—considering their many savage encounters on the floor of the Senate—of onlookers. At Baltimore he was mobbed by well-wishers, who offered a special train (which he graciously declined) to take him to Philadelphia.

another. He was forced to come to the balcony of the home of Henry White, where he was staying, to speak to a large crowd of Whigs who had assembled outside and shouted to see and hear him. He obliged them with patriotic nothings delivered in his inimitable style. And of course, he insisted that his visit was private and that he did not want to create a public disturbance. But all his receptions were enthusiastic, both in Philadelphia and elsewhere. "I was almost crushed by their kindness," he told Lucretia.[9]

He arrived at Cape May by special boat on August 17 and took the "Sea bath" he wanted so much to experience. "The air, the water, and the whole scene greatly interested me," he wrote to his wife. He quickly adjusted to sea bathing, swimming on top of the breakers, dunking the ladies (who dunked him in turn), and grabbing hands with them and frolicking like a man half his age. Only with difficulty was he finally persuaded to abandon the surf.[10]

At Cape May Clay gave an emotionally charged address to several delegations of citizens from Philadelphia, Trenton, New York City, and New Haven. He naturally mentioned his dead son and how everything at Ashland was associated with his memory. "The very trees which his hands assisted me to plant," the emotional man half-audibly muttered, "served to remind me of my loss." The crowd listened intently, hardly making a sound. Then, with unbelievable sadness written all over his face and his voice reflecting his grief, he spoke of his eleven children and how only four remained. "Of six lovely daughters," he sobbed, "not one is left."

Clay broke the spell he had conjured by shaking himself and clearing his voice and renouncing "that theatre of sadness." He admitted he had come to the ocean shore to seek relief from all the tragedy that had surrounded him. He came as a "private and humble citizen, without an army, without a navy, without even a constable's staff," and had been greeted at every step of his journey "with the kindest manifestations of feeling—manifestations of which, at present, a monarch or an emperor might well be proud."[11]

It was vintage Clay. He still retained all his powers to move and persuade an audience. He was irresistible, and people loved him. At this point he, more than anyone else, had become "the most popular man in this broad nation."[12]

Clay returned to Ashland on September 19 via New Castle, Delaware, Baltimore, and White Sulphur Springs, receiving ovations wherever he appeared. He contracted "a very bad cold" along the way and was involved in a carriage accident, which was variously reported around the country. He pro-

9. *National Intelligencer,* August 18, 1847; Lexington *Observer and Kentucky Reporter,* August 8, 14, 28, 1847; Clay to Lucretia, August 18, 1847, Thomas J. Clay Papers, LC.

10. Clay to Lucretia, August 18, 1847, Thomas J. Clay Papers, LC; Lexington *Observer and Kentucky Reporter,* August 28, 1847.

11. *National Intelligencer,* August 26, 1847. The speech was widely circulated, and Clay received many congratulatory letters for his "beautiful and touching address." See Elizabeth Sloan to Clay, September 12, 1847, Thomas J. Clay Papers, LC.

12. French, *Witness to the Young Republic,* p. 213.

tested that he was not "in any very imminent danger at the Cape from the oversetting carriage. Nor did I leap out of it, with a young lady in my arms, although after getting out of it myself I did assist her."[13] Otherwise the trip went exceedingly well, and he was more determined than ever to advance his candidacy.

But when he reached home, he found a letter waiting for him from his friend Joseph L. White of New York that expressed regret over the efforts of John Crittenden to advance the candidacy of General Taylor. Knowing "Mr Crittenden's former devotion to your interests," White assumed that it was a diversionary tactic. If it was not a diversion and he acted without Clay's knowledge, then, said White, "he has separated himself from his friends in this region without warning & I fear without just excuse."

The letter no doubt staggered Clay. He sent a copy to Crittenden with the comment that he did so out of their "mutual friendship & the candour and confidence which have ever existed between us" and with an assurance that he did not endorse any of the conjectures in the letter. He asked Crittenden to give it such consideration as he thought it merited and to please return it.

Crittenden had indeed deserted Clay for the simple reason that he did not believe his friend could win the election. He therefore turned to Taylor and began as cautiously as possible to drum up support. Of course, Clay's old enemies in Kentucky—like the Wickliffes and Ben Hardin—joined the cause, all of them convinced that the Old Coon could be defeated. Without Crittenden's aid the Taylor bandwagon would no doubt have halted abruptly. Crittenden's defection proved to be one more agony for Clay to endure. Their friendly relationship subsequently broke off.[14]

Crittenden replied as diplomatically as possible, but Clay saw right through him. In a second letter Clay frankly told the senator that the movements in Kentucky for Taylor "have occasioned me some mortification." He thought a more dignified silence on the part of Kentucky would best promote its character instead of embarrassing him and leading the way in advancing the candidacy of someone else. "I am not a stranger to the arts and to the instruments which have been employed to get up most of these meetings," he snapped at Crittenden. "They have been not infrequently prompted or promoted by the malignity of some of my personal enemies . . . [who] care less for Genl. Taylor than the gratification of their malevolence towards me." The purpose of giving offense "and wounding my feelings has not been accomplished to the extent designed."[15]

Despite the "treachery" in his own backyard, or maybe because of it, Clay

13. Clay to Henry White, September 4, 1847, Clay to Mary S. Bayard, September 22, 1847, copies CPP.

14. Joseph L. White to Clay, September 4, 1847, Clay to Crittenden, September 21, 1847, Crittenden Papers, LC; Kirwan, *Crittenden,* p. 200ff. The estrangement between Clay and Crittenden ended before Clay's death.

15. Clay to Crittenden, September 26, 1847, Crittenden Papers, LC.

decided to forge ahead with his undeclared candidacy by giving a major address on the war and its probable effects on the nation for the immediate future. He shrewdly chose Lexington for the speech not only because it was his hometown but because of popular feeling in favor of the war. And in view of the ruckus over the Wilmot Proviso, he intended to face the slavery question squarely and say precisely what he thought and believed. It was an especially courageous speech. Once again he gambled. Conceivably it could win or lose him the nomination.

He spoke at a general meeting on November 13, 1847. In the audience sat the newly elected Whig representative from Illinois Abraham Lincoln, listening intently to his political idol. The young Illinoisan Whig revered the Great Compromiser because of the Kentuckian's great love of the Union, his economic nationalism, and his commitment to the eventual disappearance of slavery.[16]

Clay began by saying that the day was dark and gloomy (he rather liked that figure of speech), unsettled and uncertain, because of the "unnatural" war with Mexico. He had come before his fellow Kentuckians "to address you, earnestly, calmly, seriously and plainly." War, pestilence, and famine were the three greatest calamities that could befall a nation, he reminded his audience, but of these three, war was the most frightful and "direful." War unhinges society, disturbs regular industry, and scatters poisonous seeds of disease and immorality. Its pageantry, glitter and pomp deceive the youthful and romantic and often make them useless to society when they return from the bloody battlefields. He then traced the history of U.S. involvement in this struggle with Mexico, citing the mistakes, the lies, the treachery, and the stupidity of the administration. He himself would never have voted for the declaration of war had he been a member of Congress since it had palpable falsehood stamped all over it. "Almost idolizing truth, as I do, I never, never, could have voted for that bill."

Must we blindly continue this dreadful conflict, he asked, without any visible object in sight or any prospect of a definite termination? It was up to congressmen to determine the objects and purposes of this war. They should speak up—loudly and clearly. If their determinations are left to the President and he decides to pursue objects against the will of Congress, "where is the difference between our free government and that of any other nation which may be governed by an absolute Czar, Emperor, or King?" If Congress acted as he recommended, the nation would then know for what ends its blood was to be further shed and its treasure further expended, instead of being locked up and concealed in the bosom of one man.

And shall we fight on for the purpose of conquering Mexico and annexing it? We could do it, he continued, but not without frightful carnage, dreadful

16. "During my whole political life," Lincoln later wrote, "I have loved and revered [Clay] as a teacher and leader." Lincoln to James Sulgrove et al., January 28, 1861, in Basler, ed., *Collected Works of Lincoln*, IV, 184. On this occasion Lincoln had come to visit his in-laws in Lexington.

sacrifices of human life, the creation of a monstrous national debt, and the raising of a standing army of one hundred thousand men to keep the peace.

And how shall Mexico be governed? Like Roman provinces, by proconsuls? What a mockery that would be to our lofty ideals of free institutions. Shall it be annexed? Does anyone believe that two nations dissimilar in race, language, religion, and laws could be blended together into one harmonious mass? "Murmurs, discontent, insurrections, rebellion, would inevitably ensue, until the incompatible parts would be broken asunder, and . . . our present glorious Union itself would be dissevered or dissolved."

History warns against such foreign adventures. Look at Canada. The English conquered the French nearly one hundred years ago, yet they remain "a foreign land in the midst of the British provinces, foreign in feelings and attachment, and foreign in laws, language and religion." Ireland was another example. "Every Irishman hates, with a mortal hatred, his Saxon oppressor." If we conquer Mexico, we can expect to elicit the same hatred.

Mexico could not at this time be a partner with this country in self-government. The population, on account of its habits, customs, laws, and religion, was not prepared for such a responsibility. Why, then, expand an already immense nation like the United States? "We do not want the mines, the mountains, the morasses, and the sterile lands of Mexico." But what about the Bay of San Francisco and Upper California? Surely they could provide great benefit to our commercial and navigating interests. Clay agreed. "If we can obtain it [California] by fair purchase with a just equivalent, I should be happy to see it so acquired."

And what of the claim that the southern states wanted the war to acquire territory for the purpose of introducing slavery into it?

I have ever regarded slavery as a great evil, a wrong, for the present, I fear, an irremediable wrong to its unfortunate victims. I should rejoice if not a single slave breathed the air or was within the limits of our country. But here they are, to be dealt with as well as we can, with a due consideration of all circumstances affecting the security, safety and happiness of all races. Every State has the supreme, uncontrolled and exclusive power to decide for itself whether slavery shall cease or continue within its limits, without any exterior intervention from any quarter. In States, where the slaves outnumber the whites, as is the case with several, the blacks could not be emancipated and invested with all the rights of freemen, without becoming the governing race in those States. Collisions and conflicts, between the two races, would be inevitable, and, after shocking scenes of rapine and carnage, the extinction or expulsion of the blacks would certainly take place.

Fifty years ago Kentucky considered gradual emancipation—to wit, all slaves born subsequent to a specified day were to become free at the age of twenty-eight and, during their service, to be taught to read, write, and cipher. Thus, instead of an ignorant and unprepared freeman being thrown into society, as would be the case by immediate emancipation, he would enter society capable of enjoying and participating in it. Regrettably the proposed system was defeated. It might be worth another try.

Clay concluded his address by proposing a series of resolutions in which members of the meeting would call on the Congress to determine the objects and purposes of the war, declare their opposition to any purpose of annexing or dismembering Mexico except to get a proper determination of the boundary of Texas, and "positively and emphatically" disclaim and disavow "any wish or desire, on our part, to acquire any foreign territory whatever, for the purpose of propagating slavery, or of introducing slaves from the United States, into such foreign territory." Finally Clay called on "our fellow citizens of the United States" to hold meetings and express their "views, feelings, and opinions."[17]

It was a clear, strong, courageous, and powerful statement that elicited applause from a wide range of northern Whigs, increasingly called Conscience Whigs because of their opposition to slavery. Almost unanimously they praised his speech. He had come forward as spokesman of the party and articulated all the deep sentiments and feelings pent up inside northern Whigs about the war and what it was doing to the country.

By the miracle of the newly invented telegraph the speech flashed eastward in a matter of minutes and was published a day or two later. Whigs called meetings everywhere, such as the one in New York on December 20 at the Tabernacle, where they denounced the war, blamed Polk for inciting it, and voted support of Clay's resolutions. Those resolutions virtually became the party's platform on the war.

Many of these Whig meetings expressly disavowed any attempt to acquire territory that would increase slave landholding. Even some Barnburners (the radical wing of the New York Democratic party who supposedly were so uncompromising in their antislavery views that they would even burn down the barn to get rid of the rats)[18] applauded Clay's resolutions, although they would have preferred a stronger statement on slavery, such as "No more Slave Territory at any rate." This objection to his position rather surprised Clay. "I have gone for no more territory for any purpose; and expressly for none for the purpose of Slavery. Ought not that to have satisfied them?"[19]

In any event, the speech definitely improved Clay's chances for the nomination, except among southern proslavery Whigs, of course, sometimes called Cotton Whigs.[20] If nothing else, the speech temporarily slowed the drift to-

17. Clay requested that reporters present not take notes on his speech but rather wait until he could provide them with a revised copy. The speech first appeared in the Lexington *Observer and Kentucky Reporter,* November 20, 1847, and was subsequently published in other newspapers around the country.

18. The Barnburners allied with the Locofocos.

19. Clay to Greeley, November 22, December 10, 1847, copies CPP.

20. For an excellent study of Conscience and Cotton Whigs, see Kinley J. Brauer, *Cotton versus Conscience: Massachusetts Whig Politics and Southwestern Expansion, 1843–1848* (Lexington, Ky., 1967).

ward Taylor among Kentucky Whigs. Conscience Whigs, particularly in New York, strenuously opposed Taylor's candidacy because he was a slaveholder who was seen as representing the southern agricultural wing of the Whig party as opposed to the northern wing, which emphasized support of manufactures and commerce. Those less concerned about Taylor's slaveholding found his unwillingness to express his commitment to Whig principles more trouble-some. In several published letters Taylor seemed to place himself above party. If Whigs, therefore, were compelled to choose a military candidate in order to win the election, they preferred Scott. But as Clay told Horace Greeley, Scott had no following among western Whigs. His published letters, especially those to Secretary of War William L. Marcy, subjected him to ridicule as something of scold. "Old Fuss and Feathers," he was called.

It is interesting that Clay did not mention the Wilmot Proviso specifically in his November 13 speech. But he had a reason, as he told Greely. "I did not touch eo nomini the Wilmot proviso," he wrote, "because in my view of things, it was not necessary to touch it. And sufficient for the day is the evil thereof."[21]

Not unexpectedly the speech brought renewed demands from northern friends and supporters that he formally declare his candidacy for President. He even received a request from members of the Native American party to stand as their candidate in 1848, but he turned them down. "I will decide next Spring," Clay told his Whig supporters, and then, after a moment's thought, he added: "or earlier if necessary."[22] Since he had to go to Washington around the first of the year to argue a case before the U.S. Supreme Court, he decided that he would have a better understanding of the political situation after talking with his political friends in Washington.[23]

He left Ashland the day after Christmas, endured another horrible jour-ney on the Ohio River, which was covered with floating ice, spent considera-ble time with his friends in Virginia and Baltimore, listened to their enthusias-tic comments about his Lexington speech, and reached the capital on January 10.[24]

Clay took the railroad from Baltimore—whenever possible, he had been using this newest form of transportation for the past several years—and the wildly cheering crowds that greeted him at the station on his arrival in Wash-ington gave fresh hope to his desire for another presidential run. Furthermore, "upon my arrival, I was most earnestly appealed to, chiefly from the Free States

21. Clay to Greeley, November 22, December 10, 1847, copies CPP; Greeley to Clay, November 30, 1847, Clay Papers, LC; Poage, *Clay and Whig Party,* pp. 166–168; Robert E. Rayback, *Millard Fillmore* (Buffalo, 1959), pp. 182–184; Herbert D. A. Donovan, *The Barnburners* (New York, 1925), p. 91ff.; Glyndon G. Van Deusen, *Horace Greeley* (Philadelphia, 1953), pp. 119–122.
22. Clay to Greeley, November 22, December 10, 1847, copies CPP. The Native American party subsequently nominated Zachary Taylor.
23. The case was *Houston* v. *City Bank of New Orleans.* Clay to Robert Letcher, December 22, 1847, copy CPP.
24. Clay to Lucretia, December 30, 1847, Thomas J. Clay Papers, LC.

but not exclusively, to abandon or suspend" any announcement that he would
not be a candidate. He was told that such an announcement would split the
party and lose the election. Even if Taylor could win, and that they doubted,
such a victory would constitute a loss, especially if he continued to maintain his
"present non-committal position as to parties and measures." Everyone was so
encouraged by Clay's healthy—almost youthful—physical appearance that
they pleaded with him to announce his candidacy. "HENRY CLAY," trumpeted the New York *Daily Tribune,* on February 17. "That name has magic in
it far exceeding that of any Caesar or conqueror."

Such reassurances buoyed his spirits to such an extent that he got through
a bleak Washington winter with fewer "colds (my great affliction) than usual."
He finally "consented not to abandon but to *suspend*" a final decision.[25] Meanwhile, with renewed vigor and zest, he threw himself into his duties as an
attorney arguing before the Supreme Court and into rallying his Washington
friends to check the activities of the "Young Indians," formed by Alexander H.
Stephens of Georgia among congressmen to advance the cause of General
Taylor. He also attended the wedding of Thomas Hart Benton's third daughter, Sarah, who married the brother of Clay's daughter-in-law.[26] Not surprisingly Clay escorted the bride to the supper table. It proved to be a grand sight
for those in attendance to see two old rivals, Benton and Clay, who used to
scream and rant at each other on the Senate floor, shaking hands, toasting the
bridal couple, and carrying on like long-lost brothers.[27]

The next day Clay attended the annual meeting of the American Colonization Society and gave an address, even though he had not come prepared to
do so and had no wish to trouble himself with its preparation. But he was the
president and felt obliged to make the effort. In his address he repeated his
belief that the white and black races could never live together on terms of
equality. Even though some thought his belief showed prejudice, he nonetheless felt that he spoke a simple truth. He still believed in equality as pronounced in the Declaration of Independence but only as "principle," not in
actuality. Where throughout "this entire nation . . . does the black man . . .
enjoy an equality with his white neighbor in social and political rights? In
none: no where. As to social rights, they are out of the question. In no city,
town, or hamlet throughout the entire land is he regarded as on an equal

25. Clay to James B. Clay, February 1, 1848, Clay Papers, LC; Clay to John Sloane, February 12,
1848, Clay to William N. Mercer, February 7, 1848, Clay to Richard Collins, February 20, 1848,
Clay to Anna Mercer, April 5, 1848, copies CPP. The New York *Daily Tribune,* January 26, 1848,
urged Clay not to withdraw from the presidential race. "Mr. Clay you know is here," reported
Senator Mangum, "& seems passive & indifferent, aiming at nothing, caring for nothing, & in that
respect, desiring & hoping for nothing. I say, *seems,* & yet his appearance not only throws much
consternation among Taylor men but is blocking their movements effectually, in various important quarters." Mangum to William A. Graham, January 23, February 15, 1848, in Mangum,
Papers, V, 92, 98.
26. Richard T. Jacob, brother of Susan Jacob Clay, the wife of James Brown Clay, married Sarah
McDowell Benton on January 17, 1848.
27. Poore, *Reminiscences,* I, 338; Clay to James B. Clay, January 16, 1848, Clay Papers, LC.

footing with us." Again he insisted that the solution to the problem consisted of the return of black people to Africa.[28]

Clay certainly reinvigorated his friends in Washington by his presence and swift action in taking control of his forces in Congress. "In the worst and darkest hours of political trouble, one feels a sense of safety when he is present," reported Horace Greeley.[29] "I watched him with interest," remarked another devoted observer, "as he lingered in the Senate Chamber . . . surrounded by admirers over whom the sway of his personal magnetism was as irresistible as that of Napoleon over his Old Guard."[30] They attended him in such great numbers at his lodgings in the United States Hotel that "to get a little rest, and to catch some breath," he accepted the invitation of Joseph Gales, editor of the *National Intelligencer,* to reside with him at the old Clarke house "on the Square of the Presidents." Clay even accepted an invitation to dine with President Polk, and he "was entertained with the greatest civility." But he found "too much political fog here for me yet to see any thing clearly and distinctly," for the "Whig party has not settled definitively on any course in regard to the Mexican War."[31]

Clay caused another sensation in arguing a New Orleans bank case before the Supreme Court.[32] Presiding over the Court was the chief justice, Roger B. Taney, whom Clay had "denounced in the Senate as one of the great scoundrels of the century." Dolley Madison sat beside Prince Hal, and he fussed over her and complimented her on her appearance. She in turn showed her enormous pride in him, no doubt reciprocating his own deep devotion to her late husband.

Mobs crowded their way into the tiny chamber to hear Prince Hal; many of them were women who knew nothing of the law but wished to claim the honor of witnessing what might be one of his last public performances. Again, he did not disappoint them. His "sonorous voice pealed through the corridors," reported one admirer, "and delighted a great throng." Clay himself was pleased. "My friends were highly gratified with it, and I was well satisfied." Quite unexpectedly, in view of the past hostility between Clay and Taney, the justices *unanimously* found in his favor, and he received a six-thousand-dollar fee for his efforts.[33]

Clay paid a formal visit to Justice Peter V. Daniel and was "extremely courteous indeed," reported the jurist. The Old Coon claimed he had argued his last case before the High Court, that he never "expected again to be east of

28. *National Intelligencer,* January 24, 1848.

29. New York *Daily Tribune,* February 23, 1848.

30. Stanton, *Random Recollections,* p. 154.

31. Clay to Christopher Hughes, January 12, 15, 1848, copies CPP; Clay to Lucretia, February 18, 1848, Clay Papers, LC.

32. *Houston* v. *City Bank of New Orleans.*

33. Stanton, *Random Recollections,* p. 152; Clay to Lucretia, February 18, 1848, Clay Papers, LC; Clay to William Mercer, March 18, 1848, copy CPP.

the mountains. But the declarations of hackneyed politicians are like 'Dicers oaths,' "[34] snickered Daniel. "He would no doubt avoid the mortification of again being a candidate with the prospect of defeat—but should the demonstrations of the federalists induce a belief of success, my opinion is that he would enter the contest with all the eagerness he has ever manifested."[35]

During Clay's stay in Washington, Nicholas Trist negotiated a treaty of peace with Mexico. According to the terms of the Treaty of Guadalupe Hidalgo, Mexico accepted the Rio Grande as the Texas border and ceded New Mexico and California. In return, the United States was to pay Mexico $15 million and, in addition, assume claims of American citizens against Mexico of up to $3.25 million.[36] Some members of the cabinet, including Secretary of State James Buchanan, hoped to take all or a large part of Mexico proper. But Clay advised Polk to accept Trist's treaty and end the abominable war. Polk agreed, submitted the treaty to the Senate, and on March 10, 1848, the upper house gave its consent by a vote of thirty-eight to fourteen, only three votes more than the necessary two-thirds.[37]

While Clay cavorted in the adulation and applause of his friends and admirers in Washington, his political fortunes in Kentucky took a turn for the worse. His refusal to commit himself publicly only encouraged the admirers of Zachary Taylor to organize their forces in an effort to win a nomination for the general at the state convention. The movement attracted early foes of Clay, like the Wickliffes, who realized they now had a supreme opportunity to topple the Old Coon from his lofty position as party chief as well as embarrass him in the bargain. Even men who loved Clay and had supported him in all his previous campaigns began deserting him because they were convinced he would again lead the party to defeat. They were realists, and they understood that the old questions like banks, internal improvements, and distribution with which Clay had been so long identified no longer attracted public interest. The people had moved on; they cared about expansion and slavery. For this very reason, John J. Crittenden continued to led the Taylor defection, but he still tried to be quiet about it. "Our friend Crittenden is in great distress," Senator Mangum noticed.

Robert Letcher was another defector and it tortured him to "betray" his mentor. "Great G——d," he moaned, if Clay had only foreseen "the predicament in which he had placed his friends and his party," he would not "have hesitated a moment about declining."[38]

---

34. "Such an act . . . makes marriage-vows as false as dicers' oaths." *Hamlet,* Act III, scene 4.

35. Daniel to Elizabeth Randolph Daniel, February 19, 1848, Daniel Family Papers, Virginia Historical Society, Richmond.

36. Trist negotiated the treaty even though he had been recalled by Polk.

37. Clay to James B. Clay, February 21, 1848, Thomas J. Clay Papers, LC; James K. Polk, *The Diary of a President, 1845–1849,* ed. Allan Nevins (New York, 1929), pp. 312–313; Eisenhower, *So Far from God,* p. 354. I do not mean to imply that Clay's advice was decisive in determining Polk's decision. Polk had California under the terms of the treaty, which was essential to him, along with the termination of the war. So he accepted the treaty.

38. "Mr. Crittenden is the head, the heart & soul of Taylorism *here;* with all respect however, for

The split in the Kentucky Whig party worsened because of the approaching gubernatorial contest. William J. Graves, absent from office since his frightful killing of Jonathan Cilley, wanted the Whig nomination, and he was backed by Governor William Owsley. But Archibald Dixon also coveted the post, and he was supported by Letcher. To avoid an open split and thereby guarantee a Democratic victory in the election, both sides at a state convention in Frankfort settled on a compromise candidate and selected Senator John Crittenden, without his knowledge or consent.[39] They also agreed not to place either Clay or Taylor in nomination for the presidency.[40] Instead, they chose two uninstructed delegates at large to attend the National Whig Convention to be held in Philadelphia on June 7, 1848, and directed county organizations to choose the remaining ten. And because of the superior state organization of the Taylor men—Clay was still not an announced candidate at this time—all ten delegates subsequently went to the general. It proved to be a fatal blow to Clay's candidacy. Also, the Taylor men held a rump "convention" the very day the state convention adjourned and nominated Old Rough and Ready, thereby creating the false impression that the Kentucky Whigs had dumped Clay and officially nominated Taylor.[41]

Poor Crittenden. He had thrust upon him the nomination of the relatively insignificant and unwanted office of governor, which he felt he could not refuse. He loved the Senate and did not wish to leave it, but he understood his duty to the party and so resigned from Congress. "It was cruel to take him from a theatre where he is winning an immortality of fame," said one. But others reckoned it just punishment for his abandonment of the Great Pacificator.[42]

Three days before Clay was scheduled to leave Washington for Philadelphia on business for Isaac Shelby, John Quincy Adams "was stricken . . . in his seat in the H. of R. with paralysis." The sudden shock of it saddened Clay, who visited the family and held the dying man's hand, his eyes filled with tears. John Quincy Adams never recovered consciousness and died a few days later. "So we go!" sighed the Kentuckian. He continued on his journey but later wrote to the Adams family and expressed his sympathy. "No surviving friend of your father," he declared to Charles Francis Adams, "sympathizes and condoles with you all, with more sincerity and cordiality than I do." Throughout his life John Quincy Adams's career "was patriotic, bright and glorious." For nearly a

---

his old friend Clay, whom he sincerely thinks, unavailable." Mangum to William A. Graham, January 23, 1848, Mangum to James F. Simmons, May 11, 1848, in Mangum, *Papers,* V, 93; Letcher to Crittenden, February 21, 1848, Crittenden Papers, LC.

39 Kirwan, *Crittenden,* pp. 211–214.

40. The delegates chose not to embarrass Clay by nominating Taylor, expecting the Old Coon to announce his retirement in the immediate future. But the failure of the convention to nominate him was in itself a defeat for the great man and seen as such throughout the state.

41. Poage, *Clay and Whig Party,* pp. 171–173.

42. Coleman, ed., Life of *Crittenden,* I, 293; Francis P. Blair to Van Buren, March 3, 1848, Van Buren Papers, LC; Kirwan, *Crittenden,* pp. 213–214.

century, Clay continued, the name of Adams has "shone out, with the brightest beams, at home and abroad. . . . May its lustre, in their descendants,
continue undiminished."[43]

Clay took the five o'clock railroad train (the "cars," as he called it) for
Baltimore on February 23, remained overnight with his friend Christopher
Hughes, and then proceeded to Philadelphia. At Elkton, Maryland, a committee of one hundred men from Philadelphia met him and escorted him the rest
of the way. At Wilmington he was saluted with flags, cannons, and martial
music. And an enormous mob greeted him at the railroad station in Philadelphia when he arrived on February 25 and accompanied him on the short ride
to the mayor's residence. The following day he gave a speech at Independence
Hall and delivered a eulogy for his late friend. Their associations together over
many years were now remembered, he said, "with feelings and emotions of
friendship, admiration, and affection for his memory, which he should in vain
endeavor to describe."[44]

Clay remained in Philadelphia for more than a week attending formal
receptions and concluding the Shelby business. Rather than return to Washington, he decided, at the urging of friends, to head north to New York.
Accompanied by a retinue of one hundred, he first stopped off at Perth
Amboy, New Jersey, attended more receptions, and then took a steamboat for
New York City,[45] where Horace Greeley and others had organized a large rally
at Castle Garden to cheer and proclaim his candidacy. Over the next six days he
visited the Institution for the Blind, another for the Deaf and Dumb, spoke to
a Young Ladies Institute where the ladies had to line up around the park in
order to meet him, and paid courtesy calls on Albert Gallatin, Martin Van
Buren, and John Jacob Astor. The crowds, the receptions, the formal and
informal appearances, and the speeches nearly overwhelmed him, but they all
heightened his sense of coming victory in winning the Whig presidential nomination.

On one occasion "tens of thousands of females" in New York, according
to Philip Hone, were presented to Prince Hal. "They all pressed his hands;
many kissed him; and one hand . . . prompted by a spirit of Amazonian
hardiness and armed with 'the glittering forfex'[scissors] . . . did actually commit a new 'Rape of the Lock.' " Even when he went to church at St. Bartholo-
mew's, the congregation rose when he entered to demonstrate its affection and
regard. On leaving the church, "with Mrs. Brady on his arm," the parishioners
repeated their "marks of homage."[46]

---

43. Clay to James Clay, February 21, 1848, Thomas J. Clay Papers, LC; Clay to Christopher
Hughes, February 22, 1848, copy CPP; Poore, *Reminiscences,* p. 341; Clay to Charles Francis
Adams, May 15, 1848, Massachusetts Historical Society, copy CPP.
44. New York *Daily Tribune,* February 28, 1848; *National Intelligencer,* March 1, 1848.
45. "Capt. Vanderbilt" offered his "splendid, newly-painted boat, free of charge" to the Common
Council to bring Clay to the city. New York *Daily Tribune,* March 7, 1848.
46. New York *Daily Tribune,* March 10, 11, 13, 1848; Hone, *Diary,* II, 845. A lock of Clay's hair

When Clay left New York for Baltimore, via Newark, New Jersey, and Philadelphia, he begged his friend Hughes in Baltimore to forgo all demonstrations and receptions. "My greatest want is rest & peace. Do keep the crowd off me; and if you cannot I shall hasten away from you."[47]

But arrangements had already been made for his appearance in Baltimore, and they could not be altered. Besides, he was programed for a St. Patrick's Day speech to the Hibernian Society of Baltimore, and since the Irish had abandoned him en masse in 1844, it behooved him to court their favor. And with his power of speech he was sure to delight them—and perhaps win them over—as he did by way of a testimonial to Father Theobald Mathew, the Irish temperance reformer. His efforts were rewarded with an honorary membership in the society, to which he responded: "[O]n no occasion have I regarded the voluntary extension of such an honor to me with more gratification than I now feel"—which is what he always said when an honor was conferred upon him.[48]

Clay departed for home on March 18. "I am returning after receiving the most enthusiastic demonstrations of affectionate attachment of which I was ever in my life before the object," he told William Mercer. Because of them, he had pretty much decided to make a public announcement when he reached Lexington on whether he would allow his name to be advanced as a presidential candidate, although he persisted in his contention that he regarded it as a dubious honor to engage in another "doubtful contest."[49]

On his way home he learned about the new upheavals breaking out all over Europe, especially France. Louis Philippe had abdicated, and the nation seemed in turmoil. "Poor France," Clay moaned. "I fear she is destined to undergo another bloody Revolution. It is preposterous to suppose her capable of establishing and maintaining a Republic."[50]

At Pittsburgh a wild and enthusiastic greeting awaited him. "As I approached it in a Steamboat on the Monongahela, filled with passengers and resounding with music, one of the most brilliant scenes opened on me that I ever beheld. In front a beautiful wire bridge was gracefully suspended over the river, crowded with people. The bend of the river, from the waters' edge, to its summit, for many hundred yards, was chock full with people." The entire population of the city seemed to be present. "All this was accompanied with the display of numerous flags, the roar of Cannon, the ringing of bells and the sound of music, and the enthusiastic cheers of the countless multitude."

(there are several in existence) is presently in the possession of Professor Sarah McMahon of Bowdoin College, whose grandmother's great-uncle purchased it at auction in 1864. Professor McMahon kindly presented me with several strands, and they are a light blond color.

47. New York *Tribune,* March 1, 6, 1848; Clay to Hughes, March 12, 1848, copy CPP.
48. *National Intelligencer,* March 24, 1848.
49. Clay to Mercer, March 18, 1848, copy CPP.
50. Clay to Hughes, March 19, 1848, copy CPP.

If Clay had difficulty believing he was beloved, he doubted no longer as he stared at these happy, smiling faces beaming at him. He actually wept. The flood of emotion that overtook him can best be imagined, he said. That night there was a torchlight procession through the city of all the fire companies. "Bands of music, flags, firing of rockets &c &c" accompanied them. Hordes of people screamed their admiration and devotion at him. It seemed that as a *private* individual, not a presidential candidate, the Old Coon had now risen to a new level of affection and esteem and popularity among the people. He had transcended past political limitations and achieved a place among the nation's immortals. They hailed him as the "Sage of Ashland," the beloved "Star of the West."

These wildly emotional demonstrations were repeated from Pittsburgh to Maysville as he descended the river. "At all the towns and villages, the whole surrounding population seemed to have gathered together, to greet to cheer and welcome me, amidst the incessant roar of Cannon."[51]

But these scenes also excited the passions of his enemies, who kept reassuring themselves (and publicly contending) that the Sage would eventually withdraw from the race for the good of the party. "You have no idea how I am tortured here with anxious inquiries whether you *will* withdraw," wrote a Cincinnati newspaper editor. To counter the claims of your enemies, wrote a Whig friend in Ohio, you must announce your candidacy, and you must "publicly declare against the extension of slavery in the new territories. This is inferred . . . not only from your general opinions and public *acts* respecting slavery, but also from your resolutions at the Lexington meeting." These staunch friends were particularly disturbed by Taylor's letter to Peter Sken Smith on January 30, 1848, in which he said that he would accept any nomination, provided it had been made "entirely independent of party considerations." He followed up that astounding announcement with a response to a "no-party" political meeting that had nominated him in Montgomery County, Alabama, that he would not oppose its use of his name provided it was used "independent of party distinction."[52]

Obviously, said Clay's friends, Taylor abjures political parties; he cares nothing about Whig principles; he simply wants to be President, and he will ride any party or no party to achieve his ambition. That said, they urged the Sage to declare his candidacy. Otherwise the Whig party is finished, they argued. If Taylor wins the nomination and the election, it will mean that party and measures and principles mean nothing. Military glory would be the sole prerequisite for presidential office.

51. Clay to Mary S. Bayard, March 31, 1848, University of Kentucky Library, copy CPP.
52. Thomas B. Stevenson to Clay, April 8, 1848, Clay Papers, LC; Lexington *Observer and Kentucky Reporter,* March 4, April 8, 1848; Taylor to William B. Preston, March 28, 1848, Taylor Papers, Virginia Historical Society, Richmond; Holman Hamilton, *Zachary Taylor: Soldier in the White House* (Indianapolis and New York, 1951), pp. 66–72; Bauer, *Zachary Taylor,* pp. 215–238.

Many of these friends, especially those in Ohio, also begged Clay to declare against the extension of slavery. "We cannot carry Ohio for you, unless you take ground satisfactorily against extending slavery in new territories, or, in less exceptionable phrase, *for free soil remaining free.*" The sentiment in Ohio on this subject, they delcared, "is resistless as the flow of the waters."[53]

On April 10, 1848, the Sage of Ashland finally committed himself. His announcement to the public was published two days later in the Lexington *Observer and Kentucky Reporter* and then telegraphed around the country. With malice no doubt intended, Clay sent a copy to John J. Crittenden. "I can add nothing to the reasons which it assigns for the course which I have finally felt it to be my duty to adopt; but I shall be most happy if they meet with the concurrence of your judgement."[54]

In his announcement to the public Clay claimed an unwillingness to run again but that over the past three months many friends had convinced him "that the withdrawal of my name would be fatal to the success, and perhaps lead to the dissolution, of the party with which I have been associated, especially in the free States," that if he would consent to the use of his name, the "great States of New York and Ohio" would vote for him, especially Ohio, which "would give her vote to no candidate . . . but me." He therefore finally decided to leave the consideration of his name to the Whig National Convention in June in Philadelphia. Whatever its decision, "it will meet with my prompt and cheerful acquiescence."

But the statement proved a great disappointment. It was a namby-pamby kind of announcement, hardly the sort of thing his friends expected from the great man. He would leave it to the convention to decide indeed. What kind of announcement was that? And he said nothing about slavery in the territories, as his Ohio supporters begged him to do. Perhaps as the "Sage of Ashland" and with his new status of national icon, Clay felt that a more politically charged announcement would be inappropriate. He probably thought he was playing the role that would best advance his cause.

In any event, Crittenden, in a courteous response to his note, thanked him for the copy of the declaration and said that he hoped "it may turn out for the best" but that he would stick with Taylor because, frankly, "there was not that *certainty* of success" which would warrant Clay's friends supporting his name.[55]

Acting more like a hard-nosed politician than a revered sage, Clay expressed greater commitment to his own candidacy in his letters to several confidential friends, urging them to attend the national convention as delegates. "What will be wanted there will be bold decided and good Speakers. For

53. Stevenson to Clay, April 8, 1848, Clay Papers, LC.
54. Clay to Crittenden, April 10, 1848, Crittenden Papers, LC.
55. Crittenden to Clay, May 4, 1848, Thomas J. Clay Papers, LC.

the want of such, I lost the nomination at Harrisburg in 1839, and that was the original cause of all the subsequent difficulties of the Whig party." Carefully calculating his strategy, Clay reckoned that as the Whig candidate he could count "absolutely" on the electoral votes of Kentucky, Tennessee, North Carolina, New York, and Maryland, with a fair prospect of Louisiana and Florida, leaving him with a deficiency of some five or six votes. These might be obtained from Pennsylvania, Indiana, Iowa, Georgia, and possibly Michigan. Massachusetts could be forgotten, he said. "Some of our friends there have been tickled with the feather of the Vice Presidency" to rally to Taylor. Much, of course, would depend on the nominee of the Democratic party. Lewis Cass of Michigan, James Buchanan of Pennsylvania, and Levi Woodbury of New Hampshire were the likeliest candidates. "The two first," said Clay, "I regard as the weakest."[56]

Clay knew about the strong organization of "Young Indians" in Washington formed to win the nomination for General Taylor, so he wrote to a number of his congressional friends and advised them to form a "counter organization, to operate on the Convention." The Young Indians included mostly southern Whigs, like Robert Toombs, Alexander H. Stephens, John S. Pendleton, Thomas S. Flournoy, and William C. Preston, but they had northern support as well. Truman Smith of Connecticut was a prominent leader of the group, Abraham Lincoln of Illinois less so.[57]

What enhanced Clay's candidacy was the curious, if not foolish, public statement Taylor made on April 20, published in the Richmond *Whig,* reaffirming his stand as a no-party candidate. Regardless of who the Democratic and Whig candidates might be, the statement read, he, "Old Rough and Ready," would run for the presidency.

Whigs did not take kindly to that mindless declaration, and even Crittenden admitted to Clay that "I am at a loss to conjecture" what the result of Taylor's announcement would be. "It makes the future still more impenetrable, & dark—I can hardly contemplate it without despondency." Fortunately for Taylor, Crittenden did something about it. Together with Toombs and Stephens, he drafted a statement to be published over Taylor's signature and then hurried it to the general in Baton Rouge for his approval. At the same time Taylor's Louisiana lieutenants anticipated Crittenden's letter with one of their own. The two letters were identical in content, and on April 23 the letter by the Louisiana group, addressed to Taylor's brother-in-law Captain John S. Allison of Louisville, appeared in the New Orleans *Picayune.* In it Old Rough and Ready professed to be "a Whig but not ultra Whig"—whatever that

56. Clay to Kenneth Rayner, April 12, 1848, Clay to Thomas Stevenson, April 12, May 20, 1848, Clay to William Mercer, April 18, 1848, copies CPP.
57. Clay to James E. Harvey, April 18, 1848, private collection, copy CPP; Hamilton, *Taylor,* II, 63–64. Clay was still Lincoln's "beau ideal of a statesman," but the young man did not believe the Sage could win in 1848. Basler, ed., *Collected Works of Lincoln,* III, 29, IV, 184; II, 125.

meant. If elected, he would be the President of all the people, not simply the
Whig President. He would be "independent of party domination," and he
pledged not to use the veto power, except in case of a clear violation of the
Constitution.[58]

Taylor also wrote to Clay in response to a letter from the Great Pacificator. He explained that a number of the Kentuckian's "warm political & personal friends" had assured him that Clay would not run again and that no other
Whig but he himself was likely to win the election. Be that as it may, Taylor
was in the race to stay. "I therefore now consider myself in the hands of the
people a portion of whom have placed my name before the Country . . . [but]
should you [Clay] receive the nomination . . . & should be elected in Novr, but
few of your friends will be more gratified than myself."[59]

Taylor's Allison letter brought sighs of relief from his party supporters.
Presumably they could now present him as a certified Whig—if not an "ultra"
Whig—and the general's "availability" rose considerably, especially in Kentucky. Horace Greeley, editor of the New York *Tribune* and presumably one
of Clay's staunchest supporters, believed the Old Coon's cause had been lost.
"I believe we are doomed to be beaten," he told Clay, because of "the men who
control the counsel of the Whig party through the machinery existing at
Washington." James Harlan agreed. He arrived in the capital to find "things in
a very bad condition. . . . The Palo Alto Club [Taylor's victory at Palo Alto
furnished the name] have regular meetings and are as well drilled, as any Corps
of Regulars Genl T. ever commanded." They had a committee to meet delegates when they arrived for the Whig National Convention to indoctrinate
them in the belief that Clay was "not available." And, to a very large extent,
they had already succeeded in conveying that impression to the public at large.
"The delegation of both Houses of Kentucky," with two exceptions, Harlan
told Clay, "being known to be against your nomination, has, I fear, laid the
foundation of your defeat in the Convention." They mean "to Tomahawk
you."[60]

Apart from Clay's reputation as a loser, what apparently hurt him most
among professional politicians was his stand on the slavery question. His Lexington speech completely alienated southern Whigs yet did not go far enough

58. Crittenden to Clay, May 4, 1848, Thomas J. Clay Papers, LC; Taylor to Crittenden, November
15, 1848, Crittenden Papers, LC; Kirwan, *Crittenden*, pp. 216–219; Poage, *Clay and Whig Party*,
pp. 176–177; Bauer, *Taylor*, pp. 222–223. The letter composed by the Louisiana group had the
cooperation of Taylor himself. Hamilton, *Taylor*, II, 74–75. Clay thought Taylor's Allison letter
"began with the silly if not presumtuous hope that the two parties would vie with each other in
supporting him." Clay to Stevenson, October 9, 1848, in Clay, *Works*, III, 485.
59. Taylor to Clay, April 30, 1848, Clay Papers, LC. Clay's letter to Taylor has apparently disappeared.
60. Henry S. Le Vert and Charles C. Langdon to Clay, May 29, 1848, Greeley to Clay, May 29,
1848, Harlan to Clay, June 2, 1848, Clay Papers, LC. Harlan was the only Kentucky delegate to
vote for Clay on all four ballots at the convention.

to satisfy many northern Whigs, like Thomas Corwin of Ohio and his followers and William H. Seward of New York and his friends.

In the meantime, the Democrats held their convention in Baltimore and
selected as their presidential candidate the senator from Michigan Lewis Cass,
who supported the doctrine of squatter sovereignty, or popular sovereignty,
which contended that local government in the territories should decide the
question of slavery. The New York delegation to the convention was split
between Barnburners and their rival Hunker[61] faction, and when Cass was
nominated, the Barnburners walked out. They held their own convention in
Utica, New York, endorsed the Wilmot Proviso, and nominated Martin Van
Buren. The old Liberty party men joined them and at Buffalo formed the Free
Soil party, which nominated Van Buren for President and Charles Francis
Adams for Vice President on a platform of "free soil, free speech, free labor,
and free men."[62]

The Whig Convention gathered in Philadelphia in the salon of the Chi-
nese Museum on June 7. Clay's friend and former governor of North Carolina
John M. Morehead was chosen president without opposition from the Palo
Alto Club. When the delegates began balloting, a motion was advanced stating
that no candidate could be offered unless he pledged to carry out Whig principles; but Morehead ruled this out of order, and the delegates sustained him.
Then a Louisiana delegate was permitted to read a letter from Taylor in which
he agreed to abide by the decision of the convention and to withdraw from the
campaign if someone else was chosen.

On the first ballot Taylor received 111 votes. Clay followed with 97, Scott
next with 43, then Webster with 22, with scattered votes for Clayton and
McLean. The winning candidate needed 140 votes for nomination. Kentucky
gave 5 votes to Clay and 7 to Taylor. On the second ballot Clay lost 11 and
Taylor gained 7. Then, on the third ballot, Connecticut, which had cast all its
votes for Clay, now split them with Taylor.

Applause, hisses, and cries of "Order! gentlemen! order! rap! knock!"
sounded throughout the salon after the announcement of Connecticut's action. Then 3 of Clay's Maryland votes switched to Taylor. That started the
stampede. At the end of the third ballot Taylor needed only 8 votes for a
majority, and he got them on the fourth and final ballot. Even Kentucky, as
might have been expected, deserted Clay; among the delegates, only Harlan
remained loyal. Taylor was nominated with 171 votes to Clay's 32. Clay obtained only 6 votes from the slave states, while Taylor took 105; of the dele-

61. Conservative Democrats so named because they "hunkered" after spoils, while Barnburners,
the more radical Democrats, opposed slavery.
62. Poage, *Clay and Whig Party,* p. 178; Donovan, *Barnburners* (New York, 1925), pp. 98–109;
John Mayfield, *Rehearsal for Republicanism: Free Soil and the Politics of Antislavery* (Port Washington, N.Y., 1980) pp. 101–125; Frederick J. Blue, *The Free Soilers: Third Party Politics* (Urbana, Ill.,
1973), pp. 70–80; Cole, *Van Buren,* pp. 414–415. See also Robert G. Rayback, *Free Soil: The
Election of 1848* (Lexington, Ky., 1970) and Richard H. Seward, *Ballots for Freedom: Antislavery
Politics in the United States, 1837–1860* (New York, 1976);

gates from free states, only 66 out of 169 voted for Taylor. Millard Fillmore of New York was then nominated for Vice President.[63]

It was another bitter defeat for the Sage of Ashland. Except for Harlan, wrote Leslie Combs to Clay, there was not "one *true* friend" among the Kentucky delegation. The others? "All rotten." Ohio voted for Scott consistently and gave Clay only one vote. The delegation "played false from first to last." Combs summed up the convention with this comment: "They would not take a true *ultra* Whig & a constitutional, conservative Slave holder—and they have gotten—an *Ultra* Slave holder & no particular Whig." The party had no soul, he lamented. It wanted office, no matter how obtained. "Guerilleras—and Bedouin Arabs, looking out for plunder, were thick as Blackberries from every State—far & near."[64]

"Great God," cried another, "what are we coming to—I feel disgraced that I ever was called a Whig. . . . A party no longer of principle, but of availability and expediency." Some swore they would go home and work to prevent Taylor's election. Others said they would hold a separate convention and nominate "an ultra Whig," like Clay. "D——n Kentucky," grumbled one. "The unhappy complexion of the Kentucky delegation," wrote John Lawrence to Clay, "had a malign influence from the start, and was still more pernicious when, upon the very first vote, it was found to be *one* in number worse than all our fears had calculated." But loyal Harlan credited it all to the Palo Alto Club. "I wrote to you the triggers were all Set at Washington before the Convention met," he told Clay, "and it was impossible to counteract the movements made by Members of Congress."[65]

Many newspapers carried cartoons in which they declared that Clay had been politically "assassinated" in Baltimore. "The Whig party as such is dead," moaned Willis Hall, a New York party leader. "The very name will be abandoned should Taylor be elected, for the Taylor party.' The last Whig convention committed the double crime of *suicide* & homicide."[66]

Clay could scarcely believe the reports he received. The treachery in Kentucky he knew about and understood. But Ohio? He had been assured of Ohio's vote and on that account been urged to announce his candidacy. In fact, his public letter of April 10 specifically mentioned the support he had in Ohio as one of the reasons for his announcement. So Clay wrote to several Ohio friends and demanded an explanation. "Among the most powerful considerations which induced me to consent to the submission of my name to the recent Whig Convention at Philada. was that derived from the assurance, again and again made, in every form and from the highest sources, in Ohio, that I would

63. "Whig National Convention of 1848," *History of U.S. Political Parties*, ed. Arthur M. Schlesinger, Jr., (New York, 1973), I, 433–439.

64. Combs to Clay, June 10, 1848, Clay Papers, LC.

65. George C. Collins to Clay, June 10, 1848, John C. Proud to Clay, June 11, 1848, John Lawrence to Clay, June 9, 1848, James Harlan to Clay, June 15, 1848, Clay Papers, LC.

66. Hall to Clay, June, 1848, Clay Papers, LC.

receive the vote of a majority of the delegates. . . . But for that convention . . . I never would have yielded that consent."

One Ohioan said that the treachery "emanated from the Cabal at Washington." Horace Greeley added that "we were overborne by the immense influence of that central position [Washington], and by the combined power of politicians, presses and money." Another Ohioan said it was "the search for that new fangled thing which, in the brainless cant of the day, is flippantly termed 'availability.'" Also, it was learned that the Webster men had assured the Ohio delegation that they would not go for Scott any more than they would for Clay, thus "stabbing you for the benefit of Taylor, or of breeding a difficulty to favor the chances of some third man," like Thomas Corwin. And Corwin, of course, had pretended all along there could be no one but the Kentuckian. He kept saying of Clay, "I esteem him, revere him, love him, just as I have since I lived in his mess. I only wish it had pleased God to make one *million* of such men, instead of *one.*"[67]

After gathering all this information, Clay summed it up in a letter to Horace Greeley: "I lost the nomination from three causes 1st. the course of the Kentucky delegation. 2 My very great disappointment in not obtaining, as I had every reason to suppose I should, the support of the Ohio delegation. And 3dly. the persevering adherence of the Massachusetts delegation to Mr. Webster." The Ohio action totally surprised him, but he would be eternally grateful to New Yorkers "for their zealous and constant support." He also allowed as how his residence in a slave state cost him dearly. Ironically the final result of the convention produced the nomination of one "far more deeply imbued with the doctrines of Slavery than ever I was or shall be."[68]

In the midst of his speculations over the causes for his loss of the nomination, Governor William Owsley invited him to fill the Senate seat left vacant by Crittenden's resignation. No one in the state, the governor wrote, can render more service to Kentucky "and, I may add, to the whole Union, as yourself." Europe is convulsed in revolution, and this might involve the United States in war or induce "great commercial revulsions." Owsley appreciated that Clay had taken a formal and final leave of the Senate; still, "a patriot is never discharged but by death."

Despite these flattering sentiments, Clay graciously refused the offer, citing age, long public service, and possible personal embarrassment. Were there an emergency he would certainly make any sacrifice. Besides, the current congressional session was drawing to a close, and by the time he reached Washington it might all be over. Once the general assembly reconvened, it would elect Crittenden's successor, and he had no wish to be placed "in a position that

67. Hall to Clay, June, 1848, Clay Papers, LC; Clay to Sloane, June 13, 1848, Clay to Stevenson, June 14, 1848, Clay to Hughes, June 14, 1848, copies CPP; Stevenson to Clay, May 22, June 12, 19, 1848, Sloane to Clay, June 22, 1848, Harlan to Clay, June 22, 1848, Greeley to Clay, June 21, 1848, Lawrence to Clay, June 23, 1848, Clay Papers, LC.
68. Clay to Greeley, June 15, 1848, private collection, copy CPP.

might occasion it the least embarrassment in the choice of that successor."[69] Owsley accepted the rejection and appointed Thomas Metcalfe to the post.

Meanwhile, more and more Ohioans were coming forward with explanations for their behavior in Philadelphia. Lewis D. Campbell in a speech reported in the Cincinnati *Herald* on July 27 said he favored Thomas Corwin first and Clay second, but when he got to the convention, he found a strong Taylor organization that insisted that only a military man could defeat General Cass, the Democratic nominee. And because Kentucky had abandoned Clay, the Ohioans decided to vote for General Scott. Philadelphia Van Trump, a three-term Ohio congressman, blamed "the double-dealing of Ex-Govr. Vance; who, though professedly an anti-Taylor man in Convention, done all he could to secure his nomination." He prevailed on the "20 [Ohio] delegates to go together, and to promise that none would break unless all did so." He "was probably associated with the clique at Washington, in favor of Genl Taylor," said Van Trump.[70]

Then Scott told Clay that upon his return to the United States from the war in early May 1848, suffering "with a Mexican *diarrhoea*," he had offered to run as Vice President with Clay but was told that the Old Coon's Kentucky friends in Congress had given him up "on some calculation of a want of availability."[71]

Clay shook with rage when he read this letter. "Thus you see a false suggestion as to those who were friendly to me in Congress," he stormed, "and the suppression of the truth." Supposedly he then wrote a scathing denunciation of the Kentucky delegation and entrusted its publication to his son James. However, James concealed it until his father had cooled down and then prevailed upon his parent to suppress it.[72] Also, throughout the summer the Sage received countless pleas from Whigs in many states, particularly New York and Ohio, to run despite the action of their convention. Even the "Slash Church in Hanover," Virginia, his place of birth, begged him to run. "The Democrats, have their candidates, the Abolitionists theirs, and the *No party* have their candidates but sir, the *honest Whigs,* who so nobly fought for you, our gallant leader in 44, have no candidate." You must *"save* our *glorious* party, from dissolution."[73]

69. Owsley to Clay, June 20, 1848, Clay to Owsley, June 22, 1848, copies CPP. Earlier Clay had recommended Adam Beatty for the vacant post. See Clay to Beatty, May 28, 1848, copy CPP.

70. Stevenson to Clay, July 26, September 9, 1848, Van Trump to Clay, July 26, 1848, Clay Papers, LC; Clay to Stevenson, August 14, 1848, copy CPP. A year later Clay had decided upon the principal culprit for his loss of Ohio. "Circumstances have compelled me most reluctantly to believe," he wrote John Sloane on April 10, 1849, "that Genl. [and ex-Governor of the state Joseph] Vance was the Agent or instrument in carrying off from me to Genl Scott, the twenty Ohio delegates who acted with him in the Convention." Copy CPP.

71. Scott to Clay, July 19, 1848, Clay Papers, LC.

72. Clay to Stevenson, August 5, 1848, copy CPP. Clay's letter denouncing the Kentucky delegation no longer exists. George Poage claims that a copy was read to him in August 1920 by James's son, who related the circumstances. Poage, *Clay and Whig Party,* p. 181 and note 27.

73. John M. Botts to Clay, July 3, 1848, Clay to George W. Curtis, July 4, 1848, Clay Papers, LC;

All this deeply depressed the great man. "I fear that the Whig party is dissolved," he sighed, "and that no longer are there Whig principles to animate zeal and to stimulate exertion. I am compelled, most painfully, to believe that the Whig party has been succeeded by a mere *personal* party, as much a Taylor party, as was the Jackson party." Throughout his long public service he had fought against the "cult" of personality and tried to instill in his followers the necessity of principles and issues as the reasons for the existence of parties. Everything he represented and believed now seemed overthrown, rejected, utterly destroyed by the Jacksonian approach to politics. Even Whigs, who should know better, had abandoned their principles for a military chieftain because he was "available" and could win the election. Instead of a proven statesman, they had chosen a man whose qualifications for "civil services" consisted of "sleeping forty years in the woods, and cultivating moss in the calves of his legs." The Whig party could never last under such purpose and direction.[74]

Although the movement for an independent Whig nomination had strong support in New York and Ohio, Clay refused to countenance it, and the movement finally dissipated and faded away. "I consider my public career as forever terminated," he said. Just what he would do in the election he had not yet decided. He would never vote for Cass, but whether he would vote for the "no party" candidate remained to be seen. In any event, he had no intention of coming out publicly in support of Taylor despite the urgings of many. Why should he? The general had threatened to run no matter whom the Whigs nominated; why, then, should Clay betray his deepest beliefs and encourage the electorate to vote for such a candidate? If, as President, Taylor betrayed Whig principles, then Clay would be forever disgraced for having invited his party to rally behind the general. He was willing to endorse Millard Fillmore, whom he knew to be "able, enlightened, indefatigable . . . and patriotic," but not Taylor. Old Rough and Ready was "exclusively a military man," without any experience in "civil affairs, bred up and always living in the camp with his sword by his side, and his Epoulettes on his shoulders." No, the Sage of Ashland would remain silent.[75]

In one private statement rejecting an independent candidacy, Clay blasted

N. B. Meade, J. W. King et al. to Clay, August 31, 1848, Thomas J. Clay Papers, LC; Clay to Stevenson, August 5, 14, 1848, Thomas G. Clarke to Clay, August 22, 1848, Clay to Clarke, September 12, 1848, Clay to James Brooks, September 8, 1848, Daniel Ullmann, September 9, 1848, copies CPP.

74. Clay to William W. Worsley et al., June 27, 1848, Thomas J. Clay Papers, LC; Thomas B. Stevenson to Clay, May 22, 1848, Clay Papers, LC.

75. Clay to Nicholas Dean, August 24, 1848, in Clay, *Works,* IV, 572–573; Clay to Cincinnati Whigs, September 1, 1848, Clay to James Brooks, September 8, 1848, Clay to Henry White, September 10, 1848, Clay to William G. Payne, September 19, 1848, copies CPP; Clay to Daniel Ullmann, September 16, 1848, Clay to James Lynch et al., September 20, 1848, Clay, *Works,* IV, 574–577.

Taylor as "wholly incompetent to the office. I lament to say that . . . he has practised duplicity that he is vascillating and instable." The convention allowed itself "to be menaced or frightened into [his] nomination, which it ought never to have made." It has placed the Whig party "in a humiliating condition" by yielding to the "overbearing influence of some Southern & S. Western members of Congress." It accepted his "hocus pocus explanation of his position made by the Louisiana delegation, upon an unproduced letter alleged to be from him." Out of deference to friends Clay said he would not come out publicly and oppose him. "I remain silent and passive. My great solicitude now, that my public career is terminated, is to preserve unsullied my character."[76]

Clay suffered another terrible jolt when he was informed that a "favorite grandson," James Erwin, Jr., "a most promising" young man, had shot himself to death. The circumstances "greatly aggravated our grief," Clay conceded. Then a niece whom Lucretia "dearly loved" died, and in September his son-in-law Martin Duralde, Jr., also died. "Ah! my dear Hughes," he later wrote his friend Christopher Hughes, "we must all soon follow them. We ought to be prepared for it, and I hope that you think seriously on that momentus matter."[77]

To add to his grief, a letter, supposedly written by John Crittenden, which said that Henry Clay was a millstone around the neck of the Whig party and had been for the past quarter century, that any Whig but Clay could have won in 1844, and that "everybody had beat him, and anybody could," circulated during the summer. It naturally caused quite a sensation. Later Crittenden denied writing any such letter, and it was subsequently learned to be fraudulent. Despite this latest insult, Clay voted for Crittenden in the August election probably because he knew that Crittenden was innocent of the charges brought against him and indeed had acted honorably throughout the contest. Clay never came out against him, and Crittenden won the election by more than eight thousand votes.[78] But in the presidential election the Old Coon did not vote for Taylor because he was confined to his bed for most of November for an unspecified illness.[79]

Clay would not and could not face the fact that many Whigs rejoiced in his latest defeat. "Thank God, we have got rid of the old tyrant at last!" exulted William S. Archer of Virginia. They hoped his perpetual domination of the party was broken at last and forever. But others shared Clay's pain in suffering

---

76. Clay to Morton McMichael, September 16, 1848, copy CPP.

77. Clay to Susan Allibone, July 19, 1848, Clay, *Works,* IV, 569–570; Clay to Mary S. Bayard, October 19, 1848, Clay to Hughes, September 30, 1848, copies CPP. It is not clear whether Erwin's death was a suicide or an accident.

78. Clay to James Harlan, August 5, 1848, Clay, *Works,* IV, 571; James Erwin to A. T. Burnley, July 18, 1848, Crittenden Papers, LC; Kirwan, *Crittenden,* pp. 228–231.

79. Lexington *Observer and Kentucky Reporter,* November 15, 18, 29, 1848.

through yet another rejection. They hoped he would rise above it. Northern Whigs particularly wished he would turn his attention toward emancipating slaves in Kentucky. "I could wish also," wrote his Cincinnati editor friend Thomas Stevenson, "that the Sage of Ashland should distinctly (now that no electioneering motive can be ascribed) denounce the scheme . . . [of] extending the curse of [slavery] into free territory."[80]

But Clay would not oblige them. He believed that the North was overly apprehensive about slavery in the territories just acquired from Mexico. The area was simply not conducive to slavery, he said. Even so, he did think that the South ought "magnanimously to assent" to the exclusion of slavery from the new territories. It would prevail sooner or later, he prophetically predicted, and if the South resists it, "the conflict . . . will either lead to a dissolution of the Union, or deprive it of that harmony which alone can make the Union desirable. It will lead to the formation of a sectional and Northern party, which will, sooner or later, take permanent and exclusive possession of the government."[81]

Although by late October Clay believed that Cass would be elected, "contrary to my wishes," Taylor fooled him and eked out a slim victory. He carried New York—thanks to Van Buren's candidacy, which took enough votes away from Cass to give the state to Taylor—and Pennsylvania, along with four New England and six southern states for a total of 163 electoral votes. The West went almost solidly for Cass, and he garnered five southern and southwestern states, giving him 127 electoral votes. In the popular election Taylor had 1,360,099 to Cass's 1,220,544 and Van Buren's 291,263. The switch of either New York or Pennsylvania would have reversed the results.[82]

Although former President John Tyler voted for Cass, the result of the election gave him enormous satisfaction. "Poor Van!" he wrote. "He is literally a used-up man; and Clay, let him shed tears over the fact that anybody can be elected but himself."[83]

After studying the returns, Clay convinced himself he could have won if he had been nominated. He believed he would have taken all the states Taylor had received, with the possible exception of Georgia, and gained Ohio and probably Indiana. Another might have been. It troubled him for a time, but he got over it, as he always did. Some Whigs urged him to emulate John Quincy Adams and return to the Senate, but he did not relish the idea. Besides, "I do not think that Mr. Adams added anything to his fame, by his services in Congress after his retirement from the Presidency." No, he would stay at home, tend his farm and cattle, and try to recover his health. However, if circum-

80. "Recollections of an Old Stager," *Harper's Magazine*, XLV (1872), p. 448; Stevenson to Clay, June 12, 1848, Clay Papers, LC.
81. Clay to James E. Harvey, August, 1848, in Schurz, *Clay*, II, 325–326.
82. Clay to Stevenson, October 29, 1848, in Clay, *Works*, III, 490–491; Schlesinger and Israel, eds., *History of American Presidential Elections*, II, 918. Van Buren did not receive any electoral votes.
83. Tyler to Alexander Gardiner, November 14, 1848, in Tyler, *Letters*, II, 462.

stances changed and he "could be persuaded that I could materially contribute to the proper adjustment of the momentous question which has grown out of the acquisition of New Mexico and California," then he would come out of retirement and seek again a seat in the United States Senate.[84]

84. Clay to Charles Fenton Mercer, December 10, 1848, Clay to Hughes, December 16, 1848, copies CPP.

Return to the Senate

CLAY PLANNED to winter in New Orleans. Before his departure there was increasing talk about his returning to the United States Senate when the Kentucky legislature got around to naming Crittenden's successor. And the more the subject was broached, the less resistance Clay offered. Perhaps he realized that he must reassert his claim to party leadership or accept a retirement that would totally divorce him from national affairs. Perhaps he wanted to provide a ready and self-serving comparison with the new President, who had no qualification for office except a popularity based on military success. Perhaps he could not overcome the unquenchable need for the exhilaration and excitement of national politics.

More than anything else, however, was a growing sense that he could "materially contribute" to the solution of the "momentous question" that had developed because of the acquisition of New Mexico and California. Without question, the nation now faced a growing crisis over the issue of slavery in the territories that could easily escalate into civil conflict. And who in the past had come forward with the compromises that spared the Union this calamity? Who but Henry Clay always seemed to find the solution to seemingly intractable national problems? "If I could be persuaded," he wrote, that my efforts could make a difference, then "I should cease to feel any repugnance to the resumption of a seat in the Senate."[1]

Clay repeated this thought to a great number of friends. Horace Greeley told him that the free-soil question would *"certainly"* be adjusted during the

---

1. Clay to Charles Fenton Mercer, December 10, 1848, copy CPP. An excellent study of the impact of slavery on politics is William J. Cooper, Jr., *The South and the Politics of Slavery 1828–1856* (Baton Rouge, 1978). For the developing crisis resulting from the acquisition of territory from Mexico, see David Potter, *The Impending Crisis, 1848–1861* (New York, 1976), and Michael F. Holt, *The Political Crisis of the 1850s* (New York, 1978).

next Congress on the basis of admitting the newly acquired territory as one or two states into the Union. Should that be true, said Clay, "it will exercise some influence on my disposition to return to the Senate." As it so happened, Senator Stephen A. Douglas of Illinois introduced a bill in the upper house on December 11, 1848, providing for the admission of California and New Mexico as a single state, and this action surely made a profound impression on the great man. Of course, to one and all, Clay repeated his honest conviction that he had no overwhelming desire to resume his senatorial duties, that the thought of it was really repugnant to him. Still, he felt a powerful sense of duty to return if he could lend a useful voice and a practical political head in resolving this treacherous question, and he therefore placed himself in the hands of his Kentucky friends and the will of the state legislature.[2]

Clay left Ashland for New Orleans on December 20, heading first for Louisville, where he picked up the steamship *Alexander Scott* to sail down the Ohio and Mississippi rivers. He wanted to escape Kentucky and its wintry blasts and recuperate from his long and debilitating illness. He arrived in Natchez on January 5 and, because of the cholera outbreak in New Orleans, decided to pause awhile before going on. Then, when he heard that the epidemic had greatly abated, he continued his journey and reached the Crescent City on January 13.[3]

Along the way he ran into the President-elect aboard the steamship *Princess* at the Baton Rouge landing, and they conversed briefly, both making a serious effort to appear friendly. The meeting came about as General Taylor passed the dinner table and recognized Clay. He bowed and continued on his way. Taylor was an ordinary-looking man, muscular, broad-shouldered, with prominent checkbones, a long nose, and deeply lined cheeks, who gave an appearance of authority only when astride a horse.[4] Clay obviously did not know who was bowing to him, so another gentleman whispered to him: "Mr. Clay, that is General Taylor."

"It is," cried the surprised Clay. And with that he rose from his place, swiftly pursued the general into the adjacent hall, and extended his hand.

"Why, General," said Clay, "you have grown out of my recollection!"

Taylor grasped Clay's hand and shook it energetically. "You can never grow out of mine," came the gracious reply.[5] And that was the extent of their exchange.

2. By January 1849 Clay was telling his friends that "I suppose that I shall be elected to the Senate . . . in which case I shall hardly feel myself at liberty to decline." Clay to Thomas B. Stevenson, December 19, 1848, January 31, 1849, Clay to James Harlan, January 26, 1849, in Clay, *Works*, III, 492, 583–584; *Congressional Globe*, 30th Congress, 2d session, pp. 52, 67; Robert W. Johannsen, *Stephen A. Douglas* (New York, 1973), pp. 242–248.
3. Clay to Christopher Hughes, December 16, 1848, copy CPP; Clay to James Brown Clay, January 10, 1849, Thomas J. Clay Papers, LC.
4. Hamilton, *Zachary Taylor*, II, 21.
5. Clay to Thomas B. Stevenson, January 31, 1849, in Clay, *Works*, IV, 584; Hamilton, *Taylor*, II, 141.

Upon his arrival in New Orleans, Clay took particular precautions to guard himself against cholera, especially in view of his recent illness and general poor health. The epidemic had returned to the United States from Europe at the ports of New Orleans and New York in December 1848 and quickly spread across the country, killing as much as 10 percent of the population in the largest cities. Kentucky was especially hard hit during the following summer; some 217 persons in Lexington and another 141 in Louisville died from the disease.[6]

To add to his physical discomfort, Clay took a "violent" fall while descending a flight of stairs to greet a visitor at the home of Dr. William N. Mercer, where he was staying. "I got terribly bruised," he wrote; his injuries confined him to his room for "five or six weeks" since he could not walk without assistance. Even writing became a problem. "I don't know but the fall was of service to me," he jokingly remarked, "in arousing some of my sleeping interior organs, and stimulating them to the performance of their duties." Fortunately he broke no bones.[7]

About mid-February Clay received word that the Kentucky legislature had elected him to the U.S. Senate by a vote of ninety-two to forty-five over the Democrat, Richard M. Johnson. His election terrified some. It especially aroused fears among the "Young Indians" in Washington that he would use his position to embarrass and humiliate the new administration out of revenge over his loss of the Whig presidential nomination. Indeed, many in Kentucky who supported the President-elect worried about Clay's future conduct, but Robert P. Letcher wrote a letter that was read in the legislature, assuring everyone that Clay would provide Taylor with his wholehearted support. Both Letcher and Crittenden convinced themselves that the Old Coon would show his true Whig colors and do everything in his power to guarantee success to the incoming administration. Besides, after all that had happened in the past year, how could these worriers deny the Sage of Ashland this final tribute? The people of Kentucky seemed to expect his election as recognition for his outstanding services over many decades to the state and nation.[8]

6. Charles Rosenberg, *The Cholera Years: The United States in 1832, 1849, and 1866* (Chicago, 1962), pp. 101, 172.

7. Clay to James Harlan, January 26, 1849, in Clay, *Works*, IV, 583–584; Clay to Christopher Hughes, April 16, 1849, copy CPP. During his entire stay in New Orleans Clay did not receive a visit from his grandson and namesake Henry Clay Duralde. Nearly a year later Duralde explained his "shameful neglect and inattention." He had been indulging "in pleasures of all kinds," theater, balls, and other pleasures. He gave himself up to the gratification of "my passions, make, pleasure & dissipation, my idols, neglecting to visit my relations, and almost ruining my constitution." Apparently there was something of Prince Hal in young Duralde. Since he feared that Clay would ask him about his activities, he simply stayed away rather than lie. But his pleasure seeking nearly reduced him "to a state of beggary," so he shipped out to California in the great gold rush of 1849. Nearly a year later Clay was informed that young Duralde had drowned in the Sacramento River on September 5, 1850. Clay paid between three and four hundred dollars for money advanced to his grandson and for his funeral expenses. Duralde to Clay, November 22, 1849, Thomas J. Clay Papers, LC; Isaac Owen to Clay, September 11, 1850, copy CPP; Clay to Lucretia, December 26, 1850, Clay Papers, LC.

8. Robert Toombs to Crittenden, December 3, 1848, J. Pendleton to Crittenden, December 22,

Upon learning of his election, Clay let out a long sigh. "I . . . shall go back with some thing like the feelings which the day laborer may be supposed to have," he wrote, "who having worked hard all day by sun shine, is sent again at night into the field to work by moon light." Then he added with a wink: "I do not however apprehend any danger from lunacy."[9]

Because of his recent illness and injury, Clay decided against attending the "Call Session" of the Senate on March 4 to confirm the cabinet appointments of the new President. And Taylor came up with a truly lackluster list of department heads. He had hoped to name Crittenden for the State Department, but the recently elected governor refused. In part his refusal was based on Clay's momentous mistake in accepting the same post from John Quincy Adams in 1825. In his place, Taylor appointed John M. Clayton, with William M. Meredith of Pennsylvania heading the Treasury, George W. Crawford of Georgia the War Department, William B. Preston of Virginia the Navy Department, Thomas Ewing of Ohio to the newly created Department of the Interior, and Reverdy Johnson of Maryland as attorney general. Clay was rather surprised by the uniform level of mediocrity of this cabinet, despite the presence of Clayton. "I think that he might have made one of greater strength," he commented. Then Taylor compounded his mistakes by turning over the executive patronage to these department heads and watching as Whigs from around the country scrambled and begged and connived for offices. The party almost tore itself apart in the wild rush to share and control the patronage.[10]

While recuperating from his violent fall, Clay spent much of his time composing a statement he had been asked to write by his Kentucky friends on the question of emancipating slaves within the state. The statement was intended to influence the delegates to a convention to be held in the fall to amend the present constitution.[11] In view of the frightening arguments over slavery and its extension precipitated by the recent acquisition of California and New Mexico, Clay knew that his own position was becoming more and more unpopular within Kentucky. Indeed, doubts about whether he could win a popular election if one were held for his senatorial seat had been expressed in several quarters. The Sage might have national acclaim, but back home a lot of slavery

---

1848, Crittenden Papers, LC; Crittenden to John M. Clayton, January 7, 30, 1849, Letcher to Clayton, May 8, 1849, Clayton Papers, LC; Thomas B. Stevenson to Clay, April 30, 1849, Clay Papers, LC; Poage, *Clay and Whig Party*, pp. 189–190.

9. Clay to Joseph R. Underwood, February 11, 1849, copy CPP. Clay's certificate of election was signed by the governor and secretary of state of Kentucky and dated February 5, 1849.

10. Kirwan, *Crittenden*, pp. 235–240; Hamilton, *Taylor*, II, 136–141; Bauer, *Taylor*, pp. 250–251; Poage, *Clay and Whig Party*, pp. 183–189; Clay to James Harlan, March 13, 1849, Clay, *Works*, IV, 586. "From the general character of the appointments, which I have observed," Clay wrote to Thomas B. Stevenson, "I apprehend that they have been pretty much confined to the Taylor men to the exclusion of the friends of other Candidates. Such a course if it be adopted, will be both unwise and unjust." April 21, 1849, in Clay, *Works*, III, 492.

11. The convention sat from October 1 to December 21, 1849. Clay did not choose to run as a delegate. For one thing, the convention partially coincided with the congressional session. Colonel Henry Clay of Bourbon County, Kentucky, did attend and presided over the convention.

sympathizers actively resented his constant call for gradual emancipation. Still, he went right ahead and publicly acknowledged his support for the "gradual and ultimate extinction" of slavery within Kentucky. His statement was published by the Frankfort *Commonwealth* and the Lexington *Observer and Kentucky Reporter* in early March and then throughout the country.

The letter, for that is the form the statement took, repeated many of his previous ideas, but a few new observations merit attention. He first noted the proslavery argument which claimed that black intellectual inferiority gave whites the right to enslave them. If that were true, Clay wrote, "then the wisest man in the world would have a right to make slaves of all the rest of mankind!" And if true, that fact alone should "require us not to subjugate or deal unjustly by our fellow men, who are less blessed than we are, but to instruct, to improve, and to enlighten them."

Clay had long favored gradual emancipation, and "my opinion has never changed," he wrote. Emancipation should be slow, gradual, and cautious; blacks should be removed to some "colony" outside the United States because "the color, passions, and prejudices would forever prevent the two races from living together in a state of cordial union"; and all expenses involved in transportation should be defrayed from a fund to be raised from the labor of each freed slave. He further proposed that slaves born after 1855 or 1860 be freed upon reaching a specified age, say, twenty-five. He did not care what date was selected so long as "a day should be permanently *fixed*, from which we could look forward, with confidence, to the final termination of slavery within the limits of the Commonwealth." As for those born before the specified date, Clay said they would remain slaves for life.

But why should the Kentucky slaveholder consent to the emancipation of his property? The reasons "can be summed up in a few words," wrote Clay.

We shall remove from among us the contaminating influence of a servile and degraded race of different color; we shall enjoy the proud and conscious satisfaction of placing that race where they can enjoy the great blessings of liberty, and civil, political and social equality; we shall acquire the advantage of the diligence, the fidelity, and the constancy of free labor, instead of the carelessness, the infidelity and the unsteadiness of slave labor; we shall elevate the character of white labor, and elevate the social condition of the white laborer; augment the value of our lands, improve the agriculture of the State, attract capital from abroad to all the pursuits of commerce, manufactures and agriculture; redress, as far and as fast as we safely and prudently could, any wrongs which the descendants of Africa have suffered at our hands, and we should demonstrate the sincerity with which we pay indiscriminate homage to the great cause of the liberty of the human race.[12]

The publication of this statement outraged both the slaveholder and the abolitionist. William Lloyd Garrison in Boston read Clay's appeal for gradual

12. Clay to Richard Pindell, February 17, 1849, in Clay, *Works*, III, 346–352. The convention chose to disregard Clay's call for gradual emancipation. Clay to James Harlan, April 20, 1849, copy CPP.

emancipation in the hope of finding him "less selfish, less inhuman, less cow-ardly" than he had been when he made his "detestable speech" on this same subject in the Senate on February 7, 1839. "But I see no evidence of this in your epistle," he wrote the Great Pacificator. "Nay . . . it is remorseless in purpose, cruel in spirit, delusive in expectation, sophistical in reasoning, tyran-nous in principle." As the author of the Missouri Compromise you stand "at the head of as cruel a conspiracy against God and man as was ever contrived." If the acquisition of California and New Mexico means the extension of slavery into those territories, then "the criminality is eminently yours." Slavery "is pollution, concubinage, adultery—it is theft, robbery, kidnapping." Yet you dare to "affirm that its continuance *is a matter* of 'necessity'! Ah! this is ever 'the tyrants plea,' and you are a tyrant."[13]

Clay had been warned that because of rising passions around the nation over the issue, his letter could do him infinite harm and undercut his support both in Kentucky and throughout the country. But that did not faze him in the least. "As I regret to hear that [it is] not popular, I suppose that my letter will bring on me some od[ium]. I nevertheless wish it published. I owe that to the cause and [to] myself, and to posterity." He realized there were strong preju-dices against his position reinforced by long habit and "powerful interests." The "truth is that many of our leading men, who had been favorable to gradual emancipation, have suppressed, modified, or abandoned their opinions. The Governor [Crittenden] is quite dumb on the perilous subject."[14]

Clay returned to Ashland in time to celebrate with Lucretia their golden wedding anniversary on April 11. To mark the occasion, a daguerreotype of the happy couple may have been taken. Clay seemed in relatively good health after his vacation of three months and immediately resumed his legal responsi-bilities with his son James by unsuccessfully arguing a case in Clark County. He had been thinking a great deal about James lately, especially with regard to the complaints of James's wife, Susan, about the young man's "roving" spirit. In response, Clay tried to discount its importance. "You ought to be recon-ciled to it," he counseled the wife, "if he will not float off to California." Perhaps his health will benefit from it, he jokingly added. But making light of James's situation hardly provided an answer.

"I do wish that he had some permanent & agreeable employment," Clay wistfully wrote.[15] To that end the concerned father finally decided to approach

13. Garrison to Clay, March 16, 1849, copy CPP. There were, of course, those who praised Clay for his stand, like the former governor of Illinois, for example. See Edward Coles to Clay, June 15, 1849, copy CPP. The Cincinnati *Daily Atlas* of March 6 called Clay's statement "strictly an Anti-Slavery document." The New York *Daily Tribune* of March 10 disagreed with the mode of emancipation proposed by Clay but commended him for wanting to end the "peculiar institution" in Kentucky.

14. Clay to James Brown Clay, March 3, 1849, Thomas J. Clay Papers, LC; Clay to Stevenson, June 18, 1849, in Clay, *Works,* III, 493–494. See also Clay to Mary S. Bayard, June 16, 1849, copy CPP.

15. Clay to Susan Jacob Clay, March 10, April 15, 1849, Thomas J. Clay Papers, LC.

President Taylor. He had never done such a thing before, he said, and it galled him to feel he must do it now. "During my long connection with public affairs, I have never employed any official influence . . . to promote the appointment to public office of any relations of mine." Still, James needed "permanent" employment, so Clay wrote to Taylor and asked him for an appointment for his son.

It is a delicate subject for a father to speak of the qualifications of a son; but I think that I can describe those of James with perfect truth. He is entirely free from all habits of dissipation whatever, and he has great industry, with remarkable capacity for the trans-action of business, in which he displays much quickness. I practised law with him several years, and in some of the departments of the profession, I found him better informed and more conversant than I was. I think he has very respectable talents. He has a wife and three children.[16]

As a matter of fact, in 1821 Clay had intervened to get an appointment at West Point for his son Thomas, and on December 14, 1848, he had asked for an appointment to the military academy for his grandson Henry Clay III, the eldest son of Henry Clay, Jr. True, neither of these requests involved a "public office," nor were they directed to the chief executive. Thomas failed mathematics and was dismissed. Henry Clay III received the appointment, but on January 19, 1853, the academy recommended his discharge for accumulating 289 demerits over a seven-month period. Young Henry resigned.[17]

In his request for James, the father mentioned the mission to Brussels, Rome, Naples, or Lisbon. President Taylor responded favorably and immediately. "It will afford me much pleasure to comply with your wishes . . . by conferring on him the appointment referred to." James received the Lisbon mission.[18]

For Taylor, accommodating Clay made a great deal of political sense. By placing the Kentucky senator in his debt, he could nullify in one stroke any potential for trouble from that quarter when Congress convened in December. Indeed, Clay felt profoundly grateful. "We are both very thankful," he wrote the new secretary of state, John M. Clayton, "and deeply penetrated with sentiments of gratitude, for this high proof of the goodness and the confidence of the President."[19]

Unfortunately the President foolishly chose to publicize his political "masterstroke." There was even the suggestion of publishing the correspondence between Taylor and Clay regarding James's appointment. "I have no objection," Clay loftily retorted, but of course, he understood the strategy behind this ploy and rightfully resented it. In any event, the senator thereafter

16. Clay to Taylor, May 12, 1849, copy CPP.
17. Calhoun to Clay, May 19, 1821, in Clay, *Papers,* III, 82–83; Clay to Charles S. Morehead, December 14, 1848, copy CPP.
18. Taylor to Clay, May 28, 1849, Clay Papers, LC.
19. Clay to Clayton, June 7, 1849, Clayton Papers, LC.

felt free of any obligation toward the chief executive. "The mission to Portugal," he declared, "which in fact only rectifies in one son [James], an injustice which was done by Tyler to another, Col. Clay,[20] will not weigh a feather with me." The President had written to him in a perfectly friendly manner, he blandly admitted. "I have made no commitment of myself, nor descended to any unmanly or unbecoming solicitation." All along he had insisted that his behavior in Congress would be studiously correct and consistent with his political ideals and philosophy. "I shall go there . . . with no view blindly to oppose or blindly to support the Administration." Public duty, if nothing else, would "restrain me from offering any opposition to the course of the Administration, if, as I hope and anticipate, it should be conducted on principles which we have so long cherished and adhered to."[21]

Because his health continued to be precarious—his cough never seemed to leave him—and because of the real and fancied benefits he received at various spas and in bathing at the seashore, Clay decided to spend the summer in the East, particularly Saratoga and Newport. At the same time James and his family could accompany him as they commenced the first leg of their trip to Europe. "I have been breathing a Cholera Atmosphere, living upon Cholera diet. . . . The effect is, that I am somewhat reduced in flesh, and debilitated in strength. . . . I trust that the mineral water, followed by the Sea bath will restore me."[22]

So he set out by carriage, boat, and rail on July 24, swung by Cincinnati, Sandusky, and Cleveland, and arrived in Saratoga on August 4. For two weeks he luxuriated in the mineral water of that renowned spa, although he did not derive the benefit he expected. Worse, on August 10, he suffered "one of the severest attacks that I ever experienced. It was a bilious cholick and I suffered excruciating pain for several hours. Some fears were even entertained for my safety. I have been relieved," he told his wife three days later, "but am left very weak." Once the attack passed, Clay decided to push on to Newport, convinced that the "Sea bath" would work wonders. Indeed, "the bracing sea air" provided some benefit although he was "as yet afraid to enter" the water. "This island is a most healthy place . . . where I have enjoyed more repose than I have done since I left home."[23]

During his sojourn in Newport, Clay's personal servant, Levi, who had replaced the emancipated Charles Dupuy, ran away, enticed by three hundred dollars paid him by abolitionists. But on reaching Boston, Levi changed his

20. Clay always mentioned the fact that the appointment of a mission to Brussels had been promised his son Henry, Jr., by President Harrison but that Tyler refused to honor it. "If Mr. Tyler had fulfilled [that promise] . . . Col. Clay would be yet living; but he would not fulfill it." Clay to Reverdy Johnson, March 17, 1849, copy CPP.
21. Clay to Thomas B. Stevenson, June 18, 30, July 21, 1849, Clay to Combs, March 7, 1849, in Clay, Works, III, 493–496, IV, 585–586; Clay to Jesse M. Christopher, April 19, 1849, copy CPP; Hamilton, Taylor, II, 215; Kirwan, Crittenden, p. 250; Poage, Clay and Whig Party, p. 192.
22. Clay to Christopher Hughes, August 4, 1849, copy CPP.
23. Clay to Lucretia, August 13, 23, 1849, Thomas J. Clay Papers, LC.

mind, gave the money back, and returned to Clay. The plan by the abolitionists to embarrass the great man backfired. Levi's decision to return to his master said a great deal about Henry Clay as master.[24]

A few days later he decided to risk a swim in the ocean, and to his delight he not only enjoyed it but felt much better. "My health began to improve . . . immediately after I went into the sea," he told Lucretia. "I am now better than I have been since I left home; and but for a cough which still hangs on me, I should be quite well." He was only sorry he did not have enough time to remain at Newport for several more days.

On his return home he swung through New York City, switching within half an hour from a steamboat on the East River to another on the Hudson River, and headed for Syracuse and Utica. Clay had received an invitation to visit his old rival Martin Van Buren, and since his route would take him within four miles of Lindenwald, the Van Buren home, just outside Albany, he decided to accept the invitation.[25]

The two old foes, mellowed with age but still feisty enough to argue for their ideas and principles—Van Buren a little less strenuously perhaps—spent three days together. They "talked over old scenes without reserve" in what Van Buren called "unrestricted and family chats." They even discussed the election of 1825! "The feuds of the past and the asperities caused by them," the Magician later recorded, "were as completely ignored in these conversations as if they had never existed." Many of Van Buren's neighbors came to "our vicinage to give him a cordial shake by the hand," delighted that he and his host had finally gotten together and put away all their past differences. At the conclusion of the visit Van Buren's sons escorted Clay to Albany, and the former President went with him as far as the railroad station, "where we parted never to see each other again."[26]

Continuing homeward, Clay attended the state fair at Syracuse, spent a day or two at Utica, and arrived at Ashland on September 18, his health much improved, except for his cough.

Throughout his tour the public continually demonstrated their affection for this extraordinary statesman. Crowds gathered wherever he appeared, screaming, waving at him, calling his name, demanding a few words. In New York City, for example, the mobs "pester him to death," reported Philip Hone,

---

24. Clay to James Brown Clay, September 3, 1849, Clay Papers, LC; Clay to Lucretia, September 5, 1849, Thomas J. Clay Papers, LC. Levi ran away a second time at Buffalo and again returned home to Ashland a few days later. Clay to James Brown Clay, October 2, 1849, Thomas J. Clay Papers, LC. When Clay first realized that Levi had run away again, he could not be sure if he disappeared voluntarily or against his wishes. "If voluntarily, I will take no trouble about him, as it is probably that in a reversal of our conditions I would have done the same thing." Clay to L. Hodges, September 15, 1849, copy CPP.

25. Clay to Lucretia, September 5, 1849, Thomas J. Clay Papers, LC; Horace Greeley to Clay, September 4, 1849, Clay Papers, LC;

26. Van Buren, *Autobiography,* pp. 153, 534, 664–665.

"haunt him by day, serenade him by night, follow him in his walks, shouting, hurrahing, Henry Claying him wherever he goes." At Syracuse he "went through some trying scenes" when a mob pursued him. "To escape the over-whelming crowd, I sought an asylum, and, for more than half an hour, was locked up with Mrs. Phillips at the Globe Hotel, the multitude thundering all the time to get in!" By this time the glow and excitement of popular approval no longer worked its magic on him. He now tried his best to avoid situations that would produce these demonstrations. He was too old, too tired, and too weak from his many bouts of illness to experience any real joy from them or think that they made any difference in his life. Still, it was always encouraging to believe that the people continued to recognize and applaud his efforts to serve them and the nation.[27]

Back home Clay got something of a surprise when Lucretia Erwin, the daughter of his beloved Anne, informed him of her decision to enter a Catholic convent and "adopt the veil." He had no prejudice against Catholics, he wrote in reply, even though most of them had probably voted against him in 1844. "On the contrary, I sincerely believe that Catholics, who are truly religious, are as sure of eternal happiness in another world as the most pious Protestants." What disturbed him was the "awful separation" from family and friends in-volved in becoming a nun, and he could not help but "feel intense distress. Adieu, my dear grand child. May God enlighten guide and direct you; and, if we never meet again in this world, may we meet in the regions of eternal bliss, and there join my beloved daughter, your lamented mother."[28]

But apparently Lucretia changed her mind about adopting the veil. She married Frederick A. Cowles in the late 1850s.

Clay spent much of the fall resting and preparing himself for a return to Washington for the opening of Congress in early December. Like everyone else, he was truly worried over the newest twist to the slavery question now agitating the nation—namely, the right of slaveowners to introduce their "pe-culiar institution" into California and New Mexico. "No one can be more opposed than I am to the extension of slavery into those new territories," he wrote, and he hoped the Congress could address the question "in a spirit of calmness and candor" and the exercise of "mutual and friendly forbearance." Recent elections in northern states held out little prospect for calmness, and Whigs had suffered losses in Ohio and Pennsylvania that would make the situation more difficult for the administration in legislating its program, if one could assume, of course, it had a program to offer the country.[29]

Clay decided to leave Ashland on November 1, not to go to Washington

27. Hone, *Diary*, II, 877; Clay to Mr. and Mrs. Frederick Hollister, September 19, 1849, copy CPP.

28. Clay to Lucretia Erwin, October 27, 1849, copy CPP.

29. Clay to John C. Vaughan and Thomas Brown, June 16, 1849, copy CPP; Clay to James Brown Clay, October 15, 1849, in Clay, *Works*, IV, 589–590.

immediately but to visit friends in Pennsylvania and New York. Along the way his stagecoach had an accident near Uniontown, Pennsylvania, but fortunately he suffered no injury.

After visiting his friends in the East,[30] Clay headed back to Washington to resume his senatorial career. At the railroad depot in Baltimore, just before his departure for the capital, a crowd gathered "without preconcert or arrangement." The people seemed to appear suddenly as a last-minute attempt not only to pay him tribute but to express to him their need of and confidence in his ability to find the solution to the nation's developing crisis and keep it from plunging forward into disunion and possible civil war. This enormous crowd followed his carriage from the railroad station to his hotel, cheering and waving to him. And the people would not give up, even after he had entered the hotel. Not until he appeared at the second-floor window did the chanting abate. Now they hushed in the hope that he would speak to them. "We are too far apart," he called to them. It was impossible to speak. He would meet them all the next day, he promised, and shake each one by the hand.

And he did. At 11:00 A.M. Clay took up a position between two parlors on the first floor of the Barnum City Hotel, and after telling the assembled populace how delighted he was with its reception, he received every one who came forward to greet him.

In his remarks to various crowds he met on his long journey from Ashland to Washington, Clay made it clear that he understood the "great, threatening and alarming questions" facing them, that he did not believe slavery could be extended into California and New Mexico because of the climate and character of the country and its inhabitants, that he stood pledged "under all circumstances and in all storms . . . TO STAND BY THE UNION," and that he would do all in his power to prevent "the dissolution of the Union . . . and all the horrors of civil war."[31]

Upon his arrival in Washington, which touched off more demonstrations, Clay went immediately to the White House, where he left his card. Then he settled in at the National Hotel, where he had a "good parlour and bedroom opening into each other," for which he paid $30 a week. He was tended by "an excellent Valet, a freeman" by the name of James Marshall, whom Clay had hired as a personal servant after Levi ran away. "I am as comfortable as I can be," he reported. In another apartment in the same hotel lived the British minister, Henry L. Bulwer, and his wife, Georgiana Wellesley Bulwer, a niece of the Iron Duke's, with whom Clay occasionally dined.

Visitors crowded into his rooms every day. "It seemed to me," wrote

30. Clay stayed at the home of Richard Henry Bayard in Philadelphia from November 8 to 19 and attended the wedding of Bayard's daughter. Then he traveled to New York City and spent the period from the nineteenth to the twenty-fourth at the home of Egbert Benson. He returned to Philadelphia, where he remained until the twenty-ninth, when he left for Washington, where he arrived on December 1.

31. Lexington *Observer and Kentucky Reporter,* December 5, 1849, copy CPP.

Benjamin Brown French, "as if he was 'the observed of all observers' instead of the President." Clay called upon the various members of the cabinet, and he dined with Taylor on December 13. As he passed through the East Room of the White House, a crowd quickly surrounded him. "I could not but think," continued French, "that, after all, he was the idol of the occasion. 'Henry Clay' is a political war cry that will at any time and in any part of this Union create more sensation among men of all parties than any other name that can be uttered. . . . He now stands, at the age of three score years & ten, the *beau ideal* of a patriot, a statesman, a great man!"[32]

Although a large company attended the White House dinner, Clay found an opportunity to tell Taylor straight to his face that there was considerable dissatisfaction among Whigs from all sections of the country against the administration. After several weeks in session Congress had undertaken no public business. The House was divided between the two parties (112 Democrats and 105 Whigs) and could not even select a Speaker. Thirteen Free Soilers held the balance of power. In the Senate Democrats controlled the body with a margin of 10 votes. To make matters worse, the southern Whigs, led by Alexander H. Stephens and Robert Toombs, opposed the Whig choice for Speaker, Robert C. Winthrop, because the Whig caucus had failed to take a stand against the Wilmot Proviso. The party seemed to be in disarray, and since elections during the past year had gone so badly for the Whigs and were not likely to get better in the immediate future, there was danger during this session of Congress of a total stalemate. From both parties, Clay later admitted, "strong expressions are made to me of hopes that I may be able to calm the raging elements."[33]

During his brief discussion with Clay, President Taylor admitted that he knew of the dissatisfaction and that he believed it arose out of an "inordinate pursuit of office." The senator wholeheartedly agreed with the President but added that the "character" of the appointments had produced much displeasure and discontent, by which he meant that the President had not sufficiently involved himself in this important matter and that control of the patronage had fallen into the hands of those, like William H. Seward, the recently elected senator from New York, and his mentor Thurlow Weed, who used it improperly by giving the appointments a distinctly northern and antislavery bias.

The two men could not speak at length, and Taylor ended the conversation by assuring Clay that he would invite him back for a long interview. Not much later the senator admitted that his relations with Taylor and the cabinet were "Civil and amicable, but with all of them not very confidential."[34]

32. French, *Witness to the Young Republic,* p. 213.

33. Clay to James Brown Clay, December 4, 1849, Clay to Lucretia, December 5, 28, 1849, Clay to Susan Jacob Clay, December 15, 1849, Thomas J. Clay Papers, LC; Clay to Leslie Combs, December 10, 1849, Clay to Mary S. Bayard, December 14, 1849, copies CPP.

34. Clay to Mary Bayard, December 14, 1849, copy CPP; Clay to Thomas B. Stevenson, Decem-

As a doting parent Clay could not resist intruding into diplomatic affairs upon his arrival in Washington in order to advance his son's budding career in the Foreign Service. Not only did he engage in "a long, long interview" with the Portuguese minister in which he demanded "satisfaction of our claims" against Portugal over seizures of ships, but he constructively criticized his son's note to the Portuguese foreign minister concerning one of the incidents growing out of the seizures. He even advised his son to read to the foreign minister "passages from my letter to show the serious apprehensions entertained here" over the issue and cautioned James to "observe the greatest courtesy, and speak gravely with[ou]t threatening."[35]

But the "great moment" after Clay's return to Washington came with his reappearance in the Senate on Monday, December 3. He created a sensation. A thunderous ovation echoed around the chamber on his arrival. There was much handshaking and kissing as he greeted old friends and former colleages. The ladies, of course, received his special salute. "Much deference and consideration are shown me," he pridefully noted, "by even political opponents." Some felt reassured about the fate of the Union now that the Great Pacificator was back. Everybody expected him to perform miracles. "I wish I could," he lamented, "but I fear I cannot, realize their hopes."

Seated in his usual place, Clay looked old and worn. And he coughed a great deal. His head was partially bald on top, his hair fringed with iron gray streaks; his cheeks were shrunken, his nose looked pinched, but his wide mouth was "wreathed in genial smiles," just as in years past. He always dressed in black with a white shirt, the collar of which stood high, covering his long neck and reaching to his ears. Nearly seventy-three years of age, Clay was back where he belonged, and little of importance seemed to have changed during his absence. He "generally kissed the prettiest girls wherever he went," played cards in his room, and enjoyed a large glass of bourbon whenever he relaxed.[36]

Seated around him were many old friends and enemies, prominent men of the Jacksonian era who still influenced national affairs. Thomas Hart Benton of Missouri, Willie P. Mangum of North Carolina, Lewis Cass of Michigan, John Berrien of Georgia, and, of course, the other two members of the old triumvirate, Daniel Webster and John C. Calhoun, still commanded the respect and attention of the nation. Some junior members of the Senate also gained prominence over the next several congressional sessions by virtue of

ber 21, 1849, in Clay, *Works*, III, 497; Poage, *Clay and Whig Party*, pp. 184–187, 194–196; Kirwan, *Crittenden*, pp. 247–251.

35. Clay to Susan Jacob Clay, December 13, 1849, Clay to James Clay, December 29, 1849, January 2, 1850, in Clay, *Works*, IV, 591–593, 595–597, 582–583; Clay to James Clay, January 8, 1850, undated note, ca. December 1849, Thomas J. Clay Papers. For Clay's involvement in this matter, see Sara Bearss, "Henry Clay and the American Claims against Portugal, 1850," *Journal of the Early American Republic*, VII (Summer 1987), p. 173ff.

36. Clay to Stevenson, December 21, 1849, in Clay, *Works*, III, 497; Clay to Mary Bayard, December 14, 1849, copy CPP; Poore, *Reminiscences*, I, 363.

their intelligence, integrity, diligence, leadership, and commitment to the ideals and demands of their respective sections. Jefferson Davis of Mississippi, Stephen A. Douglas of Illinois, Salmon P. Chase of Ohio, and William H. Seward of New York were to replace the Great Triumvirate in shaping the direction of the nation's future.

Clay took his time about reassuming his position as a senior member of the august upper house. In one of his first remarks on the floor he asked to be excused from serving on any of the standing committees. He was quite prepared to shoulder his share of senatorial work but said that he would appreciate a respite from regular chores of committee drudgery. Then, with a smile, he allowed as there was no danger of his being assigned to chair a committee in view of his recent arrival in the upper house. Naturally the Senate graciously acceded to his request.[37]

The political situation in Washington turned out to be worse than Clay expected. "The feeling for disunion, among some intemperate Southern politicians," he lamented, "is stronger than I supposed it could be." Already a call had gone out for a convention of slave states to meet in Nashville to demand their rights as well as promote southern unity. It was all terribly frightening, and Clay alerted his friends in Kentucky to take steps to counteract this apparent drive toward disunion. He specifically mentioned public meetings throughout Kentucky of *both* parties to express in the strongest language possible the determination of the people of the state to "stand by the Union." He enclosed for possible passage at these meetings a set of resolutions that would declare that no matter what happened over the slavery issue the Union must not be dissolved. Knowing how his own popularity had declined in many parts of the state, Clay wisely urged his friends not to use his name in getting up these meetings.[38]

For weeks Congress could not get down to business because of the wrangling over the speakership. The Representatives even had trouble deciding on a doorkeeper without first knowing the candidate's position on slavery. Finally, on December 22, after sixty-three ballots, Howell Cobb of Georgia, a Democrat, was elected Speaker over the Whig Robert C. Winthrop, by a vote of 102 to 99. Clay was greatly relieved. It was far more important to get the House organized and working, he said, than that a Whig be chosen as Speaker.[39]

It was also important to get the country headed in some direction to address the California and New Mexico questions. Because of the discovery of

37. *Congressional Globe*, 31st Congress, 1st session, pp. 39–40, 45.

38. Clay to Leslie Combs, December 22, 1849, in Clay, *Works*, IV, 593; the resolutions were later printed in the Louisville *Daily Journal*, July 21, 1860, copy CPP. On the convention that met in Nashville in June 1850, see Thelma Jennings, *The Nashville Convention: Southern Movement for Unity, 1848–1851* (Memphis, 1980).

39. Clay to James Brown Clay, December 29, 1849, Clay Papers, LC; *Congressional Globe*, 31st Congress, 1st session, pp. 61–67.

gold and the gold rush of '49, California had swelled in population and now prepared to ask Congress for immediate admission as a state, bypassing the usual period of territorial status. President Taylor thought he could put forward a "plan" advising Congress to do nothing until California submitted its request for admission together with a completed and ratified constitution. He expected New Mexico to do the same shortly thereafter. Since both areas under Mexican rule had excluded slavery, presumably both would come into the Union as free states, totally disrupting the equal balance presently existing between the slave and free states. Naturally southerners had no intention of approving what would in effect deny them any benefit from the Mexican War.

If Taylor's so-called plan meant to address the mounting crisis in the country over slavery and its extension into the territories, it was totally inadequate and unrealistic. For one thing, it made no mention of the fact that Texas claimed a large portion of New Mexico, including Santa Fe. Drawing the boundary lines would cause a monumental problem and add to the sectional conflict. Moreover, the Texas debt, amounting to more than eleven million dollars, was involved in the question because the state held the United States partially responsible for its failure to redeem its bonds resulting from the loss of income from customs as a consequence of annexation. Boundary and debt were intertwined. But once more the President failed to provide an adequate scheme to solve this problem. In a special message to Congress in January 1850 he reiterated his "plan" for California and New Mexico. As for the boundary question he requested immediate action by Congress on New Mexico, thereby creating a conflict between two states and throwing the burden of solution on the Supreme Court.

Complicating matters was the presence of Mormons, or members of the Church of Jesus Christ of the Latter-day Saints, who had created a large and prosperous community around the Great Salt Lake in Utah and had drafted a constitution for a provisional state to be called Deseret. Since Deseret did not involve any dispute over its boundary with Texas or permit slavery, its admission into the Union could prove much easier—except, of course, for the practice of polygamy by Mormons, which could prove intolerable to Christian communities in other states.[40]

Southerners prepared to scuttle any effort at admission or consideration of any of these issues unless the South received an adequate compensation. As chief participants in the Mexican War they seethed over the disregard of their interests and the great possibility that the sectional balance in the Senate would soon be upset with the admission of free states. Some of them demanded an extension of the 36°30' line to the Pacific Ocean, with slavery permitted south of the line, including California. Others sought an improved fugitive slave law

40. Allan Nevins, *Ordeal of the Union* (New York, 1958), I, 257; Holman Hamilton, *Prologue to Conflict: The Crisis and Compromise of 1850* (Lexington, Ky., 1964), pp. 17–21; Holt, *Political Crisis of the 1850s,* pp. 77–78; Elbert B. Smith, *The Presidencies of Zachary Taylor & Millard Fillmore* (Lawrence, Kan., 1988), pp. 95–101.

so that southerners would obtain greater assistance in recovering runaways. Indeed, James M. Mason of Virginia came forward during the first week of 1850 with a fugitive slave bill that was far stronger than the old 1793 law.

Northern Free Soil congressmen responded to these demands with some of their own. They demanded the termination of the slave trade as well as the abolition of slavery in the District of Columbia. The idea of foreigners (and other sensitive persons) perpetually witnessing the appalling sight of human beings on an auction block in the capital city of a so-called democratic, civilized, and Christian country was intolerable. Both practices had to end immediately—to which southerners replied that the day slaves were emancipated in Washington was the day the South would secede from the Union. "I . . . avow before this House and country, and in the presence of the living God," stormed Robert Toombs of Georgia, "that if by your legislation you seek to drive us from the territories of California and New Mexico . . . and to abolish slavery in this District . . . *I am for disunion.*"[41]

The crisis was indeed grave, graver than Clay had imagined. The nation seemed headed on a course of disruption and chaos. And as the crisis deepened, many Americans naturally expected Henry Clay to come up with yet another compromise and save the Union from destruction.

41. Cooper, *The South and the Politics of Slavery,* pp. 290–295; *Congressional Globe,* 31st Congress, 1st session, pp. 27–28.

The Compromise
of 1850

T HE FAILURE of presidential leadership immediately opened
up to Clay the unanticipated opportunity to reassume control
of the Whig party and hammer out a series of proposals satisfactory to both North and South that would address each of the issues involved in the territorial and slavery questions. And in searching for a solution
Clay worried particularly over the fact that Protestant denominations had already split over the issue of slavery. Five years earlier the Methodist and Baptist
churches had cracked apart, and the split roared an apocalyptic message of
doom across the nation. If Christian churches could not maintain their unity in
the face of this momentous question, could the Union itself long endure? It
was a frightening apprehension that no doubt speeded Clay's determination to
seek an amicable resolution to the immediate problem.

There seems little doubt that in attempting this formidable task the Great
Compromiser wished to remind everyone in the country that twice before he
had rescued the nation from seeming disaster and that he still retained the wit
and will to do it again. The President's plan called for Congress to do nothing
except wait for the formal application by California and New Mexico for
admission into the Union.[1] The Star of the West would provide something
more substantial.

But more than pride or a need for vindication motivated the senator. He
truly sought to rescue his country from disaster. His love of the Union, his
intense patriotism, his desire to harmonize and bring peace and tranquillity to
the nation prompted him to lay everything else aside and grapple with this
enormous problem. For what he attempted was truly heroic: the settlement of
the slavery issue in a way that would cause no just complaint from either the

---

1. For a defense of Taylor's plan, see Smith, *Presidencies of Taylor & Fillmore,* pp. 91–122. Daniel
Walker Howe also regards the President's policy as "straightforward and statesmanlike" and not
proslavery. *The Political Culture of the American Whigs,* pp. 146, 147.

North or the South. Whatever he did and however he proceeded to work through the tangled and conflicting difficulties, he faced the immense task of addressing *all* the acute questions troubling the country. In his present state of health he could no longer act in the hope of generating popular demand for a fourth presidential campaign. By this time and after many heartbreaks he had gone beyond that once-obsessive dream. Instead, he felt the overwhelming desire, as Webster later said, "to accomplish something for the good of the country during the little time he had left upon earth." So he made a valiant effort in energy, in time, in hard work. He unhesitatingly rushed forward to do what he could to avert the "great evil" he saw looming ahead. In the process he further undermined his already weakened physical condition.

He alerted both friends and family that he had started to formulate his plans. "I have been thinking much of proposing some comprehensive scheme of settling amicably the whole question, in all its bearings," he told his son James in early January, "but I have not yet positively determined to do so." Apparently there was a momentary hesitation in deciding whether he could physically cope with the burden of responsibility. By this time he had undoubtedly contracted an active case of tuberculosis[2]—his earlier colds may have been due to chronic bronchitis and regular bouts of influenza or possibly bronchiectasis—and the drain on his energies was constant and considerable. But whatever doubts he initially entertained on account of his health soon disappeared as he became more and more troubled by the ever-mounting danger.

Early in this congressional session Henry Foote of Mississippi brought forward the first bill for the organization of the new territories. Then, on January 4, 1850, James M. Mason of Virginia introduced a tougher fugitive slave bill by which southerners would be assisted in recovering their runaway slaves. Less than two weeks later Senator Benton produced a Texas boundary bill. The great drama was about to unfold.

What Clay conceived in these early weeks of January was a plan by which all these issues would be brought before the Congress for examination, discussion, and resolution. He believed that any solution to the present crisis must necessarily embrace each one of these issues. By doing so, he would provide a totally new and more realistic basis for debate.

By Monday, January 21, 1850, he had conceived the principal parts of his "comprehensive scheme." That evening he braved the inclement weather and went to the home of Daniel Webster to enlist Black Dan's support. Relations between the two men had been strained for years—to put it mildly—but that did not deter the tortured statesman. And although he rarely went out at night because of his hacking cough and weakened condition, let alone a rainy night,

---

2. I once suspected that Clay had contracted tuberculosis in the 1820s, when he first showed signs of pulmonary problems, but I have been assured by Dr. Bernard Adelson of Winnetka, Illinois, that Clay would never have survived thirty years with an active case of the disease. Just when he did become tubercular is unknown.

he showed up unannounced at 7:00 P.M. looking "very feeble." The two men spoke for an hour, with Clay expressing his anxieties about the condition of the country and outlining his scheme to deal with it. Webster "thought Mr. Clay's objects were great and highly patriotic," and without committing himself totally, until he had time to study the proposals, he assured his former rival of his general support. The long interview exhausted the Kentuckian, but he came away invigorated by his sense of accomplishment. Two members of the Great Triumvirate would at least fight for another compromise to preserve the Union. The third member had already drifted in another direction.[3]

Clay spoke to no other northerner about his scheme, but he did consult several of his friends from the South, probably because he realized his need for greater support from that section of the country if he expected to win acceptance of his plan. He later said that he had learned a lesson in 1833, when he consulted too many congressmen in devising the Compromise Tariff and thereby endangered its final passage. He would not make that mistake again. He therefore carefully selected the southerners with whom he now divulged the details of his newest compromise.[4]

On Tuesday, January 29, 1850, Clay rose in the Senate to set forth his "comprehensive scheme." "Mr. President," Clay called out in his still-strong and vibrant voice, "I hold in my hand a series of resolutions which I desire to submit to the consideration of this body." Taken together, "in combination," he went on, they propose an "amicable arrangement of all questions in controversy between the free and slave States." It was, he hoped, a "great national scheme of compromise and harmony," and he asked each senator to give it the same amount of "care and deliberation" as he had done in preparing the resolutions.

There were eight in all. The first called for the admission of California as a state without any mention of slavery; the second provided for the organization of territorial governments for the remaining portion of the Mexican cessation without any congressional restriction or condition on the subject of slavery since the institution did not exist under Mexican law and was not likely to be introduced. In effect Clay proposed popular sovereignty for New Mexico and Utah (or Deseret), allowing the residents of the respective areas to decide the question themselves at any time.[5] The third and fourth resolutions provided

3. The interview was recorded by a "gentleman" visiting Webster at the time. George Ticknor Curtis, *Life of Daniel Webster* (New York, 1870), II, 397–398. Clay's intention to formulate a scheme may be found in Clay to James Clay, January 2, 1850, Clay to James Harlan, January 24, 1850, in Clay, *Works,* IV, 582–583, 599–600. Clay's recognition that his presidential availability had passed may be inferred from his letter to James Harlan, March 22, 1850, copy CPP.

4. Speech of February 20, 1850, *Congressional Globe,* 31st Congress, 1st session, p. 403.

5. Although Clay believed that settlers in the territories could decide the slavery question at any time, southern extremists insisted that settlers could not decide the question until the territory formally applied for admission as a state. Prior to that moment, they argued, slave property in the territories was part of the national domain and as such was protected by the Constitution. Clay's position is made clear by his statements and voting in the Senate during this session. *Congressional Globe,* 31st Congress, 1st session, pp. 948–950, 955, appendix, pp. 902, 1463. See Potter, *Impending Crisis,* pp. 58–60.

for the settlement of the Texas boundary and the assumption by the United States of the Texas debt acquired before annexation, on condition that Texas formally "relinquish to the United States any claim which it has to any part of New Mexico." These two resolutions, he said, should be "read and considered together" since they were intimately connected. Clay also linked the fifth and sixth resolutions. The fifth declared it "inexpedient" to abolish slavery in the District of Columbia without the consent of Maryland[6] and the people living in the District and without just compensation to the slaveowners in the area. And the sixth pronounced it "expedient" to abolish the slave trade in the District, forbidding the sale of slaves or their transportation to other markets outside Washington. It was truly shocking, he declared, to see "a long train of slaves passing through the avenue leading from this Capitol to the house of the Chief Magistrate."[7] The seventh resolution called for a more effective fugitive slave law, a problem so obvious that he did not wish at this time to comment further upon it. Finally, the eighth resolution stated that Congress had no power to interfere in the interstate slave trade, leaving it to the particular laws of the respective states involved.

Clay summed up his comprehensive scheme by insisting that no sacrifice of principle was proposed in any of the resolutions. Rather, it was founded on "mutual forbearance" and originated from a spirit of "conciliation and concession." It contained, he believed, an equal amount of compromise on both sides.[8]

Clay made no elaborate speech when he presented his resolutions. That would come later after the other senators had had time to study his scheme. So he asked that his proposals be made the order of the day for Tuesday next, February 5. And he hoped his colleagues would have suggestions for modifications and improvements, anything which would placate both sides and get the nation through its present crisis.

Although parts of his comprehensive scheme came from other congressmen, Clay's important contributions to the whole included his attempt to bring all the issues together, to be treated not as a *single bill* but as a *single problem;* his effort to balance the gains and losses of the two major sections in the overall package so that there would be a fair compromise; his recognition of the validity of Mexican law with respect to slavery; and his inclusion of a bill to prohibit the slave trade in the District of Columbia.

When Clay finally returned to his seat, several southern senators grumbled complaints over one or another aspect of the resolutions, with Jefferson Davis denying that the South really gained any benefit from Clay's compro-

6. Previously Clay had called for the consent of Maryland and Virginia. He dropped Virginia at this time, he explained, because the District of Columbia had recently returned all the Virginia land originally ceded. The capital rested solely on former Maryland land; therefore, only Maryland's consent was needed.

7. However, he would not forbid "private" sales between neighbors. Private sales, he contended, often joined husbands and wives.

8. *Congressional Globe,* 31st Congress, 1st session, pp. 244–252.

mise. This would be the southern complaint to the very end—namely, that the North got everything, the South nothing. Nevertheless, full-scale debate was scheduled to begin the following week, and immediately word shot around Washington and beyond that Clay was to deliver a major address on his compromise scheme next Tuesday.[9]

Clay spent the remainder of the week not only preparing his forthcoming speech but writing to political friends and allies about the necessity of generating popular support for compromise. The hotspurs of the South, called ultras, seemed intent on opposing any settlement of the slavery question, he said, and too many "timid" northerners hesitate to speak out about the necessity of finding a solution to their present problems. "I shall need, therefore, popular support. Large public meetings (one at New York especially), indorsing my plan substantially, would do much good. Perhaps the last of next week," after he had given his speech, "or the week after may be early enough." But he wisely warned his correspondents against the appearance of intervention from Congress or any other distant quarter in initiating these meetings. "Its beneficial effects will depend much upon its being conducted and regarded as a local and spontaneous assemblage, without any ground for the imputation of its being prompted from any exterior source."

For the next six months Clay constantly strove to whip up public demand for a compromise solution in order to bolster his own efforts, stiffen the will of the "timid" in Congress, and overwhelm the disunionists. And he succeeded. His subsequent speeches on the compromise were "applauded by all parties, and [sent] flying in pamphlet form the length and breadth of the land," reported one Whig leader. Several thousand people turned out at the Castle Garden in New York City on February 25 to endorse Clay's resolutions and reaffirm their commitment to the Union. Other cities imitated the action of New York. Slowly but steadily an outpouring of vocal demand for compromise swelled and spread across the nation. And each time that the resolutions of these meetings were sent to Clay, he presented them in the Senate with the admonition that the American people demanded action and the preservation of the Union. "Nineteen-twentieths, if not ninety-nine out of a hundred people of the United States," he declared at one point, "desire most anxiously a settlement of this question . . . and the restoration once more of peace, and harmony, and fraternity."[10]

Most important of all, starting in early February and continuing through July, Clay assembled in daily caucus both Whigs and Democrats committed to preserving the Union. Serving as chairman of this group, he guided, advised, and encouraged their efforts to legislate a compromise that would address and resolve all the issues driving the nation toward disunion. In managing this

9. *Congressional Globe,* 31st Congress, 1st session, p. 252.

10. Clay to Daniel Ullmann, February 2, 15, 1850, in Clay, *Works,* IV, 600–601; Hone, *Diary,* II, 885; *National Intelligencer,* February 27, 1850; New York *Herald,* February 26, 1850; *Congressional Globe,* 31st Congress, 1st session, pp. 1107, 1139–1142, 1202–1203, 1263–1264.

highly diverse group of congressmen he tended to approach conservative
Democrats through Lewis Cass of Michigan and liberal Democrats through
Stephen A. Douglas of Illinois. He later said he spent more time "in conference and consultation" with Democrats about his compromise scheme than he
did with Whigs.[11]

The following Tuesday, February 5, Clay prepared to go to the Senate to
give his first major address since his return. He had a cold, as always, but at
least the usual fever did not accompany it. Still, he coughed a great deal,
despite his efforts to suppress it. And walking to the Capitol weakened him.
"Will you lend me your arm?" he asked a friend who accompanied him. "I feel
myself quite weak and exhausted this morning." He ascended the stairs of the
Capitol with great difficulty and frequently paused to catch his breath. Perhaps
he should postpone his speech, said the friend. Clay shook his head. "I consider our country in danger," he replied, "and if I can be the means in any
measure of averting that danger, my health and life is of little consequence."

When he arrived at the Senate chamber, he beheld a spectacle that may
have startled him. An enormous crowd had jammed its way into the galleries,
the corridors, the Rotunda, and the floor of the chamber itself. From as far as
Boston, New York, Philadelphia, Baltimore, "and places more distant" had
come mobs of people to hear the Great Pacificator and by their cheers and
applause salute his efforts at compromise. They had squeezed into every corner, cranny, door, window, and avenue to hear him, to hear the "lion of the
day" roar his imprecations against those who would destroy the Union. The
atmosphere in the room crackled with excitement. Everyone expected to witness a momentous and historic address.[12]

The Senate was called to order at 1:00 P.M. Preliminary business was
quickly dispensed with and the senator from Kentucky recognized. The haggard man slowly got to his feet but immediately drew himself to his full height.
As he did so, the chamber suddenly thundered with applause. The noise rose
to such a level that the chair ordered the entrances cleared. Clay waited until
the din subsided, and then he spoke. The speech took two days to deliver
because his strength gave out after several hours. In all he figured he spoke for
nearly four and three-quarter hours on his compromise plan.[13]

As he started to speak, his voice momentarily faltered, but then he cleared
his throat and let the mighty organ ring out with all its old power and reso-
nance.

"Never, on any occasion," he began, "have I risen under feelings of such
deep solicitude. . . . I have never before arisen to address any assembly so

11. Speech of Douglas, September 9, 1859, quoted in James Ford Rhodes, *History of the United
States since the Compromise of 1850* (New York, 1902), I, 173, note; Speech to the General Assembly, November 15, 1850, *National Intelligencer,* November 27, 1850.
12. Schurz, *Clay,* II, 335–336; New York *Tribune,* February 8, 1840; New York *Herald,* February
7, 1840; Baltimore *Sun,* February 6, 1840.
13. Clay to Lucretia, February 7, 1850, copy CPP.

oppressed, so appalled, so anxious." After that necessary introduction he next implored the deity to bless the nation, calm the violence and rage of partisan politics, still passion, and allow reason to resume its empire.

He had "two or three general purposes" in submitting his resolutions, he admitted: first, to settle all the questions arising from slavery; then to frame "a scheme of accommodation" so that neither North nor South would "make a sacrifice of any great principle"; and finally, to extract from both sides some concession, "not of principle . . . but of feeling, of opinion" in relation to the present controversy.

On the matter of the Wilmot Proviso, which so many northerners seemed determined to engraft on any bill dealing with the territories, Clay begged them to look at the facts and listen to reason. Neither California nor New Mexico wishes to introduce slavery. New Mexico's "soil, its barrenness, its unproductive character" will never allow slavery to flourish there. "You have got what is worth more than a thousand Wilmot provisos," he cried. "You have nature on your side—facts upon your side—and this truth staring you in the face, that there is no slavery in those territories." What more can you want? What more can you demand? "Elevate yourselves from the mud and mire of mere party contentions." Act like responsible men, "as lovers of liberty, and lovers, above all, of this Union."

Clay proceeded through his resolutions one by one, pausing frequently for dramatic effect and to rest. Often his arms flew up from his sides to point, to reach out, to embrace. He rejected the President's plea to allow the Supreme Court to decide the Texas boundary issue. "There are questions too large for any tribunal of that kind to decide—great political, national, and territorial questions, which transcend their limits, and to which they are utterly incompetent." As for the Texas debt, his resolution proposed to pay a portion of it, amounting to not less than three million dollars, and he felt confident that the people of that state themselves would readily accede to the settlement.

On slavery in the District of Columbia, Clay insisted that Congress had full power to abolish it. Such power "is here" in this legislature, he declared, as he pointed to the floor, "or it is nowhere." But in good faith and conscience Congress must not exercise that power as long as slavery is legal in Maryland, the state that ceded the land to form the District in the first place. Nor can it be done without compensating the slaveholders. "Congress cannot, without forfeiture of all those obligations of honor which men of honor, and nations of honor will respect . . . interfere with slavery in this District."

But the slave trade is another matter. What an abominable sight to witness in the capital. Its abolition, he said, should not be regarded as a concession by one side or the other but as an object "conformable to the wishes and feelings of both." Clay noted that delegates were to be sent to a convention in Nashville in June because of this issue.[14] "That is to be cause . . . for consider-

14. Some likened the Nashville Convention to the Hartford Convention. See *National Intelligencer,* March 16, 20, 1850.

ing whether this Union ought to be dissolved or not. Is it possible to contemplate a greater extent of wildness and extravagance to which men can be carried by the indulgence of their passions?"

As for fugitive slaves, Clay believed every man in the nation, every officer of every state had an obligation to assist in the recovery of runaways.[15] The Supreme Court in the case *Prigg* v. *Pennsylvania* had exempted state officials from helping enforce federal fugitive slave laws. Clay disagreed with the Court on this point and thought it had exceeded its authority. As a result, the free states had acted in an unkind and unneighborly manner in the matter of apprehending runaway slaves and "not in the spirit of that fraternal connection existing between all parts of this Confederacy." It was the duty of Congress to make the Fugitive Slave Law more effective, "and I will go with the furthest Senator from the South in this body to make penal laws, to impose the heaviest sanctions upon the recovery of fugitive slaves, and the restoration of them to their owners."

On the second day Clay spent considerable time recalling the Missouri Compromise debates, how a joint committee of the two houses worked out a solution, and why extending the 36°30' line to the Pacific in the present situation would not serve the interest of the South. Jefferson Davis had said that he would not be satisfied with anything less than recognition of slavery south of the line, but Clay assured him that "non-action" would be better. "If you adopt the Missouri line . . . you do legislate upon the subject of slavery, and you legislate for its restriction" to the north of the line without obtaining any "action for admission" to the South, "I know it has been said . . . that non-legislation . . . implies . . . exclusion of slavery. That we cannot help. . . . If nature has pronounced the doom of slavery in these territories . . . who can you reproach but nature and nature's God?"

Clay ended with a plea for the Union. The nation was like a marriage, and no human authority can dissolve it. "I am directly opposed to any purpose of secession, of separation. . . . Here I am within it, and here I mean to stand and die." The alternative was war and the "extermination" of liberty within all "dissevered portions of the Union." To prevent such a catastrophe, he begged both northerners and southerners "by all their love of liberty—by all their veneration for their ancestors—by all their regard for posterity . . . to pause—solemnly to pause—at the edge of the precipice, before the fearful and disastrous leap is taken into the yawning abyss below. . . . Finally . . . I implore" the Almighty that "if the direful and sad event of the dissolution of the Union shall happen, I may not survive to behold the sad and heart-rending spectacle."[16]

Men and women rushed forward as he concluded this nearly five-hour marathon to shake his hand and kiss him. He sank back into his seat completely exhausted, his strength totally drained. It was not one of his greatest speeches.

15. On reading this remark, William Furness wrote to Webster: "Mr. Clay tells us we should all consider ourselves bound to help slave catchers. May our right hands fester first!" Furness to Webster, [February 1850], in Webster, *Papers, Correspondence,* VII, 18.

16. *Congressional Globe,* 31st Congress, 1st session, appendix, pp. 115–127.

It did not have the dash and verve and exuberance of his best efforts, but the sight of a desperately ill seventy-three-year-old man pleading for the life of his country in a performance of heroic length electrified his audience. "There seemed to be a solemnity, and a grandeur in his appeal," recorded one observer, "that lifted him as it were from the earth, and seemed as a voice speaking from Heaven." The imagination, cleverness, daring, and sweep of his compromise plan staggered both his listeners and the nation at large over the possibility that at last an agreeable settlement which could prevent disunion had been found. Though feeble, Henry Clay was the only man in Washington with the moral strength, courage, and intelligence to provide a compromise. Thanks to him, an agenda finally existed to settle the slavery question amicably. Congress could now begin its work.[17]

Clay's old rival Martin Van Buren summoned up the thinking of the majority of Americans. "Tell Clay for me," the Magician wrote to the former editor of the Washington *Globe* Francis P. Blair, "that he added a crowning grace to his public life . . . more honorable & durable than his election to the Presidency could possibly have been."[18] Indeed.

Other Democrats, including Senators Cass and Douglas, offered similar praise. And when Blair sent Van Buren's letter to Clay in the Senate chamber and included one of his own, the Kentuckian rose from his seat, walked over to Blair, and extended his hand. Andrew Jackson must have turned over in his grave!

"Henry Clay," proclaimed the New York *Herald,* "may never reap the reward of his devotion to the United States, to the Union, and to the constitution; but posterity will do him justice, if the present generation do not."[19]

"In five hundred years to come," prophesized the Frankfort, Kentucky, *Commonwealth,* "it is not probable that an opportunity will occur to elevate his equal. Greece produced but one Demosthenes; Rome but one Cicero; and America, we fear, will never see another Clay."[20]

One unexpected ally in the good cause appeared four days later. Thomas Ritchie, accompanied by General Thomas H. Bayly of Virginia, called on Clay at his hotel on Sunday, February 10, at 1:00 P.M. At Ritchie's request the interview had been arranged by James W. Simonton, a journalist. The editor had already expressed his approval of the compromise in the Washington *Union* and had suggested to Senator Henry S. Foote of Mississippi the idea of proposing a special committee of thirteen to work out details for a final statement. Now he had come to wipe away years of resentment and disagreement between the two men in the cause of preserving the Union. Thereafter Ritchie argued forcibly and ably for Clay's compromise proposals.

17. Schurz, *Clay,* II, 336; Clay to Lucretia, February 7, 1850, copy CPP; New York *Express,* February 7, 1850, quoted in Poage, *Clay and the Whig Party,* p. 203.
18. Van Buren to Francis P. Blair, February 9, 1850, Blair Papers, LC.
19. November 21, 1850, copy CPP.
20. December 16, 1851, copy CPP.

Several weeks later the two men made their reconciliation public and official. They dined at the home of a mutual friend, John T. Sullivan, and at one point Ritchie jokingly turned to the Old Coon and said: "Look here, Mr. Clay, if you will really save the Union, we will all forgive you for having had Mr. Adams elected in 1825 by *bargain, intrigue, and management.*'"

"Shut your mouth!" Clay snapped in reply. "Shut your mouth, Tom Ritchie; you know perfectly well that there never was a word of truth in that charge."

"Very well, very well," Ritchie laughed. "I say to you now . . . that if you succeed in rescuing the Republic from ruin, and I should survive you, Tom Ritchie will plant a sprig of laurel upon your grave."[21]

Others applauded Clay's efforts at conciliation. The speech, commented Philip Hone, "was worthy of the statesman and patriot who has always succeeded in cases of national emergency in calming the rage of contending factions; but will it do now?" Sadly Hone doubted that it would. "Alas! the demon of party listens not to the voice of the charmer, charm he ever so wisely."[22]

And there were other doubters. Extremists, of course, in both parties— the "Northern & Southern Ultraists"—roundly condemned the compromise proposals, both denying that they obtained anything substantial from them. "Sentiment" for the North, sneered Senator Salmon P. Chase of Ohio, and "substance" for the South, "just like the Missouri Compromise." Beverley Tucker of Virginia believed the South would lose everything if it supported the resolutions, and he called Clay the "prince of humbugs, charlatans and traitors."[23]

Debate on the proposals formally opened on February 11 and extended to March 27, with all the leading men in the Senate giving powerful voice to their approval or disapproval. As the other senators spoke, Clay frequently interrupted to explain what he meant by a particular resolution or to reject ideas or words falsely attributed to him. When President Taylor on February 13 forwarded an authenticated copy of California's constitution to the Senate and requested admission for the area as a state, the matter should have been referred to the Committee on Territories, but Senator Foote of Mississippi proposed a special committee to consider it, along with all the other sectional problems encompassed in Clay's resolutions, and unite them into a single bill.

The Great Pacificator immediately objected. He did not intend his resolutions to be considered as a single measure. "I do not think it would be right to

21. Clay to James W. Simonton, February 8, 1850, copy CPP; Ambler, *Ritchie,* pp. 280–282; Henry S. Foote, *Casket of Reminiscences* (New York, 1968), p. 27.

22. Hone, *Diary,* II, 886.

23. Clay to Elijah F. Nuttall, June 18, 1850, copy CPP; Chase to E. S. Hamlin, February 2, 1850, in *Diary and Correspondence of Salmon P. Chase* (Washington, 1903), II, 200–201; Tucker to James H. Hammond, February 2, 1850, Hammond Papers, LC; Hamilton, *Prologue to Conflict,* pp. 60–61.

confound or to combine all these subjects," he said. The question of California ought to stand by itself.

Foote pretended astonishment at what he called Clay's reversal of course. "I am grieved—I am mortified," he protested. The resolutions had been presented to "cover the *whole* ground of controversy" as a means of adopting a compromise.

In response Clay referred to Foote's remarks as a "sort of omnibus speech," thereby adding the name of the newest form of urban transportation into the congressional (and ultimately popular) vocabulary. Into this omnibus, snickered Clay, "he introduces all sorts of things and every kind of passenger, and myself among them." The galleries guffawed. But "I have risen rather to vindicate myself from the charge of inconsistency."[24] On slavery, Clay declared, "I have made no change. . . . I shall go to the grave" believing that slavery "is an evil, a social and political evil." As for the omnibus idea, "my desire was that the Senate should express its sense upon each of the resolutions. . . . I never did contemplate . . . bringing them all into one measure."

With respect to favoring one section over another in the resolutions, said Clay, the charge was false. "I intend, so help me God, to propose a plan of doing equal and impartial justice to the South and to the North. . . . I consider us all as one family, all as friends, all as brethren. I consider us all as united in one common destiny; and those efforts which I shall continue to employ will be to keep us together as one family, in concord and harmony; and above all, to avoid that direful day when one part of the Union can speak of the other as an enemy."

Foote also accused Clay of failing, as a native son, in his responsibilities to the South. "The persecuted South has looked to him as one of her safest, most influential and distinguished sons," and what has he done? He has given our adversaries "all the *trump cards* in the pack."

In a near-classic statement Clay responded:

> I know whence I came, and I know my duty, and I am ready to submit to any responsibility which belongs to me as a senator from a slaveholding State. Sir, I have heard something said on this and on a former occasion about allegiance to the South. I know no South, no North, no East, no West, to which I owe my allegiance. . . . My allegiance is to this Union and to my own State; but if gentlemen suppose they can exact from me an acknowledgment of allegiance to any ideal or future contemplated confederacy of the South, I here declare that I own no allegiance to it; nor will I, for one, come under any such allegiance if I can avoid it.

It was a statement of "towering grandeur," reported the New York *Express* on February 18. "It withered all the plotters of a Southern Confederacy that heard him. It actually made them tremble."[25]

---

24. Senator Jefferson Davis later repeated this charge.

25. *Congressional Globe,* 31st Congress, 1st session, pp. 353–355, 365–369, 399–405; Clay, *Works,* VI, 394–409 At the conclusion of this speech Webster reportedly said to Clay: "You improve in eloquence, Sir: you are a younger man than ever." Poage, *Clay and the Whig Party,* p. 203.

As the debate heated up over the next several weeks, Clay seemed to draw renewed strength from the contest. His old sense of humor returned in full force, and he never failed to take advantage of any opportunity to lighten the mood of the chamber with a snappy comeback or joke. "It cannot be denied, however, that he oftener parried the attacks of his opponents with wit," noted one man, "than met them in argument." When Senator Jeremiah Clemens of Alabama, for example, commented on the unlikely cooperation between Clay and Benton by noting that the "lion and the lamb had got together," Clay shot back: "I do not know to which of these quadrupeds he assigned me; I should make a very poor lamb I am afraid, and I am very far from being ambitious of claiming prowess of the lion." Clemens added to the lighter mood when he called out that he considered Clay the lion. But Clay denied there was any "cooperation." A "Senator came to me this morning, (I will not tell whom—that is a matter between the Senator and myself) . . . and we had a very long and interesting conversation. . . . Now, suppose that some northern man had watched the motions of the honorable Senator from Miss—ah! I beg pardon, I was just going to name him." The other senators and the visitors in the galleries chuckled. Clay contended, of course, that there was no impropriety for the "private intercourse" between any two senators.

So invigorated by the debate did Clay feel that he informed his wife that his health was "pretty good," all things considered. "I eat and drink, perhaps too much, I sleep well, going to bed regularly about 10 o'clock, and I never worked harder. I still have bad colds, but without any fever. I think I have grown fatter."[26]

Even old adversaries noted Clay's indulgent and less combative mood. "In relation to your Senior in that Body [Clay] during the days I was at Washington," wrote Isaac Hill to Webster, "I was struck with admiration at the temper which would not be provoked into controversy when taunts were thrown as to the maintainance of favorite theories and opinions."[27]

In late February Clay decided to take a short "furlough" to Philadelphia "to breathe a little more pure air" and get away for a short while from the "grating and doleful sounds of dissolution of the Union, treason, and War." He may also have wished to get a better "feel" for public reaction to his proposals. Northern newspapers had been most favorable, a fact noted by Foote on the Senate floor. If the people at large concurred with his ideas, then a ground swell of demand for compromise could bring a resolution to all their problems.

To his delight, Clay found that his speech and compromise plan had "produced a powerful & salutory effect in the Country and in Congress." If any compromise were adopted, he reckoned, it would be "substantially mine."

In Philadelphia a committee received him and arranged a ball in his

26. Greenwood, *Greenwood Leaves,* p. 302; *Congressional Globe,* 31st Congress, 1st session, pp. 399–401; Clay to Lucretia, February 19, March 7, 1850, Thomas J. Clay Papers, LC.
27. Hill to Webster, April 17, 1850, in Webster, *Papers, Correspondence,* VII, 70.

honor. He "appeared at the head of the staircase" to make his entrance at the ball, "having a lady on each arm, when a tremendous cheer of welcome broke forth. . . . The ladies waved their hankerchiefs . . . and clustered around him at once." He kissed them, of course, and they gushed their congratulations and good wishes. The display so delighted him that he did not retire until eleven o'clock.

Lithographs of the great man delivering his magnificent compromise speech soon appeared around the country. He received encouraging letters from friends and strangers in every section and from opposing political views, congratulating him on his proposals and expressing their "approbation of my humble endeavors." He began to hope that the poisonous atmosphere in the nation had begun to dissipate. He was especially pleased that Kentucky refused to be represented in the Nashville Convention scheduled to meet in June and had given him no instructions concerning the present crisis. "All this is well," he wrote his son.[28]

But when Clay returned to the capital from Philadelphia,[29] he found that the more radical southerners who criticized his proposals as yielding too many concessions to the North had backed proposals put forward by John Bell of Tennessee. Bell adopted the omnibus principle, but his scheme dealt only with the territory acquired from Mexico and the Texas boundary. Also, President Taylor had grown increasingly annoyed with Clay over the compromise because *his* plan had been virtually shunted aside without getting serious consideration. As President he felt he deserved more attention and courtesy, and he suspected Clay of deliberately acting to usurp his role as leader of the Whig party. His wounded pride festered throughout the long debate on the compromise, and he listened avidly to any rumor or gossip brought to him by troublemakers that indicted the Great Pacificator for disloyalty. Getting a compromise past him with Clay's name written on it might prove impossible.

In March the debate intensified. All the big cannons spat out their fire. And John C. Calhoun led off. The dying man could not deliver his speech, and it was read for him by Senator James M. Mason of Virginia, while the "cast-iron man," wrapped in his black cloak and looking like a ghostly apparition,

28. Clay to John Pendleton Kennedy, February 24, 1850, copy CPP; *Congressional Globe,* 31st Congress, 1st session, pp. 400–401; Clay to A. D. Chaloner et al., March 9, 1850, Lexington *Observer and Kentucky Reporter,* March 27, 1850, copy CPP; *National Intelligencer,* February 26, 1850; Clay to Reuben H. Walworth, March 11, 1850, Clay to Thomas O. Larkin, June 10, 1850, Edmund Dillahunty et al. to Clay, June 14, 1850, J. W. Morrow to Clay, June 15, 1850, copies CPP; Clay to James Clay, March 6, 13, 1850, in Clay, *Works,* IV, 601–603; Clay to Edward Coles, March 15, 1850, copy CPP.

29. Upon his return he learned that his younger brother, Porter, had died in Arkansas. A cabinetmaker and a man of great piety, Porter became a Baptist minister late in life and moved to Missouri, where he was credited with giving the first sermon in English west of the Mississippi River. He died on December 30, 1849, in Camden, Arkansas. Thomas Hart Clay, *Henry Clay,* p. 20. "My greatest consolation in the loss which I have sustained," Clay wrote, "arises out of the fact that my brother had long been a sincere, pious, and zealous Christian." Clay to N. L. Farris, March 11, 1850, copy CPP.

listened motionless. Offering no plan of his own, Calhoun simply excoriated the North for fomenting the crisis. He demanded a constitutional amendment that would somehow restore the South's power to protect itself. And so this bitter, frustrated, and disappointed genius went to his death proclaiming the inevitable breakup of the Union. "Disunion is the only alternative that is left us," he said.[30] He died on March 31.

The following day Clay gave a brief eulogy in the Senate. "No man with whom I have ever been acquainted, exceeded him in habits of temperance and regularity, and in all the freedom, frankness, and affability of social intercourse, and in all the tenderness and respect and affection which he manifested" toward his wife, Floride. "No more shall we witness . . . the flashes of that keen and penetrating eye of his" or "that torrent of clear, concise, compact logic . . . which, if it did not always carry conviction to our judgement, commanded our great admiration. . . . I was his senior . . . in years—in nothing else."[31]

Prior to Calhoun's death, Daniel Webster delivered his justly famous Seventh of March Speech on the compromise proposals—but in a different style and mood and purpose from those of the old nullifier. "I wish to speak today," he began, "not as a Massachusetts man, nor as a Northern man, but as an American. . . . I speak today for the preservation of the Union. Hear me for my cause.'" He continued for three hours, repeating many of Clay's arguments and denunciation of secession.[32]

Equally famous (some said infamous because it invoked "a higher law than the Constitution" to block the extension of slavery into the territories) was a speech delivered on March 11 by Senator William H. Seward. He expressed his faith in an unshakable Union, leaving it to the timid to make compromises to rescue it. For himself he would vote for California's admission "without conditions, without qualifications, and without compromise."[33]

Among the younger corps of senators, Salmon Chase condemned the compromise, but Stephen A. Douglas, chairman of the Committee on Territories, adopted several principles of the Clay plan. The youngest man in the Senate at age thirty-six, Douglas was undoubtedly the shortest, standing only five feet four inches tall. But he had a massive head, broad shoulders, and a muscular trunk atop two stumps for legs. He exuded strength and self-confidence. Douglas not only helped halt a filibuster in the House over the admission of California and served as Clay's liaison to liberal Democrats but worked out an agreement with Toombs, Stephens, and others by which he brought in two bills from his committee on March 25 for the admission of California and the organization of territorial governments for New Mexico and Utah. These bills essentially followed Clay's compromise scheme—although they were not

30. Calhoun to James H. Hammond, February 16, 1850, Calhoun to Thomas G. Clemson, March 10, 1850, in Jameson, ed., *Correspondence of John C. Calhoun*, II, 781, 784.

31. Calhoun, *Works*, IV, p. 542–573; *Congressional Globe*, 31st Congress, 1st session, pp. 624–625.

32. Webster, *Writings*, X, 57–98.

33. *Congressional Globe*, 31st Congress, 1st session, appendix, pp. 260–269.

as comprehensive—in that they applied the principle of popular sovereignty to the slavery question.[34]

Then Senator Foote moved the formation of a select committee of thirteen to prepare a solution to their problems. Clay expressed little hope that such a committee's recommendation could command a majority, but he was willing to try it.

Unfortunately the administration provided no direction in all the maneuvering going on in Congress. It seemed to be drifting without any other thought than the President's "no action" plan. Should there be one omnibus bill or many bills? Should California be held distinct and separate from the others? And was the committee of thirteen the route to take to achieve a solution? "I have never before seen such an Administration," exclaimed Clay. "There is very little co-operation or concord between the two ends of the avenue." Not a single prominent Whig in either House had any "confidential intercourse" with Taylor. "Seward, it is said, had; but his late Abolition speech has, I presume, cut him off from any such intercourse, as it has eradicated the respect of almost all men for him."[35]

Clay faced a dilemma in deciding between an omnibus bill or separate bills. With separate bills, as he originally proposed, he now began to fear that there existed not only a "strenuous minority" opposed to the admission of California but real doubt about the passage of the other territorial bills without the Wilmot Proviso. Most particularly, he came to understand how committed southern Whigs seemed to be to the omnibus idea. Also, it provided a measure of protection against a presidential veto. So, over the course of several weeks, and probably on the advice of the regular caucus of Whigs and Democrats over which he presided, Clay steadily edged his way to the Foote strategy, finally reversed himself, and opted for an omnibus bill to be prepared by a select committee of thirteen. It was the only way to achieve success, he reckoned.[36]

On April 8 he announced his switch on the Senate floor. He said he found "little practicability in this idea of total separation of subjects." After all, tariff bills contain hundreds of items, and no tariff bill in which all provisions met the approval of every congressman had ever passed. We face a similar problem now, he declared. "You may vote against it if you please in toto, because of the bad there is in it, or you may vote for it, because you approve of the greater amount of good there is in it."

Benton quarreled with him over this change of strategy. He wanted a separate bill on California and saw no need for a select committee. As Benton thundered out his demand, virtually shaking the walls with the power of his

34. Johannsen, *Douglas,* pp. 273, 281–282.

35. *Congressional Globe,* 31st Congress, 1st session, p. 510, appendix, pp. 364–375; Clay to James Harlan, March 16, 1850, Clay to Thomas B. Stevenson, April 3, 1850, in Clay, *Works,* IV, 603–604; III, 498. "Aleck, this is a nice mess Governor Seward has got us into," said President Taylor. "The speech must be disclaimed at once, authoritatively and decidedly." Nevins, *Ordeal of the Union,* I, 301–302.

36. Clay to Thomas B. Stevenson, April 3, 1850, in Clay, *Works,* III, 498; Poage, *Clay and Whig Party,* p. 216.

voice, Clay leaned forward, cupped his hand around his ear, and said, "Speak a little louder." The chamber rocked with laughter.

When Benton finally quieted and sat down, Clay rebutted the argument. Separate bills might get vetoed, he said, and he now feared that the attempt to consider California separately was a ploy by some to satisfy their "own wants" and forget the other parts of his plan. No, he concluded, an omnibus bill brought forward by a select committee could bring compromise.

I go for honorable compromise whenever it can be made. Life itself is but a compromise between death and life, the struggle continuing throughout our whole existence, until the great Destroyer finally triumphs. All legislation, all government, all society, is formed upon the principle of mutual concession, politeness, comity, courtesy; upon these, every thing is based. . . . Compromises have this recommendation, that if you concede any thing, you have something conceded to you in return.[37]

Having found an ally in Clay, Foote returned the compliment, in a manner of speaking, by attacking Benton. Among other things he attacked the Missouri senator for having denounced Calhoun's 1849 Southern Address, in the course of which attack Benton lost his temper, sprang from his seat, and charged forward.

Foote blanched when he spotted Benton rushing toward him. Fearful of a physical thrashing, he retreated toward the Vice President's dais and then pulled out a pistol, loaded and cocked. The chamber resounded with screams and shouts as colleagues rushed forward to prevent a tragedy. Clay, along with several others, called for order.

Benton stopped in his tracks, restrained by Senator Henry Dodge. "Let the assassin fire!" he screamed. "A pistol has been brought here to assassinate me."

"I brought it here to defend myself," the Mississippi senator protested as he surrendered his weapon to Senator Daniel Dickinson.

"Nothing of the kind, sir," Benton rasped. ". . . No assassin has a right to draw a pistol on me."

Indeed not—at least not in the august Senate chamber. An investigation followed, and despite calls for Foote's expulsion, nothing came of the incident.[38]

The language and action in the debate had suddenly become vicious. Explosive words frequently ricocheted around the room as these highly excited, highly opinionated, highly verbal senators struggled to find a solution to the crisis. Clay himself indulged in one verbal blast when he struck out against abolitionists.

Sir, of all the bitterest enemies toward the unfortunate negro race, there are none to compare with these Abolitionists, pretended friends of theirs; but who, like, the Siamese twins, connect themselves with the negro, or, like the centaur of old, mount

37. Greenwood, *Greenwood Leaves,* p. 302; Clay, *Works,* VI, 410–418.
38. *Congressional Globe,* 31st Congress, 1st session, pp. 760–763. Chambers, *Old Bullion Benton,* pp. 359–362, carries a complete account of the altercation.

not the back of a horse, but the back of the negro to ride themselves into power; and in order to display a friendship they feel only for themselves, and not for the negro race. No, sir; there are not worse enemies in the country of the negro race than the ultra abolitionists. To what sorts of extremity have they not driven the slaveholding States in defence of their own rights, and in guarding against those excesses to which they have a constant tendency.[39]

Clay's seventy-third birthday on April 12 provided an appropriate occasion for demonstrations around the country in favor of compromise. Popular demand for a settlement based on Clay's proposals found voice in rallies, public celebrations, and newspaper editorials. Clay himself was paid "the compliment of a grand Serenade" in Washington. At 10:00 P.M. some friends, accompanied by the Marine Corps Band, came under the windows of his hotel and saluted him with a variety of patriotic airs. The streets around the hotel soon crowded with people, and when he appeared at his window, they started screaming and begging him to say a few words. He obliged the mob by speaking solemnly about his love of the Union and his desire to calm the agitation threatening to tear the nation apart. His actions were now judged so patriotic that they transcended personal ambition and party consideration; his efforts were described as those of a consummate statesman; his name and reputation were hailed in extravagant terms befitting the exalted rank he now occupied in the hearts of his countrymen.[40]

By mid-April, as a result of his regular caucus meetings of Whigs and Democrats, Clay had fused a coalition under his leadership of border state and southern Whigs, joined most often by conservative northern Democrats, who followed Lewis Cass, and less frequently by the more liberal Democrats, led by Stephen A. Douglas. These separate factions voted approval in the Senate for the formation of the Committee of Thirteen on April 18 to consider all the questions dealing with the territories and slavery. The members of this committee (six Democrats and six Whigs) were elected the next day. As the thirteenth member and chairman Henry Clay received twenty-eight votes, with three others (Bell, Benton, and Mangum) receiving one vote each. It was a rather extraordinary tribute to Prince Hal's stature and the respect accorded him by his colleagues.[41]

As always, Clay exercised considerable control of the committee and the

39. *Congressional Globe,* 31st Congress, 1st session, pp. 685, 772. Some tried to joke about what was happening in Congress. A "United States lunatic asylum for the immediate treatment of some worthy Senators and Representatives" should be established, wrote one constituent, especially for abolitionist congressmen, who should be bled, placed on a water diet, and have their heads "shaved and blistered."

40. *National Intelligencer,* April 15, 1850; New York *Tribune,* April 15, 1850.

41. There were also four blank ballots cast. In addition to Clay, the committee consisted of Webster, Samuel S. Phelps, and James Cooper (northern Whigs); Mangum, Bell, and Berrien (southern Whigs); Cass, Dickinson, and Jesse D. Bright (northern Democrats); William R. King, Mason, and Solomon W. Downs (southern Democrats). *Congressional Globe,* 31st Congress, 1st session, p. 781.

writing of its final report, although he was so anxious to keep both sides content and agreeable to compromise that he frequently gave in on points raised by the other members of the committee that seemed to him more procedural than substantive.

But Clay, Cass, and others on the committee were outvoted on one important point. The majority agreed that slavery was a "rightful" subject of legislation but forbade territorial legislatures to touch it, thereby eliminating Clay's recognition of the binding force of Mexican law and apparently affirming the extreme southern position that the Constitution protected slave property until a territory became a state.[42]

For one solid week the committee argued and debated and finally agreed on a majority recommendation. On April 25 Clay retreated to the Riverdale home of his friend Charles Benedict Calvert, near Bladensburg, Maryland, where he prepared the committee's report and hoped to recover from a debilitating cold that had plagued him for weeks.[43]

On Wednesday, May 8, to a packed chamber, Clay presented the report. It took the form of an omnibus bill. It linked together as one measure the admission of California as a free state, establishment of territorial governments for New Mexico and Utah without the right to legislate on slavery, and adjustment of the boundary of Texas with compensation for relinquishing all claim to any part of New Mexico. As a separate item the report called for a fugitive slave law with two amendments, one requiring slaveholders to produce documentation for their claim of loss and the other providing trial by jury if the alleged fugitive so desired in the state from which he or she had fled. Finally the report recommended the abolition of the slave trade in the District of Columbia.

Although members of the committee disagreed over certain proposals, and they themselves would speak to the Senate of their differences, Clay commended them on their performance. "I have never been associated with gentlemen on any great and momentous occasion in which a spirit of more kindness, more conciliation, and more of a disposition to listen and to give effect . . . than was presented during the whole of our session."[44]

The following Monday Clay spoke at length on the report. He said the committee had linked the two bills introduced by Douglas on March 25. Then he pretended that the change by the committee of the provisions concerning slavery in the territories hardly mattered. Actually he had every intention of restoring popular sovereignty to the bill in the ensuing debate, but for the

42. *Congressional Globe,* 31st Congress, 1st session, pp. 948–950; Frank H. Hodder, "The Authorship of the Compromise of 1850," *Mississippi Valley Historical Review,* XXII (March 1936), 529; Robert R. Russell, "What Was the Compromise of 1850?", *Journal of Southern History,* XXII (August 1956), pp. 296–297. Clay claimed the committee could not agree on provisions concerning slavery prior to a territory's admission as a state.

43. Clay to Lucretia, April 25, 1850, Thomas J. Clay Papers, LC.

44. *Congressional Globe,* 31st Congress, 1st session, pp. 944–951. For comments of the other members, see ibid., pp. 951–956.

moment he chose to be less than candid, so he flooded the chamber with emotional eloquence and with such extravagant praise for both the North and South that cynical listeners could hardly keep from laughing out loud. Despite his fears, he declared, that no measure regarding the territories could be advanced without producing "scenes of the most painful and unpleasant character," he had witnessed a "gratifying change." The "North, the glorious North, has come to the rescue of this Union of ours. She has displayed a disposition to abate in her demands." And the "South, the glorious South—not less glorious than her neighbor section of the Union—has also come to the rescue. The minds of men have moderated; passion has given place to reason everywhere." Instead of allowing the territories to "shift for themselves," as the President recommended, the committee felt an obligation to provide them with appropriate governments.

Clay followed up his snide remark about Taylor's plan with another aimed at Senator Seward. The fugitive bill will not conciliate those in the free states, he said, who assert "that there is a higher law—a divine law—a natural law— which entitles a man, under whose roof a runaway has come, to give him assistance, and succor, and hospitality." What is the difference between harboring a fugitive and going to a plantation and stealing him outright? He denounced the "wild, reckless, and abominable theories, which strike at the foundation of all property and threaten to crush in ruins the fabric of civilized society."[45]

The ultras immediately expressed their opposition to the omnibus bill. Other senators, like Douglas, doubted it could pass as a package. A majority in its favor could simply not be mustered in its present form, he insisted. Its strongest support came from southern Whigs and northern Democrats. Southern Democrats and northern Whigs attacked it, with the opposition led by two cunning strategists, Jefferson Davis for the ultras of the South and William H. Seward for the ultras of the North. Both opposed compromise in any form. They demanded virtual capitulation to their demands by the other side.

When the debate began two days later, their strategy became immediately evident. Amendments, including amendments on amendments, calls for adjournment, recess, and postponement, questions on the meaning or interpretation of clauses in each of the proposals, and the introduction of extraneous business—all these and more kept Clay on his feet day after day, fighting off these disunionists, as he called them. The omnibus was most vulnerable in two places: drawing a boundary for Texas and preventing those determined to detach California's admission from the other parts of the package, after which they would pass it and then scrap the rest.

Senator Benton, who favored the detachment of California, tangled repeatedly with Clay, and their language grew sharper as the debate intensified over the next two months. At one point Clay accused Old Bullion of calumny

45. Clay, *Works,* VI, 426–451.

and "hurled it back at him" with "scorn and indignation" that he may stick it "in his casket of calumnies, where he has many other things of the same sort."[46]

When Jefferson Davis argued for the extension of the 36°30' line to the Pacific, Clay tried to reason with him. If Congress has the power to introduce slavery into New Mexico and California, where the institution did not now exist, did it not follow that Congress also had the right to prohibit its introduction into the territories? Was that what he wanted to achieve? And to the complaint that the South would get nothing from the compromise, Clay denied Davis's charge by pointing to the "total absence" of all congressional action on slavery. For the past several years the South had been intent on putting down the Wilmot Proviso. Well, said Clay, it has been done. "The proviso is not in the bill." And the committee report distinctly declared the proviso to be "[t]otally destitute . . . of any practical import." Congress must refrain from legislating on slavery in the territories, said Clay, and leave it to the people of each territory to decide. "The bill is neither southern nor northern. It is equal; it is fair; it is a compromise."

And the nation demanded compromise, Clay thundered. It cannot survive another year of "this agitation, this distraction, this exasperation" between sections over slavery. We must harmonize the country. Unless compromise prevails, nothing will be done for California, the territories, the fugitive slavery bill, and the rest. Nonaction would be disastrous. "Instead of healing and closing the wounds of the country, instead of stopping the effusion of blood, it will flow in still greater quantities."[47]

Although Clay dragged himself to his feet every day to counter the attacks of the opposition, although he caucused daily with other congressmen in seeking a solution to the crisis, although he displayed some of his old political skills in timing roll call votes on amendments, in counting heads, and in ensuring the presence of his allies on crucial votes, and although he did more than any other man in Congress to muster popular support around the country for compromise, still he sometimes overplayed his hand, sometimes grew testy, and sometimes needlessly offended moderates. No longer caring about reasserting his leadership of the Whig party, no longer concerned about winning another presidential nomination, no longer intent on advancing his "popularity," he became relentless and obsessed with the determination to bring the issues to a satisfactory conclusion. "Mr. Clay with all his talents, is not a good leader, for want of temper," exclaimed Daniel Webster. "He is irritable, impatient, and occasionally overbearing; & he drives people off."[48]

One of Clay's more unfortunate political mistakes at this crucial moment

46. Holt, *Crisis of the 1850s*, p. 88; Smith, *Presidencies of Taylor & Fillmore*, pp. 139–140; *Congressional Globe*, 31st Congress, 1st session, appendix, p. 867. See also the exchanges between Clay and Benton on July 16. Ibid., pp. 1261–1265.

47. *Congressional Globe*, 31st Congress, 1st session, p. 1005, appendix, pp. 612–616, 897–899, 902–903..

48. Clay to Willie P. Mangum, June 25, 1850 in Mangum, *Papers*, V, 178; Webster to Franklin Haven, July 4, 1850, in Webster, *Papers, Correspondence*, VII, 121.

was the speech he gave on May 21 in which he blistered the President and thereby openly acknowledged the split within the Whig party. It lacked some of the pungency and nastiness of his efforts against earlier opponents, like Old Hickory, but in view of the temper of the times it was bad enough. Taylor had invited it, of course, not only by again insisting on his own plan—thereby suggesting a veto of any other—but by engineering the resignation of the editor of the administration's own newspaper, the *Republic,* which had shown sympathy and support for the compromise and frequently lauded Clay for his untiring efforts to save the Union. The new editor, Allen A. Hall, reversed the policy of the newspaper and savaged the work of the Committee of Thirteen. As for Clay, wrote Hall, he had clearly come to Washington "to lead, not to follow."[49]

In his May 21 speech Clay announced that it was a "very painful duty," but one he would perform nonetheless—that is, contrast the President's plan with that of the committee—and let the chips fall where they may. What is Taylor's plan? So that it may be fully understood, Clay continued, "I will describe it by a simile." The nation has sustained five wounds, bleeding and threatening its life. Here Clay raised his hand and ticked them off—"one, two, three, four, five"—as the galleries watched in fascination. What will the President do? Heal only one, cried Clay, and leave the others to continue bleeding, "even if it should produce death itself." With profound surprise and regret Clay said that he had watched the persistence of Taylor in his own "peculiar plan. I think that in the spirit of compromise . . . in a spirit of peace and concord, and of mutual confidence and co-operation," the President ought to unite with the Congress and save the Union. But no, he will follow none but his own plan, no matter what Congress thinks or does. His plan for New Mexico, for example, allows a lieutenant colonel, "a mere subordinate of the army of the United States," to hold the governmental power. And "in a time of profound peace!" What a mockery of American institutions. "Stand up, Whig who can," shouted Clay, "stand up, Democrat who can, and defend the establishment of a military government in this free and glorious Republic, in a time of profound peace!" He brought his speech to a roaring conclusion by calling upon newspapers around the country to print in parallel columns the respective plans of the chief executive and the committee so that the people could judge for themselves which would prevent disunion and civil war.[50]

Friends rushed forward when Clay resumed his seat to shake his hand and assure him that it was the greatest speech of his career. Clay knew better. "My

---

49. Quoted in Hamilton, *Prologue to Conflict,* p. 98. Sara B. Bearss argues convincingly that one additional reason for Clay's delay in openly breaking with Taylor involved the negotiations his son James was conducting in Portugal. The father did not wish to jeopardize his son's efforts at bringing the negotiations to a successful conclusion. Clay finally broke with Taylor, Bearss contends, when he decided that the negotiations had already collapsed. Bearss, "Henry Clay and the American Claims against Portugal, 1850," pp. 168, 178.

50. Clay, *Works,* VI, 458–478.

friends speak in terms of extravagant praise of my Speeches," he told his son, "and especially of the last." Whatever doubts he may have had about his now-open breach with the President he dismissed as unfortunate but necessary. "I had to attack the plan of the Administration for Compromising our Slavery difficulties," he said. "Its course left me no other alternative." In any event, the rupture had now been revealed to the entire country, and strangely the supporters of the President's plan thought it might prove advantageous to their cause. "Mr. Clay is sustaining all his former reputation and power in Congress," wrote one, "and true to his hates he has flung down the defiance to the friends of General Taylor." So be it. "I am glad myself that he has at last stept out with his armor on—an avowed enemy though formidable can be met." Daniel Webster shook his head in surprise and disappointment. "I think Mr. Clay is in danger of eclipsing his glory. Why attack the President?"[51]

Clay's assault on Taylor became sharper with each succeeding speech. "War, open war, undisguised war, was made by the Administration," he bellowed. His speech on May 21 was nothing but "a vindication of the plan of the committee." At that Senator John Bell of Tennessee leaped to his feet to deride Clay's "exercise of this moral despotism." When he considered the differences between the President's and the committee's plans, Bell wondered "whether Mahomet will go to the mountain, or the mountain shall come to Mahomet."

"I only wanted the mountain to let me alone," interrupted Clay. With that the audience laughed out loud.[52]

Over the next month attacks upon the omnibus in the Senate intensified, and something like twenty-eight amendments to its provisions were put forward, each one requiring time and energy to accept or reject. Frequently Clay admitted that he did not care which way a particular amendment was decided—"I should not care the pinch of snuff I hold in my fingers, whether I vote pro or con"—because it made so little difference to the larger questions. But he recognized the strategy, and all he could do was hope that his strength would hold out to the end. When weary senators asked for a recess to allow the removal of the chamber's carpets and draperies for the summer, Clay objected. "He said that he did not care about having the matting put down. . . . He would be content with the carpet all summer. It was of the utmost importance to push the Compromise bill through." So the debate continued, and Clay succeeded in getting the senators to approve his motion to begin their sessions at eleven o'clock rather than noon. "The Administration, the Abolitionists, the Ultra Southern men, and the timid Whigs of the North are all combined against it [the omnibus bill]," he told his family. "Against such a combination, it will be wonderful if it should succeed."[53]

51. Clay to James Clay, May 27, 1850, Thomas J. Clay Papers, LC; Orlando Brown to Crittenden, May 23, 1850, Crittenden Papers, LC; Webster to Moses Stuart, May 30, 1850 in Webster, *Papers, Correspondence,* VII, 105.

52. *Congressional Globe,* 31st Congress, 1st session, appendix, pp. 1091–1093.

53. Hamilton, *Prologue to Conflict,* p. 98; *Congressional Globe,* 31st Congress, 1st session, pp.

As Clay had warned, delay in reaching a final vote on the compromise only intensified the crisis in the country. The convention in Nashville met during the first week of June to assert the rights of the South. Fortunately the ultras could not convince the delegates to opt for secession—perhaps, suggested one man, because the remains of General Andrew Jackson lay buried only twelve miles away—but would try again when the delegates reconvened in the fall. Worse, the New Mexico authorities, confident of Taylor's support, pushed for immediate statehood under a free-state constitution with proposed boundaries that triggered a Texas threat to send troops to Santa Fe to establish its territorial claims. Bloody conflict seemed inevitable.[54]

And the "breach between the Administration and me," wrote Clay to his wife, ". . . is getting wider and wider. Their conduct is generally condemned. They seem utterly regardless of public feeling and opinion, and blindly rushing on to their own ruin, if not the ruin of their Country."[55]

What might have happened next can only be conjectured because something totally unforeseen occurred on July 9. President Taylor suddenly died. On a blisteringly hot and muggy Fourth of July, the President returned from ceremonies marking the occasion and consumed large quantities of raw fruit and vegetables—the kind "made for four footed animals & not Bipeds" washed down with ice water.[56] Five days later he died in agony, and some said that had he lived, there would have been civil war. At the funeral the Great Pacificator served as one of the twenty pallbearers.[57]

In any event, a powerful enemy of Clay's compromise had been eliminated. Indeed, the Kentuckian contended that the event "will favor the passage of the Compromise bill." For the Star of the West the accession of Millard Fillmore of New York to the presidency brought enormous satisfaction, and he could barely hide his elation. The two men were old friends, and the new President showed the senator all the respect and deference denied him by the previous administration. "My relations to the new Chief are intimate and confidential," Clay admitted.[58] They met frequently and privately. The old cabinet was sent packing, and Clay exercised considerable influence in the selection of a new one, including the appointment of Daniel Webster as secretary of state. Moreover, he offered no objection to Fillmore's choice of John J. Crittenden as attorney general.[59] The influence of Seward, which had fostered administration opposition to compromise ended abruptly since the two New Yorkers

---

1298–1299, appendix, pp. 1398–1402; Clay to Thomas Hart Clay, May 31, 1850, Clay Papers, LC. The vote on Clay's motion to begin sessions at eleven o'clock was thirty to seventeen.
54. Jennings, *Nashville Convention,* pp. 135–166; Nevins, *Ordeal of the Union,* I, 327–332.
55. Clay to Lucretia, July 6, 1850, Thomas J. Clay Papers, LC.
56. Mangum to Charity A. Mangum, July 10, 1850, in Mangum, *Papers,* V, 181. According to Mangum, cabbages and cucumbers were not fit for "Bipeds."
57. *National Intelligencer,* July 9, 1850 (In 1991, Clay was one of a few accused of poisoning Taylor, but an exhumation and medical examination proved the accusation false.)
58. Clay to James Clay, July 18, 1850, Thomas J. Clay Papers, LC.
59. Clay to Thomas Hart Clay, August 6, 1850, in Clay, *Works,* IV, 611.

(Fillmore and Seward) thoroughly detested each other. Clay became the new White House spokesman in Congress, and executive patronage and influence were now employed on the side of compromise. "The government," wrote Seward, "is in the hands of Mr. Webster, and Mr. Clay is its organ in Congress."[60]

And the change mellowed Clay a little. He conceded points more readily and agreed to certain changes in particular portions of his bill. The "celebrated 'driver' [of the omnibus], Old Hal," wrote one observer, "thinks, it is said, of putting on new gearing, rearranging his horses, and changing his load a little." But it was a little late in the day to undertake any major overhaul of the omnibus. Besides, the months of "toil and arduous labor" he had expended to bring about a compromise had slowed him down considerably. He was not about to initiate important revisions.

But there did occur one change, one he had been quietly engineering for the past several months. It dealt with the slavery provisions in the proposed territories. The Committee of Thirteen had rejected the principle of popular sovereignty. Clay was determined to restore it because he believed the compromise would otherwise fail on the final vote. Stephen A. Douglas had made an earlier attempt to restore the principle but been voted down. Now Clay asked him to renew his effort and reintroduce a motion to strike out the amendment prohibiting slavery legislation by territorial legislatures. Conditions for its passage, he said, had improved considerably in the past several weeks.

But Douglas chose to have Moses Norris, the Democratic senator of New Hampshire, make the motion for him, and at the last moment it passed by the vote of thirty-two to twenty. No doubt the fact that Fillmore was now President and known to favor compromise with popular sovereignty, no doubt the heightened popular demand for compromise, thanks to Clay's constant efforts to arouse the public to pressure Congress, no doubt the lessening of tension since the adjournment of the Nashville Convention, and no doubt the fact that New Mexico had already fashioned a free-state constitution—all these reasons probably account for the success of Norris's motion. In any case, territorial legislatures could now forbid or permit slavery subject only to a possible veto by the governor or disallowance by Congress.[61]

During these hectic summer months, as the great debate continued, Clay fled to Riversdale, the home of his friend Charles Calvert, whenever possible to escape the oppressive heat of Washington and "breathe the Country air." But with the passage of time he needed to get away for a more extended rest. "As soon as the compromise measure is disposed of," he told William Mercer, and

60. Clay to Lucretia, July 6, 1850, Clay to James Clay, July 18, 1850, Thomas J. Clay Papers, LC; Clay to Mary Clay, July 13, 1850, in Clay, *Works*, IV, 610–611; Blair to Van Buren, July 15, 1850, Van Buren Papers, LC; Rayback, *Fillmore*, pp. 224–247; Smith, *Presidencies of Taylor & Fillmore*, pp. 167–169; Frederick W. Seward, *Seward at Washington* (New York, 1891), II, 147.

61. *Congressional Globe*, 31st Congress, 1st session, appendix, pp. 306, 1473; Johannsen, *Douglas*, p. 292; Hodder, "The Authorship of the Compromise of 1850," pp. 532, 533.

"without waiting the adjournment of Congress, I purpose passing two or three weeks at New Port where my health derived so much benefit last summer."[62]

Still, he continued the struggle throughout the month of July. "Mr. Clay bears up bravely against the extreme heat . . . the wearying delays . . . and the opposition . . . of both parties, North and South," wrote Grace Greenwood in one of her letters to the Philadelphia *Saturday Evening Post*. "He may be seen every morning at his post in the Senate, sitting quiet and erect, now and then turning to shake hands with a friend, smiling always as he does so, in his own illuminating way." His voice carried the same "impassioned sound," still emitting the "old beguiling music. When in moments of excitement he rises to speak, and stands so firm and proud, with his eye all a-gleam, while his voice rings out clear and strong, it almost seems that his apparent physical debility was but a sort of Richelieu *ruse,* and that the hot blood of youth was yet coursing through his veins, and the full vigor of manhood yet strong in every limb. The wonderful old man!"[63]

Clay made one final effort to drive his omnibus through the Senate. It turned out to be his last great oration in Congress. He delivered it on Monday, July 22, and it was undoubtedly his best of the entire debate. "I never heard Clay more eloquent," Francis Blair later told Van Buren. He never exhibited "greater resources of mind."

In an emotional outburst Clay appealed to the patriotic, nationalistic, moralistic sense of his audience and frequently elicited loud and long applause for what he said, so much so that the president of the Senate repeatedly threatened to clear the galleries. He expressed the feelings of the American people about the need to remain a whole, undivided nation. "We have no Africans or Abolitionists in our omnibus—no disunionists or Free-Soilers, no Jew or Gentile. Our passengers consist of Democrats and Whigs, who, seeing the crisis of their common country . . . have met together . . . to compare their opinions upon this great measure of reconciliation and harmony." Several times he took aim at particular senators—the abolitionist John P. Hale of New Hampshire was a favorite—and lashed them for resisting conciliation. He found Jefferson Davis's remark about using the territories to "breed slaves" disgusting. This sort of talk was suitable for "bar-rooms of cross-road taverns," not the Senate of the United States. Then he attempted to demonstrate one last time what would be "gained and lost" by each section from supporting compromise. The North gained California as a free state and the high probability that Utah and New Mexico would also remain free, and it secured the end of the slave trade in the District of Columbia. The South gained "a virtual abandonment of the Wilmot proviso," obtained an "efficient" fugitive slave bill, ended agitation

62. Hamilton, *Prologue to Conflict,* p. 108; Poage, *Clay and Whig Party,* p. 246; Clay to Lucretia, July 6, 1850, Thomas J. Clay Papers, LC; Clay to Calvert, July 19, 1850, Clay to Mercer, July 21, 1850, copies CPP.
63. Greenwood, *Greenwood Leaves,* letter of July 6, 1850, p. 317.

about the abolition of slavery in the District, and secured nine hundred miles of territory within Texas. The South would not get territory in Utah, New Mexico, or California. However, "she cannot blame Congress, but must upbraid Nature's law and Nature's God!" From the "bottom of my soul," he cried, the compromise "is the reunion of this Union. I believe it is the dove of peace, taking its aerial flight from the dome of the Capitol, carries the glad tidings of assured peace and restored harmony to all the remotest extremities of this distracted land."

One magnificent moment came toward the end of the speech when Senator Robert Barnwell of South Carolina "rushed into the lion's mouth with a fool-hardiness absolutely appalling" and accused Clay of using "disrespectful" expressions about a friend, Robert Barnwell Rhett, the principal secessionist speaker at the Nashville Convention. In a "grand exhibition of power and spirit," said one, Clay shattered the charge. "But, if he [Rhett] pronounced the sentiment attributed to him of raising the standard of disunion and of resistance to the common government, whatever he has been, if he follows up that declaration by a corresponding overt act, he will be a traitor, and I hope he will meet the fate of the traitor."

The galleries applauded wildly and shouted approval. The whooping and yelling became deafening. The presiding officer gaveled for order, threatening once again to remove all visitors. "The Senate chamber is not a theater," he lectured.

Clay concluded with these words:

If Kentucky to-morrow unfurls the banner of resistance unjustly, I never will fight under that banner. I owe a permanent allegiance to the whole Union—a subordinate one to my own State. When my State is right—when it has a cause for resistance, when tyranny, and wrong, and oppression insufferable arise—I will then share her fortunes; but if she summons me to the battle-field or to support her in any cause which is unjust against the Union, never, never will I engage with her in such a cause.

Should South Carolina or any other state "hoist the flag of disunion and rebellion," gallant men and devoted patriots in every other state would respond. "Thousands, tens of thousands, of Kentuckians would flock to the standard of their country to dissipate and repress their rebellion. These are my sentiments," and then Clay flung his outstretched arm down to his side and cried, "[M]ake the most of them."[64]

The Senate exploded, thundering its approval. A great man and a great cause had been joined. The result had the audience reeling. According to the *National Intelligencer,* Clay "surpassed even his ancient fame as a powerful, impassioned and impressive debater." Men and women wept. The eloquence of an old man standing tall and imploring his fellow senators in the name of

64. Clay, *Works,* VI, 529–567. Senator Davis denied the accusation about breeding, but Clay said he heard him distinctly, even though the published record had been altered.

their countrymen to preserve the Union "penetrated the minds and souls" of virtually everyone in the chamber. The hall shook with cheers.

Clay slumped into his seat, perspiration pouring down his face. What "a magnificent effort," exclaimed Grace Greenwood. "At his advanced age, to be able to stand up and speak so eloquently and so powerfully for three hours of an oppressively hot day, proves the Kentucky statesman to be one of the wonders of our time and country."[65]

A few days later William Seward assured his mentor, Thurlow Weed, that the game was up. "The Compromise is now to pass," he gloomily wrote.[66] And for a few days it did indeed seem that Clay's efforts had finally brought the success he had worked so hard and so long to achieve.

Then, in a moment, the omnibus "went to pieces all at once," just like Oliver Wendell Holmes's "wonderful one-hoss shay." The Texas boundary question knocked it apart. To the excellent amendment proposed by Senator James W. Bradbury of Maine that the boundary question be entrusted to a joint U.S.-Texas commission, Georgia Senator William C. Dawson added a modification that New Mexico would not have jurisdiction east of the Rio Grande until the commission settled on the dividing line. But fearful that New Mexico might object, Senator James A. Pearce of Maryland, a staunch advocate of compromise, who contended that Dawson's proposition was "cranky, lop-eared, crippled, deformed," moved to strike it out until he could offer something better. Sensing the danger because it might alienate southern support, Clay immediately jumped to his feet, expressing surprise and regret at the suggestion. He begged Pearce to withdraw his motion. Other means existed, he said, to right any imbalances. But Pearce persisted, and a vote to strike carried thirty-three to twenty-two.

Florida Senator David L. Yulee then moved to strike everything related to Texas, and it narrowly passed, twenty-nine to twenty-eight. Once Texas was eliminated, California followed on a motion by Missouri's David R. Atchison, thereby wrecking the omnibus. The vote: thirty-four to twenty-five. The omnibus lay in a heap.

The shattered Clay sat "as melancholy as Caius Marius over the ruins of Carthage." Then he silently rose from his chair and walked out of the chamber.[67]

"The omnibus is overturned," Benton gleefully shouted, "and all the passengers spilled out but one. We have but Utah left—all gone but Utah!" The "Mormons alone got thru' living," laughed another; "the Christians all jumped out." Abolitionists and ultras congratulated each other, and Seward danced

---

65. *National Intelligencer,* July 23, 1850; Greenwood, *Greenwood Leaves,* letter of July 25, 1850, p. 328.

66. Seward to Weed, July 26, 1850, Weed Papers, University of Rochester Library.

67. *Congressional Globe,* 31st Congress, 1st session, appendix, pp. 1449, 1458–1459, 1473–1474; Hamilton, *Prologue to Conflict,* pp. 108–112; Smith, *Presidencies of Taylor & Fillmore,* pp. 171–181; Poage, *Clay and Whig Party,* p. 257, quoting the New York *Express,* August 2, 1850. The voting that smashed the omnibus occurred on July 31.

around the room like a little top. Benton could hardly restrain himself. *"He had routed Clay! He had smashed his Omnibus to atoms!"*[68]

Poor Clay. Everyone knew his "heart is bound up with this measure" and "feared that his energies, his very life, would die out, or be laid on the table with it." Although shocked, angered, and "shaken to his soul," he fought on. He returned to the Senate the next day and excoriated Pearce for wantonly defeating the bill. He was especially "indignant at his Southern allies." Nevertheless, he announced his readiness to pursue another route to bring about compromise. "I was willing to take the measures united," he declared. "I am willing now to see them pass separate and distinct, and I hope they may be passed so without that odious [Wilmot] proviso which has created such a sensation in every quarter of the Union." But he himself no longer had the heart or energy or strength to continue leading the compromise forces. He had to get away for some rest or suffer the dire consequences. The tuberculosis had begun to kill him. He "has gone north," reported the *National Intelligencer,* "in order to recruit, by a few days rest, his exhausted strength."[69]

Later Clay publicly acknowledged the efforts of Webster, Cass, Foote, Dickinson, Cooper, Bright, Downs, Mangum, and the other members of the Committee of Thirteen in trying to help him win passage of his compromise.[70] On the other side, nineteen northerners and fourteen southerners voted for Pearce's amendment; only six Whigs, including Clay, voted against it. Sixteen northern and thirteen southern votes accounted for the passage of Yulee's amendment, while ten northern and twenty-four southern senators agreed with the Atchison amendment. This kaleidoscopic voting pattern signaled to everyone, including Clay,[71] that the various territorial bills of the omnibus might stand a better chance of passage if taken separately. That was the reason he returned the following day and asked for the passage of separate bills for each part of his compromise. Stephen A. Douglas had always maintained that the omnibus technique would break down. Now he came forward, as chairman of the Committee on Territories, and separated the parts of Clay's compromise and wrote each into a individual bill.[72]

Clay did not participate. He had left Washington on August 5, for Newport, Rhode Island, accompanied by Charles Calvert and his wife. In Philadelphia an omnibus tried to get through the crowd that formed to greet Clay but was stopped. "That omnibus is like the omnibus I left at Washington," laughed Clay; "it didn't get through." He explained to the crowd that he had

68. *Congressional Globe,* 31st Congress, 1st session, p. 1504, appendix, pp. 1482–1485; Elizabeth Blair Lee to Samuel Phillips Lee, August 1, 1850, quoted in Smith, *Blair,* p. 206; *National Intelligencer,* August 1, 1850; Poage, *Clay and Whig Party,* p. 257

69. Greenwood, *Greenwood Leaves,* p. 329; Oramus B. Matteson to Weed, August 1, 1850, Weed Papers, University of Rochester Library; Clay, *Works,* VI, 568–575, which also carries the exchange between Clay and Pearce; *National Intelligencer,* August 6, 1850.

70. Clay to John R. Thomson et al., August 14, 1850, copy CPP.

71. Clay to Caleb Cushing, August 3, 1850, copy CPP.

72. Smith, *Presidencies of Taylor & Fillmore,* pp. 179–180.

adopted the omnibus technique because many thought it had a better chance of passage. Now, he said, he placed his hopes in the separate passage of each bill.

In New York City another large crowd greeted him, demanding a speech. But he begged off. "I am fatigued and broken down," he admitted. Still, these extraordinarily large crowds and the homage they paid him proved the success of his efforts to generate popular support for the compromise. The people thanked him for his devotion to a cause they shared; they assured him his exertions for the Union had not failed. They would increase pressure on Congress,[73] and "he would indeed be a bold man, if not a rash one, who should take upon himself the responsibility of dashing this cup of conciliation from the eager lips of the American people."

On reaching Newport, feeling "very much worn down," he proceeded directly to the Bellevue House, where a large levee was held in his honor. Almost immediately he went "seabathing" and kept at it each day. By the end of the week he reported to President Fillmore that he felt much refreshed. He planned to stay several weeks so that the "invigorating air" and water could restore his health completely. Meanwhile, he regularly promenaded about town, to the delight of onlookers, and visited friends in the neighborhood.[74]

While Clay splashed in the seawater off Newport, Senator Douglas took up the Kentuckian's unfinished agenda and within seven working days had five separate bills ready for consideration. He and Pearce fashioned a new Texas boundary bill, which conceded 33,333 more square miles of territory to the state than had been allowed by the omnibus, and left New Mexico all its occupied territory. For its "sacrifice," Texas would receive ten million dollars. The Senate gave its collective consent to this bill on August 9. "Hail Liberty and Union and Domestic Peace!" cried the *National Intelligencer.* "Hail the return of Government from its long aberration back to its just sphere of action and usefulness!"[75]

Four days later the Senate agreed to California's admission, the following day the New Mexico bill passed, and on August 23, the fugitive slave bill went to its third reading by a vote of twenty-seven to twelve, passing three days later on a simple voice vote. The House concurred with these measures on September 7, 9, and 12. By the time Clay returned to Washington on August 27, after a three-week holiday, only the District slave trade bill awaited action. It, too, won approval on September 16 under Clay's "personal guidance."[76]

---

73. "Arouse the Northern public mind," demanded the New York *Express,* "to awaken their Representatives in Congress to the importance of settling the boundary line [of Texas] . . . at all hazards." August 9, 1850.

74. *National Intelligencer,* August 6, 12, 14, 21, 1850; New York *Herald,* August 8, 9, 1850; New York *Tribune,* August 6, 1850; Clay to Fillmore, August 10, 1850, copy CPP.

75. August 10, 1850.

76. Holman Hamilton, "Democratic Senate Leadership and the Compromise of 1850," *Mississippi Valley Historical Review,* XLI (December 1954), pp. 407–412.

But Douglas took no credit for these achievements. The important labor had been exerted by Clay. Indeed, Douglas told friends at the time he introduced the separate bills that when "they are all passed you see they will be collectively Mr Clays compromise."[77] And several years later in a speech in Cincinnati Douglas acknowledged that "All the Union men, North and South, Whigs and Democrats, for the period of six months were assembled in Caucus every day, with Clay in the chair, Cass upon his right hand, Webster upon his left hand, and the Whigs and Democrats arranged on either side." And, under the Great Pacificator, they worked ceaselessly and harmoniously and finally forged and won approval for the compromise that averted disunion.[78]

The people credited Clay with the victory as well, and Old Hal appreciated the recognition. "Every measure which I proposed in Feby last has substantially passed; and the Country seems to be disposed generally to give me quite as much credit as I deserve."[79]

With the passage of the most crucial bills of the compromise in early September, the people of Washington wildly celebrated the victory by firing one hundred guns at Washington Monument Square and discharging rockets from the Mall east of Seventh Street. Then they marched to Clay's hotel with the Marine Corps Band to acknowledge and thank him for his central role in restoring peace to the country. Unfortunately the Great Pacificator had gone to Calvert's country home once again to rest so the joyful mob demonstrated their gratitude before the residences of Foote, Cass, Webster, and Douglas.[80]

The failure of the omnibus followed almost immediately by the passage of each of its parts in separate bills caused bewilderment in many quarters. Why the one and not the other? A number of senators—Douglas most particularly—argued that the omnibus technique could never muster majority support. What it mustered was the majority *opposition*. "By combining the measures into one Bill," he wrote, "the Committee united the opponents of each measure instead of securing the friends of each." Taken individually, he went on, the measures could have been enacted from the very beginning.

Not likely. If nothing else, the omnibus brought over southern support and permitted the formation of the Committee of Thirteen. The committee played an important role in the solution because it provided the initial forum where all elements of the dispute could be analyzed, discussed, and finally hammered into a single legislative program, which was then presented to the

77. Smith, *Presidencies of Taylor & Fillmore,* pp. 181, 185; *Congressional Globe,* 31st Congress, 1st session, p. 1543ff.; Douglas to Charles H. Lanphier and George Walker, August 3, 1850, in Robert Johannsen, ed., *The Letters of Stephen A. Douglas* (Urbana, Ill., 1961), p. 192.

78. Speech by Douglas at Cincinnati on September 9, 1859, quoted in Rhodes, *History of the United States,* I, 173, note.

79. Clay to James Clay, September 20, 1850, Thomas J. Clay Papers, LC.

80. The people of Washington went to Clay's hotel first to express their appreciation for the compromise. It is interesting that they did not go to Douglas's residence until they had first saluted Foote, Cass, and Webster. Could it be that they did not regard his contribution in winning passage of the compromise as important as that of the others? *National Intelligencer,* September 9, 1850.

Senate for debate. And passage of the final Compromise of 1850 required the many months of intensive debate that resulted from the committee's report. But the omnibus, as a package, could not win passage through the Senate because, as Douglas said, it simply lacked a majority. Since feelings ran so high, senators could not be expected to vote affirmatively across the board. They needed the option to support one measure but oppose another. Only the "Free Soils & disun[ion]ists & the administration of Gen'l Taylor," said Douglas, labored to defeat the entire compromise, and they constituted a minority. Only sixteen senators voted for all the compromise bills, but the shifting back and forth on each roll call vote produced a majority for each of the five bills. In the long run, success of the compromise depended in the beginning on the omnibus strategy, and in the end on the individual approach to each measure. One or the other could not succeed by itself.[81]

Another thing. Combining the several bills into an omnibus package provided the surest protection against a presidential veto. But once that threat was removed by the demise of President Taylor, it made more sense to enact each bill separately and thereby allow senators the privilege of shifting sides according to their individual preferences.

One other reason exists for the collapse of the omnibus: Clay's failure of leadership. He irritated, annoyed, exasperated, and alienated any number of people during the long and trying months the Congress took to resolve the crisis, despite his intermittent efforts to lighten the mood of the Senate. He never lessened the pressure on his colleagues, forcing them to disregard other legislative business and lengthening their workday. More important, he assumed a patriotic and moralistic stance and, in so doing, seemed to impugn the patriotism and loyalty of those who disagreed with him. To his mind, abolitionists and ultras were intent on the destruction of the Union—or so he implied—and many individual senators in both groups resented it. His interminable warnings about what might happen in the nation (delivered frequently "with ponderous force"), his "severe morality," his regular invocation "of the Deity" to attest to the justice of his cause, his "want of temper," as Webster declared, his frequent irritability, his overbearing manner—all contributed to a failure of leadership that drove off needed support from his omnibus.[82]

Furthermore, Clay's not-too-disguised attempt at seizing the leadership of Congress and the Whig party was resented by President Taylor and his friends. And their anger manifested itself in their determination to kill his

81. Douglas to Lanphier and Walker, August 3, 1850, in Johannsen, ed., *Letters of Douglas,* p. 191. For an analysis of the Senate and House votes on the separate bills, see Holman Hamilton, "Democratic Senate Leadership and the Compromise of 1850," pp. 407–415, and " 'The Cave of the Winds' and the Compromise of 1850," *Journal of Southern History,* XXIII (August 1957), pp. 331–353.
82. Greenwood, *Greenwood Leaves,* p. 344; Webster to Haven, July 4, 1850, in Webster, *Papers, Correspondence,* VII, 121.

compromise. "If Mr Clays name had not been associated with the Bills," said Douglas, "they would have passed long ago. The administration were jealous of him & hated him & some democrats were weak enough to fear that the success of his Bill would make him President."[83]

Not that any of these negative factors diminish Clay's right to recognition as the one person most responsible for the ultimate solution to the crisis of 1850. As Douglas said, the measures were his. He set the agenda; he led the debate; he organized the meetings of the congressional friends of his "comprehensive scheme"; his speeches, more than any of the others, produced an enormous ground swell of public support for the compromise in every state, with the exception of South Carolina. Congressmen in both houses felt the popular reaction, particularly as the long and much publicized debates continued over nine months.[84] In the final analysis they could not fly in the face of public demand for a settlement and risk their political future.

"Let it always be said of old Hal," saluted Douglas, "that he fought a glorious & a patriotic battle. No man was ever governed by higher & purer motives."[85]

The nation paid fitting tribute to Henry Clay for resolving the impasse.[86] Once again the people dubbed him the Great Compromiser. As long as he lived, they happily contended, he could always find a solution to reconcile conflicting sectional interests. But when he was gone, what then? Who could replace him?

Twenty-five years later Senator Foote thought about what the loss of Henry Clay meant to the nation. "Had there been one such man in the Congress of the United States as Henry Clay in 1860–'61," he wrote, "there would, I feel sure, have been no civil war."[87]

83. Douglas to Lanphier and Walker, August 3, 1850, in Johannsen, ed., *Letters of Douglas,* pp. 192–193.

84. See the many editorials from newspapers around the country reprinted in the Washington *National Intelligencer,* February 27, 28, March 20, August 10, 22, 24, 27, September 2, 5, 7, 1850.

85. Douglas to Lanphier and Walker, August 3, 1850, in Johannsen, ed., *Letters of Douglas,* p. 193.

86. *National Intelligencer,* September 16, 1850. William W. Freehling in his *Road to Disunion,* I, 477, does not agree with this assessment. He thinks that Clay provoked a controversy within the South as important as the one between the two warring sections.

87. Foote, *Casket of Reminiscences,* p. 30.

FORTY-ONE

"My Political Life Is Over"

THE COMPROMISE of 1850 postponed secession and civil war by ten years, and many historians have argued that had secession and war occurred in 1850, the South would undoubtedly have won its independence. By giving the North ten years to develop further its enormous industrial potential and "find" Abraham Lincoln to lead the nation, the Compromise of 1850 did, in a very real sense, prevent the permanent separation of the Union—thanks to Henry Clay.

The country quieted after its near brush with disaster. The Nashville Convention reconvened on schedule, but because the compromise had proved acceptable to both sides, the delegates took no further action and adjourned. Only the Fugitive Slave Act, the one bill that infuriated many northerners, met their total approbation. Still peace had been achieved, and for that most Americans expressed their gratitude and delight.[1]

Clay sat out the final weeks of the congressional session, but he could hardly wait to return home. "Never have I been so tired of a Session of Congress or so anxious to get home," he told his wife. He should have stayed longer at Newport, where he had gained so much benefit, he added. Already the healthy effects of his "seabathing" had worn off, and "I am again getting very much exhausted." He would start as soon as possible for home, "where I desire to be more than I ever did in my life."[2]

Clay left Washington on Saturday, September 28, and arrived back in Lexington on October 2, a journey of incredible speed, thanks to the railroad.

---

1. For the hostility aroused by this law, see Stanley W. Campbell, *The Slave Catchers: Enforcement of the Fugitive Slave Law, 1850–1860* (Chapel Hill, N.C., 1970), and Thomas D. Morris, *Free Men All: The Personal Liberty Laws of the North, 1780–1861* (Baltimore, 1971).

2. Jennings, *Nashville Convention*, pp. 187–211; Clay to Lucretia, August 27, 1850, Clay to James Clay, September 20, 1850, Thomas J. Clay Papers, LC; Clay to Thomas Hart Clay, September 6, 1850, Clay Papers, LC.

At various stops along the way people recognized him and shouted their congratulations and appreciation. Everyone wanted to shake his hand, but he begged them to respect his feeble condition and allow him to resume his homeward trip without further delay. When he reached Lexington, an enormous crowd greeted him and escorted him to the Phoenix Hotel. Obviously all the rancor expressed by Kentuckians in the past few years on account of his emancipation ideas had vanished. Once again he was their idol and hero, the personification of Kentucky's finest.

Clay spoke briefly to this crowd, declaring his belief that the Union had been saved by the compromise. Then he lifted his arm slowly and pointed in the direction of Ashland. "There lives an old lady about a mile-and-a-half from here, whom I would rather see than any of you." The crowd laughed and applauded but seemed appreciative of his need to get home.[3]

Over the next several weeks Clay tried to relax and enjoy his family surroundings at Ashland and attend to his financial interests. More and more of late he felt an obligation to give more heed to his fiscal situation. His taxable property now included Ashland and its 515 acres, valued at $40,800; the Mansfield property with 125 acres, at $6,250; 33 slaves, at $9,600; half ownership of a house and lot in Frankfort, at $1,500; 35 mares and mules and 2 jennies; 16 head of cattle; "17 Black tith[e]s"; and a stud horse and 2 carriages among a number of other listed but less valuable items. His nontaxable property included furniture, plate, paintings, wines, and library, valued at $7,500; Frankfort Bridge stock, valued at $4,500; Maysville Road stock, at $1,900; Lexington & Richmond Turnpike, at $4,000; Lexington & Frankfort Railroad, at $10,000; several other railroad stock, interest in saltworks, and notes owed him from the sale of his Illinois property and from the Agricultural Bank in Natchez amounting to several thousand dollars.[4] Not a great estate, but adequate for himself and his wife and those dependent upon him. His executor later estimated its total worth at $100,000.[5]

Despite his best efforts to avoid attracting attention, well-wishers constantly called on him at home and intruded with their personal concerns. They seemed to need to tell him how much they appreciated what he had done for them, as though to make up for the many times they had failed him by rejecting his bid for the White House. He was continually urged to attend public meetings and barbecues. "During your long and eventful career," he was told in one invitation to a "Free Barbecue," the people of Kentucky, both "Democrats and Whigs alike . . . have never welcomed your return with such unanimous and affectionate manifestations of their regard as now." In the past the state had always been "divided into two great parties. . . . Now her people . . .

3. Clay to Mary S. Bayard, September 26, 1850, Lexington *Kentucky Statesman,* October 5, 1850, copy CPP.
4. "H. Clay's List of Taxable Property," 1851, statement of assets of Henry Clay, July 10, 1851, copy CPP.
5. Harrison, "Henry Clay, Reminiscences by His Executor," p. 177.

[stand] shoulder to shoulder." The crisis the compromise had averted produced a triumph, "the most glorious in our annals." In that struggle "you were a great actor." Your courage, patriotism, and eloquence "have not only extorted the admiration of the country and of mankind, but placed you above and beyond the region of party. Upon this lofty eminence may your fame rest forever."

What especially delighted Clay about the invitation to the Free Barbecue was the fact that it celebrated the coming together of Whigs and Democrats in support of the Union. That meant a great deal to him. To that end he had expended all his energies during the recent crisis. So he accepted the invitation, despite his infirmities and "delicate health."

It took place on the fairgrounds at Lexington on October 17. Thousands attended, and six resolutions, praising Clay and his compromise and reaffirming Kentucky's allegiance to the Union, were passed. John C. Breckinridge, a Democrat, gave the principal speech, and Clay responded. In his remarks Old Hal expressed his belief that the great body of Americans would acquiesce in all the measures of the compromise. He hoped that their compliance would "lead to quiet and tranquility. Malcontents, at the North and in the South, may seek to continue or revive agitation, but, rebuked and discountenanced by the Masses, they will ultimately be silenced generally, and induced to keep the peace."[6]

Other invitations followed, but Clay took pains to protect himself since he had to return to Washington for the second session of Congress scheduled to begin in early December. His son James had returned from Lisbon, where he succeeded in negotiating a claims settlement with the Portuguese. In his first message to Congress President Fillmore acknowledged young Clay's contribution in reaching the agreement.[7] This pleased the father very much, although, by and large, his children continued to disappoint him. Both Thomas and John constantly dunned him for money, and John, who spent most of his time racing horses, suffered a recurring mental problem. When James later complained that Lucretia seemed to care more for John than for any of her other children, the father tried to reassure him. John's "great afflictions," he wrote, "undoubtedly deeply affect her; but I believe that she affectionately feels for all her children. Her manner does not always truly indicate the intensity of her actual feelings."[8]

6. Clay to Benjamin Gratz et al., October 10, 1850, Frankfort *Commonwealth,* October 22, 1850, Kentucky *Statesman,* October 19, 1850, copies CPP. Clay's remarks at the barbecue are inferred from his letter to Gratz.

7. The Taylor administration rejected this settlement and ordered James home. But the Fillmore administration accepted it, although James did not complete the final treaty because he had already started for home. "He acquitted himself very well in his mission," wrote Clay to Lucretia. "I should have been glad if James could have concluded the treaty himself and so have acquired the merit of the negotiation, which he deserves. The President is very kindly disposed towards him." August 27, 1850, Thomas J. Clay Papers, LC.

8. Clay to James Clay, February 18, 1851, March 14, 1852, Thomas J. Clay Papers, LC. It is

Decades earlier the "hard featured" Lucretia had given up accompanying Clay to Washington. Not surprisingly, therefore, Clay's reputation in the capital for getting involved with "loose women" during those years caused widespread comment among gossipmongers.[9] As he said, Lucretia's manner often seemed cold and distant, perhaps with good reason. For a man as ardent and passionate as Clay, that attribute in his wife must have been a burden, although he never complained. Nor did she write him. In the entire corpus of Clay correspondence there is only a single letter from Lucretia to her husband, dated March 10 [1814]—and even this one is doubtful. Apparently she wrote an earlier letter in 1814 to notify him of his reelection to the House of Representatives. But that is all there is—as far as one can determine. Clay admitted that she never wrote, but that, too, did not faze him. He said he understood.

But what should be remembered about Lucretia is the difficult life she led. Not only did she contend with an absent husband, whose career did not particularly engage her deepest interests or sympathies, and rebellious and (in a few cases) mentally disturbed children, but she was forced by circumstances to raise many of her grandchildren.[10] The loss of all her daughters was another cruel blow. And like Rachel Jackson, she spent a good deal of her time running the estate. Moreover, she ran it extremely well, not that Clay ever said so directly.

Several of Clay's grandchildren also gave him grief. One had devoted himself "to the gratification of his sensual appetite" while another took off, "without my permission," to join a filibustering expedition to Cuba in which some seventy Americans were later killed and another fifty captured. "His conduct has given me great pain and anxiety," said Clay. "It is not yet time for us to get Cuba. It will come to us in due season if we are wise, prudent and

---

interesting and curious that there are no letters from John in the vast Clay correspondence, although in his own letters home the father acknowledges receipt of them. Obviously they were removed and possibly destroyed. John later married Josephine Russell, daughter of William Henry Russell, one of Clay's good friends. Josephine first married Andrew Eugene Erwin, son of Clay's daughter Anne Brown Clay Erwin, in 1853. Her first husband died at Vicksburg in 1863, after which she married John. John died in 1887.

9. Edward Bates to Julia Bates, December 4, 1829, Bates Papers, Virginia Historical Society, Richmond; Bleser, ed., *Secret and Sacred*, p. 172. Even during one eulogy after Clay died it was alluded to. Of Clay's moral life it "has been for years most slanderously and wilfully misrepresented," said Charles Anderson. *A Funeral Oration on the Character, Life and Public Services of Henry Clay* (Cincinnati, 1852), p. 34.

10. There was a total of twenty-nine grandchildren. Susan Clay Duralde had two children: Martin III (1823–1846), and Henry Clay (1824–1850). Anne Brown Clay Erwin had seven children: Julia (1825–1828), Henry Clay (1827–1859), James, Jr. (1828–1848), Andrew (1830–1863), Lucretia (1830–1866), Mary (1832), and Charles (1835–1860). Thomas had five children: Lucretia (1838–1860), Henry (d. 1906?), Thomas (1843–1907), Rose Victoire, and Mary Russell. Henry, Jr., had five children: Henry III (1833–1862), Matilda (b. 1835), Martha (b. 1838), Anne (1837–1917), and Thomas (1840–1863). James had ten children: James (1846–1906), John (1848–1872), Henry (1849–1884), Thomas (1853–1939), Charles, George, Nathaniel, Lucy, Susan (1855–1863), and Lucretia (b. 1851).

united." Clay also worried about Henry Clay III, son of Henry Clay, Jr. The young man hated the confinement and discipline of West Point and managed to get himself expelled.[11]

In mid-November Clay spoke to the general assembly of Kentucky. Again, the fact that the invitation had been "dictated by no party feelings" and had won a unanimous vote from both Whigs and Democrats prompted his acceptance. Once more he spoke of the good effect of the compromise in tranquilizing the country. "At all event," he assured them, "the field of excitement and agitation has been greatly circumscribed." Moreover, it had "thrown together in free and friendly intercourse" members of both political parties. He admitted that throughout the debates "I was in conference and consultation quite as often, if not oftener, with Democrats than Whigs; and I found in the Democratic party quite as much patriotism, devotion to the Union, honor, and probity, as in the other party."

Clearly the old warrior had mellowed. He had transcended party politics, as everyone recognized. Party strife alarmed him for the danger it posed to the continued life of the Union. For himself, he concluded, "I want no office, no station in the gift of man"—and here he paused—except "a warm place in your hearts." The entire assembly broke out in spontaneous applause.[12]

Clay's speech was given national coverage. Newspapers everywhere now treated him like a second father of his country, above party, above faction, above sectional rivalry. Old political foes readily forgave him for his past "sins" and errors. All acknowledged his privileged station as elder statesman. Marble and plaster busts of Old Hal were turned out in great quantities by Mahlon J. Pruden of Lexington to satisfy popular demand. The best likeness, in Clay's own opinion, was still the one done by Joel T. Hart in 1845. His portraits also circulated widely,[13] and his speeches, especially those that glowed with passion about his love for the Union, were reproduced.[14]

Clay did not arrive back in Washington for the start of the second session of the Thirty-first Congress until December 13, nearly two weeks after the

11. Clay to William Mercer, August 1, 1851, Clay to Andrew Erwin, September 14, 1851, Clay to Octavia Walton Le Vert, November 14, 1851, Clay to Henry Clay III, October 22, 1850, November 22, 1850, December 23, 1850, January 18, 1851, June 27, 1851, copies CPP.
12. Speech to the general assembly, November 15, 1850, *National Intelligencer,* November 27, 1850.
13. Clay to Peter V. Hasted, April 29, 1851, Clay to Henry Williams, March 30, 1852, copies CPP. There were five portraits of Clay: two in Philadelphia and one each in Washington, Pittsburgh, and New Orleans. The Neagle portrait hangs in the Union League Club in Philadelphia, and the John Wood Dodge protrait hangs in the Pennsylvania Academy of Fine Arts. Late in December 1851 Neagle offered the Clay portrait to the Kentucky general assembly for $1,060, but the legislature did not act on the offer.
14. When asked to provide excerpts of his speeches for publication, Clay declined because he lacked the time. However, he did indicate which speeches the publisher might choose. "I would say that from my speeches in January 1812, on the War, on South American Independence, on Greece, on the removal of the deposits, during Gen Jackson's Administration, in answer to Mr. Rives, in 1841, on Tyler's Veto of the Bank, and my speech of September last on the Compromise." Clay to Richard G. Parker, February 23, 1851, copy CPP.

session had begun, again suffering from a bad cold, which turned into "one of the worst colds I ever had." Although his tuberculosis was surely terminal, he had no idea of his disease.[15]

Along the route to Washington he just missed meeting his son James, who was headed for Kentucky on his way home from Europe. "He passed me in the stage wednesday night, whilst I was asleep in the mountains." Clay tried to contact him by telegraph at three different places "but could not do it, the wires being every where out of order."[16]

Despite his cold and a promise to Lucretia to stay indoors as much as possible, Clay could never resist an important dinner party or a gala social affair in Washington. And he regularly attended theatrical performances and concerts in the capital whenever possible. He had become a fan of the nineteenth-century Norwegian composer-violinist Ole Bornemann Bull, who toured the United States several times starting in 1843 and even visited Clay at Ashland. Because of a bad cold and inclement weather, the statesman could not attend a Bull concert in Lexington, so the next morning the violinist went to Ashland and from an adjoining room softly played Clay's favorite composition, "The Last Rose of Summer." "Ah, that must be Ole Bull," exclaimed the delighted invalid; "no one but he could play the old familiar air in that manner." As Bull finished playing the final strains of the melody, the doors separating the two rooms were suddenly thrown open, and the two men "embraced."[17]

When the celebrated soprano Jenny Lind, the "Swedish Nightingale," arrived in the capital for a concert in 1850, she visited the Supreme Court and heard Clay argue a case. He so fascinated her that she sent him a special invitation to attend her concert. He was delighted by her invitation but at a loss as to her interest in "such an old fellow." Francis P. Blair, now completely reconciled with his former foe, told him that she had fallen in "love with his voice box."

At Lind's concert Clay scored another triumph. When General Scott entered the hall, he was only "feebly cheered." Webster and Crittenden came next, and they, too, hardly roused the audience—and for "Fillmore & family just so so." As a consummate actor Clay waited until the overture had concluded before making his grand entrance. Then he strode down the aisle.

15. Clay to Lucretia, December 14, 1850, Thomas J. Clay Papers, LC; Clay to Lucretia, December 26, 1850, Clay Papers, LC.

16. Clay to Lucretia, December 14, 1850, Thomas J. Clay Papers, LC. Upon his return James took up farming in Missouri, where he lived until his father's death. Then he returned to Kentucky, purchased Ashland, and served in the U.S. House of Representatives. He fought on the Confederate side during the Civil War and died in Montreal, Canada, of tuberculosis in 1864.

17. Clay to Bull, no date, in Sara C. Bull, *Ole Bull: A Memoir* (Boston and New York, 1882), pp. 213–214. Later Clay gave Bull a daguerreotype portrait of himself taken by Frederick De Bourg Richards, a landscape painter turned photographer, ca. 1850. In 1990 the daguerreotype was purchased at auction by the National Portrait Gallery. Bull's "The Herdsmaid's Sunday," a popular song in the nineteenth century, is available today in a recording by the great Norwegian soprano Kirsten Flagstad.

Immediately the crowd cried out its delight at seeing him, and "amidst sounds" of unprecedented volume "the whole house rose" to its feet. Naturally the demonstration thrilled him, and he could not resist telling Blair that he "was delighted at the triumph he had won over Scott, the President and the Cabinet." His pride, if nothing else, was still strong and vibrant.[18]

So, too, his acting ability. On another occasion he was conversing with Colonel John W. Forney and the celebrated actor Edwin Forrest, and Forney chanced to remark that Senator Pierre Soulé of Louisiana had given a fine speech during the compromise debates. Suddenly Clay's eyes flashed, he angrily corrected Forney, and he ended up by stating that Soulé was "nothing but an actor, sir—a mere actor!" Then, realizing the presence of the famed tragedian, Clay turned to Forrest and, with a graceful gesture, said: "I mean, my dear sir, a mere French actor!"

Later Forrest laughingly remarked to Forney: "Mr. Clay has proved by the skill with which he can change his manner, and the grace with which he can make an apology, that he is a better actor than Soulé."[19]

Clay attended one public function on January 21, 1851, that meant a great deal to him: the annual meeting of the American Colonization Society, of which he was still president. He gave a speech in which he had little to say that was new about emancipation and colonization, but he felt obliged to offer some explanation for the "misbehavior" of blacks in society. He did not wish to "wound their feelings," he declared, since it was not their fault "that they are a debased and degraded set . . . more addicted to crime, and vice, and dissolute manners than any other portion of the people of the United States. It is the inevitable result of the law of their condition." In view of the "nature of our [whites] feelings and prejudices" toward them, he continued, "they can never be incorporated, and stand upon an equal platform." Thus, they would benefit by a return to Africa.[20]

No doubt Clay regarded these lamentable comments as an enlightened view of a social problem. Still, their tone bespeaks an abominable racist attitude toward blacks, and it reflected not only Clay's thinking but that of most white Americans of the antebellum period, including many abolitionists. And such beliefs only intensified the national problem of dealing with the ongoing problem of slavery.

The Fugitive Slave Act provided the immediate difficulty. And Clay worried over it. Although he reduced his appearances and vocal participation in the Senate proceedings this session, he did give one speech in which he doubted that "there is any man in Congress who has watched with more anxious attention the operation of the fugitive act of the last session than I have." The law had been generally and faithfully executed, in Indiana, Ohio,

18. Blair to Van Buren, December 26, 1850, Van Buren Papers, LC.
19. Poore, *Reminiscences,* I, 388–389.
20. *African Repository,* April 1851, copy CPP.

Pennsylvania, and New York, he averred, but in the city of Boston "there has been a failure there upon two occasions to execute the law." Such resistance, he warned, could "lead to the most dangerous consequences." Not that Boston alone jeopardized the compromise.

He also worried over the continuing attempts by such ultras in the South as Robert Barnwell Rhett to initiate the secession of South Carolina, thereby "threatening more immediately the safety of the Union." And if resistance to the laws and rebellion against the government should result in a bloody civil war, "I have no doubt that it will be promptly & effectually put down, and that the moral effect would be to add greater strength & stability to our glorious Union."[21]

So alarmed had Clay become about the extremists on both sides and in both parties that he freely talked with both Whigs and Democrats in Congress about the necessity of strictly enforcing all the terms of the compromise and stoutly resisting the determined efforts of abolitionists and secessionists to trigger a breakup of the Union. Moderation was his plea, and he even unwittingly allowed his name to be used in the New York senatorial election against the Whig candidate, Hamilton Fish, who had refused to endorse the Fugitive Slave Act. So persistent were his efforts at conciliation that some wondered whether he intended to form a new party. "There seems to be a settled plan among the omnibus men of the last session," wrote Blair to Van Buren, "to get up an omnibus party. . . . Clay is the prime mover." The Great Compromiser appeared determined to appeal to "all honest men" to sacrifice their commitments and allegiances to the Whig and Democratic parties "to save the Union."[22]

Actually Clay had no such intention. But he did continue through the session to appeal to both sides to unite behind the compromise. To southerners he swore in one speech that from birth he had been "emphatically in the true, legitimate, full sense of the term, a States-rights man." That school of thought preached that no power that could not be found in the Constitution may be exercised. But where in the Constitution, he cried, does it give one state the power to nullify the acts of all the other states? Where does it empower a state to secede? "You find that whenever you press them on these

21. *Congressional Globe,* 31st Congress, 2d session, appendix, pp. 293–298; Clay to Francis Lathrop et al., February 17, 1851, copy CPP. One of the cases in Boston referred to by Clay involved William and Ellen Craft, a slave couple who had fled Georgia. When an attempt was made to reclaim them, a vigilante committee, headed by Theodore Parker and Wendell Phillips, prevented their recapture. The representatives of the owners, the "slave-catchers," were briefly jailed. See Nevins, *Ordeal of the Union,* I, 388; Smith, *Presidencies of Taylor & Fillmore,* pp. 211–212; Campbell, *Slave Catchers,* pp. 199–207.
22. Clay to Hugh Maxwell, February 15, 1851, Hamilton Fish to Clay, February 18, 1851, Clay to Hamilton Fish, February 23, 1851, copies CPP; Blair to Van Buren, December 30, 1850, Van Buren Papers, LC. Fish was subsequently elected. See Allan Nevins, *Hamilton Fish: The Inner History of the Grant Administration* (New York, 1957), I, 41. Clay and forty-three others signed a round robin letter pledging not to support anyone for office who rejected the terms of the compromise.

points, they fly from the Constitution and talk about the mode of its formation, its compact character, its being formed by the States." Only when it suits their purpose do they find justification "without the least difficulty . . . in the interpretation of the Constitution."

As for abolitionists who denounced the compromise and argued that it had failed to bring "peace and tranquility" to the nation, Clay sketched for the Senate and the American people the immediate benefits of the compromise bills: the termination of agitation over the Wilmot Proviso, over the admission of California, over the Texas boundary, and over the abolition of the slave trade in the District of Columbia. Only enforcement of the Fugitive Slave Law in Boston generated excitement. Not since the Whiskey Rebellion, argued Clay, had there been an instance "in which there was so violent and forcible obstruction to the laws of the United States since the commencement of the Government."[23]

Regarding emancipation, he still relied on the work of the American Colonization Society, but he had long since given up hope of "the possibility of establishing a system of gradual emancipation of the slaves of the United States." After the failure of his attempt to initiate it in Kentucky, "I confess I despair of obtaining the object by legal enactment. I nevertheless confidently believe that slavery will ultimately be extinguished when there shall be a great increase of our population, and a great diminution in the value of labor."[24]

Thus Clay's final solution to the slavery problem lay in his hope and faith in what he called the "laws of economics and population." Eventually, he said, every state would become predominantly white, thereby driving down the price of labor so that free labor would become more economically profitable than slave labor in both the North and the South. The nation, North and South, would thereafter abandon slavery as too costly. This hardly constituted a program for emancipation, but it was the best the tired old man could produce at the moment.

These efforts in the Senate placed an enormous physical and emotional burden on Clay. By mid-February he talked of returning home. He generally referred to himself, even in his Senate speeches, as "an old man," tired and debilitated. "I cannot live a great while longer," he told his wife. He had been thinking of returning to Ashland by way of Cuba (a trip that had been on his mind for several years), "on account of a cough which has hung by me too long." Perhaps the warm climate of the island would improve it. That cough had persisted for months. "I am never free from colds," he complained. "And what distresses me is that Nature seems less & less competent to carry them off, or to resist them. Expectoration is tough and difficult, and I have frequent fits of coughing at night." The weather in March and the condition of the

---

23. *Congressional Globe,* 31st Congress, 2d session, pp. 675–676, appendix, pp. 320–323.
24. Clay to Benjamin Coates, October 18, 1851, copy CPP. This position was expressed several years earlier in Clay to Robert S. Hamilton, October 2, 1849, copy CPP.

roads over the mountains were another consideration in favor of his going to Cuba, instead of directly home.[25]

So Clay went to Cuba, taking his servant James Marshall with him. "I hope that I may be benefitted by the softer climate of Cuba," he declared. He left Washington on March 10—the session ended three days later—and headed for New York City to catch the steamship *Georgia* for Havana. He attended a dinner and ball at Niblo's in New York, where he greeted and kissed "eight hundred ladies and gentlemen. The most touching appeals were made to his worshippers to not shake the hand of their divinity too violently, nor crowd too closely about his person, as his health was too feeble to admit of those lively demonstrations."

After this reception he boarded his ship. He got seasick the first day out "and was glad of it" since the nausea of seasickness was believed at the time to be a cure for pulmonary diseases, including tuberculosis. In any event, on March 17 he reached Cuba, where he found, "very much to my gratification," his old friend Dr. William N. Mercer and family. He remained on the island for three weeks and remarked that it was "different from any thing I had ever seen before." He felt better at the end of his stay, although his cough persisted. He headed for home via New Orleans with the Mercers in early April.[26]

New Orleans still delighted him, and he lingered in the city for a few days in order to take a "good and safe boat," the *Peytona,* to journey up the Mississippi River. Of course, he was bombarded with invitations to public meetings, all of which he refused, and on April 9 a group of citizens gathered at Mercer's home on Canal Street, where he was staying, to pay their respects. Unfortunately he was indisposed and could not greet his visitors or speak to them. Two days later he left for home, celebrating his seventy-fourth birthday along the way. He arrived at Ashland on April 20.[27]

Clay spent the rest of the spring, summer, and fall "rusticating" and struggling to improve his health. By this time, if not earlier, he was spitting blood, yet he continued to believe he would recover. Dr. Benjamin W. Dudley assured him that he had not contracted the dreaded disease tuberculosis. He said "my lungs are unaffected, and that it proceeds from some derangement in the functions of the stomach. Be that as it may I must get rid of the cough or it will dispose of me."[28]

During the summer he decided to write his will and buy a plot in the Lexington cemetery. He consulted A. T. Skillman, chairman of the board of

25. *Congressional Globe,* 31st Congress, 1st session, appendix, pp. 329–330; Clay to Lucretia, February 11, 27, March 7, 1851, Clay to James Clay, March 5, 1851, Thomas J. Clay Papers, LC

26. Clay to Lucretia, March 7, 8, 18, April 7, 1851, Thomas J. Clay Papers, LC; Hone, *Diary,* II, 915; *National Intelligencer,* March 13, April 2, 12, 1851.

27. Clay to Lucretia, April 7, 1851, Thomas J. Clay Papers, LC; Clay to Randall Hunt, April 9, 1851, *Daily Picayune,* April 10, 1851, copy CPP.

28. Clay to James Clay, May 9, 1851, Clay to Octavia Walton Le Vert, November 14, 1851, copies CPP.

the newly opened Lexington cemetery in Boswell's Woods, near the western edge of the city, about his intention, but when word of it circulated in the neighborhood, John Lutz, an engineer who had laid out the tract for the cemetery, offered him four lots as "a token of that high esteem in which I am proud to participate with your countrymen." Clay acknowledged that he had been thinking about purchasing a plot since "my age, and other circumstances, admonished me that the day could not be very distant when I should have occasion for it." He thanked Lutz and accepted his offer with "grateful feelings" for his kindness.[29]

His last will and testament was executed on July 10. In it he left the "use and occupation" of Ashland to Lucretia, with the exception of 200 acres set aside for his son John. Lucretia also received all the furniture, plate, paintings, library, cattle, and carriages. Thomas received the 125-acre estate known as Mansfield, where he and his family had been living, along with five thousand dollars, the cancellation of any debts owed the father, and stock in the Lexington and Richmond Turnpike Road Company.[30] In addition to the 200 acres, John received four slaves (he had already received other slaves[31]) and several valuable horses. Theodore was to be "decently and comfortably supported in whatever situation it may be deemed best to place him," and if "God restore him to reason," he would receive ten thousand dollars from the sale of Ashland after Lucretia's death.[32] It was Clay's hope that James would buy Ashland, as he did, and the father directed that two-thirds of the purchase money might, during Lucretia's lifetime, remain in his hands. To the children of his beloved daughter Anne and his son Henry Clay, Jr., he bequeathed seventy-five hundred dollars each. In a special bequest he left his breast pin containing the hair of Henry Clay, Jr., to Henry Clay III. The rest of the estate went into a trust fund with the annual interest from it to be divided equally between Thomas and James.

The most interesting provision of the will concerned his slaves. All children born of his female slaves after January 1, 1850, would be freed at the age of twenty-eight if male, and twenty-five if female. Three years prior to the arrival of "the age of freedom" they would be entitled to wages for those years to pay for the expense of their transportation to Africa and furnish "them with an outfit on their arrival there." They would also be taught to read, write, and cipher. The children of the females set free at age twenty-five would be free at

29. J. Winston Coleman, Jr., *Last Days, Death and Funeral of Henry Clay* (Lexington, Ky., 1951), p. 1. Lutz offered lots no. 38, 39 and 54, 55 in Section 1. On October 27, 1851, Clay removed his mother's remains from Woodford County to the family's new lot no. 38 in the Lexington cemetery and erected a monument over it. Ibid., p. 2 and note 1. Lutz to Clay, May 23, 1851, Clay to Lutz, May 26, 1851, copies CPP.

30. During the Civil War Thomas Hart Clay was elected to the Kentucky legislature from Fayette County, and President Lincoln later appointed him minister to Nicaragua. He died at Mansfield on March 18, 1871.

31. Clay to John Clay, April 30, 1851, copy CPP.

32. Theodore died in 1870.

birth and bound out as apprentices to learn a useful trade before their removal to Africa. Clay then named Lucretia as executrix and Thomas A. Marshall and James O. Harrison as executors.[33]

It gave Clay great peace of mind to conclude the drawing of his will and the acquisition of a cemetery plot.[34] He felt he could return to Washington in late fall to attend the opening of Congress without having to worry about his family if anything happened to him along the way. Although his health did not really permit him to undertake another trip over the mountains, the prospect of extremely handsome fees for arguing two cases before the Supreme Court prompted him to make the effort. And he felt he must still do everything possible to encourage the "omnibus men" and defeat the wicked designs of the secessionists and abolitionists in Congress.

Of course, he had many invitations to attend unionist meetings throughout the autumn months. One in Mississippi particularly elicited his interest because of the efforts of the South Carolina secessionists to spread their disease into that state. Begging off because of his health, he wished the unionists great success in realizing "all their anticipations, and that Mississippi may continue to manifest her fidelity to the Union." Secession, he now told all who wrote him, "is treason," just as Jackson had said in his Proclamation of December 10, 1832, "and if it were not, if it were a legitimate and rightful exercise of power, it would be a virtual dissolution of the Union. For if one State may secede every State may secede." It might take physical force to hold the Union together, just as Jackson threatened in the nullification controversy, but Clay now accepted that possibility. "There are those who think the Union may be preserved and kept together, by an exclusive reliance upon love and reason." Nonsense. "No human government can exist without the power of applying force, and the application of it in extreme cases."[35]

But his best, and what turned out to be his last, great appeal to the American people to cherish and protect the Union came in response to an invitation signed by 311 New Yorkers to attend a rally in support of the compromise. Clay had great affection for the people of New York because of their undeviating support and loyalty over the years. Indeed, his many friends in the city wanted him to declare again for the presidency in 1852; he had already declined in view of his age, health, and "the frequency and the unsuc-

33. Last will and testament of Henry Clay, July 10, 1851, copy CPP. Marshall was a nephew of Chief Justice John Marshall's, and Harrison a longtime friend. The will was probated in Fayette County on July 12, 1852. After Clay's death Lucretia lived with her youngest son, John. James purchased Ashland in the spring of 1854 for $45,408. Two and half years later he razed Ashland, which had become uninhabitable because of large cracks in the walls and foundations. He then erected the present structure on the same site, using the same materials and design of the original. After James fled to Canada, Colonel H. C. McDowell, husband of the only surviving child of Henry Clay, Jr., assumed ownership of Ashland. The final settlement of the will was executed at the October term of the probate court in 1860.

34. Clay to James Clay, January 3, 1852, Thomas J. Clay Papers, LC.

35. Clay to Unionists of Mississippi, September 20, 1851, Clay to Thomas B. Stevenson, May 17, 1851, copies CPP.

cessful presentations of my name on former occasions." So in declining the
invitation to attend the union rally, he wrote a long, very moving, and heartfelt
statement about the obligations of both North and South to unite in directing
the nation farther along the road to ultimate greatness.

Since the adoption of the Constitution, he said, the Union, blessed by
"Providence," had advanced in population, power, wealth, internal improvements, and physical size with such rapidity as to excite "the astonishment and
. . . admiration of mankind." New York City itself "illustrates our surprising
progress." He continued:

Such are the gratifying results which have been obtained under the auspices of that
Union, which some rash men, prompted by ambition, passion and frenzy, would seek
to dissolve and subvert. To revolt against such a government, for any thing which has
passed, would be so atrocious, and characterized by such extreme folly and madness,
that we may search in vain for an example of it in human annals. We can look for its
prototype only (if I may be pardoned the allusion) to that diabolical revolt which,
recorded on the pages of Holy Writ, has been illustrative and commemorated by the
sublime genius of the immortal Milton.[36]

Clay left for Washington on November 15 despite the fears and worry of
his family. "My political life is ended," he wrote, "but I wish once more, and
for the last time, to visit Washington;—and yet, I hesitate, for I do not like to
go there to be *brought* back!"[37] Nevertheless, he set out once again[38] and took
the boat from Maysville, arriving in Pittsburgh on the nineteenth. "I have
borne the journey so far as well as I could have expected," he informed his wife
on reaching Pittsburgh, "but as usual I have caught a cold this morning I spit
up more blood than I have done for many weeks. I hope the Alum water will
relieve me." Weakened and fatigued by driving across the mountains in a
snowstorm, he reached Washington on November 23 and again took up residence in room 32, the second floor of the National Hotel at the northeast
corner of Pennsylvania Avenue and Sixth Street—"Gadsbys old stand," he
called it—where he had lived the previous winter.[39]

Clay attended the opening of the first session of the Thirty-second Congress on Monday, December 1, and even made a short and successful speech
against seating Senator David L. Yulee of Florida in favor of Stephen R.
Mallory. It no doubt gave him enormous pleasure to oust one of the men who
had wrecked his omnibus. As it turned out, the speech proved to be his final
appearance in the United States Senate, for the effort totally exhausted him,

36. Clay to Daniel Ullmann, June 14, 1851, copy CPP; Clay to Fellow Citizens of New York City,
October 3, 1851, in Clay, *Works,* III, 400–412.
37. Clay to J. D. H., November, 1851, copy CPP.
38. Just before Clay left home, he spoke to the youngest executor of his estate. "Remember," he
said, "that my will is in the custody of my wife." He really worried that he would die before he
returned. Harrison, "Henry Clay, Reminiscences by His Executor," p. 175.
39. Clay to Lucretia, November 19, 23, 1851, Thomas J. Clay Papers, LC; New York *Tribune,*
June 30, 1852.

and he returned to his hotel "very weak," so weak in fact that Dr. William W. Hall was summoned to attend him.[40]

The next several days proved extremely difficult. The weather was blustery, so he did not venture outside. "My strength, my flesh, and my appetite have continued to decline," he informed his son James, "and I feel weaker than I did when I left home. I regret now that I ever left it at all, and my utmost wish is to live to return." Indeed, he told his wife, "if I should live, I should come here no more." When he declined an invitation to dine at the White House, Fillmore came to his hotel to see him and learn his condition firsthand. In the next few months the President visited him at least three times and showed him the greatest kindness and affection. Only when the weather cooperated did Clay risk a carriage ride in the hope that it would improve his condition. But the winter of 1851–1852 turned out to be harsh and blustery, forcing Clay to remain closeted in his apartment for weeks. He finally sent for the eminent physician Dr. Francis Jackson of Philadelphia for consultation. Jackson stayed two days and with Hall's assistance gave Clay a thorough examination. They "pronounced my cough not consumption," the dying man happily reported, "but bronchitas. They think that they can so far check or abate it as to make life more comfortable than it is, and I am now pursuing the system of treatment which they adopted."[41]

But he could not continue an active career in the Senate. Accordingly, on December 17, Clay resigned his seat, beginning the first Monday of September 1852. The date selected for the resignation to go into effect was Clay's last political maneuver. In the state elections the previous August a Democrat had been elected governor. Worse, another Democrat, John C. Breckinridge, had been elected to Congress from the Ashland district. But the Whigs still controlled the legislature, and by delaying the date when his resignation would take effect, Clay provided the Whig majority in the general assembly with the opportunity to select his successor. If he resigned immediately, the Democratic governor, Lazarus W. Powell, would make the choice. Much as he implored Democrats and Whigs to forget their differences, Clay himself still retained enough party spirit to engineer this final political coup de main. Clay wrote to the legislature: "I felt it to be my duty to return again to the Senate and to contribute my humble aid, by an amicable settlement of those questions, to avert the calamities with which we were threatened." But a "feeble state of health" now forced him to resign.[42]

Members of his family offered to come to Washington to nurse him, but

40. *Congressional Globe*, 32d Congress, 1st session, pp. 2, 4; Clay to Lucretia, December 1, 1851, Thomas J. Clay Papers, LC; Clay to John Clay, December 3, 1851, copy CPP.

41. Clay to James Clay, December 6, 1851, Clay to Lucretia, December 18, 1851, Thomas J. Clay Papers, LC; Clay to Lucretia, December 9, 1851, Clay Papers, LC; Rayback, *Fillmore*, p. 350. There is disagreement over Dr. Jackson's first name, but in the memorandum he wrote before his death Clay directed the payment of "Dr. Francis Jackson's bill of Philadelphia." Harrison, "Henry Clay, Reminiscences by His Executor," p. 176.

42. Clay to the general assembly of Kentucky, December 17, 1851, copy CPP.

he still thought he would get better and stronger. "Every want, every wish, every attention which I need is supplied" by the hotel, he told his daughter-in-law Marie, Thomas's wife. Some thirty or forty dishes adorned the hotel's menu, and "if I want anything which is not on the bill of fare, it is promptly procured for me." His servant constantly attended him, and his two-room apartment was kept at a comfortable temperature of seventy degrees, so he really had no need at this time for further assistance.[43]

Francis Blair came to see Clay and invited him to his home in Silver Spring, where his wife and family could look after him until he recovered. "I found him extremely kind," Blair reported to Van Buren. "He asked very kindly after you." Clay went on to express his regret over some of the things he had said in public about the Magician, especially on one occasion during the debate on the West Indian treaty when he had yielded to "high party excitement." He also mentioned Benton and declared that he felt no malice toward the Missouri senator despite their many collisions in "senatorial tournaments." The strongly held positions of many "brave men" had frequently "excited his impetuosity," but there was no hatred in him, reported Blair, only "a lofty spirit."

"You must not despond," Blair cautioned the dying man.

"Sir (he replied, with his marked emphasis) there is no such word in my vocabulary."

If by despondency Blair meant a fear of death, Clay felt not the slightest apprehension of its approach. He thanked Blair for his invitation but thought he would wait until spring before making a move. As he turned to leave, the journalist felt his old adversary had little time left. "He has a dreadful cough & is reduced to a shadow," Blair commented. "I fear he will not live through the session."[44]

On a second visit Blair told Clay that Benton was writing his memoirs and that he had read the chapter on the election of 1824–1825 involving the corrupt bargain charge. Apparently Blair led Clay to believe that the account was favorable, for "a beam of sunshine went over his face with many expressions of gratification." When Benton heard about Clay's reaction, he declared that what the chapter showed was "that there is a time when political animosities are to be obliterated under the great duties of historic truth." Other incidents to be recorded in the memoirs might bear down hard on Clay, he admitted, "but without malice and always preferring to say what is honorable when the

43. Clay to Mary Clay, December 25, 1851, Clay Papers, LC; Clay to James Clay, January 3, 1852, Thomas J. Clay Papers, LC.
44. Blair to Van Buren, December 11, 21, 1851, Van Buren Papers, LC. "You think I am despondent," Clay wrote to his son, "but if you could witness my Coughing for twenty four hours, And how much I have been reduced since we parted, you would not think so—"Besides despondency implies apprehension of death; I entertain none. I am ready to go whenever it is the will of God that I should be summoned hence. And I do most sincerely desire that my present Critical Condition should be brought to a speedy issue one way or the other." Clay to James Clay, January 3, 1852, Thomas J. Clay Papers, LC.

veracity of history will permit." Benton urged Van Buren to write the dying man and "express your own feelings." It would be "proper I think under the circumstances."[45]

Van Buren took Benton's advice. He also forwarded Benton's letter to Blair to be shown to Clay. "We ought not to hesitate, I think," wrote the former President, "in employing the means which have been accidentally placed in our power to ameliorate the effects of past estrangements, if we cannot remove them altogether, to which I would be most happy to contribute all in my power." Van Buren concluded by asking Blair to assure Clay of "my respect, esteem & confidence and add that no one can have derived more satisfaction from his noble bearing whilst confined to the sick bed than I have done."

Blair carried out the mission. "Mr Blair," responded Clay, "I opened my heart truly to you when we talked before. If it were unfolded before you at this moment you would see in it no unkindness."

Blair almost wept. A little later he admitted to Van Buren that "you know I always (perhaps you will think extravagantly) admired" Henry Clay.

So the past estrangement between three of the most powerful Jacksonians of the past three decades and their most formidable Whig opponent dissolved in the closing months of Clay's life as they completed their final reconciliation. George Bancroft later wrote that "Clay left not an enemy behind him."[46]

His weakened condition and the impossibility of his venturing outside in inclement weather forced Clay to cancel his appearances before the Supreme Court. With the consent of his client, he engaged Joseph R. Underwood to represent the client, promising him one-half of the fee. Underwood won the case and received $1,250. In the second case Clay submitted a written argument for the plaintiffs.[47]

Clay received many other visitors during the months of his confinement. In January the great Hungarian revolutionary Louis Kossuth came to his hotel to beg his assistance in helping Hungary to achieve independence from Austria. Clay's well-known reputation of lending vital support to all nations seeking freedom prompted Kossuth to seek him out. The Hungarian patriot

45. Benton to Van Buren, January 11, 1852, Van Buren Papers, LC.

46. Blair to Van Buren, January 11, August 11, 1852, Van Buren to Blair, January 16, 1852, Van Buren Papers, LC; Blair to Clay, January 22, 1852, in Van Buren, *Autobiography,* p. 669. This did not keep Clay from warning his son James, now living in Missouri: "unless you Consent to become a partizan of the Colonel's [Benton] you will not long retain relations of friendship with him." Clay to James Clay, January 3, 1852, Thomas J. Clay Papers, LC. Bancroft, "A Few Words about Henry Clay," p. 480. After Clay's death, even John Tyler said that his "feelings of anger towards him are all buried in his grave. We were once intimate, and I had a warm attachment and admiration for him, but he broke the silver cord with a reckless hand, and his arm, became too short to reach the golden fruit for which he gave up friendship and everything." Tyler to John S. Cunningham, July 15, 1852, in Tyler, *Letters,* II, 499–500.

47. The first case, *Gilbert C. Russell* v. *Daniel R. Southard et al.,* was argued by Underwood and his associate Charles S. Morehead; the second was the Fire Insurance Company of Louisville case. Clay to Lucretia, January 4, March 22, 1852, Thomas J. Clay Papers, LC.

had failed in his initial revolutionary attempt, and he had fled to the United States in search of aid. Americans enthusiastically hailed him for his efforts but would do nothing more. He got pious encouragement but little else. He now hoped, and probably expected, that Clay would rally to his cause and issue a ringing call to the American people to supply Kossuth with the means of renewing the revolution.

Though constantly coughing, Clay turned on his old charm. "Your wonderful and fascinating eloquence," he told the Hungarian, "has mesmerized" everyone, even members of Congress, "that I feared to come under its influence, lest you might shake my faith in some principles . . . I have long and constantly cherished." Sympathy has been extended to you, also encouragement, but it is not enough. "You require material aid." Sir, to extend such aid would mean war, and to transport men and arms across the ocean to fight Austria would be impossible. It would mean abandoning our policy of non-intervention in the affairs of other nations, with the result that the despots of Europe would turn on the United States and say: "You have set us the example. You have quit your own to stand on foreign ground. . . . We [who hate your republican ideas and believe] that monarchical principles are essential to the peace, security and happiness of our subjects . . . will crush you as the propagandist of doctrines so destructive of the peace and good order of the world." The recent subversion of the republican government of France with the seizure of power by Emperor Napoleon III "teaches us to despair of any present success for liberal institutions in Europe. Far better is it for ourselves, for Hungary, and for the cause of liberty, that, adhering to our wise, pacific system, and avoiding the distant wars of Europe, we should keep our lamp burning brightly on this western shore as a light to all nations, than to hazard its utter extinction amid the ruins of fallen or falling republics in Europe."

Encouragement, sympathy, good wishes were all Clay, just like the rest of the country, held out to Kossuth. Actual involvement by the United States in any material way, he said, "would be terrible." These were his honest thoughts and feelings, "the expression of a dying man."[48]

Kossuth left his bedside, deeply discouraged. As he did so, Clay reached out, grasped his hand, and supposedly said: "God bless you and your family! God bless your country! May she yet be free!"

Clay's remarks appeared in the newspapers, much to Kossuth's distress because he thought their interview was private and privileged. The dying man denied the charge that he had violated a privileged conversation since other men, including several congressmen, were present in the room at the time.[49]

Another visitor remembered finding Clay sitting in an easy chair near a coal fire in a darkened room with the windows covered by heavy curtains. But Old Hal still joked and told funny stories. He playfully commented on the

48. Speech to Louis Kossuth, January 9, 1852, in Clay, *Works*, III, 221–224.
49. Clay to a New Orleans gentleman, March 30, 1852, in *National Intelligencer,* April 16, 1852.

visitor's cold hand as they greeted each other. Hardly the appropriate way to approach "an invalid such as I am. Come," he said, "draw up a chair, and sit near me; I am compelled to use my voice but little, and very carefully."

All his visitors came away with a profound sense of personal loss. They also appreciated what a towering statesman he was, what his passing would mean to the nation. "Poor Mr. Clay, is about closing his political and I fear natural Life," wrote Jabez D. Hammond, the New York politician and historian. "I can not but regard him as a great and good man."[50]

These politicians who visited Clay during this period—and they included both Whigs and Democrats—kept him abreast of events in Congress and hoped to draw him out on the presidential election scheduled for the fall. Clay preferred Fillmore as the Whig candidate, over Webster and Scott, and hoped that Cass, whom he admired because of his help in winning passage of the compromise, would run as the Democratic candidate. He still wanted a Whig in the White House but he doubted the party could win. Besides, he cared more about the President's devotion to the Union than that he wear the correct party label.[51]

But the Whigs, clearly pursuing now a course leading to inevitable extinction, preferred another "military chieftain" and nominated Winfield Scott. The Democrats fielded Franklin Pierce.

During the final months left to his life, Clay also received a New York delegation that presented him with a large and costly gold medal commemorating his public life. One side accommodated his likeness; the other, "all the great public measures" he had authored. The New Yorkers noted that all American national medals heretofore commemorated military victories. "Let the first American victor of peace," they said, also be "thus commemorated."

In accepting the gift, Clay again noted how the citizens of New York City had shown greater "zeal, constancy and fidelity" in their affection for and attachment to him than any others in the nation. Accept "my cordial and heartfelt thanks," he whispered, "and my grateful and profound acknowledgments, for this rich tribute." Later the delegation asked for the return of the medallion to make a more accurate impression of Clay's features. Unfortunately he gave it to a woman to deliver, and it was stolen. The New Yorkers substituted another, this one executed in bronze. They also celebrated his seventy-fifth birthday on April 12, which he protested because he believed that only George Washington deserved that honor.[52]

50. "Henry Clay: Personal Anecdotes, Incidents, etc.," p. 397; Hammond to Van Buren, March 29, 1852, Van Buren Papers, LC.
51. Clay to Daniel Ullmann, June 14, 1851, in Clay, *Works*, IV, 617–620. "You rightly understood me in expressing a preference for Mr. Fillmore as the Whig candidate for the Presidency. . . . He has been tried and found true, faithful, honest, and conscientious." Clay to Ullmann, March 6, 1852, ibid., IV, 628.
52. Daniel Ullmann et al. to Clay, February 9, 1852, speech to the citizens of New York, February 9, 1852, *National Intelligencer*, February 10, 1852; Clay to Ullmann, March 18, 1852, in Clay,

To keep up his spirits and, he hoped, to benefit his health, Clay managed a few closed carriage rides of five or six miles around town when the weather occasionally improved. He read a good deal, although "I take less and less interest as to what is passing in the world, out side of my own family, children and personal affairs." He wrote occasionally; but the effort proved too exhausting, and he resorted to a secretary to attend his correspondence. Because of a loss of appetite, he had lost a considerable amount of weight, "but still I eat quite enough to sustain life." His biggest problem was lack of sleep. Each night he took an opiate; even so, "I lay for hours and hours without any sleep. I sit up four or five hours every day, and for the rest I am on a Couch." He retired at eight o'clock and rose around ten in the morning. "I take two or three kinds of medicine every day," he told his son John, "& have nearly emptied an apothecary's shop." Each day Dr. Hall visited him and reassured him that his lungs showed no signs of disease. Clay was dying, and he knew he was dying; but he did not know the cause. And the doctors could offer no adequate explanation.[53]

In March 1852 Clay's condition worsened. He took a carriage ride—and climbing stairs greatly fatigued him—caught another cold and began "spitting some blood, the first for some time." He suffered chills, for which he took quinine, and constipation. Dreadfully weakened and getting worse, he knew he now needed help from home, and he sent for his son Thomas to come and get him. He wanted to return to Ashland in May or early June, when the weather—"we have had the vilest spring I ever knew for invalids"—would cooperate, he hoped.[54]

By late April his condition had turned critical. He dispatched an urgent telegraph home: "Tell Thomas to come as soon as he can." To James, he wrote: "I cannot hold out much longer." He then settled accounts with his servant James G. Marshall and directed his Washington bankers to forward any balances to Ashland.[55]

Thomas arrived in Washington on May 5 and found his father so debilitated that he could not talk five minutes without great exhaustion and noted that "he has now to be carried from his bed to his couch." The younger Clay realized at once that all hope of getting him back to Kentucky alive was gone. It now became a death watch.

John J. Crittenden came one last time to complete their reconciliation.

Works, IV, 629; Clay to Clay Festival Association of New York City, April 5, 1852, in *National Intelligencer,* April 15, 1852. On Easter, the day before his seventy-fifth birthday, ministers in several Washington churches offered up prayers for his recovery. Clay to Clement M. Butler, April 12, 1852, copy CPP.

53. Clay to Lucretia, January 12, 1852, Clay Papers, LC; Clay to Lucretia, March 3, 22, 1852, Clay to James Clay, March 14, 1852, Thomas J. Clay Papers, LC; Clay to John Clay, February 28, 1852, copy CPP; Benton to Van Buren, January 11, 1852, Van Buren Papers, LC.

54. Clay to Lucretia, March 22, April 2, 1852, Thomas J. Clay Papers, LC; Clay to Mary Clay, April 7, 1852, in Clay, *Works,* IV, 630; Clay to Thomas Clay, April 21, 1852, copy CPP.

55. Telegraph to James O. Harrison, his executor, April 28, 1852, memoranda of H. Clay, late June 1852, copies CPP; Clay to James Clay, April 28, 1852, Thomas J. Clay Papers, LC.

When the attorney general had left, Clay turned to Thomas and said, "Treat him kindly."

On May 7 the chaplain of the Senate, Dr. Clement M. Butler, administered the sacrament and sat by Clay's side for several hours. The great man had been in full communion with Trinity Parish in Washington, and during their brief conversations he "averred to me," said Butler, "his full faith in the great leading doctrines of the Gospel." It was difficult for them to converse because the dying man's coughing never ceased. It also prevented him from sleeping. "I never before imagined that any one could live in the extreme state of debility under which my father is now suffering," wrote Thomas. It was painful to watch him and hear him as he coughed and wheezed and gasped for air. At one point, his mind wandering, he murmured: *"My mother! mother! mother!,* and then, *My dear wife,"* as though she were present in the room.[56]

Unfortunately Clay suffered a deep depression during the following weeks. He looked for letters from home and listened attentively as they were read to him. At one point he broke into a cold sweat after dinner, and his servant and Thomas took turns rubbing him all over with brandy and alum. And even though in late May his coughing was constant and his breathing terribly labored, his doctor still assured Thomas that "his lungs are not at all affected."

Then his appetite disappeared altogether. For a week he could be persuaded to take only a few mouthfuls of soup. Finally, on Tuesday, June 29, 1852, after Marshall had shaved him, Clay summoned Thomas to his bedside. "Sit near me, my dear son," he whispered, "I do not wish you to leave me for any time today." He then lapsed into silence.

An hour passed. "Give me some water," he hoarsely cried. Thomas quickly brought half a glassful. "I believe, my son, I am going," he gasped. Moments later he asked to have his shirt collar unbuttoned. Thomas loosened it. Then Clay clasped his son's hand and held it as tightly as he could. Suddenly his hand relaxed and slipped away. Harry of the West, Prince Hal, the Great Compromiser, the most popular man in America, died at 11:17 A.M. of tuberculosis, his lungs totally ravaged.[57] He was seventy-five years, two months, and seventeen days old.

Within the hour bells had begun their mournful tolling as the news of Clay's death quickly spread throughout Washington. At 12:30 P.M. the President issued an executive order closing all federal offices for the rest of the day. "I am sure all hearts are too sad at this moment to attend to business," he declared. Congress met at noon and immediately adjourned. Thomas sent word home via the telegraph. In Lexington shops immediately closed and church bells tolled.[58]

56. Butler's eulogy in the Senate, in Clay, *Works,* III, 259, 261.

57. Excerpts of Thomas Clay's letters to his wife and probably his mother, May 8, 13, 18, 20, June 4, 7, 29, 1852, in Clay, *Private Correspondence* (Cincinnati, 1856), pp. 633–636; "Henry Clay, Personal Anecdotes, Incidents, etc.," p. 398.

58. Executive order of Millard Fillmore, June 29, 1852, copy CPP; Thomas Clay to Mary Clay,

"No formal annunciation of the sad event was necessary," wrote one Washingtonian. "A short walk along our main avenue suffices to show the least observant that a great national sorrow hung over us."

The following day a large crowd jammed its way into the Senate chamber to hear what the members might say about their fallen colleague. The President, Supreme Court judges, foreign ministers, the cabinet, and members of the House also attended, in part out of respect for the diseased, in part out of curiosity about who would speak and what they would say. Never had there been so many eulogies given in Congress before. Predictably members of both parties spoke, and none so eloquently as the Democrats or the men, like William H. Seward and John P. Hale, who had most recently opposed the Great Pacificator. "I must believe," wrote Blair, who watched the proceedings, "that Clay's melancholy fate & lingering suffering cancelled all his faults in the eyes of . . . [those] who were hostile towards him while he lived." The "Democratic Eulogies in the two Houses," he went on, "(and they made the best speeches) seem to have forgotten in their praises of Clay . . . that there had ever been any good men of their party in Congress!" John C. Breckinridge, "who is a good democrat, seems to feel that Clay, Webster & Calhoun were the real glories of the Senate." "But, *as a whole man,*" said another, "HENRY CLAY, *was the greatest of the Triumvirate—nay—the greatest of his Age!*"[59]

William Seward declared that whether people agreed with Henry Clay or not, "they are nevertheless unanimous in acknowledging that he was at once the greatest, the most faithful, and the most reliable of their statesmen." He needed only to come out in favor of a measure or against it in the Senate, "and immediately popular enthusiasm, excited as by a magic wand, was felt, overcoming and dissolving all opposition in the Senate Chamber." His eloquence, his conversation, his gestures, his very look were "magisterial, persuasive, seductive, irresistible."[60]

Irresistible! Indeed. All his public life Henry Clay fascinated both men and women, and although they denied him the White House, they yielded to him their respect, love, and veneration.

When the speeches concluded, pallbearers, a committee of arrangements, and a committee to accompany the body back to Kentucky were appointed.[61]

The following day, July 1, a procession of military and civilian authorities,

June 29, 1852, in Clay, *Private Correspondence,* p. 636; James C. Hogan Diary, entry for June 29, 1852, Manuscript Department, Filson Club, Louisville, Kentucky.

59. *National Intelligencer,* June 30, July 1, 1852; Anderson, *Funeral Oration on . . . Clay,* p. 36; Blair to Van Buren, July 4, 1852, Van Buren Papers, LC. Such senators as Benton, Wright, "& yourself," Blair told Van Buren, "were really men of no mark," according to the eulogists.

60. Clay, *Works,* III, 250–251; Sargent, *Clay,* includes all the eulogies in both the House and Senate, as well as the chaplain's funeral sermon, pp. 371–421.

61. Arrangements included Hunter, Dawson, Jones of Iowa, Cooper, Bright, and Smith; pallbearers, Cass, Mangum, Dodge of Wisconsin, Pratt, Atchison, and Bell; committee to accompany the body, Underwood, Jones of Tennessee, Cass, Fish, Houston, and Stockton.

both foreign and American, formed at the National Hotel and carried the casket bearing Clay's remains up Pennsylvania Avenue to the portico, through the "rotundo" to the Senate and placed it in the center of the chamber. A wreath of flowers was placed on the sarcophagus. The casket, made of cast iron and highly ornamented, resembled the outlines of the human body; its handles and the plate for inscribing Clay's name, as well as other plates on the coffin, all were made of massive silver and appropriately decorated. A covering of "the finest broadcloth" was thrown over the casket like a cloth coat, and twelve tassels dangled from each side.[62]

The chaplain, Dr. Butler, in "full canonicals," read part of the Episcopal funeral ritual and delivered the sermon. "A great mind," he said, "a great heart, a great orator, a great career, have been consigned to history." Then the coffin was carried to the Rotunda of the Capitol, where Clay lay in state until 3:30 P.M., the first person accorded that honor in American history. The silver faceplate was removed from the coffin so that mourners could view the face of their departed savior.[63]

"But when will be forgotten the memory of his chivalrous character," editorialized the *National Intelligencer*, "his gallant bearing, his melodious voice 'whose every tone was music's own?' His proudest epitaph would be his own words that he knew no North, no South, nothing but his country."

At 3:30 P.M. the cortege, again accompanied by a large procession of dignitaries, proceeded to the railroad station. Along the route people stood in silence to express their sympathy and grief. The black-draped funeral train moved slowly to Baltimore, remained overnight, then stopped briefly at Wilmington before reaching Philadelphia. "It is needless to say," recorded Calvin Colton, "that the great heart of Philadelphia was moved with sorrow as never before. Ever honored there while living, he was wept there by tens of thousands as he was borne through their midst in his coffin." The remains were taken for the night to Independence Hall, where a military guard of honor was posted. On Saturday citizens filed past the bier to pay their respects.[64]

The cortege continued to New York City via steamboat and railroad and was brought to City Hall, again under a guard of honor. "It was not the weeping flags at half-mast throughout the city," wrote one commentator, "not the tolling of the bells, the solemn booming of the minute-guns, nor the plaintive strains of funeral music, which brought the tears to the eyes of thousands, as the mournful cavalcade passed on." It was the realization that Henry Clay "is no more." For "here were the lifeless limbs, the dimmed eye, the hushed voice, that never should move, nor sparkle, nor resound in eloquent tones again!" Some one hundred thousand New Yorkers, "in solemn silence,"

62. Coleman, *Last Days*, pp. 7–8.

63. *National Intelligencer*, July 1, 2, 1852. Epes Sargent in his biography of Clay states that the "body was removed to the Rotunda, that his sorrowing countrymen might gaze upon that face in death which has cheered them so much while living." p. 421. See also Coleman, *Last Days*, p. 9.

64. *National Intelligencer*, July 2, 1852; Colton, *Last Seven Years*, p. 438.

viewed the casket on Saturday and all day Sunday, July 4.[65]

Early Monday morning the steamboat *Santa Claus,* bedecked "with all the habiliments of mourning," carried the body up the Hudson River to Albany, and booming guns in every village and town along the way saluted as it passed. From Albany to Buffalo the cortege resumed its way on the Erie Railroad and stopped at all the principal cities—Schenectady, Utica, Rome, Syracuse, Rochester—in response to the demand of the public. In Buffalo the cortege was received by torchlight, and there followed "another sad and funeral pageant suited to the occasion." Then the remains were transported to Cleveland on the Lake Erie steamer *Buckeye State* and from there by railroad to Columbus, Xenia, and Cincinnati. Again the remains were transferred to the U.S. mail boat *Ben Franklin,* and they reached Louisville at 6:00 A.M. Friday, July 9. All along this route thousands of mourners stood by the roadside and riverbank and silently watched. Bells tolled; guns fired; crepe decorated doors and windows; shops closed.[66]

On Friday, at ten o'clock, the Senate committee, accompanied by committees from New York and Dayton, Ohio, the Clay Guards of Cincinnati, a deputation of seventy-six men from Louisville, and several military contingents gathered at the Odd Fellows Hall in Louisville and accompanied the body on its last railroad journey to Frankfort, the state capital, and finally Lexington. Upon its arrival at the depot at sunset in Lexington a local committee took charge, placed the remains in a hearse, and walked it by torchlight to Ashland behind a procession headed by a cavalcade of horsemen under a series of funeral arches and through streets lined by a silent multitude. At Ashland the body lay in state in Clay's study, watched over by the Clay Guard of Cincinnati. Thomas, James, and John, several grandchildren and nephews, and the seventy-two-year-old Lucretia gathered around the bier. The silver faceplate on the coffin had not been removed since the obsequies in Washington. In view of the intense July heat over the past nine days it was wisely decided not to expose the face of the deceased, even to members of the family.[67]

Thousands of vehicles poured into Lexington for the burial on Saturday, July 10. At 9:00 A.M. the coffin was taken outside and was covered with a black cloth. Flowers were strewn over it. The Reverend Edward F. Berkeley, rector of Christ Church in Lexington, conducted the services, including a eulogy,[68] after which the coffin was placed in a special funeral car lined with velvet and satin and overhung with black crepe. A large silver urn decorated the top of the car, which was surmounted by an eagle with "outstretched pinions," holding in its beak a pall of black crepe which covered the entire vehicle. Eight white horses, each covered with black crepe and silver fringe, drew the funeral car. It

65. A public funeral was solemnized in New York on July 20, 1852. Colton, *Last Seven Years,* p. 439; Lexington *Observer and Kentucky Reporter,* July 14, 1852.
66. Coleman, *Last Days,* pp. 10–12; Colton, *Last Seven Years,* p. 439.
67. *Colton, Last Seven Years*, pp. 439–444; Coleman, *Last Days,* pp. 12–13.
68. The eulogy is recorded in Colton, *Last Seven Years,* pp. 445–449.

moved from Ashland into the city, where it was joined by the main procession of mourners. Lucretia's health was too feeble to permit her to follow the remains to the cemetery, so she stayed at home.

The order of procession began with marshals, a military corps, military officers, the committee of arrangements, the Senate committee and the state and city committees, and the Masonic fraternity. The military marched with reversed arms, muffled drums, and colors furled and draped in mourning. Then came the funeral car and pallbearers, followed by members of the family, the clergy, the governor, the mayor, judges of state and federal courts, and other dignitaries.

At ten o'clock a signal gun put the procession in motion. Minute guns and tolling church bells kept up a steady din until the mourners reached the cemetery. Business establishments closed, and virtually every house along the way was draped in black. A crowd numbering thirty thousand jammed the streets and streamed into the cemetery. Part of the cemetery's fence had to be removed to accommodate the crowd.

At the cemetery the Episcopal service was read, followed by ceremonies performed by Masons of the local lodge. A handsome Masonic apron given to Clay by Lafayette was thrown over the coffin. Then the body was placed in a vault by the Masonic fraternity, to be removed upon the completion of a monument to be built specially for Clay.[69]

Nine years later, on July 4, 1861, just as the Civil War commenced, a towering 130-foot column with a Corinthian capital, topped by a 12.5-foot statue of the great man, made from a model by Joel T. Hart and facing Ashland, was completed, at a cost of approximately fifty-eight thousand dollars. After the war, on April 8, 1864, both Clay and his wife, who had died only a few days before, on April 4, were placed in the vault of the monument at the foot of the column.[70] But as one man wrote, "They may lay their pedestals of granite—they may cover their marble pillars all over with the blazoning of his deeds, the trophies of his triumphant genius, and surmount them with images of his form wrought by the cunningest hands—it matters not—he is not there. . . . He is not dead—he lives. . . . He needs no statue—he desired none. . . . He carved his own statue, built his own monument."[71]

An obscure Richmond poet, Thomas Watson, like a number of other

69. Lexington *Observer and Kentucky Reporter,* July 14, 1852; "Order of Arrangements for the Funeral of Henry Clay," James C. Hogan Diary, entry for July 10, 1852, Manuscript Department, Filson Club, Louisville, Kentucky; Coleman, *Last Days,* pp. 15, 19.

70. Coleman, *Last Days,* pp. 20, 22. The elaborately carved iron coffin containing Clay's body was placed in a handsome marble sarcophagus, the gift of William Struthers, a Philadelphia marble mason. The sarcophagus was opened in January 1951, and the coffin was found to be in excellent condition. During a violent storm on July 21, 1903, the head of the statue on top of the column was knocked to the ground. In 1910 a new statue by Charles J. Mulligan of Chicago replaced the old one. The monument was extensively restored in 1976. See Burton Milward, *A History of the Lexington Cemetery* (Lexington, 1989), pp. 33–42.

71. Quoted in Peterson, *Great Triumvirate,* p. 489.

artists, composed a six-stanza verse, entitled "Lines on the Death of Henry Clay," the concluding section of which reads:

> He sleeps, yes, let the mighty Statesman sleep,
> His name shall live while time shall count a day,
> Columbian's children shall, for ages keep,
> The great and glorious name of Henry Clay.[72]

In Springfield, Illinois, on July 6 Abraham Lincoln delivered a eulogy in which he contended that Clay's "predominant sentiment, from first to last, was a deep devotion to the cause of human liberty." It was his primary and all controlling passion, said Lincoln. He loved his country because it was a free country, and he desired nothing more than to see it advance in "prosperity and glory."

Fortunately, during the nation's earliest moments of profound and intense adversity, it produced a man who repeatedly rescued it from destruction. He was *"the* man for a crisis," acknowledged Lincoln. Now he was gone. May the nation always be blessed with statesmen such as he, the Great Emancipator concluded, to emerge during future national crises and again save the Union and insure the security and liberty of all.

During the height of the Civil War, President Lincoln could still hear Prince Hal's majestic voice, still hear the compelling pleas for the life of his country. "I recognize his voice," Lincoln declared, "speaking as it ever spoke, for the Union, the Constitution, and the freedom of mankind."[73]

72. "Poems of Thomas Watson," Virginia Historical Society, Richmond. The self-proclaimed "prototype bard and poet laureate of the world" may have been a black man.

73. Basler, ed., *Collected Works of Lincoln,* II, 121–132; Lincoln to John M. Clay, August 9, 1862, ibid., V, 363–364.

Bibliographical Essay

IT IS IMPOSSIBLE to cite all the manuscript sources and books consulted in the preparation of this biography. However, a great many of the manuscript collections and secondary sources for the antebellum era are listed in the third volume of my biography of Andrew Jackson. In addition, Robert O. Rupp and I compiled a bibliography of all sources available on Andrew Jackson personally, as part of the Meckler's Bibliographies of the Presidents of the United States Series, and entitled *Andrew Jackson: A Bibliography* (Westport, Conn., 1991). See also Robert V. Remini and Edwin A. Miles, *The Era of Good Feelings and the Age of Jackson, 1816–1841* (Arlington Heights, Ill., 1979) for a more comprehensive listing for the era that extends over a longer time period but obviously does not include works published since 1979. Also, in preparing a short college textbook, *The Jacksonian Era* (Arlington Heights, Ill., 1989), I wrote an extended historiographical essay that attempted to delineate all the major interpretations about this unique period of American history, starting with the earliest contemporary opinions and coming down to the present day.

Basic to the writing of this biography is the vast collection of letters, papers, and other documents written by or to Henry Clay that are scattered in libraries and archives around the country and abroad. The largest single collection of these manuscripts, the Clay Family Papers, as it is presently designated, may be found in the Manuscript Division of the Library of Congress and includes the Henry and Thomas J. Clay Papers plus manuscripts of other members of the Clay family. In all, approximately twenty thousand documents are contained in this collection, and they occupy thirty-four volumes and forty-one boxes. An excellent guide to the Kentucky and Kentucky-related collections in the Manuscript Division of the Library of Congress is John J. McDonough, "Kentuckiana in the Manuscript Division, Library of Congress," *Filson Club History Quarterly,* LXII (July 1988), pp. 356–379.

Other relatively large collections of Clay manuscripts may be found in the libraries of the Chicago Historical Society, Duke University, the Filson Club, Indiana University, the New-York Historical Society, the University of Kentucky, and the University of Virginia. Smaller collections are located in the Boston Public Library, the Historical Society of Pennsylvania, the Indiana Historical Society, the Kentucky Historical Society, the Pierpont Morgan Library, and Rutgers University.

Fortunately for my research, copies of virtually all known Clay documents in public repositories plus those held in private hands have been collected at the Clay Papers Project in the King Library of the University of Kentucky. The most important items in this corpus have been published under the title *The Papers of Henry Clay* (Lexington, Ky., 1959–). The first volume begins with 1797, and the ninth volume concludes with 1843. A tenth volume is now in press and will carry forward to the end of Clay's life in 1852. Projected for the future is an eleventh volume that will include documents obtained after the initial volumes were published. James F. Hopkins edited the first five volumes; Mary W. M. Hargreaves, the sixth volume; Robert Seager II, the seventh, eighth, and ninth volumes; and Melba Porter Hay, the tenth. All these fine editors and their associates expended enormous amounts of time and energy in bringing these materials to publication, and they deserve the everlasting gratitude of Clay scholars everywhere.

Until the publication of *The Papers of Henry Clay* is complete, two additional sources are indispensable: Calvin Colton, ed., *The Works of Henry Clay* (New York, 1857), 6 volumes; and Calvin Colton, ed., *The Private Correspondence of Henry Clay* (Cincinnati, 1856).

There are also comprehensive publication projects for all the leading figures of the antebellum era, with the single exception of Martin Van Buren. The Jackson Papers Project consists at present of two published volumes with a third in press. The period covered by these three volumes extends from 1770 to 1815. A microfilm edition of the entire corpus of Jackson Papers exists on thirty-nine reels with a *Guide and Index to the Microfilm Editions* (Wilmington, Del., 1987) prepared by the director of the Jackson Papers Project, Harold Moser. For students and scholars, the *Correspondence of Andrew Jackson* (Washington, D.C., 1926–1935), edited in 6 volumes by John Spencer Bassett, remains an indispensable source, and it contains many of the best letters from several collections of Jackson manuscripts.

The Calhoun and Webster papers constitute another important source for any study of this period, and their publication has progressed further along than the Jackson Papers Project. For the Calhoun documents, see W. Edwin Hamphill et al., eds., *The Papers of John C. Calhoun* (Columbia, S.C., 1959–), 19 volumes. There are three series to the Webster papers, two of which proved essential in the writing of this biography: Charles M. Wiltse et al., *The Papers of Daniel Webster, Correspondence* (Hanover, N.H., 1974–1986), complete in 7 volumes, and *Speeches and Formal Writings* (Hanover, N.H., 1986, 1988), complete in 2 volumes. Other published primary sources essential to this work include: Charles Francis Adams, ed., *Memoirs of John Quincy Adams* (Philadelphia, 1874–1877), 12 volumes; Thomas Hart Benton, *Thirty Years' View* (New

York, 1865), 2 volumes; Allan Nevins, ed., *The Diary of Philip Hone, 1828–1851* (New York, 1927), 2 volumes; Herbert Weaver et al., eds., *Correspondence of James K. Polk* (Nashville, 1969–), 7 volumes; Lyon G. Tyler, *The Letters and Times of the Tylers* (New York, 1896, 1970), 3 volumes; and John C. Fitzpatrick, ed., *Autobiography of Martin Van Buren* (Washington, D.C., 1920).

Of published Clay material, the Library of Congress presently holds 226 individual titles, most of them currently out of print. Among the earliest biographies the most useful and still valuable is Calvin Colton, *The Life and Times of Henry Clay* (New York, 1842), 2 volumes, which he concluded with *The Last Seven Years of the Life of Henry Clay* (New York, 1856). This complete work contains information not found in any other source, but it is totally uncritical and excessively "panegyric," as Clay himself described it. Of other early studies, many of them campaign biographies, George Denison Prentice, *Biography of Henry Clay* (Hartford, 1831); Epes Sargent, *The Life and Public Services of Henry Clay Down to 1848* (New York, 1848); and Nathan Sargent, *Life of Henry Clay* (Philadelphia, 1844) frequently provide useful nuggets of historical information. Thomas Hart Clay also wrote a study of his grandfather, which was completed by E. P. Oberholtzer, entitled *Henry Clay* (Philadelphia, 1910). Of particular interest is the now-classic two-volume biography *Life of Henry Clay* (Boston, 1887) written by Carl Schurz and recently (New York, 1980) made available in a paperback reprint.

In the modern period Bernard Mayo began an excellent multivolume study, *Henry Clay: Spokesman of the New West* (Boston, 1937), but unfortunately did not complete it. The volume ends with the outbreak of the War of 1812. Glyndon G. Van Deusen, *The Life of Henry Clay* (Boston, 1937) is unquestionably the best and most scholarly account of the Kentuckian's life, while Clement Eaton, *Henry Clay and the Art of American Politics* (Boston, 1957) is a short, well-written narrative, as well as the most recent. Of special importance, although limited to the last period of Clay's life, is George R. Poage, *Henry Clay and the Whig Party* (Chapel Hill, 1936). Robert Seager II, "Henry Clay and the Politics of Compromise and Non-Compromise," *Register of the Kentucky Historical Society,* LXXXV (Winter 1987), pp. 1–28, is an interesting assessment of Clay's political motivations.

The other two members of the Great Triumvirate have been handsomely served by historians over the past few decades. Charles M. Wiltse's beautifully written and massive 3-volume *John C. Calhoun* (Indianapolis and New York, 1944–1951) is a splendid work, but for a more in-depth treatment of Calhoun's character and personality, consult John Niven, *John C. Calhoun and the Price of Union* (Baton Rouge, 1988). Another finely written treatment is the Pulitzer Prize-winning study by Margaret L. Coit *John C. Calhoun, American Portrait* (Boston, 1950). Maurice C. Baxter, *One and Inseparable: Daniel Webster and the Union* (Cambridge, Mass., 1984) is excellent, but I think Irving Bartlett, *Daniel Webster* (New York, 1978) shows more of the darker side of "Black

Dan." Of special merit because of its reliability and overall balance is the recent Merrill D. Peterson, *The Great Triumvirate: Webster, Clay, and Calhoun* (New York, 1987). To achieve such scholarly precision and accuracy in researching three major figures is a notable achievement in itself.

No one should miss the magnificent *Jefferson and His Time* (Boston, 1948–1981), 6 volumes, by Dumas Malone, my *beau ideal* of a biographer and southern gentleman. And Irving Brant, *James Madison* (Indianapolis and New York, 1948–1961), 6 volumes, was particularly useful to me in writing Clay's life. For Madison's ideological thinking on a variety of major issues, Drew R. McCoy, *The Last of the Fathers: James Madison and the Republican Legacy* (Cambridge, Mass., 1989) proved both stimulating and illuminating.

In addition to his life of Clay, Glyndon G. Van Deusen has provided us with biographies of three other notable Whigs: *Horace Greeley: Nineteenth-Century Crusader* (New York, 1953); *Thurlow Weed: Wizard of the Lobby* (New York, 1947); and *William Henry Seward* (New York, 1967). I also found Richard Current, *Old Thad Stevens* (Madison, Wis., 1942) especially valuable in understanding what happened at the Whig convention in 1839 that cost Clay the nomination.

Biographies of other notable figures of the antebellum period who directly figured in Clay's life include: John Niven, *Martin Van Buren and the Romantic Age of American Politics* (New York, 1983); Donald B. Cole, *Martin Van Buren and the American Political System* (Princeton, 1984); William N. Chambers, *Old Bullion Benton, Senator from the New West* (Boston, 1956); Samuel Flagg Bemis, *John Quincy Adams and the Foundations of American Foreign Policy* and *John Quincy Adams and the Union* (New York, 1949, 1956), 2 volumes; Harry Ammon, *James Monroe: The Quest for National Identity* (New York, 1971); Chase Mooney, *William H. Crawford* (Lexington, Ky., 1974); Raymond Walters, Jr., *Albert Gallatin: Jeffersonian Financier and Diplomat* (New York, 1957); William Cabell Bruce, *John Randolph of Roanoke, 1773–1833* (New York, 1922), 2 volumes; Charles H. Ambler, *Thomas Ritchie: A Study in Virginia Politics* (Richmond, 1913); the unfinished biography of James K. Polk by Charles G. Sellers, Jr., *James K. Polk, Jacksonian, 1795–1843* (Princeton, 1957) and *James K. Polk, Continentalist, 1843–1846* (Princeton, 1966); Thomas P. Govan, *Nicholas Biddle, Nationalist and Public Banker* (Chicago, 1959); Carl B. Swisher, *Roger B. Taney* (New York, 1935); Albert D. Kirwan, *John J. Crittenden: The Struggle for the Union* (Lexington, Ky., 1962); Ann Mary Butler Coleman, *Life of John J. Crittenden* (Philadelphia, 1871), 2 volumes; Philip S. Klein, *President James Buchanan* (University Park, Pa., 1962); Elbert Smith, *Francis Preston Blair* (New York, 1980); Robert Seager II, *And Tyler Too: A Biography of John and Julia Gardiner Tyler* (New York, 1963); Oliver Perry Chitwood, *John Tyler: Champion of the Old South* (New York, 1939); John Munroe, *Louis McLane, Federalist and Jacksonian* (New Brunswick, 1973); Freeman Cleaves, *Old Tippecanoe: William Henry Harrison and His Time* (New York, 1939); Joseph H. Parks, *John Bell of Tennessee*

(Baton Rouge, 1950); Holman Hamilton, *Zachary Taylor* (Indianapolis and New York, 1941, 1951), 2 volumes; K. Jack Bauer, *Zachary Taylor* (Baton Rouge, 1986); Robert J. Rayback, *Millard Fillmore* (Buffalo, 1959); and Robert W. Johannsen, *Stephen A. Douglas* (New York, 1973). My own *Andrew Jackson and the Course of American Empire, 1767–1821* (New York, 1977); *Andrew Jackson and the Course of American Freedom, 1822–1832* (New York, 1981); and *Andrew Jackson and the Course of American Democracy, 1833–1845* (New York, 1984) allowed me to examine most of the political events of the antebellum period from a Democratic point of view. A one-volume condensation of this three-volume study is entitled *The Life of Andrew Jackson* (New York, 1988).

For Clay's American System and other aspects of his political thinking, I found Daniel Walker Howe, *The Political Culture of the American Whigs* (Chicago, 1979) outstandingly valuable. There is a brilliant analysis of Clay in the chapter entitled "Henry Clay, Ideologue of the Center." See also Howe's edition *The American Whigs: An Anthology* (New York, 1973). Equally impressive and valuable is Thomas Brown, *Politics and Statesmanship: Essays on the American Whig Party* (New York, 1985), especially Chapter Five entitled "Henry Clay and the Politics of Consensus." In my judgment, the most detailed statement on the American System is Marie-Luise Frings, *Henry Clays American System und die sektionale Kontroverse in den Vereinigten Staaten von Amerika, 1815–1829* (Frankfurt, 1979). However, I cannot agree with her that Clay's motive for initiating the American System rose primarily to serve the interests of Kentucky. My own opinion is that it came from his experiences in Europe during the peace and trade negotiations and his own profound nationalistic feelings. Frings also contends that Clay exacerbated sectional tensions in urging his American System so forcefully. Unfortunately her study has not yet been translated into English but should be.

Glyndon G. Van Deusen's article "Some Aspects of Whig Thought and Theory in the Jacksonian Period," *American Historical Review*, LXIII (1958), pp. 305–322, is very useful. In addition, see Thomas Brown, *Politics and Statesmanship: Essays on the American Whig Party* (New York, 1985), Rush Welter, *The Mind of America, 1830–1860* (New York, 1975), and John Ashworth, *"Agrarians & Aristocrats": Party Political Ideology in the United States, 1837–1846* (London, 1983). Major L. Wilson, *Space, Time, and Freedom: The Quest for Nationality and the Irrepressible Conflict* (Westport, Conn., 1974) contrasts the goals and purposes of the Whigs and Democrats. For the Democrats, see Jean H. Baker, *Affairs of Party* (Ithaca, N.Y., 1983) and Marvin Meyers's classic study *The Jacksonian Persuasion* (Stanford, Calif., 1957).

There is a fine sketch of Clay's early career in Peterson's *Great Triumvirate* and in George Dangerfield, *The Era of Good Feelings* (New York, 1952). For background material treating the War of 1812 and Clay's participation in the peace negotiations, the following are among the most recent and accessible: J. C. A. Stagg, *Mr. Madison's War: Politics, Diplomacy, and Warfare in the Early*

American Republic, 1783–1830 (Princeton, 1983); Donald R. Hickey, *The War of 1812: A Forgotten Conflict* (Urbana, Ill., 1989); Bradford Perkins, *Castlereagh and Adams: England and the United States, 1812–1823* (Berkeley, 1964); Lawrence Kaplan, *Entangling Alliances with None: American Foreign Policy in the Age of Jefferson* (Kent, Ohio, 1987); and Fred L. Engelman, *The Peace of Christmas Eve* (New York, 1962). Older but still valuable is Frank A. Updyke, *The Diplomacy of the War of 1812* (Baltimore, 1915).

The market revolution that embraced the many economic changes occurring in the nation following the War of 1812 may be traced in Christopher Clark, "The Household Economy, Market Exchange, and the Rise of Capitalism in the Connecticut Valley, 1800–1860," *Journal of Social History,* XIII (1979), pp. 169–190. Harry L. Watson, *Liberty and Power: The Politics of Jacksonian America* (New York, 1990) explains the market revolution in a broader historical context, even though it is primarily concerned with the politics of the 1820s and 1830s. For the individual economic concerns of the antebellum period, consult Murray Rothbard, *The Panic of 1819* (New York, 1962); Peter Temin, *The Jacksonian Economy* (New York, 1969); Ralph C. H. Catterall, *The Second Bank of the United States* (Chicago, 1902); Bray Hammond, *Banks and Politics in America from the Revolution to the Civil War* (Princeton, 1957); Larry Schweikart, *Banking in the American South from the Age of Jackson to Reconstruction* (Baton Rouge, 1987); Joseph Hobson Harrison, "Internal Improvements in the Politics of the Union, 1783–1835," doctoral dissertation, University of Virginia, 1954; Gavin Wright, *The Political Economy of the Cotton South* (New York, 1978); Malcolm J. Rohrbough, *The Land Office Business* (New York, 1968); Daniel Feller, *Public Lands and Jacksonian Politics* (Madison, Wis., 1984); Stephen Hahn, *The Roots of Southern Populism* (New York, 1983); Frank W. Taussig, *The Tariff History of the United States* (New York, 1893); David Montgomery, "The Working Classes of the Pre-Industrial American City, 1780–1830," *Labor History,* IX (1968), pp. 3–22; and Sean Wilentz, *Chants Democratic: New York City and the Rise of the American Working Class, 1788–1850* (New York, 1984).

The standard study of the compromises involving Missouri's admission into the Union is Glover Moore, *The Missouri Controversy, 1819–1821* (Lexington, Ky., 1953). A provocative examination of the consequences of the compromise is Richard H. Brown, "The Missouri Crisis, Slavery, and the Politics of Jacksonianism," *South Atlantic Quarterly,* LXV (1966), pp. 55–72. However, my own *The Legacy of Andrew Jackson: Essays on Democracy, Indian Removal and Slavery* (Baton Rouge, 1988) challenges some of Brown's conclusions.

Attitudes toward political parties and how they changed from the first to the second party system are brilliantly explained in Richard Hofstadter, *The Idea of a Party System* (Berkeley, Calif., 1972). See also Michael Wallace, "Changing Concepts of Party in the United States: New York, 1815–1825," *American Historical Review,* LXXIV (1968), pp. 453–491, and Ralph Katcham,

Presidents above Party (Chapel Hill, N.C., 1984). My own *Martin Van Buren and the Making of the Democratic Party* (New York, 1959) explored the Magician's unique contribution to the structuring of the party and the motivation behind it. Richard P. McCormick's two books *The Second American Party System: Party Formation in the Jacksonian Era* (Chapel Hill, N.C., 1966) and *The Presidential Game: The Origins of American Presidential Politics* (New York, 1982) are outstanding in explaining party development and operation. On the Federalists, Shaw Livermore, Jr., *The Twilight of Federalism: The Disintegration of the Federalist Party, 1815–1830* (Princeton, 1962) is excellent. For all the presidential elections in this antebellum period, see Arthur M. Schlesinger, Jr., and Fred J. Israel, eds., *History of American Presidential Elections, 1789–1968* (New York, 1971), 4 volumes.

The corrupt bargain charge is analyzed in two articles by William G. Morgan: "The 'Corrupt Bargain' Charge against Clay and Adams: An Historiographical Analysis," *Filson Club Historical Quarterly*, XLII (April 1968), pp. 132–149, and "Henry Clay's Biographers and the 'Corrupt Bargain' Charge," *Register of the Kentucky Historical Society*, LXVI (1968), pp. 242–258. Of special importance is M. J. Heale's *The Presidential Quest: Candidates and Images in American Political Culture, 1787–1852* (London, 1982).

Among secondary sources treating the Jacksonian era none can compare with Arthur M. Schlesinger, Jr., *The Age of Jackson* (New York, 1945), a remarkable, brilliantly written, and imperishable study. This classic work is a landmark in Jacksonian scholarship and will undoubtedly continue to stimulate discussion and debate among historians as long as they struggle to understand the total Zeitgeist of this period. Taking an altogether different tack, Glyndon G. Van Deusen, *The Jacksonian Era, 1828–1848* (New York, 1959) stresses the role of Henry Clay in explaining the direction of national politics. As Clay's biographer his approach should surprise no one. But more recent studies of Whig and Democratic ideology and politics include Bruce Collins, "The Ideology of the Ante-Bellum Northern Democrats," *Journal of American Studies*, IX (April 1977), pp. 103–121; Jean Elizabeth Friedman, "The Revolt of the Conservative Democrats: An Essay on American Political Culture and Political Development, 1837–1844," doctoral dissertation, Lehigh University, 1976; Perry M. Goldman, "The Republic of Virtue and Other Essays on the Politics of the Early National Republic," doctoral dissertation, Columbia University, 1970; Louis Hartz, *The Liberal Tradition in America: An Interpretation of American Political Thought since the Revolution* (New York, 1955); Robert Kelley, *The Cultural Pattern in American Politics: The First Century* (New York, 1979); Lawrence F. Kohl, *The Politics of Individualism: Parties and the American Character in the Jacksonian Era* (New York, 1989); Richard L. McCormick, *The Party Period from the Age of Jackson to the Progressive Era* (New York, 1986); Roy Nichols, *The Invention of the American Political Parties* (New York, 1967); and Joel Silbey, *The Partisan Imperative: The Dynamics of American Politics before the Civil War* (New York, 1985).

For the administration of John Quincy Adams, Mary W. M. Hargreaves, *The Presidency of John Quincy Adams* (Lawrence, Kan., 1985) is a most valuable and reliable study. Thoroughly researched, this work is particularly informative concerning Clay's role as secretary of state. On Clay and Latin American independence, the most useful works include Halford L. Hoskins, "The Hispanic American Policy of Henry Clay, 1816–1828," *Hispanic American Historical Review,* VII (1927), pp. 460–478; William S. Robertson, "The Recognition of the Hispanic American Nations by the United States," *Hispanic-American Historical Review,* I (1918), pp. 239–269; Joseph B. Lockey, *Pan-Americanism: Its Beginnings* (New York, 1920); J. Fred Rippy, *Rivalry of the United States and Great Britain over Latin America (1808–1830)* (Baltimore, 1928); and Arthur Preston Whitaker, *The United States and the Independence of Latin America, 1800–1830* (Baltimore, 1941).

Vernon G. Setser, *The Commercial Reciprocity Policy of the United States, 1774–1829* (New York, 1937) examines the administration's commercial policy and goals. For the colonial trade controversy, see F. Lee Benns, *The American Struggle for the British West Indian Carrying Trade, 1815–1830* (Bloomington, Ind., 1923). A unique study is Margaret Ruth Morley, "The Edge of Empire: Henry Clay's American System and the Formulation of American Foreign Policy, 1810–1833," doctoral dissertation, University of Wisconsin, Madison, 1972, but unfortunately it has not been published. Also useful is Thomas B. Jones, "Henry Clay and Continental Expansion, 1820–1844," *Register of the Kentucky Historical Society,* LXXIII (1975), pp. 241–262.

A splendid account of the Jackson presidency is Richard B. Latner, *The Presidency of Andrew Jackson* (Athens, Ga., 1979). It is especially good in demonstrating western influence on Jackson's behavior, particularly through the contributions of those two former Kentuckians Amos Kendall and Francis P. Blair. Jackson's use of the patronage is analyzed in Sidney H. Aronson, *Status and Kinship in the Higher Civil Service: Standards of Selection in the Administrations of John Adams, Thomas Jefferson, and Andrew Jackson* (Cambridge, Mass., 1964); Frank Freidel, "Jackson's Political Removals as Seen by Historians," *Historian,* II (Winter 1939), pp. 41–52; William F. Mugleston, "Andrew Jackson and the Spoils System: An Historiographical Survey," *Mid-America,* LIX (April–July 1977), pp. 113–125; and Leonard D. White, *The Jacksonians: A Study in Administrative History, 1829–1861* (New York, 1954).

The best overall evaluation of Indian removal is Ronald N. Satz, *American Indian Policy in the Jacksonian Era* (Lincoln, Neb., 1975). A critical and controversial study of the problem is Michael Paul Rogin, *Fathers and Children: Andrew Jackson and the Subjugation of the American Indian* (New York, 1975). Francis Paul Prucha has written ably and extensively on Indian policy and provides the best defense for removal in his article "Andrew Jackson's Indian Policy: A Reassessment," *Journal of American History,* LVI, (December 1969), pp. 527–539. For Clay and the Indian question, see Rickey L. Hendricks, "Henry Clay and Jacksonian Indian Policy: A Political Anachronism," *Filson Club Historical Quarterly,* LX (April 1986), pp. 218–238.

On the nullification crisis and the Compromise Tariff of 1833, the most recent and best account is Richard E. Ellis, *The Union at Risk: Jacksonian Democracy, States' Rights, and the Nullification Crisis* (New York, 1987). But Merrill D. Peterson provides important insights into the arrival of a compromise in *The Olive Branch and Sword: The Compromise of 1833* (Baton Rouge, 1982). An older but still useful account of the nullification controversy is William W. Freehling, *Prelude to Civil War: The Nullification Movement in South Carolina, 1816–1836* (New York, 1966). His more recent study of the secession movement, *The Road to Disunion: Secessionists at Bay, 1776–1854* (New York, 1990), is particularly illuminating. Important in understanding the political domination of slavery in southern thinking and behavior and Clay's concessions to the South to win support is William J. Cooper, Jr., *The South and the Politics of Slavery, 1828–1856* (Baton Rouge, 1978).

The Bank War has been the subject of innumerable studies, and my own *Andrew Jackson and the Bank War* (New York, 1968) provides a general survey. Various aspects of this war may be traced in John M. McFaul, *The Politics of Jacksonian Finance* (Ithaca, N.Y., 1972); James Roger Sharp, *The Jacksonians versus the Banks: Politics in the States after the Panic of 1837* (New York, 1970); Walter B. Smith, *Economic Aspects of the Second Bank of the United States* (Cambridge, 1953); and Jean Alexander Wilburn, *Biddle Bank: The Crucial Years* (New York, 1967).

The presidential election of 1832 and the rise of Anti-Masonry are examined in Samuel R. Gammon, Jr., *The Presidential Campaign of 1832* (Baltimore, 1922); Charles McCarthy, *A Study of Political Antimasonry in the United States, 1827–1840*, in American Historical Association, *Annual Report, 1902* (Washington, 1903); Paul Goodman, *Towards a Christian Republic: Antimasonry and the Great Transition in New England, 1826–1836* (New York, 1988); and William P. Vaughn, *The Antimasonic Party in the United States, 1826–1843* (Lexington, Ky., 1983).

On the Whig party there are several informative studies, including E. Malcolm Carroll, *Origins of the Whig Party* (Durham, N.C., 1925); Arthur C. Cole, *The Whig Party in the South* (Washington, D.C., 1913); Charles G. Sellers, Jr., "Who Were the Southern Whigs?," *American Historical Review,* LIX (January 1954), pp. 341–346; Thomas Brown, "Southern Whigs and the Politics of Statesmanship, 1833–41," *Journal of Southern History,* XLVI (August 1980), pp. 361–380; Lynn L. Marshall, "The Strange Stillbirth of the Whig Party," *American Historical Review,* LXXII (January 1967), pp. 445–468, William S. Stokes, "Whig Conceptions of Executive Power," *Presidential Studies Quarterly,* VI (Winter 1976), pp. 16–35; Franklin Arthur Walker, "The Whig Party and Domestic Politics, 1830–1841," doctoral dissertation, Cornell University, 1954; and Glyndon G. Van Deusen, "The Whig Party," *History of U.S. Political Parties,* ed. Arthur M. Schlesinger, Jr. (New York, 1973), I, 333–496, along with numerous studies of the party in individual states, especially in the South.

On the ties between urban wealth and Whiggery, see Frank Otto Gatell,

"Money and Party in Jacksonian America," *Political Science Quarterly*, LXXXII (1967), pp. 235–252, and Robert Rich, "A Wilderness of Whigs," *Journal of Social History*, IV (1971), pp. 263–276. Richard L. McCormick, "Ethno-Cultural Interpretations of Nineteenth-Century American Voting Behavior," *Political Science Quarterly*, LXXXIX (1974), pp. 351–377, provides a sane and balanced critique of the ethnocultural approach to Jacksonian politics. Valuable, too, is McCormick's article "The Party Period and Public Policy," *Journal of American History*, LXVI (1979), pp. 279–298.

Major L. Wilson, *The Presidency of Martin Van Buren* (Lawrence, Kan., 1984) is the most useful study of its subject, as is Reginald C. McGrane, *The Panic of 1837* (Chicago, 1924). All the fun and nonsense of the campaign of 1840 are captured in Robert Gray Gunderson, *The Log-Cabin Campaign* (Lexington, Ky., 1957). For the economic issues involved in the campaign, see Michael F. Holt, "The Election of 1840, Voter Mobilization and the Emergence of Jacksonian Voting Behavior," in *A Master's Due*, ed. William J. Cooper, Jr., et al. (Baton Rouge, 1985), pp. 16–58. An invaluable study of the development of partisan congressional voting is Joel Silbey, *The Shrine of Party: Congressional Voting Behavior, 1841–1852* (Pittsburgh, 1967). See also Silbey's *Political Ideology and Voting Behavior in the Age of Jackson* (Englewood Cliffs, N.J., 1967).

A fair and balanced treatment of the Tyler administration is Robert J. Morgan, *A Whig Embattled: The Presidency under John Tyler* (Lincoln, Neb., 1954). The individual presidencies of Harrison, Tyler, Polk, and Taylor are extensively covered in the American Presidencies Series published by the University of Kansas Press. These include Norma Lois Peterson, *The Presidencies of William Henry Harrison & John Tyler* (Lawrence, Kan, 1989); Paul Bergeron, *The Presidency of James K. Polk* (Lawrence, Kan., 1987); and Elbert B. Smith, *The Presidencies of Zachary Taylor & Millard Fillmore* (Lawrence, Kan., 1989). For Polk, Charles A. McCoy, *Polk and the Presidency* (Austin, Texas, 1960) is especially good.

Several significant works treat the expansionist impulse that swept the nation and led to the Mexican War. These include the classic statement by Albert K. Weinberg, *Manifest Destiny* (Baltimore, 1935); two works by Frederick Merk, *Manifest Destiny and Mission in American History* (New York, 1963) and *Slavery and the Annexation of Texas* (New York, 1972); Justin H. Smith, *The Annexation of Texas* (New York, 1911); David M. Pletcher, *The Diplomacy of Annexation: Texas, Oregon, and the Mexican War* (Bloomington, Ind., 1973); Norman A. Graebner, *Empire on the Pacific: A Study in American Continental Expansion* (New York, 1955); and Dexter Perkins, *The Monroe Doctrine, 1826–1867* (Baltimore, 1933).

The Mexican War is splendidly detailed in Justin H. Smith, *The War with Mexico* (New York, 1919), 2 volumes, and remains the best account available. More recent studies include Otis A. Singletary, *The Mexican War* (New York, 1960); K. Jack Bauer, *The Mexican-American War, 1846–1848* (New York,

1974); and John S. D. Eisenhower, *So Far from God: The U.S. War with Mexico, 1846–1848* (New York, 1989). Robert W. Johannsen explains the popular enthusiasm for the war in his *To the Halls of the Montezumas: The War with Mexico in the American Imagination* (New York, 1985), while John H. Schroeder, *Mr. Polk's War: American Opposition and Dissent, 1846–1848* (Madison, Wis., 1973) presents the strong opposition to it by Whigs.

On the question of slavery, the list of available studies is extensive, and much of it is relatively recent. John Niven provides an excellent bibliographical essay on the subject at the conclusion of his short text *The Coming of the Civil War, 1837–1861* (Arlington Heights, Ill., 1990). I have always found Kenneth M. Stampp, *The Peculiar Institution: Slavery in the Ante-Bellum South* (New York, 1956) an especially fine introduction to the subject. Most notable are Eugene D. Genovese, *The Political Economy of Slavery* (New York, 1965); John W. Blassingame, *The Slave Community: Plantation Life in the Ante-Bellum South* (New York, 1979); and James Oakes, *The Ruling Race: A History of American Slaveholders* (New York, 1982).

On the colonizing of free blacks, consult Early Lee Fox, *The American Colonization Society, 1817–1840* (Baltimore, 1919); Peter Kent Opper, "The Mind of the White Participant in the African Colonization Movement, 1816–1840," doctoral dissertation, University of North Carolina, Chapel Hill, 1972; Phil S. Sigler, "The Attitudes of Free Blacks towards Emigration to Liberia," doctoral dissertation, Boston University, 1969; and P. J. Staudenraus, *The African Colonization Movement, 1816–1865* (New York, 1961).

For the abolition movement, an older but still valuable study is Gilbert H. Barnes, *The Antislavery Impulse, 1830–1844* (New York, 1933). It should be supplemented with Dwight Dumond, *Antislavery: The Crusade for Freedom in America* (Ann Arbor, Mich., 1961); Carleton Mabee, *Black Freedom: The Nonviolent Abolitionists from 1830 through the Civil War* (New York, 1970); Thomas D. Morris, *Free Men All: The Personal Liberty Laws of the North, 1780–1861* (Baltimore, 1974); Richard H. Sewall, *Ballots for Freedom: Antislavery Politics in the United States, 1837–1860* (New York, 1976); Theodore C. Smith, *The Liberty and Free Soil Parties in the Northwest* (New York, 1897); James Brewer Stewart, *Holy Warriors: The Abolitionists and American Slavery* (New York, 1976); William L. Van Deburg, "Henry Clay, the Right of Petition, and Slavery in the Nation's Capital," *Register of the Kentucky Historical Society*, LXVIII (1970), pp. 132–146; and Louis Filler, *The Crusade against Slavery, 1830–1860* (New York, 1960). For an interesting (because it concerns one of Clay's best and earliest biographers) sidelight on the question, see Alfred A. Cave, "The Case of Calvin Colton: White Racism in Northern Anti-slavery Thought," *New-York Historical Society Quarterly*, XLIX (1969), pp. 209–230.

The consequences of the Mexican War with respect to the slavery question are fully detailed in Allan Nevins, *Ordeal of the Union* (New York, 1947), 2 volumes; Michael F. Holt, *The Political Crisis of the 1850s* (New York, 1978); David Potter, *The Impending Crisis 1848–1861* (New York, 1976); Reginald

Horsman, *Race and Manifest Destiny: The Origins of American Racial Anglo-Saxonism* (Cambridge, Mass., 1981); Joseph G. Rayback, *Free Soil: The Election of 1848* (Lexington, Ky., 1970); and Frederick J. Blue, *The Free Soilers: Third Party Politics 1848–1854* (Urbana, Ill., 1964). The best single work on the Compromise of 1850 is Holman Hamilton, *Prologue to Conflict: The Crisis and Compromise of 1850* (Lexington, Ky., 1964). Stanley W. Campbell, *The Slave Catchers: Enforcement of the Fugitive Slave Law 1850–1860* (Chapel Hill, N.C., 1970) traces the violence generated by one of the component parts of the compromise.

When I first began to research the Age of Jackson as a graduate student, I never realized what a delightful, indeed fascinating, lighthearted, and charming man Henry Clay was to his contemporaries. Not until I began to probe his life and career more intensely, especially by reading all his great speeches in Congress and on the stump as well as his enormous correspondence, did I begin to fathom the full dimension of his personal attractiveness, his insouciance, his audacity, and his wonderful sense of humor. Several books also helped in this regard because of their valuable anecdotal material. The most important of these includes Ben: Perley Poore, *Perley's Reminiscences of Sixty Years in the National Metropolis* (Philadelphia, 1886), 2 volumes; Nathan Sargent, *Public Men and Events* (Philadelphia, 1875), 2 volumes; and Gaillard Hunt, ed., *The First Forty Years of Washington Society Portrayed by the Family Letters of Mrs. Samuel Harrison Smith* (New York, 1906). They frequently spring Clay and his contemporaries to life, far better than any secondary account can hope to achieve.

Index